COLLINS GEM

ENGLISH *School* DICTIONARY

HarperCollins*Publishers*

HarperCollins Publishers
PO Box, Glasgow G4 0NB
First Published in this Edition 1995

ISBN 0 00470903-9

A catalogue record for this book is available
from the British Library.

Typeset by Morton Word Processing Ltd,
Scarborough, England

Printed and bound in Great Britain
by HarperCollins Manufacturing

EDITORIAL TEAM

Managing Editor
Marian Makins

Chief Lexicographer
Diana Adams

Lexicographers
Elspeth Summers
Sheila Ferguson · Andrew Holmes
Ian Brookes · Alice Grandison · Mary O'Neill
Danielle McGinley · Thomas Shearer

Computing Staff
Jane Creevy

Corpus Acknowledgements

We would like to thank those authors and publishers who kindly gave permission for copyright material to be used in the Bank of English. We would also like to thank Times Newspapers Ltd for providing valuable data.

GUIDE TO THE DICTIONARY

venerate, venerates, venerating, venerated (verb; a formal word) If you venerate someone, you feel great respect for them. **veneration** (noun). — Label

Entry Word — **vengeance** **1** (noun) Vengeance is the act of harming someone because they have harmed you. **2** (phrase) If something happens **with a vengeance,** it happens to a much greater extent than was expected, e.g *It began to rain again with a vengeance.* — Example

venom **1** (noun) The venom of a snake, scorpion, or spider is its poison. **2** Venom is a feeling of great bitterness or spitefulness towards someone, e.g. *He was glaring at me with venom.* **venomous** (adjective). — Definition

vent, vents, venting, vented **1** (noun) A vent is a hole in something through which gases and smoke can escape and fresh air can enter, e.g. *air vents.* **2** (verb) If you vent strong feelings, you express them, e.g. *She wanted to vent her anger upon me.* **3** (phrase) If you **give vent** to strong feelings, you express them, e.g. *Pamela gave vent to a lot of bitterness.* — Other forms of Entry Word; Sense Number; Phrase

ventriloquist, ventriloquists (pronounced ven-**trill**-o-kwist) (noun) A ventriloquist is an entertainer who can speak without moving their lips so that the words seem to come from a dummy or a puppet. **ventriloquism** (noun). — Pronunciation; Part of Speech; Related Word

A a

a, an (adjective) The indefinite articles 'a' and 'an' are used when you are talking about one of something, especially something that you have not mentioned before, e.g. *a train... an apple... There was a car parked behind the hedge.*

aback (adverb) If you are taken aback, you are very surprised and slightly shocked.

abacus, abacuses (noun) An abacus is a frame with beads that slide along rods, used for calculating.

abandon, abandons, abandoning, abandoned 1 (verb) If you abandon someone or something, you leave them or give them up permanently. **2** (noun) If you do something with abandon, you do it in a rather wild uncontrolled way. **abandoned** (adjective), **abandonment** (noun).

abate, abates, abating, abated (verb) If something abates, it becomes less, e.g. *The rain did not abate.*

abattoir, abattoirs (pronounced **ab**-a-twah) (noun) An abattoir is a place where animals are killed for meat.

abbess, abbesses (noun) An abbess is a nun in charge of all the nuns in a convent.

abbey, abbeys (noun) An abbey is a church with buildings attached to it in which monks or nuns live.

abbot, abbots (noun) An abbot is the monk or priest in charge of all the monks in a monastery.

abbreviate, abbreviates, abbreviating, abbreviated (verb) To abbreviate something means to make it shorter.

abbreviation, abbreviations (noun) An abbreviation is a short form of a word or phrase.

abdicate, abdicates, abdicating, abdicated (verb) If a king or queen abdicates, he or she resigns. **abdication** (noun).

abdomen, abdomens (noun) Your abdomen is the front part of your body below your chest, containing your stomach and intestines. **abdominal** (adjective).

abduct, abducts, abducting, abducted (verb) To abduct someone means to take them away by force. **abduction** (noun).

aberration, aberrations (noun) An aberration is something that is not normal or usual, e.g. *a statistical aberration.*

abet, abets, abetting, abetted (verb) If you abet someone, you help them to do something wrong.

abhor, abhors, abhorring, abhorred (verb; a formal word) If you abhor something, you hate it. **abhorrence** (noun), **abhorrent** (adjective).

abide, abides, abiding, abided 1 (verb) If you can't abide something, you dislike it very much. **2** If you abide by a de- cision, agreement, or law, y accept it and act in accordance with it.

ability, abilities (noun) Your ability to do something is the quality of intelligence or skill that you have that enables you to do it, e.g. *the ability to get on with others.*

abject (adjective) very bad, e.g. *abject failure.* **abjectly** (adverb).

ablaze (adjective) on fire or in flames.

able, abler, ablest 1 (adjective) If you are able to do something, you can do it. **2** Someone who is able is very clever or talented.

ably (pronounced **ay**-blee) (adverb) skilfully and successfully, e.g. *He is ably supported by an accomplished cast.*

abnormal (adjective) not normal or usual, e.g. *The disorder is caused by abnormal levels of chemicals in the brain.* **abnormally** (adverb).

abnormality, abnormalities (noun) An abnormality is something that is not normal or usual.

aboard (preposition or adverb) on a ship or plane.

abode, abodes (noun; an old-fashioned word) Your abode is your home.

abolish, abolishes, abolishing, abolished (verb) To abolish something means to put an end to it officially. **abolition** (noun).

abominable (adjective) very unpleasant or shocking. **abominably** (adverb).

Aborigine, Aborigines (pronounced ab-or-**rij**-in-ee) (noun) An Aborigine is someone descended from the people who lived in Australia before Europeans arrived. **Aboriginal** (adjective).

abort, aborts, aborting, aborted 1 (verb) If a pregnant woman aborts, the pregnancy ends too soon and the baby dies. **2** If a plan or activity is aborted, it is stopped before it is finished.

abortion, abortions (noun) If a woman has an abortion, the pregnancy is ended deliberately and the baby dies.

abortive (adjective) unsuccessful, e.g. *their abortive attempts.*

abound, abounds, abounding, abounded (verb) If things abound, there are very large numbers of them.

about 1 (preposition or adverb) of or concerning. **2** approximately and not exactly. **3** (adverb) in different directions, e.g. *There were some bottles scattered about.* **4** (adjective) present or in a place, e.g. *Is Jane about?* **5** (phrase) If you are **about to** do something, you are just going to do it.

above 1 (preposition or adverb) directly over or higher than something, e.g. *above the clouds.* **2** greater than a level or amount, e.g. *The temperature didn't rise above freezing point.*

above board (adjective) completely open, honest, and legal, e.g. *They assured me it was above board and properly licensed.*

abrasion, abrasions (noun) An abrasion is an area where your skin has been broken or scraped.

abrasive 1 (adjective) An abrasive substance is rough and can be used to clean hard surfaces. **2** Someone who is abrasive is unpleasant and rude, e.g. *his abrasive manner.*

abroad (adverb) in a foreign country.

abrupt 1 (adjective) sudden, quick, and unexpected, e.g. *His career came to an abrupt end.* **2** rude, unfriendly, and impolite. **abruptly** (adverb), **abruptness** (noun).

abscess, abscesses (pronounced **ab**-sess) (noun) An abscess is a painful swelling that contains pus.

abseiling (noun) Abseiling is the activity of going down cliffs or mountains by sliding down ropes.

absent (adjective) Something that is absent is not present in a place or situation. **absence** (noun).

absentee, absentees (noun) An absentee is someone who is not present in a place when they should be present.

absent-minded (adjective) rather vague and forgetful.

absolute 1 (adjective) total and complete, e.g. *absolute honesty.* **2** having complete and unlimited power and authority, e.g. *an absolute monarchy.* **absolutely** (adverb).

absolve, absolves, absolving, absolved (verb) To absolve someone of something means to state officially that they are not guilty of it or not to blame for it.

absorb, absorbs, absorbing, absorbed (verb) If something absorbs liquid or gas, it soaks it up.

absorbent (adjective) Absorbent materials soak up liquid easily.

absorption 1 (noun) An absorption is a great interest in something, e.g. *my father's absorption in his business affairs.* **2** Absorption is the soaking up of a liquid.

abstain, abstains, abstaining, abstained 1 (verb) If you abstain from something, you do not do it or have it, e.g. *The patients had to abstain from alcohol.* **2** If you abstain in a vote, you do not vote. **abstention** (noun).

abstinence (noun) Abstinence is deliberately not doing something that you enjoy.

abstract (adjective) based on thoughts and ideas rather than physical objects or events. **abstraction** (noun).

absurd (adjective) ridiculous and stupid. **absurdly** (adverb), **absurdity** (noun).

abundance (noun) Something that exists in abundance exists in large numbers, e.g. *an abundance of wildlife.* **abundant** (adjective), **abundantly** (adverb).

abuse, abuses, abusing, abused 1 (noun) Abuse is cruel and violent treatment of someone, e.g. *child abuse.* **2** Abuse is rude and unkind remarks directed towards someone. **3** The abuse of something is the wrong use of it, e.g. *an abuse of power... alcohol abuse.* **4** (verb) If you abuse someone, you speak insultingly to them. **5** To abuse someone also means to treat them cruelly and violently. **6** If you abuse something, you use it wrongly or for a bad purpose, e.g. *He had abused his position of* *trust.*

abusive (adjective) rude, offensive, and unkind. **abusively** (adverb), **abusiveness** (noun).

abysmal (pronounced ab-**biz**-ml) (adjective) very bad indeed, e.g. *an abysmal performance.* **abysmally** (adverb).

abyss, abysses (noun) An abyss is a very deep hole.

academic, academics 1 (adjective) Academic work is work done in a school, college, or university. **2** (noun) An academic is someone who teaches or does research in a college or university. **academically** (adverb).

academy, academies (noun) An academy is a school or college, usually one that specializes in one particular subject, e.g. *the Royal Academy of Dramatic Art.*

accelerate, accelerates, accelerating, accelerated (verb) To accelerate means to go faster.

acceleration (noun) Acceleration is the rate at which the speed of something is increasing.

accelerator, accelerators (noun) The accelerator in a vehicle is the pedal which you press to make it go faster.

accent, accents 1 (noun) An accent is a way of pronouncing a language, e.g. *He had an Australian accent.* **2** An accent is also a mark placed above or below a letter in some languages, which affects the way the letter is pronounced. **3** An accent on something is an emphasis on it, e.g. *The accent is on action and special effects.*

accentuate, accentuates, accentuating, accentuated (verb) To accentuate a feature of something means to make it more noticeable.

accept, accepts, accepting, accepted 1 (verb) If you accept something, you say yes to it or take it from someone. **2** If you accept a situation, you realize that it cannot be changed, e.g. *He accepts criticism as part of his job.* **3** If you accept a statement or story, you believe that it is true, e.g. *The board accepted his explanation.* **acceptance** (noun), **acceptable** (adjective), **acceptably** (adverb).

access, accesses, accessing, accessed 1 (noun) Access is the right or opportunity to use something or to enter a place. **2** (verb) If you access information from a computer, you get it.

accessible 1 (adjective) easily reached or seen, e.g. *The village was accessible by foot only.* **2** easily understood or used, e.g. *an accessible writing style.* **accessibility** (noun).

accession (noun) A ruler's accession is the time when he or she becomes the ruler of a country.

accessory, accessories 1 (noun) An accessory is an extra part. **2** An accessory to a crime is someone who helps another person commit the crime.

accident, accidents 1 (noun) An accident is an event in which people are injured or killed. **2** Something that happens by accident happens by chance.

accidental (adjective) happening by chance. **accidentally** (adverb).

acclaimed (adjective) If someone or something is acclaimed, they are praised enthusiastically.

accolade, accolades (noun; a formal word) An accolade is great praise or an award that is given to someone.

accommodate, accommodates, accommodating, accommodated 1 (verb) If you accommodate someone, you provide them with a place to sleep, live, or work. **2** If a place can accommodate a number of things or people, it has enough room for them.

accommodation (noun) Accommodation is a place provided for someone to sleep, live, or work in.

accompaniment, accompaniments 1 (noun) The accompaniment to a song or tune is the music that is played to go with it. **2** An accompaniment to something is another thing that comes with it, e.g. *This wine is the perfect accompaniment to winter dishes.*

accompany, accompanies, accompanying, accompanied 1 (verb) If you accompany someone, you go with them. **2** If one thing accompanies another, the two things exist at the same time, e.g. *severe pain accompanied by fever.*

accomplice, accomplices (noun) An accomplice is a person who helps someone else to commit a crime.

accomplish, accomplishes, accomplishing, accomplished (verb) If you accomplish something, you succeed in doing it.

accomplished (adjective) very talented at something, e.g. *an accomplished cook.*

accomplishment, accomplishments (noun) Someone's accomplishments are the skills that they have acquired.

accord, accords, according, accorded 1 (verb) If you accord someone or something a particular treatment, you treat them in that way, e.g. *He was accorded a proper respect for his status.* **2** (noun) Accord is agreement. **3** (phrase) If you do something **of your own accord,** you do it willingly and not because you have been forced to do it.

accordance (phrase) If you act **in accordance with** a rule or belief, you act in the way that the rule or belief says you should.

according to 1 (preposition) If something is true according to a particular person, that person says that it is true. **2** If something is done according to a principle or plan, that principle or plan is used as the basis for it.

accordion, accordions (noun) An accordion is a musical instrument shaped like an expanding box. It is played by squeezing the two sides together while pressing the keys on it.

accost, accosts, accosting, accosted (verb) If someone accosts you, especially someone you do not know, they come up and speak to you.

account, accounts, accounting, accounted 1 (noun) An account is a written or spoken report of something. **2** (plural noun) Accounts are records of money spent and received by a person or business. **3** (noun)

If you have a bank account, you can leave money in the bank and take it out when you need it. **4** (phrase) **On account of** means because of. **5** (verb) To account for something means to explain it, e.g. *This might account for her strange behaviour.* **6** If something accounts for a particular amount of something, it is that amount, e.g. *The brain accounts for three per cent of body weight.*

accountable (adjective) If you are accountable for something, you are responsible for it and have to explain your actions, e.g. *The agency is accountable to the Scottish Office.* **accountability** (noun).

accountancy (noun) Accountancy is the job of keeping or inspecting financial accounts.

accountant, accountants (noun) An accountant is a person whose job is to keep or inspect financial accounts.

accounting (noun) Accounting is the process of keeping and checking financial accounts.

accrue, accrues, accruing, accrued (verb) If money or interest accrues, it increases or accumulates gradually.

accumulate, accumulates, accumulating, accumulated (verb) If you accumulate things or they accumulate, they collect over a period of time.

accurate (adjective) completely true, correct, or precise. **accurately** (adverb), **accuracy** (noun).

accuse, accuses, accusing, accused (verb) If you accuse someone of doing something wrong, you say that they have done it. **accusation** (noun), **accuser** (noun).

accustom, accustoms, accustoming, accustomed (verb) If you accustom yourself to something new or different, you get used to it.

ace, aces 1 (noun) In a pack of cards, an ace is a card with a single symbol on it. **2** (adjective; an informal use) good or skilful, e.g. *an ace squash player.*

acerbic (pronounced as-**ser**-bik) (adjective; a formal word) Acerbic remarks are harsh and bitter.

ache, aches, aching, ached 1 (verb) If you ache, you feel a continuous dull pain in a part of your body. **2** If you are aching for something or aching to do something, you want it very much. **3** (noun) An ache is a continuous dull pain.

achieve, achieves, achieving, achieved (verb) If you achieve something, you successfully do it or cause it to happen.

achievement, achievements (noun) An achievement is something which you succeed in doing, especially after a lot of effort.

acid, acids 1 (noun) An acid is a chemical liquid that turns litmus paper red. Strong acids can damage skin, cloth, and metal. **2** (adjective) Acid tastes are sharp or sour. **acidic** (adjective), **acidity** (noun).

acid rain (noun) Acid rain is rain polluted by acid in the atmosphere which has come from factories.

acknowledge, acknowledges, acknowledging, acknowledged 1 (verb) If you acknowledge a fact or situation, you agree or admit that it is true. **2** If you acknowledge someone, you show that you have seen and recognized them. **acknowledgment** or **acknowledgement** (noun).

acne (pronounced **ak**-nee) (noun) Acne consists of painful, lumpy spots that cover someone's face.

acorn, acorns (noun) An acorn is the fruit of the oak tree, consisting of a pale oval nut in a cup-shaped base.

acoustic (pronounced a-**koo**-stik) **1** (adjective) relating to sound or hearing. **2** An acoustic guitar does not have its sound amplified electronically.

acoustics (noun) The acoustics of a room are its structural features which determine how clearly you can hear sounds made in it.

acquaintance, acquaintances (noun) An acquaintance is someone you know slightly but not well.

acquainted (adjective) If you are acquainted with someone, you know them slightly but not well.

acquire, acquires, acquiring, acquired (verb) If you acquire something, you obtain it.

acquisition, acquisitions (noun) An acquisition is something that you have obtained.

acquit, acquits, acquitting, acquitted (verb) If someone is acquitted of a crime, they have been tried in a court and found not guilty. **acquittal** (noun).

acre, acres (noun) An acre is a unit for measuring areas of land. One acre is equal to 4840 square yards or about 4047 square metres.

acrid (adjective) sharp and bitter, e.g. *an acrid smell.*

acrimony (pronounced **ak**-rim-on-ee) (noun; a formal word) Acrimony is bitterness and anger. **acrimonious** (adjective).

acrobat, acrobats (noun) An acrobat is an entertainer who performs gymnastic tricks. **acrobatic** (adjective), **acrobatics** (plural noun).

acronym, acronyms (noun) An acronym is a word made up of the initial letters of a phrase. An example of an acronym is OPEC, which stands for 'Organization of Petroleum Exporting Countries'.

across 1 (preposition or adverb) going from one side of something to the other. **2** on the other side of a road or river.

acrylic (pronounced a-**kril**-lik) (noun) Acrylic is a type of man-made cloth.

act, acts, acting, acted 1 (verb) If you act, you do something, e.g. *It would be irresponsible not to act swiftly.* **2** If you act in a particular way, you behave in that way. **3** If one thing acts as something else, it has the function or does the job of the second thing, e.g. *She was able to act as an interpreter.* **4** If you act in a play or film, you play a part. **5** (noun) An act is a single thing that someone does, e.g. *It was an act of disloyalty to the King.* **6** An Act of Parliament is a law passed by the government. **7** In a play, ballet, or opera, an act is one of the main parts that it is divided into.

acting (noun) Acting is the profession of performing in plays or films.

action, actions 1 (noun) An action is something you do for a particular purpose, e.g. *He had to take evasive action to avoid being hit.* **2** An action is also a physical movement. **3** In law, an action is a legal proceeding, e.g. *a libel action.*

activate, activates, activating, activated (verb) To activate something means to cause it to start working.

active 1 (adjective) Active people are full of energy and are always busy. **2** If someone is active in an organization or cause, they are involved in it and work hard for it. **3** In grammar, a verb in the active voice is one where the subject does the action, rather than having it done to them. **actively** (adverb).

activist, activists (noun) A political activist is a person who tries to bring about political and social change.

activity, activities 1 (noun) Activity is a situation in which a lot of things are happening at the same time. **2** An activity is something that you do for pleasure, e.g. *sport and leisure activities.*

actor, actors (noun) An actor is a man or woman whose profession is acting.

actress, actresses (noun) An actress is a woman whose profession is acting.

actual (adjective) real or genuine, and not imaginary. **actually** (adverb).

actuary, actuaries (noun) An actuary is a person whose job is to calculate insurance risks.

acumen (noun) Acumen is the ability to make good decisions quickly, e.g. *business acumen.*

acupuncture (noun) Acupuncture is the treatment of illness or pain by sticking small needles into specific places in a person's body.

acute 1 (adjective) severe or intense, e.g. *an acute shortage of accommodation.* **2** very bright and intelligent, e.g. *an acute mind.* **3** An acute angle is less than 90°. **4** In French and some other languages, an acute accent is an upward-sloping line placed over a vowel to indicate a change in pronunciation, as in the word *blasé.*

ad, ads (noun; an informal word) An ad is an advertisement.

AD You use AD in dates to indicate the number of years after the birth of Jesus Christ.

adage, adages (pronounced **ad**-dij) (noun) An adage is a saying or proverb that expresses some general truth about life.

adamant (adjective) If you are adamant, you are determined not to change your mind. **adamantly** (adverb).

adapt, adapts, adapting, adapted 1 (verb) If you adapt to a new situation, you change so that you can deal with it successfully. **2** If you adapt something, you change it so that it is suitable for a new purpose or situation. **adaptable** (adjective), **adaptation** (noun).

adaptor, adaptors; also spelled **adapter** (noun) An adaptor is a type of electric plug which can be used to connect two or more plugs to one socket.

add, adds, adding, added 1 (verb) If you add something to a number of things, you put it with the things. **2** If you add numbers together or add them up, you calculate the total.

adder, adders (noun) An adder is a small poisonous snake with a black zigzag pattern on its back.

addict, addicts (noun) An addict is someone who cannot stop taking harmful drugs. **addicted** (adjective), **addiction** (noun).

addictive (adjective) If a drug is addictive, the people who take it find that they cannot stop taking it.

addition, additions 1 (noun) An addition is something that has been added to something else, e.g. *Carrots are a welcome addition to a horse's diet.* **2** Addition is the process of adding numbers together.

additional (adjective) extra or more, e.g. *They made the decision to take on additional staff.* **additionally** (adverb).

additive, additives (noun) Additives are things that are added to something, usually in order to improve it.

address, addresses, addressing, addressed 1 (noun) Your address is the number of the house where you live, together with the name of the street and the town or village. **2** (verb) If a letter is addressed to you, it has your name and address written on it. **3** (noun) An address is also a speech given to a group of people. **4** (verb) If you address a problem or task, you start to deal with it.

adept (adjective) very skilful or clever at doing something, e.g. *She is adept at motivating others.*

adequate (adjective) enough in amount or good enough for a purpose, e.g. *an adequate diet.* **adequately** (adverb), **adequacy** (noun).

adhere, adheres, adhering, adhered 1 (verb) If one thing adheres to another, it sticks firmly to it. **2** If you adhere to a rule or agreement, you do exactly what it says. **3** If you adhere to an opinion or belief, you firmly hold that opinion or belief. **adherence** (noun).

adherent, adherents (noun) An adherent of a particular belief is someone who holds that belief.

adhesive, adhesives 1 (noun) Adhesive is any substance that is used to stick two things together, for example glue. **2** (adjective) Adhesive substances are sticky and able to stick to things.

adjacent (pronounced ad-**jay**-sent) (adjective; a formal word) If two things are adjacent, they are next to each other, e.g. *a hotel adjacent to the beach.*

adjective, adjectives (noun) An adjective is a word that adds to the description given by a noun. For example, in 'They live in a large white Georgian house', 'large', 'white', and 'Georgian' are all adjectives. **adjectival** (adjective).

adjoining (adjective) If two rooms are next to each other and are connected, they are adjoining.

adjourn, adjourns, adjourning, adjourned 1 (verb) If a meeting or trial is adjourned, it stops for a time, e.g. *The case was adjourned until September.* **2** If people adjourn to another place, they go there together after a meeting, e.g. *We adjourned to the lounge.* **adjournment** (noun).

adjust, adjusts, adjusting, adjusted 1 (verb) If you adjust something, you slightly change its position or alter it in some other way. **2** If you adjust to a new situation, you get used to it, often by slightly changing your attitude. **adjustment** (noun), **adjustable** (adjective).

ad-lib, ad-libs, ad-libbing, ad-libbed 1 (verb) If you ad-lib, you say something that has not been prepared beforehand, e.g. *I ad-lib on radio but use a script on TV.* **2** (noun) An ad-lib is a comment that has not been prepared beforehand.

administer, administers, administering, administered 1 (verb) To administer an organization means to be responsible for managing it. **2** To administer the law or administer justice means to put it into practice and apply it. **3** If medicine is administered to someone, it is given to them.

administration, administrations 1 (noun) Administration is the work of organizing and supervising an organization. **2** Administration is also the process of administering something, e.g. *the administration of criminal justice.* **3** The administration is the group of people that manages an organization or a country. **administrative** (adjective), **administrator** (noun).

admirable (adjective) very good and deserving to be admired. **admirably** (adverb).

admiral, admirals (noun) An admiral is the commander of a navy.

admire, admires, admiring, admired (verb) If you admire someone or something, you like, respect, and approve of them. **admiration** (noun), **admirer** (noun), **admiring** (adjective), **admiringly** (adverb).

admission, admissions 1 (noun) If you are allowed admission to a place, you are allowed to go in. **2** If you make an admission of something bad such as guilt or laziness, you agree, often reluctantly, that it is true.

admit, admits, admitting, admitted 1 (verb) If you admit something, you agree, often reluctantly, that it is true. **2** To admit someone or something to a place means to allow them to enter it. **3** If you are admitted to hospital, you are taken there to stay there until you are better.

admittedly (adverb) People use admittedly to show that what they are saying contrasts with something they have already said, and weakens their argument, e.g. *Admittedly, economists often disagree among each other.*

adolescent, adolescents (noun) An adolescent is a young person who is no longer a child but who is not yet an adult. **adolescence** (noun).

adopt, adopts, adopting, adopt-

ed **1** (verb) If you adopt a child that is not your own, you take him or her into your family as your son or daughter. **2** (a formal use) If you adopt a particular attitude, you start to have it. **adoption** (noun).

adorable (adjective) sweet, pretty, and attractive.

adore, adores, adoring, adored (verb) If you adore someone, you feel deep love and admiration for them. **adoration** (noun).

adorn, adorns, adorning, adorned (verb) To adorn someone or something means to decorate them or make them beautiful, e.g. *The cathedral is adorned with statues.* **adornment** (noun).

adrenalin or **adrenaline** (pronounced a-**dren**-al-in) (noun) Adrenalin is a substance which is produced by your body when you are angry, nervous, or excited. It makes your heart beat faster, and gives you more energy.

adrift 1 (adjective or adverb) If a boat is adrift, it is floating on the water without being controlled. **2** If a plan goes adrift, it goes wrong.

adulation (pronounced ad-yoo-**lay**-shn) (noun) Adulation is excessive admiration and praise for someone. **adulatory** (adjective).

adult, adults (noun) An adult is a mature and fully developed person or animal.

adultery (noun) Adultery is sexual intercourse between a married person and someone who he or she is not married to. **adulterer** (noun), **adulterous** (adjective).

adulthood (noun) Someone's adulthood is the time during their life when they are an adult.

advance, advances, advancing, advanced 1 (verb) To advance means to move forward. **2** (noun) Advance in something is progress in it, e.g. *scientific advance.* **3** (verb) To advance a cause or interest means to help it to be successful. **4** If you advance someone a sum of money, you lend it to them. **5** (noun) An advance is also a sum of money that is lent to someone. **6** (adjective) done or happening before an event, e.g. *He arrived without any advance notice.* **7** (phrase) If you do something **in advance,** you do it before something else happens, e.g. *We booked up the room well in advance.*

advantage, advantages 1 (noun) An advantage is a benefit or something that puts you in a better position. **2** (phrase) If you **take advantage of** someone, you treat them unfairly for your own benefit. **3** If you **take advantage of** something, you make use of it.

advantageous (adjective) likely to be useful or to benefit you in some way, e.g. *an advantageous marriage.*

advent 1 (noun) The advent of something is its start or its coming into existence, e.g. *The advent of the submarine changed naval warfare.* **2** Advent is the season just before Christmas in the Christian calendar.

adventure, adventures (noun) An adventure is a series of events that are unusual, exciting, and often dangerous.

adventurer, adventurers (noun) An adventurer is someone who enjoys doing dangerous and exciting things.

adventurous (adjective) willing to take risks and do new and exciting things. **adventurously** (adverb).

adverb, adverbs (noun) An adverb is a word that adds information about a verb or a following adjective or other adverb, for example saying how, when, or where something is done. 'Slowly', 'now', and 'here' are all adverbs. **adverbial** (adjective).

adversary, adversaries (pronounced **ad**-ver-sar-ee) (noun) Your adversary is someone who is your enemy or who opposes what you are doing.

adverse (adjective) unfavourable to you or opposite to what you want or need, e.g. *adverse weather conditions.* **adversely** (adverb).

adversity, adversities (noun) Adversity is a time of danger or difficulty.

advert, adverts (noun; an informal word) An advert is an advertisement.

advertise, advertises, advertising, advertised 1 (verb) If you advertise something, you tell people about it in a newspaper or poster, or on TV. **2** To advertise means to make an announcement in a newspaper or poster, or on TV. **advertiser** (noun), **advertising** (noun).

advertisement, advertisements (pronounced ad-**ver**-tiss-ment) (noun) An advertisement is an announcement about something in a newspaper or poster, or on TV, e.g. *an advertisement for a new magazine.*

advice (noun) Advice is an opinion or suggestion from someone about what you should do.

advisable (adjective) sensible and likely to achieve the result you want, e.g. *It is advisable to buy the visa before travelling.* **advisably** (adverb), **advisability** (noun).

advise, advises, advising, advised 1 (verb) If you advise someone to do something, you tell them that you think they should do it. **2** (a formal use) If you advise someone of something, you inform them of it. **adviser** (noun), **advisory** (adjective).

advocate, advocates, advocating, advocated 1 (verb) If you advocate a course of action or plan, you support it publicly. **2** (noun) An advocate of something is someone who supports it publicly. **3** (a formal use) An advocate is a lawyer who represents clients in court. **advocacy** (noun).

aerial, aerials (pronounced **air**-ee-al) **1** (adjective) Aerial means happening in the air or above the ground, e.g. *aerial combat.* **2** (noun) An aerial is a piece of wire for receiving television or radio signals.

aerobics (noun) Aerobics is a type of fast physical exercise, which increases the oxygen in your blood and strengthens your heart and lungs. **aerobic** (adjective).

aerodynamic (adjective) having a streamlined shape that

moves easily through the air.

aeroplane, aeroplanes (noun) An aeroplane is a vehicle with wings and engines that enable it to fly.

aerosol, aerosols (noun) An aerosol is a small metal container in which liquid is kept under pressure so that it can be forced out as a spray.

aerospace (adjective) involved in making and designing aeroplanes, rockets, and spacecraft.

aesthetic or **esthetic** (pronounced eess-**thet**-ik) (adjective; a formal word) relating to the appreciation of beauty or art. **aesthetically** (adverb), **aesthetics** (noun).

afar (adjective; a literary word) From afar means from a long way away.

affable (adjective) pleasant and easy to talk to. **affably** (adverb), **affability** (noun).

affair, affairs 1 (noun) An affair is an event or series of events, e.g. *The function was a rather drunken affair.* **2** (plural noun) Your affairs are your private and personal life, e.g. *Why had he meddled in her affairs?* **3** (noun) To have an affair means to have a secret sexual or romantic relationship, especially when one of the people is married.

affect, affects, affecting, affected 1 (verb) If something affects you, it influences you or changes you in some way. **2** (a formal use) If you affect a particular way of behaving, you behave in that way, e.g. *He affected a Cockney accent.*

affectation, affectations (noun) An affectation is behaviour that is not genuine but is put on to impress people.

affection, affections 1 (noun) Affection is a feeling of love and fondness for someone. **2** (plural noun) Your affections are feelings of love that you have for someone.

affectionate (adjective) full of love, care, and fondness for someone, e.g. *an affectionate embrace.* **affectionately** (adverb).

affiliate, affiliates, affiliating, affiliated (verb) If a group affiliates itself to another, larger group, it forms a close association with it, e.g. *There are over 70 unions affiliated to the TUC.* **affiliation** (noun).

affinity, affinities (noun) An affinity is a close similarity or understanding between two things, groups, or people, e.g. *There is are affinities between the two poets.*

affirm, affirms, affirming, affirmed (verb) If you affirm an idea or belief, you clearly indicate your support for it, e.g. *We affirm our commitment to broadcast quality programmes.* **affirmation** (noun).

affirmative (adjective) An affirmative word or gesture is one that means yes.

afflict, afflicts, afflicting, afflicted (verb) If pain, illness, or sorrow afflicts someone, it causes them to suffer, e.g. *She was afflicted by depression.* **affliction** (noun).

affluent (adjective) having a lot of money and possessions. **affluence** (noun).

afford, affords, affording, afforded 1 (verb) If you can afford to do something, you have enough money to do it. **2** If you afford the time or energy to do something, you find the time or energy to do it.

affront, affronts, affronting, affronted 1 (verb) If you are affronted by something, you are insulted and angered by it. **2** (noun) An affront is something that you feel is an insult, e.g. *Our prisons are an affront to civilized society.*

afield (adverb) Far afield means a long way away, e.g. *competitors from as far afield as Russia and China.*

afloat 1 (adverb or adjective) floating on water. **2** successful and not likely to fail, e.g. *Companies are struggling hard to stay afloat.*

afoot (adjective or adverb) happening or being planned, especially secretly, e.g. *Plans are afoot to build a new museum.*

afraid 1 (adjective) If you are afraid, you are very frightened. **2** If you are afraid that something might happen, you are worried that it might happen.

afresh (adverb) again and in a new way, e.g. *The couple moved abroad to start life afresh.*

Africa (noun) Africa is the second largest continent. It is almost surrounded by sea, with the Atlantic on its west side, the Mediterranean to the north and the Indian Ocean and the Red Sea to the east.

African, Africans 1 (adjective) belonging or relating to Africa. **2** (noun) An African is someone, especially a black person, who comes from Africa.

African-American, African-Americans (noun) An African-American is an American whose ancestors came from Africa.

Afrikaans (pronounced af-rik-**ahns**) (noun) Afrikaans is a language spoken in South Africa, based on 17th century Dutch.

Afrikaner, Afrikaners (noun) An Afrikaner is a white South African of Dutch descent.

aft (adverb or adjective) towards the back of a ship or boat.

after 1 (preposition or adverb) later than a particular time, date, or event. **2** behind and following someone or something, e.g. *They ran after her.*

afterlife (noun) The afterlife is a life that some people believe begins when you die.

aftermath (noun) The aftermath of a disaster is the situation that comes after it.

afternoon, afternoons (noun) The afternoon is the part of the day between noon and about six o'clock.

aftershave (noun) Aftershave is a pleasant-smelling liquid that men put on their faces after shaving.

afterthought, afterthoughts (noun) An afterthought is something that you do or say as an addition to something else that you have already done or said.

afterwards (adverb) after an event, date, or time.

again 1 (adverb) happening one more time, e.g. *He looked forward to becoming a father again.* **2** returning to the same state or place as before, e.g.

Her back began to hurt her again.

against 1 (preposition) touching and leaning on, e.g. *He leaned against the wall.* **2** in opposition to, e.g. *a World Cup match against Holland.* **3** in order to prevent, e.g. *precautions against fire.* **4** in comparison with, e.g. *The pound is now at its lowest rate against the dollar.*

age, ages, ageing, aged 1 (noun) The age of something or someone is the number of years that they have lived or existed. **2** Age is the quality of being old, e.g. *a wine capable of improving with age.* **3** (verb) To age means to grow old or to appear older. **4** (noun) An age is a particular period in history, e.g. *the Iron Age.* **5** (plural noun; an informal use) Ages means a very long time, e.g. *He's been talking for ages.*

aged 1 (rhymes with **raged**) having a particular age, e.g. *people aged 16 to 24.* **2** (pronounced **ay**-dgid) very old, e.g. *an aged invalid.*

agency, agencies (noun) An agency is an organization or business which provides certain services on behalf of other businesses, e.g. *a detective agency.*

agenda, agendas (noun) An agenda is a list of items to be discussed at a meeting.

agent, agents 1 (noun) An agent is someone who arranges work or business for other people, especially actors or singers. **2** An agent is also someone who works for their country's secret service.

aggravate, aggravates, aggravating, aggravated 1 (verb) To aggravate a bad situation means to make it worse. **2** (an informal use) If someone or something aggravates you, they make you annoyed. **aggravating** (adjective), **aggravation** (noun).

aggregate, aggregates (noun) An aggregate is a total that is made up of several smaller amounts.

aggression (noun) Aggression is violent and hostile behaviour.

aggressive (adjective) full of anger, hostility, and violence. **aggressively** (adverb), **aggressiveness** (noun).

aggressor, aggressors (noun) An aggressor is a person or country that starts a fight or a war.

aggrieved (adjective) upset and angry about the way you have been treated.

aghast (pronounced a-**gast**) (adjective) shocked and horrified.

agile 1 (adjective) able to move quickly and easily, e.g. *He is as agile as a cat.* **2** quick and intelligent, e.g. *an agile mind.* **agilely** (adverb), **agility** (noun).

agitate, agitates, agitating, agitated 1 (verb) If you agitate for something, you campaign energetically to get it. **2** If something agitates you, it worries you. **agitation** (noun), **agitator** (noun).

agnostic, agnostics (noun or adjective) Someone who is an agnostic believes that it is impossible to know definitely whether God exists or not. **agnosticism** (noun).

ago (adverb) in the past, e.g. *She bought her flat three years* *ago.*

agog (adjective) excited and eager to know more about an event or situation, e.g. *She was agog to hear his news.*

agonizing or **agonising** (adjective) extremely painful, either physically or mentally, e.g. *an agonizing decision.*

agony (noun) very great physical or mental pain.

agrarian (pronounced ag-**rare**-ee-an) (adjective; a formal word) relating to farming and agriculture, e.g. *agrarian economies.*

agree, agrees, agreeing, agreed 1 (verb) If you agree with someone, you have the same opinion as them. **2** If you agree to do something, you say that you will do it. **3** If two stories or totals agree, they are the same. **4** Food that doesn't agree with you makes you ill.

agreeable 1 (adjective) pleasant or enjoyable, e.g. *Two nearby hotels offer agreeable menus for dinner.* **2** If you are agreeable to something, you are willing to allow it or to do it, e.g. *She was agreeable to the project.* **agreeably** (adverb).

agreement, agreements 1 (noun) An agreement is a joint decision that has been reached by two or more people. **2** Two people who are in agreement have the same opinion about something.

agriculture (noun) Agriculture means the same as farming. **agricultural** (adjective).

aground (adverb) If a boat runs aground, it becomes stuck in a shallow part of the sea, a lake, or a river.

ahead 1 (adverb) in front, e.g. *He looked ahead.* **2** more advanced than someone or something else, e.g. *We are five years ahead of the competition.* **3** in the future, e.g. *I haven't had time to think far ahead.*

aid, aids, aiding, aided 1 (noun) Aid is money, equipment, or services that are provided for people in need, e.g. *food and medical aid.* **2** An aid is something that makes a task easier, e.g. *teaching aids.* **3** (verb) If you aid a person or an organization, you help or support them.

aide, aides (noun) An aide is an assistant to an important person, especially in the government or the army, e.g. *the Prime Minister's closest aides.*

AIDS (noun) AIDS is a disease which destroys the body's natural system of immunity to diseases. AIDS is an abbreviation for 'acquired immune deficiency syndrome'.

ailing 1 (adjective) sick or ill, and not getting better. **2** getting into difficulties, especially financially, e.g. *an ailing company.*

ailment, ailments (noun) An ailment is a minor illness.

aim, aims, aiming, aimed 1 (verb) If you aim an object or weapon at someone or something, you point it at them. **2** If you aim to do something, you are planning or hoping to do it. **3** (noun) Your aim is what you intend to achieve. **4** If you take aim, you point an object or weapon at someone or something.

aimless (adjective) having no clear purpose or plan. **aimless-**

ly (adverb), **aimlessness** (noun).

air, airs, airing, aired 1 (noun) Air is the mixture of oxygen and other gases which we breathe and which forms the earth's atmosphere. **2** An air that someone or something has is the impression that they give, e.g. *an air of defiance.* **3** Air is used to refer to travel in aircraft, e.g. *I have to travel by air a great deal.* **4** (verb) If you air your opinions, you talk about them to other people.

airborne (adjective) in the air and flying.

air-conditioning (noun) Air-conditioning is a system of providing cool, dry, clean air in buildings. **air-conditioned** (adjective).

aircraft (noun) An aircraft is any vehicle which can fly.

airfield, airfields (noun) An airfield is an open area of ground with runways where small aircraft take off and land.

air force, air forces (noun) An air force is the part of a country's armed services that fights using aircraft.

air gun, air guns (noun) An air gun is a gun which fires pellets by means of air pressure.

air hostess, air hostesses (noun) An air hostess is a woman whose job is to look after passengers on an aircraft.

airless (adjective) having no wind, breeze, or fresh air.

airlift, airlifts (noun) An airlift is an operation to move people or goods by air, especially in an emergency.

airline, airlines (noun) An airline is a company which provides air travel.

air mail (noun) Air mail is the system of sending letters and parcels by air.

airman, airmen (noun) An airman is a man who serves in his country's air force.

airport, airports (noun) An airport is a place where people go to catch planes.

air raid, air raids (noun) An air raid is an attack by enemy aircraft, in which bombs are dropped.

airship, airships (noun) An airship was a large, light aircraft, consisting of a rigid balloon filled with gas and powered by an engine, with a passenger compartment underneath.

airstrip, airstrips (noun) An airstrip is a stretch of land that has been cleared for aircraft to take off and land.

airtight (adjective) not letting air in or out.

airy, airier, airiest (adjective) full of fresh air and light. **airily** (adverb).

aisle, aisles (rhymes with **mile**) (noun) An aisle is a long narrow gap that people can walk along between rows of seats or shelves.

ajar (adjective) A door or window that is ajar is slightly open.

akin (adjective; a formal word) similar, e.g. *The wine was more akin to a dry French white.*

alabaster (noun) Alabaster is a type of smooth stone used for making ornaments.

alacrity (noun; a formal word) Alacrity is eager willingness, e.g. *He seized this offer with alacrity.*

alarm, alarms, alarming, alarmed 1 (noun) Alarm is a feeling of fear, anxiety, and worry, e.g. *The cat sprang back in alarm.* **2** An alarm is an automatic device used to warn people of something, e.g. *a car alarm.* **3** (verb) If something alarms you, it makes you worried and anxious. **alarming** (adjective).

alas (adverb) unfortunately or regrettably, e.g. *but, alas, it would not be true.*

Albanian, Albanians 1 (adjective) belonging or relating to Albania. **2** (noun) An Albanian is someone who comes from Albania. **3** Albanian is the main language spoken in Albania.

albatross, albatrosses (noun) An albatross is a large white sea bird.

albeit (pronounced awl-**bee**-it) (conjunction; a formal word) although, e.g. *The society continued to flourish, albeit in secret.*

albino, albinos (noun) An albino is a person or animal with very white skin, white hair, and pink eyes.

album, albums 1 (noun) An album is a record with about 25 minutes of music or speech on each side. **2** An album is also a book in which you keep a collection of things such as photographs or stamps.

alchemy (pronounced **al**-kem-ee) (noun) Alchemy was a medieval science that attempted to change ordinary metals into gold. **alchemist** (noun).

alcohol (noun) Alcohol is any drink that can make people drunk; also the colourless flammable liquid found in these drinks, produced by fermenting sugar.

alcoholic, alcoholics 1 (adjective) An alcoholic drink contains alcohol. **2** (noun) An alcoholic is someone who is addicted to alcohol. **alcoholism** (noun).

alcove, alcoves (noun) An alcove is an area of a room which is set back slightly from the main part.

ale (noun) Ale is a type of beer.

alert, alerts, alerting, alerted 1 (adjective) paying full attention to what is happening, e.g. *The criminal was spotted by an alert member of the public.* **2** (noun) An alert is a situation in which people prepare themselves for danger, e.g. *The troops were on a war alert.* **3** (verb) If you alert someone to a problem or danger, you warn them of it. **alertness** (noun).

algae (pronounced **al**-jee) (plural noun) Algae are plants that grow in water or on damp surfaces. They have no roots, stems, or leaves.

algebra (noun) Algebra is a branch of mathematics in which symbols and letters are used instead of numbers, in order to express general relationships between quantities. **algebraic** (adjective).

Algerian, Algerians 1 (adjective) belonging or relating to Algeria. **2** (noun) An Algerian is someone who comes from Algeria.

alias, aliases (pronounced **ay**-lee-ass) (noun) An alias is a false name used by a criminal, e.g. *Bryan Procter, alias Barry Cornwall.*

alibi, alibis (pronounced **al**-li-bye) (noun) An alibi is evidence proving that you were somewhere else when a crime was committed.

alien, aliens (pronounced **ay**-lee-an) **1** (adjective) not normal, and therefore strange and slightly frightening, e.g. *a totally alien culture.* **2** If something is alien to your beliefs or behaviour, it is not the way you normally think or behave. **3** (noun) An alien is someone who is not a citizen of the country in which he or she lives. **4** In science fiction, an alien is a creature from outer space.

alienate, alienates, alienating, alienated (verb) If you alienate someone, you do something that makes them become unsympathetic to you, e.g. *The Council's approach alienated many local residents.* **alienation** (noun).

alight, alights, alighting, alighted 1 (adjective) Something that is alight is burning. **2** (verb) If a bird or insect alights somewhere, it lands there. **3** (a formal use) When passengers alight from a vehicle, they get out of it at the end of a journey.

align, aligns, aligning, aligned (pronounced a-**line**) **1** (verb) If you align yourself with a particular group, you support them politically. **2** If you align things, you place them in a straight line, e.g. *The spirit level makes sure the camera is aligned correctly.* **alignment** (noun).

alike 1 (adjective) Things that are alike are similar in some way. **2** (adverb) If people or things are treated alike, they are treated in a similar way.

alimony (pronounced **al**-li-mon-ee) (noun) Alimony is money that someone has to pay regularly to their wife or husband after they are divorced.

alive 1 (adjective) living. **2** lively and active, and full of interest.

alkali, alkalis (pronounced **al**-kal-eye) (noun) An alkali is a chemical substance that turns litmus paper blue. **alkaline** (adjective), **alkalinity** (noun).

all 1 (adjective, pronoun, or adverb) used when referring to the whole of something, e.g. *Why did he have to say all that?.. She managed to finish it all.* **2** (adverb) All is also used when saying that the two sides in a game or contest have the same score, e.g. *The final score was six points all.*

Allah (proper noun) Allah is the Muslim name for God.

allay, allays, allaying, allayed (verb) To allay someone's fears or suspicions means to cause them to be felt less strongly.

allege, alleges, alleging, alleged (pronounced a-**lej**) (verb) If you allege that something is true, you say it is true but do not provide any proof, e.g. *It is alleged that she died as a result of neglect.* **allegation** (noun), **alleged** (adjective).

allegiance, allegiances (pronounced al-**lee**-jenss) (noun) Allegiance is loyal support for a person or organization.

allergy, allergies (pronounced **al**-er-jee) (noun) An allergy is an abnormal physical sensitivity that someone has to something, so that they become ill when they eat it or are exposed to it, e.g. *an allergy to cows' milk.*

alleviate, alleviates, alleviating, alleviated (verb) To alleviate pain or a problem means to make it less severe, e.g. *measures to alleviate poverty.* **alleviation** (noun).

alley, alleys (noun) An alley is a narrow passage between buildings.

alliance, alliances (noun) An alliance is a group of people, organizations, or countries working together for similar aims.

alligator, alligators (noun) An alligator is a large animal, similar to a crocodile.

allocate, allocates, allocating, allocated (verb) If you allocate something, you decide that it should be given to a person or place, or used for a particular purpose, e.g. *funds allocated for nursery education.* **allocation** (noun).

allot, allots, allotting, allotted (verb) If something is allotted to you, it is given to you as your share, e.g. *Space was allotted for visitors' cars.*

allotment, allotments 1 (noun) An allotment is a piece of land which people can rent to grow vegetables on. **2** An allotment of something is a share of it.

allow, allows, allowing, allowed 1 (verb) If someone in authority allows you to do something, they say that it is all right for you to do it. **2** If you allow something to happen, you let it happen. **3** If you allow a period of time or an amount of something, you set it aside for a particular purpose, e.g. *Allow four hours for the paint to dry.* **allowable** (adjective).

allowance, allowances 1 (noun) An allowance is money that is given regularly to someone for a particular purpose, e.g. *a petrol allowance.* **2** (phrase) If you **make allowances** for something, you take it into account in your plans or actions, e.g. *The school made allowances for Muslim cultural customs.*

alloy, alloys (noun) An alloy is a mixture of two or more metals, e.g. *nickel alloys.*

all right or **alright** Some people say that **all right** is the only correct spelling. **1** (adjective) If something is all right, it is satisfactory or acceptable. **2** If someone is all right, they are safe and not harmed. **3** You say 'all right' to agree to something.

allude, alludes, alluding, alluded (verb) If you allude to something, you refer to it in an indirect way.

allure (noun) The allure of something is a pleasing or exciting quality that makes it attractive, e.g. *the allure of foreign travel.* **alluring** (adjective).

allusion, allusions (noun) An allusion to something is an indirect reference to it or comment about it, e.g. *English literature is full of classical allusions.*

ally, allies, allying, allied 1

(noun) An ally is a person, organization, or country that helps and supports another. **2** (verb) If you ally yourself with someone, you agree to help and support each other.

almanac, almanacs (noun) An almanac is a book published every year giving information about a particular subject.

almighty 1 (adjective) very great or serious, e.g. *I've just had an almighty row with the chairman.* **2** (proper noun) The Almighty is another name for God.

almond, almonds (noun) An almond is a pale brown oval nut.

almost (adverb) very nearly, but not completely or exactly, e.g. *Over the past decade their wages have almost doubled.*

alms (plural noun; an old-fashioned word) Alms are gifts of money, food, or clothing to poor people.

aloft (adverb) up in the air or in a high position, e.g. *He held aloft the trophy.*

alone (adjective or adverb) not with other people or things, e.g. *He just wanted to be alone... She brought up three children alone.*

along 1 (preposition) moving, happening, or existing continuously from one end to the other of something, or at various points beside it, e.g. *Put rivets along the top edge.* **2** (adverb) moving forward or making progress, e.g. *We marched along.* **3** with someone, e.g. *Why could she not take her along?* **4** (phrase) **All along** means from the beginning of a period of time right up to now, e.g. *You've known that all along.*

alongside 1 (preposition or adverb) next to something, e.g. *They had a house in the park alongside the river.* **2** (preposition) If you work alongside other people, you are working in the same place and cooperating with them, e.g. *He was thrilled to work alongside Robert De Niro.*

aloof (adjective) separate from someone or something, distant, and not involved with them.

aloud (adverb) When you read or speak aloud, you speak loudly enough for other people to hear you.

alphabet, alphabets (noun) An alphabet is a set of letters in a fixed order that is used in writing a language. **alphabetical** (adjective), **alphabetically** (adverb).

alpine (adjective) existing in or relating to high mountains, e.g. *alpine flowers.*

already (adverb) having happened before the present time or earlier than expected, e.g. *She has already gone to bed.*

alright another spelling of **all right.**

Alsatian, Alsatians (pronounced al-**say**-shn) (noun) An Alsatian is a large wolflike dog. They are used as police dogs.

also (adverb) in addition to an action, situation, person, or thing that has just been mentioned.

altar, altars (noun) An altar is a holy table in a church or temple.

alter, alters, altering, altered (verb) If something alters or if you alter it, it changes. **alteration** (noun).

altercation, altercations (noun; a formal word) An altercation is a noisy argument or disagreement.

alternate, alternates, alternating, alternated 1 (verb) If one thing alternates with another, the two things regularly occur one after the other. **2** (adjective) If something happens on alternate days, it happens on the first day but not the second, and happens again on the third day but not the fourth, and so on, e.g. *The two teams use the pitch on alternate Saturdays.* **alternately** (adverb), **alternation** (noun).

alternative, alternatives 1 (noun) An alternative is something that you can do or have instead of something else, e.g. *alternatives to prison such as community service.* **2** (adjective) Alternative plans, arrangements, or processes can happen or be done instead of what is already happening or being done. **alternatively** (adverb).

although (conjunction) in spite of the fact that, e.g. *He wasn't well known in America, although he did make a film there.*

altitude, altitudes (noun) The altitude of something is its height above sea level, e.g. *The mountain range reaches an altitude of 1330 metres.*

altogether 1 (adverb) completely or entirely, e.g. *She wasn't altogether sorry to be leaving.* **2** in total; used of amounts, e.g. *I get paid £800 a month altogether.*

aluminium (noun) Aluminium is a silvery-white lightweight metal.

always (adverb) all the time or for ever, e.g. *She's always moaning.*

am the first person singular, present tense of **be**.

a.m. used to specify times between 12 midnight and 12 noon, e.g. *I get up at 6 a.m.* It is an abbreviation for the Latin phrase 'ante meridiem', which means 'before noon'.

amalgamate, amalgamates, amalgamating, amalgamated (verb) If two organizations amalgamate, they join together to form one new organization. **amalgamation** (noun).

amass, amasses, amassing, amassed (verb) If you amass something such as money, information, or goods, you collect large quantities of it, e.g. *He amassed a huge fortune.*

amateur, amateurs (noun) An amateur is someone who does something as a hobby rather than as a job.

amateurish (adjective) not skilfully made or done. **amateurishly** (adverb).

amaze, amazes, amazing, amazed (verb) If something amazes you, it surprises you very much. **amazement** (noun).

amazing (adjective) very surprising, remarkable, or difficult to believe. **amazingly** (adverb).

ambassador, ambassadors (noun) An ambassador is a person sent to a foreign country as the representative of his or her own government.

amber 1 (noun) Amber is a

hard, yellowish-brown fossilized resin. It is used for making jewellery and ornaments. **2** (noun or adjective) orange-brown.

ambidextrous (adjective) Someone who is ambidextrous is able to use both hands equally skilfully.

ambience (noun; a formal word) The ambience of a place is its atmosphere.

ambiguous (adjective) A word or phrase that is ambiguous has more than one meaning. **ambiguously** (adverb), **ambiguity** (noun).

ambition, ambitions 1 (noun) If you have an ambition to achieve something, you want very much to achieve it. **2** Ambition is a great desire for success, power, and wealth, e.g. *He's talented and full of ambition.*

ambitious 1 (adjective) Someone who is ambitious has a strong desire for success, power, and wealth. **2** An ambitious plan or project is on a large scale and requires a lot of effort and work, e.g. *an ambitious rebuilding schedule.*

ambivalent (adjective) having or showing two conflicting attitudes or emotions. **ambivalence** (noun).

amble, ambles, ambling, ambled (verb) If you amble, you walk slowly and in a relaxed and leisurely manner.

ambulance, ambulances (noun) An ambulance is a vehicle for taking sick and injured people to hospital.

ambush, ambushes, ambushing, ambushed 1 (verb) To ambush someone means to attack them after hiding and lying in wait for them. **2** (noun) An ambush is an attack on someone after hiding and lying in wait for them.

amen (interjection) Amen is said by Christians at the end of a prayer.

amenable (pronounced am-**mee**-na-bl) (adjective) willing to listen to comments and suggestions, or to cooperate with someone, e.g. *Both brothers were amenable to the arrangement.* **amenably** (adverb), **amenability** (noun).

amend, amends, amending, amended 1 (verb) To amend something that has been written or said means to alter it slightly, e.g. *Our constitution had to be amended.* **2** (plural noun) If you make amends for something bad that you have done, you say you are sorry and try to make up for it in some way. **amendment** (noun).

amenity, amenities (pronounced am-**mee**-nit-ee) (noun) Amenities are things that are available for the public to use, such as sports facilities, cinemas, or shopping centres.

America (noun) America refers to the United States, or to the whole of North, South, and Central America.

American, Americans 1 (adjective) belonging or relating to the United States, or to the whole of North, South, and Central America. **2** (noun) An American is someone who comes from the United States.

amethyst, amethysts (noun) An amethyst is a type of purple semiprecious stone.

amiable (adjective) pleasant, friendly, and kind, e.g. *The hotel staff were very amiable.* **amiably** (adverb), **amiability** (noun).

amicable (adjective) fairly friendly. **amicably** (adverb).

amid or **amidst** (preposition; a formal word) surrounded by, e.g. *Pine trees were scattered amid the grass.*

amiss (adjective) If something is amiss, there is something wrong.

ammonia (noun) Ammonia is a colourless, strong-smelling gas or liquid. It is used in household cleaning materials.

ammunition (noun) Ammunition is anything that can be fired from a gun or other weapon, for example bullets, rockets, and shells.

amnesia (noun) Amnesia is loss of memory.

amnesty (noun) An amnesty is an official pardon for political or other prisoners.

amoeba, amoebas or **amoebae** (pronounced am-**mee**-ba); also spelled **ameba** (noun) Amoebas are the smallest kind of living creature. They consist of one cell, which reproduces by dividing into two.

amok (pronounced am-**muk**) (phrase) If a person or animal **runs amok,** they behave in a violent and uncontrolled way.

among or **amongst 1** (preposition) surrounded by, e.g. *The bike lay among piles of chains and pedals.* **2** in the company of, e.g. *He was among friends.* **3** between more than two, e.g. *The money will be divided among seven charities.*

amoral (adjective) Someone who is amoral has no moral standards by which to live or on which to base their behaviour.

amorous (adjective) passionately affectionate, e.g. *He was always sweet, welcoming, and amorous.* **amorously** (adverb), **amorousness** (noun).

amount, amounts, amounting, amounted 1 (noun) An amount of something is how much there is of it. **2** (verb) If something amounts to a particular total, all the parts of it add up to that total, e.g. *His expenses amounted to £14,000.*

amp, amps (noun) An amp is the same as an ampere.

ampere, amperes (pronounced **am**-pair) (noun) The ampere is a unit which is used for measuring electric current.

amphetamine, amphetamines (noun) Amphetamine is a drug that increases people's energy and makes them excited. It can have dangerous and unpleasant side effects.

amphibian, amphibians (noun) An amphibian is a creature that lives partly on land and partly in water. Frogs, toads, and newts are amphibians.

amphibious (adjective) An amphibious animal, such as a frog, lives partly on land and partly in the water.

amphitheatre, amphitheatres (noun) An amphitheatre is a large, semicircular open area with sloping sides covered with rows of seats.

ample (adjective) If there is an ample amount of something, there is more than enough of it. **amply** (adverb).

amplifier, amplifiers (noun) An

amplifier is a piece of equipment in a radio or stereo system which causes sounds or signals to become louder.

amplify, amplifies, amplifying, amplified (verb) If you amplify a sound, you make it louder. **amplification** (noun).

amputate, amputates, amputating, amputated (verb) To amputate an arm or a leg means to cut it off as a surgical operation. **amputation** (noun).

amuse, amuses, amusing, amused **1** (verb) If something amuses you, you think it is funny. **2** If you amuse yourself, you find things to do which stop you from being bored. **amused** (adjective), **amusing** (adjective).

amusement, amusements **1** (noun) Amusement is the state of thinking that something is funny. **2** Amusement is also the pleasure you get from being entertained or from doing something interesting. **3** Amusements are ways of passing the time pleasantly.

an (adjective) 'An' is used instead of 'a' in front of words that begin with a vowel sound.

anachronism, anachronisms (pronounced an-**ak**-kron-izm) (noun) An anachronism is something that belongs or seems to belong to another time. **anachronistic** (adjective).

anaemia (pronounced a-**nee**-mee-a) (noun) Anaemia is a medical condition resulting from too few red cells in a person's blood. People with anaemia look pale and feel very tired. **anaemic** (adjective).

anaesthetic, anaesthetics (pronounced an-niss-**thet**-ik) (noun) An anaesthetic is a substance that stops you feeling pain. A general anaesthetic stops you from feeling pain in the whole of your body by putting you to sleep, and a local anaesthetic makes just one part of your body go numb.

anaesthetist, anaesthetists (noun) An anaesthetist is a doctor who is specially trained to give anaesthetics.

anagram, anagrams (noun) An anagram is a word or phrase formed by reordering the letters of another word or phrase. For example, 'triangle' is an anagram of 'integral'.

anal (pronounced **ay**-nl) (adjective) relating to the anus.

analgesic, analgesics (pronounced an-al-**jee**-sik) (noun) An analgesic is a substance that relieves pain.

analogy, analogies (pronounced an-**al**-o-jee) (noun) An analogy is a comparison showing that two things are similar in some ways. **analogous** (adjective).

analyse, analyses, analysing, analysed (verb) To analyse something means to investigate it carefully in order to understand it or find out what it consists of.

analysis, analyses (noun) Analysis is the process of investigating something in order to understand it or find out what it consists of, e.g. *statistical analysis... a full analysis of the problem.*

analyst, analysts (noun) An analyst is a person whose job is to analyse things to find out about them.

analytic or **analytical** (adjective) using logical reasoning, e.g. *Planning in detail requires an acute analytical mind.* **analytically** (adverb).

anarchy (pronounced **an**-nar-kee) (noun) Anarchy is a situation where nobody obeys laws or rules.

anatomy, anatomies 1 (noun) Anatomy is the study of the structure of the human body or of the bodies of animals. **2** An animal's anatomy is the structure of its body. **anatomical** (adjective), **anatomically** (adverb).

ancestor, ancestors (noun) Your ancestors are the members of your family who lived many years ago and from whom you are descended. **ancestral** (adjective).

ancestry, ancestries (noun) Your ancestry consists of the people from whom you are descended, e.g. *a French citizen of Greek ancestry.*

anchor, anchors, anchoring, anchored 1 (noun) An anchor is a heavy, hooked object that is dropped from a boat into the water at the end of a chain, to keep the boat in one place. **2** (verb) To anchor a boat or another object means to stop it from moving by dropping an anchor or attaching it to something solid.

anchorage, anchorages (noun) An anchorage is a place where a boat or ship can safely anchor.

anchovy, anchovies (noun) An anchovy is a type of small edible fish with a very strong salty taste.

ancient (pronounced **ayn**-shent) **1** (adjective) existing or happening in the distant past, e.g. *ancient Greece.* **2** very old or having a very long history, e.g. *an ancient monastery.*

ancillary (pronounced an-**sil**-lar-ee) (adjective) The ancillary workers in an institution are the people such as cooks and cleaners, whose work supports the main work of the institution.

and (conjunction) You use 'and' to link two or more words or phrases together.

androgynous (pronounced an-**droj**-in-uss) (adjective; a formal word) having both male and female characteristics.

anecdote, anecdotes (noun) An anecdote is a short, entertaining story. **anecdotal** (adjective).

anemone, anemones (pronounced an-**em**-on-ee) (noun) An anemone is a plant with red, purple, or white flowers.

anew (adverb) If you do something anew, you do it again, e.g. *They left their life in Britain to start anew in France.*

angel, angels (noun) Angels are spiritual beings that some people believe live in heaven and act as messengers for God. **angelic** (adjective).

anger, angers, angering, angered 1 (noun) Anger is the strong feeling that you get when you feel that someone has behaved in an unfair, cruel, or insulting way. **2** (verb) If something angers you, it makes you feel angry.

angina (pronounced an-**jy**-na) (noun) Angina is a brief but very severe heart pain, caused by lack of blood supply to the heart.

angle, angles 1 (noun) An angle is the distance between two lines at the point where they join together. Angles are measured in degrees. **2** An angle is also the direction from which you look at something, e.g. *He had painted the vase from all angles.* **3** An angle on something is a particular way of considering it, e.g. *the story's feminist angle.*

angler, anglers (noun) An angler is someone who fishes with a fishing rod as a hobby. **angling** (noun).

Anglican, Anglicans (noun or adjective) An Anglican is a member of one of the churches belonging to the Anglican Communion, a group of Protestant churches which includes the Church of England.

Angolan, Angolans (pronounced ang-**goh**-ln) **1** (adjective) belonging or relating to Angola. **2** (noun) An Angolan is someone who comes from Angola.

angry, angrier, angriest (adjective) very cross or annoyed. **angrily** (adverb).

anguish (noun) Anguish is extreme mental or physical suffering. **anguished** (adjective).

angular (adjective) Angular things have straight lines and sharp points, e.g. *He has an angular face and pointed chin.*

animal, animals (noun) An animal is any living being except a plant, or any mammal except a human being.

animate, animates, animating, animated (verb) To animate something means to make it lively and interesting.

animated (adjective) lively and interesting, e.g. *an animated conversation.*

animation 1 (noun) Animation is a method of film-making in which a series of drawings are photographed. When the film is projected, the characters in the drawings appear to move. **2** Someone who has animation shows liveliness in the way they speak and act, e.g. *The crowd showed no sign of animation.* **animator** (noun).

animosity, animosities (noun) Animosity is a feeling of strong dislike and anger towards someone.

ankle, ankles (noun) Your ankle is the joint which connects your foot to your leg.

annex, annexes, annexing, annexed; also spelled **annexe 1** (noun) An annex is an extra building which is joined to a larger main building. **2** (verb) If one country annexes another, it seizes the other country and takes control of it. **annexation** (noun).

annihilate, annihilates, annihilating, annihilated (pronounced an-**nye**-ill-ate) (verb) If something is annihilated, it is completely destroyed. **annihilation** (noun).

anniversary, anniversaries (noun) An anniversary is a date which is remembered or celebrated because something special happened on that date in a previous year.

announce, announces, announcing, announced (verb) If you announce something, you tell people about it publicly or officially, e.g. *The team was announced on Friday.* **announcement** (noun).

announcer, announcers (noun) An announcer is someone who introduces programmes on radio and television.

annoy, annoys, annoying, annoyed (verb) If someone or something annoys you, they irritate you and make you fairly angry. **annoyance** (noun), **annoyed** (adjective).

annual, annuals 1 (adjective) happening or done every year or once a year, e.g. *their annual conference.* **2** happening or calculated over a period of one year, e.g. *annual rental costs of £12,000.* **3** (noun) An annual is a book or magazine published regularly once a year. **annually** (adverb).

annuity, annuities (noun) An annuity is a fixed sum of money paid to someone every year from an investment or insurance policy.

annul, annuls, annulling, annulled (verb) If a marriage or contract is annulled, it is declared invalid, so that legally it is considered never to have existed. **annulment** (noun).

anoint, anoints, anointing, anointed (verb) To anoint someone means to put oil on them as part of a ceremony. **anointment** (noun).

anomaly, anomalies (pronounced an-**nom**-al-ee) (noun) Something is an anomaly if it is unusual or different from what is considered normal. **anomalous** (adjective).

anon. an abbreviation for **anonymous.**

anonymous (adjective) If something is anonymous, nobody knows who did it or who is responsible for it, e.g. *The police received an anonymous phone call.* **anonymously** (adverb), **anonymity** (noun).

anorak, anoraks (noun) An anorak is a warm waterproof jacket, usually with a hood.

anorexia (noun) Anorexia is a psychological illness in which the person refuses to eat because they are frightened of becoming fat. It often leads to great weakness and sometimes death.

another (adjective or pronoun) Another thing or person means an additional thing or person.

answer, answers, answering, answered 1 (verb) If you answer someone, you reply to them using words or actions or in writing. **2** If you answer a letter or advertisement, you write to the person who wrote it. **3** (noun) An answer is the reply you give when you answer someone. **4** An answer is also a solution to a problem.

answerable (adjective) If you are answerable to someone for something, you are responsible for it, e.g. *The Home Secretary is answerable to Parliament.*

answering machine, answering machines (noun) An answering machine is a machine which records phone calls while you are out.

ant, ants (noun) Ants are small insects that live in large groups.

antagonism (noun) Antagonism is hatred or hostility.

antagonist, antagonists (noun)

An antagonist is an enemy or opponent.

antagonistic (adjective) Someone who is antagonistic towards you shows hate or hostility. **antagonistically** (adverb).

antagonize, antagonizes, antagonizing, antagonized; also spelled **antagonise** (verb) If someone is antagonized, they are made to feel anger and hostility.

Antarctic (noun) The Antarctic is the region south of the Antarctic Circle.

Antarctic Circle (noun) The Antarctic Circle is an imaginary circle around the southern part of the world at latitude 66° 32′ S.

ante- (prefix) Ante- means before, e.g. *antenatal.*

antecedent, antecedents (pronounced an-tis-**see**-dent) **1** (noun) An antecedent of a thing or event is something which happened or existed before it and is related or similar to it in some way, e.g. *the prehistoric antecedents of the horse.* **2** Your antecedents are your ancestors, the relatives from whom you are descended.

antelope, antelopes (noun) An antelope is an animal which looks like a deer.

antenatal (adjective) concerned with the care of pregnant women and their unborn children, e.g. *an antenatal clinic.*

antenna, antennae or **antennas** **1** (noun) The antennae of insects and certain other animals are the two long, thin parts attached to their heads which they use to feel with. The plural is 'antennae'. **2** In American English, an antenna is a radio or television aerial. The plural is 'antennas'.

anthem, anthems (noun) An anthem is a hymn written for a special occasion such as a coronation.

anthology, anthologies (noun) An anthology is a collection of poems, songs, or extracts from literature written by various authors and published in one book.

anthropology (noun) Anthropology is the study of human beings and their society and culture. **anthropological** (adjective), **anthropologist** (noun).

anti- (prefix) opposed to, against, or opposite to something, e.g. *antiwar marches.*

antibiotic, antibiotics (noun) Antibiotics are drugs or chemicals that are used in medicines to kill bacteria and cure infections.

antibody, antibodies (noun) Antibodies are proteins produced in the blood which can kill the harmful bacteria that cause disease.

anticipate, anticipates, anticipating, anticipated (verb) If you anticipate an event, you are expecting it and are prepared for it, e.g. *She had anticipated his visit.* **anticipation** (noun).

anticlimax, anticlimaxes (noun) If something is an anticlimax, it disappoints you because it is not as exciting as expected, or because it occurs after something that was very exciting.

anticlockwise (adjective or adverb) moving in the opposite direction to the hands of a clock.

antics (plural noun) Antics are funny or silly ways of behaving.

antidote, antidotes (noun) An antidote is a chemical substance that counteracts the effect of a poison.

antihistamine, antihistamines (noun) An antihistamine is a drug used to treat an allergy.

antipathy (noun) Antipathy is a strong feeling of dislike or hostility towards something or someone.

antiperspirant, antiperspirants (noun) An antiperspirant is a substance which stops you sweating when you put it on your skin.

antipodes (pronounced an-**tip**-pod-eez) (plural noun) The antipodes are any two points on the earth's surface that are situated directly opposite each other. Australia and New Zealand are sometimes called the Antipodes. **antipodean** (adjective).

antiquarian (adjective) relating to or involving old and rare objects, e.g. *antiquarian books.*

antiquated (adjective) very old-fashioned and out of date.

antique, antiques (pronounced an-**teek**) **1** (noun) An antique is an object from the past that is collected because of its value or beauty. **2** (adjective) from or concerning the past, e.g. *antique furniture.*

antiquity, antiquities 1 (noun) Antiquity is the distant past, especially the time of the ancient Egyptians, Greeks, and Romans. **2** Antiquities are interesting works of art and buildings from the distant past.

anti-Semitism (noun) Anti-Semitism is hatred of Jewish people. **anti-Semitic** (adjective), **anti-Semite** (noun).

antiseptic (adjective) Something that is antiseptic kills germs.

antisocial 1 (adjective) An antisocial person is unwilling to meet and be friendly with other people. **2** Antisocial behaviour is annoying or upsetting to other people, e.g. *Smoking in public is antisocial.*

antithesis, antitheses (pronounced an-**tith**-iss-iss) (noun; a formal word) The antithesis of something is its exact opposite, e.g. *Style is the antithesis of fashion.*

antler, antlers (noun) A male deer's antlers are the branched horns on its head.

antonym, antonyms (noun) An antonym is a word which means the opposite of another word. For example, 'hot' is the antonym of 'cold'.

anus, anuses (noun) The anus is the hole between the buttocks.

anvil, anvils (noun) An anvil is a heavy iron block on which hot metal is beaten into shape.

anxiety, anxieties (noun) Anxiety is nervousness or worry.

anxious 1 (adjective) If you are anxious, you are nervous or worried. **2** If you are anxious to do something or anxious that something should happen, you very much want to do it or want it to happen, e.g. *She was anxious to have children.* **anxiously** (adverb).

any 1 (adjective or pronoun) one, some, or several, e.g. *Do you have any paperclips I could borrow?* **2** even the smallest amount or even one, e.g. *He was unable to tolerate any dairy products.* **3** whatever or whichever, no matter what or which, e.g. *Any type of cooking oil will do.*

anybody (pronoun) any person.

anyhow 1 (adverb) in any case. **2** in a careless or untidy way, e.g. *They were all shoved in anyhow.*

anyone (pronoun) any person.

anything (pronoun) any object, event, situation, or action.

anyway (adverb) in any case.

anywhere (adverb) in, at, or to any place.

aorta (pronounced ay-**or**-ta) (noun) The aorta is the main artery in the body, which carries blood away from the heart.

apart 1 (adverb or adjective) When something is apart from something else, there is a space or a distance between them, e.g. *The couple separated and lived apart for four years... The gliders landed about seventy metres apart.* **2** (adverb) If you take something apart, you separate it into pieces.

apartheid (pronounced ap-**par**-tide) (noun) In South Africa, until it was abolished in 1994, apartheid was the government policy and laws which kept people of different races apart.

apartment, apartments (noun) An apartment is a set of rooms for living in, usually on one floor of a building.

apathetic (adjective) not interested in anything.

apathy (pronounced **ap**-path-ee) (noun) Apathy is a state of mind in which you do not care about anything.

ape, apes, aping, aped 1 (noun) Apes are primates with a very short tail or no tail. They are closely related to man. Apes include chimpanzees, gorillas, and gibbons. **2** (verb) If you ape someone's speech or behaviour, you imitate it.

aphid, aphids (noun) An aphid is a small insect that feeds by sucking the juices from plants.

aphrodisiac, aphrodisiacs (noun) An aphrodisiac is a food, drink, or drug which makes people want to have sex.

apiece (adverb) If people have a particular number of things apiece, they have that number each.

aplomb (pronounced uh-**plom**) (noun) If you do something with aplomb, you do it with great confidence.

apocalypse (pronounced uh-**pok**-ka-lips) (noun) The Apocalypse is the total destruction and end of the world. **apocalyptic** (adjective).

apocryphal (adjective) A story that is apocryphal is generally believed not to have really happened.

apolitical (pronounced ay-poll-**it**-i-kl) (adjective) not interested in politics.

apologetic (adjective) showing or saying that you are sorry for what you have said or done. **apologetically** (adverb).

apologize, apologizes, apologizing, apologized; also spelled

apologise (verb) When you apologize to someone, you say that you are sorry for something that you have said or done.

apology, apologies (noun) An apology is something you say or write to tell someone that you are sorry for something you have said or done.

apostle, apostles (noun) The Apostles are the twelve disciples who were chosen by Christ.

apostrophe, apostrophes (pronounced ap-**poss**-troff-ee) (noun) An apostrophe is a punctuation mark that is used to show that one or more letters have been missed out of a word. An example is 'he's' for 'he is'.

appal, appals, appalling, appalled (verb) If something appals you, it shocks you because it is very bad.

appalling (adjective) so bad as to be shocking, e.g. *She escaped with appalling injuries.*

apparatus (noun) The apparatus for a particular task is the equipment used for it.

apparent 1 (adjective) seeming real rather than actually being real, e.g. *the apparent success of their marriage.* **2** clear and obvious, e.g. *It was apparent that he had lost interest.* **apparently** (adverb).

apparition, apparitions (noun) An apparition is something that you think you see but that is not really there, e.g. *a ghostly apparition on the windscreen.*

appeal, appeals, appealing, appealed 1 (verb) If you appeal for something, you make a serious and urgent request for it, e.g. *The police appealed for witnesses to come forward.* **2** If you appeal to someone in authority against a decision, you formally ask them to change it. **3** If something appeals to you, you find it attractive or interesting. **4** (noun) The appeal of something is the quality it has which people find attractive or interesting, e.g. *the rugged appeal of the Scottish Highlands.* **appealing** (adjective).

appear, appears, appearing, appeared 1 (verb) When something which you could not see appears, it moves (or you move) so that you can see it. **2** When something new appears, it begins to exist. **3** When an actor or actress appears in a film, play, or show, they take part in it. **4** If something appears to be a certain way, it seems or looks that way, e.g. *He appeared to be searching for something.*

appearance, appearances 1 (noun) The appearance of someone in a place is their arrival there, especially when it is unexpected. **2** The appearance of something new is the time when it begins to exist, e.g. *the appearance of computer technology.* **3** Someone's or something's appearance is the way they look to other people, e.g. *His gaunt appearance had sparked fears for his health.*

appease, appeases, appeasing, appeased (verb) If you try to appease someone, you try to calm them down when they are angry, for example by giving them what they want. **ap-**

peasement (noun).

appendage, appendages (noun) An appendage is a less important part attached to a main part.

appendicitis (pronounced append-i-**site**-uss) (noun) Appendicitis is a painful illness in which a person's appendix becomes infected.

appendix, appendices 1 (noun) Your appendix is a small closed tube forming part of your digestive system. It has no particular purpose. **2** An appendix to a book is extra information that is placed after the end of the main text.

appetite, appetites 1 (noun) Your appetite is your desire to eat. **2** If you have an appetite for something, you have a strong desire for it and enjoyment of it, e.g. *She had lost her appetite for air travel.*

appetizing or **appetising** (adjective) Food that is appetizing looks and smells good, and makes you want to eat it.

applaud, applauds, applauding, applauded 1 (verb) When a group of people applaud, they clap their hands in approval or praise. **2** When an action or attitude is applauded, people praise it.

applause (noun) Applause is clapping by a group of people.

apple, apples (noun) An apple is a round fruit with smooth skin and firm white flesh.

appliance, appliances (noun) An appliance is any device or machine that is designed to do a particular job, especially in the home, e.g. *kitchen appliances.*

applicable (adjective) Something that is applicable to a situation is relevant to it, e.g. *The rules are applicable to everyone.*

applicant, applicants (noun) An applicant is someone who is applying for something, e.g. *We had problems recruiting applicants for the post.*

application, applications 1 (noun) An application for something is a formal request for it, usually in writing. **2** The application of a rule, system, or skill is the use of it in a particular situation.

apply, applies, applying, applied 1 (verb) If you apply for something, you formally ask for it, usually by writing a letter. **2** If you apply a rule, system, or skill, you use it in a situation or an activity, e.g. *He applied his mind to the problem.* **3** If something applies to a person or a situation, it is relevant to that person or situation, e.g. *The legislation applies only to people living in England and Wales.* **4** If you apply something to a surface, you put it on, e.g. *She applied lipstick to her mouth.*

appoint, appoints, appointing, appointed 1 (verb) If you appoint someone to a job or position, you formally choose them for it. **2** If you appoint a time or place for something to happen, you decide when or where it will happen. **appointed** (adjective).

appointment, appointments 1 (noun) An appointment is an arrangement you have with someone to meet or visit them. **2** The appointment of a person to do a particular job is the choosing of that person to do it. **3** An appointment is also a job or a position of responsibility, e.g. *He applied for an appointment in Russia.*

apposite (pronounced **app**-o-zit) (adjective) well suited for a particular purpose, e.g. *He went before I could think of anything apposite to say.*

appraise, appraises, appraising, appraised (verb) If you appraise something, you think about it carefully and form an opinion about it. **appraisal** (noun).

appreciable (pronounced a-**pree**-shuh-bl) (adjective) large enough or important enough to be noticed, e.g. *an appreciable difference.* **appreciably** (adverb).

appreciate, appreciates, appreciating, appreciated 1 (verb) If you appreciate something, you like it because you recognize its good qualities, e.g. *He appreciates fine wines.* **2** If you appreciate a situation or problem, you understand it and know what it involves. **3** If you appreciate something that someone has done for you, you are grateful to them for it, e.g. *I really appreciate you coming to visit me.* **4** If something appreciates over a period of time, its value increases, e.g. *The property appreciated by 50% in two years.* **appreciation** (noun).

appreciative (adjective) thankful and grateful, e.g. *They were a very appreciative audience.* **appreciatively** (adverb).

apprehend, apprehends, apprehending, apprehended (a formal word) **1** (verb) When the police apprehend someone, they arrest them and take them into custody. **2** If you apprehend something, you understand it fully, e.g. *They were unable to apprehend his hidden meaning.*

apprehensive (adjective) afraid that something bad may happen, e.g. *I was very apprehensive about the birth.* **apprehensively** (adverb), **apprehension** (noun).

apprentice, apprentices (noun) An apprentice is a person who works for a period of time with a skilled craftsman in order to learn a skill or trade. **apprenticeship** (noun).

approach, approaches, approaching, approached 1 (verb) To approach something means to come nearer to it. **2** When a future event approaches, it gradually gets nearer, e.g. *As winter approached, tents were set up to accommodate refugees.* **3** (noun) The approach of something is the process of it coming closer, e.g. *the approach of spring.* **4** (verb) If you approach someone about something, you ask them about it. **5** If you approach a situation or problem in a particular way, you think about it or deal with it in that way. **6** (noun) An approach to a situation or problem is a way of thinking about it or dealing with it. **7** (verb) If something approaches a particular level or state, it almost reaches that level or state, e.g. *The train approached speeds of 200 kilometres per hour.* **8** (noun) An approach to a place is a road or path that leads to it. **approaching** (adjective).

appropriate, appropriates, appropriating, appropriated 1 (adjective) suitable or acceptable for a particular situation, e.g. *He didn't think jeans were appropriate for a vice-president.* **2** (verb; a formal use) If you appropriate something which does not belong to you, you take it without permission. **appropriately** (adverb), **appropriation** (noun).

approval 1 (noun) Approval is agreement given to a plan or request, e.g. *The plan will require approval from the local authority.* **2** Approval is also admiration for someone, e.g. *She looked at James with approval.*

approve, approves, approving, approved 1 (verb) If you approve of something, you think that it is right or good. **2** If you approve of someone, you like them and think they are all right, e.g. *I'm sure your father would never approve of me.* **3** If someone in a position of authority approves a plan or idea, they formally agree to it. **approved** (adjective), **approving** (adjective).

approximate (adjective) almost accurate or exact, e.g. *What was the approximate distance between the cars?* **approximately** (adverb).

apricot, apricots (noun) An apricot is a small, soft, yellowish-orange fruit.

April (noun) April is the fourth month of the year. It has 30 days.

apron, aprons (noun) An apron is a piece of clothing worn over the front of normal clothing to protect it.

apt 1 (adjective) suitable or relevant, e.g. *a very apt description.* **2** having a particular tendency, e.g. *They are apt to jump to the wrong conclusions.*

aptitude (noun) Someone's aptitude for something is their ability to learn it quickly and to do it well, e.g. *I have a natural aptitude for painting.*

aquarium, aquaria or **aquariums** (noun) An aquarium is a glass tank filled with water in which fish are kept.

Aquarius (noun) Aquarius is the eleventh sign of the zodiac, represented by a person carrying water. People born between January 20th and February 18th are born under this sign.

aquatic 1 (adjective) An aquatic animal or plant lives or grows in water. **2** involving water, e.g. *aquatic sports.*

aqueduct, aqueducts (noun) An aqueduct is a long bridge with many arches carrying a water supply over a valley.

Arab, Arabs (noun) An Arab is a member of a group of people who used to live in Arabia but who now live throughout the Middle East and North Africa.

Arabic (noun) Arabic is a language spoken by many people in the Middle East and North Africa. It is the official language of several countries including Egypt and Iraq.

arable (adjective) Arable land is suitable for growing crops.

arbitrary (adjective) An arbitrary decision or action is one that is not based on a plan or system. **arbitrarily** (adverb).

arbitrate, arbitrates, arbitrating, arbitrated (verb) When someone arbitrates between two people or groups who are in disagreement, they consider the facts and decide who is right. **arbitration** (noun), **arbitrator** (noun).

arc, arcs 1 (noun) An arc is a smoothly curving line. **2** In geometry, an arc is a section of the circumference of a circle.

arcade, arcades (noun) An arcade is a covered passageway where there are shops or market stalls.

arcane (adjective) mysterious and difficult to understand.

arch, arches, arching, arched 1 (noun) An arch is a structure that has a curved top supported on either side by a pillar or wall. **2** An arch is also anything that is curved like an arch, e.g. *the arch of your foot.* **3** (verb) When something arches, it forms a curved line or shape. **4** (adjective) most important, e.g. *my arch enemy.*

archaeology or **archeology** (pronounced ar-kee-**ol**-loj-ee) (noun) Archaeology is the study of the past by digging up and examining the remains of buildings, tools, and other things. **archaeological** (adjective), **archaeologist** (noun).

archaic (pronounced ar-**kay**-ik) (adjective) very old or old-fashioned.

archangel, archangels (pronounced ark-**ain**-jel) (noun) An archangel is an angel of the highest rank.

archbishop, archbishops (noun) An archbishop is a bishop of the highest rank in a Christian Church.

archdeacon, archdeacons (noun) An archdeacon is an Anglican clergyman ranking just below a bishop.

archeology another spelling of **archaeology.**

archer, archers (noun) An archer is someone who shoots with a bow and arrow.

archery (noun) Archery is a sport in which people shoot at a target with a bow and arrow.

archipelago, archipelagos (pronounced ar-kip-**pel**-lag-oh) (noun) An archipelago is a group of small islands.

architect, architects (pronounced **ar**-kit-tekt) (noun) An architect is a person who designs buildings.

architecture (noun) Architecture is the art or practice of designing buildings. **architectural** (adjective).

archive, archives (pronounced **ar**-kive) (noun) Archives are collections of documents and records about the history of a family, organization, or some other group of people.

arctic 1 (noun) The Arctic is the region north of the Arctic Circle. **2** (adjective) Arctic means very cold indeed, e.g. *arctic conditions.*

Arctic Circle (noun) The Arctic Circle is an imaginary circle around the northern part of the world at latitude 66° 32′ N.

ardent (adjective) full of enthusiasm and passion. **ardently** (adverb).

ardour (noun) Ardour is a strong and passionate feeling of love or enthusiasm.

arduous (pronounced **ard**-yoo-uss) (adjective) tiring and needing a lot of effort, e.g. *the arduous task of rebuilding the country.*

are the plural form of the present tense of **be.**

area, areas 1 (noun) An area is a particular part of a place, country, or the world, e.g. *a built-up area of London.* **2** The area of a piece of ground or a surface is the amount of space that it covers, measured in square metres or square feet.

arena, arenas 1 (noun) An arena is a place where sports and other public events take place. **2** A particular arena is the centre of attention or activity in a particular situation, e.g. *the political arena.*

Argentinian, Argentinians (pronounced ar-jen-**tin**-ee-an) **1** (adjective) belonging or relating to Argentina. **2** (noun) An Argentinian is someone who comes from Argentina.

arguable 1 (adjective) An arguable idea, point, or comment is not necessarily true or correct and should be questioned. **2** If you say that something is arguable, you mean that it is possible to argue that it is true. **arguably** (adverb).

argue, argues, arguing, argued 1 (verb) If you argue with someone about something, you disagree with them about it, sometimes in an angry way. **2** If you argue that something is the case, you give reasons why you think it is so, e.g. *She argued that her client had been wrongly accused.*

argument, arguments 1 (noun) An argument is a disagreement between two people which causes a quarrel. **2** An argument is also a point or a set of reasons that you use to try to convince people about something.

argumentative (adjective) An argumentative person is always arguing or disagreeing with other people.

aria, arias (pronounced **ah**-ree-a) (noun) An aria is a song sung by one of the leading singers in an opera.

arid (adjective) Arid land is very dry because it has very little rain.

Aries (pronounced **air**-reez) (noun) Aries is the first sign of the zodiac, represented by a ram. People born between March 21st and April 19th are born under this sign.

arise, arises, arising, arose, arisen 1 (verb) When something such as an opportunity, problem, or new state of affairs arises, it begins to exist. **2** (a formal use) To arise also means to stand up from a sitting or lying position.

aristocracy, aristocracies (noun) The aristocracy is a class of people who have a high social rank and special titles.

aristocrat, aristocrats (noun) An aristocrat is someone whose family has a high social rank, and who has a title. **aristocratic** (adjective).

arithmetic (noun) Arithmetic is the part of mathematics which is to do with the addition, subtraction, multiplication, and division of numbers. **arithmetical** (adjective), **arithmetically** (adverb).

ark (noun) In the Bible, the ark

was the boat built by Noah for his family and the animals during the Flood.

arm, arms, arming, armed 1 (noun) Your arms are the part of your body between your shoulder and your wrist. **2** The arms of a chair are the parts on which you rest your arms. **3** An arm of an organization is a section of it, e.g. *the political arm of the Students' Union.* **4** (plural noun) Arms are weapons used in a war. **5** (verb) To arm someone means to provide them with weapons as a preparation for war.

armada, armadas (pronounced ar-**mah**-da) (noun) An armada is a large fleet of warships.

armadillo, armadillos (noun) An armadillo is a mammal from South America which is covered with strong bony plates like armour.

Armageddon (noun) In Christianity, Armageddon is the final battle between good and evil at the end of the world.

armament, armaments (noun) Armaments are the weapons and military equipment that belong to a country.

armchair, armchairs (noun) An armchair is a comfortable chair with a support on each side for your arms.

armed (adjective) A person who is armed is carrying a weapon or weapons.

armistice, armistices (pronounced **ar**-miss-tiss) (noun) An armistice is an agreement in a war to stop fighting in order to discuss peace.

armour (noun) In the past, armour was metal clothing worn for protection in battle.

armoured (adjective) covered with thick steel for protection from gunfire and other missiles, e.g. *an armoured car.*

armoury, armouries (noun) An armoury is a place where weapons are stored.

armpit, armpits (noun) Your armpit is the area under your arm where your arm joins your shoulder.

army, armies (noun) An army is a large group of soldiers organized into divisions for fighting on land.

aroma, aromas (noun) An aroma is a strong, pleasant smell. **aromatic** (adjective).

around 1 (preposition) placed at various points in a place or area, e.g. *There are many seats around the building.* **2** from place to place inside an area, e.g. *We walked around the showroom.* **3** at approximately the time or place mentioned, e.g. *The attacks began around noon.* **4** (adverb) here and there, e.g. *His papers were scattered around.*

arouse, arouses, arousing, aroused (verb) If something arouses a feeling in you, it causes you to begin to have this feeling, e.g. *She aroused in him a hatred bordering on insanity.* **arousal** (noun).

arrange, arranges, arranging, arranged 1 (verb) If you arrange to do something, you make plans for it. **2** If you arrange something for someone, you make it possible for them to have it or do it, e.g. *The bank has arranged a loan for her.* **3** If you arrange objects, you set them out in a particular position, e.g. *A spider's eyes are arranged in pairs.* **arrangement** (noun).

array, arrays (noun) An array of different things is a large number of them displayed together.

arrears 1 (plural noun) Arrears are amounts of money that you owe, e.g. *mortgage arrears.* **2** (phrase) If you are paid **in arrears,** you are paid at the end of the period for which the payment is due.

arrest, arrests, arresting, arrested 1 (verb) If the police arrest someone, they take them into custody to decide whether to charge them with an offence. **2** (noun) An arrest is the act of taking a person into custody.

arrival, arrivals 1 (noun) An arrival is the act or time of arriving, e.g. *The arrival of the train was delayed.* **2** An arrival is something or someone that has arrived, e.g. *The tourist authority reported record arrivals over Christmas.*

arrive, arrives, arriving, arrived 1 (verb) When you arrive at a place, you reach it at the end of your journey. **2** When a letter or a piece of news arrives, it is brought to you, e.g. *A letter arrived at her lawyer's office.* **3** When you arrive at an idea, decision, or conclusion, you reach it or decide on it, e.g. *The board finally arrived at a decision.* **4** When a moment, event, or new thing arrives, it begins to happen, e.g. *The Easter holidays arrived.*

arrogant (adjective) Someone who is arrogant behaves as if they are better than other people. **arrogantly** (adverb), **arrogance** (noun).

arrow, arrows (noun) An arrow is a long, thin weapon with a sharp point at one end, shot from a bow.

arsenal, arsenals (noun) An arsenal is a place where weapons and ammunition are stored or produced.

arsenic (noun) Arsenic is a very strong poison which can kill people.

arson (noun) Arson is the crime of deliberately setting fire to something, especially a building.

art, arts 1 (noun) Art is the creation of objects such as paintings and sculptures, which are thought to be beautiful or which express a particular idea; also used to refer to the objects themselves. **2** (plural noun) The arts are literature, music, painting, and sculpture, considered together. **3** (noun) An activity is called an art when it requires special skill or ability, e.g. *the art of diplomacy.*

artefact, artefacts (pronounced **ar**-tif-fact) (noun) An artefact is any ornament, tool, or other object that is made by people.

artery, arteries (noun) Your arteries are the tubes that carry blood from your heart to the rest of your body.

artful (adjective) clever and skilful, often in a cunning way. **artfully** (adverb).

arthritis (noun) Arthritis is a condition in which the joints in someone's body become swollen and painful. **arthritic** (adjective).

artichoke, artichokes 1 (noun) A globe artichoke is a round green vegetable that has a cluster of fleshy leaves, the bottom part of which you can eat. **2** A Jerusalem artichoke is a small yellowish-white vegetable that looks like a potato.

article, articles 1 (noun) An article is a piece of writing in a newspaper or magazine. **2** An article is also a particular object or item, e.g. *an article of clothing.* **3** In English grammar, 'a' and 'the' are sometimes called articles: 'a' (or 'an') is the indefinite article; 'the' is the definite article.

articulate, articulates, articulating, articulated 1 (verb) When you articulate your ideas or feelings, you express in words what you think or feel, e.g. *She could not articulate her grief.* **2** When you articulate a sound or word, you speak it clearly and distinctly. **3** (adjective) If you are articulate, you are able to express yourself well in words. **articulation** (noun).

artificial 1 (adjective) created by people rather than occurring naturally, e.g. *artificial colouring.* **2** pretending to have attitudes and feelings which other people realize are not real, e.g. *an artificial smile.* **artificially** (adverb).

artillery 1 (noun) Artillery consists of large, powerful guns such as cannons. **2** The artillery is the branch of an army which uses large, powerful guns.

artist, artists 1 (noun) An artist is a person who draws or paints or produces other works of art. **2** An artist is also a person who is very skilled at a particular activity.

artiste, artistes (pronounced ar-**teest**) (noun) An artiste is a professional entertainer, for example a singer or a dancer.

artistic 1 (adjective) able to create good paintings, sculpture, or other works of art. **2** concerning or involving art or artists. **artistically** (adverb).

artistry (noun) Artistry is the degree of creative skill of an artist, writer, actor, or musician, e.g. *a demonstration of his artistry as a cellist.*

arty (adjective; an informal word) interested in painting, sculpture, and other works of art.

as 1 (conjunction) at the same time that, e.g. *She waved at fans as she arrived for the concert.* **2** in the way that, e.g. *They had talked as only the best of friends can.* **3** because, e.g. *As I won't be back tonight, don't bother to cook a meal.* **4** You use the structure **as ... as** when you are comparing things that are similar, e.g. *It was as big as four football pitches.* **5** (preposition) You use 'as' when you are saying what role someone or something has, e.g. *She worked as a waitress.* **6** You use **as if** or **as though** when you are giving a possible explanation for something, e.g. *He looked at me as if I were mad.*

asbestos (noun) Asbestos is a grey heat-resistant material used in the past to make fireproof articles.

ascend, ascends, ascending, ascended (pronounced ass-**end**) (verb; a formal word) To ascend means to move or lead upwards, e.g. *We finally ascended to the brow of a steep hill.*

ascendancy (noun; a formal word) If one group has ascendancy over another, it has more power or influence than the other.

ascendant (adjective) rising or moving upwards.

ascent, ascents (noun) An ascent is an upward journey, for example up a mountain.

ascertain, ascertains, ascertaining, ascertained (pronounced ass-er-**tain**) (verb; a formal word) If you ascertain that something is the case, you find out that it is the case, e.g. *He had ascertained that she had given up smoking.*

ascribe, ascribes, ascribing, ascribed **1** (verb) If you ascribe an event or state of affairs to a particular factor, you consider that it is caused by that factor, e.g. *His stomach pains were ascribed to his intake of pork.* **2** If you ascribe a quality to someone, you consider that they possess it.

ash, ashes **1** (noun) Ash is the grey or black powdery remains of anything that has been burnt. **2** An ash is a tree with grey bark and hard tough wood used for timber.

ashamed **1** (adjective) feeling embarrassed or guilty. **2** If you are ashamed of someone, you feel embarrassed to be connected with them.

ashen (adjective) grey or pale, e.g. *Her face was ashen with fatigue.*

ashore (adverb) on land or onto the land.

ashtray, ashtrays (noun) An ashtray is a small dish for ash from cigarettes.

Asia (noun) Asia is the largest continent. It has Europe on its western side, with the Arctic to the north, the Pacific to the east, and the Indian Ocean to the south. Asia includes several island groups, including Japan, Indonesia, and the Philippines.

Asian, Asians **1** (adjective) belonging or relating to Asia. **2** (noun) An Asian is someone who comes from India, Pakistan, Bangladesh, or from some other part of Asia.

aside, asides **1** (adverb) If you move something aside, you move it to one side. **2** (noun) An aside is a comment that does not form part of the conversation or dialogue.

ask, asks, asking, asked **1** (verb) If you ask someone a question, you put a question to them. **2** If you ask someone to do something, you tell them that you want them to do it. **3** If you ask for something, you say that you would like to have it. **4** If you ask someone's permission or forgiveness, you try to obtain it. **5** If you ask someone somewhere, you invite them there, e.g. *Not everybody had been asked to the wedding.*

askew (adjective) not straight or level.

asleep (adjective) sleeping.

asparagus (noun) Asparagus is a vegetable that has long soft-tipped shoots which are cooked and eaten.

aspect, aspects **1** (noun) An aspect of something is one of its distinctive features, e.g. *Exam results illustrate only one aspect of a school's success.* **2** The aspect of a building is the direction it faces, e.g. *The southern aspect of the cottage faces over fields.*

asphalt (noun) Asphalt is a black substance used to make road surfaces.

aspiration, aspirations (noun) Someone's aspirations are their desires and ambitions.

aspire, aspires, aspiring, aspired (verb) If you aspire to something, you have an ambition to achieve it, e.g. *He aspired to work in music journalism.* **aspiring** (adjective).

aspirin, aspirins 1 (noun) Aspirin is a white drug used to relieve pain, fever, and colds. **2** An aspirin is a tablet of this drug.

ass, asses 1 (noun) An ass is a donkey. **2** (an informal use) You can call someone an ass if you think they are stupid.

assailant, assailants (noun) An assailant is someone who attacks another person.

assassin, assassins (noun) An assassin is someone who has murdered a political or religious leader.

assassinate, assassinates, assassinating, assassinated (verb) To assassinate a political or religious leader means to murder him or her. **assassination** (noun).

assault, assaults, assaulting, assaulted 1 (noun) An assault is a violent physical attack on someone. **2** (verb) To assault someone means to attack them violently.

assemble, assembles, assembling, assembled 1 (verb) To assemble means to gather together. **2** If you assemble something, you fit the parts of it together.

assembly, assemblies 1 (noun) An assembly is a group of people who have gathered together for a meeting. **2** The assembly of an object is the fitting together of its parts, e.g. *Laser technology was used to ensure the exact assembly of the hull and deck.*

assent, assents, assenting, assented (pronounced as-**sent**) **1** (noun) If you give your assent to something, you agree to it or say yes to it. **2** (verb) If you assent to something, you agree to it or say yes to it.

assert, asserts, asserting, asserted 1 (verb) If you assert a fact, belief, or opinion, you state it firmly and forcefully. **2** If you assert yourself, you speak and behave in a confident and direct way, so that people pay attention to you and your opinions.

assertive (adjective) If you are assertive, you speak and behave in a confident and direct way, so that people pay attention to you and your opinions. **assertively** (adverb), **assertiveness** (noun).

assess, assesses, assessing, assessed (verb) If you assess something, you consider it carefully and make a judgment about it. **assessment** (noun).

assessor, assessors (noun) An assessor is someone whose job is to assess the value of something.

asset, assets 1 (noun) An asset is a person or thing that is considered useful, e.g. *He will be a great asset to the club.* **2** (plural noun) The assets of a person or company are all the things they own that could be sold to raise money.

assign, assigns, assigning, assigned 1 (verb) To assign something to someone means to give it to them officially or to make them responsible for it. **2** If someone is assigned to do something, they are officially told to do it.

assignation, assignations (pronounced ass-ig-**nay**-shn) (noun; a literary word) An assignation is a secret meeting with someone.

assignment, assignments (noun) An assignment is a job or task that someone is given to do.

assimilate, assimilates, assimilating, assimilated 1 (verb) If you assimilate ideas or experiences, you learn and understand them. **2** When people are assimilated into a group or community, they become part of it. **assimilation** (noun).

assist, assists, assisting, assisted (verb) To assist someone means to help them do something. **assistance** (noun).

assistant, assistants (noun) An assistant is someone whose job is to help another person in their work.

associate, associates, associating, associated 1 (verb) If you associate one thing with another, you connect the two things in your mind. **2** If you associate with a group of people, you spend a lot of time with them, e.g. *I'm not supposed to associate with westerners.* **3** (noun) Your associates are the people you work with or spend a lot of time with.

association, associations 1 (noun) An association is an organization for people who have similar interests, jobs, or aims. **2** Your association with a person, group, or organization is the connection or involvement that you have with them. **3** An association between two things is a link that you make in your mind between them, e.g. *The place contained associations for her.*

assorted (adjective) Assorted things vary in size, shape, and colour, e.g. *swimsuits in assorted sizes.*

assortment, assortments (noun) An assortment is a group of similar things that vary in size, shape, and colour, e.g. *an amazing assortment of old toys.*

assume, assumes, assuming, assumed 1 (verb) If you assume that something is true, you accept that it is true even though you have not thought about it, e.g. *I assumed that he would turn up.* **2** To assume responsibility for something means to put yourself in charge of it.

assumption, assumptions 1 (noun) An assumption is a belief that something is true, without thinking about it. **2** Assumption of power is the taking of it.

assurance, assurances 1 (noun) An assurance is something said about a situation which is intended to make people less worried, e.g. *She was emphatic in her assurances that she wanted to stay.* **2** Assurance is a feeling of confidence, e.g. *He handled the car with ease and assurance.* **3** Life assurance is a type of insurance that pays money to your dependants when you die.

assure, assures, assuring, assured (verb) If you assure someone that something is true, you tell them that it is true.

asterisk, asterisks (noun) An asterisk is the symbol (*) used in printing and writing.

astern (adverb or adjective; a nautical word) backwards or at the back.

asteroid, asteroids (noun) An asteroid is one of the large number of very small planets that move around the sun.

asthma (pronounced **ass**-ma) (noun) Asthma is a disease of the chest which causes wheezing and difficulty in breathing. **asthmatic** (adjective).

astonish, astonishes, astonishing, astonished (verb) If something astonishes you, it surprises you very much. **astonished** (adjective), **astonishing** (adjective), **astonishingly** (adverb), **astonishment** (noun).

astound, astounds, astounding, astounded (verb) If something astounds you, it shocks and amazes you. **astounded** (adjective), **astounding** (adjective).

astray 1 (phrase) To **lead someone astray** means to influence them to do something wrong. **2** If something **goes astray,** it gets lost, e.g. *The money had gone astray.*

astride (preposition) with one leg on either side of something, e.g. *He is pictured astride his new motorbike.*

astringent, astringents (pronounced ass-**trin**-jent) (noun) An astringent is a substance that causes body tissues to contract. It stops bleeding.

astrology (noun) Astrology is the study of the sun, moon, and stars in order to predict the future. **astrological** (adjective), **astrologer** (noun).

astronaut, astronauts (noun) An astronaut is a person who operates a spacecraft.

astronomical 1 (adjective) involved with or relating to astronomy. **2** extremely large in amount or value, e.g. *astronomical legal costs.* **astronomically** (adverb).

astronomy (noun) Astronomy is the scientific study of stars and planets. **astronomer** (noun).

astute (adjective) clever and quick at understanding situations and behaviour, e.g. *an astute diplomat.*

asunder (adverb; a literary word) If something is torn asunder, it is violently torn apart.

asylum, asylums (pronounced ass-**eye**-lum) **1** (noun; an old-fashioned use) An asylum was a hospital for mental patients. **2** Political asylum is protection given by a government to someone who has fled from their own country for political reasons.

asymmetrical or **asymmetric** (pronounced ay-sim-**met**-ri-kl) (adjective) not symmetrical or unbalanced. **asymmetry**

(noun).

at 1 (preposition) used to say where someone or something is, e.g. *A meeting was arranged at Victoria Station.* **2** used to mention the direction something is going in, e.g. *He threw his plate at the wall.* **3** used to say when something happens, e.g. *The game starts at 3 o'clock.* **4** used to mention the rate, price, or value of something, e.g. *The shares were priced at fifty pence.*

atheist, atheists (pronounced **ayth**-ee-ist) (noun) An atheist is someone who believes that there is no God. **atheistic** (adjective), **atheism** (noun).

athlete, athletes (noun) An athlete is someone who is good at sport and takes part in sporting events.

athletic 1 (adjective) strong, healthy, and good at sports. **2** involving athletes or athletics, e.g. *I lost two years of my athletic career due to injury.*

athletics (noun) Sporting events such as running, jumping, and throwing are called athletics.

Atlantic (noun) The Atlantic is the ocean separating North and South America from Europe and Africa.

atlas, atlases (noun) An atlas is a book of maps.

atmosphere, atmospheres 1 (noun) The atmosphere is the air and other gases that surround a planet; also the air in a particular place, e.g. *a musty atmosphere.* **2** The atmosphere of a place is its general mood, e.g. *a relaxed atmosphere.* **atmospheric** (adjective).

atom, atoms (noun) An atom is the smallest part of an element that can take part in a chemical reaction.

atom bomb, atom bombs (noun) An atom bomb is an extremely powerful bomb which explodes because of nuclear energy that comes from splitting atoms.

atomic (adjective) relating to atoms or to the power released by splitting atoms, e.g. *atomic energy.*

atone, atones, atoning, atoned (verb; a formal word) If you atone for something wrong that you have done, you say you are sorry and try to make up for it.

atrocious (adjective) extremely bad, e.g. *The game was abandoned because of atrocious weather.*

atrocity, atrocities (noun) An atrocity is an extremely cruel and shocking act.

attach, attaches, attaching, attached (verb) If you attach something to something else, you join or fasten the two things together.

attaché, attachés (pronounced at-**tash**-ay) (noun) An attaché is a member of staff in an embassy, e.g. *the Russian Cultural Attaché.*

attached (adjective) If you are attached to someone, you are very fond of them.

attachment, attachments 1 (noun) Attachment to someone is a feeling of love and affection for them. **2** Attachment to a cause or ideal is a strong belief in it and support for it. **3** An attachment for a tool or machine is a piece of equipment that can be attached to it to do a particular job.

attack, attacks, attacking, attacked 1 (verb) To attack someone means to use violence against them so as to hurt or kill them. **2** (noun) An attack is violent physical action against someone. **3** (verb) If you attack someone or their ideas, you criticize them strongly, e.g. *He attacked the government's economic policies.* **4** (noun) An attack on someone or on their ideas is strong criticism of them. **5** (verb) If a disease or chemical attacks something, it damages or destroys it, e.g. *fungal diseases that attack crops.* **6** (noun) An attack of an illness is a short time in which you suffer badly with it. **7** (verb) In a game such as football or hockey, to attack means to get the ball into a position from which a goal can be scored. **attacker** (noun).

attain, attains, attaining, attained (verb; a formal word) If you attain something, you manage to achieve it, e.g. *He eventually attained the rank of major.* **attainable** (adjective), **attainment** (noun).

attempt, attempts, attempting, attempted 1 (verb) If you attempt to do something, you try to do it or achieve it, but may not succeed, e.g. *They attempted to escape.* **2** (noun) An attempt is an act of trying to do something, e.g. *He made no attempt to go for the ball.*

attend, attends, attending, attended 1 (verb) If you attend an event, you are present at it. **2** To attend school, church, or hospital means to go there regularly. **3** If you attend to something, you deal with it, e.g. *We have business to attend to.* **attendance** (noun).

attendant, attendants (noun) An attendant is someone whose job is to serve people in a shop, museum, or garage.

attention (noun) Attention is the thought, care, or interest that you give to something, e.g. *The woman needed medical attention.*

attentive (adjective) paying close attention to something, e.g. *an attentive audience.* **attentively** (adverb), **attentiveness** (noun).

attest, attests, attesting, attested (verb; a formal word) To attest something means to show or declare that it is true. **attestation** (noun).

attic, attics (noun) An attic is a room at the top of a house immediately below the roof.

attire (noun; a formal word) Attire is clothing, e.g. *traditional wedding attire.*

attitude, attitudes (noun) Your attitude to someone or something is the way you think and feel about them and behave towards them.

attorney, attorneys (pronounced at-**turn**-ee) (noun; an American word) An attorney is the same as a lawyer.

attract, attracts, attracting, attracted 1 (verb) If something attracts people, it interests them and makes them want to go to it, e.g. *The trials have attracted many leading riders.* **2** If someone attracts you, you like and admire them, e.g. *He was attracted to her outgoing* *personality.* **3** If something attracts support or publicity, it gets it.

attraction, attractions 1 (noun) Attraction is a feeling of liking someone very much and wanting to be with them, e.g. *physical attraction.* **2** An attraction is something that people visit for interest or pleasure, e.g. *The temple is a major tourist attraction.*

attractive 1 (adjective) interesting and possibly advantageous, e.g. *an attractive proposition.* **2** pleasant to look at or be with, e.g. *an attractive woman... an attractive personality.* **attractively** (adverb), **attractiveness** (noun).

attribute, attributes, attributing, attributed 1 (verb) If you attribute something to a circumstance, person, or thing, you believe that it was caused or created by that circumstance, person, or thing, e.g. *Water pollution was attributed to the use of fertilizers... a painting attributed to Raphael.* **2** (noun) An attribute is a quality or feature that someone or something has. **attribution** (noun), **attributable** (adjective).

attrition (noun) Attrition is the constant wearing down of an enemy, e.g. *a long war of attrition.*

attuned (adjective) accustomed or well adjusted to something, e.g. *His eyes quickly became attuned to the dark.*

aubergine, aubergines (pronounced **oh**-ber-jeen) (noun) An aubergine is a dark purple, pear-shaped vegetable with shiny skin and pale flesh. It is also called an **egg-plant.**

auburn (adjective) Auburn hair is reddish brown.

auction, auctions, auctioning, auctioned 1 (noun) An auction is a public sale in which goods are sold to the person who offers the highest price. **2** (verb) To auction something means to sell it in an auction.

auctioneer, auctioneers (noun) An auctioneer is the person in charge of an auction.

audacious (adjective) very daring, e.g. *an audacious escape from jail.* **audaciously** (adverb), **audacity** (noun).

audible (adjective) loud enough to be heard, e.g. *She spoke in a barely audible whisper.* **audibly** (adverb), **audibility** (noun).

audience, audiences 1 (noun) An audience is the group of people who are watching or listening to a performance. **2** An audience is also a private or formal meeting with an important person, e.g. *an audience with the Queen.*

audio (adjective) used in recording and reproducing sound, e.g. *audio equipment.*

audit, audits, auditing, audited 1 (verb) To audit a set of financial accounts means to examine them officially to check that they are correct. **2** (noun) An audit is an official examination of an organization's accounts. **auditor** (noun).

audition, auditions (noun) An audition is a short performance given by an actor or musician, so that a director can decide whether they are suitable for a part in a play or film or for a place in an orchestra.

auditorium, auditoriums or **auditoria** (noun) In a theatre or concert hall, the auditorium is the part where the audience sits.

augment, augments, augmenting, augmented (verb; a formal word) To augment something means to add something to it.

August (noun) August is the eighth month of the year. It has 31 days.

aunt, aunts (noun) Your aunt is the sister of your mother or father, or the wife of your uncle.

au pair, au pairs (pronounced oh **pair**) (noun) An au pair is a young foreign girl who lives with a family to help with the children and housework and to learn the language.

aura, auras (noun) An aura is an atmosphere that surrounds a person or thing, e.g. *She has a great aura of calmness.*

aural (rhymes with **floral**) (adjective) relating to or done through the sense of hearing, e.g. *an aural comprehension test.*

auspices (pronounced **aw**-spiss-eez) (plural noun; a formal word) If you do something under the auspices of a person or organization, you do it with their support, e.g. *military intervention under the auspices of the United Nations.*

auspicious (adjective; a formal word) favourable and seeming to promise success, e.g. *It was an auspicious start to the month.*

austere (adjective) plain and simple, and without luxury, e.g. *the austere post-war years.* **austerity** (noun).

Australasia (pronounced ost-ral-**lay**-sha) (noun) Australasia consists of Australia, New Zealand, and neighbouring islands in the Pacific. **Australasian** (adjective).

Australia (noun) Australia is the smallest continent and the largest island in the world, situated between the Indian Ocean and the Pacific.

Australian, Australians 1 (adjective) belonging or relating to Australia. **2** (noun) An Australian is someone who comes from Australia.

Austrian, Austrians 1 (adjective) belonging or relating to Austria. **2** (noun) An Austrian is someone who comes from Austria.

authentic (adjective) real and genuine. **authenticity** (noun).

author, authors (noun) The author of a book is the person who wrote it.

authoritarian (adjective) believing in strict obedience, e.g. *thirty years of authoritarian government.* **authoritarianism** (noun).

authoritative 1 (adjective) having authority, e.g. *his deep, authoritative voice.* **2** generally accepted as being reliable and accurate, e.g. *an authoritative biography of the President.* **authoritatively** (adverb).

authority, authorities 1 (noun) Authority is the power to control people, e.g. *Henry VIII refused to accept papal authority... He spoke with authority.* **2** (plural noun) The authorities are the people who have the power to make decisions. **3** (noun) An authority is a local government department, e.g. *local health authorities.* **4** Someone who is an authority on something knows a lot about it, e.g. *He is an authority on Irish history.*

authorize, authorizes, authorizing, authorized; also spelled **authorise** (verb) To authorize something means to give official permission for it to happen. **authorization** (noun).

autobiography, autobiographies (noun) Someone's autobiography is an account of their life which they have written themselves. **autobiographical** (adjective).

autograph, autographs (noun) An autograph is the signature of a famous person.

automated (adjective) If a factory or industrial process is automated, it works using machinery rather than people. **automation** (noun).

automatic 1 (adjective) An automatic machine is programmed to perform tasks without needing a person to operate it, e.g. *The plane was flying on automatic pilot.* **2** Automatic actions or reactions take place without involving conscious thought. **3** A process or punishment that is automatic always happens as a direct result of something, e.g. *The penalty for murder is an automatic life sentence.* **automatically** (adverb).

automobile, automobiles (noun; an American or formal word) An automobile is a car.

autonomous (pronounced aw-**ton**-nom-uss) (adjective) self-controlling or self-governing, e.g. *The country has two autonomous regions.* **autonomy** (noun).

autopsy, autopsies (noun) An autopsy is a medical examination of a dead body to discover the cause of death.

autumn, autumns (noun) Autumn is the season between summer and winter, when the weather becomes cooler. **autumnal** (adjective).

auxiliary, auxiliaries 1 (noun) An auxiliary is a person employed to help other members of staff, e.g. *nursing auxiliaries.* **2** (adjective) Auxiliary equipment is used when necessary in addition to the main equipment, e.g. *Auxiliary fuel tanks were stored in the bomb bay.*

avail (phrase) If something that you do is **of no avail** or **to no avail,** it is not successful or helpful.

available 1 (adjective) Something that is available can be obtained, e.g. *Artichokes are available in supermarkets.* **2** Someone who is available is ready for work or free for people to talk to, e.g. *She will no longer be available at weekends.* **availability** (noun).

avalanche, avalanches (pronounced **av**-a-lahnsh) (noun) An avalanche is a huge mass of snow and ice that falls down a mountain side.

avant-garde (pronounced av-vong-**gard**) (adjective) extremely modern or experimental, especially in art, literature, or music.

avarice (noun; a formal word)

Avarice is greed for money and possessions. **avaricious** (adjective).

avenge, avenges, avenging, avenged (verb) If you avenge something harmful that someone has done to you or your family, you punish or harm the other person in return, e.g. *He was prepared to avenge the death of his friend.* **avenger** (noun).

avenue, avenues (noun) An avenue is a street, especially one with trees along it.

average, averages, averaging, averaged 1 (noun) An average is a result obtained by adding several amounts together and then dividing the total by the number of different amounts, e.g. *Six pupils were examined in a total of 39 subjects, an average of 6.5 subjects per pupil.* **2** (adjective) Average means standard, normal, or usual, e.g. *the average American teenager.* **3** (verb) To average a number means to produce that number as an average over a period of time, e.g. *Monthly sales averaged more than 110,000.* **4** (phrase) You say **on average** when mentioning what usually happens in a situation, e.g. *Men are, on average, taller than women.*

averse (adjective) unwilling to do something, e.g. *He was averse to taking painkillers.*

aversion, aversions (noun) If you have an aversion to someone or something, you dislike them very much.

avert, averts, averting, averted 1 (verb) If you avert an unpleasant event, you prevent it from happening. **2** If you avert your eyes from something, you turn your eyes away from it.

aviary, aviaries (noun) An aviary is a large cage or group of cages in which birds are kept.

aviation (noun) Aviation is the science of flying aircraft.

aviator, aviators (noun; an old-fashioned word) An aviator is a pilot of an aircraft.

avid (adjective) eager and enthusiastic for something. **avidly** (adverb).

avocado, avocados (noun) An avocado is a pear-shaped fruit, with dark green skin, soft greenish yellow flesh, and a large stone.

avoid, avoids, avoiding, avoided 1 (verb) If you avoid doing something, you make a deliberate effort not to do it. **2** If you avoid someone, you keep away from them. **avoidable** (adjective), **avoidance** (noun).

avowed 1 (adjective; a formal word) If you are an avowed supporter or opponent of something, you have declared that you support it or oppose it. **2** An avowed belief or aim is one that you hold very strongly.

avuncular (adjective) friendly and helpful in manner towards younger people.

await, awaits, awaiting, awaited 1 (verb) If you await something, you expect it. **2** If something awaits you, it will happen to you in the future.

awake, awakes, awaking, awoke, awoken 1 (adjective) Someone who is awake is not sleeping. **2** (verb) When you awake, you wake up. **3** If you are awoken by something, it wakes you up.

awaken, awakens, awakening, awakened (verb) If something awakens an emotion or interest in you, you start to feel this emotion or interest.

award, awards, awarding, awarded 1 (noun) An award is a prize or certificate for doing something well. **2** An award is also a sum of money that an organization gives to students for training or study. **3** (verb) If you award someone something, you give it to them formally or officially.

aware (adjective) If you are aware of something, you know about it or realize that it is there. **awareness** (noun).

awash (adjective or adverb) covered with water, e.g. *After the downpour the road was awash.*

away 1 (adverb) moving from a place, e.g. *I saw them walk away.* **2** at a distance from a place, e.g. *Our nearest vet is 12 miles away.* **3** in its proper place, e.g. *He put his chequebook away.* **4** not at home, school, or work, e.g. *She had been away from home for years.*

awe (noun; a formal word) Awe is a feeling of great respect mixed with amazement and sometimes slight fear.

awesome 1 (adjective) Something that is awesome is very impressive and frightening. **2** (an informal use) Awesome also means excellent or outstanding.

awful 1 (adjective) very unpleasant or very bad. **2** (an informal use) very great, e.g. *It took an awful lot of courage.* **awfully** (adverb).

awkward 1 (adjective) clumsy and uncomfortable, e.g. *an awkward gesture.* **2** embarrassed, shy, or nervous, e.g. *He was a shy, awkward young man.* **3** difficult to deal with, e.g. *My lawyer is in an awkward situation.*

awning, awnings (noun) An awning is a large roof of canvas or plastic attached to a building or vehicle, to shelter people from the sun and rain.

awry (pronounced a-**rye**) (adjective) wrong or not as planned, e.g. *Why had their plans gone so badly awry?*

axe, axes, axing, axed 1 (noun) An axe is a tool with a handle and a sharp blade, used for chopping wood. **2** (verb) To axe something means to end it.

axiom, axioms (noun) An axiom is a statement or saying that is generally accepted to be true.

axis, axes (pronounced **ak**-siss) **1** (noun) An axis is an imaginary line through the centre of something, around which it moves. **2** An axis is also one of the two sides of a graph.

axle, axles (noun) An axle is the long bar that connects a pair of wheels on a vehicle.

ayatollah, ayatollahs (noun) An ayatollah is an Islamic religious leader in Iran.

azure (pronounced az-**yoor**) (adjective; a literary word) bright blue.

B b

babble, babbles, babbling, babbled (verb) When someone babbles, they talk in a confused or excited way.

baboon, baboons (noun) A baboon is an African monkey with a pointed face, large teeth, and a long tail.

baby, babies (noun) A baby is a child in the first year or two of its life. **babyhood** (noun), **babyish** (adjective).

baby-sit, baby-sits, baby-sitting, baby-sat (verb) To baby-sit for someone means to look after their children while that person is out. **baby-sitter** (noun), **baby-sitting** (noun).

bachelor, bachelors (noun) A bachelor is a man who has never been married.

back, backs, backing, backed 1 (adverb) When people or things move back, they move in the opposite direction from the one they are facing, e.g. *I leaned back.* **2** When people or things go back to a place or situation, they return to it, e.g. *She went back to sleep.* **3** If you get something back, it is returned to you. **4** If you do something back to someone, you do to them what they have done to you, e.g. *I smiled back at them.* **5** Back also means in the past, e.g. *It happened back in the early eighties.* **6** (noun) Your back is the rear part of your body. **7** The back of something is the part that is behind the front. **8** (adjective) The back parts of something are the ones near the rear, e.g. *an animal's back legs.* **9** (verb) If a building backs onto something, its back faces in that direction. **10** When a car backs, it moves backwards. **11** To back a person or organization means to support, encourage, or finance that person or organization. **12** (phrase) If something is **back to front,** the back part is where the front should be. **back down** (verb) If you back down on a demand or claim, you withdraw and give up. **back out** (verb) If you back out of a promise or commitment, you decide not to do what you had promised or agreed to do. **back up 1** (verb) If you back up a claim or story, you produce evidence to show that it is true. **2** If you back someone up, you support them against their critics or enemies.

backbone, backbones 1 (noun) A backbone is the column of linked bones along the middle of a person's or animal's back. **2** Backbone is also strength of character.

backdate, backdates, backdating, backdated (verb) If an arrangement is backdated, it is made effective from a date earlier than the one on which it is completed or signed.

backdrop, backdrops (noun) A backdrop is the background to a situation or event, e.g. *The visit occurred against the backdrop of the political crisis.*

backer, backers (noun) The

backers of a project are the people who give it financial help.

backfire, backfires, backfiring, backfired 1 (verb) If a plan backfires, it produces an opposite result to the one intended. **2** When a car backfires, there is a small but noisy explosion in its exhaust pipe.

background, backgrounds 1 (noun) The background to an event is the circumstances which help to explain it or caused it to happen. **2** Your background is the kind of home you come from and your education and experience, e.g. *a rich background.* **3** If sounds are in the background, they are there but no one really pays any attention to them, e.g. *She could hear voices in the background.*

backing, backings (noun) Backing is support or help, e.g. *The project got government backing.*

backlash (noun) A backlash is a hostile reaction to a new development or a new policy.

backlog, backlogs (noun) A backlog is a number of things that have accumulated and that must be dealt with.

backpack, backpacks (noun) A backpack is a large bag that hikers or campers carry on their backs.

backside, backsides (noun; an informal word) Your backside is the part of your body that you sit on.

backward 1 (adjective) Backward means directed behind you, e.g. *without a backward glance.* **2** A backward country or society is one that does not have modern industries or technology. **3** A backward child is one who is unable to learn as quickly as other children of the same age. **backwardness** (noun).

backwards 1 (adverb) Backwards means behind you, e.g. *Lucille looked backwards.* **2** If you do something backwards, you do it the opposite of the usual way, e.g. *He instructed them to count backwards.*

bacon (noun) Bacon is meat from the back or sides of a pig, which has been cured with salt and sometimes smoked.

bacteria (plural noun) Bacteria are very tiny organisms which can cause disease. **bacterial** (adjective).

bad, worse, worst 1 (adjective) Anything harmful or upsetting can be described as bad, e.g. *I have some bad news... Is the pain bad?* **2** insufficient or of poor quality, e.g. *bad roads.* **3** evil or immoral in character or behaviour, e.g. *a bad person.* **4** lacking skill in something, e.g. *I was bad at sports.* **5** Bad language consists of swearwords. **6** If you have a bad temper, you become angry easily. **7** People who have bad manners behave in a rude and unacceptable way. **badly** (adverb), **badness** (noun).

bade a form of the past tense of **bid**.

badge, badges (noun) A badge is a piece of plastic or metal with a design or message on it that you can pin to your clothes.

badger, badgers, badgering,

badgered 1 (noun) A badger is a wild animal that has a white head with two black stripes on it. Badgers live underground and come out to feed at night. **2** (verb) If you badger someone, you keep asking them questions or pestering them to do something.

badminton (noun) Badminton is a game in which two or four players use rackets to hit a shuttlecock over a high net.

baffle, baffles, baffling, baffled (verb) If something baffles you, you cannot understand it or cannot think of an answer to it, e.g. *The symptoms baffled the doctors.* **baffled** (adjective), **baffling** (adjective).

bag, bags 1 (noun) A bag is a container, usually made of plastic, cloth, or paper, for carrying things in. **2** (plural noun; an informal use) Bags of something is a lot of it, e.g. *bags of fun.*

baggage (noun) Your baggage is all the suitcases and bags that you take when you are travelling.

baggy, baggier, baggiest (adjective) Baggy clothing hangs loosely because it is too big.

bagpipes (plural noun) Bagpipes are a musical instrument played by squeezing air out of a leather bag through pipes, on which a tune is played.

bail, bails, bailing, bailed 1 (noun) Bail is a sum of money paid to a court to allow an accused person to go free until the time of his or her trial, e.g. *He was released on bail.* **2** (verb) If you bail water from a boat, you remove it using a container.

bailiff, bailiffs 1 (noun) A bailiff is a law officer who makes sure that the decisions of a court are obeyed, especially by removing someone's property if they fail to pay money that they owe. **2** A bailiff is also a person employed to look after land or property for the owner.

bait, baits, baiting, baited 1 (noun) Bait is a small amount of food placed on a hook or in a trap, to attract a fish or wild animal so that it gets caught. **2** (verb) If you bait a hook or trap, you put some food on it to catch a fish or wild animal.

baize (noun) Baize is a thick woollen material, usually green, used for covering snooker tables.

bake, bakes, baking, baked 1 (verb) To bake food means to cook it in an oven without using liquid or fat. **2** To bake earth or clay means to heat it until it becomes hard.

baker, bakers (noun) A baker is a person who makes and sells bread and cakes.

bakery, bakeries (noun) A bakery is a building where bread and cakes are baked and sold.

balaclava, balaclavas (noun) A balaclava is a close-fitting woollen hood that covers every part of your head except your face.

balance, balances, balancing, balanced 1 (verb) When someone or something balances, they remain steady and do not fall over. **2** (noun) Balance is the state of being upright and steady, e.g. *He lost his balance.* **3** Balance is also a situation in which all the parts involved have a stable relationship with each other, e.g. *the chemical balance of the brain.* **4** The balance in someone's bank account is the amount of money that they have in it.

balcony, balconies 1 (noun) A balcony is a platform on the outside of a building with a wall or railing round it. **2** In a theatre or cinema, the balcony is an area of upstairs seats.

bald, balder, baldest 1 (adjective) A bald person has little or no hair on their head. **2** A bald statement or question is made in the simplest way without any attempt to be polite. **baldly** (adverb), **baldness** (noun).

bale, bales, baling, baled 1 (noun) A bale is a large quantity of something such as cloth, paper, or hay tied in a tight bundle. **2** (verb) If you bale water from a boat, you remove it using a container; also spelled **bail**.

balk, balks, balking, balked; also spelled **baulk** (verb) If you balk at something, you object to it and may refuse to do it, e.g. *He balked at the cost.*

ball, balls 1 (noun) A ball is any object shaped like a sphere, especially one used in games such as tennis, cricket, and football. **2** The ball of your foot or thumb is the rounded part where your toes join your foot or your thumb joins your hand. **3** A ball is also a large formal social event at which people dance.

ballad, ballads 1 (noun) A ballad is a long song or poem which tells a story. **2** A ballad is also a slow, romantic pop song.

ballast (noun) Ballast is any heavy material placed in a ship to make it more stable.

ballerina, ballerinas (noun) A ballerina is a woman ballet dancer.

ballet (pronounced **bal**-lay) (noun) Ballet is a type of very skilled expressive dancing with carefully planned movements.

balloon, balloons 1 (noun) A balloon is a small bag made of thin rubber that you blow into until it becomes larger and rounder. Balloons are used as toys or decorations. **2** A balloon is also a large, strong bag filled with gas or hot air, which travels through the air carrying passengers in a basket or compartment underneath.

ballot, ballots, balloting, balloted 1 (noun) A ballot is a secret vote in which people choose a candidate in an election or express their opinion about something. **2** (verb) When a group of people are balloted, they are asked questions to find out what they think about a particular problem or question.

ballpoint, ballpoints (noun) A ballpoint is a pen with a small metal ball at the end which transfers the ink onto the paper.

ballroom, ballrooms (noun) A ballroom is a very large room used for dancing or formal balls.

balm (pronounced **bahm**) (noun; an old-fashioned word) Balm is a soothing ointment made from a fragrant oily resin produced by certain kinds of tropical trees.

balmy, balmier, balmiest (adjective) mild and pleasant, e.g. *balmy summer evenings.*

balsa (noun) Balsa is very lightweight wood from a South American tree, used to make such things as model aeroplanes.

balustrade, balustrades (noun) A balustrade is a railing or wall on a balcony or staircase.

bamboo (noun) Bamboo is a tall tropical grass with hard, hollow stems used for making furniture.

ban, bans, banning, banned 1 (verb) If something is banned, or if you are banned from doing it or using it, you are not allowed to do it or use it. **2** (noun) If there is a ban on something, it is not allowed.

banal (pronounced ba-**nahl**) (adjective) very ordinary or obvious, and therefore not effective or interesting, e.g. *He made some banal remark.* **banality** (noun).

banana, bananas (noun) A banana is a long curved fruit with a yellow skin and cream-coloured flesh.

band, bands 1 (noun) A band is a group of musicians who play jazz or pop music together, or a group who play brass instruments together. **2** A band is also any group of people who share a common purpose, e.g. *a select band of illustrious sportsmen.* **3** A band is a narrow strip of something used to hold things together or worn as a decoration round someone's head or wrist, e.g. *an elastic band... a pink headband.*

bandage, bandages, bandaging, bandaged 1 (noun) A bandage is a strip of cloth wrapped round a wound to protect it. **2** (verb) If you bandage a wound, you tie a bandage round it.

bandit, bandits (noun; an old-fashioned word) A bandit was a member of an armed gang who lived by robbing travellers.

bandstand, bandstands (noun) A bandstand is a platform, usually with a roof, where a band can play in the open air.

bandwagon (phrase) To **jump on the bandwagon** means to become involved in something because it is fashionable or likely to be successful.

bandy, bandies, bandying, bandied (verb) If a word, name, or idea is bandied about, many people use it or mention it.

bane (noun; a literary word) Someone or something that is the bane of a person or organization causes a lot of trouble for them, e.g. *the bane of my life.*

bang, bangs, banging, banged 1 (verb) If you bang something, you hit it or put it somewhere violently, so that it makes a loud noise, e.g. *He banged down the receiver.* **2** If you bang a part of your body against something, you accidentally bump it, e.g. *I banged my knee on the table.* **3** (noun) A bang is a sudden, short, loud noise. **4** A bang is also a hard or painful bump against something.

Bangladeshi, Bangladeshis

(pronounced bang-glad-**desh**-ee) **1** (adjective) belonging or relating to Bangladesh. **2** (noun) A Bangladeshi is someone who comes from Bangladesh.

bangle, bangles (noun) A bangle is an ornamental band or chain worn round someone's wrist or ankle.

banish, banishes, banishing, banished 1 (verb) To banish someone means to send them into exile. **2** To banish something means to get rid of it, e.g. *It will be a long time before cancer is banished.* **banishment** (noun).

banister, banisters; also spelled **bannister** (noun) A banister is a rail supported by posts along the side of a staircase.

banjo, banjos or **banjoes** (noun) A banjo is a musical instrument with a long neck, a hollow circular body, and four or more strings.

bank, banks, banking, banked 1 (noun) A bank is an institution where you can keep your money, and which lends money and offers other financial services. **2** (verb) When you bank money, you pay it into a bank. **3** (noun) A bank of something is a store of it kept ready for use, e.g. *a blood bank.* **4** The bank of a river or lake is the raised ground along its edge. **5** A bank is also the sloping side of an area of raised ground. **6** (verb) If you bank on something happening, you expect it and rely on it. **banker** (noun), **banking** (noun).

bank holiday, bank holidays (noun) A bank holiday is a public holiday, when banks are closed by law.

banknote, banknotes (noun) A banknote is a piece of paper money.

bankrupt, bankrupts, bankrupting, bankrupted 1 (adjective) When someone is declared bankrupt, they are legally recognized as not having enough money to pay their debts. Their property can then be sold, and the money used to repay some of what they owe. **2** (noun) A bankrupt is someone who has been declared bankrupt. **3** (verb) To bankrupt someone means to make them bankrupt, e.g. *Restoring the house nearly bankrupted them.* **bankruptcy** (noun).

banner, banners (noun) A banner is a strip of cloth with a message or slogan on it.

bannister another spelling of **banister**.

banquet, banquets (noun) A banquet is a grand formal dinner, often followed by speeches.

banter (noun) Banter is friendly joking and teasing.

baptism (noun) Baptism is the ceremony in which someone is baptized.

Baptist, Baptists (noun or adjective) Baptists are members of a Protestant church who believe that people should be baptized when they are adults rather than when they are babies.

baptize, baptizes, baptizing, baptized; also spelled **baptise** (verb) In the Christian religion, when someone is baptized, water is sprinkled on them, or they are immersed in water, as a sign that they have become a Christian.

bar, bars, barring, barred 1 (noun) A bar is a room in a pub or hotel where drinks are served; also used of the counter on which drinks are served. **2** A bar is a long, straight piece of metal. **3** Bars are strong, thin, vertical pieces of metal fixed over a window to make it secure, or made into a door or cage. **4** A bar is a piece of something made in a rectangular shape, e.g. *a bar of soap.* **5** (verb) If you bar a door, you place something across it to prevent it being opened. **6** If you bar someone's way, you stop them going somewhere by standing in front of them. **7** (noun) The bars in a piece of music are the many short parts of equal length that the piece is divided into.

barb, barbs (noun) A barb is a sharp curved point on the end of an arrow or fish-hook.

barbarian, barbarians (noun) A barbarian was a member of a wild and uncivilized tribe in former times.

barbaric (adjective) cruel or brutal, e.g. *Ban the barbaric sport of deer hunting.* **barbarity** (noun).

barbecue, barbecues, barbecuing, barbecued 1 (noun) A barbecue is a grill with a charcoal fire on which you cook food, usually outdoors; also an outdoor party where you eat food cooked on a barbecue. **2** (verb) When food is barbecued, it is cooked over a charcoal grill.

barbed (adjective) A barbed remark is one that seems straightforward but is really malicious or spiteful.

barbed wire (noun) Barbed wire is strong wire with sharp points sticking out of it, used to make fences.

barber, barbers (noun) A barber is a man who cuts men's hair.

barbiturate, barbiturates (noun) A barbiturate is a drug that people take to make them calm or to put them to sleep.

bard, bards (noun; a literary word) A bard is a poet. Some people call Shakespeare the Bard.

bare, bares, baring, bared 1 (adjective) If a part of your body is bare, it is not covered by any clothing. **2** If something is bare, it has nothing on top of it or inside it, e.g. *bare floorboards... a small bare office.* **3** When trees are bare, they have no leaves on them. **4** (verb) If you bare something, you uncover or show it. **5** (adjective) The bare minimum or bare essentials means the very least that is needed, e.g. *They were fed the bare minimum.*

barefoot (adjective or adverb) not wearing anything on your feet.

barely (adverb) only just, e.g. *The girl was barely sixteen.*

bargain, bargains, bargaining, bargained 1 (noun) A bargain is an agreement in which two people or groups discuss and agree what each will do, pay, or receive in a matter which affects them both. **2** (verb) When people bargain with each other, they discuss and agree terms about what each will do, pay, or receive in a matter which involves both. **3** (noun) A bargain is also something which is sold at a low price and which is good value.

barge, barges, barging, barged **1** (noun) A barge is a boat with a flat bottom. Barges are used for carrying heavy loads, especially on canals. **2** (verb; an informal use) If you barge into a place, you push into it in a rough or rude way.

baritone, baritones (noun) A baritone is a man with a fairly deep singing voice.

bark, barks, barking, barked **1** (verb) When a dog barks, it makes a short, loud noise, once or several times. **2** (noun) A bark is the short, loud noise that a dog makes. **3** The bark of a tree is the tough material that covers the outside.

barley (noun) Barley is a cereal that is grown for food. It is also used for making beer and whisky.

bar mitzvah (noun) A Jewish boy's bar mitzvah is a ceremony that takes place on his 13th birthday, after which he is regarded as an adult.

barmy, barmier, barmiest (adjective; an informal word) mad or very foolish.

barn, barns (noun) A barn is a large farm building used for storing crops or animal food, and sometimes for keeping animals in.

barnacle, barnacles (noun) A barnacle is a small shellfish that fixes itself to rocks and to the bottom of boats.

barometer, barometers (noun) A barometer is an instrument that measures atmospheric pressure and shows when the weather is changing.

baron, barons (noun) A baron is a member of the lowest rank of the nobility. **baronial** (adjective).

baroness, baronesses (noun) A baroness is a woman who has the rank of baron, or who is the wife of a baron.

baronet, baronets (noun) A baronet is a man who has this title which has been passed to him from his father.

barracks (noun) A barracks is a building where soldiers live.

barracuda, barracudas (noun) A barracuda is a large, fierce tropical fish with sharp teeth.

barrage, barrages **1** (noun) A barrage of questions or complaints is a lot of them all coming at the same time. **2** A barrage is continuous artillery fire over a wide area, to prevent the enemy from moving.

barrel, barrels **1** (noun) A barrel is a wooden container with rounded sides and flat ends. **2** The barrel of a gun is the long tube through which the bullet is fired.

barren **1** (adjective) Barren land has soil of such poor quality that plants cannot grow on it. **2** If a female is barren, she is physically incapable of having offspring.

barricade, barricades, barricading, barricaded **1** (noun) A barricade is a temporary barrier put up to stop people getting past. **2** (verb) If you barricade yourself inside a room or building, you put something heavy against the door to stop people getting in.

barrier, barriers (noun) A barrier is a fence or wall that prevents people or animals getting from one area to another.

barrister, barristers (noun) A barrister is a lawyer who can speak in a higher court on behalf of the defence or the prosecution.

barrow, barrows 1 (noun) A barrow is the same as a wheelbarrow. **2** A barrow is a large cart, from which fruit or other goods are sold in the street.

barter, barters, bartering, bartered 1 (verb) If you barter goods, you exchange them for other goods, rather than selling them for money. **2** (noun) Barter is the activity of exchanging goods.

base, bases, basing, based 1 (noun) The base of something is its lowest part, which often supports the rest. **2** A base is a place which part of an army, navy, or air force works from. **3** (verb) To base something on something else means to use the second thing as a foundation or starting point of the first, e.g. *The opera is based on a work by Pushkin.* **4** If you are based somewhere, you live there or work from there.

baseball (noun) Baseball is a game played by two teams of nine players. Each player hits a ball with a bat and tries to run round four points, called bases, before the other team can get the ball back.

basement, basements (noun) The basement of a building is a floor built completely or partly below the ground.

bases 1 (pronounced **bay**-seez) the plural of **basis**. **2** (pronounced **bay**-siz) the plural of **base**.

bash, bashes, bashing, bashed (verb; an informal word) If you bash someone or bash into them, you hit them hard.

bashful (adjective) shy and easily embarrassed.

basic, basics 1 (adjective) The basic aspects of something are the most necessary ones, e.g. *the basic necessities of life.* **2** (plural noun) The basics of something are the most necessary aspects of it, e.g. *the basics of map-reading.* **3** (adjective) Something that is basic has only the necessary features without any extras or luxuries, e.g. *The accommodation is pretty basic.* **basically** (adverb).

basilica, basilicas (noun) A basilica is an oblong church with a rounded end called an apse.

basin, basins 1 (noun) A basin is a round wide container which is open at the top. **2** The basin of a river is a bowl of land from which water runs into the river.

basis, bases 1 (noun) The basis of something is the essential main principle from which it can be developed, e.g. *The same colour theme is used as the basis for several patterns.* **2** The basis for a belief is the facts that support it, e.g. *There is no basis for this assumption.*

bask, basks, basking, basked (verb) If you bask in the sun, you sit or lie in it, enjoying its warmth.

basket, baskets (noun) A basket is a container made of thin strips of cane woven together.

basketball (noun) Basketball is a game in which two teams of five players try to score goals by throwing a large ball through one of two circular nets suspended high up at each end of the court.

bass, basses (rhymes with **lace**) **1** (noun) A bass is a man who sings the lowest part in four-part harmony. **2** A bass is also a musical instrument that provides the rhythm and lowest part in the harmonies

bass, basses (rhymes with **gas**) (noun) A bass is a type of edible sea fish.

basset hound, basset hounds (noun) A basset hound is a smooth-haired dog with a long body and ears, and short legs.

bassoon, bassoons (noun) A bassoon is a large woodwind instrument that can produce a wide range of notes, including very low ones.

bastard, bastards 1 (noun; an offensive use) People sometimes call someone a bastard when they dislike them or are very angry with them. **2** (an old-fashioned use) A bastard is someone whose parents were not married when he or she was born.

baste, bastes, basting, basted (verb) When you baste meat that is roasting, you pour hot fat over it so that it does not become dry while cooking.

bastion, bastions (noun; a literary word) A bastion is something that protects a system or way of life, e.g. *The country is the last bastion of Communism.*

bat, bats, batting, batted 1 (noun) A bat is a specially shaped piece of wood with a handle, used for hitting the ball in a game such as cricket, baseball, or table tennis. **2** (verb) In certain sports, when someone is batting, it is their turn to try to hit the ball and score runs. **3** (noun) A bat is also a small, flying nocturnal animal that looks like a mouse with wings.

batch, batches (noun) A batch is a group of things of the same kind produced or dealt with together.

bated (phrase) **With bated breath** means very anxiously.

bath, baths (noun) A bath is a long container which you fill with water and sit in to wash yourself.

bathe, bathes, bathing, bathed 1 (verb) When you bathe, you swim or play in the sea or in a river or lake. **2** When you bathe a wound, you wash it gently. **3** (a literary use) If a place is bathed in light, a lot of light reaches it, e.g. *The room was bathed in spring sunshine.* **bather** (noun), **bathing** (noun).

bathroom, bathrooms (noun) A bathroom is a room with a bath or shower, a washbasin, and often a toilet in it.

baths (noun) The baths is a public swimming pool.

baton, batons 1 (noun) A baton is a light, thin stick that a conductor uses to direct an orchestra or choir. **2** In athletics, the baton is a short stick passed from one runner to another in a relay race.

batsman, batsmen (noun) In cricket, the batsman is the person who is batting.

battalion, battalions (noun) A battalion is an army unit consisting of three or more companies.

batten, battens, battening, battened (noun) A batten is a strip of wood that is fixed to something to strengthen it or hold it firm. **batten down** (verb) If you batten something down, you make it secure by fixing battens across it.

batter, batters, battering, battered 1 (verb) To batter someone or something means to hit them many times, e.g. *The waves kept battering the life raft.* **2** (noun) Batter is a mixture of flour, eggs, and milk, used to make pancakes, or to coat food before frying it. **battering** (noun).

battery, batteries 1 (noun) A battery is an apparatus for storing and producing electricity, for example in a torch, a radio, or a car. **2** A battery of things or people is a large group of them. **3** (adjective) A battery hen is one of a large number of hens kept in small cages for the mass production of eggs.

battle, battles 1 (noun) A battle is a fight between armed forces; also used of a struggle between two people or groups with conflicting aims, e.g. *the battle between town and country.* **2** A battle for something difficult is a determined attempt to obtain or achieve it, e.g. *the battle for equality.*

battlefield, battlefields (noun) A battlefield is a place where a battle is or has been fought.

battlements (plural noun) The battlements of a castle or fortress consist of a wall built round the top, with gaps through which guns or arrows could be fired.

battleship, battleships (noun) A battleship is a large, heavily armoured warship.

batty, battier, battiest (adjective; an informal word) crazy or eccentric.

bauble, baubles (noun) A bauble is a pretty but cheap ornament or piece of jewellery.

bawdy, bawdier, bawdiest (adjective) A bawdy joke, story, or song contains humorous references to sex.

bawl, bawls, bawling, bawled 1 (verb; an informal word) To bawl at someone means to shout at them loudly and harshly. **2** When a child is bawling, it is crying very loudly and angrily.

bay, bays, baying, bayed 1 (noun) A bay is a part of a coastline where the land curves inwards. **2** A bay is also a space or area used for a particular purpose, e.g. *a loading bay.* **3** Bay is a kind of tree similar to the laurel. Bay leaves are used for flavouring in cooking. **4** (phrase) If you **keep something at bay,** you prevent it from reaching you, e.g. *Eating oranges keeps colds at bay.* **5** (verb) When a hound or wolf bays, it makes a deep howling noise.

bayonet, bayonets (noun) A bayonet is a sharp blade that can be fixed to the end of a rifle and used for stabbing.

bazaar, bazaars 1 (noun) A bazaar is an area with many small shops and stalls, especially in Eastern countries. **2** A bazaar is also a sale of various goods to raise money for charity.

BC BC means 'before Christ', e.g. *in 49 BC.*

be, am, is, are; being; was, were; been 1 (auxiliary verb) Be is used with a present participle to form the continuous tense, e.g. *Crimes of violence are increasing.* **2** Be is also used to say that something will happen, e.g. *We are going to Italy next month.* **3** Be is used to form the passive voice, e.g. *The walls are being repaired.* **4** (verb) Be is used to give more information about the subject of a sentence, e.g. *Her name is Melanie.*

beach, beaches (noun) A beach is an area of sand or pebbles beside the sea.

beacon, beacons (noun) In the past, a beacon was a light or fire on a hill, which acted as a signal or warning.

bead, beads 1 (noun) Beads are small pieces of coloured glass, wood, or plastic with a hole through the middle, strung together to make necklaces and bracelets. **2** Beads of liquid are drops of it.

beady (adjective) Beady eyes are small and bright like beads.

beagle, beagles (noun) A beagle is a short-haired dog with long ears and short legs.

beak, beaks (noun) A bird's beak is the hard part of its mouth that sticks out.

beaker, beakers 1 (noun) A beaker is a cup for drinking out of, usually made of plastic and without a handle. **2** A beaker is also a glass container with a lip which is used in laboratories.

beam, beams, beaming, beamed 1 (noun) A beam is a broad smile. **2** A beam of light is a band of light that shines from something such as a torch. **3** A beam is also a long, thick bar of wood, concrete, or metal, especially one that supports a roof. **4** (verb) If you beam, you smile because you are happy.

bean, beans (noun) Beans are the seeds or pods of a climbing plant, which are eaten as a vegetable; also used of some other seeds, for example the seeds from which coffee is made.

bear, bears, bearing, bore, borne 1 (noun) A bear is a large, strong wild animal with thick fur and sharp claws. **2** (verb; a formal use) To bear something means to carry it or support its weight, e.g. *Ensure your balcony is strong enough to bear the weight of plants and containers.* **3** If something bears a mark or typical feature, it has it, e.g. *The game bore the hallmarks of his artistry.* **4** If you bear something difficult, you accept it and are able to deal with it, e.g *He bore his last illness with remarkable courage.* **5** If you can't bear someone or something, you dislike them very much. **6** (a formal use) When a plant or tree bears flowers, fruit, or leaves, it produces them. **bearable** (adjective).

beard, beards (noun) A man's beard is the hair that grows on the lower part of his face. **bearded** (adjective).

bearer, bearers (noun) The bearer of something is the person who carries, presents, or upholds it, e.g. *the bearer of bad news.*

bearing 1 (noun) If something has a bearing on a situation, it is relevant to it. **2** Someone's bearing is the way in which they move or stand.

beast, beasts 1 (noun; an old-fashioned use) A beast is a large wild animal. **2** (an informal use) If you call someone a beast, you mean that they are unkind, cruel, or spiteful.

beastly, beastlier, beastliest (adjective; an old-fashioned informal word) unkind, cruel, or spiteful.

beat, beats, beating, beat, beaten 1 (verb) To beat someone or something means to hit them hard and repeatedly, e.g. *He threatened to beat her.* **2** If you beat someone in a race, game, or competition, you defeat them or do better than them. **3** When a bird or insect beats its wings, it moves them up and down. **4** When your heart is beating, it is pumping blood with a regular rhythm. **5** If you beat eggs, cream, or butter, you mix them vigorously using a fork or a whisk. **6** (noun) The beat of your heart is its regular pumping action. **7** The beat of a piece of music is its main rhythm. **8** A police officer's beat is the area which he or she patrols and is responsible for. **beater** (noun), **beating** (noun). **beat up** (verb) To beat someone up means to hit or kick them repeatedly until they are severely hurt.

beautiful (adjective) very attractive or pleasing, e.g. *a beautiful girl... beautiful music.* **beautifully** (adverb).

beauty, beauties 1 (noun) Beauty is the quality of being beautiful. **2** (a rather old-fashioned use) A beauty is a very attractive woman. **3** The beauty of an idea or plan is what makes it attractive or worthwhile, e.g. *The beauty of the fund is its simplicity.*

beaver, beavers (noun) A beaver is an amphibious rodent with a big, flat tail and webbed hind feet which it uses to build dams.

because 1 (conjunction) Because is used with a clause that gives the reason for something, e.g. *I went home because I was tired.* **2** (preposition) **Because of** is used with a noun that gives the reason for something, e.g. *He quit playing because of a knee injury.*

beck (noun) If you are at someone's beck and call, you are always available to do what they ask.

beckon, beckons, beckoning, beckoned 1 (verb) If you beckon to someone, you signal with your hand that you want them to come to you. **2** If you say that something beckons, you mean that you find it very attractive, e.g. *A career in journalism beckons.*

become, becomes, becoming,

became, become (verb) To become something means to start feeling or being that thing, e.g. *I became very angry... He became an actor.*

bed, beds 1 (noun) A bed is a piece of furniture that you lie on when you sleep. **2** A bed in a garden is an area of ground in which plants are grown. **3** The bed of a sea or river is the ground at the bottom of it.

bedclothes (plural noun) Bedclothes are the sheets and covers that you put over you when you get into bed.

bedding (noun) Bedding is sheets, blankets, and other covers that are used on beds.

bedlam (noun) You can refer to a noisy and disorderly place or situation as bedlam, e.g. *The delay caused bedlam at the crowded station.*

bedpan, bedpans (noun) A bedpan is a shallow bowl shaped like a toilet seat, which is used as a toilet by people who are too ill to get out of bed.

bedraggled (adjective) A bedraggled person or animal is in a messy or untidy state.

bedridden (adjective) Someone who is bedridden is too ill or disabled to get out of bed.

bedrock 1 (noun) Bedrock is the solid rock under the soil. **2** The bedrock of something is the foundation and principles on which it is based, e.g. *His life was built on the bedrock of integrity.*

bedroom, bedrooms (noun) A bedroom is a room used for sleeping in.

bedspread, bedspreads (noun) A bedspread is a cover put over a bed, on top of the sheets and blankets.

bedstead, bedsteads (noun) A bedstead is the metal or wooden frame of an old-fashioned bed.

bee, bees (noun) A bee is an insect that buzzes as it flies. Bees make honey and live in large groups.

beech, beeches (noun) A beech is a deciduous tree with a smooth grey trunk and shiny leaves.

beef (noun) Beef is the meat of a cow, bull, or ox.

beefy, beefier, beefiest (adjective; an informal word) A beefy person is strong and muscular.

beehive, beehives (noun) A beehive is a natural or artificial structure in which bees live and make their honey.

beeline (phrase; an informal use) If you **make a beeline** for a place, you go there as quickly and directly as possible.

been the past participle of **be.**

beer (noun) Beer is an alcoholic drink made from malt and flavoured with hops.

beet (noun) Beet is a plant with an edible root and leaves.

beetle, beetles (noun) A beetle is a flying insect with hard wings which cover its body when it is not flying.

beetroot, beetroots (noun) A beetroot is the edible, round, dark red root of a type of beet.

befall, befalls, befalling, befell, befallen (verb; an old-fashioned word) If something befalls you, it happens to you, e.g. *A similar fate befell my cousin.*

before 1 (adverb, preposition,

or conjunction) Before is used to refer to a previous time, e.g. *Apply the ointment before going to bed.* **2** (adverb) If you have done something before, you have done it on a previous occasion, e.g. *Never before had I seen such a moon.* **3** (preposition; a formal use) Before also means in front of, e.g. *He grabbed the beer before him on the table.*

beforehand (adverb) before, e.g. *It had been agreed beforehand that they would spend the night there.*

befriend, befriends, befriending, befriended (verb) If you befriend someone, you act in a kind and helpful way and so become friends with them.

beg, begs, begging, begged 1 (verb) When people beg, they ask for food or money, because they are very poor. **2** If you beg someone to do something, you ask them very earnestly to do it.

beggar, beggars (noun) A beggar is someone who lives by asking people for money or food.

begin, begins, beginning, began, begun (verb) If you begin to do something, you start doing it. When something begins, it starts.

beginner, beginners (noun) A beginner is someone who has just started learning to do something and cannot do it very well yet.

beginning, beginnings (noun) The beginning of something is the first part of it or the time when it starts, e.g. *They had now reached the beginning of the city.*

begonia, begonias (pronounced be-**go**-nya) (noun) A begonia is a garden plant or house plant with brightly coloured flowers.

begrudge, begrudges, begrudging, begrudged (verb) If you begrudge someone something, you are angry or envious because they have it, e.g. *No one could begrudge him the glory.*

beguiling (rhymes with **smiling**) (adjective) charming, but often in a deceptive way.

behalf (phrase) To do something **on behalf of** someone or something means to do it for their benefit or as their representative.

behave, behaves, behaving, behaved 1 (verb) If you behave in a particular way, you act in that way, e.g. *They were behaving like animals.* **2** To behave yourself means to act correctly or properly.

behaviour (noun) Your behaviour is the way in which you behave.

behead, beheads, beheading, beheaded (verb) To behead someone means to cut their head off.

beheld the past tense of **behold**.

behind 1 (preposition) at the back of, e.g. *He was seated behind the desk.* **2** responsible for or causing, e.g. *He was the driving force behind the move.* **3** supporting someone, e.g. *The whole country was behind him.* **4** (adverb) If you stay behind, you remain after other people have gone. **5** If you leave something behind, you do not take it with you.

behold (interjection; a literary word) You say 'behold' when you want someone to look at something. **beholder** (noun).

beige (pronounced **bayj**) (noun or adjective) pale creamy-brown.

being, beings 1 Being is the present participle of **be. 2** (noun) Being is the state or fact of existing, e.g. *He was a politician to the last fibre of his being... The eleven plus was still in being then.* **3** A being is a living creature, either real or imaginary, e.g. *alien beings with oblong heads.*

belated (adjective; a formal word) A belated action happens later than it should have done, e.g. *a belated birthday present.* **belatedly** (adverb).

belch, belches, belching, belched 1 (verb) If you belch, you make a sudden noise in your throat because air has risen up from your stomach. **2** (noun) A belch is the noise you make when you belch. **3** (verb) If something belches smoke or fire, it sends it out in large amounts, e.g. *Smoke belched from the steelworks.*

beleaguered 1 (adjective) struggling against difficulties or criticism, e.g. *the beleaguered England boss.* **2** besieged by an enemy, e.g. *the beleaguered garrison.*

belfry, belfries (noun) The belfry is the part of a church tower where the bells are.

Belgian, Belgians 1 (adjective) belonging or relating to Belgium. **2** (noun) A Belgian is someone who comes from Belgium.

belief, beliefs 1 (noun) A belief is a feeling of certainty that something exists or is true. **2** A belief is also one of the principles of a religion or moral system.

believe, believes, believing, believed 1 (verb) If you believe that something is true, you accept that it is true. **2** If you believe someone, you accept that they are telling the truth. **3** If you believe in things such as God and miracles, you accept that they exist or happen. **4** If you believe in something such as a plan or system, you are in favour of it, e.g. *They really believe in education.* **believable** (adjective), **believer** (noun).

belittle, belittles, belittling, belittled (verb) If you belittle someone or something, you make them seem unimportant, e.g. *He derided my taste and belittled my opinions.*

bell, bells 1 (noun) A bell is a hollow metal object shaped like an inverted cup. It has a piece inside called a clapper that hits the sides, producing a loud ringing sound. **2** A bell is also an electrical device that rings or buzzes in order to attract attention.

belligerent (adjective) aggressive and keen to start a fight or an argument. **belligerence** (noun).

bellow, bellows, bellowing, bellowed 1 (verb) When an animal such as a bull bellows, it makes a loud, deep roaring noise. **2** If someone bellows, they shout in a loud, deep voice. **3** (plural noun) Bellows are a piece of equipment used for blowing air into a fire to make it burn more fiercely.

belly, bellies 1 (noun) Your belly is your stomach or the front of your body below your chest. **2** An animal's belly is the underneath part of its body.

belong, belongs, belonging, belonged 1 (verb) If something belongs to you, it is yours and you own it. **2** To belong to a group means to be a member of it. **3** If something belongs in a particular place, that is where it should be, e.g. *It did not belong in the music room.*

belongings (plural noun) Your belongings are the things that you own.

beloved (pronounced bil-**luv**-id) (adjective) A beloved person or thing is one that you feel a great affection for.

below 1 (preposition or adverb) If something is below a line or the surface of something else, it is lower down, e.g. *six inches below soil level.* **2** Below also means at or to a lower point, level, or rate, e.g. *The temperature fell below the legal minimum.*

belt, belts, belting, belted 1 (noun) A belt is a strip of leather or cloth that you fasten round your waist to hold your trousers or skirt up. **2** In a machine, a belt is a circular strip of rubber that drives moving parts or carries objects along. **3** A belt is also a specific area, e.g. *Scotland's central belt.* **4** (verb; an informal use) To belt someone means to hit them very hard.

bemused (adjective) If you are bemused, you are puzzled or confused.

bench, benches 1 (noun) A bench is a long seat that two or more people can sit on. **2** A bench is also a long, narrow worktable.

bend, bends, bending, bent (verb) When you bend something, you use force to make it curved or angular. **2** When you bend, you move your head and shoulders forward and downwards. **3** (noun) A bend in a road, river, or pipe is a curved part of it. **bent** (adjective).

beneath 1 an old-fashioned word for **underneath**. **2** (preposition) If someone thinks something is beneath them they think that it is too trivial or unimportant for them to bother with it.

benefactor, benefactors (noun) A benefactor is a person who helps to support a person or institution by giving money.

beneficial (adjective) Something that is beneficial is good for people, e.g. *the beneficial effects of exercise.* **beneficially** (adverb).

beneficiary, beneficiaries (noun) A beneficiary of something is someone who receives money or other benefits from it, e.g. *She is the chief beneficiary of her father's will.*

benefit, benefits, benefiting, benefited 1 (noun) The benefits of something are the advantages that it brings to people, e.g. *the benefits of relaxation.* **2** (verb) If you benefit from something, it helps you. **3** (noun) Benefit is money given by the government to people who are poor, ill, or unemployed.

benevolent (adjective) kind and helpful. **benevolence**

(noun), **benevolently** (adverb).

benign (pronounced be-**nine**) **1** (adjective) Someone who is benign is kind, gentle, and harmless. **2** A benign tumour is one that will not cause death or serious illness. **benignly** (adverb).

bent 1 Bent is the past participle and past tense of **bend. 2** (phrase) If you are **bent on** doing something, you are determined to do it.

bequeath, bequeaths, bequeathing, bequeathed (verb; a formal word) If someone bequeaths money or property to you, they give it to you in their will, so that it is yours after they have died.

bequest, bequests (noun; a formal word) A bequest is money or property that has been left to someone in a will.

berate, berates, berating, berated (verb; a formal word) If you berate someone, you scold them angrily, e.g. *He berated them for getting caught.*

bereaved (adjective; a formal word) You say that someone is bereaved when a close relative of theirs has recently died. **bereavement** (noun).

bereft (adjective; a literary word) If you are bereft of something, you no longer have it, e.g. *The government seems bereft of ideas.*

beret, berets (pronounced **ber**-ray) (noun) A beret is a circular flat hat with no brim.

berry, berries (noun) Berries are small, round fruits that grow on bushes or trees.

berserk (phrase) If someone **goes berserk,** they lose control of themselves and become very violent.

berth, berths 1 (noun) A berth is a space in a harbour where a ship stays when it is being loaded or unloaded. **2** In a boat, train, or caravan, a berth is a bed.

beseech, beseeches, beseeching, beseeched or **besought** (verb; a literary word) If you beseech someone to do something, you ask them very earnestly to do it, e.g. *Her eyes beseeched him to show mercy.* **beseeching** (adjective).

beset (adjective; a formal word) If you are beset by difficulties, problems, or doubts, you have a lot of them.

beside (preposition) If one thing is beside something else, they are next to each other.

besiege, besieges, besieging, besieged 1 (verb) When soldiers besiege a place, they surround it and wait for the people inside to surrender. **2** If you are besieged by people, problems, or questions, there are too many of them around you and they keep troubling you.

besought a past tense and past participle of **beseech.**

best 1 the superlative of **good** and **well. 2** (adverb) The thing that you like best is the thing that you prefer to everything else.

best man (noun) The best man at a wedding is the man who acts as the bridegroom's attendant and supporter.

bestow, bestows, bestowing, bestowed (verb; a formal word) If you bestow something on someone, you give it to them.

bet, bets, betting, bet 1 (verb) If you bet on the result of an event, you will win money if something happens and lose money if it does not. **2** (noun) A bet is the act of betting on something, or the amount of money that you agree to risk. **3** (an informal phrase) You say **I bet** to indicate that you are sure that something is or will be so, e.g. *I bet the answer is no.* **betting** (noun).

betray, betrays, betraying, betrayed 1 (verb) If you betray someone who trusts you, you do something which harms them, such as helping their enemies. **2** If you betray a secret, you tell it to someone you should not tell it to. **3** If you betray your feelings or thoughts, you show them without intending to. **betrayal** (noun), **betrayer** (noun).

betrothal, betrothals (noun; an old-fashioned word) A betrothal is an engagement to be married. **betrothed** (adjective or noun).

better 1 the comparative of **good** and **well**. **2** (adverb) If you like one thing better than another, you like it more than the other thing. **3** (adjective) If you are better after an illness, you are no longer ill.

between 1 (preposition or adverb) If something is between two other things, it is situated or happens in the space or time that separates them, e.g. *Reading is between London and Bristol.* **2** A relationship, discussion, or difference between two people or things involves only those two.

beverage, beverages (noun; a formal word) A beverage is a drink.

bevy, bevies (noun) A bevy of things or people is a group of them, e.g. *a bevy of lawyers.*

beware (verb) If you tell someone to beware of something, you are warning them that it might be dangerous or harmful.

bewilder, bewilders, bewildering, bewildered (verb) If something bewilders you, it is too confusing or difficult for you to understand. **bewildered** (adjective), **bewildering** (adjective), **bewilderingly** (adverb), **bewilderment** (noun).

bewitch, bewitches, bewitching, bewitched 1 (verb) To bewitch someone means to cast a spell on them. **2** If something bewitches you, you are so excited or attracted by it that you cannot pay attention to anything else. **bewitched** (adjective), **bewitching** (adjective).

beyond 1 (preposition) If something is beyond a certain place, it is on the other side of it, e.g. *Beyond the hills was the Sahara.* **2** If something extends or continues beyond a particular point, it extends or continues further than that point, e.g. *an education beyond the age of 16.* **3** If someone or something is beyond understanding or help, they cannot be understood or helped.

bias (noun) Someone who shows bias favours one person or thing unfairly.

biased or **biassed** (adjective) favouring one person or thing unfairly, e.g. *biased attitudes.*

bib, bibs (noun) A bib is a

piece of cloth or plastic which is tied under the chin of very young children when they are eating, to keep their clothes clean.

ble, Bibles (noun) The Bible is the sacred book of the Christian religion. **biblical** (adjective).

icentenary, bicentenaries (noun) The bicentenary of an event is its two-hundredth anniversary.

iceps (noun) Your biceps are the large muscles on your upper arms.

icker, bickers, bickering, bickered (verb) When people bicker, they argue or quarrel about unimportant things.

icycle, bicycles (noun) A bicycle is a two-wheeled vehicle which you ride by sitting on it and pushing two pedals with your feet.

id, bids, bidding, bade, bidden, bid In paragraph 3, the past tense and past participle is **bid**; in paragraph 4, the past tense is **bade** and the past participle is **bidden**. **1** (noun) A bid is an attempt to obtain or do something, e.g. *He made a bid for freedom.* **2** A bid is also an offer to buy something for a certain sum of money. **3** (verb) If you bid for something, you offer to pay a certain sum of money for it. **4** (an old-fashioned use) If you bid someone a greeting or a farewell, you say it to them.

bide, bides, biding, bided (phrase) If you **bide your time,** you wait for a good opportunity before doing something.

bidet, bidets (pronounced **bee**-day) (noun) A bidet is a low basin in a bathroom which is used for washing your bottom in.

big, bigger, biggest (adjective) large in size, extent, or importance. **biggish** (adjective), **bigness** (noun).

bigamy (noun) Bigamy is the crime of marrying someone when you are already married to someone else. **bigamist** (noun).

bigot, bigots (noun) A bigot is someone who has strong and unreasonable opinions which they refuse to change. **bigoted** (adjective), **bigotry** (noun).

bike, bikes (noun; an informal word) A bike is a bicycle or motorcycle.

bikini, bikinis (noun) A bikini is a small two-piece swimming costume worn by women.

bilateral (adjective) A bilateral agreement is one made between two groups or countries.

bile (noun) Bile is a bitter yellow liquid produced by the liver which helps the digestion of fat.

bilge (noun) The bilge of a ship is its lowest part, where dirty water collects.

bilingual (adjective) involving or using two languages, e.g. *bilingual street signs.*

bill, bills 1 (noun) A bill is a written statement of how much is owed for goods or services. **2** In Parliament, a bill is a formal statement of a proposed new law that is discussed and then voted on. **3** A bill is also a notice or a poster. **4** A bird's bill is its beak.

billboard, billboards (noun) A billboard is a large board on which advertisements are displayed.

billet, billets, billeting, billeted (verb) When soldiers are billeted in a building, arrangements are made for them to stay there.

billiards (noun) Billiards is a game in which a long cue is used to move balls on a table.

billion, billions (noun) A billion is a thousand million. Formerly, a billion was a million million.

billow, billows, billowing, billowed 1 (verb) When things made of cloth billow, they swell out and flap slowly in the wind. **2** When smoke or cloud billows, it spreads upwards and outwards. **3** (noun) A billow is a large wave.

bin, bins (noun) A bin is a container, especially one that you put rubbish in.

binary (pronounced **by**-nar-ee) (adjective) The binary system expresses numbers using only two digits, 0 and 1.

bind, binds, binding, bound 1 (verb) If you bind something, you tie rope or string round it so that it is held firmly. **2** If something binds you to a course of action, it compels you to act in that way, e.g. *He was bound by that decision.*

binding, bindings 1 (adjective) If a promise or agreement is binding, it must be obeyed or carried out. **2** (noun) The binding of a book is its cover.

binge, binges (noun; an informal word) A binge is a wild bout of excessive drinking or eating.

bingo (noun) Bingo is a game in which each player has card with numbers on Someone calls out numb and the first person to ha all their numbers called wi a prize.

binoculars (plural noun) B oculars are an instrume with lenses for both ey which you look through in der to see distant objects.

biochemistry (noun) Bioche istry is the study of the che istry of living things. **bi chemical** (adjective), **biocher ist** (noun).

biodegradable (adjective) c pable of being decompos naturally by the action of ba teria, e.g. *biodegradable clea ing products.*

biography, biographies (nou A biography is an account someone's life, written b someone else. **biograph** (noun), **biographical** (adje tive).

biology (noun) Biology is th study of living things. **biolog cal** (adjective), **biologically** (ac verb), **biologist** (noun).

bionic (adjective) having a pa of the body that is operate electronically.

biopsy, biopsies (noun) A biop sy is an examination under microscope of tissue from living body to determine th cause or extent of a disease.

birch, birches (noun) A birch i a tall deciduous tree with thi branches and thin bark.

bird, birds (noun) A bird is two-legged creature wit feathers and wings. Mos birds can fly; female birds la eggs.

birth, births 1 (noun) The birth

of a baby is its emergence from its mother's womb at the beginning of its life. **2** The birth of something is its beginning, e.g. *the birth of modern art.*

birthday, birthdays (noun) Your birthday is the anniversary of the date on which you were born.

birthmark, birthmarks (noun) A birthmark is a mark on someone's skin that has been there since they were born.

biscuit, biscuits (noun) A biscuit is a small flat cake made of baked dough.

bisect, bisects, bisecting, bisected (verb) To bisect a line, angle, or area means to divide it in half.

bisexual (adjective) sexually attracted by members of both sexes.

bishop, bishops 1 (noun) A bishop is a high-ranking clergyman in some Christian Churches. **2** In chess, a bishop is a piece that is moved diagonally across the board.

bison (noun) A bison is a large hairy animal related to cattle.

bistro, bistros (pronounced **bee**-stroh) (noun) A bistro is a small informal restaurant.

bit, bits 1 (noun) A bit of something is a small amount of it, e.g. *a bit of coal.* **2** (an informal phrase) **A bit** means slightly or to a small extent, e.g. *That's a bit tricky.* **3** Bit is also the past tense of **bite.**

bitch, bitches 1 (noun) A bitch is a female dog. **2** (an offensive use) If someone refers to a woman as a bitch, it means that they think she behaves in a spiteful way. **bitchy** (adjective).

bite, bites, biting, bit, bitten 1 (verb) If you bite something, you use your teeth to cut into it or through it. **2** (noun) A bite is a small amount that you bite off something with your teeth. **3** (verb) When an animal or insect bites you, it pierces your skin with its teeth or mouth. **4** (noun) A bite is also the injury you get when an animal or insect bites you.

bitter, bitterest 1 (adjective) If someone is bitter, they feel angry and resentful. **2** A bitter disappointment or experience makes people feel angry or unhappy for a long time afterwards. **3** In a bitter argument or war, people argue or fight fiercely and angrily, e.g. *a bitter power struggle.* **4** A bitter wind is an extremely cold wind. **5** Something that tastes bitter has a sharp, unpleasant taste. **bitterly** (adverb), **bitterness** (noun).

bivouac, bivouacs (pronounced **biv**-oo-ak) (noun) A bivouac is a temporary camp in the open air.

bizarre (pronounced biz-**zahr**) (adjective) very strange or eccentric.

blab, blabs, blabbing, blabbed (verb; an informal word) When someone blabs, they give away secrets by talking carelessly.

black, blacker, blackest; blacks 1 (noun or adjective) Black is the darkest possible colour. A surface that is completely black reflects no light at all. **2** Someone who is black is a member of a dark-skinned race. **3** (adjective) Black coffee or tea has no milk or cream added to it. **4** Black humour involves jokes about death or suffering. **blackness** (noun).

blackberry, blackberries (noun) Blackberries are small black fruits that grow on prickly bushes called brambles.

blackbird, blackbirds (noun) A blackbird is a common European bird. The male has black feathers and a bright yellow beak.

blackboard, blackboards (noun) A blackboard is a dark-coloured board in a classroom, which teachers write on using chalk.

black box, black boxes (noun) A black box is an electronic device in an aircraft which collects and stores information during flights.

blackcurrant, blackcurrants (noun) Blackcurrants are very small dark purple fruits that grow in bunches on bushes.

blacken, blackens, blackening, blackened (verb) To blacken something means to make it black, e.g. *The great ridge of cloud blackened the western sky.*

blackhead, blackheads (noun) A blackhead is a very small black spot on the skin caused by a pore being blocked with dirt.

blacklist, blacklists, blacklisting, blacklisted 1 (noun) A blacklist is a list of people or organizations who are thought to be untrustworthy or to have done something wrong. **2** (verb) When someone is blacklisted, they are put on a blacklist.

blackmail, blackmails, blackmailing, blackmailed 1 (verb) If someone blackmails another person, they threaten to reveal an unpleasant secret about them unless that person gives them money or does something for them. **2** (noun) Blackmail is the practice of blackmailing people. **blackmailer** (noun).

black market (noun) If something is bought or sold on the black market, it is bought or sold illegally.

blackout, blackouts (noun) If you have a blackout, you temporarily lose consciousness.

blacksmith, blacksmiths (noun) A blacksmith is a person whose job is making things out of iron, such as horseshoes.

bladder, bladders (noun) Your bladder is the part of your body where urine is held until it leaves your body.

blade, blades 1 (noun) The blade of a knife, axe, or saw is the sharp part that is used for cutting. **2** The blades of a propeller are the thin, flat parts that turn round. **3** A blade of grass is a single piece of it.

blame, blames, blaming, blamed 1 (verb) If someone blames you for something bad that has happened, they believe you caused it or are responsible for it. **2** (noun) The blame for something bad that happens is the responsibility for causing it or letting it happen.

blameless (adjective) Someone who is blameless has not done anything wrong.

blanch, blanches, blanching,

blanched (verb) If you blanch, you suddenly become very pale.

bland, blander, blandest (adjective) mild, tasteless, and dull, e.g. *a bland diet... her bland round face.* **blandly** (adverb).

blank, blanker, blankest 1 (adjective) Something that is blank has nothing on it, e.g. *a blank sheet of paper.* **2** If you look blank, your face shows no feeling, understanding, or interest. **3** (noun) If your mind or memory is a blank, you cannot think of anything or remember anything.

blanket, blankets 1 (noun) A blanket is a large rectangle of thick cloth that is put on a bed to keep people warm. **2** A blanket of something such as snow is a thick covering of it.

blare, blares, blaring, blared (verb) To blare means to make a loud, unpleasant noise, e.g. *The radio blared pop music.*

blaspheme, blasphemes, blaspheming, blasphemed (verb) When people blaspheme, they say rude or disrespectful things about God, or they use God's name as a swearword.

blasphemy, blasphemies (noun) Blasphemy is speech or behaviour that shows disrespect for God or for things people regard as holy. **blasphemous** (adjective).

blast, blasts, blasting, blasted 1 (verb) When people blast a hole in something, they make the hole with an explosion. **2** (noun) A blast is a big explosion, especially one caused by a bomb. **3** A blast of air or wind is a sudden strong rush of it.

blatant (adjective) done in an obvious way, without any attempt at concealment, e.g. *a blatant disregard for the law.*

blaze, blazes, blazing, blazed 1 (noun) A blaze is a large, hot fire. **2** A blaze of light or colour is a great or strong amount of it, e.g. *a blaze of red.* **3** A blaze of publicity or attention is a lot of it. **4** (verb) When a fire blazes, it burns strongly and brightly. **5** If something blazes with light or colour, it is extremely bright.

blazer, blazers (noun) A blazer is a jacket, especially one worn as part of a uniform by schoolchildren or members of a sports team.

bleach, bleaches, bleaching, bleached 1 (verb) To bleach material or hair means to make it white or pale, usually by using a chemical. **2** (noun) Bleach is a chemical that is used to make material white or to clean thoroughly and kill germs.

bleak, bleaker, bleakest 1 (adjective) If a situation is bleak, it is bad and depressing and seems unlikely to improve. **2** If a place is bleak, it is cold, bare, and exposed to the wind.

bleat, bleats, bleating, bleated 1 (verb) When sheep or goats bleat, they make a high-pitched pitiful sound. **2** (noun) A bleat is the high-pitched pitiful sound that a sheep or goat makes.

bleed, bleeds, bleeding, bled (verb) When you bleed, you lose blood as a result of an injury or illness.

bleep, bleeps (noun) A bleep is

a short high-pitched sound made by an electrical device such as an alarm.

blemish, blemishes (noun) A blemish is a mark that spoils the appearance of something.

blend, blends, blending, blended 1 (verb) When you blend two or more substances, you mix them together to form a single substance. **2** When colours or sounds blend, they combine in a pleasing way. **3** (noun) A blend of things is a mixture of them, especially one that is pleasing.

blender, blenders (noun) A blender is a machine used for mixing liquids and foods at high speed.

bless, blesses, blessing, blessed or **blest** (verb) When a priest blesses people or things, he or she asks for God's favour and protection for them.

blessed 1 (adjective; pronounced **bless**-id) People use blessed to describe something that they are glad about, e.g. *She walked into the blessed cool of the lobby.* **2** (pronounced **blest**) If someone is blessed with a particular quality or skill, they have it, e.g. *He was blessed with a sense of humour.* **blessedly** (adverb).

blessing, blessings 1 (noun) A blessing is something good that you are thankful for, e.g. *Good health is the greatest blessing.* **2** (phrase) If something is done **with someone's blessing,** they approve of it and support it.

blew the past tense of **blow.**

blight, blights, blighting, blighted 1 (noun) A blight is something that damages or spoils other things, e.g. *the blight of the recession.* **2** (verb) When something is blighted, it is spoiled or seriously harmed, e.g. *His life had been blighted by sickness.*

blind, blinds, blinding, blinded 1 (adjective) Someone who is blind cannot see. **2** If someone is blind to a particular fact, they fail to recognize it or understand it. **3** (verb) If something blinds you, you become unable to see, either for a short time or permanently. **4** If something blinds you to a fact or situation, it prevents you from realizing that it exists. **5** (noun) A blind is a roll of cloth or paper that you pull down over a window to keep out the light. **blindly** (adverb), **blindness** (noun).

blindfold, blindfolds, blindfolding, blindfolded 1 (noun) A blindfold is a strip of cloth tied over someone's eyes so that they cannot see. **2** (verb) To blindfold someone means to cover their eyes with a strip of cloth.

blinding (adjective) A blinding light is so bright that it hurts your eyes, e.g. *There was a blinding flash.*

blindingly (adverb; an informal use) If something is blindingly obvious, it is very obvious indeed.

blink, blinks, blinking, blinked (verb) When you blink, you close your eyes rapidly for a moment, usually involuntarily.

blinkers (plural noun) Blinkers are two pieces of leather placed at the side of a horse's eyes so that it can only see straight ahead.

bliss (noun) Bliss is a state of complete happiness. **blissful** (adjective), **blissfully** (adverb).

blister, blisters, blistering, blistered 1 (noun) A blister is a small bubble on your skin containing watery liquid, caused by a burn or rubbing. **2** (verb) If someone's skin blisters, blisters appear on it as result of burning or rubbing.

blithe (adjective) casual and done without serious thought, e.g. *They could not share her blithe confidence.* **blithely** (adverb).

blitz, blitzes, blitzing, blitzed 1 (noun) A blitz is a sudden intensive bombing attack by aircraft on a city or town. **2** (verb) When a city, town, or building is blitzed, it is bombed by aircraft and is damaged or destroyed.

blizzard, blizzards (noun) A blizzard is a heavy snowstorm with strong winds.

bloated (adjective) Something that is bloated is much larger than normal, often because there is a lot of liquid or gas inside it.

blob, blobs (noun) A blob of a thick or sticky substance is a small amount of it.

bloc, blocs (noun) A group of countries with similar aims and interests acting together is often called a bloc, e.g. *the Eastern bloc.*

block, blocks, blocking, blocked 1 (noun) A block of flats or offices is a large building containing flats or offices. **2** In a town, a block is a group of buildings with streets on all its sides, e.g. *He lives a few blocks down.* **3** A block of something is a large rectangular piece of it, e.g. *a block of marble.* **4** (verb) To block a road, channel, or pipe means to put something across it so that nothing can get through. **5** If something blocks your view, it is in the way and prevents you from seeing what you want to see. **6** If someone blocks something, they prevent it from happening, e.g. *The council blocked his plans.*

blockade, blockades, blockading, blockaded 1 (noun) A blockade is an action that prevents goods from reaching a place. **2** (verb) When a place is blockaded, goods are prevented from reaching it.

blockage, blockages (noun) When there is a blockage in a pipe, tube, or tunnel, something is clogging it.

bloke, blokes (noun; an informal word) A bloke is a man.

blonde, blondes 1 (adjective) Blonde hair is pale yellow in colour. The spelling 'blond' is used when referring to men. **2** (noun) A blonde, or blond, is a person with light-coloured hair.

blood 1 (noun) Blood is the red liquid that is pumped by the heart round the bodies of human beings and other mammals. **2** (phrase) If something cruel is done **in cold blood,** it is done deliberately and without emotion.

bloodhound, bloodhounds (noun) A bloodhound is a large dog with an excellent sense of smell.

bloodless 1 (adjective) If someone's face or skin is

bloodless, it is very pale. **2** In a bloodless coup or revolution, nobody is killed.

blood pressure (noun) Your blood pressure is a measure of the force with which your blood is being pumped round your body.

bloodshed (noun) When there is bloodshed, people are killed or wounded.

bloodshot (adjective) If a person's eyes are bloodshot, the white parts have become red because tiny blood vessels have burst in their eyes.

bloodstained (adjective) covered with blood.

bloodstream (noun) Your bloodstream is the flow of blood through your body.

bloodthirsty (adjective) Someone who is bloodthirsty enjoys using or watching violence.

blood transfusion, blood transfusions (noun) A blood transfusion is a process in which blood is injected into the body of someone who has lost a lot of blood.

blood vessel, blood vessels (noun) Your blood vessels are the narrow tubes in your body through which your blood flows.

bloody, bloodier, bloodiest 1 (adjective or adverb) Bloody is a common swearword, used to express anger or annoyance. **2** (adjective) A bloody event is one in which a lot of people are killed, e.g. *a bloody revolution.* **3** Bloody also means covered with blood, e.g. *a bloody gash on his head.*

bloom, blooms, blooming, bloomed 1 (noun) A bloom is a flower on a plant. **2** (verb) When a plant blooms, it produces flowers. **3** When something like a feeling blooms, it grows, e.g. *Romance can bloom where you least expect it.*

blossom, blossoms, blossoming, blossomed 1 (noun) Blossom is the growth of flowers that appears on a tree before the fruit. **2** (verb) When a tree blossoms, it produces blossom.

blot, blots, blotting, blotted 1 (noun) A blot is a drop of ink that has been spilled on a surface. **2** A blot on someone's reputation is a mistake or piece of bad behaviour that spoils their good name. **blot out** (verb) To blot something out means to be in front of it and prevent it from being seen, e.g. *The smoke blotted out the sky.*

blotch, blotches (noun) A blotch is a discoloured area or stain. **blotchy** (adjective).

blouse, blouses (noun) A blouse is a light garment, like a shirt, worn by a girl or a woman.

blow, blows, blowing, blew, blown 1 (verb) When the wind blows, the air moves. **2** If something blows or is blown somewhere, the wind moves it there. **3** If you blow a whistle or horn, you make a sound by blowing into it. **4** (noun) If you receive a blow, someone or something hits you. **5** A blow is also something that makes you very disappointed or unhappy, e.g. *Marc's death was a terrible blow.* **blow up 1** (verb) To blow something up means to destroy it with an explosion. **2** To blow up a balloon or a tyre means to fill it with air.

blubber (noun) Blubber is the thick insulating layer of fat beneath the skin of animals such as whales and seals.

bludgeon, bludgeons, bludgeoning, bludgeoned (verb) To bludgeon someone means to hit them several times with a heavy object.

blue, bluer, bluest 1 (adjective or noun) Blue is the colour of the sky on a clear, sunny day. **2** (phrase) If something happens **out of the blue,** it happens suddenly and unexpectedly. **3** (adjective) Blue films, stories, and jokes are about sex. **bluish** or **blueish** (adjective).

bluebell, bluebells (noun) A bluebell is a woodland plant with blue, bell-shaped flowers.

bluebottle, bluebottles (noun) A bluebottle is a large fly with a shiny dark-blue body.

blue-collar (adjective) Blue-collar workers do manual work as opposed to office work.

blueprint, blueprints (noun) A blueprint for something is a plan of how it is expected to work, e.g. *the blueprint for successful living.*

bluff, bluffs, bluffing, bluffed; bluffer, bluffest 1 (noun) A bluff is an attempt to make someone wrongly believe that you are in a strong position. **2** (verb) If you are bluffing, you are trying to make someone believe that you are in a position of strength. **3** (adjective) If someone has a bluff manner, they are rather rough and outspoken but they mean to be kind and friendly.

blunder, blunders, blundering, blundered 1 (verb) If you blunder, you make a silly mistake. **2** (noun) A blunder is a silly mistake.

blunt, blunter, bluntest 1 (adjective) A blunt object has a rounded point or edge, rather than a sharp one. **2** If you are blunt, you say exactly what you think, without trying to be polite.

blur, blurs, blurring, blurred 1 (noun) A blur is a shape or area which you cannot see clearly because it has no distinct outline or because it is moving very fast. **2** (verb) To blur the differences between things means to make them no longer clear, e.g. *The dreams blurred confusingly with her memories.* **blurred** (adjective).

blurb (noun) The blurb about a product is information about it, written to make people interested in it.

blurt out, blurts out, blurting out, blurted out (verb) If you blurt something out, you say it suddenly, after trying to keep quiet or keep it a secret, e.g. *He foolishly blurted out that he was rich.*

blush, blushes, blushing, blushed 1 (verb) If you blush, your face becomes redder than usual, because you are embarrassed or ashamed. **2** (noun) A blush is the red colour on someone's face when they are embarrassed or ashamed.

bluster, blusters, blustering, blustered 1 (verb) When someone blusters, they behave noisily and aggressively because they are angry or frightened. **2** (noun) Bluster is aggressive behaviour by someone who is angry or frightened.

blustery (adjective) Blustery weather is rough and windy.

boa, boas (noun) A boa, or a boa constrictor, is a large snake that kills its prey by coiling round it and crushing it.

boar, boars (noun) A boar is a male wild pig, or a male domestic pig used for breeding.

board, boards, boarding, boarded 1 (noun) A board is a long, flat piece of wood. **2** The board of a company or organization is the group of people who control it. **3** Board is the meals provided when you stay somewhere, e.g. *The price includes full board.* **4** (verb) If you board a train, ship, or aircraft, you get on it. **5** (phrase) If you are **on board** a train, ship, or aircraft, you are on it or in it.

boarder, boarders (noun) A boarder is a pupil who lives at school during term time.

boarding school, boarding schools (noun) A boarding school is a school where the pupils live during the term.

boardroom, boardrooms (noun) A boardroom is a room where the board of a company meets.

boast, boasts, boasting, boasted 1 (verb) If you boast about your possessions or achievements, you talk about them proudly, especially to impress other people. **2** (noun) A boast is something that you say which shows that you are proud of what you own or have done. **boastful** (adjective).

boat, boats (noun) A boat is a small vehicle for travelling across water.

bob, bobs, bobbing, bobbed 1 (verb) When something bobs, it moves up and down. **2** (noun) A bob is a woman's hair style in which her hair is cut level with her chin.

bobbin, bobbins (noun) A bobbin is a small round object on which thread or wool is wound.

bobby, bobbies (noun; an old-fashioned informal word) A bobby is a policeman.

bode, bodes, boding, boded (phrase; a literary use) If something **bodes ill**, or **bodes well**, it makes you think that something bad, or good, will happen.

bodice, bodices (noun) A bodice is the upper part of a dress.

bodily 1 (adjective) relating to the body, e.g. *bodily contact.* **2** (adverb) involving the whole of someone's body, e.g. *He was carried bodily up the steps.*

body, bodies 1 (noun) Your body is either all your physical parts or just your trunk, excluding your head and limbs. **2** A body is a person's dead body. **3** The body of a car or aircraft is the main part of it, excluding the engine. **4** A body of people is also an organized group.

bodyguard, bodyguards (noun) A bodyguard is a person or group of people employed to protect someone.

bodywork (noun) The bodywork of a motor vehicle is the outer part of it.

bog, bogs (noun) A bog is an area of land which is wet and permanently spongy.

boggle, boggles, boggling, boggled (verb) If your mind boggles at something, you find it difficult to imagine or understand.

bogus (adjective) not genuine, e.g. *a bogus doctor.*

bohemian (pronounced boh-**hee**-mee-an) (adjective) Someone who is bohemian lives in an exotic and unconventional way, and is usually involved with music, art, or literature.

boil, boils, boiling, boiled 1 (verb) When a hot liquid boils, bubbles appear in it and it starts to change into vapour. **2** When you boil a kettle, you heat it until the water in it boils. **3** When you boil food, you cook it in boiling water. **4** (noun) A boil is a red swelling on your skin.

boiler, boilers (noun) A boiler is a piece of equipment which burns fuel to provide hot water.

boiling (adjective; an informal word) very hot.

boisterous (adjective) Someone who is boisterous is noisy, lively, and rather rough.

bold, bolder, boldest 1 (adjective) confident and not shy or embarrassed, e.g. *He was not bold enough to ask them.* **2** not afraid of risk or danger. **3** clear and noticeable, e.g. *bold colours.* **boldly** (adverb), **boldness** (noun).

bollard, bollards (noun) A bollard is a short, thick post used to keep vehicles out of a road.

bolster, bolsters, bolstering, bolstered (verb) To bolster something means to support it or make it stronger, e.g. *She relied on others to bolster her self-esteem.*

bolt, bolts, bolting, bolted 1 (noun) A bolt is a metal bar that you slide across a door or window in order to fasten it. **2** A bolt is also a metal object which screws into a nut and is used to fasten things together. **3** (verb) If you bolt a door or window, you fasten it using a bolt. If you bolt things together, you fasten them together using a bolt. **4** To bolt means to escape or run away. **5** To bolt food means to eat it very quickly.

bomb, bombs, bombing, bombed 1 (noun) A bomb is a container filled with material that explodes when it hits something or is set off by a timing mechanism. **2** (verb) When a place is bombed, it is attacked with bombs.

bombard, bombards, bombarding, bombarded 1 (verb) To bombard a place means to attack it with heavy gunfire or bombs. **2** If you are bombarded with something you are constantly subjected to it, e.g *I was bombarded with complaints.* **bombardment** (noun).

bomber, bombers (noun) A bomber is an aircraft that drops bombs.

bombshell, bombshells (noun) A bombshell is a sudden piece of shocking or upsetting news.

bona fide (pronounced boh-na **fie**-dee) (adjective) genuine, e.g. *This competition is open to bona fide amateurs.*

bond, bonds, bonding, bonded **1** (noun) A bond is a close relationship between people, e.g. *Females have a wonderful bond with their babies.* **2** (a literary use) Bonds are chains or ropes used to tie a prisoner up. **3** A bond is also a certificate which records that you have lent money to a business and that it will repay you the loan with interest. **4** Bonds are also feelings or obligations that force you to behave in a particular way, e.g. *the social bonds of community.* **5** (verb) When two things bond or are bonded, they become closely linked or attached.

bondage (noun) Bondage is the condition of being someone's slave.

bone, bones (noun) Bones are the hard parts that form the framework of a person's or animal's body. **boneless** (adjective).

bonfire, bonfires (noun) A bonfire is a large fire made outdoors, often to burn rubbish.

bonnet, bonnets **1** (noun) The bonnet of a car is the metal cover over the engine. **2** A bonnet is also a baby's or woman's hat tied under the chin.

bonny, bonnier, bonniest (adjective; a Scottish and Northern English word) nice to look at.

bonus, bonuses **1** (noun) A bonus is an amount of money added to your usual pay. **2** Something that is a bonus is a good thing that you get in addition to something else, e.g. *The view from the hotel was an added bonus.*

bony, bonier, boniest (adjective) Bony people or animals are thin, with very little flesh covering their bones.

boo, boos, booing, booed **1** (noun) A boo is a shout of disapproval. **2** (verb) When people boo, they shout 'boo' to show their disapproval.

book, books, booking, booked **1** (noun) A book is a number of pages held together inside a cover. **2** (verb) When you book something such as a room, you arrange to have it or use it at a particular time.

bookcase, bookcases (noun) A bookcase is a piece of furniture with shelves for books.

bookie, bookies (noun; an informal word) A bookie is a bookmaker.

booking, bookings (noun) A booking is an arrangement to book something such as a hotel room.

book-keeping (noun) Book-keeping is the keeping of a record of the money spent and received by a business or other organization.

booklet, booklets (noun) A booklet is a small book with a paper cover.

bookmaker, bookmakers (noun) A bookmaker is a person who makes a living by taking people's bets and paying them when they win.

bookmark, bookmarks (noun) A bookmark is a piece of card or other material which you put between the pages of a book to mark your place.

boom, booms, booming, boomed **1** (noun) A boom is a rapid increase in something, e.g. *the baby boom.* **2** (verb) When something booms, it increases rapidly, e.g. *Sales are booming.* **3** (noun) A boom is also a loud deep echoing sound, e.g. *the boom of heavy metal music.* **4** (verb) To boom means to make a loud deep echoing sound, e.g. *The clock boomed out the hour.*

boomerang, boomerangs (noun) A boomerang is a curved piece of wood thrown as a weapon by Australian Aborigines. It is supposed to come back to you if you throw it correctly.

boon, boons (noun) Something that is a boon makes life better or easier, e.g. *Credit cards have been a boon to shoppers.*

boost, boosts, boosting, boosted **1** (verb) To boost something means to cause it to improve or increase, e.g. *It was designed to boost profits.* **2** (noun) A boost is an improvement or increase, e.g. *a boost to the economy.* **booster** (noun).

boot, boots, booting, booted **1** (noun) Boots are strong shoes that come up over your ankle and sometimes your calf. **2** (verb; an informal use) If you boot something, you kick it. **3** (noun) The boot of a car is a covered space, usually at the back, for carrying things in. **4** (phrase) **To boot** means also or in addition, e.g. *The story was compelling and well-written to boot.*

booth, booths **1** (noun) A booth is a small partly enclosed area, e.g. *a telephone booth.* **2** A booth is a stall where you can buy goods.

booty (noun) Booty is valuable things taken from a place, especially by soldiers after a battle.

booze, boozes, boozing, boozed (an informal word) **1** (noun) Booze is alcoholic drink. **2** (verb) When people booze, they drink alcohol. **boozer** (noun), **boozy** (adjective).

border, borders, bordering, bordered **1** (noun) The border between two countries is the dividing line between them. **2** A border is also a strip or band round the edge of something, e.g. *They carried banners with a black border.* **3** In a garden, a border is a long flower bed. **4** (verb) To border something means to form a border or boundary along the side of it, e.g. *Tall poplar trees bordered the fields.*

borderline (adjective) only just acceptable as a member of a class or group, e.g. *a borderline case.*

bore, bores, boring, bored **1** (verb) If something bores you, you find it dull and uninteresting. **2** (noun) A bore is someone or something that bores you. **3** (verb) If you bore a hole in something, you make it using a tool such as a drill.

bored (adjective) If you are bored, you are impatient because you find something uninteresting or because you have nothing to do. **boredom** (noun).

boring (adjective) dull and uninteresting.

born **1** (verb) When a baby is born, it comes out of its mother's womb at the beginning of its life. **2** (adjective) You use born to mean that someone has a particular quality from birth, e.g. *He was a born pessimist.*

borne the past participle of **bear**.

borough, boroughs (pronounced **bur**-uh) (noun) A borough is a town, or a district within a large town, that has its own council.

borrow, borrows, borrowing, borrowed (verb) If you borrow something that belongs to someone else, they let you have it for a period of time. **borrower** (noun).

Bosnian, Bosnians 1 (adjective) belonging to or relating to Bosnia. **2** (noun) A Bosnian is someone who comes from Bosnia.

bosom, bosoms 1 (noun) A woman's bosom is her breasts. **2** (adjective) A bosom friend is a very close friend.

boss, bosses, bossing, bossed 1 (noun) Someone's boss is the person in charge of the place where they work. **2** (verb) If someone bosses you around, they keep telling you what to do.

bossy, bossier, bossiest (adjective) A bossy person enjoys telling other people what to do. **bossiness** (noun).

botany (noun) Botany is the scientific study of plants. **botanic** or **botanical** (adjective), **botanist** (noun).

botch, botches, botching, botched (verb; an informal word) If you botch something, you do it badly or clumsily.

both (adjective or pronoun) Both is used when saying something about two things or people.

bother, bothers, bothering, bothered 1 (verb) If you do not bother to do something, you do not do it because it takes too much effort or it seems unnecessary. **2** If something bothers you, you are worried or concerned about it. If you do not bother about it, you are not concerned about it, e.g. *She is not bothered about money.* **3** If you bother someone, you interrupt them when they are busy. **4** (noun) Bother is trouble, fuss, or difficulty. **bothersome** (adjective).

bottle, bottles, bottling, bottled 1 (noun) A bottle is a glass or plastic container for keeping liquids in. **2** (verb) To bottle something means to store it in bottles.

bottleneck, bottlenecks (noun) A bottleneck is a narrow section of road or an awkward junction where traffic has to slow down or stop.

bottom, bottoms 1 (noun) The bottom of something is its lowest part. **2** Your bottom is your buttocks. **3** (adjective) The bottom thing in a series of things is the lowest one. **bottomless** (adjective).

bough, boughs (rhymes with **now**) (noun) A bough is a large branch of a tree.

bought the past tense and past participle of **buy**.

boulder, boulders (noun) A boulder is a large rounded rock.

boulevard, boulevards (pronounced **boo**-le-vard) (noun) A boulevard is a wide street in a city, usually with trees along each side.

bounce, bounces, bouncing, bounced 1 (verb) When an object bounces, it springs back from something after hitting it. **2** To bounce also means to move up and down, e.g. *Her long black hair bounced as she walked.* **3** If a cheque bounces, the bank refuses to accept it because there is not enough money in the account.

bouncy (adjective) Someone who is bouncy is lively and enthusiastic.

bound, bounds, bounding, bounded 1 (adjective) If you say that something is bound to happen, you mean that it is certain to happen. **2** If a person or a vehicle is bound for a place, they are going there. **3** If someone is bound by an agreement or regulation, they must obey it. **4** (plural noun) Bounds are limits which restrict or control something, e.g. *Their enthusiasm knew no bounds.* **5** (noun) A bound is a large leap. **6** (phrase) If a place is **out of bounds,** you are forbidden to go there. **7** (verb) When animals or people bound, they move quickly with large leaps, e.g. *He bounded up the stairway.* **8** Bound is also the past tense and past participle of **bind**.

boundary, boundaries (noun) A boundary is something that indicates the farthest limit of anything, e.g *the city boundary... the accepted boundaries of social norms.*

boundless (adjective) without end or limit, e.g. *her boundless energy.*

bountiful (adjective; a literary word) freely available in large amounts, e.g. *a bountiful harvest of local produce.*

bounty 1 (noun; a literary word) Bounty is a generous supply, e.g. *autumn's bounty of fruits.* **2** Someone's bounty is their generosity in giving a lot of something.

bouquet, bouquets (pronounced boo-**kay**) (noun) A bouquet is an attractively arranged bunch of flowers.

bourgeois (pronounced **boor**-jhwah) (adjective) belonging to or typical of the urban middle class in a society.

bourgeoisie (pronounced boor-jhwah-**zee**) (noun) The bourgeoisie is the urban middle class in a society.

bout, bouts 1 (noun) If you have a bout of something such as an illness, you have it for a short time, e.g. *a disagreeable bout of jaundice.* **2** If you have a bout of doing something, you do it enthusiastically for a short time. **3** A bout is also a boxing or wrestling match.

boutique, boutiques (pronounced boo-**teek**) (noun) A boutique is a small shop that sells fashionable clothes, shoes, or jewellery.

bovine (adjective; a technical use) relating to cattle.

bow, bows, bowing, bowed (rhymes with **now**) **1** (verb) When you bow, you bend your body or lower your head as a sign of respect, greeting, shame, or agreement. **2** (noun) A bow is the movement you make when you bow. **3** (verb) If you bow to something, you give in to it, e.g. *He bowed to public pressure.* **4** (noun) The bow of a ship is its front part.

bow, bows (rhymes with **low**) **1** (noun) A bow is a knot with two loops and two loose ends. **2** A bow is a long piece of wood with horsehair stretched along it, which you use to play a stringed instrument like a violin. **3** A bow is also a long flexible piece of wood used for shooting arrows.

bowel, bowels (noun) Your bowels are the tubes leading from your stomach, through which waste matter passes before it leaves your body.

bowl, bowls, bowling, bowled 1 (noun) A bowl is a round container with a wide uncovered top, used for holding liquid or for serving food. **2** A bowl is also the hollow, rounded part of something, e.g. *a toilet bowl.* **3** A bowl is a large heavy ball used in the game of bowls or tenpin bowling. **4** (verb) In cricket, to bowl means to throw the ball towards the batsman. **bowler** (noun).

bowling (noun) Bowling is a game in which you roll a heavy ball down a narrow track towards a group of wooden objects called pins and try to knock them down.

bowls (noun) Bowls is a game in which the players try to roll large wooden balls as near as possible to a small ball.

bow tie, bow ties (rhymes with **low**) (noun) A bow tie is a man's tie in the form of a bow, worn especially on formal occasions.

box, boxes, boxing, boxed 1 (noun) A box is a container with a firm base and sides and usually a lid. **2** On a form, a box is a rectangular space which you have to fill in. **3** In a theatre, a box is a small separate area where a few people can watch the performance together. **4** (verb) To box means to fight someone according to the rules of boxing.

boxer, boxers 1 (noun) A boxer is a man who boxes. **2** A boxer is also a breed of medium-sized, smooth-haired dog with a flat face.

boxing (noun) Boxing is a sport in which two men fight using their fists, wearing padded gloves.

box office, box offices (noun) In a theatre or cinema, the box office is the place where tickets are sold.

boy, boys (noun) A boy is a male child. **boyhood** (noun), **boyish** (adjective).

boycott, boycotts, boycotting, boycotted 1 (verb) If you boycott an organization, product, or event, you refuse to have anything to do with it, e.g. *Many people boycotted the meeting.* **2** (noun) A boycott is the boycotting of a person, organization, product, or event, e.g. *a boycott of the movie.*

boyfriend, boyfriends (noun) Someone's boyfriend is the man or boy with whom they are having a romantic or sexual relationship.

bra, bras (noun) A bra is a piece of underwear worn by a woman to support her breasts.

brace, braces, bracing, braced 1 (verb) When you brace yourself, you stiffen your body in order to steady yourself or avoid falling over, e.g. *The ship lurched and he braced himself.* **2** If you brace yourself for something unpleasant or difficult, you prepare yourself to deal with it, e.g. *The police are braced for violent reprisals.* **3** (plural noun) Braces are a pair of straps worn over the shoulders and fastened to the trousers to hold them up. **4** (noun) A brace is an object fastened to something to straighten or support it.

bracelet, bracelets (noun) A bracelet is a chain or band worn around someone's wrist as an ornament.

bracing (adjective) Something that is bracing makes you feel fit and full of energy, e.g. *the bracing sea air.*

bracken (noun) Bracken is a plant like a large fern that grows on hills and in woods.

bracket, brackets 1 (noun) Brackets are a pair of written marks, ( ), [ ], or { }, placed round a word, expression, or sentence that is not part of the main text, or to show that the items inside the brackets belong together. **2** A bracket is a range, for example of ages or prices, e.g. *the four-figure price bracket.* **3** A bracket is also a piece of metal or wood fastened to a wall to support something such as a shelf.

brag, brags, bragging, bragged (verb) When someone brags, they talk in a boastful way about something that they own or something that they have done, e.g. *Both leaders bragged they could win by a landslide.*

brahmin, brahmins (pronounced **brah**-min) (noun) A brahmin is a member of the highest or priestly caste in Hindu society.

braid, braids, braiding, braided 1 (noun) Braid is a strip of contrasting cloth or twisted threads used to decorate clothes or curtains. **2** A braid is a length of hair which has been plaited and tied. **3** (verb) To braid hair or thread means to plait it.

Braille (noun) Braille is a system of printing for blind people in which letters are represented by raised dots that can be felt with the fingers.

brain, brains 1 (noun) Your brain is the mass of nerve tissue inside your head that controls your body and enables you to think and feel; also used to refer to your mind and the way that you think, e.g. *I admired his legal brain.* **2** If you say that someone has brains, you mean that they are very intelligent.

brainchild (noun; an informal word) Someone's brainchild is something that they have invented or created.

brainwash, brainwashes, brainwashing, brainwashed (verb) If people are brainwashed into believing something, they accept it unthinkingly because it is repeatedly or systematically presented to them. **brainwashing** (noun).

brainwave, brainwaves (noun; an informal expression) If you have a brainwave, you suddenly think of a clever idea.

brainy, brainier, brainiest (adjective; an informal word) clever.

braise, braises, braising, braised

(verb) To braise food means to fry it for a short time, then cook it slowly in a little liquid.

brake, brakes, braking, braked 1 (noun) A brake is a device for making a vehicle stop or slow down. **2** (verb) When a driver brakes, he or she makes a vehicle stop or slow down by using its brakes.

bramble, brambles (noun) A bramble is a wild, thorny bush that produces blackberries.

bran (noun) Bran is the ground husks that are left over after flour has been made from wheat grains.

branch, branches, branching, branched 1 (noun) The branches of a tree are the parts that grow out from its trunk. **2** A branch of an organization is one of a number of its offices, shops, or local groups. **3** A branch of a subject is one of its areas of study or activity, e.g. *specialists in certain branches of medicine.* **4** (verb) A road that branches off from another road splits off from it to lead in a different direction.

brand, brands, branding, branded 1 (noun) A brand of something is a particular kind or make of it, e.g. *a popular brand of malt whisky.* **2** (verb) When an animal is branded, a mark is burned on its skin to show who owns it.

brandish, brandishes, brandishing, brandished (verb; a literary word) If you brandish something, you wave it vigorously, e.g. *He brandished his sword over his head.*

brand-new (adjective) completely new.

brandy (noun) Brandy is a strong alcoholic drink, usually made from wine.

brash, brasher, brashest (adjective) If someone is brash, they are overconfident or rather rude, e.g. *a brash young man.*

brass 1 (noun or adjective) Brass is a yellow-coloured metal made from copper and zinc. **2** In an orchestra, the brass section consists of brass wind instruments such as trumpets and trombones.

brat, brats (noun; an informal word) A badly behaved child may be referred to as a brat.

bravado (pronounced bra-**vah**-doh) (noun) Bravado is a display of courage intended to impress other people.

brave, braver, bravest; braves, braving, braved 1 (adjective) A brave person is willing to do dangerous things and does not show any fear. **2** (verb) If you brave an unpleasant or dangerous situation, you face up to it in order to do something, e.g. *His fans braved the rain to hear him sing.* **bravely** (adverb), **bravery** (noun).

bravo (interjection) People shout 'Bravo!' to express appreciation when something has been done well.

brawl, brawls, brawling, brawled 1 (noun) A brawl is a rough fight. **2** (verb) When people brawl, they take part in a rough fight.

brawn (noun) Brawn is physical strength, e.g. *brains as well as brawn.* **brawny** (adjective).

bray, brays, braying, brayed 1

(verb) When a donkey brays, it makes a loud, harsh sound. **2** (noun) A bray is the sound a donkey makes.

brazen (adjective) When someone's behaviour is brazen, they do not care if other people think they are behaving wrongly. **brazenly** (adverb).

brazier, braziers (noun) A brazier is a metal container in which coal or charcoal is burned to keep people warm out of doors.

Brazilian, Brazilians 1 (adjective) belonging or relating to Brazil. **2** (noun) A Brazilian is someone who comes from Brazil.

breach, breaches, breaching, breached 1 (verb; a formal word) If you breach an agreement or law, you break it. **2** (noun) A breach of an agreement or law is an action that breaks it, e.g. *a breach of contract.* **3** A breach is a gap or break. **4** (verb) To breach a barrier means to make a gap in it, e.g. *The river breached its banks.*

bread (noun) Bread is a basic food made from flour and water, usually raised with yeast, and baked.

breadth (noun) The breadth of something is the distance between its two sides.

breadwinner, breadwinners (noun) The breadwinner in a family is the person who earns the money.

break, breaks, breaking, broke, broken 1 (verb) When an object breaks, it is damaged and separates into pieces. **2** If you break a rule, promise, or agreement, you fail to keep it. **3** When a boy's voice breaks, it becomes permanently deeper. **4** (noun) A break is a short period during which you rest or do something different. **breakable** (adjective). **break down 1** (verb) When a machine or a vehicle breaks down, it stops working. **2** When a system, plan, or negotiation breaks down, it ends because of problems or disagreements. **break up** (verb) If something breaks up, it ends, e.g. *The marriage broke up after a year.*

breakage, breakages (noun) A breakage is the act of breaking something; also a thing that has been broken.

breakaway (adjective) A breakaway group is one that has separated from a larger group.

breakdown, breakdowns 1 (noun) The breakdown of something such as a system is its failure, e.g. *a breakdown in communications.* **2** If someone has a breakdown, they become so depressed that they cannot cope with life. **3** If a driver has a breakdown, his or her car stops working.

breaker, breakers (noun) Breakers are big sea waves.

breakfast, breakfasts (noun) Breakfast is the first meal of the day.

break-in, break-ins (noun) A break-in is the illegal entering of a building, especially by a burglar.

breakneck (adjective; an informal word) Someone or something that is travelling at breakneck speed is travelling dangerously fast.

breakthrough, breakthroughs (noun) A breakthrough is a sudden important development, e.g. *a medical breakthrough.*

breakwater, breakwaters (noun) A breakwater is a wall extending into the sea which protects a harbour or beach from the force of the waves.

breast, breasts (noun) A woman's breasts are the two soft, fleshy parts on her chest, which produce milk after she has had a baby.

breath, breaths 1 (noun) Your breath is the air you take into your lungs and let out again when you breathe. **2** (phrase) If you are **out of breath,** you are breathing with difficulty after doing something energetic. **3** If you say something **under your breath,** you say it in a very quiet voice.

breathe, breathes, breathing, breathed (verb) When you breathe, you take air into your lungs and let it out again.

breathless (adjective) If you are breathless, you are breathing fast or with difficulty. **breathlessly** (adverb), **breathlessness** (noun).

breathtaking (adjective) If you say that something is breathtaking, you mean that it is very beautiful or exciting.

bred the past tense and past participle of **breed.**

breeches (pronounced **brit**-chiz) (plural noun) Breeches are trousers reaching to just below the knee, nowadays worn especially for riding.

breed, breeds, breeding, bred 1 (noun) A breed of a species of domestic animal is a particular type of it. **2** (verb) Someone who breeds animals or plants keeps them in order to produce more animals or plants with particular qualities. **3** When animals breed, they mate and produce offspring.

breeze, breezes (noun) A breeze is a gentle wind.

brevity (noun; a formal word) Brevity means shortness, e.g. *the brevity of his account.*

brew, brews, brewing, brewed 1 (verb) If you brew a pot of tea or coffee, you make it by pouring hot water over it. **2** To brew beer means to make it, by boiling and fermenting malt. **3** If an unpleasant situation is brewing, it is about to happen, e.g. *Another scandal is brewing.* **brewer** (noun).

brewery, breweries (noun) A brewery is a place where beer is made, or a company that makes it.

briar, briars (noun) A briar is a wild rose that grows on a dense prickly bush.

bribe, bribes, bribing, bribed 1 (noun) A bribe is money or something valuable given to an official to persuade him or her to make a favourable decision. **2** (verb) To bribe someone means to give them a bribe. **bribery** (noun).

bric-a-brac (noun) Bric-a-brac consists of small ornaments or pieces of furniture of no great value.

brick, bricks (noun) Bricks are rectangular blocks of baked clay used in building.

bricklayer, bricklayers (noun) A bricklayer is someone whose job is to build with bricks.

bride, brides (noun) A bride is a woman who is getting married or who has just got married. **bridal** (adjective).

bridegroom, bridegrooms (noun) A bridegroom is a man who is getting married or who has just got married.

bridesmaid, bridesmaids (noun) A bridesmaid is a girl or woman who helps and accompanies a bride on her wedding day.

bridge, bridges 1 (noun) A bridge is a structure built over a river, road, or railway so that vehicles and people can cross. **2** A ship's bridge is the high part from which it is steered and controlled. **3** The bridge of your nose is the hard ridge at the top of it. **4** Bridge is a card game for four players based on whist.

bridle, bridles, bridling, bridled 1 (noun) A bridle is a set of straps round a horse's head and mouth, which the rider uses to control the horse. **2** (verb) If a person bridles, they show that they are offended by drawing back their head stiffly.

brief, briefer, briefest; briefs, briefing, briefed 1 (adjective) Something that is brief lasts only a short time. **2** (verb) When you brief someone on a task, you give them all the necessary instructions and information about it. **briefly** (adverb).

briefcase, briefcases (noun) A briefcase is a small flat case for carrying papers.

briefing, briefings (noun) A briefing is a meeting at which information and instructions are given.

brier another spelling of **briar**.

brigade, brigades (noun) A brigade is an army unit consisting of three battalions.

brigadier, brigadiers (pronounced brig-ad-**ear**) (noun) A brigadier is an army officer of the rank immediately above colonel.

bright, brighter, brightest 1 (adjective) strong and startling, e.g. *a bright light.* **2** clever, e.g. *my brightest student.* **3** cheerful, e.g. *a bright smile.* **brightly** (adverb), **brightness** (noun).

brighten, brightens, brightening, brightened 1 (verb) If something brightens, it becomes brighter, e.g. *The weather had brightened.* **2** If someone brightens, they suddenly look happier. **brighten up** (verb) To brighten something up means to make it more attractive and cheerful, e.g. *ways to brighten up a child's room.*

brilliant 1 (adjective) A brilliant light or colour is extremely bright. **2** A brilliant person is extremely clever. **3** A brilliant career is extremely successful. **brilliantly** (adverb), **brilliance** (noun).

brim, brims 1 (noun) The brim of a hat is the wide part that sticks outwards at the bottom. **2** (phrase) If a container is filled **to the brim**, it is filled right to the top.

brine (noun) Brine is salt water.

bring, brings, bringing, brought 1 (verb) If you bring something or someone with you when you go to a place, you take them with you, e.g. *You can bring a friend to the party.* **2** To bring something to a particular state or condition means to cause it to be like that, e.g. *Bring the vegetables to the boil.* **bring about** (verb) To bring something about means to cause it to happen, e.g. *We must try to bring about a better world.* **bring up 1** (verb) To bring up children means to look after them while they grow up. **2** If you bring up a subject, you introduce it into the conversation, e.g. *She brought up the subject at dinner.*

brink (noun) If you are on the brink of something, you are just about to do it or to experience it.

brisk, brisker, briskest 1 (adjective) A brisk action is done quickly and energetically, e.g. *A brisk walk restores your energy.* **2** If someone's manner is brisk, it shows that they want to get things done quickly and efficiently. **briskly** (adverb), **briskness** (noun).

bristle, bristles, bristling, bristled 1 (noun) Bristles are strong animal hairs used to make brushes. **2** (verb) If the hairs on an animal's body bristle, they rise up, because it is frightened. **bristly** (adjective).

British (adjective) belonging or relating to the United Kingdom of Great Britain and Northern Ireland.

Briton, Britons (noun) A Briton is someone who comes from the United Kingdom of Great Britain and Northern Ireland.

brittle (adjective) An object that is brittle is hard but breaks easily.

broach, broaches, broaching, broached (verb) When you broach a subject, you introduce it into a discussion.

broad, broader, broadest 1 (adjective) wide, e.g. *a broad smile.* **2** having many different aspects or concerning many different people, e.g. *He had the broad support of the public.* **3** general rather than detailed, e.g. *the broad concerns of the movement.* **4** If someone has a broad accent, the way that they speak makes it very clear where they come from, e.g. *She spoke in a broad Yorkshire accent.*

broad bean, broad beans (noun) Broad beans are light-green beans with thick flat edible seeds.

broadcast, broadcasts, broadcasting, broadcast 1 (noun) A broadcast is a programme or announcement on radio or television. **2** (verb) To broadcast something means to send it out by radio waves, so that it can be seen on television or heard on radio. **broadcaster** (noun), **broadcasting** (noun).

broaden, broadens, broadening, broadened 1 (verb) When something broadens, it becomes wider, e.g. *His smile broadened.* **2** To broaden something means to cause it to involve more things or concern more people, e.g. *We must broaden the scope of this job.*

broadly (adverb) true to a large extent or in most cases, e.g.

There are broadly two schools of thought on this.

broad-minded (adjective) Someone who is broad-minded is tolerant of behaviour that other people may find upsetting or immoral.

brocade (noun) Brocade is a heavy, expensive material, often made of silk, with a raised pattern.

broccoli (noun) Broccoli is a vegetable with green stalks and green or purple flower buds.

brochure, brochures (pronounced **broh**-sher) (noun) A brochure is a booklet which gives information about a product or service.

brogue, brogues (pronounced **broag**) **1** (noun) A brogue is a strong accent, especially an Irish one. **2** Brogues are thick leather shoes.

broke 1 the past tense of **break**. **2** (adjective; an informal use) If you are broke, you have no money.

broken the past participle of **break**.

broker, brokers (noun) A broker is a person whose job is to buy and sell shares for other people.

brolly, brollies (noun; an informal word) A brolly is an umbrella.

bronchitis (noun) Bronchitis is an illness in which the two tubes which connect your windpipe to your lungs become infected, making you cough.

brontosaurus, brontosauruses (noun) A brontosaurus was a type of very large, four-footed, plant-eating dinosaur, with a long neck and a long tail.

bronze (noun) Bronze is a yellowish-brown metal which is a mixture of copper and tin; also the yellowish-brown colour of this metal.

brooch, brooches (rhymes with **coach**) (noun) A brooch is a piece of jewellery with a pin at the back for attaching to a dress or blouse.

brood, broods, brooding, brooded 1 (noun) A brood is a family of baby birds. **2** (verb) If you brood about something, you keep thinking about it in a serious or unhappy way.

brook, brooks (noun) A brook is a stream.

broom, brooms 1 (noun) A broom is a long-handled brush. **2** Broom is a shrub with yellow flowers.

broth (noun) Broth is soup, usually with vegetables in it.

brothel, brothels (noun) A brothel is a house where men pay to have sex with prostitutes.

brother, brothers (noun) Your brother is a boy or man who has the same parents as you. **brotherly** (adjective).

brotherhood, brotherhoods 1 (noun) Brotherhood is the affection and loyalty that brothers or close male friends feel for each other. **2** A brotherhood is an organization or group of men with common interests, jobs, or beliefs.

brother-in-law, brothers-in-law (noun) Someone's brother-in-law is the brother of their husband or wife, or their sister's husband.

brought the past tense and past participle of **bring**.

brow, brows 1 (noun) Your brow is your forehead. **2** Your brows are your eyebrows. **3** The brow of a hill is the top of it.

brown, browner, brownest (adjective or noun) Brown is the colour of earth or wood.

brownie, brownies (noun) A brownie is a junior member of the Guides.

browse, browses, browsing, browsed 1 (verb) If you browse through a book, you look through it in a casual way. **2** If you browse in a shop, you look at the things in it for interest rather than because you want to buy something.

bruise, bruises, bruising, bruised 1 (noun) A bruise is a purple mark that appears on your skin after something has hit it. **2** (verb) If something bruises you, it hits you so that a bruise appears on your skin.

brunette, brunettes (noun) A brunette is a girl or woman with dark brown hair.

brunt (phrase) If you **bear the brunt** of something unpleasant, you are the person who suffers most, e.g. *Women bear the brunt of crime.*

brush, brushes, brushing, brushed 1 (noun) A brush is an object with bristles which you use for cleaning things, painting, or tidying your hair. **2** (verb) If you brush something, you clean it or tidy it with a brush. **3** To brush against something means to touch it while passing it, e.g. *Her lips brushed his cheek.*

brusque (pronounced **broosk**) (adjective) Someone who is brusque deals with people quickly and without considering their feelings. **brusquely** (adverb).

brussels sprout, brussels sprouts (noun) Brussels sprouts are vegetables that look like tiny cabbages.

brutal (adjective) Brutal behaviour is cruel and violent, e.g. *Their action led to brutal reprisals by enemy forces.* **brutally** (adverb), **brutality** (noun).

brute, brutes 1 (noun) A man who is a brute is rough and insensitive. **2** (adjective) Brute force is strength alone, without any skill, e.g. *You have to open the lock gates using brute force.* **brutish** (adjective).

bubble, bubbles, bubbling, bubbled 1 (noun) A bubble is a ball of air in a liquid. **2** A bubble is also a hollow, delicate ball of soapy liquid floating on the surface of a liquid or in the air. **3** (verb) When a liquid bubbles, bubbles form in it. **4** If you are bubbling with something like excitement, you are full of it. **bubbly** (adjective).

buck, bucks, bucking, bucked 1 (noun) A buck is the male of various animals, including the deer and the rabbit. **2** (verb) If a horse bucks, it jumps straight up in the air with all four feet off the ground.

bucket, buckets (noun) A bucket is a cylindrical container with an open top and a handle.

buckle, buckles, buckling, buckled 1 (noun) A buckle is a fastening on the end of a belt or strap. **2** (verb) If you buckle a belt or strap, you fasten it. **3** If something buckles, it becomes bent because of severe heat or pressure.

bud, buds, budding, budded 1 (noun) A bud is a small, tight swelling on a tree or plant, consisting of overlapping undeveloped petals or leaves which develop into a flower or a cluster of leaves. **2** (verb) When a tree or plant buds, new buds appear on it.

Buddhism (noun) Buddhism is a religion, founded by the Buddha, which teaches that the way to end suffering is by overcoming your desires. **Buddhist** (noun or adjective).

budding (adjective) just beginning to develop, e.g. *a budding artist.*

budge, budges, budging, budged (verb) If something will not budge, you cannot move it.

budgerigar, budgerigars (noun) A budgerigar is a small brightly coloured pet bird.

budget, budgets, budgeting, budgeted 1 (noun) A budget is a plan showing how much money will be available in a given period, usually a year, and how it will be spent. **2** (verb) If you budget for something, you plan your money carefully, so as to be able to afford it. **budgetary** (adjective).

budgie, budgies (noun; an informal word) A budgie is a budgerigar.

buff, buffs 1 (adjective) a pale brown colour. **2** (noun; an informal use) A buff is someone who knows a lot about a subject, e.g. *a film buff.*

buffalo, buffaloes (noun) A buffalo is a wild animal like a large cow with long curved horns.

buffer, buffers 1 (noun) Buffers on a train or at the end of a railway line are metal discs on springs that reduce shock when they are hit. **2** A buffer is also a person or thing that provides protection between two things, e.g *The council provides a buffer between the clients and the government.*

buffet, buffets (pronounced **boof**-ay) **1** (noun) A buffet is a café at a station. **2** A buffet is also a cold meal to which guests help themselves at a party or public occasion.

buffet, buffets, buffeting, buffeted (pronounced **buff**-it) (verb) If the wind or sea buffets a place or person, it strikes them violently and repeatedly.

bug, bugs, bugging, bugged 1 (noun) A bug is an insect, especially one that infests dirty houses. **2** A bug in a computer program is a small error which means that the program will not work properly. **3** (an informal use) A bug is also a virus or minor infection, e.g. *He was recovering from a stomach bug.* **4** (verb) If a place is bugged, tiny microphones are hidden there to pick up what people are saying.

bugle, bugles (noun) A bugle is a simple brass instrument that looks like a small trumpet. **bugler** (noun).

build, builds, building, built 1 (verb) To build something such as a house or a bridge means to make it from its parts. **2** To build something such as an organization means to form it and develop it gradually. **3** (noun) Your build is the shape and size of your body. **builder** (noun).

building, buildings (noun) A building is a structure with walls and a roof.

building society, building societies (noun) A building society is an organization in which some people invest their money, while others borrow from it to buy a house.

bulb, bulbs 1 (noun) A bulb is the glass part of an electric lamp. **2** A bulb is also an onion-shaped root that grows into a flower or plant.

Bulgarian, Bulgarians 1 (adjective) belonging or relating to Bulgaria. **2** (noun) A Bulgarian is someone who comes from Bulgaria. **3** Bulgarian is the main language spoken in Bulgaria.

bulge, bulges, bulging, bulged 1 (verb) If something bulges, it swells out from a surface. **2** (noun) A bulge is a lump on a normally flat surface.

bulk, bulks 1 (noun) A bulk is a large mass of something, e.g. *The book is more impressive for its bulk than its content.* **2** The bulk of something is most of it, e.g. *He has taken responsibility for the bulk of the debt.* **3** (phrase) To buy something **in bulk** means to buy it in large quantities.

bulky, bulkier, bulkiest (adjective) large and heavy, e.g. *a bulky package.*

bull, bulls (noun) A bull is the male of some species of animals, including domestic cattle, elephants, seals, and whales.

bulldog, bulldogs (noun) A bulldog is a dog with a large square head, muscular body, and short hair.

bulldozer, bulldozers (noun) A bulldozer is a large, powerful tractor with a broad blade in front, which is used for moving earth or knocking things down.

bullet, bullets (noun) A bullet is a small piece of metal fired from a gun.

bulletin, bulletins 1 (noun) A bulletin is a short news report on radio or television. **2** A bulletin is also a leaflet or small newspaper regularly produced by a group or organization.

bullion (noun) Bullion is gold or silver in the form of lumps or bars.

bullock, bullocks (noun) A bullock is a young castrated bull.

bully, bullies, bullying, bullied 1 (noun) A bully is someone who uses their strength or power to hurt or frighten other people. **2** (verb) If someone bullies you into doing something, they make you do it by using force or threats.

bump, bumps, bumping, bumped 1 (verb) If you bump into something, you knock into it with a jolt. **2** (noun) A bump is a soft or dull noise made by something knocking into something else. **3** A bump on a surface is a raised, uneven part. **bumpy** (adjective).

bumper, bumpers 1 (noun) Bumpers are bars on the front and back of a vehicle which protect it if there is a collision. **2** (adjective) A bumper crop or harvest is larger than usual.

bun, buns (noun) A bun is a small, round cake.

bunch, bunches, bunching, bunched 1 (noun) A bunch of people or things is a group of them. **2** A bunch of flowers is a number of them held or tied together. **3** A bunch of bananas or grapes is a group of them growing on the same stem. **4** (verb) When people bunch together or bunch up, they stay very close to each other.

bundle, bundles, bundling, bundled 1 (noun) A bundle is a number of things tied together or wrapped up in a cloth. **2** (verb) If you bundle someone or something somewhere, you push them there quickly and roughly.

bung, bungs, bunging, bunged 1 (noun) A bung is a piece of wood, cork, or rubber used to close a hole in something such as a barrel. **2** (verb; an informal use) If you bung something somewhere, you put it there quickly and carelessly.

bungalow, bungalows (noun) A bungalow is a one-storey house.

bungle, bungles, bungling, bungled (verb) To bungle something means to make mistakes and fail to do it properly.

bunion, bunions (noun) A bunion is a painful lump on the first joint of a person's big toe.

bunk, bunks (noun) A bunk is a bed fixed to a wall in a ship or caravan.

bunker, bunkers 1 (noun) On a golf course, a bunker is a large hole filled with sand. **2** A coal bunker is a storage place for coal. **3** A bunker is also an underground shelter with strong walls to protect it from bombing and gunfire.

bunting (noun) Bunting is a series of rows of small coloured flags displayed on streets and buildings on special occasions.

buoy, buoys (pronounced **boy**) (noun) A buoy is a floating object anchored to the bottom of the sea, marking a channel or warning of an obstruction.

buoyant 1 (adjective) able to float. **2** lively and cheerful, e.g. *She was in a buoyant mood.* **buoyancy** (noun).

burble, burbles, burbling, burbled (verb) To burble means to makes an indistinct, continuous bubbling sound.

burden, burdens 1 (noun) A burden is a heavy load. **2** If something is a burden to you, it causes you a lot of worry or hard work. **burdensome** (adjective).

bureau, bureaux (pronounced **byoo**-roh) **1** (noun) A bureau is an office that provides a service, e.g. *an employment bureau.* **2** A bureau is also a writing desk with shelves and drawers.

bureaucracy (noun) Bureaucracy is the complex system of rules and routine procedures which operate in government departments. **bureaucratic** (adjective).

bureaucrat, bureaucrats (noun) A bureaucrat is a person who works in a government department, especially one who is excessively concerned with rules and procedures.

burgeoning (adjective) growing or developing rapidly, e.g. *a burgeoning political crisis.*

burglar, burglars (noun) A burglar is a thief who breaks into a building. **burglary** (noun).

burgle, burgles, burgling, burgled (verb) If your house is burgled, someone breaks into it and steals things.

burial, burials (noun) A burial is a ceremony held when a dead person is buried.

burly, burlier, burliest (adjective) A burly man has a broad body and strong muscles.

burn, burns, burning, burned or **burnt 1** (verb) If something is burning, it is on fire. **2** To burn something means to destroy it with fire. **3** If you burn yourself or are burned, you are injured by fire or by something hot. **4** (noun) A burn is an injury caused by fire or by something hot.

burp, burps, burping, burped 1 (verb) If you burp, you make a noise because air from your stomach has been forced up through your throat. **2** (noun) A burp is the noise that you make when you burp.

burrow, burrows, burrowing, burrowed 1 (noun) A burrow is a tunnel or hole in the ground dug by a rabbit or other small animal. **2** (verb) When an animal burrows, it digs a burrow.

bursary, bursaries (noun) A bursary is a sum of money given to someone to enable them to study in a college or university.

burst, bursts, bursting, burst 1 (verb) When something bursts, it splits open because of pressure from inside it. **2** If you burst into a room, you enter it suddenly. **3** To burst means to happen or come suddenly and with force, e.g. *The aircraft burst into flames.* **4** (an informal use) If you are bursting with something, you find it difficult to keep it to yourself, e.g. *We were bursting with joy.* **5** (noun) A burst of something is a short period of it, e.g. *He had a sudden burst of energy.*

bury, buries, burying, buried 1 (verb) When a dead person is buried, their body is put into a grave and covered with earth. **2** To bury something means to put it in a hole in the ground and cover it up. **3** If something is buried under something, it is covered by it, e.g. *My bag was buried under a pile of old newspapers.*

bus, buses (noun) A bus is a large motor vehicle that carries passengers.

bush, bushes (noun) A bush is a thick plant with many stems branching out from ground level.

bushy, bushier, bushiest (adjective) Bushy hair or fur grows very thickly, e.g. *bushy eyebrows.*

business, businesses 1 (noun) Business is work relating to the buying and selling of goods and services. **2** A business is an organization which produces or sells goods or provides a service. **3** You can refer to any event, situation, or activity as a business, e.g.

This whole business has upset me. **businessman** (noun), **businesswoman** (noun).

businesslike (adjective) dealing with things in an efficient way.

busker, buskers (noun) A busker is someone who plays music or sings for money in the street or in some other public place.

bust, busts, busting, bust or **busted 1** (noun) A bust is a statue of someone's head and shoulders, e.g. *a bust of Mozart.* **2** A woman's bust is her chest and her breasts. **3** (verb; an informal use) If you bust something, you break it. **4** (adjective; an informal use) If a business goes bust, it becomes bankrupt and closes down.

bustle, bustles, bustling, bustled 1 (verb) When people bustle, they move in a busy, hurried way. **2** (noun) Bustle is busy, noisy activity.

busy, busier, busiest; busies, busying, busied 1 (adjective) If you are busy, you are in the middle of doing something. **2** A busy place is full of people doing things or moving about, e.g. *a busy seaside resort.* **3** (verb) If you busy yourself with something, you occupy yourself by doing it. **busily** (adverb).

but 1 (conjunction) used to introduce an idea that is contrary to what has gone before, e.g. *I don't miss teaching but I miss the pupils.* **2** used when apologizing, e.g. *I'm sorry, but I can't come tonight.* **3** except, e.g. *We can't do anything but wait.*

butcher, butchers (noun) A butcher is a shopkeeper who sells meat.

butler, butlers (noun) A butler is the chief male servant in a rich household.

butt, butts, butting, butted 1 (noun) The butt of a weapon is the thick end of its handle. **2** If you are the butt of teasing or criticism, you are the target of it. **3** (verb) If you butt something, you ram it with your head. **butt in** (verb) If you butt in, you join in a private conversation or activity without being asked to.

butter, butters, buttering, buttered 1 (noun) Butter is a yellowish substance made from cream, which is spread on bread and used in cooking. **2** (verb) To butter bread means to spread butter on it.

buttercup, buttercups (noun) A buttercup is a wild plant with bright yellow flowers.

butterfly, butterflies (noun) A butterfly is a type of insect with large colourful wings and a thin body.

buttocks (plural noun) Your buttocks are the part of your body that you sit on.

button, buttons, buttoning, buttoned 1 (noun) Buttons are small, hard objects sewn on to clothing, and used to fasten two surfaces together. **2** (verb) If you button a piece of clothing, you fasten it using its buttons. **3** (noun) A button is also a small object on a piece of equipment that you press to make it work.

buttonhole, buttonholes 1 (noun) A buttonhole is a hole that you push a button through to fasten a piece of clothing. **2** A buttonhole is also a flower worn in your lapel.

buxom (adjective) A buxom woman is large, healthy, and attractive.

buy, buys, buying, bought (verb) If you buy something, you obtain it by paying money for it. **buyer** (noun).

buzz, buzzes, buzzing, buzzed 1 (verb) If something buzzes, it makes a continuous humming sound, like a bee. **2** (noun) A buzz is the sound something makes when it buzzes.

buzzard, buzzards (noun) A buzzard is a large brown and white bird of prey with broad rounded wings.

buzzer, buzzers (noun) A buzzer is a device that makes a buzzing sound, to attract attention.

by 1 (preposition) used to indicate who or what has done something, e.g. *The statement was issued by his solicitor.* **2** used to indicate how something is done, e.g. *He frightened her by hiding behind the door.* **3** located next to, e.g. *I sat by her bed.* **4** before a particular time, e.g. *It should be ready by next spring.* **5** (preposition or adverb) going past, e.g. *We drove by his house.*

by-election, by-elections (noun) A by-election is an election held to choose a new member of parliament after the previous member has resigned or died.

bygone (adjective; a literary word) happening or existing a long time ago, e.g. *the ceremonies of a bygone era.*

bypass, bypasses (noun) A bypass is a main road which takes traffic round a town rather than through it.

bystander, bystanders (noun) A bystander is someone who sees something happen but does not take part in it.

byte, bytes (noun) A byte is a unit of storage in a computer, often representing a single letter or figure.

C c

cab, cabs 1 (noun) A cab is a taxi. **2** In a lorry, bus, or train, the cab is where the driver sits.

cabaret, cabarets (pronounced **kab**-bar-ray) (noun) A cabaret is a show consisting of dancing, singing, or comedy acts.

cabbage, cabbages (noun) A cabbage is a large green leafy vegetable.

cabin, cabins 1 (noun) A cabin is a room in a ship where a passenger sleeps. **2** A cabin is also a small wooden house.

cabinet, cabinets 1 (noun) A cabinet is a small cupboard. **2** The cabinet in a government is a group of ministers who advise the leader and decide policies.

cable, cables 1 (noun) A cable is a strong, thick rope or chain. **2** An electric cable is a bundle of wires with a rubber covering, which carries electricity. **3** A cable is also a message sent abroad by using electricity.

cable car, cable cars (noun) A cable car is a vehicle pulled by a moving cable, for taking people up mountains.

cache, caches (pronounced **kash**) (noun) A cache is a store of things hidden away, e.g. *a cache of guns.*

cachet (pronounced **kash**-shay) (noun; a formal word) Cachet is a quality of distinction and prestige, e.g. *the cachet of shopping at Smythson.*

cackle, cackles, cackling, cackled 1 (verb) If you cackle, you laugh harshly. **2** (noun) A cackle is a harsh triumphant laugh.

cacophony (pronounced kak-**koff**-fon-nee) (noun; a formal word) A cacophony is a loud, unpleasant noise, e.g. *a cacophony of barking dogs.*

cactus, cacti or **cactuses** (noun) A cactus is a thick, fleshy plant that grows in deserts and is usually covered in spikes.

cad, cads (noun; an old-fashioned word) If you describe a man as a cad, you mean that he treats people badly and unfairly.

caddie, caddies; also spelled **caddy 1** (noun) A caddie is a person who carries golf clubs for a golf player. **2** A tea caddy is a box for keeping tea in.

cadence, cadences (noun) The cadence of someone's voice is the way it goes up and down as they speak.

cadet, cadets (noun) A cadet is a young person being trained in the armed forces or police.

cadge, cadges, cadging, cadged (verb) If you cadge something off someone, you get it from them and don't give them anything in return, e.g. *I cadged a lift ashore.*

caesarean, caesareans (pronounced siz-**air**-ee-an) (noun) A caesarean or caesarean section is an operation in which a baby is lifted out of a woman's womb through an opening cut in her abdomen.

café, cafés (pronounced **kaf**-fay) (noun) A café is a place where you can buy light meals, snacks, and drinks.

cafeteria, cafeterias (pronounced kaf-fit-**ee**-ree-ya) (noun) A cafeteria is a restaurant where you serve yourself.

caffeine or **caffein** (pronounced **kaf**-feen) (noun) Caffeine is a substance found in coffee, tea, and cocoa, which makes you more active.

cage, cages (noun) A cage is a boxlike structure made of wire or bars in which birds or animals are kept. **caged** (adjective).

cagey, cagier, cagiest (pronounced **kay**-jee) (adjective; an informal word) cautious and not direct or open, e.g. *They're very cagey when they talk to me.*

cagoule, cagoules (pronounced ka-**gool**) (noun) A cagoule is a lightweight waterproof jacket with a hood.

cahoots (phrase; an informal use) If you are **in cahoots** with someone, you are working closely with them on a secret plan.

cairn, cairns (noun) A cairn is a pile of stones built as a memorial or a landmark.

cajole, cajoles, cajoling, cajoled

(verb) If you cajole someone into doing something, you persuade them to do it by saying nice things to them.

cake, cakes, caking, caked 1 (noun) A cake is a sweet food made by baking flour, eggs, fat, and sugar. **2** A cake of a hard substance such as soap is a block of it. **3** (verb) If something cakes or is caked, it forms or becomes covered with a solid layer, e.g. *caked with mud.*

calamity, calamities (noun) A calamity is an event that causes disaster or distress. **calamitous** (adjective).

calcium (pronounced **kal**-see-um) (noun) Calcium is a soft white element found in bones and teeth.

calculate, calculates, calculating, calculated 1 (verb) If you calculate something, you work it out, usually by doing some arithmetic. **2** If something is calculated, it is deliberately planned to have a particular effect, e.g. *It's calculated to shut us up.* **calculation** (noun).

calculating (adjective) carefully planning situations to get what you want, e.g. *Toby was always a calculating type.*

calculator, calculators (noun) A calculator is a small electronic machine used for doing mathematical calculations.

calculus (noun) Calculus is a branch of mathematics concerned with variable quantities.

calendar, calendars 1 (noun) A calendar is a chart showing the date of each day in a particular year. **2** A particular calendar is a system of dividing time into fixed periods of days, months, and years, e.g. *the Jewish calendar.*

calf, calves 1 (noun) A calf is a young cow, bull, elephant, whale, or seal. **2** Your calf is the thick part at the back of your leg below your knee.

calibre, calibres (pronounced **kal**-lib-ber) **1** (noun) A person's calibre is their ability or intelligence, e.g. *a player of her calibre.* **2** The calibre of a gun is the width of the inside of its barrel.

call, calls, calling, called 1 (verb) If someone or something is called by a particular name, that is their name, e.g. *a man called Jeffrey.* **2** If you call people or situations something, you use words to describe your opinion of them, e.g. *They called me crazy.* **3** If you call something, you say it loudly. **4** If you call someone, you telephone them. **5** If you call on someone, you pay them a short visit, e.g. *Don't hesitate to call on me.* **6** (noun) If you get a call from someone, they telephone you or pay you a visit. **7** A call is a cry or shout, e.g. *a call for help.* **8** A call for something is a demand or desire for it, e.g. *The call for art teachers was small.* **call off** (verb) If you call something off, you cancel it. **call up** (verb) If someone is called up, they are ordered to join the army, navy, or air force.

call box, call boxes (noun) A call box is a telephone kiosk.

calling 1 (noun) A calling is a profession or career. **2** If you have a calling to a particular job, you have a strong feeling that you should do it.

callous (adjective) cruel and showing no concern for other people's feelings. **callously** (adverb), **callousness** (noun).

calm, calmer, calmest; calms, calming, calmed 1 (adjective) Someone who is calm is quiet and does not show any worry or excitement. **2** If the weather or the sea is calm, it is still because there is no strong wind. **3** (noun) Calm is a state of quietness and peacefulness, e.g. *He liked the calm of the evening.* **4** (verb) To calm someone means to make them less upset or excited. **calmly** (adverb), **calmness** (noun).

calorie, calories (noun) A calorie is a unit of measurement for the energy value of food, e.g. *Alcohol is high in calories.*

calves the plural of **calf**.

calypso, calypsos (pronounced kal-**lip**-soh) (noun) A calypso is a type of song from the West Indies, with a topical subject.

camaraderie (pronounced kam-mer-**rah**-der-ree) (noun) Camaraderie is a feeling of trust and friendship between a group of people.

camber, cambers (noun) A camber is a gradual downwards slope from the centre of a road to each side of it.

camel, camels (noun) A camel is a large mammal with either one or two humps on its back. Camels live in hot desert areas and are used for carrying things.

cameo, cameos 1 (noun) A cameo is a brooch with a raised stone design on a flat stone of another colour. **2** A cameo is also a small but important part in a play or film played by a well-known actor or actress.

camera, cameras (noun) A camera is a piece of equipment used for taking photographs or for filming.

camomile (noun) Camomile is a plant with a strong smell and daisy-like flowers which are used to make herbal tea.

camouflage, camouflages, camouflaging, camouflaged (pronounced **kam**-mof-flahj) **1** (noun) Camouflage is a way of avoiding being seen by having the same colour or appearance as the surroundings. **2** (verb) To camouflage something means to hide it or disguise it using camouflage.

camp, camps, camping, camped 1 (noun) A camp is a place where people live in tents or stay in tents on holiday. **2** A camp is also a collection of buildings used for a particular group of people such as soldiers or prisoners. **3** A particular camp is a group of people who support a particular idea or belief. **4** (verb) If you camp, you stay in a tent. **camper** (noun), **camping** (noun).

campaign, campaigns, campaigning, campaigned (pronounced kam-**pane**) **1** (noun) A campaign is a planned set of actions aimed at achieving a particular result, e.g. *a campaign to educate people.* **2** (verb) To campaign means to carry out a campaign, e.g. *He has campaigned against smoking.* **campaigner** (noun).

campus, campuses (noun) A campus is the area of land and the buildings that make up a university or college.
can, could 1 (verb) If you can do something, it is possible for you to do it or you are allowed to do it, e.g. *Can I walk you home?.. He can't work tomorrow.* **2** If you can do something, you have the skill or ability to do it, e.g. *I can speak Italian.*
can, cans, canning, canned 1 (noun) A can is a metal container, often a sealed one with food or drink inside. **2** (verb) To can food or drink means to seal it in cans.
Canadian, Canadians 1 (adjective) belonging or relating to Canada. **2** (noun) A Canadian is someone who comes from Canada.
canal, canals (noun) A canal is a long, narrow man-made stretch of water.
canary, canaries (noun) A canary is a small yellow bird, often kept in a cage as a pet.
can-can, can-cans (noun) The can-can is a lively dance in which women kick their legs high in the air to fast music.
cancel, cancels, cancelling, cancelled 1 (verb) If you cancel something that has been arranged, you stop it from happening. **2** If you cancel a cheque or an agreement, you make sure that it is no longer valid. **cancellation** (noun).
cancer, cancers 1 (noun) Cancer is a serious disease in which abnormal cells in a part of the body increase rapidly, producing growths. **2** Cancer is also the fourth sign of the zodiac, represented by a crab. People born between June 21st and July 22nd are born under this sign. **cancerous** (adjective).
candelabra or **candelabrum, candelabras** (noun) A candelabra is an ornamental holder for a number of candles.
candid (adjective) honest and frank. **candidly** (adverb), **candour** (noun).
candidate, candidates 1 (noun) A candidate for a job is a person who is being considered for that job. **2** A candidate is also a person taking an examination. **candidacy** (noun).
candied (adjective) covered or cooked in sugar, e.g. *candied fruit.*
candle, candles (noun) A candle is a stick of hard wax with a wick through the middle. The lighted wick gives a flame that provides light.
candlestick, candlesticks (noun) A candlestick is a holder for a candle.
candy, candies (noun; used especially in American English) Candies are sweets.
cane, canes, caning, caned 1 (noun) Cane is the long, hollow stems of a plant such as bamboo. **2** Cane is also strips of cane used for weaving things such as baskets and chairs. **3** A cane is a long narrow stick, often one used to beat people as a punishment. **4** (verb) To cane someone means to beat them with a cane as a punishment.
canine (pronounced **kay**-nine) (adjective) relating to dogs.
canister, canisters (noun) A canister is a container with a

lid, used for storing foods such as sugar or tea.

cannabis (noun) Cannabis is a drug which some people smoke. It is illegal in many countries.

canned (adjective) Canned food is preserved in cans.

cannibal, cannibals (noun) A cannibal is a person who eats the flesh of other human beings. **cannibalism** (noun).

cannon, cannons or **cannon** (noun) A cannon is a large gun, usually on wheels, used in battles to fire heavy metal balls.

cannot (verb) Cannot is the same as can not, e.g. *She cannot come home yet.*

canny (adjective) clever and cautious, e.g. *canny business people.* **cannily** (adverb).

canoe, canoes (pronounced ka-**noo**) (noun) A canoe is a small, narrow boat that you row using a paddle. **canoeing** (noun).

canon, canons 1 (noun) A canon is a member of the clergy who is attached to a cathedral. **2** A canon is also a basic rule or principle, e.g. *the canons of political economy.*

canopy, canopies (noun) A canopy is a cover for something, used for shelter or decoration, e.g. *the new canopy above the tomb.*

cantankerous (adjective) Cantankerous people are quarrelsome and bad-tempered.

canteen, canteens 1 (noun) A canteen is the part of a factory or other workplace where the workers can go to eat. **2** A canteen of cutlery is a set of cutlery in a box.

canter, canters, cantering, cantered (verb) When a horse canters, it moves at a speed between a gallop and a trot.

canton, cantons (noun) A canton is a political and administrative region of a country, especially in Switzerland.

canvas, canvases 1 (noun) Canvas is strong, heavy cotton or linen cloth used for making things such as sails, tents, and bags. **2** A canvas is a piece of canvas on which an artist does a painting.

canvass, canvasses, canvassing, canvassed 1 (verb) If you canvass people or a place, you go round trying to persuade people to vote for a particular candidate or party in an election. **2** If you canvass opinion, you find out what people think about a particular subject by asking them.

canyon, canyons (noun) A canyon is a narrow river valley with steep sides.

cap, caps, capping, capped 1 (noun) A cap is a soft, flat hat usually worn by men or boys, often with a peak at the front. **2** A cap is also the lid or top of a bottle. **3** Caps are small explosives used in toy guns. **4** (verb) To cap something means to cover it with something.

capable 1 (adjective) able to do something, e.g. *a man capable of extreme violence.* **2** skilful or talented, e.g. *She was a very capable woman.* **capably** (adverb), **capability** (noun).

capacity, capacities (pronounced kap-**pas**-sit-tee) **1** (noun) The capacity of something is the maximum amount that it can hold or produce, e.g. *a seating capacity of eleven thousand.* **2** A person's capacity is their power or ability to do something, e.g. *his capacity for consuming hamburgers.* **3** You can also refer to someone's position or role as their capacity, e.g. *in his capacity as councillor.*

cape, capes 1 (noun) A cape is a short cloak with no sleeves. **2** A cape is also a large piece of land sticking out into the sea, e.g. *Cape Cod.*

caper, capers 1 (noun) Capers are the flower buds of a spiky Mediterranean shrub, which are pickled and used to flavour food. **2** A caper is also a light-hearted practical joke, e.g. *Jack would have nothing to do with such capers.*

capillary, capillaries (pronounced kap-**pill**-lar-ree) (noun) Capillaries are very thin blood vessels.

capital, capitals 1 (noun) The capital of a country is the city where the government meets. **2** Capital is the amount of money or property owned or used by a business. **3** Capital is also a sum of money that you save or invest in order to gain interest. **4** A capital or capital letter is a larger letter used at the beginning of a sentence or a name. **5** (adjective) involving or requiring the punishment of death.

capitalism (noun) Capitalism is an economic and political system where business and industry are owned by private individuals and not by the state. **capitalist** (adjective or noun).

capitalize, capitalizes, capitalizing, capitalized; also spelled **capitalise** (verb) If you capitalize on a situation, you use it to get an advantage.

capitulate, capitulates, capitulating, capitulated (verb) To capitulate means to give in and stop fighting or resisting, e.g. *The Finns capitulated in 1940.* **capitulation** (noun).

capricious (pronounced kap-**prish**-uss) (adjective) often changing unexpectedly, e.g. *capricious English weather.*

Capricorn (noun) Capricorn is the tenth sign of the zodiac, represented by a goat. People born between December 22nd and January 19th are born under this sign.

capsize, capsizes, capsizing, capsized (verb) If a boat capsizes, it turns upside down.

capsule, capsules 1 (noun) A capsule is a small container with medicine inside which you swallow. **2** A capsule is also the part of a spacecraft in which astronauts travel.

captain, captains, captaining, captained 1 (noun) The captain of a ship or aeroplane is the officer in charge of it. **2** In the army, a captain is an officer of the rank immediately above lieutenant. **3** In the navy, a captain is an officer of the rank immediately above commander. **4** The captain of a sports team is its leader, e.g. *captain of the staff cricket team.* **5** (verb) If you captain a group of people, you are their leader.

caption, captions (noun) A caption is a title printed underneath a picture or photograph.

captivate, captivates, captivating, captivated (verb) To captivate someone means to fascinate them or attract them so that they cannot take their attention away, e.g. *I was captivated by her.* **captivating** (adjective).

captive, captives 1 (noun) A captive is a person who has been captured and kept prisoner. **2** (adjective) imprisoned or enclosed, e.g. *a captive bird.* **captivity** (noun).

captor, captors (noun) The captor of a person or animal is someone who has captured them.

capture, captures, capturing, captured 1 (verb) To capture someone means to take them prisoner. **2** To capture a quality or mood means to succeed in representing or describing it, e.g. *capturing the mood of the riots.* **3** (noun) The capture of someone or something is the capturing of them, e.g. *the fifth anniversary of his capture.*

car, cars 1 (noun) A car is a four-wheeled road vehicle with room for a small number of people. **2** A car is also a railway carriage used for a particular purpose, e.g. *the buffet car.*

carafe, carafes (pronounced kar-**raf**) (noun) A carafe is a glass bottle for serving water or wine.

caramel, caramels 1 (noun) A caramel is a chewy sweet made from sugar, butter, and milk. **2** Caramel is burnt sugar used for colouring or flavouring food.

carat, carats 1 (noun) A carat is a unit for measuring the weight of diamonds and other precious stones. **2** A carat is also a unit for measuring the purity of gold.

caravan, caravans 1 (noun) A caravan is a vehicle pulled by a car in which people live or spend their holidays. **2** A caravan is also a group of people and animals travelling together across a desert.

carbohydrate, carbohydrates (noun) Carbohydrate is a substance that gives you energy. It is found in foods like sugar and bread.

carbon (noun) Carbon is a chemical element that is pure in diamonds and also found in coal.

carburettor, carburettors (pronounced **kahr**-bur-ret-ter) (noun) The carburettor in a vehicle is the part of the engine in which air and petrol are mixed together.

carcass, carcasses; also spelled **carcase** (noun) A carcass is the body of a dead animal.

card, cards 1 (noun) A card is a piece of stiff paper, plastic, or thin cardboard with information or a message on it, e.g. *a birthday card.* **2** A card is also a playing card, e.g. *a pack of cards.* **3** When you play cards, you play any game using playing cards. **4** Card is strong, stiff paper or thin cardboard.

cardboard (noun) Cardboard is thick, stiff paper.

cardiac (adjective; a medical word) relating to the heart, e.g. *cardiac disease.*

cardigan, cardigans (noun) A cardigan is a knitted jacket that fastens up the front.

cardinal, cardinals 1 (noun) In the Roman Catholic church, a cardinal is one of the high-ranking members of the clergy who choose and advise the Pope. **2** (adjective) extremely important, e.g. *a cardinal principle of English law.*

care, cares, caring, cared 1 (verb) If you care about something, you are concerned about it and interested in it. **2** If you care about someone, you feel affection towards them. **3** If you care for someone, you look after them. **4** (noun) Care is a feeling of concern or worry. **5** Care of someone or something is treatment for them or looking after them, e.g. *the care of the elderly.* **6** If you do something with care, you do it with close attention.

career, careers, careering, careered 1 (noun) Someone's career is the series of jobs that they have in life, usually in the same occupation, e.g. *a career in insurance.* **2** (verb) To career somewhere means to move very quickly, often out of control, e.g. *His car careered off the road.*

carefree (adjective) having no worries or responsibilities.

careful 1 (adjective) acting sensibly and with care, e.g. *Be careful what you say to him.* **2** complete and well done, e.g. *It needs very careful planning.* **carefully** (adverb).

careless 1 (adjective) doing something badly without enough attention, e.g. *careless driving.* **2** relaxed and unconcerned, e.g. *careless laughter.* **carelessly** (adverb), **carelessness** (noun).

caress, caresses, caressing, caressed 1 (verb) If you caress someone, you stroke them gently and affectionately. **2** (noun) A caress is a gentle, affectionate stroke.

caretaker, caretakers 1 (noun) A caretaker is a person whose job is to look after a large building such as a school. **2** (adjective) having an important position for a short time until a new person is appointed, e.g. *He was named caretaker manager.*

cargo, cargoes (noun) Cargo is the goods carried on a ship or plane.

Caribbean (noun) The Caribbean consists of the Caribbean Sea east of Central America and the islands in it.

caricature, caricatures, caricaturing, caricatured 1 (noun) A caricature is a drawing or description of someone that exaggerates striking parts of their appearance or personality. **2** (verb) To caricature someone means to give a caricature of them.

carjack, carjacks, carjacking, carjacked (verb) If a car is carjacked, its driver is attacked and robbed, or the car is stolen.

carnage (pronounced **kahr**-nij) (noun) Carnage is the violent killing of large numbers of people.

carnal (adjective; a formal word) sexual and sensual rather than spiritual, e.g. *carnal pleasure.*

carnation, carnations (noun) A carnation is a plant with long stems and white, pink, or red flowers.

carnival, carnivals (noun) A carnival is a public festival with music, processions, and dancing.

carnivore, carnivores (noun) A carnivore is an animal that eats meat. **carnivorous** (adjective).

carol, carols (noun) A carol is a religious song sung at Christmas time.

carousel, carousels (pronounced kar-ros-**sel**) (noun) A carousel is a merry-go-round.

carp, carps, carping, carped 1 (noun) A carp is a large edible freshwater fish. **2** (verb) To carp means to complain about unimportant things.

carpenter, carpenters (noun) A carpenter is a person whose job is making and repairing wooden structures. **carpentry** (noun).

carpet, carpets, carpeting, carpeted 1 (noun) A carpet is a thick covering for a floor, usually made of a material like wool. **2** (verb) To carpet a floor means to cover it with a carpet.

carriage, carriages 1 (noun) A carriage is one of the separate sections of a passenger train. **2** A carriage is also an old-fashioned vehicle for carrying passengers, usually pulled by horses.

carriageway, carriageways (noun) A carriageway is one of the sides of a road which traffic travels along in one direction only.

carrier, carriers 1 (noun) A carrier is a vehicle or other structure that is used for carrying things, e.g. *a troop carrier.* **2** A carrier of a germ or disease is a person or animal that can pass it on to others.

carrier bag, carrier bags (noun) A carrier bag is a paper or plastic bag with handles.

carrion (noun) Carrion is the decaying flesh of dead animals.

carrot, carrots (noun) A carrot is a long, thin orange root vegetable.

carry, carries, carrying, carried 1 (verb) To carry something means to hold it and take it somewhere. **2** When a vehicle carries people, they travel in it. **3** A person or animal that carries a germ is capable of passing it on to other people or animals, e.g. *I still carry the disease.* **4** If a sound carries, it can be heard far away, e.g. *Jake's voice carried over the cheering.* **5** In a meeting, if a proposal is carried, it is accepted by a majority of the people there. **carry away** (verb) If you are carried away, you are so excited by something that you do not behave sensibly. **carry on** (verb) To carry on doing something means to continue doing it. **carry out** (verb) To carry something out means to do it and complete it, e.g. *The conversion was carried out by a local builder.*

cart, carts (noun) A cart is a vehicle with wheels, used to carry goods and often pulled by horses or cattle.

cartilage (noun) Cartilage is strong, flexible body tissue found around the joints and in the nose and ears.

carton, cartons (noun) A carton

is a cardboard or plastic container.

cartoon, cartoons 1 (noun) A cartoon is a drawing or a series of drawings which are funny or make a political point. **2** A cartoon is also a film in which the characters and scenes are drawn rather than being real people and objects. **cartoonist** (noun).

cartridge, cartridges 1 (noun) A cartridge is a tube containing a bullet and an explosive substance, used in guns. **2** A cartridge is also a thin plastic tube containing ink that you put in a pen.

cartwheel, cartwheels (noun) A cartwheel is an acrobatic movement in which you throw yourself sideways onto one hand and move round in a circle with arms and legs stretched until you land on your feet again.

carve, carves, carving, carved 1 (verb) To carve an object means to cut it out of a substance such as stone or wood. **2** To carve meat means to cut slices from it.

carving, carvings (noun) A carving is a carved object.

cascade, cascades, cascading, cascaded 1 (noun) A cascade is a waterfall or group of waterfalls. **2** (verb) To cascade means to flow downwards quickly, e.g. *Thousands of gallons of water cascaded from the attic.*

case, cases 1 (noun) A case is a particular situation, event, or example, e.g. *a clear case of mistaken identity.* **2** A case is also a container for something, or a suitcase, e.g. *a camera case.* **3** Doctors sometimes refer to a patient as a case. **4** Police detectives refer to a crime they are investigating as a case. **5** In an argument, the case for an idea is the facts and reasons used to support it. **6** In law, a case is a trial or other legal inquiry. **7** In grammar, the case of a noun or pronoun is the form of it which shows its relationship with other words in a sentence, e.g. *the accusative case.* **8** (phrase) You say **in case** to explain something that you do because a particular thing might happen, e.g. *I didn't want to shout in case I startled you.* **9** You say **in that case** to indicate that you are assuming something to be true, e.g. *In that case we won't do it.*

casement, casements (noun) A casement is a window that opens on hinges at one side.

cash, cashes, cashing, cashed 1 (noun) Cash is money in the form of notes and coins rather than cheques. **2** (verb) If you cash a cheque, you take it to a bank and exchange it for money.

cashew, cashews (pronounced **kash**-oo) (noun) Cashews are curved, edible nuts.

cashier, cashiers (noun) A cashier is the person that customers pay in a shop or get money from in a bank.

cashmere (noun) Cashmere is very soft, fine wool from goats.

cash register, cash registers (noun) A cash register is a machine in a shop which records sales, and where the money is kept.

casing, casings (noun) A casing is a protective covering for something.

casino, casinos (pronounced kass-**ee**-noh) (noun) A casino is a place where people go to play gambling games.

cask, casks (noun) A cask is a wooden barrel.

casket, caskets (noun) A casket is a small decorative box for jewellery.

casserole, casseroles (noun) A casserole is a dish made by cooking a mixture of meat and vegetables slowly in an oven; also used of the pot a casserole is cooked in.

cassette, cassettes (noun) A cassette is a small flat container with magnetic tape inside, which is used for recording and playing back sounds.

cassette recorder, cassette recorders (noun) A cassette recorder or cassette player is a machine used for recording and playing cassettes.

cassock, cassocks (noun) A cassock is a long robe that is worn by some members of the clergy.

cast, casts, casting, cast 1 (noun) The cast of a play or film is all the people who act in it. **2** (verb) To cast actors means to choose them for roles in a play or film. **3** When people cast their votes in an election, they vote. **4** To cast something means to throw it. **5** If you cast your eyes somewhere, you look there, e.g. *I cast my eyes down briefly.* **6** To cast an object means to make it by pouring liquid into a mould and leaving it to harden, e.g. *An image of him has been cast in bronze.* **7** (noun) A cast is an object made in this way, e.g. *the casts of classical sculptures.* **8** A cast is a stiff plaster covering put on broken bones to keep them still so that they heal properly.

castanets (plural noun) Castanets are a Spanish musical instrument consisting of two small round pieces of wood that are clicked together with the fingers.

castaway, castaways (noun) A castaway is a person who has been shipwrecked.

caste, castes 1 (noun) A caste is one of the four hereditary classes into which Hindu society is divided. **2** Caste is a system of social classes decided according to family, wealth, and position.

caster sugar or **castor sugar** (noun) Caster sugar is very fine white sugar.

castigate, castigates, castigating, castigated (verb; a formal word) To castigate someone means to criticize them severely.

cast iron 1 (noun) Cast iron is iron which is made into objects by casting. It contains carbon. **2** (adjective) A cast-iron excuse or guarantee is absolutely certain and firm.

castle, castles 1 (noun) A castle is a large building with walls or ditches round it to protect it from attack. **2** In chess, a castle is the same as a rook.

cast-off, cast-offs (noun) A cast-off is a piece of outgrown or discarded clothing that has been passed on to someone else.

castor, castors; also spelled **caster** (noun) A castor is a small wheel fitted to furniture so that it can be moved easily.

castor oil (noun) Castor oil is a thick oil that comes from the seeds of the castor oil plant. It is used as a laxative.

castrate, castrates, castrating, castrated (verb) To castrate a male animal means to remove its testicles so that it can no longer produce sperm. **castration** (noun).

casual 1 (adjective) happening by chance without planning, e.g. *a casual remark.* **2** careless or without interest, e.g. *a casual glance over his shoulder.* **3** Casual clothes are suitable for informal occasions. **4** Casual work is not regular or permanent. **casually** (adverb), **casualness** (noun).

casualty, casualties (noun) A casualty is a person killed or injured in an accident or war, e.g. *Many of the casualties were office workers.*

cat, cats 1 (noun) A cat is a small furry mammal kept as a pet. **2** A cat is also any of the family of mammals that includes lions and tigers.

catacomb, catacombs (pronounced **kat**-a-koom) (noun) Catacombs are underground passages with places where dead bodies are buried.

catalogue, catalogues, cataloguing, catalogued 1 (noun) A catalogue is a book containing a list of goods that you can buy in a shop or through the post, together with pictures and descriptions. **2** A catalogue is also a list of things such as the objects in a museum. **3** (verb) To catalogue a collection of things means to list them in a catalogue.

catalyst, catalysts (pronounced **kat**-a-list) (noun) A catalyst is something that causes a change to happen, e.g. *the catalyst which provoked war.*

catamaran, catamarans (noun) A catamaran is a sailing boat with two hulls connected to each other.

catapult, catapults, catapulting, catapulted 1 (noun) A catapult is a Y-shaped object with a piece of elastic tied between the two top ends used for shooting small stones. **2** (verb) To catapult something means to throw it violently through the air. **3** If someone is catapulted into a situation, they suddenly find themselves unexpectedly in that situation, e.g. *Tony has been catapulted into the limelight.*

cataract, cataracts (noun) A cataract is an area of the lens of someone's eye that has become white instead of clear, so that they cannot see properly.

catarrh (pronounced kat-**tahr**) (noun) Catarrh is a condition in which you get a lot of mucus in your nose and throat.

catastrophe, catastrophes (pronounced kat-**tass**-trif-fee) (noun) A catastrophe is a terrible disaster. **catastrophic** (adjective).

catch, catches, catching, caught 1 (verb) If you catch a ball moving in the air, you grasp hold of it when it comes near you. **2** To catch an animal means to stop it from moving freely after chasing or trapping it, e.g. *I caught ten fish.* **3** When the police catch criminals, they find them and arrest them. **4** If you catch someone doing something they should not be doing, you discover them doing it, e.g. *He caught me playing the church organ.* **5** If you catch a bus or train, you get on it and travel somewhere. **6** If you catch a cold or a disease, you become infected with it. **7** If something catches on an object, it sticks to it or gets trapped, e.g. *The white fibres caught on the mesh.* **8** (noun) A catch is a hook that fastens or locks a door or window. **9** If there is a catch in something, there is a problem or hidden complication. **catch on 1** (verb) If you catch on to something, you understand it. **2** If something catches on, it becomes popular, e.g. *This drink has never really caught on in England.* **catch out** (verb) To catch someone out means to trick them or trap them. **catch up 1** (verb) To catch up with someone in front of you means to reach the place where they are by moving slightly faster than them. **2** To catch up with someone also means to reach the same level or standard as them.

catching (adjective) tending to spread very quickly, e.g. *Measles is catching.*

catchy, catchier, catchiest (adjective) attractive and easily remembered, e.g. *a catchy little tune.*

catechism, catechisms (pronounced **kat**-ik-kizm) (noun) A catechism is a set of questions and answers which summarizes the main beliefs of a religion.

categorical (adjective) absolutely certain and direct, e.g. *a categorical denial.* **categorically** (adverb).

categorize, categorizes, categorizing, categorized; also spelled **categorise** (verb) To categorize things means to arrange them in different categories.

category, categories (noun) A category of things is a set of them with a particular characteristic in common, e.g. *Occupations can be divided into four categories.*

cater, caters, catering, catered (verb) To cater for people means to provide them with what they need, especially food.

caterer, caterers (noun) A caterer is a person or business that provides food for parties.

caterpillar, caterpillars (noun) A caterpillar is the larva of a butterfly or moth. It looks like a small coloured worm.

catharsis, catharses (pronounced kath-**ar**-siss) (noun; a formal word) Catharsis is the release of strong emotions and feelings by expressing them through drama, art, or literature.

cathedral, cathedrals (noun) A cathedral is an important church with a bishop in charge of it.

Catholic, Catholics 1 (noun or adjective) A Catholic is a Roman Catholic. **2** (adjective) If a person has catholic interests, then they have a wide range of interests. **Catholicism**

(noun).

cattle (plural noun) Cattle are cows and bulls kept by farmers.

catty, cattier, cattiest (adjective) unpleasant and spiteful. **cattiness** (noun).

catwalk, catwalks (noun) A catwalk is a narrow pathway that people walk along, for example over a stage.

Caucasian, Caucasians (pronounced kaw-**kayz**-yn) (noun) A Caucasian is a person belonging to the race of people with fair or light-brown skin.

caught the past tense and past participle of **catch**.

cauldron, cauldrons (noun) A cauldron is a large, round metal cooking pot, especially one that sits over a fire.

cauliflower, cauliflowers (noun) A cauliflower is a large, round, white vegetable surrounded by green leaves.

cause, causes, causing, caused **1** (noun) The cause of something is the thing that makes it happen, e.g. *the most common cause of back pain.* **2** A cause is an aim or principle which a group of people are working for, e.g. *He was committed to the cause.* **3** If you have cause for something, you have a reason for it, e.g. *They gave us no cause to believe that.* **4** (verb) To cause something means to make it happen, e.g. *This can cause delays.* **causal** (adjective).

causeway, causeways (noun) A causeway is a raised path or road across water or marshland.

caustic 1 (adjective) capable of destroying substances by chemical action, e.g. *caustic liquids such as acids.* **2** bitter or sarcastic, e.g. *your caustic sense of humour.*

caution, cautions, cautioning, cautioned 1 (noun) Caution is great care which you take to avoid danger, e.g. *You will need to proceed with caution.* **2** A caution is a warning, e.g. *Sutton was let off with a caution.* **3** (verb) If someone cautions you, they warn you, usually not to do something again, e.g. *A man has been cautioned by police.* **cautionary** (adjective).

cautious (adjective) acting very carefully to avoid danger, e.g. *a cautious approach.* **cautiously** (adverb).

cavalcade, cavalcades (noun) A cavalcade is a procession of people on horses or in cars.

cavalier (pronounced kav-val-**eer**) (adjective) arrogant and behaving without sensitivity, e.g. *a cavalier attitude to children.*

cavalry (noun) The cavalry is the part of an army that uses armoured vehicles or horses.

cave, caves, caving, caved 1 (noun) A cave is a large hole in rock, that is underground or in the side of a cliff. **2** (verb) If a roof caves in, it collapses inwards.

caveman, cavemen (noun) Cavemen were people who lived in caves in prehistoric times.

cavern, caverns (noun) A cavern is a large cave.

cavernous (adjective) large, deep, and hollow, e.g. *a cavernous warehouse... cavernous eyes.*

caviar or **caviare** (pronounced **kav**-vee-ar) (noun) Caviar is the tiny salted eggs of a fish called the sturgeon.

cavity, cavities (noun) A cavity is a small hole in something solid, e.g. *There were dark cavities in his back teeth.*

cavort, cavorts, cavorting, cavorted (verb) When people cavort, they jump around excitedly.

caw, caws, cawing, cawed (verb) When a crow or rook caws, it makes a harsh sound.

cc an abbreviation for 'cubic centimetres'.

cease, ceases, ceasing, ceased 1 (verb) If something ceases, it stops happening. **2** If you cease to do something, you stop doing it.

cease-fire, cease-fires (noun) A cease-fire is an agreement between groups that are fighting each other to stop for a period and discuss peace.

ceaseless (adjective) going on without stopping, e.g. *the ceaseless movement of the streets.* **ceaselessly** (adverb).

cedar, cedars (noun) A cedar is a large evergreen tree with needle-shaped leaves.

cede, cedes, ceding, ceded (pronounced **seed**) (verb) To cede something means to give it up to someone else, e.g. *Haiti was ceded to France in 1697.*

ceiling, ceilings (noun) A ceiling is the top inside surface of a room.

celebrate, celebrates, celebrating, celebrated 1 (verb) If you celebrate or celebrate something, you do something special and enjoyable in honour of it, e.g. *a party to celebrate the end of the exams.* **2** When a priest celebrates Mass, he performs the actions and ceremonies of the Mass. **celebration** (noun), **celebratory** (adjective).

celebrated (adjective) famous, e.g. *the celebrated Italian mountaineer.*

celebrity, celebrities (noun) A celebrity is a famous person.

celery (noun) Celery is a vegetable with long pale green stalks.

celestial (pronounced sil-**lest**-yal) (adjective; a formal word) concerning the sky or heaven, e.g. *celestial bodies.*

celibate (pronounced **sel**-lib-bit) (adjective) Someone who is celibate does not marry or have sex. **celibacy** (noun).

cell, cells 1 (noun) In biology, a cell is the smallest part of an animal or plant that can exist by itself. Each cell contains a nucleus. **2** In a prison or police station, a cell is a small room where a prisoner is kept. **3** A cell is also a small group of people set up to work together as part of a larger organization.

cellar, cellars (noun) A cellar is a room underneath a building, often used to store wine.

cello, cellos (pronounced **chel**-loh) (noun) A cello is a large musical stringed instrument which you play sitting down, holding the instrument upright with your knees. **cellist** (noun).

cellophane (noun; a trademark) Cellophane is thin, transparent plastic material used to wrap food or other things to protect them.

cellular (adjective) Cellular

means relating to the cells of animals or plants.

celluloid (pronounced **sel**-yul-loyd) (noun) Celluloid is a type of plastic which was once used to make photographic film.

Celsius (pronounced **sel**-see-yuss) (noun) Celsius is a scale for measuring temperature in which water freezes at 0 degrees (0°C) and boils at 100 degrees (100°C). Celsius is the same as 'Centigrade'.

Celtic (pronounced **kel**-tik) (adjective) A Celtic language is one of a group of languages that includes Gaelic and Welsh.

cement, cements, cementing, cemented 1 (noun) Cement is a fine powder made from limestone and clay, which is mixed with sand and water to make mortar or concrete. **2** (verb) To cement things means to stick them together with cement or cover them with cement. **3** Something that cements a relationship makes it stronger, e.g. *to cement relations between them.*

cemetery, cemeteries (noun) A cemetery is a place where dead people are buried.

cenotaph, cenotaphs (pronounced **sen**-not-ahf) (noun) A cenotaph is a monument built in memory of dead people, especially soldiers buried elsewhere.

censor, censors, censoring, censored 1 (noun) A censor is a person officially appointed to examine books or films and to cut or ban parts that are considered unsuitable. **2** (verb) If someone censors a book or film, they cut or ban parts of it that are considered unsuitable for the public. **censorship** (noun).

censure, censures, censuring, censured (pronounced **sen**-sher) **1** (noun) Censure is strong disapproval of something. **2** (verb) To censure someone means to criticize them severely.

census, censuses (noun) A census is an official survey of the population of a country.

cent, cents (noun) The cent is a unit of currency in the USA and in some other countries. In the USA, a cent is worth one hundredth of a dollar.

centaur, centaurs (pronounced **sen**-tawr) (noun) In Greek mythology, a centaur is a creature with the top half of a man and the lower body and legs of a horse.

centenary, centenaries (pronounced sen-**teen**-er-ee) (nouns) A centenary is the 100th anniversary of something.

centi- (prefix) Centi- is used to form words that have 'hundred' as part of their meaning, e.g. *centimetre.*

Centigrade Centigrade is another name for **Celsius.**

centilitre, centilitres (noun) A centilitre is a unit of liquid volume equal to one hundredth of a litre.

centimetre, centimetres (noun) A centimetre is a unit of length equal to ten millimetres or one hundredth of a metre.

centipede, centipedes (noun) A centipede is a long, thin insect with many pairs of legs.

central 1 (adjective) in or near the centre of an object or area, e.g. *central ceiling lights.* **2** main or most important, e.g. *the central idea of this work.* **centrally** (adverb), **centrality** (noun).

Central America (noun) Central America is another name for the Isthmus of Panama, the area of land joining North America to South America.

central heating (noun) Central heating is a system of heating a building in which water or air is heated in a tank and travels through pipes and radiators round the building.

centralize, centralizes, centralizing, centralized; also spelled **centralise** (verb) To centralize a system means to bring the organization of it under the control of one central group. **centralization** (noun).

centre, centres, centring, centred 1 (noun) The centre of an object or area is the middle of it. **2** A centre is a building where people go for activities, meetings, or help, e.g. *a health centre.* **3** Someone or something that is the centre of attention attracts a lot of attention. **4** (verb) To centre something means to move it so that it is balanced or at the centre of something else. **5** If something centres on or around a particular thing, that thing is the main subject of attention, e.g. *The discussion centred on his request for British aid.*

centrifugal (pronounced sen-trif-**yoo**-gl) (adjective) In physics, centrifugal force is the force that makes rotating objects move outwards.

centurion, centurions (noun) A centurion was a Roman officer in charge of a hundred soldiers.

century, centuries 1 (noun) A century is a period of one hundred years. **2** In cricket, a century is one hundred runs scored by a batsman.

ceramic, ceramics (pronounced sir-**ram**-mik) (noun) Ceramic is a hard material made by baking clay to a very high temperature.

cereal, cereals 1 (noun) A cereal is a food made from grain, often eaten with milk for breakfast. **2** A cereal is a plant that produces edible grain, such as wheat or oats.

cerebral (pronounced **ser**-reb-ral) (adjective; a formal word) relating to the brain, e.g. *a cerebral haemorrhage.*

cerebral palsy (noun) Cerebral palsy is an illness caused by damage to a baby's brain before it is born, which makes its muscles and limbs very weak.

ceremonial (adjective) relating to a ceremony, e.g. *ceremonial dress.* **ceremonially** (adverb).

ceremony, ceremonies 1 (noun) A ceremony is a set of formal actions performed at a special occasion or important public event, e.g. *his recent coronation ceremony.* **2** Ceremony is very formal and polite behaviour, e.g. *He hung up without ceremony.*

certain 1 (adjective) definite and with no doubt at all, e.g. *He is certain to be in Italy.* **2** You use certain to refer to a specific person or thing, e.g. *certain aspects of the job.* **3**

You use certain to suggest that a quality is noticeable but not clearly definable, e.g. *There's a certain resemblance to the man.*

certainly 1 (adverb) without doubt, e.g. *My boss was certainly interested.* **2** of course, e.g. *'Will you be there?' – 'Certainly.'*

certainty, certainties 1 (noun) Certainty is the state of being certain. **2** A certainty is something that is known without doubt, e.g. *There are no certainties and no guarantees.*

certificate, certificates (noun) A certificate is a document stating particular facts, for example of someone's birth or death, e.g. *a marriage certificate.*

certify, certifies, certifying, certified 1 (verb) To certify something means to declare formally that it is true, e.g. *certifying the cause of death.* **2** To certify someone means to declare officially that they are insane.

cervix, cervixes or **cervices** (noun; a technical word) The cervix is the entrance to the womb at the top of the vagina. **cervical** (adjective).

cessation (noun; a formal word) The cessation of something is the stopping of it, e.g. *a swift cessation of hostilities.*

cf. cf. means 'compare'. It is written to mention something that should be considered in connection with the subject being discussed.

CFC, CFCs (noun) CFCs are man-made chemicals that are used in aerosol sprays. They damage the ozone layer. CFC is an abbreviation for 'chlorofluorocarbon'.

chaff (noun) Chaff is the outer parts of grain separated from the seeds by beating.

chaffinch, chaffinches (noun) A chaffinch is a small European bird with black and white wings.

chagrin (pronounced **shag**-rin) (noun; a formal word) Chagrin is a feeling of annoyance or disappointment.

chain, chains, chaining, chained 1 (noun) A chain is a number of metal rings connected together in a line, e.g. *a bicycle chain.* **2** A chain of things is a number of them in a series or connected to each other, e.g. *a chain of shops.* **3** (verb) If you chain one thing to another, you fasten them together with a chain, e.g. *They had chained themselves to railings.*

chain saw, chain saws (noun) A chain saw is a large saw with teeth fixed in a chain that is driven round by a motor.

chain-smoke, chain-smokes, chain-smoking, chain-smoked (verb) To chain-smoke means to smoke cigarettes continually.

chair, chairs, chairing, chaired 1 (noun) A chair is a seat with a back and four legs for one person. **2** The chair of a meeting is the person in charge who decides when each person may speak. **3** (verb) The person who chairs a meeting is in charge of it.

chair lift, chair lifts (noun) A chair lift is a line of chairs that hang from a moving cable and carry people up and down a mountain.

chairman, chairmen 1 (noun) The chairman of a meeting is the person in charge who decides when each person may speak. **2** The chairman of a company or committee is the head of it. **chairperson** (noun), **chairwoman** (noun), **chairmanship** (noun).

chalet, chalets (pronounced **shall**-lay) (noun) A chalet is a wooden house with a sloping roof, especially in a mountain area or a holiday camp.

chalice, chalices (pronounced **chal**-liss) (noun) A chalice is a gold or silver cup used in Christian churches to hold the Communion wine.

chalk, chalks, chalking, chalked 1 (noun) Chalk is a soft white rock. Small sticks of chalk are used for writing or drawing on a blackboard. **2** (verb) To chalk up a result means to achieve it, e.g. *He chalked up his first win.* **chalky** (adjective).

challenge, challenges, challenging, challenged 1 (noun) A challenge is something that is new and exciting but requires a lot of effort, e.g. *It's a new challenge at the right time in my career.* **2** A challenge is also a suggestion from someone to compete with them. **3** A challenge to something is a questioning of whether it is correct or true, e.g. *a challenge to authority.* **4** (verb) If someone challenges you, they suggest that you compete with them in some way. **5** If you challenge something, you question whether it is correct or true. **challenger** (noun), **challenging** (adjective).

chamber, chambers 1 (noun) A chamber is a large room, especially one used for formal meetings, e.g. *the Council Chamber.* **2** A chamber is also a group of people appointed to decide laws or administrative matters. **3** A chamber is also a hollow place or compartment inside something, especially inside an animal's body or inside a gun, e.g. *the chambers of the heart.*

chambermaid, chambermaids (noun) A chambermaid is a woman who cleans and tidies rooms in a hotel.

chameleon, chameleons (pronounced kam-**mee**-lee-on) (noun) A chameleon is a lizard which is able to change the colour of its skin to match the colour of its surroundings.

chamois leather, chamois leathers (pronounced **sham**-mee) (noun) A chamois leather is a soft leather cloth used for polishing.

champagne, champagnes (pronounced sham-**pain**) (noun) Champagne is a sparkling white wine made in France.

champion, champions, championing, championed 1 (noun) A champion is a person who wins a competition. **2** A champion of a cause or principle is someone who supports or defends it, e.g. *a champion of women's causes.* **3** (verb) Someone who champions a cause or principle supports or defends it.

championship, championships (noun) A championship is a competition to find the champion of a sport; also the title or status of a champion.

chance, chances, chancing, chanced 1 (noun) The chance of something happening is how possible or likely it is, e.g. *There's a chance of rain later.* **2** A chance to do something is an opportunity to do it. **3** A chance is also a possibility that something dangerous or unpleasant may happen, e.g. *Don't take chances, he's armed.* **4** Chance is also the way things happen unexpectedly without being planned, e.g. *I only found out by chance.* **5** (verb) If you chance something, you try it although you are taking a risk.

chancellor, chancellors 1 (noun) In some European countries, the Chancellor is the head of government. **2** In Britain, the Chancellor is the Chancellor of the Exchequer. **3** A chancellor is also the honorary head of a British university.

Chancellor of the Exchequer (noun) The Chancellor of the Exchequer is the minister responsible for finance and taxes.

chandelier, chandeliers (pronounced shan-del-**leer**) (noun) A chandelier is an ornamental light fitting which hangs from the ceiling.

change, changes, changing, changed 1 (noun) A change in something is a difference or alteration, e.g. *Steven soon noticed a change in Penny's attitude.* **2** (verb) When something changes or when you change it, it becomes different, e.g. *It changed my life.* **3** (noun) A change of something is a replacement by something else, e.g. *a change of clothes.* **4** (verb) If you change something, you exchange it for something else. **5** When you change, you put on different clothes. **6** (noun) Change is money you get back when you have paid more than the actual price of something.

changeable (adjective) likely to change all the time.

changeover, changeovers (noun) A changeover is a change from one system or activity to another, e.g. *the changeover to the council tax.*

channel, channels, channelling, channelled 1 (noun) A channel is a wavelength used to receive programmes broadcast by a television or radio station; also the station itself, e.g. *I was watching the other channel.* **2** A channel is also a passage along which water flows or along which something is carried. **3** The Channel or the English Channel is the stretch of sea between England and France. **4** A channel is also a method of achieving something, e.g. *We have tried to do things through the right channels.* **5** (verb) To channel something such as money or energy means to control and direct it in a particular way, e.g. *Their efforts are being channelled into worthy causes.*

chant, chants, chanting, chanted 1 (noun) A chant is a group of words repeated over and over again, e.g. *a rousing chant.* **2** A chant is also a religious song sung on only a few notes. **3** (verb) If people chant a group of words, they repeat them over and over again, e.g. *Crowds chanted his name.*

chaos (pronounced **kay**-oss) (noun) Chaos is a state of complete disorder and confusion. **chaotic** (adjective).

chap, chaps, chapping, chapped **1** (noun; an informal use) A chap is a man. **2** (verb) If your skin chaps, it becomes dry and cracked, usually as a result of cold or wind.

chapel, chapels **1** (noun) A chapel is a section of a church or cathedral with its own altar. **2** A chapel is also a type of small church.

chaperone, chaperones (pronounced **shap**-per-rone); also spelled **chaperon** (noun) A chaperone is an older woman who accompanies a young unmarried woman on social occasions, or any person who accompanies a group of younger people.

chaplain, chaplains (noun) A chaplain is a member of the Christian clergy attached to an institution such as a hospital, school, or prison. **chaplaincy** (noun).

chapter, chapters **1** (noun) A chapter is one of the parts into which a book is divided. **2** A chapter in someone's life or in history is a particular period in it.

char, chars, charring, charred (verb) If something chars, it gets partly burned and goes black. **charred** (adjective).

character, characters **1** (noun) The character of a person or place is all the qualities which combine to form their personality or atmosphere. **2** A person or place that has character has an interesting, attractive, or admirable quality, e.g. *an inn of great character and simplicity.* **3** The characters in a film, play, or book are the people in it. **4** You can refer to a person as a character, e.g. *an odd character.* **5** A character is also a letter, number, or other written symbol.

characteristic, characteristics **1** (noun) A characteristic is a quality that is typical of a particular person or thing, e.g. *Silence is the characteristic of the place.* **2** (adjective) Characteristic means typical of a particular person or thing, e.g. *Two things are characteristic of his driving.* **characteristically** (adverb).

characterize, characterizes, characterizing, characterized; also spelled **characterise** (verb) A quality that characterizes something is typical of it, e.g. *a condition characterized by muscle stiffness.*

characterless (adjective) dull and uninteresting, e.g. *a tiny characterless London flat.*

charade, charades (pronounced shar-**rahd**) (noun) A charade is a ridiculous and unnecessary activity or pretence.

charcoal (noun) Charcoal is a black form of carbon made by burning wood without air, used as a fuel and also for drawing.

charge, charges, charging, charged **1** (verb) If someone charges you money, they ask you to pay it for something that you have bought or received, e.g. *The company charged £150 on each loan.* **2** (noun) A charge is the price that you have to pay for something. **3** A charge is a formal accusation that a person is guilty of a crime and has to go to court. **4** (verb) To charge someone means to accuse them formally of having committed a crime. **5** (noun) To have charge or be in charge of someone or something means to be responsible for them and be in control of them. **6** A charge is also an explosive put in a gun or other weapon. **7** An electrical charge is the amount of electricity that something carries. **8** (verb) To charge a battery means to pass an electrical current through it to make it store electricity. **9** To charge somewhere means to rush forward, often in order to attack someone, e.g. *The rhino charged at her*.

charger, chargers (noun) A charger is a device for charging or recharging batteries.

chariot, chariots (noun) A chariot is a two-wheeled open vehicle pulled by horses.

charisma (pronounced kar-**riz**-ma) (noun) Charisma is a special ability to attract or influence people by your personality. **charismatic** (adjective).

charity, charities 1 (noun) A charity is an organization that raises money to help people who are ill, poor, or disabled. **2** Charity is money or other help given to poor, disabled, or ill people, e.g. *to help raise money for charity*. **3** Charity is also a kind, sympathetic attitude towards people. **charitable** (adjective).

charlatan, charlatans (pronounced **shar**-lat-tn) (noun) A charlatan is someone who pretends to have skill or knowledge that they do not really have.

charm, charms, charming, charmed 1 (noun) Charm is an attractive and pleasing quality that some people and things have, e.g. *a man of great personal charm*. **2** (verb) If you charm someone, you use your charm to please them. **3** (noun) A charm is a small ornament worn on a bracelet. **4** A charm is also a magical spell or an object that is supposed to bring good luck.

charmer, charmers (noun) A charmer is someone who uses their personal charm to influence people.

charming (adjective) very pleasant and attractive, e.g. *a rather charming man*. **charmingly** (adverb).

chart, charts, charting, charted 1 (noun) A chart is a diagram or table showing information, e.g. *He noted the score on his chart*. **2** A chart is also a map of the sea or stars. **3** (verb) If you chart something, you observe and record it carefully.

charter, charters, chartering, chartered 1 (noun) A charter is a document stating the rights or aims of a group or organization as laid down by the government, e.g. *the new charter for commuters*. **2** (verb) To charter transport such as a plane or boat means to hire it for private use. **chartered** (adjective).

chase, chases, chasing, chased 1 (verb) If you chase someone or something, you run or go after them in order to catch them or drive them away. **2** (noun) A chase is the activity of chasing or hunting someone or something, e.g. *a high-speed car chase.*

chasm, chasms (pronounced **kazm**) **1** (noun) A chasm is a deep crack in the earth's surface. **2** A chasm is also a very large difference between two ideas or groups of people, e.g. *the chasm between rich and poor in America.*

chassis (pronounced **shas**-ee) The plural is also **chassis**. (noun) The chassis of a vehicle is the frame on which it is built.

chaste (pronounced **chayst**) (adjective; an old-fashioned use) not having sex outside marriage. **chastity** (noun).

chastise, chastises, chastising, chastised (verb; a formal word) If someone chastises you, they scold you or punish you for something that you have done.

chat, chats, chatting, chatted 1 (noun) A chat is a friendly talk with someone, usually about things that are not very important. **2** (verb) When people chat, they talk to each other in a friendly way. **chat up** (verb; an informal use) If you chat up a member of the opposite sex, you talk to them in a friendly way, because you are attracted to them.

chateau, chateaux (pronounced **shat**-toe) (noun) A chateau is a large country house or castle in France.

chatter, chatters, chattering, chattered 1 (verb) When people chatter, they talk very fast. **2** (noun) Chatter is a lot of fast unimportant talk. **3** (verb) If your teeth are chattering, they are knocking together and making a clicking noise because you are cold.

chatty, chattier, chattiest (adjective) talkative and friendly.

chauffeur, chauffeurs (pronounced **show**-fur) (noun) A chauffeur is a person whose job is to drive another person's car.

chauvinist, chauvinists 1 (noun) A chauvinist is a person who thinks their country is always right. **2** A male chauvinist is a man who believes that men are superior to women. **chauvinistic** (adjective), **chauvinism** (noun).

cheap, cheaper, cheapest 1 (adjective) Something that is cheap costs very little money, and is sometimes of poor quality. **2** A cheap joke or cheap remark is unfair and unkind. **cheaply** (adverb).

cheat, cheats, cheating, cheated 1 (verb) If someone cheats, they do wrong or unfair things in order to win or get something that they want. **2** If you are cheated of or out of something, you do not get what you are entitled to. **3** (noun) A cheat is a person who cheats.

check, checks, checking, checked 1 (verb) To check something means to examine it in order to make sure that everything is all right. **2** (noun) A check is an inspection to make sure that everything is all right. **3** (verb) To check the growth, movement, or spread of something means to make it stop, e.g. *a policy to check fast population growth.* **4** (noun) Checks are different coloured squares which form a pattern. **5** (adjective) Check or checked means marked with a pattern of squares, e.g. *check design.*

checkmate (noun) In chess, checkmate is a situation where one player cannot stop their king being captured and so loses the game.

checkout, checkouts (noun) A checkout is a counter in a supermarket where the customers pay for their goods.

checkpoint, checkpoints (noun) A checkpoint is a place where traffic has to stop in order to be checked.

checkup, checkups (noun) A checkup is an examination by a doctor to see if your health is all right.

cheek, cheeks 1 (noun) Your cheeks are the sides of your face below your eyes. **2** Cheek is speech or behaviour that is rude or disrespectful, e.g. *an expression of sheer cheek.*

cheeky, cheekier, cheekiest (adjective) rather rude and disrespectful.

cheer, cheers, cheering, cheered 1 (verb) When people cheer, they shout with approval or in order to show support for a person or team. **2** (noun) A cheer is a shout of approval or support. **cheer up** (verb) When you cheer up, you feel more cheerful.

cheerful 1 (adjective) happy and in good spirits, e.g. *I had never seen her so cheerful.* **2** bright and pleasant-looking, e.g. *a cheerful and charming place.* **cheerfully** (adverb), **cheerfulness** (noun).

cheerio (interjection) Cheerio is a friendly way of saying goodbye.

cheery, cheerier, cheeriest (adjective) happy and cheerful, e.g. *He gave me a cheery nod.*

cheese, cheeses (noun) Cheese is a hard or creamy food made from milk.

cheesecake, cheesecakes (noun) Cheesecake is a dessert made of biscuit covered with cream cheese.

cheetah, cheetahs (noun) A cheetah is a wild animal like a large cat with black spots. Cheetahs can run very fast.

chef, chefs (noun) A chef is a head cook in a restaurant or hotel.

chemical, chemicals 1 (noun) Chemicals are substances manufactured by chemistry. **2** (adjective) involved in chemistry or using chemicals, e.g. *chemical weapons.* **chemically** (adverb).

chemist, chemists 1 (noun) A chemist is a person who is qualified to make up drugs and medicines prescribed by a doctor. **2** A chemist or a chemist's is a shop where medicines and cosmetics are sold. **3** A chemist is also a scientist who does research in chemistry, e.g. *a research chemist.*

chemistry (noun) Chemistry is the scientific study of substances and the ways in which they change when they are combined with other substances.

chemotherapy (pronounced keem-oh-**ther**-a-pee) (noun)

Chemotherapy is a way of treating diseases such as cancer by using chemicals.

cheque, cheques (noun) A cheque is a printed form on which you write an amount of money that you have to pay. You sign the cheque and your bank pays the money from your account.

chequered (pronounced **chek**-kerd) **1** (adjective) covered with a pattern of squares. **2** A chequered career is a varied career that has both good and bad parts.

cherish, cherishes, cherishing, cherished 1 (verb) If you cherish something, you care deeply about it and want to keep it or look after it lovingly. **2** If you cherish a memory or hope, you have it in your mind and care deeply about it, e.g. *I cherish the good memories I have of him.*

cherry, cherries 1 (noun) A cherry is a small, juicy fruit with a red or black skin and a hard stone in the centre. **2** A cherry is also a tree that produces cherries.

cherub, cherubs or **cherubim** (noun) A cherub is an angel, shown in pictures as a plump, naked child with wings. **cherubic** (adjective).

chess (noun) Chess is a board game for two people in which each player has 16 pieces and tries to move his or her pieces so that the other player's king cannot escape.

chest, chests 1 (noun) Your chest is the front part of your body between your shoulders and your waist. **2** A chest is a large wooden box with a hinged lid.

chestnut, chestnuts 1 (noun) Chestnuts are reddish-brown nuts that grow inside a prickly green outer covering. **2** A chestnut is a tree that produces these nuts. **3** (adjective) Something that is chestnut is reddish-brown.

chest of drawers, chests of drawers (noun) A chest of drawers is a piece of furniture with drawers in it.

chew, chews, chewing, chewed (verb) When you chew something, you use your teeth to break it up in your mouth before swallowing it. **chewy** (adjective).

chewing gum (noun) Chewing gum is a kind of sweet that you chew for a long time, but which you do not swallow.

chic (pronounced **sheek**) (adjective) elegant and fashionable, e.g. *chic French women... a chic restaurant.*

chick, chicks (noun) A chick is a young bird.

chicken, chickens, chickening, chickened 1 (noun) A chicken is a bird kept on a farm for its eggs and meat; also the meat of this bird, e.g. *roast chicken.* **2** (verb; an informal use) If you chicken out of something, you do not do it because you are afraid.

chickenpox (noun) Chickenpox is an illness which produces a fever and blister-like spots on the skin.

chicory (noun) Chicory is a plant with bitter leaves that are used in salads.

chide, chides, chiding, chided (verb; an old-fashioned word) To chide someone means to tell them off.

chief, chiefs 1 (noun) The leader of a group or organization is its chief. **2** (adjective) most important, e.g. *the chief source of success.* **chiefly** (adverb).

chieftain, chieftains (noun) A chieftain is the leader of a tribe or clan.

chiffon (pronounced **shif**-fon) (noun) Chiffon is a very thin lightweight cloth made of silk or nylon.

chihuahua, chihuahuas (pronounced chi-**wah**-wah) (noun) A chihuahua is a breed of very small dog with short hair and pointed ears.

chilblain, chilblains (noun) A chilblain is a sore, itchy swelling on a finger or toe.

child, children 1 (noun) A child is a young person who is not yet an adult. **2** Someone's child is their son or daughter.

childhood, childhoods (noun) Someone's childhood is the time when they are a child.

childish (adjective) immature and foolish, e.g. *I don't have time for childish arguments.* **childishly** (adverb), **childishness** (noun).

childless (adjective) having no children.

childlike (adjective) like a child in appearance or behaviour, e.g. *childlike enthusiasm.*

childminder, childminders (noun) A childminder is a person who is paid to look after other people's children while they are at work.

Chilean, Chileans 1 (adjective) belonging or relating to Chile. **2** (noun) A Chilean is someone who comes from Chile.

chill, chills, chilling, chilled 1 (verb) To chill something means to make it cold, e.g. *Chill the cheesecake.* **2** If something chills you, it makes you feel worried or frightened, e.g. *The thought chilled her.* **3** (noun) A chill is a feverish cold. **4** A chill is also a feeling of cold, e.g. *the chill of the night air.*

chilli, chillies (noun) A chilli is the red or green seed pod of a type of pepper which has a very hot, spicy taste.

chilly, chillier, chilliest 1 (adjective) rather cold, e.g. *the chilly November breeze.* **2** unfriendly and without enthusiasm, e.g. *his chilly relationship with Stephens.*

chime, chimes, chiming, chimed (verb) When a bell chimes, it makes a clear ringing sound.

chimney, chimneys (noun) A chimney is a vertical pipe or other hollow structure above a fireplace or furnace through which smoke from a fire escapes.

chimpanzee, chimpanzees (noun) A chimpanzee is a small ape with dark fur that lives in forests in Africa.

chin, chins (noun) Your chin is the part of your face below your mouth.

china (noun) China is items like cups, saucers, and plates made from very fine clay.

Chinese 1 (adjective) belonging or relating to China. **2** (noun) A Chinese is someone who comes from China. **3** Chinese refers to any of a group of related languages and dialects spoken by Chinese people.

chink, chinks 1 (noun) A chink is a small, narrow opening, e.g. *a chink in the roof.* **2** A chink is also a short, light, ringing sound, like one made by glasses touching each other.

chintz (noun) Chintz is a type of brightly patterned cotton fabric.

chip, chips, chipping, chipped 1 (noun) Chips are thin strips of fried potato. **2** In electronics, a chip is a tiny piece of silicon inside a computer which is used to form electronic circuits. **3** A chip is also a small piece broken off an object, or the mark made when a piece breaks off. **4** (verb) If you chip an object, you break a small piece off it.

chipmunk, chipmunks (noun) A chipmunk is a small rodent with a striped back.

chiropodist, chiropodists (pronounced kir-**rop**-pod-dist) (noun) A chiropodist is a person whose job is treating people's feet. **chiropody** (noun).

chirp, chirps, chirping, chirped (verb) When a bird chirps, it makes a short, high-pitched sound.

chisel, chisels, chiselling, chiselled 1 (noun) A chisel is a tool with a long metal blade and a sharp edge at the end which is used for cutting and shaping wood, stone, or metal. **2** (verb) To chisel wood, stone, or metal means to cut or shape it using a chisel.

chivalry (pronounced **shiv**-val-ree) (noun) Chivalry is polite, kind, helpful behaviour, especially by men towards women. **chivalrous** (adjective).

chive, chives (noun) Chives are grasslike hollow leaves that taste like onions

chlorine (pronounced **klaw**-reen) (noun) Chlorine is a poisonous greenish-yellow gas with a strong, unpleasant smell. It is used as a disinfectant for water, and to make bleach.

chloroform (pronounced **klor**-rof-form) (noun) Chloroform is a colourless liquid with a strong, sweet smell used in cleaning products.

chlorophyll (pronounced **klor**-rof-fil) (noun) Chlorophyll is a green substance in plants which enables them to use the energy from sunlight in order to grow.

chock-a-block or **chock-full** (adjective) completely full.

chocolate, chocolates 1 (noun) Chocolate is a sweet food made from cacao seeds. **2** A chocolate is a sweet made of chocolate.

choice, choices 1 (noun) A choice is a range of different things that are available to choose from, e.g. *a wider choice of treatments.* **2** A choice is also something that you choose, e.g. *You've made a good choice.* **3** Choice is the power or right to choose, e.g. *I had no choice.*

choir, choirs (pronounced **kwire**) (noun) A choir is a group of singers, for example in a church.

choke, chokes, choking, choked 1 (verb) If you choke, you stop being able to breathe properly, usually because something is blocking your windpipe, e.g. *the diner who choked on a fish bone.* **2** If things choke a place, they fill it so much that it is blocked or clogged up, e.g. *The canal was choked with old tyres.*

cholera (pronounced **kol**-ler-ra) (noun) Cholera is a serious disease causing severe diarrhoea and vomiting. It is caused by infected food or water.

cholesterol (pronounced kol-**less**-ter-rol) (noun) Cholesterol is a substance found in all animal fats, tissues, and blood.

choose, chooses, choosing, chose, chosen (verb) To choose something means to decide to have it or do it, e.g. *He chose to live in England.*

choosy, choosier, choosiest (adjective) fussy and difficult to satisfy, e.g. *Policemen are very choosy about their partners.*

chop, chops, chopping, chopped **1** (verb) To chop something means to cut it with quick, heavy strokes using an axe or a knife. **2** (noun) A chop is a small piece of lamb or pork containing a bone, usually cut from the ribs.

chopper, choppers (noun; an informal word) A chopper is a helicopter.

choppy, choppier, choppiest (adjective) Choppy water has a lot of waves because it is windy.

chopstick, chopsticks (noun) Chopsticks are a pair of thin sticks used by people in the Far East for eating food.

choral (adjective) relating to singing by a choir, e.g. *choral music.*

chord, chords (noun) A chord is a group of three or more musical notes played together.

chore, chores (noun) A chore is an unpleasant job that has to be done, e.g. *the chore of food preparation.*

choreography (pronounced kor-ree-**og**-raf-fee) (noun) Choreography is the art of composing dance steps and movements. **choreographer** (noun).

chortle, chortles, chortling, chortled (verb) To chortle means to laugh with amusement.

chorus, choruses, chorusing, chorused **1** (noun) A chorus is a large group of singers. **2** The chorus of a song is a part which is repeated after each verse. **3** (verb) If people chorus something, they all say or sing it at the same time.

Christ (noun) Christ is the name for Jesus. Christians believe that Jesus is the son of God.

christen, christens, christening, christened (verb) When a baby is christened, it is named by a clergyman in a religious ceremony as a sign that it is a member of the Christian church.

Christian, Christians **1** (noun) A Christian is a person who believes in Jesus Christ and his teachings. **2** (adjective) relating to Christ and his teachings, e.g. *the Christian faith.* **3** good, kind, and considerate, e.g. *a good Christian woman.* **Christianity** (noun).

Christian name, Christian names (noun) Someone's Christian name is the name given to them when they were born or christened.

Christmas, Christmases (noun) Christmas is the Christian festival celebrating the birth of Christ, falling on December 25th.

chrome (pronounced **krome**) (noun) Chrome is metal plated with chromium, a hard grey metal.

chromosome, chromosomes (noun) In biology, a chromosome is a part of a cell which contains genes that determine the characteristics of an animal or plant.

chronic (pronounced **kron**-nik) (adjective) lasting a very long time or never stopping, e.g. *a chronic illness.* **chronically** (adverb).

chronicle, chronicles, chronicling, chronicled 1 (noun) A chronicle is a record of a series of events described in the order in which they happened. **2** (verb) To chronicle a series of events means to record or describe them in the order in which they happened.

chronological (pronounced kron-nol-**loj**-i-kl) (adjective) arranged in the order in which things happened, e.g. *Tell me the whole story in chronological order.* **chronologically** (adverb).

chrysalis, chrysalises (pronounced **kriss**-sal-liss) (noun) A chrysalis is a butterfly or moth when it is developing from being a caterpillar to being a fully grown adult.

chrysanthemum, chrysanthemums (pronounced kriss-**an**-thim-mum) (noun) A chrysanthemum is a plant with large, bright flowers.

chubby, chubbier, chubbiest (adjective) plump and round, e.g. *his chubby cheeks.*

chuck, chucks, chucking, chucked (verb; an informal word) To chuck something means to throw it casually.

chuckle, chuckles, chuckling, chuckled (verb) When you chuckle, you laugh quietly.

chug, chugs, chugging, chugged (verb) When a machine or engine chugs, it makes a continuous dull thudding sound.

chum, chums (noun; an informal word) A chum is a friend.

chunk, chunks (noun) A chunk of something solid is a thick piece of it.

chunky, chunkier, chunkiest (adjective) Someone who is chunky is broad and heavy but usually short.

church, churches 1 (noun) A church is a building where Christians go for religious services and worship. **2** In the Christian religion, a church is one of the groups with their own particular beliefs, customs, and clergy, e.g. *the Catholic Church.*

Church of England (noun) The Church of England is the Anglican church in England, where it is the state church, with the King or Queen as its head.

churchyard, churchyards (noun) A churchyard is an area of land around a church, often used as a graveyard.

churn, churns (noun) A churn is a container used for making milk or cream into butter.

chute, chutes (pronounced **shoot**) (noun) A chute is a steep slope or channel used to slide things down, e.g. *a rubbish chute.*

chutney (noun) Chutney is a strong-tasting thick sauce made from fruit, vinegar, and spices.
cider (noun) Cider is an alcoholic drink made from apples.
cigar, cigars (noun) A cigar is a roll of dried tobacco leaves which people smoke.
cigarette, cigarettes (noun) A cigarette is a thin roll of tobacco covered in thin paper which people smoke.
cinder, cinders (noun) Cinders are small pieces of burnt material left after wood or coal has burned.
cinema, cinemas 1 (noun) A cinema is a place where people go to watch films. **2** Cinema is the business of making films.
cinnamon (noun) Cinnamon is a sweet spice used for flavouring food.
cipher, ciphers (pronounced **sy**-fer); also spelled **cypher** (noun) A cipher is a secret code or system of writing used to send secret messages.
circa (pronounced **sir**-ka) (preposition; a formal word) about or approximately; used especially before dates, e.g. *portrait of a lady, circa 1840.*
circle, circles, circling, circled 1 (noun) A circle is a completely regular round shape. Every point on its edge is the same distance from the centre. **2** (verb) To circle means to move round and round as though going round the edge of a circle, e.g. *A police helicopter circled above.* **3** (noun) A circle of people is a group of them with the same interest or profession, e.g. *a character well known in yachting circles.* **4** In a theatre, the circle is an area of seats on an upper floor.
circuit, circuits (pronounced **sir**-kit) **1** (noun) A circuit is any closed line or path, often circular, for example a racing track; also the distance round this path, e.g. *three circuits of the 26-lap race remaining.* **2** An electrical circuit is a complete route around which an electric current can flow.
circular, circulars 1 (adjective) in the shape of a circle. **2** A circular argument or theory is not valid because it uses a statement to prove a conclusion and the conclusion to prove the statement. **3** (noun) A circular is a letter or advert sent to a lot of people at the same time. **circularity** (noun).
circulate, circulates, circulating, circulated 1 (verb) When something circulates or when you circulate it, it moves easily around an area, e.g. *an open position where the air can circulate freely.* **2** When you circulate something among people, you pass it round or tell it to all the people, e.g. *We circulate a regular newsletter.*
circulation, circulations 1 (noun) The circulation of something is the act of circulating it or the action of it circulating, e.g. *traffic circulation.* **2** The circulation of a newspaper or magazine is the number of copies that are sold of each issue. **3** Your circulation is the movement of blood through your body.
circumference, circumferences (noun) The circumference of a circle is its outer line or edge;

also the length of this line.

circumstance, circumstances 1 (noun) The circumstances of a situation or event are the conditions that affect what happens, e.g. *He did well in the circumstances.* **2** Someone's circumstances are their position and conditions in life, e.g. *Her circumstances had changed.*

circus, circuses (noun) A circus is a show given by a travelling group of entertainers such as clowns, acrobats, and specially trained animals.

CIS (noun) The CIS is a group of countries which used to be part of the USSR. CIS is an abbreviation for 'Commonwealth of Independent States'.

cistern, cisterns (noun) A cistern is a tank in which water is stored, for example one in the roof of a house or above a toilet.

citadel, citadels (noun) A citadel is a fortress in or near a city.

cite, cites, citing, cited 1 (verb; a formal word) If you cite something, you quote it or refer to it, e.g. *He cited a letter written by Newall.* **2** If someone is cited in a legal action, they are officially summoned to appear in court.

citizen, citizens (noun) The citizens of a country or city are the people who live in it or belong to it, e.g. *American citizens.* **citizenship** (noun).

citrus fruit, citrus fruits (noun) Citrus fruits are juicy, sharp-tasting fruits such as oranges, lemons, and grapefruit.

city, cities (noun) A city is a large town where many people live and work.

civic (adjective) relating to a city or citizens, e.g. *Wolverhampton Civic Hall.*

civil 1 (adjective) relating to the citizens of a country, e.g. *civil rights.* **2** relating to people or things that are not connected with the armed forces, e.g. *the history of civil aviation.* **3** polite. **civilly** (adverb), **civility** (noun).

civil engineering (noun) Civil engineering is the design and construction of roads, bridges, and public buildings.

civilian, civilians (noun) A civilian is a person who is not in the armed forces.

civilization, civilizations; also spelled **civilisation 1** (noun) A civilization is a society which has a highly developed organization, culture, and way of life, e.g. *the tale of a lost civilization.* **2** Civilization is an advanced state of social organization, culture, and way of life.

civilized 1 (adjective) A civilized society is one with a developed social organization and way of life. **2** A civilized person is polite and reasonable.

civil servant, civil servants (noun) A civil servant is a person who works in the civil service.

civil service (noun) The civil service is the staff who work in government departments responsible for the administration of a country.

civil war, civil wars (noun) A civil war is a war between groups of people who live in the same country.

cl an abbreviation for 'centilitres'.

clad (adjective; a literary word) Someone who is clad in particular clothes is wearing them.

claim, claims, claiming, claimed 1 (verb) If you claim that something is true or is the case, you say that it is, although some people may not believe you, e.g. *He claims to have lived in the same house all his life.* **2** If you claim something, you ask for it because it belongs to you or you have a right to it, e.g. *Cartier claimed the land for the King of France.* **3** (noun) A claim is a statement that something is the case, or that you have a right to something, e.g. *I intend to make a claim for damages.*

claimant, claimants (noun) A claimant is someone who is making a claim, especially for money.

clairvoyant, clairvoyants 1 (adjective) able to know about things that will happen in the future. **2** (noun) A clairvoyant is a person who is, or claims to be, clairvoyant.

clam, clams (noun) A clam is a kind of shellfish. Many types of clam are edible.

clamber, clambers, clambering, clambered (verb) If you clamber somewhere, you climb there with difficulty.

clammy, clammier, clammiest (adjective) unpleasantly damp and sticky, e.g. *clammy hands.*

clamour, clamours, clamouring, clamoured 1 (verb) If people clamour for something, they demand it noisily or angrily, e.g. *We clamoured for an explanation.* **2** (noun) Clamour is noisy or angry shouts or demands by a lot of people.

clamp, clamps, clamping, clamped 1 (noun) A clamp is an object with movable parts that are used to hold two things firmly together. **2** (verb) To clamp things together means to fasten them or hold them firmly with a clamp. **clamp down on** (verb) To clamp down on something means to become stricter in controlling it, e.g. *The Queen has clamped down on all Palace expenditure.*

clan, clans (noun) A clan is a group of families related to each other by being descended from the same ancestor.

clandestine (adjective) secret and hidden, e.g. *a clandestine meeting with friends.*

clang, clangs, clanging, clanged (verb) When something metal clangs or when you clang it, it makes a loud, deep sound.

clank, clanks, clanking, clanked (verb) If something metal clanks, it makes a loud noise.

clap, claps, clapping, clapped 1 (verb) When you clap, you hit your hands together loudly to show your appreciation. **2** If you clap someone on the back or shoulder, you hit them in a friendly way. **3** If you clap something somewhere, you put it there quickly and firmly, e.g. *I clapped a hand over her mouth.* **4** (noun) A clap is a sound made by clapping your hands. **5** A clap of thunder is a sudden loud noise of thunder.

claret, clarets (noun) Claret is a

type of red wine.

clarify, clarifies, clarifying, clarified (verb) To clarify something means to make it clear and easier to understand, e.g. *The Danish government has clarified its position on what it intends to do.* **clarification** (noun).

clarinet, clarinets (noun) A clarinet is a woodwind instrument with a straight tube and a single reed in its mouthpiece.

clarity (noun) The clarity of something is its clearness.

clash, clashes, clashing, clashed **1** (verb) If people clash with each other, they fight or argue. **2** Ideas or styles that clash are so different that they do not go together. **3** If two events clash, they happen at the same time so you cannot go to both. **4** When metal objects clash, they hit each other with a loud noise. **5** (noun) A clash is a fight or argument. **6** A clash of ideas, styles, or events is a situation in which they do not go together.

clasp, clasps, clasping, clasped **1** (verb) To clasp something means to hold it tightly or fasten it, e.g. *He clasped his hands.* **2** (noun) A clasp is a fastening such as a hook or catch.

class, classes, classing, classed **1** (noun) A class of people or things is a group of them of a particular type or quality, e.g. *the old class of politicians.* **2** A class is a group of pupils or students taught together, or a lesson that they have together. **3** Someone who has class is elegant in appearance or behaviour. **4** (verb) To class something means to arrange it in a particular group or to consider it as belonging to a particular group, e.g. *They are officially classed as visitors.*

classic, classics **1** (adjective) typical and therefore a good model or example of something, e.g. *a classic case of misuse.* **2** of very high quality, e.g. *one of the classic films of all time.* **3** simple in style and form, e.g. *the classic English suit.* **4** (noun) Something that is considered a classic is of the highest quality, e.g. *one of the great classics of rock music.*

classical **1** (adjective) traditional in style, form, and content, e.g. *classical ballet.* **2** Classical music is serious music considered to be of lasting value. **3** characteristic of the style of ancient Greece and Rome, e.g. *Classical friezes decorate the walls.* **classically** (adverb).

classified (adjective) officially declared secret by the government, e.g. *access to classified information.*

classify, classifies, classifying, classified (verb) To classify things means to arrange them into groups with similar characteristics, e.g. *We can classify the differences into three groups.* **classification** (noun).

classy, classier, classiest (adjective; an informal word) stylish and elegant.

clatter, clatters, clattering, clattered **1** (verb) When things clatter, they hit each other with a loud rattling noise. **2** (noun) A clatter is a loud rattling noise made by hard things hitting each other.

clause, clauses 1 (noun) A clause is a section of a legal document. **2** In grammar, a clause is a group of words with a subject and a verb, which may be a complete sentence or one of the parts of a sentence.

claustrophobia (pronounced klos-trof-**foe**-bee-ya) (noun) Claustrophobia is a fear of being in enclosed spaces. **claustrophobic** (adjective).

claw, claws, clawing, clawed 1 (noun) An animal's claws are hard, curved nails at the end of its feet. **2** The claws of a crab or lobster are the two jointed parts, used for grasping things. **3** (verb) If an animal claws something, it digs its claws into it.

clay (noun) Clay is a type of earth that is soft and sticky when wet and hard when baked dry. It is used to make pottery and bricks.

clean, cleaner, cleanest; cleans, cleaning, cleaned 1 (adjective) free from dirt or other unwanted substances or marks. **2** (verb) To clean something means to remove dirt from it. **3** (adjective) If humour is clean it is not rude and does not involve bad language. **4** A clean movement is skilful and accurate. **5** Clean also means free from fault or error, e.g. *a clean driving licence.* **cleanly** (adverb), **cleaner** (noun).

cleanliness (pronounced **klen**-lin-ness) (noun) Cleanliness is the practice or habit of keeping yourself and your surroundings clean.

cleanse, cleanses, cleansing, cleansed (pronounced **klenz**) (verb) To cleanse something means to make it completely free from dirt.

clear, clearer, clearest; clears, clearing, cleared 1 (adjective) easy to understand, see, or hear, e.g. *He made it clear he did not want to talk.* **2** easy to see through, e.g. *a clear liquid.* **3** free from obstructions or unwanted things, e.g. *clear of snow.* **4** (verb) To clear an area means to remove unwanted things from it. **5** If you clear a fence or other obstacle, you jump over it without touching it. **6** When fog or mist clears, it disappears. **7** If someone is cleared of a crime, they are proved to be not guilty. **clearly** (adverb). **clear up 1** (verb) If you clear up, you tidy a place and put things away. **2** When a problem or misunderstanding is cleared up, it is solved or settled.

clearance 1 (noun) Clearance is the removal of old buildings in an area. **2** If someone is given clearance to do something, they get official permission to do it.

clearing, clearings (noun) A clearing is an area of bare ground in a forest.

cleavage, cleavages (noun) A woman's cleavage is the space between her breasts.

cleaver, cleavers (noun) A cleaver is a knife with a large square blade, used especially by butchers.

cleft, clefts (noun) A cleft in a rock is a narrow opening.

clementine, clementines (noun)

A clementine is a type of small citrus fruit.

clench, clenches, clenching, clenched 1 (verb) When you clench your fist, you curl your fingers up tightly. **2** When you clench your teeth, you squeeze them together tightly.

clergy (plural noun) The clergy are the ministers of the Christian Church.

clergyman, clergymen (noun) A clergyman is a male member of the clergy.

clerical 1 (adjective) relating to work done in an office, e.g. *clerical work at a hospital.* **2** relating to the clergy.

clerk, clerks (pronounced **klahrk**) (noun) A clerk is a person whose job is keeping records or accounts in an office, bank, or law court.

clever, cleverer, cleverest 1 (adjective) intelligent and quick to understand things. **2** very effective or skilful, e.g. *a clever plan.* **cleverly** (adverb), **cleverness** (noun).

cliché, clichés (pronounced **klee**-shay) (noun) A cliché is an idea or phrase which is no longer effective because it has been used so much.

click, clicks, clicking, clicked 1 (verb) When something clicks or when you click it, it makes a short snapping sound. **2** (noun) A click is a sound of something clicking, e.g. *I heard the click of a bolt.*

client, clients (noun) A client is someone who pays a professional person or company to receive a service.

clientele (pronounced klee-on-**tell**) (plural noun) The clientele of a place are its customers.

cliff, cliffs (noun) A cliff is a steep high rock face by the sea.

climate, climates 1 (noun) The climate of a place is the typical weather conditions there, e.g. *The climate was dry in the summer.* **2** The climate of opinion is the general attitude and opinion of people at a particular time. **climatic** (adjective).

climax, climaxes (noun) The climax of a process, story, or piece of music is the most exciting moment in it, usually near the end.

climb, climbs, climbing, climbed 1 (verb) To climb means to move upwards. **2** (noun) A climb is a movement upwards, e.g. *this long climb up the slope... the rapid climb in murders.* **3** (verb) If you climb somewhere, you move there with difficulty, e.g. *She climbed out of the driving seat.* **climber** (noun).

clinch, clinches, clinching, clinched (verb) If you clinch an agreement or an argument, you settle it in a definite way, e.g. *Peter has clinched a deal.*

cling, clings, clinging, clung (verb) To cling to something means to hold onto it or stay closely attached to it, e.g. *still clinging to old-fashioned values.*

clingfilm (noun; a trademark) Clingfilm is a clear thin plastic used for wrapping food.

clinic, clinics (noun) A clinic is a building where people go for medical treatment.

clinical 1 (adjective) relating to the medical treatment of patients, e.g. *clinical tests.* **2** Clinical behaviour or thought is logical and unemotional, e.g. *the cold, clinical attitudes of his colleagues.* **clinically** (adverb).

clip, clips, clipping, clipped 1 (noun) A clip is a small metal or plastic object used for holding things together. **2** (verb) If you clip things together, you fasten them with clips. **3** If you clip something, you cut bits from it to shape it, e.g. *clipped hedges.* **4** (noun) A clip of a film is a short piece of it shown by itself.

clippers (plural noun) Clippers are tools used for cutting.

clipping, clippings (noun) A clipping is an article cut from a newspaper or magazine.

clique, cliques (rhymes with **seek**) (noun) A clique is a small group of people who stick together and do not mix with other people.

clitoris, clitorises (pronounced **klit**-tor-riss) (noun) A woman's clitoris is a small highly sensitive piece of flesh near the opening of her vagina.

cloak, cloaks, cloaking, cloaked 1 (noun) A cloak is a wide, loose coat without sleeves. **2** (verb) To cloak something means to cover or hide it, e.g. *a land permanently cloaked in mist.*

cloakroom, cloakrooms (noun) In a public building, a cloakroom is a room for coats, or a room with toilets and washbasins.

clock, clocks 1 (noun) A clock is an instrument that measures and shows the time. **2** (phrase) If you work **round the clock,** you work all day and night.

clockwise (adjective or adverb) in the same direction as the hands on a clock.

clockwork 1 (noun) Toys that work by clockwork move when they are wound up with a key. **2** (phrase) If something happens **like clockwork,** it happens with no problems or delays.

clog, clogs, clogging, clogged 1 (verb) When something clogs a hole, it blocks it, e.g. *The nostrils were clogged with wet sand.* **2** (noun) Clogs are heavy wooden shoes.

cloister, cloisters (noun) A cloister is a covered area for walking around a square in a monastery or a cathedral.

clone, clones, cloning, cloned 1 (noun) In biology, a clone is an animal or plant that has been produced artificially from the cells of another animal or plant and is therefore identical to it. **2** (verb) To clone an animal or plant means to produce it as a clone.

close, closes, closing, closed; closer, closest 1 (verb) To close something means to shut it. **2** To close a road or entrance means to block it so that no-one can go in or out. **3** If a shop closes at a certain time, then it does not do business after that time. **4** (adjective or adverb) near to something, e.g. *a restaurant close to their home.* **5** (adjective) People who are close to each other are very friendly and know each other well. **6** You say the weather is close when it is uncomfortably warm and there is not enough air. **closely** (adverb), **closeness** (noun), **closed** (adjective). **close down** (verb) If a business closes down, all work stops there permanently.

closed shop, closed shops (noun) A closed shop is a factory or other business whose employees have to be members of a trade union.

closet, closets, closeting, closeted **1** (noun) A closet is a cupboard. **2** (verb) If you are closeted somewhere, you shut yourself away alone or in private with another person. **3** (adjective) Closet beliefs or habits are kept private and secret, e.g. *He's a closet conservative.*

close-up, close-ups (noun) A close-up is a detailed close view of something, especially a photograph taken close to the subject.

closure, closures (pronounced **klohz**-yur) **1** (noun) The closure of a business is the permanent shutting of it. **2** The closure of a road is the blocking of it.

clot, clots, clotting, clotted **1** (noun) A clot is a lump, especially one that forms when blood thickens. **2** (verb) When a substance such as blood clots, it thickens and forms a lump.

cloth, cloths **1** (noun) Cloth is fabric made by a process such as weaving. **2** A cloth is a piece of material used for wiping or protecting things.

clothe, clothes, clothing, clothed **1** (plural noun) Clothes are the things people wear on their bodies. **2** (verb) To clothe someone means to give them clothes to wear.

clothing (noun) Clothing is the clothes people wear.

cloud, clouds, clouding, clouded **1** (noun) A cloud is a mass of water vapour that forms in the air and is seen as a white or grey patch in the sky. **2** A cloud of smoke or dust is a mass of it floating in the air. **3** (verb) If something clouds or is clouded, it becomes cloudy or difficult to see through, e.g. *The sky clouded over.* **4** Something that clouds an issue makes it more confusing.

cloudy, cloudier, cloudiest **1** (adjective) full of clouds, e.g. *the cloudy sky.* **2** difficult to see through, e.g. *a glass of cloudy liquid.*

clout (noun; an informal word) Someone who has clout has influence.

clove, cloves **1** (noun) Cloves are small, strong-smelling dried flower buds from a tropical tree, used as a spice in cooking. **2** A clove of garlic is one of the separate sections of the bulb.

clover (noun) Clover is a small plant with leaves made up of three lobes.

clown, clowns, clowning, clowned **1** (noun) A clown is a circus performer who wears funny clothes and make-up and does silly things to make people laugh. **2** (verb) If you clown, you do silly things to make people laugh.

cloying (adjective) unpleasantly sickly, sweet, or sentimental, e.g. *something less cloying than whipped cream.*

club, clubs, clubbing, clubbed **1**

(noun) A club is an organization of people with a particular interest, who meet regularly; also the place where they meet. **2** A club is also a thick, heavy stick used as a weapon. **3** In golf, a club is a stick with a shaped head that a player uses to hit the ball. **4** (verb) To club someone means to hit them hard with a heavy object. **5** (noun) Clubs is one of the four suits in a pack of playing cards. It is marked by a black symbol in the shape of a clover leaf. **club together** (verb) If people club together, they all join together to give money to buy something.

cluck, clucks, clucking, clucked (verb) When a hen clucks, it makes a short repeated high-pitched sound.

clue, clues (noun) A clue to a problem, mystery, or puzzle is something that helps to solve it.

clump, clumps, clumping, clumped 1 (noun) A clump of plants, people, or buildings is a small group of them close together. **2** (verb) If you clump about, you walk with heavy footsteps.

clumsy, clumsier, clumsiest 1 (adjective) moving awkwardly and carelessly. **2** said or done without thought or tact, e.g. *his clumsy attempts to catch her out.* **clumsily** (adverb), **clumsiness** (noun).

cluster, clusters, clustering, clustered 1 (noun) A cluster of things is a group of them together, e.g. *a cluster of huts at the foot of the mountains.* **2** (verb) If people cluster together, they stay together in a close group.

clutch, clutches, clutching, clutched 1 (verb) If you clutch something, you hold it tightly or seize it. **2** (plural noun) If you are in someone's clutches, they have power or control over you.

clutter, clutters, cluttering, cluttered 1 (noun) Clutter is an untidy mess. **2** (verb) Things that clutter a place fill it and make it untidy.

cm an abbreviation for 'centimetres'.

co- (prefix) Co- means together, e.g. *Paula is now co-writing a book with Pierre.*

coach, coaches, coaching, coached 1 (noun) A coach is a long motor vehicle used for taking passengers on long journeys. **2** The coaches of a train are the separate sections that carry passengers. **3** A coach is also a four-wheeled enclosed vehicle pulled by horses, which people used to travel in. **4** (verb) If someone coaches you, they teach you and help you to get better at a sport or a subject. **5** (noun) Someone's coach is a person who coaches them in a sport or a subject.

coal, coals 1 (noun) Coal is a hard black rock obtained from under the earth and burned as a fuel. **2** Coals are burning pieces of coal.

coalition, coalitions (noun) A coalition is a temporary alliance, especially between different political parties in order to form a government.

coarse, coarser, coarsest 1 (adjective) Something that is coarse is rough in texture, often consisting of large particles, e.g. *a coarse blanket.* **2** Someone who is coarse talks or behaves in a rude or rather offensive way. **coarsely** (adverb), **coarseness** (noun).

coast, coasts, coasting, coasted **1** (noun) A coast is the edge of the land where it meets the sea. **2** (verb) A vehicle that is coasting is moving without engine power. **coastal** (adjective).

coastguard, coastguards (noun) A coastguard is an official who watches the sea near a coast to get help for sailors when they need it.

coastline, coastlines (noun) A coastline is the outline of a coast, especially as it looks from the sea or air.

coat, coats, coating, coated **1** (noun) A coat is a piece of clothing with sleeves which you wear outside over your other clothes. **2** An animal's coat is the fur or hair on its body. **3** A coat of paint or varnish is a layer of it. **4** (verb) To coat something means to cover it with a thin layer of a something, e.g. *Walnuts are coated with chocolate and cocoa.* **coating** (noun).

coax, coaxes, coaxing, coaxed (verb) If you coax someone to do something, you gently persuade them to do it.

cobalt (noun) Cobalt is a hard silvery-white metal which produced a blue dye.

cobble, cobbles (noun) Cobbles or cobblestones are stones with a rounded surface that were used in the past for making roads.

cobbler, cobblers (noun; an old-fashioned word) A cobbler is a person whose job is making or mending shoes.

cobra, cobras (pronounced **koh**-bra) (noun) A cobra is a type of large poisonous snake from Africa and Asia.

cobweb, cobwebs (noun) A cobweb is the very thin net that a spider spins for catching insects.

cocaine (noun) Cocaine is an addictive drug. It is sometimes used as an anaesthetic.

cock, cocks (noun) A cock is an adult male chicken; also used of any male bird.

cockatoo, cockatoos (noun) A cockatoo is a type of parrot with a crest on its head.

cockerel, cockerels (noun) A cockerel is a young cock.

Cockney, Cockneys (noun) A Cockney is a person born in the East End of London.

cockpit, cockpits (noun) The cockpit of a small plane is the place where the pilot sits.

cockroach, cockroaches (noun) A cockroach is a large dark-coloured insect often found in dirty rooms.

cocktail, cocktails (noun) A cocktail is an alcoholic drink made from several ingredients.

cocky, cockier, cockiest (adjective; an informal word) cheeky or too self-confident. **cockiness** (noun).

cocoa (noun) Cocoa is a brown powder made from the seeds of a tropical tree and used for making chocolate; also a hot drink made from this powder.

coconut, coconuts (noun) A coconut is a very large nut with white flesh, milky juice, and a hard hairy shell.

cocoon, cocoons (noun) A cocoon is a silky covering over the larvae of moths and some other insects.

cod The plural is also **cod**. (noun) A cod is a large edible fish.

code, codes 1 (noun) A code is a system of replacing the letters or words in a message with other letters or words, so that nobody can understand the message unless they know the system. **2** A code is also a group of numbers and letters which is used to identify something, e.g. *the telephone code for Guildford.* **coded** (adjective).

coffee (noun) Coffee is a substance made by roasting and grinding the beans of a tropical shrub; also a hot drink made from this substance.

coffin, coffins (noun) A coffin is a box in which a dead body is buried or cremated.

cog, cogs (noun) A cog is a wheel with teeth which turns another wheel or part of a machine.

cognac (pronounced **kon**-yak) (noun) Cognac is a kind of brandy.

coherent 1 (adjective) If something such as a theory is coherent, its parts fit together well and do not contradict each other. **2** If someone is coherent, what they are saying makes sense and is not jumbled or confused. **coherence** (noun).

cohesive (adjective) If something is cohesive, its parts fit together well and form a united whole, e.g. *The team must work as a cohesive unit.* **cohesion** (noun).

coil, coils, coiling, coiled 1 (noun) A coil of rope or wire is a length of it wound into a series of loops; also one of the loops. **2** (verb) If something coils, it turns into a series of loops.

coin, coins, coining, coined 1 (noun) A coin is a small metal disc which is used as money. **2** (verb) If you coin a word or a phrase, you invent it.

coinage (noun) The coinage of a country is the coins that are used there.

coincide, coincides, coinciding, coincided 1 (verb) If two events coincide, they happen at about the same time. **2** When two people's ideas or opinions coincide, they agree, e.g. *What she said coincided exactly with his own thinking.*

coincidence, coincidences 1 (noun) A coincidence is what happens when two similar things occur at the same time by chance, e.g. *I had moved to London, and by coincidence, Helen had too.* **2** A coincidence is also the fact that two things are surprisingly the same. **coincidental** (adjective), **coincidentally** (adverb).

coke (noun) Coke is a grey fuel produced from coal.

colander, colanders (pronounced **kol**-an-der) (noun) A colander is a bowl-shaped container with holes in it, used for washing or draining food.

cold, colder, coldest; colds 1 (adjective) Something that is cold has a very low temperature. **2** If it is cold, the air temperature is very low. **3**

(noun) You can refer to cold weather as the cold, e.g. *She was complaining about the cold.* **4** (adjective) Someone who is cold does not show much affection. **5** (noun) A cold is a minor illness in which you sneeze and may have a sore throat. **coldly** (adverb), **coldness** (noun).

cold-blooded 1 (adjective) Someone who is cold-blooded does not show any pity, e.g. *two cold-blooded killers.* **2** A cold-blooded animal has a body temperature that changes according to the surrounding temperature.

cold war (noun) Cold war is a state of extreme unfriendliness between countries not actually at war.

coleslaw (noun) Coleslaw is a salad of chopped cabbage and other vegetables in mayonnaise.

colic (noun) Colic is pain in a baby's stomach and bowels.

collaborate, collaborates, collaborating, collaborated (verb) When people collaborate, they work together to produce something, e.g. *The two bands have collaborated in the past.* **collaboration** (noun), **collaborator** (noun).

collage, collages (pronounced **kol**-lahj) (noun) A collage is a picture made by sticking pieces of paper or cloth onto a surface.

collapse, collapses, collapsing, collapsed 1 (verb) If something such as a building collapses, it falls down suddenly. If a person collapses, they fall down suddenly because they are ill. **2** If something such as a system or a business collapses, it suddenly stops working, e.g. *50,000 small firms collapsed last year.* **3** (noun) The collapse of something is what happens when it stops working, e.g. *the collapse of his marriage.*

collapsible (adjective) A collapsible object can be folded flat when it is not in use, e.g. *a collapsible ironing board.*

collar, collars 1 (noun) The collar of a shirt or coat is the part round the neck which is usually folded over. **2** A collar is also a leather band round the neck of a dog or cat.

collateral (noun) Collateral is money or property which is used as a guarantee that someone will repay a loan.

colleague, colleagues (noun) A person's colleagues are the people he or she works with.

collect, collects, collecting, collected 1 (verb) To collect things means to gather them together for a special purpose or as a hobby, e.g. *collecting money for charity.* **2** If you collect someone or something from a place, you call there and take them away, e.g. *We had to collect her from school.* **3** When things collect in a place, they gather there over a period of time, e.g. *Food collects in holes in the teeth.* **collector** (noun).

collected (adjective) calm and self-controlled.

collection, collections 1 (noun) A collection of things is a group of them acquired over a period of time, e.g. *a collection of paintings.* **2** Collection is the collecting of something, e.g. *tax collection.* **3** A collection is also the organized collecting of money, for example for charity, or the sum of money collected.

collective, collectives 1 (adjective) involving every member of a group of people, e.g. *The wine growers took a collective decision.* **2** (noun) A collective is a group of people who share the responsibility both for running something and for doing the work. **collectively** (adverb).

college, colleges 1 (noun) A college is a place where students study after they have left school. **2** A college is also one of the institutions into which some universities are divided, e.g. *Trinity College, Cambridge.*

collide, collides, colliding, collided (verb) If a moving object collides with something, it hits it.

collie, collies (noun) A collie is a dog that is used for rounding up sheep.

colliery, collieries (noun) A colliery is a coal mine.

collision, collisions (noun) A collision occurs when a moving object hits something.

cologne (pronounced kol-**lone**) (noun) Cologne is a kind of weak perfume.

colon, colons 1 (noun) A colon is the punctuation mark (:). **2** Your colon is a part of your intestine.

colonel, colonels (pronounced **kur**-nl) (noun) A colonel is an army officer with a fairly high rank.

colony, colonies (noun) A colony is a country controlled by a more powerful country. **colonial** (adjective).

colossal (adjective) very large indeed.

colour, colours, colouring, coloured 1 (noun) The colour of something is the appearance that it has as a result of reflecting light. **2** Someone's colour is the normal colour of their skin. **3** Colour is also a quality that makes something interesting or exciting, e.g. *some local colour.* **4** (verb) If something colours your opinion, it affects the way you think about something. **coloured** (adjective), **colourful** (adjective), **colourfully** (adverb), **colourless** (adjective), **colouring** (noun).

colour blind (adjective) Someone who is colour blind cannot distinguish between colours.

colt, colts (noun) A colt is a young male horse.

column, columns 1 (noun) A column is a tall solid upright cylinder, especially one supporting a part of a building. **2** A column is also a group of people moving in a long line.

columnist, columnists (noun) A columnist is a journalist who writes a regular article in a newspaper or magazine.

coma, comas (noun) Someone who is in a coma is in a state of deep unconsciousness.

comb, combs, combing, combed 1 (noun) A comb is a flat object with pointed teeth used for tidying your hair. **2** (verb) When you comb your hair, you tidy it with a comb.

combat, combats, combating, combated 1 (noun) Combat is

fighting, e.g. *his first experience of combat.* **2** (verb) To combat something means to try to stop it happening or developing, e.g. *a way to combat crime.*

combination, combinations 1 (noun) A combination of things is a mixture of them, e.g. *a combination of charm and skill.* **2** A combination is a series of letters or numbers used to open a special lock.

combine, combines, combining, combined 1 (verb) To combine things means to cause them to exist together, e.g. *to combine a career with being a mother.* **2** To combine things also means to join them together to make a single thing, e.g. *Combine all the ingredients.* **3** If something combines two qualities or features, it has them both, e.g. *a film that combines great charm and scintillating performances.*

combustion (noun) Combustion is the act of burning something or the process of burning.

come, comes, coming, came, come 1 (verb) To come to a place means to move there or arrive there. **2** To come to a place also means to reach as far as that place, e.g. *The sea water came up to his waist.* **3** Come is used to say that someone or something enters or reaches a particular state, e.g. *They came to power in 1982... We had come to a decision.* **4** When a particular time or event comes, it happens, e.g. *The peak of his career came early in 1990.* **5** If you come from a place, you were born there or it is your home. **6** (phrase) A time or event **to come** is a future time or event, e.g. *The public will thank them in years to come.* **come about** (verb) The way something comes about is the way it happens, e.g. *The discussion came about because of the proposed changes.* **come across** (verb) If you come across something, you find it by chance. **come off** (verb) If something comes off, it succeeds, e.g. *His rescue plan had come off.* **come on** (verb) If something is coming on, it is making progress, e.g. *Let's go and see how the grapes are coming on.*

comeback, comebacks (noun) To make a comeback means to be popular or successful again.

comedian, comedians (noun) A comedian is an entertainer whose job is to make people laugh.

comedienne, comediennes (pronounced kom-mee-dee-**en**) (noun) A comedienne is a female comedian.

comedy, comedies (noun) A comedy is a light-hearted play or film with a happy ending.

comet, comets (noun) A comet is an object that travels around the sun leaving a bright trail behind it.

comfort, comforts, comforting, comforted 1 (noun) Comfort is the state of being physically relaxed, e.g. *He settled back in comfort.* **2** Comfort is also a feeling of relief from worries or unhappiness, e.g. *The thought is a great comfort to me.* **3** (plural noun) Comforts are things which make your life easier and more pleasant, e.g. *all the comforts of home.* **4** (verb) To comfort someone means to make them less worried or unhappy.

comfortable 1 (adjective) If you are comfortable, you are physically relaxed. **2** Something that is comfortable makes you feel relaxed, e.g. *a comfortable bed.* **3** If you feel comfortable in a particular situation, you are not afraid or embarrassed. **comfortably** (adverb).

comic, comics 1 (adjective) funny, e.g. *a comic monologue.* **2** (noun) A comic is someone who tells jokes. **3** A comic is also a magazine that contains stories told in pictures.

comical (adjective) funny, e.g. *a comical sight.*

comma, commas (noun) A comma is the punctuation mark (,).

command, commands, commanding, commanded 1 (verb) To command someone to do something means to order them to do it. **2** (noun) A command is an order to do something. **3** (verb) If you command something such as respect, you receive it because of your personal qualities. **4** An officer who commands part of an army or navy is in charge of it. **5** (noun) Your command of something is your knowledge of it and your ability to use this knowledge, e.g. *a good command of English.*

commandant, commandants (pronounced **kom**-man-dant) (noun) A commandant is an army officer in charge of a place or group of people.

commander, commanders (noun) A commander is an officer in charge of a military operation or organization.

commandment, commandments (noun) The commandments are ten rules of behaviour that, according to the Old Testament, we should obey.

commando, commandos (noun) Commandos are soldiers who have been specially trained to carry out raids.

commemorate, commemorates, commemorating, commemorated 1 (verb) An object that commemorates a person or an event is intended to remind people of that person or event. **2** If you commemorate an event, you do something special to show that you remember it. **commemorative** (adjective), **commemoration** (noun).

commence, commences, commencing, commenced (verb; a formal word) To commence means to begin. **commencement** (noun).

commend, commends, commending, commended (verb) To commend someone or something means to praise them, e.g. *He has been commended for his work.* **commendation** (noun), **commendable** (adjective).

comment, comments, commenting, commented 1 (verb) If you comment on something, you make a remark about it. **2** (noun) A comment is a remark about something, e.g. *She received many comments about her appearance.*

commentary, commentaries (noun) A commentary is a description of an event which is broadcast on radio or television while the event is happening.

commentator, commentators (noun) A commentator is someone who gives a radio or television commentary.

commerce (noun) Commerce is the buying and selling of goods.

commercial, commercials 1 (adjective) relating to commerce. **2** Commercial activities involve producing goods on a large scale in order to make money, e.g. *the commercial fishing world.* **3** (noun) A commercial is an advertisement on television or radio. **commercially** (adverb).

commission, commissions, commissioning, commissioned 1 (verb) If someone commissions a piece of work, they formally ask someone to do it, e.g. *a study commissioned by the government.* **2** (noun) A commission is a piece of work that has been commissioned. **3** Commission is money paid to a salesman each time a sale is made. **4** A commission is also an official body appointed to investigate or control something.

commit, commits, committing, committed 1 (verb) To commit a crime or sin means to do it. **2** If you commit yourself, you state an opinion or state that you will do something. **3** If someone is committed to hospital or prison, they are officially sent there. **committal** (noun).

commitment, commitments 1 (noun) Commitment is a strong belief in an idea or system. **2** A commitment is something that regularly takes up some of your time, e.g. *business commitments.*

committed (adjective) A committed person has strong beliefs, e.g. *a committed feminist.*

committee, committees (noun) A committee is a group of people who make decisions on behalf of a larger group.

commodity, commodities (noun; a formal word) Commodities are things that are sold.

common, commoner, commonest; commons 1 (adjective) Something that is common exists in large numbers or happens often, e.g. *a common complaint.* **2** If something is common to two or more people, they all have it or use it, e.g. *I realized we had a common interest.* **3** Common is used to indicate that something is of the ordinary kind and not special. **4** If you describe someone as common, you mean they do not have good taste or good manners. **5** (noun) A common is an area of grassy land where everyone can go. **6** (phrase) If two things or people have something **in common,** they both have it. **commonly** (adverb).

commoner, commoners (noun) A commoner is someone who is not a member of the nobility.

commonplace (adjective) Something that is commonplace happens often, e.g. *Foreign holidays have become* *commonplace.*

common sense (noun) Your common sense is your natural ability to behave sensibly and make good judgments.

Commonwealth (noun) The Commonwealth consists of an association of countries around the world that are or used to be ruled by Britain.

commotion (noun) A commotion is a lot of noise and excitement.

communal (adjective) shared by a group of people, e.g. *a communal canteen.*

commune, communes (pronounced **kom**-yoon) (noun) A commune is a group of people who live together and share everything.

communicate, communicates, communicating, communicated 1 (verb) When people communicate with each other, they exchange information, usually by talking or writing to each other. **2** If you communicate an idea or a feeling to someone, you make them aware of it.

communication, communications 1 (noun) Communication is the process by which people or animals exchange information. **2** (plural noun) Communications are the systems by which people communicate or broadcast information, especially using electricity or radio waves. **3** (noun; a formal use) A communication is a letter or telephone call.

communicative (adjective) Someone who is communicative is willing to talk to people.

communion 1 (noun) Communion is the sharing of thoughts and feelings. **2** In Christianity, Communion is a religious service in which people share bread and wine in remembrance of the death and resurrection of Jesus Christ.

communism (noun) Communism is the doctrine that the state should control the means of production and that there should be no private property. **communist** (adjective or noun).

community, communities (noun) A community is all the people living in a particular area; also used to refer to particular groups within a society, e.g. *the heart of the local community... the Asian community.*

commute, commutes, commuting, commuted (verb) People who commute travel a long distance to work every day. **commuter** (noun).

compact (adjective) taking up very little space, e.g. *a compact microwave.*

compact disc, compact discs (noun) A compact disc is a type of record with superior sound reproduction, played using a laser on a special machine.

companion, companions (noun) A companion is someone you travel or spend time with. **companionship** (noun).

company, companies 1 (noun) A company is a business that sells goods or provides a service, e.g. *the record company.* **2** A company is also a group of actors, opera singers, or dancers, e.g. *the Royal Shakespeare Company.* **3** If you have company, you have a friend or visitor with you, e.g. *I enjoyed her company.*

comparable (pronounced **kom**-pra-bl) (adjective) If two things are comparable, they are similar in size or quality, e.g. *The skill is comparable to playing the violin.* **comparably** (adverb).

comparative, comparatives 1 (adjective) You add comparative to indicate that something is true only when compared with what is normal, e.g. *eight years of comparative calm.* **2** (noun) In grammar, the comparative is the form of an adjective which indicates that the person or thing described has more of a particular quality than someone or something else. For example, 'quicker', 'better', and 'easier' are all comparatives. **comparatively** (adverb).

compare, compares, comparing, compared 1 (verb) When you compare things, you consider them together and see in what ways they are different or similar. **2** If you compare one thing to another, you say it is like the other thing, e.g. *His voice is often compared to Michael Stipe.*

comparison, comparisons (noun) When you make a comparison, you consider two things together and see in what ways they are different or similar.

compartment, compartments 1 (noun) A compartment is a section of a railway carriage. **2** A compartment is also one of the separate parts of an object, e.g. *a special compartment inside your vehicle.*

compass, compasses 1 (noun) A compass is an instrument with a magnetic needle for finding directions. **2** (plural noun) Compasses are a hinged instrument for drawing circles.

compassion (noun) Compassion is pity and sympathy for someone who is suffering. **compassionate** (adjective).

compatible (adjective) If people or things are compatible, they can live, exist, or work together successfully. **compatibility** (noun).

compatriot, compatriots (noun) Your compatriots are people from your own country.

compel, compels, compelling, compelled (verb) To compel someone to do something means to force them to do it.

compelling 1 (adjective) If a story or event is compelling, it is extremely interesting, e.g. *a compelling novel.* **2** A compelling argument or reason makes you believe that something is true or should be done, e.g. *compelling new evidence.*

compensate, compensates, compensating, compensated 1 (verb) To compensate someone means to give them money to replace something lost or damaged. **2** If one thing compensates for another, it cancels out its bad effects, e.g. *The trip more than compensated for the hardship.* **compensatory** (adjective), **compensation** (noun).

compere, comperes, compering, compered (pronounced **kom**-pare) **1** (noun) The compere of a show is the person who introduces the guests or performers. **2** (verb) To compere a show means to act as its compere.

compete, competes, competing, competed 1 (verb) When people or firms compete, each tries to prove that they or their products are the best. **2** If you compete in a contest or game, you take part in it.

competent (adjective) Someone who is competent at something can do it satisfactorily, e.g. *a very competent engineer.* **competently** (adverb), **competence** (noun).

competition, competitions 1 (noun) When there is competition between people or groups, they are all trying to get something that not everyone can have, e.g. *There's a lot of competition for places.* **2** A competition is an event in which people take part to find who is best at something. **3** When there is competition between firms, each firm is trying to get people to buy its own goods.

competitive 1 (adjective) A competitive situation is one in which people or firms are competing with each other, e.g. *a crowded and competitive market.* **2** A competitive person is eager to be more successful than others. **3** Goods sold at competitive prices are cheaper than other goods of the same kind. **competitively** (adverb).

competitor, competitors (noun) A competitor is a person or firm that is competing to become the most successful.

compilation, compilations (noun) A compilation is a book, record, or programme consisting of several items that were originally produced separately, e.g. *this compilation of his solo work.*

compile, compiles, compiling, compiled (verb) When someone compiles a book or report, they make it by putting together several items.

complacent (adjective) If someone is complacent, they are self-satisfied and unconcerned about a serious situation. **complacency** (noun).

complain, complains, complaining, complained 1 (verb) If you complain, you say that you are not satisfied with something. **2** If you complain of pain or illness, you say that you have it.

complaint, complaints (noun) If you make a complaint, you complain about something.

complement, complements, complementing, complemented 1 (verb) If one thing complements another, the two things go well together, e.g. *The tiled floor complements the pine furniture.* **2** (noun) If one thing is a complement to another, it goes well with it. **complementary** (adjective).

complete, completes, completing, completed 1 (adjective) to the greatest degree possible, e.g. *a complete mess.* **2** If something is complete, none of it is missing, e.g. *a complete set of tools.* **3** When a task is complete, it is finished, e.g. *The planning stage is now complete.* **4** (verb) If you complete something, you finish it. **5** If you complete a form, you fill it in. **completely** (adverb), **completion** (noun).

complex, complexes 1 (adjective) Something that is complex has many different parts, e.g. *a very complex problem.* **2** (noun) A complex is a group of buildings, roads, or other things connected with each other in some way, e.g. *a hotel and restaurant complex.* **3** If someone has a complex, they have a continuing emotional problem because of a past experience, e.g. *an inferiority complex.* **complexity** (noun).

complexion, complexions (noun) Your complexion is the quality of the skin on your face, e.g. *a healthy glowing complexion.*

complicate, complicates, complicating, complicated (verb) To complicate something means to make it more difficult to understand or deal with.

complicated (adjective) Something that is complicated has so many parts or aspects that it is difficult to understand or deal with.

complication, complications (noun) A complication is a circumstance that makes a situation more difficult to deal with, e.g. *One possible complication was that it was late in the year.*

compliment, compliments, complimenting, complimented 1 (noun) If you pay someone a compliment, you tell them you admire something about them. **2** (verb) If you compliment someone, you pay them a compliment.

complimentary 1 (adjective) If you are complimentary about something, you express admiration for it. **2** A complimentary seat, ticket, or publication is given to you free.

comply, complies, complying, complied (verb) If you comply with an order or rule, you obey it. **compliance** (noun).

component, components (noun) The components of something are the parts it is made of.

compose, composes, composing, composed 1 (verb) If something is composed of particular things or people, it is made up of them. **2** To compose a piece of music, letter, or speech means to write it. **3** If you compose yourself, you become calm after being angry, excited, or upset.

composed (adjective) calm and in control of your feelings.

composer, composers (noun) A composer is someone who writes music.

composition, compositions 1 (noun) The composition of something is the things it consists of, e.g. *the composition of the ozone layer.* **2** The composition of a poem or piece of music is the writing of it. **3** A composition is a piece of music or writing.

compost (noun) Compost is a mixture of decaying plants and manure added to soil to help plants grow.

composure (noun) Someone's composure is their ability to stay calm, e.g. *Jarvis was able to recover his composure.*

compound, compounds, compounding, compounded 1

(noun) A compound is an enclosed area of land with buildings used for a particular purpose, e.g. *the prison compound.* **2** In chemistry, a compound is a substance consisting of two or more different substances or chemical elements. **3** (verb) To compound something means to put together different parts to make a whole. **4** To compound a problem means to make it worse by adding to it, e.g. *Hangovers are compounded by lack of sleep.*

comprehend, comprehends, comprehending, comprehended (verb; a formal word) To comprehend something means to understand or appreciate it, e.g. *He did not fully comprehend what was puzzling me.* **comprehension** (noun).

comprehensible (adjective) able to be understood.

comprehensive, comprehensives 1 (adjective) Something that is comprehensive includes everything necessary or relevant, e.g. *a comprehensive guide.* **2** (noun) A comprehensive is a school where children of all abilities are taught together. **comprehensively** (adverb).

compress, compresses, compressing, compressed (verb) To compress something means to squeeze it or shorten it so that it takes up less space, e.g. *compressed air.* **compression** (noun).

comprise, comprises, comprising, comprised (verb; a formal word) What something comprises is what it consists of, e.g. *The district then comprised 66 villages.*

compromise, compromises, compromising, compromised 1 (noun) A compromise is an agreement in which people accept less than they originally wanted, e.g. *In the end they reached a compromise.* **2** (verb) When people compromise, they agree to accept less than they originally wanted. **compromising** (adjective).

compulsion, compulsions (noun) A compulsion is a very strong desire to do something.

compulsive 1 (adjective) You use compulsive to describe someone who cannot stop doing something, e.g. *a compulsive letter writer.* **2** If you find something such as a book or television programme compulsive, you cannot stop reading or watching it.

compulsory (adjective) If something is compulsory, you have to do it, e.g. *compulsory redundancies.*

computer, computers (noun) A computer is an electronic machine that can quickly make calculations or store and retrieve information.

computerize, computerizes, computerizing, computerized; also spelled **computerise** (verb) When a system or process is computerized, the work starts being done by computers.

computing (noun) Computing is the use of computers and the writing of programs for them.

comrade, comrades (noun) A soldier's comrades are his fellow soldiers, especially in battle. **comradeship** (noun).

con, cons, conning, conned (an informal word) **1** (verb) If someone cons you, they trick you into doing or believing something. **2** (noun) A con is a trick in which someone deceives you into doing or believing something.

concave (adjective) A concave surface curves inwards, rather than being level or bulging outwards.

conceal, conceals, concealing, concealed (verb) To conceal something means to hide it, e.g. *He had concealed his gun.* **concealment** (noun).

concede, concedes, conceding, conceded (pronounced kon-**seed**) **1** (verb) If you concede something, you admit that it is true, e.g. *I conceded that he was entitled to his views.* **2** When someone concedes defeat, they accept that they have lost something such as a contest or an election.

conceit (noun) Conceit is someone's excessive pride in their appearance, abilities, or achievements.

conceited (adjective) Someone who is conceited is too proud of their appearance, abilities, or achievements.

conceivable (adjective) If something is conceivable, you can believe that it could exist or be true, e.g. *It's conceivable that you also met her.* **conceivably** (adverb).

conceive, conceives, conceiving, conceived 1 (verb) If you can conceive of something, you can imagine it or believe it, e.g. *Could you conceive of doing such a thing yourself?* **2** If you conceive something such as a plan, you think of it and work out how it could be done. **3** When a woman conceives, she becomes pregnant.

concentrate, concentrates, concentrating, concentrated 1 (verb) If you concentrate on something, you give it all your attention. **2** When something is concentrated in one place, it is all there rather than being distributed among several places, e.g. *They are mostly concentrated in the urban areas.* **concentration** (noun).

concentrated (adjective) A concentrated liquid has been made stronger by having water removed from it, e.g. *concentrated apple juice.*

concentration camp, concentration camps (noun) A concentration camp is a prison camp, especially one in Nazi Germany during World War Two.

concept, concepts (noun) A concept is an abstract or general idea, e.g. *the concept of tolerance.* **conceptual** (adjective), **conceptually** (adverb).

conception, conceptions 1 (noun) Your conception of something is the idea you have of it. **2** Conception is the process by which a woman becomes pregnant.

concern, concerns, concerning, concerned 1 (noun) Concern is a feeling of worry about something or someone, e.g. *public concern about violence.* **2** (verb) If something concerns you or if you are concerned about it, it worries you. **3** (phrase) If something is **of concern** to you, it is important to you. **4** (verb) You say that something concerns you if it affects or involves you, e.g. *It concerns you and me.* **5** (noun) If something is your concern, it is your responsibility. **6** A concern is also a business, e.g. *a large aircraft manufacturing concern.* **concerned** (adjective).

concerning (preposition) You use concerning to indicate what something is about, e.g. *documents concerning arm sales to Iraq.*

concert, concerts (noun) A concert is a public performance by musicians.

concerted (adjective) A concerted action is done by several people together, e.g. *concerted action to cut interest rates.*

concerto, concertos or **concerti** (pronounced kon-**cher**-toe) (noun) A concerto is a piece of music for a solo instrument and an orchestra.

concession, concessions (noun) If you make a concession, you agree to let someone have or do something, e.g. *Her one concession was to let me come into the building.*

concise (adjective) giving all the necessary information using the minimum number of words, e.g. *a concise guide.*

conclude, concludes, concluding, concluded 1 (verb) If you conclude something, you decide that it is so because of the other things that you know, e.g. *An inquiry concluded that this was untrue.* **2** When you conclude something, you finish it, e.g. *At that point I intend to conclude the interview.* **concluding** (adjective), **conclusion** (noun).

conclusive (adjective) Facts that are conclusive show that something is certainly true. **conclusively** (adverb).

concoct, concocts, concocting, concocted 1 (verb) If you concoct an excuse or explanation, you invent one. **2** If you concoct something, you make it by mixing several things together. **concoction** (noun).

concourse, concourses (noun) A concourse is a wide hall in a building where people walk about or gather together.

concrete 1 (noun) Concrete is a solid building material made by mixing cement, sand, and water. **2** (adjective) definite, rather than general or vague, e.g. *I don't really have any concrete plans.* **3** real and physical, rather than abstract, e.g. *concrete evidence.*

concubine, concubines (pronounced **kong**-kyoo-bine) (noun; an old-fashioned word) A man's concubine is his mistress.

concur, concurs, concurring, concurred (verb; a formal word) To concur means to agree, e.g. *She concurred with me.*

concurrent (adjective) If things are concurrent, they happen at the same time. **concurrently** (adverb).

concussed (adjective) confused or unconscious because of a blow to the head. **concussion** (noun).

condemn, condemns, condemning, condemned 1 (verb) If you condemn something, you say it is bad and unacceptable, e.g. *Teachers condemned the new plans.* **2** If someone is condemned to a punishment, they are given it, e.g. *She was condemned to death.* **3** If you are condemned to something unpleasant, you must suffer it, e.g. *Many women are condemned to poverty.* **4** When a building is condemned, it is going to be pulled down because it is unsafe. **condemnation** (noun).

condensation (noun) Condensation is a coating of tiny drops formed on a surface by steam or vapour.

condense, condenses, condensing, condensed 1 (verb) If you condense a piece of writing or a speech, you shorten it. **2** When a gas or vapour condenses, it changes into a liquid.

condescending (adjective) If you are condescending, you show by your behaviour that you think you are superior to other people.

condition, conditions, conditioning, conditioned 1 (noun) The condition of someone or something is the state they are in. **2** (plural noun) The conditions in which something is done are the location and other factors likely to affect it, e.g. *The very difficult conditions continued to affect our performance.* **3** A condition is a requirement that must be fulfilled for something else to be possible, e.g. *He had been banned from drinking alcohol as a condition of bail.* **4** You can refer to an illness or other medical problem as a condition, e.g. *a heart condition.* **5** (phrase) If you are **out of condition,** you are unfit. **6** (verb) If someone is conditioned to behave or think in a certain way, they do it as a result of their upbringing or training.

conditional (adjective) If one thing is conditional on another, it can only happen if the other thing happens, e.g. *You feel his love is conditional on you pleasing him.*

condolence, condolences (noun) Condolence is sympathy expressed for a bereaved person.

condom, condoms (noun) A condom is a rubber sheath worn by a man on his penis or by a woman inside her vagina as a contraceptive.

condone, condones, condoning, condoned (verb) If you condone someone's bad behaviour, you accept it and do not try to stop it, e.g. *We cannot condone violence.*

conducive (pronounced kon-**joo**-siv) (adjective) If something is conducive to something else, it makes it likely to happen, e.g. *a situation that is conducive to relaxation.*

conduct, conducts, conducting, conducted 1 (verb) To conduct an activity or task means to carry it out, e.g. *He seemed to be conducting a conversation.* **2** (noun) If you take part in the conduct of an activity or task, you help to carry it out, e.g. *the conduct of the trial.* **3** Your conduct is your behaviour. **4** (verb; a formal use) The way you conduct yourself is the way you behave. **5** When someone conducts an orchestra or choir, they stand in front of it and direct it. **6** If something conducts heat or electricity, heat or electricity can pass through it.

conductor, conductors 1 (noun) A conductor is someone who conducts an orchestra or choir. **2** A bus conductor is someone who moves round a bus selling tickets. **3** A conductor of heat or electricity is a substance that conducts it.

cone, cones 1 (noun) A cone is a regular three-dimensional shape with a circular base and a point at the top. **2** A fir cone or pine cone is the fruit of a fir or pine tree.

confectionery (noun) Confectionery is sweets.

confederation, confederations (noun) A confederation is an organization or alliance formed for business or political purposes.

confer, confers, conferring, conferred (verb) When people confer, they discuss something in order to make a decision.

conference, conferences (noun) A conference is a meeting at which formal discussions take place.

confess, confesses, confessing, confessed (verb) If you confess to something, you admit it, e.g. *Your son has confessed to his crimes.*

confession, confessions 1 (noun) If you make a confession, you admit you have done something wrong. **2** Confession is the act of confessing something, especially a religious act in which people confess their sins to a priest.

confessional, confessionals (noun) A confessional is a small room in some churches where people confess their sins to a priest.

confetti (noun) Confetti is small pieces of coloured paper thrown over the bride and groom at a wedding.

confidant, confidants (pronounced **kon**-fid-dant); spelled **confidante** for a female. (noun; a formal word) Your confidant is a person you discuss your private problems with.

confide, confides, confiding, confided (verb) If you confide a secret to someone, you tell it to them, e.g. *Felicity confided in me that she was very worried.*

confidence, confidences 1 (noun) If you have confidence in someone, you feel you can trust them. **2** Someone who has confidence is sure of their own abilities, qualities, or ideas. **3** A confidence is a secret you tell someone.

confident 1 (adjective) If you are confident about something, you are sure it will happen the way you want it to. **2** People who are confident are sure of their own abilities, qualities, or ideas. **confidently** (adverb).

confidential (adjective) Confidential information is meant to be kept secret. **confidentially** (adverb), **confidentiality** (noun).

confine, confines, confining, confined 1 (verb) If something is confined to one place, person, or thing, it exists only in that place or affects only that person or thing. **2** If you confine yourself to doing or saying something, it is the only thing you do or say, e.g. *They* *confined themselves to discussing the weather.* **3** If you are confined to a place, you cannot leave it, e.g. *She was confined to bed for two days.* **4** (plural noun) The confines of a place are its boundaries, e.g. *outside the confines of the prison.* **confinement** (noun).

confined (adjective) A confined space is small and enclosed by walls.

confirm, confirms, confirming, confirmed 1 (verb) To confirm something means to say or show that it is true, e.g. *Police confirmed that they had received a call.* **2** If you confirm an arrangement or appointment, you say it is definite. **confirmation** (noun).

confirmed (adjective) You use confirmed to describe someone who has a habit, belief, or way of life that is unlikely to change, e.g. *a confirmed bachelor.*

confiscate, confiscates, confiscating, confiscated (verb) To confiscate something means to take it away from someone as a punishment.

conflict, conflicts, conflicting, conflicted 1 (noun) Conflict is disagreement and argument, e.g. *conflict between workers and management.* **2** A conflict is a war or battle. **3** When there is a conflict of ideas or interests, people have different ideas or interests which cannot all be satisfied. **4** (verb) When ideas or interests conflict, they are different and cannot all be satisfied.

conform, conforms, conforming, conformed 1 (verb) If you conform, you behave the way people expect you to. **2** If something conforms to a law or to someone's wishes, it is what is required or wanted. **conformist** (noun or adjective).

confront, confronts, confronting, confronted 1 (verb) If you are confronted with a problem or task, you have to deal with it. **2** If you confront someone, you meet them face to face like an enemy. **3** If you confront someone with evidence or a fact, you present it to them in order to accuse them of something.

confrontation, confrontations (noun) A confrontation is a serious dispute or fight, e.g. *a confrontation between police and fans.*

confuse, confuses, confusing, confused 1 (verb) If you confuse two things, you mix them up and think one of them is the other, e.g. *You are confusing facts with opinion.* **2** To confuse someone means to make them uncertain about what is happening or what to do. **3** To confuse a situation means to make it more complicated. **confused** (adjective), **confusing** (adjective), **confusion** (noun).

congeal, congeals, congealing, congealed (pronounced kon-**jeel**) (verb) When a liquid congeals, it becomes very thick and sticky.

congenial (pronounced kon-**jeen**-yal) (adjective) If something is congenial, it is pleasant and suits you, e.g. *We wanted to talk in congenial surroundings.*

congenital (adjective; a medical word) If someone has a congenital disease or handicap, they have had it from birth but did not inherit it.

congested 1 (adjective) When a road is congested, it is so full of traffic that normal movement is impossible. **2** If your nose is congested, it is blocked and you cannot breathe properly. **congestion** (noun).

conglomerate, conglomerates (noun) A conglomerate is a large business organization consisting of several companies.

congratulate, congratulates, congratulating, congratulated (verb) If you congratulate someone, you express pleasure at something good that has happened to them, or praise them for something they have achieved. **congratulation** (noun), **congratulatory** (adjective).

congregate, congregates, congregating, congregated (verb) When people congregate, they gather together somewhere.

congregation, congregations (noun) In a church, the congregation are the people attending a service.

congress, congresses (noun) A congress is a large meeting held to discuss ideas or policies, e.g. *a medical congress.*

conical (adjective) shaped like a cone.

conifer, conifers (noun) A conifer is any type of evergreen tree that produces cones. **coniferous** (adjective).

conjecture (noun) Conjecture is guesswork about the nature of something, e.g. *There was no evidence, only conjecture.*

conjunction, conjunctions 1 (phrase) If two or more things are done **in conjunction,** they are done together. **2** (noun) In grammar, a conjunction is a word that links two other words or two clauses, for example 'and', 'but', 'while', and 'that'.

conjurer, conjurers (noun) A conjurer is someone who entertains people by doing magic tricks.

conker, conkers (noun) Conkers are hard brown nuts from a horse chestnut tree.

connect, connects, connecting, connected 1 (verb) To connect two things means to join them together. **2** If you connect something with something else, you think of them as being linked, e.g. *High blood pressure is closely connected to heart disease.*

connection, connections; also spelled **connexion 1** (noun) A connection is a link or relationship that exists between things. **2** A connection is also the point where two wires or pipes are joined together, e.g. *a loose connection.* **3** (plural noun) Someone's connections are the people they know, e.g. *He had powerful connections in the army.*

connoisseur, connoisseurs (pronounced kon-nis-**sir**) (noun) A connoisseur is someone who knows a lot about the arts, or about food or drink, e.g. *a great connoisseur of champagne.*

connotation, connotations (noun) The connotations of a word or name are what it makes you think of, e.g. *a* *grey man for whom grey has no connotation of dullness.*

conquer, conquers, conquering, conquered 1 (verb) To conquer people means to take control of their country by force. **2** If you conquer something difficult or dangerous, you succeed in controlling it, e.g. *I could conquer the pain.* **conqueror** (noun).

conquest, conquests (noun) Conquest is the conquering of a country or group of people.

conscience, consciences (noun) Your conscience is the part of your mind that tells you what is right and wrong.

conscientious (pronounced kon-shee-**en**-shus) (adjective) Someone who is conscientious is very careful to do their work properly. **conscientiously** (adverb).

conscious 1 (adjective) If you are conscious of something, you are aware of it, e.g. *She was not conscious of the time.* **2** A conscious action or effort is done deliberately, e.g. *I made a conscious decision not to hide.* **3** Someone who is conscious is awake, rather than asleep or unconscious, e.g. *Still conscious, she was taken to hospital.* **consciously** (adverb), **consciousness** (noun).

consecrated (adjective) A consecrated building or place is one that has been officially declared to be holy.

consecutive (adjective) Consecutive events or periods of time happen one after the other, e.g. *eight consecutive games.*

consensus (noun) Consensus is general agreement among a group of people, e.g. *The consensus was that it could be done.*

consent, consents, consenting, consented 1 (noun) Consent is permission to do something, e.g. *Sir Thomas reluctantly gave his consent to my writing this book.* **2** Consent is also agreement between two or more people, e.g. *By common consent it was the best game of these championships.* **3** (verb) If you consent to something, you agree to it or allow it, e.g. *The council had consented to the operations.*

consequence, consequences 1 (noun) The consequences of something are its results or effects, e.g. *the dire consequences of major war.* **2** (a formal use) If something is of consequence, it is important.

consequent (adjective) Consequent describes something as being the result of something else, e.g. *an earthquake in 1980 and its consequent damage.* **consequently** (adverb).

conservation (noun) Conservation is the preservation of the environment. **conservationist** (noun or adjective).

conservative, conservatives 1 (adjective) Conservative views and policies are right-wing ones. **2** (noun) A Conservative is someone with right-wing views. **3** (adjective) Someone who is conservative is not willing to accept changes or new ideas. **4** A conservative estimate or guess is a cautious or moderate one. **conservatively** (adverb), **conservatism** (noun).

conservatory, conservatories

(noun) A conservatory is a room with glass walls and a glass roof in which plants are kept.

conserve, conserves, conserving, conserved (verb) If you conserve a supply of something, you make it last, e.g. *the way to conserve energy.*

consider, considers, considering, considered 1 (verb) If you consider something to be the case, you think or judge it to be so, e.g. *The manager does not consider him an ideal team member.* **2** To consider something means to think about it carefully, e.g. *If an offer were made, we would consider it.* **3** If you consider someone's needs, wishes, or feelings, you take account of them.

considerable (adjective) A considerable amount of something is a lot of it, e.g. *a considerable sum of money.* **considerably** (adverb).

considerate (adjective) Someone who is considerate pays attention to other people's needs, wishes, and feelings.

consideration, considerations 1 (noun) Consideration is careful thought about something, e.g. *a decision demanding careful consideration.* **2** If you show consideration for someone, you take account of their needs, wishes, and feelings. **3** A consideration is something that has to be taken into account, e.g. *Money was also a consideration.*

considered (adjective) A considered opinion or judgment is arrived at by careful thought.

considering (conjunction or preposition) You say considering to indicate that you are taking something into account, e.g. *I know that must sound callous, considering that I was married to the man for seventeen years.*

consign, consigns, consigning, consigned (verb; a formal word) To consign something to a particular place means to send or put it there.

consignment, consignments (noun) A consignment of goods is a load of them being delivered somewhere.

consist, consists, consisting, consisted (verb) What something consists of is its different parts or members, e.g. *The brain consists of millions of nerve cells.*

consistency, consistencies 1 (noun) Consistency is the quality of being consistent. **2** The consistency of a substance is how thick or smooth it is, e.g. *the consistency of single cream.*

consistent 1 (adjective) If you are consistent, you keep doing something the same way, e.g. *one of our most consistent performers.* **2** If something such as a statement or argument is consistent, there are no contradictions in it. **consistently** (adverb).

console, consoles, consoling, consoled 1 (verb) To console someone who is unhappy means to make them more cheerful. **2** (noun) A console is a panel with switches or knobs for operating a machine. **consolation** (noun).

consolidate, consolidates, consolidating, consolidated (verb)

To consolidate something you have gained or achieved means to make it more secure. **consolidation** (noun).

consonant, consonants (noun) A consonant is a sound such as 'p' or 'm' which you make by stopping the air flowing freely through your mouth.

consort, consorts, consorting, consorted **1** (verb; a formal word) If you consort with someone, you spend a lot of time with them. **2** (noun) The wife or husband of the ruling monarch is his or her consort.

consortium, consortia or **consortiums** (noun) A consortium is a group of businesses working together.

conspicuous (adjective) If something is conspicuous, people can see or notice it very easily. **conspicuously** (adverb).

conspiracy, conspiracies (noun) When there is a conspiracy, a group of people plan something illegal, often for a political purpose.

conspirator, conspirators (noun) A conspirator is someone involved in a conspiracy.

conspire, conspires, conspiring, conspired **1** (verb) When people conspire, they plan together to do something illegal, often for a political purpose. **2** (a literary use) When events conspire towards a particular result, they seem to work together to cause it, e.g. *Circumstances conspired to doom the business.*

constable, constables (noun) A constable is a police officer of the lowest rank.

constabulary, constabularies (noun) The constabulary of an area is its police force.

constant **1** (adjective) Something that is constant happens all the time or is always there, e.g. *a city under constant attack.* **2** If an amount or level is constant, it stays the same. **3** People who are constant remain loyal to a person or idea. **constantly** (adverb), **constancy** (noun).

constellation, constellations (noun) A constellation is a group of stars.

consternation (noun) Consternation is anxiety or dismay, e.g. *There was some consternation when it began raining.*

constipated (adjective) Someone who is constipated is unable to defecate. **constipation** (noun).

constituency, constituencies (noun) A constituency is a town or area represented by an MP.

constituent, constituents **1** (noun) An MP's constituents are the voters who live in his or her constituency. **2** The constituents of something are its parts, e.g. *the major constituents of bone.*

constitute, constitutes, constituting, constituted (verb) If a group of things constitute something, they are what it consists of, e.g. *Jewellery constitutes 80 per cent of the stock.*

constitution, constitutions **1** (noun) The constitution of a country is the system of laws which formally states people's rights and duties. **2** Your constitution is your health, e.g. *a very strong constitution.* **constitutional** (adjective), **constitu-**

tionally (adverb).

constrained (adjective) If a person feels constrained to do something, they feel that they should do that, even if they do not want to.

constraint, constraints (noun) A constraint is something that limits someone's freedom of action, e.g. *constraints on trade union power.*

constrict, constricts, constricting, constricted (verb) To constrict something means to squeeze it tightly. **constriction** (noun).

construct, constructs, constructing, constructed (verb) To construct something means to build or make it.

construction, constructions 1 (noun) The construction of something is the building or making of it, e.g. *the construction of the harbour.* **2** A construction is something built or made, e.g. *The lightweight construction saves damage to decks and toes.*

constructive (adjective) Constructive criticisms and comments are helpful. **constructively** (adverb).

consul, consuls (noun) A consul is an official who lives in a foreign city and who looks after people there who are citizens of his or her own country. **consular** (adjective).

consulate, consulates (noun) A consulate is the place where a consul works.

consult, consults, consulting, consulted 1 (verb) If you consult someone, you ask for their opinion or advice. **2** If you consult a book or map, you refer to it for information.

consultancy, consultancies (noun) A consultancy is an organization whose members give expert advice on a subject.

consultant, consultants 1 (noun) A consultant is an experienced doctor who specializes in one type of medicine. **2** A consultant is also someone who gives expert advice, e.g. *a management consultant.*

consultation, consultations 1 (noun) A consultation is a meeting held to discuss something. **2** Consultation is discussion or the seeking of advice, e.g. *There has to be much better consultation with the public.* **consultative** (adjective).

consume, consumes, consuming, consumed 1 (verb; a formal word) If you consume something, you eat or drink it. **2** To consume fuel or energy means to use it up.

consumer, consumers (noun) A consumer is someone who buys things or uses services, e.g. *two new magazines for teenage consumers.*

consuming (adjective) A consuming passion or interest is more important to you than anything else.

consummate, consummates, consummating, consummated (pronounced **kons**-yum-mate) **1** (verb; a formal word) If two people consummate a marriage or relationship, they make it complete by having sex. **2** To consummate something means to make it complete. **3** (adjective; pronounced kon-**sum**-mit) You use consummate to describe someone who is very good at something, e.g. *a consummate artist.* **consummation** (noun).

consumption (noun) The consumption of fuel or food is the using of it, or the amount used.

contact, contacts, contacting, contacted 1 (noun) If you are in contact with someone, you regularly meet them, talk to them, or write to them. **2** When things are in contact, they are touching each other. **3** (verb) If you contact someone, you telephone them or write to them. **4** (noun) A contact is someone you know in a place or organization from whom you can get help or information.

contact lens, contact lenses (noun) Contact lenses are small plastic lenses that you put in your eyes instead of wearing glasses, to help you see better.

contagious (adjective) A contagious disease can be caught by touching people or things infected with it.

contain, contains, containing, contained 1 (verb) If a substance contains something, that thing is a part of it, e.g. *Alcohol contains sugar.* **2** The things a box or room contains are the things inside it. **3** (a formal use) To contain something also means to stop it increasing or spreading, e.g. *efforts to contain the widespread violence.* **containment** (noun).

container, containers 1 (noun) A container is something such as a box or a bottle that you keep things in. **2** Containers are also large sealed metal boxes for transporting things.

contaminate, contaminates, contaminating, contaminated (verb) If something is contaminated by dirt, chemicals, or radiation, it is made impure and harmful, e.g. *foods contaminated with lead.* **contamination** (noun).

contemplate, contemplates, contemplating, contemplated 1 (verb) To contemplate means to think carefully about something for a long time. **2** If you contemplate doing something, you consider doing it, e.g. *I never contemplated marrying the Prince of Wales.* **3** If you contemplate something, you look at it for a long time, e.g. *He contemplated his drawings.* **contemplation** (noun), **contemplative** (adjective).

contemporary, contemporaries 1 (adjective) functioning, produced, or happening now, e.g. *contemporary literature.* **2** functioning, produced, or happening at the time you are talking about, e.g. *contemporary descriptions of Lizzie Borden.* **3** (noun) Someone's contemporaries are other people living or active at the same time as them, e.g. *Shakespeare and his contemporaries.*

contempt (noun) If you treat someone or something with contempt, you show no respect for them at all.

contemptible (adjective) not worthy of any respect, e.g. *this contemptible piece of nonsense.*

contemptuous (adjective) showing contempt. **contemptuously** (adverb).

contend, contends, contending,

contended 1 (verb) To contend with a difficulty means to deal with it, e.g. *They had to contend with injuries.* **2** (a formal use) If you contend that something is true, you say firmly that it is true. **3** When people contend for something, they compete for it. **contender** (noun).

content, contents, contenting, contented 1 (plural noun) The contents of something are the things inside it. **2** (noun) The content of an article or speech is what is expressed in it. **3** Content is used to refer to the proportion of something that a substance contains, e.g. *White bread is inferior in vitamin content.* **4** (adjective) happy and satisfied with your life. **5** willing to do or have something, e.g. *He would be content to telephone her.* **6** (verb) If you content yourself with doing something, you do it and do not try to do anything else, e.g. *He contented himself with an early morning lecture.*

contented (adjective) happy and satisfied with your life. **contentedly** (adverb), **contentment** (noun).

contention, contentions (noun; a formal word) Someone's contention is the idea or opinion they are expressing, e.g. *It is our contention that the 1980s mark a turning point in planning.*

contest, contests, contesting, contested 1 (noun) A contest is a competition or game, e.g. *a boxing contest.* **2** A contest is also a struggle for power, e.g. *a presidential contest.* **3** (verb) If you contest a statement or decision, you object to it formally.

contestant, contestants (noun) The contestants in a competition are the people taking part in it.

context, contexts 1 (noun) The context of something consists of matters related to it which help to explain it, e.g. *English history is treated in a European context.* **2** The context of a word or sentence consists of the words or sentences before and after it.

continent, continents 1 (noun) A continent is a very large area of land, such as Africa or Asia. **2** The Continent is the mainland of Europe. **continental** (adjective).

contingency, contingencies (pronounced kon-**tin**-jen-see) (noun) A contingency is something that might happen in the future, e.g. *I need to examine all possible contingencies.*

contingent, contingents 1 (noun) A contingent is a group of people representing a country or organization, e.g. *a strong British contingent.* **2** A contingent is also a group of police or soldiers.

continual 1 (adjective) happening all the time without stopping, e.g. *continual headaches.* **2** happening again and again, e.g. *the continual snide remarks.* **continually** (adverb).

continuation, continuations 1 (noun) The continuation of something is the continuing of it. **2** Something that is a continuation of an event follows it and seems like a part of it.

continue, continues, continuing, continued 1 (verb) If you continue to do something, you keep doing it. **2** If something continues, it does not stop. **3** You also say something continues when it starts again after stopping, e.g. *She continued after a pause.*

continuous 1 (adjective) Continuous means happening or existing without stopping. **2** A continuous line or surface has no gaps or holes in it. **continuously** (adverb), **continuity** (noun).

contorted (adjective) twisted into an unnatural, unattractive shape.

contour, contours 1 (noun) The contours of something are its general shape. **2** On a map, a contour is a line joining points of equal height.

contra- (prefix) Contra- means against or opposite to, e.g. *contraflow.*

contraception (noun) Contraception refers to methods of preventing pregnancy.

contraceptive, contraceptives (noun) A contraceptive is a device or pill for preventing pregnancy.

contract, contracts, contracting, contracted 1 (noun) A contract is a written legal agreement concerning the sale of something or work done for money. **2** (verb) When something contracts, it gets smaller or shorter. **3** (a formal use) If you contract an illness, you get it, e.g. *Her husband contracted a virus.* **contractual** (adjective), **contraction** (noun).

contractor, contractors (noun) A contractor is a person or company who does work for other people or companies, e.g. *a building contractor.*

contradict, contradicts, contradicting, contradicted (verb) If you contradict someone, you say that what they have just said is not true, and that something else is. **contradiction** (noun), **contradictory** (adjective).

contraption, contraptions (noun) A contraption is a strange-looking machine or piece of equipment.

contrary 1 (adjective) Contrary ideas or opinions are opposed to each other and cannot be held by the same person, e.g. *There isn't any contrary evidence?* **2** (phrase) You say **on the contrary** when you are contradicting what someone has just said, e.g. *On the contrary, her parents have complained to the press.*

contrast, contrasts, contrasting, contrasted 1 (noun) A contrast is a great difference between things, e.g. *the real contrast between the two poems.* **2** If one thing is a contrast to another, it is very different from it, e.g. *I couldn't imagine a greater contrast to Maxwell.* **3** (verb) If you contrast things, you describe or emphasize the differences between them. **4** If one thing contrasts with another, it is very different from it, e.g. *The interview contrasted completely with the one she gave after Tokyo.*

contravene, contravenes, contravening, contravened (verb; a formal word) If you contravene a law or rule, you do something that it forbids.

contribute, contributes, contributing, contributed 1 (verb) If you contribute to something, you do things to help it succeed, e.g. *The elderly have much to contribute to the community.* **2** If you contribute money, you give it to help to pay for something. **3** If something contributes to an event or situation, it is one of its causes, e.g. *The dry summer has contributed to perfect conditions.* **contribution** (noun), **contributor** (noun), **contributory** (adjective).

contrive, contrives, contriving, contrived (verb; a formal word) If you contrive to do something difficult, you succeed in doing it, e.g. *Anthony contrived to escape with a few companions.*

contrived (adjective) Something that is contrived is unnatural, e.g. *a contrived compliment.*

control, controls, controlling, controlled 1 (noun) Control of a country or organization is the power to make the important decisions about how it is run. **2** Your control over something is your ability to make it work the way you want it to. **3** (verb) To control a country or organization means to have the power to make decisions about how it is run. **4** To control something such as a machine or system means to make it work the way you want it to. **5** If you control yourself, you make yourself behave calmly when you are angry or upset. **6** (noun) The controls on a machine are knobs or other devices used to work it. **7** (phrase) If something is **out of control,** nobody has any power over it. **controller** (noun).

controversial (adjective) Something that is controversial causes a lot of discussion and argument, because many people disapprove of it.

controversy, controversies (pronounced **kon**-triv-ver-see) (noun) Controversy is discussion and argument because many people disapprove of something.

conundrum, conundrums (noun; a formal word) A conundrum is a puzzling problem.

convene, convenes, convening, convened 1 (verb; a formal word) To convene a meeting means to arrange for it to take place. **2** When people convene, they come together for a meeting.

convenience, conveniences 1 (noun) The convenience of something is the fact that it is easy to use or that it makes something easy to do, e.g. *for the convenience of the customers.* **2** A convenience is something useful, e.g. *every modern convenience.*

convenient (adjective) If something is convenient, it is easy to use or it makes something easy to do. **conveniently** (adverb).

convent, convents (noun) A convent is a building where nuns live, or a school run by nuns.

convention, conventions 1 (noun) A convention is an accepted way of behaving or doing something. **2** A convention is also a large meeting of an organization or political group, e.g. *the Democratic Con-*

vention.

conventional 1 (adjective) You say that people are conventional when there is nothing unusual about their way of life. **2** Conventional methods and products are the ones that are usually used. **conventionally** (adverb).

converge, converges, converging, converged (verb) To converge means to meet or join at a particular place.

conversation, conversations (noun) If you have a conversation with someone, you spend time talking to them. **conversational** (adjective), **conversationalist** (noun).

converse, converses, conversing, conversed 1 (verb; a formal use) When people converse, they talk to each other. **2** (noun) The converse of something is its opposite, e.g. *Don't you think that the converse might also be possible?* **conversely** (adverb).

convert, converts, converting, converted 1 (verb) To convert one thing into another means to change it so that it becomes the other thing. **2** If someone converts you, they persuade you to change your religious or political beliefs. **3** (noun) A convert is someone who has changed their religious or political beliefs. **conversion** (noun), **convertible** (adjective).

convex (adjective) A convex surface bulges outwards, rather than being level or curving inwards.

convey, conveys, conveying, conveyed 1 (verb) To convey information or ideas means to cause them to be known or understood. **2** (a formal use) To convey someone or something to a place means to transport them there.

conveyor belt, conveyor belts (noun) A conveyor belt is a moving strip used in factories for moving objects along.

convict, convicts, convicting, convicted 1 (verb) To convict someone of a crime means to find them guilty, e.g. *He was convicted of arson.* **2** (noun) A convict is someone serving a prison sentence.

conviction, convictions 1 (noun) A conviction is a strong belief or opinion. **2** The conviction of someone is what happens when they are found guilty in a court of law.

convince, convinces, convincing, convinced (verb) To convince someone of something means to persuade them that it is true.

convincing (adjective) Convincing is used to describe things or people that can make you believe something is true, e.g. *a convincing argument.* **convincingly** (adverb).

convoluted (pronounced kon-vol-**yoo**-tid) (adjective) Something that is convoluted has many twists and bends, e.g. *the convoluted patterns of these designs.*

convoy, convoys (noun) A convoy is a group of vehicles or ships travelling together.

convulsion, convulsions (noun) If someone has convulsions, their muscles move violently and uncontrollably.

coo, coos, cooing, cooed (verb) When pigeons and doves coo, they make a soft flutelike sound.

cook, cooks, cooking, cooked 1 (verb) To cook food means to prepare it for eating by heating it. **2** (noun) A cook is someone who prepares and cooks food, often as their job.

cooker, cookers (noun) A cooker is a device for cooking food.

cookery (noun) Cookery is the activity of preparing and cooking food.

cool, cooler, coolest; cools, cooling, cooled 1 (adjective) Something cool has a low temperature but is not cold. **2** (verb) When something cools or when you cool it, it becomes less warm. **3** (adjective) If you are cool in a difficult situation, you stay calm and unemotional. **coolly** (adverb), **coolness** (noun).

coop, coops (noun) A coop is a cage for chickens or rabbits.

cooperate, cooperates, cooperating, cooperated (pronounced koh-**op**-er-rate) **1** (verb) When people cooperate, they work or act together. **2** To cooperate also means to do what someone asks. **cooperation** (noun).

cooperative, cooperatives (pronounced koh-**op**-er-ut-tiv) **1** (noun) A cooperative is a business or organization run by the people who work for it, and who share its benefits or profits. **2** (adjective) A cooperative activity is done by people working together. **3** Someone who is cooperative does what you ask them to.

coordinate, coordinates, coordinating, coordinated (pronounced koh-**or**-din-ate) (verb) To coordinate an activity means to organize the people or things involved in it, e.g. *to coordinate the campaign.* **coordination** (noun), **coordinator** (noun).

cop, cops (noun; an informal word) A cop is a policeman.

cope, copes, coping, coped (verb) If you cope with a problem or task, you deal with it successfully.

copious (adjective; a formal word) existing or produced in large quantities, e.g. *I wrote copious notes for the solicitor.*

copper, coppers 1 (noun) Copper is a soft reddish-brown metal. **2** Coppers are brown metal coins of low value. **3** (an informal use) A copper is also a policeman.

copse, copses (noun) A copse is a small group of trees growing close together.

copulate, copulates, copulating, copulated (verb; a formal word) To copulate means to have sex. **copulation** (noun).

copy, copies, copying, copied 1 (noun) A copy is something made to look like something else. **2** A copy of a book, newspaper, or record is one of many identical ones produced at the same time. **3** (verb) If you copy what someone does, you do the same thing. **4** If you copy something, you make a copy of it. **copier** (noun).

copyright, copyrights (noun) If someone has the copyright on a piece of writing or music, it cannot be copied or performed without their permission.

coral, corals (noun) Coral is a hard substance that forms in the sea from the skeletons of tiny animals called corals.

cord, cords 1 (noun) Cord is strong, thick string. **2** Electrical wire covered in rubber or plastic is also called cord.

cordial, cordials 1 (adjective) warm and friendly, e.g. *the cordial greeting.* **2** (noun) Cordial is a sweet drink made from fruit juice.

cordon, cordons, cordoning, cordoned 1 (noun) A cordon is a line or ring of police or soldiers preventing people entering or leaving a place. **2** (verb) If police or soldiers cordon off an area, they stop people entering or leaving by forming themselves into a line or ring.

corduroy (noun) Corduroy is a thick cloth with parallel raised lines on the outside.

core, cores 1 (noun) The core of a fruit such as an apple is its hard central part. **2** The core of an object or a place is its most central part, e.g. *the earth's core.* **3** The core of something is its most important part, e.g. *the core of Britain's problems.*

cork, corks 1 (noun) Cork is the very light, spongelike bark of a Mediterranean tree. **2** A cork is a piece of cork pushed into the end of a bottle to close it.

corkscrew, corkscrews (noun) A corkscrew is a device for pulling corks out of bottles.

cormorant, cormorants (noun) A cormorant is a dark-coloured bird with a long neck.

corn, corns 1 (noun) Corn refers to crops such as wheat and barley and to their seeds. **2** A corn is a small painful area of hard skin on your foot.

cornea, corneas (pronounced **kor**-nee-a) (noun) The cornea is the transparent skin that covers the outside of your eyeball.

corner, corners, cornering, cornered 1 (noun) A corner is a place where two sides or edges of something meet, e.g. *a small corner of one shelf... a street corner.* **2** (verb) To corner a person or animal means to get them into a place they cannot escape from.

cornet, cornets (noun) A cornet is a small brass instrument used in brass and military bands.

cornflour (noun) Cornflour is a fine white flour made from maize and used in cooking to thicken sauces.

cornflower, cornflowers (noun) A cornflower is a small plant with bright flowers, usually blue.

cornice, cornices (noun) A cornice is a decorative strip of plaster, wood, or stone along the top edge of a wall.

corny, cornier, corniest (adjective) very obvious or sentimental and not at all original, e.g. *corny old love songs.*

coronary, coronaries (noun) If someone has a coronary, blood cannot reach their heart because of a blood clot.

coronation, coronations (noun) A coronation is the ceremony at which a king or queen is crowned.

coroner, coroners (noun) A coroner is an official who investigates the deaths of people who have died in a violent or unusual way.

coronet, coronets (noun) A coronet is a small crown.

corporal, corporals (noun) A corporal is an officer of low rank in the army or air force.

corporal punishment (noun) Corporal punishment is the punishing of people by beating them.

corporate (adjective; a formal word) belonging to or done by all members of a group together, e.g. *a corporate decision.*

corporation, corporations 1 (noun) A corporation is a large business. **2** A corporation is also a group of people responsible for running a city.

corps (rhymes with **more**) The plural is also **corps. 1** (noun) A corps is a part of an army with special duties, e.g. *the Royal Army Ordnance Corps.* **2** A corps is also a small group of people who do a special job, e.g. *the press corps.*

corpse, corpses (noun) A corpse is a dead body.

corpuscle, corpuscles (pronounced **kor**-pus-sl) (noun) A corpuscle is a red or white blood cell.

correct, corrects, correcting, corrected 1 (adjective) If something is correct, there are no mistakes in it. **2** The correct thing in a particular situation is the right one, e.g. *Each has the correct number of coins.* **3** Correct behaviour is considered to be socially acceptable. **4** (verb) If you correct something which is wrong, you make it right. **correctly** (adverb), **correction** (noun), **corrective** (adjective or noun).

correlate, correlates, correlating, correlated (verb) If two things correlate or are correlated, they are closely connected or strongly influence each other, e.g. *Obesity correlates with increased risk of stroke and diabetes.* **correlation** (noun).

correspond, corresponds, corresponding, corresponded 1 (verb) If one thing corresponds to another, it has a similar purpose, function, or status. **2** If numbers or amounts correspond, they are the same. **3** When people correspond, they write to each other.

correspondence 1 (noun) Correspondence is the writing of letters; also the letters written. **2** If there is a correspondence between two things, they are closely related or very similar.

correspondent, correspondents (noun) A correspondent is a newspaper, television, or radio reporter.

corresponding 1 (adjective) You use corresponding to describe a change that results from a change in something else, e.g. *the rise in interest rates and corresponding fall in house values.* **2** You also use corresponding to describe something which has a similar purpose or status to something else, e.g. *Alfard is the corresponding Western name for the star.* **correspondingly** (adverb).

corridor, corridors (noun) A corridor is a passage in a building or train.

corrode, corrodes, corroding, corroded (verb) When metal corrodes, it is gradually destroyed by a chemical or rust. **corrosion** (noun), **corrosive** (adjective).

corrugated (adjective) Corrugated metal or cardboard is produced in parallel folds to make it stronger.

corrupt, corrupts, corrupting, corrupted 1 (adjective) Corrupt people act dishonestly or illegally in return for money or power, e.g. *corrupt ministers.* **2** (verb) To corrupt someone means to make them dishonest or immoral. **corruptible** (adjective).

corruption (noun) Corruption is dishonesty and illegal behaviour by people in positions of power.

corset, corsets (noun) Corsets are stiff underwear worn by some women round their hips and waist to make them look slimmer.

cosmetic, cosmetics 1 (noun) Cosmetics are substances such as lipstick and face powder which improve a person's appearance. **2** (adjective) Cosmetic measures or changes improve the appearance of something without changing its basic character.

cosmic (adjective) belonging or relating to the universe.

cosmopolitan (adjective) A cosmopolitan place is full of people from many countries.

cosmos (noun) The cosmos is the universe.

cosset, cossets, cosseting, cosseted (verb) If you cosset someone, you spoil them and protect them too much.

cost, costs, costing, cost 1 (noun) The cost of something is the amount of money needed to buy it, do it, or make it. **2** The cost of achieving something is the loss or injury in achieving it, e.g. *the total cost in human misery.* **3** (verb) You use cost to talk about the amount of money you have to pay for things, e.g. *The air fares were going to cost a lot.* **4** If a mistake costs you something, you lose that thing because of the mistake, e.g. *a reckless gamble that could cost him his job.*

costly, costlier, costliest (adjective) expensive, e.g. *the most costly piece of furniture.*

costume, costumes 1 (noun) A costume is a set of clothes worn by an actor. **2** Costume is the clothing worn in a particular place or during a particular period, e.g. *eighteenth-century costume.*

cosy, cosier, cosiest; cosies 1 (adjective) warm and comfortable, e.g. *her cosy London flat.* **2** Cosy activities are pleasant and friendly, e.g. *a cosy chat.* **3** (noun) A cosy is a soft cover put over a teapot to keep the tea warm. **cosily** (adverb), **cosiness** (noun).

cot, cots (noun) A cot is a small bed for a baby, with bars or panels round it to stop the baby falling out.

cottage, cottages (noun) A cottage is a small house in the country.

cottage cheese (noun) Cottage cheese is a type of soft white lumpy cheese.

cotton, cottons 1 (noun) Cotton is cloth made from the soft fibres of the cotton plant. **2** Cotton is also thread used for sewing.

cotton wool (noun) Cotton wool is soft fluffy cotton, often used for dressing wounds.

couch, couches, couching, couched 1 (noun) A couch is a long, soft piece of furniture which more than one person can sit on. **2** (verb) If a statement is couched in a particular type of language, it is expressed in that language, e.g. *a comment couched in impertinent terms.*

cough, coughs, coughing, coughed 1 (verb) When you cough, you force air out of your throat with a sudden harsh noise. **2** (noun) A cough is an illness that makes you cough a lot; also the noise you make when you cough.

could 1 (verb) You use could to say that you were able or allowed to do something, e.g. *He could hear voices... She could come and go as she wanted.* **2** You also use could to say that something might happen or might be the case, e.g. *It could rain.* **3** You use could when you are asking for something politely, e.g. *Could you tell me the name of that film?*

council, councils 1 (noun) A council is a group of people elected to look after the affairs of a town, district, or county, e.g. *Manchester City Council.* **2** Some other groups have Council as part of their name, e.g. *the Irish Council on Alcoholism.*

councillor, councillors (noun) A councillor is an elected member of a local council.

council tax (noun) The council tax is a tax on property that raises money to pay for local services like libraries.

counsel, counsels, counselling, counselled 1 (noun; a formal use) To give someone counsel means to give them advice. **2** (verb) To counsel people means to give them advice about their problems. **counselling** (noun), **counsellor** (noun).

count, counts, counting, counted 1 (verb) To count means to say all the numbers in order up to a particular number. **2** If you count all the things in a group, you add them up to see how many there are. **3** (noun) A count is a number reached by counting. **4** (verb) What counts in a situation is whatever is most important. **5** To count as something means to be regarded as that thing, e.g. *I'm not sure whether this counts as harassment.* **6** (noun; a formal use) If something is wrong on a particular count, it is wrong in that respect. **7** (verb) If you can count on someone or something, you can rely on them. **8** (noun) A count is a European nobleman.

countdown, countdowns (noun) Countdown is the counting aloud of numbers in reverse order before something happens, especially before a spacecraft is launched.

countenance, countenances (noun; a formal word) Someone's countenance is their face.

counter, counters, countering, countered 1 (noun) A counter in a shop is a long, flat surface over which goods are sold. **2** A counter is a small, flat, round object used in board games. **3** (verb) If you counter something that is being done, you take action to make it less effective, e.g. *I countered that argument with a reference to our sales report.*

counteract, counteracts, counteracting, counteracted (verb) To counteract something means to reduce its effect by producing an opposite effect.

counterfeit, counterfeits, counterfeiting, counterfeited (pronounced **kown**-ter-fit) **1** (adjective) Something counterfeit is not genuine but has been made to look genuine to deceive people, e.g. *counterfeit money.* **2** (verb) To counterfeit something means to make a counterfeit version of it.

counterpart, counterparts (noun) The counterpart of a person or thing is another person or thing with a similar function in a different place, e.g. *Unlike his British counterpart, the French mayor is an important personality.*

countess, countesses (noun) A countess is the wife of a count or earl, or a woman with the same rank as a count or earl.

counting (preposition) You say 'counting' when including something in a calculation, e.g. *nearly 4000 of us, not counting women and children.*

countless (adjective) too many to count, e.g. *There had been countless demonstrations.*

country, countries 1 (noun) A country is one of the political areas the world is divided into. **2** The country is land away from towns and cities. **3** Country is used to refer to an area with particular features or associations, e.g. *the heart of wine country.*

countryman, countrymen (noun) Your countrymen are people from your own country.

countryside (noun) The countryside is land away from towns and cities.

county, counties (noun) A county is a region with its own local government.

coup, coups (rhymes with **you**) (noun) When there is a coup, a group of people seize power in a country.

couple, couples, coupling, coupled 1 (noun) You refer to two people as a couple when they are married or are having a sexual or romantic relationship. **2** A couple of things or people means two of them, e.g. *a couple of weeks ago.* **3** (verb) If one thing is coupled with another, the two things are done or dealt with together, e.g. *Its stores combine high quality coupled with low prices.*

couplet, couplets (noun) A couplet is two lines of poetry together, especially two that rhyme.

coupon, coupons 1 (noun) A coupon is a piece of printed paper which, when you hand it in, entitles you to pay less than usual for something. **2** A coupon is also a form you fill in to ask for information or to enter a competition.

courage (noun) Courage is the quality shown by people who do things knowing they are dangerous or difficult. **coura-**

geous (adjective), **courageously** (adverb).

courgette, courgettes (pronounced koor-**jet**) (noun) A courgette is a type of small marrow with dark green skin.

courier, couriers (pronounced **koo**-ree-er) **1** (noun) A courier is someone employed by a travel company to look after people on holiday. **2** A courier is also someone employed to deliver special letters quickly.

course, courses 1 (noun) A course is a series of lessons or lectures. **2** A series of medical treatments is also called a course, e.g. *a course of injections.* **3** A course is one of the parts of a meal. **4** A course or a course of action is one of the things you can do in a situation. **5** A course is also a piece of land where a sport such as golf is played. **6** The course of a ship or aircraft is the route it takes. **7** If something happens in the course of a period of time, it happens during that period, e.g. *Ten people died in the course of the day.* **8** (phrase) If you say **of course,** you are showing that something is totally expected or that you are sure about something, e.g. *Of course she wouldn't do that.*

court, courts, courting, courted 1 (noun) A court is a place where legal matters are decided by a judge and jury or a magistrate. The judge and jury or magistrate can also be referred to as the court. **2** A court is a place where a game such as tennis or badminton is played. **3** A king or queen's court is the place where they live and carry out ceremonial duties. **4** (verb; an old-fashioned use) If a man and woman are courting, they are spending a lot of time together because they intend to get married.

courteous (pronounced **kur**-tee-yuss) (adjective) Courteous behaviour is polite, respectful, and considerate.

courtesy (noun) Courtesy is polite, respectful, considerate behaviour.

courtier, courtiers (noun) Courtiers were noblemen and noblewomen at the court of a king or queen.

court-martial, court-martials, court-martialling, court-martialled 1 (noun) A court martial is a military trial. **2** (verb) If a member of the armed forces is court-martialled, he or she is tried by a court martial.

courtship (noun; a formal word) Courtship is the activity of courting or the period of time during which a man and a woman are courting.

courtyard, courtyards (noun) A courtyard is a flat area of ground surrounded by buildings or walls.

cousin, cousins (noun) Your cousin is the child of your uncle or aunt.

cove, coves (noun) A cove is a small bay.

covenant, covenants (pronounced **kuv**-vi-nant) (noun) A covenant is a formal written agreement or promise.

cover, covers, covering, covered 1 (verb) If you cover something, you put something else over it to protect it or hide it.

2 If something covers something else, it forms a layer over it, e.g. *Tears covered his face.* **3** (noun) A cover is something put over an object to protect it or keep it warm. **4** The cover of a book or magazine is its outside. **5** (verb) If you cover a particular distance, you travel that distance, e.g. *He covered 52 kilometres in 210 laps.* **6** (noun) Insurance cover is a guarantee that money will be paid if something is lost or harmed. **7** In the open, cover consists of trees, rocks, or other places where you can shelter or hide. **cover up** (verb) If you cover up something you do not want people to know about, you hide it from them, e.g. *She was trying to cover up for someone.* **cover-up** (noun).

coverage (noun) The coverage of something in the news is the reporting of it.

covert (pronounced **kuv**-vert) (adjective; a formal word) Covert activities are secret, rather than open. **covertly** (adverb).

covet, covets, coveting, coveted (pronounced **kuv**-vit) (verb; a formal word) If you covet something, you want it very much.

cow, cows (noun) A cow is a large animal kept on farms for its milk.

coward, cowards (noun) A coward is someone who is easily frightened and who avoids dangerous or difficult situations. **cowardly** (adjective), **cowardice** (noun).

cowboy, cowboys (noun) A cowboy is a man employed to look after cattle in America.

cower, cowers, cowering, cowered (verb) When someone cowers, they crouch or move backwards because they are afraid.

cox, coxes (noun) A cox is a person who steers a boat.

coy, coyer, coyest (adjective) If someone is coy, they pretend to be shy and modest. **coyly** (adverb).

coyote, coyotes (pronounced koy-**ote**-ee) (noun) A coyote is a North American animal like a small wolf.

crab, crabs (noun) A crab is a sea creature with four pairs of legs, two pincers, and a flat, round body covered by a shell.

crack, cracks, cracking, cracked 1 (verb) If something cracks, it becomes damaged, with lines appearing on its surface. **2** (noun) A crack is one of the lines appearing on something when it cracks. **3** A crack is also a narrow gap. **4** (verb) If you crack a joke, you tell it. **5** If you crack a problem or code, you solve it. **6** (adjective) A crack soldier or sportsman is highly trained and skilful.

cracker, crackers 1 (noun) A cracker is a thin, crisp biscuit that is often eaten with cheese. **2** A cracker is also a paper-covered tube that pulls apart with a bang and usually has a toy and paper hat inside.

crackle, crackles, crackling, crackled 1 (verb) If something crackles, it makes a rapid series of short, harsh noises. **2** (noun) A crackle is a short, harsh noise.

cradle, cradles, cradling, cradled **1** (noun) A cradle is a box-shaped bed for a baby. **2** (verb) If you cradle something in your arms or hands, you hold it there carefully.

craft, crafts The plural of sense 3 is **craft**. **1** (noun) A craft is an activity such as weaving, carving, or pottery. **2** Any skilful occupation can be referred to as a craft, e.g. *the writer's craft.* **3** You can refer to a boat, plane, or spacecraft as a craft.

craftsman, craftsmen (noun) A craftsman is a man whose job is to make things skilfully with his hands. **craftsmanship** (noun), **craftswoman** (noun).

crafty, craftier, craftiest (adjective) Someone who is crafty gets what they want by tricking people in a clever way.

crag, crags (noun) A crag is a steep rugged rock or peak.

craggy, craggier, craggiest (adjective) A craggy mountain or cliff is steep and rocky.

cram, crams, cramming, crammed (verb) If you cram people or things into a place, you put more in than there is room for.

cramp, cramps (noun) Cramp or cramps is a pain caused by a muscle contracting.

cramped (adjective) If a room or building is cramped, it is not big enough for the people or things in it.

cranberry, cranberries (noun) Cranberries are sour-tasting red berries, often made into a sauce.

crane, cranes, craning, craned **1** (noun) A crane is a machine that moves heavy things by lifting them in the air. **2** A crane is also a large bird with a long neck and long legs. **3** (verb) If you crane your neck, you extend your head in a particular direction to see or hear something better.

crank, cranks, cranking, cranked **1** (noun; an informal use) A crank is someone with strange ideas who behaves in an odd way. **2** A crank is a device you turn to make something move, e.g. *The adjustment is made by turning the crank.* **3** (verb) If you crank something, you make it move by turning a handle. **cranky** (adjective).

cranny, crannies (noun) A cranny is a very narrow opening in a wall or rock, e.g. *nooks and crannies.*

crash, crashes, crashing, crashed **1** (noun) A crash is an accident in which a moving vehicle hits something violently. **2** (verb) When a vehicle crashes, it hits something and is badly damaged. **3** (noun) A crash is a sudden loud noise, e.g. *the crash of the waves on the rocks.* **4** The sudden failure of a business or financial institution is also called a crash.

crash helmet, crash helmets (noun) A crash helmet is a helmet worn by motor cyclists for protection when they are riding.

crate, crates (noun) A crate is a large box used for transporting or storing things.

crater, craters (noun) A crater is a wide hole in the ground caused by something hitting it or by an explosion.

cravat, cravats (noun) A cravat is a piece of cloth a man wears round his neck tucked into his shirt collar.

crave, craves, craving, craved (verb) If you crave something, you want it very much, e.g. *I crave her approval.* **craving** (noun).

crawl, crawls, crawling, crawled **1** (verb) When you crawl, you move forward on your hands and knees. **2** When a vehicle crawls, it moves very slowly. **3** (an informal use) If a place is crawling with people or things, it is full of them, e.g. *The place is crawling with drunks.* **crawler** (noun).

crayfish, crayfishes or **crayfish** (noun) A crayfish is a small shellfish like a lobster.

crayon, crayons (noun) A crayon is a coloured pencil or a stick of coloured wax.

craze, crazes (noun) A craze is something that is very popular for a short time.

crazy, crazier, craziest (an informal word) **1** (adjective) very strange or foolish, e.g. *The guy is probably crazy... a crazy idea.* **2** If you are crazy about something, you are very keen on it, e.g. *I was crazy about dancing.* **crazily** (adverb), **craziness** (noun).

creak, creaks, creaking, creaked **1** (verb) If something creaks, it makes a harsh sound when it moves or when you stand on it. **2** (noun) A creak is a harsh squeaking noise. **creaky** (adjective).

cream, creams **1** (noun) Cream is a thick, yellowish-white liquid taken from the top of milk. **2** Cream is also a substance people can rub on their skin to make it soft. **3** (adjective) yellowish-white. **creamy** (adjective).

crease, creases, creasing, creased **1** (noun) Creases are irregular lines that appear on cloth or paper when it is crumpled. **2** Creases are also straight lines on something that has been pressed or folded neatly. **3** (verb) To crease something means to make lines appear on it. **creased** (adjective).

create, creates, creating, created **1** (verb) To create something means to cause it to happen or exist, e.g. *This is absolutely vital but creates a problem.* **2** When someone creates a new product or process, they invent it. **creator** (noun), **creation** (noun).

creative **1** (adjective) Creative people are able to invent and develop original ideas. **2** Creative activities involve the inventing and developing of original ideas, e.g. *creative writing.* **creatively** (adverb), **creativity** (noun).

creature, creatures (noun) Any living thing that moves about can be referred to as a creature.

crèche, crèches (pronounced **kresh**) (noun) A crèche is a place where small children are looked after while their parents are working.

credence (noun; a formal word) If something lends credence to a theory or story, it makes it easier to believe.

credentials (plural noun) Your credentials are your past achievements or other things in your background that make you qualified for something.

credible (adjective) If someone or something is credible, you can believe or trust them. **credibility** (noun).

credit, credits, crediting, credited 1 (noun) If you are allowed credit, you can take something and pay for it later, e.g. *to buy goods on credit.* **2** (phrase) If someone or their bank account is **in credit**, their account has money in it. **3** (noun) If you get the credit for something, people praise you for it. **4** (verb) If you are credited with an achievement, people believe that you were responsible for it. **5** (noun) If you say someone is a credit to their family or school, you mean that their family or school should be proud of them.

creditable (adjective) satisfactory or fairly good, e.g. *a creditable performance.*

credit card, credit cards (noun) A credit card is a card that allows someone to buy goods on credit.

creditor, creditors (noun) Your creditors are the people you owe money to.

creed, creeds 1 (noun) A creed is a religion. **2** You can refer to any set of beliefs as a creed, e.g. *the feminist creed.*

creek, creeks (noun) A creek is a narrow inlet where the sea comes a long way into the land.

creep, creeps, creeping, crept (verb) To creep means to move quietly and slowly.

creepy, creepier, creepiest (adjective; an informal word) strange and frightening, e.g. *a creepy feeling.*

cremate, cremates, cremating, cremated (verb) When someone is cremated, their dead body is burned during a funeral service. **cremation** (noun).

crematorium, crematoriums or **crematoria** (noun) A crematorium is a building in which the bodies of dead people are burned.

crepe (pronounced **krayp**) **1** (noun) Crepe is a thin ridged material made from cotton, silk, or wool. **2** Crepe is also a type of rubber with a rough surface.

crescendo, crescendos (pronounced krish-**en**-doe) (noun) When there is a crescendo in a piece of music, the music gets louder.

crescent, crescents (noun) A crescent is a curved shape that is wider in its middle than at the ends, which taper to a point.

cress (noun) Cress is a plant with small, strong-tasting leaves. It is used in salads.

crest, crests 1 (noun) The crest of a hill or wave is its highest part. **2** A bird's crest is a tuft of feathers on top of its head. **3** A crest is also a small picture or design that is the emblem of a noble family, a town, or an organization. **crested** (adjective).

crevice, crevices (noun) A crevice is a narrow crack or gap in rock.

crew, crews 1 (noun) The crew of a ship, aeroplane, or spacecraft are the people who operate it. **2** Other people with special technical skills who work together are called crews, e.g. *the camera crew.*

crib, cribs, cribbing, cribbed 1 (verb; an informal use) If you crib, you copy what someone else has written and pretend it is your own work. **2** (noun; an old-fashioned use) A crib is a baby's cot.

crick, cricks (noun) A crick in your neck or back is a pain caused by muscles becoming stiff.

cricket, crickets 1 (noun) Cricket is an outdoor game played by two teams who take turns at scoring runs by hitting a ball with a bat. **2** A cricket is a small jumping insect that produces sounds by rubbing its wings together. **cricketer** (noun).

crime, crimes (noun) A crime is an action for which you can be punished by law, e.g. *a serious crime.*

criminal, criminals 1 (noun) A criminal is someone who has committed a crime. **2** (adjective) involving or related to crime, e.g. *criminal activities.* **criminally** (adverb).

crimson (noun or adjective) dark purplish-red.

cringe, cringes, cringing, cringed (verb) If you cringe, you back away from someone or something because you are afraid or embarrassed.

crinkle, crinkles, crinkling, crinkled 1 (verb) If something crinkles, it becomes slightly creased or folded. **2** (noun) Crinkles are small creases or folds.

cripple, cripples, crippling, crippled 1 (noun) A cripple is someone who cannot move their body properly because it is weak or affected by disease. **2** (verb) To cripple someone means to injure them severely so that they can never move properly again. **crippled** (adjective), **crippling** (adjective).

crisis, crises (pronounced **kry**-seez in the plural) (noun) A crisis is a serious or dangerous situation.

crisp, crisper, crispest; crisps 1 (adjective) Something that is crisp is pleasantly fresh and firm, e.g. *crisp lettuce leaves.* **2** If the air or the weather is crisp, it is pleasantly fresh, cold, and dry, e.g. *crisp wintry days.* **3** (noun) Crisps are thin slices of potato fried until they are hard and crunchy.

crispy, crispier, crispiest (adjective) Crispy food is pleasantly hard and crunchy, e.g. *a crispy salad.*

criterion, criteria (pronounced kry-**teer**-ee-on) (noun) A criterion is a standard by which you judge or decide something.

critic, critics 1 (noun) A critic is someone who writes reviews of books, films, plays, or musical performances. **2** A critic of a person or system is someone who criticizes them publicly, e.g. *the government's critics.*

critical 1 (adjective) A critical time is one which is very important in determining what happens in the future, e.g. *critical months in the history of the world.* **2** A critical situation is a very serious one, e.g. *Rock music is in a critical state.* **3** If an ill or injured person is critical, they are in danger of dying. **4** If you are critical of something or someone, you express severe judgments or opinions about them. **5** If you are critical, you examine and judge something carefully, e.g. *a critical look at the way he led his life.* **critically** (adverb).

criticism, criticisms 1 (noun) When there is criticism of someone or something, people express disapproval of them. **2** If you make a criticism, you point out a fault you think someone or something has.

criticize, criticizes, criticizing, criticized; also spelled **criticise** (verb) If you criticize someone or something, you say what you think is wrong with them.

croak, croaks, croaking, croaked 1 (verb) When animals and birds croak, they make harsh, low sounds. **2** (noun) A croak is a harsh, low sound.

Croatian, Croatians 1 (adjective) belonging to or relating to Croatia. **2** (noun) A Croatian is someone who comes from Croatia. **3** Croatian is the form of Serbo-Croat spoken in Croatia.

crochet (pronounced **kroh**-shay) (noun) Crochet is a way of making clothes and other things out of thread using a needle with a small hook at the end.

crockery (noun) Crockery is plates, cups, and saucers.

crocodile, crocodiles (noun) A crocodile is a large scaly meat-eating reptile which lives in tropical rivers.

crocus, crocuses (noun) Crocuses are yellow, purple, or white flowers that grow in early spring.

croft, crofts (noun) A croft is a small piece of land, especially in Scotland, which is farmed by one family. **crofter** (noun).

croissant, croissants (pronounced **krwus**-son) (noun) A croissant is a light, crescent-shaped roll eaten at breakfast.

crony, cronies (noun; an old-fashioned word) Your cronies are the friends you spend a lot of time with.

crook, crooks 1 (noun; an informal use) A crook is a criminal. **2** The crook of your arm or leg is the soft inside part where you bend your elbow or knee.

crooked (pronounced **kroo**-kid) **1** (adjective) bent or twisted. **2** Someone who is crooked is dishonest.

croon, croons, crooning, crooned (verb) To croon means to sing or hum quietly and gently, e.g. *He crooned a love song.*

crop, crops, cropping, cropped 1 (noun) Crops are plants such as wheat and potatoes that are grown for food. **2** The plants collected at harvest time are called a crop, e.g. *You should have two crops in the year.* **3** (verb) To crop someone's hair means to cut it very short.

croquet (pronounced **kroh**-kay) (noun) Croquet is a game in which the players use long-handled mallets to hit balls through metal arches pushed into a lawn.

cross, crosses, crossing, crossed; crosser, crossest 1 (verb) If you cross something such as a room or a road, you go to the other side of it. **2** Lines or roads that cross meet and go across each other. **3** If a thought crosses your mind, you think of it. **4** If you cross your arms, legs, or fingers, you put one on top of the other. **5** (noun) A cross consists of a vertical bar or line crossed by a shorter horizontal bar or line; also used to describe any object shaped like this. **6** The Cross is the cross-shaped structure on which Jesus Christ was crucified. A cross is also any symbol representing Christ's Cross. **7** A cross is also a written mark shaped like an X, e.g. *I drew a small bicycle and put a cross by it.* **8** Something that is a cross between two things is neither one thing nor the other, but a mixture of both. **9** (adjective) Someone who is cross is rather angry. **crossly** (adverb).

crossbow, crossbows (noun) A crossbow is a weapon consisting of a small bow fixed at the end of a piece of wood.

cross-country 1 (noun) Cross-country is the sport of running across open countryside, rather than on roads or on a track. **2** (adverb or adjective) across country.

cross-eyed (adjective) A cross-eyed person has eyes that seem to look towards each other.

crossfire (noun) Crossfire is gunfire crossing the same place from opposite directions.

crossing, crossings 1 (noun) A crossing is a place where you can cross a road safely. **2** A crossing is also a journey by ship to a place on the other side of the sea.

cross-legged (adjective) If you are sitting cross-legged, you are sitting on the floor with your knees pointing outwards and your feet tucked under them.

crossword, crosswords (noun) A crossword or a crossword puzzle is a puzzle in which you work out the answers to clues and write them in the white squares of a pattern of black and white squares.

crotch, crotches (noun) Your crotch is the part of your body between the tops of your legs.

crouch, crouches, crouching, crouched (verb) If you are crouching, you are leaning forward with your legs bent under you.

crow, crows, crowing, crowed 1 (noun) A crow is a large black bird which makes a loud, harsh noise. **2** (verb) When a cock crows, it utters a loud squawking sound.

crowbar, crowbars (noun) A crowbar is a heavy iron bar used as a lever or for forcing things open.

crowd, crowds, crowding, crowded 1 (noun) A crowd is a large group of people gathered together. **2** (verb) When people crowd somewhere, they gather there close together or in large numbers.

crowded (adjective) A crowded place is full of people.

crown, crowns, crowning, crowned 1 (noun) A crown is a circular ornament worn on a royal person's head. **2** (verb) When a king or queen is crowned, a crown is put on their head during their coronation ceremony. **3** (noun) The crown of something such as your head is the top part of it. **4** (verb) When something crowns an event, it is the final part of it, e.g. *The news crowned a dreadful week.*

crucial (pronounced **kroo**-shl) (adjective) If something is crucial, it is very important in determining how something else will be in the future.

crucifix, crucifixes (noun) A crucifix is a cross with a figure representing Jesus Christ being crucified on it.

crucify, crucifies, crucifying, crucified (verb) To crucify someone means to tie or nail them to a cross and leave them there to die. **crucifixion** (noun).

crude, cruder, crudest 1 (adjective) rough and simple, e.g. *a crude weapon... a crude method of entry.* **2** A crude person speaks or behaves in a rude and offensive way, e.g. *You can be quite crude at times.* **crudely** (adverb), **crudity** (noun).

cruel, crueller, cruellest (adjective) Cruel people deliberately cause pain or distress to other people or to animals. **cruelly** (adverb), **cruelty** (noun).

cruise, cruises, cruising, cruised 1 (noun) A cruise is a holiday in which you travel on a ship and visit places. **2** (verb) When a vehicle cruises, it moves at a constant moderate speed.

cruiser, cruisers 1 (noun) A cruiser is a motor boat with a cabin you can sleep in. **2** A cruiser is also a large, fast warship.

crumb, crumbs (noun) Crumbs are very small pieces of bread or cake.

crumble, crumbles, crumbling, crumbled (verb) When something crumbles, it breaks into small pieces.

crumbly (adjective) Something crumbly easily breaks into small pieces.

crumpet, crumpets (noun) A crumpet is a round, flat, breadlike cake which you eat toasted.

crumple, crumples, crumpling, crumpled (verb) To crumple paper or cloth means to squash it so that it is full of creases and folds.

crunch, crunches, crunching, crunched (verb) If you crunch something, you crush it noisily, for example between your teeth or under your feet.

crunchy, crunchier, crunchiest (adjective) Crunchy food is hard or crisp and makes a noise when you eat it.

crusade, crusades (noun) A crusade is a long and determined attempt to achieve something, e.g. *the crusade for human rights.* **crusader** (noun).

crush, crushes, crushing, crushed 1 (verb) To crush something means to destroy its shape by squeezing it. **2** To crush a substance means to turn it into liquid or powder by squeezing or grinding it. **3** To crush an army or political organization means to defeat it completely. **4** (noun) A crush is a dense crowd of people.

crust, crusts 1 (noun) The crust

of a loaf is the hard outside part. **2** A crust is also a hard layer on top of something, e.g. *The snow had a fine crust on it.*

crusty, crustier, crustiest 1 (adjective) Something that is crusty has a hard outside layer. **2** Crusty people are impatient and irritable.

crutch, crutches (noun) A crutch is a support like a long stick which you lean on to help you walk when you have an injured foot or leg.

crux (noun) The crux of a problem or argument is the most important or difficult part.

cry, cries, crying, cried 1 (verb) When you cry, tears appear in your eyes. **2** (noun) If you have a cry, you cry for a period of time. **3** (verb) To cry something means to shout it or say it loudly, e.g. *'See you soon!' they cried.* **4** (noun) A cry is a shout or other loud sound made with your voice. **5** A cry is also a loud sound made by some birds, e.g. *the cry of a seagull.*

crypt, crypts (noun) A crypt is an underground room beneath a church, usually used as a burial place.

cryptic (adjective) A cryptic remark or message has a hidden meaning.

crystal, crystals 1 (noun) A crystal is a piece of a mineral that has formed naturally into a regular shape. **2** Crystal is a type of transparent rock, used in jewellery. **3** Crystal is also a kind of very high quality glass. **crystalline** (adjective).

crystallize, crystallizes, crystallizing, crystallized; also spelled **crystallise 1** (verb) If a substance crystallizes, it turns into crystals. **2** If an idea crystallizes, it becomes clear in your mind.

cub, cubs 1 (noun) Some young wild animals are called cubs, e.g. *a lion cub.* **2** The Cubs is an organization for young boys before they join the Scouts.

Cuban, Cubans (pronounced **kyoo**-ban) **1** (adjective) belonging or relating to Cuba. **2** (noun) A Cuban is someone who comes from Cuba.

cube, cubes, cubing, cubed 1 (noun) A cube is a three-dimensional shape with six equally-sized square surfaces. **2** If you multiply a number by itself twice, you get its cube. **3** (verb) To cube a number means to multiply it by itself twice.

cubic (adjective) used in measurements of volume, e.g. *cubic centimetres... cubic feet.*

cubicle, cubicles (noun) A cubicle is a small enclosed area in a place such as a sports centre, where you can dress and undress.

cuckoo, cuckoos (noun) A cuckoo is a grey bird with a two-note call that lays its eggs in other birds' nests.

cucumber, cucumbers (noun) A cucumber is a long, thin, green-skinned vegetable eaten raw.

cuddle, cuddles, cuddling, cuddled 1 (verb) If you cuddle someone, you hold them affectionately in your arms. **2** (noun) If you give someone a cuddle, you hold them affectionately in your arms.

cuddly, cuddlier, cuddliest (adjective) Cuddly people, animals, or toys are soft or pleasing in some way so that you want to cuddle them.

cue, cues 1 (noun) A cue is something said or done by a performer that is a signal for another performer to begin, e.g. *Lettie never misses a cue.* **2** In snooker and billiards, a cue is a long stick used to hit the balls.

cuff, cuffs (noun) A cuff is the end part of a sleeve.

cufflink, cufflinks (noun) Cufflinks are small objects for holding shirt cuffs together.

cuisine (pronounced kwiz-**een**) (noun) The cuisine of a region is the style of cooking that is typical of it.

cul-de-sac, cul-de-sacs (pronounced **kul**-des-sak) (noun) A cul-de-sac is a road that does not lead to any other roads because one end is blocked off.

culinary (adjective; a formal word) connected with the kitchen, food, or cooking.

cull, culls, culling, culled 1 (verb) If you cull things, you gather them from different places or sources, e.g. *information culled from movies.* **2** (noun) When there is a cull, weaker animals are killed to reduce the numbers in a group.

culminate, culminates, culminating, culminated (verb) To culminate in something means to finally develop into it, e.g. *a campaign that culminated in a stunning success.* **culmination** (noun).

culprit, culprits (noun) A culprit is someone who has done something harmful or wrong.

cult, cults 1 (noun) A cult is a religious group with special rituals, usually connected with the worship of a particular person. **2** Cult is used to refer to any situation in which someone or something is very popular with a large group of people, e.g. *the American sports car cult.*

cultivate, cultivates, cultivating, cultivated 1 (verb) To cultivate land means to grow crops on it. **2** If you cultivate a feeling or attitude, you try to develop it in yourself or other people. **cultivation** (noun).

culture, cultures 1 (noun) Culture refers to the arts and to people's appreciation of them, e.g. *He was a man of culture.* **2** The culture of a particular society is its ideas, customs, and art, e.g. *Japanese culture.* **3** In science, a culture is a group of bacteria or cells grown in a laboratory. **cultured** (adjective), **cultural** (adjective).

cumulative (adjective) Something that is cumulative keeps being added to.

cunning 1 (adjective) Someone who is cunning uses clever and deceitful methods to get what they want. **2** (noun) Cunning is the ability to get what you want using clever and deceitful methods. **cunningly** (adverb).

cup, cups, cupping, cupped 1 (noun) A cup is a small, round container with a handle, which you drink out of. **2** A cup is also a large metal container with two handles, given as a prize. **3** (verb) If you cup your hands, you put them together to make a shape like a cup.

cupboard, cupboards (noun) A cupboard is a piece of furniture with doors and shelves.

curable (adjective) If a disease or illness is curable, it can be cured.

curate, curates (noun) A curate is a clergyman who helps a vicar or a priest.

curator, curators (noun) The curator of a museum or art gallery is the person in charge of its contents.

curb, curbs, curbing, curbed 1 (verb) To curb something means to keep it within definite limits, e.g. *policies designed to curb inflation.* **2** (noun) If a curb is placed on something, it is kept within definite limits, e.g. *the curb on spending.*

curdle, curdles, curdling, curdled (verb) When milk curdles, it turns sour.

curds (plural noun) Curds are the thick white substance formed when milk turns sour.

cure, cures, curing, cured 1 (verb) To cure an illness means to end it. **2** To cure a sick or injured person means to make them well. **3** (noun) A cure for an illness is something that cures it. **4** (verb) If something cures you of a habit or attitude, it stops you having it. **5** To cure food, tobacco, or animal skin means to treat it in order to preserve it.

curfew, curfews (noun) If there is a curfew, people must stay indoors between particular times at night.

curiosity, curiosities 1 (noun) Curiosity is the desire to know about something or about many things. **2** A curiosity is something unusual and interesting.

curious 1 (adjective) Someone who is curious wants to know more about something. **2** Something that is curious is unusual and hard to explain. **curiously** (adverb).

curl, curls, curling, curled 1 (noun) Curls are lengths of hair shaped in tight curves and circles. **2** A curl is a curved or spiral shape, e.g. *the curls of morning fog.* **3** (verb) If something curls, it moves in a curve or spiral. **curly** (adjective).

curler, curlers (noun) Curlers are plastic or metal tubes that women roll their hair round to make it curly.

curlew, curlews (pronounced **kur**-lyoo) (noun) A curlew is a large brown bird with a long curved beak and a loud cry.

currant, currants 1 (noun) Currants are small dried grapes often put in cakes and puddings. **2** Currants are also blackcurrants or redcurrants.

currency, currencies 1 (noun) A country's currency is its coins and banknotes, or its monetary system generally, e.g. *foreign currency... a strong economy and a weak currency.* **2** If something such as an idea has currency, it is used a lot at a particular time.

current, currents 1 (noun) The current in a river or in the sea is a strong continuous movement of the water. **2** An air current is a flowing movement in the air. **3** An electric current is a flow of electricity through a wire or circuit. **4** (adjective) Something that is current is happening, being done, or being used now. **currently** (adverb).

current affairs (plural noun) Current affairs are political and social events discussed in newspapers and on television and radio.

curriculum, curriculums or **curricula** (pronounced kur-**rik**-yoo-lum) (noun) The curriculum at a school or university consists of the different courses taught there.

curriculum vitae, curricula vitae (pronounced **vee**-tie) (noun) Someone's curriculum vitae is a written account of their personal details, education, and work experience which they send when they apply for a job.

curried (adjective) Curried food has been flavoured with hot spices, e.g. *curried lamb.*

curry, curries (noun) Curry is an Indian dish made with hot spices.

curse, curses, cursing, cursed 1 (verb) To curse means to swear because you are angry. **2** If you curse someone or something, you say angry things about them using rude words. **3** (noun) A curse is what you say when you curse. **4** A curse is also something supernatural that is supposed to cause unpleasant things to happen to someone. **5** A thing or person that causes a lot of distress can also be referred to as a curse, e.g. *the curse of recession.* **cursed** (adjective).

cursor, cursors (noun) A cursor is an indicator on a computer monitor which indicates where the next letter or symbol is.

cursory (adjective) When you give something a cursory glance or examination, you look at it briefly without paying attention to detail.

curt, curter, curtest (adjective) If someone is curt, they speak in a brief and rather rude way. **curtly** (adverb).

curtail, curtails, curtailing, curtailed (verb; a formal word) To curtail something means to reduce or restrict it, e.g. *Injury curtailed his career.*

curtain, curtains 1 (noun) A curtain is a hanging piece of material which can be pulled across a window for privacy or to keep out the light. **2** In a theatre, the curtain is a large piece of material which hangs in front of the stage until a performance begins.

curtsy, curtsies, curtsying, curtsied; also spelled **curtsey 1** (verb) When a woman curtsies, she lowers her body briefly, bending her knees, to show respect. **2** (noun) A curtsy is the movement a woman makes when she curtsies, e.g. *She gave a mock curtsy.*

curve, curves, curving, curved 1 (noun) A curve is a smooth, gradually bending line. **2** (verb) When something curves, it moves in a curve or has the shape of a curve, e.g. *The track curved away below him... His mouth curved slightly.* **curved** (adjective).

cushion, cushions, cushioning, cushioned 1 (noun) A cushion is a soft object put on a seat to make it more comfortable.

2 (verb) To cushion something means to reduce its effect, e.g. *We might have helped to cushion the shock for her.*

custard (noun) Custard is a sweet yellow sauce made from milk and eggs or milk and a powder.

custodian, custodians (noun) The custodian of a collection in an art gallery or a museum is the person in charge of it.

custody 1 (noun) To have custody of a child means to have the legal right to keep it and look after it, e.g. *She won custody of her younger son.* **2** (phrase) Someone who is **in custody** is being kept in prison until they can be tried in a court. **custodial** (adjective).

custom, customs 1 (noun) A custom is a traditional activity, e.g. *an ancient Chinese custom.* **2** A custom is also something usually done at a particular time or in particular circumstances by a person or by the people in a society, e.g. *It was also my custom to do Christmas shows.* **3** Customs is the place at a border, airport, or harbour where you have to declare goods. **4** (a formal use) If a shop or business has your custom, you buy things or go there regularly, e.g. *Banks are desperate to get your custom.*

customary (adjective) usual, e.g. *his customary modesty... her customary greeting.* **customarily** (adverb).

custom-built (adjective) Something that is custom-built or custom-made is made to someone's special requirements.

customer, customers 1 (noun) A shop's or firm's customers are the people who buy its goods. **2** (an informal use) You can use customer to refer to someone when describing what they are like to deal with, e.g. *a tough customer... a cool customer.*

cut, cuts, cutting, cut 1 (verb) If you cut something, you use a knife, scissors, or some other sharp tool to mark it, damage it, or remove parts of it. **2** (noun) If you make a cut in something, you mark it with a knife or other sharp tool. **3** (verb) If you cut yourself, you injure yourself on a sharp object. **4** (noun) A cut is an injury caused by a sharp object. **5** (verb) If you cut the amount of something, you reduce it, e.g. *Some costs could be cut.* **6** (noun) A cut in something is a reduction in it, e.g. *another cut in interest rates.* **7** (verb) When writing is cut, parts of it are not printed or broadcast. **8** (noun) A cut in something written is a part that is not printed or broadcast. **9** (adjective) Well cut clothes have been well designed and made, e.g. *this beautifully cut coat.* **10** (noun) A cut of meat is a large piece ready for cooking. **cut back** (verb) To cut back expenditure or cut back on it means to reduce it. **cutback** (noun). **cut down** (verb) If you cut down on an activity, you do it less often, e.g. *cutting down on smoking.* **cut off 1** (verb) To cut someone or something off means to separate them from things they are normally connected with, e.g. *The President had cut himself off from the people.* **2** If a supply of something is cut off, you no longer get it, e.g. *The water had been cut off.* **3** If your telephone or telephone call is cut off, it is disconnected. **cut out 1** (verb) If you cut out something you are doing, you stop doing it, e.g. *Cut out drinking.* **2** If an engine cuts out, it suddenly stops working.

cute, cuter, cutest (adjective) pretty or attractive.

cuticle, cuticles (noun) Your cuticles are the pieces of skin that cover the base of your fingernails and toenails.

cutlass, cutlasses (noun) A cutlass was a curved sword used by sailors.

cutlery (noun) Cutlery is knives, forks, and spoons.

cutlet, cutlets (noun) A cutlet is a small piece of meat which you fry or grill.

cutting, cuttings 1 (noun) A cutting is something cut from a newspaper or magazine. **2** A cutting from a plant is a part cut from it and used to grow a new plant. **3** (adjective) A cutting remark is unkind and likely to hurt someone.

CV an abbreviation for **curriculum vitae.**

cyanide (pronounced **sigh**-an-nide) (noun) Cyanide is an extremely poisonous chemical.

cycle, cycles, cycling, cycled 1 (verb) When you cycle, you ride a bicycle. **2** (noun) A cycle is a bicycle or a motorcycle. **3** A cycle is also a series of events which is repeated again and again in the same order, e.g. *the cycle of births and deaths.* **4** A cycle in an electrical, electronic, mechanical, or organic process is a single complete series of movements or events. **5** A cycle of songs or poems is a series of them intended to be performed or read together.

cyclical or **cyclic** (adjective) happening over and over again in cycles, e.g. *a clear cyclical pattern.*

cyclist, cyclists (noun) A cyclist is someone who rides a bicycle.

cyclone, cyclones (noun) A cyclone is a violent tropical storm.

cygnet, cygnets (pronounced **sig**-net) (noun) A cygnet is a young swan.

cylinder, cylinders 1 (noun) A cylinder is a regular three-dimensional shape with two equally-sized flat circular ends joined by a curved surface. **2** The cylinder in a motor engine is the part in which the piston moves backwards and forwards. **cylindrical** (adjective).

cymbal, cymbals (noun) A cymbal is a circular brass plate used as a percussion instrument. Cymbals are clashed together or hit with a stick.

cynic, cynics (pronounced **sin**-nik) (noun) A cynic is a cynical person.

cynical (adjective) believing that people always behave selfishly or dishonestly. **cynically** (adverb), **cynicism** (noun).

cypher another spelling of **cipher.**

cypress, cypresses (noun) A cypress is a type of evergreen tree with small dark green leaves and round cones.

cyst, cysts (pronounced **sist**) (noun) A cyst is a growth containing liquid that can form under your skin or inside your body.

czar another spelling of **tsar**.

czarina another spelling of **tsarina**.

Czech, Czechs (pronounced **chek**) **1** (adjective) belonging or relating to the Czech Republic. **2** (noun) A Czech is someone who comes from the Czech Republic. **3** Czech is the language spoken in the Czech Republic.

Czechoslovak, Czechoslovaks (pronounced chek-oh-**slow**-vak) **1** (adjective) belonging to or relating to the country that used to be Czechoslovakia. **2** (noun) A Czechoslovak was someone who came from the country that used to be Czechoslovakia.

D d

dab, dabs, dabbing, dabbed 1 (verb) If you dab something, you touch it with quick light strokes, e.g. *He dabbed some disinfectant on to the gash.* **2** (noun) A dab of something is a small amount that is put on a surface, e.g. *a dab of perfume.*

dabble, dabbles, dabbling, dabbled (verb) If you dabble in something, you work or play at it without being seriously involved in it, e.g. *dabbling in the paranormal.*

dachshund, dachshunds (pronounced **daks**-hoond) (noun) A dachshund is a small dog with a long body and very short legs.

dad, dads or **daddy, daddies** (noun; an informal word) Your dad or your daddy is your father.

daddy-long-legs (noun) A daddy-long-legs is a flying insect with very long legs.

daffodil, daffodils (noun) A daffodil is a plant with a yellow trumpet-shaped flower.

daft, dafter, daftest (adjective) foolish or slightly insane.

dagger, daggers (noun) A dagger is a weapon like a knife with a sharp pointed blade.

dahlia, dahlias (pronounced **dale**-ya) (noun) A dahlia is a type of brightly coloured garden flower.

daily 1 (adjective) occurring every day, e.g *our daily visit to the gym.* **2** of or relating to a single day or to one day at a time, e.g. *the average daily wage.*

dainty, daintier, daintiest (adjective) very delicate and pretty. **daintily** (adverb).

dairy, dairies 1 (noun) A dairy is a shop or company that supplies milk and milk products. **2** (adjective) Dairy products are foods made from milk, such as butter, cheese, cream, and yogurt. **3** A dairy farm is one which keeps cattle to produce milk.

dais (pronounced **day**-is) (noun) A dais is a raised platform, normally at one end of a hall and used by a speaker.

daisy, daisies (noun) A daisy is

a small wild flower with a yellow centre and small white petals.

dale, dales (noun) A dale is a valley.

dalmatian, dalmatians (noun) A dalmatian is a large dog with short smooth white hair and black or brown spots.

dam, dams (noun) A dam is a wall built across a river to hold back water.

damage, damages, damaging, damaged 1 (verb) To damage something means to harm or spoil it. **2** (noun) Damage to something is injury or harm done to it. **3** Damages is the sum of money claimed, or awarded by a court, to compensate someone for loss or harm. **damaging** (adjective).

dame, dames (noun) Dame is the title given to a woman who has been awarded the OBE or one of the other British orders of chivalry.

damn, damns, damning, damned (pronounced **dam**) **1** (verb) To damn something or someone means to curse or condemn them. **2** (interjection) 'Damn' is a swearword. **damned** (adjective).

damnation (pronounced dam-**nay**-shun) (noun) Damnation is everlasting punishment in Hell after death.

damp, damper, dampest 1 (adjective) slightly wet. **2** (noun) Damp is slight wetness or moisture, especially in the air or in the walls of a building. **dampness** (noun).

dampen, dampens, dampening, dampened 1 (verb) If you dampen something, you make it slightly wet. **2** To dampen something also means to reduce its liveliness, energy, or strength.

damper (an informal phrase) To **put a damper on** something means to stop it being enjoyable.

damson, damsons (noun) A damson is a small blue-black plum; also the tree that the fruit grows on.

dance, dances, dancing, danced 1 (verb) To dance means to move your feet and body rhythmically in time to music. **2** (noun) A dance is a series of rhythmic movements or steps in time to music. **3** A dance is also a social event where people dance with each other. **dancer** (noun), **dancing** (noun).

dandelion, dandelions (noun) A dandelion is a wild plant with yellow flowers which form a ball of fluffy seeds.

dandruff (noun) Dandruff is small, loose scales of dead skin in someone's hair.

dandy, dandies (noun; an old-fashioned use) A dandy is a man who dresses in smart clothes and is very concerned with his appearance.

Dane, Danes (noun) A Dane is someone who comes from Denmark.

danger, dangers 1 (noun) Danger is the possibility that someone may be harmed or killed. **2** A danger is something or someone that can hurt or harm you.

dangerous (adjective) able to or likely to cause hurt or harm. **dangerously** (adverb).

dangle, dangles, dangling, dangled (verb) When something dangles or when you dangle it, it swings or hangs loosely.

Danish 1 (adjective) belonging or relating to Denmark. **2** (noun) Danish is the main language spoken in Denmark.

dank, danker, dankest (adjective) A dank place is unpleasantly damp and chilly.

dapper (adjective) slim and neatly dressed.

dappled (adjective) marked with spots or patches of a different or darker shade.

dare, dares, daring, dared 1 (verb) To dare someone means to challenge them to do something in order to prove their courage. **2** To dare to do something means to have the courage to do it. **3** (noun) A dare is a challenge to do something dangerous or frightening.

daredevil, daredevils (noun) A daredevil is a person who enjoys doing dangerous things.

dark, darker, darkest 1 (adjective) If it is dark, there is not enough light to see properly. **2** (noun) The dark is the lack of light in a place. **3** (adjective) Dark colours or surfaces reflect little light and therefore look deep-coloured or dull. **4** Dark is also used to describe thoughts, ideas, or looks which are sinister, unpleasant, or frightening. **darkly** (adverb), **darkness** (noun).

darken, darkens, darkening, darkened (verb) If something darkens, or if you darken it, it becomes darker than it was.

darkroom, darkrooms (noun) A darkroom is a room from which daylight is shut out so that photographic film can be developed and processed.

darling, darlings 1 (noun) Someone who is lovable or a favourite may be called a darling. **2** (adjective) much admired or loved, e.g. *his darling daughter.*

darn, darns, darning, darned 1 (verb) To darn a hole in a garment means to mend it with a series of crossing stitches. **2** (noun) A darn is a part of a garment that has been darned.

dart, darts, darting, darted 1 (noun) A dart is a small pointed arrow. **2** Darts is a game in which the players throw a number of darts at a dartboard. **3** (verb) To dart about means to move quickly and suddenly from one place to another.

dash, dashes, dashing, dashed 1 (verb) To dash somewhere means to rush there. **2** If something is dashed against something else, it strikes it or is thrown violently against it. **3** If hopes or ambitions are dashed, they are ruined or frustrated. **4** (noun) A dash is a sudden movement or rush. **5** A dash of something is a small quantity of it. **6** In writing, a dash is the punctuation mark (–) which shows a change of subject, or which may be used instead of brackets.

dashboard, dashboards (noun) A dashboard is the instrument panel in a motor vehicle.

dashing (adjective) stylish, and giving an impression of confidence, e.g. *He was a dashing figure in his youth.*

data (noun) Data is information, usually in the form of

facts or statistics.

database, databases (noun) A database is a collection of information stored in a computer, that can easily be accessed and used.

date, dates, dating, dated 1 (noun) A date is a particular day or year that can be named. **2** If you have a date, you have an appointment to meet someone; also used to refer to the person you are meeting. **3** (verb) If you are dating someone, you have a romantic relationship with them. **4** If you date something, you find out the time when it began or was made. **5** If something dates from a particular time, that is when it happened or was made. **6** (phrase) If something is **out of date,** it is old-fashioned or no longer valid. **7** (noun) A date is a small dark-brown sticky fruit which grows on palm trees.

datum the singular form of **data.**

daub, daubs, daubing, daubed (verb) If you daub a substance such as mud or paint on a surface, you smear it there.

daughter, daughters (noun) Someone's daughter is their female child.

daughter-in-law, daughters-in-law (noun) Someone's daughter-in-law is the wife of their son.

daunt, daunts, daunting, daunted (verb) If something daunts you, you feel afraid or worried about whether you can succeed in doing it, e.g. *He was not the type of man to be daunted by adversity.* **daunting** (adjective).

dawn, dawns, dawning, dawned 1 (noun) Dawn is the time in the morning when light first appears in the sky. **2** The dawn of something is the beginning of it. **3** (verb) If day is dawning, morning light is beginning to appear. **4** If an idea or fact dawns on you, it gradually becomes apparent.

day, days 1 (noun) A day is one of the seven 24-hour periods of time in a week, measured from one midnight to the next. **2** Day is the period of light between sunrise and sunset. **3** You can refer to a particular day or days meaning a particular period in history, e.g. *in Gladstone's day.*

daybreak (noun) Daybreak is the time in the morning when light first appears in the sky.

daydream, daydreams, daydreaming, daydreamed 1 (noun) A daydream is a series of pleasant thoughts about things that you would like to happen. **2** (verb) When you daydream, you drift off into a daydream.

daylight 1 (noun) Daylight is the period during the day when it is light. **2** Daylight is also the light from the sun.

day-to-day (adjective) happening every day as part of ordinary routine life.

day trip, day trips (noun) A day trip is a journey for pleasure to a place and back again on the same day.

daze (phrase) If you are **in a daze,** you are confused and bewildered.

dazed (adjective) If you are dazed, you are stunned and unable to think clearly.

dazzle, dazzles, dazzling, dazzled 1 (verb) If someone or something dazzles you, you are extremely impressed by their brilliance. **2** If a bright light dazzles you, it blinds you for a moment. **dazzling** (adjective).

de- (prefix) When de- is added to a noun or verb, it changes the meaning to its opposite, e.g. *de-ice.*

deacon, deacons 1 (noun) In the Church of England or Roman Catholic Church, a deacon is a member of the clergy below the rank of priest. **2** In some other churches, a deacon is a church official appointed to help the minister. **deaconess** (noun).

dead 1 (adjective) no longer living or supporting life. **2** no longer used or no longer functioning, e.g. *a dead language.* **3** If part of your body goes dead, it loses sensation and feels numb. **4** (noun) The dead of night is the middle part of it, when it is most quiet and at its darkest.

dead end, dead ends (noun) A dead end is a street that is closed off at one end.

deadline, deadlines (noun) A deadline is a time or date before which a job or activity must be completed.

deadlock, deadlocks (noun) A deadlock is a situation in which neither side in a dispute is willing to give in.

deadly, deadlier, deadliest 1 (adjective) likely or able to cause death. **2** (adverb or adjective) Deadly is used to emphasize how serious or unpleasant a situation is, e.g. *deadly boring.*

deadpan (adjective or adverb) showing no emotion or expression.

deaf, deafer, deafest 1 (adjective) partially or totally unable to hear. **2** refusing to listen or pay attention to something, e.g. *He was deaf to all pleas for financial help.* **deafness** (noun).

deafening (adjective) If a noise is deafening, it is so loud that you cannot hear anything else.

deal, deals, dealing, dealt 1 (noun) A deal is an agreement or arrangement, especially in business. **2** (verb) If you deal with something, you do what is necessary to sort it out, e.g. *He must learn to deal with stress.* **3** If you deal in a particular type of goods, you buy and sell those goods. **4** If you deal someone or something a blow, you hurt or harm them, e.g. *Competition from abroad dealt a heavy blow to the industry.*

dealer, dealers (noun) A dealer is a person or firm whose business involves buying or selling things.

dealings (plural noun) Your dealings with people are the relations you have with them or the business you do with them.

dean, deans 1 (noun) In a university or college, a dean is a person responsible for administration or for the welfare of students. **2** In the Church of England, a dean is a clergyman who is responsible for the administration of a cathedral or a group of parishes.

dear, dears; dearer, dearest 1 (noun) Dear is used as a sign of affection, e.g *What's the matter, dear?* **2** (adjective) much loved, e.g. *my dear son.* **3** Something that is dear is very expensive. **4** You use dear at the beginning of a letter before the name of the person you are writing to. **dearly** (adverb).

dearth (pronounced **derth**) (noun) A dearth of something is a shortage of it.

death, deaths (noun) Death is the end of the life of a person or animal.

debacle, debacles (pronounced day-**bah**-kl) (noun; a formal word) A debacle is a sudden disastrous failure.

debase, debases, debasing, debased (verb) To debase something means to reduce its value or quality.

debatable (adjective) not absolutely certain, e.g. *The justness of these wars is debatable.*

debate, debates, debating, debated 1 (noun) Debate is argument or discussion, e.g. *There is much debate as to what causes depression.* **2** A debate is a formal discussion in which opposing views are expressed. **3** (verb) When people debate something, they discuss it in a fairly formal manner. **4** If you are debating whether or not to do something, you are considering it, e.g. *He was debating whether or not he should tell her.*

debilitating (adjective; a formal word) If something is debilitating, it makes you very weak, e.g. *a debilitating illness.*

debit, debits, debiting, debited 1 (verb) To debit a person's bank account means to take money from it. **2** (noun) A debit is a record of the money that has been taken out of a person's bank account.

debrief, debriefs, debriefing, debriefed (verb) When someone such as a soldier, astronaut, or diplomat is debriefed, they are asked to give a report on a task they have just completed. **debriefing** (noun).

debris (pronounced **day**-bree) (noun) Debris is fragments or rubble left after something has been destroyed.

debt, debts (pronounced **det**) **1** (noun) A debt is money that is owed to one person by another. **2** Debt is the state of owing money.

debtor, debtors (noun) A debtor is a person who owes money.

debut, debuts (pronounced **day**-byoo) (noun) A performer's debut is his or her first public appearance.

debutante, debutantes (pronounced **deb**-yoo-tant) (noun) A debutante is a girl from the upper classes who has started going to social events.

decade, decades (noun) A decade is a period of ten years.

decadence (noun) Decadence is a decline in standards of morality and behaviour. **decadent** (adjective).

decaffeinated (pronounced dee-**kaf**-in-ate-ed) (adjective) Decaffeinated coffee or tea has had most of the caffeine removed.

decanter, decanters (noun) A decanter is a glass bottle with a stopper, from which wine and other drinks are served.

decapitate, decapitates, decapitating, decapitated (verb) To decapitate someone means to cut off their head.

decathlon, decathlons (pronounced de-**cath**-lon) (noun) A decathlon is a sports contest in which athletes compete in ten different events.

decay, decays, decaying, decayed 1 (verb) When things decay, they rot or go bad. **2** (noun) Decay is the process of decaying.

deceased (a formal word) **1** (adjective) A deceased person is someone who has recently died. **2** (noun) The deceased is someone who has recently died.

deceit (noun) Deceit is behaviour that is intended to mislead people into believing something that is not true. **deceitful** (adjective).

deceive, deceives, deceiving, deceived (verb) If you deceive someone, you make them believe something that is not true, especially by lying or being dishonest.

December (noun) December is the twelfth and last month of the year. It has 31 days.

decency 1 (noun) Decency is behaviour that is respectable and follows accepted moral standards. **2** Decency is also behaviour which shows kindness and respect towards people, e.g. *No one had the decency to tell me to my face.*

decent 1 (adjective) of an acceptable standard or quality, e.g. *He gets a decent pension.* **2** Decent people are honest and respectable, e.g. *a decent man.* **decently** (adverb).

deception, deceptions 1 (noun) A deception is something that is intended to trick or deceive someone. **2** Deception is the act of deceiving someone.

deceptive (adjective) likely to make people believe something that is not true. **deceptively** (adverb).

decibel, decibels (noun) A decibel is a unit of the intensity of sound.

decide, decides, deciding, decided (verb) If you decide to do something, you choose to do it.

deciduous (adjective) Deciduous trees lose their leaves in the autumn every year.

decimal, decimals 1 (adjective) The decimal system expresses numbers using all the digits from 0 to 9. **2** (noun) A decimal is a fraction in which a dot called a decimal point is followed by numbers representing tenths, hundredths, and thousandths. For example, 0.5 represents $\frac{5}{10}$ (or $\frac{1}{2}$); 0.05 represents $\frac{5}{100}$ (or $\frac{1}{20}$).

decimate, decimates, decimating, decimated (verb) To decimate a group of people or animals means to kill or destroy a large number of them.

decipher, deciphers, deciphering, deciphered (verb) If you decipher a piece of writing or a message, you work out its meaning.

decision, decisions (noun) A decision is a choice or judgment that is made about something, e.g. *The editor's decision is final.*

decisive (pronounced dis-**sigh**-

siv) **1** (adjective) having great influence on the result of something, e.g. *It was the decisive moment of the race.* **2** A decisive person is able to make decisions firmly and quickly. **decisively** (adverb), **decisiveness** (noun).

deck, decks 1 (noun) A deck is a floor or platform built into a ship, or one of the two floors on a bus. **2** A deck of cards is a pack of them.

deck chair, deck chairs (noun) A deck chair is a light portable folding chair which is used outdoors.

declaration, declarations (noun) A declaration is a firm, forceful statement, often an official announcement, e.g. *a declaration of war.*

declare, declares, declaring, declared 1 (verb) If you declare something, you say it firmly and forcefully, e.g *He declared early he was going to be famous.* **2** To declare something means to announce it officially or formally, e.g. *Catholicism was declared the state religion.* **3** If you declare goods or earnings, you state what you have bought or earned, in order to pay tax or duty.

decline, declines, declining, declined 1 (verb) If something declines, it becomes smaller, weaker, or less important. **2** (noun) A decline is a gradual weakening or decrease, e.g. *a decline in the birth rate.* **3** (verb) If you decline something, you politely refuse to accept it or do it.

decode, decodes, decoding, decoded (verb) If you decode a coded message, you convert it into ordinary language.

decompose, decomposes, decomposing, decomposed (verb) If something decomposes, it decays through chemical or bacterial action.

decor (pronounced **day**-kor) (noun) The decor of a room or house is the style in which it is decorated and furnished.

decorate, decorates, decorating, decorated 1 (verb) If you decorate something, you make it more attractive by adding some ornament or colour to it. **2** If you decorate a room or building, you paint or wallpaper it.

decoration, decorations 1 (noun) Decorations are features or ornaments added to something to make it more attractive. **2** The decoration in a building or room is the style of the furniture, wallpaper, and ornaments.

decorative (adjective) intended to look attractive.

decorator, decorators (noun) A decorator is a person whose job is painting and wallpapering rooms and buildings.

decorum (pronounced dik-**ore**-um) (noun; a formal word) Decorum is polite and correct behaviour.

decoy, decoys (noun) A decoy is a person or object that is used to lead someone or something into danger.

decrease, decreases, decreasing, decreased 1 (verb) If something decreases or if you decrease it, it becomes less in quantity, size, or strength. **2** (noun) A decrease is a lessening in the amount of something; also the amount by which something becomes less. **decreasing** (adjective).

decree, decrees, decreeing, decreed 1 (verb) If someone decrees something, they state formally that it will happen. **2** (noun) A decree is an official decision or order, usually by governments or rulers.

dedicate, dedicates, dedicating, dedicated (verb) If you dedicate yourself to something, you devote your time and energy to it. **dedication** (noun).

deduce, deduces, deducing, deduced (verb) If you deduce something, you work it out from other facts that you know are true.

deduct, deducts, deducting, deducted (verb) To deduct an amount from a total amount means to subtract it from the total.

deduction, deductions 1 (noun) A deduction is an amount which is taken away from a total. **2** A deduction is also a conclusion that you have reached because of other things that you know are true.

deed, deeds 1 (noun) A deed is something that is done. **2** A deed is also a legal document, especially concerning the ownership of land or buildings.

deem, deems, deeming, deemed (verb; a formal use) If you deem something to be true, you judge or consider it to be true, e.g. *His ideas were deemed unacceptable.*

deep, deeper, deepest 1 (adjective) situated or extending a long way down from the top surface of something, or a long way inwards, e.g. *a deep hole.* **2** great or intense, e.g. *deep suspicion.* **3** low in pitch, e.g. *a deep voice.* **4** strong and fairly dark in colour, e.g. *The claret was deep ruby in colour.* **deeply** (adverb).

deepen, deepens, deepening, deepened (verb) If something deepens or is deepened, it becomes deeper or more intense.

deer (noun) A deer is a large, hoofed mammal that lives wild in parts of Britain.

deface, defaces, defacing, defaced (verb) If you deface a wall or notice, you spoil it by writing or drawing on it, e.g. *She spitefully defaced her sister's poster.*

default, defaults, defaulting, defaulted 1 (verb) If you default on an obligation, you fail to do what you are supposed to do, e.g. *He defaulted on repayment of the loan.* **2** (phrase) If something happens **by default,** it happens because something else which might have prevented it has failed to happen.

defeat, defeats, defeating, defeated 1 (verb) If you defeat someone or something, you win a victory over them, or cause them to fail. **2** (noun) Defeat is the state of being beaten or of failing, e.g. *He was gracious in defeat.* **3** A defeat is an occasion on which someone is beaten or fails to achieve something, e.g. *It was a crushing defeat for the government.*

defecate, defecates, defecating, defecated (verb) To defecate means to get rid of waste matter from the bowels through the anus.

defect, defects, defecting, de-

fected 1 (noun) A defect is a fault or flaw in something. **2** (verb) If someone defects, they leave their own country or organization and join an opposing one. **defection** (noun).

defective (adjective) imperfect or faulty, e.g. *defective eyesight.*

defence, defences 1 (noun) Defence is action that is taken to protect someone or something from attack. **2** A defence is any arguments, writing, or speech used in support of something that has been criticized or questioned. **3** In a court of law, the defence is the case presented by a lawyer for the person on trial; also the person on trial and his or her lawyers. **4** A country's defences are its military resources, such as its armed forces.

defend, defends, defending, defended 1 (verb) To defend someone or something means to protect them from harm or danger. **2** If you defend a person or their ideas and beliefs, you argue in support of them. **3** To defend someone in court means to represent them and argue their case for them. **4** In a game such as football or hockey, to defend means to try to prevent goals being scored by your opponents. **defender** (noun).

defendant, defendants (noun) A defendant is a person who has been accused of a crime in a court of law.

defensible (adjective) able to be defended or justified against criticism or attack.

defensive 1 (adjective) intended or designed for protection, e.g. *defensive weapons.* **2** Someone who is defensive feels unsure and threatened by other people's opinions and attitudes, e.g. *Don't get defensive, I was only joking.* **defensively** (adverb), **defensiveness** (noun).

defer, defers, deferring, deferred 1 (verb) If you defer something, you delay or postpone it until a future time. **2** If you defer to someone, you agree with them or do what they want because you respect them.

deference (pronounced **def**-erense) (noun) Deference is polite and respectful behaviour. **deferential** (adjective).

defiance (noun) Defiance is behaviour which shows that you are not willing to obey someone or behave in the expected way, e.g. *a gesture of defiance.* **defiant** (adjective), **defiantly** (adverb).

deficiency, deficiencies (noun) A deficiency is a lack of something, e.g. *vitamin deficiency.* **deficient** (adjective).

deficit, deficits (pronounced **def**-iss-it) (noun) A deficit is the amount by which money received by an organization is less than money spent.

define, defines, defining, defined (verb) If you define something, you describe its nature, e.g. *Culture can be defined in hundreds of different ways.*

definite 1 (adjective) firm, clear, and unlikely to be changed, e.g. *The answer is a definite 'yes'.* **2** certain or true rather than guessed or imagined, e.g. *definite proof.* **definitely** (adverb).

definition, definitions (noun) A definition is a statement explaining the meaning of a word, expression, or idea.

definitive 1 (adjective) final and unable to be questioned or altered, e.g. *a definitive answer.* **2** most complete, or the best of its kind, e.g. *a definitive history of science fiction.* **definitively** (adverb).

deflate, deflates, deflating, deflated 1 (verb) If you deflate something such as a tyre or balloon, you let out all the air or gas in it. **2** If you deflate someone, you take away their confidence or make them seem less important.

deflect, deflects, deflecting, deflected (verb) To deflect something means to turn it aside, divert it, or make it change direction. **deflection** (noun).

deformed (adjective) disfigured or abnormally shaped.

defraud, defrauds, defrauding, defrauded (verb) If someone defrauds you, they cheat you out of something that should be yours.

defrost, defrosts, defrosting, defrosted 1 (verb) If you defrost a freezer or refrigerator, you remove the ice from it. **2** If you defrost frozen food, you let it thaw out.

deft, defter, deftest (adjective) Someone who is deft is quick and skilful in their movements. **deftly** (adverb).

defunct (adjective) no longer existing or functioning.

defuse, defuses, defusing, defused 1 (verb) To defuse a dangerous or tense situation means to make it less dangerous or tense. **2** To defuse a bomb means to remove its fuse or detonator so that it cannot explode.

defy, defies, defying, defied 1 (verb) If you defy a person or a law, you openly refuse to obey. **2** (a formal use) If you defy someone to do something that you think is impossible, you challenge them to do it.

degenerate, degenerates, degenerating, degenerated 1 (verb) If something degenerates, it becomes worse, e.g. *The election campaign degenerated into farce.* **2** (adjective) having low standards of morality. **3** (noun) A degenerate is someone whose standards of morality are so low that people find their behaviour shocking or disgusting. **degeneration** (noun).

degradation (noun) Degradation is a state of poverty and misery.

degrade, degrades, degrading, degraded (verb) If something degrades people, it humiliates or corrupts them. **degrading** (adjective).

degree, degrees 1 (noun) A degree is an amount of a feeling or quality, e.g. *a degree of pain.* **2** A degree is a unit of measurement of temperature; often written as ° after a number, e.g. *20°C.* **3** A degree is also a unit of measurement of angles in mathematics, and of latitude and longitude, e.g. *The yacht was 20° off course.* **4** A degree at a university or college is a course of study there; also the qualification obtained after passing the course.

dehydrated (adjective) If someone is dehydrated, they are weak or ill because they have lost too much water from their body.

deign, deigns, deigning, deigned (pronounced **dane**) (verb; a formal word) If you deign to do something, you do it even though you think you are too important to do such a thing.

deity, deities (noun) A deity is a god or goddess.

deja vu (pronounced **day**-ja **voo**) (noun) Deja vu is the feeling that you have already experienced in the past exactly the same sequence of events as is happening now.

dejected (adjective) miserable and unhappy. **dejection** (noun).

delay, delays, delaying, delayed 1 (verb) If you delay doing something, you put it off until a later time. **2** If something delays you, it hinders you or slows you down. **3** (noun) Delay is time during which something is delayed.

delectable (adjective) very pleasing or delightful.

delegate, delegates, delegating, delegated 1 (noun) A delegate is a person appointed to vote or to make decisions on behalf of a group of people. **2** (verb) If you delegate duties or power, you give them to someone who can then act on your behalf.

delegation, delegations 1 (noun) A delegation is a group of people chosen to represent a larger group of people. **2** Delegation is the giving of duties, responsibilities, or power to someone who can then act on your behalf.

delete, deletes, deleting, deleted (verb) To delete something written means to cross it out or remove it. **deletion** (noun).

deliberate, deliberates, deliberating, deliberated 1 (adjective) done on purpose or planned in advance, e.g. *It was a deliberate insult.* **2** careful and not hurried in speech and action, e.g. *She was very deliberate in her movements.* **3** (verb) If you deliberate about something, you think about it seriously and carefully. **deliberately** (adverb).

deliberation, deliberations (noun) Deliberation is careful and often lengthy consideration of a subject.

delicacy, delicacies 1 (noun) Delicacy is grace and attractiveness. **2** Something said or done with delicacy is said or done carefully and tactfully so that nobody is offended. **3** Delicacies are rare or expensive foods that are considered especially nice to eat.

delicate 1 (adjective) fine, graceful, or subtle in character, e.g. *a delicate fragrance.* **2** fragile and needing to be handled carefully, e.g. *delicate antique lace.* **3** precise or sensitive, and able to notice very small changes, e.g. *a delicate instrument.* **delicately** (adverb).

delicatessen, delicatessens (noun) A delicatessen is a shop selling unusual or imported foods.

delicious (adjective) very pleasing, especially to taste. **deliciously** (adverb).

delight, delights, delighting, delighted 1 (noun) Delight is great pleasure or joy. **2** (verb) If something delights you or if you are delighted by it, it gives you a lot of pleasure. **delighted** (adjective).

delightful (adjective) very pleasant and attractive.

delinquent, delinquents (noun) A delinquent is a young person who repeatedly commits minor crimes. **delinquency** (noun).

delirious 1 (adjective) unable to speak or act in a rational way because of illness or fever. **2** wildly excited and happy. **deliriously** (adverb).

deliver, delivers, delivering, delivered 1 (verb) If you deliver something to someone, you take it to them and give them it. **2** To deliver a lecture or speech means to give it.

delivery, deliveries 1 (noun) Delivery or a delivery is the bringing of letters, parcels, or goods to a person or firm. **2** Someone's delivery is the way in which they give a speech.

dell, dells (noun; a literary word) A dell is a small wooded valley.

delta, deltas (noun) A delta is a low, flat area at the mouth of a river where silt has been deposited and where the river has split into several branches to enter the sea.

delude, deludes, deluding, deluded (verb) To delude people means to deceive them into believing something that is not true.

deluge, deluges, deluging, deluged 1 (noun) A deluge is a sudden, heavy downpour of rain. **2** (verb) To be deluged with things means to be overwhelmed by a great number of them.

delusion, delusions (noun) A delusion is a mistaken or misleading belief or idea.

de luxe (pronounced de **luks**) (adjective) rich, luxurious, or of superior quality.

delve, delves, delving, delved (verb) If you delve into something, you seek out more information about it.

demand, demands, demanding, demanded 1 (verb) If you demand something, you ask for it forcefully and urgently. **2** If a job or situation demands a particular quality, it needs it, e.g. *This situation demands hard work.* **3** (noun) A demand is a forceful request for something. **4** If there is a demand for something, a lot of people want to buy it or have it.

demean, demeans, demeaning, demeaned (verb) If you demean yourself, you do something which lowers your dignity and makes people have less respect for you. **demeaning** (adjective).

demeanour (noun) Your demeanour is the way you behave and the impression that this creates.

demented (adjective) Someone who is demented behaves in a wild or violent way.

dementia (pronounced dee-**men**-sha) (noun; a medical word) Dementia is a serious illness of the mind.

demi- (prefix) Demi- means half.

demise (pronounced dee-**myz**)

(noun; a formal word) Someone's demise is their death.

demo, demos (noun; an informal word) A demo is a demonstration.

democracy, democracies (noun) Democracy is a system of government in which the people choose their leaders by voting for them in elections.

democrat, democrats (noun) A democrat is a person who believes in democracy, personal freedom, and equality.

democratic (adjective) having representatives elected by the people. **democratically** (adverb).

demolish, demolishes, demolishing, demolished (verb) To demolish a building means to pull it down or break it up. **demolition** (noun).

demon, demons 1 (noun) A demon is an evil spirit or devil. **2** (adjective) skilful, keen, and energetic, e.g. *a demon squash player*. **demonic** (adjective).

demonstrate, demonstrates, demonstrating, demonstrated 1 (verb) To demonstrate a fact, theory, or principle means to prove or show it to be true. **2** If you demonstrate something to somebody, you show and explain it by using or doing the thing itself, e.g. *She demonstrated how to apply the make-up.* **3** If people demonstrate, they take part in a march, meeting, or rally to show their opposition to something or their support for something.

demonstration, demonstrations 1 A demonstration is a talk or explanation to show how to do or use something. **2** Demonstration is proof that something exists or is true. **3** A demonstration is also a public march, meeting, or rally in support of or opposition to something. **demonstrator** (noun).

demote, demotes, demoting, demoted (verb) A person who is demoted is put in a lower rank or position, often as a punishment. **demotion** (noun).

demure (adjective) Someone who is demure is quiet, shy, and behaves very modestly. **demurely** (adverb).

den, dens (noun) A den is the home of some wild animals such as lions or foxes.

denial, denials 1 (noun) A denial of something is a statement that it is untrue, e.g. *He published a firm denial of the report.* **2** The denial of a request or something to which you have a right is the refusal of it, e.g. *the denial of human rights.*

denigrate, denigrates, denigrating, denigrated (verb; a formal word) To denigrate someone or something means to criticize them in order to damage their reputation.

denim, denims 1 (noun) Denim is strong cotton cloth, used for making clothes. **2** (plural noun) Denims are jeans made from denim.

denomination, denominations 1 (noun) A religious denomination is a particular group which has slightly different beliefs from other groups within the same faith. **2** A denomination is a unit in a system of weights, values, or measures, e.g. *a high denomination note.*

denominator, denominators (noun) In maths, the denominator is the bottom part of a fraction.

denote, denotes, denoting, denoted (verb) If one thing denotes another, it is a sign of it or it represents it, e.g. *Formerly, a tan denoted wealth.*

denounce, denounces, denouncing, denounced 1 (verb) If you denounce someone or something, you express very strong disapproval of them, e.g. *He publicly denounced government nuclear policy.* **2** If you denounce someone, you give information against them, e.g. *He was denounced as a dangerous agitator.*

dense, denser, densest 1 (adjective) thickly crowded or packed together, e.g. *the dense crowd.* **2** difficult to see through, e.g. *dense black smoke.* **densely** (adverb).

density, densities (noun) The density of something is the degree to which it is filled, concentrated, or occupied, e.g. *a very high population density.*

dent, dents, denting, dented 1 (verb) To dent something means to damage it by hitting it and making a hollow in its surface. **2** (noun) A dent is a hollow in the surface of something.

dental (adjective) relating to the teeth.

dentist, dentists (noun) A dentist is a person who is qualified to treat people's teeth.

dentistry (noun) Dentistry is the branch of medicine concerned with disorders of the teeth.

denture, dentures (noun) Dentures are false teeth.

denunciation, denunciations (noun) A denunciation of someone or something is severe public criticism of them.

deny, denies, denying, denied 1 (verb) If you deny something that has been said, you state that it is untrue. **2** If you deny that something is the case, you refuse to believe it or accept it, e.g. *He denied the existence of the human soul.* **3** If you deny someone something, you refuse to give it to them or you prevent them from having it, e.g. *They were denied freedom.*

deodorant, deodorants (noun) A deodorant is a substance or spray used to hide or prevent the smell of perspiration.

depart, departs, departing, departed (verb) When you depart, you leave. **departure** (noun).

department, departments (noun) A department is one of the sections into which an organization is divided, e.g. *the history department.* **departmental** (adjective).

depend, depends, depending, depended 1 (verb) If you depend on someone or something, you trust them and rely on them. **2** If one thing depends on another, it is influenced or determined by it, e.g. *Success depends on the quality of the workforce.*

dependable (adjective) reliable and trustworthy.

dependant, dependants (noun) A dependant is someone who relies on another person for financial support.

dependence (noun) Dependence is a constant and regular need that someone has for something or someone in order to survive or operate properly, e.g. *He was flattered by her dependence on him.*

dependency, dependencies (noun) A dependency is a country or province controlled by another country.

dependent (adjective) reliant on someone or something.

depict, depicts, depicting, depicted (verb) To depict someone or something means to represent them in painting or sculpture.

deplete, depletes, depleting, depleted (verb) To deplete something means to reduce greatly the amount of it available. **depletion** (noun).

deplorable (adjective) shocking or regrettable, e.g. *deplorable conditions.*

deplore, deplores, deploring, deplored (verb) If you deplore something, you condemn it because you feel it is wrong.

deploy, deploys, deploying, deployed (verb) To deploy troops or resources means to organize or position them so that they can be used effectively. **deployment** (noun).

deport, deports, deporting, deported (verb) If a government deports someone, it sends them out of the country because they have committed a crime or because they do not have the right to be there. **deportation** (noun).

depose, deposes, deposing, deposed (verb) If someone is deposed, they are removed from a position of power.

deposit, deposits, depositing, deposited 1 (verb) If you deposit something, you put it down or leave it somewhere. **2** If you deposit money or valuables, you put them somewhere for safekeeping. **3** (noun) A deposit is money given in part payment for goods or services.

depot, depots (pronounced **dep**-oh) (noun) A depot is a place where large supplies of materials or equipment may be stored.

depraved (adjective) morally bad.

depress, depresses, depressing, depressed 1 (verb) If something depresses you, it makes you feel sad and gloomy. **2** If wages or prices are depressed, their value falls. **depressive** (adjective or noun).

depressant, depressants (noun) A depressant is a drug which reduces nervous activity and so has a calming effect.

depressed 1 (adjective) unhappy and gloomy. **2** A place that is depressed has little economic activity and therefore low incomes and high unemployment, e.g. *depressed industrial areas.*

depression, depressions 1 (noun) Depression is a state of mind in which someone feels unhappy and has no energy or enthusiasm. **2** A depression is a time of industrial and economic decline.

deprive, deprives, depriving, deprived (verb) If you deprive someone of something, you take it away or prevent them from having it. **deprived** (adjective), **deprivation** (noun).

depth, depths 1 (noun) The depth of something is the measurement or distance between its top and bottom, or between its front and back. **2** The depth of something such as emotion is its intensity, e.g. *the depth of her hostility.*

deputation, deputations (noun) A deputation is a small group of people sent to speak or act on behalf of others.

deputy, deputies (noun) Someone's deputy is a person appointed to act in their place.

deranged (adjective) mad, or behaving in a wild and uncontrolled way.

derby, derbies (pronounced **dar**-bee) (noun) A local derby is a sporting event between two teams from the same area.

derelict (adjective) abandoned and falling into ruins.

deride, derides, deriding, derided (verb) To deride someone or something means to mock or jeer at them with contempt.

derision (noun) Derision is an attitude of contempt or scorn towards something or someone.

derivation, derivations (noun) The derivation of something is its origin or source.

derivative, derivatives 1 (noun) A derivative is something which has developed from an earlier source. **2** (adjective) not original, but based on or copied from something else, e.g. *The record was not deliberately derivative.*

derive, derives, deriving, derived 1 (verb; a formal use) If you derive something from someone or something, you get it from them, e.g. *He derived so much joy from life.* **2** If something derives from something else, it develops from it.

derogatory (adjective) critical and scornful, e.g. *He made derogatory remarks about them.*

descant, descants (noun) The descant to a tune is another tune played at the same time and at a higher pitch.

descend, descends, descending, descended 1 (verb) To descend means to move downwards. **2** If you descend on people or on a place, you arrive unexpectedly.

descendant, descendants (noun) A person's descendants are the people in later generations who are descended from them.

descended (adjective) If you are descended from someone who lived in the past, your family originally derived from them.

descent, descents 1 (noun) A descent is a movement or slope from a higher to a lower position or level. **2** Your descent is your family's origins.

describe, describes, describing, described (verb) To describe someone or something means to give an account or a picture of them in words.

description, descriptions (noun) A description is an account or picture of something in words. **descriptive** (adjective).

desert, deserts, deserting, deserted For sense 1, the pronunciation is **dez**-ert. Sense 2 is pronounced diz-**zert**. **1**

(noun) A desert is a region of land with very little plant life, usually because of low rainfall. **2** (verb) To desert a person means to leave or abandon them, e.g. *His clients had deserted him.* **desertion** (noun).

deserter, deserters (noun) A deserter is someone who leaves the army, navy, or air force without permission.

deserve, deserves, deserving, deserved (verb) If you deserve something, you are entitled to it or earn it because of your qualities, achievements, or actions, e.g. *He deserved a rest.*

deserving (adjective) worthy of being helped, rewarded, or praised, e.g. *a deserving charity.*

design, designs, designing, designed 1 (verb) To design something means to plan it, especially by preparing a detailed sketch or drawings from which it can be built or made. **2** (noun) A design is a drawing or plan from which something can be built or made. **3** The design of something is its shape and style. **designer** (noun).

designate, designates, designating, designated (pronounced **dez**-ig-nate) **1** (verb) To designate someone or something means to formally label or name them, e.g. *The room was designated a no smoking area.* **2** If you designate someone to do something, you appoint them to do it, e.g. *He designated his son as his successor.*

designation, designations (noun) A designation is a name or title.

designing (adjective) crafty and cunning.

desirable 1 (adjective) worth having or doing, e.g. *a desirable job.* **2** sexually attractive. **desirability** (noun).

desire, desires, desiring, desired 1 (verb) If you desire something, you want it very much. **2** (noun) A desire is a strong feeling of wanting something. **3** Desire for someone is a strong sexual attraction to them.

desist, desists, desisting, desisted (verb; a formal word) To desist from doing something means to stop doing it.

desk, desks 1 (noun) A desk is a piece of furniture, often with drawers, designed for working at or writing on. **2** A desk is also a counter or table in a public building behind which a receptionist sits.

desktop (adjective) of a convenient size to be used on a desk or table, e.g. *a desktop computer.*

desolate 1 (adjective) deserted and bleak, e.g. *a desolate mountainous region.* **2** lonely, very sad, and without hope, e.g. *He was desolate without her.* **desolation** (noun).

despair, despairs, despairing, despaired 1 (noun) Despair is a total loss of hope. **2** (verb) If you despair, you lose hope, e.g. *He despaired of finishing it.* **despairing** (adjective).

despatch another spelling of **dispatch.**

desperate 1 (adjective) If you are desperate, you are so worried or frightened that you will try anything to improve your situation, e.g. *a desperate* *attempt to save their marriage.* **2** A desperate person is violent and dangerous. **3** A desperate situation is extremely dangerous, difficult, or serious. **desperately** (adverb), **desperation** (noun).

despicable (adjective) deserving contempt.

despise, despises, despising, despised (verb) If you despise someone or something, you have a very low opinion of them and dislike them.

despite (preposition) in spite of, e.g. *He fell asleep despite all the coffee he'd drunk.*

despondent (adjective) dejected and unhappy. **despondency** (noun).

dessert, desserts (pronounced diz-**ert**) (noun) A dessert is sweet food served after the main course of a meal.

destination, destinations (noun) A destination is a place to which someone or something is going or is being sent.

destined (adjective) meant or intended to happen, e.g. *I was destined for fame and fortune.*

destiny, destinies 1 (noun) Your destiny is all the things that happen to you in your life, especially when they are considered to be outside human control. **2** Destiny is the force which some people believe controls everyone's life.

destitute (adjective) without money or possessions, and therefore in great need. **destitution** (noun).

destroy, destroys, destroying, destroyed 1 (verb) To destroy something means to damage it so much that it is completely ruined. **2** To destroy something means to put an end to it, e.g. *The holiday destroyed their friendship.*

destruction (noun) Destruction is the act of destroying something or the state of being destroyed.

destructive (adjective) causing or able to cause great harm, damage, or injury. **destructiveness** (noun).

desultory (pronounced **dez**-ul-tree) (adjective) unplanned, disorganized, and without enthusiasm, e.g. *A desultory, embarrassed chatter began.*

detach, detaches, detaching, detached (verb) To detach something means to remove or unfasten it, e.g. *The hood can be detached.* **detachable** (adjective).

detached 1 (adjective) separate or standing apart, e.g. *a detached house.* **2** having no real interest or emotional involvement in something, e.g. *He observed me with a detached curiosity.*

detachment, detachments 1 (noun) Detachment is the feeling of not being personally involved with something, e.g. *A stranger can view your problems with detachment.* **2** A detachment is a small group of soldiers sent to do a special job.

detail, details 1 (noun) A detail is an individual fact or feature of something, e.g. *We discussed every detail of the performance.* **2** Detail is all the small features that make up the whole of something, e.g. *Look at the detail.* **detailed** (adjective).

detain, detains, detaining, detained **1** (verb) To detain someone means to force them to stay, e.g. *She was being detained for interrogation.* **2** If you detain someone, you delay them, e.g. *I mustn't detain you.*

detect, detects, detecting, detected **1** (verb) If you detect something, you notice it, e.g. *I detected a glimmer of interest in his eyes.* **2** To detect something means to find it, e.g. *Cancer can be detected by X-rays.* **detectable** (adjective).

detection (noun) Detection is the act of noticing, discovering, or sensing something.

detective, detectives (noun) A detective is a person, usually a police officer, whose job is to investigate crimes.

detector, detectors (noun) A detector is an instrument which is used to detect the presence of something, e.g. *a metal detector.*

detention (noun) The detention of someone is their arrest or imprisonment.

deter, deters, deterring, deterred (verb) To deter someone means to discourage or prevent them from doing something by creating a feeling of fear or doubt, e.g. *99 per cent of burglars are deterred by the sight of an alarm box.*

detergent, detergents (noun) A detergent is a chemical substance used for washing or cleaning things.

deteriorate, deteriorates, deteriorating, deteriorated (verb) If something deteriorates, it gets worse, e.g. *My father's health has deteriorated lately.* **deterioration** (noun).

determination (noun) Determination is great firmness, after you have made up your mind to do something, e.g. *They shared a determination to win the war.*

determine, determines, determining, determined **1** (verb) If something determines a situation or result, it causes it or controls it, e.g. *The track surface determines his tactics in a race.* **2** To determine something means to decide or settle it firmly, e.g. *The date has still to be determined.* **3** To determine something means to find out or calculate the facts about it, e.g. *He bit the coin to determine whether it was genuine.*

determined (adjective) firmly decided, e.g. *She was determined not to repeat her error.* **determinedly** (adverb).

deterrent, deterrents (noun) A deterrent is something that prevents you from doing something by making you afraid of what will happen if you do it, e.g. *Capital punishment was no deterrent to domestic murders.* **deterrence** (noun).

detest, detests, detesting, detested (verb) If you detest someone or something, you strongly dislike them.

detonate, detonates, detonating, detonated (verb) To detonate a bomb or mine means to cause it to explode. **detonator** (noun).

detour, detours (noun) A detour is an alternative, less direct route.

detract, detracts, detracting, de-

tracted (verb) To detract from something means to make it seem less good or valuable.

detriment (noun) Detriment is disadvantage or harm, e.g. *a detriment to their health.* **detrimental** (adjective).

deuce, deuces (pronounced **joos**) (noun) In tennis, deuce is the score of forty all.

devalue, devalues, devaluing, devalued (verb) To devalue something means to lower its status, importance, or worth. **devaluation** (noun).

devastate, devastates, devastating, devastated (verb) To devastate an area or place means to damage it severely or destroy it. **devastation** (noun).

devastated (adjective) very shocked or upset, e.g. *The family are devastated by the news.*

develop, develops, developing, developed 1 (verb) When something develops or is developed, it grows or becomes more advanced, e.g. *The sneezing developed into a full blown cold.* **2** To develop an area of land means to build on it. **3** To develop an illness or a fault means to become affected by it.

developer, developers (noun) A developer is a person or company that builds on land.

development, developments 1 (noun) Development is gradual growth or progress. **2** The development of land or water is the process of making it more useful or profitable by the expansion of industry or housing, e.g. *the development of London's docklands.* **3** A development is a new stage in a series of events, e.g. *developments in technology.* **developmental** (adjective).

deviant, deviants 1 (adjective) Deviant behaviour is unacceptable or different from what people consider as normal. **2** (noun) A deviant is someone whose behaviour or beliefs are different from what people consider to be acceptable.

deviate, deviates, deviating, deviated (verb) To deviate means to differ or depart from what is usual or acceptable. **deviation** (noun).

device, devices 1 (noun) A device is a machine or tool that is used for a particular purpose, e.g. *a device to warn you when the batteries need changing.* **2** A device is also a plan or scheme, e.g. *Another favourite CIA device was economic sabotage.*

devil, devils 1 (noun) In Christianity and Judaism, the Devil is the spirit of evil and enemy of God **2** A devil is any evil spirit.

devious (adjective) insincere and dishonest. **deviousness** (noun).

devise, devises, devising, devised (verb) To devise something means to work it out, e.g. *Besides diets, he devised punishing exercise routines.*

devoid (adjective) lacking in a particular thing or quality, e.g. *His glance was devoid of expression.*

devolution (noun) Devolution is the transfer of power or authority from a central government or organization to smaller organizations or to local government departments.

devote, devotes, devoting, devoted (verb) If you devote yourself to something, you give all your time, energy, or money to it, e.g. *She has devoted herself to women's causes.*

devoted (adjective) very loving and loyal.

devotee, devotees (noun) A devotee of something is a fanatical or enthusiastic follower of it.

devotion (noun) Devotion to someone or something is great love or affection for them. **devotional** (adjective).

devour, devours, devouring, devoured (verb) If you devour something, you eat it hungrily or greedily.

devout (adjective) deeply and sincerely religious, e.g. *a devout Buddhist.* **devoutly** (adverb).

dew (noun) Dew is drops of moisture that form on the ground and other cool surfaces at night.

dexterity (noun) Dexterity is skill or agility in using your hands or mind, e.g. *He had learned to use the crutches with dexterity.* **dexterous** (adjective).

diabetes (pronounced dy-a-**bee**-tiss) (noun) Diabetes is a disease in which someone has too much sugar in their blood, because they do not produce enough insulin to absorb it. **diabetic** (noun or adjective).

diabolical 1 (adjective; an informal use) dreadful and very annoying, e.g. *The pain was diabolical.* **2** extremely wicked and cruel.

diagnose, diagnoses, diagnosing, diagnosed (verb) To diagnose an illness or problem means to identify exactly what is wrong.

diagnosis, diagnoses (noun) A diagnosis is the identification of what is wrong with someone who is ill. **diagnostic** (adjective).

diagonal (adjective) in a slanting direction. **diagonally** (adverb).

diagram, diagrams (noun) A diagram is a drawing that shows or explains something.

dial, dials, dialling, dialled 1 (noun) A dial is the face of a clock or meter, with divisions marked on it so that a time or measurement can be recorded and read. **2** A dial is also the part on some equipment, such as a radio or time switch, by which the equipment is tuned or controlled. **3** (verb) To dial a telephone number means to press the number keys to select the required number.

dialect, dialects (noun) A dialect is a form of a language spoken in a particular geographical area.

dialogue, dialogues 1 (noun) In a novel, play, or film, dialogue is conversation. **2** Dialogue is communication or discussion between people or groups of people, e.g. *The union sought dialogue with the council.*

dialysis (noun) Dialysis is a treatment used for some kidney diseases, in which blood is filtered by means of a special machine to remove waste products.

diameter, diameters (noun) The diameter of a circle is the length of a straight line drawn across it through its centre.

diamond, diamonds 1 (noun) A diamond is a precious stone made of pure carbon. **2** A diamond is also a shape with four straight sides of equal length forming two opposite angles less than 90° and two opposite angles greater than 90°. **3** Diamonds is one of the four suits in a pack of playing cards. It is marked by a red diamond-shaped symbol. **4** (adjective) A diamond anniversary is the 60th anniversary of an event.

diaphragm, diaphragms (pronounced **dy**-a-fram) (noun) In mammals, the diaphragm is the muscular wall that separates the lungs from the stomach.

diarrhoea (pronounced dy-a-**ree**-a) (noun) Diarrhoea is a condition in which the faeces are more liquid and frequent than usual.

diary, diaries (noun) A diary is a book which has a separate space or page for each day of the year on which to keep a record of appointments. **diarist** (noun).

dice, dices, dicing, diced 1 (noun) A dice is a small cube which has each side marked with dots representing the numbers one to six. **2** (verb) To dice food means to cut it into small cubes. **diced** (adjective).

dictate, dictates, dictating, dictated 1 (verb) If you dictate something, you say or read it aloud for someone else to write down. **2** To dictate something means to command or state what must happen, e.g. *What we wear is largely dictated by our daily routine.* **dictation** (noun).

dictator, dictators (noun) A dictator is a ruler who has complete power in a country, especially one who has taken power by force. **dictatorial** (adjective).

diction (noun) Someone's diction is the clarity with which they speak or sing.

dictionary, dictionaries (noun) A dictionary is a book in which words are listed alphabetically and explained, or equivalent words are given in another language.

die, dies, dying, died 1 (verb) When people, animals, or plants die, they stop living. **2** When things die or die out, they cease to exist, e.g. *That custom has died out now.* **3** When something dies, dies away, or dies down, it gradually fades away, e.g. *The footsteps died away.* **4** (an informal use) If you are dying to do something, you are longing to do it. **5** (noun) A die is a dice.

diesel (pronounced **dee**-zel) **1** (noun) Diesel is a heavy fuel used in trains, buses, and lorries. **2** A diesel is a vehicle with a diesel engine.

diet, diets 1 (noun) Someone's diet is the usual food that they eat, e.g. *a vegetarian diet.* **2** A diet is a special restricted selection of foods that someone eats to improve their health or regulate their weight. **dietary** (adjective).

dietician, dieticians; also spelled **dietitian** (noun) A dietician is someone trained to advise people about healthy eating.

differ, differs, differing, differed 1 (verb) If two or more things differ, they are unlike each other. **2** If people differ, they have opposing views or disagree about something.

difference, differences 1 (noun) The difference between things is the way in which they are unlike each other. **2** The difference between two numbers is the amount by which one is less than another. **3** A difference in someone or something is a significant change in them, e.g. *You wouldn't believe the difference in her.*

different 1 (adjective) unlike something else. **2** unusual and out of the ordinary. **3** distinct and separate, although of the same kind, e.g. *The lunch supports a different charity each year.* **differently** (adverb).

differentiate, differentiates, differentiating, differentiated 1 (verb) To differentiate between things means to recognize or show how one is unlike the other. **2** Something that differentiates one thing from another makes it distinct and unlike the other. **differentiation** (noun).

difficult 1 (adjective) not easy to do, understand, or solve. **2** hard to deal with or troublesome, especially because of being unreasonable or unpredictable, e.g. *a difficult child.*

difficulty, difficulties 1 (noun) A difficulty is a problem, e.g. *The central difficulty is his drinking.* **2** Difficulty is the fact or quality of being difficult.

diffident (adjective) timid and lacking in self-confidence. **diffidently** (adverb), **diffidence** (noun).

diffuse, diffuses, diffusing, diffused 1 (verb; pronounced dif-**yooz**) If something diffuses, it spreads out or scatters in all directions. **2** (adjective; pronounced dif-**yoos**) spread out over a wide area. **diffusion** (noun).

dig, digs, digging, dug 1 (verb) If you dig, you break up soil or sand, especially with a spade or garden fork. **2** To dig something into an object means to push, thrust, or poke it in. **3** (noun) A dig is a prod or jab, especially in the ribs. **4** (an informal use) A dig at someone is a spiteful or unpleasant remark intended to hurt, anger, or embarrass them. **5** (plural noun) Digs are lodgings in someone else's house.

digest, digests, digesting, digested 1 (verb) To digest food means to break it down in the gut so that it can be easily absorbed and used by the body. **2** If you digest information or a fact, you understand it and take it in. **digestible** (adjective).

digestion, digestions 1 (noun) Digestion is the process of digesting food. **2** Your digestion is your ability to digest food, e.g. *Camomile tea aids poor digestion.* **digestive** (adjective).

digit, digits (pronounced **dij**-it) **1** (noun; a formal use) Your digits are your fingers or toes. **2** A digit is a written symbol for any of the numbers from 0 to 9.

digital (adjective) displaying information, especially time, by numbers, rather than by a pointer moving round a dial, e.g. *a digital watch.* **digitally** (adverb).

dignified (adjective) full of dignity.

dignitary, dignitaries (noun) A dignitary is a person who holds a high official position.

dignity (noun) Dignity is behaviour which is serious, calm, and controlled, e.g. *She conducted herself with dignity.*

digression, digressions (noun) A digression in speech or writing is leaving the main subject for a while.

dilapidated (adjective) falling to pieces and generally in a bad condition, e.g. *a dilapidated castle.*

dilate, dilates, dilating, dilated (verb) To dilate means to become wider and larger, e.g. *The pupil of the eye dilates in the dark.* **dilated** (adjective), **dilation** (noun).

dilemma, dilemmas (noun) A dilemma is a situation in which a choice has to be made between alternatives that are equally difficult or unpleasant.

diligent (adjective) hard-working, and showing care and perseverance. **diligently** (adverb), **diligence** (noun).

dill (noun) Dill is a herb with yellow flowers and a strong sweet smell.

dilute, dilutes, diluting, diluted (verb) To dilute a liquid means to add water or another liquid to it to make it less concentrated. **dilution** (noun).

dim, dimmer, dimmest; dims, dimming, dimmed 1 (adjective) badly lit and lacking in brightness. **2** very vague and unclear in your mind, e.g. *dim recollections.* **3** (an informal use) stupid or mentally dull, e.g. *He is rather dim.* **4** (verb) If lights dim or are dimmed, they become less bright. **dimly** (adverb), **dimness** (noun).

dimension, dimensions 1 (noun) A dimension of a situation is an aspect or factor that influences the way you understand it, e.g. *This process had a domestic and a foreign dimension.* **2** You can talk about the size or extent of something as its dimensions, e.g. *It was an explosion of major dimensions.* **3** The dimensions of something are also its measurements, for example its length, breadth, height, or diameter.

diminish, diminishes, diminishing, diminished (verb) If something diminishes or if you diminish it, it becomes reduced in size, importance, or intensity.

diminutive (adjective) very small.

dimple, dimples (noun) A dimple is a small hollow in someone's cheek or chin.

din, dins (noun) A din is a loud and unpleasant noise.

dinar, dinars (pronounced **dee**-nar) (noun) The dinar is a unit of currency in several countries in Southern Europe, North Africa and the Middle East.

dine, dines, dining, dined (verb; a formal use) To dine means to eat dinner in the evening, e.g. *We dined together in the hotel.*

diner, diners 1 (noun) A diner is someone who is having dinner in a restaurant. **2** A diner is also a small restaurant or railway restaurant car.

dinghy, dinghies (pronounced **ding**-ee) (noun) A dinghy is a small boat which is rowed, sailed, or powered by outboard motor.

dingo, dingoes (noun) A dingo is an Australian wild dog.

dingy, dingier, dingiest (pronounced **din**-jee) (adjective) dusty, dark, and rather depressing, e.g. *a dingy bedsit.*

dinner, dinners 1 (noun) Dinner is the main meal of the day, eaten either in the evening or at lunchtime. **2** A dinner is a formal social occasion in the evening, at which a meal is served.

dinosaur, dinosaurs (pronounced **dy**-no-sor) (noun) A dinosaur was a large reptile which lived in prehistoric times.

dint (phrase) **By dint of** means by means of, e.g. *He succeeds by dint of hard work.*

diocese, dioceses (noun) A diocese is a district controlled by a bishop. **diocesan** (adjective).

dip, dips, dipping, dipped 1 (verb) If you dip something into a liquid, you lower it or plunge it quickly into the liquid. **2** (noun) A dip is a rich creamy mixture which you scoop up with biscuits or raw vegetables and eat, e.g. *an avocado dip.* **3** (an informal use) A dip is also a swim. **4** (verb) If something dips, it slopes downwards or goes below a certain level, e.g. *The sun dipped below the horizon.* **5** To dip also means to make a quick, slight downward movement, e.g. *She dipped her fingers into the cool water.*

diploma, diplomas (noun) A diploma is a certificate awarded to a student who has successfully completed a course of study.

diplomacy 1 (noun) Diplomacy is the managing of relationships between countries. **2** Diplomacy is also skill in dealing with people without offending or upsetting them. **diplomatic** (adjective), **diplomatically** (adverb).

diplomat, diplomats (noun) A diplomat is an official who negotiates and deals with another country on behalf of his or her own country.

dire, direr, direst (adjective) disastrous, urgent, or terrible, e.g. *dire warnings... people in dire need.*

direct, directs, directing, directed 1 (adjective) moving or aimed in a straight line or by the shortest route, e.g. *the direct route.* **2** straightforward, and without delay or evasion, e.g. *his direct manner.* **3** without anyone or anything intervening, e.g. *Schools can take direct control of their own funding.* **4** exact, e.g. *the direct opposite.* **5** (verb) To direct something means to guide and control it. **6** To direct people or things means to send them, tell them, or show them the way. **7** To direct a film, a play, or a television or radio programme means to organize the way it is made and performed.

direction, directions 1 (noun) A direction is the general line that someone or something is moving or pointing in. **2** Direction is the controlling and guiding of something, e.g. *He was chopping vegetables under the chef's direction.* **3** (plural noun) Directions are instructions that tell you how to do something or how to get somewhere.

directive, directives (noun) A directive is an instruction that must be obeyed, e.g. *a directive banning cigarette advertising.*

directly (adverb) in a straight line or immediately, e.g. *He looked directly at Rose.*

director, directors 1 (noun) A director is a member of the board of a company or institution. **2** A director is also the person responsible for the making and performance of a programme, play, or film. **directorial** (adjective).

directorate, directorates (noun) A directorate is a board of directors of a company or organization.

directory, directories (noun) A directory is a book which gives lists of facts, such as names and addresses.

dirge, dirges (noun) A dirge is a slow, sad, or mournful piece of music, sometimes played or sung at funerals.

dirt 1 (noun) Dirt is any unclean substance, such as dust, mud, or stains. **2** Dirt is also earth or soil.

dirty, dirtier, dirtiest 1 (adjective) marked or covered with dirt. **2** unfair or dishonest, e.g. *a dirty fight.* **3** referring to sex in a way that many people find offensive, e.g. *dirty jokes.*

dis- (prefix) Dis- is added to the beginning of words to form a word that means the opposite, e.g. *discontented.*

disability, disabilities (noun) A disability is a physical or mental inability or illness that restricts someone's way of life.

disable, disables, disabling, disabled (verb) If something disables someone, it injures or harms them physically or mentally and severely affects their life. **disablement** (noun).

disabled (adjective) lacking one or more physical powers, such as the ability to walk or to coordinate one's movements.

disadvantage, disadvantages (noun) A disadvantage is an unfavourable or harmful circumstance. **disadvantaged** (adjective).

disaffected (adjective) If someone is disaffected with an idea or organization, they no longer believe in it or support it, e.g. *disaffected Tory voters.*

disagree, disagrees, disagreeing, disagreed 1 (verb) If you disagree with someone, you have a different view or opinion from theirs. **2** If you disagree with an action or proposal, you disapprove of it and believe it is wrong, e.g. *He detested her and disagreed with her policies.* **disagreement** (noun).

disagreeable (adjective) unpleasant or unhelpful and unfriendly, e.g. *a disagreeable odour.*

disappear, disappears, disap-

pearing, disappeared 1 (verb) If something or someone disappears, they go out of sight or become lost. **2** To disappear also means to stop existing or happening, e.g. *The pain has disappeared.* **disappearance** (noun).

disappoint, disappoints, disappointing, disappointed (verb) If someone or something disappoints you, it fails to live up to what you expected of it. **disappointed** (adjective), **disappointment** (noun).

disapprove, disapproves, disapproving, disapproved (verb) To disapprove of something or someone means to believe they are wrong or bad, e.g. *Everyone disapproved of their marrying so young.* **disapproval** (noun), **disapproving** (adjective).

disarm, disarms, disarming, disarmed 1 (verb) To disarm means to get rid of weapons. **2** If someone disarms you, they overcome your anger or hostility, by charming or soothing you, e.g. *Mahoney was almost disarmed by the frankness.* **disarming** (adjective).

disarmament (noun) Disarmament is the reducing or getting rid of military forces and weapons.

disarray (noun) Disarray is a state of disorder and confusion, e.g. *Our army was in disarray and practically weaponless.*

disaster, disasters 1 (noun) A disaster is an event or accident that causes great distress or destruction. **2** A disaster is also a complete failure. **disastrous** (adjective), **disastrously** (adverb).

disband, disbands, disbanding, disbanded (verb) When a group of people disbands, it officially ceases to exist.

disc, discs; also spelled **disk 1** (noun) A disc is a flat round object, e.g. *a tax disc... a compact disc.* **2** A disc is one of the thin circular pieces of cartilage which separate the bones in your spine. **3** A disc is also a storage device used in computers.

discard, discards, discarding, discarded (verb) To discard something means to get rid of it, because you no longer want it or find it useful.

discern, discerns, discerning, discerned (pronounced dis-**ern**) (verb; a formal word) To discern something means to notice or understand it clearly, e.g. *The film had no plot that I could discern.*

discernible (adjective) able to be seen or recognized, e.g. *no discernible talent.*

discerning (adjective) having good taste and judgment. **discernment** (noun).

discharge, discharges, discharging, discharged 1 (verb) If something discharges or is discharged, it is given or sent out, e.g. *Oil discharged into the world's oceans.* **2** To discharge someone from hospital means to allow them to leave. **3** If someone is discharged from a job, they are dismissed from it. **4** (noun) A discharge is a substance that is released from the inside of something, e.g. *a thick nasal discharge.* **5** A discharge is also dismissal or release from a job or an institution.

disciple, disciples (pronounced dis-**sigh**-pl) (noun) A disciple is a follower of someone or something.

discipline, disciplines, disciplining, disciplined 1 (noun) Discipline is the imposing of order by making people obey rules and punishing them when they break them. **2** Discipline is the ability to behave and work in a controlled way. **3** (verb) If you discipline yourself, you train yourself to behave and work in an ordered way. **4** To discipline someone means to punish them. **disciplinary** (adjective), **disciplined** (adjective).

disc jockey, disc jockeys (noun) A disc jockey is someone who introduces and plays pop records on the radio or at a disco.

disclose, discloses, disclosing, disclosed (verb) To disclose something means to make it known or allow it to be seen. **disclosure** (noun).

disco, discos (noun) A disco is a party or a club where people go to dance to pop records.

discomfort, discomforts 1 (noun) Discomfort is distress or slight pain. **2** Discomfort is also a feeling of worry or embarrassment.

disconcert, disconcerts, disconcerting, disconcerted (verb) If something disconcerts you, it makes you feel flustered or embarrassed. **disconcerting** (adjective).

disconnect, disconnects, disconnecting, disconnected 1 (verb) To disconnect something means to detach it from something else. **2** If someone disconnects your fuel supply or telephone, they cut you off.

discontent (noun) Discontent is a feeling of dissatisfaction with conditions or with life in general, e.g. *He was aware of the discontent this policy had caused.* **discontented** (adjective).

discontinue, discontinues, discontinuing, discontinued (verb) To discontinue something means to stop doing it.

discord (noun) Discord is an argument or unpleasantness between people.

discount, discounts, discounting, discounted 1 (noun) A discount is a reduction in the price of something. **2** (verb) If you discount an idea or theory, you reject it as being unsuitable or untrue, e.g. *I haven't discounted her connection with the kidnapping case.*

discourage, discourages, discouraging, discouraged (verb) To discourage someone means to take away their enthusiasm or confidence to do something. **discouraging** (adjective), **discouragement** (noun).

discourse, discourses (a formal word) **1** (noun) A discourse is a formal talk or piece of writing intended to teach or explain something. **2** Discourse is serious conversation between people on a particular subject.

discover, discovers, discovering, discovered (verb) When you discover something, you find it or find out about it. **discovery** (noun), **discoverer** (noun).

discredit, discredits, discrediting, discredited 1 (verb) To discredit someone means to damage their reputation. **2** To discredit an idea or theory means to cause it to be doubted or not believed.

discreet (adjective) If you are discreet, you avoid causing embarrassment when dealing with secret or private matters. **discreetly** (adverb).

discrepancy, discrepancies (noun) A discrepancy is a difference between two things which ought to be the same.

discrete (adjective; a formal word) separate and distinct, e.g. *two discrete sets of nerves.*

discretion 1 (noun) Discretion is the quality of behaving with care and tact so as to avoid embarrassment or distress to other people, e.g. *You can count on my discretion.* **2** Discretion is also freedom and authority to make decisions and take action according to your own judgment, e.g. *Class teachers have very limited discretion in decision-making.* **discretionary** (adjective).

discriminate, discriminates, discriminating, discriminated 1 (verb) To discriminate between things means to recognize and understand the differences between them. **2** To discriminate against a person or group means to treat them badly or unfairly, usually because of their race, colour, or sex. **3** To discriminate in favour of a person or group means to treat them more favourably than others. **discrimination** (noun), **discriminatory** (adjective).

discus, discuses (noun) The discus is a disc-shaped object with a heavy middle, thrown by athletes.

discuss, discusses, discussing, discussed (verb) When people discuss something, they talk about it in detail and consider different aspects of it.

discussion, discussions (noun) A discussion is a conversation or piece of writing in which a subject is considered in detail, from several points of view.

disdain (noun) Disdain is a feeling of superiority over or contempt for someone or something, e.g. *The candidates shared an equal disdain for the press.* **disdainful** (adjective).

disease, diseases (noun) A disease is an unhealthy condition in people, animals, or plants. **diseased** (adjective).

disembark, disembarks, disembarking, disembarked (verb) To disembark means to land or unload from a ship, aircraft, or bus.

disembodied 1 (adjective) separate from or existing without a body, e.g. *a disembodied skull.* **2** seeming not to be attached or to come from anyone, e.g. *disembodied voices.*

disenchanted (adjective) disappointed with something, and no longer believing that it is good or worthwhile, e.g. *She is very disenchanted with the marriage.* **disenchantment** (noun).

disfigure, disfigures, disfiguring, disfigured (verb) To disfigure something means to spoil its appearance, e.g. *Graffiti or posters disfigured every wall.*

disgrace, disgraces, disgracing, disgraced 1 (noun) Disgrace is a state in which people disapprove of someone. **2** If something is a disgrace, it is unacceptable, e.g. *The overcrowded prisons were a disgrace.* **3** If someone is a disgrace to a group of people, their behaviour is unacceptable and makes the group feel ashamed, e.g. *You're a disgrace to the school.* **4** (verb) If you disgrace yourself or disgrace someone else, you cause yourself or them to be strongly disapproved of by other people.

disgraceful (adjective) If something is disgraceful, people disapprove of it strongly and think that those who are responsible for it should be ashamed. **disgracefully** (adverb).

disgruntled (adjective) discontented or in a bad mood.

disguise, disguises, disguising, disguised 1 (verb) To disguise something means to change it so that people do not recognize it. **2** To disguise a feeling means to hide it, e.g. *I tried to disguise my relief.* **3** (noun) A disguise is something you wear or something you do to alter your appearance so that you cannot be recognized by other people.

disgust, disgusts, disgusting, disgusted 1 (noun) Disgust is the feeling aroused in you by something that is morally wrong, shameful, or very unpleasant. **2** (verb) To disgust someone means to make them feel sickened and disapproving. **disgusted** (adjective).

dish, dishes 1 (noun) A dish is a shallow container for cooking or serving food. **2** A dish is also food cooked in a particular way.

disheartened (adjective) If you are disheartened, you feel disappointed.

dishevelled (pronounced dish-**ev**-ld) (adjective) If someone looks dishevelled, their hair or clothes look untidy.

dishonest (adjective) not truthful or able to be trusted. **dishonestly** (adverb).

dishonesty (noun) Dishonesty is behaviour which is meant to deceive people.

disillusioned (adjective) If you are disillusioned with something, you are disappointed because it is not as good as you had expected.

disinfectant, disinfectants (noun) A disinfectant is a chemical substance that kills germs.

disintegrate, disintegrates, disintegrating, disintegrated 1 (verb) If something disintegrates, it becomes weakened and is not effective, e.g. *My confidence disintegrated.* **2** If an object disintegrates, it shatters into many pieces and so is destroyed. **disintegration** (noun).

disinterest 1 (noun) Disinterest is a lack of interest. **2** Disinterest is also a lack of personal involvement in a situation.

disinterested (adjective) If someone is disinterested, they are not going to gain or lose from the situation they are involved in, and so can act in a way that is fair to both sides, e.g. *a disinterested judge.*

disjointed (adjective) If thought or speech is disjointed, it jumps from subject to subject and so is difficult to follow or understand.

disk another spelling of **disc.**

dislike, dislikes, disliking, disliked 1 (verb) If you dislike something or someone, you think they are unpleasant and do not like them. **2** (noun) Dislike is a feeling that you have when you do not like someone or something.

dislocate, dislocates, dislocating, dislocated (verb) To dislocate your bone or joint means to put it out of place.

dislodge, dislodges, dislodging, dislodged (verb) To dislodge something means to move it or force it out of place.

dismal (pronounced **diz**-mal) (adjective) rather gloomy and depressing, e.g. *dismal weather.* **dismally** (adverb).

dismantle, dismantles, dismantling, dismantled (verb) To dismantle something means to take it apart.

dismay, dismays, dismaying, dismayed 1 (noun) Dismay is a feeling of fear and worry. **2** (verb) If someone or something dismays you, it fills you with alarm and worry.

dismember, dismembers, dismembering, dismembered (verb; a formal word) To dismember a person or animal means to cut or tear their body into pieces.

dismiss, dismisses, dismissing, dismissed 1 (verb) If you dismiss something, you decide to ignore it because it is not important enough for you to think about. **2** To dismiss an employee means to ask that person to leave their job. **3** If someone in authority dismisses you, they tell you to leave. **dismissal** (noun).

dismissive (adjective) If you are dismissive of something or someone, you show that you think they are of little importance or value, e.g. *a dismissive gesture.*

disorder, disorders 1 (noun) Disorder is a state of untidiness. **2** Disorder is also a lack of organization, e.g. *The men fled in disorder.* **3** A disorder is a disease, e.g. *a stomach disorder.*

disorganized or **disorganised** (adjective) If something is disorganized, it is confused and badly prepared or badly arranged. **disorganization** (noun).

disown, disowns, disowning, disowned (verb) To disown someone or something means to refuse to admit any connection with them.

disparaging (adjective) critical and scornful, e.g. *disparaging remarks.*

disparate (adjective; a formal word) Things that are disparate are utterly different from one another. **disparity** (noun).

dispatch, dispatches, dispatching, dispatched; also spelled **despatch 1** (verb) To dispatch someone or something to a particular place means to send them there for a special reason, e.g. *The president dispatched him on a fact-finding visit.* **2** (noun) A dispatch is an official written message, often sent to an army or government headquarters.

dispel, dispels, dispelling, dispelled (verb) To dispel fears or beliefs means to drive them away or to destroy them, e.g. *The myths are being dispelled.*

dispensary, dispensaries (noun) A dispensary is a place where medicines are prepared and given out.

dispense, dispenses, dispensing, dispensed 1 (verb; a formal use) To dispense something means to give it out, e.g. *They dispense advice.* **2** To dispense medicines means to prepare them and give them out. **3** To dispense with something means to do without it or do away with it, e.g. *We'll dispense with formalities.*

dispenser, dispensers (noun) A dispenser is a machine or container from which you can get things, e.g. *a cash dispenser.*

disperse, disperses, dispersing, dispersed 1 (verb) When something disperses, it scatters over a wide area. **2** When people disperse or when someone disperses them, they move apart and go in different directions. **dispersion** (noun).

dispirited (adjective) depressed and having no enthusiasm for anything.

dispiriting (adjective) Something dispiriting makes you depressed and unenthusiastic, e.g. *a dispiriting defeat.*

displace, displaces, displacing, displaced 1 (verb) If one thing displaces another, it forces the thing out of its usual place or position and occupies that place itself. **2** If people are displaced, they are forced to leave their home or country.

displacement (noun) Displacement is the removal of something from its usual or correct place or position.

display, displays, displaying, displayed 1 (verb) If you display something, you show it or make it visible to people. **2** If you display something such as an emotion, you behave in a way that shows you feel it. **3** (noun) A display is an arrangement of things designed to attract people's attention.

displease, displeases, displeasing, displeased (verb) If someone or something displeases you, they make you annoyed, dissatisfied, or offended. **displeasure** (noun).

disposable (adjective) designed to be thrown away after use, e.g. *disposable nappies.*

disposal (noun) Disposal is the act of getting rid of something that is no longer wanted or needed.

dispose, disposes, disposing, disposed 1 (verb) To dispose of something means to get rid of it. **2** If you are not disposed to do something, you are not willing to do it.

disprove, disproves, disproving, disproved (verb) If someone disproves an idea, belief, or theory, they show that it is not true.

dispute, disputes, disputing, disputed 1 (noun) A dispute is an argument. **2** (verb) To dispute a fact or theory means to question the truth of it.

disqualify, disqualifies, disqualifying, disqualified (verb) If someone is disqualified, their right to take part in a competition or activity is removed, e.g. *He was disqualified from driving.* **disqualification** (noun).

disquiet (noun) Disquiet is

worry or anxiety. **disquieting** (adjective).

disregard, disregards, disregarding, disregarded 1 (verb) To disregard something means to pay little or no attention to it. **2** (noun) Disregard is a lack of attention or respect for something, e.g. *He exhibited a flagrant disregard of the law.*

disrepair (phrase) If something is **in disrepair**, it is broken or in poor condition.

disrespect (noun) Disrespect is contempt or lack of respect, e.g. *his disrespect for authority.* **disrespectful** (adjective).

disrupt, disrupts, disrupting, disrupted (verb) To disrupt something such as an event or system means to break it up or throw it into confusion, e.g. *Strikes disrupted air and rail traffic in Italy.* **disruption** (noun), **disruptive** (adjective).

dissatisfied (adjective) not pleased or not contented. **dissatisfaction** (noun).

dissect, dissects, dissecting, dissected (verb) To dissect a plant or a dead body means to cut it up so that it can be scientifically examined. **dissection** (noun).

dissent, dissents, dissenting, dissented 1 (noun) Dissent is strong difference of opinion, e.g. *political dissent.* **2** (verb) When people dissent, they express a difference of opinion about something. **dissenting** (adjective).

dissertation, dissertations (noun) A dissertation is a long essay, especially for a university degree.

disservice (noun) To do someone a disservice means to do something that harms them.

dissident, dissidents (noun) A dissident is someone who disagrees with and criticizes their government.

dissimilar (adjective) If things are dissimilar, they are unlike each other.

dissipate, dissipates, dissipating, dissipated 1 (verb; a formal word) When something dissipates or is dissipated, it completely disappears, e.g. *The cloud seemed to dissipate there.* **2** If someone dissipates time, money, or effort, they waste it.

dissipated (adjective) Someone who is dissipated shows signs of indulging too much in alcohol or other physical pleasures.

dissolve, dissolves, dissolving, dissolved 1 (verb) If you dissolve something or if it dissolves in a liquid, it becomes mixed with and absorbed in the liquid. **2** To dissolve an organization or institution means to officially end it.

dissuade, dissuades, dissuading, dissuaded (pronounced dis-**wade**) (verb) To dissuade someone from doing something or from believing something means to persuade them not to do it or not to believe it.

distance, distances, distancing, distanced 1 (noun) The distance between two points is how far it is between them. **2** Distance is the fact of being far away in space or time. **3** (verb) If you distance yourself from someone or something or are distanced from them, you become less involved with them.

distant 1 (adjective) far away in space or time. 2 A distant relative is one who is not closely related to you. 3 Someone who is distant is cold and unfriendly. **distantly** (adverb).

distaste (noun) Distaste is a dislike of something which you find offensive.

distasteful (adjective) If you find something distasteful, you think it is unpleasant or offensive.

distil, distils, distilling, distilled (verb) When a liquid is distilled, it is heated until it evaporates and then cooled to enable purified liquid to be collected. **distillation** (noun).

distillery, distilleries (noun) A distillery is a place where whisky or other strong alcoholic drink is made, using a process of distillation.

distinct 1 (adjective) If one thing is distinct from another, it is recognizably different from it, e.g. *A word may have two quite distinct meanings.* 2 If something is distinct, you can hear, smell, or see it clearly and plainly, e.g. *There was a distinct buzzing noise.* 3 If something such as a fact, idea, or intention is distinct, it is clear and definite, e.g. *She had a distinct feeling someone was watching them.* **distinctly** (adverb).

distinction, distinctions 1 (noun) A distinction is a difference between two things, e.g. *a distinction between the body and the soul.* 2 Distinction is a quality of excellence and superiority, e.g. *a man of distinction.* 3 A distinction is also a special honour or claim, e.g. *It had the distinction of being the largest square in Europe.*

distinctive (adjective) Something that is distinctive has a special quality which makes it recognizable, e.g. *a distinctive voice.* **distinctively** (adverb).

distinguish, distinguishes, distinguishing, distinguished 1 (verb) To distinguish between things means to recognize the difference between them, e.g. *I've learned to distinguish business and friendship.* 2 To distinguish something means to make it out by seeing, hearing, or tasting it, e.g. *I heard shouting but was unable to distinguish the words.* 3 If you distinguish yourself, you do something that makes people think highly of you. **distinguishable** (adjective), **distinguishing** (adjective).

distort, distorts, distorting, distorted 1 (verb) If you distort a statement or an argument, you change it so as to give a wrong emphasis or interpretation to it. 2 If something is distorted, it is changed so that it seems strange or unclear, e.g. *His voice was distorted.* 3 If an object is distorted, it is twisted or pulled out of shape. **distorted** (adjective), **distortion** (noun).

distract, distracts, distracting, distracted (verb) If something distracts you, your attention is taken away from what you are doing. **distracted** (adjective), **distractedly** (adverb), **distracting** (adjective).

distraction, distractions 1

(noun) A distraction is something that takes people's attention away from something. **2** A distraction is also an activity that is intended to amuse or relax someone.

distraught (adjective) so upset and worried that you cannot think clearly, e.g. *He was still distraught about her death.*

distress, distresses, distressing, distressed 1 (noun) Distress is great suffering caused by pain, sorrow, or hardship. **2** Distress is also the state of needing help because of difficulties or danger. **3** (verb) To distress someone means to make them feel alarmed or unhappy, e.g. *Her death had profoundly distressed me.*

distressing (adjective) very worrying or upsetting.

distribute, distributes, distributing, distributed 1 (verb) To distribute something such as leaflets means to hand them out or deliver them, e.g. *They publish and distribute brochures.* **2** If things are distributed, they are spread throughout an area or space, e.g. *Distribute the cheese evenly on top of the quiche.* **3** To distribute something means to divide it and share it out among a number of people.

distribution, distributions 1 (noun) Distribution is the delivering of something to various people or organizations, e.g. *the distribution of vicious leaflets.* **2** Distribution is the sharing out of something, e.g. *distribution of power.*

distributor, distributors (noun) A distributor is a person or company that supplies goods to other businesses who then sell them to the public.

district, districts (noun) A district is an area which has special or recognizable features, e.g. *a residential district.*

district nurse, district nurses (noun) A district nurse is a nurse who treats people in their own homes.

distrust, distrusts, distrusting, distrusted 1 (verb) If you distrust someone, you are suspicious of them because you are not sure whether they are honest. **2** (noun) Distrust is suspicion. **distrustful** (adjective).

disturb, disturbs, disturbing, disturbed 1 (verb) If you disturb someone, you break their rest, peace, or privacy. **2** If something disturbs you, it makes you feel upset or worried. **3** If something is disturbed, it is moved out of position or meddled with. **disturbing** (adjective).

disturbance, disturbances 1 (noun) Disturbance is the state of being disturbed. **2** A disturbance is a violent or unruly incident in public.

disuse (noun) Something that has fallen into disuse is neglected or no longer used. **disused** (adjective).

ditch, ditches (noun) A ditch is a channel at the side of a road or field, usually to drain away excess water.

dither, dithers, dithering, dithered (verb) To dither means to be unsure and hesitant.

ditto Ditto means 'the same'. In written lists, ditto is represented by a mark („) to avoid repetition.

ditty, ditties (noun; an old-fashioned word) A ditty is a short simple song or poem.

dive, dives, diving, dived 1 (verb) To dive means to jump into water with your arms held straight above your head. **2** If you go diving, you go down under the surface of the sea or a lake using special breathing equipment. **3** If an aircraft or bird dives, it flies in a steep downward path, or drops sharply. **diver** (noun), **diving** (noun).

diverge, diverges, diverging, diverged 1 (verb) If opinions or facts diverge, they differ, e.g. *Theory and practice sometimes diverged.* **2** If two things such as roads or paths which have been going in the same direction diverge, they separate and go off in different directions. **divergence** (noun), **divergent** (adjective).

diverse 1 (adjective) If a group of things is diverse, it is made up of different kinds of things, e.g. *a diverse range of goods and services.* **2** People, ideas, or objects that are diverse are very different from each other. **diversity** (noun).

diversify, diversifies, diversifying, diversified (verb) To diversify means to increase the variety of something, e.g. *Has the company diversified into new areas?* **diversification** (noun).

diversion, diversions 1 (noun) A diversion is a special route arranged for traffic when the usual route is closed. **2** A diversion is something that takes your attention away from what you should be concentrating on, e.g. *A break for tea created a welcome diversion.* **3** A diversion is also a pleasant or amusing pastime or activity.

divert, diverts, diverting, diverted (verb) To divert something means to change the course or direction it is following. **diverting** (adjective).

divide, divides, dividing, divided 1 (verb) When something divides or is divided, it is split up and separated into two or more parts. **2** If something divides two areas, it forms a barrier between them. **3** If people divide over something or if something divides them, it causes strong disagreement between them. **4** In mathematics, when you divide, you calculate how many times one number contains another. **5** (noun) A divide is a separation, e.g. *the class divide.*

dividend, dividends (noun) A dividend is a portion of a company's profits that is paid to shareholders.

divine, divines, divining, divined 1 (adjective) having the qualities of a god or goddess. **2** (verb) To divine something means to discover it by guessing. **divinely** (adverb).

divinity, divinities 1 (noun) Divinity is the study of religion. **2** Divinity is the state of being a god. **3** A divinity is a god or goddess.

division, divisions 1 (noun) Division is the separation of something into two or more distinct parts. **2** Division is also the process of dividing one number by another. **3** A division is a difference of opinion that causes separation between ideas or groups of people, e.g. *There were divisions in the Party on economic policy.* **4** A division is also any one of the parts into which something is split, e.g. *the Research Division.* **divisional** (adjective).

divisive (adjective) causing hostility between people so that they split into different groups, e.g. *Inflation is economically and socially divisive.*

divisor, divisors (noun) A divisor is a number by which another number is divided.

divorce, divorces, divorcing, divorced 1 (noun) Divorce is the formal and legal ending of a marriage. **2** (verb) When a married couple divorce, their marriage is legally ended. **divorced** (adjective), **divorcee** (noun).

divulge, divulges, divulging, divulged (verb) To divulge information means to reveal it.

DIY (noun) DIY is the activity of making or repairing things yourself. DIY is an abbreviation for 'do-it-yourself'.

dizzy, dizzier, dizziest (adjective) having or causing a whirling sensation. **dizziness** (noun).

DNA (noun) DNA is deoxyribonucleic acid, which is found in the cells of all living things. It is responsible for passing on characteristics from parents to their children.

do, does, doing, did, done; dos 1 (verb) Do is an auxiliary verb, which is used to form questions, negatives, and to give emphasis to the main verb of a sentence. **2** If someone does a task, chore, or activity, they perform it and finish it, e.g. *He just didn't want to do any work.* **3** If you ask what people do, you want to know what their job is, e.g. *What will you do when you leave school?* **4** If you do well at something, you are successful. If you do badly, you are unsuccessful. **5** If something will do, it is adequate but not the most suitable option, e.g. *Home-made stock is best, but cubes will do.* **6** (noun; an informal use) A do is a party or other social event.

docile (adjective) quiet, calm, and easily controlled.

dock, docks, docking, docked 1 (noun) A dock is an enclosed area in a harbour where ships go to be loaded, unloaded, or repaired. **2** (verb) When a ship docks, it is brought into dock at the end of its voyage. **3** To dock someone's wages means to deduct an amount from the sum they would normally receive. **4** To dock an animal's tail means to cut part of it off. **5** (noun) In a court of law, the dock is the place where the accused person stands or sits. **docker** (noun).

doctor, doctors, doctoring, doctored 1 (noun) A doctor is a person who is qualified in medicine and treats people who are ill. **2** A doctor of an academic subject is someone who has been awarded the highest academic degree, e.g. *She is a doctor of philosophy.* **3** (verb) To doctor something means to alter it in order to deceive people, e.g. *Stamps can be doctored.*

doctorate, doctorates (noun) A doctorate is the highest university degree. **doctoral** (adjective).

doctrine, doctrines (noun) A doctrine is a set of beliefs or principles held by a group. **doctrinal** (adjective).

document, documents, documenting, documented 1 (noun) A document is a piece of paper which provides an official record of something. **2** (verb) If you document something, you make a detailed record of it. **documentation** (noun).

documentary, documentaries 1 (noun) A documentary is a radio or television programme, or a film, which provides information on a particular subject. **2** (adjective) Documentary evidence is made up of written or official records.

dodge, dodges, dodging, dodged 1 (verb) If you dodge or dodge something, you move suddenly to avoid being seen, hit, or caught. **2** If you dodge something such as an issue or accusation, you avoid dealing with it.

dodgy 1 (adjective; an informal word) dangerous, risky, or unreliable, e.g. *He has a dodgy heart.* **2** suspected of being illegal or untrustworthy, e.g. *There's some very dodgy business going on.*

dodo, dodos (noun) A dodo was a large, flightless bird which is now extinct.

doe, does (noun) A doe is a female deer, rabbit, or hare.

does the third person singular of the present tense of **do**.

dog, dogs, dogging, dogged 1 (noun) A dog is a four-legged, meat-eating animal, kept as a pet, or to guard property or go hunting. **2** (verb) If you dog someone, you follow them very closely and never leave them.

dog collar, dog collars (noun; an informal word) A dog collar is a white collar worn by Christian clergy.

dog-eared (adjective) A book that is dog-eared has been used so much that the corners of the pages are turned down or worn.

dogged (pronounced **dog**-ged) (adjective) showing determination to continue with something, even if it is very difficult, e.g. *dogged persistence.* **doggedly** (adverb).

dogma, dogmas (noun) A dogma is a belief or system of beliefs held by a religious or political group.

dogmatic (adjective) Someone who is dogmatic about something is convinced that they are right about it and will not consider other points of view. **dogmatism** (noun).

doldrums (an informal phrase) If you are **in the doldrums,** you are depressed or bored.

dole, doles, doling, doled (verb) If you dole something out, you give a certain amount of it to each individual in a group.

doll, dolls (noun) A doll is a child's toy which looks like a baby or person.

dollar, dollars (noun) The dollar is the main unit of currency in the USA, Canada, Australia, and some other countries. A dollar is worth 100 cents.

dollop, dollops (noun) A dollop

of food is an amount of it served casually in a lump.

dolphin, dolphins (noun) A dolphin is a mammal which lives in the sea and looks like a large fish with a long pointed snout.

domain, domains 1 (noun) A domain is a particular area of activity or interest, e.g. *the domain of science.* **2** A domain is also an area over which someone has control or influence, e.g. *This reservation was the largest of the Apache domains.*

dome, domes (noun) A dome is a round roof. **domed** (adjective).

domestic 1 (adjective) happening or existing within one particular country, e.g. *domestic and foreign politics.* **2** involving or concerned with the home and family, e.g. *routine domestic tasks.*

domesticated (adjective) If a wild animal or plant has been domesticated, it has been controlled or cultivated.

domesticity (noun; a formal word) Domesticity is life at home with your family.

dominance 1 (noun) Dominance is power or control. **2** If something has dominance over other similar things, it is more powerful, important, or noticeable than they are, e.g. *the dominance of the United States in the film business.* **dominant** (adjective).

dominate, dominates, dominating, dominated 1 (verb) If something or someone dominates a situation or event, they are the most powerful or important thing in it and have control over it, e.g. *The civil service dominated public affairs.* **2** If a person or country dominates other people or places, they have power or control over them. **3** If something dominates an area, it towers over it, e.g. *The medieval city is dominated by the cathedral.* **dominating** (adjective), **domination** (noun).

domineering (adjective) Someone who is domineering tries to control other people, e.g. *a domineering mother.*

dominion (noun) Dominion is control or authority that a person or a country has over other people, e.g. *They have dominion over us.*

domino, dominoes (noun) Dominoes are small rectangular blocks marked with two groups of spots on one side, used for playing the game called dominoes.

don, dons, donning, donned 1 (noun) A don is a lecturer at Oxford or Cambridge university. **2** (verb; a literary use) If you don clothing, you put it on.

donate, donates, donating, donated (verb) To donate something to a charity or organization means to give it as a gift. **donation** (noun).

done the past participle of **do**.

donkey, donkeys (noun) A donkey is an animal related to the horse, but smaller and with longer ears.

donor, donors 1 (noun) A donor is someone who gives some of their blood while they are alive or an organ after their death to be used for medical purposes, e.g. *a kidney donor.* **2** A donor is also someone who gives something such as money to a charity or other organization.

doodle, doodles, doodling, doodled 1 (noun) A doodle is a pattern or a drawing done when you are thinking about something else or when you are bored. **2** (verb) To doodle means to draw doodles.

doom (noun) Doom is a terrible fate or event in the future which you can do nothing to prevent.

doomed (adjective) If someone or something is doomed to an unpleasant or unhappy experience, they are certain to suffer it, e.g. *doomed to failure.*

doomsday (noun) Doomsday is the end of the world.

door, doors (noun) A door is a swinging or sliding panel for opening or closing the entrance to a building, room, or cupboard; also the entrance itself.

doorway, doorways (noun) A doorway is an opening in a wall for a door.

dope, dopes, doping, doped 1 (noun) Dope is an illegal drug. **2** (verb) If someone dopes you, they put a drug into your food or drink.

dormant (adjective) Something that is dormant is not active, growing, or being used, e.g. *The virus remains dormant in nerve tissue until activated.*

dormitory, dormitories (noun) A dormitory is a large bedroom where several people sleep.

dormouse, dormice (noun) A dormouse is a mouselike rodent with a furry tail. It sleeps for several months a year.

dosage, dosages (noun) The dosage of a medicine or a drug is the amount of it that should be taken.

dose, doses (noun) A dose of a medicine or drug is a measured amount of it.

dossier, dossiers (pronounced **doss**-ee-ay) (noun) A dossier is a collection of papers containing information on a particular subject or person.

dot, dots, dotting, dotted 1 (noun) A dot is a very small, round mark. **2** (verb) If things dot an area, they are scattered all over it, e.g. *Fishing villages dot the coastline.* **3** (phrase) If you arrive somewhere **on the dot,** you arrive there at exactly the right time.

dote, dotes, doting, doted (verb) If you dote on someone, you love them very much. **doting** (adjective).

double, doubles, doubling, doubled 1 (adjective) twice the usual size, e.g. *a double whisky.* **2** consisting of two parts, e.g. *a double album.* **3** (verb) If something doubles, it becomes twice as large. **4** To double as something means to have a second job or use as well as the main one, e.g. *Their beautiful home doubles as an office.* **5** (noun) Your double is someone who looks exactly like you. **6** Doubles is a game of tennis or badminton which two people play against two other people. **doubly** (adverb).

double bass, double basses (noun) The double bass is the largest instrument in the violin family.

double-cross, double-crosses, double-crossing, double-crossed (verb) If someone double-crosses you, they cheat you by pretending to do what you both planned, when in fact they do the opposite.

double-decker, double-deckers (noun) A double-decker is a bus with two floors.

double glazing (noun) Double glazing is a second layer of glass fitted to windows to keep the building quieter or warmer.

doubt, doubts, doubting, doubted **1** (noun) Doubt is a feeling of uncertainty about whether something is true or possible. **2** (verb) If you doubt something, you think that it is probably not true or possible.

doubtful (adjective) unlikely or uncertain.

dough **1** (noun) Dough is a mixture of flour and water and sometimes other ingredients, used to make bread, pastry, or biscuits. **2** (an informal use) Dough is money.

doughnut, doughnuts (noun) A doughnut is a piece of sweet dough cooked in hot fat and usually covered with sugar.

dour (rhymes with **poor**) (adjective) severe and unfriendly, e.g. *a dour portrait of his personality.*

douse, douses, dousing, doused; also spelled **dowse** (verb) If you douse a fire, you stop it burning by throwing water over it.

dove, doves (noun) A dove is a bird like a small pigeon.

dovetail, dovetails, dovetailing, dovetailed (verb) If two things dovetail together, they fit together closely or neatly.

dowager, dowagers (noun) A dowager is a woman who has inherited a title from her dead husband, e.g. *the Empress Dowager.*

dowdy, dowdier, dowdiest (adjective) wearing dull and unfashionable clothes.

down, downs, downing, downed **1** (preposition or adverb) Down means towards the ground, towards a lower level, or in a lower place. **2** (adverb) If you put something down, you place it on a surface. **3** (preposition or adverb) If you go down a road or river, you go along it. **4** (adverb) If an amount of something goes down, it decreases. **5** (adjective) If you feel down, you feel depressed. **6** (verb) If you down a drink, you drink it quickly. **7** (noun) Down is the small, soft feathers on young birds.

downcast **1** (adjective) feeling sad and dejected. **2** If your eyes are downcast, they are looking towards the ground.

downfall **1** (noun) The downfall of a successful or powerful person or institution is their failure. **2** Something that is someone's downfall is the thing that causes their failure, e.g. *His pride may be his downfall.*

downgrade, downgrades, downgrading, downgraded (verb) If you downgrade something, you give it less importance or make it less valuable.

downhill **1** (adverb) moving down a slope. **2** becoming worse, e.g. *The press has gone downhill in the last 10 years.*

downpour, downpours (noun) A downpour is a heavy fall of rain.

downright (adjective or adverb) You use downright to emphasize that something is extremely unpleasant or bad, e.g. *Staff are often discourteous and sometimes downright rude.*

downstairs **1** (adverb) going down a staircase towards the ground floor. **2** (adjective or adverb) on a lower floor or on the ground floor.

downstream (adjective or adverb) Something that is downstream or moving downstream is nearer or moving nearer to the mouth of a river from a point further up.

down-to-earth (adjective) sensible and practical, e.g. *a down-to-earth approach.*

downtrodden (adjective) People who are downtrodden are treated badly by those with power and do not have the energy or ability to fight back.

downturn, downturns (noun) A downturn is a decline in the success of a company or industry.

downwards or **downward** **1** (adverb or adjective) If you move or look downwards, you move or look towards the ground or towards a lower level, e.g. *His eyes travelled downwards... She slipped on the downward slope.* **2** If an amount or rate moves downwards, it decreases.

downwind (adverb) If something moves downwind, it moves in the same direction as the wind, e.g. *Sparks drifted downwind.*

dowry, dowries (noun) A woman's dowry is money or property which her father gives to the man she marries.

doze, dozes, dozing, dozed **1** (verb) When you doze, you sleep lightly for a short period. **2** (noun) A doze is a short, light sleep.

dozen, dozens (noun) A dozen things are twelve of them.

drab, drabber, drabbest (adjective) dull and unattractive. **drabness** (noun).

draft, drafts, drafting, drafted **1** (noun) A draft of a document or speech is an early rough version of it. **2** (verb) When you draft a document or speech, you write the first rough version of it. **3** To draft people somewhere means to move them there so that they can do a specific job, e.g. *Various different presenters were drafted in.*

drag, drags, dragging, dragged **1** (verb) If you drag a heavy object somewhere, you pull it slowly and with difficulty. **2** If you drag someone somewhere, you make them go although they may be unwilling. **3** If things drag behind you, they trail along the ground as you move along. **4** If an event or a period of time drags, it is boring and seems to last a long time.

dragon, dragons (noun) In stories and legends, a dragon is a fierce animal like a large lizard with wings and claws that breathes fire.

dragonfly, dragonflies (noun) A dragonfly is a colourful insect which is often found near water.

dragoon, dragoons, dragooning, dragooned 1 (noun) Dragoons are soldiers. Originally, they were mounted infantry soldiers. **2** (verb) If you dragoon someone into something, you force them to do it.

drain, drains, draining, drained 1 (verb) If you drain something or if it drains, liquid gradually flows out of it or off it. **2** If you drain a glass, you drink all its contents. **3** If something drains strength, energy, or resources, it gradually uses them up, e.g. *The prolonged boardroom battle drained him of energy and money.* **4** (noun) A drain is a pipe or channel that carries water or sewage away from a place. **5** A drain in a road is a metal grid through which rainwater flows.

drainage 1 (noun) Drainage is the system of pipes, drains, or ditches used to drain water or other liquid away from a place. **2** Drainage is also the process of draining water away, or the way in which a place drains, e.g. *To grow these well, all you need is good drainage.*

drake, drakes (noun) A drake is a male duck.

drama, dramas 1 (noun) A drama is a serious play for the theatre, television, or radio. **2** Drama is plays and the theatre in general, e.g. *Elizabethan drama.* **3** You can refer to the exciting events or aspects of a situation as drama, e.g. *the drama of real life.*

dramatic (adjective) A dramatic change or event happens suddenly and is very noticeable, e.g. *a dramatic departure from tradition.* **dramatically** (adverb).

dramatist, dramatists (noun) A dramatist is a person who writes plays.

drape, drapes, draping, draped (verb) If you drape a piece of cloth, you arrange it so that it hangs down or covers something in loose folds.

drastic (adjective) A drastic course of action is very strong and severe and is usually taken urgently, e.g. *It's time for drastic action.* **drastically** (adverb).

draught, draughts (pronounced **draft**) **1** (noun) A draught is a current of cold air. **2** A draught of liquid is an amount that you swallow. **3** (adjective) Draught beer is served straight from barrels rather than in bottles. **4** (noun) Draughts is a game for two people played on a chessboard with round pieces.

draughtsman, draughtsmen (noun) A draughtsman is someone who prepares detailed drawings or plans.

draughty, draughtier, draughtiest (adjective) A place that is draughty has currents of cold air blowing through it.

draw, draws, drawing, drew, drawn 1 (verb) When you draw, you use a pen, pencil, or crayon to make a picture or diagram. **2** To draw near means to move closer. To draw away or draw back means to move away. **3** If you draw something in a particular direction, you pull it there smoothly and gently, e.g. *He drew his feet under the chair.* **4**

If you draw a deep breath, you breathe in deeply. **5** If you draw the curtains, you pull them so that they cover or uncover the window. **6** If something such as money, water, or energy is drawn from a source, it is taken from it. **7** If you draw a conclusion, you arrive at it from the facts you know. **8** If you draw a distinction or a comparison between two things, you point out that it exists. **9** (noun) A draw is the result of a game or competition in which nobody wins. **draw up** (verb) To draw up a plan, document, or list means to prepare it and write it out.

drawback, drawbacks (noun) A drawback is a problem that makes something less acceptable or desirable, e.g. *Shortcuts usually have a drawback.*

drawbridge, drawbridges (noun) A drawbridge is a bridge that can be pulled up or lowered.

drawer, drawers (noun) A drawer is a sliding box-shaped part of a piece of furniture used for storage.

drawing, drawings 1 (noun) A drawing is a picture made with a pencil, pen, or crayon. **2** Drawing is the skill or work of making drawings.

drawing room, drawing rooms (noun; an old-fashioned word) A drawing room is a room in a house where people sit and relax or entertain guests.

drawl, drawls, drawling, drawled (verb) If someone drawls, they speak slowly with long vowel sounds.

drawn Drawn is the past participle of **draw**.

dread, dreads, dreading, dreaded 1 (verb) If you dread something, you feel very worried and frightened about it, e.g. *He was dreading the journey.* **2** (noun) Dread is a feeling of great fear or anxiety. **dreaded** (adjective).

dreadful (adjective) very bad or unpleasant. **dreadfully** (adverb).

dream, dreams, dreaming, dreamed or **dreamt 1** (noun) A dream is a series of pictures or events that you experience in your mind while asleep. **2** A dream is a situation or event which you often think about because you would very much like it to happen, e.g. *The trust helped people to fulfil their dream of becoming self-employed.* **3** (verb) When you dream, you see pictures and events in your mind while you are asleep. **4** When you dream about something happening, you often think about it because you would very much like it to happen. **5** If someone dreams up a plan or idea, they invent it. **6** If you say you would not dream of doing something, you are emphasizing that you would not do it, e.g. *I wouldn't dream of giving the plot away.* **7** (adjective) too good to be true, e.g. *a dream holiday.* **dreamer** (noun).

dreamy, dreamier, dreamiest (adjective) Someone with a dreamy expression looks as if they are thinking about something very pleasant.

dreary, drearier, dreariest (adjective) dull or boring.

dregs (plural noun) The dregs of a liquid are the last drops left at the bottom of a container, and any sediment left with it.

drenched (adjective) soaking wet.

dress, dresses, dressing, dressed 1 (noun) A dress is a piece of clothing for women or girls made up of a skirt and top attached. **2** Dress is any clothing worn by men or women. **3** (verb) When you dress, you put clothes on. **4** If you dress for a special occasion, you put on formal clothes. **5** To dress a wound means to clean it up and treat it.

dresser, dressers (noun) A dresser is a piece of kitchen or dining room furniture with cupboards or drawers in the lower part and open shelves in the top part.

dribble, dribbles, dribbling, dribbled 1 (verb) When liquid dribbles down a surface, it trickles down it in drops or a thin stream. **2** If a person or animal dribbles, saliva trickles from their mouth. **3** (noun) A dribble of liquid is a small quantity of it flowing in a thin stream or drops. **4** (verb) In sport, to dribble a ball means to move it along by repeatedly tapping it with your hand, foot, or a stick.

drift, drifts, drifting, drifted 1 (verb) When something drifts, it is carried along by the wind or by water. **2** When people drift, they move aimlessly from one place or activity to another. **3** If you drift off to sleep, you gradually fall asleep. **4** (noun) A snow drift is a pile of snow heaped up by the wind. **5** The drift of an argument or speech is its main point. **drifter** (noun).

drill, drills, drilling, drilled 1 (noun) A drill is any of various tools for making holes, e.g. *an electric drill.* **2** (verb) To drill into something means to make a hole in it using a drill. **3** (noun) Drill is a routine exercise or routine training, e.g. *lifeboat drill.* **4** (verb) If you drill people, you teach them to do something by repetition.

drink, drinks, drinking, drank, drunk 1 (verb) When you drink, you take liquid into your mouth and swallow it. **2** To drink also means to drink alcohol, e.g. *He drinks little and eats carefully.* **3** (noun) A drink is an amount of liquid suitable for drinking. **4** A drink is also an alcoholic drink. **drinker** (noun).

drip, drips, dripping, dripped 1 (verb) When liquid drips, it falls in small drops. **2** When an object drips, drops of liquid fall from it. **3** (noun) A drip is a drop of liquid falling from something. **4** A drip is also a device for allowing liquid food to enter the bloodstream of a person who cannot eat properly because they are ill.

drive, drives, driving, drove, driven 1 (verb) To drive a vehicle means to operate it and control its movements. **2** If something or someone drives you to do something, they force you to do it, e.g. *The illness of his daughter drove him* *to religion.* **3** If you drive a post or nail into something, you force it in by hitting it with a hammer. **4** If something drives a machine, it supplies the power that makes it work. **5** (noun) A drive is a journey in a vehicle such as a car. **6** A drive is also a private road that leads from a public road to a person's house. **7** Drive is energy and determination. **driver** (noun), **driving** (noun).

drivel (noun) Drivel is nonsense, e.g. *Never heard such patent drivel in my life.*

drizzle (noun) Drizzle is light rain.

dromedary, dromedaries (noun) A dromedary is a camel which has one hump.

drone, drones, droning, droned **1** (verb) If something drones, it makes a low, continuous humming noise. **2** If someone drones on, they keep talking or reading aloud in a boring way. **3** (noun) A drone is a continuous low dull sound.

drool, drools, drooling, drooled (verb) If someone drools, saliva dribbles from their mouth without them being able to stop it.

droop, droops, drooping, drooped (verb) If something droops, it hangs or sags downwards with no strength or firmness.

drop, drops, dropping, dropped **1** (verb) If you drop something, you let it fall. **2** If something drops, it falls straight down. **3** If a level or amount drops, it becomes less. **4** If you drop something that you are doing or dealing with, you stop doing it or dealing with it, e.g. *She dropped the subject and never mentioned it again.* **5** If you drop a hint, you give someone a hint in a casual way. **6** If you drop something or someone somewhere, you deposit or leave them there. **7** (noun) A drop of liquid is a very small quantity of it that forms or falls in a spherical shape. **8** A drop is a decrease, e.g. *a huge drop in income.* **9** A drop is also the vertical distance between the top and bottom of something tall, such as a cliff or building, e.g. *It is a sheer drop to the foot of the cliff.*

droplet, droplets (noun) A droplet is a small drop.

droppings (plural noun) Droppings are the faeces of birds and small animals.

drought, droughts (rhymes with **shout**) (noun) A drought is a long period during which there is no rain.

drove Drove is the past tense of **drive**.

drown, drowns, drowning, drowned **1** (verb) When someone drowns or is drowned, they die because they have gone under water and cannot breathe. **2** If a noise drowns a sound, it is louder than the sound and makes it impossible to hear it.

drowsy, drowsier, drowsiest (adjective) feeling sleepy.

drudgery (noun) Drudgery is hard uninteresting work.

drug, drugs, drugging, drugged **1** (noun) A drug is a chemical given to people to treat disease. **2** Drugs are chemical substances that some people smoke, swallow, smell, or inject because of their stimulating effects. **3** (verb) To drug a person or animal means to give them a drug to make them unconscious. **4** To drug food or drink means to add a drug to it in order to make someone unconscious. **drugged** (adjective).

druid, druids (pronounced **droo**-id) (noun) A druid was a priest of an ancient religion in Northern Europe.

drum, drums, drumming, drummed 1 (noun) A drum is a musical instrument consisting of a skin stretched tightly over a round frame. **2** A drum is also any object shaped like a drum, e.g. *an oil drum.* **3** (verb) If something is drumming on a surface, it is hitting it regularly, making a continuous beating sound. **4** If you drum something into someone, you keep saying it to them until they understand it or remember it.

drumstick, drumsticks 1 (noun) A drumstick is a stick used for beating a drum. **2** A chicken drumstick is the lower part of the leg of a chicken, which is cooked and eaten.

drunk, drunks 1 Drunk is the past participle of **drink**. **2** (adjective) If someone is drunk, they have drunk so much alcohol that they cannot speak clearly or behave sensibly. **3** (noun) A drunk is a person who is drunk, or who often gets drunk. **drunken** (adjective), **drunkenly** (adverb), **drunkenness** (noun).

dry, drier or **dryer, driest; dries, drying, dried 1** (adjective) Something that is dry contains or uses no water or liquid. **2** (verb) When you dry something, or when it dries, liquid is removed from it. **3** (adjective) Dry bread or toast is eaten without jam, butter, or any other kind of topping. **4** Dry sherry or wine does not taste sweet. **5** Dry also means plain and sometimes boring, e.g. *the dry facts.* **6** Dry humour is subtle and sarcastic. **dryness** (noun), **drily** (adverb).

dry up 1 (verb) If something dries up, it becomes completely dry. **2** (an informal use) If you dry up, you forget what you were going to say, or find that you have nothing left to say.

dry-clean, dry-cleans, dry-cleaning, dry-cleaned (verb) When clothes are dry-cleaned, they are cleaned with a liquid chemical rather than with water.

dryer, dryers; also spelled **drier** (noun) A dryer is any device for removing moisture from something by heating or by hot air, e.g. *a hair dryer.*

dual (adjective) having two parts, functions, or aspects, e.g. *a dual-purpose trimmer.*

dub, dubs, dubbing, dubbed 1 (verb) If something is dubbed a particular name, it is given that name, e.g. *Smiling has been dubbed 'nature's secret weapon'.* **2** If a film is dubbed, the voices on the soundtrack are not those of the actors, but those of other actors speaking in a different language.

dubious (pronounced **dyoo**-bee-uss) **1** (adjective) not entirely honest, safe, or reliable, e.g. *dubious sales techniques.* **2** doubtful, e.g. *I felt dubious about the entire proposition.* **dubiously** (adverb).

duchess, duchesses (noun) A duchess is a woman who has the same rank as a duke, or who is a duke's wife or widow.

duchy, duchies (pronounced **dut**-shee) (noun) A duchy is the land owned and ruled by a duke or duchess.

duck, ducks, ducking, ducked 1 (noun) A duck is any of various birds that live in water and have short legs, webbed feet, a short neck, and a large flat bill. **2** (verb) If you duck, you move your head quickly downwards in order to avoid being hit by something. **3** If you duck a duty or responsibility, you avoid it. **4** To duck someone means to push them briefly under water.

duckling, ducklings (noun) A duckling is a young duck.

duct, ducts 1 (noun) A duct is a pipe, tube, or channel through which liquid or gas is sent. **2** A duct is also any bodily passage through which liquid such as tears can pass.

dud, duds (noun) A dud is something which does not function properly.

due, dues 1 (adjective) expected to happen or arrive, e.g. *The baby is due at Christmas.* **2** If you give something due consideration, you give it the consideration that it needs. **3** (phrase) **Due to** means because of, e.g. *Headaches can be due to stress.* **4** (adverb) Due means exactly in a particular direction, e.g. *About a mile due west lay the ocean.* **5** (plural noun) Dues are sums of money that you pay regularly to an organization you belong to.

duel, duels 1 (noun) A duel is a fight arranged between two people using deadly weapons, for the purpose of settling a quarrel. **2** Any contest or conflict between two people can be referred to as a duel.

duet, duets (noun) A duet is a piece of music sung or played by two people.

dug Dug is the past tense and past participle of **dig.**

dugout, dugouts 1 (noun) A dugout is a canoe made by hollowing out a log. **2** (a military word) A dugout is also a shelter dug in the ground for protection.

duke, dukes (noun) A duke is a nobleman with a rank just below that of a prince.

dull, duller, dullest; dulls, dulling, dulled 1 (adjective) not at all interesting in any way. **2** slow to learn or understand. **3** not bright, sharp, or clear. **4** A dull day or dull sky is very cloudy. **5** Dull feelings are weak and not intense, e.g. *He should have been angry but felt only dull resentment.* **6** (verb) If something dulls or is dulled, it becomes less bright, sharp, or clear. **dully** (adverb), **dullness** (noun).

duly 1 (adverb; a formal use) If something is duly done, it is done in the correct way, e.g. *I wish to record my support for the duly elected council.* **2** If something duly happens, it is something that you expected to happen, e.g. *Two chicks duly emerged from their eggs.*

dumb, dumber, dumbest 1 (adjective) unable to speak. **2** (an informal use) slow to understand or stupid.

dumbfounded (adjective) speechless with amazement, e.g *She was too dumbfounded to answer.*

dummy, dummies 1 (noun) A baby's dummy is a rubber teat which it sucks or bites on. **2** A dummy is also an imitation or model of something which is used for display. **3** (adjective) imitation or substitute.

dump, dumps, dumping, dumped 1 (verb) When unwanted waste matter is dumped, it is left somewhere. **2** If you dump something, you throw it down or put it down somewhere in a careless way. **3** (noun) A dump is a place where rubbish is left. **4** A dump is also a storage place, especially used by the military for storing supplies. **5** (an informal use) You refer to a place as a dump when it is unattractive and unpleasant to live in.

dumpling, dumplings (noun) A dumpling is a small lump of dough that is cooked and eaten with meat and vegetables.

dunce, dunces (noun) A dunce is a person who cannot learn what someone is trying to teach them.

dune, dunes (noun) A dune or sand dune is a hill of sand near the sea or in the desert.

dung (noun) Dung is the faeces from large animals, sometimes called manure.

dungarees (plural noun) Dungarees are trousers which have a bib covering the chest and straps over the shoulders.

dungeon, dungeons (pronounced **dun**-jen) (noun) A dungeon is an underground prison.

dunk, dunks, dunking, dunked (verb) To dunk something means to dip it briefly into a liquid, e.g. *He dunked a single tea bag into two cups.*

duo, duos 1 (noun) A duo is a pair of musical performers; also a piece of music written for two players. **2** Any two people doing something together can be referred to as a duo.

dupe, dupes, duping, duped 1 (verb) If someone dupes you, they trick you. **2** (noun) A dupe is someone who has been tricked.

duplicate, duplicates, duplicating, duplicated 1 (verb) To duplicate something means to make an exact copy of it. **2** (noun) A duplicate is something that is identical to something else. **3** (adjective) identical to or an exact copy of, e.g. *a duplicate key.* **duplication** (noun).

durable (adjective) strong and lasting for a long time. **durability** (noun).

duration (noun) The duration of something is the length of time during which it happens or exists.

duress (pronounced dyoo-**ress**) (noun) If you do something under duress, you are forced to do it, and you do it very unwillingly.

during (preposition) happening

throughout a particular time or at a particular point in time, e.g. *The mussels will open naturally during cooking.*

dusk (noun) Dusk is the time just before nightfall when it is not completely dark.

dust, dusts, dusting, dusted 1 (noun) Dust is dry fine powdery material such as particles of earth, dirt, or pollen. **2** (verb) When you dust furniture or other objects, you remove dust from them using a duster. **3** If you dust a surface with powder, you cover it lightly with the powder.

dustbin, dustbins (noun) A dustbin is a large container for rubbish.

duster, dusters (noun) A duster is a cloth used for removing dust from furniture and other objects.

dustman, dustmen (noun) A dustman is someone whose job is to collect the rubbish from people's houses.

dusty, dustier, dustiest (adjective) covered with dust.

Dutch 1 (adjective) belonging or relating to Holland. **2** (noun) Dutch is the main language spoken in Holland.

dutiful (adjective) doing everything you are expected to do. **dutifully** (adverb).

duty, duties 1 (noun) Duties are things you ought to do or feel you should do, because it is your responsibility to do them, e.g. *We have a duty as adults to listen to children.* **2** (plural noun) Your duties are the tasks which you do as part of your job. **3** (noun) Duty is tax paid to the government on some goods, especially imports.

duty-free (adjective) Duty-free goods are goods which are not subject to customs duty and can be bought cheaply at airports or on planes and ships.

duvet, duvets (pronounced **doo**-vay) (noun) A duvet is a bed cover consisting of a cotton quilt filled with feathers or other material, used in place of a sheet and blankets.

dwarf, dwarfs, dwarfing, dwarfed 1 (verb) If one thing dwarfs another, it is so much bigger that it makes it look very small. **2** (adjective) smaller than average. **3** (noun) A dwarf is a person who is much smaller than average size.

dwell, dwells, dwelling, dwelled or **dwelt 1** (verb; a literary use) To dwell somewhere means to live there. **2** If you dwell on something or dwell upon it, you think, speak, or write about it a lot.

dwelling, dwellings (noun; a formal word) Someone's dwelling is the house or other place where they live.

dwindle, dwindles, dwindling, dwindled (verb) If something dwindles, it becomes less in size, strength, or number.

dye, dyes, dyeing, dyed 1 (verb) To dye something means to change its colour by applying coloured liquid to it. **2** (noun) Dye is a staining or colouring substance which is mixed into a liquid and used to change the colour of something such as cloth or hair.

dyke, dykes; also spelled **dike** (noun) A dyke is a thick wall that prevents water flooding onto land from a river or from the sea.

dynamic, dynamics 1 (adjective) A dynamic person is full of energy, ambition, personality, and new ideas. **2** (noun) In physics, dynamics is the study of the forces that change or produce the motion of bodies or particles. **3** (adjective) relating to energy or forces which produce motion. **4** (plural noun) The dynamics of a society or a situation are the forces that cause it to change.

dynamite (noun) Dynamite is a kind of explosive.

dynamo, dynamos (noun) A dynamo is a device that converts mechanical energy into electricity.

dynasty, dynasties (noun) A dynasty is a series of rulers of a country all belonging to the same family.

dysentery (pronounced **diss**-en-tree) (noun) Dysentery is an infection of the bowel which causes fever, stomach pain, and severe diarrhoea.

E e

each 1 (adjective or pronoun) every one taken separately, e.g. *Each time she went out, she would buy a plant... She thrust a bag at each of us.* **2** (phrase) If people do something to **each other,** each person does it to the other or others, e.g. *She and Chris smiled to each other.*

eager (adjective) wanting very much to do or have something. **eagerly** (adverb), **eagerness** (noun).

eagle, eagles (noun) An eagle is a large bird which hunts and kills other animals for food.

ear, ears 1 (noun) Your ears are the parts of your body on either side of your head with which you hear sounds. **2** An ear of corn or wheat is the top part of the stalk which contains seeds.

eardrum, eardrums (noun) Your eardrums are thin pieces of tightly stretched skin inside your ears which vibrate so that you can hear sounds.

earl, earls (noun) An earl is a British nobleman.

early, earlier, earliest 1 (adjective or adverb) before the arranged or expected time, e.g. *He wasn't late for our meeting, I was early.* **2** near the beginning of a day, evening, or other period of time, e.g. *the early 1970s.*

earmark, earmarks, earmarking, earmarked (verb) If you earmark something for a special purpose, you keep it for that purpose.

earn, earns, earning, earned 1 (verb) If you earn money, you get it in return for work that you do. **2** If you earn something such as praise, you receive it because you deserve it. **earner** (noun).

earnest 1 (adjective) sincere in what you say or do, e.g. *I answered with an earnest smile.* **2** (phrase) If something begins **in earnest,** it happens to a greater or more serious extent than before, e.g. *The battle began in earnest.* **earnestly** (adverb).

earnings (plural noun) Your earnings are money that you earn.

earphones (plural noun) Earphones are small speakers which you wear on your ears to listen to a radio or cassette player without other people hearing it.

earring, earrings (noun) Earrings are pieces of jewellery that you wear on your ears.

earshot (phrase) If you are **within earshot** of something, you can hear it.

earth, earths 1 (noun) The earth is the planet on which we live. **2** Earth is the dry land on the surface of the earth, especially the soil in which things grow. **3** An earth is a hole in the ground where a fox lives. **4** The earth in a plug or piece of electrical equipment is the wire through which electricity can pass into the ground and so make the equipment safe for use.

earthenware (noun) Earthenware is pottery made of baked clay.

earthly (adjective) concerned with life on earth rather than heaven or life after death.

earthquake, earthquakes (noun) An earthquake is a series of vibrations along the surface of the earth caused by a build-up of pressure deep within the earth.

earthworm, earthworms (noun) An earthworm is a worm that lives under the ground.

earthy, earthier, earthiest 1 (adjective) looking or smelling like earth. **2** Someone who is earthy is open and direct, often in a crude way, e.g. *earthy language.*

earwig, earwigs (noun) An earwig is a small, thin, brown insect which has a pair of pincers at the end of its body.

ease, eases, easing, eased 1 (noun) Ease is lack of difficulty, worry, or hardship, e.g. *He had sailed through life with relative ease.* **2** (verb) When something eases, or when you ease it, it becomes less severe or less intense, e.g. *to ease the pain.* **3** If you ease something somewhere, you move it there slowly and carefully, e.g. *He eased himself into his chair.*

easel, easels (noun) An easel is an upright frame which supports a picture that someone is painting.

easily 1 (adverb) without difficulty. **2** without a doubt, e.g. *The song is easily one of their finest.*

east 1 (noun) East is the direction in which you look to see the sun rise. **2** The east of a place or country is the part which is towards the east when you are in the centre, e.g. *the east of England.* **3** (adjective or adverb) East means in or towards the east, e.g. *East London.* **4** (adjective) An east wind blows from the east. **5** (noun) The East is the countries in the south and east of Asia.

Easter (noun) Easter is a Christian religious festival celebrating the resurrection of Christ.

easterly 1 (adjective) Easterly means to or towards the east. **2** An easterly wind blows from the east.

eastern (adjective) in or from the east, e.g. *a remote eastern corner of the country.*

eastward or **eastwards** **1** (adverb) Eastward or eastwards means towards the east, e.g. *the eastward expansion of the City of London.* **2** (adjective) The eastward part of something is the east part.

easy, easier, easiest **1** (adjective) able to be done without difficulty, e.g. *It's easy to fall.* **2** comfortable and without any worries, e.g. *an easy life.*

eat, eats, eating, ate, eaten **1** (verb) To eat means to chew and swallow food. **2** When you eat, you have a meal, e.g. *We like to eat early.* **eat away** (verb) If something is eaten away, it is slowly destroyed, e.g. *The sea had eaten away at the headland.*

eaves (plural noun) The eaves of a roof are the lower edges which jut out over the walls.

eavesdrop, eavesdrops, eavesdropping, eavesdropped (verb) If you eavesdrop, you listen secretly to what other people are saying.

ebb, ebbs, ebbing, ebbed **1** (verb) When the sea or the tide ebbs, it flows back. **2** If a person's feeling or strength ebbs, it gets weaker, e.g. *The strength ebbed from his body.*

ebony **1** (noun) Ebony is the hard, dark-coloured wood of a tropical tree, used for making furniture. **2** (noun or adjective) very deep black.

ebullient (adjective; a formal word) lively and full of enthusiasm. **ebullience** (noun).

EC (noun) The EC is an old name for the European Union. EC is an abbreviation for 'European Community'.

eccentric, eccentrics (pronounced ik-**sen**-trik) **1** (adjective) having habits or opinions which other people think are odd or peculiar. **2** (noun) An eccentric is someone who is eccentric. **eccentricity** (noun), **eccentrically** (adverb).

ecclesiastical (pronounced ik-leez-ee-**ass**-ti-kl) (adjective) of or relating to the Christian church.

echelon, echelons (pronounced **esh**-el-on) (noun) An echelon is a level of power or responsibility in an organization.

echo, echoes, echoing, echoed **1** (noun) An echo is a sound which is caused by sound waves reflecting off a surface. **2** An echo is also a repetition, imitation, or reminder of something, e.g. *Echoes of the past are everywhere.* **3** (verb) If a sound echoes, it is reflected off a surface so that you can hear it again after the original sound has stopped.

eclipse, eclipses (noun) An eclipse occurs when one planet passes in front of another and hides it from view for a short time.

ecology (noun) Ecology is the relationship between plants, animals, people, and their environment; also used of the study of this relationship. **ecological** (adjective), **ecologically** (adverb), **ecologist** (noun).

economic **1** (adjective) concerning the management of the money, industry, and trade of a country. **2** concerning making a profit, e.g. *economic to* *produce.*

economical 1 (adjective) Something that is economical is cheap to use or operate. **2** Someone who is economical spends money sensibly. **economically** (adverb).

economics (noun) Economics is the study of the production and distribution of goods, services, and wealth in a society and the organization of its money, industry, and trade.

economist, economists (noun) An economist is a person who studies or writes about economics.

economy, economies 1 (noun) The economy of a country is the system it uses to organize and manage its money, industry, and trade; also used of the wealth that a country gets from business and industry. **2** Economy is the careful use of things to save money, time, or energy, e.g. *Max dished up deftly, with an economy of movement.*

ecstasy, ecstasies 1 (noun) Ecstasy is a feeling of extreme happiness. **2** (an informal use) Ecstasy is a strong illegal drug that can cause hallucinations. **ecstatic** (adjective), **ecstatically** (adverb).

eczema (pronounced **ek**-sim-ma) (noun) Eczema is a skin disease that causes the surface of the skin to become rough and itchy.

eddy, eddies (noun) An eddy is a circular movement in water or air.

edge, edges, edging, edged 1 (noun) The edge of something is a border or line where it ends or meets something else. **2** The edge of a blade is its thin, sharp side. **3** If you have the edge over someone, you have an advantage over them. **4** (verb) If you edge something, you make a border for it, e.g. *The veil was edged with matching lace.* **5** If you edge somewhere, you move there very gradually, e.g. *The ferry edged its way out into the river.*

edgy, edgier, edgiest (adjective) nervous, anxious, and irritable.

edible (adjective) safe and pleasant to eat.

edifice, edifices (pronounced **ed**-if-iss) (noun; a formal word) An edifice is a large and impressive building.

edit, edits, editing, edited 1 (verb) If you edit a piece of writing, you correct it so that it is fit for publishing. **2** To edit a film or a radio or television programme means to select different parts of it and arrange them in a particular order. **3** Someone who edits a newspaper or magazine is in charge of it.

edition, editions 1 (noun) An edition of a book, magazine, or newspaper is a particular version of it printed at one time. **2** An edition of a television or radio programme is a single programme that is one of a series.

editor, editors 1 (noun) An editor is a person who is responsible for the content of a newspaper or magazine. **2** An editor is also a person who checks books and makes corrections to them before they are published. **3** An editor of a film or television or radio programme is a person who selects different parts and arranges them in a particular order. **editorship** (noun).

editorial, editorials 1 (adjective) involved in preparing a newspaper, book, or magazine for publication. **2** involving the contents and the opinions of a newspaper or magazine, e.g. *an editorial comment.* **3** (noun) An editorial is an article in a newspaper or magazine which gives the opinions of the editor or publisher on a particular topic. **editorially** (adverb).

educate, educates, educating, educated (verb) To educate someone means to teach them so that they acquire knowledge and understanding about something.

educated (adjective) having a high standard of learning and culture.

education 1 (noun) Education is the process of gaining knowledge and understanding through learning. **2** Education also refers to the system of teaching people at school, college, or university. **educational** (adjective), **educationally** (adverb).

eel, eels (noun) An eel is a long, thin, snakelike fish.

eerie, eerier, eeriest (adjective) strange and frightening, e.g. *the eerie silence of the still, ghostly water.* **eerily** (adverb).

effect, effects 1 (noun) An effect is a direct result of someone or something on another person or thing, e.g. *He was treated for burns, shock, and the effects of the smoke.* **2** An effect that someone or something has is the overall impression or result that they have, e.g. *The effect of the decor was cosy and antique.*

effective 1 (adjective) working well and producing the intended results. **2** coming into operation or beginning officially, e.g. *The agreement has become effective immediately.* **effectively** (adverb).

effeminate (adjective) A man who is effeminate behaves or looks like a woman.

efficient (adjective) capable of doing something well without wasting time or energy. **efficiently** (adverb), **efficiency** (noun).

effigy, effigies (pronounced **ef**-fij-ee) (noun) An effigy is a statue, carving, or other figure of a person.

effluent, effluents (pronounced **ef**-loo-ent) (noun) Effluent is liquid waste that comes out of factories or sewage works.

effort, efforts 1 (noun) Effort is the physical or mental energy needed to do something. **2** An effort is an attempt or struggle to do something, e.g. *She went to keep-fit classes in an effort to fight the flab.*

effortless (adjective) done easily. **effortlessly** (adverb).

e.g. e.g. means 'for example', and is abbreviated from the Latin expression 'exempli gratia'.

egalitarian (adjective) favouring equality for all people, e.g. *an egalitarian country.*

egg, eggs 1 (noun) An egg is an oval or rounded object laid by female birds, reptiles, fishes, and insects. A baby creature develops inside the egg until it is ready to be born. **2** An egg is also a hen's egg used as food. **3** In a female animal, an egg is a cell produced in its body which can develop into a baby if it is fertilized.

ego, egos (pronounced **ee**-goh) (noun) Your ego is your opinion of what you are worth, e.g. *It'll do her good and boost her ego.*

egocentric (adjective) only thinking of yourself and your own interests.

egoism or **egotism** (noun) Egoism is behaviour and attitudes which show that you believe that you are more important than other people. **egoist** or **egotist** (noun), **egoistic, egotistic** or **egotistical** (adjective).

Egyptian, Egyptians (pronounced ij-**jip**-shn) **1** (adjective) belonging or relating to Egypt. **2** (noun) An Egyptian is someone who comes from Egypt.

eight, eights the number 8. **eighth**

eighteen the number 18. **eighteenth**

eighty, eighties the number 80. **eightieth**

either 1 (adjective, pronoun, or conjunction) one or the other of two possible alternatives, e.g. *You can spell it either way... Either of these schemes would cost billions of pounds... Either take it or leave it.* **2** (adjective) both one and the other, e.g. *on either side of your forehead.*

ejaculate, ejaculates, ejaculating, ejaculated 1 (verb) When a man ejaculates, he discharges semen from his penis. **2** If you ejaculate, you suddenly say something. **ejaculation** (noun).

eject, ejects, ejecting, ejected (verb) If you eject something or someone, you forcefully push or send them out, e.g. *He was ejected from the canteen.* **ejection** (noun).

elaborate, elaborates, elaborating, elaborated 1 (adjective) having many different parts, e.g. *an elaborate system of drains.* **2** carefully planned, detailed, and exact, e.g. *elaborate plans.* **3** highly decorated and complicated, e.g. *elaborate designs.* **4** (verb) If you elaborate on something, you add more information or detail about it. **elaborately** (adverb), **elaboration** (noun).

elapse, elapses, elapsing, elapsed (verb) When time elapses, it passes by, e.g. *Eleven years elapsed before you got this job.*

elastic 1 (adjective) able to stretch easily. **2** (noun) Elastic is rubber material which stretches and returns to its original shape. **elasticity** (noun).

elation (noun) Elation is a feeling of great happiness. **elated** (adjective).

elbow, elbows, elbowing, elbowed 1 (noun) Your elbow is the joint between the upper part of your arm and your forearm. **2** (verb) If you elbow someone aside, you push them away with your elbow.

elder, eldest; elders 1 (adjective) Your elder brother or sister is older than you. **2** (noun) An elder is a senior member of a group who has influence or authority. **3** An elder is also a bush or small tree with dark purple berries.

elderly 1 (adjective) Elderly is a polite way to describe an old person. **2** (noun) The elderly are old people, e.g. *Priority should be given to services for the elderly.*

elect, elects, electing, elected 1 (verb) If you elect someone, you choose them to fill a position, by voting, e.g. *He's just been elected president.* **2** (a formal use) If you elect to do something, you choose to do it, e.g. *I have elected to stay.* **3** (adjective; a formal use) voted into a position, but not yet carrying out the duties of the position, e.g. *the vice-president elect.*

election, elections (noun) An election is the selection of one or more people for an official position by voting. **electoral** (adjective).

electorate, electorates (noun) The electorate is all the people who have the right to vote in an election.

electric 1 (adjective) powered by, produced by, or carrying electricity. **2** very tense or exciting, e.g. *The atmosphere is electric.*

electrical (adjective) using, producing, or concerning electricity, e.g. *electrical goods.* **electrically** (adverb).

electrician, electricians (noun) An electrician is a person whose job is to install, maintain, and repair electrical equipment.

electricity (noun) Electricity is a form of energy used for heating and lighting, and to provide power for machines.

electrified (adjective) A piece of equipment that is electrified is connected to a supply of electricity.

electrifying (adjective) Something that is electrifying makes you feel very excited.

electrocute, electrocutes, electrocuting, electrocuted (verb) If someone is electrocuted, they are killed by touching something that is connected to electricity. **electrocution** (noun).

electrode, electrodes (noun) An electrode is a small piece of metal which allows an electric current to pass between a source of power and a piece of equipment.

electron, electrons (noun) In physics, an electron is a tiny particle of matter, smaller than an atom.

electronic (adjective) having transistors, silicon chips, or valves which control an electric current. **electronically** (adverb).

electronics (noun) Electronics is the technology of electronic devices such as radios, televisions, and computers; also the study of how these devices work.

elegant (adjective) attractive and graceful or stylish, e.g. *an elegant and beautiful city.* **elegantly** (adverb), **elegance** (noun).

elegy, elegies (pronounced **el**-lij-ee) (noun) An elegy is a sad poem or song about someone who has died.

element, elements 1 (noun) An element of something is a part which combines with others to make a whole. **2** In chemistry, an element is a substance that is made up of only one type of atom. **3** A particular element within a large group of people is a section of it which is similar, e.g. *the undesirable elements of the population.* **4** An element of a quality is a certain amount of it, e.g. *Their attack has largely lost the element of surprise.* **5** The elements of a subject are the basic and most important points. **6** The elements are the weather conditions, e.g. *He battled against the elements of the Great British weather.*

elemental (adjective; a formal word) simple and basic, but powerful, e.g. *elemental emotions.*

elementary (adjective) simple, basic, and straightforward, e.g. *an elementary course in woodwork.*

elephant, elephants (noun) An elephant is a very large four-legged mammal with thick leathery skin, a long trunk, large ears, and ivory tusks.

elevate, elevates, elevating, elevated 1 (verb) To elevate someone to a higher status or position means to give them greater status or importance, e.g. *He was elevated to the rank of major in the army.* **2** To elevate something means to raise it up.

elevation, elevations 1 (noun) The elevation of someone or something is the raising of them to a higher level or position. **2** The elevation of a place is its height above sea level or above the ground.

eleven, elevens 1 Eleven is the number 11. **2** (noun) An eleven is a team of cricket or football players. **eleventh**

elf, elves (noun) In folklore, an elf is a small mischievous fairy.

elicit, elicits, eliciting, elicited (pronounced il-**iss**-it) **1** (verb; a formal use) If you elicit information, you find it out by asking careful questions. **2** If you elicit a response or reaction, you make it happen, e.g. *He elicited sympathy from the audience.*

eligible (pronounced **el**-lij-i-bl) (adjective) suitable or having the right qualifications for something, e.g. *You will be eligible for a grant in the future.* **eligibility** (noun).

eliminate, eliminates, eliminating, eliminated 1 (verb) If you eliminate something or someone, you get rid of them, e.g. *They eliminated him from their inquiries.* **2** If a team or a person is eliminated from a competition, they can no longer take part. **elimination** (noun).

elite, elites (pronounced ill-**eet**) (noun) An elite is a group of the most powerful, rich, or talented people in a society.

Elizabethan (adjective) Someone or something that is Elizabethan lived or was made during the reign of Elizabeth I.

elk, elks (noun) An elk is the largest type of deer, found in North Europe, Asia, and North America.

ellipse, ellipses (noun) An ellipse is a regular oval shape, like a circle seen from an angle.

elm, elms (noun) An elm is a tall tree with broad leaves.
elocution (noun) Elocution is the art or study of speaking clearly or well in public with a standard accent.
elongated (adjective) long and thin.
elope, elopes, eloping, eloped (verb) If someone elopes, they run away secretly with their lover to get married.
eloquent (adjective) skilfully expressive and fluent in speech or writing, e.g. *an eloquent politician.* **eloquently** (adverb), **eloquence** (noun).
else 1 (adverb) other than this or more than this, e.g. *Can you think of anything else?* **2** (phrase) You say **or else** to introduce a possibility or an alternative, e.g. *You have to go with the flow or else be left behind in the rush.*
elsewhere (adverb) in or to another place, e.g. *He would rather be elsewhere.*
elude, eludes, eluding, eluded (pronounced ill-**ood**) **1** (verb) If a fact or idea eludes you, you cannot understand it or remember it. **2** If you elude someone or something, you avoid them or escape from them, e.g. *He eluded the authorities.*
elusive (adjective) difficult to find, achieve, describe, or remember, e.g. *the elusive million dollar prize.*
elves the plural of **elf.**
emaciated (pronounced im-**may**-see-ate-ed) (adjective) extremely thin and weak, because of illness or lack of food.
emancipation (noun) The emancipation of a person means the act of freeing them from harmful or unpleasant restrictions.
embargo, embargoes (noun) An embargo is an order made by a government to stop trade with another country.
embark, embarks, embarking, embarked 1 (verb) If you embark, you go onto a ship at the start of a journey. **2** If you embark on something, you start it, e.g. *He embarked on a huge spending spree.*
embarrass, embarrasses, embarrassing, embarrassed (verb) If you embarrass someone, you make them feel shy, ashamed, or uncomfortable, e.g. *I won't embarrass you by asking for details.* **embarrassed** (adjective), **embarrassing** (adjective), **embarrassment** (noun).
embassy, embassies (noun) An embassy is the building in which an ambassador and his or her staff work.
embedded (adjective) Something that is embedded is fixed firmly and deeply, e.g. *glass decorated with embedded threads.*
ember, embers (noun) Embers are glowing or smouldering pieces of coal or wood from a dying fire.
embittered (adjective) If you are embittered, you are angry and resentful about things that have happened to you.
emblazoned (pronounced im-**blaze**-nd) (adjective) If something is emblazoned with designs, it is decorated with them, e.g. *vases emblazoned with colourful images.*

emblem, emblems (noun) An emblem is an object or a design chosen to represent an organization or an idea, e.g. *a flower emblem of Japan.*

embody, embodies, embodying, embodied 1 (verb) To embody a particular quality or idea means to contain it or express it, e.g. *A young dancer embodies the spirit of fun.* **2** If a number of things are embodied in one thing, they are contained in it, e.g. *the principles embodied in his report.* **embodiment** (noun).

embossed (adjective) decorated with designs that stand up slightly from the surface, e.g. *embossed wallpaper.*

embrace, embraces, embracing, embraced 1 (verb) If you embrace someone, you hug them to show affection or as a greeting. **2** (noun) An embrace is a hug. **3** (verb) If you embrace an idea, religion, or political system, you accept it and believe in it.

embroider, embroiders, embroidering, embroidered (verb) If you embroider fabric, you sew a decorative design onto it.

embroidery (noun) Embroidery is decorative designs sewn onto fabric; also the art or skill of embroidery.

embroiled (adjective) If someone is embroiled in an argument, conflict, or trouble, they are deeply involved in it and cannot get out of it, e.g. *The two companies are now embroiled in the courts.*

embryo, embryos (pronounced **em**-bree-oh) (noun) An embryo is an animal or human being in the very early stages of development in the womb. **embryonic** (adjective).

emerald, emeralds 1 (noun) An emerald is a bright green precious stone. **2** (noun or adjective) bright green.

emerge, emerges, emerging, emerged 1 (verb) If someone emerges from a place, they come out of it so that they can be seen. **2** If something emerges, it becomes known or begins to be recognized as existing, e.g. *It later emerged that he faced bankruptcy proceedings.* **emergence** (noun), **emergent** (adjective).

emergency, emergencies (noun) An emergency is an unexpected and serious event which needs immediate action to deal with it.

emigrant, emigrants (noun) An emigrant is a person who leaves their native country and goes to live permanently in another one.

emigrate, emigrates, emigrating, emigrated (verb) If you emigrate, you leave your native country and go to live permanently in another one. **emigration** (noun).

eminence 1 (noun) Eminence is the quality of being well known and respected for what you do, e.g. *lawyers of eminence.* **2** 'Your Eminence' is a title of respect used to address a Roman Catholic cardinal.

eminent (adjective) well known and respected for what you do, e.g. *an eminent scientist.*

eminently (adverb; a formal word) very, e.g. *eminently reasonable.*

emir, emirs (pronounced em-**eer**) (noun) An emir is a Muslim ruler or nobleman.

emission, emissions (noun; a formal word) The emission of something such as gas or radiation is the release of it into the atmosphere.

emit, emits, emitting, emitted (verb) To emit something means to give it out or release it, e.g. *Bullfrogs emit an occasional croak from the pond.*

emotion, emotions (noun) An emotion is any strong feeling, such as love or fear.

emotional 1 (adjective) causing strong feelings, e.g. *an emotional appeal for help.* **2** to do with feelings rather than your physical condition, e.g. *emotional support.* **3** showing your feelings openly, e.g. *The child is in a very emotional state.* **emotionally** (adverb).

emotive (adjective) concerning emotions, or stirring up strong emotions, e.g. *emotive language.*

emperor, emperors (noun) An emperor is a male ruler of an empire.

emphasis, emphases (noun) Emphasis is special importance or extra stress given to something.

emphasize, emphasizes, emphasizing, emphasized; also spelled **emphasise** (verb) If you emphasize something, you make it known that it is very important, e.g. *It was emphasized that the matter was of international concern.*

emphatic (adjective) expressed strongly and with force to show how important something is, e.g. *I answered both questions with an emphatic 'Yes'.* **emphatically** (adverb).

empire, empires 1 (noun) An empire is a group of countries controlled by one country. **2** An empire is also a powerful group of companies controlled by one person.

employ, employs, employing, employed 1 (verb) If you employ someone, you pay them to work for you. **2** If you employ something for a particular purpose, you make use of it, e.g. *the techniques employed in turning grapes into wine.*

employee, employees (noun) An employee is a person who is paid to work for another person or for an organization.

employer, employers (noun) Someone's employer is the person or organization that they work for.

employment (noun) Employment is the state of having a paid job, or the activity of recruiting people for a job.

empower, empowers, empowering, empowered (verb) If you are empowered to do something, you have the authority or power to do it.

empress, empresses (noun) An empress is a woman who rules an empire, or the wife of an emperor.

empty, emptier, emptiest; empties, emptying, emptied 1 (adjective) having nothing or nobody inside. **2** without purpose, value, or meaning, e.g. *empty promises.* **3** (verb) If you empty something, or empty its contents, you remove the contents. **emptiness** (noun).

emu, emus (pronounced **ee**-myoo) (noun) An emu is a large greyish-brown Australian bird with long legs and three-toed feet. It can run fast, but cannot fly.

emulate, emulates, emulating, emulated (verb) If you emulate someone or something, you imitate them because you admire them. **emulation** (noun).

emulsion, emulsions (noun) Emulsion is a water-based paint.

enable, enables, enabling, enabled (verb) To enable something to happen means to make it possible.

enact, enacts, enacting, enacted 1 (verb) If a government enacts a law or bill, it officially passes it so that it becomes law. **2** If you enact a story or play, you act it out. **enactment** (noun).

enamel, enamels, enamelling, enamelled 1 (noun) Enamel is a substance like glass, used to decorate or protect metal, glass, or china. **2** The enamel on your teeth is the hard, white substance that forms the outer part. **3** (verb) If you enamel something, you decorate or cover it with enamel. **enamelled** (adjective).

enamoured (pronounced in-**am**-erd) (adjective) If you are enamoured of someone or something, you like them very much.

encapsulate, encapsulates, encapsulating, encapsulated (verb) If something encapsulates facts or ideas, it contains or represents them in a small space.

encased (adjective) Something that is encased is surrounded or covered with a substance, e.g. *encased in plaster.*

enchanted (adjective) If you are enchanted by something or someone, you are fascinated or charmed by them.

enchanting (adjective) attractive, delightful, or charming, e.g. *an enchanting baby.*

encircle, encircles, encircling, encircled (verb) To encircle something or someone means to completely surround or enclose them.

enclave, enclaves (noun) An enclave is a place that is surrounded by areas that are completely different from it in some important way, for example because the people who live there are of a different race.

enclose, encloses, enclosing, enclosed (verb) To enclose an object or area means to surround it with something solid. **enclosed** (adjective).

enclosure, enclosures (noun) An enclosure is an area of land surrounded by a wall or fence and used for a particular purpose.

encompass, encompasses, encompassing, encompassed (verb) To encompass a number of things means to include all of those things, e.g. *The book encompassed all aspects of maths.*

encore, encores (pronounced **ong**-kor) (noun) An encore is a short extra performance given by an entertainer because the audience asks for it.

encounter, encounters, encountering, encountered 1 (verb) If you encounter someone or something, you meet them or are faced with them, e.g. *She was the most gifted child he* *ever expected to encounter.* **2** (noun) An encounter is a meeting, especially when it is difficult or unexpected.

encourage, encourages, encouraging, encouraged 1 (verb) If you encourage someone, you give them courage and confidence to do something. **2** If someone or something encourages a particular activity, they support it, e.g. *The government will continue to encourage the creation of nursery places.* **encouraging** (adjective), **encouragement** (noun).

encroach, encroaches, encroaching, encroached (verb) If something encroaches on a place or on your time or rights, it gradually takes up or takes away more and more of it. **encroachment** (noun).

encrusted (adjective) covered with a crust or layer of something, e.g. *a necklace encrusted with gold.*

encyclopedia, encyclopedias (pronounced en-sigh-klop-**ee**-dee-a); also spelled **encyclopaedia** (noun) An encyclopedia is a book or set of books giving information and facts about many different subjects, places, and things.

encyclopedic or **encyclopaedic** (adjective) knowing or giving information about many different things.

end, ends, ending, ended 1 (noun) The end of a period of time, an event, or an experience is the last part. **2** The end of something is the farthest point of it, e.g. *the room at the end of the passage.* **3** An end is the purpose for which something is done, e.g. *the use of taxpayers' money for overt political ends.* **4** (verb) If something ends or if you end it, it comes to a finish.

endanger, endangers, endangering, endangered (verb) To endanger something means to cause it to be in a dangerous and harmful situation, e.g. *a driver who endangers the safety of others.*

endear, endears, endearing, endeared (verb) If someone's behaviour endears them to you, it makes you fond of them. **endearing** (adjective), **endearingly** (adverb).

endeavour, endeavours, endeavouring, endeavoured (pronounced in-**dev**-er) **1** (verb; a formal word) If you endeavour to do something, you try very hard to do it. **2** (noun) An endeavour is an effort to do or achieve something.

endless (adjective) having or seeming to have no end. **endlessly** (adverb).

endorse, endorses, endorsing, endorsed 1 (verb) If you endorse someone or something, you give approval and support to them. **2** If you endorse a document, you write your signature or a comment on it, usually to show that you approve of it. **endorsement** (noun).

endowed (adjective) If someone is endowed with a quality or ability, they have it or are given it, e.g. *He was endowed with great willpower.*

endurance (noun) Endurance is the ability to put up with a difficult situation for a period of time.

endure, endures, enduring, en-

dured 1 (verb) If you endure a difficult or unpleasant situation, you put up with it calmly and patiently. **2** If something endures, it lasts or continues to exist, e.g. *The old alliance still endures.* **enduring** (adjective).

enema, enemas (noun) An enema is a liquid that is put into a person's rectum in order to empty their bowels.

enemy, enemies (noun) An enemy is a person or group that is hostile or opposed to another person or group.

energetic (adjective) having or showing energy or enthusiasm. **energetically** (adverb).

energy, energies 1 (noun) Energy is the physical strength to do active things. **2** Energy is the power which drives machinery.

enforce, enforces, enforcing, enforced (verb) If you enforce a law or a rule, you make sure that it is obeyed. **enforceable** (adjective), **enforcement** (noun).

engage, engages, engaging, engaged 1 (verb) If you engage in an activity, you take part in it, e.g. *Officials have declined to engage in a debate.* **2** To engage someone or their attention means to make or keep someone interested in something, e.g. *He engaged the driver in conversation.*

engaged 1 (adjective) When two people are engaged, they have agreed to marry each other. **2** If someone or something is engaged, they are occupied or busy, e.g. *Mr Anderson was otherwise engaged.*

engagement, engagements 1 (noun) An engagement is an appointment that you have with someone. **2** An engagement is an agreement that two people have made with each other to get married.

engine, engines 1 (noun) An engine is any machine designed to convert heat or other kinds of energy into mechanical movement. **2** An engine is a railway locomotive.

engineer, engineers, engineering, engineered 1 (noun) An engineer is a person trained in designing and constructing machinery, engines, and electrical devices, or roads and bridges. **2** An engineer is also a person who repairs mechanical or electrical devices. **3** (verb) If you engineer an event or situation, you arrange it cleverly, usually for your own advantage.

engineering (noun) Engineering is the profession of designing and constructing machinery, engines, and electrical devices, or roads and bridges.

English 1 (adjective) belonging or relating to England. **2** (noun) English is the main language spoken in the United Kingdom, the USA, Canada, Australia, and many other countries.

Englishman, Englishmen (noun) An Englishman is a man who comes from England. **Englishwoman** (noun).

engrave, engraves, engraving, engraved (verb) To engrave means to cut marks, such as letters or designs, into a hard surface with a tool.

engraving, engravings (noun) An engraving is a picture or design that has been cut into a hard surface. **engraver** (noun).

engrossed (adjective) If you are engrossed in something, it holds all your attention, e.g. *He was engrossed in a video game.*

engulf, engulfs, engulfing, engulfed (verb) To engulf something means to completely cover or surround it, e.g. *Black smoke engulfed him.*

enhance, enhances, enhancing, enhanced (verb) To enhance something means to make it more valuable or attractive, e.g. *an outfit that really enhances his good looks.* **enhancement** (noun).

enigma, enigmas (noun) An enigma is anything which is puzzling or difficult to understand.

enigmatic (adjective) mysterious, puzzling, or difficult to understand, e.g. *an enigmatic stranger.* **enigmatically** (adverb).

enjoy, enjoys, enjoying, enjoyed **1** (verb) If you enjoy something, you find pleasure and satisfaction in it. **2** If you enjoy something, you are lucky to have it or experience it, e.g. *The mother has enjoyed a long life.*

enjoyable (adjective) giving pleasure or satisfaction.

enjoyment (noun) Enjoyment is the feeling of pleasure or satisfaction you get from something you enjoy.

enlarge, enlarges, enlarging, enlarged **1** (verb) When you enlarge something, it gets bigger. **2** If you enlarge on a subject, you give more details about it.

enlargement, enlargements (noun) An enlargement of something is the action or process of making it bigger.

enlighten, enlightens, enlightening, enlightened (verb) To enlighten someone means to give them more knowledge or understanding of something. **enlightening** (adjective), **enlightenment** (noun).

enlightened (adjective) well-informed and willing to consider different opinions, e.g. *an enlightened government.*

enlist, enlists, enlisting, enlisted **1** (verb) If someone enlists, they join the army, navy, or air force. **2** If you enlist someone's help, you persuade them to help you in something you are doing.

enliven, enlivens, enlivening, enlivened (verb) To enliven something means to make it more lively or more cheerful.

en masse (pronounced **on mass**) (adverb) If a group of people do something en masse, they do it together and at the same time.

enormity, enormities **1** (noun) The enormity of a problem or difficulty is its great size and seriousness. **2** An enormity is something that is thought to be a terrible crime or offence.

enormous (adjective) very large in size, amount, or degree. **enormously** (adverb).

enough **1** (adjective or adverb) as much or as many as required, e.g. *He did not have enough money for a cab.* **2** (noun) Enough is the quantity necessary for something, e.g. *There's not enough to go* *round.* **3** (adverb) very or fairly, e.g. *She could manage well enough without me.*

enquire, enquires, enquiring, enquired; also spelled **inquire** (verb) If you enquire about something or someone, you ask about them.

enquiry, enquiries; also spelled **inquiry 1** (noun) An enquiry is a question that you ask in order to find something out. **2** An enquiry is also an investigation into something that has happened and that needs explaining.

enrage, enrages, enraging, enraged (verb) If something enrages you, it makes you very angry. **enraged** (adjective).

enrich, enriches, enriching, enriched (verb) To enrich something means to improve the quality or value of it, e.g. *new woods to enrich our countryside.* **enriched** (adjective), **enrichment** (noun).

enrol, enrols, enrolling, enrolled (verb) If you enrol for something such as a course or a college, you sign your name on a list or register to join or become a member of it. **enrolment** (noun).

en route (pronounced on **root**) (adverb) If something happens en route to a place, it happens on the way there.

ensconced (adjective) If you are ensconced in a particular place, you are settled there firmly and comfortably.

ensemble, ensembles (pronounced on-**som**-bl) **1** (noun) An ensemble is a group of things or people considered as a whole rather than separately. **2** An ensemble is also a small group of musicians who play or sing together.

enshrine, enshrines, enshrining, enshrined (verb) To enshrine something such as an idea or a thought means to cherish and keep it, e.g. *Memories of Julia were enshrined in his heart.*

ensign, ensigns (noun) An ensign is a flag flown by a ship to show what country that ship belongs to.

ensue, ensues, ensuing, ensued (pronounced en-**syoo**) (verb) If something ensues, it happens after another event, usually as a result of it, e.g. *He entered the house and an argument ensued.* **ensuing** (adjective).

ensure, ensures, ensuring, ensured (verb) To ensure that something happens means to make certain that it happens, e.g. *We make every effort to ensure the information given is correct.*

entangled (adjective) If you are entangled in problems or difficulties, you are involved in them.

enter, enters, entering, entered 1 (verb) To enter a place means to go into it. **2** If you enter an organization or institution, you join and become a member of it, e.g. *He entered the Commons in 1979.* **3** If you enter a competition, race, or examination, you take part in it. **4** If you enter something in a diary or a list, you write it down.

enterprise, enterprises 1 (noun) An enterprise is a business or company. **2** An enterprise is also a project or task, especially one requiring boldness and effort.

enterprising (adjective) ready to start new projects and tasks and full of boldness and initiative, e.g. *an enterprising company.*

entertain, entertains, entertaining, entertained 1 (verb) If you entertain people, you keep them amused, interested, or attentive. **2** If you entertain guests, you receive them into your house and give them food and hospitality.

entertainer, entertainers (noun) An entertainer is someone whose job is to amuse and please audiences.

entertainment, entertainments (noun) Entertainment is anything that people watch for pleasure, such as shows and films.

enthral, enthrals, enthralling, enthralled (pronounced in-**thrawl**) (verb) If you enthral someone, you hold their attention and interest completely. **enthralling** (adjective).

enthuse, enthuses, enthusing, enthused (pronounced inth-**yooz**) (verb) If you enthuse about something, you talk about it with enthusiasm and excitement.

enthusiasm, enthusiasms (noun) Enthusiasm is interest, eagerness, or delight in something that you enjoy.

enthusiastic (adjective) showing great excitement, eagerness, or approval for something, e.g. *She was enthusiastic about poetry.* **enthusiastically** (adverb).

entice, entices, enticing, enticed (verb) If you entice someone to do something, you tempt them to do it, e.g. *We tried to entice the mouse out of the hole.*

enticing (adjective) extremely attractive and tempting.

entire (adjective) all of something, e.g. *the entire month of July.*

entirely (adverb) wholly and completely, e.g. *He and I were entirely different.*

entirety (pronounced en-**tire**-ittee) (phrase) If something happens to something **in its entirety,** it happens to all of it, e.g. *This message will now be repeated in its entirety.*

entitle, entitles, entitling, entitled (verb) If something entitles you to have or do something, it gives you the right to have or do it. **entitlement** (noun).

entity, entities (pronounced **en**-tit-ee) (noun) An entity is any complete thing that is not divided and not part of anything else.

entourage, entourages (pronounced **on**-too-rahj) (noun) An entourage is the group of people who follow or travel with a famous or important person.

entrails (plural noun) Entrails are the inner parts, especially the intestines, of people or animals.

entrance, entrances (pronounced **en**-trunss) **1** (noun) The entrance of a building or area is its doorway or gate. **2** A person's entrance is their arrival in a place, or the way in which they arrive, e.g. *Each creation is designed for you to make a dramatic entrance.* **3** Entrance is the right to enter a place, e.g. *He had gained entrance to the Hall by pretending to be a heating engineer.*

entrance, entrances, entrancing, entranced (pronounced **en**-trahnss) (verb) If something entrances you, it gives you a feeling of wonder and delight. **entrancing** (adjective).

entrant, entrants (noun) An entrant is a person who officially enters a competition or an organization.

entrenched (adjective) If a belief, custom, or power is entrenched, it is firmly and strongly established.

entrepreneur, entrepreneurs (pronounced on-tre-pren-**ur**) (noun) An entrepreneur is a person who sets up business deals, especially ones in which risks are involved, in order to make a profit. **entrepreneurial** (adjective).

entrust, entrusts, entrusting, entrusted (verb) If you entrust something to someone, you give them the care and protection of it, e.g. *Miss Conway was entrusted with the children's education.*

entry, entries 1 (noun) Entry is the act of entering a place. **2** An entry is any place through which you enter somewhere. **3** An entry is also anything which is entered or recorded, e.g. *Send your entry to the address below.*

envelop, envelops, enveloping, enveloped (verb) To envelop something means to cover or surround it completely, e.g. *A dense fog enveloped the area.*

envelope, envelopes (noun) An envelope is a flat covering of paper with a flap that can be folded over to seal it, which is used to hold a letter.

enviable (adjective) If you describe something as enviable, you mean that you wish you had it yourself.

envious (adjective) full of envy. **enviously** (adverb).

environment, environments 1 (noun) Your environment is the circumstances and conditions in which you live, e.g. *You are only concerned with your immediate family and environment.* **2** The environment is the natural world around us, e.g. *the waste which is dumped in the environment.* **environmental** (adjective), **environmentally** (adverb).

environmentalist, environmentalists (noun) An environmentalist is somebody who is concerned with the problems of the natural environment, such as pollution.

envisage, envisages, envisaging, envisaged (verb) If you envisage a situation or state of affairs, you can picture it in your mind as being true or likely to happen.

envoy, envoys (noun) An envoy is as a messenger, sent especially from one government to another.

envy, envies, envying, envied 1 (noun) Envy is a feeling of resentment you have when you wish you could have what someone else has. **2** (verb) If you envy someone, you wish that you had what they have.

enzyme, enzymes (noun) An enzyme is a chemical substance, usually a protein, produced by cells in the body.

ephemeral (pronounced if-**em**-er-al) (adjective) lasting only a short time.

epic, epics 1 (noun) An epic is a long story of heroic events and actions in the form of a book, poem, or film. **2** (adjective) very impressive or ambitious, e.g. *epic adventures.*

epidemic, epidemics 1 (noun) An epidemic is the occurrence of a disease in one area, spreading quickly and affecting many people. **2** An epidemic is a rapid development or spread of something, e.g. *the country's crime epidemic.*

epilepsy (noun) Epilepsy is a condition of the brain which causes fits and periods of unconsciousness. **epileptic** (noun or adjective).

episode, episodes 1 (noun) An episode is an event or period, e.g. *After this episode, she found it impossible to trust him.* **2** An episode is also one of several parts of a novel or drama appearing for example on television, e.g. *I never miss an episode of Neighbours.*

epistle, epistles (pronounced ip-**piss**-sl) (noun; a formal word) An epistle is a letter.

epitaph, epitaphs (pronounced **ep**-it-ahf) (noun) An epitaph is a short inscription on a gravestone about the person who has died.

epithet, epithets (noun) An epithet is a word or short phrase used to describe some characteristic of a person.

epitome (pronounced ip-**pit**-om-ee) (noun; a formal word) The epitome of something is the most typical example of its sort, e.g. *She was the epitome of the successful woman.*

epoch, epochs (pronounced **ee**-pok) (noun) An epoch is a long period of time.

eponymous (pronounced ip-**on**-im-uss) (adjective; a formal word) The eponymous hero or heroine of a play, film, or book is the person whose name forms its title, e.g. *the eponymous hero of 'Eric the Viking'.*

equal, equals, equalling, equalled 1 (adjective) having the same size, amount, value, or standard. **2** (noun) Your equals are people who have the same ability, status, or rights as you. **3** (adjective) If you are equal to a task, you have the necessary ability to deal with it. **4** (verb) If one thing equals another, it is as good or remarkable as the other, e.g. *He equalled the course record of 64.* **equally** (adverb), **equality** (noun).

equate, equates, equating, equated (verb) If you equate a particular thing with something else, you believe that it is similar or equal, e.g. *You can't equate lives with money.*

equation, equations (noun) An equation is a mathematical formula stating that two amounts or values are the same.

equator (pronounced ik-**way**-tor) (noun) The equator is an imaginary line drawn round the middle of the earth, lying halfway between the North and South poles. **equatorial** (adjective).

equestrian (pronounced ik-**west**-ree-an) (adjective) relating to or involving horses.

equilibrium, equilibria (noun) Equilibrium is a state of balance or rest existing between different influences or aspects of a situation.

equine (adjective) relating to horses.

equinox, equinoxes (noun) An equinox is one of the two days in the year when the day and night are of equal length, occurring in September and March.

equip, equips, equipping, equipped (verb) If a person or thing is equipped with something, they have it or are provided with it, e.g. *The test boat was equipped with a folding propeller.*

equipment (noun) Equipment is all the things that are needed or used for a particular job or activity.

equitable (adjective) fair and reasonable.

equity (noun) Equity is the quality of being fair and reasonable, e.g. *It is important to distribute income with some sense of equity.*

equivalent, equivalents 1 (adjective) equal in use, size, value, or effect. **2** (noun) An equivalent is something that has the same use, size, value, or effect as something else, e.g. *Lieutenant Commander is the Navy equivalent to an Army Major.* **equivalence** (noun).

era, eras (pronounced **ear**-a) (noun) An era is a period of time distinguished by a particular feature, e.g. *a new era of prosperity.*

eradicate, eradicates, eradicating, eradicated (verb) To eradicate something means to get rid of it or destroy it completely. **eradication** (noun).

erase, erases, erasing, erased (verb) To erase something means to remove it.

erect, erects, erecting, erected 1 (verb) To erect something means to put it up or construct it, e.g. *The building was erected in 1900.* **2** (adjective) in a straight and upright position, e.g. *She held herself erect and looked directly at him.*

erection, erections 1 (noun) The erection of something is the process of erecting it. **2** An erection is anything which has been erected. **3** When a man has an erection, his penis is stiff, swollen, and in an upright position.

ermine (noun) Ermine is expensive white fur.

erode, erodes, eroding, eroded (verb) If something erodes or is eroded, it is gradually worn or eaten away and destroyed.

erosion (noun) Erosion is the gradual wearing away and destruction of something, e.g. *soil erosion.*

erotic (adjective) relating to sexual desire or intended to arouse sexual pleasure. **erotically** (adverb), **eroticism** (noun).

err, errs, erring, erred (verb) If you err, you make a mistake.

errand, errands (noun) An errand is a short trip you make in order to do a job for someone.

erratic (adjective) not following a regular pattern or a fixed course, e.g. *Police officers noticed his erratic driving.* **erratically** (adverb).

erroneous (pronounced ir-**rone**-ee-uss) (adjective) Ideas, beliefs, or methods that are erroneous are incorrect or only partly correct. **erroneously** (adverb).

error, errors (noun) An error is a mistake or something which you have done wrong.

erudite (pronounced **eh**-roo-dite) (adjective) having great academic knowledge.

erupt, erupts, erupting, erupted **1** (verb) When a volcano erupts, it violently throws out a lot of hot lava, ash, and steam. **2** When a situation erupts, it starts up suddenly and violently, e.g. *A family row erupted outside.* **eruption** (noun).

escalate, escalates, escalating, escalated (verb) If a situation escalates, it becomes greater in size, seriousness, or intensity.

escalator, escalators (noun) An escalator is a mechanical moving staircase.

escapade, escapades (noun) An escapade is an adventurous or daring incident that causes trouble.

escape, escapes, escaping, escaped **1** (verb) To escape means to get free from a person, place, or thing. **2** If you escape something unpleasant or difficult, you manage to avoid it, e.g. *He escaped the death penalty.* **3** If something escapes you, you cannot remember it, e.g. *It was an actor whose name escapes me for the moment.* **4** (noun) An escape is an act of escaping from a particular place or situation, e.g. *our escape from Warsaw.* **5** An escape is a situation or activity which distracts you from something unpleasant, e.g. *Television provides an escape.*

escapee, escapees (pronounced is-kay-**pee**) (noun) An escapee is someone who has escaped, especially an escaped prisoner.

escapism (noun) Escapism is the tendency to avoid the real and unpleasant things in life by thinking about pleasant or fantastic things, e.g. *Acting is a form of escapism.* **escapist** (adjective).

eschew, eschews, eschewing, eschewed (pronounced is-**chew**) (verb; a formal word) If you eschew something, you deliberately avoid or keep away from it.

escort, escorts, escorting, escorted **1** (noun) An escort is a person or vehicle that travels with another in order to protect or guide them. **2** An escort is also a person who accompanies another person of the opposite sex to a social event. **3** (verb) If you escort someone, you go with them somewhere, especially in order to protect or guide them.

Eskimo, Eskimos (noun) An Eskimo is a member of a group of people who live in Northern Canada, Greenland, Alaska, and Eastern Siberia.

especially (adverb) You say especially to show that something applies more to one thing, person, or situation than to any other, e.g. *Regular eye tests are very important, especially for the elderly.*

espionage (pronounced **ess**-pee-on-ahj) (noun) Espionage is the act of spying to get secret information, especially to find out military or political secrets.

espouse, espouses, espousing, espoused (verb; a formal word) If you espouse a particular policy, cause, or plan, you give your support to it, e.g. *They espoused the rights of man.*

espresso (noun) Espresso is strong coffee made by forcing steam or boiling water through ground coffee.

essay, essays (noun) An essay is a short piece of writing on a particular subject, for example one done as an exercise by a student.

essence, essences 1 (noun) The essence of something is its most basic and most important part, which gives it its identity, e.g. *the very essence of being a woman.* **2** Essence is a concentrated liquid used for flavouring food, e.g. *vanilla essence.*

essential, essentials 1 (adjective) vitally important and absolutely necessary, e.g. *Good ventilation is essential in the greenhouse.* **2** very basic, important, and typical, e.g. *the essential aspects of international banking.* **3** (noun) An essential is something that is very important or necessary, e.g. *the bare essentials of furnishing.* **essentially** (adverb).

establish, establishes, establishing, established 1 (verb) To establish something means to create it or set it up in a permanent way. **2** If you establish yourself or become established as something, you achieve a strong reputation for a particular activity, e.g. *He had just established himself as a film star.* **3** If you establish a fact or establish the truth of something, you discover it and can prove it, e.g. *Our first priority is to establish the cause of her death.* **established** (adjective).

establishment, establishments 1 (noun) The establishment of an organization or system is the act of creating it or setting it up. **2** An establishment is a shop, business, or some other sort of organization or institution. **3** The Establishment is the group of people in a country who have power and influence.

estate, estates 1 (noun) An estate is a large area of privately owned land in the country, together with all the property on it. **2** An estate is also an area of land, usually in or near a city, which has been developed for housing or industry. **3** (a legal use) A person's estate consists of all the possessions they leave behind when they die.

estate agent, estate agents (noun) An estate agent is someone who works for a company that sells houses and land.

esteem (noun) Esteem is admiration and respect that you feel for another person. **esteemed** (adjective).

estimate, estimates, estimating, estimated 1 (verb) If you estimate an amount or quantity, you calculate it approximately. **2** If you estimate something, you make a guess about it based on the evidence you have available, e.g. *Often it's possible to estimate a person's age just by knowing their name.* **3** (noun) An estimate is an approximate calculation of an amount or quantity. **4** An estimate is also a guess you make about something based on the evidence you have available. **5** An estimate is also a formal statement from a company who may do some work for you, telling you how much it is likely to cost.

estimation, estimations 1 (noun) An estimation is an approximate calculation of something that can be measured. **2** Your estimation of a person or situation is the opinion or impression you have formed.

estranged 1 (adjective) If someone is estranged from their husband or wife, they no longer live with them. **2** If someone is estranged from their family or friends, they have quarrelled with them and no longer keep in touch with them.

estrogen (noun) Estrogen is a female sex hormone which regulates the reproductive cycle.

estuary, estuaries (pronounced **est**-yoo-ree) (noun) An estuary is the wide part of a river near where it joins the sea and where fresh water mixes with salt water.

etc. a written abbreviation for **et cetera**.

et cetera (pronounced it **set**-ra) Et cetera is used at the end of a list to indicate that other items of the same type you have mentioned could have been mentioned if there had been time or space.

etch, etches, etching, etched 1 (verb) If you etch a design or pattern on a surface, you cut it into the surface by using acid or a sharp tool. **2** If something is etched on your mind or memory, it has made such a strong impression on you that you feel you will never forget it. **etched** (adjective).

etching, etchings (noun) An etching is a picture printed from a metal plate that has had a design cut into it.

eternal (adjective) lasting forever, or seeming to last forever, e.g. *eternal life.* **eternally** (adverb).

eternity, eternities 1 (noun) Eternity is time without end, or a state of existing outside time, especially the state some people believe they will pass into when they die. **2** An eternity is also a period of time which seems to go on for ever, e.g. *We arrived there after an eternity.*

ether (pronounced **eeth**-er) (noun) Ether is a colourless liquid that burns easily. It is used in industry as a solvent and in medicine as an anaesthetic.

ethereal (pronounced ith-**ee**-ree-al) (adjective) light and delicate, e.g. *misty ethereal landscapes.* **ethereally** (adverb).

ethical (adjective) in agreement with accepted principles of behaviour that are thought to be right, e.g. *teenagers who become vegetarian for ethical reasons.* **ethically** (adverb).

ethics (plural noun) Ethics are

moral beliefs about right and wrong, e.g. *The medical profession has a code of ethics.*

Ethiopian, Ethiopians (pronounced eeth-ee-**oh**-pee-an) **1** (adjective) belonging to or relating to Ethiopia. **2** (noun) An Ethiopian is someone who comes from Ethiopia.

ethnic 1 (adjective) involving different racial groups of people, e.g. *ethnic minorities.* **2** relating to or characteristic of a particular racial or cultural group, especially when very different from modern western culture, e.g. *ethnic food.* **ethnically** (adverb).

ethos (pronounced **eeth**-oss) (noun) An ethos is a set of ideas and attitudes that is characteristic of a particular group of people, e.g. *the ethos of journalism.*

etiquette (pronounced **et**-ik-ket) (noun) Etiquette is a set of rules for behaviour in a particular social situation.

etymology (pronounced et-tim-**ol**-loj-ee) (noun) Etymology is the study of the origin, development, and changes of form in words.

EU (noun) EU is an abbreviation for 'European Union'.

eucalyptus, eucalyptus or **eucalyptuses** (noun) A eucalyptus is an evergreen tree grown, mostly in Australia, to provide timber, gum, and medicinal oil; also the wood and oil obtained from this tree.

Eucharist, Eucharists (pronounced **yoo**-kar-rist) (noun) The Eucharist is a religious ceremony in which Christians remember and celebrate Christ's last meal with his disciples.

eunuch, eunuchs (pronounced **yoo**-nuk) (noun) A eunuch is a man who has been castrated.

euphemism, euphemisms (noun) A euphemism is a polite word or expression that you can use instead of one that might offend or upset people, e.g. *action movies, a euphemism for violence.* **euphemistic** (adjective), **euphemistically** (adverb).

euphoria (noun) Euphoria is a feeling of great happiness. **euphoric** (adjective).

Europe (noun) Europe is the second smallest continent. It has Asia on its eastern side, with the Arctic to the north, the Atlantic to the west, and the Mediterranean and Africa to the south.

European, Europeans 1 (adjective) belonging or relating to Europe. **2** (noun) A European is someone who comes from Europe.

European Union (noun) The group of countries who have joined together under the Treaty of Rome for economic and trade purposes are officially known as the European Union.

euthanasia (pronounced yooth-a-**nay**-zee-a) (noun) Euthanasia is the act of killing someone painlessly in order to stop their suffering when nothing can be done to help them, for example when they have an incurable illness.

evacuate, evacuates, evacuating, evacuated (verb) If someone is evacuated, they are removed from a place of danger to a place of safety, e.g. *a* *crowd of shoppers had to be evacuated from a store after a bomb scare.* **evacuation** (noun), **evacuee** (noun).

evade, evades, evading, evaded 1 (verb) If you evade something or someone, you keep moving in order to keep out of their way, e.g. *For two months he evaded police.* **2** If you evade a problem or question, you avoid dealing with it.

evaluate, evaluates, evaluating, evaluated (verb) If you evaluate something, you assess its quality, value, or significance. **evaluation** (noun).

evangelical (pronounced ee-van-**jel**-ik-kl) (adjective) Evangelical beliefs are Christian beliefs that stress the importance of the gospels and a personal belief in Christ.

evangelist, evangelists (pronounced iv-**van**-jel-ist) (noun) An evangelist is a person who travels from place to place preaching Christianity. **evangelize** (verb), **evangelism** (noun).

evaporate, evaporates, evaporating, evaporated 1 (verb) When a liquid evaporates, it gradually becomes less and less because it has changed from a liquid into a gas. **2** If a substance has been evaporated, all the liquid has been taken out so that it is dry or concentrated. **evaporation** (noun).

evasion, evasions (noun) Evasion is deliberately avoiding doing something, e.g. *evasion of arrest.*

evasive (adjective) deliberately trying to avoid talking about or doing something, e.g. *usually he was evasive to the point of secretiveness.*

eve, eves (noun) The eve of an event or occasion is the evening or day before it, e.g. *on the eve of the battle.*

even, evens, evening, evened 1 (adjective) flat and level, e.g. *an even layer of chocolate.* **2** regular and without variation, e.g. *an even temperature.* **3** In maths, numbers that are even can be divided exactly by two, e.g. *4 is an even number.* **4** Scores that are even are exactly the same. **5** (adverb) Even is used to suggest that something is unexpected or surprising, e.g. *I haven't even got a bank account.* **6** Even is also used to say that something is greater in degree than something else, e.g. *This was an opportunity to obtain even more money.* **7** (phrase) **Even if** or **even though** is used to introduce something that is surprising in relation to the main part of the sentence, e.g. *She was too kind to say anything, even though she was jealous.* **evenly** (adverb).

evening, evenings (noun) Evening is the part of the day between late afternoon and the time you go to bed.

event, events 1 (noun) An event is something that happens, especially when it is unusual or important. **2** An event is also one of the races or competitions that are part of an organized occasion, especially in sports. **3** (phrase) If you say **in any event,** you mean whatever happens, e.g. *In any event we must get on with our own lives.*

eventful (adjective) full of interesting, exciting, and important events.

eventual (adjective) happening or being achieved in the end, e.g. *He remained confident of eventual victory.*

eventuality, eventualities (noun) An eventuality is a possible future event or result, e.g. *equipment to cope with most eventualities.*

eventually (adverb) in the end, e.g. *Eventually I got to Berlin.*

ever 1 (adverb) at any time, e.g. *Have you ever seen anything like it?* **2** all the time, e.g. *The Prime Minister will come under ever more pressure to concede.* **3** Ever is used to give emphasis to what you are saying, e.g. *I'm as strange here as ever I was in England.* **4** (phrase; an informal use) **Ever so** means very, e.g. *Thank you ever so much.*

evergreen, evergreens (noun) An evergreen is a tree or bush which has green leaves all the year round.

everlasting (adjective) never coming to an end.

every 1 (adjective) Every is used to refer to all the members of a particular group, separately and one by one, e.g. *We eat out every night.* **2** Every is used to mean the greatest or the best possible degree of something, e.g. *He has every reason to avoid the subject.* **3** Every is also used to indicate that something happens at regular intervals, e.g. *renewable every five years.* **4** (phrase) **Every other** means each alternate, e.g. *I see Lisa at least every other week.*

everybody 1 (pronoun) all the people in a group, e.g. *He obviously thinks everybody in the place knows him.* **2** all the people in the world, e.g. *Everybody has a hobby.*

everyday (adjective) usual or ordinary, e.g. *the drudgery of everyday life.*

everyone 1 (pronoun) all the people in a group. **2** all the people in the world.

everything 1 (pronoun) all or the whole of something. **2** the most important thing, e.g. *When I was 20, friends were everything to me.*

everywhere (adverb) in or to all places.

evict, evicts, evicting, evicted (verb) To evict someone means to officially force them to leave a place they are occupying. **eviction** (noun).

evidence 1 (noun) Evidence is anything you see, experience, read, or are told which gives you reason to believe something. **2** Evidence is the information used in court to attempt to prove or disprove something.

evident (adjective) easily noticed or understood, e.g. *His love of nature is evident in his paintings.* **evidently** (adverb).

evil, evils 1 (noun) Evil is a force or power that is believed to cause wicked or bad things to happen. **2** An evil is a very unpleasant or harmful situation or activity, e.g. *the evils of war.* **3** (adjective) Someone or something that is evil is morally wrong or bad, e.g. *evil influences.*

evoke, evokes, evoking, evoked (verb) To evoke an emotion, memory, or reaction means to cause it, e.g. *enthusiasm was evoked by the appearance of the Prince.*

evolution (pronounced ee-vol-**oo**-shn) **1** (noun) In biology, evolution is a process of gradual change taking place over many generations during which animals, plants, and insects slowly change as they adapt to different environments. **2** Evolution is also any process of gradual change and development over a period of time, e.g. *the evolution of the European Union.* **evolutionary** (adjective).

evolve, evolves, evolving, evolved 1 (verb) If something evolves or if you evolve it, it develops gradually over a period of time, e.g. *I was given a brief to evolve a system of training.* **2** When plants, animals, and insects evolve, they gradually change and develop into different forms over a period of time.

ewe, ewes (pronounced **yoo**) (noun) A ewe is a female sheep.

ex- (prefix) former, e.g. *her ex-husband.*

exacerbate, exacerbates, exacerbating, exacerbated (pronounced ig-**zass**-er-bate) (verb) To exacerbate something means to make it worse.

exact, exacts, exacting, exacted 1 (adjective) correct and complete in every detail, e.g. *an exact replica of the Santa Maria.* **2** accurate and precise, as opposed to approximate, e.g. *Mystery surrounds the exact circumstances of his death.* **3** (verb; a formal word) If somebody or something exacts something from you, they demand or obtain it from you, especially through force, e.g. *The British Navy was on its way to exact a terrible revenge.*

exactly 1 (adverb) with complete accuracy and precision, e.g. *That's exactly what happened.* **2** You can use exactly to emphasize the truth of a statement, or a similarity or close relationship between one thing and another, e.g. *It's exactly the same colour.*

exaggerate, exaggerates, exaggerating, exaggerated 1 (verb) If you exaggerate, you make the thing you are describing seem better, worse, bigger, or more important than it really is. **2** To exaggerate something means to make it more noticeable than usual, e.g. *His Irish brogue was exaggerated for the benefit of the joke he was telling.* **exaggeration** (noun).

exalted (adjective; a formal word) Someone who is exalted is very important.

exam, exams (noun) An exam is an official test set to assess your knowledge or skill in a subject.

examination, examinations 1 (noun) An examination is the same as an exam. **2** If you make an examination of something, you inspect it very carefully, e.g. *I carried out a very careful examination of the hull surface.* **3** A medical examination is a check by a doctor in order to assess the state of your health.

examine, examines, examining, examined 1 (verb) If you examine something, you inspect it very carefully. **2** To examine someone means to assess their knowledge or skill in a particular subject by testing them. **3** If a doctor examines you, he or she checks your body to assess the state of your health.

examiner, examiners (noun) An examiner is a person who sets or marks an exam.

example, examples 1 (noun) An example is something which represents or is typical of a group or set, e.g. *some examples of early Spanish music.* **2** If you say someone or something is an example to people, you mean that people can imitate and learn from them. **3** (phrase) You use **for example** to give an example of something you are talking about.

exasperate, exasperates, exasperating, exasperated (verb) If someone or something exasperates you, they irritate you and make you angry. **exasperating** (adjective), **exasperation** (noun).

excavate, excavates, excavating, excavated (verb) To excavate means to remove earth from the ground by digging. **excavation** (noun).

exceed, exceeds, exceeding, exceeded (verb) To exceed something such as a limit means to go beyond it or to become greater than it, e.g. *Most of us have exceeded the speed limit.*

exceedingly (adverb) extremely or very much.

excel, excels, excelling, excelled (verb) If someone excels in something, they are very good at doing it.

Excellency, Excellencies (noun) Excellency is a title used to address or refer to an official of very high rank, such as an ambassador or a governor.

excellent (adjective) very good indeed. **excellence** (noun).

except (preposition) Except or except for means other than or apart from, e.g. *All my family were musicians except my father.*

exception, exceptions (noun) An exception is somebody or something that is not included in a general statement or rule, e.g. *English, like every language, has exceptions to its rules.*

exceptional 1 (adjective) unusually talented or clever. **2** unusual and likely to happen very rarely. **exceptionally** (adverb).

excerpt, excerpts (noun) An excerpt is a short piece of writing or music which is taken from a larger piece.

excess, excesses 1 (noun) Excess is behaviour which goes beyond normally acceptable limits, e.g. *a life of excess.* **2** An excess is a larger amount of something than is needed, usual, or healthy, e.g. *an excess of energy.* **3** (adjective) more than is needed, allowed, or healthy, e.g. *excess weight.* **4** (phrase) **In excess of** a particular amount means more than that amount, e.g. *He has a fortune in excess of £150 million.* **5** If you do something **to excess**, you do it too much, e.g. *She drank to excess.*

excessive (adjective) too great in amount or degree, e.g. *using excessive force.* **excessively** (adverb).

exchange, exchanges, exchang-

ing, exchanged 1 (verb) To exchange things means to give or receive one thing in return for another, e.g. *They exchange small presents on Christmas Eve.* **2** (noun) An exchange is the act of giving or receiving something in return for something else, e.g. *an exchange of letters... exchanges of gunfire.* **3** An exchange is also a place where people trade and do business, e.g. *the stock exchange.*

exchequer (pronounced iks-**chek**-er) (noun) The exchequer is the department in the government which is responsible for money belonging to the state.

excise (noun) Excise is a tax put on goods produced for sale in the country that produces them.

excitable (adjective) easily excited.

excite, excites, exciting, excited 1 (verb) If somebody or something excites you, they make you feel very happy and nervous or very interested and enthusiastic. **2** If something excites a particular feeling, it causes somebody to have that feeling, e.g. *This excited my suspicion.* **excited** (adjective), **excitedly** (adverb), **exciting** (adjective), **excitement** (noun).

exclaim, exclaims, exclaiming, exclaimed (verb) When you exclaim, you cry out or speak suddenly or loudly because you are excited, shocked, or angry.

exclamation, exclamations (noun) An exclamation is a word or phrase spoken suddenly to express a strong feeling such as surprise, pain, or anger.

exclamation mark, exclamation marks (noun) An exclamation mark is a punctuation mark (!) used in writing to express shock, surprise, or anger.

exclude, excludes, excluding, excluded 1 (verb) If you exclude something, you deliberately do not include it or do not consider it. **2** If you exclude somebody from a place or an activity, you prevent them from entering the place or taking part in the activity. **exclusion** (noun).

exclusive, exclusives 1 (adjective) available to or for the use of a small group of rich or privileged people, e.g. *an exclusive club.* **2** belonging to a particular person or group only, e.g. *exclusive rights to coverage of the Olympic Games.* **3** (noun) An exclusive is a story or interview which appears in only one newspaper or magazine or on only one television programme. **exclusively** (adverb).

excrement (pronounced **eks**-krim-ment) (noun) Excrement is the solid waste matter that is passed out of a person's or animal's body through their bowels.

excruciating (pronounced iks-**kroo**-shee-ate-ing) (adjective) unbearably painful. **excruciatingly** (adverb).

excursion, excursions (noun) An excursion is a short journey or outing.

excuse, excuses, excusing, excused 1 (noun) An excuse is a reason which you give to explain why something has been done, has not been done, or will not be done. **2** (verb) If you excuse yourself or something that you have done, you give reasons defending your actions or behaviour. **3** If you excuse somebody for something wrong they have done, you forgive them for it. **4** If you excuse somebody from a duty or responsibility, you free them from it, e.g. *He was excused from standing trial because of ill health.* **5** (phrase) You say **excuse me** to try to catch somebody's attention or to apologize for an interruption or for rude behaviour.

execute, executes, executing, executed 1 (verb) To execute somebody means to kill them as a punishment for a crime. **2** If you execute something such as a plan or an action, you carry it out or perform it, e.g. *The crime had been planned and executed in Montreal.* **execution** (noun).

executioner, executioners (noun) An executioner is a person whose job is to execute criminals.

executive, executives 1 (noun) An executive is a person who is employed by a company at a senior level. **2** The executive of an organization is a committee which has the authority to make decisions and ensure that they are carried out, e.g. *a powerful executive headed by the president.* **3** (adjective) concerned with making important decisions and ensuring that they are carried out, e.g. *the commission's executive director.*

executor, executors (pronounced ig-**zek**-yoo-tor) (noun) An executor is a person you appoint to carry out the instructions in your will.

exemplary 1 (adjective) being a good example and worthy of imitation, e.g. *an exemplary performance.* **2** serving as a warning, e.g. *an exemplary tale.*

exemplify, exemplifies, exemplifying, exemplified 1 (verb) To exemplify something means to be a typical example of it, e.g. *The monarchy exemplifies traditional English values.* **2** If you exemplify something, you give an example of it.

exempt, exempts, exempting, exempted 1 (adjective) excused from a rule, duty, or obligation, e.g. *people exempt from prescription charges.* **2** (verb) To exempt someone from a rule, duty, or obligation means to excuse them from it. **exemption** (noun).

exercise, exercises, exercising, exercised 1 (noun) Exercise is any activity which you do to get fit or remain healthy. **2** Exercises are also activities which you do to practise and train for a particular skill, e.g. *piano exercises... a mathematical exercise.* **3** (verb) When you exercise, you do activities which help you to get fit and remain healthy. **4** If you exercise your authority, rights, or responsibilities, you use them.

exert, exerts, exerting, exerted 1 (verb) To exert pressure means to apply it. **2** If you exert yourself, you make a physical or mental effort to do something.

exertion, exertions (noun) Exertion is vigorous physical effort or exercise.

exhale, exhales, exhaling, exhaled (verb) When you exhale, you breathe out.

exhaust, exhausts, exhausting, exhausted 1 (verb) To exhaust somebody means to make them very tired, e.g. *Several laps in the pool left her exhausted.* **2** If you exhaust a supply of something such as money or food, you use it up completely. **3** If you exhaust a subject, you talk about it so much that there is nothing else to say about it. **4** (noun) An exhaust is a pipe which carries the gas or steam out of the engine of a vehicle. **exhaustion** (noun).

exhaustive (adjective) thorough and complete, e.g. *an exhaustive series of tests.* **exhaustively** (adverb).

exhibit, exhibits, exhibiting, exhibited 1 (verb) To exhibit things means to show them in a public place for people to see. **2** If you exhibit your feelings or abilities, you display them so that other people can see them. **3** (noun) An exhibit is anything which is put on show for the public to see.

exhibition, exhibitions (noun) An exhibition is a public display of works of art, products, skills, or activities.

exhibitor, exhibitors (noun) An exhibitor is a person whose work is being shown in an exhibition.

exhilarating (adjective) Something that is exhilarating makes you feel very happy and excited.

exile, exiles, exiling, exiled 1 (noun) If somebody lives in exile, they live in a foreign country because they cannot live in their own country, usually for political reasons. **2** An exile is somebody who lives in exile. **3** (verb) If somebody is exiled, they are sent away from their own country and not allowed to return.

exist, exists, existing, existed (verb) If something exists, it is present in the world as a real or living thing.

existence 1 (noun) Existence is the state of being or existing. **2** An existence is a way of living or being, e.g. *They live an idyllic existence.*

exit, exits, exiting, exited 1 (noun) An exit is a way out of a place. **2** If you make an exit, you leave a place. **3** (verb) To exit means to go out.

exodus (noun) An exodus is the departure of a large number of people from a place.

exotic 1 (adjective) attractive or interesting through being unusual, e.g. *exotic fabrics.* **2** coming from a foreign country, e.g. *exotic plants.*

expand, expands, expanding, expanded 1 (verb) If something expands or you expand it, it becomes larger in number or size. **2** If you expand on something, you give more details about it, e.g. *The minister's speech expanded on the aims which he outlined last month.* **expansion** (noun).

expanse, expanses (noun) An expanse is a very large or widespread area, e.g. *a vast expanse of pine forests.*

expansive 1 (adjective) Something that is expansive is very wide or extends over a very large area, e.g. *the expansive North Devon countryside.* **2** Someone who is expansive is friendly, open, or talkative.

expatriate, expatriates (pronounced eks-**pat**-ree-it) (noun) An expatriate is someone who is living in a country which is not their own.

expect, expects, expecting, expected 1 (verb) If you expect something to happen, you believe that it will happen, e.g. *The trial is expected to end today.* **2** If you are expecting somebody or something, you believe that they are going to arrive or to happen, e.g. *The Queen was expecting the chambermaid.* **3** If you expect something, you believe that it is your right to get it or have it, e.g. *He seemed to expect a reply.*

expectancy (noun) Expectancy is the feeling that something is about to happen, especially something exciting.

expectant 1 (adjective) If you are expectant, you believe that something is about to happen, especially something exciting. **2** An expectant mother or father is someone whose baby is going to be born soon. **expectantly** (adverb).

expectation, expectations (noun) Expectation or an expectation is a strong belief or hope that something will happen.

expedient, expedients (pronounced iks-**pee**-dee-ent) **1** (noun) An expedient is an action or plan that achieves the desired result but that may not be morally acceptable. **2** (adjective) Something that is expedient is useful or convenient in a particular situation. **expediency** (noun).

expedition, expeditions 1 (noun) An expedition is an organized journey made for a special purpose, such as to explore; also the party of people who make such a journey. **2** An expedition is also a short journey or outing, e.g. *shopping expeditions.* **expeditionary** (adjective).

expel, expels, expelling, expelled 1 (verb) If someone is expelled from a school or club, they are officially told to leave because they have behaved badly. **2** If a gas or liquid is expelled from a place, it is forced out of it.

expend, expends, expending, expended (verb) To expend energy, time, or money means to use it up or spend it.

expendable (adjective) no longer useful or necessary, and therefore able to be got rid of.

expenditure (noun) Expenditure is the total amount of money spent on something.

expense, expenses 1 (noun) Expense is the money that something costs, e.g. *the expense of installing a burglar alarm.* **2** (plural noun) Expenses are the money somebody spends while doing something connected with their work, which is paid back to them by their employer, e.g. *travelling expenses.*

expensive (adjective) costing a lot of money. **expensively** (adverb).

experience, experiences, experiencing, experienced 1 (noun)

Experience consists of all the things that you have done or that have happened to you. **2** An experience is something that you do or something that happens to you, especially something new or unusual. **3** (verb) If you experience a situation or feeling, it happens to you or you are affected by it.

experiment, experiments, experimenting, experimented 1 (noun) An experiment is the testing of something, either to find out its effect or to prove something. **2** (verb) If you experiment with something, you do a scientific test on it to prove or discover something. **experimentation** (noun), **experimental** (adjective), **experimentally** (adverb).

expert, experts 1 (noun) An expert is a person who is very skilled at doing something or very knowledgeable about a particular subject. **2** (adjective) having, showing, or requiring special skill or knowledge, e.g. *expert advice.* **expertly** (adverb).

expertise (pronounced eks-per-**teez**) (noun) Expertise is special skill or knowledge.

expire, expires, expiring, expired (verb) When something expires, it reaches the end of the period of time for which it is valid, e.g. *The striker's current contract expires in the summer.* **expiry** (noun).

explain, explains, explaining, explained (verb) If you explain something, you give details about it or reasons for it so that it can be understood. **explanation** (noun), **explanatory** (adjective).

explicit (adjective) shown or expressed clearly, openly, and precisely, e.g. *an explicit death threat.* **explicitly** (adverb).

explode, explodes, exploding, exploded 1 (verb) If something such as a bomb explodes, it bursts loudly and with great force, often causing damage. **2** If somebody explodes, they express strong feelings suddenly or violently, e.g. *I half expected him to explode in anger.* **3** When something increases suddenly and rapidly, it can be said to explode, e.g. *Sales of men's toiletries have exploded.*

exploit, exploits, exploiting, exploited 1 (verb) If somebody exploits a person or a situation, they take advantage of them for their own ends, e.g. *When the government is in trouble, the opposition is always tempted to exploit its difficulties.* **2** If you exploit something, you make the best use of it, often for profit, e.g. *exploiting the power of computers.* **3** (noun) An exploit is something daring or interesting that somebody has done, e.g. *His courage and exploits were legendary.* **exploitation** (noun).

explore, explores, exploring, explored 1 (verb) If you explore a place, you travel in it to find out what it is like. **2** If you explore an idea, you think about it carefully. **exploration** (noun), **exploratory** (adjective), **explorer** (noun).

explosion, explosions (noun) An explosion is a sudden violent burst of energy, for example one caused by a bomb.

explosive, explosives 1 (adjective) capable of exploding or likely to explode. **2** happening suddenly and making a loud noise. **3** An explosive situation is one which is likely to have serious or dangerous effects. **4** (noun) An explosive is a substance or device that can explode.

exponent, exponents 1 (noun) An exponent of an idea, theory, or plan is someone who puts it forward. **2** (a formal use) An exponent of a skill or activity is someone who is good at it.

export, exports, exporting, exported 1 (verb) To export goods means to sell them to another country and send them there. **2** (noun) Exports are goods which are sold and sent to another country. **exporter** (noun).

expose, exposes, exposing, exposed 1 (verb) To expose something means to uncover it and make it visible. **2** To expose a person to something dangerous means to put them in a situation in which it might harm them, e.g. *exposed to tobacco smoke*. **3** To expose a person or situation means to reveal the truth about them, especially when it involves dishonest or shocking behaviour.

exposition, expositions (noun) An exposition is a detailed explanation of a particular subject.

exposure, exposures 1 (noun) Exposure is the exposing of something. **2** Exposure is the harmful effect on the body caused by very cold weather.

express, expresses, expressing, expressed 1 (verb) When you express an idea or feeling, you show what you think or feel by saying or doing something. **2** If you express a quantity in a particular form, you write it down in that form, e.g. *the result of the equation is usually expressed as a percentage*. **3** (adjective) very fast, e.g. *express delivery service*. **4** (noun) An express is a fast train or coach which stops at only a few places.

expression, expressions 1 (noun) Your expression is the look on your face which shows what you are thinking or feeling. **2** The expression of ideas or feelings is the showing of them through words, actions, or art. **3** An expression is a word or phrase used in communicating, e.g. *the expression 'nosey parker'*.

expressive 1 (adjective) showing feelings clearly. **2** full of expression.

expulsion, expulsions (noun) Expulsion is the act of expelling.

exquisite 1 (adjective) extremely beautiful and pleasing. **2** intense, but pleasant and satisfying, e.g. *the exquisite pleasure of the ice cold water*.

extend, extends, extending, extended 1 (verb) If something extends for a distance, it continues and stretches into the distance. **2** If something extends from a surface or object, it sticks out from it. **3** If you extend something, you make it larger or longer, e.g. *the table had been extended to seat* *fifty.*

extension, extensions 1 (noun) An extension is a room or building which is added to an existing building. **2** An extension is an extra period of time for which something continues to exist or be valid. **3** An extension is also an additional telephone connected to the same line as another telephone.

extensive 1 (adjective) covering a large area. **2** very great in effect, e.g. *extensive repairs.* **extensively** (adverb).

extent, extents (noun) The extent of something is its length, area, size, or scale.

exterior, exteriors 1 (noun) The exterior of something is its outside. **2** Your exterior is your outward appearance.

exterminate, exterminates, exterminating, exterminated (verb) When animals or people are exterminated, they are deliberately killed. **extermination** (noun).

external, externals (adjective) existing or happening on the outside or outer part of something. **externally** (adverb).

extinct 1 (adjective) An extinct species of animal or plant is no longer in existence. **2** An extinct volcano is no longer likely to erupt. **extinction** (noun).

extinguish, extinguishes, extinguishing, extinguished (verb) To extinguish a light or fire means to put it out.

extortionate (adjective) more expensive than you consider to be fair.

extra, extras 1 (adjective) more than is usual, necessary, or expected. **2** (noun) An extra is anything which is additional. **3** An extra in a film is a person who is hired to play a very small and unimportant part in it.

extract, extracts, extracting, extracted 1 (verb) To extract something from a place means to take it out or get it out, often by force. **2** If you extract information from someone, you get it from them with difficulty. **3** (noun) An extract is a small section taken from a book, piece of music, play, or film.

extraction 1 (noun) Your extraction is the country or people that your family originally comes from, e.g. *a Malaysian citizen of Australian extraction.* **2** Extraction is the process of taking or getting something out of a place.

extraordinary (adjective) unusual or surprising. **extraordinarily** (adverb).

extravagant 1 (adjective) spending or costing more money than is reasonable or affordable. **2** going beyond reasonable limits. **extravagantly** (adverb), **extravagance** (noun).

extravaganza, extravaganzas (noun) An extravaganza is a very elaborate and expensive public activity or performance.

extreme, extremes 1 (adjective) very great in degree or intensity, e.g. *extreme caution.* **2** going beyond what is usual or reasonable, e.g. *extreme weather conditions.* **3** at the furthest point or edge of something, e.g. *the extreme northern cor-*

ner of Spain. **4** (noun) An extreme is the highest or furthest degree of something. **extremely** (adverb).

extremist, extremists (noun) An extremist is a person who uses severe or unreasonable methods or behaviour, especially to bring about political change. **extremism** (noun).

extremity, extremities (noun) The extremities of something are its furthest ends or edges.

extricate, extricates, extricating, extricated (verb) To extricate someone from a place or a situation means to free them from it.

extrovert, extroverts (noun) An extrovert is a person who is more interested in other people and the world around them than their own thoughts and feelings.

exuberant (adjective) full of energy, excitement, and cheerfulness. **exuberantly** (adverb), **exuberance** (noun).

exude, exudes, exuding, exuded (verb) If someone exudes a quality or feeling, they seem to have it to a great degree.

eye, eyes, eyeing or **eying, eyed** **1** (noun) The eye is the organ of sight. **2** The eye of a needle is the small hole at the end through which you pass the thread. **3** (verb) To eye something means to look at it carefully or suspiciously.

eyeball, eyeballs (noun) The eyeball is the whole of the ball-shaped part of the eye.

eyebrow, eyebrows (noun) Your eyebrows are the lines of hair which grow on the ridges of bone above your eyes.

eyelash, eyelashes (noun) Your eyelashes are hairs that grow on the edges of your eyelids.

eyelid, eyelids (noun) Your eyelids are the folds of skin which cover your eyes when they are closed.

eyesight (noun) Your eyesight is your ability to see.

eyesore, eyesores (noun) Something that is an eyesore is extremely ugly.

eyewitness, eyewitnesses (noun) An eyewitness is a person who has seen an event and can describe what happened.

eyrie, eyries (pronounced **ear**-ee) (noun) An eyrie is the nest of an eagle or other bird of prey, usually built on a cliff or mountain.

F f

fable, fables (noun) A fable is a story intended to teach a moral lesson.

fabled (adjective) well known because many stories have been told about it, e.g. *the fabled city of Troy.*

fabric, fabrics 1 (noun) Fabric is cloth, e.g. *tough fabric for tents.* **2** The fabric of a building is its walls, roof, and other parts. **3** The fabric of a society or system is its structure, laws, and customs, e.g. *the democratic fabric of American society.*

fabricate, fabricates, fabricating, fabricated 1 (verb) If you fabricate a story or an explanation, you invent it in order to deceive people. **2** To fabricate something means to make or manufacture it. **fabrication** (noun).

fabulous 1 (adjective) wonderful or very impressive, e.g. *a fabulous picnic.* **2** not real, but happening or occurring in stories and legends, e.g *fabulous creatures.*

facade, facades (pronounced fas-**sahd**) **1** (noun) A facade is the front outside wall of a building. **2** A facade is also a false outward appearance, e.g. *the facade of honesty.*

face, faces, facing, faced 1 (noun) Your face is the front part of your head from your chin to your forehead. **2** A face is the expression someone has or is making, e.g. *a grim face.* **3** A face of something is a surface or side of it, especially the most important side, e.g. *the north face of Everest.* **4** (verb) To face something or someone means to be opposite them or to look at them or towards them, e.g. *a room that faces on to the street.* **5** (noun) The face of something is its main aspect or general appearance, e.g. *We have changed the face of language study.* **6** (verb) If you face something difficult or unpleasant, you have to deal with it, e.g. *She faced a terrible dilemma.*

faceless (adjective) without character or individuality, e.g. *anonymous shops and faceless coffee-bars.*

face-lift, face-lifts 1 (noun) A face-lift is an operation to tighten the skin on someone's face to make them look younger. **2** If you give something a face-lift, you clean it or improve its appearance.

facet, facets (pronounced **fas**-it) **1** (noun) A facet of something is a single part or aspect of it, e.g. *the many facets of his talent.* **2** A facet is also one of the flat, cut surfaces of a precious stone.

facetious (pronounced fas-**see**-shuss) (adjective) witty or amusing but in a rather silly or inappropriate way, e.g. *He didn't appreciate my facetious suggestion.*

facial (pronounced **fay**-shal) (adjective) Facial means appearing on or being part of the face, e.g. *facial expressions.*

facilitate, facilitates, facilitating, facilitated (verb) To facilitate something means to make it easier for it to happen or be done, e.g. *a process that will facilitate individual development.*

facility, facilities 1 (noun) A facility is a service, opportunity, or piece of equipment which makes it possible to do something, e.g. *excellent shopping facilities.* **2** A facility for something is an ability to do it easily or well, e.g. *a facility for novel-writing.*

fact, facts 1 (noun) A fact is a piece of knowledge or information that is true or something that has actually happened. **2** (phrases) **In fact, as a matter of fact,** and **in point of fact** mean 'actually' or 'really' and are used for emphasis or when making an additional comment, e.g. *Very few people, in fact, have this type of skin.*

factual (adjective), **factually** (adverb).

faction, factions (noun) A faction is a small group of people belonging to a larger group, but differing from it in some aims or ideas.

fact of life, facts of life 1 (noun) The facts of life are details about sexual intercourse and how babies are conceived and born. **2** If you say that something is a fact of life, you mean that it is something that people expect to happen, even though they might find it shocking or unpleasant, e.g. *War is a fact of life.*

factor, factors 1 (noun) A factor is something that helps to cause a result, e.g. *House dust mites are a major factor in asthma.* **2** The factors of a number are the whole numbers that will divide exactly into it. For example, 2 and 5 are factors of 10. **3** If something increases by a particular factor, it is multiplied that number of times, e.g. *The amount of energy used has increased by a factor of eight.*

factory, factories (noun) A factory is a building or group of buildings where goods are made in large quantities.

faculty, faculties 1 (noun) Your faculties are your physical and mental abilities, e.g. *My mental faculties are as sharp as ever.* **2** In some universities, a Faculty is a group of related departments, e.g. *the Science Faculty.*

fad, fads (noun) A fad is an intense but temporary fashion or craze, e.g. *the latest exercise fad.*

fade, fades, fading, faded (verb) If something fades, the intensity of its colour, brightness, or sound is gradually reduced.

faeces or **feces** (pronounced **fee**-seez) (plural noun) Faeces are the solid waste substances discharged from a person's or animal's body.

fag, fags (noun; an informal word) A fag is a cigarette.

Fahrenheit (pronounced **far**-ren-hite) (noun) Fahrenheit is a scale of temperature in which the freezing point of water is 32° and the boiling point is 212°.

fail, fails, failing, failed 1 (verb) If someone fails to achieve something, they are not successful. **2** If you fail an exam, your marks are too low and you do not pass. **3** (noun) In an exam, a fail is a piece of work that is not good enough to pass. **4** (verb) If you fail to do something that you should have done, you do not do it, e.g. *They failed to phone her.* **5** If something fails, it becomes less strong or effective or stops working properly, e.g. *The power failed... His grandmother's eyesight began to fail.* **6** (phrase) **Without fail** means definitely or regularly, e.g. *Every Sunday her mum would ring without fail.*

failing, failings 1 (noun) A failing is a fault or unsatisfactory feature in something or someone. **2** (preposition) used to introduce an alternative, e.g. *Failing that, get a market stall.*

failure, failures 1 (noun) Failure is a lack of success, e.g. *Not all conservation programmes* *ended in failure.* **2** A failure is an unsuccessful person, thing, action, or event, e.g. *The venture was a complete failure.* **3** Your failure to do something is not doing something that you were expected to do, e.g. *a statement explaining his failure to turn up as a speaker.*

faint, fainter, faintest; faints, fainting, fainted 1 (adjective) A sound, colour, or feeling that is faint has little strength or intensity. **2** (verb) If you faint, you lose consciousness for a short time. **3** (adjective) If you feel faint, you feel weak, dizzy, and unsteady. **faintly** (adverb).

fair, fairer, fairest; fairs 1 (adjective) reasonable or equal according to generally accepted ideas about what is right and just, e.g. *fair and prompt trials for political prisoners.* **2** quite large, e.g. *a fair size envelope.* **3** moderately good or likely to be correct, e.g. *He had a fair idea of what to expect.* **4** having light coloured hair or pale skin. **5** with pleasant, dry, and fine weather, e.g *Ireland's fair weather months.* **6** (noun) A fair is a form of entertainment that takes place outside, with stalls, sideshows, and machines to ride on. **7** A fair is also an exhibition of goods produced by a particular industry, e.g. *International Wine and Food Fair.* **fairly** (adverb), **fairness** (noun).

fairway, fairways (noun) On a golf course, the fairway is the area of trimmed grass between a tee and a green.

fairy, fairies (noun) In stories, fairies are small, supernatural creatures with magical powers.

fairy tale, fairy tales (noun) A fairy tale is a story of magical events.

faith, faiths 1 (noun) Faith is a feeling of confidence, trust or optimism about something. **2** A faith is a particular religion.

faithful 1 (adjective) loyal to someone or something and remaining firm in support of them. **2** accurate and truthful, e.g. *a faithful copy of an original.* **faithfully** (adverb), **faithfulness** (noun).

fake, fakes, faking, faked 1 (noun) A fake is an imitation of something made to trick people into thinking that it is genuine. **2** (adjective) Fake means imitation and not genuine, e.g. *fake fur.* **3** (verb) If you fake an emotion or feeling, you pretend that you are experiencing it.

falcon, falcons (noun) A falcon is a bird of prey that can be trained to hunt other birds or small animals.

fall, falls, falling, fell, fallen 1 (verb) If someone or something falls or falls over, they drop towards the ground. **2** (noun) If you have a fall, you accidentally fall over. **3** A fall of snow, soot, or other substance is a quantity of it that has fallen to the ground. **4** (verb) If something falls somewhere, it lands there, e.g. *The spotlight fell on her.* **5** If something falls in amount or strength, it becomes less or weaker, e.g. *Steel production fell about 25%.* **6** (noun) A fall in something is a reduction in its amount or strength. **7** (verb) If a person or group in a position of power falls, they lose their position and someone else takes control. **8** Someone who falls in battle is killed. **9** If, for example, you fall asleep, fall ill, or fall in love, you change quite quickly to that new state. **10** If you fall for someone, you become strongly attracted to them and fall in love. **11** If you fall for a trick or lie, you are deceived by it. **12** Something that falls on a particular date occurs on that date. **13** (noun) In America, autumn is called the fall. **fall down** (verb) An argument or idea that falls down on a particular point is weak in that area and as a result will be unsuccessful. **fall out** (verb) If people fall out, they disagree and quarrel. **fall through** (verb) If an arrangement or plan falls through, it fails or is abandoned.

fallacy, fallacies (pronounced **fal**-lass-ee) (noun) A fallacy is something false that is generally believed to be true.

fallopian tube, fallopian tubes (pronounced fal-**loh**-pee-an) (noun) The fallopian tubes in a woman's body are the pair of tubes along which the eggs pass from the ovaries to the uterus.

fallout (noun) Fallout is radioactive particles that fall to the earth after a nuclear explosion.

fallow (adjective) Land that is fallow is not being used for crop growing so that it has the chance to rest and improve.

false 1 (adjective) untrue, mistaken, or incorrect, e.g. *I think that's a false argument.* **2** not real or genuine but intended to seem real, e.g. *false hair.* **3** unfaithful or deceitful. **falsely** (adverb), **falsity** (noun).

falsehood, falsehoods 1 (noun) Falsehood is the quality or fact of being untrue, e.g. *the difference between truth and falsehood.* **2** A falsehood is a lie.

falsify, falsifies, falsifying, falsified (verb) If you falsify something, you change or misrepresent it in order to deceive people. **falsification** (noun).

falter, falters, faltering, faltered (verb) If someone or something falters, they hesitate or become unsure or unsteady, e.g. *Her voice faltered.*

fame (noun) Fame is the state of being very well known.

famed (adjective) very well known, e.g. *an area famed for its beauty.*

familiar 1 (adjective) well known or easy to recognize, e.g. *familiar faces.* **2** knowing or understanding something well, e.g. *Most children are familiar with stories.* **familiarity** (noun), **familiarize** (verb).

family, families 1 (noun) A family is a group consisting of parents and their children; also all the people who are related to each other, including aunts and uncles, cousins, and grandparents. **2** A family is also a group of related species of animals or plants. **familial** (adjective).

family planning (noun) Family planning is the practice of controlling the number of children you have, usually by using contraception.

famine, famines (noun) A famine is a serious shortage of food which may cause many deaths.

famished (adjective; an informal word) very hungry.

famous (adjective) very well known.

famously (adverb; an old-fashioned word) If people get on famously, they enjoy each other's company very much.

fan, fans, fanning, fanned 1 (noun) If you are a fan of someone or something, you like them very much and are very enthusiastic about them. **2** A fan is a hand-held or mechanical object which creates a draught of cool air when it moves. **3** (verb) To fan someone or something means to create a draught in their direction, e.g. *The gentle wind fanned her from all sides.* **fan out** (verb) If things or people fan out, they move outwards from a point in different directions.

fanatic, fanatics (noun) A fanatic is a person who is very extreme in their support for a cause or in their enthusiasm for a particular sport or activity. **fanaticism** (noun).

fanatical (adjective) If you are fanatical about something, you are very extreme in your enthusiasm or support for it. **fanatically** (adverb).

fancy, fancies, fancying, fancied; fancier, fanciest 1 (verb) If you fancy something, you want to have it or do it, e.g *She fancied living in Scotland.* **2** (adjective) Something that is fancy is special and elaborate, e.g. *dressed up in some fancy clothes.* **fanciful** (adjective).

fancy dress (noun) Fancy dress is clothing worn for a party at which people dress up to look like a particular character or animal.

fanfare, fanfares (noun) A fanfare is a short, loud, musical introduction to a special event, usually played on trumpets.

fang, fangs (noun) Fangs are long, pointed teeth.

fantasize, fantasizes, fantasizing, fantasized; also spelled **fantasise** (verb) If you fantasize, you imagine pleasant but unlikely events or situations.

fantastic 1 (adjective) wonderful and very pleasing, e.g. *a fantastic view of the sea.* **2** extremely large in degree or amount, e.g. *fantastic debts.* **3** strange and difficult to believe, e.g. *fantastic animals found nowhere else on earth.* **fantastically** (adverb).

fantasy, fantasies 1 (noun) A fantasy is an imagined story or situation. **2** Fantasy is the activity of imagining things or the things that you imagine, e.g. *She can't distinguish between fantasy and reality.*

far, farther, farthest; further, furthest 1 (adverb) If something is far away from other things, it is a long distance away. **2** (adjective) Far means very distant, e.g. *in the far south of England.* **3** Far also describes the more distant of two things rather than the nearer one, e.g. *the far corner of the goal.* **4** (adverb) Far also means very much or to a great extent or degree, e.g. *far more important.* **5** (phrase) **By far** and **far and away** are used to say that something is the best, e.g. *Walking is by far the best way to get around.* **6 So far** means up to the present moment, e.g. *So far, it's been good news.* **7 As far as, so far as,** and **in so far as** mean to the degree or extent that something is true, e.g. *As far as I know he is progressing well.*

farce, farces 1 (noun) A farce is a humorous play in which ridiculous and unlikely situations occur. **2** A farce is also a disorganized and ridiculous situation. **farcical** (adjective).

fare, fares, faring, fared 1 (noun) A fare is the amount charged for a journey on a bus, train, or plane. **2** (verb) How someone fares in a particular situation is how they get on, e.g. *The team have not fared well in this tournament.*

Far East (noun) The Far East consists of the countries of East Asia, including China, Japan, and Malaysia. **Far Eastern** (adjective).

farewell 1 (interjection) Farewell means goodbye. **2** (adjective) A farewell act is performed by or for someone who is leaving a particular job or career, e.g. *a farewell speech.*

far-fetched (adjective) unlikely to be true.

farm, farms, farming, farmed 1 (noun) A farm is an area of land together with buildings, used for growing crops and raising animals. **2** (verb) Someone who farms uses land to grow crops and raise animals. **farmer** (noun), **farming** (noun).

farmhouse, farmhouses (noun) A farmhouse is the main house on a farm.

farmyard, farmyards (noun) A farmyard is an area surrounded by farm buildings.

fascinate, fascinates, fascinating, fascinated (verb) If something fascinates you, it interests and delights you so much that your thoughts concentrate on it and nothing else. **fascinating** (adjective).

fascism (pronounced **fash**-izm) (noun) Fascism is an extreme right-wing political ideology or system of government with a powerful dictator and state control of most activities. Nationalism is encouraged and political opposition is not allowed. **fascist** (noun or adjective).

fashion, fashions, fashioning, fashioned 1 (noun) A fashion is a style of dress or way of behaving that is popular at a particular time. **2** The fashion in which someone does something is the way in which they do it. **3** (verb) If you fashion something, you make or shape it.

fashionable (adjective) Something that is fashionable is very popular with a lot of people at the same time. **fashionably** (adverb).

fast, faster, fastest; fasts, fasting, fasted 1 (adjective or adverb) moving, doing something, or happening quickly or with great speed. **2** If a clock is fast, it shows a time that is later than the real time. **3** (adverb) Something that is held fast is firmly fixed. **4** (phrase) If you are **fast asleep,** you are in a deep sleep. **5** (verb) If you fast, you eat no food at all for a period of time, usually for religious reasons. **6** (noun) A fast is a period of time during which someone does not eat food.

fasten, fastens, fastening, fastened 1 (verb) To fasten something means to close it, do it up, or attach it firmly to something else. **2** If you fasten your hands or teeth around or onto something, you hold it tightly with them. **fastener** (noun), **fastening** (noun).

fast food (noun) Fast food is hot food that is prepared and served quickly after you have ordered it.

fastidious (adjective) extremely choosy and concerned about neatness and cleanliness.

fat, fatter, fattest; fats 1 (adjective) Someone who is fat has too much weight on their body. **2** (noun) Fat is the greasy, cream-coloured substance that animals and humans have under their skin, which is used to store energy and to help keep them warm. **3** Fat is also the greasy solid or liquid substance obtained from animals and plants and used in cooking. **4** (adjective) large or great, e.g. *a fat pile of letters.* **fatness** (noun), **fatty** (adjective).

fatal 1 (adjective) causing death, e.g. *fatal injuries.* **2** very important or significant and likely to have an undesirable effect, e.g. *The mistake was fatal to my plans.* **fatally** (adverb).

fatality, fatalities (noun) A fatality is a death caused by accident or violence.

fate, fates 1 (noun) Fate is a power that is believed to control events. **2** Someone's fate is what happens to them, e.g. *She was resigned to her fate.*

fateful (adjective) having an important, often disastrous, effect, e.g. *fateful political decisions.*

father, fathers, fathering, fathered 1 (noun) A person's father is their male parent. **2** (verb; a literary use) When a man fathers a child, he makes a woman pregnant. **3** (noun) The father of something is the man who invented or started it, e.g. *the father of Italian painting.* **4** Father is used to address a priest in some Christian churches. **5** Father is another name for God. **fatherly** (adjective), **fatherhood** (noun).

father-in-law, fathers-in-law (noun) A person's father-in-law is the father of their husband or wife.

fathom, fathoms, fathoming, fathomed 1 (noun) A fathom is a unit for measuring the depth of water. It is equal to 6 feet or about 1.83 metres. **2** (verb) If you fathom something, you understand it after careful thought, e.g. *Daisy tries to fathom what it means.*

fatigue, fatigues, fatiguing, fatigued (pronounced fat-**eeg**) **1** (noun) Fatigue is extreme tiredness. **2** (verb) If you are fatigued by something, it makes you extremely tired.

fault, faults, faulting, faulted 1 (noun) If something bad is your fault, you are to blame for it. 2 (phrase) If you are **at fault**, you are mistaken or are to blame for something, e.g. *If you were at fault, you accept it.* 3 (noun) A fault in something or in someone's character is a weakness or imperfection in it. 4 (verb) If you cannot fault someone, you cannot criticize them for what they are doing because they are doing it so well. 5 (noun) A fault is a large crack in rock caused by movement of the earth's crust. **faultless** (adjective), **faulty** (adjective).

favour, favours, favouring, favoured 1 (noun) If you regard someone or something with favour, you like or support them. 2 If you do someone a favour, you do something helpful for them. 3 (phrase) Something that is **in someone's favour** is a help or advantage to them, e.g. *The arguments seemed to be in our favour.* 4 If you are **in favour of** something, you agree with it and think it should happen. 5 (verb) If you favour something or someone, you prefer that person or thing. **favourable** (adjective), **favourably** (adverb).

favourite, favourites 1 (adjective) Your favourite person or thing is the one you like best. 2 (noun) Someone's favourite is the person or thing they like best. 3 In a race or contest, the favourite is the animal or person expected to win.

favouritism (noun) Favouritism is behaviour in which you are unfairly more helpful or more generous to one person than to other people.

fawn, fawns, fawning, fawned 1 (noun or adjective) pale yellowish-brown. 2 (noun) A fawn is a very young deer. 3 (verb) To fawn on someone means to seek their approval by flattering them.

fax, faxes (noun) A fax is an exact copy of a document sent by a telegraph system.

fear, fears, fearing, feared 1 (noun) Fear is an unpleasant feeling of danger. 2 A fear is a thought that something undesirable or unpleasant might happen, e.g. *You have a fear of failure.* 3 (verb) If you fear someone or something, you are frightened of them. 4 If you fear something unpleasant, you are worried that it is likely to happen, e.g. *Artists feared that their pictures would be forgotten.* **fearless** (adjective), **fearlessly** (adverb).

fearful 1 (adjective) afraid and full of fear. 2 extremely unpleasant or worrying, e.g. *The world's in such a fearful mess.* **fearfully** (adverb).

fearsome (adjective) terrible or frightening, e.g. *a powerful, fearsome weapon.*

feasible (adjective) possible and likely to be done or likely to happen, e.g. *The proposal is just not feasible.* **feasibility** (noun).

feast, feasts (noun) A feast is a large and special meal for many people.

feat, feats (noun) A feat is an impressive and difficult achievement, e.g. *It was an astonishing feat for Leeds to score six.*

feather, feathers (noun) A feather is one of the light fluffy structures covering a bird's body. **feathery** (adjective).

feature, features, featuring, featured 1 (noun) A feature of something is an interesting or important part or characteristic of it. **2** Someone's features are the various parts of their face. **3** A feature is a special article or programme dealing with a particular subject or the main film in a cinema programme. **4** (verb) To feature something means to include it or emphasize it as an important part or subject. **featureless** (adjective).

February (noun) February is the second month of the year. It has 28 days, except in a leap year, when it has 29 days.

fed the past tense and past participle of **feed**.

federal (adjective) relating to a system of government in which a group of states is controlled by a central government, but each state has its own local powers, e.g. *The United States of America is a federal country.*

federation, federations (noun) A federation is a group of organizations or states that have joined together for a common purpose.

fed up (adjective; an informal expression) unhappy or bored.

fee, fees (noun) A fee is a charge or payment for a job, service, or activity.

feeble, feebler, feeblest (adjective) weak or lacking in power, strength, or influence, e.g. *feeble and stupid arguments.*

feed, feeds, feeding, fed 1 (verb) To feed a person or animal means to give them food. **2** When an animal or baby feeds, it eats. **3** (noun) Feed is food for animals or babies. **4** (verb) To feed something means to supply what is needed for it to operate, develop, or exist, e.g. *The information was fed into a computer database.*

feedback 1 (noun) Feedback is comments and information about the quality or success of something. **2** Feedback is also a condition in which some of the power, sound, or information produced by electronic equipment goes back into it.

feel, feels, feeling, felt 1 (verb) If you feel an emotion or sensation, you experience it, e.g. *I felt a bit ashamed.* **2** If you feel that something is the case, you believe it to be so, e.g. *She feels that she is in control of her life.* **3** If you feel something, you touch it. **4** If something feels warm or cold, for example, you experience its warmth or coldness through the sense of touch, e.g. *Real marble feels cold to the touch.* **5** (noun) The feel of something is how it feels to you when you touch it, e.g. *skin with a velvety smooth feel.* **6** (verb) To feel the effect of something means to be affected by it, e.g. *The shock waves of this fire will be felt by people from all over the world.* **7** (phrase) If you **feel like** doing something, you want to do it.

feeler, feelers (noun) An insect's feelers are the two thin antennae on its head with which it senses things around it.

feeling, feelings 1 (noun) A feeling is an emotion or reaction, e.g. *feelings of envy.* **2** A feeling is also a physical sensation, e.g. *a feeling of pain.* **3** Feeling is the ability to experience the sense of touch in your body, e.g. *He had no feeling in his hands.* **4** Your feelings about something are your general attitudes, impressions, or thoughts about it, e.g. *He has strong feelings about our national sport.*

feet the plural of **foot.**

feign, feigns, feigning, feigned (rhymes with **rain**) (verb) If you feign an emotion, feeling, or state, you pretend to experience it, e.g. *I feigned a headache.*

feline (pronounced **fee**-line) (adjective) belonging or relating to the cat family.

fell, fells, felling, felled 1 the past tense of **fall. 2** (verb) To fell a tree means to cut it down.

fellow, fellows 1 (noun; a rather old-fashioned informal use) A fellow is a man, e.g. *I knew a fellow by that name.* **2** (adjective) You use fellow to describe people who have something in common with you, e.g. *his fellow editors.* **3** (noun) A fellow is also a senior member of a learned society or a university college. **4** Your fellows are the people who share work or an activity with you.

fellowship, fellowships 1 (noun) Fellowship is a feeling of friendliness that a group of people have when they are doing things together. **2** A fellowship is a society or other group of people that join together because they have interests in common, e.g. *the Dickens Fellowship.* **3** A fellowship is also an academic post at a university which involves research work.

felt 1 the past tense and past participle of **feel. 2** (noun) Felt is a thick cloth made by pressing short threads together.

female, females 1 (noun) A female is a person or animal that belongs to the sex that can have babies or young. **2** (adjective) concerning or relating to females.

feminine (adjective) relating to women or considered to be typical of women. **femininity** (noun).

feminism (noun) Feminism is the belief that women should have the same rights, power, and opportunities as men. **feminist** (noun or adjective).

fen, fens (noun) The fens are an area of low, flat, very wet land in the east of England.

fence, fences, fencing, fenced 1 (noun) A fence is a wooden or wire barrier between two areas of land. **2** (verb) To fence an area of land means to surround it with a fence. **3** (noun) A fence in horse racing or show jumping is a barrier or hedge for the horses to jump over. **4** (verb) When two people fence, they use special swords to fight each other as a sport.

fend, fends, fending, fended 1 (phrase) If you have to **fend for yourself,** you have to look after yourself. **2** (verb) If you fend off an attack or unwelcome questions or attention, you defend and protect yourself.

ferment, ferments, fermenting, fermented (verb) When wine, beer, or fruit ferments, a chemical change takes place in it, often producing alcohol. **fermentation** (noun).

fern, ferns (noun) A fern is a plant with long feathery leaves, having no flowers and reproducing by spores.

ferocious (adjective) violent and fierce, e.g. *ferocious dogs... ferocious storms.* **ferociously** (adverb), **ferocity** (noun).

ferret, ferrets (noun) A ferret is a small, white, fierce animal related to the weasel and kept for hunting rats and rabbits.

ferry, ferries, ferrying, ferried 1 (noun) A ferry is a boat that carries people and vehicles across short stretches of water. **2** (verb) To ferry people or goods somewhere means to transport them there, usually on a short, regular journey.

fertile 1 (adjective) capable of producing strong, healthy plants, e.g. *fertile soil.* **2** creative, e.g. *fertile minds.* **3** able to have babies or young. **fertility** (noun).

fertilize, fertilizes, fertilizing, fertilized; also spelled **fertilise 1** (verb) When an egg, plant, or female is fertilized, the process of reproduction begins by sperm joining with the egg, or by pollen coming into contact with the reproductive part of a plant. **2** To fertilize land means to put manure or chemicals onto it to feed the plants.

fertilizer, fertilizers; also spelled **fertiliser** (noun) Fertilizer is a substance put onto soil to improve plant growth.

fervent (adjective) showing strong, sincere, and enthusiastic feeling, e.g. *a fervent nationalist.* **fervently** (adverb).

fervour (noun) Fervour is a very strong feeling for or belief in something, e.g. *a wave of religious fervour.*

fester, festers, festering, festered (verb) If a wound festers it becomes infected and produces pus.

festival, festivals 1 (noun) A festival is an organized series of events and performances, e.g. *the Cannes Film Festival.* **2** A festival is also a day or period of religious celebration.

festive (adjective) full of happiness and celebration, e.g. *a festive time of singing and dancing.*

festivity, festivities (noun) Festivity is celebration and happiness, e.g. *the wedding festivities.*

festooned (adjective) If something is festooned with objects, the objects are hanging across it in large numbers.

fetch, fetches, fetching, fetched 1 (verb) If you fetch something, you go to where it is and bring it back. **2** If something fetches a particular sum of money, it is sold for that amount, e.g. *Bronzes fetch the highest prices.*

fetching (adjective) attractive in appearance, e.g. *a fetching purple frock.*

fete, fetes, feting, feted (rhymes with **date**) **1** (noun) A fete is an outdoor event with competitions, displays, and goods for sale. **2** (verb) Someone who is feted receives a public welcome or entertainment as an honour.

feud, feuds, feuding, feuded (pronounced **fyood**) **1** (noun) A feud is a long-term and very bitter quarrel, especially between families. **2** (verb) When people feud, they take part in a feud.

feudalism (noun) Feudalism is a social and political system that was common in the Middle Ages in Europe. Under this system, ordinary people were given land and protection by a lord, and in return they worked and fought for him. **feudal** (adjective).

fever, fevers 1 (noun) Fever is a condition occurring during illness, in which the patient has a very high body temperature. **2** A fever is extreme excitement or agitation, e.g. *a fever of impatience.*

feverish 1 (adjective) in a state of extreme excitement or agitation, e.g. *increasingly feverish activity.* **2** suffering from a high body temperature. **feverishly** (adverb).

few, fewer, fewest 1 (adjective or noun) used to refer to a small number of things, e.g. *I saw him a few moments ago... one of only a few.* **2** (phrases) **Quite a few** or **a good few** means quite a large number of things.

fiancé, fiancés (pronounced fee-**on**-say) (noun) A woman's fiancé is the man to whom she is engaged.

fiancée, fiancées (noun) A man's fiancée is the woman to whom he is engaged.

fiasco, fiascos (pronounced fee-**ass**-koh) (noun) A fiasco is an event or attempt that fails completely, especially in a ridiculous or disorganized way, e.g. *The game ended in a complete fiasco.*

fib, fibs, fibbing, fibbed 1 (noun) A fib is a small, unimportant lie. **2** (verb) If you fib, you tell a small lie.

fibre, fibres 1 (noun) A fibre is a thin thread of a substance used to make cloth. **2** Fibre is also a part of plants that can be eaten but not digested; it helps food pass quickly through the body. **fibrous** (adjective).

fickle (adjective) A fickle person keeps changing their mind about who or what they like or want.

fiction, fictions 1 (noun) Fiction is stories about people and events that have been invented by the author. **2** A fiction is something that is not true. **fictional** (adjective), **fictitious** (adjective).

fiddle, fiddles, fiddling, fiddled 1 (verb) If you fiddle with something, you keep moving it or touching it restlessly. **2** (an informal use) If someone fiddles something such as an account, they alter it dishonestly to get money for themselves. **3** (noun; an informal use) A fiddle is a dishonest action or scheme to get money. **4** A fiddle is also a violin. **fiddler** (noun).

fiddly, fiddlier, fiddliest (adjective) small and difficult to do, use, or handle, e.g. *fiddly nuts and bolts.*

fidelity (noun) Fidelity is the quality of remaining firm in your beliefs, friendships, or loyalty to another person.

fidget, fidgets, fidgeting, fidgeted 1 (verb) If you fidget, you keep changing your position because of nervousness or boredom. **2** (noun) A fidget is someone who fidgets. **fidgety** (adjective).

field, fields, fielding, fielded 1 (noun) A field is an area of land where crops are grown or animals are kept. **2** A sports field is an area of land where sports are played, e.g. *a hockey field.* **3** A coal field, oil field, or gold field is an area where coal, oil, or gold is found. **4** A particular field is a subject or area of interest, e.g. *He was doing well in his own field of advertising.* **5** (adjective) A field trip or a field study involves research or activity in the natural environment rather than theoretical or laboratory work. **6** In an athletics competition, the field events are the events such as the high jump and the javelin which do not take place on a running track. **7** (verb) In cricket, when you field the ball, you stop it after the batsman has hit it. **8** To field questions means to answer or deal with them skilfully.

fielder, fielders (noun) In cricket, the fielders are the team members who stand at various parts of the pitch and try to get the batsmen out or to prevent runs from being scored.

field marshal, field, marshals (noun) A field marshal is an army officer of the highest rank.

fiend, fiends (pronounced **feend**) **1** (noun) A fiend is a devil or evil spirit. **2** A fiend is also a very wicked or cruel person. **3** (an informal use) You can describe someone who is very keen on a particular thing as a fiend, e.g. *a fitness fiend.*

fierce, fiercer, fiercest 1 (adjective) very aggressive or angry. **2** extremely strong or intense, e.g. *a sudden fierce pain... a fierce storm.* **fiercely** (adverb).

fiery, fierier, fieriest 1 (adjective) involving fire or seeming like fire, e.g. *a huge fiery sun.* **2** showing great anger, energy, or passion, e.g. *a fiery debate.*

fifteen the number 15. **fifteenth**

fifth, fifths 1 The fifth item in a series is the one counted as number five. **2** (noun) A fifth is one of five equal parts.

fifty, fifties the number 50. **fiftieth**

fifty-fifty 1 (adverb) divided equally into two portions. **2** (adjective) just as likely not to happen as to happen, e.g. *You've got a fifty-fifty chance of being right.*

fig, figs (noun) A fig is a soft, sweet fruit full of tiny seeds. It grows in hot countries and is often eaten dried.

fight, fights, fighting, fought 1 (verb) When people fight, they take part in a battle, a war, a boxing match, or in some other attempt to hurt or kill someone. **2** (noun) A fight is a situation in which people hit or try to hurt each other. **3** (verb) To fight for something means to try in a very determined way to achieve it, e.g. *I must fight for respect.* **4** (noun) A fight is a determined attempt to prevent or achieve something, e.g. *the fight for independence.* **fighter** (noun).

figurative (adjective) If you use a word or expression in a figurative sense, you use it with a more abstract or imaginative meaning than its ordinary one. **figuratively** (adverb).

figure, figures, figuring, figured **1** (noun) A figure is a written number or the amount expressed by a number. **2** A figure is a geometrical shape. **3** In written texts, a figure is a diagram or table. **4** A figure is the shape of a person whom you cannot see clearly, e.g. *A human figure leaped at him.* **5** Your figure is the shape of your body, e.g. *his slim and supple figure.* **6** A figure is also a person, e.g. *He was a major figure in the trial.* **7** (verb) To figure in something means to appear or be included in it, e.g. *the many people who have figured in his life.* **8** (an informal use) If you figure that something is the case, you guess or conclude this, e.g. *We figure the fire broke out around four in the morning.*

figurehead, figureheads (noun) A figurehead is the leader of a movement or organization who has no real power.

figure of speech, figures of speech (noun) A figure of speech is an expression such as a simile or idiom in which the words are not used in their literal sense.

file, files, filing, filed **1** (noun) A file is a box or folder in which a group of papers or records is kept; also used of the information kept in the file. **2** In computing, a file is a stored set of related data with its own name. **3** A file is a line of people one behind the other. **4** A file is also a long steel tool with a rough surface, used for smoothing and shaping hard materials. **5** (verb) When someone files a document, they put it in its correct place with similar documents. **6** When a group of people file somewhere, they walk one behind the other in a line. **7** If you file something, you smooth or shape it with a file.

fill, fills, filling, filled **1** (verb) If you fill something or if it fills up, it becomes full. **2** If something fills a need, it satisfies the need, e.g. *Ella had in some small way filled the gap left by Molly's absence.* **3** To fill a job vacancy means to appoint someone to do that job. **4** (noun) If you have had your fill of something, you do not want any more. **fill in** **1** (verb) If you fill in a form, you write information in the appropriate spaces. **2** If you fill someone in, you give them information to bring them up to date.

fillet, fillets, filleting, filleted **1** (noun) Fillet is a strip of tender, boneless beef, veal, or pork. **2** A fillet of fish is a piece of fish with the bones removed. **3** (verb) To fillet meat or fish means to prepare it by cutting out the bones.

filling, fillings **1** (noun) The filling in a sandwich, cake, or pie is the soft food mixture inside it. **2** A filling is a small amount of metal or plastic put into a hole in a tooth by a dentist.

filly, fillies (noun) A filly is a female horse or pony under the age of four.

film, films, filming, filmed 1 (noun) A film is a series of moving pictures projected onto a screen and shown at the cinema or on television. **2** A film is also a thin flexible strip of plastic used in a camera to record images when exposed to light. **3** (verb) If you film someone, you use a cine camera or a video camera to record their movements on film. **4** (noun) A film of powder or liquid is a very thin layer of it on a surface. **5** Plastic film is a very thin sheet of plastic used for wrapping things.

filter, filters, filtering, filtered 1 (noun) A filter is a device that allows some substances, lights, or sounds to pass through it, but not others, e.g. *a filter against the harmful rays of the sun.* **2** (verb) To filter a substance means to pass it through a filter. **3** If something filters somewhere, it gets there slowly, gradually, or faintly, e.g. *Traffic filtered into the city.* **filtration** (noun).

filth 1 (noun) Filth is disgusting dirt and muck. **2** People often use the word filth to refer to excessively bad language or to sexual material that is thought to be crude and offensive. **filthy** (adjective).

fin, fins (noun) A fin is a thin, angular structure on the body of a fish, used to help guide it and push it through the water.

final, finals 1 (adjective) last in a series or happening at the end of something. **2** A decision that is final cannot be changed or questioned. **3** (noun) A final is the last game or contest in a series which decides the overall winner. **4** (plural noun) Finals are the last and most important examinations of a university or college course.

finale, finales (pronounced fin-**nah**-lee) (noun) The finale is the last section of a piece of music or show.

finalist, finalists (noun) A finalist is a person taking part in the final of a competition.

finalize, finalizes, finalizing, finalized; also spelled **finalise** (verb) If you finalize something, you complete all the arrangements for it.

finally (adverb) If something finally happens, it happens after a long delay.

finance, finances, financing, financed 1 (verb) To finance a project or a large purchase means to provide the money for it. **2** (noun) Finance for something is the money or loans used to pay for it. **3** Finance is also the management of money, loans, and investments.

financial (adjective) relating to or involving money. **financially** (adverb).

financier, financiers (noun) A financier is a person who organizes and deals with the finance for large businesses.

finch, finches (noun) A finch is a small bird with a short strong beak for crushing seeds.

find, finds, finding, found 1 (verb) If you find someone or something, you discover them, either as a result of searching or by coming across them unexpectedly. **2** If you find that something is the case, you become aware of it or realize it, e.g. *I found my fists were clenched.* **3** Something that is found in a particular place typically lives or exists there. **4** When a court or jury finds a person guilty or not guilty, they decide that the person is guilty or innocent, e.g. *He was found guilty and sentenced to life imprisonment.* **5** (noun) If you describe something or someone as a find, you mean that you have recently discovered them and they are valuable, interesting, or useful. **finder** (noun). **find out 1** (verb) If you find out something, you learn or discover something that you did not know. **2** If you find someone out, you discover that they have been doing something they should not have been doing.

findings (plural noun) Someone's findings are the conclusions they reach as a result of investigation.

fine, finer, finest; fines, fining, fined 1 (adjective) very good or very beautiful, e.g *a fine school... fine clothes.* **2** satisfactory or suitable, e.g *Pasta dishes are fine if not served with a rich sauce.* **3** very narrow or thin, e.g. *fine paper.* **4** A fine net or sieve has very small holes. Fine powder or dust consists of very small particles. **5** A fine detail, adjustment, or distinction is very delicate, exact, or subtle. **6** When the weather is fine, it is not raining and is bright or sunny. **7** (noun) A fine is a sum of money paid as a punishment. **8** (verb) Someone who is fined has to pay a specific sum of money as a punishment.

finery (noun) Finery is very beautiful clothing and jewellery.

finesse (pronounced fin-**ness**) (noun) If you do something with finesse, you do it with skill, elegance, and subtlety.

finger, fingers, fingering, fingered 1 (noun) Your fingers are the four long jointed parts of your hands, sometimes including the thumbs. **2** (verb) If you finger something you feel it with your fingers.

fingernail, fingernails (noun) Your fingernails are the hard coverings at the ends of your fingers.

fingerprint, fingerprints (noun) A fingerprint is a mark made showing the pattern on the skin at the tip of a person's finger.

finish, finishes, finishing, finished 1 (verb) When you finish something, you reach the end of it and complete it. **2** When something finishes, it ends or stops. **3** (noun) The finish of something is the end or last part of it. **4** The finish that something has is the texture or appearance of its surface, e.g. *a healthy, glossy fin-*

ish.

finite (pronounced **fie**-nite) (adjective) having a particular size or limit which cannot be increased, e.g. *There's only finite money to spend.*

Finn, Finns (noun) A Finn is someone who comes from Finland.

Finnish 1 (adjective) belonging or relating to Finland. **2** (noun) Finnish is the main language spoken in Finland.

fir, firs (noun) A fir is a tall pointed evergreen tree that has thin needle-like leaves and produces cones.

fire, fires, firing, fired 1 (noun) Fire is the flames produced when something burns. **2** A fire is a pile or mass of burning material. **3** A fire is also a piece of equipment that is used as a heater, e.g. *a gas fire.* **4** (verb) If you fire a weapon or fire a bullet, you operate the weapon so that the bullet or missile is released. **5** (phrase) If someone **opens fire,** they start shooting. **6** (verb) If you fire questions at someone, you ask them a lot of questions very quickly. **7** (an informal use) If an employer fires someone, he or she dismisses that person from their job.

firearm, firearms (noun) A firearm is a gun.

fire brigade, fire brigades (noun) The fire brigade is the organization which has the job of putting out fires.

fire engine, fire engines (noun) A fire engine is a large vehicle that carries equipment for putting out fires.

fire escape, fire escapes (noun) A fire escape is an emergency exit or staircase for use if there is a fire.

fire extinguisher, fire extinguishers (noun) A fire extinguisher is a metal cylinder containing water or chemical foam for spraying onto a fire.

firefighter, firefighters (noun) A firefighter is a person whose job is to put out fires and rescue trapped people.

firefly, fireflies (noun) A firefly is an insect belonging to the beetle family that glows in the dark.

fireplace, fireplaces (noun) A fireplace is the opening beneath a chimney where a domestic fire can be lit.

fireproof (adjective) designed to be resistant to fire.

fire station, fire stations (noun) A fire station is a building where fire engines are kept and where firefighters wait to be called out.

firework, fireworks (noun) A firework is a small container of gunpowder and other chemicals which explodes or produces coloured sparks or smoke when lit.

firing squad, firing squads (noun) A firing squad is a group of soldiers ordered to shoot a person condemned to death.

firm, firmer, firmest; firms 1 (adjective) Something that is firm does not move easily when pressed, pushed, or shaken, or when weight is put on it. **2** A firm grasp or push is one with controlled force or pressure. **3** A firm decision is definite. **4** Someone who is firm behaves with authority that shows they will not change their mind. **5** (noun) A firm is a business selling or producing something. **firmly** (adverb), **firmness** (noun).

first 1 (adjective or adverb) happening, coming, or done before everything or everyone else. **2** (adjective) more important than anything else, e.g. *Her pig won first prize.* **3** (noun) A first is something that has never happened or been done before. **firstly** (adverb).

first aid (noun) First aid is medical treatment given to an injured person.

first class 1 (adjective) Something that is first class is of the highest quality or standard. **2** First-class accommodation on a train, aircraft, or ship is the best and most expensive type of accommodation. **3** First-class postage is quick but more expensive.

first-hand (adjective) First-hand knowledge or experience is gained directly rather than from books or other people.

First Lady, First Ladies (noun) The First Lady of a country is the wife of a president.

first-rate (adjective) excellent.

fiscal (adjective) relating to or involving government or public money, especially taxes.

fish, fishes, fishing, fished The plural of the noun can be either **fish** or **fishes** but is normally **fish. 1** (noun) A fish is a cold-blooded creature living in water and having a spine, gills, fins, and a scaly skin. **2** Fish is the flesh of fish eaten as food. **3** (verb) To fish means to try to catch fish for food or sport. **4** If you fish for information, you try to get it in an indirect way. **fishing** (noun), **fisherman** (noun).

fishery, fisheries (noun) A fishery is an area of the sea where fish are caught commercially.

fishmonger, fishmongers (noun) A fishmonger is a shopkeeper who sells fish; also the shop itself.

fishy, fishier, fishiest 1 (adjective) smelling of fish. **2** (an informal use) suspicious or doubtful, e.g. *He spotted something fishy going on.*

fission (rhymes with **mission**) **1** (noun) Fission is the splitting or breaking of something into parts. **2** Fission is also nuclear fission.

fissure, fissures (noun) A fissure is a deep crack in rock.

fist, fists (noun) A fist is a hand with the fingers curled tightly towards the palm.

fit, fits, fitting, fitted; fitter, fittest 1 (verb) Something that fits is the right shape or size for a particular person or position. **2** If you fit something somewhere, you put it there carefully or securely, e.g. *Very carefully he fitted the files inside the compartment.* **3** If something fits a particular situation, person, or thing, it is suitable or appropriate, e.g. *a sentence that fitted the crime.* **4** (noun) The fit of something is how it fits, e.g. *This bolt must be a good fit.* **5** (adjective) good enough or suitable, e.g. *Housing fit for frail elderly people.* **6** Someone who is fit is healthy and has strong muscles as a result of regular exercise. **7** (noun) If someone has a fit, their muscles suddenly start contracting violently and they may lose consciousness. **8** A fit of laughter, coughing, anger, or panic is a sudden uncontrolled outburst. **fitness** (noun).

fitful (adjective) happening at irregular intervals and not continuous, e.g. *a fitful breeze.* **fitfully** (adverb).

fitter, fitters (noun) A fitter is a person whose job is to assemble or install machinery.

fitting, fittings 1 (adjective) right or suitable, e.g. *a fitting reward for his efforts.* **2** (noun) A fitting is a small part that is fixed to a piece of equipment or furniture. **3** If you have a fitting, you try on a garment that is being made to see whether it fits properly.

five the number 5.

fix, fixes, fixing, fixed 1 (verb) If you fix something somewhere, you attach it or put it there firmly and securely. **2** If you fix something broken, you mend it. **3** If you fix your attention on something, you concentrate on it. **4** If you fix something, you make arrangements for it, e.g. *The opening party is fixed for the 24th September.* **5** (an informal use) To fix something means to arrange the outcome unfairly or dishonestly. **6** (noun; an informal use) Something that is a fix has been unfairly or dishonestly arranged. **7** (an informal use) If you are in a fix, you are in a difficult situation. **8** A fix is an injection of a drug such as heroin. **fixed** (adjective), **fixedly** (adverb).

fixation, fixations (noun) A fixation is an extreme and obsessive interest in something.

fixture, fixtures 1 (noun) A fixture is a piece of furniture or equipment that is fixed into position in a house. **2** A fixture is also a sports event due to take place on a particular date.

fizz, fizzes, fizzing, fizzed (verb) Something that fizzes makes a hissing sound.

fizzle, fizzles, fizzling, fizzled (verb) Something that fizzles makes a weak hissing or spitting sound.

fizzy, fizzier, fizziest (adjective) Fizzy drinks have carbon dioxide in them to make them bubbly.

fjord, fjords (pronounced fee-**ord**); also spelled **fiord** (noun) A fjord is a long narrow inlet of the sea between very high cliffs, especially in Norway.

flab (noun) Flab is large amounts of surplus fat on someone's body.

flabbergasted (adjective) extremely surprised.

flabby, flabbier, flabbiest (adjective) Someone who is flabby is rather fat and unfit, with loose flesh on their body.

flag, flags, flagging, flagged 1 (noun) A flag is a rectangular or square cloth of a particular colour and design which is used as the symbol of a nation, or as a signal. **2** (verb) If you or your spirits flag, you start to lose energy or enthusiasm.

flagrant (pronounced **flay**-grant) (adjective) very shocking and bad in an obvious way, e.g. *a flagrant defiance of the rules.*

flagship, flagships 1 (noun) A flagship is a ship carrying the commander of the fleet. **2** The flagship of an organization is its most modern or impressive product or asset.

flail, flails, flailing, flailed (verb) If someone's arms or legs flail about, they move in a wild, uncontrolled way.

flair (noun) Flair is a natural ability to do something well or stylishly.

flak 1 (noun) Flak is anti-aircraft fire. **2** If you get flak for doing something, you get a lot of severe criticism.

flake, flakes, flaking, flaked 1 (noun) A flake is a small thin piece of something. **2** (verb) When something such as paint flakes, small thin pieces of it come off. **flaky** (adjective), **flaked** (adjective).

flamboyant (adjective) behaving in a very showy, confident, and exaggerated way. **flamboyance** (noun).

flame, flames 1 (noun) A flame is a flickering tongue or blaze of fire. **2** A flame of passion, desire, or anger is a sudden strong feeling.

flamenco (noun) Flamenco is a type of very lively, fast Spanish dancing, accompanied by guitar music.

flamingo, flamingos or **flamingoes** (noun) A flamingo is a long-legged wading bird with pink feathers and a long neck.

flammable (adjective) likely to catch fire and burn easily.

flan, flans (noun) A flan is an open sweet or savoury tart with a pastry or cake base.

flank, flanks, flanking, flanked 1 (noun) An animal's flank is its side between the ribs and the hip. **2** (verb) Someone or something that is flanked by a particular thing or person has them at their side, e.g. *He was flanked by four bodyguards.*

flannel, flannels 1 (noun) Flannel is a lightweight woollen fabric. **2** A flannel is a small square of towelling, used for washing yourself. **3** (an informal use) Flannel is also indirect or evasive talk or explanations.

flap, flaps, flapping, flapped 1 (verb) Something that flaps moves up and down or from side to side with a snapping sound. **2** (noun) A flap of something such as paper or skin is a loose piece that is attached at one edge.

flare, flares, flaring, flared 1 (noun) A flare is a device that produces a brightly coloured flame, used especially as an emergency signal. **2** (verb) If a fire flares, it suddenly burns much more vigorously. **3** If violence or a conflict flares or flares up, it suddenly starts or becomes more serious.

flash, flashes, flashing, flashed 1 (noun) A flash is a sudden short burst of light. **2** (verb) If a light flashes, it shines for a very short period, often repeatedly. **3** Something that flashes past moves or happens so fast that you almost miss it. **4** If you flash something, you show it briefly, e.g. *Michael Jackson flashed his face at the crowd.* **5** (phrase) Something that happens **in a flash** happens suddenly and lasts a very short time.

flashback, flashbacks (noun) A

flashback is a scene in a film, play, or book that returns to events in the past.

flashlight, flashlights (noun) A flashlight is a large, powerful torch.

flashy, flashier, flashiest (adjective) expensive and fashionable in appearance, in a vulgar way, e.g. *flashy clothes.*

flask, flasks (noun) A flask is a bottle used for carrying alcoholic or hot drinks around with you.

flat, flats; flatter, flattest 1 (noun) A flat is a self-contained set of rooms, usually on one level, for living in. **2** (adjective) Something that is flat is level and smooth. **3** A flat object is not very tall or deep, e.g. *a low flat building.* **4** A flat tyre or ball has not got enough air in it. **5** A flat battery has lost its electrical charge. **6** A flat refusal or denial is complete and firm. **7** Something that is flat is without emotion, variety, or interest. **8** A flat rate or price is fixed and the same for everyone whatever their circumstances, e.g. *The company charges a flat fee for its advice.* **9** A musical instrument or note that is flat is slightly too low in pitch. **10** (noun) In music, a flat is a note or key a semitone lower than that described by the same letter. It is represented by the symbol (♭). **11** (adverb) Something that is done in a particular time flat, takes exactly that time, e.g. *They would find them in two minutes flat.* **flatly** (adverb), **flatness** (noun).

flatten, flattens, flattening, flattened (verb) If you flatten something or if it flattens, it becomes flat or flatter.

flatter, flatters, flattering, flattered 1 (verb) If you flatter someone, you praise them in an exaggerated way, either to please them or to persuade them to do something. **2** If you are flattered by something, it makes you feel pleased and important, e.g. *He was very flattered because she liked him.* **3** If you flatter yourself that something is the case, you believe, perhaps mistakenly, something good about yourself or your abilities. **4** Something that flatters you makes you appear more attractive. **flattering** (adjective).

flattery (noun) Flattery is flattering words or behaviour.

flatulence (noun) Flatulence is the uncomfortable state of having too much gas in your stomach or intestine.

flaunt, flaunts, flaunting, flaunted (verb) If you flaunt your possessions or talents, you display them too obviously or proudly.

flautist, flautists (noun) A flautist is someone who plays the flute.

flavour, flavours, flavouring, flavoured 1 (noun) The flavour of food is its taste. **2** (verb) If you flavour food with a spice or herb, you add it to the food to give it a particular taste. **3** (noun) The flavour of something is its distinctive characteristic or quality. **flavouring** (noun).

flaw, flaws 1 (noun) A flaw is a fault or mark in a piece of fabric, china, or glass, or in a decorative pattern. **2** A flaw is also a weak point or undesirable quality in a theory, plan, or person's character. **flawed** (adjective), **flawless** (adjective).

flax (noun) Flax is a plant used for making rope and cloth.

flay, flays, flaying, flayed 1 (verb) To flay a dead animal means to cut off its skin. **2** To flay someone means to criticize them severely.

flea, fleas (noun) A flea is a small wingless jumping insect which feeds on blood.

fleck, flecks (noun) A fleck is a small coloured mark or particle. **flecked** (adjective).

fled the past tense and past participle of **flee.**

fledgling, fledglings 1 (noun) A fledgling is a young bird that is learning to fly. **2** (adjective) Fledgling means new, or young and inexperienced, e.g. *the fledgling American President.*

flee, flees, fleeing, fled (verb) To flee from someone or something means to run away from them.

fleece, fleeces, fleecing, fleeced 1 (noun) A sheep's fleece is its coat of wool. **2** (verb) To fleece someone means to overcharge or swindle them.

fleet, fleets (noun) A fleet is a group of ships or vehicles owned by the same organization or travelling together.

fleeting (adjective) lasting for a very short time.

Flemish (noun) Flemish is a language spoken in many parts of Belgium.

flesh 1 (noun) Flesh is the soft part of the body. **2** The flesh of a fruit or vegetable is the soft inner part that you eat. **fleshy** (adjective).

flew the past tense of **fly.**

flex, flexes, flexing, flexed 1 (noun) A flex is a length of wire covered in plastic, which carries electricity to an appliance. **2** (verb) If you flex your muscles, you bend and stretch them.

flexible 1 (adjective) able to be bent easily without breaking. **2** able to adapt to changing circumstances. **flexibility** (noun).

flick, flicks, flicking, flicked 1 (verb) If you flick something, you move it sharply with your finger. **2** If something flicks somewhere, it moves with a short sudden movement, e.g. *His foot flicked forward.* **3** (noun) A flick is a sudden quick movement or sharp touch with the finger, e.g. *a sideways flick of the head.*

flicker, flickers, flickering, flickered 1 (verb) If a light or a flame flickers, it shines and moves unsteadily. **2** (noun) A flicker is a short unsteady light or movement of light, e.g. *the flicker of candlelight.* **3** A flicker of emotion or feeling is a very brief experience of it, e.g. *a flicker of interest.*

flight, flights 1 (noun) A flight is a journey made by aeroplane. **2** Flight is the action of flying or the ability to fly. **3** Flight is also the act of running away. **4** A flight of stairs or steps is a set running in a single direction.

flimsy, flimsier, flimsiest 1 (adjective) made of something very thin or weak and not providing much protection. **2** not very convincing, e.g. *flimsy evidence.*

flinch, flinches, flinching, flinched (verb) If you flinch, you make a sudden small movement in fear or pain.

fling, flings, flinging, flung 1 (verb) If you fling something, you throw it with a lot of force. **2** (noun) A fling is a short period of unrestricted enjoyment and activity.

flint, flints (noun) Flint is a hard greyish-black form of quartz. It produces a spark when struck with steel.

flip, flips, flipping, flipped 1 (verb) If you flip something, you turn or move it quickly and sharply, e.g. *He flipped over the first page.* **2** If you flip something, you hit it sharply with your finger or thumb.

flippant (adjective) showing an inappropriate lack of seriousness, e.g. *a flippant attitude to money.* **flippancy** (noun).

flipper, flippers 1 (noun) A flipper is one of the broad, flat limbs of sea animals, for example seals or penguins, used for swimming. **2** Flippers are broad, flat pieces of rubber that you can attach to your feet to help you swim.

flirt, flirts, flirting, flirted 1 (verb) If you flirt with someone, you behave as if you are sexually attracted to them but without serious intentions. **2** (noun) A flirt is someone who often flirts with people. **3** (verb) If you flirt with an idea, you consider it without seriously intending to do anything about it. **flirtation** (noun), **flirtatious** (adjective).

flit, flits, flitting, flitted (verb) To flit somewhere means to fly or move there with quick, light movements.

float, floats, floating, floated 1 (verb) Something that floats is supported by water. **2** (noun) A float is a light object that floats and either supports something or someone or regulates the level of liquid in a tank or cistern. **3** (verb) Something that floats through the air moves along gently, supported by the air. **4** If a company is floated, shares are sold to the public for the first time and the company gains a listing on the stock exchange.

flock, flocks, flocking, flocked 1 (noun) A flock of birds, sheep, or goats is a group of them. **2** (verb) If people flock somewhere, they go there in large numbers.

flog, flogs, flogging, flogged 1 (verb; an informal use) If you flog something, you sell it. **2** To flog someone means to beat them with a whip or stick. **flogging** (noun).

flood, floods, flooding, flooded 1 (noun) A flood is a large amount of water covering an area that is usually dry. **2** (verb) If liquid floods an area, or if a river floods, the water or liquid overflows, covering the surrounding area. **3** (noun) A flood of something is a large amount of it suddenly occurring, e.g. *a flood of angry language.* **4** (verb) If people or things flood into a place, they come there in large numbers, e.g. *Refugees have flooded into Austria in the last few months.*

floodgates (phrase) To **open the floodgates** means suddenly to give a lot of people the opportunity to do something they could not do before.

floodlight, floodlights (noun) A floodlight is a very powerful outdoor lamp used to illuminate public buildings and sports grounds. **floodlit** (adjective).

floor, floors, flooring, floored 1 (noun) The floor of a room is the part you walk on. **2** A floor of a building is one of the levels in it, e.g. *the top floor of a factory.* **3** The floor of a valley, forest, or the sea is the ground at the bottom. **4** (verb) If a remark or question floors you, you are completely unable to deal with it or answer it.

floorboard, floorboards (noun) A floorboard is one of the long planks of wood from which a floor is made.

flop, flops, flopping, flopped 1 (verb) If someone or something flops, they fall loosely and rather heavily. **2** (an informal use) Something that flops fails. **3** (noun; an informal use) Something that is a flop is completely unsuccessful.

floppy, floppier, floppiest (adjective) tending to hang downwards in a rather loose way, e.g. *a floppy, outsize jacket.*

floppy disk, floppy disks; also spelled **floppy disc** (noun) A floppy disk is a small flexible magnetic disk on which computer data is stored.

floral (adjective) patterned with flowers or made from flowers, e.g. *floral cotton dresses.*

florid (rhymes with **horrid**) **1** (adjective) highly elaborate and extravagant, e.g. *florid language.* **2** having a red face.

florist, florists (noun) A florist is a person or shop selling flowers.

floss (noun) Dental floss is soft silky threads or fibre which you use to clean between your teeth.

flotation, flotations 1 (noun) The flotation of a business is the issuing of shares in order to launch it or to raise money. **2** Flotation is the act of floating.

flotilla, flotillas (pronounced flot-**til**-la) (noun) A flotilla is a small fleet or group of small ships.

flotsam (noun) Flotsam is rubbish or wreckage floating at sea or washed up on the shore.

flounce, flounces, flouncing, flounced 1 (verb) If you flounce somewhere, you walk there with exaggerated movements suggesting that you are feeling angry or impatient about something, e.g. *She flounced out of the office.* **2** (noun) A flounce is a big frill around the bottom of a dress or skirt.

flounder, flounders, floundering, floundered 1 (verb) To flounder means to struggle to move or stay upright, for example in water or mud. **2** If you flounder in a conversation or situation, you find it difficult to decide what to say or do. **3** (noun) A flounder is a type of edible flatfish.

flour (noun) Flour is a powder made from finely ground

grain, usually wheat, and used for baking and cooking. **floured** (adjective), **floury** (adjective).

flourish, flourishes, flourishing, flourished 1 (verb) Something that flourishes continues, develops, or functions successfully or healthily. **2** If you flourish something, you wave or display it so that people notice it. **3** (noun) A flourish is a bold sweeping or waving movement.

flout, flouts, flouting, flouted (verb) If you flout a convention, law, or order, you deliberately disobey it.

flow, flows, flowing, flowed 1 (verb) If something flows, it moves, happens, or occurs in a steady continuous stream. **2** (noun) A flow of something is a steady continuous movement of it; also the rate at which it flows, e.g. *a steady flow of complaints.*

flower, flowers, flowering, flowered 1 (noun) A flower is the part of a plant containing the reproductive organs from which the fruit or seeds develop. **2** (verb) When a plant flowers, it produces flowers.

flowery (adjective) Flowery language is full of elaborate literary expressions.

flown the past participle of **fly**.

flu (noun) Flu is an illness similar to a very bad cold, which causes headaches, sore throat, weakness, and aching muscles. Flu is short for 'influenza'.

fluctuate, fluctuates, fluctuating, fluctuated (verb) Something that fluctuates is irregular and changeable, e.g. *fluctuating between feeling well and not so well.*

flue, flues (noun) A flue is a pipe which takes fumes and smoke away from a stove or boiler.

fluent 1 (adjective) able to speak a foreign language correctly and without hesitation. **2** able to express yourself clearly and without hesitation. **fluently** (adverb).

fluff, fluffs, fluffing, fluffed 1 (noun) Fluff is soft, light, woolly threads or fibres bunched together. **2** (verb) If you fluff something up or out, you brush or shake it to make it seem larger and lighter, e.g. *Fluff the rice up with a fork before serving.* **fluffy** (adjective).

fluid, fluids 1 (noun) A fluid is a liquid. **2** (adjective) Fluid movement is smooth and flowing. **3** A fluid arrangement, plan, or idea is flexible and without a fixed structure. **fluidity** (noun).

fluke, flukes (noun) A fluke is an accidental success or piece of good luck.

flung the past tense of **fling**.

fluorescent (pronounced floo-er-**ess**-nt) **1** (adjective) having a very bright appearance when light is shone on it, as if it is shining itself, e.g. *fluorescent yellow dye.* **2** A fluorescent light is in the form of a tube and shines with a hard bright light.

fluoride (noun) Fluoride is a mixture of chemicals that is meant to prevent tooth decay.

flurry, flurries (noun) A flurry is a short rush of vigorous activity or movement.

flush, flushes, flushing, flushed **1** (noun) A flush is a rosy red colour, e.g. *The flowers are cream with a pink flush.* **2** In cards, a flush is a hand all of one suit. **3** (verb) If you flush, your face goes red. **4** If you flush a toilet or something such as a pipe, you force water through it to clean it. **5** (adjective; an informal use) Someone who is flush has plenty of money. **6** Something that is flush with a surface is level with it or flat against it.

flustered (adjective) If you are flustered, you feel confused, nervous, and rushed.

flute, flutes (noun) A flute is a musical wind instrument consisting of a long metal tube with holes and keys. It is held sideways to the mouth and played by blowing across a hole in its side.

fluted (adjective) decorated with long grooves.

flutter, flutters, fluttering, fluttered **1** (verb) If something flutters, it flaps or waves with small, quick movements. **2** (noun) If you are in a flutter, you are excited and nervous. **3** (an informal use) If you have a flutter, you have a small bet.

flux (noun) Flux is a state of constant change, e.g. *stability in a world of flux.*

fly, flies, flying, flew, flown **1** (noun) A fly is an insect with two pairs of wings. **2** The front opening on a pair of trousers is the fly or the flies. **3** The fly or fly sheet of a tent is either a flap at the entrance or an outer layer providing protection from rain. **4** (verb) When a bird, insect, or aircraft flies, it moves through the air. **5** If someone or something flies, they move or go very quickly. **6** If you fly at someone or let fly at them, you attack or criticize them suddenly and aggressively. **flying** (adjective or noun), **flyer** (noun).

fly-fishing (noun) Fly-fishing is a method of fishing using imitation flies as bait.

flying saucer, flying saucers (noun) A flying saucer is believed to be a large disc-shaped spacecraft.

flyover, flyovers (noun) A flyover is a structure carrying one road over another at a junction or intersection.

foal, foals, foaling, foaled **1** (noun) A foal is a young horse. **2** (verb) When a female horse foals, she gives birth.

foam, foams, foaming, foamed **1** (noun) Foam is a mass of tiny bubbles. **2** (verb) When something foams, it forms a mass of small bubbles. **3** (noun) Foam is light spongy material used, for example, in furniture or packaging.

fob off, fobs off, fobbing off, fobbed off (verb; an informal use) If you fob someone off, you provide them with something that is not very good or not adequate.

focus, focuses, focusing, focused The plural of the noun is either **foci** or **focuses.** **1** (verb) If you focus your eyes or an instrument on an object, you adjust them so that the image is clear. **2** (noun) The focus of something is its centre of attention, e.g. *The focus* *of the conversation had moved around during the meal.* **focal** (adjective).

fodder (noun) Fodder is food for farm animals or horses.

foe, foes (noun) A foe is an enemy.

foetus, foetuses (pronounced **fee**-tus); also spelled **fetus** (noun) A foetus is an unborn child or animal in the womb. **foetal** (adjective).

fog, fogs, fogging, fogged 1 (noun) Fog is a thick mist of water droplets suspended in the air. **2** (verb) If glass fogs up, it becomes clouded with steam or condensation. **foggy** (adjective).

foil, foils, foiling, foiled 1 (verb) If you foil someone's attempt at something, you prevent them from succeeding. **2** (noun) Foil is thin, paper-like sheets of metal used to wrap food. **3** Something that is a good foil for something else contrasts with it and makes its good qualities more noticeable. **4** A foil is a thin, light sword with a button on the tip, used in fencing.

foist, foists, foisting, foisted (verb) If you foist something on someone, you force or impose it on them.

fold, folds, folding, folded 1 (verb) If you fold something, you bend it so that one part lies over another. **2** (an informal use) If a business folds, it fails and closes down. **3** In cooking, if you fold one ingredient into another, you mix it in gently. **4** (noun) A fold in paper or cloth is a crease or bend. **5** A fold is a small enclosed area for sheep.

folder, folders (noun) A folder is a thin piece of folded cardboard for keeping loose papers together.

foliage (noun) Foliage is leaves and plants.

folk, folks 1 (noun) Folk or folks are people. **2** (adjective) Folk music, dance, or art is traditional or representative of the ordinary people of an area.

folklore (noun) Folklore is the traditional stories and beliefs of a community.

follicle, follicles (noun) A follicle is a small sac or cavity in the body, e.g. *hair follicles.*

follow, follows, following, followed 1 (verb) If you follow someone, you move along behind them. If you follow a path or a sign, you move along in that direction. **2** Something that follows a particular thing happens after it. **3** Something that follows is true or logical as a result of something else being the case, e.g. *Just because she is pretty, it doesn't follow that she can sing.* **4** If you follow instructions or advice, you do what you are told.

follower, followers (noun) The followers of a person or belief are the people who support them.

folly, follies (noun) Folly is a foolish act or foolish behaviour.

fond, fonder, fondest 1 (adjective) If you are fond of someone or something, you like them. **2** A fond hope or belief is thought of with happiness but is unlikely to happen. **fondly** (adverb), **fondness**

(noun).

fondle, fondles, fondling, fondled (verb) To fondle something means to stroke it affectionately.

font, fonts (noun) A font is a large stone bowl in a church that holds the water for baptisms.

food, foods (noun) Food is any substance consumed by an animal or plant to provide energy.

foodstuff, foodstuffs (noun) A foodstuff is anything used for food.

fool, fools, fooling, fooled 1 (noun) Someone who is a fool behaves in a silly and unintelligent way. **2** A fool is also a dessert made from fruit, eggs, cream, and sugar whipped together. **3** (verb) If you fool someone, you deceive or trick them.

foolhardy (adjective) foolish and involving too great a risk.

foolish (adjective) very silly or unwise. **foolishly** (adverb), **foolishness** (noun).

foolproof (adjective) Something that is foolproof is so well designed or simple to use that it cannot fail.

foot, feet 1 (noun) Your foot is the part of your body at the end of your leg. **2** The foot of something is the bottom, base, or lower end of it, e.g. *the foot of the mountain.* **3** A foot is a unit of length equal to 12 inches or about 30.5 centimetres. **4** In poetry, a foot is the basic unit of rhythm containing two or three syllables. **5** (adjective) A foot brake, pedal, or pump is operated by your foot.

footage (noun) Footage is a length of film, e.g. *library footage of prison riots.*

football, footballs 1 (noun) Football is a game played by two teams of eleven players kicking a ball in an attempt to score goals. **2** A football is a ball used in football. **footballer** (noun).

foothills (plural noun) Foothills are hills at the base of mountains.

foothold, footholds 1 (noun) A foothold is a place where you can put your foot when climbing. **2** A foothold is also a favourable position from which further progress can be made.

footing 1 (noun) Footing is a secure grip by or for your feet, e.g. *He missed his footing and fell flat.* **2** A footing is the basis or nature of a relationship or situation, e.g. *Steps to put the nation on a war footing.*

footman, footmen (noun) A footman is a male servant in a large house who wears uniform.

footnote, footnotes (noun) A footnote is a note at the bottom of a page or an additional comment giving extra information.

footpath, footpaths (noun) A footpath is a path for people to walk on.

footprint, footprints (noun) A footprint is a mark left by a foot or shoe.

footstep, footsteps (noun) A footstep is the sound or mark made by someone walking.

for 1 (preposition) intended to be given to or used by a particular person, or done in order to help or benefit them, e.g. *private beaches for their exclusive use.* **2** For is used when explaining the reason, cause, or purpose of something, e.g. *This is my excuse for going to Italy.* **3** You use for to express a quantity, time, or distance, e.g. *I'll play for ages... the only house for miles around.* **4** If you are for something, you support it or approve of it, e.g. *votes for or against independence.*

forage, forages, foraging, foraged (verb) When a person or animal forages, they search for food.

foray, forays 1 (noun) A foray is a brief attempt to do or get something. **2** A foray is also an attack or raid by soldiers.

forbid, forbids, forbidding, forbade, forbidden (verb) If you forbid someone to do something, you order them not to do it. **forbidden** (adjective).

force, forces, forcing, forced 1 (verb) To force someone to do something means to make them do it. **2** To force something means to use violence or great strength to move, push, or open it. **3** (noun) The use of force is the use of violence or great strength. **4** The force of something is its strength or power, e.g. *The force of the explosion shook buildings.* **5** A force is a person or thing that has considerable influence or effect, e.g. *She became the dominant force in tennis.* **6** A force is also an organized group of soldiers or police. **7** (phrase) A law or rule that is **in force** is currently valid and must be obeyed.

forceful (adjective) powerful and convincing, e.g. *a forceful, highly political lawyer.* **forcefully** (adverb).

forceps (plural noun) Forceps are a pair of long tongs or pincers used by a doctor or surgeon.

forcible 1 (adjective) involving physical force or violence. **2** convincing and making a strong impression, e.g. *a forcible reminder.* **forcibly** (adverb).

ford, fords, fording, forded 1 (noun) A ford is a shallow place in a river where it is possible to cross on foot or in a vehicle. **2** (verb) To ford a river means to cross it on foot or in a vehicle.

fore (phrase) Someone or something that comes **to the fore** becomes important or popular.

forearm, forearms (noun) Your forearm is the part of your arm between your elbow and your wrist.

forebear, forebears (noun) Your forebears are your ancestors.

foreboding, forebodings (noun) A foreboding is a strong feeling of approaching disaster.

forecast, forecasts, forecasting, forecast or **forecasted 1** (noun) A forecast is a prediction of what will happen, especially a statement about what the weather will be like. **2** (verb) To forecast an event means to predict what will happen.

forecourt, forecourts (noun) A forecourt is an open area at the front of a petrol station or large building.

forefather, forefathers (noun) Your forefathers are your ancestors.

forefinger, forefingers (noun) Your forefinger is the finger next to your thumb.

forefront (noun) The forefront of something is the most important and progressive part of it.

forego, foregoes, foregoing, forewent, foregone; also spelled **forgo** (verb) If you forego something pleasant, you give it up or do not insist on having it.

foregoing (a formal phrase) You can say **the foregoing** when talking about something that has just been said, e.g. *The foregoing discussion has highlighted the difficulties.*

foregone conclusion, foregone conclusions (noun) A foregone conclusion is an inevitable or predictable result or conclusion.

foreground (noun) In a picture, the foreground is the part that seems nearest to you.

forehand, forehands (noun or adjective) Forehand is a stroke in tennis, squash, or badminton made with the palm of your hand facing in the direction that you hit the ball.

forehead, foreheads (noun) Your forehead is the area at the front of your head, above your eyebrows and below your hairline.

foreign 1 (adjective) belonging to, relating to, or involving countries other than your own, e.g. *foreign coins... foreign travel.* **2** unfamiliar or uncharacteristic, e.g. *Such daft enthusiasm was foreign to him.* **3** A foreign object has got into something, usually by accident, and should not be there, e.g. *a foreign object in my eye.* **foreigner** (noun).

foreman, foremen 1 (noun) A foreman is a person in charge of a group of workers, for example on a building site. **2** The foreman of a jury is the spokesman.

foremost (adjective) The foremost of a group of things is the most important or the best.

forensic 1 (adjective) relating to or involving the scientific examination of objects involved in a crime. **2** relating to or involving the legal profession.

forerunner, forerunners (noun) The forerunner of something is the person who first introduced or achieved it, or the first example of it.

foresee, foresees, foreseeing, foresaw, foreseen (verb) If you foresee something, you predict or expect that it will happen. **foreseeable** (adjective).

foresight (noun) Foresight is the ability to know what is going to happen in the future.

foreskin, foreskins (noun) A man's foreskin is the fold of skin covering the end of his penis.

forest, forests (noun) A forest is a large area of trees growing close together.

forestry (noun) Forestry is the study and work of growing and maintaining forests.

foretaste, foretastes (noun) A foretaste of something is a slight taste or experience of it in advance.

foretell, foretells, foretelling,

foretold (verb) If you foretell something, you predict that it will happen.

forever (adverb) permanently or continually.

forewarn, forewarns, forewarning, forewarned (verb) If you forewarn someone, you warn them in advance about something.

foreword, forewords (noun) A foreword is an introduction in a book.

forfeit, forfeits, forfeiting, forfeited 1 (verb) If you forfeit something, you have to give it up as a penalty. **2** (noun) A forfeit is something that you have to give up or do as a penalty.

forge, forges, forging, forged 1 (noun) A forge is a place where a blacksmith works making metal goods by hand. **2** (verb) To forge metal means to hammer and bend it into shape while hot. **3** To forge a relationship means to create a strong and lasting relationship. **4** Someone who forges money, documents, or paintings makes illegal copies of them. **5** To forge ahead means to progress quickly.

forgery, forgeries (noun) Forgery is the crime of forging money, documents, or paintings; also something that has been forged. **forger** (noun).

forget, forgets, forgetting, forgot, forgotten 1 (verb) If you forget something, you fail to remember or think about it. **2** If you forget yourself, you behave in an unacceptable, uncontrolled way. **forgetful** (adjective).

forget-me-not, forget-me-nots (noun) A forget-me-not is a small plant with tiny blue flowers.

forgive, forgives, forgiving, forgave, forgiven (verb) If you forgive someone for doing something bad, you stop feeling angry and resentful towards them. **forgiveness** (noun), **forgiving** (adjective).

forgo another spelling of **forego.**

fork, forks, forking, forked 1 (noun) A fork is a pronged instrument used for eating food. **2** A fork is also a large garden tool with three or four prongs. **3** (verb) To fork something means to move or turn it with a fork. **4** (noun) A fork in a road, path, river, or branch is a y-shaped junction or division. **fork out** (verb; an informal use) If you fork out for something, you pay for it, often unwillingly.

forlorn 1 (adjective) lonely, unhappy, and uncared for. **2** desperate and without any expectation of success, e.g. *a forlorn fight for a draw.* **forlornly** (adverb).

form, forms, forming, formed 1 (noun) A particular form of something is a type or kind of it, e.g. *a new form of weapon.* **2** The form of something is its shape or pattern. **3** (verb) The things that form something are the things it consists of, e.g. *events that were to form the basis of her novel.* **4** When someone forms something or when it forms, it is created, organized, or started. **5** (noun) A form is a sheet of paper with questions and spaces for you to fill in the answers. **6** In a school, a form is a class.

formal 1 (adjective) correct, serious, and conforming to accepted conventions, e.g. *a very formal letter of apology.* **2** official and publicly recognized, e.g. *the first formal agreement of its kind.* **formally** (adverb).

formaldehyde (pronounced for-**mal**-di-hide) (noun) Formaldehyde is a poisonous, strong-smelling gas, used for preserving biological specimens.

formality, formalities (noun) A formality is an action or process that is carried out as part of an official procedure.

format, formats (noun) The format of something is the way in which it is arranged or presented.

formation, formations 1 (noun) The formation of something is the process of developing and creating it. **2** A formation is the pattern or shape of something.

formative (adjective) having an important and lasting influence on character and development, e.g. *the formative days of his young manhood.*

former 1 (adjective) happening or existing before now or in the past, e.g. *a former tennis champion.* **2** (noun) You use the former to refer to the first of two things just mentioned, e.g. *If I had to choose between happiness and money, I would have the former.* **formerly** (adverb).

formidable (adjective) very difficult to deal with or overcome, and therefore rather frightening or impressive, e.g. *formidable enemies.*

formula, formulae or **formulas 1** (noun) A formula is a group of letters, numbers, and symbols representing a mathematical or scientific rule. **2** A formula is also a list of quantities of substances that when mixed make another substance, for example in chemistry. **3** A formula is also a plan or set of rules for dealing with a particular problem, e.g. *my secret formula for keeping in trim.*

formulate, formulates, formulating, formulated (verb) If you formulate a plan or thought, you create it and express it in a clear and precise way.

fornication (noun; a formal word) Fornication is the sin of having sex with someone when you are not married to them.

forsake, forsakes, forsaking, forsook, forsaken (verb) To forsake someone or something means to desert, give up, or abandon them.

fort, forts 1 (noun) A fort is a strong building built for defence. **2** (phrase) If you **hold the fort** for someone, you manage their affairs while they are away.

forte, fortes (pronounced **for**-tay) **1** In music, forte is an instruction to play or sing something loudly. **2** (noun) If something is your forte, you are particularly good at doing it.

forth 1 (adverb) out and forward from a starting place, e.g. *Ashdown's stated resolution to go forth among the workers.* **2** into view, e.g. *Nature herself brings forth new forms of life.*

forthcoming 1 (adjective) planned to happen soon, e.g. *their forthcoming holiday.* **2** given or made available, e.g. *Medical aid might be forthcoming.* **3** willing to give information, e.g. *He was not too forthcoming about this.*

forthright (adjective) Someone who is forthright is direct and honest about their opinions and feelings.

fortification, fortifications (noun) Fortifications are buildings, walls, and ditches used to protect a place.

fortitude (noun) Fortitude is calm and patient courage.

fortnight, fortnights (noun) A fortnight is a period of two weeks. **fortnightly** (adverb or adjective).

fortress, fortresses (noun) A fortress is a castle or well-protected town built for defence.

fortuitous (pronounced for-**tyoo**-it-uss) (adjective) happening by chance or good luck, e.g. *a fortuitous winning goal.*

fortunate 1 (adjective) Someone who is fortunate is lucky. **2** Something that is fortunate brings success or advantage. **fortunately** (adverb).

fortune, fortunes 1 (noun) Fortune or good fortune is good luck. **2** (phrase) If someone **tells your fortune,** they predict your future. **3** (noun) A fortune is a large amount of money.

forty, forties the number 40. **fortieth**

forum, forums 1 (noun) A forum is a place or meeting in which people can exchange ideas and discuss public issues. **2** In Roman towns, a forum was a square where people met to discuss business and politics.

forward, forwards, forwarding, forwarded 1 (adverb or adjective) Forward or forwards means in the front or towards the front, e.g. *A photographer moved forward to capture the moment.* **2** Forward means in or towards a future time, e.g. *a positive atmosphere of looking forward and making fresh starts.* **3** Forward or forwards also means developing or progressing, e.g. *The new committee would push forward government plans.* **4** (adverb) If someone or something is put forward, they are suggested as being suitable for something. **5** (verb) If you forward a letter that you have received, you send it on to the person to whom it is addressed at their new address. **6** (noun) In a game such as football or hockey, a forward is a player in an attacking position.

fossil, fossils (noun) A fossil is the remains or impression of an animal or plant of a previous geological age, preserved in rock. **fossilize** (verb).

foster, fosters, fostering, fostered 1 (verb) If someone fosters a child, they are paid to look after the child for a period, but do not become its legal parent. **2** If you foster something such as an activity or an idea, you help its development and growth by encouraging people to do or think it, e.g. *to foster and maintain this good will.* **foster child** (noun), **foster home** (noun), **foster par-**

ent (noun).

fought the past tense and past participle of **fight.**

foul, fouler, foulest; fouls, fouling, fouled 1 (adjective) Something that is foul is very unpleasant, especially because it is dirty, wicked, or obscene. **2** (verb) To foul something means to make it dirty, especially with faeces, e.g. *Dogs must not be allowed to foul the pavement.* **3** (noun) In sport, a foul is an act of breaking the rules.

found, founds, founding, founded 1 Found is the past tense and past participle of **find. 2** (verb) If someone founds an organization or institution, they start it and set it up.

foundation, foundations 1 (noun) The foundation of a belief or way of life is the basic ideas or attitudes on which it is built. **2** A foundation is a solid layer of concrete or bricks in the ground, on which a building is built to give it a firm base. **3** A foundation is also an organization set up by a legacy to provide money for research or charity.

founder, founders, foundering, foundered 1 (noun) The founder of an institution or organization is the person who sets it up. **2** (verb) If something founders, it fails.

foundry, foundries (noun) A foundry is a factory where metal is melted and cast.

fountain, fountains (noun) A fountain is an ornamental feature consisting of a jet of water forced into the air by a pump.

fountain pen, fountain pens (noun) A fountain pen is a pen which is supplied with ink from a container inside the pen.

four, fours 1 Four is the number 4. **2** (phrase) If you are **on all fours,** you are on your hands and knees.

four-poster, four-posters (noun) A four-poster is a bed with a tall post at each corner supporting a canopy and curtains.

fourteen the number 14. **fourteenth**

fourth The fourth item in a series is the one counted as number four.

fowl, fowls (noun) A fowl is a bird such as chicken or duck that is kept or hunted for its meat or eggs.

fox, foxes, foxing, foxed 1 (noun) A fox is a dog-like wild animal with reddish-brown fur, a pointed face and ears, and a thick tail. **2** (verb) If something foxes you, it is too confusing or puzzling for you to understand.

foxglove, foxgloves (noun) A foxglove is a plant with a tall spike of purple or white trumpet-shaped flowers.

foxhound, foxhounds (noun) A foxhound is a dog trained for hunting foxes.

foyer, foyers (pronounced **foy**-ay) (noun) A foyer is a large area just inside the main doors of a cinema, hotel, or public building.

fracas (pronounced **frak**-ah) (noun) A fracas is a rough noisy quarrel or fight.

fraction, fractions 1 (noun) In arithmetic, a fraction is a part of a whole number. **2** A fraction is a tiny proportion or amount of something, e.g. *an area a fraction of the size of London.* **fractional** (adjective), **fractionally** (adverb).

fractious (adjective) When small children are fractious, they become upset or angry very easily, often because they are tired.

fracture, fractures, fracturing, fractured 1 (noun) A fracture is a crack or break in something, especially a bone. **2** (verb) If something fractures, it breaks.

fragile (adjective) easily broken or damaged, e.g. *fragile glass... a fragile relationship.* **fragility** (noun).

fragment, fragments, fragmenting, fragmented 1 (noun) A fragment of something is a small piece or part of it. **2** (verb) If something fragments, it breaks into small pieces or different parts. **fragmentation** (noun), **fragmented** (adjective).

fragmentary (adjective) made up of small or unconnected pieces, e.g. *fragmentary notes in a journal.*

fragrance, fragrances (noun) A fragrance is a sweet or pleasant smell.

fragrant (adjective) Something that is fragrant smells sweet or pleasant.

frail, frailer, frailest 1 (adjective) Someone who is frail is not strong or healthy. **2** Something that is frail is easily broken or damaged. **frailty** (noun).

frame, frames, framing, framed 1 (noun) The frame of a door, window, or picture is the structure surrounding it. **2** A frame is also an arrangement of connected bars over which something is formed or built. **3** The frames of a pair of glasses are the wire or plastic parts that hold the lenses. **4** Your frame is your body, e.g. *his large frame.* **5** A frame in a cinema film is one of the many separate photographs of which it is made up. **6** (verb) To frame a picture means to put it into a frame, e.g. *I've framed pictures I've pulled out of magazines.*

framework, frameworks 1 (noun) A framework is a structure acting as a support or frame. **2** A framework of rules, beliefs, or ideas is a set of them which you use to decide what to do.

franc, francs (noun) The franc is the main unit of currency in France, Belgium, Switzerland, and some other countries. A franc is worth 100 centimes.

franchise, franchises 1 (noun) The franchise is the right to vote in an election, e.g. *a franchise that gave the vote to less than 2% of the population.* **2** A franchise is the right given by a company to someone to allow them to sell its goods or services.

frank, franker, frankest (adjective) If you are frank, you say things in an open and honest way. **frankly** (adverb), **frankness** (noun).

frantic (adjective) If you are frantic, you behave in a wild, desperate way because you are anxious or frightened. **frantically** (adverb).

fraternal (adjective) Fraternal is used to describe friendly actions and feelings between groups of people, e.g. *an affectionate fraternal greeting.*

fraternity, fraternities 1 (noun) Fraternity is friendship between groups of people. **2** You can refer to a group of people with something in common as a particular fraternity, e.g. *the football fraternity.*

fraud, frauds 1 (noun) Fraud is the crime of getting money by deceit or trickery. **2** A fraud is something that deceives people in an illegal or immoral way. **3** Someone who is a fraud is not what they pretend to be.

fraudulent (adjective) dishonest or deceitful, e.g. *fraudulent cheques.*

fraught (adjective) If something is fraught with problems or difficulties, it is full of them, e.g. *Modern life was fraught with hazards.*

fray, frays, fraying, frayed 1 (verb) If cloth or rope frays, its threads or strands become worn and it is likely to tear or break. **2** (noun) You can refer to a fight or argument as the fray.

freak, freaks 1 (noun) A freak is someone whose appearance or behaviour is very unusual. **2** (adjective or noun) A freak event is very unusual and unlikely to happen, e.g. *a freak allergy to peanuts.*

freckle, freckles (noun) Freckles are small, light brown spots on someone's skin, especially their face. **freckled** (adjective).

free, freer, freest; frees, freeing, freed 1 (adjective) not restricted, controlled, or limited, e.g. *the free flow of aid... free trade.* **2** Someone who is free is no longer a prisoner. **3** To be free of something unpleasant means not to have it, e.g. *She wanted her aunt's life to be free of worry.* **4** If someone is free, they are not busy or occupied. If a place, seat, or machine is free, it is not occupied or not being used, e.g. *Are you free for dinner?* **5** If something is free, you can have it without paying for it. **6** (verb) If you free something that is fastened or trapped, you release it, e.g. *a campaign to free captive animals.* **7** When a prisoner is freed, he or she is released.

freedom 1 (noun) If you have the freedom to do something, you have the scope or are allowed to do it, e.g. *We have the freedom to decide our own futures.* **2** When prisoners gain their freedom, they escape or are released. **3** When there is freedom from something unpleasant, people are not affected by it, e.g. *freedom from guilt.*

freehold, freeholds (noun) The freehold of a house or piece of land is the right to own it for life without conditions.

freelance (adjective or adverb) A freelance journalist or photographer is not employed by one organization, but is paid for each job he or she does.

freely (adverb) Freely means without restriction, e.g. *the pleasure of being able to walk about freely.*

free-range (adjective) Free-range eggs are laid by hens

that can move and feed freely on an area of open ground.

freestyle (noun) Freestyle refers to sports competitions, especially swimming, in which competitors can use any style or method.

free will (phrase) If you do something **of your own free will,** you do it by choice and not because you are forced to.

freeze, freezes, freezing, froze, frozen 1 (verb) When a liquid freezes, it becomes solid because it is very cold. **2** If you freeze, you suddenly become still and quiet, because there is danger. **3** If you freeze food, you put it in a freezer to preserve it. **4** When wages or prices are frozen, they are officially prevented from rising. **5** (noun) A wage or price freeze is an official action taken to prevent wages or prices from rising. **6** A freeze is a period of freezing weather.

freezer, freezers (noun) A freezer is a large refrigerator which runs at a specially low temperature in order to freeze and store food for a long time.

freezing (adjective) extremely cold.

freight (noun) Freight is goods moved by lorries, ships, or other transport; also the moving of these goods.

French 1 (adjective) belonging or relating to France. **2** (noun) French is the main language spoken in France, and is also spoken by many people in Belgium, Switzerland, and Canada.

French bean, French beans (noun) French beans are green pods eaten as a vegetable, which grow on a climbing plant with white or mauve flowers.

French horn, French horns (noun) A French horn is a brass musical wind instrument consisting of a tube wound in a circle.

Frenchman, Frenchmen (noun) A Frenchman is a man who comes from France. **Frenchwoman** (noun).

french window, french windows (noun) French windows are glass doors that lead into a garden or onto a balcony.

frenetic (adjective) Frenetic behaviour is wild, excited, and uncontrolled.

frenzy, frenzies (noun) If someone is in a frenzy, their behaviour is wild and uncontrolled. **frenzied** (adjective).

frequency, frequencies 1 (noun) The frequency of an event is how often it happens, e.g. *He was not known to call anyone with great frequency.* **2** The frequency of a sound or radio wave is the rate at which it vibrates.

frequent, frequents, frequenting, frequented 1 (adjective) often happening, e.g. *His visits were frequent... They move at frequent intervals.* **2** (verb) If you frequent a place, you go there often. **frequently** (adverb).

fresco, frescoes (noun) A fresco is a picture painted on a plastered wall while the plaster is still wet.

fresh, fresher, freshest 1 (adjective) A fresh thing replaces a previous one, or is added to it, e.g. *footprints filled in by fresh snow... fresh evidence.* **2** Fresh food is newly made or obtained, and not tinned or frozen. **3** Fresh water is not salty, for example the water in a stream. **4** If the weather is fresh, it is fairly cold and windy. **5** If you are fresh from something, you have experienced it recently, e.g. *a teacher fresh from college.* **freshly** (adverb), **freshness** (noun).

freshwater 1 (adjective) A freshwater lake or pool contains water that is not salty. **2** A freshwater creature lives in a river, lake, or pool that is not salty.

fret, frets, fretting, fretted 1 (verb) If you fret about something, you worry about it. **2** (noun) The frets on a stringed instrument, such as a guitar, are the metal ridges across its neck. **fretful** (adjective).

friar, friars (noun) A friar is a member of a Catholic religious order.

friction 1 (noun) Friction is the force that prevents things from moving freely when they rub against each other. **2** Friction between people is disagreement and quarrels.

Friday, Fridays (noun) Friday is the day between Thursday and Saturday.

fridge, fridges (noun) A fridge is the same as a refrigerator.

friend, friends (noun) Your friends are people you know well and like to spend time with.

friendly, friendlier, friendliest 1 (adjective) If you are friendly to someone, you behave in a kind and pleasant way to them. **2** People who are friendly with each other like each other and enjoy spending time together. **friendliness** (noun).

friendship, friendships 1 (noun) Your friendships are the special relationships that you have with your friends. **2** Friendship is the state of being friends with someone.

frieze, friezes (noun) A frieze is a strip of decoration, carving, or pictures along the top of a wall.

frigate, frigates (noun) A frigate is a small, fast warship.

fright (noun) Fright is a sudden feeling of fear.

frighten, frightens, frightening, frightened (verb) If something frightens you, it makes you afraid. **frightened** (adjective), **frightening** (adjective).

frightful (adjective) very bad or unpleasant, e.g. *a frightful bully.*

frigid (adjective) Frigid behaviour is cold and unfriendly, e.g. *frigid stares.*

frill, frills (noun) A frill is a strip of cloth with many folds, attached to something as a decoration. **frilly** (adjective).

fringe, fringes 1 (noun) If someone has a fringe, their hair is cut to hang over their forehead. **2** A fringe is also a decoration on clothes and other objects, consisting of a row of hanging strips or threads. **3** The fringes of a place are the parts farthest from its centre, e.g. *the western fringe of Britain.* **fringed** (adjective).

frisk, frisks, frisking, frisked (verb; an informal use) If someone frisks you, they search you quickly with their hands to see if you are hiding a weapon in your clothes.

frisky, friskier, friskiest (adjective) A frisky animal or child is energetic and wants to have fun.

fritter, fritters, frittering, frittered 1 (noun) Fritters consist of food dipped in batter and fried, e.g. *apple fritters.* **2** (verb) If you fritter away your time or money, you waste it on unimportant things.

frivolous (adjective) Someone who is frivolous behaves in a silly or light-hearted way, especially when they should be serious or sensible. **frivolity** (noun).

frizzy, frizzier, frizziest (adjective) Frizzy hair has stiff, wiry curls.

frock, frocks (noun; an old-fashioned word) A frock is a dress.

frog, frogs (noun) A frog is a small amphibious creature with smooth skin, prominent eyes, and long back legs which it uses for jumping.

frolic, frolics, frolicking, frolicked (verb) When animals or children frolic, they run around and play in a lively way.

from 1 (preposition) You use from to say what the source, origin, or starting point of something is, e.g. *a call from a public telephone... people from a city 100 miles away.* **2** If you take something from an amount, you reduce the amount by that much, e.g. *£570 was wrongly taken from his account.* **3** You also use from when stating the range of something, e.g. *a score from one to five.*

frond, fronds (noun) Fronds are long feathery leaves.

front, fronts, fronting, fronted 1 (noun) The front of something is the part that faces forward. **2** In a war, the front is the place where two armies are fighting. **3** In meteorology, a front is the line where a mass of cold air meets a mass of warm air. **4** A front is an outward appearance, often one that is false, e.g. *I put up a brave front... He's no more than a respectable front for some very dubious happenings.* **5** (phrase) **In front** means ahead or further forward. **6** If you do something **in front of** someone, you do it when they are present. **frontal** (adjective).

frontage, frontages (noun) A frontage of a building is one of its walls that faces a street.

frontier, frontiers (noun) A frontier is a border between two countries.

frontispiece, frontispieces (noun) The frontispiece of a book is a picture opposite the title page.

frost, frosts (noun) When there is a frost, the temperature outside falls below freezing.

frostbite (noun) Frostbite is damage to your fingers, toes, or ears caused by extreme cold.

frosty, frostier, frostiest 1 (adjective) If it is frosty, the temperature outside is below freezing point. **2** If someone is frosty, they are unfriendly or disapproving.

froth, froths, frothing, frothed 1 (noun) Froth is a mass of small bubbles on the surface of a liquid. **2** (verb) If a liquid froths, small bubbles appear on its surface. **frothy** (adjective).

frown, frowns, frowning, frowned 1 (verb) If you frown, you move your eyebrows closer together, because you are annoyed, worried, or concentrating. **2** (noun) A frown is a cross expression on someone's face.

froze the past tense of **freeze**.

frozen 1 Frozen is the past participle of **freeze**. **2** (adjective) If you are frozen, you are extremely cold.

frugal 1 (adjective) Someone who is frugal spends very little money. **2** A frugal meal is small and cheap. **frugality** (noun).

fruit, fruits 1 (noun) A fruit is the part of a plant that develops after the flower and contains the seeds. Many fruits are edible. **2** (plural noun) The fruits of something are its good results, e.g. *It will be a few years before the fruits of this work are apparent.*

fruitful (adjective) Something that is fruitful has good and useful results, e.g. *a fruitful experience.*

fruitless (adjective) Something that is fruitless does not achieve anything, e.g. *a fruitless effort.*

fruit machine, fruit machines (noun) A fruit machine is a coin-operated gambling machine which pays out money when a particular series of symbols, usually fruit, appears on a screen.

fruit salad, fruit salads (noun) A fruit salad is a mixture of pieces of different fruits served in a juice as a dessert.

fruity, fruitier, fruitiest (adjective) Something that is fruity smells or tastes of fruit.

frustrate, frustrates, frustrating, frustrated 1 (verb) If something frustrates you, it prevents you doing what you want and makes you upset and angry, e.g. *Everyone gets frustrated with their work.* **2** To frustrate something such as a plan means to prevent it, e.g. *She hopes to frustrate the engagement of her son.* **frustrated** (adjective), **frustrating** (adjective), **frustration** (noun).

fry, fries, frying, fried (verb) When you fry food, you cook it in a pan containing hot fat or oil.

fuchsia, fuchsias (pronounced **fyoo**-sha) (noun) A fuchsia is a plant or small bush with pink, purple, or white flowers that hang downwards.

fudge, fudges, fudging, fudged 1 (noun) Fudge is a soft brown sweet made from butter, milk, and sugar. **2** (verb) If you fudge something, you avoid making clear or definite decisions or statements about it, e.g. *He was carefully fudging his message.*

fuel, fuels, fuelling, fuelled 1 (noun) Fuel is a substance such as coal or petrol that is burned to provide heat or power. **2** (verb) A machine or vehicle that is fuelled by a substance works by burning the substance as a fuel, e.g. *power stations fuelled by wood.*

fug (noun) A fug is an airless, smoky atmosphere.

fugitive, fugitives (pronounced **fyoo**-jit-tiv) (noun) A fugitive is someone who is running away or hiding, especially from the police.

fulcrum, fulcrums or **fulcra** (noun) A fulcrum is the point at which something is balancing or pivoting.

fulfil, fulfils, fulfilling, fulfilled 1 (verb) If you fulfil a promise, hope, or duty, you carry it out or achieve it. **2** If something fulfils you, it gives you satisfaction. **fulfilling** (adjective), **fulfilment** (noun).

full, fuller, fullest 1 (adjective) containing or having as much as it is possible to hold, e.g. *His room is full of posters.* **2** complete or whole, e.g. *They had taken a full meal... a full 20 years later.* **3** loose and made from a lot of fabric, e.g. *full sleeves.* **4** rich and strong, e.g. *a full, fruity wine.* **5** (adverb) completely and directly, e.g. *Turn the taps full on.* **6** (phrase) Something that has been done or described **in full** has been dealt with completely. **fullness** (noun), **fully** (adverb).

full-blooded (adjective) having great commitment and enthusiasm, e.g. *a full-blooded sprint for third place.*

full-blown (adjective) complete and fully developed, e.g. *a full-blown love of music.*

full moon, full moons (noun) The full moon is the moon when it appears as a complete circle.

full stop, full stops (noun) A full stop is the punctuation mark (.) used at the end of a sentence and after an abbreviation or initial.

full-time 1 (adjective) involving work for the whole of each normal working week. **2** (noun) In games such as football, full time is the end of the match.

fully-fledged (adjective) completely developed, e.g. *I was a fully-fledged and mature human being.*

fulsome (adjective) exaggerated and elaborate, and often sounding insincere, e.g. *His most fulsome praise was reserved for his mother.*

fumble, fumbles, fumbling, fumbled (verb) If you fumble, you feel or handle something clumsily.

fume, fumes, fuming, fumed 1 (noun) Fumes are unpleasant-smelling gases and smoke, often toxic, that are produced by burning and by some chemicals. **2** (verb) If you are fuming, you are very angry.

fun 1 (noun) Fun is pleasant, enjoyable and light-hearted activity or amusement. **2** (phrase) If you **make fun** of someone, you tease them or make jokes about them.

function, functions, functioning, functioned 1 (noun) The function of something is its purpose or role, e.g. *The proper function of criticism is to bring about change for the better.* **2** A function is a large formal dinner, reception, or party. **3** (verb) When something functions, it operates or works.

functional 1 (adjective) relating to the way something works. **2** designed for practical use rather than for decoration or attractiveness, e.g. *Feminine clothing has never been designed to be functional.* **3**

working properly, e.g. *fully functional smoke alarms.*

fund, funds, funding, funded 1 (noun) A fund is an amount of available money, usually for a particular purpose, e.g. *a pension fund.* **2** A fund of something is a lot of it, e.g. *He had a fund of hilarious tales on the subject.* **3** (verb) Someone who funds something provides money for it, e.g. *research funded by pharmaceutical companies.*

fundamental, fundamentals 1 (adjective) basic and central, e.g. *the fundamental right of freedom of choice... fundamental changes.* **2** (noun) The fundamentals of something are its most basic and important parts, e.g. *teaching small children the fundamentals of road safety.*

funeral, funerals (pronounced **fyoo**-ner-al) (noun) A funeral is a religious service or ceremony for the burial or cremation of a dead person.

funereal (pronounced few-**nee**-ree-al) (adjective) depressing and gloomy.

fungicide, fungicides (noun) A fungicide is a chemical used to kill or prevent fungus.

fungus, fungi or **funguses** (noun) A fungus is a plant such as a mushroom or mould that does not have leaves and grows on other living things. **fungal** (adjective).

funk, funks, funking, funked 1 (verb; an old-fashioned informal use) If you funk something, you fail to do it because of fear. **2** (noun) Funk is a style of music with a strong rhythm based on jazz and blues.

funnel, funnels, funnelling, funnelled 1 (noun) A funnel is an open cone tapering to a narrow tube, used to pour substances into containers. **2** A funnel is also a metal chimney on a ship or steam engine. **3** (verb) If something is funnelled somewhere, it is directed through a narrow space into that place.

funny, funnier, funniest 1 (adjective) strange or puzzling, e.g. *You get a lot of funny people coming into the libraries.* **2** causing amusement or laughter, e.g. *a funny old film.* **funnily** (adverb).

fur, furs 1 (noun) Fur is the soft thick body hair of many animals. **2** A fur is a coat made from an animal's fur. **furry** (adjective).

furious 1 (adjective) extremely angry. **2** involving great energy, effort, or speed, e.g. *the furious speed of technological development.* **furiously** (adverb).

furlong, furlongs (noun) A furlong is a unit of length equal to 220 yards or about 201.2 metres. Furlong originally referred to the length of the average furrow.

furnace, furnaces (noun) A furnace is a container for a very large, hot fire used, for example, in the steel industry for melting ore.

furnish, furnishes, furnishing, furnished 1 (verb) If you furnish a room, you put furniture into it. **2** (a formal use) If you furnish someone with something, you supply or provide it for them.

furnishings (plural noun) The

furnishings of a room or house are the furniture and fittings in it.

furniture (noun) Furniture is movable objects such as tables, chairs and wardrobes.

furore (pronounced fyoo-**roh**-ree) (noun) A furore is an angry and excited reaction or protest.

furrow, furrows, furrowing, furrowed 1 (noun) A furrow is a long, shallow trench made by a plough. **2** (verb) When someone furrows their brow, they frown.

further, furthers, furthering, furthered 1 a comparative form of **far. 2** (adjective) additional or more, e.g. *There was no further rain.* **3** (verb) If you further something, you help it to progress, e.g. *He is desperately keen to further his England career.*

further education (noun) Further education is education at a college after leaving school, but not at a university.

furthermore (adverb; a formal use) used to introduce additional information, e.g. *There is no record of such a letter. Furthermore it is company policy never to send such letters.*

furthest a superlative form of **far.**

furtive (adjective) secretive, sly, and cautious, e.g. *a furtive smile.* **furtively** (adverb).

fury (noun) Fury is violent or extreme anger.

fuse, fuses, fusing, fused 1 (noun) In a plug or electrical appliance, a fuse is a safety device consisting of a piece of wire which melts to stop the electric current if a fault occurs. **2** In some types of simple bomb, a fuse is a long cord attached to the bomb which is lit to detonate it. **3** (verb) When an electrical appliance fuses, it stops working because the fuse has melted to protect it. **4** If two things fuse, they join or become combined, e.g. *Christianity slowly fused with existing beliefs.*

fuselage, fuselages (pronounced **fyoo**-zil-ahj) (noun) The fuselage of an aeroplane or rocket is its main part.

fusion (noun) Fusion is what happens when two substances join by melting together.

fuss, fusses, fussing, fussed 1 (noun) Fuss is unnecessarily anxious or excited behaviour. **2** (verb) If someone fusses, they behave with unnecessary anxiety and concern for unimportant things.

fussy, fussier, fussiest 1 (adjective) likely to fuss a lot, e.g. *He was unusually fussy about keeping things perfect.* **2** with too much elaborate detail or decoration, e.g. *fussy chiffon evening wear.*

futile (adjective) having no chance of success, e.g. *a futile attempt to calm the storm.* **futility** (noun).

future, futures 1 (noun) The future is the period of time after the present. **2** Something that has a future is likely to succeed, e.g. *She sees no future in a modelling career.* **3** (adjective) relating to or occurring at a time after the present, e.g. *to predict future events.* **4** The future tense of a verb is the form used to express something that will happen in the future.

futuristic (adjective) very modern and strange, as if belonging to a time in the future, e.g. *futuristic cars.*

fuzz 1 (noun) Fuzz is short fluffy hair. **2** (plural noun; an informal use) The fuzz are the police.

G g

g an abbreviation for 'grams'.

gabble, gabbles, gabbling, gabbled (verb) If you gabble, you talk so fast that it is difficult for people to understand you.

gable, gables (noun) Gables are the triangular parts at the top of the outside walls at each end of a house.

gadget, gadgets (noun) A gadget is a small machine or tool. **gadgetry** (noun).

Gaelic (pronounced **gay**-lik) (noun) Gaelic is a language spoken in some parts of Scotland and Ireland.

gaffe, gaffes (pronounced **gaf**) (noun) A gaffe is a social blunder or mistake.

gaffer, gaffers (noun; an informal word) A gaffer is a boss.

gag, gags, gagging, gagged 1 (noun) A gag is a strip of cloth that is tied round or put inside someone's mouth in order to stop them speaking. **2** (verb) To gag someone means to put a gag round or in their mouth. **3** (noun; an informal use) A gag is also a joke told by a comedian. **4** (verb) If you gag, you choke and nearly vomit.

gaggle, gaggles 1 (noun) A gaggle is a group of geese. **2** (an informal use) A gaggle is a noisy group, e.g. *a gaggle of schoolboys.*

gaiety (pronounced **gay**-yet-tee) (noun) Gaiety is liveliness and fun.

gaily (adverb) in a happy and cheerful way.

gain, gains, gaining, gained 1 (verb) If you gain something, you get it gradually, e.g. *I spent years at night school trying to gain qualifications.* **2** (noun) A gain is an increase, e.g. *a gain in speed.* **3** (verb) If you gain from a situation, you get some advantage from it. **4** (noun) Gain is an advantage that you get for yourself, e.g. *People use whatever influence they have for personal gain.* **5** (verb) If you gain on someone, you gradually catch them up.

gait, gaits (noun) Someone's gait is their way of walking, e.g. *an awkward gait.*

gala, galas (noun) A gala is a special public celebration, entertainment, or performance, e.g. *the Olympics' opening gala.*

galaxy, galaxies (noun) A galaxy is an enormous group of stars that extends over many millions of miles. **galactic** (adjective).

gale, gales (noun) A gale is an extremely strong wind.

gall, galls, galling, galled (rhymes with **ball**) **1** (noun) If someone has the gall to do something, they have enough courage or impudence and daring to do it, e.g. *He even has the gall to visit her.* **2** (verb) If something galls you, it makes you extremely annoyed.

gallant (adjective) brave and honourable, e.g. *They have put up a gallant fight for pensioners' rights.* **gallantly** (adverb), **gallantry** (noun).

gall bladder, gall bladders (noun) Your gall bladder is an organ in your body which stores bile and which is next to your liver.

galleon, galleons (noun) A galleon is a large sailing ship used in the past.

gallery, galleries 1 (noun) A gallery is a building or room where works of art are exhibited. **2** In a theatre or large hall, the gallery is a raised area at the back or sides, e.g. *the public gallery.*

galley, galleys 1 (noun) A galley is a kitchen in a ship or aircraft. **2** A galley is also a ship, propelled by oars and sometimes sails, which was used in the past.

Gallic (pronounced **gal**-lik) (adjective; a formal or literary word) French.

gallon, gallons (noun) A gallon is a unit of liquid volume equal to eight pints or about 4.55 litres.

gallop, gallops, galloping, galloped 1 (verb) When a horse gallops, it runs very fast, so that all four feet are off the ground at the same time. **2** (noun) A gallop is a very fast run.

gallows (noun) A gallows is a framework on which criminals used to be hanged.

gallstone, gallstones (noun) A gallstone is a small painful lump that can develop in your gall bladder.

galore (adjective) in very large numbers, e.g. *chocolates galore.*

galoshes (plural noun) Galoshes are waterproof rubber shoes which you wear over your ordinary shoes to stop them getting wet.

galvanized or **galvanised** (adjective) Galvanized metal has been coated with zinc to protect it from rust.

gambit, gambits (noun) A gambit is something which someone does to gain an advantage in a situation.

gamble, gambles, gambling, gambled 1 (verb) When people gamble, they bet money or play games like roulette in order to try and win money. **2** (noun) If you take a gamble, you take a risk in the hope of gaining an advantage. **3** (verb) If you gamble something, you risk losing it in the hope of gaining an advantage, e.g. *The company gambled everything on the new factory.* **gambler** (noun), **gambling** (noun).

game, games 1 (noun) A game is an enjoyable activity with a set of rules which is played by individuals or teams against each other. **2** A game is also an enjoyable imaginative activity played by small children, e.g. *childhood games of cowboys and Indians.* **3** (plural noun) Games are sports played at school or in a competition. **4** You might describe something as a game when it is designed to gain advantage, e.g. *This is the political game we have entered here.* **5** (adjective; an informal use) Someone who is game is willing to try something unusual or difficult. **6** (noun) Game is wild animals or birds that are hunted for sport or for food. **gamely** (adverb).

gamekeeper, gamekeepers (noun) A gamekeeper is a person employed to look after game animals and birds on a country estate.

gammon (noun) Gammon is cured meat from a pig, similar to bacon.

gamut (pronounced **gam**-mut) (noun; a formal word) The gamut of something is the whole range of things that can be included in it, e.g. *the whole gamut of human emotions.*

gander, ganders (noun) A gander is a male goose.

gang, gangs, ganging, ganged 1 (noun) A gang is a group of people who join together for some purpose, for example to commit a crime. **2** (verb; an informal use) If people gang up on you, they join together to oppose you.

gangplank, gangplanks (noun) A gangplank is a plank used for boarding and leaving a ship or boat.

gangrene (pronounced **gang**-green) (noun) Gangrene is decay in the tissues of part of the body, caused by inadequate blood supply. **gangrenous** (adjective).

gangster, gangsters (noun) A gangster is a violent criminal who is a member of a gang.

gannet, gannets (noun) A gannet is a large sea bird.

gaol another spelling of **jail**.

gap, gaps 1 (noun) A gap is a space between two things or a hole in something solid. **2** A gap between things, people, or ideas is a great difference between them, e.g. *the gap between fantasy and reality.*

gape, gapes, gaping, gaped 1 (verb) If you gape at someone or something, you stare at them with your mouth open in surprise. **2** Something that gapes is wide open, e.g. *gaping holes in the wall.*

garage, garages 1 (noun) A garage is a building where a car can be kept. **2** A garage is also a place where cars are repaired and where petrol is sold.

garb (noun; a formal word) Someone's garb is their clothes, e.g. *his usual garb of a dark suit.*

garbage (noun) Garbage is rubbish, especially household rubbish.

garbled (adjective) Garbled messages are jumbled and the details may be wrong.

garden, gardens 1 (noun) A garden is an area of land next to a house, where flowers, fruit, or vegetables are grown. **2** (plural noun) Gardens are a type of park in a town or around a large house. **gardening** (noun).

gardener, gardeners (noun) A gardener is a person who looks after a garden as a job or as a hobby.

gargle, gargles, gargling, gargled (verb) When you gargle, you rinse the back of your throat by putting some liquid in your mouth, tilting your head back, and making a bubbling sound at the back of your throat without swallowing the liquid.

gargoyle, gargoyles (noun) A gargoyle is a large stone carving under the roof of a building, in the shape of an ugly person or animal.

garish (pronounced **gair**-rish) (adjective) bright and harsh to look at, e.g. *garish bright red boots.*

garland, garlands (noun) A garland is a circle of flowers and leaves which is worn around the neck or head.

garlic (noun) Garlic is the small white bulb of an onion-like plant which has a strong taste and smell. It is used for flavouring in cooking.

garment, garments (noun) A garment is a piece of clothing.

garnet, garnets (noun) A garnet is a type of gemstone, usually red in colour.

garnish, garnishes, garnishing, garnished 1 (noun) A garnish is something such as a wedge of lemon or a sprig of parsley, that is used in cooking for decoration. **2** (verb) To garnish food means to decorate it with a garnish.

garret, garrets (noun) A garret is an attic.

garrison, garrisons (noun) A garrison is a group of soldiers stationed in a town in order to guard it.

garrotte, garrottes, garrotting, garrotted (pronounced gar-**rot**); also spelled **garotte** (verb) To garrotte someone means to strangle them with a piece of wire.

garter, garters (noun) A garter is a piece of elastic worn round the top of a stocking or sock to stop it slipping.

gas, gases, gasses, gassing, gassed The form **gases** is the plural of the noun. The verb forms are spelled with a double 's'. **1** (noun) A gas is any airlike substance that is not liquid or solid, such as oxygen or hydrogen or the gas used as a fuel in heating. **2** In American English, gas is petrol. **3** (verb) To gas people or animals means to kill them with poisonous gas.

gas chamber, gas chambers (noun) A gas chamber is a room in which people or animals are killed with poisonous gas.

gash, gashes, gashing, gashed 1 (noun) A gash is a long, deep cut. **2** (verb) If you gash something, you make a long, deep cut in it.

gas mask, gas masks (noun) A gas mask is a large mask with special filters attached which people wear over their face to protect them from poisonous gas.

gasoline (noun) In American English, gasoline is petrol.

gasp, gasps, gasping, gasped 1 (verb) If you gasp, you quickly draw in your breath through your mouth because you are surprised, shocked, or in pain. **2** (noun) A gasp is a sharp intake of breath through the mouth.

gastric (adjective) occurring in the stomach or involving the stomach, e.g. *gastric pain.*

gate, gates 1 (noun) A gate is a barrier which can open and shut and is used to close the entrance to a garden or field. **2** The gate at a sports event such as a football match is the total number of people who have attended it.

gateau, gateaux (pronounced **gat**-toe) (noun) A gateau is a rich layered cake with cream in it.

gatecrash, gatecrashes, gatecrashing, gatecrashed (verb) If you gatecrash a party, you go to it when you have not been invited.

gateway, gateways 1 (noun) A gateway is an entrance through a wall, fence, or hedge where there is a gate. **2** Something that is considered to be the entrance to a larger or more important thing can be described as the gateway to the larger thing, e.g. *New York is the great gateway to America.*

gather, gathers, gathering, gathered 1 (verb) When people gather, they come together in a group. **2** If you gather a number of things, you collect them or bring them together in one place. **3** If something gathers speed, momentum, or strength, it gets faster or stronger. **4** If you gather something, you learn it, often from what someone says.

gathering, gatherings (noun) A gathering is a meeting of people who have come together for a particular purpose.

gauche (pronounced **gohsh**) (adjective; a formal word) socially awkward.

gaudy, gaudier, gaudiest (pronounced **gaw**-dee) (adjective) very colourful in a vulgar way.

gauge, gauges, gauging, gauged (pronounced **gayj**) **1** (verb) If you gauge something, you estimate it or calculate it, e.g. *It is very difficult to gauge how people are going to react.* **2** (noun) A gauge is a piece of equipment that measures the amount of something, e.g. *a rain gauge.* **3** A gauge is also something that is used as a standard by which you judge a situation, e.g. *seeking people's approval as a gauge of personal achievement.* **4** On railways, the gauge is the distance between the two rails on a railway line.

gaunt (adjective) A person who looks gaunt is thin and bony.

gauntlet, gauntlets (noun) Gauntlets are long thick gloves worn for protection, for example by motorcyclists.

gave the past tense of **give**.

gay, gayer, gayest; gays 1 (adjective) Someone who is gay is homosexual. **2** (noun) A gay is a homosexual person. **3** (adjective; an old-fashioned use) Gay people or places are lively and full of fun.

gaze, gazes, gazing, gazed (verb) If you gaze at something, you look steadily at it for a long time.

gazelle, gazelles (noun) A gazelle is a small antelope found in Africa and Asia.

gazette, gazettes (noun) A gazette is an official newspaper or other publication.

GB an abbreviation for **Great Britain**.

GCE, GCEs The GCE is an advanced level examination taken by school students aged seventeen and eighteen. GCE is an abbreviation for 'General Certificate of Education'.

GCSE, GCSEs The GCSE is an examination taken by school students aged fifteen and sixteen. GCSE is an abbreviation for 'General Certificate of Secondary Education'.

gear, gears, gearing, geared 1 (noun) A gear is a piece of machinery which controls the rate at which energy is converted into movement. Gears in vehicles control the speed and power of the vehicle. **2** The gear for an activity is the clothes and equipment that you need for it. **3** (verb) If someone or something is geared to a particular event or purpose, they are prepared or organized for it.

geese the plural of **goose.**

gel, gels, gelling, gelled (pronounced **jel**) **1** (noun) A gel is a smooth soft jelly-like substance, e.g. *shower gel.* **2** (verb) If a liquid gels, it turns into a gel. **3** If a vague thought or plan gels, it becomes more definite.

gelatine or **gelatin** (pronounced **jel**-lat-tin) (noun) Gelatine is a clear tasteless substance used to make liquids firm and jelly-like. It is obtained from meat and bones, and used in cooking, medicine, and photography.

gelding, geldings (pronounced **gel**-ding) (noun) A gelding is a horse which has been castrated.

gem, gems 1 (noun) A gem is a jewel or precious stone. **2** You can describe something or someone that is extremely good, pleasing, or beautiful as a gem, e.g. *A gem of a novel.*

Gemini (pronounced **jem**-in-nye) (noun) Gemini is the third sign of the zodiac, represented by a pair of twins. People born between May 21st and June 20th are born under this sign.

gen (noun; an informal word) The gen on something is information about it.

gender, genders (noun) Gender is the sex of a person or animal, e.g. *The female gender.*

gene, genes (pronounced **jeen**) (noun) A gene is one of the parts of a living cell which controls the physical characteristics of an organism, for example its eye colour. Genes are passed on from one generation to the next.

general, generals 1 (adjective) relating to the whole of something or to most things in a group, e.g. *your general health.* **2** true, suitable, or relevant in most situations, e.g. *the general truth of science.* **3** including or involving a wide range of different things, e.g. *a general hospital.* **4** having complete responsibility over a wide area of work or a large number of people, e.g. *the general secretary.* **5** (noun) A general is an army officer of very high rank. **6** (phrase) **In general** means usually. **generally** (adverb).

general election, general elections (noun) A general election is an election for a new government, which all the people of a country may vote in.

generalize, generalizes, general-

izing, generalized; also spelled **generalise** (verb) To generalize means to say that something is true in most cases, ignoring minor details. **generalization** (noun).

general practitioner, general practitioners (noun) A general practitioner is a doctor who works in the community rather than in a hospital.

generate, generates, generating, generated (verb) To generate something means to create or produce it, e.g. *using wind power to generate electricity.*

generation, generations (noun) A generation is all the people of about the same age; also the period of time between one generation and the next, usually considered to be about 25-30 years.

generator, generators (noun) A generator is a machine which produces electricity from another form of energy such as wind or water power.

generic (adjective) A generic term is a name that applies to all the members of a group of similar things.

generous 1 (adjective) A generous person is very willing to give money, time, or gifts. **2** Something that is generous is very large, e.g. *a generous waist.* **generously** (adverb), **generosity** (noun).

genesis (noun; a formal word) The genesis of something is its beginning.

genetics (noun) Genetics is the science of the way that characteristics are passed on from generation to generation by means of genes. **genetic** (adjective), **genetically** (adverb).

genial (adjective) cheerful, friendly, and kind. **genially** (adverb).

genie, genies (pronounced **jee**-nee) (noun) In stories from Arabia and Persia, a genie is a magical being that obeys the wishes of the person who controls it.

genitals (plural noun) The genitals are the reproductive organs. Technical name: genitalia. **genital** (adjective).

genius, geniuses 1 (noun) A genius is a highly intelligent, creative, or talented person. **2** Genius is great intelligence, creativity, or talent, e.g. *a poet of genius.*

genocide (pronounced **jen**-nos-side) (noun; a formal word) Genocide is the systematic murder of all members of a particular race or group.

genre, genres (pronounced **jahn**-ra) (noun; a formal word) A genre is a particular style in art, literature, or music.

genteel (adjective) excessively polite and refined.

Gentile, Gentiles (pronounced **jen**-tile) (noun) A Gentile is a person who is not Jewish.

gentility (noun) Gentility is excessive politeness and refinement.

gentle, gentler, gentlest (adjective) mild and calm; not violent or rough, e.g. *a gentle man.* **gently** (adverb), **gentleness** (noun).

gentleman, gentlemen (noun) A gentleman is a man from the upper middle classes, or a man who is polite and well-educated. Gentleman is also a polite way of referring to any man. **gentlemanly** (adjective).

gentry (plural noun) The gentry are people from the upper classes.

genuine (pronounced **jen**-yoo-in) **1** (adjective) real and not false or pretend, e.g. *a genuine smile... genuine silver.* **2** A genuine person is sincere and honest. **genuinely** (adverb), **genuineness** (noun).

genus, genera (pronounced **jee**-nuss) (noun) In biology, a genus is a class of animals or closely related plants.

geography (noun) Geography is the study of the physical features of the earth, together with the climate, natural resources and population in different parts of the world. **geographic** or **geographical** (adjective), **geographically** (adverb).

geology (noun) Geology is the study of the earth's structure, especially the layers of rock and soil that make up the surface of the earth. **geological** (adjective), **geologist** (noun).

geometric or **geometrical** **1** (adjective) consisting of regular lines and shapes, such as squares, triangles, and circles, e.g. *bold geometric designs.* **2** involving geometry.

geometry (noun) Geometry is the branch of mathematics that deals with lines, angles, curves, and spaces.

Georgian (adjective) belonging to or typical of the time from 1714 to 1830, when George I to George IV reigned in Britain.

geranium, geraniums (noun) A geranium is a garden plant with strongly scented leaves and clusters of red, pink, or white flowers.

gerbil, gerbils (pronounced **jer**-bil) (noun) A gerbil is a small rodent with long back legs. Gerbils come from desert regions and are often kept as pets.

geriatric (pronounced jer-ree-**at**-rik) **1** (adjective) relating to the medical care of old people, e.g. *a geriatric nurse.* **2** Someone or something that is geriatric is very old, e.g. *a geriatric donkey.* **geriatrics** (noun).

germ, germs **1** (noun) A germ is a very small organism that causes disease. **2** (a formal use) The germ of an idea, plan, or theory is the beginning of it.

German, Germans **1** (adjective) belonging or relating to Germany. **2** (noun) A German is someone who comes from Germany. **3** German is the main language spoken in Germany and Austria and is also spoken by many people in Switzerland.

Germanic **1** (adjective) typical of Germany or the German people. **2** The Germanic group of languages includes English, Dutch, German, Danish, Swedish, and Norwegian.

German measles (noun) German measles is a contagious disease that gives you a cough, sore throat, and red spots.

germinate, germinates, germinating, germinated **1** (verb) When a seed germinates, it starts to grow. **2** When an idea or plan germinates, it starts to develop. **germination** (noun).

gestation (pronounced jes-**tay**-shn) (noun; a technical word)

Gestation is the time during which a foetus is growing inside its mother's womb.

gesticulate, gesticulates, gesticulating, gesticulated (pronounced jes-**stik**-yoo-late) (verb) If you gesticulate, you move your hands and arms around while you are talking. **gesticulation** (noun).

gesture, gestures, gesturing, gestured 1 (noun) A gesture is a movement of your hands or head that conveys a message or feeling. **2** (verb) If you gesture, you move your hands or head in order to convey a message or feeling. **3** (noun) A gesture is also an action symbolizing something, e.g. *a gesture of support.*

get, gets, getting, got 1 (verb) Get often means the same as become, e.g. *People usually draw the curtains once it gets dark.* **2** If you get into a particular situation, you put yourself in that situation, e.g. *We are going to get into a hopeless muddle.* **3** If you get something done, you do it or you persuade someone to do it, e.g. *You can get your homework done in time.* **4** If you get somewhere, you go there, e.g. *I must get home.* **5** If you get something, you fetch it, receive it, or are given it, e.g. *I'll get us all a cup of coffee... I got your message.* **6** If you get a joke or get the point of something, you understand it. **7** If you get a train, bus, or plane, you travel on it, e.g. *You can get a bus.* **get across** (verb) If you get an idea across, you make people understand it. **get at 1** (verb) If someone is getting at you, they are criticizing you in an unkind way. **2** If you ask someone what they are getting at, you are asking them to explain what they mean. **get away with** (verb) If you get away with something dishonest or naughty, you are not found out or punished for doing it. **get by** (verb) If you get by, you have just enough money, food, and clothing to live on. **get on 1** (verb) If two people get on well together, they like each other's company. **2** If you get on with a job or task, you do it. **3** If someone is getting on, they are old. **4** (phrase) **Getting on for** means the same as nearly, e.g. *It's getting on for two o'clock.* **get over with** (verb) If you want to get something unpleasant over with, you want it to be finished quickly. **get through 1** (verb) If you get through to someone, you make them understand what you are saying. **2** If you get through to someone on the telephone, you succeed in talking to them.

getaway, getaways (noun) A getaway is an escape made by criminals.

get-together, get-togethers (noun; an informal word) A get-together is an informal meeting or party.

geyser, geysers (pronounced **gee**-zer) (noun) A geyser is a spring through which hot water and steam gush up in spurts.

Ghanaian, Ghanaians (pronounced gah-**nay**-an) **1** (adjective) belonging or relating to

Ghana. **2** (noun) A Ghanaian is someone who comes from Ghana.

ghastly, ghastlier, ghastliest (adjective) extremely horrible and unpleasant, e.g. *a ghastly crime... ghastly food.*

gherkin, gherkins (noun) A gherkin is a small pickled cucumber.

ghetto, ghettoes or **ghettos** (noun) A ghetto is a part of a city where many poor people of a particular race or nationality live.

ghost, ghosts (noun) A ghost is the spirit of a dead person, believed to haunt people or places.

ghoulish (pronounced **gool**-ish) (adjective) very interested in unpleasant things such as death and murder.

giant, giants 1 (noun) In stories and legends, a giant is a huge person who is very strong, and often very cruel or stupid. **2** (adjective) much larger than other similar things, e.g. *giant prawns... a giant wave.*

gibberish (noun) Gibberish is speech that makes no sense at all.

gibbon, gibbons (noun) A gibbon is an ape with very long arms. Gibbons live in forests in southern Asia.

gibe, gibes; also spelled **jibe** (noun) A gibe is an insulting remark.

giddy, giddier, giddiest (adjective) If you feel giddy, you feel unsteady on your feet because you are ill, tired, or very excited. **giddily** (adverb).

gift, gifts 1 (noun) A gift is a present. **2** A gift is also a natural skill or ability, e.g. *a gift for comedy.*

gifted (adjective) having a special ability, e.g. *gifted tennis players.*

gig, gigs (noun) A gig is a rock or jazz concert.

gigantic (adjective) extremely large.

giggle, giggles, giggling, giggled 1 (verb) To giggle means to laugh in a nervous or embarrassed way. **2** (noun) A giggle is a short, nervous laugh. **giggly** (adjective).

gilded (adjective) Something which is gilded is covered with a thin layer of gold.

gill, gills 1 (noun; pronounced **gil**) The gills of a fish are the organs on its sides which it uses for breathing. **2** (pronounced **jil**) A gill is a unit of liquid volume equal to one quarter of a pint or about 0.142 litres.

gilt, gilts 1 (noun) Gilt is a thin layer of gold. **2** (adjective) covered with a thin layer of gold, e.g. *a gilt writing-table.*

gimmick, gimmicks (noun) A gimmick is a device that is not really necessary but is used to attract interest, e.g. *All pop stars need a good gimmick.* **gimmicky** (adjective).

gin (noun) Gin is a strong, colourless alcoholic drink made from grain and juniper berries.

ginger 1 (noun) Ginger is a plant root with a hot, spicy flavour, used for flavouring in cooking, often in a powder form. **2** (adjective) bright orangey-brown, e.g. *ginger hair.*

gingerbread (noun) Gingerbread is a sweet, ginger-flavoured cake.

gingerly (adverb) If you move gingerly, you move cautiously, e.g. *They walked gingerly down the stairs.*

gingham (noun) Gingham is checked cotton cloth.

gipsy another spelling of **gypsy**.

giraffe, giraffes (noun) A giraffe is a tall, four-legged African mammal with a very long neck and dark patches on its skin.

girder, girders (noun) A girder is a large metal beam used in the framework of a structure.

girdle, girdles (noun) A girdle is a woman's corset.

girl, girls (noun) A girl is a female child. **girlish** (adjective), **girlhood** (noun).

girlfriend, girlfriends (noun) Someone's girlfriend is the woman or girl with whom they are having a romantic or sexual relationship.

giro, giros (pronounced **jie**-roh) **1** (noun) Giro is a system of transferring money from one account to another through a bank or post office. **2** A giro is a cheque received regularly from the government by unemployed or sick people.

girth (noun) The girth of something is the measurement round it.

gist (pronounced **jist**) (noun) The gist of a piece of writing or speech is the general meaning or most important points in it.

give, gives, giving, gave, given **1** (verb) If you give someone something, you hand it to them or provide it for them, e.g. *I gave her a tape... George gave me my job.* **2** Give is also used to express physical actions and speech, e.g. *He gave a fierce smile... Rosa gave a lovely performance.* **3** If you give a party or a meal, you are the host at it. **4** If something gives, it collapses under pressure. **5** (noun) If material has give, it will bend or stretch when pulled or put under pressure. **6** (phrase) You use **give or take** to indicate that an amount you are mentioning is not exact, e.g. *About two years, give or take a month or so.* **7** If something **gives way** to something else, it is replaced by it. **8** If something **gives way,** it collapses. **give in** (verb) If you give in, you admit that you are defeated. **give out** (verb) If something gives out, it stops working, e.g. *the electricity gave out.* **give up** **1** (verb) If you give something up, you stop doing it, e.g. *I can't give up my job.* **2** If you give up, you admit that you cannot do something. **3** If you give someone up, you let the police know where they are hiding.

given **1** the past participle of **give**. **2** (adjective) fixed or specified, e.g. *My style can change at any given moment.*

glacé (pronounced **glass**-say) (adjective) Glacé fruits are fruits soaked and coated with sugar, e.g. *glacé cherries.*

glacier, glaciers (pronounced **glass**-yer) (noun) A glacier is a huge frozen river of slow-moving ice.

glad, gladder, gladdest (adjective) happy and pleased, e.g. *They'll be glad to get away from it all.* **gladly** (adverb),

gladness (noun).

glade, glades (noun) A glade is a grassy space in a forest.

gladiator, gladiators (noun) At the time of the Roman Empire, gladiators were slaves trained to fight with various weapons.

gladiolus, gladioli (noun) A gladiolus is a garden plant with spikes of brightly coloured flowers on a long stem.

glamour (noun) The glamour of a fashionable or attractive person or place is the charm and excitement that they have, e.g. *the glamour of Paris.* **glamorous** (adjective).

glance, glances, glancing, glanced 1 (verb) If you glance at something, you look at it quickly. **2** If one object glances off another, it hits it at an angle and bounces away in another direction. **3** (noun) A glance is a quick look.

gland, glands (noun) A gland is one of several organs in your body, such as the thyroid gland and the sweat glands, which either produce chemical substances for your body to use, or which help to get rid of waste products from your body. **glandular** (adjective).

glare, glares, glaring, glared 1 (verb) If you glare at someone, you look at them angrily. **2** (noun) A glare is a hard, angry look. **3** Glare is extremely bright light.

glass, glasses 1 (noun) Glass is a hard, transparent substance that is easily broken, used to make windows and bottles. **2** A glass is a container for drinking out of, made from glass.

glasses (plural noun) Glasses are two lenses in a frame, which some people wear over their eyes to improve their eyesight.

glassy 1 (adjective) smooth and shiny like glass, e.g. *glassy water.* **2** A glassy look shows no feeling or expression.

glaze, glazes, glazing, glazed 1 (noun) A glaze on pottery or on food is a smooth shiny surface. **2** (verb) To glaze pottery or food means to cover it with a glaze. **3** To glaze a window means to fit a sheet of glass into a window frame. **glaze over** (verb) If your eyes glaze over, they lose all expression, usually because you are bored.

glazed (adjective) Someone who has a glazed expression looks bored.

gleam, gleams, gleaming, gleamed 1 (verb) If something gleams, it shines and reflects light. **2** (noun) A gleam is a pale shining light.

glean, gleans, gleaning, gleaned (verb) To glean information means to collect it from various sources.

glee (noun; an old-fashioned word) Glee is joy and delight. **gleeful** (adjective), **gleefully** (adverb).

glen, glens (noun) A glen is a deep, narrow valley, especially in Scotland or Ireland.

glide, glides, gliding, glided 1 (verb) To glide means to move smoothly, e.g. *cygnets gliding up the stream.* **2** When birds or aeroplanes glide, they float on air currents.

glider, gliders (noun) A glider

is an aeroplane without an engine, which flies by floating on air currents.

glimmer, glimmers, glimmering, glimmered 1 (noun) A glimmer is a faint, unsteady light. **2** A glimmer of a feeling or quality is a faint sign of it, e.g. *a glimmer of intelligence.*

glimpse, glimpses, glimpsing, glimpsed 1 (noun) A glimpse of something is a brief sight of it, e.g. *They caught a glimpse of their hero.* **2** (verb) If you glimpse something, you see it very briefly.

glint, glints, glinting, glinted 1 (verb) If something glints, it reflects quick flashes of light. **2** (noun) A glint is a quick flash of light. **3** A glint in someone's eye is a brightness expressing some emotion, e.g. *A glint of mischief in her blue-grey eyes.*

glisten, glistens, glistening, glistened (pronounced **gliss**-sn) (verb) If something glistens, it shines or sparkles.

glitter, glitters, glittering, glittered 1 (verb) If something glitters, it shines in a sparkling way, e.g. *a glittering crown.* **2** (noun) Glitter is sparkling light.

gloat, gloats, gloating, gloated (verb) If you gloat, you cruelly show your pleasure about your own success or someone else's failure, e.g. *Rivals United were gloating over their triumph.*

global (adjective) concerning the whole world, e.g. *a global tour.*

globe, globes 1 (noun) A globe is a spherical object, especially one with a map of the earth on it. **2** You can refer to the world as the globe.

gloom 1 (noun) Gloom is darkness or dimness. **2** Gloom is also a feeling of unhappiness or despair. **gloomy** (adjective), **gloomily** (adverb).

glorify, glorifies, glorifying, glorified (verb) If you glorify someone or something, you make them seem better or more important than they really are, e.g. *Their aggressive music glorifies violence.* **glorification** (noun).

glorious 1 (adjective) beautiful and impressive to look at, e.g. *glorious beaches.* **2** very pleasant and giving a feeling of happiness, e.g. *glorious sunshine.* **3** involving great fame and success, e.g. *a glorious career.* **gloriously** (adverb).

glory, glories, glorying, gloried 1 (noun) Glory is fame and admiration for an achievement. **2** A glory is something considered splendid or admirable, e.g. *the true glories of Scotland.* **3** (verb) If you glory in something, you take great delight in it.

gloss, glosses, glossing, glossed 1 (noun) Gloss is a bright shine on a surface. **2** Gloss is also an attractive appearance which may hide less attractive qualities, e.g. *to put a positive gloss on the events.* **3** If you gloss over a problem or fault, you try to ignore it or deal with it very quickly.

glossary, glossaries (noun) A glossary is a list of explanations of specialist words, usually found at the back of a book.

glossy, glossier, glossiest 1 (adjective) smooth and shiny, e.g. *glossy lipstick.* **2** Glossy magazines and photographs are produced on expensive, shiny paper.

glove, gloves (noun) Gloves are coverings which you wear over your hands for warmth or protection.

glow, glows, glowing, glowed 1 (verb) If something glows, it shines with a dull, steady light, e.g. *A light glowed behind the curtains.* **2** (noun) A glow is a dull, steady light. **3** (verb) If you are glowing, you look very happy or healthy. **4** (noun) A glow is also a strong feeling of pleasure or happiness.

glower, glowers, glowering, glowered (rhymes with **shower**) (verb) If you glower, you stare angrily.

glowing (adjective) A glowing description praises someone or something very highly, e.g. *a glowing character reference.*

glucose (noun) Glucose is a type of sugar found in plants and that animals and people make in their bodies from food. Glucose provides energy.

glue, glues, gluing or **glueing, glued 1** (noun) Glue is a substance used for sticking things together. **2** (verb) If you glue one object to another, you stick them together using glue.

glum, glummer, glummest (adjective) miserable and depressed. **glumly** (adverb).

glut, gluts (noun) A glut of things is a greater quantity than is needed.

glutton, gluttons 1 (noun) A glutton is a person who eats too much. **2** If you are a glutton for something, such as punishment or hard work, you seem very eager for it. **gluttony** (noun).

gnarled (pronounced **narld**) (adjective) old, twisted, and rough, e.g. *gnarled fingers.*

gnat, gnats (pronounced **nat**) (noun) A gnat is a tiny flying insect that bites.

gnaw, gnaws, gnawing, gnawed (pronounced **naw**) **1** (verb) To gnaw something means to bite at it repeatedly. **2** If a feeling gnaws at you, it keeps worrying you, e.g. *Lillian's anguish gnawed.*

gnome, gnomes (pronounced **nome**) (noun) A gnome is a tiny old man in fairy stories.

gnu, gnus (pronounced **noo**) (noun) A gnu is a large African antelope.

go, goes, going, went, gone 1 (verb) If you go somewhere, you move or travel there. **2** You can use go to mean become, e.g. *She felt she was going mad.* **3** You can use go to describe the state that someone or something is in, e.g. *Our arrival went unnoticed.* **4** If something goes well, it is successful. If it goes badly, it is unsuccessful. **5** If you are going to do something, you will do it. **6** If a machine or clock goes, it works and is not broken. **7** You use go before giving the sound something makes or before quoting a poem, song, or saying, e.g. *The bell went ding-dong.* **8** If something goes on something or to someone, it is allotted to them. **9** If one thing goes with another, they are appropriate or suitable together. **10** If one number goes into another, it can be divided into it. **11** If you go back on a promise or agreement, you do not do what you promised or agreed. **12** If someone goes for you, they attack you. **13** If you go in for something, you decide to do it as your job. **14** If you go out with someone, you have a romantic relationship with them. **15** If you go over something, you think about it or discuss it carefully. **16** (noun) A go is an attempt at doing something. **17** (phrase) If someone is always **on the go,** they are always busy and active. **18** **To go** means remaining, e.g. *I've got one more year of my course to go.* **go down 1** (verb) If something goes down well, people like it. If it goes down badly, they do not like it. **2** If you go down with an illness, you catch it. **go off 1** (verb) If you go off someone or something, you stop liking them. **2** If a bomb goes off, it explodes. **go on 1** (verb) If you go on doing something, you continue to do it. **2** If you go on about something, you keep talking about it in a rather boring way. **3** Something that is going on is happening. **go through 1** (verb) If you go through an unpleasant event, you experience it. **2** If a law, agreement, or decision goes through, it is approved and becomes official. **3** If you go through with something, you do it even though it is unpleasant.

goad, goads, goading, goaded (verb) If you goad someone, you encourage them to do something by making them angry or excited, e.g. *He had goaded the man into near violence.*

go-ahead (noun) If someone gives you the go-ahead for something, they give you permission to do it.

goal, goals 1 (noun) In games like football or hockey, the goal is the space into which the players try to get the ball in order to score a point. **2** A goal is an instance of this. **3** Your goal is something that you hope to achieve.

goalkeeper, goalkeepers (noun) In games like football or hockey, the goalkeeper is the player who stands in the goal and tries to stop the other team from scoring.

goat, goats (noun) A goat is an animal with shaggy hair, a beard, and horns. Goats live in mountainous areas, but are sometimes kept on farms for their milk or meat.

gob, gobs (noun; an informal use) Your gob is your mouth.

gobble, gobbles, gobbling, gobbled 1 (verb) If you gobble food, you eat it very quickly. **2** When a turkey gobbles, it makes a loud gurgling sound.

gobbledygook or **gobbledegook** (noun) Gobbledygook is language that is impossible to understand because it is so formal or complicated.

goblet, goblets (noun) A goblet is a glass with a long stem and a base.

goblin, goblins (noun) A goblin is an ugly, mischievous creature in fairy stories.

god, gods 1 (noun) The name

God is given to the being who is worshipped by Christians, Jews, and Muslims as the creator and ruler of the world. **2** A god is any of the beings that are believed in many religions to have power over an aspect of life or a part of the world. **3** If someone is your god, you admire them very much. **4** (plural noun) In a theatre, the gods are the highest seats farthest from the stage.

godchild, godchildren (noun) If you are someone's godchild, they agreed to be responsible for your religious upbringing when you were baptized in a Christian church. **goddaughter** (noun), **godson** (noun).

goddess, goddesses (noun) A goddess is a female god.

godparent, godparents (noun) A person's godparent is someone who agrees to be responsible for their religious upbringing when they are baptized in a Christian church. **godfather** (noun), **godmother** (noun).

godsend, godsends (noun) A godsend is something that comes unexpectedly and helps you very much.

goggles (plural noun) Goggles are special glasses that fit closely round your eyes to protect them.

going (noun) The going is the conditions that affect your ability to do something, e.g. *He found the going very slow indeed.*

gold 1 (noun) Gold is a valuable, yellow-coloured metal. It is used for making jewellery and as an international currency. **2** Gold is also used to mean things that are made of gold. **3** (adjective) bright yellow.

golden 1 (adjective) gold in colour, e.g. *golden syrup.* **2** made of gold, e.g. *a golden chain.* **3** excellent or ideal, e.g. *a golden hero.*

golden rule, golden rules (noun) A golden rule is a very important rule to remember in order to be able to do something successfully.

golden wedding, golden weddings (noun) Someone's golden wedding is their fiftieth wedding anniversary.

goldfish (noun) A goldfish is a small orange-coloured fish. Goldfish are often kept in ponds or bowls.

goldsmith, goldsmiths (noun) A goldsmith is a person whose job is making jewellery and other objects out of gold.

golf (noun) Golf is a game in which players use special clubs to hit a small ball into holes that are spread out over a large area of grassy land. **golfer** (noun).

golf course, golf courses (noun) A golf course is an area of grassy land where people play golf.

gondola, gondolas (pronounced **gon**-dol-la) (noun) A gondola is a long narrow boat used in Venice, which is propelled with a long pole.

gone the past participle of **go**.

gong, gongs (noun) A gong is a flat, circular piece of metal that is hit with a hammer to make a loud sound, often as a signal for something.

good, better, best; goods 1 (adjective) pleasant, acceptable, or satisfactory, e.g. *good news... a good film.* **2** skilful or successful, e.g. *good at art.* **3** kind, thoughtful, and loving, e.g. *She was grateful to him for being so good to her.* **4** well-behaved, e.g. *Have the children been good?* **5** used to emphasize something, e.g. *a good few million pounds.* **6** (noun) Good is moral and spiritual justice and rightness, e.g. *the forces of good and evil.* **7** Good also refers to anything that is desirable, useful, or beneficial as opposed to harmful, e.g. *The break has done me good.* **8** (plural noun) Goods are objects that people own or that are sold in shops, e.g. *leather goods.* **9** (phrase) **For good** means for ever. **10** **As good as** means almost, e.g. *The election is as good as decided.*

goodbye You say goodbye when you are leaving someone or ending a telephone conversation.

Good Friday (noun) Good Friday is the Friday before Easter, when Christians remember the crucifixion of Christ.

good-natured (adjective) friendly, pleasant and even-tempered.

goodness 1 (noun) Goodness is the quality of being kind. **2** (interjection) People say 'Goodness!' or 'My goodness!' when they are surprised.

good will (noun) Good will is kindness and helpfulness, e.g. *Messages of good will were exchanged.*

goody, goodies 1 (noun; an informal word) Goodies are enjoyable things, often food. **2** You can call a hero in a film or book a goody.

goose, geese (noun) A goose is a fairly large bird with webbed feet and a long neck. Geese make a loud honking noise, and are sometimes kept on farms for their meat and eggs.

gooseberry, gooseberries (noun) A gooseberry is a round, green edible berry that grows on a bush and has a sharp taste.

gore, gores, goring, gored 1 (verb) If an animal gores someone, it wounds them badly with its horns or tusks. **2** (noun) Gore is clotted blood from a wound.

gorge, gorges, gorging, gorged 1 (noun) A gorge is a deep, narrow valley. **2** (verb) If you gorge yourself, you eat a lot of food greedily.

gorgeous (adjective) extremely pleasant or attractive, e.g. *a gorgeous man.*

gorilla, gorillas (noun) A gorilla is a very large, strong ape with very dark fur. Gorillas live in forests in central Africa.

gorse (noun) Gorse is a dark green wild shrub that has sharp prickles and small yellow flowers.

gory, gorier, goriest (adjective) Gory situations involve people being injured in horrible ways.

gosling, goslings (pronounced **goz**-ling) (noun) A gosling is a young goose.

gospel, gospels 1 (noun) The Gospels are the four books in the New Testament which describe the life and teachings of Jesus Christ. **2** A gospel is a set of ideas that someone strongly believes in, e.g. *the so-called gospel of work.* **3** (phrase) If you take something **as gospel** or **gospel truth**, you believe that it is true. **4** (adjective) Gospel music is a style of religious music popular among Black Christians in the United States.

gossip, gossips, gossiping, gossiped 1 (noun) Gossip is informal conversation, often concerning people's private affairs. **2** (verb) If you gossip, you talk informally with someone, especially about other people. **3** (noun) Someone who is a gossip enjoys talking about other people's private affairs.

got 1 Got is the past tense and past participle of **get**. **2** You can use 'have got' instead of the more formal 'have' when talking about possessing things, e.g. *The director has got a map.* **3** You can use 'have got to' instead of the more formal 'have to' when talking about something that must be done, e.g. *He has got to win.*

gouge, gouges, gouging, gouged (pronounced **gowj**) **1** (verb) If you gouge a hole in something, you make a hole in it with a pointed object. **2** If you gouge something out, you force it out of position with your fingers or a sharp tool.

gourd, gourds (pronounced **goord**) (noun) A gourd is a large fruit with a hard outside.

gourmet, gourmets (pronounced **goor**-may) (noun) A gourmet is a person who enjoys good food and drink and knows a lot about it.

gout (noun) Gout is a disease which causes someone's joints to swell painfully, especially in their toes.

govern, governs, governing, governed 1 (verb) To govern a country means to control it. **2** Something that governs a situation influences it, e.g. *Our thinking is as much governed by habit as by behaviour.*

governess, governesses (noun) A governess is a woman who is employed to teach the children in a family and who lives with the family.

government, governments 1 (noun) The government is the group of people who govern a country. **2** Government is the control and organization of a country. **governmental** (adjective).

governor, governors (noun) A governor is a person who controls and organizes a state or an institution.

gown, gowns 1 (noun) A gown is a long, formal dress. **2** A gown is also a special long, dark cloak worn by people such as judges and lawyers.

GP an abbreviation for **general practitioner**.

grab, grabs, grabbing, grabbed 1 (verb) If you grab something, you take it or pick it up roughly. **2** If you grab an opportunity, you take advantage of it eagerly. **3** (an informal use) If an idea grabs you, it interests you or excites you. **4**

(noun) A grab at an object is an attempt to grab it.

grace, graces, gracing, graced 1 (noun) Grace is an elegant way of moving. **2** Grace is also a pleasant, kind way of behaving. **3** (verb) Something that graces a place makes it more attractive. **4** If someone important graces an event, they kindly agree to be present at it. **5** (noun) Grace is also a short prayer of thanks said before a meal. **6** Dukes and archbishops are addressed as 'Your Grace' and referred to as 'His Grace'. **graceful** (adjective), **gracefully** (adverb).

gracious 1 (adjective) kind, polite, and pleasant. **2** 'Good gracious' is an exclamation of surprise. **graciously** (adverb).

grade, grades, grading, graded 1 (verb) To grade things means to arrange them according to quality, size, or colour. **2** (noun) The grade of something is its quality. **3** A grade in an exam or piece of written work is the mark that you get for it. **4** Your grade in a company or organization is your level of importance or your rank.

gradient, gradients (noun) A gradient is a slope or the steepness of a slope.

gradual (adjective) happening or changing slowly over a long period of time rather than suddenly.

gradually (adverb) happening or changing slowly over a long period of time.

graduate, graduates, graduating, graduated 1 (noun) A graduate is a person who has completed a first degree at a university or college. **2** (verb) When students graduate, they complete a first degree at a university or college. **3** To graduate from one thing to another means to progress gradually towards the second thing. **graduation** (noun).

graffiti (pronounced graf-**fee**-tee) (noun) Graffiti is slogans or drawings scribbled on walls, posters, trains, and buses.

graft, grafts, grafting, grafted 1 (noun) A graft is a piece of healthy flesh or a healthy organ which is used to replace by surgery a damaged or unhealthy part of a person's body. **2** (verb) To graft one thing to another means to attach it. **3** (noun; an informal use) Graft is hard work.

grain, grains 1 (noun) Grain is a cereal plant, such as wheat or corn, that is grown as a crop and used for food. **2** Grains are seeds of a cereal plant. **3** A grain of sand or salt is a tiny particle of it. **4** The grain of a piece of wood is the pattern of lines made by the fibres in it. **5** (phrase) If something **goes against the grain,** you find it difficult to accept because it is against your principles.

gram, grams; also spelled **gramme** (noun) A gram is a unit of weight equal to one thousandth of a kilogram.

grammar (noun) Grammar is the rules of a language relating to the ways you can combine words to form sentences.

grammar school, grammar schools (noun) A grammar

school is a secondary school for pupils of high academic ability.

grammatical 1 (adjective) relating to grammar, e.g. *grammatical knowledge.* 2 following the rules of grammar correctly, e.g. *grammatical sentences.* **grammatically** (adverb).

gran, grans (noun; an informal word) Your gran is your grandmother.

granary, granaries 1 (noun) A granary is a building for storing grain. 2 (adjective; a trademark) Granary bread contains whole grains of wheat.

grand, grander, grandest 1 (adjective) magnificent in appearance and size, e.g. *a grand house.* 2 very important, e.g. *the grand scheme of your life.* 3 (an informal use) very pleasant or enjoyable, e.g. *It was a grand day.* 4 A grand total is the final complete amount. 5 (noun; an informal use) A grand is a thousand pounds or dollars. **grandly** (adverb).

grandad, grandads (noun; an informal word) Your grandad is your grandfather.

grandchild, grandchildren (noun) Someone's grandchildren are the children of their son or daughter.

granddaughter, granddaughters (noun) Someone's granddaughter is the daughter of their son or daughter.

grandeur (pronounced **grand**-yer) (noun) Grandeur is great beauty and magnificence.

grandfather, grandfathers (noun) Your grandfather is your father's father or your mother's father.

grandfather clock, grandfather clocks (noun) A grandfather clock is a clock in a tall wooden case that stands on the floor.

grandiose (pronounced **gran**-dee-ose) (adjective) intended to be very impressive, but seeming ridiculous, e.g. *a grandiose gesture of love.*

grandma, grandmas (noun; an informal word) Your grandma is your grandmother.

grandmother, grandmothers (noun) Your grandmother is your father's mother or your mother's mother.

grandparent, grandparents (noun) Your grandparents are your parents' parents.

grand piano, grand pianos (noun) A grand piano is a large flat piano with horizontal strings.

grandson, grandsons (noun) Someone's grandson is the son of their son or daughter.

grandstand, grandstands (noun) A grandstand is a structure with a roof and seats for spectators at a sports ground.

granite (pronounced **gran**-nit) (noun) Granite is a very hard rock used in building.

granny, grannies (noun; an informal word) Your granny is your grandmother.

grant, grants, granting, granted 1 (noun) A grant is an amount of money that the government or local council gives to someone for a particular purpose, e.g. *a grant to carry out repairs.* 2 (verb) If you grant something to someone, you allow them to have it. 3 If you grant that something is true, you admit that it is true. **4** (phrases) If you **take something for granted,** you believe it without thinking about it. If you **take someone for granted,** you benefit from them without showing that you are grateful.

granule, granules (noun) A granule is a very small piece of something, e.g. *granules of salt.*

grape, grapes (noun) A grape is a small green or purple fruit. Grapes are eaten raw, dried to make raisins, sultanas, and currants, or used to make wine.

grapefruit, grapefruits (noun) A grapefruit is a large, round, yellow citrus fruit with a thick skin and bitter taste.

grapevine, grapevines 1 (noun) A grapevine is a climbing plant which grapes grow on. **2** If you hear some news on the grapevine, it has been passed on from person to person, usually unofficially or secretly.

graph, graphs (noun) A graph is a diagram in which a straight, curved, or zigzag line shows how two sets of numbers or measurements are related.

graphic, graphics 1 (adjective) A graphic description is very detailed and lifelike. **2** relating to drawing or painting. **3** (plural noun) Graphics are drawings and pictures composed of simple lines and strong colours, e.g. *computerized graphics.* **graphically** (adverb).

grapple, grapples, grappling, grappled 1 (verb) If you grapple with someone, you struggle with them while fighting. **2** If you grapple with a problem, you try hard to solve it.

grasp, grasps, grasping, grasped 1 (verb) If you grasp something, you hold it firmly. **2** If you grasp an idea, you understand it. **3** (noun) A grasp is a firm hold. **4** Your grasp of something is your understanding of it.

grass, grasses (noun) Grass is the common green plant that grows on lawns and in parks. **grassy** (adjective).

grasshopper, grasshoppers (noun) A grasshopper is an insect with long back legs which it uses for jumping and making a high-pitched vibrating sound.

grate, grates, grating, grated 1 (noun) A grate is a framework of metal bars in a fireplace. **2** (verb) To grate food means to shred it into small pieces by rubbing it against a grater. **3** When something grates on something else, it rubs against it making a harsh sound. **4** If something grates on you, it irritates you.

grateful (adjective) If you are grateful for something, you are glad you have it and want to thank the person who gave it to you. **gratefully** (adverb).

grater, graters (noun) A grater is a small metal tool used for grating food.

gratify, gratifies, gratifying, gratified 1 (verb) If you are gratified by something, you are pleased by it. **2** If you gratify a wish or feeling, you satisfy it.

grating, gratings 1 (noun) A grating is a metal frame with bars across it fastened over a hole in a wall or in the ground. **2** (adjective) A grating sound is harsh and unpleasant, e.g. *grating melodies.*

gratis (pronounced **grah**-tis) (adverb or adjective) free, e.g. *food and drink supplied gratis.*

gratitude (noun) Gratitude is the feeling of being grateful.

gratuitous (pronounced grat-**yoo**-it-tuss) (adjective) unnecessary, e.g. *a gratuitous attack.* **gratuitously** (adverb).

grave, graves; graver, gravest 1 (noun) A grave is a place where a corpse is buried. **2** (adjective; a formal use) very serious, e.g. *grave danger.*

grave (pronounced **grahv**) (adjective) In French and some other languages, a grave accent is a downward-sloping line placed over a vowel to indicate a change in pronunciation, as in the word *lèvre.*

gravel (noun) Gravel is small stones used for making roads and paths.

gravestone, gravestones (noun) A gravestone is a large stone placed over someone's grave, with their name and other information on it.

graveyard, graveyards (noun) A graveyard is an area of land where corpses are buried.

gravitate, gravitates, gravitating, gravitated (verb) When people gravitate towards something, they go towards it because they are attracted by it.

gravitation (noun) Gravitation is the force which causes objects to be attracted to each other.

gravity 1 (noun) Gravity is the force that makes things fall when you drop them. **2** (a formal use) The gravity of a situation is its seriousness.

gravy (noun) Gravy is a brown sauce made from the juice that comes out of meat when you cook it.

graze, grazes, grazing, grazed 1 (verb) When animals graze, they eat grass. **2** If something grazes a part of your body, it scrapes against it, injuring you slightly. **3** (noun) A graze is a slight injury caused by something scraping against your skin.

grease, greases, greasing, greased 1 (noun) Grease is an oily substance used for lubricating machines. **2** Grease is also melted animal fat, used in cooking. **3** Grease is also an oily substance produced by your skin and found in your hair. **4** (verb) If you grease something, you lubricate it with grease. **greasy** (adjective).

great, greater, greatest 1 (adjective) very large, e.g. *a great sea... great efforts.* **2** very important, e.g. *a great artist.* **3** (an informal use) very good, e.g. *Paul had a great time.* **greatly** (adverb), **greatness** (noun).

Great Britain (noun) Great Britain is the largest of the British Isles, consisting of England, Scotland, and Wales.

Great Dane, Great Danes (noun) A Great Dane is a very large dog with short hair.

great-grandfather, great-grandfathers (noun) Your great-grandfather is your father's or mother's grandfather.

great-grandmother, great-grandmothers (noun) Your great-grandmother is your father's or mother's grandmother.

greed (noun) Greed is a desire for more of something, such as food, than you really need.

greedy, greedier, greediest (adjective) wanting more of something, such as food, than you really need. **greedily** (adverb), **greediness** (noun).

Greek, Greeks 1 (adjective) belonging or relating to Greece. **2** (noun) A Greek is someone who comes from Greece. **3** Greek is the main language spoken in Greece.

green, greener, greenest; greens 1 (adjective or noun) Green is a colour between yellow and blue on the spectrum. **2** (noun) A green is an area of grass in the middle of a village. **3** A putting green or bowling green is a grassy area on which putting or bowls is played. **4** In golf, a green is an area of smooth short grass around each hole on the course. **5** (plural noun) Greens are green vegetables. **6** (adjective) Green is used to describe political movements which are concerned with environmental issues. **7** (an informal use) Someone who is green is young and inexperienced.

greenery (noun) Greenery is a lot of trees, bushes, or other green plants together in one place.

greenfly (noun) Greenfly are small green insects that damage plants.

greengrocer, greengrocers (noun) A greengrocer is a shopkeeper who sells vegetables and fruit.

greenhouse, greenhouses (noun) A greenhouse is a glass building in which people grow plants that need to be kept warm.

greet, greets, greeting, greeted 1 (verb) If you greet someone, you say something friendly like 'hello' to them when you meet them. **2** If you greet something in a particular way, you react to it in that way, e.g. *He was greeted with deep suspicion.*

greeting, greetings (noun) A greeting is something friendly that you say to someone when you meet them or when they arrive somewhere, e.g. *Her greeting was warm.*

gregarious (pronounced grig-**air**-ee-uss) (adjective; a formal word) Someone who is gregarious enjoys being with other people.

grenade, grenades (noun) A grenade is a small bomb, containing explosive or tear gas, which can be thrown by hand.

grew the past tense of **grow**.

grey, greyer, greyest; greys; greying 1 (adjective or noun) Grey is a colour between black and white. **2** (adjective) dull and boring, e.g. *He's a bit of a grey man.* **3** (verb) If someone is greying, their hair is going grey. **greyness** (noun).

greyhound, greyhounds (noun) A greyhound is a thin dog with long legs that can run very fast. People bet on greyhounds in races.

grid, grids 1 (noun) A grid is a pattern of lines crossing each other to form squares. **2** The grid is the network of wires and cables by which electricity is distributed throughout a country.

grief **1** (noun) Grief is extreme sadness. **2** (phrase) If someone or something **comes to grief,** they fail or are injured.

grievance, grievances (noun) A grievance is a reason for complaining.

grieve, grieves, grieving, grieved **1** (verb) If you grieve, you are extremely sad, especially because someone has died. **2** If something grieves you, it makes you feel very sad.

grievous (adjective; a formal word) extremely serious, e.g. *grievous damage.* **grievously** (adverb).

grill, grills, grilling, grilled **1** (noun) A grill is a part on a cooker where food is cooked by strong heat from above. **2** A grill is also a metal frame on which you cook food over a fire. **3** (verb) If you grill food, you cook it on or under a grill. **4** (an informal use) If you grill someone, you ask them a lot of questions in a very intense way.

grille, grilles (rhymes with **pill**) (noun) A grille is a metal framework over a window or piece of machinery, used for protection.

grim, grimmer, grimmest **1** (adjective) If a situation or piece of news is grim, it is very unpleasant and worrying, e.g. *There are grim times ahead.* **2** Grim places are unattractive and depressing, e.g. *The streets were grim and sunless.* **3** If someone is grim, they are very serious, e.g. *The man looked grim and thoughtful.* **grimly** (adverb).

grimace, grimaces, grimacing, grimaced (pronounced grim-**mace**) **1** (noun) A grimace is a twisted facial expression indicating annoyance, disgust, or pain. **2** (verb) When someone grimaces, they make a grimace.

grime (noun) Grime is thick dirt which gathers on the surface of something. **grimy** (adjective).

grin, grins, grinning, grinned **1** (verb) If you grin, you smile broadly. **2** (noun) A grin is a broad smile. **3** (phrase) If you **grin and bear it,** you accept a difficult situation without complaining.

grind, grinds, grinding, ground **1** (verb) If you grind something such as corn or pepper, you crush it into a fine powder. **2** If you grind your teeth, you rub your upper and lower teeth together. **3** (phrase) If something **grinds to a halt,** it stops, e.g. *Progress ground to a halt.*

grip, grips, gripping, gripped **1** (verb) If you grip something, you hold it firmly. **2** (noun) A grip is a firm hold. **3** Your grip on a situation is your control over it. **4** (phrase) If you **get to grips with** a situation or problem, you start to deal with it effectively. **5** If you **are losing your grip,** you are becoming less able to deal with things.

grisly, grislier, grisliest (adjective) very nasty and horrible, e.g. *a grisly murder scene.*

grit, grits, gritting, gritted 1 (noun) Grit consists of very small stones. It is put on icy roads to make them less slippery. **2** (verb) When workmen grit an icy road, they put grit on it. **3** (phrase) To **grit your teeth** means to decide to carry on in a difficult situation. **gritty** (adjective).

grizzled (adjective) Grizzled hair is grey. A grizzled person has grey hair.

grizzly bear, grizzly bears (noun) A grizzly bear or a grizzly is a large, greyish-brown bear from North America.

groan, groans, groaning, groaned 1 (verb) If you groan, you make a long, low sound of pain, unhappiness, or disapproval. **2** (noun) A groan is the sound you make when you groan.

grocer, grocers (noun) A grocer is a shopkeeper who sells many kinds of food and other household goods.

grocery, groceries 1 (noun) A grocery is a grocer's shop. **2** (plural noun) Groceries are the goods that you buy in a grocer's shop.

groin, groins (noun) Your groin is the area where your legs join the main part of your body at the front.

groom, grooms, grooming, groomed 1 (noun) A groom is someone who looks after horses in a stable. **2** At a wedding, the groom is the bridegroom. **3** (verb) To groom an animal means to clean its fur. **4** If you groom someone for a particular job, you prepare them for it by teaching them the skills they will need.

groove, grooves (noun) A groove is a deep line cut into a surface. **grooved** (adjective).

grope, gropes, groping, groped 1 (verb) If you grope for something you cannot see, you search for it with your hands. **2** If you grope for something such as the solution to a problem, you try to think of it.

gross, grosser, grossest; grosses, grossing, grossed 1 (adjective) extremely bad, e.g. *a gross betrayal.* **2** Gross speech or behaviour is very rude. **3** Gross things are ugly, e.g. *gross holiday outfits.* **4** Someone's gross income is their total income before any deductions are made. **5** The gross weight of something is its total weight including the weight of its container. **6** (verb) If you gross an amount of money, you earn that amount in total. **grossly** (adverb).

grotesque (pronounced groh-**tesk**) **1** (adjective) exaggerated and absurd, e.g. *It was the most grotesque thing she had ever heard.* **2** very strange and ugly, e.g. *grotesque animal puppets.* **grotesquely** (adverb).

grotto, grottoes or **grottos** (noun) A grotto is a small cave that people visit because it is attractive.

ground, grounds, grounding, grounded 1 (noun) The ground is the surface of the earth. **2** A ground is a piece of land that is used for a particular purpose, e.g. *the training ground.* **3** The ground covered by a book or course is the range of subjects it deals with. **4** (plural noun) The grounds of a large building are the land belonging to it and surrounding it. **5** (a formal use) The grounds for something are the reasons for it, e.g. *genuine grounds for caution.* **6** (verb; a formal use) If something is grounded in something else, it is based on it. **7** If an aircraft is grounded, it has to remain on the ground. **8** Ground is the past tense and past participle of **grind.**

ground floor, ground floors (noun) The ground floor of a building is the floor that is approximately level with the ground.

grounding (noun) If you have a grounding in a skill or subject, you have had basic instruction in it.

groundless (adjective) not based on reason or evidence, e.g. *groundless accusations.*

group, groups, grouping, grouped 1 (noun) A group of things or people is a number of them that are linked together in some way. **2** A group is also a number of musicians who perform pop music together. **3** (verb) When things or people are grouped together, they are linked together in some way.

grouping, groupings (noun) A grouping is a number of things or people that are linked together in some way.

grouse, grouse (noun) A grouse is a fat brown or grey bird. Grouse are shot for sport and can be eaten.

grove, groves (noun; a literary word) A grove is a group of trees growing close together.

grovel, grovels, grovelling, grovelled (verb) If you grovel, you behave in an unpleasantly humble way towards someone you regard as important.

grow, grows, growing, grew, grown 1 (verb) To grow means to increase in size, amount, or degree. **2** If a tree or plant grows somewhere, it is alive there. **3** When people grow plants, they plant them and look after them. **4** If a man grows a beard or moustache, he lets it develop by not shaving. **5** If you grow to have a particular feeling, you eventually have it. **6** If one thing grows from another, it develops from it. **7** (an informal use) If something grows on you, you gradually get to like it. **grow up** (verb) When a child grows up, he or she becomes an adult.

growl, growls, growling, growled 1 (verb) When an animal growls, it makes a low rumbling sound, usually because it is angry. **2** (noun) A growl is the sound an animal makes when it growls. **3** (verb) If you growl something, you say it in a low, rough, rather angry voice.

grown-up, grown-ups 1 (noun; an informal use) A grown-up is an adult. **2** (adjective) Someone who is grown-up is adult, or behaves like an adult.

growth, growths 1 (noun) When there is a growth in something, it gets bigger, e.g. *the growth of the fishing industry.* **2** Growth is the process by which something develops to its full size. **3** A growth is an abnormal lump on the outside or inside of a person, animal, or plant.

grub, grubs 1 (noun) A grub is a wormlike insect that has just hatched from its egg. **2** (an informal use) Grub is food.

grubby, grubbier, grubbiest (adjective) rather dirty.

grudge, grudges, grudging, grudged 1 (noun) If you have a grudge against someone, you resent them because they have harmed you in the past. **2** (verb) If you grudge someone something, you give it to them unwillingly, or are displeased that they have it.

grudging (adjective) done or felt unwillingly, e.g. *grudging admiration.* **grudgingly** (adverb).

gruel (noun) Gruel was oatmeal boiled in water or milk.

gruelling (adjective) difficult and tiring, e.g. *a gruelling race.*

gruesome (adjective) shocking and horrible, e.g. *gruesome pictures.*

gruff, gruffer, gruffest (adjective) If someone's voice is gruff, it sounds rough and unfriendly.

grumble, grumbles, grumbling, grumbled 1 (verb) If you grumble, you complain in a bad-tempered way. **2** (noun) A grumble is a bad-tempered complaint.

grumpy, grumpier, grumpiest (adjective) bad-tempered and fed-up.

grunt, grunts, grunting, grunted 1 (verb) If a person or a pig grunts, they make a short, low, gruff sound. **2** (noun) A grunt is the sound a person or a pig makes when they grunt.

guarantee, guarantees, guaranteeing, guaranteed 1 (verb) If something or someone guarantees something, they make certain that it will happen, e.g. *Money may not guarantee success.* **2** (noun) If something is a guarantee of something else, it makes it certain that it will happen. **3** A guarantee is also a written promise that if a product develops a fault within a specified period of time, it will be replaced or repaired free. **guarantor** (noun).

guard, guards, guarding, guarded 1 (verb) If you guard a person or object, you stay near to them either to protect them or to make sure they do not escape. **2** If you guard against something, you are careful to avoid it happening. **3** (noun) A guard is a person or group of people who guard a person, object, or place. **4** A guard is also a railway official in charge of a train. **5** Any object which covers something to prevent it causing harm can be called a guard, e.g. *a fire guard.*

guardian, guardians 1 (noun) A guardian is someone who has been legally appointed to look after an orphaned child. **2** A guardian of something is someone who protects it, e.g. *a guardian of the law.* **guardianship** (noun).

guerrilla, guerrillas (pronounced ger-**ril**-la); also spelled **guerilla** (noun) A guerrilla is a member of a small unofficial army fighting an official army.

guess, guesses, guessing,

guessed 1 (verb) If you guess something, you form or express an opinion that it is the case, without having much information. **2** (noun) A guess is an attempt to give the correct answer to something without having much information.

guest, guests 1 (noun) A guest is someone who stays at your home or who attends an occasion because they have been invited. **2** The guests in a hotel are the people staying there.

guest house, guest houses (noun) A guest house is a private house which has rooms where people can pay to stay and which usually provides some meals.

guest of honour, guests of honour (noun) The guest of honour at a dinner or social occasion is the most important guest.

guffaw (noun) A guffaw is a loud, coarse laugh.

guidance (noun) Guidance is help and advice.

guide, guides, guiding, guided 1 (noun) A guide is someone who shows you round places, or leads the way through difficult country. **2** A guide is also a book which gives you information or instructions, e.g. *a London street guide.* **3** A Guide is a girl who is a member of an organization that encourages discipline and practical skills. **4** (verb) If you guide someone in a particular direction, you lead them in that direction. **5** If you are guided by something, it influences your actions or decisions.

guidebook, guidebooks (noun) A guidebook is a book which gives information about a place.

guide dog, guide dogs (noun) A guide dog is a dog that has been trained to lead a blind person.

guideline, guidelines (noun) A guideline is a piece of advice about how something should be done.

guild, guilds (noun) A guild is a society of people, e.g. *Townswomen's Guild.*

guile (rhymes with **mile**) (noun) Guile is cunning and deceit. **guileless** (adjective).

guillotine, guillotines (pronounced **gil**-lot-teen) (noun) In the past, the guillotine was a machine used for beheading people, especially in France.

guilt 1 (noun) Guilt is an unhappy feeling of having done something wrong. **2** Someone's guilt is the fact that they have done something wrong, e.g. *The law will decide their guilt.*

guilty, guiltier, guiltiest 1 (adjective) If you are guilty of doing something wrong, you did it, e.g. *He was guilty of theft.* **2** If you feel guilty, you are unhappy because you have done something wrong. **guiltily** (adverb).

guinea, guineas (pronounced **gin**-ee) (noun) A guinea is an old British unit of money, worth 21 shillings.

guinea pig, guinea pigs 1 (noun) A guinea pig is a small furry animal without a tail, often kept as a pet. **2** A guinea pig is also a person used to try something out on, e.g. *a guinea pig for a new tech-*

nique.

guise, guises (rhymes with **prize**) (noun) A guise is a misleading appearance, e.g. *political statements in the guise of religious talk.*

guitar, guitars (noun) A guitar is a musical instrument with six strings which are strummed or plucked. **guitarist** (noun).

gulf, gulfs 1 (noun) A gulf is a very large bay. **2** A gulf is a wide gap or difference between two things, people, or groups.

gull, gulls (noun) A gull is a very common sea bird with long wings, white and grey or black feathers, and webbed feet.

gullet, gullets (noun) Your gullet is the tube that goes from your mouth to your stomach.

gullible (adjective) easily tricked. **gullibility** (noun).

gully, gullies (noun) A gully is a long, narrow valley.

gulp, gulps, gulping, gulped 1 (verb) If you gulp food or drink, you swallow large quantities of it. **2** (noun) A gulp of food or drink is a large quantity of it swallowed at one time. **3** (verb) If you gulp, you swallow air, because you are nervous.

gum, gums 1 (noun) Gum is a soft flavoured substance that people chew but do not swallow. **2** Gum is also glue for sticking paper. **3** Your gums are the firm flesh in which your teeth are set.

gun, guns (noun) A gun is a weapon which fires bullets or shells.

gunpowder (noun) Gunpowder is an explosive powder made from a mixture of potassium nitrate and other substances.

gunshot, gunshots (noun) A gunshot is the sound of a gun being fired.

guppy, guppies (noun) A guppy is a small, brightly-coloured tropical fish.

gurgle, gurgles, gurgling, gurgled 1 (verb) To gurgle means to make a bubbling sound. **2** (noun) A gurgle is a bubbling sound.

guru, gurus (pronounced **goo**-rooh) (noun) A guru is a spiritual leader and teacher, especially in India.

gush, gushes, gushing, gushed 1 (verb) When liquid gushes from something, it flows out of it in large quantities. **2** When people gush, they express admiration or pleasure in an exaggerated way. **gushing** (adjective).

gust, gusts (noun) A gust is a sudden rush of wind. **gusty** (adjective).

gusto (noun) Gusto is energy and enthusiasm, e.g. *Her gusto for life was amazing.*

gut, guts, gutting, gutted 1 (plural noun) Your guts are your internal organs, especially your intestines. **2** (verb) To gut a dead fish means to remove its internal organs. **3** (noun; an informal use) Guts is courage. **4** (verb) If a building is gutted, the inside of it is destroyed, especially by fire.

gutter, gutters 1 (noun) A gutter is the edge of a road next to the pavement, where rain collects and flows away. **2** A gutter is also a channel fixed to the edge of a roof, where rain collects and flows away. **guttering** (noun).

guttural (pronounced **gut**-ter-al) (adjective) Guttural sounds are produced at the back of a person's throat and are often considered to be unpleasant.

guy, guys (noun; an informal use) A guy is a man or boy.

guzzle, guzzles, guzzling, guzzled (verb) To guzzle something means to drink or eat it quickly and greedily.

gym, gyms 1 (noun) A gym is a gymnasium. **2** Gym is gymnastics.

gymkhana, gymkhanas (pronounced jim-**kah**-na) (noun) A gymkhana is an event in which people take part in horse-riding contests.

gymnasium, gymnasiums (noun) A gymnasium is a room with special equipment for physical exercises.

gymnast, gymnasts (noun) A gymnast is someone who is trained in gymnastics. **gymnastic** (adjective).

gymnastics (noun) Gymnastics is physical exercises, especially ones using equipment such as bars and ropes.

gynaecology or **gynecology** (pronounced gie-nak-**kol**-loj-ee) (noun) Gynaecology is the branch of medical science concerned with the female reproductive system. **gynaecologist** (noun), **gynaecological** (adjective).

gypsy, gypsies; also spelled **gipsy** (noun) A gypsy is a member of a race of people, originally from India but now found mainly in Europe, who travel around in caravans.

H h

habit, habits 1 (noun) A habit is something that you do often, e.g. *He got into the habit of eating out.* **2** A habit is also something that you keep doing and find it difficult to stop doing, e.g. *a 20-a-day smoking habit.* **3** A monk's or nun's habit is a garment like a loose dress. **habitual** (adjective), **habitually** (adverb).

habitat, habitats (noun) The habitat of a plant or animal is its natural home.

hack, hacks, hacking, hacked 1 (verb) If you hack at something, you cut it using rough strokes. **2** (noun) A hack is a writer or journalist who produces work fast without worrying about quality.

hacker, hackers (noun; an informal word) A hacker is someone who uses a computer to break into the computer system of a company or government.

hackles (plural noun) A dog's hackles are the hairs on the back of its neck which rise when it is angry.

hackneyed (adjective) A hackneyed phrase is meaningless because it has been used too often.

hacksaw, hacksaws (noun) A hacksaw is a small saw with a narrow blade set in a frame.

haddock (noun) A haddock is an edible sea fish.

haemoglobin (pronounced hee-moh-**gloh**-bin) (noun) Haemoglobin is a substance in red blood cells which carries oxygen round the body.

haemorrhage (pronounced **hem**-er-rij) (noun) A haemorrhage is serious bleeding especially inside a person's body.

haemorrhoids (pronounced **hem**-er-roydz) (plural noun) Haemorrhoids are painful lumps around the anus that are caused by swollen veins.

hag, hags (noun; an offensive word) A hag is an ugly old woman.

haggard (adjective) A person who is haggard looks very tired and ill.

haggis (noun) Haggis is a Scottish dish made of the internal organs of a calf or sheep, chopped up and boiled together with oatmeal and spices in a skin.

haggle, haggles, haggling, haggled (verb) If you haggle with someone, you argue with them, usually about the cost of something.

hail, hails, hailing, hailed 1 (noun) Hail is frozen rain. **2** (verb) When it is hailing, frozen rain is falling. **3** (noun) A hail of things is a lot of them falling together, e.g. *a hail of bullets... a hail of protest.* **4** (verb) If someone hails you, they call you to attract your attention or greet you, e.g. *He hailed a taxi.*

hair, hairs (noun) Hair consists of the long, threadlike strands that grow from the skin of animals and humans.

haircut, haircuts (noun) A haircut is the cutting of someone's hair; also the style in which it is cut.

hairdo, hairdos (noun) A hairdo is a hairstyle.

hairdresser, hairdressers (noun) A hairdresser is someone who is trained to cut and style people's hair; also a shop where this is done. **hairdressing** (noun or adjective).

hairline, hairlines 1 (noun) Your hairline is the edge of the area on your forehead where your hair grows. **2** (adjective) A hairline crack is so fine that you can hardly see it.

hairpin, hairpins 1 (noun) A hairpin is a U-shaped wire used to hold hair in position. **2** (adjective) A hairpin bend is a U-shaped bend in the road.

hair-raising (adjective) very frightening or exciting.

hairstyle, hairstyles (noun) Someone's hairstyle is the way in which their hair is arranged or cut.

hairy, hairier, hairiest 1 (adjective) covered in a lot of hair. **2** (an informal use) difficult, exciting, and rather frightening, e.g. *He had lived through many hairy adventures.*

hake, hakes (noun) A hake is an edible sea fish related to the cod.

halcyon (pronounced **hal**-see-on) **1** (adjective; a literary word) peaceful, gentle, and calm, e.g *halcyon hues of ochre and olive.* **2** (phrase) **Halcyon days** are a happy and carefree time in the past, e.g *memories of halcyon days in the sun.*

half, halves 1 (noun, adjective, or adverb) Half refers to one of two equal parts that make up a whole, e.g. *the two halves* *of the brain... They chatted for another half hour... The bottle was only half full.* **2** (adverb) You can use half to say that something is only partly true, e.g. *I half expected him to explode in anger.*

half-baked (adjective; an informal word) Half-baked ideas or plans have not been properly thought out.

half board (noun) Half board at a hotel includes breakfast and dinner but not lunch.

half-brother, half-brothers (noun) Your half-brother is the son of either your mother or your father but not of your other parent.

half-hearted (adjective) showing no real effort or enthusiasm.

half-sister, half-sisters (noun) Your half-sister is the daughter of either your mother or your father but not of your other parent.

half-timbered (adjective) A half-timbered building has a framework of wooden beams showing in the walls.

half-time (noun) Half-time is a short break between two parts of a game when the players have a rest.

halfway (adverb) at the middle of the distance between two points in place or time, e.g. *He stopped halfway down the ladder... We were halfway through the term.*

halibut, halibuts (noun) Halibut is a large edible fish.

hall, halls 1 (noun) A hall is the room just inside the front entrance of a house which leads into other rooms. **2** A hall is also a large room or building used for public meetings, concerts, plays, and exhibitions.

hallmark, hallmarks 1 (noun) The hallmark of a person, group, or organization is their most typical quality or feature, e.g. *A warm, hospitable welcome is the hallmark of island people.* **2** A hallmark is an official mark on gold or silver indicating the quality of the metal.

hallowed (pronounced **hal**-lode) (adjective) respected as being holy, e.g. *hallowed ground.*

Halloween (noun) Halloween is October 31st, and is celebrated by children dressing up, often as ghosts and witches.

hallucinate, hallucinates, hallucinating, hallucinated (pronounced hal-**loo**-sin-ate) (verb) If you hallucinate, you see strange things in your mind because of illness or drugs. **hallucination** (noun), **hallucinatory** (adjective).

halo, haloes or **halos** (noun) A halo is a circle of light around the head of a holy figure.

halt, halts, halting, halted 1 (verb) To halt when moving means to stop. **2** To halt growth, development, or action means to stop it. **3** (noun) A halt is a short standstill.

halter, halters (noun) A halter is a strap fastened round a horse's head so that it can be led easily.

halve, halves, halving, halved (pronounced **hahv**) **1** (verb) If you halve something, you divide it into two equal parts. **2** To halve something also means to reduce its size or amount by half.

ham, hams 1 (noun) Ham is

meat from the hind leg of a pig, salted, cured, and usually bought ready-cooked. **2** A ham is a bad actor who exaggerates emotions and gestures. **3** A ham is also someone who is very interested in amateur radio.

hamburger, hamburgers (noun) A hamburger is a flat disc of minced meat, seasoned and fried; often eaten in a bread roll.

hammer, hammers, hammering, hammered 1 (noun) A hammer is a tool consisting of a heavy piece of metal at the end of a handle, used for hitting nails into things. **2** (verb) If you hammer something, you hit it repeatedly, with a hammer or with your fist. **3** If you hammer an idea into someone, you keep repeating it and telling them about it. **4** (an informal use) If you hammer someone, you criticize, attack, or defeat them severely.

hammock, hammocks (noun) A hammock is a piece of net or canvas hung between two supports and used as a bed.

hamper, hampers, hampering, hampered 1 (noun) A hamper is a rectangular wicker basket with a lid, used for carrying food. **2** (verb) If you hamper someone, you make it difficult for them to move or progress.

hamster, hamsters (noun) A hamster is a small furry rodent which is often kept as a pet.

hamstring, hamstrings (noun) Your hamstring is a tendon behind your knee joining your thigh muscles to the bones of your lower leg.

hand, hands, handing, handed 1 (noun) Your hand is the part of your body beyond the wrist, with four fingers and a thumb. **2** Your hand is also your writing style. **3** The hand of someone in a situation is their influence or the part they play in it, e.g. *He had a hand in its design.* **4** If you give someone a hand, you help them to do something. **5** When an audience gives someone a big hand, they applaud. **6** The hands of a clock or watch are the pointers that point to the numbers. **7** In cards, your hand is the cards you are holding. **8** (verb) If you hand something to someone, you give it to them. **9** (phrases) Something that is **at hand, to hand,** or **on hand** is available, close by, and ready for use. **10** You use **on the one hand** to introduce the first part of an argument or discussion with two different points of view. **11** You use **on the other hand** to introduce the second part of an argument or discussion with two different points of view. **12** If you do something **by hand,** you do it using your hands rather than a machine. **hand down** (verb) Something that is handed down is passed from one generation to another.

handbag, handbags (noun) A handbag is a small bag used mainly by women to carry money and personal items.

handbook, handbooks (noun) A handbook is a book giving information and instructions about something.

handcuff, handcuffs (noun)

Handcuffs are two metal rings linked by a chain which are locked around a prisoner's wrists.

handful, handfuls 1 (noun) A handful of something is the amount of it you can hold in your hand, e.g. *He picked up a handful of seeds.* **2** A handful is also a small quantity, e.g. *Only a handful of people knew.* **3** Someone who is a handful is difficult to control, e.g. *He is a bit of a handful.*

handicap, handicaps, handicapping, handicapped 1 (noun) A handicap is a physical or mental disability. **2** A handicap is also something that makes it difficult for you to achieve something. **3** In sport or a competition, a handicap is a disadvantage or advantage given to competitors according to their skill, in order to give them an equal chance of winning. **4** (verb) If something handicaps someone, it makes it difficult for them to achieve something.

handicraft, handicrafts (noun) Handicrafts are activities such as embroidery or pottery which involve making things with your hands; also the items produced.

handiwork (noun) Your handiwork is something that you have done or made yourself.

handkerchief, handkerchiefs (noun) A handkerchief is a small square of fabric used for blowing your nose.

handle, handles, handling, handled 1 (noun) The handle of an object is the part by which it is held or controlled. **2** A handle is also a small lever used to open and close a door or window. **3** (verb) If you handle an object, you hold it in your hands to examine it. **4** If you handle something, you deal with it or control it, e.g. *I have learned how to handle pressure.*

handlebar, handlebars (noun) Handlebars are the bar and handles at the front of a bicycle, used for steering.

handout, handouts 1 (noun) A handout is a gift of food, clothing, or money given to a poor person. **2** A handout is also a piece of paper giving information about something.

hand-picked (adjective) carefully chosen, e.g. *a hand-picked team of superfit men and women.*

handset, handsets (noun) The handset of a telephone is the part that you speak into and listen with.

handshake, handshakes (noun) A handshake is the grasping and shaking of a person's hand by another person.

handsome 1 (adjective) very attractive in appearance. **2** large and generous, e.g. *a handsome profit.* **handsomely** (adverb).

handwriting (noun) Someone's handwriting is their style of writing as it looks on the page.

handy, handier, handiest 1 (adjective) conveniently near. **2** easy to handle or use. **3** skilful.

hang, hangs, hanging, hung The past tense and past participle of sense 5 is **hanged. 1** (verb) If you hang something somewhere, you attach it to a high point. If it is hanging there, it is attached by its top to something, e.g. *His jacket hung from a hook behind the door.* **2** If a future event or possibility is hanging over you, it worries or frightens you, e.g. *She has an eviction notice hanging over her.* **3** When you hang wallpaper, you stick it onto a wall. **4** (phrase) When you **get the hang of something,** you understand it and are able to do it. **5** (verb) To hang someone means to kill them by suspending them by a rope around the neck. **hang about** or **hang around 1** (verb; an informal use) To hang about or hang around means to wait somewhere. **2** To hang about or hang around with someone means to spend a lot of time with them. **hang on 1** (verb) If you hang on to something, you hold it tightly or keep it. **2** (an informal use) To hang on means to wait. **hang up** (verb) When you hang up, you put down the receiver to end a telephone call.

hangar, hangars (noun) A hangar is a large building where aircraft are kept.

hanger, hangers (noun) A hanger is a coat hanger.

hanger-on, hangers-on (noun) A hanger-on is an unwelcome follower of an important person.

hang-glider, hang-gliders (noun) A hang-glider is an unpowered aircraft consisting of a large frame covered in fabric, from which the pilot hangs in a harness.

hangover, hangovers (noun) A hangover is a feeling of sickness and headache after drinking too much alcohol.

hang-up, hang-ups (noun) A hang-up about something is a continual feeling of embarrassment or fear about it.

hanker, hankers, hankering, hankered (verb) If you hanker after something, you continually want it. **hankering** (noun).

hanky, hankies (noun) A hanky is a handkerchief.

haphazard (pronounced hap-**haz**-ard) (adjective) not organized or planned. **haphazardly** (adverb).

hapless (adjective; a literary word) unlucky.

happen, happens, happening, happened 1 (verb) When something happens, it occurs or takes place. **2** If you happen to do something, you do it by chance. **happening** (noun).

happiness (noun) Happiness is a feeling of great contentment or pleasure.

happy, happier, happiest 1 (adjective) feeling, showing, or producing contentment or pleasure, e.g. *a happy smile... a happy atmosphere.* **2** satisfied that something is right, e.g. *I wasn't very happy about the layout.* **3** willing, e.g. *I would be happy to help.* **4** fortunate or lucky, e.g. *a happy coincidence.* **happily** (adverb).

happy-go-lucky (adjective) carefree and unconcerned.

harangue, harangues, haranguing, harangued (pronounced har-**rang**) **1** (noun) A harangue is a long, forceful, passionate speech. **2** (verb) To harangue someone means to talk to them at length passionately and forcefully about something.

harass, harasses, harassing, harassed (pronounced **har**-rass) (verb) If someone harasses you, they trouble or annoy you continually. **harassed** (adjective), **harassment** (noun).

harbinger, harbingers (pronounced **har**-bin-jer) (noun) A harbinger of a future event is a person or thing that announces or indicates the approach of something.

harbour, harbours, harbouring, harboured 1 (noun) A harbour is a protected area of deep water where boats can be moored. **2** (verb) To harbour someone means to hide them secretly in your house. **3** If you harbour a feeling, you have it for a long time, e.g. *She's still harbouring great bitterness towards him.*

hard, harder, hardest 1 (adjective or adverb) Something that is hard is firm, solid, or stiff, e.g. *a hard piece of cheese... The ground was baked hard.* **2** requiring a lot of effort, e.g. *hard work... They tried hard to attract tourists.* **3** (adjective) difficult, e.g. *These are hard times.* **4** Someone who is hard has no kindness or pity, e.g. *Don't be hard on him... She's as hard as nails.* **5** A hard colour or voice is harsh and unpleasant. **6** Hard evidence or facts can be proved to be true. **7** Hard water contains a lot of lime, leaves a coating on kettles and does not easily produce a lather. **8** Hard drugs are very strong illegal drugs. **9** Hard drink is strong alcohol. **10** (adverb) An event that follows hard upon something takes place immediately afterwards. **hardness** (noun).

hard and fast (adjective) fixed and not able to be changed, e.g. *hard and fast rules.*

hardback, hardbacks (noun) A hardback is a book with a stiff cover.

hard core (noun) The hard core in an organization is the group of people who most resist change.

harden, hardens, hardening, hardened (verb) To harden means to become hard or get harder. **hardening** (noun), **hardened** (adjective).

hard labour (noun) Hard labour is physical work which is difficult and tiring. It is used in some countries as a punishment for a crime.

hardly 1 (adverb) almost not or not quite, e.g. *I could hardly believe it.* **2** certainly not, e.g. *It's hardly a secret.*

hard-nosed (adjective) tough, practical, and realistic.

hard of hearing (adjective) not able to hear properly.

hardship, hardships (noun) Hardship is a time or situation of suffering and difficulty.

hard shoulder, hard shoulders (noun) The hard shoulder is the area at the edge of a motorway where a driver can stop in the event of a breakdown.

hard up (adjective; an informal expression) having hardly any money.

hardware 1 (noun) Hardware is tools and equipment for use in the home and garden. **2** Hardware is also computer machinery rather than computer programs.

hard-wearing (adjective) strong, well-made, and long-lasting.

hardwood, hardwoods (noun) Hardwood is strong, hard wood from a tree such as an oak; also the tree itself.

hardy, hardier, hardiest (adjective) tough and able to endure very difficult or cold conditions, e.g. *a hardy race of pioneers.*

hare, hares, haring, hared 1 (noun) A hare is an animal like a large rabbit, but with longer ears and legs. **2** (verb) To hare about means to run very fast, e.g. *He hared off down the corridor.*

harem, harems (pronounced har-**reem**) (noun) A harem is a group of wives or mistresses of one man, especially in Muslim societies.

hark, harks, harking, harked 1 (verb; an old-fashioned use) To hark means to listen. **2** To hark back to something in the past means to refer back to it or recall it.

harlequin (pronounced **har**-lik-win) (adjective) having many different colours.

harm, harms, harming, harmed 1 (verb) To harm someone or something means to injure or damage them. **2** (noun) Harm is injury or damage.

harmful (adjective) having a bad effect on something, e.g. *Whilst most stress is harmful, some is beneficial.*

harmless 1 (adjective) safe to use or be near. **2** unlikely to cause problems or annoyance, e.g. *He's harmless really.* **harmlessly** (adverb).

harmonic (adjective) using musical harmony.

harmonica, harmonicas (noun) A harmonica is a small musical instrument which you play by blowing and sucking while moving it across your lips.

harmonious (pronounced har-**moh**-nee-uss) **1** (adjective) showing agreement, peacefulness, and friendship, e.g. *a harmonious relationship.* **2** consisting of parts which blend well together making an attractive whole, e.g. *the harmonious notes of a string quartet.* **harmoniously** (adverb).

harmony, harmonies 1 (noun) Harmony is a state of peaceful agreement and cooperation, e.g. *the promotion of racial harmony.* **2** In music, harmony is the pleasant combination of two or more notes played at the same time.

harness, harnesses, harnessing, harnessed 1 (noun) A harness is a set of straps and fittings fastened round a horse so that it can pull a vehicle, or fastened round someone's body to attach something, e.g. *a safety harness.* **2** (verb) If you harness something, you bring it under control to use it, e.g. *harnessing public opinion.*

harp, harps, harping, harped 1 (noun) A harp is a musical instrument consisting of a triangular frame with vertical strings which you pluck with your fingers. **2** (verb) If someone harps on something, they keep talking about it, especially in a boring way.

harpoon, harpoons (noun) A harpoon is a barbed spear attached to a rope, thrown or fired from a gun and used for catching whales or large sea fish.

harpsichord, harpsichords (noun) A harpsichord is a keyboard instrument in which the strings are plucked mechanically when the keys are pressed.

harrowing (adjective) very upsetting or disturbing, e.g. *a harrowing experience.*

harsh, harsher, harshest (adjective) severe, difficult, and unpleasant, e.g. *harsh weather conditions... harsh criticism.* **harshly** (adverb), **harshness** (noun).

harvest, harvests, harvesting, harvested 1 (noun) The harvest is the cutting and gathering of a crop; also the ripe crop when it is gathered and the time of gathering. **2** (verb) To harvest food means to gather it when it is ripe. **harvester** (noun).

has-been, has-beens (noun; an informal expression) A has-been is a person who is no longer important or successful.

hash 1 (phrase) If you **make a hash of** a job, you do it badly. **2** (noun) Hash is a dish made of small pieces of meat and vegetables cooked together. **3** (an informal use) Hash is also hashish.

hashish (pronounced **hash**-eesh) (noun) Hashish is a drug made from the hemp plant. It is usually smoked, and is illegal in many countries.

hassle, hassles, hassling, hassled 1 (noun; an informal word) Something that is a hassle is difficult or causes trouble. **2** (verb) If you hassle someone, you annoy them by repeatedly asking them to do something.

haste (noun) Haste is doing something quickly, especially too quickly.

hasten, hastens, hastening, hastened (pronounced **hay**-sn) (verb) To hasten means to move quickly or do something quickly.

hasty, hastier, hastiest (adjective) done or happening suddenly and quickly, often without enough care or thought. **hastily** (adverb).

hat, hats (noun) A hat is a covering for the head.

hatch, hatches, hatching, hatched 1 (verb) When an egg hatches, or when a bird or reptile hatches, the egg breaks open and the young bird or reptile emerges. **2** To hatch a plot means to plan it. **3** (noun) A hatch is a covered opening in a floor, wall, or ceiling.

hatchback, hatchbacks (noun) A hatchback is a car with a door at the back which opens upwards.

hatchet, hatchets 1 (noun) A hatchet is a small axe. **2** (phrase) To **bury the hatchet** means to resolve a disagreement and become friends again.

hate, hates, hating, hated 1 (verb) If you hate someone or something, you have a strong dislike for them. **2** (noun) Hate is a strong dislike.

hatred (pronounced **hay**-trid) (noun) Hatred is an extremely strong feeling of dislike.

hat trick, hat tricks (noun) In

sport, a hat trick is a series of three achievements, for example when a footballer scores three goals in a match.

haughty, haughtier, haughtiest (rhymes with **naughty**) (adjective) showing excessive pride, e.g. *He behaved in a haughty manner.* **haughtily** (adverb).

haul, hauls, hauling, hauled 1 (verb) To haul something somewhere means to pull it with great effort. **2** (noun) A haul is a quantity of something obtained, e.g. *a good haul of fish.* **3** (phrase) Something that you describe as **a long haul** takes a lot of time and effort to achieve, e.g. *So women began the long haul to equality.*

haulage (pronounced **hawl**-lij) (noun) Haulage is the business or cost of transporting goods by road.

haunches (plural noun) Your haunches are your buttocks and the tops of your legs, e.g. *He squatted on his haunches.*

haunt, haunts, haunting, haunted 1 (verb) If a ghost haunts a place, it is seen or heard there regularly. **2** If a memory or a fear haunts you, it continually worries you. **3** (noun) A person's favourite haunt is a place they like to visit often.

haunted 1 (adjective) regularly visited by a ghost, e.g. *a haunted house.* **2** very worried or troubled, e.g. *a haunted expression.*

haunting (adjective) extremely beautiful or sad so that it makes a lasting impression on you, e.g. *haunting landscapes.*

have, has, having, had 1 (verb) Have is an auxiliary verb, used to form the past tense or to express completed actions, e.g. *They have never met... I have lost it.* **2** If you have something, you own or possess it, e.g. *We have two tickets for the concert.* **3** If you have something, you experience it, it happens to you, or you are affected by it, e.g. *I have an idea!... He had a marvellous time.* **4** To have a child or baby animal means to give birth to it, e.g. *When is she having the baby?* **5** (phrases) If you **have to** do something, you must do it. If you **had better** do something, you ought to do it.

haven, havens (pronounced **hay**-ven) (noun) A haven is a safe place.

havoc 1 (noun) Havoc is disorder and confusion. **2** (phrase) To **play havoc** with something means to cause great disorder and confusion, e.g. *Food allergies often play havoc with the immune system.*

hawk, hawks, hawking, hawked 1 (noun) A hawk is a large bird with a short, hooked bill, sharp claws and very good eyesight. Hawks hunt small birds and animals. **2** (verb) To hawk goods means to sell them by taking them around from place to place.

hawthorn, hawthorns (noun) A hawthorn is a small, thorny tree producing white blossom and red berries.

hay (noun) Hay is grass which has been cut and dried and is used as animal feed.

hay fever (noun) Hay fever is an allergy to pollen and grass, causing sneezing, a blocked nose, and watering eyes.

haystack, haystacks (noun) A haystack is a large, firmly built pile of hay, usually covered and left out in the open.

hazard, hazards, hazarding, hazarded 1 (noun) A hazard is something which could be dangerous to you. **2** (verb) If you hazard something, you put it at risk, e.g. *hazarding the health of his crew.* **3** (phrase) If you **hazard a guess,** you make a guess. **hazardous** (adjective).

haze (noun) If there is a haze, you cannot see clearly because there is moisture, dust, or smoke in the air.

hazel, hazels 1 (noun) A hazel is a small tree producing edible nuts. **2** (adjective) greenish brown in colour.

hazy, hazier, haziest (adjective) dim or vague, e.g. *hazy sunshine... a hazy memory.*

he (pronoun) 'He' is used to refer to a man, boy, or male animal or to any person whose sex is not mentioned.

head, heads, heading, headed 1 (noun) Your head is the part of your body which has your eyes, brain, and mouth in it. **2** Your head is also your mind and mental abilities, e.g. *He has a head for figures.* **3** The head of something is the top, start, or most important end, e.g. *at the head of the table.* **4** The head of a group or organization is the leader or person in charge. **5** (verb) To head a group or organization means to be the leader or be in charge, e.g. *Harmon heads the help organization.* **6** (noun) The head on beer is the layer of froth on the top. **7** The head on a computer or tape recorder is the part that can read, write, or erase information. **8** (verb) To head in a particular direction means to move in that direction, e.g. *She is heading for a breakdown.* **9** To head a ball means to hit it with your head. **10** (noun) When you toss a coin, the side called heads is the one with the head on it. **11** (phrase) If someone **bites** or **snaps your head off,** they speak to you sharply and angrily. **12** If you give some information **off the top of your head,** you give it from memory. **13** If you **lose your head,** you panic. **14** If you say that someone is **off their head,** you mean that they are mad or very stupid. **15** If something is **over someone's head,** it is too difficult for them to understand.

head off (verb) If you head off someone or something, you make them change direction or prevent something from happening, e.g. *He hopes to head off a public squabble.*

headache, headaches 1 (noun) A headache is a pain in your head. **2** Something that is a headache is causing a lot of difficulty or worry, e.g. *Delays in receiving money owed is a major headache for small firms.*

header, headers (noun) A header in football is hitting the ball with your head.

heading, headings (noun) A heading is a piece of writing that is written or printed at the top of a page.

headland, headlands (noun) A

headland is a narrow piece of land jutting out into the sea.

headlight, headlights (noun) The headlights on a motor vehicle are the large powerful lights at the front.

headline, headlines 1 (noun) A newspaper headline is the title of a newspaper article printed in large, bold type. **2** The headlines are the main points of the radio or television news.

headmaster, headmasters (noun) A headmaster is a man who is the head teacher of a school.

headmistress, headmistresses (noun) A headmistress is a woman who is the head teacher of a school.

headphones (plural noun) Headphones are a pair of small speakers which you wear over your ears to listen to recorded music or the radio without other people hearing it.

headquarters (noun) The headquarters of an organization is the main place or building from which it is run.

headroom (noun) Headroom is the amount of space below a roof or surface under which an object must pass or fit.

headstone, headstones (noun) A headstone is a large stone standing at one end of a grave and showing the name of the person buried there.

headstrong (adjective) determined to do something in your own way and ignoring other people's advice.

head teacher, head teachers (noun) The head teacher of a school is the teacher who is in charge of it.

headway (phrase) If you are **making headway,** you are making progress.

headwind, headwinds (noun) A headwind is a wind blowing in the opposite direction to the way you are travelling.

heady (adjective) extremely exciting, e.g. *the heady days of the civil rights era.*

heal, heals, healing, healed (verb) If something heals or if you heal it, it becomes healthy or normal again, e.g. *He had a nasty wound which had not healed properly.* **healer** (noun).

health (noun) Health is the normally good condition of someone's body and the extent to which it is free from illness, e.g. *Vitamins are essential for health.*

health food, health foods (noun) Health food is food which is free from added chemicals and is considered to be good for your health.

healthy, healthier, healthiest 1 (adjective) Someone who is healthy is fit and strong and does not have any diseases. **2** Something that is healthy is good for you and likely to make you fit and strong, e.g. *a healthy diet.* **3** An organization or system that is healthy is successful, e.g. *a healthy economy.* **healthily** (adverb).

heap, heaps, heaping, heaped 1 (noun) A heap of things is a pile of them. **2** (an informal use) Heaps of something means plenty of it, e.g. *His performance earned him heaps of praise.* **3** (verb) If you heap things, you pile them up. **4** To heap something such as praise on someone means to give them a lot of it.

hear, hears, hearing, heard 1 (verb) When you hear sounds, you are aware of them because they reach your ears. **2** When you hear from someone, they write to you or phone you. **3** When a judge hears a case, he or she listens to it in court in order to make a decision on it. **4** (phrase) If you say that you **won't hear of** something, you mean you refuse to allow it. **hear out** (verb) If you hear someone out, you listen to all they have to say without interrupting.

hearing, hearings 1 (noun) Hearing is the sense which makes it possible for you to be aware of sounds, e.g. *My hearing is poor.* **2** A hearing is a court trial or official meeting to hear facts about an incident. **3** If someone gives you a hearing, they let you give your point of view and listen to you.

hearsay (noun) Hearsay is information that you have heard from other people rather than something that you know personally to be true.

hearse, hearses (rhymes with **verse**) (noun) A hearse is a large car that carries the coffin at a funeral.

heart, hearts 1 (noun) Your heart is the organ in your chest that pumps the blood around your body. **2** Your heart is also thought of as the centre of your emotions. **3** Heart is courage, determination, or enthusiasm, e.g. *They were losing heart.* **4** The heart of something is the most central and important part of it. **5** A heart is a shape similar to a heart, used especially as a symbol of love. **6** Hearts is one of the four suits in a pack of playing cards. It is marked by a red heart-shaped symbol.

heartache, heartaches (noun) Heartache is very great sadness and emotional suffering.

heart attack, heart attacks (noun) A heart attack is a serious medical condition in which the heart suddenly beats irregularly or stops completely. Death can result if medical attention is not given quickly.

heartbreak, heartbreaks (noun) Heartbreak is great sadness and emotional suffering. **heartbreaking** (adjective).

heartbroken (adjective) very sad and emotionally upset, e.g. *She was heartbroken at his death.*

heartburn (noun) Heartburn is a painful burning sensation in your chest, caused by indigestion.

heartening (adjective) encouraging or uplifting, e.g. *heartening news.*

heart failure (noun) Heart failure is a serious condition in which someone's heart does not work as well as it should, sometimes stopping completely.

heartfelt (adjective) sincerely and deeply felt, e.g. *Our heartfelt sympathy goes out to the family.*

hearth, hearths (pronounced **harth**) (noun) A hearth is the floor of a fireplace.

heartless (adjective) cruel and

unkind.

heart-rending (adjective) causing great sadness and pity, e.g. *a heart-rending story.*

heart-throb, heart-throbs (noun) A heart-throb is someone who is attractive to a lot of people.

heart-to-heart, heart-to-hearts (noun) A heart-to-heart is a discussion in which two people talk about their deepest feelings.

hearty, heartier, heartiest 1 (adjective) cheerful and enthusiastic, e.g. *hearty congratulations.* **2** strongly felt, e.g. *a hearty dislike of dogs.* **3** A hearty meal is large and satisfying. **heartily** (adverb).

heat, heats, heating, heated 1 (noun) Heat is warmth or the quality of being hot; also the temperature of something that is warm or hot. **2** (verb) To heat something means to raise its temperature. **3** (noun) Heat is strength of feeling, especially of anger or excitement. **4** A heat is one of a series of contests in a competition. The winners of a heat go forward to play in the next round of the competition. **5** (phrase) When a female animal is **on heat,** she is ready for mating. **heater** (noun).

heath, heaths (noun) A heath is an area of open land covered with rough grass or heather.

heathen, heathens (noun; an old-fashioned word) A heathen is someone who has no religion or who does not believe in one of the established religions.

heather (noun) Heather is a low, spreading plant with small, spiky leaves and pink, purple, or white flowers. Heather grows wild on hills and moorland.

heating (noun) Heating is the equipment used to heat a building; also the process and cost of running the equipment to provide heat.

heatwave, heatwaves (noun) A heatwave is a period of time during which the weather is much hotter than usual.

heave, heaves, heaving, heaved 1 (verb) To heave something means to pull, push, or throw it with a lot of effort. **2** (noun) If you give something a heave, you pull, push, or throw it with a lot of effort. **3** (verb) If your stomach heaves, you vomit or suddenly feel sick. **4** If you heave a sigh, you sigh loudly.

heaven, heavens 1 (noun) Heaven is a place of happiness where God is believed to live and where good people are believed to go when they die. **2** If you describe a situation or place as heaven, you mean that it is wonderful, e.g. *The pudding was pure heaven.* **3** (phrase) You say **'Good heavens'** to express surprise.

heavenly 1 (adjective) relating to heaven, e.g. *a heavenly choir.* **2** (an informal use) wonderful, e.g. *his heavenly blue eyes.*

heavy, heavier, heaviest; heavies 1 (adjective) great in weight or force, e.g. *How heavy are you?... a heavy blow.* **2** great in degree or amount, e.g. *heavy casualties.* **3** solid and thick in appearance, e.g. *heavy shoes.* **4** using a lot of something quickly, e.g. *The van is heavy on petrol.* **5** serious and difficult to deal with or understand, e.g. *It all got a bit heavy when the police arrived... a heavy speech.* **6** Food that is heavy is solid and difficult to digest, e.g. *a heavy meal.* **7** When it is heavy, the weather is hot, humid, and still. **8** Someone with a heavy heart is very sad. **9** (noun; an informal use) A heavy is a large, strong man employed to protect someone or something. **heavily** (adverb), **heaviness** (noun).

heavy-duty (adjective) Heavy-duty equipment is strong and hard-wearing.

heavy-handed (adjective) showing a lack of care or thought and using too much authority, e.g. *heavy-handed police tactics.*

heavyweight, heavyweights 1 (noun) A heavyweight is a boxer in the heaviest weight group. **2** A heavyweight is also an important person with a lot of influence.

Hebrew, Hebrews (pronounced **hee**-broo) **1** (noun) Hebrew is an ancient language now spoken in Israel, where it is the official language. **2** In the past, the Hebrews were Hebrew-speaking Jews who lived in Israel. **3** (adjective) relating to the Hebrews and their customs.

heckle, heckles, heckling, heckled (verb) If members of an audience heckle a speaker, they interrupt and shout rude remarks. **heckler** (noun).

hectare, hectares (noun) A hectare is a unit for measuring areas of land. One hectare is equal to 10,000 square metres or about 2.471 acres.

hectic (adjective) involving a lot of rushed activity, e.g. *a hectic schedule.*

hedge, hedges, hedging, hedged 1 (noun) A hedge is a row of bushes forming a barrier or boundary. **2** (verb) If you hedge against something unpleasant happening, you protect yourself. **3** If you hedge, you avoid answering a question or dealing with a problem. **4** (phrase) If you **hedge your bets,** you support two or more people or courses of action to avoid the risk of losing a lot.

hedgehog, hedgehogs (noun) A hedgehog is a small, brown nocturnal animal with sharp spikes covering its back.

hedonism (pronounced **hee**-dn-izm) (noun) Hedonism is the belief that gaining pleasure is the most important thing in life. **hedonistic** (adjective).

heed, heeds, heeding, heeded 1 (verb) If you heed someone's advice, you pay attention to it. **2** (noun) If you take or pay heed to something, you give it careful attention.

heel, heels, heeling, heeled 1 (noun) Your heel is the back part of your foot. **2** The heel of a shoe or sock is the part that fits over your heel. **3** (verb) To heel a pair of shoes means to put a new piece on the heel. **4** (phrase) A person or place that looks **down at heel** looks untidy and in poor condition.

hefty, heftier, heftiest (adjective) of great size, force, or weight, e.g. *a hefty fine... hefty volumes.*

height, heights 1 (noun) The height of an object is its measurement from the bottom to the top. **2** A height is a high position or place, e.g. *Their nesting rarely takes place at any great height.* **3** The height of something is its peak, or the time when it is most successful or intense, e.g. *the height of the tourist season... at the height of his career.*

heighten, heightens, heightening, heightened (verb) If something heightens a feeling or experience, it increases its intensity.

heinous (pronounced **hay**-nuss or **hee**-nuss) (adjective) evil and terrible, e.g. *heinous crimes.*

heir, heirs (pronounced **air**) (noun) A person's heir is the person who is entitled to inherit their property or title.

heiress, heiresses (pronounced **air**-iss) (noun) An heiress is a female with the right to inherit property or a title.

heirloom, heirlooms (pronounced **air**-loom) (noun) An heirloom is something belonging to a family that has been passed from one generation to another.

helicopter, helicopters (noun) A helicopter is an aircraft without wings, but with rotating blades above it which enable it to take off vertically, hover, and fly.

helium (pronounced **hee**-lee-um) (noun) Helium is a gas that is lighter than air and that is used to fill balloons.

hell 1 (noun) Hell is the place where souls of evil people are believed to go to be punished after death. **2** (an informal use) If you say that something is hell, you mean it is very unpleasant. **3** (interjection) 'Hell' is also a swearword.

hell-bent (adjective) determined to do something whatever the consequences.

hellish (adjective; an informal word) very unpleasant.

hello You say 'Hello' as a greeting or when you answer the phone.

helm, helms 1 (noun) The helm on a boat is the position from which it is steered and the wheel or tiller. **2** (phrase) **At the helm** means in a position of leadership or control.

helmet, helmets (noun) A helmet is a hard hat worn to protect the head.

help, helps, helping, helped 1 (verb) To help someone means to make something easier, better, or quicker for them. **2** (noun) If you need or give help, you need or give assistance. **3** A help is someone or something that helps you, e.g. *He really is a good help.* **4** (phrase) If you **help yourself** to something, you take it. **5** If you **can't help** something, you cannot control it or change it, e.g. *I can't help feeling sorry for him.* **helper** (noun).

helpful 1 (adjective) If someone is helpful, they help you by doing something for you. **2** Something that is helpful makes a situation more pleasant or easier to tolerate. **helpfully** (adverb).

helping, helpings (noun) A helping is an amount of food

that you get in a single serving.

helpless 1 (adjective) unable to cope on your own, e.g. *a helpless child.* **2** weak or powerless, e.g. *helpless despair.* **helplessly** (adverb), **helplessness** (noun).

hem, hems, hemming, hemmed 1 (noun) The hem of a garment is an edge which has been turned over and sewn in place. **2** (verb) To hem something means to make a hem on it. **hem in** (verb) If someone is hemmed in, they are surrounded and prevented from moving.

hemisphere, hemispheres (pronounced **hem**-iss-feer) (noun) A hemisphere is one half of the earth, the brain, or a sphere.

hemp (noun) Hemp is a tall plant, originally grown in Asia. Some varieties of it are used to make rope, and others to produce the drug cannabis.

hen, hens (noun) A hen is a female chicken; also any female bird.

hence 1 (adverb; a formal word) for this reason, e.g. *It sells more papers, hence more money is made.* **2** from now or from the time mentioned, e.g. *The convention is due to start two weeks hence.*

henceforth (adverb; a formal word) from this time onward, e.g. *His life henceforth was to revolve around her.*

henchman, henchmen (noun) The henchmen of a powerful person are the people employed to do violent or dishonest work for that person.

hepatitis (noun) Hepatitis is a serious infectious disease causing inflammation of the liver.

her (pronoun or adjective) 'Her' is used to refer to a woman, girl or female animal that has already been mentioned, or to show that something belongs to a particular female.

herald, heralds, heralding, heralded 1 (noun) In the past, a herald was a messenger. **2** (verb) Something that heralds a future event is a sign of that event.

herb, herbs (noun) A herb is a plant whose leaves are used in medicine or to flavour food. **herbal** (adjective), **herbalist** (noun).

herbivore, herbivores (noun) A herbivore is an animal that eats only plants.

herd, herds, herding, herded 1 (noun) A herd is a large group of animals. **2** (verb) To herd animals or people means to make them move together as a group.

here 1 (adverb) at, to, or in the place where you are, or the place mentioned or indicated. **2** (phrase) **Here and there** means in various unspecified places, e.g. *Scattered here and there were the gaunt winter skeletons of the trees.*

hereafter (adverb; a formal word) after this time or point, e.g. *the South China Morning Post (referred to hereafter as SCMP).*

hereby (adverb; a formal word) used in documents and statements to indicate that a declaration is official, e.g. *All leave is hereby cancelled.*

hereditary (adjective) passed on to a child from a parent, e.g. *a* *hereditary disease.*

heredity (noun) Heredity is the process by which characteristics are passed from parents to their children through the genes.

herein (adverb; a formal word) in this place or document.

heresy, heresies (pronounced **herr**-ess-ee) (noun) Heresy is belief or behaviour considered to be wrong because it disagrees with what is generally accepted, especially with regard to religion. **heretic** (noun), **heretical** (adjective).

herewith (adverb; a formal word) with this letter or document, e.g. *I herewith return your cheque.*

heritage (noun) A heritage is the possessions, traditions, or conditions that have been passed from one generation to another.

hermit, hermits (noun) A hermit is a person who lives alone with a simple way of life, especially for religious reasons.

hernia, hernias (pronounced **her**-nee-a) (noun) A hernia is a medical condition in which part of the intestine sticks through a weak point in the surrounding tissue. It is caused especially by muscular strain.

hero, heroes 1 (noun) A hero is the main male character in a book, film, or play. **2** A hero is also a person who has done something brave or good.

heroic (adjective) brave, courageous, and determined. **heroically** (adverb).

heroin (pronounced **herr**-oh-in) (noun) Heroin is a powerful drug formerly used as an anaesthetic and now taken illegally by some people for pleasure.

heroine, heroines (pronounced **herr**-oh-in) **1** (noun) A heroine is the main female character in a book, film, or play. **2** A heroine is also a woman who has done something brave or good.

heroism (pronounced **herr**-oh-i-zm) (noun) Heroism is great courage and bravery.

heron, herons (noun) A heron is a wading bird with very long legs and a long beak and neck.

herpes (pronounced **her**-peez) (noun) Herpes is a virus which causes painful red spots on the skin. There are several different types of herpes.

herring, herrings (noun) A herring is a silvery fish that lives in large shoals in northern seas.

hers (pronoun) Hers refers to something that belongs to or relates to a woman, girl, or female animal.

herself 1 (pronoun) Herself is used when the same woman, girl, or female animal does an action and is affected by it, e.g. *She pulled herself out of the water.* **2** Herself is used to emphasize 'she'.

hertz (noun) A hertz is a unit of frequency equal to one cycle per second.

hesitant (adjective) If you are hesitant, you do not do something immediately because you are uncertain, worried, or embarrassed. **hesitantly** (adverb).

hesitate, hesitates, hesitating, hesitated (verb) To hesitate means to pause or show uncertainty. **hesitation** (noun).

hessian (noun) Hessian is a thick, rough fabric made from jute and used for making sacks.

heterosexual, heterosexuals (pronounced het-roh-**seks**-yool) **1** (adjective) involving a sexual relationship between a man and a woman, e.g. *heterosexual couples.* **2** (noun) A heterosexual is a person who is sexually attracted to people of the opposite sex.

hewn (adjective) carved from a substance, e.g. *a cave, hewn out of the hillside.*

hexagon, hexagons (noun) A hexagon is a shape with six straight sides. **hexagonal** (adjective).

heyday (pronounced **hay**-day) (noun) The heyday of a person or thing is the period when they are most successful, powerful, or popular, e.g. *Hollywood in its heyday.*

hi 'Hi!' is an informal greeting.

hiatus (pronounced high-**ay**-tuss) (noun; a formal word) A hiatus is a pause or gap.

hibernate, hibernates, hibernating, hibernated (verb) Animals that hibernate spend the winter in a state like deep sleep. **hibernation** (noun).

hibiscus, hibiscuses (pronounced hie-**bis**-kuss) (noun) Hibiscus is a type of tropical shrub with brightly coloured flowers.

hiccup, hiccups, hiccupping, hiccupped (pronounced **hik**-kup) **1** (noun) Hiccups are short, uncontrolled choking sounds in your throat that you sometimes get if you have been eating or drinking too quickly. **2** (verb) When you hiccup, you make these little choking sounds. **3** (noun; an informal use) A hiccup is a minor problem.

hide, hides, hiding, hid, hidden **1** (verb) To hide something means to put it where it cannot be seen, or to prevent it from being discovered, e.g. *He was unable to hide his disappointment.* **2** (noun) A hide is the skin of a large animal.

hideous (pronounced **hid**-ee-uss) (adjective) extremely ugly or unpleasant. **hideously** (adverb).

hideout, hideouts (noun) A hideout is a hiding place.

hierarchy, hierarchies (pronounced **high**-er-ar-kee) (noun) A hierarchy is a system in which people or things are ranked or positioned according to how important they are. **hierarchical** (adjective).

hi-fi, hi-fis (noun) A hi-fi is a set of stereo equipment on which you can play records, tapes, and compact discs.

high, higher, highest; highs **1** (adjective or adverb) tall or a long way above the ground. **2** great in degree, quantity, or intensity, e.g. *high interest rates... There is a high risk of malignancy.* **3** towards the top of a scale of importance or quality, e.g. *high fashion.* **4** close to the top of a range of sound or notes, e.g. *the human voice reaches a very high pitch.* **5** (adjective; an informal use) Someone who is high on a drug such as marijuana is affected by having taken it. **6** (noun) A high is a high point or level, e.g. *Morale reached a new high.* **7** (an informal use) Someone who is on a high is in a very excited and optimistic mood.

highbrow (adjective) concerned with serious, intellectual subjects.

higher education (noun) Higher education is education at universities and colleges.

high jump (noun) The high jump is an athletics event involving jumping over a high bar.

highlands (plural noun) Highlands are mountainous or hilly areas of land.

highlight, highlights, highlighting, highlighted 1 (verb) If you highlight a point or problem, you emphasize and draw attention to it. **2** (noun) The highlight of something is the most interesting part of it, e.g. *His show was the highlight of the Festival.* **3** A highlight is a lighter area of a painting, showing where light shines on things. **4** Highlights are also light-coloured streaks in someone's hair.

highly 1 (adverb) extremely, e.g. *It is highly unlikely I'll be able to replace it.* **2** towards the top of a scale of importance, admiration, or respect, e.g. *She thought highly of him... highly qualified personnel.*

high-minded (adjective) Someone who is high-minded has strong moral principles.

Highness Highness is used in titles and forms of address for members of the royal family other than a king or queen, e.g. *Her Royal Highness, Princess Alexandra.*

high-pitched (adjective) A high-pitched sound or voice is high and often rather shrill.

high-rise (adjective) High-rise buildings are very tall and modern.

high school, high schools (noun) A high school is a secondary school, especially in America.

high technology (noun) High technology is the development and use of advanced electronics, computers, and robots.

high tide (noun) On a coast, high tide is the time, usually twice a day, when the sea is at its highest level.

highway, highways (noun) A highway is a road along which vehicles have the right to pass, e.g. *He admitted obstructing the highway.*

highwayman, highwaymen (noun) In the past, highwaymen were robbers on horseback who used to rob travellers.

hijack, hijacks, hijacking, hijacked (verb) If someone hijacks a plane or vehicle, they illegally take control of it by forcing the pilot or driver and any passengers to follow their instructions. **hijacking** (noun).

hike, hikes, hiking, hiked 1 (noun) A hike is a long country walk. **2** (verb) To hike means to walk long distances in the country.

hilarious (adjective) very funny. **hilariously** (adverb).

hilarity (noun) Hilarity is great amusement and laughter, e.g. *His antics caused great hilar-*

ity.

hill, hills (noun) A hill is a rounded area of land higher than the land surrounding it. **hilly** (adjective).

hilt, hilts (noun) The hilt of a sword, dagger, or knife is its handle.

him (pronoun) 'Him' is used to refer to a man, boy, or male animal that has already been mentioned, or to any person whose sex is not known.

himself 1 (pronoun) Himself is used when the same man, boy, or male animal does an action and is affected by it, e.g. *He discharged himself from hospital.* **2** Himself is used to emphasize 'he'.

hind, hinds (rhymes with **blind**) **1** (adjective) used to refer to the back part of an animal, e.g. *the hind legs.* **2** (noun) A hind is a female deer.

hinder, hinders, hindering, hindered (pronounced **hin**-der) (verb) If you hinder someone or something, you get in their way and make something difficult for them.

Hindi (pronounced **hin**-dee) (noun) Hindi is a language spoken in northern India.

hindrance, hindrances 1 (noun) Someone or something that is a hindrance causes difficulties or is an obstruction. **2** Hindrance is the act of hindering someone or something.

hindsight (noun) Hindsight is the ability to understand an event or situation after it has actually taken place, e.g. *With hindsight, I realized how strange he'd been.*

Hindu, Hindus (pronounced **hin**-doo) (noun) A Hindu is a person who believes in Hinduism, an Indian religion which has many gods and believes that people have another life on earth after death.

hinge, hinges, hinging, hinged 1 (noun) A hinge is the movable joint which attaches a door or window to its frame. **2** (verb) Something that hinges on a situation or event depends entirely on that situation or event, e.g. *Victory or defeat hinged on her final putt.*

hint, hints, hinting, hinted 1 (noun) A hint is a suggestion, clue, or helpful piece of advice. **2** (verb) If you hint at something, you suggest it indirectly.

hinterland, hinterlands (noun) The hinterland of a coastline or a port is the area of land behind it or around it.

hip, hips (noun) Your hips are the two parts at the sides of your body between your waist and your upper legs.

hippie, hippies; also spelled **hippy** (noun) A hippie is a person who has rejected conventional ideas and lives a life based on peace and love. The hippie movement started and was most popular in the 1960s.

hippo, hippos (noun; an informal word) A hippo is a hippopotamus.

hippopotamus, hippopotamuses or **hippopotami** (noun) A hippopotamus is a large animal from tropical Africa with thick wrinkled skin. Hippopotamuses spend a lot of time in water.

hire, hires, hiring, hired 1 (verb) If you hire something, you pay money to be able to use it for a period of time. **2** If you hire someone, you pay them to do a job for you. **3** (phrase) Something that is **for hire** is available for people to hire.

hirsute (pronounced **hir**-syoot) (adjective; a formal word) hairy.

his (adjective or pronoun) His refers to something that belongs or relates to a man, boy, or male animal that has already been mentioned, or to any person whose sex is not known.

hiss, hisses, hissing, hissed 1 (verb) To hiss means to make a long 's' sound, especially to show disapproval or aggression. **2** (noun) A hiss is a long 's' sound.

historian, historians (noun) A historian is a person who studies and writes about history.

historic (adjective) important in the past or likely to be seen as important in the future.

historical 1 (adjective) occurring in the past, or relating to the study of the past, e.g. *historical events.* **2** describing or representing the past, e.g. *historical novels.* **historically** (adverb).

history, histories (noun) History is the study of the past. A history is a record of the past, e.g. *the village is steeped in Scottish history... He fabricated his family history.*

histrionic, histrionics (pronounced hiss-tree-**on**-ik) **1** (adjective) Histrionic behaviour is very dramatic and full of exaggerated emotion, e.g. *The setting was unbelievably histrionic.* **2** (noun) Histrionics are histrionic behaviour. **3** (adjective; a formal use) relating to drama and acting, e.g. *a young man of marked histrionic ability.*

hit, hits, hitting, hit 1 (verb) To hit someone or something means to strike or touch them forcefully, usually causing hurt or damage. **2** To hit a ball or other object means to make it move by hitting it with something. **3** If something hits you, it affects you badly and suddenly, e.g. *The recession has hit the tourist industry hard.* **4** If something hits a particular point or place, it reaches it, e.g. *The book hit Britain just at the right time.* **5** (noun) A hit is also a person or thing that is popular and successful. **6** A hit is the action of hitting something, e.g. *Give it a good hard hit with the hammer.* **7** (an informal phrase) If you **hit it off** with someone, you become friendly with them the first time you meet them. **8** (verb) If you hit on an idea or solution, you suddenly think of it.

hit and miss (adjective) happening in an unplanned or unpredictable way.

hit-and-run (adjective) A hit-and-run car accident is one in which the person who has caused the damage drives away without stopping.

hitch, hitches, hitching, hitched 1 (noun) A hitch is a slight problem or difficulty, e.g. *The whole process was completed without a hitch.* **2** (verb; an informal use) If you hitch, you travel by getting lifts from passing vehicles, e.g. *America is no longer a safe place to hitch round.*

hitchhiking (noun) Hitchhiking is travelling by getting free lifts from passing vehicles.

hi tech (adjective) designed using the most modern methods and equipment, especially electronic equipment.

hither (an old-fashioned word) **1** (adverb) used to refer to movement towards the place where you are. **2** (phrase) Something that moves **hither and thither** moves in all directions.

hitherto (adverb; a formal word) until now, e.g. *What he was aiming at had not hitherto been attempted.*

HIV (noun) HIV is a virus that reduces people's resistance to illness and can cause AIDS. HIV is an abbreviation for 'human immunodeficiency virus'.

hive, hives, hiving, hived 1 (noun) A hive is a beehive. **2** A place that is a hive of activity is very busy with a lot of people working hard. **3** (verb) If part of something such as a business is hived off, it is transferred to new ownership, e.g. *a proposal to hive off London Transport to the private sector.*

hoard, hoards, hoarding, hoarded 1 (verb) To hoard things means to save them even though they may no longer be useful. **2** (noun) A hoard is a store of things that has been saved or hidden.

hoarding, hoardings (noun) A hoarding is a large advertising board by the side of the road.

hoarse, hoarser, hoarsest (adjective) A hoarse voice sounds rough and unclear. **hoarsely** (adverb).

hoax, hoaxes, hoaxing, hoaxed 1 (noun) A hoax is a trick or an attempt to deceive someone. **2** (verb) To hoax someone means to trick or deceive them.

hob, hobs (noun) A hob is a surface with a set of gas or electric cooking rings, either on top of a cooker or fitted into a work surface.

hobble, hobbles, hobbling, hobbled 1 (verb) If you hobble, you walk awkwardly because of pain or injury. **2** If you hobble an animal, you tie its legs together to restrict its movement.

hobby, hobbies (noun) A hobby is something that you do for enjoyment in your spare time.

hock, hocks 1 (noun) The hock of a horse or other animal is the angled joint in its back leg. **2** Hock is a type of white German wine from the Rhine region.

hockey (noun) Hockey is an outdoor game for two teams of eleven players. They use long sticks with curved ends to try to hit a small ball into the other team's goal.

hoe, hoes, hoeing, hoed 1 (noun) A hoe is a long-handled gardening tool with a small, flat, square blade, used to remove weeds and break up the soil. **2** (verb) To hoe the ground means to use a hoe on it.

hog, hogs, hogging, hogged 1 (noun) A hog is a castrated male pig. **2** (verb; an informal use) If you hog something, you take more than your share of it, or keep it for too long. **3** (an informal phrase) If you **go the whole hog,** you do something completely or thoroughly in a bold or extravagant way.

hoist, hoists, hoisting, hoisted 1 (verb) To hoist something means to lift it, especially using a crane or other machinery. **2** (noun) A hoist is a machine for lifting heavy things.

hold, holds, holding, held 1 (verb) To hold something means to carry, support, or keep it in place, usually with your hand or arms. **2** Someone who holds power, office, or an opinion has it or possesses it. **3** If you hold something such as a meeting, a party, or an election, you arrange it and cause it to happen. **4** If something holds, it is still available, true, or valid, e.g. *The offer still holds.* **5** If you hold someone responsible for something, you consider them responsible for it. **6** If something holds a certain amount, it can contain that amount, e.g. *The theatre holds 150 people.* **7** If you hold something such as theatre tickets, a telephone call, or the price of something, you keep or reserve it for a period of time, e.g. *The line is engaged – will you hold?* **8** If you don't hold with something, you do not approve of it, e.g. *I don't hold with war.* **9** To hold something down means to keep it or to keep it under control, e.g. *How could I have children and hold down a job like this?* **10** If you hold on to something, you continue it or keep it even though it might be difficult, e.g. *They are keen to hold on to their culture.* **11** To hold something back means to prevent it, keep it under control, or not reveal it, e.g. *She failed to hold back the tears.* **12** (noun) If someone or something has a hold over you, they have power, control, or influence over you, e.g. *The party has a considerable hold over its own leader.* **13** A hold is a way of holding something or the act of holding it, e.g. *He grabbed the rope and got a hold on it.* **14** The hold in a ship or plane is the place where cargo or luggage is stored.

holdall, holdalls (noun) A holdall is a large, soft bag for carrying clothing.

hole, holes, holing, holed 1 (noun) A hole is an opening or hollow in something. **2** (an informal use) If you are in a hole, you are in a difficult situation. **3** (an informal use) A hole in a theory or argument is a weakness or error in it. **4** In golf, a hole is one of the small holes into which you have to hit the ball. **5** (verb) When you hole the ball in golf, you hit the ball into one of the holes.

holiday, holidays, holidaying, holidayed 1 (noun) A holiday is a period of time spent away from home for enjoyment. **2** A holiday is a time when you are not working or not at school or college. **3** (verb)

When you holiday somewhere, you take a holiday there, e.g. *She is currently holidaying in Italy.*

holidaymaker, holidaymakers (noun) A holidaymaker is a person who is away from home on holiday.

holiness 1 (noun) Holiness is the state or quality of being holy. **2** 'Your Holiness' and 'His Holiness' are titles used to address or refer to the Pope or to leaders of some other religions.

hollow, hollows, hollowing, hollowed 1 (adjective) Something that is hollow has space inside it rather than being solid. **2** (noun) A hollow is a hole in something or a part of a surface that is lower than the rest, e.g. *It is a pleasant village in a lush hollow.* **3** (verb) To hollow means to make a hollow, e.g. *They hollowed out crude dwellings from the soft rock.* **4** (adjective) An opinion or situation that is hollow has no real value or worth, e.g. *a hollow gesture.* **5** A hollow sound is dull and has a slight echo, e.g. *the hollow sound of his footsteps on the stairs.*

holly (noun) Holly is an evergreen tree or shrub with spiky leaves. It often has red berries in winter.

holocaust, holocausts (pronounced **hol**-o-kawst) (noun) A holocaust is a large-scale destruction or loss of life, especially the result of war or fire.

holster, holsters (noun) A holster is a holder for a pistol or revolver, worn at the side of the body or under the arm.

holy, holier, holiest 1 (adjective) relating to God or to a particular religion, e.g. *the holy city.* **2** Someone who is holy is religious and leads a pure and good life.

homage (pronounced **hom**-ij) (noun) Homage is an act of respect and admiration, e.g. *The thronging crowds paid homage to their assassinated president.*

home, homes 1 (noun) Your home is the building, place, or country in which you live or feel you belong. **2** (adjective) connected with or involving your home or country, e.g. *He gave them his home phone number... The government is expanding the home market.* **3** (noun) A home is an institution in which elderly or ill people live and are looked after, e.g. *He has been confined to a nursing home since his stroke.*

homeland, homelands (noun) Your homeland is your native country.

homeless 1 (adjective) having nowhere to live. **2** (plural noun) The homeless are people who have nowhere to live. **homelessness** (noun).

homely (adjective) simple, ordinary and comfortable, e.g. *The room was small and homely.*

homeopathy (pronounced home-ee-**op**-path-ee) (noun) Homeopathy is a way of treating illness by means of minute amounts of a substance that would normally cause illness in a healthy person. **homeopathic** (adjective).

homeowner, homeowners (noun) A homeowner is a person who owns the home in which he or she lives.

homesick (adjective) unhappy because of being away from home and missing family and friends.

homespun (adjective) simple and uncomplicated, e.g. *The book is simple homespun philosophy.*

homestead, homesteads (noun) A homestead is a house and its land and other buildings, especially a farm.

home truth, home truths (noun) Home truths are unpleasant facts about yourself that you are told by someone else.

homeward or **homewards** (adjective or adverb) towards home, e.g. *the homeward journey.*

homework 1 (noun) Homework is school work given to pupils to be done in the evening at home. **2** Homework is also research and preparation, e.g. *You certainly need to do your homework before buying a horse.*

homicide, homicides (noun) Homicide is the crime of murder. **homicidal** (adjective).

homing (adjective) A homing device is able to guide itself to a target. An animal with a homing instinct is able to guide itself home.

homo sapiens (pronounced hoh-moh **sap**-ee-enz) (noun; a formal expression) Homo sapiens is the scientific name for human beings.

homosexual, homosexuals 1 (noun) A homosexual is a person who is sexually attracted to someone of the same sex. **2** (adjective) sexually attracted to people of the same sex, e.g. *a homosexual relationship.* **homosexuality** (noun).

hone, hones, honing, honed 1 (verb) If you hone a tool, you sharpen it. **2** If you hone a quality or ability, you develop and improve it, e.g. *He had a sharply honed sense of justice.*

honest (adjective) truthful and trustworthy. **honestly** (adverb).

honesty 1 (noun) Honesty is the quality of being truthful and trustworthy. **2** Honesty is also a plant with purple flowers. In autumn, it has flat silvery pods that people use in dried flower arrangements.

honey 1 (noun) Honey is a sweet, edible, sticky substance produced by bees. **2** Honey means 'sweetheart' or 'darling', e.g. *What is it, honey?*

honeycomb, honeycombs (noun) A honeycomb is a wax structure consisting of rows of six-sided cells made by bees for storage of honey and the eggs.

honeymoon, honeymoons (noun) A honeymoon is a holiday taken by a couple who have just got married.

honeysuckle (noun) Honeysuckle is a climbing plant with fragrant pink or cream flowers.

honk, honks, honking, honked 1 (noun) A honk is a short, loud sound like that made by a car horn or a goose. **2** (verb) When something honks, it makes a short, loud sound.

honorary (adjective) An honorary title or job is given as a mark of respect or honour, and does not involve the usual qualifications, work, or payment, e.g. *She was awarded an honorary degree.*

honour, honours, honouring, honoured 1 (noun) Your honour is your good reputation and the respect that other people have for you, e.g. *This is a war fought by men totally without honour.* **2** An honour is an award or privilege given as a mark of respect. **3** (phrase) If something is done **in honour of** someone, it is done out of respect for them, e.g. *Egypt celebrated frequent minor festivals in honour of the dead.* **4** (noun) Honours is a class of university degree which is higher than a pass or ordinary degree. **5** (verb) If you honour someone, you give them special praise or attention, or an award. **6** If you honour an agreement or promise, you do what was agreed or promised, e.g. *There is enough cash to honour the existing pledges.*

honourable (adjective) worthy of respect or admiration, e.g. *He should do the honourable thing and resign.*

hood, hoods 1 (noun) A hood is a loose covering for the head, usually part of a coat or jacket. **2** A hood is also a cover on a piece of equipment or vehicle, usually curved and movable, e.g. *The mechanic had the hood up to work on the engine.* **hooded** (adjective).

hoof, hooves or **hoofs** (noun) A hoof is the hard bony part of certain animals' feet.

hook, hooks, hooking, hooked 1 (noun) A hook is a curved piece of metal or plastic that is used for catching, holding, or hanging things, e.g. *picture hooks.* **2** (verb) If you hook one thing onto another, you attach it there using a hook. **3** (noun) A hook is a curving movement, for example of the fist in boxing, or of a golf ball. **4** (phrase) If you are **let off the hook,** something happens so that you avoid punishment or a difficult situation.

hooked (adjective) addicted to something; also obsessed by something, e.g. *hooked on alcohol... I'm hooked on exercise.*

hooligan, hooligans (noun) A hooligan is a noisy, destructive, and violent young person. **hooliganism** (noun).

hoop, hoops (noun) A hoop is a large ring, often used as a toy.

hooray another spelling of **hurray.**

hoot, hoots, hooting, hooted 1 (verb) To hoot means to make a long 'oo' sound like an owl, e.g. *hooting with laughter.* **2** If a car horn hoots, it makes a loud honking noise. **3** (noun) A hoot is a sound like that made by an owl or car horn.

hoover, hoovers, hoovering, hoovered 1 (noun; a trademark) A hoover is a vacuum cleaner. **2** (verb) When you hoover, you use a vacuum cleaner to clean the floor.

hooves a plural of **hoof.**

hop, hops, hopping, hopped 1 (verb) If you hop, you jump on one foot. **2** When animals or birds hop, they jump with two feet together. **3** (an informal use) If you hop into or out of something, you move there quickly and easily, e.g. *You only have to hop on the ferry to get there.* **4** (noun) A hop is a jump on one leg. **5** Hops are flowers of the hop plant, which are dried and used for making beer.

hope, hopes, hoping, hoped 1 (verb) If you hope that something will happen or hope that it is true, you want it to happen or be true. **2** (noun) Hope is a wish or feeling of desire and expectation, e.g. *There was little hope of recovery.* **hopeful** (adjective), **hopefully** (adverb).

hopeless 1 (adjective) having no hope, e.g. *She shook her head in hopeless bewilderment.* **2** certain to fail or be unsuccessful. **3** unable to do something well, e.g. *I'm hopeless at remembering birthdays.* **hopelessly** (adverb), **hopelessness** (noun).

hopper, hoppers (noun) A hopper is a large, funnel-shaped container for storing things such as grain or sand.

horde, hordes (rhymes with **bored**) (noun) A horde is a large group or number of people, animals, or insects, e.g. *hordes of tourists.*

horizon, horizons (pronounced hor-**eye**-zn) **1** (noun) The horizon is the distant line where the sky seems to touch the land or sea. **2** (phrase) If something is **on the horizon,** it is almost certainly going to happen or be done in the future, e.g. *Political change was on the horizon.* **3** (noun) Your horizons are the limits of what you want to do or are interested in, e.g. *Travel broadens your horizons.*

horizontal (pronounced hor-riz-**zon**-tl) (adjective) flat and level with the ground or with a line considered as a base, e.g. *a patchwork of vertical and horizontal black lines.* **horizontally** (adverb).

hormone, hormones (noun) A hormone is a chemical made by one part of your body that stimulates or has a specific effect on another part of your body. **hormonal** (adjective).

horn, horns 1 (noun) A horn is one of the hard, pointed growths on the heads of animals such as sheep and goats. **2** A horn is a musical instrument made of brass, consisting of a pipe or tube that is narrow at one end and wide at the other. **3** On vehicles, a horn is a warning device which makes a loud noise.

hornet, hornets (noun) A hornet is a type of very large wasp.

horoscope, horoscopes (pronounced **hor**-ros-kope) (noun) A horoscope is a prediction about what is going to happen to someone, based on the position of the stars when they were born.

horrendous (adjective) very unpleasant and shocking, e.g. *horrendous injuries.*

horrible 1 (adjective) disagreeable and unpleasant, e.g. *A horrible nausea rose within him.* **2** causing shock, fear, or disgust, e.g. *horrible crimes.* **horribly** (adverb).

horrid (adjective) very unpleasant indeed, e.g. *He was in a horrid mess... We were all so horrid to him.*

horrific (adjective) so bad or unpleasant that people are horrified, e.g. *a horrific attack.*

horrify, horrifies, horrifying, horrified (verb) If something horrifies you, it makes you feel dismay or disgust, e.g. *She was horrified by the dirt.* **horrifying** (adjective).

horror, horrors 1 (noun) Horror is a strong feeling of alarm, dismay, and disgust, e.g. *He gazed in horror at the knife.* **2** If you have a horror of something, you dislike or fear it very much, e.g. *He had a horror of fire.*

horse, horses 1 (noun) A horse is a large animal with a mane and long tail, which is ridden for pleasure or hunting, or kept as a working animal. **2** In gymnastics, a horse is a piece of equipment with four legs, used for jumping over.

horsepower (noun) Horsepower is a unit used for measuring how powerful an engine is, equal to about 746 watts.

horseradish (noun) Horseradish is the white root of a plant made into a hot-tasting sauce, often served cold with beef.

horseshoe, horseshoes (noun) A horseshoe is a U-shaped piece of metal, nailed to the hard surface of a horse's hoof to protect it; also anything of this shape, often regarded as a good luck symbol.

horsey or **horsy 1** (adjective) very keen on horses and riding. **2** having a face similar to that of a horse.

horticulture (noun) Horticulture is the study and practice of growing flowers, fruit, and vegetables. **horticultural** (adjective).

hose, hoses, hosing, hosed 1 (noun) A hose is a long flexible tube through which liquid or gas can be passed, e.g. *He left the garden hose on.* **2** (verb) If you hose something, you wash or water it using a hose, e.g. *The street cleaners need to hose the square down.*

hosiery (pronounced **hoze**-yer-ee) (noun) Hosiery consists of tights, socks, stockings and similar items, especially in shops.

hospice, hospices (pronounced **hoss**-piss) (noun) A hospice is a type of hospital which provides care for people who are dying.

hospitable (adjective) friendly, generous, and welcoming to guests or strangers. **hospitality** (noun).

hospital, hospitals (noun) A hospital is a place where sick and injured people are treated and cared for.

host, hosts, hosting, hosted 1 (noun) The host of an event is the person or organization that welcomes guests or visitors and provides food or accommodation for them, e.g. *He is a most generous host who takes his guests to the best restaurants in town.* **2** (verb) To host an event means to organize it or act as host at it. **3** (noun) A host is a plant or animal with smaller plants or animals living on or in it. **4** A host of things is a large number of them, e.g. *a host of close friends.* **5** In the Christian church, the Host is the consecrated bread used in Mass or Holy Communion.

hostage, hostages (noun) A hostage is a person who is illegally held prisoner and threatened with injury or death unless certain demands or conditions are met by other people.

hostel, hostels (noun) A hostel is a large building in which people can stay or live, e.g. *a hostel for battered women.*

hostess, hostesses (noun) A hostess is a woman who welcomes guests or visitors and provides food or accommodation for them.

hostile 1 (adjective) unfriendly, aggressive, and unpleasant, e.g. *a hostile audience.* **2** relating to or involving the enemies of a country, e.g. *hostile territory.* **hostility** (noun).

hot, hotter, hottest 1 (adjective) having a high temperature, e.g. *a hot climate.* **2** very spicy and causing a burning sensation in your mouth, e.g. *a hot curry.* **3** new, recent, and exciting, e.g. *hot news from tinseltown.* **4** dangerous or difficult to deal with, e.g. *Animal testing is a hot issue.* **hotly** (adverb).

hotbed, hotbeds (noun) A hotbed of some type of activity is a place that seems to encourage it, e.g. *The city was a hotbed of rumour.*

hot dog, hot dogs (noun) A hot dog is a sausage served in a roll split lengthways.

hotel, hotels (noun) A hotel is a building where people stay, paying for their room and meals.

hothouse, hothouses 1 (noun) A hothouse is a large heated greenhouse. **2** A hothouse is also a place or situation of intense intellectual or emotional activity.

hot seat (noun; an informal expression) Someone who is in the hot seat has to make difficult decisions for which they will be held responsible.

hotting (noun; an informal word) Hotting is performing stunts at high speed in a stolen car. **hotter** (noun).

hound, hounds, hounding, hounded 1 (noun) A hound is a dog, especially one used for hunting or racing. **2** (verb) If someone hounds you, they constantly pursue or trouble you.

hour, hours 1 (noun) An hour is a unit of time equal to 60 minutes. There are 24 hours in a day. **2** The hour for something is the time when it happens, e.g. *The hour for launching approached.* **3** The hour is also the time of day, e.g. *What are you doing up at this hour?* **4** An hour is also an important or difficult time, e.g. *The hour has come... He is the hero of the hour.* **5** (plural noun) The hours that you keep are the times that you usually go to bed and get up. **hourly** (adjective or adverb).

house, houses, housing, housed 1 (noun) A house is a building where a family, person, or small group of people lives. **2** A house is also a building used for a particular purpose, e.g. *an auction house... the opera house.* **3** In a theatre or cinema, the house is the part where the audience sits; also the audience itself, e.g. *The show had a packed house calling for more.* **4** (verb) To house something means to keep it, contain it, or shelter it, e.g. *The west wing housed a considerable store of valuable antiques.*

houseboat, houseboats (noun) A houseboat is a small boat which people live on that is tied up at a particular place on a river or canal.

household, households 1 (noun) A household is all the people who live as a group in a house or flat. **2** (phrase) Someone who is **a household name** is very well known. **householder** (noun).

housekeeper, housekeepers (noun) A housekeeper is a person who is employed to cook, clean, and look after a house.

House of Commons (noun) The House of Commons is the more powerful of the two parts of the British Parliament. Its members are elected by the public.

House of Lords (noun) The House of Lords is the less powerful of the two parts of the British Parliament. Its members come from noble families or hold a special office.

housewife, housewives (noun) A housewife is a married woman who does the cooking, cleaning, and other chores in her home, and does not have a paid job.

housing (noun) Housing is the buildings in which people live, e.g. *the serious housing shortage.*

hovel, hovels (noun) A hovel is a small hut or house that is dirty or badly in need of repair.

hover, hovers, hovering, hovered 1 (verb) When a bird, insect, or aircraft hovers, it stays in the same position in the air. **2** If someone or something hovers, they are in an uncertain situation or frame of mind, e.g. *He was hovering ineptly over his sister... Grief hovered round the edges of her heart.*

hovercraft, hovercraft or **hovercrafts** (noun) A hovercraft is a vehicle which can travel over water or land supported by a cushion of air.

how 1 (adverb) How is used to ask about, explain, or refer to the way in which something is done, known, or experienced, e.g. *How did this happen?... He knew how quickly rumours could spread.* **2** How is used to ask about or refer to a measurement or quantity, e.g. *How much is it for the weekend?... I wonder how old he is.* **3** How is used to emphasize the following word or statement, e.g. *How odd!*

however 1 (adverb) You use 'however' when you are adding a comment that seems to contradict or contrast with what has just been said, e.g. *For all his warmth and compassion, he is, however, surprisingly restrained.* **2** You use 'however' to say that something makes no difference to a situation, e.g. *A baby under 2.5 kg will probably be put in an incubator, however lively and healthy it seems.*

howl, howls, howling, howled 1 (verb) To howl means to make a long, loud wailing noise such as that made by a dog when it is upset, e.g. *A distant coyote howled at the moon... The wind howled through the trees.* **2** (noun) A howl is a long, loud wailing noise.

HQ an abbreviation for **headquarters.**

hub, hubs 1 (noun) The hub of a wheel is the centre part of it. **2** The hub of a place or organization is the central or most important, active part of it, e.g. *The kitchen is the hub of most households.*

huddle, huddles, huddling, huddled 1 (verb) If you huddle up or are huddled, you are curled up with your arms and legs close to your body. **2** When people or animals huddle together, they sit or stand close to each other, often for warmth. **3** (noun) A huddle of people or things is a small group of them.

hue, hues 1 (noun; a literary use) A hue is a colour or a particular shade of a colour. **2** (phrase) If people raise a **hue and cry,** they are very angry about something and protest.

huff (phrase) If you are **in a huff,** you are sulking or offended about something. **huffy** (adjective).

hug, hugs, hugging, hugged 1 (verb) If you hug someone, you put your arms round them and hold them close to you. **2** (noun) If you give someone a hug, you hold them close to you. **3** (verb) To hug a surface or shoreline means to keep very close to it or in contact with it, e.g. *Dependent on water power, factories hugged the major rivers and streams.*

huge, huger, hugest (adjective) extremely large in amount, size, or degree, e.g. *a huge success... a huge crowd.* **hugely** (adverb).

hulk, hulks 1 (noun) A hulk is a large, heavy person or thing. **2** A hulk is also the body of a boat or ship that has been wrecked or abandoned. **hulking** (adjective).

hull, hulls 1 (noun) The hull of a boat is the main part of its body that sits in the water. **2** The hull on some fruit such as strawberries is the stalk and ring of leaves at the base.

hum, hums, humming, hummed 1 (verb) To hum means to make a continuous low noise, e.g. *The generator hummed faintly.* **2** If you hum, you sing with your lips closed. **3** (noun) A hum is a continuous low noise, e.g. *the hum of the fridge.*

human, humans 1 (adjective) relating to, concerning, or typical of people, e.g. *Intolerance appears deeply ingrained in human nature... The statistics do not convey the human suffering involved.* **2** (noun) A human is a person. **humanly** (adverb).

human being, human beings (noun) A human being is a person.

humane (adjective) showing kindness, thoughtfulness, and sympathy towards others, e.g. *Medicine is regarded as the most humane of professions.* **humanely** (adverb).

humanism (noun) Humanism is the belief in mankind's ability to achieve happiness and fulfilment without the need for religion.

humanitarian, humanitarians 1 (noun) A humanitarian is a person who works for the welfare of mankind. **2** (adjective) concerned with the welfare of mankind, e.g. *humanitarian aid.* **humanitarianism** (noun).

humanity 1 (noun) Humanity is people in general, e.g. *I have faith in humanity.* **2** Humanity is also the condition of being human, e.g. *He denies his humanity.* **3** Someone who has humanity is kind, thoughtful, and sympathetic.

humble, humbler, humblest; humbles, humbling, humbled 1 (adjective) A humble person is modest and thinks that he or she has very little value. **2** Something that is humble is small or not very important, e.g. *Just a splash of wine will transform a humble casserole.* **3** (verb) To humble someone means to make them feel humiliated. **humbly** (adverb), **humbled** (adjective).

humbug, humbugs 1 (noun) A humbug is a hard black and white striped sweet that tastes of peppermint. **2** Humbug is speech or writing that is obviously dishonest, untrue, or nonsense, e.g. *hypocritical humbug.*

humdrum (adjective) ordinary, dull, and uninteresting, e.g. *humdrum domestic tasks.*

humid (adjective) If it is humid, the air feels damp, heavy, and warm.

humidity (noun) Humidity is the amount of moisture in the air, or the state of being humid.

humiliate, humiliates, humiliating, humiliated (verb) To humiliate someone means to make them feel ashamed or appear stupid to other people. **humiliation** (noun).

humility (noun) Humility is the quality of being modest and humble.

hummingbird, hummingbirds (noun) A hummingbird is a very small brightly coloured bird with powerful wings that make a humming noise as they beat.

humour, humours, humouring, humoured 1 (noun) Humour is the quality of being funny, e.g. *They discussed it with tact and humour.* **2** Humour is also the ability to be amused by certain things, e.g. *She's got a peculiar sense of humour.* **3** Someone's humour is the mood they are in, e.g. *He hasn't been in a good humour lately.* **4** (verb) If you humour someone, you are especially kind to them and do whatever they want. **humorous** (adjective).

hump, humps, humping, humped 1 (noun) A hump is a small, rounded lump or mound, e.g. *a camel's hump.* **2** (verb; an informal use) If you hump something heavy, you carry or move it with difficulty.

hunch, hunches, hunching, hunched 1 (noun) A hunch is a feeling or suspicion about something, not based on facts or evidence. **2** (verb) If you hunch your shoulders, you raise your shoulders and lean forwards.

hunchback, hunchbacks (noun; an old-fashioned word) A hunchback is someone who has a large hump on their back.

hundred, hundreds the number 100. **hundredth**

Hungarian, Hungarians (pronounced hung-**gair**-ee-an) **1** (adjective) belonging or relating to Hungary. **2** (noun) A Hungarian is someone who comes from Hungary. **3** Hungarian is the main language spoken in Hungary.

hunger, hungers, hungering, hungered 1 (noun) Hunger is the need to eat or the desire to eat. **2** A hunger for something is a strong need or desire for it, e.g. *a hunger for winning.* **3** (verb) If you hunger for something, you want it very much.

hunger strike, hunger strikes (noun) A hunger strike is a refusal to eat anything at all, especially by prisoners, as a form of protest.

hungry, hungrier, hungriest (adjective) needing or wanting to eat, e.g. *People are going hungry.* **hungrily** (adverb).

hunk, hunks (noun) A hunk of something is a large piece of it.

hunt, hunts, hunting, hunted 1 (verb) To hunt means to chase wild animals to kill them for food or for sport. **2** (noun) A hunt is the act of hunting, e.g. *Police launched a hunt for an abandoned car.* **3** (verb) If you hunt for something, you search for it. **hunter** (noun), **hunting** (adjective or noun).

hurdle, hurdles 1 (noun) A hurdle is one of the frames or barriers that you jump over in an athletics race called hurdles, e.g. *She won the four hundred metre hurdles.* **2** A hurdle is also a problem or difficulty, e.g. *Several hurdles exist for anyone seeking to do postgraduate study.*

hurl, hurls, hurling, hurled 1 (verb) To hurl something means to throw it with great force. **2** If you hurl insults at someone, you insult them aggressively and repeatedly.

hurray or **hurrah** or **hooray** an exclamation of excitement or approval.

hurricane, hurricanes (noun) A hurricane is a violent wind or storm.

hurry, hurries, hurrying, hurried 1 (verb) To hurry means to move or do something as quickly as possible, e.g. *She hurried through the empty streets.* **2** To hurry something means to make it happen more quickly, e.g. *You can't hurry nature.* **3** (noun) Hurry is the speed with which you do something quickly, e.g. *He was in a hurry to leave.* **hurried** (adjective), **hurriedly** (adverb).

hurt, hurts, hurting, hurt 1 (verb) To hurt someone means to cause them physical pain. **2** If a part of your body hurts, you feel pain there. **3** If you hurt yourself, you injure yourself. **4** To hurt someone also means to make them unhappy by being unkind or thoughtless towards them, e.g. *I didn't want to hurt his feelings.* **5** (adjective) If someone feels hurt, they feel unhappy because of someone's unkindness or thoughtlessness towards them, e.g. *He felt hurt by all the lies.* **hurtful** (adjective).

hurtle, hurtles, hurtling, hurtled (verb) To hurtle means to move or travel very fast indeed, especially in an uncontrolled or violent way.

husband, husbands (noun) A woman's husband is the man she is married to.

husbandry 1 (noun) Husbandry is the art or skill of farming. **2** Husbandry is also the art or skill of managing something carefully and economically.

hush, hushes, hushing, hushed 1 (verb) If you tell someone to hush, you are telling them to be quiet. **2** (noun) If there is a hush, it is quiet and still, e.g. *A graveyard hush had fallen over the group.* **3** (verb) To hush something up means to keep it secret, especially something dishonest involving important people, e.g. *The Foreign Office has hushed up a series of scandals.* **hushed** (adjective).

husk, husks (noun) Husks are the dry outer coverings of grain or seed.

husky, huskier, huskiest; huskies 1 (adjective) A husky voice is rough or hoarse. **2** (noun) A husky is a large, strong dog with a thick coat. Teams of huskies are used to pull sledges across snow.

hustle, hustles, hustling, hustled (verb) To hustle someone means to make them move by pushing and jostling them, e.g. *The guards hustled him out of the car.*

hut, huts (noun) A hut is a small, simple building, with one or two rooms.

hutch, hutches (noun) A hutch is a wooden box with wire mesh at one side, in which rabbits, guinea pigs, or other small pets can be kept.

hyacinth, hyacinths (pronounced **high**-as-sinth) (noun) A hyacinth is a spring flower with many small, bell-shaped flowers grouped around the stem.

hybrid, hybrids 1 (noun) A hybrid is a plant or animal that has been bred from two different types of plant or animal. **2** A hybrid is also anything that is a mixture of two other things.

hydra, hydras or **hydrae** (noun) A hydra is a microscopic freshwater creature that has a slender tubular body and tentacles round the mouth.

hydrangea, hydrangeas (pronounced high-**drain**-ja) (noun) A hydrangea is a garden shrub with large clusters of pink or blue flowers.

hydraulic (pronounced high-**drol**-lik) (adjective) operated by water, oil, or other fluid which is under pressure.

hydrogen (noun) Hydrogen is the lightest gas and the simplest chemical element.

hyena, hyenas (pronounced high-**ee**-na); also spelled **hyaena** (noun) A hyena is a dog-like African and Asian animal that hunts in packs.

hygiene (pronounced **high**-jeen) (noun) Hygiene is the practice of keeping yourself and your surroundings clean, especially in order to prevent the spread of disease. **hygienic** (adjective).

hymn, hymns (noun) A hymn is a Christian song in praise of God.

hyperactive (adjective) A hyperactive person is unable to relax and is always in a state of restless activity.

hyperbole (pronounced high-**per**-bol-lee) (noun) Hyperbole is a style of speech or writing which uses exaggeration.

hypertension (noun) Hypertension is a medical condition in which a person has high blood pressure.

hyphen, hyphens (noun) A hyphen is a punctuation mark used to join together words or parts of words, as for example in the word 'left-handed'. **hyphenate** (verb), **hyphenation** (noun).

hypnosis (pronounced hip-**noh**-siss) (noun) Hypnosis is an artificially produced state of relaxation in which the mind is very receptive to suggestion.

hypnotize, hypnotizes, hypnotizing, hypnotized; also spelled **hypnotise** (verb) To hypnotize someone means to put them into a state in which they seem to be asleep but can respond to questions and suggestions. **hypnotic** (adjective), **hypnotism** (noun), **hypnotist** (noun).

hypochondriac, hypochondriacs (pronounced high-pok-**kon**-dree-ak) (noun) A hypochondriac is a person who continually worries about their health, being convinced that they are ill when there is actually nothing wrong with them.

hypocrisy, hypocrisies (noun) Hypocrisy is pretending to have beliefs, qualities, or feelings that you do not really have, so that you seem a better person than you are. **hypocritical** (adjective), **hypocrite** (noun).

hypodermic, hypodermics (noun) A hypodermic is a medical instrument with a hollow needle. It is used for giving people injections, or taking samples of their blood.

hypothermia (noun) Hypothermia is a condition in which a person is very ill because their body temperature has been unusually low for a long time.

hypothesis, hypotheses (noun) A hypothesis is an explanation or theory which has not yet been proved to be correct.

hypothetical (adjective) based on assumption rather than on fact or reality.

hysterectomy, hysterectomies (pronounced his-ter-**rek**-tom-ee) (noun) A hysterectomy is an operation to remove a woman's womb.

hysteria (pronounced hiss-**teer**-ee-a) (noun) Hysteria is a state of uncontrolled excitement, anger, or panic.

hysterical 1 (adjective) Someone who is hysterical is in a state of uncontrolled excitement, anger, or panic. **2** (an informal use) Something that is hysterical is extremely funny. **hysterically** (adverb), **hysterics** (noun).

I i

I (pronoun) A speaker or writer uses I to refer to himself or herself, e.g. *I like the colour.*

ice, ices, icing, iced 1 (noun) Ice is water that has frozen solid. **2** (verb) If you ice cakes, you cover them with icing. **3** (noun) An ice is an ice cream. **4** (verb) If something ices over or ices up, it becomes covered with a layer of ice.

Ice Age, Ice Ages (noun) An Ice Age was a period of time lasting thousands of years when a lot of the earth's surface was covered with ice.

iceberg, icebergs (noun) An iceberg is a large mass of ice floating in the sea.

icecap, icecaps (noun) An icecap is a layer of ice and snow that permanently covers the North or South Pole.

ice cream, ice creams (noun) Ice cream is a very cold sweet food made from frozen cream.

ice cube, ice cubes (noun) Ice cubes are small cubes of ice put in drinks to make them cold.

ice hockey (noun) Ice hockey is a type of hockey played on ice, with two teams of six skaters.

Icelandic (noun) Icelandic is the main language spoken in Iceland.

ice-skate, ice-skates, ice-skating, ice-skated 1 (noun) An ice-skate is a boot with a metal blade on the bottom, which you wear when skating on ice. **2** (verb) If you ice-skate, you move about on ice wearing ice-skates.

icicle, icicles (pronounced **eye**-sik-kl) (noun) An icicle is a piece of ice shaped like a pointed stick that hangs down from a surface.

icing (noun) Icing is a mixture of powdered sugar and water or egg whites, used to decorate cakes.

icon, icons (pronounced **eye**-kon) (noun) In the Orthodox Churches, an icon is a holy picture of Christ, the Virgin Mary, or a saint.

icy, icier, iciest 1 (adjective) Something which is icy is very cold, e.g. *an icy wind.* **2** An icy road has ice on it. **icily** (adverb).

idea, ideas 1 (noun) An idea is a plan, suggestion, or thought that you have after thinking about a problem. **2** An idea is also an opinion or belief, e.g. *old-fashioned ideas about women.* **3** An idea of something is what you know about it, e.g. *They had no idea of their position.*

ideal, ideals 1 (noun) An ideal is a principle or idea that you try to achieve because it seems perfect to you. **2** Your ideal of something is the person or thing that seems the best example of it. **3** (adjective) The ideal person or thing is the best possible person or thing for the situation.

idealism (pronounced eye-**dee**-il-izm) (noun) Idealism is behaviour that is based on a person's ideals. **idealist**

(noun), **idealistic** (adjective).

idealize, idealizes, idealizing, idealized; also spelled **idealise** (verb) If you idealize someone or something, you regard them as being perfect. **idealization** (noun).

ideally 1 (adverb) If you say that ideally something should happen, you mean that you would like it to happen but you know that it is not possible. **2** Ideally means perfectly, e.g. *The hotel is ideally placed for business travellers.*

identical (adjective) exactly the same, e.g. *identical twins.* **identically** (adverb).

identification 1 (noun) The identification of someone or something is the act of identifying them. **2** Identification is a document such as a driver's licence or passport, which proves who you are.

identify, identifies, identifying, identified 1 (verb) To identify someone or something means to recognize them or name them. **2** If you identify with someone, you understand their feelings and ideas. **identifiable** (adjective).

identity, identities (noun) Your identity consists of the characteristics that make you who you are.

ideology, ideologies (noun) An ideology is a set of political beliefs. **ideological** (adjective), **ideologically** (adverb).

idiom, idioms (noun) An idiom is a group of words whose meaning together is different from all the words taken individually. For example, 'It is raining cats and dogs' is an idiom.

idiosyncrasy, idiosyncrasies (pronounced id-ee-oh-**sing**-krass-ee) (noun) Someone's idiosyncrasies are their own habits and likes or dislikes. **idiosyncratic** (adjective).

idiot, idiots (noun) If you call someone an idiot, you mean that they are stupid or foolish.

idiotic (adjective) extremely foolish or silly.

idle, idles, idling, idled (adjective) If you are idle, you are doing nothing. **idleness** (noun), **idly** (adverb).

idol, idols (pronounced **eye**-doll) **1** (noun) An idol is a famous person who is loved and admired by fans. **2** An idol is also a picture or statue which is worshipped as if it were a god.

idyll, idylls (pronounced **id**-ill) (noun) An idyll is a situation which is pleasant, peaceful, and beautiful. **idyllic** (adjective).

i.e i.e. means 'that is', and is used before giving more information. It is an abbreviation for the Latin expression 'id est'.

if 1 (conjunction) on the condition that, e.g. *I shall stay if I can.* **2** whether, e.g. *I asked my friend if she wanted to come shopping.*

igloo, igloos (noun) An igloo is a dome-shaped house built out of blocks of snow by the Inuit, or Eskimo people.

ignite, ignites, igniting, ignited (verb) If you ignite something or if it ignites, it starts burning.

ignition, ignitions (noun) In a car, the ignition is the part of the engine where the fuel is ignited.

ignominious (adjective) shameful or morally unacceptable. **ignominiously** (adverb), **ignominy** (noun).

ignoramus, ignoramuses (pronounced ig-nor-**ray**-muss) (noun) An ignoramus is an ignorant person.

ignorant **1** (adjective) If you are ignorant of something, you do not know about it, e.g. *He was completely ignorant of the rules.* **2** Someone who is ignorant does not know about things in general, e.g. *I thought of asking, but didn't want to seem ignorant.* **ignorantly** (adverb), **ignorance** (noun).

ignore, ignores, ignoring, ignored (verb) If you ignore someone or something, you deliberately do not take any notice of them.

ill, ills **1** (adjective) unhealthy or sick. **2** (noun) Ills are difficulties or problems. **3** (adjective) harmful or unpleasant, e.g. *ill effects.*

ill at ease (phrase) If you feel **ill at ease,** you feel unable to relax.

illegal (adjective) forbidden by the law. **illegally** (adverb), **illegality** (noun).

illegible (pronounced il-**lej**-i-bl) (adjective) Writing which is illegible is unclear and very difficult to read.

illegitimate (pronounced il-lij-**it**-tim-it) (adjective) A person who is illegitimate was born to parents who were not married at the time. **illegitimacy** (noun).

ill-fated (adjective) doomed to end unhappily, e.g. *his ill-fated attempt on the world record.*

illicit (pronounced il-**liss**-it) (adjective) not allowed by law or not approved of by society, e.g. *illicit drugs.*

illiterate (adjective) unable to read or write. **illiteracy** (noun).

illness, illnesses **1** (noun) Illness is the experience of being ill. **2** An illness is a particular disease, e.g. *the treatment of common illnesses.*

illogical (adjective) An illogical feeling or action is not reasonable or sensible. **illogically** (adverb).

ill-treat, ill-treats, ill-treating, ill-treated (verb) If you ill-treat someone or something you hurt or damage them or treat them cruelly. **ill-treatment** (noun).

illuminate, illuminates, illuminating, illuminated (verb) To illuminate something means to shine light on it to make it easier to see.

illumination, illuminations **1** (noun) Illumination is lighting. **2** Illuminations are the coloured lights put up to decorate a town, especially at Christmas.

illusion, illusions **1** (noun) An illusion is a false belief which you think is true, e.g. *Their hopes proved to be an illusion.* **2** An illusion is also something which you think you see clearly but does not really exist, e.g. *Painters create the illusion of space.*

illusory (pronounced ill-**yoo**-ser-ee) (adjective) seeming to be true, but actually false, e.g. *an illusory truce.*

illustrate, illustrates, illustrating, illustrated **1** (verb) If you illustrate a point, you explain it or make it clearer, often by using examples. **2** If you illustrate a book, you put pictures in it. **illustrator** (noun), **illustrative** (adjective).

illustration, illustrations 1 (noun) An illustration is an example or a story which is used to make a point clear. **2** An illustration in a book is a picture.

illustrious (adjective) An illustrious person is famous and respected.

ill will (noun) Ill will is a feeling of hostility.

image, images 1 (noun) An image is a mental picture of someone or something. **2** An image is the public face of a person or organization.

imagery (noun) The imagery of a poem or book is the descriptive language used.

imaginary (adjective) Something that is imaginary exists only in your mind, not in real life.

imagination, imaginations (noun) Your imagination is your ability to form new and exciting ideas.

imaginative (adjective) Someone who is imaginative can easily form new or exciting ideas in their mind. **imaginatively** (adverb).

imagine, imagines, imagining, imagined 1 (verb) If you imagine something, you form an idea of it in your mind, or you think you have seen or heard it but you have not really. **2** If you imagine that something is the case, you believe it is the case, e.g. *I imagine that's what you aim to do.* **imaginable** (adjective).

imbalance, imbalances (noun) If there is an imbalance between things, they are unequal, e.g. *the imbalance between rich and poor.*

imbecile, imbeciles (pronounced **im**-bis-seel) (noun) If you call someone an imbecile, you think that they are stupid.

imitate, imitates, imitating, imitated (verb) To imitate someone or something means to copy them. **imitator** (noun), **imitative** (adjective).

imitation, imitations (noun) An imitation is a copy of something else.

immaculate (pronounced im-**mak**-yoo-lit) **1** (adjective) completely clean and tidy, e.g. *The flat was immaculate.* **2** without any mistakes at all, e.g. *his usual immaculate guitar accompaniment.* **immaculately** (adverb).

immaterial (adjective) Something that is immaterial is not important.

immature 1 (adjective) Something that is immature has not finished growing or developing. **2** A person who is immature does not behave in a sensible adult way. **immaturity** (noun).

immediate 1 (adjective) Something that is immediate happens or is done without delay. **2** Your immediate relatives and friends are the ones most closely connected or related to you.

immediately 1 (adverb) If something happens immediately it happens right away. **2** Immediately means very near in time or position, e.g. *immediately behind the house.*

immemorial (adjective) If something has been happening from time immemorial, it has been happening longer than anyone can remember.

immense (adjective) very large or huge. **immensely** (adverb), **immensity** (noun).

immerse, immerses, immersing, immersed 1 (verb) If you are immersed in an activity you are completely involved in it. **2** If you immerse something in a liquid, you put it into the liquid so that it is completely covered. **immersion** (noun).

immigrant, immigrants (noun) An immigrant is someone who has come to live permanently in a new country. **immigrate** (verb), **immigration** (noun).

imminent (adjective) If something is imminent, it is going to happen very soon. **imminently** (adverb), **imminence** (noun).

immobile (adjective) not moving. **immobility** (noun).

immoral (adjective) If you describe someone or their behaviour as immoral, you mean that they do not fit in with most people's idea of what is right and proper. **immorality** (noun).

immortal 1 (adjective) Something that is immortal is famous and will be remembered for a long time, e.g. *Emily Bronte's immortal love story.* **2** In stories, someone who is immortal will never die. **immortality** (noun).

immovable or **immoveable** (adjective) Something that is immovable is fixed and cannot be moved. **immovably** (adverb).

immune (pronounced im-**yoon**) **1** (adjective) If you are immune to a particular disease, you cannot catch it. **2** If someone or something is immune to something, they are able to avoid it or are not bound by it, e.g. *The captain was immune to prosecution.* **immunity** (noun).

imp, imps (noun) In fairy stories, an imp is a small mischievous creature. **impish** (adjective).

impact, impacts 1 (noun) The impact that someone or something has is the impression that they make or the effect that they have. **2** Impact is the action of one object hitting another, usually with a lot of force, e.g. *The aircraft crashed into a ditch, exploding on impact.*

impair, impairs, impairing, impaired (verb) To impair something means to damage it so that it stops working properly, e.g. *Travel had made him weary and impaired his judgement.*

impale, impales, impaling, impaled (verb) If you impale something, you pierce it with a sharp object.

impart, imparts, imparting, imparted (verb; a formal word) To impart information to someone means to pass it on to them.

impartial (adjective) Someone who is impartial has a fair and unbiased view of something. **impartially** (adverb), **impartiality** (noun).

impasse (pronounced **am**-pass) (noun) An impasse is a difficult situation in which it is impossible to find a solution.
impassioned (adjective) full of emotion, e.g. *an impassioned plea.*
impassive (adjective) showing no emotion. **impassively** (adverb).
impatient 1 (adjective) Someone who is impatient becomes annoyed easily or is quick to lose their temper when things go wrong. **2** If you are impatient to do something, you are eager and do not want to wait, e.g. *He was impatient to get back.* **impatiently** (adverb), **impatience** (noun).
impeccable (pronounced im-**pek**-i-bl) (adjective) excellent, without any faults. **impeccably** (adverb).
impede, impedes, impeding, impeded (verb) If you impede someone, you make their progress difficult.
impediment, impediments (noun) An impediment is something that makes it difficult to move, develop, or do something properly, e.g. *a speech impediment.*
impelled (adjective) If you feel impelled to do something, you feel a strong emotional force urging you to do it.
impending (adjective; a formal word) You use impending to describe something that is going to happen very soon, e.g. *a sense of impending doom.*
impenetrable (adjective) impossible to get through.
imperative 1 (adjective) Something that is imperative is extremely urgent or important. **2** (noun) In grammar, an imperative is the form of a verb that is used for giving orders.
imperfect 1 (adjective) Something that is imperfect has faults or problems. **2** (noun) In grammar, the imperfect is a tense used to describe continuous or repeated actions which happened in the past. **imperfectly** (adverb), **imperfection** (noun).
imperial 1 (adjective) Imperial means relating to an empire or an emperor or empress, e.g. *the Imperial Palace.* **2** The imperial system of measurement is the measuring system which uses inches, feet, and yards, ounces and pounds, and pints and gallons.
imperialism (noun) Imperialism is a system of rule in which a rich and powerful nation controls other nations. **imperialist** (adjective or noun).
imperious (adjective) proud and domineering, e.g. *an imperious manner.* **imperiously** (adverb).
impersonal (adjective) Something that is impersonal makes you feel that individuals and their feelings do not matter, e.g. *impersonal cold rooms.* **impersonally** (adverb).
impersonate, impersonates, impersonating, impersonated (verb) If you impersonate someone, you pretend to be that person. **impersonation** (noun), **impersonator** (noun).
impertinent (adjective) disrespectful and rude, e.g. *impertinent questions.* **impertinently** (adverb), **impertinence** (noun).
impetuous (adjective) If you are impetuous, you act quick-

ly without thinking, e.g. *an impetuous gamble.* **impetuously** (adverb), **impetuosity** (noun).

impetus (noun) An impetus is the stimulating effect that something has on a situation, which causes it to develop more quickly.

impinge, impinges, impinging, impinged (verb) If something impinges on your life, it has an effect on you and influences you, e.g. *My private life doesn't impinge on my professional life.*

implacable (pronounced im-**plak**-a-bl) (adjective) Someone who is implacable is being harsh and refuses to change their mind. **implacably** (adverb).

implant, implants, implanting, implanted 1 (verb) To implant something into a person's body means to put it there, usually by means of an operation. **2** (noun) An implant is something that has been implanted into someone's body.

implausible (adjective) very unlikely, e.g. *implausible stories.* **implausibly** (adverb).

implement, implements, implementing, implemented 1 (verb) If you implement something such as a plan, you carry it out, e.g. *The government has failed to implement promised reforms.* **2** (noun) An implement is a tool. **implementation** (noun).

implicate, implicates, implicating, implicated (verb) If you are implicated in a crime, you are shown to be involved in it.

implication, implications (noun) An implication is something that is suggested or implied but not stated directly.

implicit (pronounced im-**pliss**-it) **1** (adjective) expressed in an indirect way, e.g. *implicit criticism.* **2** If you have an implicit belief in something, you have no doubts about it, e.g. *He had implicit faith in the noble intentions of the Emperor.* **implicitly** (adverb).

implore, implores, imploring, implored (verb) If you implore someone to do something, you beg them to do it.

imply, implies, implying, implied (verb) If you imply that something is the case, you suggest it in an indirect way.

import, imports, importing, imported 1 (verb) If you import something from another country, you bring it into your country or have it sent there. **2** (noun) An import is a product that is made in another country and sent to your own country for use there. **importation** (noun), **importer** (noun).

important 1 (adjective) Something that is important is very valuable, necessary, or significant. **2** An important person has great influence or power. **importantly** (adverb), **importance** (noun).

impose, imposes, imposing, imposed 1 (verb) If you impose something on people, you force it on them, e.g. *The allies had imposed a ban on all flights over Iraq.* **2** If someone imposes on you, they unreasonably expect you to do something for them. **imposition** (noun).

imposing (adjective) having an

impressive appearance or manner, e.g. *an imposing building.*

impossible (adjective) Something that is impossible cannot happen, be done, or be believed. **impossibly** (adverb), **impossibility** (noun).

imposter, imposters; also spelled **impostor** (noun) An imposter is a person who pretends to be someone else in order to get things they want.

impotent (adjective) Someone who is impotent has no power to influence people or events. **impotently** (adverb), **impotence** (noun).

impound, impounds, impounding, impounded (verb) If something you own is impounded, the police or other officials take possession of it.

impoverished (adjective) Someone who is impoverished is poor.

impractical (adjective) not practical, sensible, or realistic.

impregnable (adjective) A building or other structure that is impregnable is so strong that it cannot be broken into or captured.

impregnated (adjective) If something is impregnated with a substance, it has absorbed the substance so that it spreads right through it, e.g. *sponges impregnated with detergent and water.*

impresario, impresarios (pronounced im-pris-**sar**-ee-oh) (noun) An impresario is a person who manages theatrical or musical events or companies.

impress, impresses, impressing, impressed 1 (verb) If you impress someone, you do something to make them admire or respect you. **2** If you impress something on someone, you make them understand the importance of it.

impression, impressions (noun) An impression of someone or something is the way they look or seem to you.

impressionable (adjective) easy to influence, e.g. *impressionable teenagers.*

impressionism (noun) Impressionism is a style of painting which is concerned with the impressions created by light and shapes, rather than with exact details. **impressionist** (noun).

impressive (adjective) If something is impressive, it impresses you, e.g. *an impressive display of old-fashioned American cars.*

imprint, imprints, imprinting, imprinted 1 (noun) If something leaves an imprint on your mind, it has a strong and lasting effect. **2** (verb) If something is imprinted on your memory, it is firmly fixed there. **3** (noun) An imprint is the mark left by the pressure of one object on another.

imprison, imprisons, imprisoning, imprisoned (verb) If you are imprisoned, you are locked up, usually in a prison. **imprisonment** (noun).

improbable (adjective) not probable or likely to happen. **improbably** (adverb).

impromptu (pronounced im-**prompt**-yoo) (adjective) An impromptu action is one done without planning or organization.

improper 1 (adjective) rude or shocking, e.g. *improper behaviour.* **2** illegal or dishonest, e.g. *improper dealings.* **3** not suitable or correct, e.g. *an improper diet.* **improperly** (adverb).

improve, improves, improving, improved (verb) If something improves or if you improve it, it gets better or becomes more valuable. **improvement** (noun).

improvise, improvises, improvising, improvised 1 (verb) If you improvise something, you make or do something without planning in advance, and with whatever materials are available. **2** When musicians or actors improvise, they make up the music or words as they go along. **improvised** (adjective), **improvisation** (noun).

impudent (adjective) If someone is impudent, they behave or speak disrespectfully. **impudently** (adverb), **impudence** (noun).

impulse, impulses (noun) An impulse is a strong urge to do something, e.g. *She felt a sudden impulse to confide in her.*

impulsive (adjective) If you are impulsive, you do things suddenly, without thinking about them carefully. **impulsively** (adverb).

in (preposition or adverb) 'In' is used to indicate position, direction, time, and manner.

in- 1 (prefix) In- is added to the beginning of some words to form a word with the opposite meaning. **2** In- also means in, into, or in the course of.

inability (noun) An inability is a lack of ability to do something.

inaccessible (adjective) impossible or very difficult to reach.

inadequate 1 (adjective) If something is inadequate, there is not enough of it, or it is not good enough in quality for a particular purpose. **2** If someone feels inadequate, they feel they do not possess the skills necessary to do a particular job or to cope with life in general. **inadequately** (adverb), **inadequacy** (noun).

inadvertent (adjective) not intentional, e.g. *his talent for inadvertent comedy.* **inadvertently** (adverb).

inane (adjective) silly or stupid. **inanely** (adverb), **inanity** (noun).

inanimate (adjective) An inanimate object is not alive.

inappropriate (adjective) not suitable for a particular purpose or occasion, e.g. *It was quite inappropriate to ask such questions.* **inappropriately** (adverb).

inarticulate (adjective) If you are inarticulate, you are unable to express yourself well or easily in speech.

inasmuch (conjunction) 'Inasmuch as' means to the extent that, e.g. *Standards have risen hugely, inasmuch as the tricks have got more and more technically brilliant.*

inaudible (adjective) not loud enough to be heard. **inaudibly** (adverb).

inaugurate, inaugurates, inaugurating, inaugurated (pronounced in-**awg**-yoo-rate) **1** (verb) To inaugurate a new scheme means to start it. **2** To inaugurate a new leader means to officially establish them in their new position in a special ceremony, e.g. *Albania's Orthodox Church inaugurated its first archbishop in 25 years.* **inauguration** (noun), **inaugural** (adjective).

inborn (adjective) An inborn quality is one that you were born with.

incandescent (adjective) Something which is incandescent gives out light when it is heated. **incandescence** (noun).

incapable 1 (adjective) Someone who is incapable of doing something is not able to do it, e.g. *He is incapable of changing a fuse.* **2** An incapable person is weak and helpless.

incarcerate, incarcerates, incarcerating, incarcerated (pronounced in-**kar**-ser-rate) (verb) To incarcerate someone means to lock them up. **incarceration** (noun).

incendiary (pronounced in-**send**-yer-ee) (adjective) An incendiary weapon is one which sets fire to things, e.g. *incendiary bombs.*

incense (noun) Incense is a spicy substance which is burned to create a sweet smell, especially during religious services.

incensed (adjective) If you are incensed by something, it makes you extremely angry.

incentive, incentives (noun) An incentive is something that encourages you to do something.

inception (noun; a formal word) The inception of a project is the start of it.

incessant (adjective) continuing without stopping, e.g. *her incessant talking.* **incessantly** (adverb).

incest (noun) Incest is the crime of two people who are closely related having sex with each other. **incestuous** (adjective).

inch, inches, inching, inched 1 (noun) An inch is a unit of length equal to about 2.54 centimetres. **2** (verb) To inch forward means to move forward slowly.

incident, incidents (noun) An incident is an event, e.g. *a shooting incident.*

incidental (adjective) occurring as a minor part of something, e.g. *vivid incidental detail.* **incidentally** (adverb).

incinerate, incinerates, incinerating, incinerated (verb) If you incinerate something, you burn it. **incineration** (noun).

incinerator, incinerators (noun) An incinerator is a furnace for burning rubbish.

incipient (adjective) beginning to happen or appear, e.g. *incipient panic.*

incision, incisions (noun) An incision is a sharp cut, usually made by a surgeon operating on a patient.

incisive (adjective) Incisive language is clear and forceful.

incite, incites, inciting, incited (verb) If you incite someone to do something, you encourage them to do it by making them angry or excited. **incitement** (noun).

inclination, inclinations (noun) If you have an inclination to do something, you want to do it.

incline, inclines, inclining, inclined 1 (verb) If you are inclined to behave in a certain way, you often behave that way or you want to behave that way. **2** (noun) An incline is a slope.

include, includes, including, included (verb) If one thing includes another, it has the second thing as one of its parts. **including** (preposition).

inclusion (noun) The inclusion of one thing in another is the act of making it part of the other thing.

inclusive (adjective) A price that is inclusive includes all the goods and services that are being offered.

incognito (pronounced in-kog-**nee**-toe) (adverb) If you are travelling incognito, you are travelling in disguise.

incoherent (adjective) If someone is incoherent, they are talking in an unclear or rambling way. **incoherently** (adverb), **incoherence** (noun).

income, incomes (noun) A person's income is the money they earn.

income tax (noun) Income tax is a part of someone's salary which they pay regularly to the government.

incoming (adjective) coming in, e.g. *incoming trains... an incoming phone call.*

incomparable (adjective) Something that is incomparable is so good that it cannot be compared with anything else. **incomparably** (adverb).

incompatible (adjective) Two things or people are incompatible if they are unable to live or exist together because they are completely different. **incompatibility** (noun).

incompetent (adjective) Someone who is incompetent does not have the ability to do something properly. **incompetently** (adverb), **incompetence** (noun).

incomplete (adjective) not complete or finished. **incompletely** (adverb).

incomprehensible (adjective) not able to be understood.

inconceivable (adjective) impossible to believe.

inconclusive (adjective) not leading to a decision or to a definite result.

incongruous (adjective) Something that is incongruous seems strange because it does not fit in to a place or situation. **incongruously** (adverb).

inconsequential (adjective) Something that is inconsequential is not very important.

inconsistent (adjective) Someone or something which is inconsistent is unpredictable and behaves differently in similar situations. **inconsistently** (adverb), **inconsistency** (noun).

inconspicuous (adjective) not easily seen or obvious. **inconspicuously** (adverb).

incontinent (adjective) Someone who is incontinent is unable to control their bladder or bowels.

inconvenience, inconveniences, inconveniencing, inconvenienced 1 (noun) If something causes inconvenience, it causes difficulty or problems. **2** (verb) To inconvenience someone means to cause them difficulty or problems. **inconvenient** (adjective), **inconveniently** (adverb).

incorporate, incorporates, incorporating, incorporated (verb) If something is incorporated into another thing, it becomes part of that thing. **incorporation** (noun).

incorrect (adjective) wrong or untrue. **incorrectly** (adverb).

increase, increases, increasing, increased 1 (verb) If something increases, it becomes larger in amount. **2** (noun) An increase is a rise in the number, level, or amount of something. **increasingly** (adverb).

incredible (adjective) totally amazing or impossible to believe. **incredibly** (adverb).

incredulous (adjective) If you are incredulous, you are unable to believe something because it is very surprising or shocking. **incredulously** (adverb), **incredulity** (noun).

increment, increments (noun) An increment is the amount by which something increases, or a regular increase in someone's salary. **incremental** (adjective).

incriminate, incriminates, incriminating, incriminated (verb) If something incriminates you, it suggests that you are involved in a crime.

incubate, incubates, incubating, incubated (pronounced **in**-kyoo-bate) (verb) When eggs incubate, they are kept warm until they are ready to hatch. **incubation** (noun).

incubator, incubators (noun) An incubator is a piece of hospital equipment in which sick or weak newborn babies are kept warm.

incumbent, incumbents (a formal word) **1** (adjective) If it is incumbent on you to do something, it is your duty to do it. **2** (noun) An incumbent is the person in a particular official position.

incur, incurs, incurring, incurred (verb) If you incur something unpleasant, you cause it to happen.

incurable 1 (adjective) An incurable disease is one which cannot be cured. **2** An incurable habit is one which cannot be changed, e.g. *an incurable romantic.* **incurably** (adverb).

indebted (adjective) If you are indebted to someone, you are grateful to them.

indecent (adjective) Something that is indecent is shocking or rude, usually because it concerns nakedness or sex. **indecently** (adverb), **indecency** (noun).

indeed (adverb) You use indeed to strengthen a point that you are making, e.g. *The puddings are very good indeed.*

indefatigable (pronounced in-dif-**fat**-ig-a-bl) (adjective) People who never get tired of doing something are indefatigable.

indefinite 1 (adjective) If something is indefinite, no time to finish has been decided, e.g. *an indefinite strike.* **2** Indefinite also means vague or not exact, e.g. *indefinite words and pictures.* **indefinitely** (adverb).

indefinite article, indefinite articles (noun) The indefinite article is the grammatical term for 'a' and 'an'.

indelible (adjective) unable to be removed, e.g. *indelible ink.* **indelibly** (adverb).

indemnity (noun; a formal word) If something provides indemnity, it gives protection against damage or loss.

indentation, indentations (noun) An indentation is a dent or a groove in a surface or on the edge of something.

independent 1 (adjective) Something that is independent happens or exists separately from other people or things, e.g. *Results are assessed by an independent panel.* **2** Someone who is independent does not need other people's help, e.g. *a fiercely independent woman.* **independently** (adverb), **independence** (noun).

indeterminate (adjective) not certain or definite, e.g. *some indeterminate point in the future.*

index, indexes (noun) An index is an alphabetical list at the back of a book, referring to items in the book.

index finger, index fingers (noun) Your index finger is your first finger, next to your thumb.

Indian, Indians 1 (adjective) belonging or relating to India. **2** (noun) An Indian is someone who comes from India. **3** An Indian is also someone descended from the people who lived in North, South, or Central America before Europeans arrived.

indicate, indicates, indicating, indicated 1 (verb) If something indicates something, it shows that it is true, e.g. *a gesture which clearly indicates his relief.* **2** If you indicate something to someone, you point to it. **3** If you indicate a fact, you mention it. **4** If the driver of a vehicle indicates, they give a signal to show which way they are going to turn.

indication, indications (noun) An indication is a sign of what someone feels or what is likely to happen.

indicative 1 (adjective) If something is indicative of something else, it is a sign of that thing, e.g. *It is indicative of a poor diet.* **2** (noun) If a verb is used in the indicative, it is in the form used for making statements.

indicator, indicators 1 (noun) An indicator is something which tells you what something is like or what is happening. **2** A car's indicators are the lights at the front and back which are used to show when it is turning left or right.

indict, indicts, indicting, indicted (pronounced in-**dite**) (verb; a formal word) To indict someone means to charge them officially with a crime. **indictment** (noun), **indictable** (adjective).

indifferent 1 (adjective) If you are indifferent to something, you have no interest in it. **2** If something is indifferent, it is of a poor quality or low standard, e.g. *a pair of rather indifferent paintings.* **indifferently** (adverb), **indifference** (noun).

indigenous (pronounced in-**dij**-in-uss) (adjective) If something is indigenous to a country, it comes from that country, e.g. *a plant indigenous to Asia.*

indigestion (noun) Indigestion is a pain you get when you find it difficult to digest food.

indignant (adjective) If you are indignant, you feel angry about something that you think is unfair. **indignantly** (adverb).

indignation (noun) Indignation is anger about something that you think is unfair.

indignity, indignities (noun) An indignity is something that makes you feel embarrassed or humiliated, e.g. *the indignity of having to flee angry protesters.*

indigo (noun or adjective) dark violet-blue.

indirect (adjective) Something that is indirect is not done or caused directly by a particular person or thing, but by someone or something else. **indirectly** (adverb).

indiscriminate (adjective) not involving careful thought or choice, e.g. *an indiscriminate bombing campaign.* **indiscriminately** (adverb).

indispensable (adjective) If something is indispensable, you cannot do without it, e.g. *A good pair of walking shoes is indispensable.*

indistinct (adjective) not clear, e.g. *indistinct voices.*

individual, individuals 1 (adjective) relating to one particular person or thing, e.g. *Each family needs individual attention.* **2** Someone who is individual behaves quite differently from the way other people behave. **3** (noun) An individual is a person, different from any other person, e.g. *wealthy individuals.* **individually** (adverb).

individualist, individualists (noun) If you are an individualist, you like to do things in your own way. **individualistic** (adjective).

individuality (noun) If something has individuality, it is different from all other things, and very interesting and noticeable.

indomitable (adjective; a formal word) impossible to overcome, e.g. *an indomitable spirit.*

Indonesian, Indonesians (pronounced in-don-**nee**-zee-an) **1** (adjective) belonging or relating to Indonesia. **2** (noun) An Indonesian is someone who comes from Indonesia. **3** Indonesian is the official language of Indonesia.

indoor (adjective) situated or happening inside a building.

indoors (adverb) If something happens indoors, it takes place inside a building.

induce, induces, inducing, induced 1 (verb) To induce a state means to cause it, e.g. *His manner was rough and suspicious but he did not induce fear.* **2** If you induce someone to do something, you persuade them to do it.

inducement, inducements (noun) An inducement is something offered to encourage someone to do something.

indulge, indulges, indulging, indulged 1 (verb) If you indulge in something, you allow yourself to do something that you enjoy. **2** If you indulge someone, you let them have or do what they want, often in a way that is not good for them.

indulgence, indulgences 1 (noun) An indulgence is something you allow yourself to have because it gives you pleasure. **2** Indulgence is the act of indulging yourself or another person.

indulgent (adjective) If you are indulgent, you treat someone with special kindness, e.g. *a rich, indulgent father.* **indulgently** (adjective).

industrial (adjective) relating to industry.

industrial action (noun) Industrial action is action taken by workers in protest over pay or working conditions.

industrialist, industrialists (noun) An industrialist is a person who owns or controls a lot of factories.

industrious (adjective) An industrious person works very hard.

industry, industries 1 (noun) Industry is the work and processes involved in manufacturing things in factories. **2** An industry is all the people and processes involved in manufacturing a particular thing.

inedible (adjective) too nasty or poisonous to eat.

inefficient (adjective) badly organized, wasteful, and slow, e.g. *a corrupt and inefficient administration.* **inefficiently** (adverb), **inefficiency** (noun).

inept (adjective) without skill, e.g. *an inept lawyer.* **ineptitude** (noun).

inequality, inequalities (noun) An inequality is a difference in size, status, wealth, or position, between different things, groups, or people.

inert (adjective) Something that is inert does not move and appears lifeless, e.g. *an inert body lying on the floor.*

inertia (pronounced in-**ner**-sha) (noun) If you have a feeling of inertia, you feel very lazy and unwilling to do anything.

inevitable (adjective) certain to happen. **inevitably** (adverb), **inevitability** (noun).

inexhaustible (adjective) Something that is inexhaustible will never be used up, e.g. *an inexhaustible supply of ideas.*

inexorable (adjective; a formal word) Something that is inexorable cannot be prevented from continuing, e.g. *the inexorable increase in the number of cars.* **inexorably** (adverb).

inexpensive (adjective) not costing much.

inexperienced (adjective) lacking experience of a situation or activity, e.g. *inexperienced drivers.* **inexperience** (noun).

inexplicable (adjective) If something is inexplicable, you cannot explain it, e.g. *For some inexplicable reason I still felt uneasy.* **inexplicably** (adverb).

inextricably (adverb) If two or more things are inextricably linked, they cannot be separated.

infallible (adjective) never wrong, e.g. *No machine is infallible.* **infallibility** (noun).

infamous (pronounced **in**-fe-muss) (adjective) well known because of something bad or evil, e.g. *a book about Scotland's most infamous murder cases.*

infant, infants 1 (noun) An infant is a baby or very young child. **2** (adjective) designed for young children, e.g. *an in-*

fant school. **infancy** (noun), **infantile** (adjective).

infantry (noun) In an army, the infantry are soldiers who fight on foot rather than in tanks or on horses.

infatuated (adjective) If you are infatuated with someone, you have such strong feelings of love or passion that you cannot think sensibly about them. **infatuation** (noun).

infect, infects, infecting, infected (verb) To infect people, animals, plants, or food means to cause disease in them.

infection, infections 1 (noun) An infection is a disease caused by germs, e.g. *a chest infection.* **2** Infection is the state of being infected, e.g. *a very small risk of infection.*

infectious (adjective) spreading from one person to another, e.g. *an infectious disease.*

infer, infers, inferring, inferred (verb) If you infer something, you work out that it is true on the basis of information that you already have. **inference** (noun).

inferior, inferiors 1 (adjective) having a lower position or worth less than something else, e.g. *inferior quality cassette tapes.* **2** (noun) Your inferiors are people in a lower position than you. **inferiority** (noun).

infernal (adjective) very unpleasant, e.g. *an infernal bore.*

inferno, infernos (noun) An inferno is a very large dangerous fire.

infertile 1 (adjective) Infertile soil is of poor quality and plants cannot grow well in it. **2** Someone who is infertile cannot have children.

infest, infests, infesting, infested (verb) When animals or insects infest something, they spread in large numbers over it or into it and cause damage. **infestation** (noun).

infested (adjective) Something that is infested has a large number of animals or insects living on it and causing damage, e.g. *The flats are damp and infested with rats.* **infestation** (noun).

infidelity, infidelities (noun) Infidelity is being unfaithful to your husband, wife, or lover.

infighting (noun) Infighting is quarrelling or rivalry between members of the same organization.

infiltrate, infiltrates, infiltrating, infiltrated (verb) If people infiltrate an organization, they gradually enter it in secret to spy on its activities. **infiltration** (noun).

infinite (adjective) without any limit or end, e.g. *an infinite number of possibilities.* **infinitely** (adverb).

infinitive, infinitives (noun) In grammar, the infinitive is the base form of the verb. It often has 'to' in front of it.

infinity 1 (noun) Infinity is a number that is larger than any other number and can never be given an exact value. **2** Infinity is also an unreachable point, further away than any other point, e.g. *skies stretching on into infinity.*

infirmary, infirmaries (noun) Some hospitals are called infirmaries.

inflamed (adjective) If part of

your body is inflamed, it is red, hot, and swollen, usually because of infection.

inflammable (adjective) An inflammable material burns easily.

inflammation (noun) Inflammation is painful redness or swelling of part of the body.

inflammatory (adjective) Inflammatory actions are likely to make people very angry.

inflate, inflates, inflating, inflated (verb) When you inflate something, you fill it with air or gas to make it swell. **inflatable** (adjective).

inflation (noun) Inflation is a general increase in the price of goods and services in a country. **inflationary** (adjective).

inflexible (adjective) fixed and unable to be altered, e.g. *an inflexible routine.*

inflict, inflicts, inflicting, inflicted (verb) If you inflict something unpleasant on someone, you make them suffer it.

influence, influences, influencing, influenced 1 (noun) Influence is power that a person has over other people. **2** An influence is also the effect that someone or something has, e.g. *under the influence of alcohol.* **3** (verb) To influence someone or something means to have an effect on them.

influential (adjective) Someone who is influential has a lot of influence over people.

influenza (noun; a formal word) Influenza is flu.

influx (noun) An influx of people or things is a steady arrival of them, e.g. *a large influx of tourists.*

inform, informs, informing, informed 1 (verb) If you inform someone of something, you tell them about it. **2** If you inform on a person, you tell the police about a crime they have committed. **informant** (noun).

informal (adjective) relaxed and casual, e.g. *an informal meeting.* **informally** (adverb), **informality** (noun).

information (noun) If you have information on or about something, you know something about it.

informative (adjective) Something that is informative gives you useful information.

informer, informers (noun) An informer is someone who tells the police that another person has committed a crime.

infringe, infringes, infringing, infringed 1 (verb) If you infringe a law, you break it. **2** To infringe people's rights means to not allow them the rights to which they are entitled. **infringement** (noun).

infuriate, infuriates, infuriating, infuriated (verb) If someone infuriates you, they make you very angry. **infuriating** (adjective).

infuse, infuses, infusing, infused 1 (verb) If you infuse someone with a feeling such as enthusiasm or joy, you fill them with it. **2** If you infuse a substance such as a herb or medicine, you pour hot water onto it and leave it for the water to absorb the flavour. **infusion** (noun).

ingenious (pronounced in-**jeen**-yuss) (adjective) very clever and using new ideas, e.g. *his* *ingenious invention.* **ingeniously** (adverb).

ingenuity (pronounced in-jen-**yoo**-it-ee) (noun) Ingenuity is cleverness and skill at inventing things or working out plans.

ingot, ingots (noun) An ingot is a brick-shaped lump of metal, especially gold.

ingrained (adjective) If habits and beliefs are ingrained, they are difficult to change or destroy.

ingredient, ingredients (noun) Ingredients are the things that something is made from, especially in cookery.

inhabit, inhabits, inhabiting, inhabited (verb) If you inhabit a place, you live there.

inhabitant, inhabitants (noun) The inhabitants of a place are the people who live there.

inhale, inhales, inhaling, inhaled (verb) When you inhale, you breathe in.

inherent (adjective) Inherent qualities or characteristics in something are a natural part of it, e.g. *her inherent common sense.* **inherently** (adverb).

inherit, inherits, inheriting, inherited 1 (verb) If you inherit money or property, you receive it from someone who has died. **2** If you inherit a quality or characteristic from a parent or ancestor, it is passed on to you at birth. **inheritance** (noun), **inheritor** (noun).

inhibit, inhibits, inhibiting, inhibited (verb) If you inhibit someone from doing something, you prevent them from doing it.

inhibited (adjective) People who are inhibited find it difficult to relax and to show their emotions.

inhibition, inhibitions (noun) Inhibitions are feelings of fear or embarrassment that make it difficult for someone to relax and to show their emotions.

inhospitable 1 (adjective) An inhospitable place is unpleasant or difficult to live in. **2** If someone is inhospitable, they do not make people who visit them feel welcome.

inhuman (adjective) not human or not behaving like a human, e.g. *the inhuman killing of their enemies.*

inhumane (adjective) extremely cruel. **inhumanity** (noun).

inimitable (adjective) If you have an inimitable characteristic, it is special to you, e.g. *her inimitable sense of style.*

initial, initials (pronounced in-**nish**-l) **1** (adjective) first, or at the beginning, e.g. *Shock and dismay were my initial reactions.* **2** (noun) An initial is the first letter of a name. **initially** (adverb).

initiate, initiates, initiating, initiated (pronounced in-**nish**-ee-ate) **1** (verb) If you initiate something, you make it start or happen. **2** If you initiate someone into a group or club, you allow them to become a member of it, usually by means of a special ceremony. **initiation** (noun).

initiative, initiatives (pronounced in-**nish**-at-ive) **1** (noun) An initiative is an attempt to get something done. **2** If you have initiative, you decide what to do and then do it, without needing the advice of other people.

inject, injects, injecting, injected 1 (verb) If a doctor or nurse injects you with a substance, they use a needle and syringe to put the substance into your body. **2** If you inject something new into a situation, you add it. **injection** (noun).

injunction, injunctions (noun) An injunction is an order issued by a court of law to stop someone doing something.

injure, injures, injuring, injured (verb) To injure someone means to damage part of their body. **injury** (noun).

injustice, injustices 1 (noun) Injustice is unfairness and lack of justice. **2** If you do someone an injustice, you judge them too harshly.

ink (noun) Ink is the coloured liquid used for writing or printing.

inkling, inklings (noun) If you have an inkling of something, you have a vague idea about it.

inlaid (adjective) decorated with small pieces of wood, metal, or stone, e.g. *decorative plates inlaid with brass.* **inlay** (noun).

inland (adverb or adjective) towards or near the middle of a country, away from the sea.

in-law, in-laws (noun) Your in-laws are members of your husband's or wife's family.

inlet, inlets (noun) An inlet is a narrow bay.

inmate, inmates (noun) An inmate is someone who lives in a prison or psychiatric hospital.

inn, inns (noun) An inn is a small old country pub or hotel.

innards (plural noun) The innards of something are its inside parts.

innate (adjective) An innate quality is one that you were born with, e.g. *an innate sense of fairness.* **innately** (adverb).

inner (adjective) contained inside a place or object, e.g. *an inner room.*

innermost (adjective) deepest and most secret, e.g. *our innermost feelings.*

innings (noun) In cricket, an innings is a period during which a particular team is batting.

innocent 1 (adjective) not guilty of a crime. **2** without experience of evil or unpleasant things, e.g. *an innocent child.* **innocently** (adverb), **innocence** (noun).

innocuous (pronounced in-**nok**-yoo-uss) (adjective) not harmful.

innovation, innovations (noun) An innovation is a completely new idea, product, or system of doing things.

innuendo, innuendos or **innuendoes** (pronounced in-yoo-**en**-doe) (noun) An innuendo is an indirect reference to something rude or unpleasant.

innumerable (adjective) too many to be counted, e.g. *innumerable cups of tea.*

input, inputs 1 (noun) Input consists of all the money, information, and other resources that are put into a job, project, or company to make it work. **2** In computing, input is information which is fed into a computer.

inquest, inquests (noun) An inquest is an official inquiry to find out what caused a person's death.

inquire, inquires, inquiring, inquired; also spelled **enquire** (verb) If you inquire about something, you ask for information about it. **inquiring** (adjective), **inquiringly** (adverb), **inquiry** (noun).

inquisition, inquisitions (noun) An inquisition is an official investigation, especially one which is very thorough and uses harsh methods of questioning.

inquisitive (adjective) Someone who is inquisitive is keen to find out about things. **inquisitively** (adverb).

inroads (plural noun) If something makes inroads on or into something, it starts affecting it or destroying it.

insane (adjective) Someone who is insane is mad. **insanely** (adverb), **insanity** (noun).

insatiable (pronounced in-**saysh**-a-bl) (adjective) A desire or urge that is insatiable is very great, e.g. *an insatiable curiosity.* **insatiably** (adverb).

inscribe, inscribes, inscribing, inscribed (verb) If you inscribe words on an object, you write or carve them on it.

inscription, inscriptions (noun) An inscription is the words that are written or carved on something.

inscrutable (pronounced in-**skroot**-a-bl) (adjective) Someone who is inscrutable does not show what they are really thinking.

insect, insects (noun) An insect is a small creature with six legs, a hard external skeleton, and usually wings.

insecticide, insecticides (noun) An insecticide is a poisonous chemical used to kill insects.

insecure 1 (adjective) If you are insecure, you feel unsure of yourself and doubt whether other people like you. **2** Something that is insecure is not safe or well protected, e.g. *People still feel their jobs are insecure.* **insecurity** (noun).

insensitive (adjective) If you are insensitive, you do not notice when you are upsetting people. **insensitivity** (noun).

insert, inserts, inserting, inserted (verb) If you insert an object into something, you put it inside. **insertion** (noun).

inshore (adjective) at sea but close to the shore.

inside, insides 1 (adverb, preposition, or adjective) Inside refers to the part of something which is surrounded by the main part and is often hidden, e.g. *Tom had to stay inside and work... inside the house... an inside pocket.* **2** (plural noun) Your insides are the parts inside your body. **3** (phrase) **Inside out** means with the inside part facing outwards.

insider, insiders (noun) An insider is a person who is involved in a situation and so knows more about it than other people.

insidious (adjective) Something that is insidious is unpleasant and develops slowly without being noticed, e.g. *the insidious progress of the disease.* **insidiously** (adverb).

insight, insights (noun) If you

gain insight into a problem, you gradually get a deep and accurate understanding of it.

insignia (pronounced in-**sig**-nee-a) (noun) An insignia is a badge or a sign showing that you belong to a particular organization.

insignificant (adjective) small and unimportant. **insignificance** (noun).

insinuate, insinuates, insinuating, insinuated (verb) If you insinuate something unpleasant, you hint about it. **insinuation** (noun).

insipid 1 (adjective) An insipid person or activity is dull and boring. **2** Food that is insipid has very little taste.

insist, insists, insisting, insisted (verb) If you insist on something, you demand it emphatically. **insistent** (adjective), **insistence** (noun).

insolent (adjective) very rude and disrespectful. **insolently** (adverb), **insolence** (noun).

insoluble (pronounced in-**soll**-yoo-bl) **1** (adjective) impossible to solve, e.g. *an insoluble problem.* **2** unable to dissolve, e.g. *substances which are insoluble in water.*

insolvent (adjective) unable to pay your debts. **insolvency** (noun).

insomnia (noun) Insomnia is difficulty in sleeping. **insomniac** (noun).

inspect, inspects, inspecting, inspected (verb) To inspect something means to examine it carefully to check that everything is all right. **inspection** (noun).

inspector, inspectors 1 (noun) An inspector is someone who inspects things. **2** In the police force, an inspector is an officer just above a sergeant in rank.

inspire, inspires, inspiring, inspired 1 (verb) If something inspires you, it gives you new ideas and enthusiasm to do something. **2** To inspire an emotion in someone means to make them feel this emotion. **inspired** (adjective), **inspiring** (adjective), **inspiration** (noun).

instability (noun) Instability is a lack of stability in a place, e.g. *political instability.*

install, installs, installing, installed 1 (verb) If you install a piece of equipment in a place, you put it there so it is ready to be used. **2** To install someone in an important job means to officially give them that position. **3** If you install yourself in a place, you settle there and make yourself comfortable. **installation** (noun).

instalment, instalments 1 (noun) If you pay for something in instalments, you pay small amounts of money regularly over a period of time. **2** An instalment of a story or television series is one of the parts that appear regularly over a period of time.

instance, instances 1 (noun) An instance is a particular example or occurrence of an event, situation, or person, e.g. *a serious instance of corruption.* **2** (phrase) You use **for instance** to give an example of something you are talking about.

instant, instants 1 (noun) An instant is a moment or short period of time, e.g. *In an instant they were gone.* **2** (adjective) immediate and without delay, e.g. *The record was an instant success.* **instantly** (adverb).

instantaneous (adjective) happening immediately and without delay, e.g. *The applause was instantaneous.* **instantaneously** (adverb).

instead (adverb) in place of something, e.g. *Take the stairs instead of the lift.*

instigate, instigates, instigating, instigated (verb) Someone who instigates a situation causes it to happen through their own efforts. **instigation** (noun), **instigator** (noun).

instil, instils, instilling, instilled (verb) If you instil an idea or feeling into someone, you make them feel or think it.

instinct, instincts (noun) An instinct is an unlearned natural tendency to behave in a certain way, e.g. *My first instinct was to protect myself.* **instinctive** (adjective), **instinctively** (adverb).

institute, institutes, instituting, instituted 1 (noun) An institute is an organization set up for teaching or research. **2** (verb; a formal use) If you institute a rule or system, you introduce it.

institution, institutions 1 (noun) An institution is a custom or system regarded as an important tradition within a society, e.g. *The family is an institution to be cherished.* **2** An institution is also a large, important organization, for example a university or bank. **institutional** (adjective).

instruct, instructs, instructing, instructed 1 (verb) If you instruct someone to do something, you tell them to do it. **2** If someone instructs you in a subject or skill, they teach you about it. **instructor** (noun), **instructive** (adjective), **instruction** (noun).

instrument, instruments 1 (noun) An instrument is a tool or device used for a particular job, especially for measuring something, e.g. *scientific instruments.* **2** A musical instrument is an object, such as a piano or flute, played to make music.

instrumental 1 (adjective) If you are instrumental in doing something, you help to make it happen. **2** Instrumental music is performed using only musical instruments, and not voices.

insufficient (adjective) not enough for a particular purpose. **insufficiently** (adverb).

insular (pronounced **inss**-yoo-lar) (adjective) Someone who is insular is unwilling to meet new people or to consider new ideas. **insularity** (noun).

insulate, insulates, insulating, insulated (verb) If you insulate something, you cover it with a layer to keep it warm or to stop electricity passing through it. **insulation** (noun), **insulator** (noun).

insulin (pronounced **inss**-yoo-lin) (noun) Insulin is a substance which controls the level of sugar in the blood. People who have diabetes do not produce insulin naturally and have to take regular doses of it.

insult, insults, insulting, insulted 1 (verb) If you insult someone, you offend them by being rude to them. **2** (noun) An insult is a rude remark which offends you. **insulting** (adjective).

insure, insures, insuring, insured 1 (verb) If you insure something or yourself, you pay money regularly to a company so that if there is an accident or damage, the company will pay for medical treatment or repairs. **2** If you do something to insure against something unpleasant happening, you do it in order to protect yourself if it does happen or to prevent it from happening. **insurance** (noun).

insurrection, insurrections (noun) An insurrection is a violent action taken against the rulers of a country.

intact (adjective) complete, and not changed or damaged in any way, e.g. *The rear of the aircraft remained intact when it crashed.*

intake, intakes (noun) A person's intake of food, drink, or air is the amount they take in.

integral (adjective) If something is an integral part of a whole thing, it is an essential part.

integrate, integrates, integrating, integrated 1 (verb) If a person integrates into a group, they become part of it. **2** To integrate things means to combine them so that they become closely linked or form one thing, e.g. *his plan to integrate the coal and steel industries.* **integration** (noun).

integrity 1 (noun) Integrity is the quality of being honest and following your principles. **2** The integrity of a group of people is the quality of their being united as one whole.

intellect, intellects (noun) Intellect is the ability to understand ideas and information.

intellectual, intellectuals 1 (adjective) involving thought, ideas, and understanding, e.g. *an intellectual exercise.* **2** (noun) An intellectual is someone who enjoys thinking about complicated ideas and theories. **intellectually** (adverb).

intelligence (noun) A person's intelligence is their ability to understand and learn things quickly and well. **intelligent** (adjective), **intelligently** (adverb).

intelligentsia (pronounced in-tell-lee-**jent**-sya) (noun) The intelligentsia are intellectual people, considered as a group.

intelligible (adjective) able to be understood, e.g. *very few intelligible remarks.*

intend, intends, intending, intended 1 (verb) If you intend to do something, you have decided or planned to do it, e.g. *She intended to move back to London.* **2** If something is intended for a particular use, you have planned that it should have this use, e.g. *The booklet is intended to be kept handy.*

intense 1 (adjective) very great in strength or amount, e.g. *intense heat.* **2** If a person is intense, they take things very seriously and have very strong feelings. **intensely** (adverb), **intensity** (noun).

intensify, intensifies, intensify-

ing, **intensified** (verb) To intensify something means to make it greater or stronger.

intensive (adjective) involving a lot of energy or effort over a very short time, e.g. *an intensive training course.*

intent, intents 1 (noun; a formal use) A person's intent is their purpose or intention. **2** (adjective) If you are intent on doing something, you are determined to do it. **intently** (adverb).

intention, intentions (noun) If you have an intention to do something, you have a plan of what you are going to do.

intentional (adjective) If something is intentional, it is done on purpose. **intentionally** (adverb).

inter- (prefix) Inter- means between, e.g. *inter-school competitions.*

interact, interacts, interacting, interacted (verb) The way two people or things interact is the way they work together, communicate, or react with each other. **interaction** (noun), **interactive** (adjective).

intercept, intercepts, intercepting, intercepted (pronounced in-ter-**sept**) (verb) If you intercept someone or something that is going from one place to another, you stop them.

interchange, interchanges (noun) An interchange is the act or process of exchanging things or ideas. **interchangeable** (adjective).

intercom, intercoms (noun) An intercom is a device consisting of a microphone and a loudspeaker, which you use to speak to people in another room.

intercourse (noun) Intercourse or sexual intercourse is the act of having sex.

interest, interests, interesting, interested 1 (noun) If you have an interest in something or if something is of interest, you want to learn or hear more about it. **2** Your interests are your hobbies. **3** (verb) Something that interests you attracts your attention so that you want to learn or hear more about it. **4** (noun) If you have an interest in something being done, you want it to be done because it will benefit you. **5** Interest is a sum of money paid as a percentage of a larger sum of money which has been borrowed or invested. **interesting** (adjective), **interestingly** (adverb), **interested** (adjective).

interface, interfaces (noun) The interface between two subjects or systems is the area in which they affect each other or are linked.

interfere, interferes, interfering, interfered 1 (verb) If you interfere in a situation, you try to influence it, although it does not really concern you. **2** Something that interferes with a situation has a damaging effect on it. **interference** (noun), **interfering** (adjective).

interim (adjective) intended for use only until something permanent is arranged, e.g. *an interim measure.*

interior, interiors 1 (noun) The interior of something is the inside part of it. **2** (adjective) Interior means inside, e.g. *They painted the interior walls* *white.*

interjection, interjections (noun) An interjection is a word or phrase spoken suddenly to express a feeling such as surprise, pain, or anger.

interlude, interludes (rhymes with **rude**) (noun) An interlude is a short break from an activity.

intermediary, intermediaries (pronounced in-ter-**meed**-yer-ee) (noun) An intermediary is someone who tries to get two groups of people to come to an agreement.

intermediate (adjective) An intermediate level occurs in the middle, between two other stages, e.g. *intermediate students.*

interminable (adjective) If something is interminable, it goes on for a very long time, e.g. *an interminable wait for the bus.* **interminably** (adverb).

intermission, intermissions (noun) An intermission is an interval between two parts of a film or play.

intermittent (adjective) happening only occasionally. **intermittently** (adverb).

internal (adjective) happening inside a person, place, or object. **internally** (adverb).

international, internationals 1 (adjective) involving different countries. **2** (noun) An international is a sports match between two countries. **internationally** (adverb).

interplay (noun) The interplay between two things is the way they react with one another.

interpret, interprets, interpreting, interpreted 1 (verb) If you interpret what someone says or does, you decide what it means. **2** If you interpret a foreign language that someone is speaking, you translate it. **interpretation** (noun), **interpreter** (noun).

interrogate, interrogates, interrogating, interrogated (verb) If you interrogate someone, you question them thoroughly to get information from them. **interrogation** (noun), **interrogator** (noun).

interrupt, interrupts, interrupting, interrupted 1 (verb) If you interrupt someone, you start talking while they are talking. **2** If you interrupt a process or activity, you stop it continuing for a time. **interruption** (noun).

intersect, intersects, intersecting, intersected (verb) When two roads intersect, they cross each other. **intersection** (noun).

interspersed (adjective) If something is interspersed with things, these things occur at various points in it.

interval, intervals 1 (noun) An interval is the period of time between two moments or dates. **2** An interval is also a short break during a play or concert.

intervene, intervenes, intervening, intervened (verb) If you intervene in a situation, you step in to prevent conflict between people. **intervention** (noun).

intervening (adjective) An intervening period of time is one which separates two events.

interview, interviews 1 (noun)

An interview is a meeting at which someone asks you questions about yourself to see if you are suitable for a particular job. **2** An interview is a conversation in which a journalist asks a famous person questions. **3** (verb) If you interview someone, you ask them questions about themselves.

intestine, intestines (noun) Your intestines are a long tube which carries food from your stomach through to your bowels, and in which the food is digested. **intestinal** (adjective).

intimate, intimates, intimating, intimated 1 (adjective) If two people are intimate, there is a close relationship between them. **2** An intimate matter is very private and personal. **3** An intimate knowledge of something is very deep and detailed. **4** (verb) If you intimate something, you hint at it, e.g. *He did intimate that he is considering legal action.* **intimately** (adverb), **intimacy** (noun), **intimation** (noun).

intimidate, intimidates, intimidating, intimidated (verb) If you intimidate someone, you frighten them in a threatening way. **intimidated** (adjective), **intimidating** (adjective), **intimidation** (noun).

into 1 (preposition) If something goes into something else, it goes inside it. **2** If you bump or crash into something, you hit it. **3** (an informal use) If you are into something, you like it very much, e.g. *Nowadays I'm really into healthy food.*

intolerable (adjective) If something is intolerable, it is so bad or extreme that it is difficult to put up with it. **intolerably** (adverb).

intoxicated (adjective) If someone is intoxicated, they are drunk. **intoxicating** (adjective), **intoxication** (noun).

intra- (prefix) Intra- means within or inside, e.g. *intra-family difficulties.*

intractable (adjective; a formal word) stubborn and difficult to deal with or control.

intransitive (adjective) An intransitive verb is one that does not have a direct object.

intravenous (pronounced in-trav-**vee**-nuss) (adjective) Intravenous foods or drugs are given to sick people through their veins. **intravenously** (adverb).

intrepid (adjective) not worried by danger, e.g. *an intrepid explorer.* **intrepidly** (adverb).

intricate (adjective) Something that is intricate has many fine details, e.g. *walls and ceilings covered with intricate patterns.* **intricately** (adverb), **intricacy** (noun).

intrigue, intrigues, intriguing, intrigued 1 (noun) Intrigue is the making of secret plans, often with the intention of harming other people, e.g. *political intrigue.* **2** (verb) If something intrigues you, you are fascinated by it and curious about it. **intriguing** (adjective).

intrinsic (adjective; a formal word) The intrinsic qualities of something are its basic qualities. **intrinsically** (adverb).

introduce, introduces, introduc-

ing, introduced 1 (verb) If you introduce one person to another, you tell them each other's name so that they can get to know each other. **2** When someone introduces a radio or television show, they say a few words at the beginning to tell you about it. **3** If you introduce someone to something, they learn about it for the first time. **introductory** (adjective).

introduction, introductions 1 (noun) The introduction of someone or something is the act of presenting them for the first time. **2** The introduction to a book is a piece of writing at the beginning of it, which usually tells you what the book is about.

intrude, intrudes, intruding, intruded (verb) To intrude on someone or something means to disturb them, e.g. *I don't want to intrude on your parents.* **intruder** (noun), **intrusion** (noun), **intrusive** (adjective).

intuition, intuitions (pronounced int-yoo-**ish**-n) (noun) Your intuition is a feeling you have about something that you cannot explain, e.g. *My intuition is right about him.* **intuitive** (adjective), **intuitively** (adverb).

Inuit, Inuits; also spelled **Innuit** (noun) An Inuit is an Eskimo who comes from North America or Greenland.

inundated (adjective) If you are inundated by letters or requests, you receive so many that you cannot deal with them all.

invade, invades, invading, invaded 1 (verb) If an army invades a country, it enters it by force. **2** If someone invades your privacy, they disturb you when you want to be alone. **invader** (noun), **invasion** (noun).

invalid, invalids (pronounced **in**-va-lid) (noun) An invalid is someone who is so ill that they need to be looked after by someone else.

invalid (pronounced in-**val**-id) **1** (adjective) If an argument or result is invalid, it is not acceptable because it is based on a mistake. **2** If a law, marriage, or election is invalid, it is illegal because it has not been carried out properly. **invalidate** (verb).

invalidity (pronounced in-va-**lid**-dit-ee) (noun) Invalidity is the condition of being very ill for a very long time.

invaluable (adjective) extremely useful, e.g. *This book contains invaluable tips.*

invariably (adverb) If something invariably happens, it almost always happens.

invective (noun; a formal word) Invective is abusive language used by someone who is angry.

invent, invents, inventing, invented 1 (verb) If you invent a machine, device, or process, you are the first person to think of it or to use it. **2** If you invent a story or an excuse, you make it up. **inventor** (noun), **invention** (noun), **inventive** (adjective), **inventiveness** (noun).

inventory, inventories (noun) An inventory is a written list of all the objects in a place.

inverse (adjective; a formal

word) If there is an inverse relationship between two things, one decreases as the other increases.

invertebrate, invertebrates (noun; a technical word) An invertebrate is a creature which does not have a spine.

inverted (adjective) upside down or back to front.

inverted comma, inverted commas (noun) Inverted commas are the punctuation marks used to show where speech begins and ends.

invest, invests, investing, invested 1 (verb) If you invest money, you pay it into a bank or buy shares so that you will receive a profit. **2** If you invest in something useful, you buy it because it will help you do something more efficiently. **3** If you invest money, time, or energy in something, you try to make it a success. **investor** (noun), **investment** (noun).

investigate, investigates, investigating, investigated (verb) To investigate something means to try to find out all the facts about it. **investigator** (noun), **investigation** (noun).

inveterate (adjective) having lasted for a long time and not likely to stop, e.g. *an inveterate gambler.*

invincible (adjective) unable to be defeated. **invincibility** (noun).

invisible (adjective) If something is invisible, you cannot see it, because it is hidden, very small, or imaginary. **invisibly** (adverb), **invisibility** (noun).

invite, invites, inviting, invited 1 (verb) If you invite someone to an event, you ask them to come to it. **2** If you invite someone to do something, you ask them to do it, e.g. *Mr Icke has been invited to speak at the conference.* **inviting** (adjective), **invitation** (noun).

invoice, invoices (noun) An invoice is a bill for services or goods.

invoke, invokes, invoking, invoked 1 (verb; a formal word) If you invoke a law, you use it to justify what you are doing. **2** If you invoke certain feelings, you cause someone to have these feelings.

involuntary (adjective) sudden and uncontrollable. **involuntarily** (adverb).

involve, involves, involving, involved (verb) If a situation involves someone or something, it includes them as a necessary part. **involvement** (noun).

inward or **inwards 1** (adjective) Your inward thoughts and feelings are private. **2** (adjective or adverb) If something moves inward or inwards, it moves towards the inside or centre of something. **inwardly** (adverb).

iodine (pronounced **eye**-oh-deen) (noun) Iodine is a bluish-black substance used in medicine and photography.

ion, ions (pronounced **eye**-on) (noun) Ions are electrically charged atoms.

iota (noun) An iota is an extremely small amount, e.g. *He did not have an iota of proof.*

IQ, IQs (noun) Your IQ is your level of intelligence shown by the results of a special test. IQ is an abbreviation for 'intelligence quotient'.

Iranian, Iranians (pronounced ir-**rain**-ee-an) **1** (adjective) belonging or relating to Iran. **2** (noun) An Iranian is someone who comes from Iran. **3** Iranian is the main language spoken in Iran. It is also known as Farsi.

Iraqi, Iraqis (pronounced ir-**ah**-kee) **1** (adjective) belonging or relating to Iraq. **2** (noun) An Iraqi is someone who comes from Iraq.

irate (pronounced eye-**rate**) (adjective) very angry.

iris, irises (pronounced **eye**-riss) **1** (noun) The iris is the round, coloured part of your eye. **2** An iris is a tall plant with long leaves and large blue, yellow, or white flowers.

Irish 1 (adjective) belonging or relating to the Irish Republic, or to the whole of Ireland. **2** (noun) Irish or Irish Gaelic is a language spoken in some parts of Ireland.

Irishman, Irishmen (noun) An Irishman is a man who comes from Ireland. **Irishwoman** (noun).

irk, irks, irking, irked (verb) If something irks you, it annoys you. **irksome** (adjective).

iron, irons, ironing, ironed 1 (noun) Iron is a hard dark metal used to make steel, and things like gates and fences. Small amounts of iron are found in blood. **2** An iron is a device which heats up and which you rub over clothes to remove creases. **3** (verb) If you iron clothes, you use a hot iron to remove creases from them. **ironing** (noun). **iron out** (verb) If you iron out difficulties, you solve them.

Iron Age (noun) The Iron Age was a time about three thousand years ago when people first started to make tools out of iron.

irony (pronounced **eye**-ron-ee) **1** (noun) Irony is a form of humour in which you say the opposite of what you really mean, e.g. *I intended a touch of irony when I asked Farley how business was.* **2** There is irony in a situation when there is an unexpected or unusual connection between things or events, e.g. *It is a great irony that when you're at sea, there is water everywhere, but never a drop to cook with.* **ironic** or **ironical** (adjective), **ironically** (adverb).

irrational (adjective) Irrational feelings are not based on logical reasons, e.g. *irrational fears.* **irrationally** (adverb), **irrationality** (noun).

irregular (adjective) Something that is irregular is not smooth or straight, or does not form a regular pattern, e.g. *irregular walls.* **irregularly** (adverb), **irregularity** (noun).

irrelevant (adjective) not directly connected with a subject, e.g. *He either ignored questions or gave irrelevant answers.* **irrelevance** (noun).

irrepressible (adjective) Someone who is irrepressible is lively, energetic, and cheerful.

irresistible 1 (adjective) unable to be controlled, e.g. *an irresistible urge to yawn.* **2** extremely attractive, e.g. *Women always found him irresistible.* **irresistibly** (adverb).

irrespective (adjective) If you

jail, jails, jailing, jailed; also spelled **gaol 1** (noun) A jail is a building where people convicted of a crime are locked up. **2** (verb) To jail someone means to lock them up in a jail.

jailer, jailers; also spelled **gaoler** (noun) A jailer is a person who works in a jail and is in charge of the prisoners in it.

jam, jams, jamming, jammed 1 (noun) Jam is a food, made by boiling fruit and sugar together until it sets. **2** A jam is a situation where there are so many things or people that it is impossible to move, e.g. *a traffic jam.* **3** (an informal phrase) If someone is **in a jam,** they are in a difficult situation. **4** (verb) If people or things are jammed into a place, they are squeezed together so closely that they can hardly move. **5** To jam something somewhere means to push it there roughly, e.g. *He jammed his foot on the brake.* **6** If something is jammed, it is stuck or unable to work properly. **7** To jam a radio or electric signal means to interfere with it and prevent it from being received clearly.

Jamaican, Jamaicans (pronounced jam-**may**-kn) **1** (adjective) belonging or relating to Jamaica. **2** (noun) A Jamaican is someone who comes from Jamaica.

jamboree, jamborees (noun) A jamboree is a party or a gathering of large numbers of people enjoying themselves.

jangle, jangles, jangling, jangled 1 (verb) If something jangles, it makes a harsh metallic ringing noise. **2** (noun) A jangle is the sound made by metal objects striking against each other.

janitor, janitors (noun) A janitor is the caretaker of a building.

January (noun) January is the first month of the year. It has 31 days.

Japanese 1 (adjective) belonging or relating to Japan. **2** (noun) A Japanese is someone who comes from Japan. **3** Japanese is the main language spoken in Japan.

jar, jars, jarring, jarred 1 (noun) A jar is a glass container with a wide top used for storing food. **2** (verb) If something jars on you, you find it unpleasant or annoying.

jargon (noun) Jargon consists of words or expressions that are used in special or technical ways by particular groups of people.

jasmine (noun) Jasmine is a climbing plant with small sweet-scented white flowers.

jaundice (noun) Jaundice is a condition in which the skin and the whites of the eyes become yellow, because of an illness affecting the liver.

jaundiced (adjective) unenthusiastic and pessimistic, e.g. *He takes a rather jaundiced view of politicians.*

jaunt, jaunts (noun) A jaunt is a journey or trip you go on for pleasure.

jaunty, jauntier, jauntiest (adjective) expressing cheerfulness and self-confidence, e.g. *a jaunty tune.* **jauntily** (adverb).

javelin, javelins (noun) A javelin is a long spear that is thrown in sports competitions.

jaw, jaws 1 (noun) A person's or animal's jaw is the bone in which the teeth are set. **2** A person's or animal's mouth and teeth are their jaws.

jay, jays (noun) A jay is a large bird with blue and black wings.

jazz, jazzes, jazzing, jazzed 1 (noun) Jazz is a style of popular music with a forceful rhythm. **2** (verb; an informal use) To jazz something up means to make it more colourful or exciting.

jazzy, jazzier, jazziest (adjective; an informal word) bright and showy.

jealous 1 (adjective) If you are jealous, you feel bitterness and anger towards someone who has something that you would like to have. **2** If you are jealous of something you have, you feel you must try to keep it from other people. **jealously** (adverb), **jealousy** (noun).

jeans (plural noun) Jeans are casual denim trousers.

jeep, jeeps (noun; a trademark) A jeep is a small road vehicle with four-wheel drive.

jeer, jeers, jeering, jeered 1 (verb) If you jeer at someone, you insult them in a loud, unpleasant way. **2** (noun) Jeers are rude and insulting remarks. **jeering** (adjective).

Jehovah (pronounced ji-**hove**-ah) (proper noun) Jehovah is the name of God in the Old Testament.

jelly, jellies 1 (noun) A jelly is a clear food made from gelatine and eaten as a dessert. **2** Jelly is a type of clear, set jam.

jellyfish, jellyfishes (noun) A jellyfish is a sea animal with a clear soft body and tentacles which may sting.

jeopardize, jeopardizes, jeopardizing, jeopardized (pronounced **jep**-par-dyz); also spelled **jeopardise** (verb) To jeopardize something means to do something which puts it at risk, e.g. *Elaine jeopardized her health.*

jeopardy (noun) If someone or something is in jeopardy, they are at risk of failing or of being destroyed.

jerk, jerks, jerking, jerked 1 (verb) To jerk something means to give it a sudden, sharp pull. **2** If something jerks, it moves suddenly and sharply. **3** (noun) A jerk is a sudden sharp movement. **4** (an informal use) If you call someone a jerk, you mean they are stupid. **jerky** (adjective), **jerkily** (adverb).

jerkin, jerkins (noun) A jerkin is a short sleeveless jacket.

jersey, jerseys 1 (noun) A jersey is a knitted garment for the upper half of the body. **2** Jersey is a type of knitted woollen or cotton fabric used to make clothing.

jest, jests, jesting, jested 1 (noun) A jest is a joke. **2** (verb) To jest means to speak jokingly.

jester, jesters (noun) In the past, a jester was a man who was kept to amuse the king or queen.

jet, jets, jetting, jetted 1 (noun) A jet is a plane which is able to fly very fast. **2** A jet is a stream of liquid, gas, or flame forced out under pressure; also the hole through which it is forced out. **3** (verb) To jet somewhere means to fly there in a plane, especially a jet. **4** (noun) Jet is a hard black stone, usually highly polished and used in jewellery and ornaments.

jet lag (noun) Jet lag is a feeling of tiredness or confusion that people experience after a long journey in an aeroplane.

jettison, jettisons, jettisoning, jettisoned (verb) If you jettison something, you throw it away because you no longer want it or need it.

jetty, jetties (noun) A jetty is a wide stone wall or wooden platform at the edge of the sea or a river, where boats can be moored.

Jew, Jews (pronounced **joo**) (noun) A Jew is a person who believes in and practises the religion of Judaism, or who is of Hebrew descent. **Jewish** (adjective).

jewel, jewels (noun) A jewel is a precious stone used to decorate valuable ornaments or jewellery. **jewelled** (adjective).

jeweller, jewellers (noun) A jeweller is a person who makes jewellery or who buys, sells, and repairs jewellery and watches.

jewellery (noun) Jewellery consists of ornaments that people wear, such as rings, bracelets, or necklaces, made of valuable metals and sometimes decorated with precious stones.

jib, jibs (noun) A jib is a small sail towards the front of a sailing boat.

jibe another spelling of **gibe**.

jig, jigs, jigging, jigged 1 (noun) A jig is a type of lively folk dance. **2** (verb) If you jig, you dance or jump around in a lively bouncy manner.

jiggle, jiggles, jiggling, jiggled (verb) If you jiggle something, you move it around with quick jerky movements.

jigsaw, jigsaws (noun) A jigsaw is a puzzle consisting of a picture on cardboard or wood that has been cut up into small pieces, which have to be put together again.

jilt, jilts, jilting, jilted (verb) If you jilt someone, you suddenly break off your relationship with them. **jilted** (adjective).

jingle, jingles, jingling, jingled 1 (noun) A jingle is a short, catchy phrase or rhyme set to music and used to advertise something on radio or television. **2** (verb) When something jingles, it makes a tinkling sound like small bells. **3** (noun) A jingle is also the sound of something jingling.

jinks (noun) High jinks is boisterous and mischievous behaviour.

jinx, jinxes (noun) A jinx is bad luck or anything that is thought to bring bad luck, e.g. *I think this car has a jinx.*

jitters (plural noun; an informal word) If you have got the jitters, you are feeling very nervous. **jittery** (adjective).

jive, jives, jiving, jived 1 (noun) The jive is a lively, energetic dance that first became popular in the 1950s, and which is performed to rock music. **2** (verb) To jive means to dance the jive.

job, jobs 1 (noun) A job is the

work that someone does to earn money. **2** A job is also a duty or responsibility, e.g. *It is a captain's job to lead from the front.* **3** (phrase) If something is **just the job,** it is exactly right or exactly what you wanted.

job centre, job centres (noun) A job centre is a government office where people can find out about job vacancies.

jobless (adjective) without any work.

jockey, jockeys, jockeying, jockeyed 1 (noun) A jockey is someone who rides a horse in a race. **2** (verb) To jockey for a position means to manoeuvre in order to gain an advantage over other people.

jocular (adjective) A jocular comment is intended to make people laugh.

jodhpurs (pronounced **jod**-purz) (plural noun) Jodhpurs are close-fitting trousers worn when riding a horse.

jog, jogs, jogging, jogged 1 (verb) To jog means to run slowly and rhythmically, often as a form of exercise. **2** (noun) A jog is a slow run. **3** (verb) If you jog something, you knock it or nudge it slightly so that it shakes or moves. **4** If someone or something jogs your memory, they remind you of something. **jogger** (noun), **jogging** (noun).

join, joins, joining, joined 1 (verb) When two things join, or when one thing joins another, they come together. **2** If you join a club or organization, you become a member of it or start taking part in it. **3** To join two things means to fasten them. **4** (noun) A join is a place where two things are fastened together. **join up** (verb) If someone joins up, they become a member of the armed forces.

joiner, joiners (noun) A joiner is a person who makes wooden window frames, door frames, or doors.

joinery (noun) Joinery is the work done by a joiner.

joint, joints, jointing, jointed 1 (adjective) shared by or belonging to two or more people, e.g. *a joint building society account.* **2** (noun) A joint is a part of the body where two bones meet and are joined together so that they can move, for example a knee or hip. **3** A joint is also a place where two things are fixed together. **4** (verb) To joint meat means to cut it into large pieces according to where the bones are. **5** (noun) A joint of meat is a large piece suitable for roasting. **6** (an informal use) A joint is any place of entertainment, such as a nightclub or pub. **jointly** (adverb), **jointed** (adjective).

joist, joists (noun) A joist is a large wooden, concrete, or metal beam used to support floors or ceilings.

joke, jokes, joking, joked 1 (noun) A joke is something that you say or do to make people laugh, such as a funny story. **2** A joke is also anything that you think is ridiculous and not worthy of respect, e.g. *The man is a joke.* **3** (verb) If you are joking, you are teasing someone. **jokingly** (adverb).

joker, jokers (noun) In a pack of cards, a joker is an extra card that does not belong to any of the four suits, but is used in some games.

jolly, jollier, jolliest 1 (adjective) happy, cheerful, and pleasant. **2** (adverb; an informal use) Jolly also means very, e.g. *jolly good fun.*

jolt, jolts, jolting, jolted 1 (verb) To jolt means to move or shake roughly and violently. **2** If you are jolted by something, it gives you an unpleasant shock or surprise. **3** (noun) A jolt is a sudden jerky movement. **4** A jolt is also an unpleasant shock or surprise.

jostle, jostles, jostling, jostled (verb) To jostle means to push or knock roughly against people in a crowd.

jot, jots, jotting, jotted 1 (verb) If you jot something down, you write it quickly in the form of a short informal note. **2** (noun) A jot means a very small amount. **jotting** (noun).

jotter, jotters (noun) A jotter is a pad or notebook.

joule, joules (rhymes with **school**) (noun) A joule is a unit of energy or work.

journal, journals 1 (noun) A journal is a magazine which is published regularly and devoted to a particular subject, trade, or profession. **2** A journal is also a diary which someone keeps regularly.

journalism (noun) Journalism is the work of collecting, writing, and publishing news in newspapers, magazines, and on television and radio. **journalist** (noun), **journalistic** (adjective).

journey, journeys, journeying, journeyed 1 (noun) A journey is the act of travelling from one place to another. **2** (verb; a formal use) To journey somewhere means to travel there, e.g. *He intended to journey up the Amazon.*

joust, jousts (noun) In medieval times, a joust was a competition between knights fighting on horseback, using lances.

jovial (adjective) cheerful and friendly. **jovially** (adverb), **joviality** (noun).

joy, joys 1 (noun) Joy is a feeling of great happiness. **2** (an informal use) Joy also means success or luck, e.g. *Any joy with your insurance claim?* **3** A joy is something that makes you happy or gives you pleasure.

joyful 1 (adjective) causing pleasure and happiness. **2** Someone who is joyful is extremely happy. **joyfully** (adverb).

joyous (adjective; a formal word) joyful. **joyously** (adverb).

joyride, joyrides (noun) A joyride is a drive in a stolen car for pleasure. **joyriding** (noun), **joyrider** (noun).

joystick, joysticks (noun) A joystick is a lever in an aircraft which the pilot uses to control height and direction.

jubilant (adjective) feeling or expressing great happiness or triumph. **jubilantly** (adverb).

jubilation (noun) Jubilation is a feeling of great happiness and triumph.

jubilee, jubilees (noun) A jubilee is a special anniversary of an event such as a coronation, e.g. *the Queen's Silver Jubilee in 1977.*

Judaism (pronounced **joo**-day-i-zm) (noun) Judaism is the religion of the Jewish people. It is based on a belief in one God, and draws its laws and authority from the Old Testament. **Judaic** (adjective).

judder, judders, juddering, juddered (verb) To judder means to shake and vibrate noisily and violently.

judge, judges, judging, judged 1 (noun) A judge is the person in a law court who has the power to decide how the law should be applied to people who appear in the court. **2** A judge is also someone who decides the winner in a contest or competition. **3** (verb) If you judge someone or something, you form an opinion about them based on the evidence or information that you have. **4** To judge a contest or competition means to decide on the winner. **judgment** or **judgement** (noun).

judicial (adjective) relating to judgment or to justice, e.g. *a judicial review.*

judiciary (noun) The judiciary is the branch of government concerned with justice and the legal system.

judicious (adjective) sensible and showing good judgment. **judiciously** (adverb).

judo (noun) Judo is a sport in which two people try to force each other to the ground using special throwing techniques.

jug, jugs (noun) A jug is a container with a lip or spout used for holding or serving liquids.

juggernaut, juggernauts (noun) A juggernaut is a large heavy lorry.

juggle, juggles, juggling, juggled (verb) To juggle means to throw balls or other objects into the air, catching them in sequence, and tossing them up again so there are several in the air at one time. **juggler** (noun).

jugular, jugulars (noun) The jugular or jugular vein is one of the veins in the neck which carry blood from the head back to the heart.

juice, juices 1 (noun) Juice is the liquid that can be squeezed or extracted from fruit, vegetables, or meat. **2** Juices in the body are fluids, e.g. *gastric juices.*

juicy, juicier, juiciest 1 (adjective) Juicy food has a lot of juice in it. **2** Something that is juicy is interesting, exciting, or scandalous, e.g. *the juicy prospect of Germany playing Brazil.*

jukebox, jukeboxes (noun) A jukebox is a large record player found in cafés and pubs which automatically plays a selected record when coins are inserted.

July (noun) July is the seventh month of the year. It has 31 days.

jumble, jumbles, jumbling, jumbled 1 (noun) A jumble is an untidy muddle of things. **2** Jumble consists of articles for a jumble sale. **3** (verb) To jumble things means to mix them up untidily.

jumble sale, jumble sales (noun) A jumble sale is an event at which cheap second-hand clothes and other articles are sold to raise money, usually for a charity.

jumbo, jumbos 1 (noun) A jumbo or jumbo jet is a large jet aeroplane that can carry several hundred passengers. **2** (adjective) very large, e.g. *jumbo packs of elastic bands.*

jump, jumps, jumping, jumped 1 (verb) To jump means to spring off the ground or some other surface using your leg muscles. **2** To jump something means to spring off the ground and move over or across it. **3** If you jump at something such as an opportunity, you accept it eagerly. **4** If you jump on someone, you criticize them suddenly and forcefully. **5** If someone jumps, they make a sudden sharp movement of surprise. **6** If an amount or level jumps, it suddenly increases. **7** (noun) A jump is a spring into the air, sometimes over an object.

jumper, jumpers (noun) A jumper is a knitted garment for the top half of the body.

jumpy, jumpier, jumpiest (adjective) nervous and worried.

junction, junctions (noun) A junction is a place where roads or railway lines meet, join, or cross.

June (noun) June is the sixth month of the year. It has 30 days.

jungle, jungles 1 (noun) A jungle is a dense tropical forest. **2** A jungle is also a tangled mass of plants or other objects.

junior, juniors 1 (adjective) Someone who is junior to other people has a lower position in an organization. **2** Junior also means younger. **3** relating to childhood, e.g. *a junior school.* **4** (noun) A junior is someone who holds an unimportant position in an organization.

juniper, junipers (noun) A juniper is an evergreen shrub with purple berries which may be used in cooking and medicine.

junk, junks 1 (noun) Junk is old or second-hand articles which are sold cheaply or are discarded. **2** If you think something is junk, you think it is worthless rubbish. **3** A junk is a Chinese sailing boat with a flat bottom and square sails.

junk food (noun) Junk food is food low in nutritional value which is eaten as well as or instead of proper meals.

junkie, junkies (noun; an informal word) A junkie is a drug addict.

Jupiter (noun) Jupiter is the largest planet in the solar system and the fifth from the sun.

jurisdiction 1 (noun; a formal word) Jurisdiction is the power or right of the courts to apply laws and make legal judgments, e.g. *The Court held that it did not have the jurisdiction to examine the merits of the case.* **2** Jurisdiction is power or authority, e.g. *The airport was under French jurisdiction.*

juror, jurors (noun) A juror is a member of a jury.

jury, juries (noun) A jury is a group of people in a court of law who have been selected to listen to the facts of a case on trial, and to decide whether the accused person is guilty or not.

just 1 (adjective) fair and impartial, e.g. *He arrived at a just decision.* **2** morally right or proper, e.g. *a just reward.* **3** (adverb) If something has just happened, it happened a very short time ago. **4** If you just do something, you do it by a very small amount, e.g. *They only just won.* **5** simply or only, e.g. *It was just an excuse not to mow the lawn.* **6** exactly, e.g. *It's just what she wanted.* **justly** (adverb).

justice, justices 1 (noun) Justice is fairness and reasonableness. **2** The system of justice in a country is the way in which laws are maintained by the courts. **3** A justice is a judge or magistrate.

justify, justifies, justifying, justified (verb) If you justify an action or idea, you prove or explain why it is reasonable or necessary. **justification** (noun), **justifiable** (adjective).

jut, juts, jutting, jutted (verb) If something juts out, it sticks out beyond or above a surface or edge.

jute (noun) Jute is a strong fibre made from the bark of an Asian plant, used to make rope and sacking.

juvenile, juveniles 1 (adjective) suitable for young people. **2** childish and rather silly, e.g. *a juvenile game.* **3** (noun) A juvenile is a young person not old enough to be considered an adult.

juxtapose, juxtaposes, juxtaposing, juxtaposed (verb) If you juxtapose things or ideas, you put them side by side or close together, often to emphasize the difference between them. **juxtaposition** (noun).

K k

kaleidoscope, kaleidoscopes (pronounced kal-**eye**-dos-skope) (noun) A kaleidoscope is a toy consisting of a tube with a hole at one end. When you look through the hole and twist the other end of the tube, you can see a changing pattern of colours.

kamikaze (noun) In the Second World War, a kamikaze was a Japanese pilot who performed a suicide mission by flying an aircraft loaded with explosives directly into an enemy target.

kangaroo, kangaroos (noun) A kangaroo is a large Australian animal with very strong back legs which it uses for jumping.

karate (pronounced kar-**rat**-ee) (noun) Karate is a sport in which people fight each other using only their hands, elbows, feet, and legs.

kayak, kayaks (pronounced **ky**-ak) (noun) A kayak is a covered canoe with a small opening for the person sitting in it, originally used by Eskimos.

kebab, kebabs (noun) A kebab consists of pieces of meat or vegetable stuck on a stick and grilled.

keel, keels, keeling, keeled 1

(noun) The keel of a ship is the specially shaped bottom which supports the sides and sits in the water. **2** (verb) If someone or something keels over, they fall down sideways.

keen, keener, keenest 1 (adjective) Someone who is keen shows great eagerness and enthusiasm. **2** If you are keen on someone or something, you are attracted to or fond of them. **3** Keen senses let you see, hear, smell, and taste things very clearly or strongly. **keenly** (adverb), **keenness** (noun).

keep, keeps, keeping, kept 1 (verb) To keep someone or something in a particular condition means to make them stay in that condition, e.g. *We'll walk to keep warm.* **2** If you keep something, you have it and look after it. **3** If you keep doing something, you do it repeatedly or continuously, e.g. *I kept phoning the hospital.* **4** If you keep a promise, you do what you promised to do. **5** If you keep a secret, you do not tell anyone else. **6** If you keep a diary, you write something in it every day. **7** If you keep someone from going somewhere, you delay them so that they are late. **8** To keep someone means to provide them with money, food, and clothing. **9** (noun) Your keep is the cost of the food you eat, your housing, and your clothing, e.g. *He does not contribute towards his keep.* **10** A keep is the main tower inside the walls of a castle. **keep up** (verb) If you keep up with other people, you move or work at the same speed as they do.

keeper, keepers 1 (noun) A keeper is a person whose job is to look after the animals in a zoo. **2** A keeper is also a goalkeeper in football or hockey.

keeping 1 (noun) If something is in your keeping, it has been given to you to look after for a while. **2** (phrase) If one thing is **in keeping with** another, the two things are suitable or appropriate together.

keepsake, keepsakes (noun) A keepsake is something that someone gives you to remind you of a particular person or event.

keg, kegs (noun) A keg is a small barrel.

kennel, kennels 1 (noun) A kennel is a shelter for a dog. **2** A kennels is a place where dogs can be kept for a time, or where they are bred.

Kenyan, Kenyans (pronounced **keen**-yan) **1** (adjective) belonging or relating to Kenya. **2** (noun) A Kenyan is someone who comes from Kenya.

kerb, kerbs (noun) A kerb is the raised edge at the point where a pavement joins onto a road.

kernel, kernels (noun) A kernel is the part of a nut that is inside the shell.

kerosene (noun) Kerosene is the same as paraffin.

kestrel, kestrels (noun) A kestrel is a type of small falcon.

ketchup (noun) Ketchup is a cold sauce, usually made from tomatoes.

kettle, kettles (noun) A kettle is a metal container with a spout, which you use to boil water in.

key, keys, keying, keyed 1 (noun) A key is a shaped piece of metal that fits into a hole so that you can unlock a door, wind a clockwork mechanism, or start a car. **2** The keys on a typewriter, piano, or cash register are the buttons that you press to use it. **3** A key is also an explanation of the symbols used in a map or diagram. **4** In music, a key is a scale of notes. **5** (verb) If you key in information on a computer keyboard, you type it.

keyboard, keyboards (noun) A keyboard is a row of levers or buttons on a piano, organ, typewriter, or computer.

kg an abbreviation for 'kilograms'.

khaki (pronounced **kah**-kee) **1** (noun) Khaki is a strong yellowish-brown material, used especially for military uniforms. **2** (noun or adjective) yellowish-brown.

kibbutz, kibbutzim (pronounced kib-**boots**) (noun) A kibbutz is a place of work in Israel, for example a farm or factory, where the workers live together and share all the duties and income.

kick, kicks, kicking, kicked 1 (verb) If you kick something, you hit it with your foot. **2** (noun) If you give something a kick, you hit it with your foot. **3** (an informal use) If you get a kick out of doing something, you enjoy doing it very much. **kick off** (verb) When players kick off, they start a football or rugby match. **kick-off** (noun).

kid, kids, kidding, kidded 1 (noun; an informal use) A kid is a child. **2** A kid is also a young goat. **3** (verb) If you kid people, you tease them by deceiving them in fun.

kidnap, kidnaps, kidnapping, kidnapped (verb) To kidnap someone means to take them away by force and demand a ransom in exchange for returning them. **kidnapper** (noun), **kidnapping** (noun).

kidney, kidneys (noun) Your kidneys are two organs in your body that remove waste products from your blood.

kill, kills, killing, killed 1 (verb) To kill a person, animal, or plant means to make them die. **2** If something is killing you, it is causing you severe pain or discomfort, e.g. *My arms are killing me.* **3** (noun) The kill is the moment when a hunter kills an animal. **killer** (noun).

kiln, kilns (noun) A kiln is an oven for baking china or pottery until it becomes hard and dry.

kilo, kilos (noun) A kilo is a kilogram.

kilogram, kilograms (noun) The kilogram is a unit of weight equal to 1000 grams.

kilohertz (noun) A kilohertz is a unit of measurement of radio waves equal to one thousand hertz.

kilometre, kilometres (noun) A kilometre is a unit of distance equal to one thousand metres.

kilowatt, kilowatts (noun) A kilowatt is a unit of power equal to one thousand watts.

kilt, kilts (noun) A kilt is a tartan skirt worn by men as part of Scottish Highland dress.

kimono, kimonos (noun) A kimono is a long, loose garment with wide sleeves and a sash, worn in Japan.

kin (plural noun) Your kin are your relatives.

kind, kinds; kinder, kindest 1 (noun) A particular kind of thing is something of the same type or sort as other things, e.g. *that kind of film.* **2** (adjective) Someone who is kind is considerate and generous towards other people. **kindly** (adverb), **kindness** (noun).

kindergarten, kindergartens (noun) A kindergarten is a school for children who are too young to go to primary school.

kindle, kindles, kindling, kindled 1 (verb) If you kindle a fire, you light it. **2** If something kindles a feeling in you, it causes you to have that feeling.

kindling (noun) Kindling is bits of dry wood or paper that you use to start a fire.

kindred (adjective) If you say that someone is a kindred spirit, you mean that they have the same interests or opinions as you.

kinetic energy (noun) Kinetic energy is the energy that is produced when something moves.

king, kings 1 (noun) The king of a country is a man who is the head of state in the country, and who inherited his position from his parents. **2** In chess, the king is a piece which can only move one square at a time. **3** In a pack of cards, a king is a card with a picture of a king on it.

kingdom, kingdoms 1 (noun) A kingdom is a country that is governed by a king or queen. **2** The divisions of the natural world are called kingdoms, e.g. *the animal kingdom.*

kingfisher, kingfishers (noun) A kingfisher is a brightly coloured bird that lives near water and feeds on fish.

king-size or **king-sized** (adjective) larger than the normal size, e.g. *a king-size bed.*

kink, kinks (noun) A kink is a dent or curve in something which is normally straight.

kinky (adjective; an informal word) having peculiar sexual tastes.

kinship (noun) Kinship is a family relationship to other people.

kiosk, kiosks (pronounced **kee**-osk) (noun) A kiosk is a covered stall on a street where you can buy sandwiches, newspapers, sweets, or cigarettes.

kip, kips, kipping, kipped (an informal word) **1** (noun) A kip is a period of sleep. **2** (verb) When you kip, you sleep.

kipper, kippers (noun) A kipper is a smoked herring.

kirk, kirks (noun) In Scotland, a kirk is a church.

kiss, kisses, kissing, kissed 1 (verb) When you kiss someone, you touch them with your lips as a sign of love or affection. **2** (noun) When you give someone a kiss, you kiss them.

kiss of life (noun) The kiss of life is a method of reviving someone by blowing air into their lungs.

kit, kits 1 (noun) A kit is a collection of things that you use for a sport or other activity. **2** A kit is also a set of parts that you put together to make something.

kitchen, kitchens (noun) A kitchen is a room used for cooking and preparing food.

kite, kites 1 (noun) A kite is a frame covered with paper or cloth which is attached to a piece of string, and which you fly in the air. **2** A kite is also a large bird of prey with a long tail and long wings.

kitten, kittens (noun) A kitten is a young cat.

kitty, kitties (noun) A kitty is a fund of money that has been given by a group of people who will use it to pay for or do things together.

kiwi, kiwis (pronounced **kee**-wee) (noun) A kiwi is a type of bird found in New Zealand. Kiwis cannot fly.

kiwi fruit, kiwi fruits (noun) A kiwi fruit is a fruit with a brown hairy skin and green flesh.

km an abbreviation for 'kilometres'.

knack (noun) A knack is an ability to do something difficult with apparent ease, e.g. *the knack of making friends.*

knead, kneads, kneading, kneaded (verb) If you knead dough, you press it and squeeze it with your hands before baking it.

knee, knees (noun) Your knee is the joint in your leg between your ankle and your hip.

kneecap, kneecaps (noun) Your kneecaps are the bones at the front of your knees.

kneel, kneels, kneeling, knelt (verb) When you kneel, you bend your legs and lower your body until your knees are touching the ground.

knell, knells (noun; a literary word) A knell is the sound of a bell rung to announce a death or at a funeral.

knickers (plural noun) Knickers are underpants worn by women and girls.

knick-knacks (plural noun) Knick-knacks are small ornaments.

knife, knives; knifes, knifing, knifed 1 (noun) A knife is a sharp metal tool that you use to cut things. **2** (verb) To knife someone means to stab them with a knife.

knight, knights, knighting, knighted 1 (noun) A knight is a man who has been given the title 'Sir' by the King or Queen. **2** In medieval Europe, a knight was a man who served a monarch or lord as a mounted soldier. **3** A knight is a chess piece that is usually in the shape of a horse's head. **4** (verb) To knight a man means to give him the title 'Sir'. **knighthood** (noun).

knit, knits, knitting, knitted 1 (verb) If you knit a piece of clothing, you make it by working lengths of wool together, either using needles held in the hand, or with a machine. **2** If you knit your brows, you frown. **knitting** (noun).

knob, knobs 1 (noun) A knob is a round handle. **2** A knob is also a round switch on a machine, e.g. *the knobs of a radio.*

knock, knocks, knocking, knocked 1 (verb) If you knock on something, you strike it with your hand or fist. **2** If you knock a part of your body against something, you bump into it quite forcefully. **3** (an informal use) To knock someone means to criticize them. **4** (noun) A knock is a firm blow on something solid, e.g. *There was a knock at the door.* **knock out** (verb) To knock someone out means to hit them so hard that they become unconscious.

knocker, knockers (noun) A knocker is a metal lever attached to a door, which you use to knock on the door.

knockout, knockouts 1 (noun) A knockout is a punch in boxing which succeeds in knocking a boxer unconscious. **2** A knockout is also a competition in which competitors are eliminated in each round until only the winner is left.

knoll, knolls (rhymes with **roll**) (noun; a literary word) A knoll is a gently sloping hill with a rounded top.

knot, knots, knotting, knotted 1 (noun) A knot is a fastening made by looping a piece of string around itself and pulling the ends tight. **2** A knot in a piece of wood is a small lump that is visible on the surface. **3** A knot of people is a small group of them. **4** (a technical use) A knot is a unit of speed used for ships and aircraft. **5** (verb) If you knot a piece of string, you tie a knot in it.

know, knows, knowing, knew, known 1 (verb) If you know a fact, you have it in your mind and you do not need to learn it. **2** People you know are not strangers because you have met them and spoken to them. **3** (an informal phrase) If you are **in the know,** you are one of a small number of people who share a secret.

know-how (noun) Know-how is the ability to do something that is quite difficult or technical.

knowing (adjective) A knowing look is one that shows that you know or understand something that other people do not. **knowingly** (adverb).

knowledge (noun) Knowledge is all the information and facts that you know.

knowledgeable (adjective) Someone who is knowledgeable knows a lot.

knuckle, knuckles (noun) Your knuckles are the joints at the end of your fingers where they join your hand.

koala, koalas (noun) A koala is an Australian animal with grey fur and small tufted ears. Koalas live in trees and eat eucalyptus leaves.

Koran (pronounced kaw-**rahn**) (noun) The Koran is the holy book of Islam.

Korean, Koreans (pronounced kor-**ree**-an) **1** (adjective) relating or belonging to Korea. **2** (noun) A Korean is someone who comes from Korea. **3** Korean is the main language spoken in Korea.

kosher (pronounced **koh**-sher) (adjective) Kosher food has been specially prepared to be eaten according to Jewish law.

kung fu (pronounced kung **foo**) (noun) Kung fu is a Chinese style of fighting which involves using your hands and feet.

Kurd, Kurds (noun) The Kurds are a group of people who live mainly in eastern Turkey, northern Iraq, and western Iran.

Kurdish 1 (adjective) belonging or relating to the Kurds. **2** (noun) Kurdish is the language spoken by the Kurds.

L l

l an abbreviation for 'litres'.

lab, labs (noun; an informal word) A lab is a laboratory.

label, labels, labelling, labelled 1 (noun) A label is a piece of paper or plastic attached to something as an identification. **2** (verb) If you label something, you put a label on it.

laboratory, laboratories (noun) A laboratory is a place where scientific experiments are carried out.

laborious (adjective) needing a lot of effort or time. **laboriously** (adverb).

labour, labours, labouring, laboured 1 (noun) Labour is hard work. **2** The workforce of a country or industry is sometimes called its labour, e.g. *unskilled labour*. **3** Labour or the Labour Party is one of the two main political parties in Britain. It believes in social equality. **4** Labour is also the last stage of pregnancy when a woman gives birth to a baby. **5** (verb; an old-fashioned use) To labour means to work hard. **labourer** (noun).

labrador, labradors (noun) A labrador is a large dog with short black or golden hair.

labyrinth, labyrinths (pronounced **lab**-er-inth) (noun) A labyrinth is a complicated series of paths or passages.

lace, laces, lacing, laced 1 (noun) Lace is a very fine decorated cloth made with a lot of holes in it. **2** Laces are cords with which you fasten your shoes. **3** (verb) When you lace up your shoes, you tie a bow in the laces. **lacy** (adjective).

lack, lacks, lacking, lacked 1 (noun) If there is a lack of something, it is not present when or where it is needed. **2** (verb) If something is lacking, it is not present when or where it is needed. **3** If someone or something is lacking something, they do not have it or do not have enough of it, e.g. *Francis was lacking in stamina*.

lacklustre (pronounced **lak**-luss-ter) (adjective) dull and unexciting.

laconic (pronounced lak-**kon** ik) (adjective) using very few words.

lacquer, lacquers (pronounced **lak**-er) (noun) Lacquer is thin, clear paint that you put on wood to protect it and make it shiny.

lacrosse (noun) Lacrosse is an outdoor ball game in which two teams try to score goals using long sticks with nets on the end of them.

lad, lads (noun) A lad is a boy or young man.

ladder, ladders 1 (noun) A ladder is a wooden or metal frame used for climbing which consists of horizontal steps fixed to two vertical poles. **2** If your stockings or tights have a ladder in them, they have a vertical, ladder-like tear in them.

laden (pronounced **lay**-den) (adjective) To be laden with something means to be carrying a lot of it, e.g. *bushes laden with ripe fruit.*

ladle, ladles, ladling, ladled 1 (noun) A ladle is a long-handled spoon with a deep, round bowl, which you use to serve soup. **2** (verb) If you ladle out food, you serve it with a ladle.

lady, ladies 1 (noun) A lady is a woman, especially one who is considered to be polite and socially correct. **2** Lady is a title used in front of the name of a woman from the nobility, such as a lord's wife.

ladybird, ladybirds (noun) A ladybird is a small flying beetle with a round red body patterned with black spots.

lady-in-waiting, ladies-in-waiting (noun) A lady-in-waiting is a woman who acts as companion to a queen.

ladylike (adjective) behaving in a polite and socially correct way.

Ladyship, Ladyships (noun) You address a woman who has the title 'Lady' as 'Your Ladyship'.

lag, lags, lagging, lagged (verb) To lag behind means to make slower progress than other people or processes.

lager, lagers (noun) Lager is light-coloured beer.

lagoon, lagoons (noun) A lagoon is an area of water separated from the sea by reefs or sand.

laid the past tense and past participle of **lay.**

lain the past participle of some meanings of **lie.**

lair, lairs (noun) A lair is a place where a wild animal lives.

laird, lairds (rhymes with **dared**) (noun) A laird is a landowner in Scotland.

lake, lakes (noun) A lake is an area of fresh water surrounded by land.

lama, lamas (noun) A lama is a Buddhist priest or monk.

lamb, lambs 1 (noun) A lamb is a young sheep. **2** Lamb is the meat from a lamb or a sheep.

lame 1 (adjective) Someone who is lame has an injured leg and cannot walk easily. **2** A lame excuse is unconvincing. **lamely** (adverb), **lameness** (noun).

lament, laments, lamenting, lamented 1 (verb) To lament something means to express sorrow or regret about it. **2** (noun) A lament is an expression of sorrow or regret. **3** A lament is also a song or poem expressing grief at someone's death.

lamentable (adjective) disappointing and regrettable.

laminated (adjective) consisting of several thin sheets or layers stuck together, e.g.

laminated glass.

lamp, lamps (noun) A lamp is a device that produces light, e.g. *a table lamp.*

lamppost, lampposts (noun) A lamppost is a tall column in a street, with a lamp at the top.

lampshade, lampshades (noun) A lampshade is a decorative covering over an electric light bulb which prevents the bulb giving out too harsh a light.

lance, lances, lancing, lanced 1 (verb) To lance a boil or abscess means to stick a sharp instrument into it in order to release the fluid. **2** (noun) A lance is a long spear that used to be used by soldiers on horseback.

land, lands, landing, landed 1 (noun) Land is an area of ground. **2** Land is also the part of the earth that is not covered by sea, lakes, or rivers. **3** A land is a country, e.g. *our native land.* **4** (verb) When a plane lands, it arrives back on the ground after a flight. **5** If you land something you have been trying to get, you succeed in getting it, e.g. *She eventually landed a job with a local radio station.* **6** To land a fish means to catch it while fishing.

landing, landings 1 (noun) A landing is a flat area in a building at the top of a flight of stairs. **2** The landing of an aeroplane is its arrival back on the ground after a flight, e.g. *a smooth landing.*

landlady, landladies (noun) A landlady is a woman who owns a house or small hotel and who lets rooms to people.

landlord, landlords (noun) A landlord is a man who owns a house or small hotel and who lets rooms to people.

landmark, landmarks 1 (noun) A landmark is a noticeable feature in a landscape, which you can use to check your position. **2** A landmark is also an important stage in the development of something, e.g. *The play is a landmark in Japanese theatre.*

landscape, landscapes 1 (noun) The landscape is the view over an area of open land. **2** A landscape is a painting of the countryside.

landslide, landslides 1 (noun) A landslide is loose earth and rocks falling down a mountain side. **2** In an election, a landslide is a victory won by a large number of votes.

lane, lanes 1 (noun) A lane is a narrow road, especially in the country. **2** A lane in a road is one of the strips marked with lines to guide drivers.

language, languages 1 (noun) A language is the system of words that the people of a country use to communicate with each other. **2** Your language is the style in which you express yourself, e.g. *His language is often obscure.* **3** Language is the study of the words and grammar of a particular language.

languid (pronounced **lang**-gwid) (adjective) slow and lacking energy. **languidly** (adverb).

languish, languishes, languishing, languished (verb) If you languish, you endure an unpleasant situation for a long time, e.g. *The majority languished in poverty.*

lanky, lankier, lankiest (adjective) Someone who is lanky is tall and thin and moves rather awkwardly.

lantern, lanterns (noun) A lantern is a lamp in a metal frame with glass sides.

lap, laps, lapping, lapped 1 (noun) Your lap is the flat area formed by your thighs when you are sitting down. **2** A lap is one circuit of a running track or racecourse. **3** (verb) When an animal laps up liquid, it drinks using its tongue to get the liquid into its mouth. **4** If you lap someone in a race, you overtake them when they are still on the previous lap. **5** When water laps against something, it gently moves against it in little waves.

lapel, lapels (pronounced lap-**el**) (noun) A lapel is a flap which is joined on to the collar of a jacket or coat.

lapse, lapses, lapsing, lapsed 1 (noun) A lapse is a moment of bad behaviour by someone who usually behaves well. **2** A lapse is also a slight mistake. **3** A lapse is also a period of time between two events. **4** (verb) If you lapse into a different way of behaving, you start behaving that way, e.g. *The offenders lapsed into a sullen silence.* **5** If a legal document or contract lapses, it is not renewed on the date when it expires.

lard (noun) Lard is fat from a pig, used in cooking.

larder, larders (noun) A larder is a room in which you store food, often next to a kitchen.

large, larger, largest 1 (adjective) Someone or something that is large is much bigger than average. **2** (phrase) If a prisoner is **at large,** he or she has escaped from prison.

largely (adverb) to a great extent, e.g. *The public are largely unaware of this.*

lark, larks 1 (noun) A lark is a small brown bird with a distinctive song. **2** If you do something for a lark, you do it in a high-spirited or mischievous way for amusement.

larva, larvae (noun) A larva is an insect at the stage before it becomes an adult. Larvae look like short, fat worms.

laryngitis (pronounced lar-in-**jie**-tiss) (noun) Laryngitis is an infection of the throat which causes you to lose your voice.

larynx, larynxes or **larynges** (noun) Your larynx is the part of your throat containing the vocal cords, through which air passes between your nose and lungs.

lasagne (pronounced laz-**zan**-ya) (noun) Lasagne is an Italian dish made with wide flat sheets of pasta, meat, and cheese sauce.

laser, lasers (noun) A laser is a machine that produces a powerful concentrated beam of light which is used to cut very hard materials and in some kinds of surgery.

lash, lashes, lashing, lashed 1 (noun) Your lashes are the hairs growing on the edge of your eyelids. **2** A lash is a strip of leather at the end of a whip. **3** Lashes are blows struck with a whip. **lash out** (verb) To lash out at someone means to criticize them severely.

lass, lasses (noun) A lass is a girl or young woman.

lasso, lassoes or **lassos, lassoing, lassoed** (pronounced las**soo**) **1** (noun) A lasso is a length of rope with a noose at one end, used by cowboys to catch cattle and horses. **2** (verb) To lasso an animal means to catch it by throwing the noose of a lasso around its neck.

last, lasts, lasting, lasted 1 (adjective) The last thing or event is the most recent one, e.g. *last year.* **2** The last thing that remains is the only one left after all the others have gone, e.g. *The last family left the island in 1950.* **3** (adverb) If you last did something on a particular occasion, you have not done it since then, e.g. *They last met in Rome.* **4** The thing that happens last in a sequence of events is the final one, e.g. *He added the milk last.* **5** (verb) If something lasts, it continues to exist or happen, e.g. *Her speech lasted for fifty minutes.* **6** To last also means to remain in good condition, e.g. *The mixture will last for up to 2 weeks in the fridge.* **7** (phrase) **At last** means after a long time, e.g. *The coffee arrived at last.* **lastly** (adverb).

last-ditch (adjective) A last-ditch attempt to do something is a final attempt to succeed when everything else has failed.

latch, latches, latching, latched 1 (noun) A latch is a simple door fastening consisting of a metal bar which falls into a hook. **2** A latch is also a type of door lock which locks automatically when you close the door and which has to be opened with a key. **3** (verb; an informal use) If you latch onto someone or something, you become attached to them.

late, later, latest 1 (adjective or adverb) Something that happens late happens towards the end of a period of time, e.g. *the late evening... late in the morning.* **2** If you arrive late, or do something late, you arrive or do it after the time you were expected to. **3** (adjective) A late event happens after the time when it usually takes place, e.g. *a late breakfast.* **4** (a formal use) Late means dead, e.g. *the late John Arlott.*

lately (adverb) Events that happened lately happened recently.

latent (adjective) A latent quality is hidden at the moment, but may emerge in the future, e.g. *a latent talent for drawing.*

lateral (adjective) relating to the sides of something, or moving in a sideways direction.

lathe, lathes (noun) A lathe is a machine which holds and turns a piece of wood or metal against a tool in order to cut and shape it.

lather, lathers (noun) Lather is the foam that you get when you rub soap in water.

Latin, Latins 1 (noun) Latin is the language of ancient Rome. **2** (noun or adjective) Latins are people who speak languages closely related to Latin, such as French, Italian, Spanish, and Portuguese.

Latin America (noun) Latin America consists of the countries in North, South, and Central America where Spanish or Portuguese is the main language. **Latin American** (adjective).

latitude, latitudes (noun) The latitude of a place is its distance north or south of the equator measured in degrees.

latrine, latrines (pronounced lat-**reen**) (noun) A latrine is a hole or trench in the ground used as a toilet at a camp.

latter 1 (adjective or noun) You use latter to refer to the second of two things that are mentioned, e.g. *They were eating sandwiches and cakes (the latter bought from Mrs Paul's bakery).* **2** (adjective) Latter also describes the second or end part of something, e.g. *The latter part of his career.*

latterly (adverb; a formal word) Latterly means recently, e.g. *It's only latterly that this has become an issue.*

lattice, lattices (noun) A lattice is a structure made of strips of wood which cross over each other diagonally leaving holes in between.

laudable (adjective; a formal word) deserving praise, e.g. *It is a laudable enough aim.*

laugh, laughs, laughing, laughed 1 (verb) When you laugh, you make a noise which shows that you are amused or happy. **2** (noun) A laugh is the noise you make when you laugh. **laughter** (noun).

laughable (adjective) quite absurd.

laughing stock (noun) A laughing stock is someone who has been made to seem ridiculous.

launch, launches, launching, launched 1 (verb) To launch a ship means to send it into the water for the first time. **2** To launch a rocket means to send it into space. **3** When a company launches a new product, they have an advertising campaign to promote it as they start to sell it. **4** (noun) A launch is a motorboat.

launch pad, launch pads (noun) A launch pad, or a launching pad, is the place from which space rockets take off.

launder, launders, laundering, laundered (verb; an old-fashioned word) To launder clothes, sheets, or towels means to wash and iron them.

laundry, laundries 1 (noun) A laundry is a business that washes and irons clothes, sheets, and towels. **2** Laundry is also the dirty clothes, sheets, and towels that are being washed, or are about to be washed.

laurel, laurels (noun) A laurel is an evergreen tree with shiny leaves.

lava (noun) Lava is the very hot liquid rock that comes shooting out of an erupting volcano, and becomes solid as it cools.

lavatory, lavatories (noun) A lavatory is a toilet.

lavender (noun) Lavender is a small bush with bluish-pink flowers that have a strong, pleasant scent.

lavish, lavishes, lavishing, lav-

ished 1 (adjective) If you are lavish, you are very generous with your time, money, or gifts. **2** A lavish amount is a large amount. **3** (verb) If you lavish presents, money, or affection on someone, you give them a lot of it. **lavishly** (adverb).

law, laws 1 (noun) The law is the system of rules developed by the government of a country, which regulate what people may and may not do and deals with people who break these rules. **2** The law is also the profession of people such as lawyers and solicitors, whose job involves the application of the laws of a country. **3** A law is one of the rules established by a government or a religion, which tells people what they may or may not do. **4** A law is also a scientific fact which allows you to explain how things work in the physical world. **lawful** (adjective), **lawfully** (adverb).

law-abiding (adjective) obeying the law and not causing any trouble.

lawless (adjective) having no regard for the law.

lawn, lawns (noun) A lawn is an area of cultivated grass.

lawnmower, lawnmowers (noun) A lawnmower is a machine for cutting grass.

lawsuit, lawsuits (noun) A lawsuit is a civil court case between two people, as opposed to the police prosecuting someone for a criminal offence.

lawyer, lawyers (noun) A lawyer is a person who is qualified in law, and whose job is to advise people about the law and represent them in court.

lax (adjective) careless and not keeping up the usual standards, e.g. *a lax accounting system.*

laxative, laxatives (noun) A laxative is something that you eat or drink to stop you being constipated.

lay, lays, laying, laid 1 (verb) When you lay something somewhere, you put it down so that it lies there. **2** If you lay the table, you put cutlery on the table ready for a meal. **3** When a bird lays an egg, it produces the egg out of its body. **4** If you lay a trap for someone, you create a situation in which you will be able to catch them out. **5** If you lay emphasis on something, you refer to it in a way that shows you think it is very important. **6** (adjective) You use lay to describe people who are involved with a Christian church but are not members of the clergy, monks, or nuns, e.g. *a lay preacher.* **7** Lay is the past tense of some senses of **lie. lay off 1** (verb) When workers are laid off, their employers tell them not to come to work for a while because there is a shortage of work. **2** (an informal use) If you tell someone to lay off, you want them to stop doing something annoying.

lay-by, lay-bys (noun) A lay-by is an area by the side of a main road where motorists can stop for a short while.

layer, layers (noun) A layer is a single thickness of something, e.g. *layers of clothing.*

layman, laymen 1 (noun) A layman is someone who does not have specialized knowledge of a subject, e.g. *a layman's guide to computers.* **2** A layman is a someone who belongs to the church but is not a member of the clergy.

layout, layouts (noun) The layout of something is the pattern in which it is arranged.

laze, lazes, lazing, lazed (verb) If you laze, you relax and do no work, e.g. *We spent a few days lazing around by the pool.*

lazy, lazier, laziest (adjective) idle and unwilling to work. **lazily** (adverb), **laziness** (noun).

lb an abbreviation for 'pounds', e.g. *3lb of sugar.*

lbw In cricket lbw is an abbreviation for 'leg before wicket', which is a way of dismissing a batsman when his legs prevent the ball from hitting the wicket.

lead, leads, leading, led (rhymes with **feed**) **1** (verb) If you lead someone somewhere, you go in front of them in order to show them the way. **2** If one thing leads to another, it causes the second thing to happen. **3** A person who leads a group of people is in charge of them. **4** (noun) A dog's lead is a length of leather or chain attached to its collar, so that the dog can be kept under control. **5** If the police have a lead, they have a clue which might help them to solve a crime. **leading** (adjective).

lead (rhymes with **fed**) (noun) Lead is a soft, grey, heavy metal.

leaden (pronounced **led**-en) **1** (adjective) dark grey, e.g. *a leaden sky.* **2** heavy and slow-moving.

leader, leaders 1 (noun) A leader is someone who is in charge of a country, an organization, or a group of people. **2** In a race or competition, the leader is the person who is winning. **3** A leader in a newspaper is a leading article.

leadership 1 (noun) A group of people in charge of an organization may be referred to as the leadership. **2** Leadership is the ability to be a good leader.

leaf, leaves; leafs, leafing, leafed 1 (noun) A leaf is the flat green growth on the end of a twig or branch of a tree or other plant. **2** (verb) If you leaf through a book, magazine, or newspaper, you turn the pages over quickly. **leafy** (adjective).

leaflet, leaflets (noun) A leaflet is a piece of paper with information or advertising printed on it.

league, leagues (pronounced **leeg**) **1** (noun) A league is group of countries, clubs, or people who have joined together for a particular purpose or because they share a common interest, e.g. *the League of Red Cross Societies... the Scottish Football League.* **2** A league was a unit of distance used in former times. In Britain, a league was equal to about 3 miles.

leak, leaks, leaking, leaked 1 (verb) If a pipe or container leaks, it has a hole which lets gas or liquid escape. **2** If liquid or gas leaks, it escapes from a pipe or container. **3** If someone in an organization leaks information, they give the information to someone who is not supposed to have it, e.g. *The letter was leaked to the press.* **4** (noun) If a pipe or container has a leak, it has a hole which lets gas or liquid escape. **5** If there is a leak in an organization, someone inside the organization is giving information to people who are not supposed to have it. **leaky** (adjective).

leakage, leakages (noun) A leakage is an escape of gas or liquid from a pipe or container.

lean, leans, leaning, leant or **leaned; leaner, leanest 1** (verb) When you lean in a particular direction, you bend your body in that direction. **2** When you lean on something, you rest your body against it for support. **3** If you lean on someone, you depend on them. **4** If you lean towards particular ideas, you approve of them and follow them, e.g. *parents who lean towards strictness.* **5** (adjective) having little or no fat, e.g. *He always looked lean and tanned... lean cuts of meat.* **6** A lean period is a time when food or money is in short supply.

leap, leaps, leaping, leapt or **leaped 1** (verb) If you leap somewhere, you jump over a long distance or high in the air. **2** (noun) A leap is a jump over a long distance or high in the air.

leap year, leap years (noun) A leap year is a year in which there are 366 days. Every fourth year is a leap year.

learn, learns, learning, learnt or **learned 1** (verb) When you learn something, you gain knowledge or a skill through studying or training. **2** If you learn of something, you find out about it, e.g. *She had first learnt of the bomb attack that morning.* **learner** (noun).

learned (pronounced **ler**-nid) (adjective) A learned person has a lot of knowledge gained from years of study.

learning (noun) Learning is knowledge that has been acquired through serious study.

lease, leases, leasing, leased 1 (noun) A lease is an agreement under which someone is allowed to use a house or flat in return for rent. **2** (verb) To lease property to someone means to allow them to use it in return for rent.

leash, leashes (noun) A leash is a length of leather or chain attached to a dog's collar so that the dog can be controlled.

least 1 (noun) The least is the smallest possible amount of something. **2** (adjective or adverb) Least is a superlative form of **little**. **3** (phrase) You use **at least** to indicate that you are referring to the minimum amount of something, and that you think the true amount is greater, e.g. *At least 200 hundred people were injured.*

leather (noun) Leather is the tanned skin of some animals, used to make shoes, bags, belts, and clothes. **leathery** (adjective).

leave, leaves, leaving, left 1

(verb) When you leave a place, you go away from it. **2** If you leave someone somewhere, they stay behind after you go away. **3** If you leave a job or organization, you stop being part of it, e.g. *He left his job shortly after Christmas.* **4** If someone leaves money or possessions to someone, they arrange for them to be given to them after their death. **5** In subtraction, when you take one number from another, it leaves a third number. **6** (noun) Leave is a period of holiday or absence from a job.

Lebanese 1 (adjective) belonging or relating to Lebanon. **2** (noun) A Lebanese is someone who comes from Lebanon.

lecherous (adjective) constantly thinking about sex.

lectern, lecterns (noun) A lectern is a sloping desk which people use to rest books or notes on.

lecture, lectures, lecturing, lectured 1 (noun) A lecture is a formal talk intended to teach people about a particular subject. **2** A lecture is also a talk intended to tell someone off. **3** (verb) Someone who lectures teaches in a college or university.

lecturer, lecturers (noun) A lecturer is a teacher in a college or university.

led the past tense and past participle of **lead.**

ledge, ledges (noun) A ledge is a narrow shelf on the side of a cliff or rock face, or on the outside of a building, directly under a window.

ledger, ledgers (noun) A ledger is a book in which accounts are kept.

lee (noun) The lee of a place is the sheltered side of it, e.g. *the lee of the mountain.*

leech, leeches (noun) A leech is a small worm that feeds by sucking the blood from other animals. Leeches live in water.

leek, leeks (noun) A leek is a long vegetable of the onion family, which is white at one end and has green leaves at the other. Leeks are sometimes used as the national symbol of Wales.

leer, leers, leering, leered 1 (verb) To leer at someone means to smile at them in an unpleasant or sexually suggestive way. **2** (noun) A leer is an unpleasant or sexually suggestive smile.

leeway (noun) If something gives you some leeway, it allows you more flexibility in your plans, for example by giving you time to finish an activity.

left 1 (noun) The left is one of two sides of something. For example, on a page, English writing begins on the left. **2** (adjective or adverb) Left means on or towards the left side of something, e.g. *Turn left down Park Road.* **3** (noun) People and political groups who hold socialist or communist views are referred to as the Left. **4** Left is the past tense and past participle of **leave.**

left-handed (adjective or adverb) Someone who is left-handed does things such as writing and painting with their left hand.

leftist, leftists (noun or adjective) A leftist is someone who holds left-wing political views.
leftovers (plural noun) The leftovers are the bits of uneaten food that remain at the end of a meal.
left wing (adjective) believing more strongly in socialism, or less strongly in capitalism or conservatism, than other members of the same party or group. **left-winger** (noun).
leg, legs 1 (noun) Your legs are the two limbs which stretch from your hips to your feet. **2** The legs of a pair of trousers are the parts that cover your legs. **3** The legs of an object such as a table are the parts which rest on the floor and support the object's weight. **4** A leg of a journey is one part of it.
legacy, legacies 1 (noun) A legacy is property or money that someone receives in the will of a person who has died. **2** A legacy is also something that exists as a result of a previous event or time, e.g. *the legacy of a Catholic upbringing.*
legal 1 (adjective) relating to the law, e.g. *the American legal system.* **2** allowed by the law, e.g. *The strike was perfectly legal.* **legally** (adverb).
legal aid (noun) Legal aid is a system which provides the services of a solicitor or lawyer free, or very cheaply, to people who cannot afford the full fees.
legality (noun) The legality of an action means whether or not it is allowed by the law, e.g. *They challenged the legality of the scheme.*
legalize, legalizes, legalizing, legalized; also spelled **legalise** (verb) To legalize something that is illegal means to change the law so that it becomes legal. **legalization** (noun).
legend, legends 1 (noun) A legend is an old story which was once believed to be true, but which is probably untrue. **2** If you refer to someone or something as a legend, you mean they are very famous, e.g. *His business career has become a legend in Hong Kong.* **legendary** (adjective).
leggings 1 (plural noun) Leggings are very close-fitting trousers made of stretch material, worn mainly by young women. **2** Leggings are also a waterproof covering worn over ordinary trousers to protect them.
legible (adjective) Writing that is legible is clear enough to be read.
legion, legions 1 (noun) In ancient Rome, a legion was a military unit of between 3000 and 6000 soldiers. **2** A legion is a large military force, e.g. *the French Foreign Legion.* **3** Legions of people are large numbers of them.
legislate, legislates, legislating, legislated (verb; a formal word) When a government legislates, it creates new laws.
legislation (noun) Legislation is a law or set of laws created by a government.
legislative (adjective) relating to the making of new laws, e.g. *a legislative council.*
legislator, legislators (noun; a formal word) A legislator is a

person involved in making or passing laws.

legislature (noun; a formal word) The legislature is the parliament or other official group in a country which is responsible for making new laws.

legitimate (pronounced lij-**it**-tim-it) (adjective) Something that is legitimate is reasonable or acceptable according to existing laws or standards, e.g. *a legitimate charge for parking the car... a legitimate excuse.* **legitimacy** (noun), **legitimately** (adverb).

leisure (rhymes with **measure**) **1** (noun) Leisure is time during which you do not have to work, and can do what you enjoy doing. **2** (phrases) If you do something **at leisure,** or **at your leisure,** you do it at a convenient time.

leisurely (adjective or adverb) A leisurely action is done in an unhurried and calm way.

lemming, lemmings (noun) A lemming is a small rodent which lives in northern and arctic areas. Traditionally, lemmings are believed to jump off cliffs to their death in large numbers.

lemon, lemons 1 (noun) A lem[illegible]on is a yell[illegible] [illegible]ective) [illegible] (noun) Lemonade is [illegible] colourless, sweet, fizzy drink.

lend, lends, lending, lent 1 (verb) If you lend someone something, you give it to them for a period of time and then they give it back to you. **2** If a bank lends money, it gives the money to someone and the money has to be repaid in the future, usually with interest. **3** (phrase) If you **lend someone a hand,** you help them. **lender** (noun).

length, lengths 1 (noun) The length of something is the horizontal distance from one end to the other. **2** The length of an event or activity is the amount of time it lasts for. **3** The length of something is also the fact that it is long rather than short, e.g. *Despite its length, it is a rewarding read.* **4** A length of something is a long piece of it.

lengthen, lengthens, lengthening, lengthened (verb) To lengthen something means to make it longer.

lengthways or **lengthwise** (adverb) If you measure something lengthways, you measure the horizontal distance from one end to the other.

lengthy, lengthier, lengthiest (adjective) Something that is lengthy lasts for a long time.

lenient (adjecti[illegible]) If someone in auth[illegible] is lenient, they ar[illegible] less severe than expected. **leniently** (adverb), **leniency** (noun).

[illegible]**, lenses 1** (noun) A lens is a curved piece of glass designed to focus light in a certain way, for example in a camera, telescope, or pair of glasses. **2** The lens in your eye is the part behind the iris, which focuses light.

lent 1 the past tense and past participle of **lend. 2** (noun) Lent is the period of forty days leading up to Easter, during which Christians give up something they enjoy.

lentil, lentils (noun) Lentils are small dried red or brown seeds which are cooked and eaten in soups and curries.

Leo (noun) Leo is the fifth sign of the zodiac, represented by a lion. People born between July 23rd and August 22nd are born under this sign.

leopard, leopards (noun) A leopard is a large wild Asian or African animal of the cat family. Leopards have yellow fur and black or brown spots.

leotard, leotards (pronounced **lee**-eh-tard) (noun) A leotard is a tight-fitting costume covering the body and legs, which is worn for dancing or exercise.

leper, lepers (noun) A leper is someone who has leprosy.

leprosy (noun) Leprosy is an infectious disease which attacks the skin and nerves, and which can lead to fingers or toes dropping off.

lesbian, lesbians (noun) A lesbian is a homosexual woman. **lesbianism** (noun).

lesion, lesions (pronounced **lee**-shen) (noun) A lesion is a wound or injury.

less 1 (adjective [illegible]) Less means a smaller amount, or not as much in quality, e.g. *They left less than three weeks ago... She had become less frightened of him now.* **2** Less is a comparative form of **little**. **3** (preposition) You use less to indicate that you are subtracting one number from another, e.g. *Eight less two leaves six.*

-less (suffix) -less means without, e.g. *tasteless tomatoes... jobless people.*

lessen, lessens, lessening, lessened (verb) If something lessens, it is reduced in amount, size, or quality.

lesser (adjective) smaller in importance, degree, or amount than something else.

lesson, lessons 1 (noun) A lesson is a fixed period of time during which a class of pupils is taught by a teacher. **2** A lesson is also an experience that makes you understand something important which you had not realized before.

lest (conjunction; an old-fashioned word) as a precaution in case something unpleasant or unwanted happens, e.g. *I was afraid to open the door lest he should follow me.*

let, lets, letting, let 1 (verb) If you let someone do something, you allow them to do it. **2** If someone lets a house or flat that they own, they rent it out. **3** You can say 'let's' or 'let us' when you want to suggest doing something with someone else, e.g. *Let's go.* **4** If you let yourself in for something, you agree to do it although you do not really want to do [illegible]

let off 1 (verb) If someone [illegible] thing you ha[illegible] you off, they [illegible] If you let off a firew[illegible] [illegible]plosive, you light it or detonate it.

lethal (pronounced **lee**-thal) (adjective) able to kill someone, e.g. *a lethal weapon.*

lethargic (pronounced lith-**ar**-jik) (adjective) If you feel lethargic, you have no energy or enthusiasm.

lethargy (pronounced **leth**-ar-jee) (noun) Lethargy is a lack of energy and enthusiasm.

letter, letters 1 (noun) Letters are written symbols which go together to make words. **2** A letter is also a piece of writing addressed to someone, and usually sent through the post.

letter box, letter boxes 1 (noun) A letter box is an oblong gap in the front door of a house or flat, through which letters are delivered. **2** A letter box is also a large metal container in the street, where you post letters.

lettering (noun) Lettering is writing, especially when you are describing the type of letters used, e.g. *bold lettering.*

lettuce, lettuces (noun) A lettuce is a vegetable with large green leaves eaten raw in salad.

leukaemia or **leukemia** (pronounced loo-**kee**-mee-a) (noun) Leukaemia is a serious illness which affects the blood.

level, levels, levelling, levelled 1 (adjective) A surface that is level is smooth, flat, and parallel to the ground. **2** (verb) To level a piece of land means to make it flat. **3** (noun) A level is a point on a scale which measures the amount, importance, or difficulty of something. **4** The level of a liquid is the height it comes up to in a container. **5** (adverb) If you draw level with someone, you get closer to them so that you are moving next to them. **6** (verb) If you level a criticism at someone, you say or write something critical about them. **level off** or **level out** (verb) If something levels off or levels out, it stops increasing or decreasing, e.g. *Profits are beginning to level off.*

level crossing, level crossings (noun) A level crossing is a place where road traffic is allowed to drive across a railway track.

level-headed (adjective) Someone who is level-headed is sensible and calm in emergencies.

lever, levers 1 (noun) A lever on a machine is a handle that you pull in order to make the machine work. **2** A lever is also a long bar that you wedge underneath a heavy object. When you press down on the lever, it makes the object move.

leverage (noun) Leverage is knowledge or influence that you can use to make someone do something.

leveret, leverets (noun) A leveret is a young hare.

levy, levies, levying, levied (pronounced **lev**-ee) **1** (noun; a formal word) A levy is an amount of money that you pay in tax. **2** (verb) When a government levies a tax, it makes people pay the tax and organizes the collection of the money.

lewd (rhymes with **rude**) (adjective) sexually coarse and crude.

liability, liabilities 1 (noun) Someone's liability is their responsibility for something they have done wrong. **2** In business, a company's liabilities are the debts which it must pay. **3** (an informal use) If you describe someone as a liability, you mean that they cause a lot of problems or embarrassment.

liable 1 (adjective) If you say that something is liable to happen, you mean that you think it will probably happen. **2** If you are liable for something you have done, you are legally responsible for it.

liaise, liaises, liaising, liaised (pronounced lee-**aze**) (verb) To liaise with someone or an organization means to cooperate with them and keep them informed.

liaison, liaisons (pronounced lee-**aze**-on) (noun) Liaison is communication between two organizations or two sections of an organization.

liar, liars (noun) A liar is a person who tells lies.

libel, libels, libelling, libelled (pronounced **lie**-bel) **1** (noun) Libel is something written about someone which is not true, and for which the writer can be made to pay damages in court. **2** (verb) To libel someone means to write or say something untrue about them. **libellous** (adjective).

liberal, liberals 1 (noun) A liberal is someone who believes in political progress, social welfare, and individual freedom. **2** (adjective) Someone who is liberal is tolerant of a wide range of behaviour, standards, or opinions. **3** To be liberal with something means to be generous with it. **4** A liberal quantity of something is a large amount of it. **liberally** (adverb), **liberalism** (noun).

Liberal Democrat, Liberal Democrats (noun) A Liberal Democrat is a member or supporter of the Liberal Democrats, a British political party that believes in individual freedom and reforming the constitution.

liberate, liberates, liberating, liberated (verb) To liberate people means to free them from prison or from an unpleasant situation. **liberation** (noun), **liberator** (noun).

liberty (noun) Liberty is the freedom to choose how you want to live, without government restrictions.

libido, libidos (pronounced lib-**bee**-doe) (noun) Someone's libido is their sexual drive.

Libra (noun) Libra is the seventh sign of the zodiac, represented by a pair of scales. People born between September 23rd and October 22nd are born under this sign.

librarian, librarians (noun) A librarian is a person who is in charge of a library or who has been trained to do responsible work in a library.

library, libraries 1 (noun) A library is a building in which books are kept for people to come and read or borrow. **2** A library is also a collection of books, records, or videos.

Libyan, Libyans 1 (adjective) belonging or relating to Libya. **2** (noun) A Libyan is someone who comes from Libya.

lice the plural of **louse**.

licence, licences 1 (noun) A licence is an official document which entitles you to carry out a particular activity, for example to drive a car or to sell alcohol. **2** Licence is the freedom to do what you want, especially when other people consider that it is being used irresponsibly.

license, licenses, licensing, licensed (verb) To license an activity means to give official permission for it to be carried out.

lichen, lichens (pronounced **lie**-ken) (noun) Lichen is a green, moss-like growth on rocks or tree trunks.

lick, licks, licking, licked 1 (verb) If you lick something, you move your tongue over it. **2** (noun) A lick is the action of licking.

lid, lids (noun) The lid of a container is the top, which you open in order to reach what is inside.

lie, lies, lying, lay, lain 1 (verb) To lie somewhere means to rest there horizontally. **2** If you say where something lies, you are describing where it is, e.g. *The farm lies between two glens.*

lie, lies, lying, lied 1 (verb) To lie means to say something that is not true. **2** (noun) A lie is something you say which is not true.

lieu (pronounced **lyoo**) (phrase) If one thing happens **in lieu** of another, it happens instead of it.

lieutenant, lieutenants (pronounced lef-**ten**-ent) (noun) A lieutenant is a junior officer in the army or navy.

life, lives 1 (noun) Life is the quality of being able to grow and develop, which is present in people, plants, and animals. **2** Your life is your existence from the time you are born until the time you die. **3** The life of a machine is the period of time for which it is likely to work and be useful. **4** If you refer to the life in a place, you are talking about the amount of activity there, e.g. *The town was full of life.* **5** If criminals are sentenced to life, they are sent to prison for the rest of their lives, or until they are granted parole.

life assurance (noun) Life assurance is an insurance which provides a sum of money in the event of the policy holder's death.

lifeblood (noun) The lifeblood of something is the most essential part of it.

lifeboat, lifeboats 1 (noun) A lifeboat is a boat kept on shore, which is sent out to rescue people who are in danger at sea. **2** A lifeboat is also a small boat kept on a ship, which is used if the ship starts to sink.

life expectancy, life expectancies (noun) Your life expectancy is the number of years you can expect to live, based on statistical evidence.

lifeguard, lifeguards (noun) A lifeguard is a person whose job is to rescue people who are in difficulty in the sea or in a swimming pool.

life jacket, life jackets (noun) A life jacket is a sleeveless inflatable jacket that keeps you afloat in water.

lifeless 1 (adjective) Someone who is lifeless is dead. **2** If you describe a place or person as lifeless, you mean that they are dull and unexciting.

lifelike (adjective) A picture or sculpture that is lifelike looks very real or alive.

lifeline, lifelines 1 (noun) A lifeline is something which helps you to survive or helps an activity to continue. **2** A lifeline is also a rope thrown to someone who is in danger of drowning.

lifelong (adjective) existing throughout someone's life, e.g. *He had a lifelong interest in music.*

life span, life spans 1 (noun) Someone's life span is the length of time during which they are alive. **2** The life span of a product or organization is the length of time it exists or is useful.

lifetime, lifetimes (noun) Your lifetime is the period of time during which you are alive.

lift, lifts, lifting, lifted 1 (verb) To lift something means to move it to a higher position. **2** When fog or mist lifts, it clears away. **3** To lift a ban on something means to remove it. **4** (an informal use) To lift things means to steal them. **5** (noun) A lift is a machine like a large box which carries passengers from one floor to another in a building. **6** If you give someone a lift, you drive them somewhere in a car or on a motorcycle.

ligament, ligaments (noun) A ligament is a piece of tough tissue in your body which connects your bones.

light, lights, lighting, lighted or **lit; lighter, lightest 1** (noun) Light is brightness from the sun, moon, fire, or lamps, that enables you to see things. **2** A light is a lamp or other device that gives out brightness. **3** If you give someone a light, you give them a match or lighter to light their cigarette. **4** (adjective) A place that is light is bright because of the sun or the use of lamps. **5** A light colour is pale. **6** A light object does not weigh much. **7** Light books or music are entertaining and are not intended to be serious. **8** (verb) To light a place means to cause it to be filled with light. **9** To light a fire means to make it start burning. **10** To light upon something means to find it by accident. **lightly** (adverb), **lightness** (noun).

lighten, lightens, lightening, lightened 1 (verb) When something lightens, it becomes less dark. **2** To lighten a load means to make it less heavy.

lighter, lighters (noun) A lighter is a device for lighting a cigarette.

light-headed (adjective) If you feel light-headed, you feel slightly dizzy or drunk.

light-hearted (adjective) Someone who is light-hearted is cheerful and has no worries.

lighthouse, lighthouses (noun) A lighthouse is a tower by the sea, which sends out a powerful light to guide ships and warn them of danger.

lighting (noun) The lighting in a room or building is the way that it is lit.

lightning (noun) Lightning is the bright flashes of light in the sky which are produced by natural electricity during a thunder storm.

lightweight, lightweights 1 (noun) A lightweight is a boxer in one of the lighter weight groups. **2** (adjective) Something that is lightweight does not weigh very much, e.g. *a lightweight jacket.*

light year, light years (noun) A light year is a unit of distance equal to the distance that light travels in a year.

likable or **likeable** (adjective) Someone who is likable is very pleasant and friendly.

like, likes, liking, liked 1 (preposition) If one thing is like another, it is similar to it. **2** (noun) 'The like' means other similar things of the sort just mentioned, e.g. *nappies, prams, cots, and the like.* **3** (phrase) If you **feel like** something, you want to do it or have it, e.g. *I feel like a walk.* **4** (verb) If you like something or someone, you find them pleasant.

-like (suffix) -like means resembling or similar to, e.g. *a balloonlike object.*

likelihood (noun) If you say that there is a likelihood that something will happen, you mean that you think it will probably happen.

likely, likelier, likeliest (adjective) Something that is likely will probably happen or is probably true.

liken, likens, likening, likened (verb) If you liken one thing to another, you say that they are similar.

likeness, likenesses (noun) If two things have a likeness to each other, they are similar in appearance.

likewise (adverb) Likewise means similarly, e.g. *He sat down and she did likewise.*

liking (noun) If you have a liking for someone or something, you like them.

lilac 1 (noun) A lilac is a shrub with large clusters of sweet-smelling pink, white, or mauve flowers. **2** (adjective) pale mauve.

lilt, lilts (noun) A lilt in someone's voice is a pleasant rising and falling sound in it. **lilting** (adjective).

lily, lilies (noun) A lily is a plant that produces trumpet-shaped flowers of various colours.

limb, limbs 1 (noun) Your limbs are your arms and legs. **2** The limbs of a tree are its branches. **3** (phrase) If you have gone **out on a limb,** you have said or done something risky.

limber up, limbers up, limbering up, limbered up (verb) If you limber up, you stretch your muscles before doing a sport or exercise.

limbo 1 (noun) If you are in limbo, you are in an uncertain situation over which you feel you have no control. **2** The limbo is a West Indian dance in which the dancer has to pass under a low bar while leaning backwards.

lime, limes 1 (noun) A lime is a small, green citrus fruit, rather like a lemon. **2** A lime tree is a large tree with pale green leaves. **3** Lime is a chemical substance that is used in cement and as a fertilizer.

limelight (noun) If someone is in the limelight, they are getting a lot of attention.

limerick, limericks (noun) A limerick is an amusing nonsense poem of five lines. The first, second, and fifth lines rhyme with each other, while the third and fourth lines rhyme with each other using a different rhyme.

limestone (noun) Limestone is a white rock which is used for building and making cement.

limit, limits, limiting, limited 1 (noun) A limit is a boundary or an extreme beyond which something cannot go, e.g. *The speed limit was 30 mph.* **2** (verb) To limit something means to prevent it from becoming bigger, spreading, or making progress, e.g. *He did all he could to limit the damage.*

limitation, limitations 1 (noun) The limitation of something is the reducing or controlling of it. **2** If you talk about the limitations of a person or thing, you are talking about the limits of their abilities.

limited (adjective) Something that is limited is rather small in amount or extent, e.g. *a limited number of bedrooms.*

limousine, limousines (pronounced **lim**-o-zeen) (noun) A limousine is a large, luxurious car, usually driven by a chauffeur.

limp, limps, limping, limped; limper, limpest 1 (verb) If you limp, you walk unevenly because you have hurt your leg or foot. **2** (noun) A limp is an uneven way of walking. **3** (adjective) Something that is limp is soft and floppy, and not stiff or firm, e.g. *a limp lettuce.*

limpet, limpets (noun) A limpet is a shellfish with a pointed shell, that attaches itself very firmly to rocks.

line, lines, lining, lined 1 (noun) A line is a long, thin mark. **2** A line of people or things is a number of them positioned one behind the other. **3** A line is also a route along which someone or something moves, e.g. *a railway line.* **4** In a piece of writing, a line is a number of words together, e.g. *I often used to change my lines as an actor.* **5** Someone's line of work is the kind of work they do. **6** The line someone takes is the attitude they have towards something, e.g. *He took a hard line with terrorism.* **7** In a shop or business, a line is a type of product, e.g. *That line has been discontinued.* **8** (verb) To line something means to cover its inside surface or edge with something, e.g. *Cottages lined the edge of the harbour.* **line up 1** (verb) When people line up, they stand in a line. **2** When you line something up, you arrange it for a special occasion, e.g. *A tour is being lined up for July.*

lineage, lineages (pronounced **lin**-ee-ij) (noun) Someone's lineage is all the people from whom they are directly descended.

linear (pronounced **lin**-ee-ar) (adjective) arranged in a line or in a strict sequence, or happening at a constant rate.

linen 1 (noun) Linen is a type of cloth made from a plant called flax. **2** Linen is also household goods made of cloth, such as sheets, teatowels, and tablecloths.

liner, liners (noun) A liner is a large passenger ship that makes long journeys.

linesman, linesmen (noun) A linesman is an official at a sports match who watches the lines of the field or court and indicates when the ball goes outside them.

linger, lingers, lingering, lingered (verb) To linger means to remain for a long time, e.g. *Economic problems lingered in the background.*

lingerie (pronounced **lan**-jer-ee) (noun) Lingerie is women's nightwear and underclothes.

lingo, lingoes (noun; an informal word) A lingo is a foreign language.

linguist, linguists (noun) A linguist is someone who studies foreign languages or the way in which language works.

lining, linings (noun) A lining is any material used to line the inside of something.

link, links, linking, linked 1 (noun) A link is a relationship or connection between two things, e.g. *the link between sunbathing and skin cancer.* **2** A link is also a physical connection between two things or places, e.g. *a high-speed rail link between Folkestone and London.* **3** A link is also one of the rings in a chain. **4** (verb) To link people, places, or things means to join them together. **linkage** (noun).

lino (noun) Lino is the same as linoleum.

linoleum (noun) Linoleum is a floor covering with a shiny surface.

lint (noun) Lint is soft cloth made from linen, used to dress wounds.

lion, lions (noun) A lion is a large member of the cat family which comes from Africa. Lions have light brown fur, and the male has a long mane. A female lion is called a lioness.

lip, lips 1 (noun) Your lips are the edges of your mouth. **2** The lip of a jug is the slightly pointed part through which liquids are poured out.

lip-read, lip-reads, lip-reading, lip-read (verb) To lip-read means to watch someone's lips when they are talking in order to understand what they are saying. Deaf people often lip-read.

lipstick, lipsticks (noun) Lipstick is a coloured substance which women wear on their lips.

liqueur, liqueurs (pronounced lik-**yoor**) (noun) A liqueur is a strong sweet alcoholic drink, usually drunk with coffee after a meal.

liquid, liquids 1 (noun) A liquid is any substance which is not a solid or a gas, and which can be poured. **2** (adjective) Something that is liquid is in the form of a liquid, e.g. *liquid nitrogen.* **3** In commerce and finance a person's or company's liquid assets are the things that can be sold quickly to raise cash.

liquidate, liquidates, liquidating, liquidated 1 (verb) To liquidate a company means to close it down and to use its assets to pay off its debts. **2** (an informal use) To liquidate a person means to murder them. **liquidation** (noun), **liqui-**

dator (noun).
liquor (noun) Liquor is any strong alcoholic drink.
liquorice (pronounced **lik**-ker-iss) (noun) Liquorice is a root used to flavour sweets; also the sweets themselves.
lira, lire (noun) The lira is the unit of currency in Italy.
lisp, lisps, lisping, lisped 1 (noun) Someone who has a lisp pronounces the sounds 's' and 'z' like 'th'. **2** (verb) To lisp means to speak with a lisp.
list, lists, listing, listed 1 (noun) A list is a set of words or items written one below the other. **2** (verb) If you list a number of things, you make a list of them.
listen, listens, listening, listened (verb) If you listen to something, you hear it and pay attention to it. **listener** (noun).
listless (adjective) lacking energy and enthusiasm. **listlessly** (adverb).
lit a past tense and past participle of **light**.
litany, litanies 1 (noun) A litany is a part of a church service in which the priest says or chants a series of prayers and the people give a series of responses. **2** A litany is also something, especially a list of things, that is repeated often or in a boring or insincere way, e.g *a tedious litany of complaints.*
literacy (noun) Literacy is the ability to read and write. **literate** (adjective).
literal 1 (adjective) The literal meaning of a word is its most basic meaning. **2** A literal translation from a foreign language is one that has been translated exactly word for word. **literally** (adverb).
literary (adjective) connected with literature, e.g. *literary critics.*
literature 1 (noun) Literature consists of novels, plays, and poetry. **2** The literature on a subject is everything that has been written about it.
lithe (adjective) supple and graceful.
litmus (noun) In chemistry, litmus is a substance that turns red under acid and blue under alkali conditions.
litre, litres (noun) A litre is a unit of liquid volume equal to about 1.76 pints.
litter, litters, littering, littered 1 (noun) Litter is rubbish in the street and other public places. **2** Cat litter is a gravelly substance you put in a container where you want your cat to urinate and defecate. **3** A litter is a number of baby animals born at the same time to the same mother. **4** (verb) If things litter a place, they are scattered all over it.
little, less, lesser, least 1 (adjective) small in size or amount. **2** (noun or adverb) A little is a small amount or degree, e.g. *Would you like a little fruit juice?* **3** Little also means not much, e.g. *He has little to say about it.*
live, lives, living, lived 1 (verb) If you live in a place, that is where your home is. **2** To live means to be alive. **3** If something lives up to your expectations, it is as good as you thought it would be. **4** (adjective) Live animals or plants

stroke in which the player hits the ball high in the air.

lobby, lobbies, lobbying, lobbied 1 (noun) The lobby in a building is the main entrance area with corridors and doors leading off it. **2** A lobby is a group of people trying to persuade an organization that something should be done, e.g. *the environmental lobby.* **3** (verb) To lobby an MP or an organization means to try to persuade them to do something, for example by writing them lots of letters.

lobe, lobes 1 (noun) The lobe of your ear is the rounded soft part at the bottom. **2** A lobe is also any rounded part of something, e.g. *the frontal lobe of the brain.*

lobster, lobsters (noun) A lobster is an edible shellfish with two front claws, eight legs, a long body, and a tail folded underneath.

local, locals 1 (adjective) Local means in, near, or belonging to the area in which you live, e.g. *the local newspaper.* **2** A local anaesthetic numbs only one part of your body and does not send you to sleep. **3** (noun) The locals are the people who live in a particular area. **4** (an informal use) Someone's local is the pub nearest their home. **locally** (adverb).

locality, localities (noun) A locality is an area of a country or city, e.g. *a large map of the locality.*

localized or **localised** (adjective) existing or happening in only one place, e.g. *localized pain.*

locate, locates, locating, located 1 (verb) To locate someone or something means to find out where they are. **2** If something is located in a place, it is in that place.

location, locations 1 (noun) A location is a place, or the position of something. **2** (phrase) If a film is made **on location,** it is made away from a studio.

loch, lochs (noun) In Scottish English, a loch is a lake.

lock, locks, locking, locked 1 (verb) If you lock something, you close it and fasten it with a key. **2** If something locks into place, it moves into place and becomes firmly fixed there. **3** (noun) A lock is a de vice on something which fas tens it and prevents it fror being opened except with key. **4** A lock on a canal is place where the water lev can be raised or lowered enable boats to go betwe two parts of the canal whi have different water levels A lock of hair is a sm bunch of hair.

locker, lockers (noun) A loc is a small cupboard for y personal belongings, for ex ple in a changing room.

locket, lockets (noun) A is a piece of jewellery c ing of a small case wh can keep a photograp which you wear or round your neck.

locksmith, locksmith locksmith is a makes or mends

locomotive, lo A locomotive i gine.

locust, locusts

is an insect similar to a large grasshopper. Locusts live in hot countries and fly in large groups, eating all the crops they find.

lodge, lodges, lodging, lodged **1** (noun) A lodge is a small house in the grounds of a large country house, or a small house used for holidays. **2** (verb) If you lodge in someone else's house, you live there and pay them rent. **3** If something lodges somewhere, it gets stuck there, e.g. *The bullet lodged in his pelvis.* **4** If you lodge a complaint, you formally make it.

lodger, lodgers (noun) A lodger is a person who lives in someone's house and pays rent.

lodgings (plural noun) If you live in lodgings, you live in someone else's house and pay them rent.

loft, lofts (noun) A loft is the space immediately under the roof of a house, often used for storing things.

lofty, loftier, loftiest **1** (adjective) very high, e.g. *a lofty hall.* **2** very noble and important, e.g. *lofty ideals.* **3** proud and superior, e.g. *her lofty manner.*

log, logs, logging, logged **1** (noun) A log is a thick branch or piece of tree trunk which has fallen or been cut down. **2** A log is also the captain's official record of everything that happens on board a ship. **3** (verb) If you log something, you officially make a record of it, for example in a ship's log. **4** To log into a computer system means to gain access to it so that you can use it, usually by giving your name and password. To log out means to finish using the system.

logic (noun) Logic is a way of reasoning involving a series of statements, each of which must be true if the statement before it is true.

logical **1** (adjective) A logical argument uses logic. **2** A logical course of action or decision is sensible or reasonable in the circumstances, e.g. *the logical conclusion.* **logically** (adverb).

logistics (noun; a formal word) The logistics of a complicated undertaking is the skilful organization of it.

logo, logos (pronounced **loh**-goh) (noun) The logo of an organization is a special design that is put on all its products.

-logy (suffix) -logy is used to form words that refer to the study of something, e.g. *biology... geology.*

loin, loins **1** (noun; an old-fashioned use) Your loins are the front part of your body between your waist and your thighs, especially your sexual parts. **2** Loin is a piece of meat from the back or sides of an animal, e.g. *loin of pork.*

loiter, loiters, loitering, loitered (verb) To loiter means stand about idly with no real purpose.

loll, lolls, lolling, lolled **1** (verb) If you loll somewhere, you sit or lie there in an idle, relaxed way. **2** If your head or tongue lolls, it hangs loosely.

lollipop, lollipops (noun) A lollipop is a hard sweet on the end of a stick.

lolly, lollies 1 (noun) A lolly is a lollipop. **2** A lolly is also a piece of flavoured ice or ice cream on a stick.

lone (adjective) A lone person or thing is the only one in a particular place, e.g. *a lone climber.*

lonely, lonelier, loneliest 1 (adjective) If you are lonely, you are unhappy because you are alone. **2** A lonely place is an isolated one which very few people visit, e.g. *a lonely hillside.* **loneliness** (noun).

loner, loners (noun) A loner is a person who likes to be alone.

lonesome (adjective) lonely and sad.

long, longer, longest; longs, longing, longed 1 (adjective or adverb) continuing for a great amount of time, e.g. *There had been no rain for a long time... The equipment will not last much longer.* **2** (adjective) great in length or distance, e.g. *a long dress... a long road.* **3** (phrase) If something **no longer** happens, it does not happen any more. **4 Before long** means soon. **5** If one thing is true **as long as** another thing is true, it is true only if the other thing is true. **6** (verb) If you long for something, you want it very much. **longing** (noun).

longevity (pronounced lon-**jev**-it-ee) (noun; a formal word) Longevity is long life.

longhand (noun) If you write something in longhand, you do it in your own handwriting rather than using shorthand or a typewriter.

longitude, longitudes (noun) The longitude of a place is its distance east or west of a line passing through Greenwich, measured in degrees.

long jump (noun) The long jump is an athletics event in which you jump as far as possible after taking a long run.

long-range 1 (adjective) able to be used over a great distance, e.g. *long-range artillery.* **2** extending a long way into the future, e.g. *a long-range weather forecast.*

long-sighted (adjective) If you are long-sighted, you have difficulty seeing things that are close.

long-standing (adjective) having existed for a long time, e.g. *a long-standing tradition.*

long-suffering (adjective) very patient, e.g. *her long-suffering husband.*

long-term (adjective) extending a long way into the future, e.g. *a long-term investment.*

long-winded (adjective) long and boring, e.g. *a long-winded letter.*

loo, loos (noun; an informal word) A loo is a toilet.

look, looks, looking, looked 1 (verb) If you look at something, you turn your eyes towards it so that you can see it. **2** If you look for someone or something, you try to find them. **3** If you look at a subject or situation, you study it or judge it. **4** If you look down on someone, you think that they are inferior to you. **5** If you are looking forward to something, you want it to happen because you think you will enjoy it. **6** If you look up to someone, you admire and respect them. **7** If you describe the way that something looks, you are describing its appearance. **8** (noun) If you have a look at something, you look at it. **9** The look on your face is the expression on it. **10** If you talk about someone's looks, you are talking about how attractive they are. **11** (interjection) You say 'look out' to warn someone of danger. **look after** (verb) If you look after someone or something, you take care of them. **look up 1** (verb) To look up information means to find it out in a book. **2** If you look someone up, you go to see them after not having seen them for a long time. **3** If a situation is looking up, it is improving.

lookalike, lookalikes (noun) A lookalike is a person who looks very like someone else, e.g. *an Elvis Presley lookalike.*

lookout, lookouts 1 (noun) A lookout is someone who is watching for danger, or a place where they watch for danger. **2** (phrase) If you are **on the lookout** for something, you are watching for it or waiting expectantly for it.

loom, looms, looming, loomed 1 (noun) A loom is a machine for weaving cloth. **2** (verb) If something looms in front of you, it suddenly appears as a tall, unclear, and sometimes frightening shape. **3** If a situation or event is looming, it is likely to happen soon and is rather worrying.

loony, loonies (an informal word) **1** (adjective) People or behaviour can be described as loony if they are mad or eccentric. **2** (noun) A loony is a mad or eccentric person.

loop, loops, looping, looped 1 (noun) A loop is a curved or circular shape in something long such as a piece of string. **2** (verb) If you loop rope or string around an object, you place it in a loop around the object.

loophole, loopholes (noun) A loophole is a small mistake or omission in the law which allows you to do something that the law really intends that you should not do.

loose, looser, loosest 1 (adjective) If something is loose, it is not firmly held, fixed, or attached. **2** Loose clothes are rather large and do not fit closely. **3** (adverb) To set animals loose means to set them free after they have been tied up or kept in a cage. **loosely** (adverb).

loosen, loosens, loosening, loosened (verb) To loosen something means to make it looser.

loot, loots, looting, looted 1 (verb) To loot shops and houses means to steal money and goods from them during a battle or riot. **2** (noun) Loot is stolen money or goods.

lop, lops, lopping, lopped (verb) If you lop something off, you cut it off with one quick stroke.

lopsided (adjective) Something that is lopsided is uneven because its two sides are different sizes or shapes.

lord, lords 1 (noun) A lord is a nobleman. **2** Lord is a title used in front of the names of some noblemen, and of bishops, archbishops, judges, and some high-ranking officials, e.g. *the Lord Mayor of London.* **3** In Christianity, Lord is a name given to God and Jesus Christ.

Lordship, Lordships (noun) You address a lord, judge, or bishop as Your Lordship.

lore (noun) The lore of a place, people, or subject is all the traditional knowledge and stories about it.

lorry, lorries (noun) A lorry is a large vehicle for transporting goods by road.

lose, loses, losing, lost 1 (verb) If you lose something, you cannot find it, or you no longer have it because it has been taken away from you, e.g. *I lost my airline ticket.* **2** If you lose a relative or friend, they die, e.g. *She lost her brother in the war.* **3** If you lose a fight or an argument, you are beaten. **4** If a business loses money, it is spending more money than it is earning. **loser** (noun).

loss, losses 1 (noun) The loss of something is the losing of it. **2** (phrase) If you are **at a loss,** you do not know what to do.

lost 1 (adjective) If you are lost, you do not know where you are. **2** If something is lost, you cannot find it. **3** Lost is the past tense and past participle of **lose.**

lot, lots 1 (noun) A lot of something, or lots of something, is a large amount of it. **2** A lot means very much or very often, e.g. *I love him a lot.* **3** A lot is an amount of something or a number of things, e.g. *He bet all his wages and lost the lot.* **4** In an auction, a lot is one of the things being sold.

lotion, lotions (noun) A lotion is a liquid that you put on your skin to protect or soften it, e.g. *suntan lotion.*

lottery, lotteries (noun) A lottery is a type of gambling game in which numbered tickets are sold. Several tickets are selected and their owners win a prize.

lotus, lotuses (noun) A lotus is a large water lily, found in Africa and Asia.

loud, louder, loudest 1 (adjective or adverb) A loud noise has a high volume of sound, e.g. *a loud explosion.* **2** If you describe clothing as loud, you mean that it is too bright and tasteless, e.g. *a loud tie.* **loudly** (adverb).

loudspeaker, loudspeakers (noun) A loudspeaker is a piece of equipment that makes your voice louder when you speak into a microphone connected to it.

lounge, lounges, lounging, lounged 1 (noun) A lounge is a room in a house or hotel with comfortable chairs where people can relax. **2** The lounge or lounge bar in a pub or hotel is a more expensive and comfortably furnished bar. **3** (verb) If you lounge around, you lean against something or sit or lie around in a lazy and comfortable way.

louse, lice (noun) Lice are small insects that live on people's bodies, e.g. *head lice.*

lousy, lousier, lousiest (an informal word) **1** (adjective) of bad quality or very unpleasant, e.g. *The weather is lousy.*

2 ill or unhappy, e.g. *I woke up feeling lousy.*

lout, louts (noun) A lout is a boy or young man who behaves in an impolite or aggressive way.

lovable or **loveable** (adjective) having very attractive qualities and therefore easy to love, e.g. *a lovable black mongrel.*

love, loves, loving, loved 1 (verb) If you love someone, you have strong emotional feelings of affection for them. **2** If you love something, you like it very much, e.g. *We both love football.* **3** (noun) Love is a strong emotional feeling of affection for someone or something. **4** (verb) If you would love to do something, you want very much to do it, e.g. *I would love to live there.* **5** (noun) In tennis, love is a score of zero. **6** (phrase) If you are **in love** with someone, you feel strongly attracted to them romantically or sexually. **7** When two people **make love,** they have sex. **loving** (adjective), **lovingly** (adverb).

love affair, love affairs (noun) A love affair is a romantic and often sexual relationship between two people who are not married to each other.

love life, love lives (noun) A person's love life is their romantic and sexual relationships.

lovely, lovelier, loveliest (adjective) very beautiful, attractive, and pleasant. **loveliness** (noun).

lover, lovers 1 (noun) A person's lover is someone that they have a sexual relationship with but are not married to. **2** Someone who is a lover of something, for example art or music, is very fond of it.

low, lower, lowest 1 (adjective or adverb) Something that is low is close to the ground, or measures a short distance from the ground to the top, e.g. *a low stool.* **2** Low is used to describe people who are considered not respectable, e.g. *mixing with low company.* **3** (noun) A low is a level or amount that is less than before, e.g. *His popularity has hit a new low.*

lower, lowers, lowering, lowered (verb) To lower something means to move it downwards or to make it less in value or amount.

lowlands (plural noun) Lowlands are an area of flat, low land. **lowland** (adjective).

lowly, lowlier, lowliest (adjective) low in importance, rank or status.

low tide (noun) On a coast, low tide is the time, usually twice a day, when the sea is at its lowest level.

loyal (adjective) firm in your friendship or support for someone or something. **loyally** (adverb), **loyalty** (noun).

loyalist, loyalists (noun) A loyalist is a person who remains firm in their support for a government or ruler.

lozenge, lozenges 1 (noun) A lozenge is a type of sweet with medicine in it, which you suck to relieve a sore throat or cough. **2** A lozenge is also a diamond shape.

LP, LPs (noun) An LP is a long-playing record. LP is short for 'long-playing record'.

LSD (noun) LSD is a very powerful drug which causes hallucinations. LSD is an abbreviation for 'lysergic acid diethylamide'.

Ltd an abbreviation for 'limited'; used after the names of limited companies.

lubricate, lubricates, lubricating, lubricated (verb) To lubricate something such as a machine means to put oil or an oily substance onto it, so that it moves smoothly and friction is reduced. **lubrication** (noun), **lubricant** (noun).

lucid 1 (adjective) Lucid writing or speech is clear and easy to understand. **2** Someone who is lucid after having been ill or delirious is able to think clearly again.

luck (noun) Luck is anything that seems to happen by chance and not through your own efforts.

luckless (adjective) unsuccessful or unfortunate, e.g. *We reduced our luckless opponents to shattered wrecks.*

lucky, luckier, luckiest 1 (adjective) Someone who is lucky has a lot of good luck. **2** Something that is lucky happens by chance and has good effects or consequences. **luckily** (adverb).

lucrative (adjective) Something that is lucrative earns you a lot of money, e.g. *a lucrative sponsorship deal.*

ludicrous (adjective) completely foolish, unsuitable, or ridiculous.

lug, lugs, lugging, lugged (verb) If you lug a heavy object around, you carry it with difficulty.

luggage (noun) Your luggage is the bags and suitcases that you take with you when you travel.

lukewarm 1 (adjective) slightly warm, e.g. *a mug of lukewarm tea.* **2** not very enthusiastic or interested, e.g. *The report was given a polite but lukewarm response.*

lull, lulls, lulling, lulled 1 (noun) A lull is a pause in something, or a short time when it is quiet and nothing much happens, e.g. *There was a temporary lull in the fighting.* **2** (verb) To lull someone means to send them to sleep or to make them feel safe and secure, e.g. *We had been lulled into a false sense of security.*

lullaby, lullabies (noun) A lullaby is a song used for sending a baby or child to sleep.

lumber, lumbers, lumbering, lumbered 1 (noun) Lumber is wood that has been roughly cut up. **2** Lumber is also old unwanted furniture and other items. **3** (verb) If you lumber around, you move heavily and clumsily. **4** (an informal use) If you are lumbered with something, you are given it to deal with even though you do not want it, e.g. *Women are still lumbered with the housework.*

luminary, luminaries (noun; a literary word) A luminary is a person who is famous or an expert in a particular subject.

luminous (adjective) Something that is luminous glows in the dark, usually because it has been treated with a special substance, e.g. *The luminous dial on her clock.* **luminosity**

(noun).

lump, lumps, lumping, lumped **1** (noun) A lump of something is a solid piece of it, of any shape or size, e.g. *a big lump of dough.* **2** A lump is also a bump on the surface of something. **3** (verb) If you lump people or things together, you combine them into one group or consider them as being similar in some way. **lumpy** (adjective).

lump sum, lump sums (noun) A lump sum is a large sum of money given or received all at once.

lunacy **1** (noun) Lunacy is extremely foolish or eccentric behaviour. **2** (an old-fashioned use) Lunacy is also severe mental illness.

lunar (adjective) relating to the moon.

lunatic, lunatics **1** (noun) If you call someone a lunatic, you mean that they are very foolish, stupid, and annoying, e.g. *He drives like a lunatic!* **2** A lunatic is also someone who is insane. **3** (adjective) Lunatic behaviour is very stupid, foolish, or dangerous.

lunch, lunches, lunching, lunched **1** (noun) Lunch is a meal eaten in the middle of the day. **2** (verb) When you lunch, you eat lunch.

luncheon, luncheons (pronounced **lun**-shen) (noun; a formal word) Luncheon is lunch.

lung, lungs (noun) Your lungs are the two organs inside your ribcage with which you breathe.

lunge, lunges, lunging, lunged **1** (noun) A lunge is a sudden forward movement, e.g. *He made a lunge for her.* **2** (verb) To lunge means to make a sudden movement in a particular direction.

lurch, lurches, lurching, lurched **1** (verb) To lurch means to make a sudden, jerky movement. **2** (noun) A lurch is a sudden, jerky movement.

lure, lures, luring, lured **1** (verb) To lure someone means to attract them into going somewhere or doing something. **2** (noun) A lure is something that you find very attractive.

lurid (pronounced **loo**-rid) **1** (adjective) involving a lot of sensational detail, e.g. *lurid stories in the press.* **2** very brightly coloured or patterned.

lurk, lurks, lurking, lurked (verb) To lurk somewhere means to remain there hidden from the person you are waiting for.

luscious (adjective) very tasty, e.g. *luscious strawberries.*

lush, lusher, lushest (adjective) In a lush field or garden, the grass or plants are healthy and growing thickly.

lust, lusts, lusting, lusted **1** (noun) Lust is a very strong feeling of sexual desire for someone. **2** A lust for something is a strong desire to have it, e.g. *a lust for money.* **3** (verb) To lust for or after someone means to desire them sexually. **4** If you lust for or after something, you have a very strong desire to possess it, e.g. *a greedy child lusting after a cream cake.*

lustre (pronounced **lus**-ter) (noun) Lustre is soft shining light reflected from the surface of something, e.g. *the lus-*

tre of silk.

lute, lutes (noun) A lute is an old-fashioned stringed musical instrument which is plucked like a guitar.

luxuriant (adjective) Luxuriant plants, trees, and gardens are large, healthy and growing strongly.

luxurious (adjective) very expensive and full of luxury. **luxuriously** (adverb).

luxury, luxuries 1 (noun) Luxury is great comfort in expensive and beautiful surroundings, e.g. *a life of luxury.* **2** A luxury is something that you enjoy very much but do not have very often, usually because it is expensive.

lying 1 (noun) Lying is telling lies. **2** Lying is also the present participle of **lie**.

lynch, lynches, lynching, lynched (verb) If a crowd lynches someone, it kills them in a violent and unpleasant way without first holding a legal trial.

lynx, lynxes (noun) A lynx is a wildcat with a short tail, tufted ears, and very good eyesight.

lyre, lyres (noun) A lyre was a stringed instrument rather like a small harp which was used in ancient Greece.

lyric, lyrics 1 (noun) The lyrics of a song are the words. **2** (adjective) Lyric poetry is written in a simple and direct style, and is usually about love.

lyrical (adjective) poetic and romantic.

M m

m an abbreviation for 'metres' or 'miles'.

macabre (pronounced mak-**kahb**-ra) (adjective) A macabre event is strange and horrible, e.g. *a macabre horror story.*

macaroni (noun) Macaroni is short hollow tubes of pasta.

macaroon, macaroons (noun) A macaroon is a sweet biscuit flavoured with almonds or coconut.

mace, maces (noun) A mace is an ornamental pole carried by an official as a ceremonial symbol of authority.

machete, machetes (pronounced mash-**ett**-ee) (noun) A machete is a large, heavy knife with a big blade.

machine, machines, machining, machined 1 (noun) A machine is a piece of equipment which uses electricity or power from an engine. **2** (verb) If you machine something, you make it or work on it using a machine.

machine-gun, machine-guns (noun) A machine-gun is a gun that works automatically, firing bullets one after the other.

machinery (noun) Machinery is machines in general.

machismo (pronounced mak-**kiz**-moe) (noun) Machismo is exaggerated aggressive male behaviour.

macho (pronounced **mat**-shoh)

(adjective) A man who is described as macho behaves in an aggressively masculine way.

mackerel, mackerels (noun) A mackerel is a sea fish with blue and silver stripes.

mackintosh, mackintoshes (noun) A mackintosh is a raincoat made from specially treated cloth.

mad, madder, maddest 1 (adjective) Someone who is mad has a mental illness which often causes them to behave in strange ways. **2** If you describe someone as mad, you mean that they are very foolish, e.g. *He said we were mad to share a flat.* **3** (an informal use) Someone who is mad is angry, e.g. *My dad was really mad when he got home.* **4** If you are mad about someone or something, you like them very much, e.g. *Alan was mad about golf.* **madness** (noun), **madman** (noun).

madam 'Madam' is a very formal way of addressing a woman.

maddening (adjective) irritating or frustrating, e.g. *She had many maddening habits.*

madly (adverb) If you do something madly, you do it in a fast, excited, and sometimes uncontrolled way.

madrigal, madrigals (noun) A madrigal is a song sung by several people without instruments.

Mafia (noun) The Mafia is a large crime organization operating in Sicily, Italy, and the USA.

magazine, magazines 1 (noun) A magazine is a weekly or monthly publication with articles, photographs, and advertisements. **2** The magazine of a gun is a compartment for cartridges.

magenta (pronounced maj-**jen**-ta) (noun or adjective) dark reddish-purple.

maggot, maggots (noun) A maggot is a creature that looks like a small worm and lives on decaying things. Maggots turn into flies.

magic 1 (noun) In fairy stories, magic is a special power that can make impossible things happen. **2** Magic is the art of performing tricks to entertain people. **magical** (adjective), **magically** (adverb).

magician, magicians 1 (noun) A magician is a person who performs tricks as a form of entertainment. **2** In fairy stories, a magician is a man with magical powers.

magistrate, magistrates (noun) A magistrate is an official who acts as a judge in a law court that deals with less serious crimes.

magnanimous (adjective) generous and forgiving.

magnate, magnates (noun) A magnate is someone who is very rich and powerful in business.

magnet, magnets (noun) A magnet is a piece of iron which attracts iron or steel towards it, and which points towards north if allowed to swing freely. **magnetic** (adjective), **magnetism** (noun).

magnificent (adjective) extremely beautiful or impressive. **magnificence** (noun).

magnify, magnifies, magnifying,

magnified (verb) When a microscope or lens magnifies something, it makes it appear bigger than it actually is. **magnification** (noun).

magnifying glass, magnifying glasses (noun) A magnifying glass is a lens which makes things appear bigger than they really are.

magnitude (noun) The magnitude of something is its great size or importance.

magnolia, magnolias (noun) A magnolia is a tree which has large white or pink flowers.

magpie, magpies (noun) A magpie is a large black and white bird with a long tail.

mahogany (noun) Mahogany is a hard reddish brown wood used for making furniture.

maid, maids (noun) A maid is a female servant.

maiden, maidens 1 (noun; a literary use) A maiden is a young woman. **2** (adjective) first, e.g. *a maiden voyage.*

maiden name, maiden names (noun) A woman's maiden name is the surname she had before she married.

mail, mails, mailing, mailed 1 (noun) Your mail is the letters and parcels delivered to you by the post office. **2** (verb) If you mail a letter, you send it by post.

mail order (noun) Mail order is a system of buying goods by post.

maim, maims, maiming, maimed (verb) To maim someone means to injure them very badly for life.

main, mains 1 (adjective) most important, e.g. *the main event.* **2** (noun) The mains are large pipes or wires that carry gas, water, electricity, or sewage. **mainly** (adverb).

mainframe, mainframes (noun) A mainframe is a large computer which can be used by many people at the same time.

mainland (noun) The mainland is the main part of a country in contrast to islands around its coast.

mainstay (noun) The mainstay of something is the most important part of it.

mainstream (noun) The mainstream is the most ordinary and conventional group of people or ideas in a society.

maintain, maintains, maintaining, maintained 1 (verb) If you maintain something, you keep it going or keep it at a particular rate or level, e.g. *I wanted to maintain our friendship.* **2** If you maintain someone, you provide them regularly with money for what they need. **3** To maintain a machine or a building means to keep it in good condition. **4** If you maintain that something is true, you believe it is true and say so.

maintenance 1 (noun) Maintenance is the process of keeping something in good condition. **2** Maintenance is also money that a person sends regularly to someone to provide for the things they need.

maize (noun) Maize is a tall plant which produces corn.

majesty, majesties 1 You say 'His Majesty' when you are talking about a king, and 'Her Majesty' when you are talking about a queen. **2** (noun) Majesty is the quality of great dignity and impressiveness. **majestic** (adjective), **majestically** (adverb).

major, majors 1 (adjective) more important or more serious or significant than other things, e.g. *There were over fifty major injuries.* **2** (noun) A major is an army officer of the rank immediately above captain.

majority, majorities 1 (noun) The majority of people or things in a group is more than half of the group. **2** In an election, the majority is the difference between the number of votes gained by the winner and the number gained by the runner-up.

make, makes, making, made 1 (verb) To make something means to produce or construct it, or to cause it to happen. **2** To make something also means to do it, e.g. *He was about to make a speech.* **3** To make something means to prepare it, e.g. *I'll make some salad dressing.* **4** If someone makes you do something, they force you to do it, e.g. *Mum made me clean the bathroom.* **5** (noun) The make of a product is the name of the company that manufactured it, e.g. *'What make of car do you drive?' – 'Mercedes'.* **make up 1** (verb) If a number of things make up something, they form that thing. **2** If you make up a story, you invent it. **3** If you make yourself up, you put make-up on. **4** If two people make it up, they become friends again after a quarrel.

make-up 1 (noun) Make-up is coloured creams and powders which women put on their faces to make themselves look more attractive. **2** Someone's make-up is their character or personality.

making (phrase) When you describe someone as something **in the making,** you mean that they are gradually becoming that thing, e.g. *a captain in the making.*

malaise (pronounced mal-**laze**) (noun; a formal word) Malaise is a feeling of dissatisfaction or unhappiness.

malaria (pronounced mal-**lay**-ree-a) (noun) Malaria is a tropical disease caught from mosquitoes which causes periods of fever and shivering.

Malaysian, Malaysians 1 (adjective) belonging or relating to Malaysia. **2** (noun) A Malaysian is someone who comes from Malaysia.

male, males 1 (noun) A male is a person or animal belonging to the sex that cannot give birth or lay eggs. **2** (adjective) concerning or affecting men rather than women.

male chauvinist, male chauvinists (noun) A male chauvinist is a man who thinks that men are better than women.

malevolent (pronounced mal-**lev**-oh-lent) (adjective; a formal word) wanting or intending to cause harm. **malevolence** (noun).

malfunction, malfunctions, malfunctioning, malfunctioned 1 (verb) If a machine malfunctions, it fails to work properly. **2** (noun) A malfunction in a machine is when it fails to work properly.

malice (noun) Malice is a desire to cause harm to people.

malicious (adjective) Malicious talk or behaviour is intended to harm someone.

malign, maligns, maligning, maligned (verb; a formal word) To malign someone means to say unpleasant and untrue things about them.

malignant 1 (adjective) harmful and cruel. **2** A malignant disease or tumour could cause death if it is allowed to continue.

mallard, mallards (noun) A mallard is a kind of wild duck.

mallet, mallets (noun) A mallet is a wooden hammer with a square head.

malnutrition (noun) Malnutrition is not eating enough healthy food.

malpractice (noun) If someone such as a doctor or lawyer breaks the rules of their profession, their behaviour is called malpractice.

malt (noun) Malt is roasted grain, usually barley, that is used in making beer and whisky.

mammal, mammals (noun) Animals that give birth to live babies and feed their young with milk from the mother's body are called mammals. Human beings, dogs, lions, and whales are all mammals.

mammoth, mammoths 1 (adjective) very large indeed, e.g. *a mammoth outdoor concert.* **2** (noun) A mammoth was a huge animal that looked like a hairy elephant with long tusks. Mammoths became extinct a long time ago.

man, men; mans, manning, manned 1 (noun) A man is an adult male human being. **2** (plural noun) Human beings in general are sometimes referred to as men, e.g. *All men are equal.* **3** (verb) To man something means to be in charge of it or operate it, e.g. *Two officers were manning the radar screens.*

manacle, manacles (noun) Manacles are metal rings or clamps attached to a prisoner's wrists or ankles.

manage, manages, managing, managed 1 (verb) If you manage to do something, you succeed in doing it, e.g. *We managed to find somewhere to sit.* **2** If you manage an organization or business, you are responsible for controlling it.

manageable (adjective) able to be dealt with.

management 1 (noun) The management of a business is the controlling and organizing of it. **2** The people who control an organization are called the management.

manager, managers (noun) A manager is a person responsible for running a business or organization, e.g. *a bank manager.*

manageress, manageresses (noun) A manageress is a woman responsible for running a business or organization.

managing director, managing directors (noun) The managing director of a company is a director who is responsible for the way the company is managed.

mandarin, mandarins (noun) A mandarin is a type of small orange which is easy to peel.

mandate, mandates (noun; a formal word) A government's mandate is the authority it has to carry out particular policies as a result of winning an election.
mandatory (adjective) If something is mandatory, there is a law or rule stating that it must be done, e.g. *a mandatory life sentence for murder.*
mandolin, mandolins (noun) A mandolin is a musical instrument like a small guitar with a deep, rounded body and four pairs of strings.
mane, manes (noun) The mane of a lion or a horse is the long hair growing from its neck.
manger, mangers (noun) A manger is a feeding box in a barn or stable.
mangle, mangles, mangling, mangled (verb) If something is mangled, it is crushed and twisted.
mango, mangoes or **mangos** (noun) A mango is a sweet yellowish fruit which grows in tropical countries.
manhole, manholes (noun) A manhole is a covered hole in the ground leading to a drain or sewer.
manhood (noun) Manhood is the state of being a man rather than a boy.
mania, manias 1 (noun) A mania for something is a strong liking for it, e.g. *my wife's mania for plant collecting.* **2** A mania is also a mental illness.
maniac, maniacs (noun) A maniac is a mad person who is violent and dangerous.
manic (adjective) energetic and excited, e.g. *his manic stage presence.*
manicure, manicures (noun) A manicure is a special treatment for the hands and nails. **manicurist** (noun).
manifest, manifests, manifesting, manifested (a formal word) **1** (adjective) obvious or easily seen, e.g. *his manifest enthusiasm.* **2** (verb) To manifest something means to make people aware of it, e.g. *Fear can manifest itself in many ways.*
manifestation, manifestations (noun; a formal word) A manifestation of something is a sign that it is happening or exists, e.g. *The illness may be a manifestation of stress.*
manifesto, manifestoes or **manifestos** (noun) A political party's manifesto is a published statement of its aims and policies.
manipulate, manipulates, manipulating, manipulated 1 (verb) To manipulate people or events means to control or influence them to produce a particular result. **2** If you manipulate a piece of equipment, you control it in a skilful way. **manipulation** (noun), **manipulator** (noun), **manipulative** (adjective).
mankind (noun) You can refer to all human beings as mankind, e.g. *a serious threat to mankind.*
manly, manlier, manliest (adjective) having qualities that are typically masculine, e.g. *He had a deep, manly laugh.*
manna (noun) If something appears like manna from heaven, it appears suddenly as if by a miracle and helps you in a difficult situation.

manner, manners 1 (noun) The manner in which you do something is the way you do it. **2** Your manner is the way in which you behave and talk, e.g. *his kind manner.* **3** (plural noun) If you have good manners, you behave very politely.

mannerism, mannerisms (noun) A mannerism is a gesture or a way of speaking which is characteristic of a person.

manoeuvre, manoeuvres, manoeuvring, manoeuvred (pronounced man-**noo**-ver) **1** (verb) If you manoeuvre something into a place, you skilfully move it there, e.g. *It took expertise to manoeuvre the boat so close to the shore.* **2** (noun) A manoeuvre is a clever move you make in order to change a situation to your advantage.

manor, manors (noun) A manor is a large country house with land.

manpower (noun) Workers can be referred to as manpower.

mansion, mansions (noun) A mansion is a very large house.

manslaughter (noun; a legal word) Manslaughter is the accidental killing of a person.

mantelpiece, mantelpieces (noun) A mantelpiece is a shelf over a fireplace.

mantle, mantles (noun; a literary word) To take on the mantle of something means to take on responsibility for it, e.g. *He has taken over the mantle of England's greatest living poet.*

manual, manuals 1 (adjective) Manual work involves physical strength rather than mental skill. **2** operated by hand rather than by electricity or by motor, e.g. *a manual typewriter.* **3** (noun) A manual is an instruction book which tells you how to use a machine. **manually** (adverb).

manufacture, manufactures, manufacturing, manufactured 1 (verb) To manufacture goods means to make them in a factory. **2** (noun) The manufacture of goods is the making of them in a factory. **manufacturer** (noun).

manure (noun) Manure is animal faeces used to fertilize the soil.

manuscript, manuscripts (noun) A manuscript is a handwritten or typed document, especially a version of a book before it is printed.

Manx (adjective) belonging or relating to the Isle of Man.

many 1 (adjective) If there are many people or things, there are a large number of them. **2** You also use many to ask how great a quantity is or to give information about it, e.g. *How many tickets do you require?* **3** (pronoun) a large number of people or things, e.g. *Many are too weak to walk.*

Maori, Maoris (noun) A Maori is someone descended from the people who lived in New Zealand before Europeans arrived.

map, maps, mapping, mapped 1 (noun) A map is a detailed drawing of an area as it would appear if you saw it from above. **2** (verb) If you map out a plan, you work out in detail what you will do.

maple, maples (noun) A maple

is a tree that has large leaves with five points.

mar, mars, marring, marred (verb) To mar something means to spoil it, e.g. *The game was marred by crowd trouble.*

marathon, marathons 1 (noun) A marathon is a race in which people run 26 miles along roads. **2** (adjective) A marathon task is a large one that takes a long time.

marble, marbles 1 (noun) Marble is a very hard, cold stone which is often polished to show the coloured patterns in it. **2** Marbles is a children's game played with small coloured glass balls. These balls are also called marbles.

march, marches, marching, marched 1 (noun) March is the third month of the year. It has 31 days. **2** (verb) When soldiers march, they walk with quick regular steps in time with each other. **3** To march somewhere means to walk quickly in a determined way, e.g. *He got up and marched out of the room.* **4** (noun) A march is an organized protest in which a large group of people walk somewhere together.

mare, mares (noun) A mare is an adult female horse.

margarine (pronounced **mar**-jar-reen) (noun) Margarine is a substance that is similar to butter but is made from vegetable oil and animal fats.

margin, margins 1 (noun) If you win a contest by a large or small margin, you win it by a large or small amount. **2** A margin is an extra amount that allows you more freedom in doing something, e.g. *a small margin of error.* **3** The margin on a written or printed page is the blank space at each side.

marginal (adjective) small and not very important, e.g. *a marginal increase.* **marginally** (adverb).

marigold, marigolds (noun) A marigold is a type of yellow or orange garden flower.

marijuana (pronounced mar-rih-**hwan**-a) (noun) Marijuana is an illegal drug which is smoked in cigarettes.

marina, marinas (noun) A marina is a harbour for pleasure boats and yachts.

marinate, marinates, marinating, marinated; also spelled **marinade** (verb) To marinate food means to soak it in a mixture of oil, wine, vinegar, herbs, and spices to flavour it before cooking.

marine, marines 1 (noun) A marine is a soldier who serves with the navy. **2** (adjective) relating to or involving the sea, e.g. *marine life.*

marital (adjective) relating to or involving marriage, e.g. *marital problems.*

maritime (adjective) relating to the sea and ships, e.g. *maritime trade.*

marjoram (noun) Marjoram is a herb with small, rounded leaves and tiny, pink flowers.

mark, marks, marking, marked 1 (noun) A mark is a small stain or damaged area on a surface, e.g. *I can't get this mark off the curtain.* **2** (verb) If something marks a surface, it damages it in some way. **3**

(noun) A mark is also a written or printed symbol, e.g. *He made a few marks with his pen.* **4** (verb) If you mark something, you write a symbol on it or identify it in some other way. **5** (noun) The mark you get for homework or for an exam is a letter or number showing how well you have done. **6** (verb) When a teacher marks your work, he or she decides how good it is and gives it a mark. **7** (noun) The mark or Deutsche Mark is the main unit of currency in Germany. A mark is worth 100 pfennigs. **8** (verb) To mark something means to be a sign of it, e.g. *The accident marked a tragic end to the day.*

marked (adjective) very obvious, e.g. *a marked improvement.* **markedly** (adverb).

market, markets, marketing, marketed 1 (noun) A market is a place where goods or animals are bought and sold. **2** A market is a place with many small stalls selling different goods. **3** The market for a product is the number of people who want to buy it, e.g. *the market for luxury cars.* **4** (verb) To market a product means to sell it on a large scale and in an organized way.

marketing (noun) Marketing is the part of a business concerned with the way a product is sold.

market research (noun) Market research is research into what people want, need, and buy.

marksman, marksmen (noun) A marksman is someone who can shoot very accurately.

marmalade (noun) Marmalade is a jam made from citrus fruit.

maroon (noun or adjective) dark reddish-purple.

marooned (adjective) If you are marooned in a place, you cannot leave it.

marquee, marquees (pronounced mar-**kee**) (noun) A marquee is a very large tent used at a fair or other outdoor entertainment.

marquis, marquises (pronounced **mar**-kwiss); also spelled **marquess** (noun) A marquis is a male member of the nobility of the rank between duke and earl.

marriage, marriages 1 (noun) A marriage is the relationship between a husband and wife. **2** Marriage is the act of marrying someone.

marrow, marrows (noun) A marrow is a long, thick green vegetable with cream-coloured flesh.

marry, marries, marrying, married 1 (verb) When a man and a woman marry, they become each other's husband and wife during a special ceremony. **2** When a clergyman or registrar marries a couple, he or she is in charge of their marriage ceremony. **married** (adjective).

Mars (noun) Mars is the planet in the solar system which is fourth from the sun.

marsh, marshes (noun) A marsh is an area of land which is permanently wet.

marshal, marshals, marshalling, marshalled 1 (verb) If you marshal things or people, you gather them together and organize them, e.g. *Shipping was being marshalled into convoys.* **2** (noun) A marshal is an official who helps to organize a public event.

marshmallow, marshmallows (noun) A marshmallow is a soft, spongy sweet.

marsupial, marsupials (pronounced mar-**syoo**-pee-al) (noun) A marsupial is an animal that carries its young in a pouch. Koala bears and kangaroos are marsupials.

martial (pronounced **mar**-shal) (adjective) relating to or involving war or soldiers, e.g. *martial music.*

martial arts (plural noun) The martial arts are the techniques of self-defence that come from the Far East, for example karate or judo.

Martian, Martians (pronounced **mar**-shan) (noun) A Martian is an imaginary creature from the planet Mars.

martyr, martyrs, martyring, martyred 1 (noun) A martyr is someone who suffers or is killed rather than change their beliefs. **2** (verb) If someone is martyred, they are killed because of their beliefs. **martyrdom** (noun).

marvel, marvels, marvelling, marvelled 1 (verb) If you marvel at something, it fills you with surprise or admiration, e.g. *Modern designers can only marvel at his genius.* **2** (noun) A marvel is something that makes you feel great surprise or admiration, e.g. *a marvel of high technology.*

marvellous (adjective) wonderful or excellent. **marvellously** (adverb).

Marxism (noun) Marxism is a political philosophy based on the writings of Karl Marx. It states that society will develop towards communism through the struggle between different social classes. **Marxist** (adjective or noun).

marzipan (noun) Marzipan is a paste made of almonds, sugar, and egg. It is used to make cakes and small sweets.

mascara (noun) Mascara is a substance that can be used to colour eyelashes and make them look longer.

mascot, mascots (noun) A mascot is a person, animal, or toy which is thought to bring good luck, e.g. *the Eurotunnel mascot, Marcus the Mole.*

masculine (adjective) typical of men, rather than women, e.g. *the masculine world of motorsport.* **masculinity** (noun).

mash, mashes, mashing, mashed (verb) If you mash vegetables, you crush them after they have been cooked.

mask, masks, masking, masked 1 (noun) A mask is something you wear over your face for protection or disguise, e.g. *a surgical mask.* **2** (verb) If you mask something, you cover it so that it is protected or cannot be seen.

masochist, masochists (pronounced **mass**-so-kist) (noun) A masochist is someone who gets pleasure from their own suffering. **masochism** (noun).

mason, masons (noun) A mason is a person who is skilled at making things with stone.

masonry (noun) Masonry is pieces of stone which form part of a wall or building.

masquerade, masquerades, masquerading, masqueraded (pronounced mass-ker-**raid**) (verb) If you masquerade as something, you pretend to be it, e.g. *He masqueraded as a doctor.*

mass, masses, massing, massed **1** (noun) A mass of something is a large amount of it. **2** (adjective) involving a large number of people, e.g. *mass unemployment.* **3** (noun) The masses are the ordinary people in society considered as a group, e.g. *opera for the masses.* **4** (verb) When people mass, they gather together in a large group. **5** (noun) In physics, the mass of an object is the amount of physical matter that it has. **6** In the Roman Catholic Church, Mass is a religious service in which people share bread and wine in remembrance of the death and resurrection of Jesus Christ.

massacre, massacres, massacring, massacred (pronounced **mass**-ik-ker) **1** (noun) A massacre is the killing of a very large number of people in a violent and cruel way. **2** (verb) To massacre people means to kill large numbers of them in a violent and cruel way.

massage, massages, massaging, massaged **1** (verb) To massage someone means to rub their body in order to help them relax or to relieve pain. **2** (noun) A massage is treatment which involves rubbing the body.

massive (adjective) extremely large in size, quantity, or extent, e.g. *a massive iceberg.* **massively** (adverb).

mass-produce, mass-produces, mass-producing, mass-produced (verb) To mass-produce something means to make it in large quantities, e.g. *Ford started mass-producing the automobile.*

mast, masts (noun) The mast of a boat is the tall upright pole that supports the sails.

master, masters, mastering, mastered **1** (noun) A master is a man who has authority over others, such as the head of a household, the employer of servants, or the owner of slaves or animals. **2** If you are master of a situation, you have control over it, e.g. *He was master of his own destiny.* **3** A master is also a male teacher at some schools. **4** (verb) If you master a difficult situation, you succeed in controlling it. **5** If you master something, you learn how to do it properly, e.g. *She found it easy to master the typewriter.*

masterful (adjective) showing control and authority.

masterly (adjective) extremely clever or well done, e.g. *a masterly exhibition of batting.*

mastermind, masterminds, masterminding, masterminded **1** (verb) If you mastermind a complicated activity, you plan and organize it. **2** (noun) The mastermind behind something is the person responsible for planning it.

masterpiece, masterpieces (noun) A masterpiece is an extremely good painting or other work of art.

masturbate, masturbates, mas-

turbating, masturbated (verb) If someone masturbates, they stroke or rub their own genitals in order to get sexual pleasure. **masturbation** (noun).

mat, mats 1 (noun) A mat is a small round or square piece of cloth, card, or plastic that is placed on a table in order to protect it from plates or glasses. **2** A mat is also a small piece of carpet or other thick material that is placed on the floor.

matador, matadors (noun) A matador is a man who fights and tries to kill bulls in a bullfight.

match, matches, matching, matched 1 (noun) A match is an organized game of football, cricket, or some other sport. **2** A match is also a small, thin stick of wood that produces a flame when you strike it against a rough surface. **3** (verb) If one thing matches another, the two things look the same or have similar qualities.

mate, mates, mating, mated 1 (noun; an informal use) Your mates are your friends. **2** The first mate on a ship is the officer who is next in importance to the captain. **3** An animal's mate is its sexual partner. **4** (verb) When a male and female animal mate, they come together sexually in order to breed.

material, materials 1 (noun) Material is cloth. **2** A material is a substance from which something is made, e.g. *raw materials.* **3** The equipment for a particular activity can be referred to as materials, e.g. *building materials.* **4** Material for a book, play, or film is the information or ideas on which it is based. **5** (adjective) involving possessions and money, e.g. *You are too concerned with material comforts.* **materially** (adverb).

materialism (noun) Materialism is an attitude held by people who think that money and possessions are the most important things in life. **materialistic** (adjective).

materialize, materializes, materializing, materialized; also spelled **materialise** (verb) If something materializes, it actually happens or appears, e.g. *Fortunately, the attack did not materialize.*

maternal (adjective) relating to or involving a mother, e.g. *her maternal instincts.*

maternity (adjective) relating to or involving pregnant women and birth, e.g. *a maternity hospital.*

mathematics (noun) Mathematics is the study of numbers, quantities, and shapes. **mathematical** (adjective), **mathematically** (adverb), **mathematician** (noun).

maths (noun) Maths is mathematics.

matinee, matinees (pronounced **mat**-in-nay); also spelled **matinée** (noun) A matinee is an afternoon performance of a play or film.

matrimony (noun; a formal word) Matrimony is marriage. **matrimonial** (adjective).

matrix, matrices (pronounced **may**-trix) **1** (noun; a formal use) A matrix is the framework in which something grows and develops. **2** In maths, a matrix is a set of numbers or elements set out in rows and columns.

matron, matrons (noun) In a hospital, a senior nurse in charge of all the nursing staff used to be known as matron.

matt (adjective) A matt surface is dull rather than shiny, e.g. *matt black plastic.*

matted (adjective) Hair that is matted is tangled with the strands sticking together.

matter, matters, mattering, mattered 1 (noun) A matter is something that you have to deal with. **2** Matter is any substance, e.g. *The atom is the smallest divisible particle of matter.* **3** Books and magazines are reading matter. **4** (verb) If something matters to you, it is important. **5** (phrase) If you ask **What's the matter?**, you are asking what is wrong.

matter-of-fact (adjective) showing no emotion.

matting (noun) Matting is thick woven material such as rope or straw, used as a floor covering.

mattress, mattresses (noun) A mattress is a thick oblong pad filled with springs or feathers that is put on a bed to make it comfortable.

mature, matures, maturing, matured 1 (verb) When a child or young animal matures, it becomes an adult. **2** When something matures, it reaches a state of complete development. **3** (adjective) Mature means fully developed and balanced in personality and emotional behaviour. **maturely** (adverb), **maturity** (noun).

maudlin (adjective) Someone who is maudlin is sad and sentimental when they are drunk.

maul, mauls, mauling, mauled (verb) If someone is mauled by an animal, they are savagely attacked and badly injured by it.

mausoleum, mausoleums (pronounced maw-sal-**lee**-um) (noun) A mausoleum is a building which contains the grave of a famous person.

mauve (rhymes with **grove**) (noun or adjective) pale purple.

maxim, maxims (noun) A maxim is a rule for good or sensible behaviour in the form of a short saying, e.g. *Instant action: that's my maxim.*

maximize, maximizes, maximizing, maximized; also spelled **maximise** (verb) To maximize something means to make it as great or effective as possible, e.g. *Their objective is to maximize profits.*

maximum 1 (adjective) The maximum amount is the most that is possible, e.g. *the maximum recommended intake.* **2** (noun) The maximum is the most that is possible, e.g. *a maximum of fifty men.*

may 1 (verb) If something may happen, it is possible that it will happen, e.g. *It may happen quite soon.* **2** If someone may do something, they are allowed to do it, e.g. *Please may I be excused?* **3** You can use 'may' when saying that, although something is true, something else is also true, e.g. *This may be true, but it is* *only part of the story.* **4** (a formal use) You also use 'may' to express a wish that something will happen, e.g. *May you live to be a hundred.* **5** (noun) May is the fifth month of the year. It has 31 days.

maybe (adverb) You use 'maybe' when you are stating a possibility that you are not certain about, e.g. *Maybe I should lie about my age.*

mayhem (noun) You can refer to a confused and chaotic situation as mayhem, e.g. *There was complete mayhem in the classroom.*

mayonnaise (pronounced may-on-**nayz**) (noun) Mayonnaise is a thick salad dressing made with egg yolks and oil.

mayor, mayors (noun) The mayor of a town is a person who has been elected to lead and represent the people.

maze, mazes (noun) A maze is a system of complicated passages which it is difficult to find your way through, e.g. *a maze of dark tunnels.*

MBE, MBEs (noun) An MBE is an honour granted by the King or Queen. MBE is an abbreviation for 'Member of the Order of the British Empire', e.g. *Ally McCoist, MBE.*

MD an abbreviation for 'Doctor of Medicine' or 'Managing Director'.

me (pronoun) A speaker or writer uses me to refer to himself or herself.

meadow, meadows (noun) A meadow is a field of grass.

meagre (pronounced **mee**-ger) (adjective) very small and poor, e.g. *He had to supplement his meagre pension.*

meal, meals (noun) A meal is an occasion when people eat, or the food they eat at that time.

mean, means, meaning, meant; meaner, meanest 1 (verb) If you ask what something means, you want it explained to you. **2** If you mean what you say, you are serious, e.g. *The boss means what he says.* **3** If something means a lot to you, it is important to you. **4** If one thing means another, it shows that the second thing is true or will happen, e.g. *Major road works will mean long delays.* **5** If you mean to do something, you intend to do it, e.g. *I meant to phone you, but didn't have time.* **6** If something is meant to be true, it is supposed to be true, e.g. *I found a road that wasn't meant to be there.* **7** (adjective) Someone who is mean is unwilling to spend much money. **8** Someone who is mean is unkind or cruel, e.g. *He apologized for being so mean to her.* **9** (noun) A means of doing something is a method or object which makes it possible, e.g. *The tests were marked by means of a computer.* **10** (plural noun) Someone's means are their money and income, e.g. *He's obviously a man of means.* **11** (noun) In mathematics, the mean is the average of a set of numbers. **meanness** (noun).

meander, meanders, meandering, meandered (pronounced mee-**an**-der) (verb) If a road or river meanders, it has a lot of bends in it.

meaning, meanings 1 (noun)

The meaning of a word, expression, or gesture is what it refers to or expresses. **2** The meaning of what someone says, or of a book or a film, is the thoughts or ideas that it is intended to express. **3** If something has meaning, it seems to be worthwhile and to have real purpose. **meaningful** (adjective), **meaningfully** (adverb), **meaningless** (adjective).

meantime (phrase) **In the meantime** means in the period of time between two events, e.g. *I'll call the nurse; in the meantime, you must rest.*

meanwhile 1 (adverb) Meanwhile means while something else is happening. **2** (noun) Meanwhile also means the time between two events.

measles (noun) Measles is an infectious illness in which you have red spots on your skin.

measly (adjective; an informal word) very small or inadequate, e.g. *a measly ten pence.*

measure, measures, measuring, measured 1 (verb) When you measure something, you find out how big it is by using a ruler or tape measure. **2** If something measures a particular distance, its length or depth is that distance, e.g. *slivers of glass measuring a few millimetres across.* **3** (noun) A measure of something is a certain amount of it, e.g. *There has been a measure of agreement.* **4** A measure is a unit in which size, speed, or depth is expressed. **5** Measures are actions carried out to achieve a particular result, e.g. *Tough measures are needed to maintain order.* **measurement** (noun).

measured (adjective) careful and deliberate, e.g. *walking at the same measured pace.*

measurement, measurements 1 (noun) A measurement is the result that you obtain when you measure something. **2** Measurement is the activity of measuring something. **3** Your measurements are the sizes of your chest, waist, and hips that you use to buy the correct size of clothes.

meat, meats (noun) Meat is the flesh of animals that is cooked and eaten. **meaty** (adjective).

mecca, meccas (noun) If a place is a mecca for people of a particular kind, many of them go there because it is of special interest to them, e.g. *The island is a mecca for whisky lovers.*

mechanic, mechanics 1 (noun) A mechanic is a person who repairs and maintains engines and machines. **2** (plural noun) The mechanics of something are the way in which it works or is done, e.g. *the mechanics of accounting.* **3** (noun) Mechanics is also the scientific study of movement and the forces that affect objects.

mechanical 1 (adjective) A mechanical device has moving parts and is used to do a physical task. **2** A mechanical action is done automatically without thinking about it, e.g. *He gave a mechanical smile.* **mechanically** (adverb).

mechanism, mechanisms 1 (noun) A mechanism is a part of a machine that does a particular task, e.g. *a locking* *mechanism.* **2** A mechanism is also part of your behaviour that is automatic, e.g. *the body's defence mechanisms.*

medal, medals (noun) A medal is a small disc of metal given as an award for bravery or as a prize for sport.

medallion, medallions (noun) A medallion is a round piece of metal worn as an ornament on a chain round the neck.

medallist, medallists (noun) A medallist is a person who has won a medal in sport, e.g. *a gold medallist at the Olympics.*

meddle, meddles, meddling, meddled (verb) To meddle means to interfere and try to change things without being asked.

media (plural noun) You can refer to the television, radio, and newspapers as the media.

mediaeval another spelling of **medieval.**

mediate, mediates, mediating, mediated (verb) If you mediate between two groups, you try to settle a dispute between them. **mediation** (noun), **mediator** (noun).

medical, medicals 1 (adjective) relating to the prevention and treatment of illness and injuries. **2** (noun) A medical is a thorough examination of your body by a doctor. **medically** (adverb).

medication, medications (noun) Medication is a substance that is used to treat illness.

medicinal (adjective) relating to the treatment of illness, e.g. *a valuable medicinal herb.*

medicine, medicines 1 (noun) Medicine is the treatment of illness and injuries by doctors and nurses. **2** A medicine is a substance that you drink or swallow to help cure an illness.

medieval or **mediaeval** (pronounced med-dee-**ee**-vul) (adjective) relating to the period between about 1100 AD and 1500 AD, especially in Europe.

mediocre (pronounced meed-dee-**oh**-ker) (adjective) of rather poor quality, e.g. *a mediocre string of performances.* **mediocrity** (noun).

meditate, meditates, meditating, meditated 1 (verb) If you meditate on something, you think about it very deeply. **2** If you meditate, you remain in a calm, silent state for a period of time, often as part of a religious training. **meditation** (noun).

Mediterranean (noun) The Mediterranean is the large inland sea between southern Europe and northern Africa.

medium, mediums or **media 1** (adjective) If something is of medium size or degree, it is neither large nor small, e.g. *a medium sized hotel.* **2** (noun) A medium is a means that you use to communicate or express something, e.g. *the medium of television.* **3** A medium is also a person who claims to be able to speak to the dead and to receive messages from them.

medley, medleys 1 (noun) A medley of different things is a mixture of them creating an interesting effect. **2** A medley is also a number of different songs or tunes sung or played one after the other.

meek, meeker, meekest (adjective) A meek person is timid and does what other people say. **meekly** (adverb).

meet, meets, meeting, met 1 (verb) If you meet someone, you happen to be in the same place as them. **2** If you meet a visitor or if you meet their train, plane, or bus, you go to be with them when they arrive. **3** When a group of people meet, they gather together for a purpose. **4** If something meets a need, it is suitable to fulfil it, e.g. *services intended to meet the needs of the elderly.* **5** If something meets with a particular reaction, it gets that reaction from people, e.g. *I was met with silence.*

meeting, meetings 1 (noun) A meeting is an event in which people discuss proposals and make decisions together. **2** A meeting is what happens when you meet someone.

melancholy (adjective or noun) If you feel melancholy, you feel sad.

mêlée, mêlées (pronounced **mel**-lay) (noun) If there are a lot of people rushing around, the situation is described as a mêlée.

mellow, mellower, mellowest; mellows, mellowing, mellowed 1 (adjective) Mellow light is soft and golden. **2** A mellow sound is smooth and pleasant to listen to, e.g. *his mellow clarinet.* **3** (verb) If someone mellows, they become more pleasant or relaxed, e.g. *He certainly hasn't mellowed with age.*

melodic (adjective) relating to melody.

melodious (adjective) pleasant to listen to, e.g. *soft melodious music.*

melodrama, melodramas (noun) A melodrama is a story or play in which people's emotions are exaggerated.

melodramatic (adjective) behaving in an exaggerated, emotional way.

melody, melodies (noun) A melody is a tune.

melon, melons (noun) A melon is a large, juicy fruit with a green or yellow skin and many seeds inside.

melt, melts, melting, melted 1 (verb) When something melts or when you melt it, it changes from a solid to a liquid because it has been heated. **2** If something melts, it disappears, e.g. *The crowd melted away.*

member, members 1 (noun) A member of a group is one of the people or things belonging to the group, e.g. *members of the family.* **2** A member of an organization is a person who has joined the organization. **3** (adjective) A country belonging to an international organization is called a member country or a member state.

Member of Parliament, Members of Parliament (noun) A Member of Parliament is a person who has been elected to represent people in a country's parliament.

membership 1 (noun) Membership of an organization is the state of being a member of it. **2** The people who belong to an organization are its membership.

membrane, membranes (noun) A membrane is a very thin

piece of skin or tissue which connects or covers plant or animal organs or cells, e.g. *the nasal membrane.*

memento, mementos (noun) A memento is an object which you keep because it reminds you of a person or a special occasion, e.g. *a lasting memento of their romance.*

memo, memos (noun) A memo is a note from one person to another within the same organization. Memo is short for 'memorandum'.

memoirs (pronounced **mem**-wahrz) (plural noun) If someone writes their memoirs, they write a book about their life and experiences.

memorable (adjective) If something is memorable, it is likely to be remembered because it is special or unusual, e.g. *a memorable victory.* **memorably** (adverb).

memorandum, memorandums or **memoranda** (noun) A memorandum is a memo.

memorial, memorials 1 (noun) A memorial is a structure built to remind people of a famous person or event, e.g. *a war memorial.* **2** (adjective) A memorial event or prize is in honour of someone who has died, so that they will be remembered.

memory, memories 1 (noun) Your memory is your ability to remember things. **2** A memory is something you remember about the past, e.g. *memories of their school days.* **3** A computer's memory is the part in which information is stored.

men the plural of **man**.

menace, menaces, menacing, menaced 1 (noun) A menace is someone or something that is likely to cause serious harm, e.g. *the menace of drugs in sport.* **2** Menace is the quality of being threatening, e.g. *an atmosphere of menace.* **3** (verb) If someone or something menaces you, they threaten to harm you. **menacingly** (adverb).

menagerie, menageries (pronounced men-**naj**-er-ree) (noun) A menagerie is a collection of different wild animals.

mend, mends, mending, mended (verb) If you mend something that is broken, you repair it.

menial (adjective) Menial work is boring and tiring and the people who do it have low status.

meningitis (noun) Meningitis is a serious infectious illness which affects your brain and spinal cord.

menopause (noun) The menopause is the time during which a woman gradually stops menstruating. This usually happens when she is about fifty.

menstruate, menstruates, menstruating, menstruated (verb) When a woman menstruates, blood comes from her womb. This normally happens once a month. **menstruation** (noun), **menstrual** (adjective).

mental 1 (adjective) relating to the process of thinking or intelligence, e.g. *mental arithmetic.* **2** relating to the health of the mind, e.g. *mental health... a mental hospital.* **mentally**

(adverb).

mentality, mentalities (noun) Your mentality is your attitude or way of thinking, e.g. *the traditional Civil Service mentality.*

mention, mentions, mentioning, mentioned **1** (verb) If you mention something, you talk about it briefly. **2** (noun) A mention of someone or something is a brief comment about them, e.g. *He made no mention of his criminal past.*

mentor, mentors (noun) Someone's mentor is a person who teaches them and gives them advice.

menu, menus **1** (noun) A menu is a list of the foods you can eat in a restaurant. **2** A menu is also a list of different options shown on a computer screen which the user must choose from.

mercenary, mercenaries **1** (noun) A mercenary is a soldier who is paid to fight for a foreign country. **2** (adjective) Someone who is mercenary is mainly interested in getting money.

merchandise (noun; a formal word) Merchandise is goods that are sold, e.g. *He had left me with more merchandise than I could sell.*

merchant, merchants (noun) A merchant is a trader who imports and exports goods, e.g. *a coal merchant.*

merchant navy (noun) The merchant navy is the shipping and seamen involved in carrying goods for trade.

merciful **1** (adjective) considered to be fortunate as a relief from suffering, e.g. *Death came as a merciful release.* **2** showing kindness and forgiveness. **mercifully** (adverb).

merciless (adjective) showing no kindness or forgiveness. **mercilessly** (adverb).

mercury **1** (noun) Mercury is a silver-coloured metallic element that is liquid at room temperature. It is used in thermometers. **2** Mercury is also the planet in the solar system which is nearest to the sun.

mercy, mercies (noun) If you show mercy, you show kindness and forgiveness and do not punish someone as severely as you could.

mere, merest (adjective) used to emphasize how unimportant or small something is, e.g. *It's a mere 7-minute journey by boat.* **merely** (adverb).

merge, merges, merging, merged (verb) When two things merge, they combine together to make one thing, e.g. *The two airlines merged in 1983.* **merger** (noun).

meringue, meringues (pronounced mer-**rang**) (noun) A meringue is a type of crisp, sweet cake made with egg whites and sugar.

merit, merits, meriting, merited **1** (noun) If something has merit, it is good or worthwhile. **2** The merits of something are its advantages or good qualities. **3** (verb) If something merits a particular treatment, it deserves that treatment, e.g. *He merits a place in the team.*

mermaid, mermaids (noun) In stories, a mermaid is a woman with a fish's tail instead of legs, who lives in the sea.

merry, merrier, merriest (adjective) happy and cheerful, e.g. *He was, for all his shyness, a merry man.* **merrily** (adverb).

merry-go-round, merry-go-rounds (noun) A merry-go-round is a large rotating platform with models of animals or vehicles on it, on which children ride at a fair.

mesh (noun) Mesh is threads of wire or plastic twisted together like a net, e.g. *a fence made of wire mesh.*

mess, messes, messing, messed **1** (noun) If something is a mess, it is untidy. **2** If a situation is a mess, it is full of problems and trouble. **3** A mess is a room or building in which members of the armed forces eat, e.g. *the officers' mess.* **4** (verb) If you mess about or mess around, you do things without any particular purpose. **5** If you mess something up, you spoil it or do it wrong. **messy** (adjective).

message, messages 1 (noun) A message is a piece of information or a request that you send someone or leave for them. **2** A message is also an idea that someone tries to communicate to people, for example in a play or a speech, e.g. *the story's anti-drugs message.*

messenger, messengers (noun) A messenger is someone who takes a message to someone for someone else.

Messiah (pronounced miss-**eye**-ah) **1** (noun) For Jews, the Messiah is the king of the Jews who will be sent by God. **2** For Christians, the Messiah is Jesus Christ.

Messrs (pronounced **mes**-serz) Messrs is the plural of **Mr.** It is often used in the names of businesses, e.g. *Messrs Brown and Humberley, Solicitors.*

met the past tense and past participle of **meet.**

metabolism, metabolisms (noun) Your metabolism is the chemical processes in your body that use food for growth and energy. **metabolic** (adjective).

metal, metals (noun) Metal is a chemical element such as iron, steel, copper, or lead. Metals are good conductors of heat and electricity. **metallic** (adjective).

metamorphosis, metamorphoses (pronounced met-am-**mor**-fiss-iss) (noun; a formal word) When a metamorphosis occurs, a person or thing changes into something completely different, e.g. *the metamorphosis of a larva into an insect.*

metaphor, metaphors (noun) A metaphor is an imaginative way of describing something by saying that it has the typical qualities of something else. For example, if you wanted to say that someone is shy, you might say they are a mouse. **metaphorical** (adjective), **metaphorically** (adverb).

meteor, meteors (noun) A meteor is a piece of rock or metal that burns very brightly when it enters the earth's atmosphere from space.

meteoric (adjective) A meteoric rise to power or success happens very quickly.

meteorite, meteorites (noun) A

meteorite is a piece of rock from space that has landed on earth.

meteorological (adjective) relating to or involving the weather or weather forecasting. **meteorology** (noun).

meter, meters (noun) A meter is a device that measures and records something, e.g. *a gas meter.*

methane (pronounced **mee**-thane) (noun) Methane is a colourless gas with no smell that is found in coal gas and produced by decaying vegetable matter. It burns easily and can be used as a fuel.

method, methods (noun) A method is a particular way of doing something, e.g. *the traditional method of making wine.*

methodical (adjective) Someone who is methodical does things carefully and in an organized way. **methodically** (adverb).

Methodist, Methodists (noun or adjective) A Methodist is someone who belongs to the Methodist Church, a Protestant church whose members worship God in a way begun by John Wesley and his followers.

meticulous (adjective) A meticulous person does things very carefully and with great attention to detail. **meticulously** (adverb).

metre, metres (noun) A metre is a unit of length equal to 100 centimetres.

metric (adjective) relating to the system of measurement that uses metres, grams, and litres.

metropolis, metropolises (noun) A metropolis is a very large city.

metropolitan (adjective) relating or belonging to a large, busy city, e.g. *metropolitan districts.*

mettle (noun) If you are on your mettle, you are ready to do something as well as you can because you know you are being tested or challenged.

mew, mews, mewing, mewed 1 (verb) When a cat mews, it makes a short high-pitched noise. **2** (noun) A mew is the short high-pitched sound that a cat makes. **3** A mews is a quiet yard or street surrounded by houses.

Mexican, Mexicans 1 (adjective) belonging or relating to Mexico. **2** (noun) A Mexican is someone who comes from Mexico.

mg an abbreviation for 'milligrams'.

mice the plural of **mouse.**

micro- (prefix) very small.

microphone, microphones (noun) A microphone is a device that is used to make sounds louder or to record them on a tape recorder.

microscope, microscopes (noun) A microscope is a piece of equipment which magnifies very small objects so that you can study them.

microscopic (adjective) very small indeed, e.g. *microscopic parasites.*

microwave, microwaves (noun) A microwave or microwave oven is a type of oven which cooks food very quickly by short-wave radiation.

mid- (prefix) Mid- is used to

form words that refer to the middle part of a place or period of time, e.g. *mid-Atlantic... the mid-70s.*

midday (noun) Midday is twelve o'clock in the middle of the day.

middle, middles 1 (noun) The middle of something is the part furthest from the edges, ends, or outside surface. **2** (adjective) The middle one in a series or a row is the one that has an equal number of people or things each side of it, e.g. *the middle child of the family.*

middle age (noun) Middle age is the period of your life when you are between about 40 and 60 years old. **middle-aged** (adjective).

Middle Ages (plural noun) In European history, the Middle Ages were the period between about 1100 AD and 1500 AD.

middle class, middle classes (noun) The middle classes are the people in a society who are not working class or upper class, for example managers, doctors, and lawyers.

Middle East (noun) The Middle East consists of Iran and the countries in Asia to the west and south-west of Iran.

middle-of-the-road (adjective) Middle-of-the-road opinions are moderate.

middle school, middle schools (noun) In England and Wales, a middle school is for children aged between about 8 and 12.

middling (adjective) of average quality or ability.

midge, midges (noun) A midge is a small flying insect which can bite people.

midget, midgets (noun) A midget is a very short person.

midnight (noun) Midnight is twelve o'clock at night.

midriff, midriffs (noun) Your midriff is the middle of your body between your waist and your chest.

midst (noun) If you are in the midst of a crowd or an event, you are in the middle of it.

midsummer (adjective) relating to the period in the middle of summer, e.g. *a lovely midsummer morning in July.*

midway (adverb) in the middle of a distance or period of time, e.g. *They scored midway through the second half.*

midwife, midwives (noun) A midwife is a nurse who is trained to help women at the birth of a baby. **midwifery** (noun).

might 1 (verb) If you say something might happen, you mean that it is possible that it will happen, e.g. *I might stay a while.* **2** If you say that someone might do something, you are suggesting that they do it, e.g. *You might like to go and see it.* **3** Might is also the past tense of **may. 4** (noun; a literary use) Might is power or strength, e.g. *the full might of the American Navy.*

mightily (adverb; a literary word) to a great degree or extent, e.g. *I was mightily relieved by the decision.*

mighty, mightier, mightiest (adjective; a literary word) very powerful or strong, e.g. *a mighty army on the march.*

migraine, migraines (pronounced **mee**-grane) (noun) A migraine is a severe headache that makes you feel very ill.

migrate, migrates, migrating, migrated 1 (verb) If people migrate, they move from one place to another, especially to find work. **2** When birds or animals migrate, they move at a particular season to a different place, usually to breed or to find new feeding grounds, e.g. *the birds migrate each year to Southern Europe.* **migration** (noun), **migratory** (adjective), **migrant** (noun or adjective).

mike, mikes (noun; an informal word) A mike is a microphone.

mild, milder, mildest 1 (adjective) Something that is mild is not strong and does not have any powerful or damaging effects, e.g. *a mild shampoo.* **2** Someone who is mild is gentle and kind. **3** Mild weather is warmer than usual, e.g. *The region has mild winters and hot summers.* **4** Mild qualities, emotions, or attitudes are not very great or extreme, e.g. *We looked at each other in mild surprise.* **mildly** (adverb).

mildew (noun) Mildew is a soft white fungus that grows on things when they are warm and damp.

mile, miles (noun) A mile is a unit of distance equal to 1760 yards or about 1.6 kilometres.

mileage, mileages 1 (noun) Your mileage is the distance that you have travelled, measured in miles. **2** The amount of mileage that you get out of something is how useful it is to you.

militant, militants 1 (adjective) A militant person is very active in trying to bring about extreme political or social change, e.g. *a militant socialist.* **2** (noun) A militant is a person who tries to bring about extreme political or social change. **militancy** (noun).

military 1 (adjective) related to or involving the armed forces of a country, e.g. *military bases.* **2** (noun) The military are the armed forces of a country. **militarily** (adverb).

militia, militias (pronounced mil-**lish**-a) (noun) A militia is an organization that operates like an army but whose members are not professional soldiers.

milk, milks, milking, milked 1 (noun) Milk is the white liquid produced by female cows, goats, and some other animals to feed their young. People drink milk and use it to make butter, cheese, and yogurt. **2** (verb) When someone milks a cow or a goat, they get milk from it by pulling its udders. **3** (noun) Milk is also the white liquid that a baby drinks from its mother's breasts. **4** (verb) If you milk a situation or place, you get as much personal gain from it as possible, e.g. *They milked money from a hospital charity.*

milk tooth, milk teeth (noun) Your milk teeth are your first teeth which fall out and are replaced by the permanent set.

milky, milkier, milkiest 1 (adjective) pale creamy white, e.g. *her milky pale flesh.* **2** containing a lot of milk, e.g. *a large mug of milky coffee.*

Milky Way (noun) The Milky

Way is a strip of stars clustered closely together, appearing as a pale band in the sky.

mill, mills 1 (noun) A mill is a building where grain is crushed to make flour. **2** A mill is also a factory for making materials such as steel, wool, or cotton. **3** A mill is also a small device for grinding coffee or spices into powder, e.g. *a pepper mill.*

millennium, millennia or **millenniums** (noun; a formal word) A millennium is a period of 1000 years.

miller, millers (noun) A miller is the person who operates a flour mill.

milligram, milligrams (noun) A milligram is a unit of weight equal to one thousandth of a gram.

millilitre, millilitres (noun) A millilitre is a unit of liquid volume equal to one thousandth of a litre.

millimetre, millimetres (noun) A millimetre is a unit of length equal to a tenth of a centimetre or one thousandth of a metre.

million, millions the number 1,000,000.

millionaire, millionaires (noun) A millionaire is a very rich person who has property worth millions of pounds or dollars.

millstone, millstones (phrase) If something is **a millstone round your neck,** it is an unpleasant problem or responsibility you cannot escape from.

mime, mimes, miming, mimed 1 (noun) Mime is the use of movements and gestures to express something or to tell a story without using speech. **2** (verb) If you mime something, you describe or express it using mime.

mimic, mimics, mimicking, mimicked 1 (verb) If you mimic someone's actions or voice, you imitate them in an amusing way. **2** (noun) A mimic is a person who can imitate other people. **mimicry** (noun).

minaret, minarets (noun) A minaret is a tall, thin tower on a mosque.

mince, minces, mincing, minced 1 (noun) Mince is meat which has been chopped into very small pieces in a mincer. **2** (verb) If you mince meat, you chop it into very small pieces. **3** To mince about means to walk with small quick steps in an affected, effeminate way.

mind, minds, minding, minded 1 (noun) Your mind is your ability to think, together with all the thoughts you have and your memory. **2** (phrase) If you **change your mind,** you change a decision that you have made or an opinion that you have. **3** (verb) If you do not mind something, you are not annoyed by it or bothered about it. **4** If you say that you wouldn't mind something, you mean that you would quite like it, e.g. *I wouldn't mind a drink.* **5** If you mind a child or mind something for someone, you look after it for a while, e.g. *My mother is minding the office.*

mindful (adjective; a formal word) If you are mindful of something, you think about it carefully before taking action, e.g. *mindful of the needs of the poor.*

mindless 1 (adjective) Mindless actions are regarded as stupid and destructive, e.g. *mindless violence.* **2** A mindless job or activity is simple, repetitive, and boring.

mine, mines, mining, mined 1 (pronoun) Mine refers to something belonging or relating to the person who is speaking or writing, e.g. *a friend of mine.* **2** (noun) A mine is a series of holes or tunnels in the ground dug in order to extract diamonds, coal, or other minerals, e.g. *a diamond mine.* **3** (verb) To mine diamonds, coal, or other minerals means to obtain these substances from underneath the ground. **4** (noun) A mine is also a bomb hidden in the ground or underwater, which explodes when people or things touch it. **miner** (noun), **mining** (noun).

minefield, minefields (noun) A minefield is an area of land or water where mines have been hidden.

mineral, minerals (noun) A mineral is a substance such as tin, salt, uranium, or coal that is formed naturally in rocks and in the earth, e.g. *rich mineral deposits.*

mineral water (noun) Mineral water is water which comes from a natural spring.

minestrone (pronounced min-nes-**strone**-ee) (noun) Minestrone is soup containing small pieces of vegetable and pasta.

minesweeper, minesweepers (noun) A minesweeper is a ship for clearing away underwater mines.

mingle, mingles, mingling, mingled (verb) If things mingle, they become mixed together, e.g. *His cries mingled with theirs.*

mini- (prefix) Mini- is used to form nouns referring to something smaller or less important than similar things, e.g. *a TV mini-series.*

miniature, miniatures (pronounced **min**-nit-cher) **1** (adjective) A miniature thing is a tiny copy of something much larger. **2** (noun) A miniature is a very small detailed painting, often of a person.

minibus, minibuses (noun) A minibus is a van with seats in the back which is used as a small bus.

minimal (adjective) very small in quality, quantity, or degree, e.g. *He has minimal experience.* **minimally** (adverb).

minimize, minimizes, minimizing, minimized; also spelled **minimise** (verb) If you minimize something, you reduce it to the smallest amount possible, e.g. *His route was changed to minimize jet lag.*

minimum 1 (adjective) The minimum amount is the smallest amount that is possible, e.g. *a minimum wage.* **2** (noun) The minimum is the smallest amount that is possible, e.g. *a minimum of three weeks.*

minister, ministers 1 (noun) A minister is a person who is in charge of a particular government department, e.g. *Portugal's deputy foreign minister.* **2** A minister in a Protestant church is a member of the clergy.

ministerial (adjective) relating to a government minister or ministry, e.g. *ministerial duties.*

ministry, ministries 1 (noun) A ministry is a government department that deals with a particular area of work, e.g. *the Ministry of Defence.* **2** Members of the clergy can be referred to as the ministry, e.g. *Her son is in the ministry.*

mink, minks (noun) Mink is an expensive fur used to make coats or hats.

minnow, minnows (noun) A minnow is a very small freshwater fish.

minor, minors 1 (adjective) not as important or serious as other things, e.g. *a minor injury.* **2** (noun; a formal use) A minor is a young person under the age of 18, e.g. *laws concerning the employment of minors.*

minority, minorities 1 (noun) The minority of people or things in a group is a number of them forming less than half of the whole, e.g. *Only a minority of people want this.* **2** A minority is a group of people of a particular race or religion living in a place where most people are of a different race or religion, e.g. *ethnic minorities.*

minstrel, minstrels (noun) A minstrel was a medieval singer and entertainer.

mint, mints, minting, minted 1 (noun) Mint is a herb used for flavouring in cooking. **2** A mint is a peppermint-flavoured sweet. **3** The mint is the place where the official coins of a country are made. **4** (verb) When coins or medals are minted, they are made. **5** (adjective) If something is in mint condition, it is in very good condition, like new.

minus 1 You use minus to show that one number is being subtracted from another, e.g. *Ten minus six equals four.* **2** (adjective) Minus is used when talking about temperatures below 0°C or 0°F.

minuscule (pronounced **min**-nus-kyool) (adjective) very small indeed.

minute, minutes, minuting, minuted (pronounced **min**-nit) **1** (noun) A minute is a unit of time equal to sixty seconds. **2** The minutes of a meeting are the written records of what was said and decided. **3** (verb) To minute a meeting means to write the official notes of it.

minute (pronounced my-**nyoot**) (adjective) extremely small, e.g. *a minute amount of pesticide.* **minutely** (adverb).

minutiae (pronounced my-**nyoo**-shee-aye) (plural noun; a formal word) Minutiae are small, unimportant details.

miracle, miracles 1 (noun) A miracle is a wonderful and surprising event, believed to have been caused by God. **2** Any very surprising and fortunate event can be called a miracle, e.g. *My father got a job. It was a miracle.* **miraculous** (adjective), **miraculously** (adverb).

mirage, mirages (pronounced mir-**ahj**) (noun) A mirage is an image which you can see in the distance in very hot weather, but which does not actually exist.

mire (noun; a literary word) Mire is swampy ground or mud.

mirror, mirrors, mirroring, mirrored 1 (noun) A mirror is a piece of glass which reflects light and in which you can see your reflection. **2** (verb) To mirror something means to have similar features to it, e.g. *His own shock was mirrored on her face.*

mirth (noun; a literary word) Mirth is great amusement and laughter.

misbehave, misbehaves, misbehaving, misbehaved (verb) If a child misbehaves, he or she is naughty or behaves badly. **misbehaviour** (noun).

miscarriage, miscarriages 1 (noun) If a woman has a miscarriage she gives birth to a baby before it is properly formed and it dies. **2** A miscarriage of justice is a wrong decision made by a court, which causes an innocent person to be punished.

miscellaneous (adjective) A miscellaneous group is made up of people or things that are different from each other.

mischief (noun) Mischief is eagerness to have fun by teasing people or playing tricks. **mischievous** (adjective).

misconception, misconceptions (noun) A misconception is a wrong idea about something, e.g. *Another misconception is that cancer is infectious.*

misconduct (noun) Misconduct is bad or unacceptable behaviour by a professional person, e.g. *The Football Association found him guilty of misconduct.*

misdemeanour, misdemeanours (pronounced miss-dem-**mee**-ner) (noun; a formal word) A misdemeanour is an act that people consider shocking or unacceptable.

miser, misers (noun) A miser is a person who enjoys saving money but hates spending it. **miserly** (adjective).

miserable 1 (adjective) If you are miserable, you are very unhappy. **2** If a place or a situation is miserable, it makes you feel depressed, e.g. *a miserable little flat.* **miserably** (adverb).

misery, miseries (noun) Misery is great unhappiness.

misfire, misfires, misfiring, misfired (verb) If a plan misfires, it goes wrong.

misfit, misfits (noun) A misfit is a person who is not accepted by other people because of being rather strange or eccentric.

misfortune, misfortunes (noun) A misfortune is an unpleasant occurrence that is regarded as bad luck, e.g. *I had the misfortune to fall off my bike.*

misgiving, misgivings (noun) If you have misgivings, you are worried or unhappy about something, e.g. *I had misgivings about his methods.*

misguided (adjective) A misguided opinion or action is wrong because it is based on a misunderstanding or bad information.

misinform, misinforms, misinforming, misinformed (verb) If you are misinformed, you are given wrong or inaccurate information. **misinformation** (noun).

misinterpret, misinterprets, misinterpreting, misinterpreted (verb) To misinterpret something means to understand it wrongly, e.g. *You completely misinterpreted what I wrote.*

misjudge, misjudges, misjudging, misjudged (verb) If you misjudge someone or something, you form an incorrect idea or opinion about them.

mislay, mislays, mislaying, mislaid (verb) If you mislay something, you lose it because you have forgotten where you put it.

mislead, misleads, misleading, misled (verb) To mislead someone means to make them believe something which is not true.

misplaced (adjective) A misplaced feeling is inappropriate or directed at the wrong thing or person, e.g. *misplaced loyalty.*

misprint, misprints (noun) A misprint is a mistake such as a spelling mistake in something that has been printed.

misrepresent, misrepresents, misrepresenting, misrepresented (verb) To misrepresent someone means to give an inaccurate or misleading account of what they have said or done. **misrepresentation** (noun).

miss, misses, missing, missed 1 (verb) If you miss something, you do not notice it, e.g. *You can't miss it. It's on the second floor.* **2** If you miss someone or something, you feel sad that they are no longer with you, e.g. *The boys miss their father.* **3** If you miss a chance or opportunity, you fail to take advantage of it. **4** If you miss a bus, plane, or train, you arrive too late to catch it. **5** If you miss something, you fail to hit it when you aim at it, e.g. *His shot missed the target and went wide.* **6** (noun) A miss is an act of missing something that you were aiming at. **7** Miss is used before the name of an unmarried woman or girl as a form of address, e.g. *Did you know Miss Smith?*

missile, missiles (noun) A missile is a weapon that moves long distances through the air and explodes when it reaches its target; also used of any object thrown as a weapon.

mission, missions 1 (noun) A mission is an important task that you have to do. **2** A mission is a group of people who have been sent to a foreign country to carry out an official task, e.g. *He became head of the Israeli mission.* **3** A mission is also a special journey made by a military aeroplane or space rocket. **4** If you have a mission, there is something that you believe it is your duty to try to achieve. **5** A mission is also the workplace of a group of Christians who are working for the Church.

missionary, missionaries (noun) A missionary is a Christian who has been sent to a foreign country to work for the Church.

missive, missives (noun; an old-fashioned word) A missive is a letter or message.

mist, mists, misting, misted 1

(noun) Mist consists of a large number of tiny drops of water in the air, which make it hard to see clearly. **2** (verb) If your eyes mist, you cannot see very far because there are tears in your eyes. **3** If glass mists over or mists up, it becomes covered with condensation so that you cannot see through it.

mistake, mistakes, mistaking, mistook, mistaken 1 (noun) A mistake is an action or opinion that is wrong or is not what you intended. **2** (verb) If you mistake someone or something for another person or thing, you wrongly think that they are the other person or thing, e.g. *I mistook him for the owner of the house.*

mistaken 1 (adjective) If you are mistaken about something, you are wrong about it. **2** If you have a mistaken belief or opinion, you believe something which is not true. **mistakenly** (adverb).

mister A man is sometimes addressed in a very informal way as 'mister', e.g. *Where do you live, mister?*

mistletoe (pronounced **mis**-sel-toe) (noun) Mistletoe is a plant which grows on trees and has white berries on it. It is used as a Christmas decoration.

mistook the past tense of **mistake.**

mistreat, mistreats, mistreating, mistreated (verb) To mistreat a person or animal means to treat them badly and make them suffer.

mistress, mistresses 1 (noun) A married man's mistress is a woman who is not his wife and who he is having a sexual relationship with. **2** A school mistress is a female teacher. **3** A servant's mistress is the woman who is the servant's employer.

mistrust, mistrusts, mistrusting, mistrusted 1 (verb) If you mistrust someone, you do not feel that you can trust them. **2** (noun) Mistrust is a feeling that you cannot trust someone.

misty, mistier, mistiest (adjective) full of or covered with mist.

misunderstand, misunderstands, misunderstanding, misunderstood (verb) If you misunderstand someone, you do not properly understand what they say or do, e.g. *They claimed he misunderstood the problem.*

misunderstanding, misunderstandings (noun) If two people have a misunderstanding, they have a slight quarrel or disagreement.

misuse, misuses, misusing, misused 1 (noun) The misuse of something is the incorrect, careless, or dishonest use of it, e.g. *the misuse of public money.* **2** (verb) To misuse something means to use it incorrectly or dishonestly.

mite, mites (noun) A mite is a very tiny creature that lives in the fur of animals.

mitigating (adjective; a formal word) Mitigating circumstances make a crime easier to understand, and perhaps justify it.

mitten, mittens (noun) Mittens are gloves which have one section that covers your thumb and another section for the rest of your fingers together.

mix, mixes, mixing, mixed (verb) If you mix things, you combine them or shake or stir them together. **mix up** (verb) If you mix up two things or people, you confuse them, e.g. *People often mix us up and greet us by each other's names.*

mixed 1 (adjective) consisting of several things of the same general kind, e.g. *a mixed salad.* **2** involving people from two or more different races, e.g. *mixed marriages.* **3** Mixed education or accommodation is for both males and females, e.g. *a mixed comprehensive.*

mixed up 1 (adjective) If you are mixed up, you are confused, e.g. *I'm mixed up about which country I want to play for.* **2** If you are mixed up in a crime or a scandal, you are involved in it.

mixer, mixers (noun) A mixer is a machine used for mixing things together, e.g. *a cement mixer.*

mixture, mixtures 1 (noun) A mixture of things consists of several different things mixed together. **2** A mixture is a substance that consists of other substances which have been stirred or shaken together, e.g. *Spoon the mixture into serving glasses.*

mix-up, mix-ups (noun) A mix-up is a mistake in something that was planned, e.g. *a mix-up with the bookings.*

ml an abbreviation for 'millilitres'.

mm an abbreviation for 'millimetres'.

moan, moans, moaning, moaned 1 (verb) If you moan, you make a low, miserable sound because you are in pain or suffering. **2** (noun) A moan is a low cry of pain or misery. **3** (verb; an informal use) If you moan about something, you complain about it.

moat, moats (noun) A moat is a wide, water-filled ditch around a building such as a castle.

mob, mobs, mobbing, mobbed 1 (noun) A mob is a large, disorganized crowd of people, e.g. *A violent mob attacked the team bus.* **2** (verb) If a lot of people mob someone, they crowd around the person in a disorderly way, e.g. *The band was mobbed by over a thousand fans.*

mobile, mobiles 1 (adjective) able to move or be moved freely and easily, e.g. *a mobile phone.* **2** If you are mobile, you are able to travel or move to another place, e.g. *a mobile workforce.* **3** (noun) A mobile is a decoration consisting of several small objects which hang from threads and move around when a breeze blows. **4** A mobile is also a mobile phone. **mobility** (noun).

moccasin, moccasins (noun) Moccasins are soft leather shoes with a low heel and a raised seam above the toe.

mock, mocks, mocking, mocked 1 (verb) If you mock someone, you say something scornful or imitate their foolish behaviour. **2** (adjective) not genuine, e.g. *mock surprise... a mock Tudor house.* **3** A mock examination is one that you do as a practice before the real examination.

mockery (noun) Mockery is the expression of scorn for someone or ridicule of their foolish behaviour.

mode, modes (noun) A mode of life or behaviour is a particular way of living or behaving.

model, models, modelling, modelled 1 (noun or adjective) A model is a physical representation that shows what something looks like or how it works, e.g. *a model aircraft*. **2** (noun) Something that is described as, for example, a model of clarity or a model of perfection, is extremely clear or absolutely perfect. **3** (adjective) Someone who is described as, for example, a model wife or a model student is an excellent wife or student. **4** (verb) If you model yourself on someone, you copy their behaviour because you admire them. **5** (noun) A particular model of a machine is a type or version of it, e.g. *Which model of washing machine did you choose?* **6** A model is a person who poses for a painter or a photographer. **7** A model at a fashion show is a person who wears the clothes that are being displayed. **8** (verb) To model clothes means to display them by wearing them. **9** To model shapes or figures means to make them out of clay or wood.

modem, modems (pronounced **moe**-dem) (noun) A modem is a piece of equipment that links a computer to the telephone system so that data can be transferred from one machine to another via the telephone line.

moderate, moderates, moderating, moderated 1 (adjective) Moderate views are not extreme, and usually favour gradual changes rather than major ones. **2** (noun) A moderate is a person whose political views are not extreme. **3** (adjective) A moderate amount of something is neither large not small. **4** (verb) If you moderate something or if it moderates, it becomes less extreme or violent, e.g. *The weather moderated.* **moderately** (adverb).

moderation (noun) Moderation is control of your behaviour that stops you acting in an extreme way, e.g. *a man of fairness and moderation.*

modern 1 (adjective) relating to the present time, e.g. *modern society*. **2** new and involving the latest ideas and equipment, e.g. *modern technology*. **modernity** (noun).

modernize, modernizes, modernizing, modernized; also spelled **modernise** (verb) To modernize something means to introduce new methods or equipment.

modest 1 (adjective) quite small in size or amount. **2** Someone who is modest does not boast about their abilities or possessions. **3** shy and easily embarrassed. **modestly** (adverb), **modesty** (noun).

modification, modifications (noun) A modification to something is a small change made to improve it, e.g. *Modi-*

fications to the undercarriage were made.

modify, modifies, modifying, modified (verb) If you modify something, you change it slightly in order to improve it.

module, modules 1 (noun) A module is one of the parts which when put together form a whole unit or object, e.g. *The college provides modules for trainees.* **2** A module is a part of a spacecraft which can do certain things independently from the main body, e.g. *the lunar module.* **modular** (adjective).

mohair (noun) Mohair is very soft, fluffy wool obtained from angora goats.

moist, moister, moistest (adjective) slightly wet.

moisten, moistens, moistening, moistened (verb) If you moisten something, you make it slightly wet.

moisture (noun) Moisture is tiny drops of water in the air or on the ground.

molar, molars (noun) Your molars are the large teeth at the back of your mouth.

mole, moles 1 (noun) A mole is a dark, slightly raised spot on your skin. **2** A mole is also a small animal with black fur. Moles live in tunnels underground. **3** (an informal use) A member of an organization who is working as a spy for a rival organization is called a mole.

molecule, molecules (noun) A molecule is the smallest amount of a substance that can exist. **molecular** (adjective).

molest, molests, molesting, molested (verb) To molest a child means to touch the child in a sexual way. This is illegal. **molester** (noun).

mollify, mollifies, mollifying, mollified (verb) To mollify someone means to do something to make them less upset or angry.

mollusc, molluscs (noun) A mollusc is an animal with a soft body and no backbone. Snails, slugs, clams, and mussels are all molluscs.

molten (adjective) Molten rock or metal has been heated to a very high temperature and has become a thick liquid.

moment, moments 1 (noun) A moment is a very short period of time, e.g. *He paused for a moment.* **2** The moment at which something happens is the point in time at which it happens, e.g. *At that moment, the doorbell rang.* **3** (phrase) If something is happening **at the moment,** it is happening now.

momentary (adjective) Something that is momentary lasts for only a few seconds, e.g. *a momentary lapse of concentration.* **momentarily** (adverb).

momentous (adjective; a formal word) very important, often because of its future effect, e.g. *a momentous occasion.*

momentum 1 (noun) Momentum is the ability that something has to keep developing, e.g. *The campaign is gaining momentum.* **2** Momentum is also the ability that an object has to continue moving as a result of the speed it already has.

monarch, monarchs (pronounced **mon**-nark) (noun) A monarch is a queen, king, or other royal person who reigns over a country.

monarchy, monarchies (noun) A monarchy is a system in which a queen or king reigns in a country.

monastery, monasteries (noun) A monastery is a building in which monks live. **monastic** (adjective).

Monday, Mondays (noun) Monday is the day between Sunday and Tuesday.

money (noun) Money is the coins or banknotes that you use to buy something.

mongrel, mongrels (noun) A mongrel is a dog with parents of different breeds.

monitor, monitors, monitoring, monitored 1 (verb) If you monitor something, you regularly check its condition and progress, e.g. *Her health will be monitored daily.* **2** (noun) A monitor is a machine used to check or record things. **3** A monitor is also the visual display unit of a computer.

monk, monks (noun) A monk is a member of a male religious community.

monkey, monkeys (noun) A monkey is an animal which has a long tail and climbs trees. Monkeys live in hot countries.

mono- (prefix) Mono- is used at the beginning of nouns and adjectives that have 'one' as part of their meaning, e.g. *monopoly... monogamy.*

monocle, monocles (noun) A monocle is a glass lens worn in front of one eye only and held in place by the curve of the eye socket.

monogamy (noun; a formal word) Monogamy is the custom of being married to only one person at a time. **monogamous** (adjective).

monologue, monologues (pronounced **mon**-nol-og) (noun) A monologue is a long speech by one person during a play or a conversation.

monopoly, monopolies (noun) A monopoly of an industry is control of most of it by one or a few large firms.

monotone, monotones (noun) A monotone is a tone which does not vary, e.g. *He droned on in a boring monotone.*

monotonous (adjective) having a regular pattern which is very dull and boring, e.g. *monotonous work.* **monotony** (noun).

monsoon, monsoons (noun) In South-east Asia, the monsoon is the season of very heavy rain.

monster, monsters 1 (noun) A monster is a large, imaginary creature that looks very frightening. **2** (adjective) extremely large, e.g. *a monster truck.* **3** (noun) If you call someone a monster, you mean they are cruel, frightening, or evil.

monstrosity, monstrosities (noun) Something that is described as a monstrosity is large and extremely ugly, e.g. *a concrete monstrosity in the middle of the city.*

monstrous (adjective) extremely shocking or unfair, e.g. *a monstrous crime against humanity.* **monstrously** (adverb).

montage, montages (pronounced mon-**tahj**) (noun) A montage is a picture or film consisting of a combination of several different items arranged to produce an unusual effect.

month, months (noun) A month is one of the twelve periods that a year is divided into.

monthly, monthlies (adjective) Monthly describes something that happens or appears once a month, e.g. *monthly staff meetings.*

monument, monuments (noun) A monument is a large stone structure built to remind people of a famous person or event, e.g. *a monument to Winston Churchill.*

monumental 1 (adjective) A monumental building or sculpture is very large, impressive, and important. **2** very large or extreme, e.g. *We face a monumental task.*

moo, moos, mooing, mooed (verb) When a cow moos, it makes a long, deep sound.

mood, moods (noun) Your mood is the way you are feeling at a particular time, e.g. *She was in a really cheerful mood.*

moody, moodier, moodiest 1 (adjective) Someone who is moody is depressed or unhappy, e.g. *Tony, despite his charm, could sulk and be moody.* **2** Someone who is moody often changes their mood for no apparent reason.

moon, moons (noun) The moon is an object moving round the earth which you see as a shining circle or crescent in the sky at night. Some other planets have moons.

moonlight, moonlights, moonlighting, moonlighted 1 (noun) Moonlight is the light that comes from the moon at night. **2** (verb; an informal use) If someone is moonlighting, they have a second job that they have not informed the tax office about. **moonlit** (adjective).

moor, moors, mooring, moored 1 (noun) A moor is a high area of open and uncultivated land. **2** (verb) If a boat is moored, it is attached to the land with a rope.

mooring, moorings (noun) A mooring is a place where a boat can be tied.

moose (noun) A moose is a large North American deer with flat antlers.

moot, moots, mooting, mooted (verb; a formal word) When something is mooted, it is suggested for discussion, e.g. *The project was first mooted in 1988.*

mop, mops, mopping, mopped 1 (noun) A mop is a tool for washing floors, consisting of a sponge or string head attached to a long handle. **2** (verb) To mop a floor means to clean it with a mop. **3** To mop a surface means to wipe it with a dry cloth to remove liquid. **4** (noun) A mop of hair is a large amount of loose or untidy hair.

mope, mopes, moping, moped (verb) If you mope, you feel miserable and not interested in anything.

moped, mopeds (pronounced **moe**-ped) (noun) A moped is a type of small motorcycle.

moral, morals 1 (plural noun) Morals are values based on beliefs about the correct and acceptable way to behave. **2** (adjective) concerned with whether behaviour is right or acceptable, e.g. *moral values.* **morality** (noun), **morally** (adverb).

morale (pronounced mor-**rahl**) (noun) Morale is the amount of confidence and optimism that you have, e.g. *The morale of the troops was high.*

morbid (adjective) having too great an interest in unpleasant things, especially death.

more 1 (adjective or pronoun) More means a greater number or extent than something else, e.g. *He's got more chips than me... I've got more than you.* **2** used to refer to an additional thing or amount of something, e.g. *He found some more clues.* **3** (adverb) to a greater degree or extent, e.g. *more amused than concerned.* **4** You can use 'more' in front of adjectives and adverbs to form comparatives, e.g. *You look more beautiful than ever.*

moreover (adverb) used to introduce a piece of information that supports or expands the previous statement, e.g. *They have accused the government of corruption. Moreover, they have named names.*

morgue, morgues (pronounced **morg**) (noun) A morgue is a building where dead bodies are kept before being buried or cremated.

moribund (adjective) no longer having a useful function and about to come to an end, e.g. *a moribund industry.*

morning, mornings 1 (noun) The morning is the early part of the day until lunchtime. **2** The part of the day between midnight and noon is also referred to as the morning, e.g. *He was born at three in the morning.*

Moroccan, Moroccans (pronounced mor-**rok**-an) **1** (adjective) belonging or relating to Morocco. **2** (noun) A Moroccan is someone who comes from Morocco.

moron, morons (noun; an informal word) If you describe someone as a moron, you mean they are very stupid. **moronic** (adjective).

morose (adjective) miserable and bad-tempered.

morphine (noun) Morphine is a drug which is used to relieve pain.

Morse or **Morse code** (noun) Morse or Morse code is a code used for sending messages in which each letter is represented by a series of dots and dashes.

morsel, morsels (noun) A morsel of food is a small piece of it.

mortal, mortals 1 (adjective) unable to live forever, e.g. *Remember that you are mortal.* **2** (noun) You can refer to an ordinary person as a mortal. **3** (adjective) A mortal wound is one that results in death.

mortality 1 (noun) Mortality is the fact that all people must die. **2** Mortality also refers to the number of people who die at any particular time, e.g. *a low infant mortality rate.*

mortar, mortars 1 (noun) A mortar is a short cannon

which fires missiles high into the air for a short distance. **2** Mortar is a mixture of sand, water, and cement used to hold bricks firmly together.

mortgage, mortgages, mortgaging, mortgaged (pronounced **mor**-gij) **1** (noun) A mortgage is a loan which you get from a bank or a building society in order to buy a house. **2** (verb) If you mortgage your house, you use it as a guarantee to a company in order to borrow money from them.

mortifying (adjective) embarrassing or humiliating, e.g. *There were some mortifying setbacks.*

mortuary, mortuaries (noun) A mortuary is a special room in a hospital where dead bodies are kept before being buried or cremated.

mosaic, mosaics (pronounced moe-**zay**-yik) (noun) A mosaic is a design made of small coloured stones or pieces of coloured glass set into concrete or plaster.

Moslem another spelling of **Muslim.**

mosque, mosques (pronounced **mosk**) (noun) A mosque is a building where Muslims go to worship.

mosquito, mosquitoes or **mosquitos** (pronounced moss-**skee**-toe) (noun) Mosquitoes are small insects which bite people in order to suck their blood.

moss, mosses (noun) Moss is a soft, low-growing, green plant which grows on damp soil, wood, or stone. **mossy** (adjective).

most 1 (adjective or pronoun) Most of a group of things or people means nearly all of them, e.g. *Most people don't share your views.* **2** The most means a larger amount than anyone or anything else, e.g. *She has the most talent.* **3** (adverb) You can use 'most' in front of adjectives or adverbs to form superlatives, e.g. *the most beautiful women in the world.*

mostly (adverb) Mostly is used to show that a statement is generally true, e.g. *Her friends are mostly men.*

MOT, MOTs (noun) An MOT is an annual test for road vehicles to check that they are safe to drive, e.g. *The car had no trouble passing its MOT.*

motel, motels (noun) A motel is a hotel providing overnight accommodation for people in the middle of a car journey.

moth, moths (noun) A moth is an insect like a butterfly which usually flies at night.

mother, mothers, mothering, mothered 1 (noun) Your mother is the woman who gave birth to you. **2** (verb) To mother someone means to look after them and bring them up.

motherhood (noun) Motherhood is the state of being a mother.

mother-in-law, mothers-in-law (noun) Someone's mother-in-law is the mother of their husband or wife.

motif, motifs (pronounced moe-**teef**) (noun) A motif is a design which is used as a decoration.

motion, motions, motioning, motioned 1 (noun) Motion is

the process of continually moving or changing position, e.g. *the motion of the ship.* **2** A motion is an action, gesture, or movement, e.g. *Apply with a brush using circular motions.* **3** A motion at a meeting is a proposal which people discuss and vote on. **4** (verb) If you motion to someone, you make a movement with your hand in order to show them what they should do, e.g. *I motioned him to proceed.*

motionless (adjective) not moving at all, e.g. *He sat motionless.*

motivate, motivates, motivating, motivated 1 (verb) If you are motivated by something, it causes you to behave in a particular way, e.g. *He is motivated by duty rather than ambition.* **2** If you motivate someone, you make them feel determined to do something. **motivated** (adjective), **motivation** (noun).

motive, motives (noun) Your motive for doing something is your reason or purpose, e.g. *There was no motive for the attack.*

motley (adjective) A motley collection is made up of people or things of very different types.

motor, motors 1 (noun) A motor is a part of a vehicle or a machine that uses electricity or fuel to produce movement so that the machine can work. **2** (adjective) concerned with or relating to vehicles with a petrol or diesel engine, e.g. *the motor industry.*

motorcycle, motorcycles (noun) A motorcycle is a two-wheeled vehicle with an engine.

motoring (adjective) relating to cars and driving, e.g. *a motoring correspondent.*

motorist, motorists (noun) A motorist is a person who drives a car.

motorway, motorways (noun) A motorway is a wide road built for fast travel over long distances.

mottled (adjective) covered with patches of different colours, e.g. *mottled leaves.*

motto, mottoes or **mottos** (noun) A motto is a short sentence or phrase that expresses a rule for good or sensible behaviour.

mould, moulds, moulding, moulded 1 (verb) To mould someone or something means to influence and change them so they develop in a particular way. **2** To mould a substance means to make it into a particular shape, e.g. *Mould the mixture into flat round cakes.* **3** (noun) A mould is a container used to make something into a particular shape, e.g. *a jelly mould.* **4** Mould is a soft grey or green substance that can form on old food or damp walls. **mouldy** (adjective).

moult, moults, moulting, moulted (verb) When an animal or bird moults, it loses its hair or feathers to make way for new growth.

mound, mounds 1 (noun) A mound is a small man-made hill. **2** A mound of things is a large, untidy pile, e.g. *a mound of blankets.*

mount, mounts, mounting, mounted 1 (verb) To mount a

campaign or event means to organize it and carry it out. **2** If something is mounting, it is increasing, e.g. *Economic problems are mounting.* **3** (a formal use) To mount something means to go to the top of it, e.g. *He mounted the steps.* **4** If you mount a horse, you climb on its back. **5** If you mount an object in a particular place, you fix it there to display it. **6** Mount is also used as part of the name of a mountain, e.g. *Mount Everest.*

mountain, mountains 1 (noun) A mountain is a very high piece of land with steep sides. **2** You can refer to a large amount of something as a mountain of it, e.g. *mountains of paperwork.*

mountaineer, mountaineers (noun) A mountaineer is a person who climbs mountains.

mountainous (adjective) A mountainous area has a lot of mountains.

mourn, mourns, mourning, mourned 1 (verb) If you mourn for someone who has died, you are very sad and think about them a lot. **2** If you mourn something, you are sad because you no longer have it, e.g. *They mourned the loss of grammar schools.*

mourner, mourners (noun) A mourner is a person who attends a funeral.

mournful (adjective) very sad.

mourning (noun) If someone is in mourning, they wear special black clothes or behave in a special way because a member of their family has died.

mouse, mice 1 (noun) A mouse is a small rodent with a long tail. **2** A mouse is also a small device moved by hand on a special mat to control the position of the cursor on a computer screen.

mousse, mousses (pronounced **moos**) (noun) Mousse is a light, fluffy food made from whipped eggs and cream.

moustache, moustaches (pronounced mus-**stahsh**) (noun) A man's moustache is hair growing on his upper lip.

mouth, mouths, mouthing, mouthed 1 (noun) Your mouth is your lips, or the space behind them where your tongue and teeth are. **2** The mouth of a cave or a hole is the entrance to it. **3** The mouth of a river is the place where it flows into the sea. **4** (verb) If you mouth something, you form words with your lips without making any sound. **mouthful** (noun).

mouthpiece, mouthpieces 1 (noun) The mouthpiece of a telephone is the part you speak into. **2** The mouthpiece of a musical instrument is the part you put to your mouth. **3** The mouthpiece of an organization is the person who publicly states its opinions and policies.

movable (adjective) Something that is movable can be moved from one place to another.

move, moves, moving, moved 1 (verb) To move means to go to a different place or position. To move something means to change its place or position. **2** (noun) A move is a change from one place or position to another, e.g. *We were watching his every move.* **3** (verb) If you move, or move house, you go to live in a different house. **4** (noun) You can refer to the act of moving house as a move. **5** A move is also the act of putting a piece or counter in a game in a different position, e.g. *It's your move next.* **6** (verb) If something moves you, it causes you to feel a deep emotion, e.g. *Her story moved us to tears.*

movement, movements 1 (noun) Movement involves changing position or going from one place to another. **2** (plural noun; a formal use) Your movements are everything you do during a period of time, e.g. *They asked him for an account of his movements during the previous morning.* **3** (noun) A movement is also a group of people who share the same beliefs or aims, e.g. *the peace movement.* **4** A movement is also one of the major sections of a piece of classical music.

moving (adjective) Something that is moving causes you to feel deep sadness or emotion. **movingly** (adverb).

mow, mows, mowing, mowed, mown 1 (verb) To mow grass means to cut it with a lawnmower. **2** To mow down a large number of people means to kill them all violently.

mower, mowers (noun) A mower is a machine for cutting grass.

MP, MPs (noun) An MP is a person who has been elected to represent people in a country's parliament. MP is an abbreviation for 'Member of Parliament'.

mpg an abbreviation for 'miles per gallon'.

mph an abbreviation for 'miles per hour'.

Mr (pronounced **miss**-ter) Mr is used before a man's name when you are speaking or referring to him.

Mrs (pronounced **miss**-iz) Mrs is used before the name of a married woman when you are speaking or referring to her.

Ms (pronounced **miz**) Ms is used before a woman's name when you are speaking or referring to her. Ms does not specify whether a woman is married or not.

much 1 (adverb) You use much to emphasize that something is true to a great extent, e.g. *I feel much better now.* **2** If something does not happen much, it does not happen very often. **3** (adjective or pronoun) You use 'much' to ask questions or give information about the size or amount of something, e.g. *How much money do you need?*

muck, mucks, mucking, mucked 1 (noun; an informal use) Muck is dirt or some other unpleasant substance. **2** Muck is also manure. **3** (verb; an informal use) If you muck about, you behave stupidly and waste time. **mucky** (adjective).

mucus (pronounced **myoo**-kuss) (noun) Mucus is a liquid produced in parts of your body, for example in your nose.

mud (noun) Mud is wet, sticky earth.

muddle, muddles, muddling, muddled 1 (noun) A muddle is a state of disorder or untidiness, e.g. *Our finances are in a muddle.* **2** (verb) If you muddle things, you mix them up.

muddy, muddier, muddiest 1 (adjective) covered in mud. **2** A muddy colour is dull and not clear, e.g. *a mottled, muddy brown.*

muesli (pronounced **myooz**-lee) (noun) Muesli is a mixture of chopped nuts, cereal flakes, and dried fruit that you can eat for breakfast with milk.

muffin, muffins (noun) A muffin is a small, round, yeast cake which you eat hot.

muffled (adjective) A muffled sound is quiet or difficult to hear, e.g. *a muffled explosion.*

mug, mugs, mugging, mugged 1 (noun) A mug is a large, deep cup with straight sides. **2** (verb; an informal use) If someone mugs you, they attack you in order to steal your money. **3** (noun; an informal use) Someone who is described as a mug is stupid and easily deceived. **mugging** (noun), **mugger** (noun).

muggy, muggier, muggiest (adjective) Muggy weather is unpleasantly warm and damp.

mule, mules (noun) A mule is the sterile offspring of a female horse and a male donkey.

mull, mulls, mulling, mulled (verb) If you mull something over, you think about it for a long time before making a decision.

multi- (prefix) Multi- is used to form words that refer to something that has many parts or aspects, e.g. *a multistorey car park.*

multinational, multinationals (noun) A multinational is a very large company with branches in many countries.

multiple, multiples 1 (adjective) having or involving many different functions or things, e.g. *He died from multiple injuries in the crash.* **2** (noun) The multiples of a number are other numbers that it will divide into exactly. For example, 6, 9, and 12 are multiples of 3.

multiple sclerosis (pronounced skler-**roe**-siss) (noun) Multiple sclerosis is a serious disease which attacks the nervous system, affecting your ability to move.

multiplication 1 (noun) Multiplication is the process of multiplying one number by another. **2** The multiplication of things is a large increase in their number, e.g. *the multiplication of universities.*

multiplicity (noun) If there is a multiplicity of things, there is a large number or variety of them.

multiply, multiplies, multiplying, multiplied 1 (verb) When something multiplies, it increases greatly in number, e.g. *The trip wore on and the hazards multiplied.* **2** When you multiply one number by another, you calculate the total you would get if you added the first number to itself a particular number of times. For example, two multiplied by three is equal to two plus two plus two, which equals six.

multitude, multitudes (noun; a formal word) A multitude of things or people is a very large number of them.

mum, mums (noun; an informal word) Your mum is your mother.

mumble, mumbles, mumbling, mumbled (verb) If you mumble, you speak very quietly and indistinctly.

mummy, mummies 1 (noun; an informal use, used especially by children) Your mummy is your mother. **2** A mummy is a dead body which was preserved long ago by being rubbed with special oils and wrapped in cloth.

mumps (noun) Mumps is a disease that causes painful swelling in the neck glands.

munch, munches, munching, munched (verb) If you munch something, you chew it steadily and thoroughly.

mundane (adjective) very ordinary and not interesting or unusual, e.g. *a mundane job.*

municipal (pronounced myoo-**nis**-si-pl) (adjective) belonging to a city or town which has its own local government, e.g. *a municipal golf course.*

munitions (plural noun) Munitions are bombs, guns, and other military supplies.

mural, murals (noun) A mural is a picture painted on a wall.

murder, murders, murdering, murdered 1 (noun) Murder is the deliberate and unlawful killing of a person. **2** (verb) To murder someone means to kill them deliberately and unlawfully. **murderer** (noun).

murderous 1 (adjective) likely to murder someone, e.g. *murderous gangsters.* **2** A murderous attack or other action results in the death of many people, e.g *murderous acts of terrorism.*

murky, murkier, murkiest (adjective) dark or dirty and unpleasant, e.g. *He rushed through the murky streets.*

murmur, murmurs, murmuring, murmured 1 (verb) If you murmur, you say something very softly. **2** (noun) A murmur is something that someone says which can hardly be heard.

muscle, muscles, muscling, muscled 1 (noun) Your muscles are pieces of flesh which you can expand or contract in order to move parts of your body. **2** (verb; an informal use) If you muscle in on something, you force your way into a situation in which you are not welcome.

muscular (pronounced **musk**-yool-lar) **1** (adjective) involving or affecting your muscles, e.g. *muscular strength.* **2** Someone who is muscular has strong, firm muscles.

muse, muses, musing, mused (verb; a literary use) To muse means to think about something for a long time.

museum, museums (noun) A museum is a building where many interesting or valuable objects are kept and displayed.

mush (noun) A mush is a thick, soft paste.

mushroom, mushrooms, mushrooming, mushroomed 1 (noun) A mushroom is a fungus with a short stem and a round top. Some types of mushroom are edible. **2** (verb) If something mushrooms, it appears and grows very quickly, e.g. *The mill towns mush-*

roomed into cities.

mushy, mushier, mushiest 1 (adjective) Mushy fruits or vegetables are too soft, e.g. *mushy tomatoes.* **2** (an informal use) Mushy stories are too sentimental.

music 1 (noun) Music is a pattern of sounds performed by people singing or playing instruments. **2** Music is also the written symbols that represent musical sounds, e.g. *I taught myself to read music.*

musical, musicals 1 (adjective) relating to playing or studying music, e.g. *a musical instrument.* **2** (noun) A musical is a play or film that uses songs and dance to tell the story. **musically** (adverb).

musician, musicians (noun) A musician is a person who plays a musical instrument as their job or hobby.

musk (noun) Musk is a substance with a strong, sweet smell. It is used to make perfume. **musky** (adjective).

musket, muskets (noun) A musket is an old-fashioned gun with a long barrel.

Muslim, Muslims; also spelled **Moslem 1** (noun) A Muslim is a person who believes in Islam and lives according to its rules. **2** (adjective) relating to Islam.

muslin (noun) Muslin is a very thin cotton material.

mussel, mussels (noun) Mussels are a kind of shellfish with black shells.

must 1 (verb) If something must happen, it is very important or necessary that it happens, e.g. *You must be over 18.* **2** If you tell someone they must do something, you are suggesting that they do it, e.g. *You must try this pudding: it's delicious.* **3** (noun) Something that is a must is absolutely necessary, e.g. *The museum is a must for all visitors.*

mustard (noun) Mustard is a hot, spicy substance made from the seeds of a plant.

muster, musters, mustering, mustered (verb) If you muster energy, you gather it together in order to do something, e.g. *as much calm as he could muster.*

mutate, mutates, mutating, mutated (verb; a technical word) If something mutates, its structure or appearance alters in some way, e.g. *Viruses react to change and can mutate fast.* **mutation** (noun), **mutant** (noun or adjective).

mute (adjective; a formal word) not giving out sound or speech, e.g. *mute amazement.*

muted 1 (adjective) Muted colours or sounds are soft and gentle. **2** A muted reaction is not very strong.

mutilate, mutilates, mutilating, mutilated 1 (verb) If someone is mutilated, their body is badly injured, e.g. *His leg was badly mutilated.* **2** If you mutilate something, you deliberately damage or spoil it, e.g *Almost every book had been mutilated.* **mutilation** (noun).

mutiny, mutinies (noun) A mutiny is a rebellion against someone in authority.

mutter, mutters, muttering, muttered (verb) To mutter means to speak in a very low and perhaps cross voice, e.g. *She muttered something under* *her breath.*

mutton (noun) Mutton is the meat of an adult sheep.

mutual (adjective) used to describe something that two or more people do to each other or share, e.g. *He didn't have a high opinion of his school, and the feeling was mutual... They had a mutual interest in rugby.*

mutually (adverb) Mutually describes a situation in which two or more people feel the same way about each other, e.g. *a mutually supportive relationship.*

muzzle, muzzles, muzzling, muzzled 1 (noun) The muzzle of an animal is its nose and mouth. **2** A muzzle is a cover or a strap for a dog's nose and mouth to prevent it from biting. **3** (verb) To muzzle a dog means to put a muzzle on it. **4** (noun) The muzzle of a gun is the open end through which the bullets come out.

my (adjective) My refers to something belonging or relating to the person speaking or writing, e.g. *I held my breath.*

mynah bird, mynah birds (noun) A mynah bird is a tropical bird which can mimic speech and sounds.

myriad, myriads (pronounced **mir**-ree-ad) (noun or adjective; a literary word) A myriad of people or things is a very large number of them.

myrrh (rhymes with **purr**) (noun) Myrrh is a fragrant substance used in perfume and incense.

myself 1 (pronoun) Myself is used when the person speaking or writing does an action and is affected by it, e.g. *I was ashamed of myself.* **2** Myself is also used to emphasize 'I', e.g. *I find it a bit odd myself.*

mysterious 1 (adjective) strange and not well understood. **2** secretive about something, e.g. *Stop being so mysterious.* **mysteriously** (adverb).

mystery, mysteries (noun) A mystery is something that is not understood or known about.

mystic, mystics 1 (noun) A mystic is a religious person who spends long hours meditating. **2** (adjective) Mystic means the same as mystical.

mystical (adjective) involving spiritual powers and influences, e.g. *a mystical experience.* **mysticism** (noun).

mystify, mystifies, mystifying, mystified (verb) If something mystifies you, you find it impossible to understand.

mystique (pronounced mis-**steek**) (noun) Mystique is an atmosphere of mystery and importance associated with a particular person or thing.

myth, myths 1 (noun) A myth is an untrue belief or explanation. **2** A myth is also a story which was made up long ago to explain natural events and religious beliefs, e.g. *Viking myths.*

mythical (adjective) imaginary, untrue, or existing only in myths, e.g. *a mythical beast.*

mythology (noun) Mythology refers to stories that have been made up in the past to explain natural events or justify religious beliefs. **mythological** (adjective).

N n

nag, nags, nagging, nagged 1 (verb) If you nag someone, you keep complaining to them about something. **2** If something nags at you, it keeps worrying you.

nail, nails, nailing, nailed 1 (noun) A nail is a small piece of metal with a sharp point at one end, which you hammer into objects to hold them together. **2** (verb) If you nail something somewhere, you fit it there using a nail. **3** (noun) Your nails are the thin hard areas covering the ends of your fingers and toes.

naive or **naïve** (pronounced ny-**eev**) (adjective) foolishly believing that things are easier or less complicated than they really are. **naively** (adverb), **naivety** (noun).

naked 1 (adjective) not wearing any clothes or not covered by anything. **2** shown openly, e.g. *naked aggression.* **nakedness** (noun).

name, names, naming, named 1 (noun) A name is a word that you use to identify a person, place, or thing. **2** (verb) If you name someone or something, you give them a name or you say their name. **3** If you name a price or a date, you say what you want it to be. **4** (noun) Someone's name is also their reputation, e.g. *My only wish now is to clear my name.*

nameless (adjective) You describe someone or something as nameless when you do not know their name.

namely (adverb) that is; used to introduce more detailed information about what you have just said, e.g. *The state stripped them of their rights, namely the right to own land.*

namesake, namesakes (noun) Your namesake is someone with the same name as you.

nanny, nannies (noun) A nanny is a woman whose job is looking after young children.

nap, naps, napping, napped 1 (noun) A nap is a short sleep. **2** (verb) When you nap, you have a short sleep.

nape, napes (noun) The nape of your neck is the back of it.

napkin, napkins (noun) A napkin is a small piece of cloth or paper used to wipe your hands and mouth after eating.

nappy, nappies (noun) A nappy is a piece of towelling or paper worn round a baby's bottom.

narcotic, narcotics (noun) A narcotic is a drug which makes you sleepy and unable to feel pain.

narrate, narrates, narrating, narrated (verb) If you narrate a story, you tell it. **narration** (noun), **narrator** (noun).

narrative, narratives (pronounced **nar**-rat-tiv) (noun) A narrative is a story or an account of events.

narrow, narrower, narrowest; narrows, narrowing, narrowed 1 (adjective) having a small distance from one side to the other, e.g. *a narrow stream.* **2**

(verb) To narrow means to become less wide, e.g. *The road narrowed.* **3** (adjective) A narrow escape or victory is one that you only just achieve. **narrowly** (adverb).

narrow-minded (adjective) unwilling to consider new ideas or opinions.

nasal (pronounced **nay**-zal) **1** (adjective) relating to the nose, e.g. *the nasal passages.* **2** Nasal sounds are made by breathing out through your nose as you speak.

nasty, nastier, nastiest (adjective) very unpleasant, e.g. *a nasty shock.* **nastily** (adverb), **nastiness** (noun).

nation, nations (noun) A nation is a large group of people sharing the same history and language and usually inhabiting a particular country.

national, nationals 1 (adjective) relating to the whole of a country, e.g. *a national newspaper.* **2** typical of a particular country, e.g. *women in Polish national dress.* **3** (noun) A national of a country is a citizen of that country, e.g. *Turkish nationals.* **nationally** (adverb).

national anthem, national anthems (noun) A country's national anthem is its official song.

nationalism 1 (noun) Nationalism is a desire for the independence of a country; also a political movement aiming to achieve such independence. **2** Nationalism is also love of your own country. **nationalist** (noun), **nationalistic** (adjective).

nationality, nationalities (noun) Nationality is the fact of belonging to a particular country.

nationalize, nationalizes, nationalizing, nationalized; also spelled **nationalise** (verb) To nationalize an industry means to bring it under the control and ownership of the state. **nationalization** (noun).

national service (noun) National service is a compulsory period of service in the armed forces.

nationwide (adjective or adverb) happening all over a country, e.g. *a nationwide search.*

native, natives 1 (adjective) Your native country is the country where you were born. **2** Your native language is the language that you first learned to speak. **3** Animals or plants that are native to a place live or grow there naturally and have not been brought there by people. **4** (noun) A native of a place is someone who was born there.

Nativity (noun) In Christianity, the Nativity is the birth of Christ or the festival celebrating this.

natter, natters, nattering, nattered (verb; an informal word) If you natter, you talk about unimportant things.

natural, naturals 1 (adjective) normal and to be expected, e.g. *It was only natural that he was tempted.* **2** not trying to pretend or hide anything, e.g. *Hannah's natural manner reassured her.* **3** existing or happening in nature, e.g. *natural disasters.* **4** A natural ability is one you were born with. **5** Your natural mother or father is your real mother or father and not someone who has adopted you. **6** (noun) A natural is someone who is born with a particular ability or talent, e.g. *She's a natural at bridge.* **7** In music, a natural is a note that is not a sharp or a flat. It is represented by the symbol (♮). **naturally** (adverb).

nature, natures 1 (noun) Nature is animals, plants, and all the other things in the world not made by people. **2** The nature of a person or thing is their basic character, e.g. *She liked his warm, generous nature.*

naughty, naughtier, naughtiest 1 (adjective) behaving badly. **2** rude or indecent, e.g. *naughty films.* **naughtiness** (noun).

nausea (pronounced **naw**-zee-ah) (noun) Nausea is a feeling in your stomach that you are going to be sick. **nauseous** (adjective).

nautical (pronounced **naw**-tik-kl) (adjective) relating to ships or navigation.

naval (adjective) relating to or having a navy, e.g. *naval officers... naval bases.*

navel, navels (noun) Your navel is the small hollow on the front of your body just below your waist.

navigate, navigates, navigating, navigated 1 (verb) When someone navigates, they work out the direction in which a ship, plane, or car should go, using maps and sometimes instruments. **2** To navigate a stretch of water means to travel safely across it, e.g. *It was the first time I had navigated the ocean.* **navigation** (noun), **navigator** (noun).

navy, navies 1 (noun) A country's navy is the part of its armed forces that fights at sea. **2** (adjective) dark blue.

Nazi, Nazis (pronounced **naht**-see) (noun) The Nazis were members of the National Socialist German Workers' Party, which was led by Adolf Hitler.

NB You write NB to draw attention to what you are going to write next. NB is an abbreviation for the Latin 'nota bene', which means 'note well'.

near, nearer, nearest; nears, nearing, neared 1 (preposition or adverb) not far from. **2** (adjective) You can also use near to mean almost, e.g. *a night of near disaster.* **3** (verb) When you are nearing something, you are approaching it and will soon reach it, e.g. *The dog began to bark as he neared the porch.*

nearby (adjective or adverb) only a short distance away.

nearly (adverb) not completely but almost.

neat, neater, neatest 1 (adjective) tidy and smart. **2** A neat alcoholic drink does not have anything added to it, e.g. *a small glass of neat gin.* **neatly** (adverb), **neatness** (noun).

necessarily (adverb) Something that is not necessarily the case is not always or inevitably the case.

necessary 1 (adjective) Something that is necessary is needed or must be done. **2** (a formal use) Necessary also means certain or inevitable, e.g. *a necessary consequence of war.*

necessity, necessities 1 (noun) Necessity is the need to do something, e.g. *There is no necessity for any of this.* **2** Necessities are things needed in order to live.

neck, necks 1 (noun) Your neck is the part of your body which joins your head to the rest of your body. **2** The neck of a bottle is the long narrow part at the top.

necklace, necklaces (noun) A necklace is a piece of jewellery which a woman wears around her neck.

nectar (noun) Nectar is a sweet liquid produced by flowers and attractive to insects.

nectarine, nectarines (noun) A nectarine is a kind of peach with a smooth skin.

née (rhymes with **day**) Née is used to indicate what a woman's surname was before she got married, e.g. *Sara Black, née Wells.*

need, needs, needing, needed 1 (verb) If you need something, you believe that you must have it or do it. **2** (noun) Your needs are the things that you need to have. **3** A need is also a strong feeling that you must have or do something, e.g. *I just felt the need to write about it.*

needle, needles 1 (noun) A needle is a small thin piece of metal with a pointed end and a hole at the other, which is used for sewing. **2** Needles are also long thin pieces of steel or plastic, used for knitting. **3** The needle in a record player is the small pointed part that touches the record and picks up the sound signals. **4** The needle of a syringe is the part which a doctor or nurse sticks into your body. **5** The needle on a dial is the thin piece of metal or plastic which moves to show a measurement. **6** The needles of a pine tree are its leaves.

needless (adjective) unnecessary. **needlessly** (adverb).

needy, needier, neediest (adjective) very poor.

negative, negatives 1 (adjective) A negative answer means 'no'. **2** Someone who is negative sees only problems and disadvantages, e.g. *Why are you so negative about everything?* **3** If a medical or scientific test is negative, it shows that something has not happened or is not present, e.g. *The pregnancy test came back negative.* **4** A negative number is less than zero. **5** (noun) A negative is the image that is first produced when you take a photograph. **negatively** (adverb).

neglect, neglects, neglecting, neglected 1 (verb) If you neglect something, you do not look after it properly. **2** (a formal use) If you neglect to do something, you fail to do it, e.g. *He had neglected to give her his address.* **3** (noun) Neglect is failure to look after something or someone properly, e.g. *Most of her plants died from neglect.* **neglectful** (adjective).

negligent (adjective) not taking enough care, e.g. *her negligent driving.* **negligence** (noun).

negligible (adjective) very small and unimportant, e.g. *a negligible amount of fat.*

negotiable (adjective) able to be changed or agreed by discussion, e.g. *All contributions are negotiable.*

negotiate, negotiates, negotiating, negotiated 1 (verb) When people negotiate, they have formal discussions in order to reach an agreement about something. **2** If you negotiate an obstacle, you manage to get over it or round it. **negotiation** (noun), **negotiator** (noun).

Negro, Negroes (noun; an old-fashioned use) A Negro is a person with black skin who comes from Africa or whose ancestors came from Africa.

neigh, neighs, neighing, neighed (rhymes with **day**) **1** (verb) When a horse neighs, it makes a loud high-pitched sound. **2** (noun) A neigh is a loud sound made by a horse.

neighbour, neighbours 1 (noun) Your neighbour is someone who lives next door to you or near you. **2** Your neighbour is also someone standing or sitting next to you, e.g. *I got chatting with my neighbour in the studio.*

neighbourhood, neighbourhoods (noun) A neighbourhood is a district where people live, e.g. *a safe neighbourhood.*

neighbouring (adjective) situated nearby, e.g. *schools in neighbouring areas.*

neither (adjective or pronoun) used to indicate that a negative statement refers to two or more things or people, e.g. *It's neither a play nor a musical... Neither of them spoke.*

neo- (prefix) new or modern, e.g. *neo-fascism.*

nephew, nephews (noun) Someone's nephew is the son of their sister or brother.

Neptune (noun) Neptune is the planet in the solar system which is eighth from the sun.

nerve, nerves 1 (noun) A nerve is a long thin fibre that sends messages between your brain and other parts of your body. **2** If you talk about someone's nerves, you are referring to how able they are to remain calm in a difficult situation, e.g. *It needs confidence and strong nerves.* **3** Nerve is courage or impudence, e.g. *She never had the nerve to ask me that question again.* **4** (an informal phrase) If someone **gets on your nerves,** they irritate you.

nerve-racking (adjective) making you feel very worried and tense, e.g. *a nerve-racking experience.*

nervous (adjective) worried and frightened. **nervously** (adverb), **nervousness** (noun).

nervous breakdown, nervous breakdowns (noun) A nervous breakdown is an illness in which someone suffers from deep depression and needs psychiatric treatment.

nest, nests, nesting, nested 1 (noun) A nest is a place that a bird makes to lay its eggs in; also a place that some insects and other animals make to rear their young in. **2** (verb) When birds nest, they build a nest and lay eggs in it.

nestle, nestles, nestling, nestled (pronounced **ness**-sl) (verb) If you nestle somewhere, you settle there comfortably, often pressing up against someone else, e.g. *A new puppy nestled in her lap.*

nestling, nestlings (noun) A nestling is a young bird that has not yet learned to fly and so has not left the nest.

net, nets 1 (noun) A net is a piece of material made of threads woven together with small spaces in between. **2** (adjective) A net result or amount is final, after everything has been considered, e.g. *a net profit of $171 million.* **3** The net weight of something is its weight without its wrapping.

netball (noun) Netball is a game played by two teams in which each team tries to score goals by throwing a ball through a net at the top of a pole.

netting (noun) Netting is material made of threads or metal wires woven together with small spaces in between.

nettle, nettles (noun) A nettle is a wild plant covered with little hairs that sting.

network, networks 1 (noun) A network is a large number of lines or roads which cross each other at many points, e.g. *a small network of side roads.* **2** A network of people or organizations is a large number of them that work together as a system, e.g. *the public telephone network.*

neurotic (pronounced nyoor-**rot**-ik) (adjective) having strong and unreasonable fears and worries, e.g. *He was neurotic about being followed.*

neuter, neuters, neutering, neutered (pronounced **nyoo**-ter) (verb) When an animal is neutered, its reproductive organs are removed.

neutral, neutrals 1 (adjective) People who are neutral do not support either side in a disagreement or war. **2** (noun) A neutral is a person or country that does not support either side in a disagreement or war. **3** Neutral is the position between the gears of a vehicle in which the gears are not connected to the engine and so the vehicle cannot move. **4** (adjective) The neutral wire in an electric plug is the one that is not earth or live. **5** A neutral colour is not definite or striking, for example pale grey. **6** In chemistry, a neutral substance is neither acid nor alkaline. **neutrality** (noun).

never (adverb) at no time in the past, present, or future.

nevertheless (adverb) in spite of what has just been said, e.g. *They dress rather plainly but nevertheless look quite smart.*

new, newer, newest 1 (adjective) recently made or created, e.g. *a new house... a new plan.* **2** only recently discovered, e.g. *a new virus.* **3** not used or owned before, e.g. *We've got a new car.* **4** different or unfamiliar, e.g. *a name which was new to me.*

newcomer, newcomers (noun) A newcomer is someone who has recently arrived in a place.

newly (adverb) recently, e.g. *the newly born baby.*

new moon, new moons (noun) The moon is a new moon when it is a thin crescent shape at the start of its four-week cycle.

news (noun) News is information about things that have happened.

newsagent, newsagents (noun) A newsagent is a person or shop that sells newspapers and magazines.

newspaper, newspapers (noun) A newspaper is a publication that is produced regularly and contains news, articles, and advertisements.

newt, newts (noun) A newt is a small amphibious creature with a moist skin, short legs, and a long tail.

New Testament (noun) The New Testament is the second part of the Bible, which deals with the life of Jesus Christ and with the early Church.

New Year (noun) New Year is the time when people celebrate the start of a year.

New Zealander, New Zealanders (noun) A New Zealander is someone who comes from New Zealand.

next 1 (adjective or adverb) coming immediately after something else, e.g. *They lived in the next street.* **2** (phrase) If one thing is **next to** another, it is at the side of it.

next door (adjective or adverb) in the house next to yours.

NHS an abbreviation for 'National Health Service'.

nib, nibs (noun) The nib of a pen is its pointed end.

nibble, nibbles, nibbling, nibbled 1 (verb) When you nibble something, you take small bites of it. **2** (noun) A nibble is a small bite of something.

nice, nicer, nicest (adjective) pleasant or attractive. **nicely** (adverb).

nicety, niceties (pronounced **nigh**-se-tee) (noun) A nicety is a small detail, e.g. *the social niceties.*

niche, niches (pronounced neesh) **1** (noun) A niche is a hollow area in a wall, e.g. *a statue in a niche in a cathedral wall.* **2** If you say that you have found your niche, you mean that you have found a job or way of life that is exactly right for you.

nick, nicks, nicking, nicked 1 (verb) If you nick something, you make a small cut in its surface, e.g. *He nicked his chin.* **2** (noun) A nick is a small cut in the surface of something. **3** (verb; an informal use) To nick something also means to steal it.

nickel (noun) Nickel is a silver-coloured metal that is used in making steel.

nickname, nicknames, nicknaming, nicknamed 1 (noun) A nickname is an informal name given to someone. **2** (verb) If you nickname someone, you give them a nickname.

nicotine (noun) Nicotine is an addictive substance found in tobacco.

niece, nieces (noun) Someone's niece is the daughter of their sister or brother.

nifty (adjective) neat and pleasing or cleverly done.

Nigerian, Nigerians (pronounced nie-**jeer**-ee-an) **1** (adjective) belonging or relating to Nigeria. **2** (noun) A Nigerian is someone who comes from Nigeria.

niggle, niggles, niggling, niggled 1 (verb) If something niggles you, it worries you slightly. **2** (noun) A niggle is a small worry that you keep thinking about.

night, nights (noun) Night is the time between sunset and sunrise when it is dark.

nightclub, nightclubs (noun) A nightclub is a place where people go late in the evening to drink and dance.

nightdress, nightdresses (noun) A nightdress is a loose dress that a woman or girl wears to sleep in.

nightfall (noun) Nightfall is the time of day when it starts to get dark.

nightie, nighties (noun; an informal word) A nightie is a nightdress.

nightingale, nightingales (noun) A nightingale is a small brown European bird. The male nightingale sings very beautifully.

nightly (adjective or adverb) happening every night, e.g. *the nightly news programme.*

nightmare, nightmares (noun) A nightmare is a very frightening dream; also used of any very unpleasant or frightening situation, e.g. *The meal itself was a nightmare.* **nightmarish** (adjective).

nil (noun) Nil means zero or nothing. It is used especially in sports scores.

nimble, nimbler, nimblest 1 (adjective) able to move quickly and easily. **2** able to think quickly and cleverly. **nimbly** (adverb).

nine the number 9. **ninth**

nineteen the number 19. **nineteenth**

ninety, nineties the number 90. **ninetieth**

nip, nips, nipping, nipped 1 (verb; an informal use) If you nip somewhere, you go there quickly. **2** To nip someone or something means to pinch, bite, or squeeze them slightly. **3** (noun) A nip is a light pinch.

nipple, nipples (noun) Your nipples are the two small pieces of projecting flesh on your chest. Babies suck milk through the nipples on their mothers' breasts.

nit, nits (noun) Nits are the eggs of a kind of louse that sometimes lives in people's hair.

nitrogen (noun) Nitrogen is a chemical element usually found as a gas. It forms about 78% of the earth's atmosphere.

no 1 (interjection) used to say that something is not true or to refuse something. **2** (adjective) none at all or not at all, e.g. *She gave no reason.* **3** (adverb) used with a comparative to mean 'not', e.g. *no later than 24th July.*

no. a written abbreviation for **number.**

nobility 1 (noun) Nobility is the quality of being noble, e.g. *the unmistakable nobility of his character.* **2** The nobility of a society are all the people who have titles and high social rank.

noble, nobler, noblest; nobles 1 (adjective) honest and brave, and deserving admiration. **2** (noun) A noble is a member of the nobility. **3** (adjective) very impressive, e.g. *a noble appearance.* **nobly** (adverb).

nobleman, noblemen (noun) A nobleman is a man who is a member of the nobility. **noblewoman** (noun).

nobody, nobodies 1 (pronoun) not a single person. **2** (noun) Someone who is a nobody is not at all important.

nocturnal 1 (adjective) happening at night, e.g. *a nocturnal journey through New York.* **2** active at night, e.g. *a nocturnal animal.*

nod, nods, nodding, nodded 1 (verb) When you nod, you move your head up and down, usually to show agreement. **2** (noun) A nod is a movement of your head up and down.

noise, noises (noun) A noise is a sound, especially one that is loud or unpleasant.

noisy, noisier, noisiest (adjective) making a lot of noise or full of noise, e.g. *a noisy crowd... the noisy room.* **noisily** (adverb), **noisiness** (noun).

nomad, nomads (noun) A nomad is a person who belongs to a tribe which travels from place to place rather than living in just one place. **nomadic** (adjective).

nominal 1 (adjective) Something that is nominal is supposed to have a particular identity or status, but in reality does not have it, e.g. *the nominal leader.* **2** A nominal amount of money is very small compared to the value of something, e.g. *I am prepared to sell my shares at a nominal price.* **nominally** (adverb).

nominate, nominates, nominating, nominated (verb) If you nominate someone for a job or position, you formally suggest that they have it. **nomination** (noun).

non- (prefix) not, e.g. *non-smoking.*

nonchalant (pronounced **non**-shal-nt) (adjective) seeming calm and not worried. **nonchalance** (noun), **nonchalantly** (adverb).

noncommissioned officer, noncommissioned officers (noun) A noncommissioned officer is an officer such as a sergeant or corporal who has been promoted from the lower ranks.

nondescript (adjective) dull and uninteresting in appearance, e.g. *a nondescript coat.*

none (pronoun) not a single thing or person, or not even a small amount of something.

nonplussed (adjective) confused and unsure about how to react.

nonsense (noun) Nonsense is foolish and meaningless words or behaviour. **nonsensical** (adjective).

nonstop (adjective or adverb) continuing without any pauses or breaks, e.g. *nonstop excitement.*

noodle, noodles (noun) Noodles are a kind of pasta shaped into long, thin pieces.

nook, nooks (noun; a literary word) A nook is a small sheltered place.

noon (noun) Noon is midday.

no-one or **no one** (pronoun) not a single person.

noose, nooses (noun) A noose is a loop at the end of a piece of rope, with a knot that tightens when the rope is pulled.

nor (conjunction) used after 'neither' or after a negative statement, to add something else that the negative statement applies to, e.g. *They had neither the time nor the money for the sport.*

norm (noun) If something is the norm, it is the usual and expected thing, e.g. *cultures where large families are the norm.*

normal (adjective) usual and ordinary, e.g. *I try to lead a normal life.* **normality** (noun).

normally 1 (adverb) usually, e.g. *I don't normally like dancing.* **2** in a way that is normal, e.g. *The foetus is developing normally.*

north 1 (noun) The north is the direction to your left when you are looking towards the place where the sun rises. **2** The north of a place or country is the part which is towards the north when you are in the centre. **3** (adverb or adjective) North means towards the north, e.g. *The helicopter took off and headed north.* **4** (adjective) A north wind blows from the north.

North America (noun) North America is the third largest continent, consisting of Canada, the United States, and Mexico. It has the Pacific Ocean on its west side, the Atlantic on the east, and the Arctic to the north. **North American** (adjective).

north-east (noun, adverb, or adjective) North-east is halfway between north and east.

north-easterly 1 (adjective) North-easterly means to or towards the north-east. **2** A north-easterly wind blows from the north-east.

north-eastern (adjective) in or from the north-east.

northerly 1 (adjective) Northerly means to or towards the north, e.g. *travelling in a northerly direction.* **2** A northerly wind blows from the north.

northern (adjective) in or from the north, e.g. *the mountains of northern Italy.*

North Pole (noun) The North Pole is the most northerly point of the earth's surface.

northward or **northwards 1** (adverb) Northward or northwards means towards the north, e.g. *We continued northwards.* **2** (adjective) The northward part of something is the north part.

north-west (noun, adverb, or adjective) North-west is halfway between north and west.

north-westerly 1 (adjective) North-westerly means to or towards the north-west. **2** A north-westerly wind blows from the north-west.

north-western (adjective) in or from the north-west.

Norwegian, Norwegians (pronounced nor-**wee**-jn) **1** (adjective) belonging or relating to Norway. **2** (noun) A Norwegian is someone who comes from Norway. **3** Norwegian is the main language spoken in Norway.

nose, noses 1 (noun) Your nose is the part of your face above your mouth which you use for smelling and breathing. **2** The nose of a car or plane is the front part of it.

nostalgia (pronounced nos-**tal**-ja) (noun) Nostalgia is a feeling of affection for the past, and sadness that things have changed. **nostalgic** (adjective).

nostril, nostrils (noun) Your nostrils are the two openings in your nose which you breathe through.

nosy, nosier, nosiest; also spelled **nosey** (adjective) trying to find out about things that do not concern you.

not (adverb) used to make a sentence negative, to refuse something, or to deny something.

notable (adjective) important or interesting, e.g. *The production is notable for some outstanding performances.* **notably** (adverb).

notch, notches (noun) A notch is a small V-shaped cut in a surface.

note, notes, noting, noted 1 (noun) A note is a short letter. **2** A note is also a written piece of information that helps you to remember something, e.g. *You should make a note of that.* **3** In music, a note is a musical sound of a particular pitch, or a written symbol that represents it. **4** A note is also an atmosphere, feeling, or quality, e.g. *There was a note of regret in his voice... I'm determined to close on an optimistic note.* **5** (verb) If you note a fact, you become aware of it or you mention it, e.g. *Suddenly, I noted that the rain had stopped.* **6** (phrase) If you **take note** of something, you pay attention to it, e.g. *The world hardly took note of this crisis.* **note down** (verb) If you note something down, you write it down so that you will remember it.

notebook, notebooks (noun) A notebook is a small book for writing notes in.

noted (adjective) well-known and admired, e.g. *a noted Hebrew scholar.*

nothing (pronoun) not anything, e.g. *There was nothing to do.*

notice, notices, noticing, noticed 1 (verb) If you notice something, you become aware of it. **2** (noun) Notice is attention or awareness, e.g. *I'm glad he brought it to my notice.* **3** A notice is a written announcement. **4** Notice is also advance warning about something, e.g. *We were lucky to get you at such short notice.* **5** (phrase) If you **hand in your notice,** you tell your employer that you intend to leave your job after a fixed period of time.

noticeable (adjective) obvious and easy to see, e.g. *a noticeable improvement.* **noticeably** (adverb).

noticeboard, noticeboards (noun) A noticeboard is a board for notices.

notify, notifies, notifying, notified (verb) To notify someone of something means to officially inform them of it, e.g. *You must notify us of any change of address.* **notification** (noun).

notion, notions (noun) A notion is an idea or belief.

notorious (adjective) well-known for something bad, e.g. *The area has become notorious for violence against tourists.* **notoriously** (adverb), **notoriety** (noun).

notwithstanding (preposition;

a formal word) in spite of, e.g. *Notwithstanding his age, he had an important job.*

nougat (pronounced **noo**-gah) (noun) Nougat is a kind of chewy sweet containing nuts and sometimes fruit.

nought the number 0.

noun, nouns (noun) A noun is a word which refers to a person, thing, or idea. Examples of nouns are 'president', 'table', 'sun', and 'beauty'.

nourish, nourishes, nourishing, nourished (pronounced **nur**-rish) (verb) To nourish people or animals means to provide them with food.

nourishing (adjective) Food that is nourishing makes you strong and healthy.

nourishment (noun) Nourishment is food that your body needs in order to remain healthy, e.g. *poor nourishment.*

novel, novels 1 (noun) A novel is a book that tells an invented story. **2** (adjective) new and interesting, e.g. *a very novel experience.*

novelist, novelists (noun) A novelist is a person who writes novels.

novelty, novelties 1 (noun) Novelty is the quality of being new and interesting, e.g. *The novelty had worn off.* **2** A novelty is something new and interesting, e.g. *Steam power was still a bit of a novelty.* **3** A novelty is also a small, unusual object sold as a gift or souvenir.

November (noun) November is the eleventh month of the year. It has 30 days.

novice, novices 1 (noun) A novice is someone who is not yet experienced at something. **2** A novice is also someone who is preparing to become a monk or nun.

now 1 (adverb) at the present time or moment. **2** (conjunction) as a result or consequence of a particular fact, e.g. *Things have got better now there is a new board.* **3** (phrase) **Just now** means very recently, e.g. *I drove Brenda back to the camp just now.* **4** If something happens **now and then,** it happens sometimes but not regularly.

nowadays (adverb) at the present time, e.g. *Nowadays most fathers choose to be present at the birth.*

nowhere (adverb) not anywhere.

nozzle, nozzles (noun) A nozzle is a spout fitted onto the end of a pipe or hose to control the flow of a liquid.

nuance, nuances (pronounced **nyoo**-ahnss) (noun) A nuance is a small difference in sound, colour, or meaning, e.g. *the nuances of his music.*

nubile (pronounced **nyoo**-bile) (adjective) A woman who is nubile is physically well-developed and attractive but still young.

nuclear 1 (adjective) relating to the energy produced when the nuclei of atoms are split, e.g. *nuclear power... the nuclear industry.* **2** relating to weapons that explode using the energy released by atoms, e.g. *nuclear war.* **3** relating to the structure and behaviour of the nuclei of atoms, e.g. *nuclear physics.*

nucleus, nuclei (pronounced

nyoo-klee-uss) **1** (noun) The nucleus of an atom or cell is the central part of it. **2** The nucleus of something is the basic central part of it to which other things are added, e.g. *Seventy scholars formed the nucleus of the school.*

nude, nudes 1 (adjective) naked. **2** (noun) A nude is a picture or statue of a naked person. **nudity** (noun).

nudge, nudges, nudging, nudged 1 (verb) If you nudge someone, you push them gently, usually with your elbow. **2** (noun) A nudge is a gentle push.

nudist, nudists (noun) A nudist is a person who believes in wearing no clothes.

nugget, nuggets (noun) A nugget is a small rough lump of something, especially gold.

nuisance, nuisances (noun) A nuisance is someone or something that is annoying or inconvenient.

null (phrase) **Null and void** means not legally valid, e.g. *Other documents were declared to be null and void.*

numb, numbs, numbing, numbed 1 (adjective) unable to feel anything, e.g. *My legs felt numb... numb with grief.* **2** (verb) If something numbs you, it makes you unable to feel anything, e.g. *The cold numbed my fingers.*

number, numbers, numbering, numbered 1 (noun) A number is a word or a symbol used for counting or calculating. **2** Someone's number is the series of numbers that you dial when you telephone them. **3** A number of things is a quantity of them, e.g. *Adrian has introduced me to a large number of people.* **4** A number is also a song or piece of music. **5** (verb) If things number a particular amount, there are that many of them, e.g. *At that time London's population numbered about 460,000.* **6** If you number something, you give it a number, e.g. *The picture is signed and numbered by the artist.* **7** To be numbered among a particular group means to belong to it, e.g. *Only the best are numbered among their champions.*

numeral, numerals (noun) A numeral is a symbol that represents a number, e.g. *a wristwatch with Roman numerals.*

numerical (adjective) expressed in numbers or relating to numbers, e.g. *a numerical value.*

numerous (adjective) existing or happening in large numbers.

nun, nuns (noun) A nun is a woman who has taken religious vows and lives in a convent.

nurse, nurses, nursing, nursed 1 (noun) A nurse is someone whose job is to look after people who are ill. **2** (verb) If you nurse someone, you look after them when they are ill. **3** If you nurse a feeling, you feel it strongly for a long time, e.g. *He nursed a grudge against the USA.*

nursery, nurseries 1 (noun) A nursery is a place where young children are looked after while their parents are working. **2** A nursery is also a room in which young children sleep and play. **3** A nursery is also a place where plants are grown and sold.

nursery school, nursery schools (noun) A nursery school is a school for children from three to five years old.

nursing home, nursing homes (noun) A nursing home is a privately run hospital, especially for old people.

nurture, nurtures, nurturing, nurtured (verb; a formal word) If you nurture a young child or a plant, you look after it carefully.

nut, nuts 1 (noun) A nut is a fruit with a hard shell and an edible centre that grows on certain trees. **2** A nut is also a piece of metal with a hole in the middle which a bolt screws into.

nutmeg (noun) Nutmeg is a spice used for flavouring in cooking.

nutrient, nutrients (noun) Nutrients are substances that help plants or animals to grow, e.g. *the nutrients in the soil.*

nutrition (noun) Nutrition is the food that you eat, considered from the point of view of how it helps you to grow and remain healthy, e.g. *The effects of poor nutrition are evident.* **nutritionist** (noun).

nutritious (adjective) containing substances that help you to grow and remain healthy.

nutty, nuttier, nuttiest 1 (adjective; an informal use) mad or very foolish. **2** tasting of nuts.

nylon, nylons 1 (noun) Nylon is a type of strong artificial material, e.g. *nylon stockings.* **2** Nylons are stockings or tights.

O o

oaf, oafs (noun) An oaf is a clumsy and stupid person.

oak, oaks (noun) An oak is a large tree which produces acorns. It has a hard wood which is often used to make furniture.

OAP, OAPs (noun) An OAP is a man over the age of 65 or a woman over the age of 60 who receives a pension. OAP is an abbreviation for 'old age pensioner'.

oar, oars (noun) An oar is a wooden pole used for rowing a boat.

oasis, oases (pronounced oh-**ay**-siss) (noun) An oasis is a small area in a desert where water and plants are found.

oat, oats (noun) Oats are a type of grain.

oath, oaths (noun) An oath is a formal promise, especially a promise to tell the truth in a court of law.

oatmeal (noun) Oatmeal is a coarse flour made from oats.

OBE, OBEs (noun) An OBE is an honour awarded by the King or Queen. OBE is an abbreviation for 'Officer of the Order of the British Empire'.

obedient (adjective) If you are obedient, you do what you are told to do. **obediently** (adverb), **obedience** (noun).

obelisk, obelisks (noun) An obelisk is a stone pillar built in honour of a person or an event.

obese (pronounced oh-**bees**) (adjective) extremely fat. **obesity** (noun).

obey, obeys, obeying, obeyed (verb) If you obey a person or an order, you do what you are told to do.

obituary, obituaries (noun) An obituary is a piece of writing about the life and achievements of someone who has just died.

object, objects, objecting, objected **1** (noun) An object is anything solid that you can touch or see, and that is not alive. **2** Someone's object is their aim or purpose. **3** The object of your feelings or actions is the person that they are directed towards. **4** In grammar, the object of a verb or preposition is the word or phrase which follows it and describes the person or thing affected. **5** (verb) If you object to something, you dislike it or disapprove of it.

objection, objections (noun) If you have an objection to something, you dislike it or disapprove of it.

objectionable (adjective) unpleasant and offensive.

objective, objectives **1** (noun) Your objective is your aim, e.g. *The protection of the countryside is their main objective.* **2** (adjective) If you are objective, you are not influenced by personal feelings or prejudices, e.g. *an objective approach.* **objectively** (adverb), **objectivity** (noun).

obligation, obligations (noun) An obligation is something that you must do because it is your duty.

obligatory (pronounced ob-**lig**-a-tree) (adjective) required by a rule or law, e.g. *Religious education was obligatory.*

oblige, obliges, obliging, obliged **1** (verb) If you are obliged to do something, you have to do it. **2** If you oblige someone, you help them. **obliging** (adjective).

oblique (pronounced o-**bleek**) **1** (adjective) An oblique remark is not direct, and is therefore difficult to understand. **2** An oblique line slopes at an angle.

obliterate, obliterates, obliterating, obliterated (verb) To obliterate something means to destroy it completely. **obliteration** (noun).

oblivion (noun) Oblivion is unconsciousness or complete unawareness of your surroundings. **oblivious** (adjective), **obliviously** (adverb).

oblong, oblongs **1** (noun) An oblong is a four-sided shape with two parallel short sides, two parallel long sides, and four right angles. **2** (adjective) shaped like an oblong.

obnoxious (pronounced ob-**nok**-shuss) (adjective) extremely unpleasant.

oboe, oboes (noun) An oboe is a woodwind musical instrument with a double reed. **oboist** (noun).

obscene (adjective) indecent and offensive, e.g. *obscene pictures.* **obscenely** (adverb), **obscenity** (noun).

obscure, obscures, obscuring, obscured **1** (adjective) Something that is obscure is known by only a few people, e.g. *an* *obscure Mongolian dialect.* **2** Something obscure is difficult to see or to understand, e.g. *The news was shrouded in obscure language.* **3** (verb) To obscure something means to make it difficult to see or understand, e.g. *His view was obscured by trees.* **obscurity** (noun).

observance (noun) The observance of a law or custom is the practice of obeying or following it.

observant (adjective) Someone who is observant notices things that are not easy to see.

observation, observations 1 (noun) Observation is the act of watching something carefully, e.g. *Success hinges on close observation.* **2** An observation is something that you have seen or noticed. **3** An observation is also a remark. **4** Observation is the ability to notice things that are not easy to see.

observatory, observatories (noun) An observatory is a room or building containing telescopes and other equipment for studying the sun, moon, and stars.

observe, observes, observing, observed 1 (verb) To observe something means to watch it carefully. **2** To observe something also means to notice it. **3** If you observe that something is the case, you make a comment about it. **4** To observe a law or custom means to obey or follow it. **observer** (noun), **observable** (adjective).

obsession, obsessions (noun) If someone has an obsession about something, they cannot stop thinking about that thing. **obsessional** (adjective), **obsessed** (adjective), **obsessive** (adjective).

obsolete (adjective) out of date and no longer used.

obstacle, obstacles (noun) An obstacle is something which is in your way and makes it difficult to do something.

obstetrics (noun) Obstetrics is the branch of medicine concerned with pregnancy and childbirth. **obstetrician** (noun).

obstinate (adjective) Someone who is obstinate is stubborn and unwilling to change their mind. **obstinately** (adverb), **obstinacy** (noun).

obstruct, obstructs, obstructing, obstructed (verb) If something obstructs a road or path, it blocks it. **obstruction** (noun), **obstructive** (adjective).

obtain, obtains, obtaining, obtained (verb) If you obtain something, you get it. **obtainable** (adjective).

obtrusive (adjective) noticeable in an unpleasant way, e.g. *a remarkably obtrusive cigar.*

obtuse 1 (adjective) Someone who is obtuse is stupid or slow to understand things. **2** An obtuse angle is between 90° and 180°.

obvious (adjective) easy to see or understand. **obviously** (adverb).

occasion, occasions, occasioning, occasioned 1 (noun) An occasion is a time when something happens. **2** An occasion is also an important event. **3** An occasion for doing something is an opportunity for doing it. **4** (verb; a formal use)

To occasion something means to cause it, e.g. *damage occasioned by fire.*

occasional (adjective) happening sometimes but not often, e.g. *an occasional outing.* **occasionally** (adverb).

occult (noun) The occult is the knowledge of supernatural and magical forces.

occupancy (noun) The occupancy of a building is the act of living or working in it.

occupant, occupants (noun) The occupants of a building are the people who live or work in it.

occupation, occupations 1 (noun) Your occupation is your job or profession. **2** An occupation is also a hobby or something you do for pleasure. **3** The occupation of a country is the act of invading it and taking control of it. **occupational** (adjective).

occupy, occupies, occupying, occupied 1 (verb) The people who occupy a building are the people who live or work there. **2** When people occupy a place, they move into it and take control of it, e.g. *Demonstrators occupied the building.* **3** To occupy a position in a system or plan means to have that position. **4** If something occupies you, you spend your time doing it, e.g. *That problem occupies me night and day.* **occupier** (noun).

occur, occurs, occurring, occurred 1 (verb) If something occurs, it happens or exists, e.g. *The second attack occurred at a swimming pool.* **2** If something occurs to you, you suddenly think of it.

occurrence, occurrences 1 (noun) An occurrence is an event. **2** The occurrence of something is the fact that it happens or exists, e.g. *the occurrence of diseases.*

ocean, oceans 1 (noun; a literary use) The ocean is the sea. **2** The five oceans are the five very large areas of sea, e.g. *the Atlantic Ocean.* **oceanic** (adjective).

o'clock (adverb) You use o'clock after the number of the hour to say what the time is.

octagon, octagons (noun) An octagon is a shape with eight straight sides. **octagonal** (adjective).

octave, octaves (noun) An octave is the difference in pitch between the first note and the eighth note of a musical scale.

October (noun) October is the tenth month of the year. It has 31 days.

octopus, octopuses (noun) An octopus is a sea creature with eight long tentacles which it uses to catch food.

odd, odder, oddest; odds 1 (adjective) Something odd is strange or unusual. **2** Odd things do not match each other, e.g. *odd socks.* **3** Odd numbers are numbers that cannot be divided exactly by two. **4** (adverb) You use odd after a number to indicate that it is approximate, e.g. *I've written twenty odd plays.* **5** (plural noun) In gambling, the probability of something happening is referred to as the odds. **oddly** (adverb), **oddness** (noun).

oddity, oddities (noun) An oddity is something very strange.

oddments (plural noun) Oddments are things that are left over after other things have been used.

odds and ends (plural noun) You can refer to a collection of small unimportant things as odds and ends.

ode, odes (noun) An ode is a poem written in praise of someone or something.

odious (adjective) extremely unpleasant.

odour, odours (noun; a formal word) An odour is a strong smell. **odorous** (adjective).

odyssey, odysseys (pronounced **od**-i-see) (noun) An odyssey is a long and eventful journey.

oesophagus, oesophaguses (pronounced ee-**sof**-fag-uss) (noun) Your oesophagus is the tube that carries food from your throat to your stomach.

oestrogen another spelling of **estrogen**.

of 1 (preposition) consisting of or containing, e.g. *a collection of short stories... a cup of tea.* **2** used when naming something or describing a characteristic of something, e.g. *the city of Lincoln... a woman of great power and influence.* **3** belonging to or connected with, e.g. *a friend of Rachel... the cover of the book.*

off 1 (preposition or adverb) indicating movement away from or out of a place, e.g. *They had just stepped off the plane... She got up and marched off.* **2** indicating separation or distance from a place, e.g. *some islands off the coast of Australia... The whole crescent has been fenced off.* **3** not working, e.g. *It was Frank's night off.* **4** (adverb or adjective) not switched on, e.g. *He turned the radio off... the off switch.* **5** (adjective) cancelled or postponed, e.g. *The concert was off.* **6** Food that is off has gone sour or bad. **7** (preposition) not liking or not using something, e.g. *He went right off alcohol.*

offal (noun) Offal is liver, kidneys, and other organs of animals, which can be eaten.

offence, offences 1 (noun) An offence is a crime, e.g. *a drink-driving offence.* **2** (phrases) If something **gives offence,** it upsets people. If you **take offence,** you are upset by someone or something.

offend, offends, offending, offended 1 (verb) If you offend someone, you upset them. **2** (a formal use) To offend or to offend a law means to commit a crime. **offender** (noun).

offensive, offensives 1 (adjective) Something offensive is rude and upsetting, e.g. *offensive behaviour.* **2** Offensive actions or weapons are used in attacking someone. **3** (noun) An offensive is an attack, e.g. *a full-scale offensive against the rebels.* **offensively** (adverb).

offer, offers, offering, offered 1 (verb) If you offer something to someone, you ask them if they would like it. **2** (noun) An offer is something that someone says they will give you or do for you if you want them to, e.g. *He refused the offer of a drink.* **3** An offer in a shop is a specially low price for a product, e.g. *You will* *need a voucher to qualify for the special offer.*

offering, offerings (noun) An offering is something that is offered or given to someone.

offhand 1 (adjective) If someone is offhand, they are unfriendly and slightly rude. **2** (adverb) If you know something offhand, you know it without having to think very hard, e.g. *I couldn't tell you offhand how long he's been here.*

office, offices 1 (noun) An office is a room where people work at desks. **2** An office is also a government department which deals with a particular area of administration, e.g. *the Office of Fair Trading.* **3** An office is also a place where people can go for information, tickets, or other services. **4** Someone who holds office has an important job or position in government or in an organization.

officer, officers (noun) An officer is a person holding a position of authority in the armed forces, the police, or a government organization.

official, officials 1 (adjective) approved by the government or by someone in authority, e.g. *the official figures.* **2** done or used by someone in authority as part of their job, e.g. *official notepaper.* **3** (noun) An official is a person who holds a position of authority in an organization. **officially** (adverb).

officialdom (noun) You can refer to officials in government or other organizations as officialdom, especially when you find them unhelpful and unfriendly.

officiate, officiates, officiating, officiated (verb) To officiate at a ceremony means to be in charge and perform the official part of the ceremony.

offing (phrase) If something is **in the offing,** it is likely to happen soon, e.g. *A change is in the offing.*

off-licence, off-licences (noun) An off-licence is a shop which sells alcoholic drinks.

offset, offsets, offsetting, offset (verb) If one thing is offset by another thing, its effect is reduced or cancelled out by that thing, e.g. *This tedium can be offset by watching the television.*

offshoot, offshoots (noun) If one thing has developed from another thing, you can say that it is an offshoot of that thing, e.g. *The technology we use is an offshoot of the motor industry.*

offshore (adjective or adverb) in or from the part of the sea near the shore, e.g. *an offshore wind... a wreck fifteen miles offshore.*

offside 1 (adjective) If a football, rugby, or hockey player is offside, they have broken the rules by moving too far forward. **2** (noun) The offside of a vehicle is the side that is furthest from the pavement.

offspring (noun) A person's or animal's offspring are their children.

often (adverb) happening many times or a lot of the time.

ogle, ogles, ogling, ogled (pronounced **oh**-gl) (verb) To ogle someone means to stare at them in a way that indicates a sexual interest.

ogre, ogres (pronounced **oh**-gur) (noun) An ogre is a cruel, frightening giant in a fairy story.

ohm, ohms (rhymes with **home**) (noun) In physics, an ohm is a unit used to measure electrical resistance.

oil, oils, oiling, oiled 1 (noun) Oil is a thick, sticky liquid used as a fuel and for lubrication. **2** (verb) If you oil something, you put oil in it or on it. **3** (noun) Oil is also a thick, greasy liquid made from plants or animals, e.g. *cooking oil... bath oil.*

oil painting, oil paintings (noun) An oil painting is a picture that has been painted with thick paints made from coloured powder and a kind of oil.

oilskin, oilskins (noun) An oilskin is a piece of clothing made from a thick, waterproof material, worn especially by fishermen.

oily (adjective) Something that is oily is covered with or contains oil, e.g. *an oily rag... oily skin.*

ointment, ointments (noun) An ointment is a smooth, thick substance that you put on sore skin to heal it.

okay or **OK** (adjective or adverb; an informal word) Okay means all right, e.g. *Tell me if this sounds okay.*

old, older, oldest 1 (adjective) having lived or existed for a long time, e.g. *an old lady... old clothes.* **2** Old is used to give the age of someone or something, e.g. *This photo is five years old.* **3** Old also means former, e.g. *my old art teacher.*

olden (phrase) **In the olden days** means long ago.

old-fashioned 1 (adjective) Something which is old-fashioned is no longer fashionable, e.g. *old-fashioned shoes.* **2** Someone who is old-fashioned believes in the values and standards of the past.

Old Testament (noun) The Old Testament is the first part of the Christian Bible. It is also the holy book of the Jewish religion and contains writings which relate to the history of the Jews.

olive, olives 1 (noun) An olive is a small green or black fruit containing a stone. Olives are usually pickled and eaten as a snack or crushed to produce oil. **2** (adjective or noun) dark yellowish-green.

-ology (suffix) -ology is used to form words that refer to the study of something, e.g. *biology... geology.*

Olympic Games (pronounced ol-**lim**-pik) (plural noun) The Olympic Games are a set of sporting contests held in a different city every four years.

ombudsman, ombudsmen (noun) The ombudsman is a person who investigates complaints against the government or a public organization.

omelette, omelettes (pronounced **om**-lit) (noun) An omelette is a dish made by beating eggs together and cooking them in a flat pan.

omen, omens (noun) An omen is something that is thought to be a sign of what will happen in the future, e.g. *John *saw this success as a good omen for his trip.*

ominous (adjective) suggesting that something unpleasant is going to happen, e.g. *an ominous sign.* **ominously** (adverb).

omission, omissions 1 (noun) An omission is something that has not been included or done, e.g. *There are some striking omissions in the survey.* **2** Omission is the act of not including or not doing something, e.g. *controversy over the omission of female novelists.*

omit, omits, omitting, omitted 1 (verb) If you omit something, you do not include it. **2** (a formal use) If you omit to do something, you do not do it.

omnibus, omnibuses 1 (noun) An omnibus is a book containing a collection of stories or articles by the same author or about the same subject. **2** (adjective) An omnibus edition of a radio or television show contains two or more programmes that were originally broadcast separately.

omnipotent (pronounced om-**nip**-a-tent) (adjective) having very great or unlimited power, e.g. *We believe that God is just, merciful, and omnipotent.* **omnipotence** (noun).

on 1 (preposition) touching or attached to something, e.g. *The woman was sitting on the sofa.* **2** If you are on a bus, plane, or train, you are inside it. **3** If something happens on a particular day, that is when it happens, e.g. *It is his birthday on Monday.* **4** If something is done on an instrument, machine, or system, it is done using that instrument, machine, or system, e.g. *He preferred to play on his computer.* **5** A book or talk on a particular subject is about that subject. **6** (adverb) If you have a piece of clothing on, you are wearing it. **7** (adjective) A machine or switch that is on is working. **8** If an event is on, it is happening or taking place, e.g. *The race is definitely on.*

once 1 (adverb) If something happens once, it happens one time only. **2** If something was once true, it was true in the past, but is no longer true. **3** (conjunction) If something happens once another thing has happened, it happens immediately afterwards. **4** (phrases) If you do something **at once,** you do it immediately. If several things happen **at once,** they all happen at the same time.

one, ones 1 One is the number 1. **2** (adjective) If you refer to the one person or thing of a particular kind, you mean the only person or thing of that kind, e.g. *My one aim is to look after the horses well.* **3** One also means 'a'; used when emphasizing something, e.g. *They got one almighty shock.* **4** (pronoun) One refers to a particular thing or person, e.g. *Alf Brown's business was a good one.* **5** One also means people in general, e.g. *One likes to have the opportunity to chat.*

one-off (noun) A one-off is something that happens or is made only once.

onerous (pronounced **ohn**-eruss) (adjective; a formal word) difficult or unpleasant, e.g. *an onerous task.*

oneself (pronoun) Oneself is used when you are talking about people in general, e.g. *One could hardly hear oneself talk.*

one-sided 1 (adjective) If an activity or relationship is one-sided, one of the people has a lot more success or involvement than the other, e.g. *a one-sided contest.* **2** A one-sided argument or report considers the facts or a situation from only one point of view.

one-way 1 (adjective) One-way streets are streets along which vehicles can drive in only one direction. **2** A one-way ticket is one that you can use to travel to a place, but not to travel back again.

ongoing (adjective) continuing to happen, e.g. *an ongoing process of learning.*

onion, onions (noun) An onion is a small, round vegetable with a brown, papery skin and a very strong taste.

onlooker, onlookers (noun) An onlooker is someone who is watching an event.

only 1 (adverb) You use only to indicate the one thing or person involved, e.g. *Only Keith knows whether he will continue.* **2** (adjective) If you talk about the only thing or person, you mean that there are no others, e.g. *their only hit single.* **3** If you are an only child, you have no brothers or sisters. **4** (adverb) You use only to emphasize that something is unimportant or small, e.g. *He's only a little boy.* **5** (conjunction) Only also means but or except, e.g. *He was like you, only blond.* **6** (adverb) You can use only to introduce something which happens immediately after something else, e.g. *She had thought of one plan, only to discard it for another.* **7** (phrase) **Only too** means extremely, e.g. *I would be only too happy to swap places.*

onset (noun) The onset of something unpleasant is the beginning of it, e.g. *the onset of war.*

onslaught, onslaughts (pronounced **on**-slawt) (noun) An onslaught is a violent attack.

onto or **on to** (preposition) If you put something onto an object, you put it on it.

onus (rhymes with **bonus**) (noun; a formal word) If the onus is on you to do something, it is your duty to do it.

onwards or **onward 1** (adverb) continuing to happen from a particular time, e.g. *He could not speak a word from that moment onwards.* **2** travelling forwards, e.g. *Duncliffe escorted the pair onwards to his own room.*

onyx (pronounced **on**-iks) (noun) Onyx is a semiprecious stone used for making ornaments and jewellery.

ooze, oozes, oozing, oozed (verb) When a thick liquid oozes, it flows slowly, e.g. *The cold mud oozed over her new footwear.*

opal, opals (noun) An opal is a pale or whitish semiprecious stone used for making jewellery.

opaque (pronounced oh-**pake**)

(adjective) If something is opaque, you cannot see through it, e.g. *opaque glass windows.*

open, opens, opening, opened 1 (verb) When you open something, or when it opens, you move it so that it is no longer closed, e.g. *She opened the door.* **2** (adjective) Something that is open is not closed or fastened, e.g. *an open box of chocolates.* **3** If you have an open mind, you are willing to consider new ideas or suggestions. **4** Someone who is open is honest and frank. **5** (verb) When a shop or office opens, the people in it start working. **6** (adjective) When a shop or office is open, the people in it are working. **7** (verb) To open something also means to start it, e.g. *He tried to open a bank account.* **8** (adjective) An open area of sea or land is a large, empty area, e.g. *open country.* **9** (phrase) **In the open** means outside. **10** (adjective) If something is open to you, it is possible for you to do it, e.g. *There is no other course open to us but to fight it out.* **11** If a situation is still open, it is still being considered, e.g. *Even if the case remains open, the full facts may never be revealed.* **openly** (adverb).

opening, openings 1 (adjective) Opening means coming first, e.g. *the opening day of the season.* **2** (noun) The opening of a book or film is the first part of it. **3** An opening is a hole or gap. **4** An opening is also an opportunity, e.g. *The two men circled around, looking for an opening to attack.*

open-minded (adjective) willing to consider new ideas and suggestions.

open-plan (adjective) An open-plan office or building has very few dividing walls.

opera, operas (noun) An opera is a play in which the words are sung rather than spoken. **operatic** (adjective).

operate, operates, operating, operated 1 (verb) To operate means to work, e.g. *We are shocked at the way that businesses operate.* **2** When you operate a machine, you make it work. **3** When surgeons operate, they cut open a patient's body to remove or repair a damaged part.

operation, operations 1 (noun) An operation is a complex, planned event, e.g. *a full-scale military operation.* **2** An operation is also a form of medical treatment in which a surgeon cuts open a patient's body to remove or repair a damaged part. **3** (phrase) If something is **in operation,** it is working or being used, e.g. *The system is in operation until the end of September.*

operational (adjective) working or able to be used, e.g. *an operational aircraft.*

operative (adjective) Something that is operative is working or having an effect.

operator, operators 1 (noun) An operator is someone who works at a telephone exchange or on a switchboard. **2** A machine operator is someone who operates a machine, e.g. *a computer operator.* **3** An operator is also someone who runs a business, e.g. *a tour op-*

erator.

opinion, opinions (noun) An opinion is a belief or view.

opinionated (adjective) Someone who is opinionated has strong views and refuses to accept that they might be wrong.

opium (noun) Opium is a drug made from the seeds of a poppy. It is used in medicine to relieve pain.

opponent, opponents (noun) Your opponent is someone who is against you in an argument, a contest, or a game.

opportune (adjective; a formal word) happening at a convenient time, e.g. *The king's death was opportune for the prince.*

opportunism (noun) Opportunism is the practice of taking advantage of any opportunity to gain money or power for yourself. **opportunist** (noun).

opportunity, opportunities (noun) An opportunity is a chance to do something.

oppose, opposes, opposing, opposed (verb) If you oppose something, you disagree with it and try to prevent it.

opposed 1 (adjective) If you are opposed to something, you disagree with it, e.g. *He was totally opposed to bullying in schools.* **2** Opposed also means opposite or very different, e.g. *two opposed schools of thought.* **3** (phrase) If you refer to one thing **as opposed to** another, you are emphasizing that it is the first thing rather than the second which concerns you, e.g. *Real spectators, as opposed to invited guests, were hard to spot.*

opposite, opposites 1 (preposition or adverb) If one thing is opposite another, it is facing it, e.g. *the shop opposite the station... the house opposite.* **2** (adjective) The opposite part of something is the part farthest away from you, e.g. *the opposite side of town.* **3** If things are opposite, they are completely different, e.g. *I take the opposite view to you.* **4** (noun) If two things are completely different, they are opposites.

opposition 1 (noun) If there is opposition to something, people disagree with it and try to prevent it. **2** The political parties who are not in power are referred to as the Opposition. **3** In a game or sports event, the opposition is the person or team that you are competing against.

oppressed (adjective) People who are oppressed are treated cruelly or unfairly. **oppress** (verb), **oppression** (noun), **oppressor** (noun).

oppressive 1 (adjective) If the weather is oppressive, it is hot and humid. **2** An oppressive situation makes you feel depressed or concerned, e.g. *The silence became oppressive.* **3** An oppressive system treats people cruelly or unfairly, e.g. *Married women were subject to oppressive laws.* **oppressively** (adverb).

opt, opts, opting, opted (verb) If you opt for something, you choose it. If you opt out of something, you choose not to be involved in it.

optical 1 (adjective) concerned with vision, light, or images, e.g. *an optical scanner.* **2** relating to the appearance of things, e.g. *an optical illusion.* **optic** (adjective).

optician, opticians (noun) An optician is someone who tests people's eyes, and makes and sells glasses and contact lenses.

optimism (noun) Optimism is a feeling of hopefulness about the future. **optimist** (noun), **optimistic** (adjective), **optimistically** (adverb).

optimum (adjective) the best that is possible, e.g. *Six is the optimum number of participants for a good meeting.*

option, options (noun) An option is a choice between two or more things. **optional** (adjective).

opulent (pronounced **op**-yool-nt) (adjective) grand and expensive-looking, e.g. *an opulent seafront estate.*

opus, opera (noun) An opus is also an artistic work, especially a piece of music.

or 1 (conjunction) used to link alternatives, e.g. *I didn't know whether to laugh or cry.* **2** used to introduce a warning, e.g. *Do what I say or else I will fire.*

oracle, oracles 1 (noun) In ancient Greece, an oracle was a place where a priest or priestess made predictions about the future. **2** An oracle is also a prophecy made by a person with great wisdom.

oral, orals 1 (adjective) spoken rather than written, e.g. *oral history.* **2** Oral describes things that are used in your mouth or done with your mouth, e.g. *an oral vaccine.* **3** (noun) An oral is an examination that is spoken rather than written. **orally** (adverb).

orange, oranges 1 (noun) An orange is a round citrus fruit that is juicy and sweet and has a thick reddish-yellow skin. **2** (adjective or noun) reddish-yellow.

orang-utan, orang-utans; also spelled **orang-utang** (noun) An orang-utan is a large ape with reddish-brown hair.

orator, orators (noun) An orator is someone who is good at making speeches.

oratory (noun) Oratory is the art and skill of making formal public speeches.

orbit, orbits, orbiting, orbited 1 (noun) An orbit is the curved path followed by an object going round a planet or the sun. **2** (verb) If something orbits a planet or the sun, it goes round and round it.

orchard, orchards (noun) An orchard is a piece of land where fruit trees are grown.

orchestra, orchestras (pronounced **or**-kess-tra) (noun) An orchestra is a large group of musicians who play musical instruments together. **orchestral** (adjective).

orchestrate, orchestrates, orchestrating, orchestrated 1 (verb) To orchestrate something means to organize it very carefully in order to produce a particular result. **2** To orchestrate a piece of music means to rewrite it so that it can be played by an orchestra. **orchestration** (noun).

orchid, orchids (pronounced **or**-kid) (noun) Orchids are plants with beautiful and unusual flowers.

ordain, ordains, ordaining, ordained (verb) When someone is ordained, they are made a member of the clergy.

ordeal, ordeals (noun) An ordeal is a difficult and extremely unpleasant experience, e.g. *the ordeal of being arrested and charged with attempted murder.*

order, orders, ordering, ordered **1** (noun) An order is a command given by someone in authority. **2** (verb) To order someone to do something means to tell them firmly to do it. **3** When you order something, you ask for it to be brought or sent to you. **4** (noun) If things are arranged or done in a particular order, they are arranged or done in that sequence, e.g. *in alphabetical order.* **5** Order is a situation in which everything is in the correct place or done at the correct time. **6** An order is something that you ask to be brought to you or sent to you. **7** (phrase) If you do something **in order to** achieve a particular thing, you do it because you want to achieve that thing.

orderly (adjective) Something that is orderly is well organized or arranged.

ordinarily (adverb) If something ordinarily happens, it usually happens.

ordinary (adjective) Ordinary means not special or different in any way.

ordination (noun) When someone's ordination takes place, they are made a member of the clergy.

ordnance (noun) Weapons and other military supplies are referred to as ordnance.

Ordnance Survey (noun) The Ordnance Survey is the British government organization that produces detailed maps of Britain and Ireland.

ore, ores (noun) Ore is rock or earth from which metal can be obtained.

oregano (pronounced or-rig-**garh**-no) (noun) Oregano is a herb used in cooking.

organ, organs **1** (noun) Your organs are parts of your body that have a particular function, for example your heart or lungs. **2** An organ is a large musical instrument with pipes of different lengths through which air is forced. It has various keyboards which are played like a piano.

organic **1** (adjective) Something that is organic is produced by or found in plants or animals, e.g. *decaying organic matter.* **2** Organic food is produced without the use of artificial fertilizers or pesticides. **organically** (adverb).

organism, organisms (noun) An organism is any living animal or plant.

organist, organists (noun) An organist is someone who plays the organ.

organization, organizations; also spelled **organisation** **1** (noun) An organization is any group, society, club, or business. **2** The organization of something is the act of planning and arranging it. **organizational** (adjective).

organize, organizes, organizing, organized; also spelled **organise** **1** (verb) If you organize an event, you plan and arrange it. **2** If you organize things, you arrange them in a sensible order. **organized** (adjective), **organizer** (noun).

orgasm, orgasms (noun) An orgasm is the moment of greatest pleasure and excitement during sexual activity.

orgy, orgies (pronounced **or**-jee) **1** (noun) An orgy is a wild, uncontrolled party involving a lot of drinking and sexual activity. **2** You can refer to a period of intense activity as an orgy of that activity, e.g. *an orgy of violence.*

orient (noun; a literary use) The Orient is eastern and south-eastern Asia.

oriental (adjective) relating to eastern or south-eastern Asia.

orientated (adjective) If someone is interested in a particular thing, you can say that they are orientated towards it, e.g. *These men are very career-orientated.*

orientation (noun) You can refer to an organization's activities and aims as its orientation, e.g. *Poland's political and military orientation.*

oriented (adjective) Oriented means the same as orientated.

orienteering (noun) Orienteering is a sport in which people run from one place to another in the countryside, using a map and compass to guide them.

origin, origins 1 (noun) You can refer to the beginning or cause of something as its origin or origins. **2** You can refer to someone's family background as their origin or origins, e.g. *She was of Swedish origin... his humble origins.*

original, originals 1 (adjective) Original describes things that existed at the beginning, rather than being added later, or things that were the first of their kind to exist, e.g. *the original owner of the cottage.* **2** (noun) An original is a work of art or a document that is the one that was first produced, and not a copy. **3** (adjective) Original means imaginative and clever, e.g. *a stunningly original idea.* **originally** (adverb), **originality** (noun).

originate, originates, originating, originated (verb) When something originates, or you originate it, it begins to happen or exist. **originator** (noun).

ornament, ornaments (noun) An ornament is a small, attractive object that you display in your home or that you wear in order to look attractive.

ornamental (adjective) designed to be attractive rather than useful, e.g. *an ornamental lake.*

ornamentation (noun) Ornamentation is decoration on a building, a piece of furniture, or a work of art.

ornate (adjective) Something that is ornate has a lot of decoration on it.

ornithology (noun) Ornithology is the study of birds. **ornithologist** (noun).

orphan, orphans, orphaning, orphaned 1 (noun) An orphan is a child whose parents are dead. **2** (verb) If a child is orphaned, its parents die.

orphanage, orphanages (noun) An orphanage is a place

where orphans are looked after.

orthodox 1 (adjective) Orthodox beliefs or methods are the ones that most people have or use and that are considered standard. **2** People who are orthodox believe in the older, more traditional ideas of their religion or political party. **3** The Orthodox church is the part of the Christian church which separated from the western European church in the 11th century and is the main church in Greece and Russia. **orthodoxy** (noun).

osprey, ospreys (pronounced **oss**-pree) (noun) An osprey is a large bird of prey which catches fish with its feet.

ostensibly (adverb) If something is done ostensibly for a reason, that seems to be the reason for it, e.g. *Byrnes submitted his resignation, ostensibly on medical grounds.*

ostentatious 1 (adjective) Something that is ostentatious is intended to impress people, for example by looking expensive, e.g. *ostentatious sculptures.* **2** People who are ostentatious try to impress other people with their wealth or importance. **ostentatiously** (adverb), **ostentation** (noun).

ostrich, ostriches (noun) The ostrich is the largest bird in the world. Ostriches cannot fly.

other, others 1 (adjective or pronoun) Other people or things are different people or things, e.g. *All the other children had gone home... One of the cabinets came from Brighton Pavilion; the other is a copy.* **2** (phrases) **The other day** or **the other week** means recently, e.g. *She had bought four pairs of shoes the other day.*

otherwise 1 (adverb) You use otherwise to say a different situation would exist if a particular fact or occurrence was not the case, e.g. *You had to learn to swim pretty quickly, otherwise you sank.* **2** Otherwise means apart from the thing mentioned, e.g. *She had written to her daughter, but otherwise refused to take sides.* **3** Otherwise also means in a different way, e.g. *The majority voted otherwise.*

otter, otters (noun) An otter is a small, furry animal with a long tail. Otters swim well and live on fish.

ouch (interjection) You say ouch when you suddenly feel pain.

ought (pronounced **awt**) (verb) If you say that someone ought to do something, you mean that they should do it, e.g. *He ought to see a doctor.*

ounce, ounces (noun) An ounce is a unit of weight equal to one sixteenth of a pound or about 28.35 grams.

our (adjective) Our refers to something belonging or relating to the speaker or writer and one or more other people, e.g. *We recently sold our house.*

ours (pronoun) Ours refers to something belonging or relating to the speaker or writer and one or more other people, e.g. *a friend of ours from Korea.*

ourselves 1 (pronoun) Ourselves is used when the same

speaker or writer and one or more other people do an action and are affected by it, e.g. *We haven't damaged ourselves too badly.* **2** Ourselves is used to emphasize 'we'.

oust, ousts, ousting, ousted (verb) If you oust someone, you force them out of a job or a place, e.g. *Cole was ousted from the board.*

out 1 (adverb) towards the outside of a place, e.g. *Two dogs rushed out of the house.* **2** not at home, e.g. *She was out when I rang last night.* **3** in the open air, e.g. *They are playing out in bright sunshine.* **4** no longer shining or burning, e.g. *The lights went out.* **5** (adjective) on strike, e.g. *1000 construction workers are out in sympathy.* **6** unacceptable or unfashionable, e.g. *Mini skirts are out.*

out-and-out (adjective) entire or complete, e.g. *an out-and-out lie.*

outback (noun) In Australia, the outback is the remote parts where very few people live.

outboard motor, outboard motors (noun) An outboard motor is a motor that can be fixed to the back of a small boat.

outbreak, outbreaks (noun) If there is an outbreak of something unpleasant, such as war, it suddenly occurs.

outburst, outbursts 1 (noun) An outburst is a sudden, strong expression of an emotion, especially anger, e.g. *John broke into an angry outburst about how unfairly the work was divided.* **2** An outburst of violent activity is a sudden occurrence of it, e.g. *an outburst of gunfire.*

outcast, outcasts (noun) An outcast is someone who is rejected by other people.

outclassed (adjective) If you are outclassed, you are much worse than your opponent at a particular activity.

outcome, outcomes (noun) The outcome of something is the result of it, e.g. *the outcome of the election.*

outcrop, outcrops (noun) An outcrop is a large piece of rock that sticks out of the ground.

outcry, outcries (noun) If there is an outcry about something, a lot of people are angry about it, e.g. *a public outcry over alleged fraud.*

outdated (adjective) no longer in fashion.

outdo, outdoes, outdoing, outdid, outdone (verb) If you outdo someone, you do a particular thing better than they do.

outdoor (adjective) happening or used outside, e.g. *outdoor activities.*

outdoors (adverb) outside, e.g. *It was too chilly to sit outdoors.*

outer (adjective) The outer parts of something are the parts furthest from the centre, e.g. *the outer door of the office.*

outer space (noun) Outer space is everything beyond the Earth's atmosphere.

outfit, outfits 1 (noun) An outfit is a set of clothes. **2** (an informal use) An outfit is also an organization.

outgoing, outgoings 1 (adjective) Outgoing describes someone who is leaving a job or place, e.g. *the outgoing President.* **2** Someone who is outgoing is friendly and not shy. **3** (noun) Your outgoings are the amount of money that you spend.

outgrow, outgrows, outgrowing, outgrew, outgrown 1 (verb) If you outgrow a piece of clothing, you grow too big for it. **2** If you outgrow a way of behaving, you stop it because you have grown older and more mature.

outhouse, outhouses (noun) An outhouse is a small building in the grounds of a house to which it belongs.

outing, outings (noun) An outing is a pleasure trip.

outlandish (adjective) very unusual or odd, e.g. *outlandish clothes.*

outlaw, outlaws, outlawing, outlawed 1 (verb) If something is outlawed, it is made illegal. **2** (noun) In the past, an outlaw was a criminal.

outlay, outlays (noun) An outlay is an amount of money spent on something, e.g. *a cash outlay of £300.*

outlet, outlets 1 (noun) An outlet for your feelings or ideas is a way of expressing them. **2** An outlet is a hole or pipe through which water or air can flow away. **3** An outlet is also a shop which sells goods made by a particular manufacturer.

outline, outlines, outlining, outlined 1 (verb) If you outline a plan or idea, you explain it in a general way. **2** (noun) An outline is a general explanation or description of something. **3** (verb) You say that something is outlined when you can see its shape because there is a light behind it. **4** (noun) The outline of something is its shape.

outlive, outlives, outliving, outlived (verb) To outlive someone means to live longer than they do.

outlook 1 (noun) Your outlook is your general attitude towards life. **2** The outlook of a situation is the way it is likely to develop, e.g. *The British economy's outlook is uncertain.*

outlying (adjective) Outlying places are far from cities.

outmoded (adjective) old-fashioned and no longer useful, e.g. *an outmoded form of transport.*

outnumber, outnumbers, outnumbering, outnumbered (verb) If there are more of one group than of another, the first group outnumbers the second.

out of 1 (preposition) If you do something out of a particular feeling, you are motivated by that feeling, e.g. *Out of curiosity she went along.* **2** Out of also means from, e.g. *old instruments made out of wood.* **3** If you are out of something, you no longer have any of it, e.g. *I do hope we're not out of fuel again.* **4** If you are out of the rain, sun, or wind, you are sheltered from it. **5** You also use out of to indicate proportion. For example, one out of five means one in every five.

out of date (adjective) old-fashioned and no longer useful.

out of doors (adverb) outside, e.g. *Sometimes we eat out of doors.*

outpatient, outpatients (noun) Outpatients are people who receive treatment in hospital without staying overnight.

outpost, outposts (noun) An outpost is a small collection of buildings a long way from a main centre, e.g. *a remote mountain outpost.*

output, outputs 1 (noun) Output is the amount of something produced by a person or organization. **2** The output of a computer is the information that it produces.

outrage, outrages, outraging, outraged 1 (verb) If something outrages you, it angers and shocks you, e.g. *His claims outraged many women.* **2** (noun) Outrage is a feeling of anger and shock. **3** You can refer to something very shocking or violent as an outrage. **outrageous** (adjective), **outrageously** (adverb).

outright 1 (adjective) absolute, e.g. *an outright rejection.* **2** (adverb) in an open and direct way, e.g. *Have you asked him outright?* **3** completely and totally, e.g. *I own the company outright.*

outset (noun) The outset of something is the beginning of it, e.g. *the outset of his journey.*

outshine, outshines, outshining, outshone (verb) If you outshine someone, you perform better than they do.

outside 1 (noun) The outside of something is the part which surrounds or encloses the rest of it. **2** (adverb, adjective, or preposition) Outside means not inside, e.g. *houses just outside the airport... He stood outside and shouted... an outside toilet.* **3** Outside also means not included in something, e.g. *outside office hours.*

outsider, outsiders 1 (noun) An outsider is someone who does not belong to a particular group. **2** An outsider is also a competitor considered unlikely to win in a race.

outsize or **outsized** (adjective) much larger than usual, e.g. *outsize feet.*

outskirts (plural noun) The outskirts of a city or town are the parts around the edge of it.

outspoken (adjective) Outspoken people give their opinions openly, even if they shock other people.

outstanding 1 (adjective) extremely good, e.g. *The collection contains hundreds of outstanding works of art.* **2** Money that is outstanding is still owed, e.g. *an outstanding mortgage of £50,000.*

outstretched (adjective) If your arms are outstretched, they are stretched out as far as possible.

outstrip, outstrips, outstripping, outstripped (verb) If one thing outstrips another thing, it becomes bigger or more successful or moves faster than the other thing.

outward 1 (adjective or adverb) Outward means away from a place or towards the outside, e.g. *the outward journey.* **2** (adjective) The outward features of someone are the ones they appear to have, rather than the ones they actually have, e.g. *He never showed any outward signs of the stress he was under.* **outwardly** (adverb).

outwards (adverb) away from a place or towards the outside, e.g. *The door opened outwards.*

outweigh, outweighs, outweighing, outweighed (verb) If you say that the advantages of something outweigh its disadvantages, you mean that the advantages are more important than the disadvantages.

outwit, outwits, outwitting, outwitted (verb) If you outwit someone, you use your intelligence to defeat them.

oval, ovals 1 (noun) An oval is a round shape, similar to a circle but wider in one direction than the other. **2** (adjective) shaped like an oval, e.g. *an oval table.*

ovary, ovaries (pronounced **oh**-var-ree) (noun) A woman's ovaries are the two organs in her body that produce eggs.

ovation, ovations (noun) An ovation is a long burst of applause.

oven, ovens (noun) An oven is the part of a cooker that you use for baking or roasting food.

over, overs 1 (preposition) Over something means directly above it or covering it, e.g. *the picture over the fireplace.* **2** A view over an area is a view across that area, e.g. *The pool and terrace look out over the sea.* **3** If something is over a road or river it is on the opposite side of the road or river. **4** (adverb) Over is used to indicate a position, e.g. *over by the window... Come over here.* **5** If something rolls or turns over, it is moved so that its other side is facing upwards, e.g. *He flipped over the envelope.* **6** (preposition) Something that is over a particular amount is more than that amount. **7** (adjective) Something that is over is completely finished. **8** (preposition) Over indicates a topic which is causing concern, e.g. *An American was arguing over the bill.* **9** If something happens over a period of time, it happens during that period, e.g. *I went to New Zealand over Christmas.* **10** (adverb or preposition) If you lean over, you bend your body in a particular direction, e.g. *He bent over and rummaged in a drawer... She was hunched over her typewriter.* **11** (phrase) **All over** a place means everywhere in that place, e.g. *studios all over America.* **12** (noun) In cricket, an over is a set of six balls bowled by a bowler from the same end of the pitch.

over- (prefix) to too great an extent or too much, e.g. *overprotective parents... overindulging in chocolate.*

overall, overalls 1 (adjective or adverb) Overall means taking into account all the parts or aspects of something, e.g. *The overall quality of pupils' work had shown a marked improvement... Overall, things are not really too bad.* **2** (plural noun) Overalls are a piece of clothing that looks like trousers and a jacket combined. You wear overalls to protect your other clothes when you are working. **3** (noun) An overall is a piece of clothing like a coat that you wear to protect your other clothes when you are working.

overawed (adjective) If you are overawed by something, you are very impressed by it and a little afraid of it.

overbearing (adjective) trying to dominate other people, e.g. *Mozart had a difficult relationship with his overbearing father.*

overboard (adverb) If you fall overboard, you fall over the side of a ship into the water.

overcast (adjective) If it is overcast, the sky is covered by cloud.

overcoat, overcoats (noun) An overcoat is a thick, warm coat.

overcome, overcomes, overcoming, overcame, overcome 1 (verb) If you overcome a problem or a feeling, you manage to deal with it or control it. **2** (adjective) If you are overcome by a feeling, you feel it very strongly.

overcrowded (adjective) If a place is overcrowded, there are too many things or people in it.

overdo, overdoes, overdoing, overdid, overdone (verb) If you overdo something, you do it too much or in an exaggerated way, e.g. *It is important never to overdo new exercises.*

overdose, overdoses (noun) An overdose is a larger dose of a drug than is safe.

overdraft, overdrafts (noun) An overdraft is an agreement with a bank that allows someone to spend more money than they have in their account.

overdrawn (adjective) If someone is overdrawn, they have taken more money from their bank account than the account has in it.

overdrive (noun) Overdrive is an extra, higher gear in a vehicle, which is used at high speeds to reduce engine wear and save petrol.

overdue (adjective) If someone or something is overdue, they are late, e.g. *The payments are overdue.*

overestimate, overestimates, overestimating, overestimated (verb) If you overestimate something, you think that it is bigger, more important, or better than it really is, e.g. *We had overestimated his popularity.*

overflow, overflows, overflowing, overflowed, overflown (verb) If a liquid overflows, it spills over the edges of its container. If a river overflows, it flows over its banks.

overgrown (adjective) A place that is overgrown is covered with weeds because it has not been looked after, e.g. *an overgrown path.*

overhang, overhangs, overhanging, overhung (verb) If one thing overhangs another, it sticks out sideways above it, e.g. *old trees whose branches overhang a footpath.*

overhaul, overhauls, overhauling, overhauled 1 (verb) If you overhaul something, you examine it thoroughly and repair any faults. **2** (noun) If you give something an overhaul, you examine it and repair or improve it.

overhead, overheads 1 (adverb or adjective) Overhead means above you, e.g. *seagulls flying overhead.* **2** (plural noun) The overheads of a business are its regular and essential expenses.

overhear, overhears, overhearing, overheard (verb) If you overhear someone's conversation, you hear what they are saying to someone else.

overjoyed (adjective) extremely pleased, e.g. *Shelley was overjoyed to see me.*

overlaid (adjective) If something is overlaid by something else, it is covered by it.

overland (adjective or adverb) travelling across land rather than going by sea or air, e.g. *an overland trek to India... Wray was returning to England overland.*

overlap, overlaps, overlapping, overlapped (verb) If one thing overlaps another, one part of it covers part of the other thing.

overleaf (adverb) on the next page, e.g. *Write to us at the address shown overleaf.*

overload, overloads, overloading, overloaded (verb) If you overload someone or something, you give them too much to do or to carry.

overlook, overlooks, overlooking, overlooked 1 (verb) If a building or window overlooks a place, it has a view over that place. **2** If you overlook something, you ignore it, do not notice it, or do not realize its importance.

overly (adverb) excessively, e.g. *I'm not overly fond of jazz.*

overnight 1 (adjective or adverb) during the night, e.g. *Further rain was forecast overnight.* **2** (adjective) for use when you go away for one or two nights, e.g. *an overnight bag.* **3** (adjective or adverb) sudden or suddenly, e.g. *an overnight success... Good players don't become bad ones overnight.*

overpower, overpowers, overpowering, overpowered 1 (verb) If you overpower someone, you seize them despite their struggles, because you are stronger than them. **2** If a feeling overpowers you, it affects you very strongly. **overpowering** (adjective).

overrate, overrates, overrating, overrated (verb) If you overrate something, you think that it is better or more important than it really is. **overrated** (adjective).

overreact, overreacts, overreacting, overreacted (verb) If you overreact, you react in an extreme way.

overriding (adjective) more important than anything else, e.g. *an overriding duty.*

overrule, overrules, overruling, overruled (verb) To overrule a person or their decisions means to decide that their decisions are incorrect.

overrun, overruns, overrunning, overran, overrun 1 (verb) If an army overruns a country, it occupies it very quickly. **2** If animals or plants overrun a place, they spread quickly over it. **3** If an event overruns, it continues for longer than it was meant to.

overseas 1 (adjective or adverb) abroad, e.g. *an overseas tour... travelling overseas.* **2** (adjective) from abroad, e.g. *overseas students.*

oversee, oversees, overseeing, oversaw, overseen (verb) To oversee a job means to make sure it is done properly. **overseer** (noun).

overshadow, overshadows, overshadowing, overshadowed (verb) If something is overshadowed, it is made unimportant by something else that is better or more important.

oversight, oversights (noun) An oversight is something which you forget to do or fail to notice.

overspill (noun or adjective) Overspill refers to the rehousing of people from overcrowded cities in smaller towns, e.g. *an East End overspill... overspill estates.*

overstate, overstates, overstating, overstated (verb) If you overstate something, you exaggerate its importance.

overstep, oversteps, overstepping, overstepped (phrase) If you **overstep the mark,** you behave in an unacceptable way.

overt (adjective) open and obvious, e.g. *overt signs of stress.* **overtly** (adverb).

overtake, overtakes, overtaking, overtook, overtaken (verb) If you overtake someone, you pass them because you are moving faster than them.

overthrow, overthrows, overthrowing, overthrew, overthrown (verb) If a government is overthrown, it is removed from power by force.

overtime 1 (noun) Overtime is time that someone works in addition to their normal working hours. **2** (adverb) If someone works overtime, they do work in addition to their normal working hours.

overtones (plural noun) If something has overtones of an emotion or attitude, it suggests it without showing it openly, e.g. *the political overtones of the trial.*

overture, overtures 1 (noun) An overture is a piece of music that is the introduction to an opera or play. **2** If you make overtures to someone, you approach them because you want to start a friendly or business relationship with them.

overturn, overturns, overturning, overturned 1 (verb) To overturn something means to turn it upside down or onto its side. **2** If someone overturns a legal decision, they change it by using their higher authority.

overview, overviews (noun) An overview of a situation is a general understanding or description of it.

overweight (adjective) too fat, and therefore unhealthy, e.g. *overweight businessmen.*

overwhelm, overwhelms, overwhelming, overwhelmed 1 (verb) If you are overwhelmed by something, it affects you very strongly, e.g. *The priest appeared overwhelmed by the news.* **2** If one group of people overwhelm another, they gain complete control or victory over them. **overwhelming** (adjective), **overwhelmingly** (adverb).

overwork, overworks, overworking, overworked (verb) If you overwork, you work too hard.

overwrought (pronounced oh-ver-**rawt**) (adjective) extremely upset, e.g. *He didn't get angry or overwrought.*

ovulate, ovulates, ovulating, ovulated (pronounced **ov**-yool-late) (verb) When a woman or female animal ovulates, she produces ova or eggs from her ovary.

ovum, ova (pronounced **oh**-vum) (noun) An ovum is a reproductive cell of a woman or female animal. The ovum is fertilized by a male sperm to produce young.

owe, owes, owing, owed 1 (verb) If you owe someone money, they have lent it to you and you have not yet paid it back. **2** If you owe a quality or skill to someone, they are responsible for giving it to you, e.g. *He owes his success to his mother.* **3** If you say that you owe someone gratitude, respect, or loyalty, you mean that they deserve it from you.

owl, owls (noun) Owls are birds of prey that hunt at night. They have large eyes and short, hooked beaks.

own, owns, owning, owned 1 (adjective) If something is your own, it belongs to you or is associated with you, e.g. *She stayed in her own house.* **2** (verb) If you own something, it belongs to you. **3** (phrase) **On your own** means alone.

owner, owners (noun) The owner of something is the person it belongs to.

ownership (noun) If you have ownership of something, you own it, e.g. *He shared the ownership of a sailing dinghy.*

ox, oxen (noun) Oxen are cattle which are used for carrying or pulling things.

oxide, oxides (noun) An oxide is a compound of oxygen and another chemical element.

oxygen (noun) Oxygen is a colourless gas in the air. It makes up about 21% of the Earth's atmosphere. All animals and plants need oxygen to live, and things cannot burn without it.

oyster, oysters (noun) Oysters are large, flat shellfish. Some oysters can be eaten, and others produce pearls.

oz an abbreviation for 'ounces'.

ozone (noun) Ozone is a form of oxygen that is poisonous and has a strong smell. There is a layer of ozone high above the Earth's surface.

ozone layer (noun) The ozone layer is that part of the Earth's atmosphere that protects living things from the harmful radiation of the sun.

P p

p 1 p is an abbreviation for 'pence'. **2** p is also a written abbreviation for 'page'. The plural is pp.

pace, paces, pacing, paced 1 (noun) The pace of something is the speed at which it moves or happens. **2** A pace is a step. **3** (verb) If you pace up and down, you continually walk around because you are anxious or impatient.

pacemaker, pacemakers (noun) A pacemaker is a small electronic device put into someone's heart to control their heartbeat.

Pacific (pronounced pas-**sif**-ik) (noun) The Pacific is the ocean separating North and South America from Asia and Australia.

pacifist, pacifists (noun) A pacifist is someone who is opposed to all violence and war. **pacifism** (noun).

pacify, pacifies, pacifying, pacified (verb) If you pacify someone who is angry, you calm them.

pack, packs, packing, packed 1 (verb) If you pack, you put things neatly into a suitcase, bag, or box. **2** If people pack into a place, it becomes crowded with them. **3** (noun) A pack is a bag or rucksack carried on your back. **4** A pack of something is a packet or collection of it, e.g. *a pack of cigarettes.* **5** A pack of playing cards is a complete set. **6** A pack of dogs or wolves is a group of them.

package, packages (noun) A package is a small parcel. **packaged** (adjective).

packaging (noun) Packaging is the container or wrapping in which an item is sold or sent.

packed (adjective) very full, e.g. *The church was packed with people.*

packet, packets (noun) A packet is a thin cardboard box or paper container in which something is sold.

pact, pacts (noun) A pact is a formal agreement or treaty.

pad, pads, padding, padded 1 (noun) A pad is a thick, soft piece of material. **2** (verb) If you pad something, you put a pad inside it or over it to protect it or change its shape. **3** (noun) A pad of paper is a number of pieces of paper fixed together at one end. **4** The pads of an animal such as a cat or dog are the soft, fleshy parts on the bottom of its paws. **5** A pad is also a flat surface from which helicopters take off or rockets are launched. **6** (verb) If you pad around, you walk softly. **padding** (noun).

paddle, paddles, paddling, paddled 1 (noun) A paddle is a short pole with a broad blade at one or both ends, used to move a small boat or a canoe. **2** (verb) If someone paddles a boat, they move it using a paddle. **3** If you paddle, you walk in shallow water.

paddock, paddocks (noun) A paddock is a small field where horses are kept.

paddy, paddies (noun) A paddy or paddy field is an area in which rice is grown.

padlock, padlocks, padlocking, padlocked 1 (noun) A padlock is a detachable lock with a U-shaped bar attached to it. One end of this bar is released when the padlock is opened. **2** (verb) If you padlock something, you lock it with a padlock.

padre, padres (pronounced **pah**-dray) (noun) A padre is a priest, especially a chaplain to the armed forces.

paediatrician, paediatricians (pronounced pee-dee-ya-**trish**-n); also spelled **pediatrician** (noun) A paediatrician is a doctor who specializes in treating children.

paediatrics (pronounced pee-dee-**ya**-triks); also spelled **pediatrics** (noun) Paediatrics is the area of medicine which deals with children's diseases. **paediatric** (adjective).

pagan, pagans (pronounced **pay**-gan) **1** (adjective) involving beliefs and worship outside the main religions of the world, e.g. *pagan myths and cults.* **2** (noun) A pagan is someone who believes in a pagan religion. **paganism** (noun).

page, pages, paging, paged 1 (noun) A page is one side of one of the pieces of paper in a book or magazine; also the sheet of paper itself. **2** (verb) To page someone means to call their name out on a loudspeaker system to give them a message.

pageant, pageants (pronounced **paj**-jent) (noun) A pageant is a grand, colourful show or parade, especially one with a historical theme.

pagoda, pagodas (noun) A pagoda is a tall, elaborately decorated temple in China or Japan.

pail, pails (noun) A pail is a bucket.

pain, pains, paining, pained 1 (noun) Pain is an unpleasant feeling of physical hurt or deep unhappiness. **2** (verb) If something pains you, it makes you very unhappy. **painless** (adjective), **painlessly** (adverb).

painful (adjective) causing emotional or physical pain. **painfully** (adverb).

painkiller, painkillers (noun) A painkiller is a drug that reduces or stops pain.

painstaking (adjective) very careful and thorough, e.g. *years of painstaking research.*

paint, paints, painting, painted 1 (noun) Paint is a coloured liquid used to decorate buildings, or to make a picture. **2** (verb) If you paint something or paint a picture of it, you make a picture of it using paint. **3** When you paint something such as a wall, you cover it with paint. **painter** (noun), **painting** (noun).

pair, pairs, pairing, paired 1 (noun) You refer to two things as a pair when they are of the same type or do the same thing. **2** You use pair when referring to certain objects which have two main matching parts, e.g. *a pair of scissors.* **3** (verb) When people pair off, they become grouped in pairs.

Pakistani, Pakistanis (pronounced pah-kiss-**tah**-nee) **1** (adjective) belonging or relating to Pakistan. **2** (noun) A Pakistani is someone who comes from Pakistan.

pal, pals (noun; an informal word) Your pal is your friend.

palace, palaces (noun) A palace is a large, grand house, especially the official home of a king or queen, or bishop.

palatable (adjective) Palatable food tastes pleasant.

palate, palates (pronounced **pall**-lat) (noun) Your palate is the top of the inside of your mouth.

pale, paler, palest (adjective) rather white and without much colour or brightness.

Palestinian, Palestinians (noun) A Palestinian is an Arab from the region formerly called Palestine situated between the River Jordan and the Mediterranean.

palette, palettes (noun) A palette is a flat piece of wood on which an artist mixes colours.

pall, palls, palling, palled (rhymes with **fall**) **1** (verb) If something palls, it becomes less interesting or less enjoyable, e.g. *This record palls after ten minutes.* **2** (noun) A pall of smoke is a thick cloud of it. **3** A pall is a cloth covering a coffin.

palm, palms 1 (noun) A palm or palm tree is a tropical tree with no branches and a crown of long leaves. **2** The palm of your hand is the flat surface which your fingers bend towards.

Palm Sunday (noun) Palm Sunday is the Sunday before Easter.

palpable (adjective) obvious and easily sensed, e.g. *Happiness was palpable in the air.* **palpably** (adverb).

paltry (pronounced **pawl**-tree) (adjective) A paltry sum of money is a very small amount.

pamper, pampers, pampering, pampered (verb) If you pamper someone, you give them too much kindness and comfort.

pamphlet, pamphlets (noun) A pamphlet is a very thin book in paper covers giving information about something.

pan, pans (noun) A pan is a round metal container with a long handle, used for cooking things in on top of a cooker.

panacea, panaceas (pronounced pan-nass-**see**-ah) (noun) A panacea is something that is supposed to cure everything.

panache (pronounced pan-**nash**) (noun) Something that is done with panache is done confidently and stylishly.

pancake, pancakes (noun) A pancake is a thin, flat round of cooked batter.

pancreas, pancreases (pronounced **pang**-kree-ass) (noun) The pancreas is an organ in the body situated behind the stomach. It helps the body to digest food.

panda, pandas (noun) A panda or giant panda is a large animal rather like a bear that lives in China. It has black fur with large patches of white.

panda car, panda cars (noun) A panda car is a police patrol car.

pandemonium (pronounced pan-dim-**moan**-ee-um) (noun) Pandemonium is a state of noisy confusion, e.g. *scenes of pandemonium.*

pander, panders, pandering, pandered (verb) If you pander to someone, you do everything they want.

pane, panes (noun) A pane is a sheet of glass in a window.

panel, panels 1 (noun) A panel is a small group of people who are chosen to do something, e.g. *a panel of judges.* **2** A panel is also a flat piece of wood forming part of a larger object, e.g. *door panels.* **3** A control panel is a surface containing switches and instruments to operate a machine. **panelled** (adjective).

panelling (noun) Panelling is rectangular pieces of wood covering an inside wall.

pang, pangs (noun) A pang is a sudden strong feeling of sadness or pain.

panic, panics, panicking, panicked 1 (noun) Panic is a sudden overwhelming feeling of fear or anxiety. **2** (verb) If you panic, you become so afraid or anxious that you cannot act sensibly.

panorama, panoramas (noun) A panorama is an extensive view over a wide area of land, e.g. *a fine panorama over the hills.* **panoramic** (adjective).

pansy, pansies (noun) A pansy is a small garden flower with large round petals.

pant, pants, panting, panted (verb) If you pant, you breathe quickly and loudly through your mouth.

panther, panthers (noun) A panther is a large wild animal belonging to the cat family, especially the black leopard.

pantomime, pantomimes (noun) A pantomime is a musical play, usually based on a fairy story and performed at Christmas.

pantry, pantries (noun) A pantry is a small room where food is kept.

pants (plural noun) Pants are a piece of underwear with holes for your legs and elastic around the waist or hips.

paper, papers, papering, papered 1 (noun) Paper is a material made from wood pulp and used for writing on or wrapping things. **2** A paper is a newspaper. **3** (plural noun) Papers are official documents, for example a passport for identification. **4** (verb) If you paper a wall, you put wallpaper on it.

paperback, paperbacks (noun) A paperback is a book with a thin cardboard cover.

paperwork (noun) Paperwork is the part of a job that involves dealing with letters, reports, and records.

papier-mâché (pronounced pap-yay **mash**-shay) (noun) Papier-mâché is a hard substance made from mashed wet paper mixed with glue and moulded when moist to make things such as bowls and ornaments.

paprika (noun) Paprika is a red powder made from a kind of pepper.

par 1 (phrase) Something that is **on a par** with something else is similar in quality or amount, e.g. *This match was on a par with the German Cup Final.* **2** Something that is **below par** or **under par** is below its normal standard.

parable, parables (noun) A parable is a short story which makes a moral or religious point.

parachute, parachutes (pronounced **par**-rash-oot) (noun) A parachute is a circular piece of fabric attached by lines to a person or package to enable them to fall safely to the ground from an aircraft.

parade, parades, parading, paraded 1 (noun) A parade is a line of people or vehicles standing or moving together as a display. **2** (verb) When people parade, they walk together in a formal group as a display.

Paradise (noun) According to some religions, Paradise is a wonderful place where good people go when they die.

paradox, paradoxes (noun) Something that is a paradox contains two ideas that seem to contradict each other, e.g. *the paradox of having to drink in order to stay sober.* **paradoxical** (adjective).

paraffin (noun) Paraffin is a strong-smelling liquid which is used as a fuel.

paragon, paragons (noun) If you describe someone as a paragon, you mean that their behaviour is perfect in some way, e.g. *a paragon of elegance.*

paragraph, paragraphs (noun) A paragraph is a section of a piece of writing. Paragraphs begin on a new line.

parallel, parallels 1 (noun) Something that is a parallel to something else has similar qualities or features to it. **2** (adjective) If two lines are parallel, they are the same distance apart along the whole of their length.

parallelogram, parallelograms (noun) A parallelogram is a four-sided shape in which each side is parallel to the opposite side.

paralyse, paralyses, paralysing, paralysed (verb) If something paralyses you, it causes loss of feeling and movement in your body.

paralysis (pronounced par-**ral**-liss-iss) (noun) Paralysis is loss of the power to move.

paramedic, paramedics (pronounced par-ram-**med**-dik) (noun) A paramedic is a person who does some types of medical work, for example for the ambulance service.

parameter, parameters (pronounced par-**ram**-met-ter) (noun) A parameter is a factor or limit which affects the way something is done, e.g. *the general parameters set by the president.*

paramilitary (adjective) A paramilitary organization has a military structure but is not the official army of a country.

paramount (adjective) more important than anything else, e.g. *Safety is paramount.*

paranoia (pronounced par-ran-**noy**-ah) (noun) Paranoia is a mental illness in which someone believes that other people are trying to harm them.

paranoid (pronounced **par**-ran-noyd) (adjective) Someone who is paranoid believes wrongly that other people are trying to harm them.

parapet, parapets (noun) A parapet is a low wall along the edge of a bridge or roof.

paraphernalia (pronounced par-raf-fan-**ale**-yah) (noun) Someone's paraphernalia consists of all their belongings or equipment.

paraphrase, paraphrases, paraphrasing, paraphrased 1 (noun) A paraphrase of a piece of writing or speech is the same thing said in a different way, e.g. *a paraphrase of the popular song.* **2** (verb) If you paraphrase what someone has said, you express it in a different way.

parasite, parasites (noun) A parasite is a small animal or plant that lives on or inside a larger animal or plant. **parasitic** (adjective).

parasol, parasols (noun) A parasol is an object like an umbrella that provides shelter from the sun.

paratroops or **paratroopers** (plural noun) Paratroops are soldiers trained to be dropped by parachute.

parcel, parcels, parcelling, parcelled 1 (noun) A parcel is something wrapped up in paper. **2** (verb) If you parcel something up, you make it into a parcel.

parched 1 (adjective) If the ground is parched, it is very dry and in need of water. **2** If you are parched, you are very thirsty.

parchment (noun) Parchment is thick yellowish paper of very good quality.

pardon, pardons, pardoning, pardoned 1 You say **pardon** or **beg your pardon** to express surprise or apology, or when you have not heard what someone has said. **2** (verb) If you pardon someone, you forgive them for doing something wrong.

pare, pares, paring, pared (verb) When you pare fruit or vegetables, you cut off the skin.

parent, parents (noun) Your parents are your father and mother. **parental** (adjective).

parentage (noun) A person's parentage is their parents and ancestors.

parish, parishes (noun) A parish is an area with its own church and clergyman, and often its own elected council.

parishioner, parishioners (noun) A clergyman's parishioners are the people who live in his parish and attend his church.

parity (noun; a formal word) If there is parity between things, they are equal, e.g. *By 1943 the USA had achieved a rough parity of power with the British.*

park, parks, parking, parked 1 (noun) In a town, a park is a public area with grass and trees. **2** A park is also a private area of grass and trees around a large country house. **3** (verb) When someone parks a vehicle, they drive it into a position where it can be left. **parked** (adjective), **parking** (noun).

parliament, parliaments (noun) A country's parliament is the group of elected representatives who make its laws. **parliamentary** (adjective).

parlour, parlours (noun; an old-fashioned word) A parlour is a sitting room.

parochial (pronounced par-**roe**-key-yal) (adjective) concerned only with local matters, e.g. *narrow parochial interests.*

parody, parodies, parodying, parodied 1 (noun) A parody is an amusing imitation of the style of an author or of a familiar situation. **2** (verb) If you parody something, you make a parody of it.

parole (noun) When prisoners are given parole, they are released early on condition that they behave well.

parrot, parrots (noun) A parrot is a brightly coloured tropical bird with a curved beak.

parry, parries, parrying, parried **1** (verb) If you parry a question, you cleverly avoid answering it, e.g. *Ryle had parried some curious inquiries.* **2** If you parry a blow, you push aside your attacker's arm to defend yourself.

parsley (noun) Parsley is a herb with curly leaves.

parsnip, parsnips (noun) A parsnip is a long, pointed, cream root vegetable.

parson, parsons (noun) A parson is a vicar or other clergyman.

part, parts, parting, parted **1** (noun) A part of something is one of the pieces, sections, or aspects that it consists of. **2** A part in a play or film is one of the roles in it, played by an actor or actress. **3** Someone's part in something is their involvement in it, e.g. *He was jailed for eleven years for his part in the plot.* **4** (phrase) If you **take part** in an activity, you do it together with other people. **5** (verb) If things that are next to each other part, they move away from each other. **6** If two people part, they leave each other.

partake, partakes, partaking, partook, partaken (verb; a formal word) If you partake of food, you eat it, e.g. *The congregation will be partaking of real wholemeal bread.*

partial **1** (adjective) not complete or whole, e.g. *a partial explanation... partial success.* **2** liking something very much, e.g. *I'm very partial to marigolds.* **3** supporting one side in a dispute, rather than being fair and unbiased. **partially** (adverb).

participate, participates, participating, participated (verb) If you participate in an activity, you take part in it. **participant** (noun), **participation** (noun).

participle, participles (noun) In grammar, a participle is a form of a verb used in compound tenses and often as an adjective. English has two participles: the past participle and the present participle.

particle, particles (noun) A particle is a very small piece of something.

particular, particulars **1** (adjective) relating or belonging to only one thing or person, e.g. *That particular place is dangerous.* **2** especially great or intense, e.g. *Pay particular attention to the forehead.* **3** Someone who is particular demands high standards and is not easily satisfied. **4** (plural noun) Particulars are facts or details. **particularly** (adverb).

parting, partings (noun) A parting is an occasion when one person leaves another.

partisan, partisans **1** (adjective) favouring or supporting one person or group, e.g. *a partisan crowd.* **2** (noun) A partisan is a member of an unofficial armed force fighting to free their country from enemy occupation, e.g. *Norwegian partisans.*

partition, partitions, partitioning, partitioned **1** (noun) A partition is a screen separating one part of a room or vehicle from another. **2** Partition is the division of a country into independent areas. **3** (verb) To partition something means to divide it into separate parts.

partly (adverb) to some extent but not completely.

partner, partners, partnering, partnered 1 (noun) Someone's partner is the person they are married to or are having a sexual relationship with. **2** Your partner is the person you are doing something with, for example in a dance or a game. **3** Business partners are joint owners of their business. **4** (verb) If you partner someone, you are their partner for a game or social occasion. **partnership** (noun).

part of speech, parts of speech (noun) A part of speech is a particular grammatical class of word.

partook the past tense of **partake.**

partridge, partridges (noun) A partridge is a brown game bird with a round body.

part-time (adjective) involving work for only a part of each normal working day or week.

party, parties 1 (noun) A party is a private social event held for people to enjoy themselves. **2** A political party is an organization whose members share the same political beliefs and campaign for election to government. **3** A party of people is a group who are doing something together.

pass, passes, passing, passed 1 (verb) To pass something means to move past it. **2** To pass in a particular direction means to move in that direction, e.g. *We passed through the gate.* **3** If you pass something to someone, you hand it to them or transfer it to them. **4** If you pass a period of time doing something, you spend it that way, e.g. *He hoped to pass the long night in meditation.* **5** When a period of time passes, it happens and finishes. **6** If you pass a test, you are considered to be of an acceptable standard. **7** When a new law or proposal is passed, it is formally approved. **8** When a judge passes sentence on someone, the judge states what the punishment will be. **9** If you pass the ball in a ball game, you throw, kick, or hit it to another player in your team. **10** (noun) A pass in a ball game is the transfer of the ball to another player in the same team. **11** A pass is an official document that allows you to go somewhere. **12** A mountain pass is a narrow route between mountains. **pass away** or **pass on** (verb) Someone who has passed away has died. **pass out** (verb) If someone passes out, they faint.

passable (adjective) of an acceptable standard, e.g. *a passable imitation of his dad.*

passage, passages 1 (noun) A passage is a long, narrow corridor or space that connects two places. **2** A passage in a book or piece of music is a section of it.

passé (pronounced **pas**-say) (adjective) no longer fashionable.

passenger, passengers (noun) A passenger is a person travelling in a vehicle, aircraft, or ship.

passer-by, passers-by (noun) A passer-by is someone who is walking past someone or something.

passing (adjective) lasting only for a short time, e.g. *a passing phase.*

passion, passions (noun) Passion is a very strong feeling, especially of sexual attraction.

passionate (adjective) expressing very strong feelings about something. **passionately** (adverb).

passive 1 (adjective) remaining calm and showing no feeling when provoked. **2** (noun) In grammar, the passive or passive voice is the form of the verb in which the recipient of an action becomes the grammatical subject of the sentence. For example, the passive of *The committee rejected your application* is *Your application was rejected by the committee.* **passively** (adverb), **passivity** (noun).

Passover (noun) The Passover is an eight day Jewish festival held in spring.

passport, passports (noun) A passport is an official identification document which you need to show when you travel abroad.

password, passwords 1 (noun) A password is a secret word known to only a few people. It allows people on the same side to recognize a friend. **2** A password is also a word you need to know to get into some computer files.

past 1 (noun) The past is the period of time before the present. **2** (adjective) Past things are things that happened or existed before the present, e.g. *the past 30 years.* **3** (preposition or adverb) You use past when you are telling the time, e.g. *It was ten past eleven.* **4** If you go past something, you move towards it and continue until you are on the other side, e.g. *They drove rapidly past their cottage.* **5** (preposition) Something that is past a place is situated on the other side of it, e.g. *It's just past the church there.*

pasta (noun) Pasta is a dried mixture of flour, eggs, and water, formed into different shapes.

paste, pastes, pasting, pasted 1 (noun) Paste is a soft, rather sticky mixture that can be easily spread, e.g. *tomato paste.* **2** (verb) If you paste something onto a surface, you stick it with glue.

pastel (adjective) Pastel colours are pale and soft.

pasteurized (pronounced **past**-yoor-ized); also spelled **pasteurised** (adjective) Pasteurized milk has been treated with a special heating process to kill bacteria.

pastime, pastimes (noun) A pastime is a hobby or something you do just for pleasure.

pastor, pastors (noun) A pastor is a clergyman in charge of a congregation.

pastoral 1 (adjective) characteristic of peaceful country life and landscape, e.g. *pastoral scenes.* **2** relating to the duties of the clergy in caring for the needs of their parishioners, e.g. *a pastoral visit,*

past participle, past participles

(noun) In grammar, the past participle of a verb is the form, usually ending in 'ed' or 'en', that is used to make some past tenses and the passive, e.g. *killed... broken.*

pastry, pastries 1 (noun) Pastry is a mixture of flour, fat, and water, rolled flat and used for making pies. **2** A pastry is a small cake.

past tense (noun) In grammar, the past tense is the tense of a verb that you use mainly to refer to things that happened or existed before the time of writing or speaking.

pasture, pastures (noun) Pasture is an area of grass on which farm animals graze.

pasty, pasties 1 (adjective; rhymes with **hasty**) Someone who is pasty looks pale and unhealthy. **2** (noun; pronounced **pass**-tee) A pasty is a small pie containing meat and vegetables.

pat, pats, patting, patted 1 (verb) If you pat something, you tap it lightly with your hand held flat. **2** (noun) A pat of butter is a small lump of it.

patch, patches, patching, patched 1 (noun) A patch is a piece of material used to cover a hole in something. **2** (verb) If you patch something, you mend it by fixing a patch over the hole. **3** (noun) A patch is an area of a surface that is different in appearance from the rest, e.g. *a bald patch.*

patchwork (adjective) **1** A patchwork quilt is made from many small pieces of material sewn together. **2** Something that is a patchwork is made up of many parts.

patchy, patchier, patchiest (adjective) Something that is patchy is unevenly spread, e.g. *patchy fog on the hills.*

pâté (pronounced **pa**-tay) (noun) Pâté is a mixture of meat, fish, or vegetables blended into a paste and spread on bread or toast.

patent, patents, patenting, patented 1 (noun) A patent is an official right given to an inventor to be the only person or company allowed to make or sell a new product. **2** (verb) If you patent something, you obtain a patent for it. **3** (adjective) obvious, e.g. *This was patent nonsense.* **patently** (adverb).

paternal (adjective) relating to a father, e.g. *paternal pride.*

paternity (noun) Paternity is the state of being a father.

path, paths 1 (noun) A path is a strip of ground for people to walk on. **2** Your path is the area ahead of you and the direction in which you are moving.

pathetic 1 (adjective) If something is pathetic, it makes you feel pity. **2** Pathetic also means very poor or unsuccessful, e.g. *a pathetic attempt.* **pathetically** (adverb).

pathological (adjective) extreme and uncontrollable, e.g. *a pathological fear of snakes.* **pathologically** (adverb).

pathology (noun) Pathology is the study of diseases and the way they develop. **pathologist** (noun).

pathos (pronounced **pay**-thoss) (noun) Pathos is a quality in literature or art that causes great sadness or pity.

pathway, pathways (noun) A pathway is a path.

patience (noun) Patience is the ability to stay calm in a difficult situation.

patient, patients 1 (adjective) If you are patient, you stay calm in a difficult situation. **2** (noun) A patient is a person receiving medical treatment from a doctor or in a hospital. **patiently** (adverb).

patio, patios (noun) A patio is a paved area close to a house.

patriarch, patriarchs (pronounced **pay**-tree-ark) (noun) A patriarch is the male head of a family or tribe. **patriarchal** (adjective).

patrician (adjective; a formal word) belonging to a family of high rank.

patriot, patriots (noun) A patriot is someone who loves their country and feels very loyal towards it. **patriotic** (adjective), **patriotism** (noun).

patrol, patrols, patrolling, patrolled 1 (verb) When soldiers, police, or guards patrol an area, they walk or drive around to make sure there is no trouble. **2** (noun) A patrol is a group of people patrolling an area.

patron, patrons 1 (noun) A patron is a person who supports or gives money to artists, writers, or musicians. **2** The patrons of a hotel, pub, or shop are the people who use it. **patronage** (noun).

patronize, patronizes, patronizing, patronized; also spelled **patronise 1** (verb) If someone patronizes you, they treat you kindly, but in a way that suggests that you are less intelligent than them or inferior to them. **2** If you patronize a hotel, pub, or shop, you are a customer there. **patronizing** (adjective).

patron saint, patron saints (noun) The patron saint of a group of people, place, or activity is a saint who is believed to look after them.

patter, patters, pattering, pattered 1 (verb) If something patters on a surface, it makes quick, light, tapping sounds. **2** (noun) A patter is a series of light tapping sounds, e.g. *a patter of light rain.*

pattern, patterns 1 (noun) A pattern is a decorative design of repeated shapes. **2** The pattern of something is the way it is usually done or happens, e.g. *a perfectly normal pattern of behaviour.* **3** A pattern is also a diagram or shape used as a guide for making something, for example clothes. **patterned** (adjective).

paunch, paunches (noun) If a man has a paunch, he has a fat stomach.

pauper, paupers (noun; an old-fashioned word) A pauper is a very poor person.

pause, pauses, pausing, paused 1 (verb) If you pause, you stop what you are doing for a short time. **2** (noun) A pause is a short period when you stop what you are doing. **3** A pause is also a short period of silence.

pave, paves, paving, paved (verb) When an area of ground is paved, it is covered with flat, regular blocks of stone or concrete.

pavement, pavements (noun) A pavement is a path with a hard surface at the side of a road.

pavilion, pavilions (noun) A pavilion is a building at a sports ground where players can wash and change.

paw, paws, pawing, pawed 1 (noun) The paws of an animal such as a cat or bear are its feet with claws and soft pads. **2** (verb) If an animal paws something, it hits it or scrapes at it with its paws.

pawn, pawns, pawning, pawned 1 (verb) If you pawn something, you leave it with a pawnbroker as security for a loan. **2** (noun) In chess, a pawn is the smallest and least valuable playing piece.

pawnbroker, pawnbrokers (noun) A pawnbroker is a dealer who lends money in return for personal property left with him or her, which may be sold if the loan is not repaid on time.

pay, pays, paying, paid 1 (verb) When you pay money to someone, you give it to them because you are buying something or owe it to them. **2** (noun) Someone's pay is their salary or wages. **3** (verb) If it pays to do something, it is to your advantage to do it, e.g. *They say it pays to advertise.* **4** If you pay attention to something, you give it your attention. **5** If you pay a visit to someone, you visit them.

payable 1 (adjective) An amount of money that is payable has to be paid or can be paid, e.g. *All fees are payable in advance.* **2** If a cheque is made payable to you, you are the person who should receive the money.

payment, payments 1 (noun) Payment is the act of paying money. **2** A payment is a sum of money paid.

payroll, payrolls (noun) Someone who is on an organization's payroll is employed and paid by them.

PC, PCs 1 (noun) A PC is a police constable. **2** A PC is also a personal computer.

PE (noun) PE is a lesson in which gymnastics or sports are taught. PE is an abbreviation for 'physical education'.

pea, peas (noun) Peas are small round green seeds that grow in pods and are eaten.

peace 1 (noun) Peace is a state of undisturbed calm and quiet. **2** When a country is at peace, it is not at war. **peaceable** (adjective).

peaceful (adjective) quiet, calm, and free from disturbance. **peacefully** (adverb).

peach, peaches 1 (noun) A peach is a soft, round, juicy fruit with yellow flesh and a yellow and red skin. **2** (adjective) pale pinky-orange.

peacock, peacocks (noun) A peacock is a large bird with green and blue feathers. The male has a long tail which it can spread out in a fan.

peak, peaks, peaking, peaked 1 (noun) The peak of an activity or process is the point at which it is strongest or most successful. **2** (verb) When something peaks, it reaches its highest value or its greatest level of success. **3** (noun) The peak of a mountain is its pointed top. **peaked** (adjective).

peal, peals, pealing, pealed 1 (noun) A peal of bells is the musical sound made by bells ringing one after another. **2** (verb) When bells peal, they ring one after the other.

peanut, peanuts (noun) Peanuts are small oval nuts that grow under the ground.

pear, pears (noun) A pear is a fruit which is narrow at the top and wide and rounded at the bottom.

pearl, pearls (noun) A pearl is a hard, round, creamy-white object used in jewellery. Pearls grow inside oysters.

peasant, peasants (noun) A peasant is a person who works on the land, especially in a poor country.

peat (noun) Peat is dark-brown decaying plant material found in cool, wet regions. Dried peat can be used as fuel.

pebble, pebbles (noun) A pebble is a smooth, round stone.

peck, pecks, pecking, pecked 1 (verb) If a bird pecks something, it bites at it quickly with its beak. **2** If you peck someone on the cheek, you give them a quick kiss. **3** (noun) A peck is a quick bite by a bird. **4** A peck is also a quick kiss on the cheek.

peculiar 1 (adjective) strange and perhaps unpleasant. **2** relating or belonging only to a particular person or thing, e.g. *a lentil soup peculiar to the town.* **peculiarly** (adverb), **peculiarity** (noun).

pedal, pedals, pedalling, pedalled 1 (noun) A pedal is a control lever on a machine or vehicle that you press with your foot. **2** (verb) When you pedal a bicycle, you push the pedals round with your feet to move along.

pedantic (adjective) If a person is pedantic, they are too concerned with unimportant details and traditional rules.

peddle, peddles, peddling, peddled (verb) Someone who peddles illegal drugs sells them.

pedestal, pedestals (noun) A pedestal is a base on which a statue stands.

pedestrian, pedestrians 1 (noun) A pedestrian is someone who is walking. **2** (adjective) Pedestrian means ordinary and rather dull, e.g. *the pedestrian plot.*

pedestrian crossing, pedestrian crossings (noun) A pedestrian crossing is a specially marked place where you can cross the road safely.

pedigree, pedigrees 1 (adjective) A pedigree animal is descended from a single breed and its ancestors are known and recorded. **2** (noun) Someone's pedigree is their background or ancestry.

peek, peeks, peeking, peeked 1 (verb) If you peek at something, you have a quick look at it, e.g. *I peeked round the corner.* **2** (noun) A peek is a quick look at something.

peel, peels, peeling, peeled 1 (noun) The peel of a fruit is the skin when it has been removed. **2** (verb) When you peel fruit or vegetables, you remove the skin. **3** If a surface is peeling, it is coming off in thin layers. **peelings** (plural noun).

peep, peeps, peeping, peeped 1 (verb) If you peep at something, you have a quick look at it. **2** (noun) A peep at something is a quick look. **3** (verb) If something peeps out from behind something else, a small part of it becomes visible, e.g. *a handkerchief peeping out of his pocket.*

peer, peers, peering, peered 1 (verb) If you peer at something, you look at it very hard. **2** (noun) A peer is a member of the nobility. **3** Your peers are the people who are of the same age and social status as yourself.

peerage, peerages 1 (noun) The peers in a country are called the peerage. **2** A peerage is also the rank of being a peer.

peerless (adjective) so magnificent or perfect that nothing can equal it, e.g. *peerless wines.*

peg, pegs, pegging, pegged 1 (noun) A peg is a plastic or wooden clip used for hanging wet clothes on a line. **2** (verb) If you peg clothes on a line, you fix them there with pegs. **3** (noun) A peg is also a hook on a wall where you can hang things. **4** (verb) If a price is pegged at a certain level, it is fixed at that level.

pejorative (pronounced pej-**jor**-ra-tiv) (adjective) A pejorative word expresses criticism.

pekinese, pekineses; also spelled **pekingese** (pronounced pee-kin-**eez**) (noun) A pekinese is a small long-haired dog with a flat nose.

pelican, pelicans (noun) A pelican is a large water bird with a pouch beneath its beak in which it stores fish.

pellet, pellets (noun) A pellet is a small ball of paper, lead, or other material.

pelt, pelts, pelting, pelted 1 (verb) If you pelt someone with things, you throw the things violently at them. **2** If you pelt along, you run very fast. **3** (noun) A pelt is the skin and fur of an animal.

pelvis, pelvises (noun) Your pelvis is the wide, curved group of bones at hip-level at the base of your spine. **pelvic** (adjective).

pen, pens, penning, penned 1 (noun) A pen is a long, thin instrument used for writing with ink. **2** (verb; a literary use) If someone pens a letter or article, they write it. **3** (noun) A pen is also a small fenced area in which farm animals are kept for a short time. **4** (verb) If you are penned in or penned up, you have to remain in an uncomfortably small area.

penal (adjective) relating to the punishment of criminals.

penalize, penalizes, penalizing, penalized; also spelled **penalise** (verb) If you are penalized, you are made to suffer some disadvantage as a punishment for something.

penalty, penalties 1 (noun) A penalty is a punishment or disadvantage that someone is made to suffer. **2** In sports such as football, a penalty is a free kick at goal that is given to the attacking team if the defending team have committed a foul near their goal.

penance (noun) If you do penance, you do something unpleasant to show that you are sorry for something wrong that you have done.

pence a plural form of **penny**.

penchant (pronounced **pon**-shon) (noun; a formal word) If you have a penchant for something, you have a particular liking for it, e.g. *a penchant for crime.*

pencil, pencils (noun) A pencil is a long thin stick of wood with graphite in the centre, used for drawing or writing.

pendant, pendants (noun) A pendant is a piece of jewellery attached to a chain and worn round the neck.

pending (a formal word) **1** (adjective) Something that is pending is waiting to be dealt with or will happen soon. **2** (preposition) Something that is done pending a future event is done until the event happens, e.g. *The army should stay in the west pending a future war.*

pendulum, pendulums (noun) A pendulum in a clock is a rod with a weight at one end which swings from side to side to control the clock.

penetrate, penetrates, penetrating, penetrated (verb) To penetrate an area that is difficult to get into means to succeed in getting into it. **penetration** (noun).

penetrating 1 (adjective) loud and high-pitched, e.g. *a penetrating voice.* **2** having or showing deep understanding, e.g. *penetrating questions.*

pen friend, pen friends (noun) A pen friend is someone living in a different place or country whom you write to regularly, although you may never have met each other.

penguin, penguins (noun) A penguin is a black and white bird with webbed feet and small wings like flippers.

penicillin (noun) Penicillin is a powerful antibiotic obtained from fungus and used to treat infections.

peninsula, peninsulas (noun) A peninsula is an area of land almost surrounded by water.

penis, penises (noun) A man's penis is the part of his body that he uses when urinating and having sexual intercourse.

penitent (adjective) Someone who is penitent is deeply sorry for having done something wrong. **penitence** (noun).

penknife, penknives (noun) A penknife is a small knife with a blade that folds back into the handle.

pennant, pennants (noun) A pennant is a triangular flag.

penniless (adjective) Someone who is penniless has no money.

penny, pennies or **pence** (noun) The penny is a unit of currency in Britain and some other countries. In Britain, a penny is worth one-hundredth of a pound.

pension, pensions (pronounced **pen**-shn) (noun) A pension is a regular sum of money paid to an old, retired, or widowed person.

pensioner, pensioners (noun) A pensioner is an old retired person receiving a pension paid by the state.

pensive (adjective) deep in thought.

pentagon, pentagons (noun) A pentagon is a shape with five straight sides.

pentathlon, pentathlons (pronounced pen-**tath**-lon) (noun) A pentathlon is a sports contest in which athletes compete in five different events.

penthouse, penthouses (noun) A penthouse is a luxurious flat at the top of a building.

pent-up (adjective) Pent-up emotions have been held back for a long time without release.

penultimate (adjective) The penultimate thing in a series is the one before the last.

peony, peonies (pronounced **pee**-yon-ee) (noun) A peony is a garden plant with large pink, white, or red flowers.

people, peoples, peopling, peopled 1 (plural noun) People are men, women, and children. **2** (noun) A people is all the men, women, and children of a particular country or race. **3** (verb) If an area is peopled by a particular group, that group of people live there.

pepper, peppers 1 (noun) Pepper is a hot-tasting powdered spice used for flavouring in cooking. **2** A pepper is a hollow green, red, or yellow vegetable, with mild, sweet-flavoured flesh.

peppermint, peppermints (noun) Peppermint is a plant with a strong taste. It is used for making sweets.

per (preposition) Per is used to mean 'each' when expressing rates and ratios, e.g. *The class meets two evenings per week.*

perceive, perceives, perceiving, perceived (verb) If you perceive something that is not obvious, you see it or realize it.

per cent (phrase) You use **per cent** to talk about amounts as a proportion of a hundred. An amount that is 10 per cent (10%) of a larger amount is equal to 10 hundredths of the larger amount, e.g. *86 per cent of Americans believe Presley is alive.*

percentage, percentages (noun) A percentage is a fraction expressed as a number of hundredths, e.g. *the high percentage of failed marriages.*

perceptible (adjective) Something that is perceptible can be seen, e.g. *a barely perceptible nod.*

perception, perceptions 1 (noun) Perception is the recognition of things using the senses, especially the sense of sight. **2** Someone who has perception realizes or notices things that are not obvious. **3** Your perception of something or someone is your understanding of them.

perceptive (adjective) Someone who is perceptive realizes or notices things that are not obvious.

perch, perches, perching, perched 1 (verb) If you perch on something, you sit on the edge of it. **2** When a bird perches on something, it stands on it. **3** (noun) A perch is a short rod for a bird to stand on. **4** A perch is also an edible freshwater fish.

percolator, percolators (noun) A percolator is a special pot for making and serving coffee.

percussion (noun or adjective) Percussion instruments are musical instruments that you hit to produce sounds. **percussionist** (noun).

perennial (adjective) continually occurring or never ending, e.g. *a perennial problem.*

perfect, perfects, perfecting, perfected 1 (adjective) of the highest standard and without fault, e.g. *His English was perfect.* **2** complete or absolute, e.g. *They have a perfect right to say so.* **3** In English grammar, the perfect tense of a verb is formed with the present tense of 'have' and the past participle of the main verb, e.g. *I have lost my home.* **4** (verb) If you perfect something, you make it as good as it can possibly be. **perfectly** (adverb), **perfection** (noun).

perfectionist, perfectionists (noun) Someone who is a perfectionist always tries to do everything perfectly.

perforated (adjective) Something that is perforated has had small holes made in it. **perforation** (noun).

perform, performs, performing, performed 1 (verb) To perform a task, action, or service means to do it. **2** To perform means to act, dance, or play music in front of an audience. **performer** (noun).

performance, performances 1 (noun) A performance is an entertainment provided for an audience. **2** The performance of a task or action is the doing of it. **3** Someone's or something's performance is how successful they are, e.g. *the poor performance of the American economy.*

perfume, perfumes 1 (noun) Perfume is a pleasant-smelling liquid which women put on their bodies. **2** The perfume of something is its pleasant smell. **perfumed** (adjective).

perfunctory (adjective) done quickly without interest or care, e.g. *a perfunctory kiss.*

perhaps (adverb) You use perhaps when you are not sure whether something is true, possible, or likely.

peril, perils (noun; a formal word) Peril is great danger. **perilous** (adjective), **perilously** (adverb).

perimeter, perimeters (noun) The perimeter of an area is the whole of its outer edge.

period, periods 1 (noun) A period is a particular length of time. **2** At school, a period is one of the parts the day is divided into. **3** A woman's period is the monthly bleeding from her womb. **4** (adjective) relating to a historical period of time, e.g. *period furniture.* **periodic** (adjective), **periodically** (adverb).

periodical, periodicals (noun) A periodical is a magazine.

peripheral (pronounced per-**rif**-fer-ral) **1** (adjective) of little importance in comparison with other things, e.g. *a peripheral activity.* **2** on or relating to the edge of an area.

periphery, peripheries (noun) The periphery of an area is its outside edge.

perish, perishes, perishing, perished 1 (verb; a formal use) If someone or something perishes, they are killed or destroyed. **2** If fruit, rubber, or fabric perishes, it rots. **perishable** (adjective).

perjury (noun; a formal or legal word) If someone commits perjury, they tell a lie in court while under oath. **perjure** (verb).

perk, perks, perking, perked **1** (noun) A perk is an extra, such as a company car, offered by an employer in addition to a salary. Perk is an abbreviation of 'perquisite'. **2** (verb; an informal expression) When someone perks up, they become more cheerful. **perky** (adjective).

perm, perms, perming, permed **1** (noun) If you have a perm, your hair is curled and treated with chemicals to keep the curls for several months. **2** (verb) To perm someone's hair means to put a perm in it.

permanent (adjective) lasting for ever, or present all the time. **permanently** (adverb), **permanence** (noun).

permeate, permeates, permeating, permeated (verb) To permeate something means to spread through it and affect every part of it, e.g. *The feeling of failure permeates everything I do.*

permissible (adjective) allowed by the rules.

permission (noun) If you have permission to do something, you are allowed to do it.

permissive (adjective) A permissive society allows things which some people disapprove of, especially freedom in sexual behaviour. **permissiveness** (noun).

permit, permits, permitting, permitted **1** (verb) To permit something means to allow it or make it possible. **2** (noun) A permit is an official document which says that you are allowed to do something.

permutation, permutations (noun) A permutation is one possible arrangement of a number of things.

pernicious (adjective; a formal word) very harmful, e.g. *the pernicious influence of TV.*

peroxide (noun) Peroxide is a chemical used for bleaching hair or as an antiseptic.

perpendicular (adjective) upright, or at right angles to a horizontal line.

perpetrate, perpetrates, perpetrating, perpetrated (verb; a formal word) To perpetrate a crime means to commit it. **perpetrator** (noun).

perpetual (adjective) never ending, e.g. *a perpetual toothache.* **perpetually** (adverb), **perpetuity** (noun).

perpetuate, perpetuates, perpetuating, perpetuated (verb) To perpetuate a situation or belief means to cause it to continue, e.g. *The TV series will perpetuate the myths.*

perplexed (adjective) If you are perplexed, you are puzzled and do not know what to do.

persecute, persecutes, persecuting, persecuted (verb) To persecute someone means to treat them with continual cruelty and unfairness. **persecution** (noun), **persecutor** (noun).

persevere, perseveres, persevering, persevered (verb) If you persevere, you keep trying to do something and do not give up. **perseverance**

(noun).

Persian (pronounced **per**-shn) (adjective or noun) an old word for **Iranian**.

persist, persists, persisting, persisted 1 (verb) If something undesirable persists, it continues to exist. **2** If you persist in doing something, you continue in spite of opposition or difficulty. **persistence** (noun), **persistent** (adjective).

person, people or **persons 1** (noun) A person is a man, woman, or child. **2** In grammar, the first person is the speaker, the second person is the person being spoken to, and the third person is anyone else being referred to.

personal 1 (adjective) Personal means belonging or relating to a particular person rather than to people in general, e.g. *my personal feeling.* **2** Personal matters relate to your feelings, relationships, and health which you may not wish to discuss with other people. **personally** (adverb).

personality, personalities 1 (noun) Your personality is your character and nature. **2** You can refer to a famous person in entertainment or sport as a personality.

personify, personifies, personifying, personified (verb) Someone who personifies a particular quality seems to be a living example of it, e.g. *Louis personified the romance of the age.* **personification** (noun).

personnel (pronounced per-son-**nell**) (noun) The personnel of an organization are the people who work for it.

perspective, perspectives (noun) A particular perspective is one way of thinking about something.

perspiration (noun) Perspiration is the moisture that appears on your skin when you are hot or frightened.

perspire, perspires, perspiring, perspired (verb) If someone perspires, they sweat.

persuade, persuades, persuading, persuaded (verb) If someone persuades you to do something or persuades you that something is true, they make you do it or believe it by giving you very good reasons. **persuasion** (noun), **persuasive** (adjective).

pertaining (adjective; a formal word) If information or questions are pertaining to a place or thing, they are about that place or thing, e.g. *issues pertaining to women.*

pertinent (adjective) especially relevant to the subject being discussed, e.g. *He asks pertinent questions.*

perturbed (adjective) Someone who is perturbed is worried.

Peruvian, Peruvians (pronounced per-**roo**-vee-an) **1** (adjective) belonging or relating to Peru. **2** (noun) A Peruvian is someone who comes from Peru.

pervade, pervades, pervading, pervaded (verb) Something that pervades a place is present and noticeable throughout it, e.g. *a fear that pervades the community.* **pervasive** (adjective).

perverse (adjective) Someone who is perverse deliberately does things that are unreasonable or harmful. **perversely**

(adverb), **perversity** (noun).

pervert, perverts, perverting, perverted 1 (verb; a formal use) To pervert something means to interfere with it so that it is no longer what it should be, e.g. *a conspiracy to pervert the course of justice.* **2** (noun) A pervert is a person whose sexual behaviour is disgusting or harmful. **perversion** (noun).

perverted 1 (adjective) Someone who is perverted has disgusting or unacceptable behaviour or ideas, especially sexual behaviour or ideas. **2** Something that is perverted is completely wrong, e.g. *a perverted sense of value.*

peseta, pesetas (pronounced pes-**say**-ta) (noun) The peseta is the main unit of currency in Spain.

peso, pesos (pronounced **pay**-soh) (noun) The peso is the main unit of currency in some South American countries.

pessimism (noun) Pessimism is the tendency to believe that bad things will happen. **pessimist** (noun), **pessimistic** (adjective).

pest, pests 1 (noun) A pest is an insect or small animal which damages plants or food supplies. **2** Someone who is a pest keeps bothering or annoying you.

pester, pesters, pestering, pestered (verb) If you pester someone, you keep bothering them or asking them to do something.

pesticide, pesticides (noun) Pesticides are chemicals sprayed onto plants to kill insects and grubs.

pet, pets, petting, petted 1 (noun) A pet is a tame animal kept at home. **2** (adjective) Someone's pet theory or pet project is something that they particularly support or feel strongly about. **3** (verb) If you pet a person or animal, you stroke them affectionately.

petal, petals (noun) The petals of a flower are the coloured outer parts.

peter out, peters out, petering out, petered out (verb) If something peters out, it gradually comes to an end.

petite (pronounced pet-**teet**) (adjective) A woman who is petite is small and slim.

petition, petitions, petitioning, petitioned 1 (noun) A petition is a document demanding official action and signed by a lot of people. **2** A legal petition is an application to a court for legal action to be taken. **3** (verb) If you petition someone in authority, you make a formal request to them, e.g. *I petitioned the Chinese government for permission to visit its country.*

petrified (adjective) If you are petrified, you are very frightened.

petrol (noun) Petrol is a liquid obtained from petroleum and used as a fuel for motor vehicles.

petroleum (noun) Petroleum is thick, dark oil found under the earth or under the sea bed.

petticoat, petticoats (noun) A petticoat is a piece of women's underwear like a very thin skirt.

petty, pettier, pettiest 1 (adjective) Petty things are small and unimportant. **2** Petty behaviour consists of doing small things which are selfish and unkind.

petulant (adjective) showing unreasonable and childish impatience or anger. **petulantly** (adverb), **petulance** (noun).

petunia, petunias (pronounced pit-**yoon**-nee-ah) (noun) A petunia is a garden plant with large trumpet-shaped flowers.

pew, pews (noun) A pew is a long wooden seat with a back, which people sit on in church.

pewter (noun) Pewter is a silvery-grey metal made from a mixture of tin and lead.

phallus, phalluses (noun) A phallus is a penis or a symbolic model of a penis. **phallic** (adjective).

phantom, phantoms 1 (noun) A phantom is a ghost. **2** (adjective) imagined or unreal, e.g. *a phantom pregnancy.*

pharaoh, pharaohs (pronounced **fair**-oh) (noun) The pharaohs were kings of ancient Egypt.

pharmaceutical (pronounced far-mass-**yoo**-tik-kl) (adjective) connected with the industrial production of medicines.

pharmacist, pharmacists (noun) A pharmacist is a person who is qualified to prepare and sell medicines.

pharmacy, pharmacies (noun) A pharmacy is a shop where medicines are sold.

phase, phases, phasing, phased 1 (noun) A phase is a particular stage in the development of something. **2** (verb) To phase something means to cause it to happen gradually in stages.

PhD, PhDs (noun) A PhD is a degree awarded to someone who has done advanced research in a subject. PhD is an abbreviation for 'Doctor of Philosophy'.

pheasant, pheasants (noun) A pheasant is a large, long-tailed game bird.

phenomenal (pronounced fin-**nom**-in-nal) (adjective) extraordinarily great or good. **phenomenally** (adverb).

phenomenon, phenomena (noun) A phenomenon is something that happens or exists, especially something remarkable or something being considered in a scientific way, e.g. *a well-known geographical phenomenon.*

philanthropist, philanthropists (pronounced fil-**lan**-throp-pist) (noun) A philanthropist is someone who freely gives help or money to people in need. **philanthropic** (adjective), **philanthropy** (noun).

philistine, philistines (noun) If you call someone a philistine, you mean that they do not like art, literature, or music.

philosophical or **philosophic** (adjective) Someone who is philosophical does not get upset when disappointing things happen.

philosophy, philosophies 1 (noun) Philosophy is the study or creation of theories about the nature of existence, knowledge, beliefs, or behaviour. **2** A philosophy is a set of beliefs that a person has. **philosopher** (noun).

phlegm (pronounced **flem**) (noun) Phlegm is a thick mucus secreted in your throat when you have a cold.

phobia, phobias (noun) A phobia is an abnormal, irrational fear or hatred of something, e.g. *He had a phobia about flying.* **phobic** (adjective).

phoenix, phoenixes (pronounced **fee**-niks) (noun) A phoenix is an imaginary bird which, according to myth, burns itself to ashes every five hundred years and rises from the fire again.

phone, phones, phoning, phoned 1 (noun) A phone is a piece of electronic equipment which allows you to speak to someone in another place by dialling their number. **2** (verb) If you phone someone, you dial their number and speak to them using a phone.

phoney, phonier, phoniest; also spelled **phony** (adjective; an informal word) false and intended to deceive.

photo, photos (noun; an informal word) A photo is a photograph.

photocopier, photocopiers (noun) A photocopier is a machine which makes instant copies of documents by photographing them.

photocopy, photocopies, photocopying, photocopied 1 (noun) A photocopy is a copy of a document produced by a photocopier. **2** (verb) If you photocopy a document, you make a copy of it using a photocopier.

photogenic (adjective) Someone who is photogenic always looks nice in photographs.

photograph, photographs, photographing, photographed 1 (noun) A photograph is a picture made using a camera. **2** (verb) When you photograph someone, you take a picture of them by using a camera. **photographer** (noun), **photography** (noun).

photographic (adjective) connected with photography.

phrase, phrases, phrasing, phrased 1 (noun) A phrase is a group of words considered as a unit, especially a saying. **2** (verb) If you phrase something in a particular way, you choose those words to express it, e.g. *I should have phrased that better.*

physical 1 (adjective) concerning the body rather than the mind. **2** relating to things that can be touched or seen, especially with regard to their size or shape, e.g. *the physical characteristics of their machinery.* **physically** (adverb).

physical education (noun) Physical education consists of the sport, gymnastics, and athletics that you do at school.

physician, physicians (noun) A physician is a doctor.

physics (noun) Physics is the scientific study of the nature and properties of matter, energy, gravity, electricity, heat, and sound. **physicist** (noun).

physiology (noun) Physiology is the scientific study of the way the bodies of living things work.

physiotherapy (noun) Physiotherapy is medical treatment which involves exercise and massage. **physiotherapist** (noun).

physique, physiques (pronounced fiz-**zeek**) (noun) A

person's physique is the shape and size of their body.

pi (rhymes with **fly**) (noun) Pi is a number, approximately 3.142 and symbolized by the Greek letter π. Pi is the ratio of the circumference of a circle to its diameter.

piano, pianos (noun) A piano is a large musical instrument with a row of black and white keys. When the keys are pressed, little hammers hit wires to produce the different notes. **pianist** (noun).

piccolo, piccolos (noun) A piccolo is a high-pitched wind instrument like a small flute.

pick, picks, picking, picked 1 (verb) To pick something means to choose it. **2** If you pick a flower or fruit, or pick something from a place, you remove it with your fingers. **3** If someone picks a lock, they open it with a piece of wire instead of a key. **4** (noun) A pick is a pickaxe.

pickaxe, pickaxes (noun) A pickaxe is a tool consisting of a curved pointed iron bar attached in the middle to a long handle.

picket, pickets, picketing, picketed 1 (verb) When a group of people picket a place of work, they stand outside to persuade other workers to join or support a strike. **2** (noun) Pickets are people who are picketing a place.

pickings (plural noun) Pickings are goods or money that can be obtained very easily, e.g. *rich pickings.*

pickle, pickles, pickling, pickled 1 (noun) Pickle or pickles consists of vegetables or fruit preserved in vinegar or salt water. **2** (verb) To pickle food means to preserve it in vinegar or salt water.

pickpocket, pickpockets (noun) A pickpocket is a thief who steals from people's pockets or handbags.

picnic, picnics, picnicking, picnicked 1 (noun) A picnic is a meal eaten out of doors. **2** (verb) People who are picnicking are having a picnic.

pictorial (adjective) relating to or using pictures, e.g. *a pictorial record of the railway.*

picture, pictures, picturing, pictured 1 (noun) A picture of someone or something is a drawing, painting, or photograph of them. **2** (verb) If someone is pictured in a newspaper or magazine, a photograph of them is printed in it. **3** (plural noun) If you go to the pictures, you go to see a film at the cinema. **4** (noun) If you have a picture of something in your mind, you have an idea or impression of it. **5** (verb) If you picture something, you think of it and imagine it clearly, e.g. *That is how I picture him.*

picturesque (pronounced pik-chur-**esk**) (adjective) A place that is picturesque is very attractive and unspoiled.

pie, pies (noun) A pie is a dish of meat, vegetables, or fruit covered with pastry.

piece, pieces, piecing, pieced 1 (noun) A piece of something is a portion, part, or section of it. **2** A piece is also something that has been written or created, such as a work of art or a musical composition. **3** A piece is also a coin, e.g. *a 50 pence piece.* **4** (verb) If you piece together a number of things, you gradually put them together to make something complete.

piecemeal (adverb or adjective) done gradually and at irregular intervals, e.g. *a piecemeal approach to career management.*

pier, piers (noun) A pier is a large structure which sticks out into the sea at a seaside town, and which people can walk along.

pierce, pierces, piercing, pierced (verb) If a sharp object pierces something, it goes through it, making a hole.

piercing 1 (adjective) A piercing sound is high-pitched, sharp, and unpleasant. **2** Someone with piercing eyes seems to look at you very intensely.

piety (pronounced **pie**-it-tee) (noun) Piety is strong and devout religious belief.

pig, pigs (noun) A pig is a farm animal kept for its meat. It has pinkish skin, short legs, and a snout.

pigeon, pigeons (noun) A pigeon is a largish bird with grey feathers, often seen in towns.

pigeonhole, pigeonholes (noun) A pigeonhole is one of the sections in a frame on a wall where letters can be left.

piggyback, piggybacks (noun) If you give someone a piggyback, you carry them on your back, supporting them under their knees.

piglet, piglets (noun) A piglet is a young pig.

pigment, pigments (noun) A pigment is a substance that gives something a particular colour. **pigmentation** (noun).

pigsty, pigsties (noun) A pigsty is a hut with a yard where pigs are kept.

pigtail, pigtails (noun) A pigtail is a length of plaited hair.

pike, pikes 1 (noun) A pike is a large freshwater fish with strong teeth. **2** A pike was a medieval weapon consisting of a pointed metal blade attached to a long pole.

pilchard, pilchards (noun) A pilchard is a small sea fish.

pile, piles, piling, piled 1 (noun) A pile of things is a quantity of them lying one on top of another. **2** (verb) If you pile things somewhere, you put them one on top of the other. **3** (noun) The pile of a carpet is its soft surface consisting of many threads standing on end.

pile-up, pile-ups (noun; an informal word) A pile-up is a road accident involving several vehicles.

pilfer, pilfers, pilfering, pilfered (verb) Someone who pilfers steals small things over a period of time.

pilgrim, pilgrims (noun) A pilgrim is a person who travels to a holy place for religious reasons. **pilgrimage** (noun).

pill, pills 1 (noun) A pill is a small, round, hard tablet of medicine that you swallow. **2** The pill is a type of drug that women can take regularly to prevent pregnancy.

pillage, pillages, pillaging, pillaged (verb) If a group of people pillage a place, they steal from it using violence.

pillar, pillars 1 (noun) A pillar is a tall, narrow, solid structure, usually supporting part of a building. **2** Someone who is described as a pillar of a particular group is an active and important member of it, e.g. *a pillar of the church.*

pillar box, pillar boxes (noun) A pillar box is a red box in which you post letters.

pillory, pillories, pillorying, pilloried (verb) If someone is pilloried, they are criticized severely by a lot of people.

pillow, pillows (noun) A pillow is a rectangular cushion which you rest your head on when you are in bed.

pillowcase, pillowcases (noun) A pillowcase is a cover for a pillow which can be removed and washed.

pilot, pilots, piloting, piloted 1 (noun) A pilot is a person who is trained to fly an aircraft. **2** A pilot is also a person who goes on board ships to guide them through local waters to a port. **3** (verb) To pilot something means to control its movement or to guide it.

pimp, pimps (noun) A pimp is a man who finds clients for prostitutes and takes a large part of their earnings.

pimple, pimples (noun) A pimple is a small spot on the skin. **pimply** (adjective).

pin, pins, pinning, pinned 1 (noun) A pin is a thin, pointed piece of metal used to fasten together things such as pieces of fabric or paper. **2** (verb) If you pin something somewhere, you fasten it there with a pin or a drawing pin. **3** If someone pins you in a particular position, they hold you there so that you cannot move. **4** If you try to pin something down, you try to get or give a clear and exact description of it or statement about it.

pinafore, pinafores (noun) A pinafore is a dress with no sleeves, worn over a blouse.

pincers 1 (plural noun) Pincers are a tool used for gripping and pulling things. They consist of two pieces of metal hinged in the middle. **2** The pincers of a crab or lobster are its front claws.

pinch, pinches, pinching, pinched 1 (verb) If you pinch something, you squeeze it between your thumb and first finger. **2** (noun) A pinch of something is the amount that you can hold between your thumb and first finger, e.g. *a pinch of salt.* **3** (verb; an informal use) If someone pinches something, they steal it.

pinched (adjective) If someone's face is pinched, it looks thin and pale.

pine, pines, pining, pined 1 (noun) A pine or pine tree is an evergreen tree with very thin leaves. **2** (verb) If you pine for something, you are sad because you cannot have it.

pineapple, pineapples (noun) A pineapple is a large, oval fruit with sweet, yellow flesh and a thick, lumpy, pale brown skin.

ping-pong (noun) Ping-pong is the same as table tennis.

pink, pinker, pinkest (adjective) pale reddish-white.

pinnacle, pinnacles 1 (noun) A

pinnacle is a tall pointed piece of stone or rock. **2** The pinnacle of something is its best or highest level, e.g. *the pinnacle of his career.*

pinpoint, pinpoints, pinpointing, pinpointed (verb) If you pinpoint something, you explain or discover exactly what or where it is.

pinstripe (adjective) Pinstripe cloth has very narrow vertical stripes.

pint, pints (noun) A pint is a unit of liquid volume equal to one eighth of a gallon or about 0.568 litres.

pioneer, pioneers, pioneering, pioneered (pronounced pie-on-**ear**) **1** (noun) Someone who is a pioneer in a particular activity is one of the first people to develop it. **2** (verb) Someone who pioneers a new process or invention is the first person to develop it.

pious (pronounced **pie**-uss) (adjective) very religious and moral.

pip, pips (noun) Pips are the hard seeds in a fruit.

pipe, pipes, piping, piped 1 (noun) A pipe is a long, round, hollow tube through which liquid or gas can flow. **2** (verb) To pipe a liquid or gas somewhere means to transfer it through a pipe. **3** (noun) A pipe is an object used for smoking tobacco. It consists of a small hollow bowl attached to a tube.

pipeline, pipelines (noun) A pipeline is a large underground pipe that carries oil or gas over a long distance.

piper, pipers (noun) A piper is a person who plays the bagpipes.

piping (noun) Piping consists of pipes and tubes.

piranha, piranhas (pronounced pir-**rah**-nah) (noun) A piranha is a small, fierce fish with sharp teeth.

pirate, pirates (noun) Pirates were sailors who attacked and robbed other ships.

pirouette, pirouettes (pronounced pir-roo-**et**) (noun) In ballet, a pirouette is a fast spinning step done on the toes.

Pisces (pronounced **pie**-seez) (noun) Pisces is the twelfth sign of the zodiac, represented by two fish. People born between February 19th and March 20th are born under this sign.

pistol, pistols (noun) A pistol is a small gun held in the hand.

piston, pistons (noun) A piston is a cylinder or disc that slides up and down inside a tube. Pistons make parts of engines move.

pit, pits 1 (noun) A pit is a large hole in the ground. **2** A pit in the surface of something is a small hollow. **3** A pit is also a coal mine.

pitch, pitches, pitching, pitched 1 (noun) A pitch is an area of ground marked out for playing a game such as football. **2** (verb) If you pitch something somewhere, you throw it with a lot of force. **3** (noun) The pitch of a sound is how high or low it is. **4** Pitch is a black substance used in road tar and also for waterproofing boats and roofs. **5** (verb) If you pitch something at a particular level of difficulty, you set it at that level, e.g. *Any film must be pitched at a level to suit its intended audience.* **6** When you pitch a tent, you fix it in an upright position.

pitcher, pitchers (noun) A pitcher is a large jug.

pitfall, pitfalls (noun) The pitfalls of a situation are its difficulties or dangers.

pith (noun) The pith of an orange or lemon is the white substance between the outer skin and the flesh.

pitiful (adjective) Someone or something that is pitiful is in such a sad or weak situation that you feel pity for them.

pittance (noun) If you receive a pittance, you receive only a very small amount of money.

pitted (adjective) covered in small hollows, e.g. *Nails often become pitted.*

pity, pities, pitying, pitied 1 (verb) If you pity someone, you feel very sorry for them. **2** (noun) Pity is a feeling of being sorry for someone. **3** If you say that it is a pity about something, you are expressing your disappointment about it.

pivot, pivots, pivoting, pivoted 1 (verb) If something pivots, it balances or turns on a central point, e.g. *The keel pivots on a large stainless steel pin.* **2** (noun) A pivot is the central point on which something balances or turns. **pivotal** (adjective).

pixie, pixies (noun) A pixie is an imaginary little creature in fairy stories.

pizza, pizzas (pronounced **peet**-sah) (noun) A pizza is a flat piece of dough covered with cheese, tomato, and other savoury food.

placard, placards (noun) A placard is a large notice carried at a demonstration or displayed in a public place.

placate, placates, placating, placated (verb) If you placate someone, you stop them feeling angry by doing something to please them.

place, places, placing, placed 1 (noun) A place is any point, building, or area. **2** You can refer to the position where something belongs as its place. **3** A place at a table is a space set with cutlery where one person can eat. **4** If you have a place in a group or at a college, you are a member or are accepted as a student. **5** A place in a sequence of things is a particular point or stage. **6** (phrase) When something **takes place,** it happens. **7** (verb) If you place something somewhere, you put it there.

placebo, placebos (pronounced plas-**see**-boh) (noun) A placebo is a harmless, inactive substance given to a patient in place of a drug.

placenta, placentas (pronounced plas-**sen**-tah) (noun) The placenta is the mass of veins and tissues in the womb of a pregnant woman or animal. It gives the foetus food and oxygen.

placid (adjective) calm and not easily excited or upset. **placidly** (adverb).

plagiarism (pronounced **play**-jer-rizm) (noun) Plagiarism is the practice of copying someone else's work or ideas and pretending that it is your own. **plagiarist** (noun), **plagiarize** (verb).

plague, plagues, plaguing, plagued (pronounced **playg**) **1** (noun) Plague is a very infectious disease that kills large numbers of people. **2** A plague of unpleasant things is a large number of them occurring at the same time, e.g. *a plague of rats.* **3** (verb) If problems plague you, they keep causing you trouble.

plaice (noun) A plaice is an edible flat fish.

plaid, plaids (pronounced **plad**) (noun) Plaid is woven material with a tartan design.

plain, plainer, plainest; plains 1 (adjective) very simple in style with no pattern or decoration, e.g. *plain walls.* **2** obvious and easy to recognize or understand, e.g. *plain language.* **3** (adverb) You can use plain before a noun or adjective to emphasize it, e.g. *You were just plain stupid.* **4** (adjective) A person who is plain is not at all beautiful or attractive. **5** (noun) A plain is a large, flat area of land with very few trees. **plainly** (adverb).

plaintiff, plaintiffs (noun) In a court case, the plaintiff is the person who has brought the case against another person.

plait, plaits, plaiting, plaited 1 (verb) If you plait three lengths of hair or rope together, you twist them over each other in turn to make one thick length. **2** (noun) A plait is a length of hair that has been plaited.

plan, plans, planning, planned 1 (noun) A plan is a method of achieving something that has been worked out beforehand. **2** A plan of something that is going to be made is a detailed diagram or drawing of it. **3** (verb) If you plan something, you decide in detail what it is to be and how to do it. **4** If you are planning to do something, you intend to do it, e.g. *They plan to marry in the summer.*

plane, planes, planing, planed 1 (noun) A plane is a vehicle with wings and engines that enable it to fly. **2** A plane is also a flat surface. **3** You can refer to a particular level of something as a particular plane, e.g. *to take the rock and roll concert to a higher plane.* **4** A plane is a tool with a flat bottom with a sharp blade in it. You move it over a piece of wood to remove thin pieces from the surface. **5** (verb) If you plane a piece of wood, you smooth its surface with a plane.

planet, planets (noun) A planet is a round object in space which moves around the sun or a star and is illuminated by light from it. **planetary** (adjective).

plank, planks (noun) A plank is a long rectangular piece of wood.

plankton (noun) Plankton is a layer of tiny plants and animals that live just below the surface of a sea or lake.

plant, plants, planting, planted 1 (noun) A plant is a living thing that grows in the earth and has stems, leaves, and roots. **2** (verb) When you plant a seed or plant, you put it into the ground. **3** (noun) A plant is also a factory or power station, e.g. *a giant bottling plant.* **4** (verb) If you plant something somewhere, you put it there firmly, deliberately, or secretly.

plantation, plantations 1 (noun) A plantation is a large area of land where crops such as tea, cotton, or sugar are grown. **2** A plantation of trees is a large number of them planted together.

plaque, plaques (rhymes with **black**) **1** (noun) A plaque is a flat piece of metal which is fixed to a wall and has an inscription in memory of a famous person or event. **2** Plaque is a substance which forms around your teeth and consists of bacteria, saliva, and food.

plasma (pronounced **plaz**-mah) (noun) Plasma is the clear fluid part of blood.

plaster, plasters, plastering, plastered 1 (noun) Plaster is a paste made of sand, lime, and water, which is used to form a smooth surface for inside walls and ceilings. **2** (verb) To plaster a wall means to cover it with a layer of plaster. **3** (noun) A plaster is a strip of sticky material with a small pad, used for covering cuts on your body. **4** (phrase) If your arm or leg is **in plaster,** it has a plaster cast on it to protect a broken bone. **plasterer** (noun).

plastered 1 (adjective) If something is plastered to a surface, it is stuck there. **2** If something is plastered with things, they are all over its surface.

plastic, plastics 1 (noun) Plastic is a substance made by a chemical process that can be moulded when soft to make a wide range of objects. **2** (adjective) made of plastic.

plastic surgery (noun) Plastic surgery is surgery to replace or repair damaged skin or to improve a person's appearance by changing the shape of their features.

plate, plates 1 (noun) A plate is a flat round or oval dish used to hold food. **2** A plate is also a flat piece of metal, glass, or other rigid material used for various purposes in machinery or building, e.g. *heavy steel plates used in shipbuilding.*

plateau, plateaus or **plateaux** (rhymes with **snow**) (noun) A plateau is a large area of high and fairly flat land.

plated (adjective) Metal that is plated is covered with a thin layer of silver or gold.

platform, platforms 1 (noun) A platform is a raised structure on which someone or something can stand. **2** A platform in a railway station is the raised area where passengers get on and off trains.

platinum (noun) Platinum is a valuable silver-grey metal.

platitude, platitudes (noun) A platitude is a statement made as if it were significant but which has become meaningless or boring because it has been used so many times before.

platonic (adjective) A platonic relationship is simply one of friendship and does not involve sexual attraction.

platoon, platoons (noun) A platoon is a small group of soldiers, commanded by a lieutenant.

platter, platters (noun) A platter is a large serving plate.

platypus, platypuses (noun) A platypus or duck-billed platypus is an Australian mammal. It has brown fur, webbed feet, and a snout like a duck.

plaudits (plural noun; a formal word) If something receives people's plaudits, they express their admiration for it.

plausible (adjective) An explanation that is plausible seems likely to be true or valid. **plausibility** (noun).

play, plays, playing, played 1 (verb) When children play, they take part in games or use toys. **2** When you play a sport or match, you take part in it, e.g. *He has only played 11 matches since February.* **3** (noun) A play is a piece of drama performed in the theatre or on television. **4** (verb) If an actor plays a character in a play or film, he or she performs that role. **5** If you play a musical instrument, you produce music from it. **6** If you play a record or tape, you listen to it. **player** (noun).

playboy, playboys (noun) A playboy is a rich man who spends his time enjoying himself.

playful 1 (adjective) friendly and light-hearted, e.g. *a playful kiss on the tip of his nose.* **2** lively, e.g. *a playful puppy.* **playfully** (adverb).

playground, playgrounds (noun) A playground is a special area for children to play in.

playgroup, playgroups (noun) A playgroup is an informal kind of school for very young children where they learn by playing.

playing card, playing cards (noun) Playing cards are cards printed with numbers or pictures which are used to play various games.

playing field, playing fields (noun) A playing field is an area of grass where people play sports.

playwright, playwrights (noun) A playwright is a person who writes plays.

plaza, plazas (pronounced **plah**-za) (noun) A plaza is an open square in a city.

plea, pleas 1 (noun) A plea is an emotional request, e.g. *a plea for help.* **2** In a court of law, someone's plea is their statement that they are guilty or not guilty.

plead, pleads, pleading, pleaded 1 (verb) If you plead with someone, you ask them in an intense emotional way to do something. **2** When a person pleads guilty or not guilty, they state in court that they are guilty or not guilty of a crime.

pleasant (adjective) enjoyable, likable, or attractive. **pleasantly** (adverb).

please, pleases, pleasing, pleased 1 You say please when you are asking someone politely to do something. **2** (verb) If something pleases you, it makes you feel happy and satisfied. **pleased** (adjective).

pleasing (adjective) attractive,

satisfying, or enjoyable, e.g. *a pleasing appearance.*

pleasure, pleasures 1 (noun) Pleasure is a feeling of happiness, satisfaction, or enjoyment. **2** A pleasure is an activity that you enjoy. **pleasurable** (adjective).

pleat, pleats (noun) A pleat is a permanent fold in fabric made by folding one part over another.

pledge, pledges, pledging, pledged 1 (noun) A pledge is a solemn promise. **2** (verb) If you pledge something, you promise that you will do it or give it.

plentiful (adjective) existing in large numbers or amounts and readily available, e.g. *Fruit and vegetables were plentiful.* **plentifully** (adverb).

plenty (noun) If there is plenty of something, there is a lot of it.

plethora (pronounced **pleth**-thor-ah) (noun) A plethora of something is an amount that is greater than you need.

pleurisy (pronounced **ploor**-ris-see) (noun) Pleurisy is a serious illness in which a person's lungs are inflamed and breathing is difficult.

pliable (adjective) If something is pliable, you can bend it without breaking it.

pliers (plural noun) Pliers are a small tool with metal jaws for holding small objects and bending wire.

plight (noun) Someone's plight is the very difficult or dangerous situation that they are in, e.g. *the plight of the refugees.*

plinth, plinths (noun) A plinth is a block of stone on which a statue or pillar stands.

plod, plods, plodding, plodded (verb) If you plod somewhere, you walk there slowly and heavily.

plonk, plonks, plonking, plonked (verb) If you plonk something down, you put it down heavily and carelessly.

plop, plops, plopping, plopped 1 (noun) A plop is a gentle sound made by something light dropping into a liquid. **2** (verb) If something plops into a liquid, it drops into it with a gentle sound.

plot, plots, plotting, plotted 1 (noun) A plot is a secret plan made by a group of people. **2** The plot of a novel or play is the story. **3** A plot of land is a small piece of it. **4** (verb) If people plot to do something, they plan it secretly, e.g. *His family is plotting to disinherit him.* **5** If someone plots the course of a plane or ship on a map, or plots a graph, they mark the points in the correct places.

plough, ploughs, ploughing, ploughed 1 (noun) A plough is a large farming tool that is pulled across a field to turn the soil over before planting seeds. **2** (verb) When someone ploughs land, they use a plough to turn over the soil.

ploy, ploys (noun) A ploy is a clever plan or way of behaving in order to get something that you want.

pluck, plucks, plucking, plucked 1 (verb) To pluck a fruit or flower means to remove it with a sharp pull. **2** To pluck a chicken or other dead bird means to pull its feathers out before cooking it. **3** When you pluck a stringed instrument, you pull the strings and let them go. **4** (noun) Pluck is courage. **plucky** (adjective).

plug, plugs, plugging, plugged 1 (noun) A plug is a plastic object with metal prongs that can be pushed into a socket to connect an appliance to the electricity supply. **2** A plug is also a disc of rubber or metal with which you block up the hole in a sink or bath. **3** (verb) If you plug a hole, you block it with something.

plum, plums (noun) A plum is a small fruit with a smooth red or yellow skin and a large stone in the middle.

plumage (pronounced **ploom**-mage) (noun) A bird's plumage is its feathers.

plumber, plumbers (noun) A plumber is a person who connects and repairs water pipes, baths, and toilets.

plumbing (noun) The plumbing in a building is the system of water pipes, sinks, baths, and toilets.

plume, plumes (noun) A plume is a large, brightly coloured feather.

plummet, plummets, plummeting, plummeted (verb) If something plummets, it falls very quickly, e.g. *Sales have plummeted.*

plump, plumper, plumpest (adjective) rather fat, e.g. *a small plump baby.*

plunder, plunders, plundering, plundered (verb) If someone plunders a place, they steal things from it.

plunge, plunges, plunging, plunged 1 (verb) If something plunges, it falls suddenly. **2** If you plunge an object into something, you push it in quickly. **3** If you plunge into an activity or state, you suddenly become involved in it or affected by it, e.g. *The United States had just plunged into the war.* **4** (noun) A plunge is a sudden fall.

plural, plurals (noun) The plural is the form of a word that is used to refer to two or more people or things, for example the plural of 'chair' is 'chairs', and the plural of 'mouse' is 'mice'.

plural noun, plural nouns (noun) In this dictionary, 'plural noun' is the name given to a noun that is normally used only in the plural, for example 'scissors' or 'police'.

plus 1 You use plus to show that one number is being added to another, e.g. *Two plus two equals four.* **2** (adjective) slightly more than the number mentioned, e.g. *a career of 25 years plus.* **3** (preposition) You can use plus when you mention an additional item, e.g. *He wrote a history of Scotland plus a history of British literature.*

plush (adjective) very expensive and smart, e.g. *a plush hotel.*

Pluto (noun) Pluto is the smallest planet in the solar system and the furthest from the sun.

ply, plies, plying, plied 1 (verb) If you ply someone with things or questions, you keep giving them things or asking them questions. **2** To ply a trade means to do a particular job as your work. **3** (noun) Ply is the thickness of wool or thread.

p.m. used to specify times between 12 noon and 12 midnight, e.g. *He went to bed at 9 p.m.* It is an abbreviation for the Latin phrase 'post meridiem', which means 'after noon'.

pneumatic (pronounced new-**mat**-ik) (adjective) operated by or filled with compressed air, e.g. *a pneumatic drill.*

pneumonia (pronounced new-**moan**-ee-ah) (noun) Pneumonia is a serious disease which affects a person's lungs and makes breathing difficult.

poach, poaches, poaching, poached 1 (verb) If someone poaches animals from someone else's land, they illegally catch the animals for food. **2** When you poach food, you cook it gently in hot liquid. **poacher** (noun).

pocket, pockets 1 (noun) A pocket is a small bag or pouch that forms part of a piece of clothing. **2** A pocket of something is a small area of it, e.g. *There are still pockets of resistance.*

pocket money (noun) Pocket money is an amount of money given regularly to children by their parents.

pod, pods (noun) A pod is a long narrow seed container that grows on plants such as peas or beans.

podium, podiums (noun) A podium is a small platform, often one on which someone stands to make a speech.

poem, poems (noun) A poem is a piece of writing in which the words are arranged in short rhythmic lines, often with a rhyme.

poet, poets (noun) A poet is a person who writes poems.

poetic 1 (adjective) very beautiful, expressive, and sensitive, e.g. *a pure and poetic love.* **2** relating to poetry. **poetically** (adverb).

poetry (noun) Poetry is poems, considered as a form of literature.

poignant (pronounced **poyn**-yant) (adjective) Something that is poignant has a strong emotional effect on you, often making you feel sad, e.g. *a moving and poignant moment.* **poignancy** (noun).

point, points, pointing, pointed 1 (noun) A point is an opinion or fact expressed by someone, e.g. *You've made a good point.* **2** A point is also a quality, e.g. *Tact was never her strong point.* **3** The point of something is its purpose, importance, or meaning, e.g. *He completely missed the point in most of his argument.* **4** A point is a position or time, e.g. *At some point during the party, a fight erupted.* **5** A point in a competition is a single mark. **6** The point of something such as a needle or knife is the thin, sharp end. **7** The points of a compass are the 32 directions indicated on it. **8** The decimal point in a number is the dot separating the whole number from the fraction. **9** On a railway track, the points are the levers and rails which enable a train to move from one track to another. **10** (verb) If you point at something, you stick out your finger to show where it is. **11**

If something points in a particular direction, it faces that way.

point-blank 1 (adverb) If you say something point-blank, you say it directly without explanation or apology. **2** (adjective) Something that is shot at point-blank range is shot with a gun held very close to it.

pointed 1 (adjective) A pointed object has a thin, sharp end. **2** Pointed comments express criticism. **pointedly** (adverb).

pointer, pointers (noun) A pointer is a piece of information which helps you to understand something, e.g. *Here are a few pointers to help you make a choice.*

pointless (adjective) Something that is pointless has no use, sense, or purpose. **pointlessly** (adverb).

point of view, points of view (noun) Your point of view is your opinion about something.

poise (noun) Someone who has poise is calm, self-controlled, and dignified.

poised (adjective) If you are poised to do something, you are ready to do it at any moment.

poison, poisons, poisoning, poisoned 1 (noun) Poison is a substance that can kill people or animals if they swallow it or absorb it. **2** (verb) To poison someone means to try to kill them with poison. **poisonous** (adjective).

poke, pokes, poking, poked 1 (verb) If you poke someone or something, you push at them quickly with your finger or a sharp object. **2** Something that pokes out of another thing appears from underneath or behind it, e.g. *roots poking out of the earth.*

poker, pokers 1 (noun) Poker is a card game in which the players make bets on the cards dealt to them. **2** A poker is a long metal rod used for moving coals in a fire.

polar (adjective) relating to the area around the North and South Poles.

polar bear, polar bears (noun) A polar bear is a large white bear which lives in the area around the North Pole.

pole, poles 1 (noun) A pole is a long rounded piece of wood or metal. **2** The earth's poles are the two opposite ends of its axis, e.g. *the North Pole.*

Pole, Poles (noun) A Pole is someone who comes from Poland.

pole vault (noun) The pole vault is an athletics event in which contestants jump over a high bar using a long flexible pole to lift themselves into the air.

police, polices, policing, policed 1 (plural noun) The police are the people who are officially responsible for making sure that people obey the law. **2** (verb) To police an area means to preserve law and order there by means of the police or an armed force.

policeman, policemen (noun) A policeman is a man who is a member of a police force. **policewoman** (noun).

policy, policies 1 (noun) A policy is a set of plans used as a basis for action, especially in politics or business, e.g. *the* *new economic policy.* **2** An insurance policy is a document which shows an agreement made with an insurance company.

polio (noun) Polio is an infectious disease that often results in paralysis. Polio is short for 'poliomyelitis'.

polish, polishes, polishing, polished 1 (verb) If you polish something, you put polish on it or rub it with a cloth to make it shine. **2** (noun) Polish is a substance that you put on an object to clean it and make it shine, e.g. *shoe polish.* **polished** (adjective).

Polish (pronounced **pole**-ish) **1** (adjective) belonging or relating to Poland. **2** (noun) Polish is the main language spoken in Poland.

polite (adjective) Someone who is polite has good manners and behaves considerately towards other people. **politely** (adverb), **politeness** (noun).

politician, politicians (noun) A politician is a person involved in the government of a country.

politics (noun) Politics is the activity and planning concerned with achieving power and control in a country or organization. **political** (adjective), **politically** (adverb).

polka, polkas (noun) A polka is a fast dance in which couples dance together in circles around the room.

poll, polls, polling, polled 1 (noun) A poll is a survey in which people are asked their opinions about something. **2** (verb) If you are polled on something, you are asked your opinion about it as part of a survey.

pollen (noun) Pollen is a fine yellow powder produced by flowers in order to fertilize other flowers.

pollinate, pollinates, pollinating, pollinated (verb) To pollinate a plant means to fertilize it with pollen. **pollination** (noun).

pollutant, pollutants (noun) A pollutant is a substance that causes pollution.

pollute, pollutes, polluting, polluted (verb) To pollute water or air means to make it dirty and dangerous to use or live in. **pollution** (noun), **polluted** (adjective).

polo (noun) Polo is a game played between two teams of players on horseback. The players use wooden hammers with long handles to hit a ball.

polo-necked (adjective) A polo-necked jumper has a deep fold of material at the neck.

polyester (noun) Polyester is a man-made fibre, used especially to make clothes.

polystyrene (noun) Polystyrene is a very light plastic, used especially to make containers.

polythene (noun) Polythene is a type of plastic that is used to make thin sheets or bags.

pomegranate, pomegranates (noun) A pomegranate is a round fruit with a thick reddish skin. It contains a lot of small seeds.

pomp (noun) Pomp is the use of ceremony, fine clothes, and decorations on special occasions, e.g. *Sir Patrick was buried with much pomp.*

pompous (adjective) behaving

in a way that is too serious and self-important. **pomposity** (noun).

pond, ponds (noun) A pond is a small area of water.

ponder, ponders, pondering, pondered (verb) If you ponder, you think about something deeply, e.g. *He was pondering the problem when Phillipson drove up.*

ponderous (adjective) dull, slow, and serious, e.g. *the ponderous commentary.*

pong, pongs (noun; an informal word) A pong is an unpleasant smell.

pontiff, pontiffs (noun; a formal word) The pontiff is the Pope.

pony, ponies (noun) A pony is a small horse.

ponytail, ponytails (noun) A ponytail is a hairstyle in which long hair is tied at the back of the head and hangs down like a tail.

pony trekking (noun) Pony trekking is a leisure activity in which people ride across country on ponies.

poodle, poodles (noun) A poodle is a type of dog with curly hair.

pool, pools, pooling, pooled 1 (noun) A pool is a small area of still water. **2** Pool is a game in which players try to hit coloured balls into pockets around the table using long sticks called cues. **3** A pool of people, money, or things is a group or collection used or shared by several people. **4** (verb) If people pool their resources, they gather together the things they have so that they can be shared or used by all of them. **5** (plural noun) The pools are a competition in which people try to guess the results of football matches.

poor, poorer, poorest 1 (adjective) Poor people have very little money and few possessions. **2** Poor places are inhabited by people with little money and show signs of neglect. **3** You use poor to show sympathy, e.g. *Poor you!* **4** Poor also means of a low quality or standard, e.g. *a poor performance.*

poorly 1 (adjective) feeling unwell or ill. **2** (adverb) badly, e.g. *a poorly planned operation.*

pop, pops, popping, popped 1 (noun) Pop is modern music played and enjoyed especially by young people. **2** You can refer to fizzy, nonalcoholic drinks as pop. **3** A pop is a short, sharp sound. **4** (verb) If something pops, it makes a sudden sharp sound. **5** If you pop something somewhere, you put it there quickly, e.g. *I'd just popped the pie in the oven.* **6** If you pop somewhere, you go there quickly, e.g. *His mother popped out to buy him an ice cream.*

popcorn (noun) Popcorn is a snack consisting of grains of maize heated until they puff up and burst.

Pope, Popes (noun) The Pope is the head of the Roman Catholic Church.

poplar, poplars (noun) A poplar is a type of tall thin tree.

poppy, poppies (noun) A poppy is a plant with a large delicate red flower.

populace (noun; a formal word) The populace of a country is its people.

popular 1 (adjective) enjoyed, approved of, or liked by a lot of people. **2** involving or intended for ordinary people, e.g. *the popular press.* **popularly** (adverb), **popularity** (noun), **popularize** (verb).

populate, populates, populating, populated (verb) The people or animals that populate an area live there.

population, populations (noun) The population of a place is the people who live there, or the number of people living there.

porcelain (noun) Porcelain is a delicate ceramic material used to make crockery.

porch, porches (noun) A porch is a covered area at the entrance to a building.

porcupine, porcupines (noun) A porcupine is a large rodent with long spines covering its body.

pore, pores, poring, pored 1 (noun) The pores in your skin or on the surface of a plant are very small holes which allow moisture to pass through. **2** (verb) If you pore over a piece of writing or a diagram, you study it carefully.

pork (noun) Pork is meat from a pig which has not been salted or smoked.

pornography (noun) Pornography refers to magazines and films that are designed to cause sexual excitement by showing naked people and sexual acts. **pornographic** (adjective).

porpoise, porpoises (pronounced **por**-pus) (noun) A porpoise is a sea mammal related to the dolphin.

porridge (noun) Porridge is a thick, sticky food made from oats cooked in water or milk.

port, ports 1 (noun) A port is a town or area which has a harbour or docks. **2** Port is a kind of strong, sweet red wine. **3** (adjective) The port side of a ship is the left side when you are facing the front.

portable (adjective) designed to be easily carried, e.g. *a portable television.*

porter, porters 1 (noun) A porter is a person whose job is to be in charge of the entrance of a building, greeting and directing visitors. **2** A porter in a railway station, airport, or hospital is a person whose job is to carry or move things.

portfolio, portfolios (noun) A portfolio is a thin, flat case for carrying papers.

porthole, portholes (noun) A porthole is a small window in the side of a ship or aircraft.

portion, portions (noun) A portion of something is a part or amount of it, e.g. *a portion of fresh fruit.*

portrait, portraits (noun) A portrait is a picture or photograph of someone.

portray, portrays, portraying, portrayed (verb) When an actor, artist, or writer portrays someone or something, they represent or describe them. **portrayal** (noun).

Portuguese (pronounced portyoo-**geez**) **1** (adjective) belonging or relating to Portugal. **2** (noun) A Portuguese is someone who comes from Portugal. **3** Portuguese is the main language spoken in Portugal and

Brazil.

pose, poses, posing, posed 1 (verb) If something poses a problem, it is the cause of the problem. **2** If you pose a question, you ask it. **3** If you pose as someone else, you pretend to be that person in order to deceive people. **4** (noun) Your pose is the way that you are standing, sitting, or lying, e.g. *Mr Clark assumes a pose for the photographer.*

poser, posers 1 (noun) A poser is someone who behaves or dresses in an exaggerated way in order to impress people. **2** A poser is also a difficult problem.

posh, posher, poshest 1 (adjective; an informal word) smart, fashionable, and expensive, e.g. *a posh restaurant.* **2** upper class, e.g. *the man with the posh voice.*

position, positions, positioning, positioned 1 (noun) The position of someone or something is the place where they are. **2** When someone or something is in a particular position, they are sitting or lying in that way, e.g. *I raised myself to a sitting position.* **3** (verb) To position something somewhere means to put it there, e.g. *Llewelyn positioned a cushion behind Joanna's back.* **4** (noun) A position in an organization is a job or post in it. **5** The position that you are in at a particular time is the situation that you are in, e.g. *This puts the president in a difficult position.*

positive 1 (adjective) completely sure about something, e.g. *I was positive he'd known about those dollars.* **2** confident and hopeful, e.g. *I felt very positive about everything.* **3** showing approval, agreement, or encouragement, e.g. *I anticipate a positive response.* **4** providing definite proof of the truth or identity of something, e.g. *positive evidence.* **5** A positive number is greater than zero. **positively** (adverb).

possess, possesses, possessing, possessed 1 (verb) If you possess something, you own it or have it. **2** If a feeling or belief possesses you, it strongly influences you, e.g. *Absolute terror possessed her.* **possessor** (noun).

possession, possessions 1 (noun) If something is in your possession or if you are in possession of it, you have it. **2** Your possessions are the things that you own or that you have with you.

possessive 1 (adjective) A person who is possessive about someone or something wants to keep them to themselves. **2** (noun) In grammar, the possessive is the form of a noun or pronoun used to show possession, e.g. *my car... That's hers.*

possibility, possibilities (noun) A possibility is something that might be true or might happen, e.g. *the possibility of a ban.*

possible 1 (adjective) likely to happen or able to be done. **2** likely or capable of being true or correct. **possibly** (adverb).

post, posts, posting, posted 1 (noun) The post is the system by which letters and parcels are collected and delivered. **2**

(verb) If you post a letter, you send it to someone by putting it into a postbox. **3** (noun) A post in an organization is a job or official position in it. **4** (verb) If you are posted somewhere, you are sent by your employers to work there. **5** (noun) A post is a strong upright pole fixed into the ground. **postal** (adjective).

post- (prefix) after a particular time or event, e.g. *his postwar career.*

postage (noun) Postage is the money that you pay to send letters and parcels by post.

postal order, postal orders (noun) A postal order is a piece of paper representing a sum of money which you can buy at a post office.

postcard, postcards (noun) A postcard is a card, often with a picture on one side, which you write on and send without an envelope.

postcode, postcodes (noun) Your postcode is a short sequence of letters and numbers at the end of your address which helps the post office to sort the mail.

poster, posters (noun) A poster is a large notice or picture that is stuck on a wall as an advertisement or for decoration.

posterior, posteriors (noun; a humorous use) A person's posterior is their bottom.

posterity (noun; a formal word) You can refer to the future and the people who will be alive then as posterity, e.g. *to record the voyage for posterity.*

posthumous (pronounced **poss**-tyum-uss) (adjective) happening or awarded after a person's death, e.g. *a posthumous medal.* **posthumously** (adverb).

postman, postmen (noun) A postman collects and delivers letters and parcels sent by post.

postmortem, postmortems (noun) A postmortem is a medical examination of a dead body to find out how the person died.

post office, post offices 1 (noun) The Post Office is the national organization responsible for postal services. **2** A post office is a building where you can buy stamps and post letters.

postpone, postpones, postponing, postponed (verb) If you postpone an event, you arrange for it to take place at a later time than was originally planned. **postponement** (noun).

posture, postures (noun) Your posture is the position or manner in which you hold your body.

posy, posies (noun) A posy is a small bunch of flowers.

pot, pots (noun) A pot is a deep round container.

potato, potatoes (noun) A potato is a white vegetable that has a brown or red skin and grows underground.

potent (adjective) effective, powerful, or strong, e.g. *a potent cocktail.* **potency** (noun).

potential 1 (adjective) capable of becoming the thing mentioned, e.g. *potential customers... potential sources of finance.* **2** (noun) Your potential is your ability to achieve success in the future. **poten-**

tially (adverb).

pothole, potholes 1 (noun) A pothole is a hole in the surface of a road caused by bad weather or traffic. **2** A pothole is also an underground cavern.

potion, potions (noun) A potion is a drink containing medicine, poison, or supposed magical powers.

potted (adjective) Potted meat or fish is cooked and put into a small sealed container to preserve it.

potter, potters, pottering, pottered 1 (noun) A potter is a person who makes pottery. **2** (verb) If you potter about, you pass the time doing pleasant, unimportant things.

pottery 1 (noun) Pottery is pots, dishes, and other items made from clay and fired in a kiln. **2** Pottery is also the craft of making pottery.

potty, potties; pottier, pottiest 1 (noun) A potty is a bowl which a small child can sit on and use instead of a toilet. **2** (adjective; an informal use) crazy or foolish.

pouch, pouches 1 (noun) A pouch is a small, soft container with a fold-over top, e.g. *a tobacco pouch.* **2** Animals like kangaroos have a pouch, which is a pocket of skin in which they carry their young.

poultry (noun) Chickens, turkeys, and other birds kept for their meat or eggs are referred to as poultry.

pounce, pounces, pouncing, pounced (verb) If an animal or person pounces on something, they leap and grab it.

pound, pounds, pounding, pounded 1 (noun) The pound is the main unit of currency in Britain and in some other countries. **2** A pound is also a unit of weight equal to 16 ounces or about 0.454 kilograms. **3** (verb) If you pound something, you hit it repeatedly with your fist, e.g. *Someone was pounding on the door.* **4** If you pound a substance, you crush it into a powder or paste, e.g. *Wooden mallets were used to pound the meat.* **5** If your heart is pounding, it is beating very strongly and quickly. **6** If you pound somewhere, you run there with heavy noisy steps.

pour, pours, pouring, poured 1 (verb) If you pour a liquid out of a container, you make it flow out by tipping the container. **2** If something pours somewhere, it flows there quickly and in large quantities, e.g. *Sweat poured down his face.* **3** When it is raining heavily, you can say that it is pouring.

pout, pouts, pouting, pouted (verb) If you pout, you stick out your lip to show disappointment or annoyance.

poverty (noun) Poverty is the state of being very poor.

powder, powders, powdering, powdered 1 (noun) Powder consists of many tiny particles of a solid substance. **2** (verb) If you powder a surface, you cover it with powder. **powdery** (adjective).

power, powers, powering, powered 1 (noun) Someone who has power has a lot of control over people and activities. **2** Someone who has the power to do something has the ability to do it, e.g. *the power of speech.* **3** The power of something is the physical strength that it has to move things. **4** Power is energy obtained, for example, by burning fuel or using the wind or waves. **5** (verb) Something that powers a machine provides the energy for it to work. **powerful** (adjective), **powerfully** (adverb).

powerless (adjective) unable to control or influence events, e.g. *I am powerless to help.*

power station, power stations (noun) A power station is a place where electricity is generated.

practicable (adjective) If a task or plan is practicable, it can be carried out successfully, e.g. *a practicable option.*

practical, practicals 1 (adjective) The practical aspects of something are those that involve direct experience and real situations rather than ideas or theories, e.g. *the practical difficulties of teaching science.* **2** Ideas, methods, tools, or clothes that are practical are sensible and likely to be effective, e.g. *practical low-heeled shoes.* **3** Someone who is practical is able to deal effectively and sensibly with problems. **4** (noun) A practical is an examination in which you make or perform something rather than just write. **practicality** (noun).

practically 1 (adverb) almost but not completely or exactly, e.g. *The house was practically a wreck.* **2** in a practical way, e.g. *practically minded.*

practice, practices 1 (noun) You can refer to something that people do regularly as a practice, e.g. *the practice of kissing hands.* **2** Practice is regular training or exercise, e.g. *I need more practice.* **3** A doctor's or lawyer's practice is his or her business.

practise, practises, practising, practised 1 (verb) If you practise something, you do it regularly in order to improve. **2** People who practise a religion, custom, or craft regularly take part in the activities associated with it, e.g. *a practising Buddhist.* **3** Someone who practises medicine or law works as a doctor or lawyer.

practised (adjective) Someone who is practised at doing something is very skilful at it, e.g. *a practised performer.*

practitioner, practitioners (noun) You can refer to someone who works in a particular profession as a practitioner, e.g. *a medical practitioner.*

pragmatic (adjective) A pragmatic way of considering or doing something is based on practical considerations rather than theoretical ones, e.g. *Rod is pragmatic about the risks.* **pragmatically** (adverb), **pragmatism** (noun).

prairie, prairies (noun) A prairie is a large area of flat, grassy land in North America.

praise, praises, praising, praised 1 (verb) If you praise someone or something, you express strong approval of their qualities or achievements. **2** (noun) Praise is what is said or written in approval of someone's qualities or achievements.

pram, prams (noun) A pram is a baby's cot on wheels.

prance, prances, prancing, pranced (verb) Someone who is prancing around is walking with exaggerated movements.

prank, pranks (noun) A prank is a childish trick.

prattle, prattles, prattling, prattled (verb) If someone prattles on, they talk a lot without saying anything important.

prawn, prawns (noun) A prawn is a small, pink, edible shellfish with a long tail.

pray, prays, praying, prayed (verb) When someone prays, they speak to God to give thanks or to ask for help.

prayer, prayers 1 (noun) Prayer is the activity of praying. **2** A prayer is the words said when someone prays.

pre- (prefix) before a particular time or event, e.g. *the pre-Christmas rush.*

preach, preaches, preaching, preached (verb) When someone preaches, they give a talk on a religious or moral subject as part of a church service. **preacher** (noun).

precarious 1 (adjective) If your situation is precarious, you may fail in what you are doing at any time. **2** Something that is precarious is likely to fall because it is not well balanced or secured. **precariously** (adverb).

precaution, precautions (noun) A precaution is an action that is intended to prevent something from happening, e.g. *It's still worth taking precautions against accidents.* **precautionary** (adjective).

precede, precedes, preceding, preceded 1 (verb) Something that precedes another thing happens or occurs before it. **2** If you precede someone somewhere, you go in front of them. **preceding** (adjective).

precedence (pronounced **press**-id-ens) (noun) If something takes precedence over other things, it is the most important thing and should be dealt with first.

precedent, precedents (noun) An action or decision that is regarded as a precedent is referred to as a guide in taking similar action or decisions later.

precinct, precincts (noun) A shopping precinct is a pedestrian shopping area.

precious (adjective) Something that is precious is valuable or very important and should be looked after or used carefully.

precipice, precipices (pronounced **press**-sip-piss) (noun) A precipice is a very steep rock face.

precipitate, precipitates, precipitating, precipitated (verb; a formal use) If something precipitates an event or situation, it causes it to happen suddenly.

precise (adjective) exact and accurate in every detail, e.g. *precise measurements.* **precisely** (adverb), **precision** (noun).

preclude, precludes, precluding, precluded (verb; a formal word) If something precludes an event or situation, it prevents it from happening, e.g. *The meal precluded serious conversation.*

precocious (adjective) Precocious children behave in a way that seems too advanced for their age.

preconceived (adjective) Preconceived ideas about something have been formed without any real experience or information. **preconception** (noun).

precondition, preconditions (noun) If something is a precondition for another thing, it must happen before the second thing can take place.

precursor, precursors (noun) A precursor of something that exists now is a similar thing that existed at an earlier time, e.g. *real tennis, an ancient precursor of the modern game.*

predator, predators (pronounced **pred**-dat-tor) (noun) A predator is an animal that kills and eats other animals. **predatory** (adjective).

predecessor, predecessors (noun) Someone's predecessor is a person who used to do their job before.

predetermined (adjective) decided in advance or controlled by previous events rather than left to chance.

predicament, predicaments (noun) If you are in a predicament, you are in a difficult situation.

predict, predicts, predicting, predicted (verb) If someone predicts an event, they say that it will happen in the future. **prediction** (noun).

predominant (adjective) more important or more noticeable than anything else in a particular set of people or things. **predominantly** (adverb).

predominate, predominates, predominating, predominated (verb) If one type of person or thing predominates, it is the most common, frequent, or noticeable. **predominance** (noun).

pre-eminent (adjective) recognized as being the most important in a particular group, e.g. *the pre-eminent experts in the area.* **pre-eminence** (noun).

pre-empt, pre-empts, pre-empting, pre-empted (verb; a formal word) If you pre-empt something, you prevent it by doing something else which makes it pointless or impossible, e.g. *a wish to pre-empt any further publicity.*

preen, preens, preening, preened (verb) When a bird preens its feathers, it cleans them using its beak.

preface, prefaces (pronounced **pref**-fiss) (noun) A preface is an introduction at the beginning of a book explaining what the book is about or why it was written.

prefect, prefects (noun) A prefect at a school is a pupil who has special duties.

prefer, prefers, preferring, preferred (verb) If you prefer one thing to another, you like it better than the other thing. **preferable** (adjective), **preferably** (adverb).

preference, preferences (pronounced **pref**-fer-enss) **1** (noun) If you have a preference for something, you like it more than other things, e.g. *a preference for white.* **2** When making a choice, if you give preference to one type of person or thing, you try to choose that type.

preferential (adjective) A person who gets preferential treatment is treated better than others.

prefix, prefixes (noun) A prefix is a letter or group of letters added to the beginning of a word to make a new word, for example 'semi-' and 'un-'.

pregnant (adjective) A woman who is pregnant has a baby developing in her womb. **pregnancy** (noun).

prehistoric (adjective) existing at a time in the past before anything was written down.

prejudice, prejudices (noun) Prejudice is an unreasonable and unfair dislike of, or preference for, a particular type of person or thing. **prejudiced** (adjective), **prejudicial** (adjective).

preliminary (adjective) Preliminary activities take place before something starts, in preparation for it, e.g. *the preliminary rounds of the competition.*

prelude, preludes (noun) Something that is an introduction to a more important event can be described as a prelude to that event.

premature (adjective) happening too early, or earlier than expected, e.g. *premature baldness.* **prematurely** (adverb).

premeditated (adjective) planned in advance, e.g. *a premeditated attack.*

premier, premiers 1 (noun) The leader of a government is sometimes referred to as the premier. **2** (adjective) considered to be the best or most important, e.g. *Edinburgh's premier jewellers.*

premiere, premieres (pronounced **prem**-mee-er) (noun) The premiere of a new play or film is its first public performance.

premise, premises (pronounced **prem**-iss) **1** (plural noun) The premises of an organization are all the buildings it occupies on one site. **2** (noun) A premise is a statement which you suppose is true and use as the basis for an idea or argument.

premium, premiums (noun) A premium is an extra sum of money that has to be paid, e.g. *Paying a premium for space is worthwhile.*

premonition, premonitions (pronounced prem-on-**ish**-on) (noun) A premonition is a feeling that something unpleasant is going to happen.

preoccupation, preoccupations (noun) If you have a preoccupation with something, it is very important to you and you keep thinking about it.

preoccupied (adjective) Someone who is preoccupied is deep in thought or totally involved with something.

preparatory (adjective) Preparatory activities are done before doing something else in order to prepare for it.

prepare, prepares, preparing, prepared (verb) If you prepare something, you make it ready for a particular purpose or event, e.g. *He was preparing the meal.* **preparation** (noun).

prepared (adjective) If you are prepared to do something, you are willing to do it.

preposition, prepositions (noun) A preposition is a

word such as 'by', 'for', 'into', or 'with', which usually has a noun as its object.

preposterous (adjective) extremely unreasonable and ridiculous, e.g. *a preposterous statement.*

prerequisite, prerequisites (pronounced pree-**rek**-wiz-zit) (noun; a formal word) Something that is a prerequisite for another thing must happen or exist before the other thing is possible.

prerogative, prerogatives (pronounced prir-**rog**-at-tiv) (noun; a formal word) Something that is the prerogative of a person is their special privilege or right.

prescribe, prescribes, prescribing, prescribed (verb) When a doctor prescribes treatment, he or she states what treatment a patient should have.

prescription, prescriptions (noun) A prescription is a piece of paper on which the doctor has written the name of a medicine needed by a patient.

presence 1 (noun) Someone's presence in a place is the fact of their being there, e.g. *His presence made me happy.* **2** If you are in someone's presence, you are in the same place as they are.

present, presents, presenting, presented 1 (adjective) If someone is present somewhere, they are there, e.g. *He had been present at the birth of his son.* **2** A present situation is one that exists now rather than in the past or the future. **3** (noun) The present is the period of time that is taking place now. **4** A present is something that you give to someone for them to keep. **5** (verb) If you present someone with something, you give it to them, e.g. *She presented a bravery award to the girl.* **6** Something that presents a difficulty or a challenge causes it or provides it. **presentation** (noun), **presenter** (noun).

presentable (adjective) neat or attractive and suitable for people to see.

present-day (adjective) existing or happening now, e.g. *present-day farming practices.*

presently 1 (adverb) If something will happen presently, it will happen soon, e.g. *I'll finish the job presently.* **2** Something that is presently happening is happening now, e.g. *Some progress is presently being made.*

present participle, present participles (noun) In grammar, the present participle of an English verb is the form that ends in '-ing'. It is used to form some tenses, and can be used to form adjectives and nouns from a verb.

present tense (noun) In grammar, the present tense is the tense of a verb that you use mainly to talk about things that happen or exist at the time of writing or speaking.

preservative, preservatives (noun) A preservative is a substance or chemical that prevents things from decaying.

preserve, preserves, preserving, preserved 1 (verb) If you preserve something, you take action to make sure that it remains as it is. **2** If you preserve food, you treat it to prevent it from decaying so that it can be stored. **3** (noun) Preserves are foods such as jam or chutney that have been made with a lot of sugar or vinegar. **preservation** (noun).

preside, presides, presiding, presided (verb) A person who presides over a formal event is in charge of it.

president, presidents 1 (noun) In a country which has no king or queen, the president is the elected leader, e.g. *the President of the United States of America.* **2** The president of an organization is the person who has the highest position. **presidency** (noun), **presidential** (adjective).

press, presses, pressing, pressed 1 (verb) If you press something, you push it or hold it firmly against something else, e.g. *Lisa pressed his hand... Press the blue button.* **2** If you press clothes, you iron them. **3** If you press for something, you try hard to persuade someone to agree to it, e.g. *She was pressing for improvements to the education system.* **4** If you press charges, you make an official accusation against someone which has to be decided in a court of law. **5** (noun) Newspapers and the journalists who work for them are called the press.

press conference, press conferences (noun) When someone gives a press conference, they have a meeting to answer questions put by reporters.

pressing (adjective) Something that is pressing needs to be dealt with immediately, e.g. *pressing needs.*

pressure, pressures, pressuring, pressured 1 (noun) Pressure is the force that is produced by pushing on something. **2** If you are under pressure, you have too much to do and not enough time, or someone is trying hard to persuade you to do something. **3** (verb) If you pressure someone, you try hard to persuade them to do something.

pressurize, pressurizes, pressurizing, pressurized; also spelled **pressurise** (verb) If you pressurize someone, you try hard to persuade them to do something.

prestige (pronounced **press-teezh**) (noun) If you have prestige, people admire you because of your position. **prestigious** (adjective).

presumably (adverb) If you say that something is presumably the case, you mean you assume that it is, e.g. *Your audience, presumably, are younger.*

presume, presumes, presuming, presumed (pronounced **priz-yoom**) (verb) If you presume something, you think that it is the case although you have no proof. **presumption** (noun).

presumptuous (adjective) Someone who behaves in a presumptuous way does things that they have no right to do.

pretence, pretences (noun) A pretence is a way of behaving that is false and intended to deceive people.

pretend, pretends, pretending, pretended (verb) If you pretend that something is the case, you try to make people believe that it is, although in fact it is not, e.g. *Latimer pretended not to notice.*

pretender, pretenders (noun) A pretender to a throne or title is someone who claims it but whose claim is disputed.

pretension, pretensions (noun) Someone with pretensions claims that they are more important than they really are.

pretentious (adjective) Someone or something that is pretentious is trying to seem important or significant when in fact they are not.

pretext, pretexts (noun) A pretext is a false reason given to hide the real reason for doing something.

pretty, prettier, prettiest 1 (adjective) nice to look at and attractive in a delicate way. **2** (adverb; an informal use) quite or rather, e.g. *He spoke pretty good English.* **prettily** (adverb), **prettiness** (noun).

prevail, prevails, prevailing, prevailed 1 (verb) If a custom or belief prevails in a particular place, it is normal or most common there, e.g. *This attitude has prevailed in Britain for many years.* **2** If someone or something prevails, they succeed in their aims, e.g. *In recent years better sense has prevailed.* **prevailing** (adjective).

prevalent (adjective) very common or widespread, e.g. *a more prevalent problem.* **prevalence** (noun).

prevent, prevents, preventing, prevented (verb) If you prevent something, you stop it from happening or being done. **preventable** (adjective), **prevention** (noun).

preventive or **preventative** (adjective) intended to help prevent things such as disease or crime, e.g. *preventive health care.*

preview, previews (noun) A preview of something such as a film or exhibition is an opportunity to see it before it is shown to the public.

previous (adjective) happening or existing before something else in time or position, e.g. *previous reports... the previous year.* **previously** (adverb).

prey, preys, preying, preyed 1 (noun) The creatures that an animal hunts and eats are called its prey. **2** (verb) An animal that preys on a particular kind of animal lives by hunting and eating it.

price, prices, pricing, priced 1 (noun) The price of something is the amount of money you have to pay to buy it. **2** (verb) To price something at a particular amount means to fix its price at that amount.

priceless (adjective) Something that is priceless is so valuable that it is difficult to assess how much it is worth.

pricey, pricier, priciest (adjective; an informal word) expensive.

prick, pricks, pricking, pricked 1 (verb) If you prick something, you stick a sharp pointed object into it. **2** (noun) A prick is a small, sharp pain caused when something pricks you.

prickle, prickles, prickling, prickled 1 (noun) Prickles are small sharp points or thorns on plants. **2** (verb) If your skin prickles, it feels as if a lot of sharp points are being stuck into it. **prickly** (adjective).

pride, prides, priding, prided 1 (noun) Pride is a feeling of satisfaction you have when you have done something well. **2** Pride is also a feeling of being better than other people. **3** (verb) If you pride yourself on a quality or skill, you are proud of it, e.g. *She prides herself on punctuality.*

priest, priests 1 (noun) A priest is a member of the clergy in some Christian Churches. **2** In many non-Christian religions, a priest is a man who has special duties in the place of worship. **priestly** (adjective).

priesthood (noun) The priesthood is the position of being a priest.

prim, primmer, primmest (adjective) Someone who is prim always behaves very correctly and is easily shocked by anything rude.

primaeval another spelling of **primeval.**

primarily (adverb) You use primarily to indicate the main or most important feature of something, e.g. *I still rated people primarily on their looks.*

primary (adjective) Primary is used to describe something that is extremely important for someone or something, e.g. *the primary aim of his research.*

primary colour, primary colours (noun) In art, the primary colours are red, yellow, and blue, from which other colours can be obtained by mixing.

primary school, primary schools (noun) A primary school is for children between the ages of 5 and 11.

primate, primates 1 (noun) A primate is an archbishop. **2** A primate is also a member of the group of animals which includes humans, monkeys, and apes.

prime, primes, priming, primed 1 (adjective) main or most important, e.g. *a prime cause of brain damage.* **2** of the best quality, e.g. *in prime condition.* **3** (noun) Someone's prime is the stage when they are at their strongest, most active, or most successful. **4** (verb) If you prime someone, you give them information about something in advance to prepare them, e.g. *Arnold primed her for her duties.*

Prime Minister, Prime Ministers (noun) The Prime Minister is the leader of the government.

primeval or **primaeval** (pronounced pry-**mee**-vl) (adjective) belonging to a very early period in the history of the world.

primitive 1 (adjective) connected with a society that lives very simply without industries or a writing system, e.g. *the primitive peoples of the world.* **2** very simple, basic, or old-fashioned, e.g. *a very small primitive cottage.*

primrose, primroses (noun) A primrose is a small plant that has pale yellow flowers.

prince, princes (noun) A prince is a male member of a royal family, especially the son of a king or queen. **princely** (adjective).

princess, princesses (noun) A princess is a female member of a royal family, usually the daughter of a king or queen, or the wife of a prince.

principal, principals 1 (adjective) main or most important, e.g. *the principal source of food.* **2** (noun) The principal of a school or college is the person in charge of it. **principally** (adverb).

principality, principalities (noun) A principality is a country ruled by a prince.

principle, principles 1 (noun) A principle is a belief you have about the way you should behave, e.g. *a woman of principle.* **2** A principle is also a general rule or scientific law which explains how something happens or works, e.g. *the principle of evolution.*

print, prints, printing, printed 1 (verb) To print a newspaper or book means to reproduce it in large quantities using a mechanical or electronic copying process. **2** (noun) The letters and numbers on the pages of a book or newspaper are referred to as the print. **3** A print is a photograph, or a printed copy of a painting. **4** Footprints and fingerprints can be referred to as prints. **5** (verb) If you print when you are writing, you do not join the letters together. **printer** (noun).

print-out, print-outs (noun) A print-out is a printed copy of information from a computer.

prior, priors 1 (adjective) planned or done at an earlier time, e.g. *I have a prior engagement.* **2** (phrase) Something that happens **prior to** a particular time or event happens before it. **3** (noun) A prior is a monk in charge of a small group of monks in a priory. **prioress** (noun).

priority, priorities (noun) Something that is a priority is the most important thing and needs to be dealt with first, e.g. *The priority is building homes.*

priory, priories (noun) A priory is a place where a small group of monks live under the charge of a prior.

prise, prises, prising, prised (verb) If you prise something open or away from a surface, you force it open or away, e.g. *She prised his fingers loose.*

prism, prisms (noun) A prism is an object made of clear glass with many flat sides. It separates light passing through it into the colours of the rainbow.

prison, prisons (noun) A prison is a building where criminals are kept in captivity.

prisoner, prisoners (noun) A prisoner is someone who is kept in prison or held in captivity against their will.

pristine (pronounced **priss**-teen) (adjective; a formal word) very clean or new and in perfect condition.

private, privates 1 (adjective) for the use of one person rather than people in general, e.g. *a private bathroom.* **2** taking place between a small number of people and kept secret from others, e.g. *a private conversation.* **3** owned or operated by individuals or companies rather than by the state, e.g. *a private company.* **4** (noun) A private is a soldier of the lowest rank. **privacy** (noun), **privately** (adverb).

private school, private schools (noun) A private school is a school that is not supported financially by the government, and which parents pay for their children to attend.

privatize, privatizes, privatizing, privatized; also spelled **privatise** (verb) If the government privatizes a state-owned industry or organization, it allows it to be bought and owned by a private individual or group.

privilege, privileges (noun) A privilege is a special right or advantage given to a person or group, e.g. *the privileges of monarchy.* **privileged** (adjective).

privy (adjective; a formal use) If you are privy to something secret, you have been told about it.

prize, prizes, prizing, prized 1 (noun) A prize is a reward given to the winner of a competition or game. **2** (adjective) of the highest quality or standard, e.g. *his prize dahlia.* **3** (verb) Something that is prized is wanted and admired for its value or quality.

pro, pros 1 (noun; an informal use) A pro is a professional. **2** (phrase) The **pros and cons** of a situation are its advantages and disadvantages.

pro- (prefix) supporting or in favour of, e.g. *pro-democracy protests.*

probability, probabilities 1 (noun) The probability of something happening is how likely it is to happen, e.g. *the probability of success.* **2** If something is a probability, it is likely to happen, e.g. *The probability is that you will be feeling better.*

probable (adjective) Something that is probable is likely to be true or correct, or likely to happen, e.g. *the most probable outcome.*

probably (adverb) Something that is probably the case is likely but not certain.

probation (noun) Probation is a period of time during which a person convicted of a crime is supervised by a probation officer instead of being sent to prison. **probationary** (adjective).

probe, probes, probing, probed 1 (verb) If you probe, you ask a lot of questions to discover the facts about something. **2** (noun) A probe is a long thin instrument used by doctors when examining a patient.

problem, problems 1 (noun) A problem is an unsatisfactory situation that causes difficulties. **2** A problem is also a puzzle or question that you solve using logical thought or mathematics. **problematic** (adjective).

procedure, procedures (noun) A procedure is a way of doing something, especially the correct or usual way, e.g. *It's standard procedure.* **procedural** (adjective).

proceed, proceeds, proceeding, proceeded 1 (verb) If you proceed to do something, you start doing it, or continue doing it, e.g. *She proceeded to tell them.* **2** (a formal use) If you proceed in a particular direction, you move in that direction, e.g. *The taxi proceeded along a lonely road.* **3** (plural noun) The proceeds from a fund-raising event are the money obtained from it.

proceedings 1 (plural noun) You can refer to an organized and related series of events as the proceedings, e.g. *She was determined to see the proceedings from start to finish.* **2** Legal proceedings are legal action taken against someone.

process, processes, processing, processed 1 (noun) A process is a series of actions intended to achieve a particular result or change. **2** (phrase) If you are **in the process** of doing something, you have started doing it but have not yet finished. **3** (verb) When something such as food or information is processed, it is treated or dealt with.

procession, processions (noun) A procession is a group of people or vehicles moving in a line, often as part of a ceremony.

proclaim, proclaims, proclaiming, proclaimed (verb) If someone proclaims something, they formally announce it or make it known, e.g. *You have proclaimed your innocence.* **proclamation** (noun).

procure, procures, procuring, procured (verb; a formal word) If you procure something, you obtain it.

prod, prods, prodding, prodded (verb) If you prod something, you give it a push with your finger or with something pointed.

prodigy, prodigies (pronounced **prod**-dij-ee) (noun) A prodigy is someone who shows an extraordinary natural ability at an early age.

produce, produces, producing, produced 1 (verb) To produce something means to make it or cause it, e.g. *a white wine produced mainly from black grapes.* **2** If you produce something from somewhere, you bring it out so it can be seen. **3** (noun) Produce is food that is grown to be sold, e.g. *fresh produce.*

producer, producers (noun) The producer of a record, film, or show is the person in charge of making it or putting it on.

product, products 1 (noun) A product is something that is made to be sold, e.g. *high-quality products.* **2** In maths, the product of two or more numbers or quantities is the result of multiplying them together.

production, productions 1 (noun) Production is the process of manufacturing or growing something in large quantities, e.g. *modern methods of production.* **2** Production is also the amount of goods manufactured or food grown by a country or company, e.g. *Production has fallen by 13.2%.*

productive (adjective) To be productive means to produce a large number of things, e.g. *Farms were more productive in these areas.*

productivity (noun) Productivity is the rate at which things are produced or dealt with.

profane (adjective; a formal

word) showing disrespect for a religion or religious things, e.g. *profane language.*

profess, professes, professing, professed 1 (verb; a formal word) If you profess to do or have something, you claim to do or have it. **2** If you profess a feeling or opinion, you express it, e.g. *He professes a lasting affection for Trinidad.*

profession, professions 1 (noun) A profession is a type of job that requires advanced education or training. **2** You can use profession to refer to all the people who have a particular profession, e.g. *the medical profession.*

professional, professionals 1 (adjective) Professional means relating to the work of someone who is qualified in a particular profession, e.g. *I think you need professional advice.* **2** Professional also describes activities when they are done to earn money rather than as a hobby, e.g. *professional football.* **3** A professional piece of work is of a very high standard. **4** (noun) A professional is a person who has been trained in a profession. **5** A professional is someone who plays a sport for money rather than as a hobby.

professor, professors (noun) In a British university, a professor is the senior teacher in a department. **professorial** (adjective).

proficient (adjective) If you are proficient at something, you can do it well. **proficiency** (noun).

profile, profiles 1 (noun) Your profile is the outline of your face seen from the side. **2** A profile of someone is a short description of their life and character.

profit, profits, profiting, profited 1 (noun) When someone sells something, the profit is the amount they gain by selling it for more than it cost them to buy or make. **2** (verb) If you profit from something, you gain or benefit from it. **profitable** (adjective).

profound 1 (adjective) great in degree or intensity, e.g. *a profound need to please.* **2** showing great and deep intellectual understanding, e.g. *a profound question.* **profoundly** (adverb), **profundity** (noun).

program, programs, programming, programmed 1 (noun) A program is a set of instructions that a computer follows to perform a particular task. **2** (verb) When someone programs a computer, they write a program and put it into the computer. **programmer** (noun).

programme, programmes 1 (noun) You can refer to a planned series of events as a programme, e.g. *a programme of official engagements.* **2** A programme on television or radio is a particular piece presented as a unit, such as a play, show, or discussion. **3** A programme is a booklet giving information about a play or concert you are attending.

progress, progresses, progressing, progressed 1 (noun) Progress is the process of gradually improving or getting near to achieving something. **2** The progress of something is the way in which it develops or continues, e.g. *news on the progress of the war.* **3** (phrase) Something that is **in progress** is happening, e.g. *A darts match was in progress.* **4** (verb) If you progress, you become more advanced or skilful. **5** To progress also means to continue, e.g. *As the evening progressed, sadness turned to rage.* **progression** (noun).

progressive 1 (adjective) having modern ideas about how things should be done. **2** happening gradually, e.g. *a progressive illness.*

prohibit, prohibits, prohibiting, prohibited (verb) If someone prohibits something, they forbid it or make it illegal. **prohibition** (noun).

prohibitive (adjective) If the cost of something is prohibitive, it is so high that people cannot afford it.

project, projects, projecting, projected 1 (noun) A project is a carefully planned attempt to achieve something or to study something over a period of time. **2** (verb) Something that is projected is planned or expected to happen in the future, e.g. *The population aged 65 or over is projected to increase.* **3** To project an image onto a screen means to make it appear there using equipment such as a projector. **4** Something that projects sticks out beyond a surface or edge. **projection** (noun).

projector, projectors (noun) A projector is a piece of equipment which produces a large image on a screen by shining light through a photographic slide or film strip.

proletariat (noun; a formal word) Working-class people are sometimes referred to as the proletariat. **proletarian** (adjective).

proliferate, proliferates, proliferating, proliferated (verb) If things proliferate, they quickly increase in number. **proliferation** (noun).

prolific (adjective) producing a lot of something, e.g. *this prolific artist.*

prologue, prologues (noun) A prologue is a speech or section that introduces a play or book.

prolong, prolongs, prolonging, prolonged (verb) If you prolong something, you make it last longer. **prolonged** (adjective).

prom, proms (noun; an informal word) A prom is a concert at which some of the audience stand.

promenade, promenades (pronounced prom-min-**ahd**) (noun) At a seaside resort, the promenade is a road or path next to the sea.

prominent 1 (adjective) Prominent people are important. **2** Something that is prominent is very noticeable, e.g. *a prominent nose.* **prominence** (noun), **prominently** (adverb).

promiscuous (pronounced prom-**misk**-yoo-uss) (adjective) Someone who is promiscuous has sex with many different people. **promiscuity** (noun).

promise, promises, promising, promised 1 (verb) If you promise to do something, you say that you will definitely do it. **2** (noun) A promise is a statement made by someone that they will definitely do something, e.g. *He made a promise to me.* **3** (verb) Something that promises to have a particular quality shows signs that it will have that quality, e.g. *This promised to be a very long night.* **4** (noun) Someone or something that shows promise seems likely to be very successful. **promising** (adjective).

promontory, promontories (pronounced **prom**-mon-tree) (noun) A promontory is an area of high land sticking out into the sea.

promote, promotes, promoting, promoted 1 (verb) If someone promotes something, they try to make it happen, increase, or become more popular, e.g. *to promote their latest film.* **2** If someone is promoted, they are given a more important job at work. **promoter** (noun), **promotion** (noun).

prompt, prompts, prompting, prompted 1 (verb) If something prompts someone to do something, it makes them decide to do it, e.g. *Curiosity prompted him to push at the door.* **2** If you prompt someone when they stop speaking, you tell them what to say next. **3** (adjective) A prompt action is done without any delay, e.g. *a prompt reply.* **4** (adverb) exactly at the time mentioned, e.g. *Wednesday morning at 10.40 prompt.* **promptly** (adverb).

prone 1 (adjective) If you are prone to something, you have a tendency to be affected by it or to do it, e.g. *She is prone to depression.* **2** If you are prone, you are lying flat and face downwards.

prong, prongs (noun) The prongs of a fork are the long, narrow, pointed parts.

pronoun, pronouns (noun) In grammar, a pronoun is a word that is used to replace a noun. 'He', 'she', and 'them' are all pronouns.

pronounce, pronounces, pronouncing, pronounced (verb) When you pronounce a word, you say it.

pronounced (adjective) very noticeable, e.g. *He talks with a pronounced lowland accent.*

pronouncement, pronouncements (noun) A pronouncement is a formal statement.

pronunciation, pronunciations (pronounced pron-nun-see-**ay**-shn) (noun) The pronunciation of a word is the way it is usually pronounced.

proof (noun) If you have proof of something, you have evidence which shows that it is true or exists.

prop, props, propping, propped 1 (verb) If you prop an object somewhere, you support it or rest it against something, e.g. *The barman propped himself against the counter.* **2** (noun) A prop is a stick or other object used to support something. **3** The props in a play are all the objects and furniture used by the actors.

propaganda (noun) Propaganda is exaggerated or false information that is published or broadcast in order to influence people.

propagate, propagates, propagating, propagated 1 (verb) If people propagate an idea, they spread it to try to influence many other people. **2** If you propagate plants, you grow more of them from an original one. **propagation** (noun).

propel, propels, propelling, propelled (verb) To propel something means to cause it to move in a particular direction.

propeller, propellers (noun) A propeller on a boat or aircraft is a device with blades which rotates and makes the boat or aircraft move.

propensity, propensities (noun; a formal word) A propensity is a tendency to behave in a particular way.

proper 1 (adjective) real and satisfactory, e.g. *He was no nearer having a proper job.* **2** correct or suitable, e.g. *Put things in their proper place.* **3** actual, e.g. *The factories are outside the town proper.* **properly** (adverb).

proper noun, proper nouns (noun) A proper noun is the name of a person, place, or institution.

property, properties 1 (noun) A person's property is the things that belong to them. **2** A property is a building and the land belonging to it. **3** A property of something is a characteristic or quality that it has, e.g. *Mint has powerful healing properties.*

prophecy, prophecies (noun) A prophecy is a statement about what someone believes will happen in the future.

prophesy, prophesies, prophesying, prophesied (verb) If someone prophesies something, they say it will happen.

prophet, prophets (noun) A prophet is a person who predicts what will happen in the future.

prophetic (adjective) correctly predicting what will happen, e.g. *a prophetic warning.*

proportion, proportions 1 (noun) A proportion of an amount or group is a part of it, e.g. *a tiny proportion of the population.* **2** The proportion of one amount to another is its size in comparison with the other amount, e.g. *the highest proportion of single women to men.* **3** (plural noun) You can refer to the size of something as its proportions, e.g. *a red umbrella of vast proportions.*

proportional or **proportionate** (adjective) If one thing is proportional to another, it remains the same size in comparison with the other, e.g. *proportional increases in profit.* **proportionally** or **proportionately** (adverb).

proposal, proposals (noun) A proposal is a plan that has been suggested, e.g. *business proposals.*

propose, proposes, proposing, proposed 1 (verb) If you propose a plan or idea, you suggest it. **2** If you propose to do something, you intend to do it, e.g. *And how do you propose to do that?* **3** When someone proposes a toast to a particular person, they ask people to drink a toast to that person. **4** If someone proposes to another person, they ask that person to marry them.

proposition, propositions 1 (noun) A proposition is a statement expressing a theory or opinion. **2** A proposition is also an offer or suggestion, e.g. *I made her a proposition.*

proprietor, proprietors (noun) The proprietor of a business is the owner.

propriety (noun; a formal word) Propriety is social or moral acceptability, e.g. *a model of propriety.*

propulsion (noun) Propulsion is the power that moves something.

prose (noun) Prose is ordinary written language in contrast to poetry.

prosecute, prosecutes, prosecuting, prosecuted (verb) If someone is prosecuted, they are charged with a crime and have to stand trial. **prosecutor** (noun).

prosecution (noun) The lawyers who try to prove that a person on trial is guilty are called the prosecution.

prospect, prospects, prospecting, prospected 1 (noun) If there is a prospect of something happening, there is a possibility that it will happen, e.g. *There was little prospect of going home.* **2** Someone's prospects are their chances of being successful in the future. **3** (verb) If someone prospects for gold or oil, they look for it. **prospector** (noun).

prospective (adjective) Prospective is used to say that someone wants to be or is likely to be something. For example, the prospective owner of something is the person who wants to own it.

prospectus, prospectuses (noun) A prospectus is a booklet giving details about a college or a company.

prosper, prospers, prospering, prospered (verb) When people or businesses prosper, they are successful and make a lot of money. **prosperous** (adjective), **prosperity** (noun).

prostitute, prostitutes (noun) A prostitute is a person, usually a woman, who has sex with men in exchange for money. **prostitution** (noun).

prostrate (adjective) lying face downwards on the ground.

protagonist, protagonists (a formal word) **1** (noun) Someone who is a protagonist of an idea or movement is a leading supporter of it. **2** The protagonists in a play or story are the main characters.

protect, protects, protecting, protected (verb) To protect someone or something means to prevent them from being harmed or damaged. **protection** (noun), **protective** (adjective).

protégé, protégés (pronounced **proh**-tij-ay) (noun) Someone who is the protégé of a more experienced person is helped and guided by that person.

protein, proteins (noun) Protein is a substance that is found in meat, eggs, and milk and that is needed by bodies for growth.

protest, protests, protesting, protested 1 (verb) If you protest about something, you say or demonstrate publicly that you disagree with it, e.g. *They protested against the killing of a teenager.* **2** (noun) A protest is a demonstration or statement showing that you disagree with something.

Protestant, Protestants (noun or adjective) A Protestant is a member of one of the Christian Churches which separated from the Catholic Church in the sixteenth century.

protestation, protestations (noun) A protestation is a strong declaration that something is true or not true, e.g. *his protestations of love.*

protocol (noun) Protocol is the system of rules about the correct way to behave in formal situations.

proton, protons (noun) A proton is a particle which forms part of the nucleus of an atom and has a positive electrical charge.

prototype, prototypes (noun) A prototype is a first model of something that is made so that the design can be tested and improved.

protracted (adjective) lasting longer than usual, e.g. *a protracted dispute.*

protractor, protractors (noun) A protractor is a flat, semicircular piece of plastic used for measuring angles.

protrude, protrudes, protruding, protruded (verb; a formal word) If something is protruding from a surface or edge, it is sticking out. **protrusion** (noun).

proud, prouder, proudest 1 (adjective) feeling pleasure and satisfaction at something you own or have achieved, e.g. *I was proud of our players today.* **2** having great dignity and self-respect, e.g. *too proud to ask for money.* **proudly** (adverb).

prove, proves, proving, proved or **proven 1** (verb) To prove that something is true means to provide evidence that it is definitely true, e.g. *A letter from Nora proved that he lived there.* **2** If something proves to be the case, it becomes clear that it is so, e.g. *His first impressions of her proved wrong.*

proverb, proverbs (noun) A proverb is a short sentence which gives advice or makes a comment about life. **proverbial** (adjective).

provide, provides, providing, provided 1 (verb) If you provide something for someone, you give it to them or make it available for them. **2** If you provide for someone, you give them the things they need.

provided or **providing** (conjunction) If you say that something will happen provided something else happens, you mean that the first thing will happen only if the second thing does.

providence (noun) Providence is God or a force which is believed to arrange the things that happen to us.

province, provinces 1 (noun) A province is one of the areas into which some large countries are divided, each province having its own administration. **2** You can refer to the parts of a country which are not near the capital as the provinces.

provincial 1 (adjective) connected with the parts of a country outside the capital, e.g. *a provincial theatre.* **2** narrow-minded and unsophisticated.

provision, provisions 1 (noun) The provision of something is the act of making it available to people, e.g. *the provision of jobs.* **2** (plural noun) Provisions are supplies of food.

provisional (adjective) A provisional arrangement has not yet been made definite and so might be changed.

proviso, provisos (pronounced prov-**eye**-zoh) (noun) A proviso is a condition in an agreement.

provocation, provocations (noun) A provocation is an act done deliberately to annoy someone.

provocative 1 (adjective) intended to annoy people or make them react, e.g. *a provocative speech.* **2** intended to make someone feel sexual desire, e.g. *provocative poses.*

provoke, provokes, provoking, provoked 1 (verb) If you provoke someone, you deliberately try to make them angry. **2** If something provokes an unpleasant reaction, it causes it, e.g. *illness provoked by worry.*

prow, prows (noun) The prow of a boat is the front part.

prowess (noun) Prowess is outstanding ability, e.g. *his prowess at tennis.*

prowl, prowls, prowling, prowled (verb) If a person or animal prowls around, they move around quietly and secretly, as if hunting.

proximity (noun; a formal word) Proximity is nearness to someone or something.

proxy (phrase) If you do something **by proxy,** someone else does it on your behalf, e.g. *voting by proxy.*

prude, prudes (noun) If you call someone a prude, you mean they are too easily shocked by sex or nudity. **prudish** (adjective).

prudent (adjective) behaving in a sensible and cautious way, e.g. *It is prudent to plan ahead.* **prudence** (noun), **prudently** (adverb).

prune, prunes, pruning, pruned 1 (noun) A prune is a dried plum. **2** (verb) When someone prunes a tree or shrub, they cut back some of the branches.

pry, pries, prying, pried (verb) If someone is prying, they are trying to find out about something secret or private.

PS PS is written before an additional message at the end of a letter. PS is an abbreviation for 'postscript'.

psalm, psalms (pronounced **sahm**) (noun) A psalm is one of the 150 songs, poems, and prayers which form the Book of Psalms in the Bible.

pseudo- (pronounced **syoo**-doh) (prefix) Pseudo- is used to form adjectives and nouns indicating that something is not what it is claimed to be, e.g. *pseudo-scientific theories.*

pseudonym, pseudonyms (pronounced **syoo**-doe-nim) (noun) A writer who uses a pseudonym uses another name as an author rather than their real name.

psyche, psyches (pronounced **sigh**-kee) (noun) Your psyche is your mind and your deepest feelings.

psychiatry (noun) Psychiatry is the branch of medicine concerned with mental illness. **psychiatrist** (noun), **psychiatric** (adjective).

psychic (adjective) having unusual mental powers such as the ability to read people's minds or predict the future.

psychology (noun) Psychology is the scientific study of the mind and of the reasons for people's behaviour. **psychological** (adjective), **psychologist** (noun).

psychopath, psychopaths (noun) A psychopath is a mentally ill person who behaves violently without feeling guilt. **psychopathic** (adjective).

pterodactyl, pterodactyls (pronounced ter-rod-**dak**-til) (noun) Pterodactyls were flying reptiles in prehistoric times.

PTO PTO is an abbreviation for 'please turn over'. It is written at the bottom of a page to indicate that the writing continues on the other side.

pub, pubs (noun) A pub is a building where people go to buy and drink alcoholic or soft drinks.

puberty (pronounced **pyoo**-ber-tee) (noun) Puberty is the stage when a person's body changes from that of a child into that of an adult.

pubic (pronounced **pyoo**-bik) (adjective) relating to the area around and above a person's genitals.

public 1 (noun) You can refer to people in general as the public. **2** (adjective) relating to people in general, e.g. *There was some public support for the idea.* **3** provided for everyone to use, or open to anyone, e.g. *public transport.* **publicly** (adverb).

publican, publicans (noun) A publican is a person who owns or manages a pub.

publication, publications 1 (noun) The publication of a book is the act of printing it and making it available. **2** A publication is a book or magazine, e.g. *medical publications.*

publicity (noun) Publicity is information or advertisements about an item or event.

publicize, publicizes, publicizing, publicized; also spelled **publicise** (verb) When someone publicizes a fact or event, they advertise it and make it widely known.

public school, public schools (noun) In Britain, a public school is a school that is privately run and that charges fees for the pupils to attend.

publish, publishes, publishing, published (verb) When a company publishes a book, newspaper, or magazine, they print copies of it and distribute it. **publisher** (noun), **publishing** (noun).

pudding, puddings 1 (noun) A pudding is a sweet cake mixture cooked with fruit or other flavouring and served hot. **2** You can refer to the sweet course of a meal as the pudding.

puddle, puddles (noun) A puddle is a small shallow pool of liquid.

puerile (pronounced **pyoo**-rile) (adjective) Puerile behaviour is silly and childish.

puff, puffs, puffing, puffed 1 (verb) To puff a cigarette or pipe means to smoke it. **2** If you are puffing, you are breathing loudly and quickly with your mouth open. **3** If something puffs out or puffs up, it swells and becomes larger and rounder. **4** (noun) A puff of air or smoke is a small amount that is released.

puffin, puffins (noun) A puffin is a black and white sea bird with a large brightly-coloured beak.

pug, pugs (noun) A pug is a small, short-haired dog with a flat nose.

puke, pukes, puking, puked (verb; an informal word) If someone pukes, they vomit.

pull, pulls, pulling, pulled 1 (verb) When you pull something, you hold it and move it towards you. **2** When something is pulled by a vehicle or animal, it is attached to it and moves along behind it, e.g. *Four oxen can pull a single plough.* **3** When you pull a curtain or blind, you move it so that it covers or uncovers the window. **4** If you pull a muscle, you injure it by stretching it too far or too quickly. **5** When a vehicle pulls away, pulls out, or pulls in, it moves in the direction indicated. **6** (noun) The pull of something is its attraction or influence, e.g. *the pull of the past.* **pull down** (verb) When a building is pulled down, it is deliberately destroyed.

pulley, pulleys (noun) A pulley is a device for lifting heavy weights. It consists of a wheel or series of wheels over which a rope passes.

pullover, pullovers (noun) A pullover is a woollen piece of clothing that covers the top part of your body.

pulmonary (adjective; a formal word) relating to the lungs or to the veins and arteries carrying blood between the lungs and the heart.

pulp (noun) If something is turned into a pulp, it is crushed until it is soft, smooth, and moist.

pulpit, pulpits (pronounced **pool**-pit) (noun) In a church, the pulpit is the small raised platform where a member of the clergy stands to preach.

pulse, pulses, pulsing, pulsed 1 (noun) Your pulse is the regular beating of blood through your body, the rate of which you can feel at your wrists and elsewhere. **2** The seeds of beans, peas, and lentils are called pulses when they are used for food. **3** (verb) If something is pulsing, it is moving or vibrating with rhythmic, regular movements, e.g. *She could feel the blood pulsing in her ears.*

puma, pumas (pronounced **pyoo**-mah) (noun) A puma is a wild animal belonging to the cat family. Pumas have brownish-grey fur.

pumice (pronounced **pum**-miss) (noun) Pumice stone is very light-weight grey stone that can be used to soften areas of hard skin.

pummel, pummels, pummelling, pummelled (verb) If you pummel something, you beat it with your fists.

pump, pumps, pumping, pumped 1 (noun) A pump is a machine that is used to force a liquid or gas to move in a particular direction. **2** (verb) To pump a liquid or gas somewhere means to force it to flow in that direction, using a pump. **3** (noun) Pumps are canvas shoes with flat soles which people wear for sport or leisure. **4** (verb) If you pump money into something, you put a lot of money into it.

pumpkin, pumpkins (noun) A pumpkin is a very large, round, orange-coloured vegetable.

pun, puns (noun) A pun is a clever and amusing use of words so that what you say has two different meanings.

punch, punches, punching, punched 1 (verb) If you punch someone, you hit them hard with your fist. **2** (noun) A punch is a hard blow with the fist. **3** A punch is also a tool used for making holes. **4** Punch is a drink made from a mixture of wine, spirits, fruit, sugar, and spices.

punctual (adjective) arriving at the correct time. **punctually** (adverb), **punctuality** (noun).

punctuate, punctuates, punctuating, punctuated 1 (verb) Something that is punctuated by a particular thing is interrupted by it at intervals, e.g. *a grey day punctuated by bouts of rain.* **2** When you punctuate a piece of writing, you put punctuation into it.

punctuation (noun) The marks in writing such as full stops, question marks, and commas are called punctuation or punctuation marks.

puncture, punctures, puncturing, punctured 1 (noun) If a tyre has a puncture, a small hole has been made in it and it has become flat. **2** (verb) To puncture something means to make a small hole in it.

pungent (adjective) having a strong, unpleasant smell or taste. **pungency** (noun).

punish, punishes, punishing, punished (verb) To punish someone who has done something wrong means to make them suffer because of it.

punishment, punishments (noun) A punishment is something unpleasant done to someone because they have done something wrong.

punitive (pronounced **pyoo**-nit-tiv) (adjective) harsh and intended to punish people, e.g. *punitive military action.*

Punjabi, Punjabis (pronounced pun-**jah**-bee) **1** (adjective) belonging or relating to the Punjab, a state in north-western India. **2** (noun) A Punjabi is someone who comes from the Punjab. **3** Punjabi is a language spoken in the Punjab.

punk (noun) Punk or punk rock is an aggressive style of rock music.

punt, punts (noun) A punt is a long, flat-bottomed boat. You move it along by pushing a pole against the river bottom.

puny, punier, puniest (adjective) very small and weak.

pup, pups (noun) A pup is a young dog. Some other young animals such as seals are also called pups.

pupil, pupils 1 (noun) The pupils at a school are the children who go there. **2** Your pupils are the small, round, black holes in the centre of your eyes.

puppet, puppets (noun) A puppet is a doll or toy animal that is moved by pulling strings or by putting your hand inside its body.

puppy, puppies (noun) A puppy is a young dog.

purchase, purchases, purchasing, purchased 1 (verb) When you purchase something, you buy it. **2** (noun) A purchase is something you have bought. **purchaser** (noun).

pure, purer, purest 1 (adjective) Something that is pure is not mixed with anything else, e.g. *pure wool... pure white.* **2** Pure also means clean and free from harmful substances, e.g. *The water is pure enough to drink.* **3** People who are pure have not done anything considered to be sinful. **4** Pure also means complete and total, e.g. *a matter of pure luck.* **purity** (noun).

purée, purées (pronounced **pyoo**-ray) (noun) A purée is a food which has been mashed or blended to a thick, smooth consistency.

purely (adverb) involving only one feature and not including anything else, e.g. *purely professional.*

Purgatory (noun) Roman Catholics believe that Purgatory is a place where spirits of the dead are sent to suffer for their sins before going to Heaven.

purge, purges, purging, purged (verb) To purge something means to remove undesirable things from it, e.g. *to purge the country of criminals.*

purify, purifies, purifying, purified (verb) To purify something means to remove all dirty or harmful substances from it. **purification** (noun).

purist, purists (noun) A purist is someone who believes that the traditional form of a subject should be maintained.

puritan, puritans (noun) A puritan is someone who believes in strict moral principles and avoids physical pleasures. **puritanical** (adjective).

purple (noun or adjective) reddish-blue.

purport, purports, purporting, purported (pronounced pur-**port**) (verb; a formal word) Something that purports to be or have a particular thing is claimed to be or have it, e.g. *a country which purports to disapprove of smokers.*

purpose, purposes 1 (noun) The purpose of something is the reason for it, e.g. *the purpose of the meeting.* **2** If you have a particular purpose, this is what you want to achieve, e.g. *To make music is my purpose in life.* **3** (phrase) If you do something **on purpose,** you do it deliberately. **purposely** (adverb), **purposeful** (adjective).

purr, purrs, purring, purred (verb) When a cat purrs, it makes a low vibrating sound because it is contented.

purse, purses, pursing, pursed 1 (noun) A purse is a small leather or fabric container for carrying money. **2** (verb) If you purse your lips, you move them into a tight, rounded shape.

purser, pursers (noun) On a ship, the purser is the officer responsible for the accounts and the paperwork.

pursue, pursues, pursuing, pursued 1 (verb) If you pursue an activity, interest, or plan, you do it or make efforts to achieve it, e.g. *I decided to pursue a career in photography.* **2** If you pursue someone, you follow them to try to catch them. **pursuer** (noun), **pursuit** (noun).

purveyor, purveyors (noun; a formal word) A purveyor of goods or services is a person who sells them or provides them.

pus (noun) Pus is a thick yellowish liquid that forms in an infected wound.

push, pushes, pushing, pushed **1** (verb) When you push something, you press it using force in order to move it. **2** If you push someone into doing something, you force or persuade them to do it, e.g. *His mother pushed him into auditioning for a part.* **3** (an informal use) Someone who pushes drugs sells them illegally.

pushchair, pushchairs (noun) A pushchair is a small folding chair on wheels in which a baby or toddler can be wheeled around.

pusher, pushers (noun; an informal word) A pusher is someone who sells illegal drugs.

pushing (preposition) Someone who is pushing a particular age is nearly that age, e.g. *pushing sixty.*

pushover (an informal word) **1** (noun) Something that is a pushover is easy. **2** Someone who is a pushover is easily persuaded or defeated.

pushy, pushier, pushiest (adjective; an informal word) behaving in a forceful and determined way.

pussy, pussies (noun; an informal use) A pussy is a cat.

put, puts, putting, put **1** (verb) When you put something somewhere, you move it into that place or position. **2** If you put an idea or remark in a particular way, you express it that way, e.g. *I think you've put that very well.* **3** To put someone or something in a particular state or situation means to cause them to be in it, e.g. *It puts us both in an awkward position.* **4** You can use put to express an estimate of the size or importance of something, e.g. *Her wealth is now put at £290 million.* **put down** **1** (verb) To put someone down means to criticize them and make them appear foolish. **2** If an animal is put down, it is killed because it is very ill or dangerous. **put off** (verb) If you put something off, you delay doing it. **put out** (verb) If you put a fire out or put the light out, you make it stop burning or shining. **put up** **1** (verb) If you put up resistance to something, you argue or fight against it, e.g. *She put up a tremendous struggle.* **2** If you put up with something, you tolerate it even though you dislike it.

putt, putts (noun) In golf, a putt is a gentle stroke made when the ball is near the hole.

putting (noun) Putting is a game played on a small grass course with no obstacles. You hit a ball gently with a club so that it rolls towards one of a series of holes around the course.

putty (noun) Putty is a paste

used to fix panes of glass into frames.

puzzle, puzzles, puzzling, puzzled 1 (verb) If something puzzles you, it confuses you and you do not understand it, e.g. *There was something about her that puzzled me.* **2** (noun) A puzzle is a game, toy, or question that requires a lot of thought to complete or solve. **puzzled** (adjective), **puzzlement** (noun).

pygmy, pygmies (pronounced **pig**-mee); also spelled **pigmy** (noun) A pygmy is a very small person, especially one who belongs to a racial group in which all the people are small.

pyjamas (plural noun) Pyjamas are loose trousers and a jacket or top that you wear in bed.

pylon, pylons (noun) Pylons are very tall metal structures which carry overhead electricity cables.

pyramid, pyramids 1 (noun) A pyramid is a three-dimensional shape with a flat base and flat triangular sides sloping upwards to a point. **2** The Pyramids are ancient stone structures built over the tombs of Egyptian kings and queens.

pyre, pyres (noun) A pyre is a high pile of wood on which a dead body or religious offering is burned.

python, pythons (noun) A python is a large snake that kills animals by squeezing them with its body.

Q q

quack, quacks, quacking, quacked (verb) When a duck quacks, it makes the loud harsh sound that ducks typically make.

quad, quads (pronounced **kwod**) (noun) Quad is the same as **quadruplet.**

quadrangle, quadrangles (pronounced **kwod**-rang-gl) (noun) A quadrangle is a courtyard with buildings all round it.

quadrilateral, quadrilaterals (pronounced kwod-ril-**lat**-ral) (noun) A quadrilateral is a shape with four straight sides.

quadruped, quadrupeds (pronounced **kwod**-roo-ped) (noun) A quadruped is any animal with four legs.

quadruple, quadruples, quadrupling, quadrupled (pronounced kwod-**roo**-pl) (verb) When an amount or number quadruples, it becomes four times as large as it was.

quadruplet, quadruplets (pronounced kwod-**roo**-plet) (noun) Quadruplets are four children born at the same time to the same mother.

quagmire, quagmires (pronounced **kwag**-mire) (noun) A quagmire is a soft, wet area of land which you sink into if you walk on it.

quail, quails, quailing, quailed 1 (noun) A quail is a type of small game bird with a round body and short tail. **2** (verb) If you quail, you feel or look afraid.

quaint, quainter, quaintest (adjective) attractively old-fashioned or unusual, e.g. *quaint customs.* **quaintly** (adverb).

quake, quakes, quaking, quaked (verb) If you quake, you shake and tremble because you are very frightened.

Quaker, Quakers (noun) A Quaker is a member of a Christian group, the Society of Friends.

qualification, qualifications 1 (noun) Your qualifications are your skills and achievements, especially as officially recognized at the end of a course of training or study. **2** A qualification is also something you add to a statement to make it less strong, e.g. *It may not be asserted without qualification.*

qualify, qualifies, qualifying, qualified 1 (verb) When you qualify, you pass the examinations that you need to pass to do a particular job, e.g. *He qualified as a pilot.* **2** If you qualify a statement, you add a detail or explanation to make it less strong. **3** If you qualify for something, you become entitled to have it, e.g. *You qualify for a discount.* **qualified** (adjective).

quality, qualities 1 (noun) The quality of something is how good it is, e.g. *The quality of food is very poor.* **2** A quality is also a characteristic, e.g. *These qualities are essential for success.*

qualm, qualms (pronounced **kwahm**) (noun) If you have qualms about what you are doing, you worry that it might not be right.

quandary, quandaries (pronounced **kwon**-dree) (noun) If you are in a quandary, you cannot decide what to do.

quantity, quantities 1 (noun) A quantity is an amount you can measure or count, e.g. *a small quantity of alcohol.* **2** Quantity is the amount of something that there is, e.g. *emphasis on quantity rather than quality.*

quarantine (pronounced **kwor**-an-teen) (noun) If an animal is in quarantine, it is kept away from other animals for a time because it might have an infectious disease.

quarrel, quarrels, quarrelling, quarrelled 1 (noun) A quarrel is an angry argument. **2** (verb) If people quarrel, they have an angry argument.

quarry, quarries, quarrying, quarried (pronounced **kwor**-ree) **1** (noun) A quarry is a place where stone is removed from the ground by digging or blasting. **2** (verb) To quarry stone means to remove it from a quarry by digging or blasting. **3** (noun) A person's or animal's quarry is the animal that they are hunting.

quart, quarts (pronounced **kwort**) (noun) A quart is a unit of liquid volume equal to two pints or about 1.136 litres.

quarter, quarters 1 (noun) A quarter is one of four equal parts. **2** A quarter is also an American coin worth 25 cents. **3** You can refer to a particular area in a city as a quarter, e.g. *the French quarter.* **4** You can use quarter to refer vaguely to a particular person or group of people, e.g. *You are very popular in certain quarters.* **5** (plural noun) A soldier's or a servant's quarters are the rooms that they live in.

quarterly, quarterlies 1 (adjective or adverb) Quarterly means happening regularly every three months, e.g. *my quarterly report.* **2** (noun) A quarterly is a magazine or journal published every three months.

quartet, quartets (pronounced kwor-**tet**) (noun) A quartet is a group of four musicians who sing or play together; also a piece of music written for four instruments or singers.

quartz (noun) Quartz is a kind of hard, shiny crystal used in making very accurate watches and clocks.

quash, quashes, quashing, quashed (pronounced **kwosh**) (verb) To quash a decision or judgment means to reject it officially, e.g. *The judges quashed their convictions.*

quasi- (pronounced **kway**-sie) (prefix) Quasi- means resembling something but not actually being that thing, e.g. *a quasi-religious order.*

quaver, quavers, quavering, quavered (pronounced **kway**-ver) (verb) If your voice quavers, it sounds unsteady, usually because you are nervous.

quay, quays (pronounced **kee**) (noun) A quay is a place where boats are tied up and loaded or unloaded.

queasy, queasier, queasiest (pronounced **kwee**-zee) (adjective) feeling slightly sick.

queen, queens 1 (noun) A queen is a female monarch or a woman married to a king. **2** A queen is also a female bee or ant which can lay eggs. **3** In chess, the queen is the most powerful piece, which can move in any direction. **4** In a pack of cards, a queen is a card with a picture of a queen on it.

Queen Mother, Queen Mothers (noun) A Queen Mother is the widow of a king and the mother of the reigning monarch.

queer, queerer, queerest (adjective) Queer means very strange.

quell, quells, quelling, quelled 1 (verb) To quell a rebellion or riot means to put an end to it by using force. **2** If you quell a feeling such as fear or grief, you stop yourself from feeling it, e.g. *trying to quell the loneliness.*

quench, quenches, quenching, quenched (verb) If you quench your thirst, you have a drink so that you are no longer thirsty.

query, queries, querying, queried (pronounced **qweer**-ree) **1** (noun) A query is a question. **2** (verb) If you query something, you ask about it because you think it might not be right, e.g. *No-one queried my decision.*

quest, quests (noun) A quest is a long search for something.

question, questions, questioning, questioned 1 (noun) A question is a sentence which asks for information. **2** (verb) If you question someone, you ask them questions. **3** If you question something, you express doubts about it, e.g. *He never stopped questioning his own beliefs.* **4** (noun) If there is some question about something, there is doubt about it. **5** A question is also a problem that needs to be discussed, e.g. *Can we get back to the question of the flat?* **6** (phrase) If something is **out of the question,** it is impossible.

questionable (adjective) possibly not true or not honest.

question mark, question marks (noun) A question mark is the punctuation mark (?) which is used at the end of a question.

questionnaire, questionnaires (noun) A questionnaire is a list of questions which asks for information for a survey.

queue, queues, queueing, queued (pronounced **kyoo**) **1** (noun) A queue is a line of people or vehicles waiting for something. **2** (verb) When people queue, they stand in a line waiting for something.

quibble, quibbles, quibbling, quibbled 1 (verb) If you quibble, you argue about something unimportant. **2** (noun) A quibble is a minor objection.

quiche, quiches (pronounced **keesh**) (noun) A quiche is a tart with a savoury filling.

quick, quicker, quickest 1 (adjective) moving with great speed. **2** lasting only a short time, e.g. *a quick chat.* **3** happening without any delay, e.g. *a quick response.* **4** intelligent and able to understand things easily. **quickly** (adverb).

quicksand, quicksands (noun) A quicksand is an area of deep wet sand that you sink into if you walk on it.

quid (noun; an informal word) A quid is a pound.

quiet, quieter, quietest 1 (adjective) Someone or something that is quiet makes very little noise or no noise at all. **2** Quiet also means peaceful, e.g. *a quiet evening at home.* **3** (noun) Quiet is silence. **4** (adjective) A quiet event happens with very little fuss or publicity, e.g. *a quiet wedding.* **quietly** (adverb).

quieten, quietens, quietening, quietened (verb) To quieten someone means to make them become quiet.

quill, quills 1 (noun) A quill is a pen made from a feather. **2** A bird's quills are the large feathers on its wings and tail. **3** A porcupine's quills are its spines.

quilt, quilts (noun) A quilt for a bed is a cover, especially a cover that is padded.

quilted (adjective) Quilted clothes or coverings are made of thick layers of material sewn together.

quin, quins (noun) Quin is the same as **quintuplet.**

quince, quinces (noun) A quince is an acid-tasting fruit used for making jam and marmalade.

quintessential (adjective; a formal word) A person or thing that is quintessential seems to represent the basic nature of something in a pure, concentrated form, e.g. *Lloyd George was the quintessential politician.*

quintet, quintets (pronounced kwin-**tet**) (noun) A quintet is a group of five musicians who sing or play together; also a piece of music written for five instruments or singers.

quintuplet, quintuplets (pronounced kwin-**tyoo**-plit) (noun) Quintuplets are five children born at the same time to the same mother.

quip, quips, quipping, quipped 1 (noun) A quip is an amusing or clever remark. **2** (verb) To quip means to make an amusing or clever remark.

quirk, quirks 1 (noun) A quirk is an odd habit or characteristic, e.g. *an interesting quirk of human nature.* **2** A quirk is also an unexpected event or development, e.g. *a quirk of fate.* **quirky** (adjective).

quit, quits, quitting, quit (verb) If you quit something, you leave it or stop doing it, e.g. *Leigh quit his job as a salesman.*

quite 1 (adverb) fairly but not very, e.g. *quite old.* **2** completely, e.g. *Jane lay quite still.* **3** (phrase) You use **quite a** to emphasize that something is large or impressive, e.g. *It was quite a party.*

quiver, quivers, quivering, quivered 1 (verb) If something quivers, it trembles. **2** (noun) A quiver is a trembling movement, e.g. *a quiver of panic.*

quiz, quizzes, quizzing, quizzed 1 (noun) A quiz is a game in which the competitors are asked questions to test their knowledge. **2** (verb) If you quiz someone, you question them closely about something.

quizzical (pronounced **kwiz**-ikl) (adjective) amused and questioning, e.g. *a quizzical smile.*

quota, quotas (noun) A quota is a number or quantity of something which is officially allowed.

quotation, quotations (noun) A quotation is an extract from a book or speech which is quoted.

quote, quotes, quoting, quoted 1 (verb) If you quote something that someone has written or said, you repeat their exact words. **2** If you quote a fact, you state it because it supports what you are saying. **3** (noun) A quote is an extract from a book or speech. **4** A quote is also an estimate of how much a piece of work will cost.

Rr

rabbi, rabbis (pronounced **rab**-by) (noun) A rabbi is a Jewish religious leader.

rabbit, rabbits (noun) A rabbit is a small animal with long ears.

rabble (noun) A rabble is a noisy, disorderly crowd.

rabid 1 (adjective) used to describe someone with strong views that you do not approve of, e.g. *a rabid Nazi.* **2** A rabid dog has rabies.

rabies (pronounced **ray**-beez) (noun) Rabies is an infectious disease which causes people and animals, especially dogs, to go mad and die.

raccoon, raccoons; also spelled **racoon** (noun) A raccoon is a small North American animal with a long striped tail.

race, races, racing, raced 1 (noun) A race is a competition to see who is fastest, for example in running, swimming, or driving. **2** (verb) If you race someone, you compete with them in a race. **3** If you race something or if it races, it goes at its greatest rate, e.g. *Her heart raced uncontrollably.* **4** If you race somewhere, you go there as quickly as possible, e.g. *The hares raced away out of sight.* **5** (noun) A race is also one of the major groups that human beings can be divided into according to their physical features. **racing** (noun).

racecourse, racecourses (noun) A racecourse is a grass track, sometimes with jumps, along which horses race.

racehorse, racehorses (noun) A racehorse is a horse trained to run in races.

racial (adjective) relating to the different races that people belong to, e.g. *racial minorities.* **racially** (adverb).

racism or **racialism** (noun) Racism or racialism is the treatment of some people as inferior because of their race. **racist** (noun or adjective).

rack, racks, racking, racked 1 (noun) A rack is a piece of equipment for holding things or hanging things on. **2** (verb) If you are racked by something, you suffer because of it, e.g. *She was racked by remorse.*

racket, rackets 1 (noun) If someone is making a racket, they are making a lot of noise. **2** A racket is also an illegal way of making money. **3** Racket is another spelling of **racquet**.

racquet, racquets; also spelled **racket** (noun) A racquet is a bat with strings across it used in tennis, squash, and badminton.

radar (noun) Radar is equipment used to track vehicles, ships, or aircraft that are out of sight by using radio signals that are reflected back from the object and shown on a screen.

radiant 1 (adjective) Someone who is radiant is so happy that it shows in their face. **2** glowing brightly. **radiance** (noun).

radiate, radiates, radiating, radiated 1 (verb) If things radiate from a place, they form a pattern like lines spreading out from the centre of a circle. **2** If you radiate a quality or emotion, it shows clearly in your face and behaviour, e.g. *He radiated health.*

radiation (noun) Radiation is the stream of particles given out by a radioactive substance.

radiator, radiators 1 (noun) A radiator is a hollow metal device for heating a room, usually connected to a central heating system. **2** A car's radiator is the part that is filled with water to cool the engine.

radical, radicals 1 (noun) Radicals are people who think there should be great changes in society, and try to make them happen. **2** (adjective) very significant, important, or basic, e.g. *a radical change in* *the law.* **radically** (adverb).

radii the plural of **radius.**

radio, radios, radioing, radioed **1** (noun) Radio is a system of sending sound over a distance by transmitting electrical signals. **2** Radio is also the broadcasting of programmes to the public by radio. **3** A radio is a piece of equipment for listening to radio programmes. **4** (verb) To radio someone means to send them a message by radio, e.g. *The pilot radioed for help.*

radioactive (adjective) giving off powerful and harmful rays. **radioactivity** (noun).

radiotherapy (noun) Radiotherapy is the treatment of diseases such as cancer using radiation. **radiotherapist** (noun).

radish, radishes (noun) A radish is a small salad vegetable with a red skin and white flesh and a strong, hot taste.

radium (noun) Radium is a radioactive element which is used in the treatment of cancer.

radius, radii (noun) The radius of a circle is the length of a straight line drawn from its centre to its circumference.

RAF an abbreviation for 'Royal Air Force'.

raffia (noun) Raffia is a material made from palm leaves and used for making mats and baskets.

raffle, raffles (noun) A raffle is a competition in which people buy numbered tickets and win a prize if they have the ticket that is chosen.

raft, rafts (noun) A raft is a floating platform made from long pieces of wood tied together.

rafter, rafters (noun) Rafters are the sloping pieces of wood that support a roof.

rag, rags 1 (noun) A rag is a piece of old cloth used to clean or wipe things. **2** If someone is dressed in rags, they are wearing old torn clothes.

rage, rages, raging, raged 1 (noun) Rage is great anger. **2** (verb) To rage about something means to speak angrily about it. **3** If something such as a storm or battle is raging, it is continuing with great force or violence, e.g. *The fire still raged out of control.*

ragged (adjective) Ragged clothes are old and torn.

raid, raids, raiding, raided 1 (verb) To raid a place means to enter it by force to attack it or steal something. **2** (noun) A raid is the raiding of a building or a place, e.g. *an armed raid on a bank.*

rail, rails 1 (noun) A rail is a fixed horizontal bar used as a support or for hanging things on. **2** Rails are the steel bars which trains run along. **3** Rail is the railway considered as a means of transport, e.g. *a journey by rail from Nottingham to Birmingham.*

railing, railings (noun) Railings are a fence made from metal bars.

railway, railways (noun) A railway is a route along which trains travel on steel rails.

rain, rains, raining, rained 1 (noun) Rain is water falling from the clouds in small drops. **2** (verb) When it is raining, rain is falling. **rainy** (adjective).

rainbow, rainbows (noun) A rainbow is an arch of different colours that sometimes appears in the sky after it has been raining.

raincoat, raincoats (noun) A raincoat is a waterproof coat.

rainfall (noun) Rainfall is the amount of rain that falls in a place during a particular period.

rainforest, rainforests (noun) A rainforest is a dense forest of tall trees in a tropical area where there is a lot of rain.

rainwater (noun) Rainwater is rain that has been stored.

raise, raises, raising, raised 1 (verb) If you raise something, you make it higher, e.g. *She went to the window and raised the blinds.* **2** If you raise your voice, you speak more loudly. **3** To raise money means to obtain it from several people or organizations. **4** To raise a child means to look after it until it is grown up.

raisin, raisins (noun) Raisins are dried grapes.

rake, rakes, raking, raked (noun) A rake is a garden tool with a row of metal teeth and a long handle. **rake up** (verb) If you rake up something distressing or embarrassing from the past, you remind someone about it.

rally, rallies, rallying, rallied 1 (noun) A rally is a large public meeting held to show support for something. **2** A rally is also a competition in which vehicles are raced over public roads. **3** In tennis or squash, a rally is a continuous series of shots exchanged by the players. **4** (verb) When people rally to something, they gather together to continue to support something.

ram, rams, ramming, rammed 1 (verb) If one vehicle rams another, it crashes into it. **2** To ram something somewhere means to push it there firmly, e.g. *He rammed his key into the lock.* **3** (noun) A ram is an adult male sheep.

RAM (noun) In computing, RAM is a temporary storage space which can be filled with data by the user but which loses its contents when the machine is switched off. RAM stands for 'random access memory'.

Ramadan (noun) Ramadan is the ninth month of the Muslim year, during which Muslims eat and drink nothing during daylight.

ramble, rambles, rambling, rambled 1 (noun) A ramble is a long walk in the countryside. **2** (verb) To ramble means to go for a ramble. **3** To ramble also means to talk in a confused way, e.g. *He started rambling and repeating himself.* **rambler** (noun).

ramification, ramifications (noun) The ramifications of a decision or plan are all its consequences and effects.

ramp, ramps (noun) A ramp is a sloping surface connecting two different levels.

rampage, rampages, rampaging, rampaged 1 (verb) To rampage means to rush about wildly causing damage. **2** (phrase) To **go on the rampage** means to rush about in a wild or violent way.

rampant (adjective) If something such as crime or disease is rampant, it is growing or spreading uncontrollably.

rampart, ramparts (noun) Ramparts are earth banks, often with a wall on top, built to protect a castle or city.

ramshackle (adjective) A ramshackle building is in poor condition, and likely to fall down.

ranch, ranches (noun) A ranch is a large farm where cattle, sheep, or horses are reared.

rancid (pronounced **ran**-sid) (adjective) Rancid food has gone bad.

rancour (pronounced **rang**-kur) (noun; a formal word) Rancour is bitter hatred. **rancorous** (adjective).

random 1 (adjective) A random choice or arrangement is not based on any definite plan. **2** (phrase) If you do something **at random,** you do it without any definite plan, e.g. *He chose his victims at random.* **randomly** (adverb).

range, ranges, ranging, ranged 1 (noun) The range of something is the maximum distance over which it can function, e.g. *This mortar has a range of 15,000 metres.* **2** A range is a number of different things of the same kind, e.g. *A wide range of colours are available.* **3** A range is also a set of values on a scale, e.g. *The average age range is between 35 and 55.* **4** A range of mountains is a line of them. **5** A rifle range or firing range is a place where people practise shooting at targets. **6** (verb) When a set of things ranges between two points, they vary within these points on a scale, e.g. *prices ranging between £370 and £1200.*

ranger, rangers (noun) A ranger is someone whose job is to look after a forest or park.

rank, ranks, ranking, ranked 1 (noun) Someone's rank is their official level in a job or profession. **2** The ranks are the ordinary members of the armed forces, rather than the officers. **3** The ranks of a group are its members, e.g. *We welcomed five new members to our ranks.* **4** (verb) To rank as something means to have that status or position on a scale, e.g. *Their relegation ranks as the worst humiliation they have ever known.* **5** (adjective) complete and absolute, e.g. *rank stupidity.* **6** having a strong, unpleasant smell, e.g. *the rank smell of unwashed clothes.*

ransack, ransacks, ransacking, ransacked (verb) To ransack a place means to disturb everything, causing complete chaos, in order to search for or steal something.

ransom, ransoms (noun) A ransom is money that is demanded to free someone who has been kidnapped.

rant, rants, ranting, ranted (verb) To rant means to talk loudly in an excited or angry way.

rap, raps, rapping, rapped 1 (verb) If you rap something, you hit it with a series of quick blows. **2** (noun) A rap is a quick knock or blow on something, e.g. *A rap on the* *door signalled his arrival.* **3** Rap is a style of poetry spoken to music with a strong rhythmic beat.

rape, rapes, raping, raped 1 (verb) If a man rapes a woman, he violently forces her to have sex with him against her will. **2** (noun) Rape is the act or crime of raping a woman, e.g. *victims of rape.* **rapist** (noun).

rapid, rapids 1 (adjective) happening or moving very quickly, e.g. *rapid industrial expansion... He took a few rapid steps.* **2** (plural noun) An area of a river where the water moves extremely fast over rocks is referred to as rapids. **rapidly** (adverb), **rapidity** (noun).

rapier, rapiers (noun) A rapier is a long thin sword with a sharp point.

rapport (pronounced rap-**por**) (noun; a formal word) If there is a rapport between two people, they find it easy to understand each other's feelings and attitudes.

rapt (adjective) If you are rapt, you are so interested in something that you are not aware of other things, e.g. *sitting with rapt attention in front of the screen.*

rapture (noun) Rapture is a feeling of extreme delight. **rapturous** (adjective), **rapturously** (adverb).

rare, rarer, rarest 1 (adjective) Something that is rare is not common or does not happen often, e.g. *a rare flower... Such major disruptions are rare.* **2** Rare meat has been lightly cooked. **rarely** (adverb).

rarefied (pronounced **rare**-if-eyed) (adjective) seeming to have little connection with ordinary life, e.g. *He grew up in a rarefied literary atmosphere.*

raring (adjective) If you are raring to do something, you are very eager to do it.

rarity, rarities 1 (noun) A rarity is something that is interesting or valuable because it is unusual. **2** The rarity of something is the fact that it is not common.

rascal, rascals (noun) If you refer to someone as a rascal, you mean that they do bad or mischievous things.

rash, rashes 1 (adjective) If you are rash, you do something hasty and foolish. **2** (noun) A rash is an area of red spots that appear on your skin when you are ill or have an allergy. **3** A rash of events is a lot of them happening in a short time, e.g. *a rash of thefts.* **rashly** (adverb).

rasher, rashers (noun) A rasher is a thin slice of bacon.

rasp, rasps, rasping, rasped 1 (verb) To rasp means to make a harsh unpleasant sound. **2** (noun) A rasp is a coarse file with rows of raised teeth, used for smoothing wood or metal.

raspberry, raspberries (noun) A raspberry is a small soft red fruit that grows on a bush.

rat, rats (noun) A rat is a long-tailed animal which looks like a large mouse.

rate, rates, rating, rated 1 (noun) The rate of something is the speed or frequency with which it happens, e.g. *New diet books appear at the rate of* *nearly one a week.* **2** The rate of interest is its level, e.g. *a further cut in interest rates.* **3** Until 1990, rates were a local tax paid by people who owned buildings. **4** (phrase) If you say **at this rate** something will happen, you mean it will happen if things continue in the same way, e.g. *At this rate we'll be lucky to get home before six.* **5** You say **at any rate** when you want to add to or amend what you have just said, e.g. *He is the least appealing character, to me at any rate.* **6** (verb) The way you rate someone or something is your opinion of them, e.g. *He was rated as one of England's top young keepers.*

rather 1 (adverb) Rather means to a certain extent, e.g. *We got along rather well... The reality is rather more complex.* **2** (phrase) If you **would rather** do a particular thing, you would prefer to do it.

ratify, ratifies, ratifying, ratified (verb; a formal word) To ratify a written agreement means to approve it formally. **ratification** (noun).

rating, ratings 1 (noun) A rating is a score based on the quality or status of something. **2** The ratings are statistics showing how popular each television or radio programme is.

ratio, ratios (noun) A ratio is a relationship which shows how many times one thing is bigger than another, e.g. *The adult to child ratio is 1 to 6.*

ration, rations, rationing, rationed 1 (noun) Your ration of something is the amount you are allowed to have. **2** (verb) When something is rationed, you are only allowed a limited amount of it, because there is a shortage. **3** (noun) Rations are the food supplied each day to a soldier or member of an expedition.

rational (adjective) When people are rational, their judgments are based on reason rather than emotion. **rationally** (adverb), **rationality** (noun).

rationale (pronounced rash-on-**nahl**) (noun) The rationale for a course of action or for a belief is the set of reasons on which it is based.

rattle, rattles, rattling, rattled 1 (verb) When something rattles, it makes short, regular knocking sounds. **2** (noun) A rattle is the noise something makes when it rattles. **3** A rattle is also a baby's toy which makes a noise when it is shaken. **4** (verb) If something rattles you, it upsets you, e.g. *He was obviously rattled by events.*

rattlesnake, rattlesnakes (noun) A rattlesnake is a poisonous American snake.

raucous (pronounced **raw**-kuss) (adjective) A raucous voice is loud and rough.

ravage, ravages, ravaging, ravaged (a formal word) **1** (verb) To ravage something means to seriously harm or damage it, e.g. *a country ravaged by floods.* **2** (noun) The ravages of something are its damaging effects, e.g. *the ravages of two world wars.*

rave, raves, raving, raved 1 (verb) If someone raves, they talk in an angry, uncontrolled way, e.g. *He started raving about being treated badly.* **2** (an informal use) If you rave about something, you talk about it very enthusiastically. **3** (adjective; an informal use) If something gets a rave review, it is praised enthusiastically. **4** (noun; an informal use) A rave is a large party with electronic dance music.

raven, ravens (noun) A raven is a large black bird with a deep, harsh call.

ravenous (adjective) very hungry.

ravine, ravines (noun) A ravine is a deep, narrow valley with steep sides.

raving, ravings 1 (adjective) If someone is raving, they are mad, e.g. *a raving lunatic.* **2** (noun) Someone's ravings are crazy things they write or say.

ravioli (pronounced rav-ee-**oh**-lee) (noun) Ravioli consists of small squares of pasta filled with meat and served with a sauce.

ravishing (adjective) Someone or something that is ravishing is very beautiful, e.g. *a ravishing landscape.*

raw 1 (adjective) Raw food is uncooked. **2** A raw substance is in its natural state, e.g. *raw sugar.* **3** If part of your body is raw, the skin has come off or been rubbed away.

raw material, raw materials (noun) Raw materials are the natural substances used to make something.

ray, rays 1 (noun) A ray is a beam of light or radiation. **2** A ray of hope is a small amount that makes an unpleasant situation seem slightly better. **3** A ray is also a large sea fish with eyes on the top of its body, and a long tail.

raze, razes, razing, razed (verb) To raze a building, town, or forest means to completely destroy it, e.g. *The town was razed to the ground during the occupation.*

razor, razors (noun) A razor is an object used for shaving.

razor blade, razor blades (noun) A razor blade is a small, sharp, flat piece of metal fitted into a razor for shaving.

re- (prefix) Re- is used to form nouns and verbs that refer to the repetition of an action or process. For example, to reread something means to read it again.

reach, reaches, reaching, reached 1 (verb) When you reach a place, you arrive there. **2** When you reach for something, you stretch out your arm to it. **3** If something reaches a place or point, it extends as far as that place or point, e.g. *She has a cloak that reaches to the ground.* **4** If something or someone reaches a stage, condition, or level, they get to it, e.g. *Unemployment has reached record levels.* **5** To reach an agreement or decision means to succeed in achieving it. **6** (phrase) If a place is **within reach,** you can get there, e.g. *a cycle route well within reach of most people.* **7** If something is **out of reach,** you cannot get it to it by stretching out your arm, e.g. *Store out of reach of children.*

react, reacts, reacting, reacted 1

(verb) When you react to something, you behave in a particular way because of it, e.g. *He reacted badly to the news.* **2** If one substance reacts with another, a chemical change takes place when they are put together.

reaction, reactions 1 (noun) Your reaction to something is what you feel, say, or do because of it, e.g. *Reaction to the visit is mixed.* **2** Your reactions are your ability to move quickly in response to something that happens, e.g. *Squash requires fast reactions.* **3** If there is a reaction against something, it becomes unpopular, e.g. *a reaction against Christianity.* **4** In a chemical reaction, a chemical change takes place when two substances are put together.

reactionary, reactionaries 1 (adjective) Someone who is reactionary tries to prevent political or social change. **2** (noun) Reactionaries are reactionary people.

reactor, reactors (noun) A reactor is a device which is used to produce nuclear energy.

read, reads, reading, read 1 (verb) When you read, you look at something written and follow it or say it aloud. **2** If you can read someone's moods or mind, you can judge what they are feeling or thinking. **3** When you read a meter or gauge, you look at it and record the figure on it.

reader, readers (noun) The readers of a newspaper or magazine are the people who read it regularly.

readership (noun) The readership of a newspaper or magazine consists of the people who read it regularly.

readily 1 (adverb) willingly and eagerly, e.g. *She readily agreed to see Alex.* **2** easily done or quickly obtainable, e.g. *Help is readily available.*

reading, readings 1 (noun) Reading is the activity of reading books. **2** The reading on a meter or gauge is the figure or measurement it shows.

readjust, readjusts, readjusting, readjusted (pronounced ree-aj-**just**) **1** (verb) If you readjust, you adapt to a new situation. **2** If you readjust something, you alter it to a different position.

ready 1 (adjective) having reached the required stage, or prepared for action or use, e.g. *In a few days time the sprouts will be ready to eat... He told his pilot to get the aircraft ready.* **2** willing or eager to do something, e.g. *She says she's not ready for marriage.* **3** If you are ready for something, you need it, e.g. *I'm ready for bed.* **4** easily produced or obtained, e.g. *ready cash.* **readiness** (noun).

ready-made (adjective) already made and therefore able to be used immediately.

reaffirm, reaffirms, reaffirming, reaffirmed (verb) To reaffirm something means to state it again, e.g. *He reaffirmed his support for the campaign.*

real 1 (adjective) actually existing and not imagined or invented. **2** genuine and not imitation, e.g. *Who's to know if they're real guns?* **3** true or actual and not mistaken, e.g. *the* *real reason for her call.*

real estate (noun) Real estate is property in the form of land and buildings rather than personal possessions.

realism (noun) Realism is the recognition and acceptance of the true nature of a situation, e.g. *a triumph of muddled thought over realism and common sense.* **realist** (noun).

realistic 1 (adjective) recognizing and accepting the true nature of a situation. **2** representing things in a way that is true to real life, e.g. *His novels are more realistic than his short stories.* **realistically** (adverb).

reality 1 (noun) Reality is the real nature of things, rather than the way someone imagines it, e.g. *Fiction and reality were increasingly blurred.* **2** If something has become reality, it actually exists or is actually happening.

realize, realizes, realizing, realized; also spelled **realise 1** (verb) If you realize something, you become aware of it. **2** (a formal use) If your hopes or fears are realized, what you hoped for or feared actually happens, e.g. *Our worst fears were realized.* **realization** (noun).

really 1 (adverb) used to add emphasis to what is being said, e.g. *I'm not really surprised.* **2** used to indicate that you are talking about the true facts about something, e.g. *What was really going on?*

realm, realms (pronounced **relm**) (a formal word) **1** (noun) You can refer to any area of thought or activity as a realm, e.g. *the realm of politics.* **2** A realm is also a country with a king or queen, e.g. *defence of the realm.*

reap, reaps, reaping, reaped 1 (verb) To reap a crop such as corn means to cut and gather it. **2** When people reap benefits or rewards, they get them as a result of hard work or careful planning. **reaper** (noun).

reappear, reappears, reappearing, reappeared (verb) When people or things reappear, you can see them again, because they have come back, e.g. *The waitress reappeared... The stolen ring reappeared three years later in a pawn shop.* **reappearance** (noun).

reappraisal, reappraisals (noun; a formal word) If there is a reappraisal, people think about something and decide whether they want to change it, e.g. *a reappraisal of the government's policies.*

rear, rears, rearing, reared 1 (noun) The rear of something is the part at the back. **2** (verb) To rear children or young animals means to bring them up until they are able to look after themselves. **3** When a horse rears, it raises the front part of its body, so that its front legs are in the air.

rear admiral, rear admirals (noun) A rear admiral is an officer in the navy.

rearrange, rearranges, rearranging, rearranged (verb) To rearrange something means to organize or arrange it in a different way.

reason, reasons, reasoning, reasoned 1 (noun) The reason for something is the fact or situation which explains why it happens or which causes it to happen. **2** If you have reason to believe or feel something, there are definite reasons why you believe it or feel it, e.g. *He had every reason to be upset.* **3** Reason is the ability to think and make judgments. **4** (verb) If you reason that something is true, you decide it is true after considering all the facts. **5** If you reason with someone, you persuade them to accept sensible arguments.

reasonable 1 (adjective) Reasonable behaviour is fair and sensible. **2** If an explanation is reasonable, there are good reasons for thinking it is correct. **3** A reasonable amount is a fairly large amount. **4** A reasonable price is fair and not too high. **reasonably** (adverb).

reasoning (noun) Reasoning is the process by which you reach a conclusion after considering all the facts.

reassess, reassesses, reassessing, reassessed (verb) If you reassess something, you consider whether it still has the same value or importance. **reassessment** (noun).

reassure, reassures, reassuring, reassured (verb) If you reassure someone, you say or do things that make them less worried. **reassurance** (noun).

rebate, rebates (noun) A rebate is money paid back to someone who has paid too much tax or rent.

rebel, rebels, rebelling, rebelled 1 (noun) Rebels are people who are fighting their own country's army in order to change the political system. **2** Someone who is a rebel rejects society's values and behaves differently from other people. **3** (verb) To rebel means to fight against authority and reject accepted values.

rebellion, rebellions (noun) A rebellion is organized and often violent opposition to authority.

rebellious (adjective) unwilling to obey and likely to rebel against authority.

rebuff, rebuffs, rebuffing, rebuffed 1 (verb) If you rebuff someone, you reject what they offer, e.g. *She rebuffed their offers of help.* **2** (noun) A rebuff is a rejection of an offer.

rebuild, rebuilds, rebuilding, rebuilt (verb) When a town or building is rebuilt, it is built again after being damaged or destroyed.

rebuke, rebukes, rebuking, rebuked (pronounced rib-**yook**) (verb) To rebuke someone means to speak severely to them about something they have done.

recall, recalls, recalling, recalled 1 (verb) To recall something means to remember it. **2** If you are recalled to a place, you are ordered to return there.

recap, recaps, recapping, recapped (verb) To recap means to repeat and summarize the main points of an explanation or discussion.

recapture, recaptures, recapturing, recaptured 1 (verb) When you recapture a pleasant feeling, you experience it again, e.g. *She may never recapture that past assurance.* **2** When soldiers recapture a place, they capture it from the people who took it from them. **3** When animals or prisoners are recaptured, they are caught after they have escaped.

recede, recedes, receding, receded 1 (verb) When something recedes, it moves away into the distance. **2** If a man's hair is receding, he is starting to go bald at the front.

receipt, receipts (pronounced ris-**seet**) **1** (noun) A receipt is a piece of paper confirming that money or goods have been received. **2** In a shop or theatre, the money received is often called the receipts, e.g. *Box-office receipts were down last month.* **3** (a formal use) The receipt of something is the receiving of it, e.g. *You have to sign here and acknowledge receipt.*

receive, receives, receiving, received 1 (verb) When you receive something, someone gives it to you, or you get it after it has been sent to you. **2** To receive something also means to have it happen to you, e.g. *injuries she received in a car crash.* **3** When you receive visitors or guests, you welcome them. **4** If something is received in a particular way, that is how people react to it, e.g. *The decision has been received with dismay.*

receiver, receivers (noun) The receiver is the part of a telephone you hold near to your ear and mouth.

recent (adjective) Something recent happened a short time ago. **recently** (adverb).

reception, receptions 1 (noun) In a hotel, office, or hospital, reception is the place near the entrance where appointments or enquiries are dealt with. **2** A reception is a formal party. **3** The reception someone or something gets is the way people react to them, e.g. *Her tour has met with a rapturous reception.*

receptionist, receptionists (noun) The receptionist in a hotel, office, or surgery deals with people when they arrive, answers the telephone, and arranges reservations or appointments.

receptive (adjective) Someone who is receptive to ideas or suggestions is willing to consider them.

recess, recesses 1 (noun) A recess is a period when no work is done by a committee or parliament, e.g. *the Christmas recess.* **2** A recess is a place where part of a wall has been built further back than the rest.

recession, recessions (noun) A recession is a period when a country's economy is less successful and more people become unemployed.

recharge, recharges, recharging, recharged (verb) To recharge a battery means to charge it with electricity again after it has been used.

recipe, recipes (pronounced **res**-sip-ee) **1** (noun) A recipe is a list of ingredients and instructions for cooking something. **2** If something is a recipe for disaster or for success, it is likely to result in disaster or success.

recipient, recipients (noun) The recipient of something is the person receiving it.

reciprocal (adjective) A reciprocal agreement involves two people, groups, or countries helping each other in a similar way, e.g. *a reciprocal agreement on trade.*

reciprocate, reciprocates, reciprocating, reciprocated (verb) If you reciprocate someone's feelings or behaviour, you feel or behave in the same way towards them.

recital, recitals (noun) A recital is a performance of music or poetry.

recite, recites, reciting, recited (verb) If you recite a poem or something you have learnt, you say it aloud. **recitation** (noun).

reckless (adjective) showing a complete lack of care about danger or damage, e.g. *a reckless tackle.* **recklessly** (adverb), **recklessness** (noun).

reckon, reckons, reckoning, reckoned 1 (verb; an informal use) If you reckon that something is true, you think it is true, e.g. *I reckoned he was still fond of her.* **2** (an informal use) If someone reckons to do something, they claim or expect to do it, e.g. *Officers on the case are reckoning to charge someone shortly.* **3** To reckon an amount means to calculate it. **4** If you reckon on something, you rely on it happening when making your plans, e.g. *He reckons on being world champion.* **5** If you had not reckoned with something, you had not expected it and therefore were unprepared when it happened, e.g. *Giles had not reckoned with the strength of Sally's feelings.*

reckoning, reckonings (noun) A reckoning is a calculation, e.g. *There were a thousand or so, by my reckoning.*

reclaim, reclaims, reclaiming, reclaimed 1 (verb) When you reclaim something, you collect it after leaving it somewhere or losing it. **2** To reclaim land means to make it suitable for use, for example by draining or clearing it. **reclamation** (noun).

recline, reclines, reclining, reclined (verb) To recline means to lie or lean back at an angle, e.g. *a photo of him reclining on his bed.*

recluse, recluses (noun) Someone who is a recluse lives alone and avoids other people. **reclusive** (adjective).

recognize, recognizes, recognizing, recognized; also spelled **recognise 1** (verb) If you recognize someone or something, you realize that you know who or what they are, e.g. *The receptionist recognized me at once.* **2** To recognize something also means to accept and acknowledge it, e.g. *The RAF recognized him as an outstanding pilot.* **recognition** (noun), **recognizable** (adjective), **recognizably** (adverb).

recommend, recommends, recommending, recommended (verb) If you recommend something to someone, you praise it and suggest they try it. **recommendation** (noun).

reconcile, reconciles, reconciling, reconciled 1 (verb) To reconcile two things that seem to oppose one another, means to make them work or exist together successfully, e.g. *The designs reconciled style with comfort.* **2** When people are reconciled, they become friendly again after a quarrel. **3** If you reconcile yourself to an unpleasant situation, you accept it. **reconciliation** (noun).

reconnaissance (pronounced rik-**kon**-iss-sanss) (noun) Reconnaissance is the gathering of military information by sending out soldiers, planes, or satellites.

reconsider, reconsiders, reconsidering, reconsidered (verb) To reconsider something means to think about it again to decide whether to change it. **reconsideration** (noun).

reconstruct, reconstructs, reconstructing, reconstructed 1 (verb) To reconstruct something that has been damaged means to build it again. **2** To reconstruct a past event means to obtain a complete description of it from small pieces of information. **reconstruction** (noun).

record, records, recording, recorded 1 (noun) If you keep a record of something, you keep a written account or store information in a computer, e.g. *medical records.* **2** (verb) If you record information, you write it down or put it into a computer. **3** To record sound means to put it on tape, record, or compact disc. **4** (noun) A record is a round, flat piece of plastic on which music has been recorded. **5** A record is also an achievement which is the best of its type. **6** (adjective) higher, lower, better, or worse than ever before, e.g. *Profits were at a record level.* **7** (noun) Your record is what is known about your achievements or past activities, e.g. *He had a distinguished record.*

recorder, recorders (noun) A recorder is a woodwind instrument that you play by blowing down one end while covering the holes with your fingers.

recording, recordings (noun) A recording of something is a record, tape, or video of it.

recount, recounts, recounting, recounted 1 (verb) If you recount a story, you tell it. **2** (noun) A recount is a second count of votes in an election when the result is very close.

recoup, recoups, recouping, recouped (pronounced rik-**koop**) (verb) If you recoup money that you have spent or lost, you get it back.

recourse (noun; a formal word) If you have recourse to something, you use it to help you, e.g. *The members settled their differences without recourse to war.*

recover, recovers, recovering, recovered 1 (verb) To recover from an illness or unhappy experience means to get well again or get over it. **2** If you recover a lost object or your ability to do something, you get it back. **recovery** (noun).

recreate, recreates, recreating, recreated (verb) To recreate something means to succeed in making it happen or exist again, e.g. *a museum that faithfully recreates an old rural farmhouse.*

recreation, recreations (noun) Recreation is all the things that you do for enjoyment in your spare time. **recreational** (adjective).

recrimination, recriminations (noun) Recriminations are accusations made by people about each other.

recruit, recruits, recruiting, recruited 1 (verb) To recruit people means to get them to join a group or help with something. **2** (noun) A recruit is someone who has joined an organization or army. **recruitment** (noun).

rectangle, rectangles (noun) A rectangle is a four-sided shape with four right angles. **rectangular** (adjective).

rectify, rectifies, rectifying, rectified (verb; a formal word) If you rectify something that is wrong, you put it right.

rector, rectors (noun) A rector is a Church of England priest in charge of a parish.

rectory, rectories (noun) A rectory is a house where a rector lives.

rectum, rectums (noun; a medical word) Your rectum is the bottom end of the tube down which waste food passes out of your body. **rectal** (adjective).

recuperate, recuperates, recuperating, recuperated (verb) When you recuperate, you gradually recover after being ill. **recuperation** (noun).

recur, recurs, recurring, recurred (verb) If something recurs, it happens or occurs again, e.g. *His hamstring injury recurred after the first game.* **recurrence** (noun), **recurrent** (adjective).

recurring (adjective) happening or occurring many times, e.g. *a recurring dream.*

recycle, recycles, recycling, recycled (verb) To recycle used products means to process them so that they can be used again, e.g. *recycled glass.*

red, redder, reddest; reds 1 (noun or adjective) Red is the colour of blood or of a ripe tomato. **2** (adjective) Red hair is between orange and brown in colour.

redcurrant, redcurrants (noun) Redcurrants are very small, bright red fruits that grow in bunches on a bush.

redeem, redeems, redeeming, redeemed 1 (verb) If a feature redeems an unpleasant thing or situation, it makes it seem less bad. **2** If you redeem yourself, you do something that gives people a good opinion of you again. **3** If you redeem something, you get it back by paying for it.

redemption (noun) Redemption is the state of being redeemed.

red-handed (phrase) To **catch someone red-handed** means to catch them doing something wrong.

red-hot (adjective) Red-hot metal has been heated to such a high temperature that it has turned red.

redress, redresses, redressing, redressed (a formal word) **1** (verb) To redress a wrong means to put it right. **2** (noun) If you get redress for harm done to you, you are compensated for it.

red tape (noun) Red tape is official rules and procedures that seem unnecessary and cause delay.

reduce, reduces, reducing, reduced 1 (verb) To reduce something means to make it smaller in size or amount. **2** You can use reduce to say that someone or something is changed to a weaker or inferior state, e.g. *She reduced them to tears... The village was reduced to rubble.*

reduction, reductions (noun) When there is a reduction in something, it is made smaller.

redundancy, redundancies 1 (noun) Redundancy is the state of being redundant. **2** The number of redundancies is the number of people made redundant.

redundant 1 (adjective) When people are made redundant, they lose their jobs because there is no more work for them or no money to pay them. **2** When something becomes redundant, it is no longer needed.

reed, reeds 1 (noun) Reeds are hollow stemmed plants that grow in shallow water or wet ground. **2** A reed is a thin piece of cane or metal inside some wind instruments. The reed vibrates when air is blown over it.

reef, reefs (noun) A reef is a long line of rocks or coral close to the surface of the sea.

reek, reeks, reeking, reeked 1 (verb) To reek of something means to smell strongly and unpleasantly of it. **2** (noun) If there is a reek of something, there is a strong unpleasant smell of it.

reel, reels, reeling, reeled 1 (noun) A reel is a cylindrical object around which you wrap something; often part of a device which you turn as a control. **2** (verb) When someone reels, they move unsteadily as if they are going to fall. **3** If your mind is reeling, you are confused because you have too much to think about. **4** (noun) A reel is also a fast Scottish dance.

re-elect, re-elects, re-electing, re-elected (verb) When someone is re-elected, they win an election again and are able to stay in power.

refer, refers, referring, referred 1 (verb) If you refer to something, you mention it. **2** If you refer to a book, document, or record, you look at it to find something out. **3** When a problem or issue is referred to someone, they are formally asked to deal with it, e.g. *The case was referred to the European Court.*

referee, referees 1 (noun) The referee is the official who controls a football game or a boxing or wrestling match. **2** A referee is also someone who gives a reference to a person who is applying for a job.

reference, references 1 (noun) A reference to something or someone is a mention of them. **2** Reference is the act of referring to something or someone for information or advice, e.g. *He makes that decision without reference to her.* **3** A reference is also a number or name that tells you where to obtain information or identifies a document. **4** If someone gives you a reference when you apply for a job, they write a letter about your character and abilities.

referendum, referendums or **referenda** (noun) A referendum is a vote in which all the people in a country are officially asked whether they agree with a policy.

refine, refines, refining, refined (verb) To refine a raw material such as oil or sugar means to process it to remove impurities.

refined (adjective) very polite and well-mannered.

refinement, refinements 1 (noun) Refinements are minor improvements. **2** Refinement is politeness and good manners.

refinery, refineries (noun) A refinery is a factory where substances such as oil or sugar are refined.

reflect, reflects, reflecting, reflected 1 (verb) If something reflects an attitude or situation, it shows what it is like, e.g. *His off-duty hobbies reflected his maritime interests.* **2** If something reflects light or heat, the light or heat bounces off it. **3** When something is reflected in a mirror or water, you can see its image in it. **4** When you reflect, you think about something. **reflective** (adjective), **reflectively** (adverb).

reflection, reflections 1 (noun) If something is a reflection of something else, it shows what it is like, e.g. *This is a terrible reflection of the times.* **2** A reflection is an image in a mirror or water. **3** Reflection is the process by which light and heat are bounced off a surface. **4** Reflection is also thought, e.g. *After days of reflection she decided to leave.*

reflex, reflexes 1 (noun) A reflex or reflex action is a sudden uncontrollable movement that you make as a result of pressure or a blow. **2** If you have good reflexes, you respond very quickly when something unexpected happens. **3** (adjective) A reflex angle is between 180° and 360°.

reflexive, reflexives (adjective or noun) In grammar, a reflexive verb or pronoun is one that refers back to the subject of the sentence, e.g. *She washed herself.*

reform, reforms, reforming, reformed 1 (noun) Reforms are major changes to laws, systems, or institutions, e.g. *a programme of economic reform.* **2** (verb) When laws, systems, or institutions are reformed, major changes are made to them. **3** When people reform, they stop committing crimes or doing unacceptable things. **reformer** (noun).

refrain, refrains, refraining, refrained 1 (verb; a formal use) If you refrain from doing something, you do not do it, e.g. *Please refrain from smoking in the hall.* **2** (noun) The refrain of a song is a short, simple part that is repeated.

refresh, refreshes, refreshing, refreshed (verb) If something refreshes you when you are hot or tired, it makes you feel cooler or more energetic, e.g. *A glass of fruit juice will refresh you.*

refreshing (adjective) You say that something is refreshing when it is pleasantly different from what you are used to, e.g. *She is a refreshing contrast to her father.*

refreshment, refreshments (noun) Refreshments are drinks and small amounts of food provided at an event.

refrigerator, refrigerators (noun) A refrigerator is an electrically cooled container in which you store food to keep it fresh.

refuel, refuels, refuelling, refuelled (verb) When an aircraft or vehicle is refuelled, it is filled with more fuel.

refuge, refuges 1 (noun) A refuge is a place where you go for safety. **2** If you take refuge, you go somewhere for safety or behave in a way that will protect you, e.g. *They took refuge in a bomb shelter... Father Rowan took refuge in silence.*

refugee, refugees (noun) Refugees are people who have been forced to leave their country and live elsewhere.

refund, refunds, refunding, refunded 1 (noun) A refund is money returned to you because you have paid too much for something or because you have returned goods. **2** (verb) To refund someone's money means to return it to them after they have paid for something with it.

refurbish, refurbishes, refurbishing, refurbished (verb; a formal word) To refurbish a building means to decorate it and repair damage. **refurbishment** (noun).

refusal, refusals (noun) A refusal is when someone says firmly that they will not do, allow, or accept something.

refuse, refuses, refusing, refused (pronounced rif-**yooz**) **1** (verb) If you refuse to do something, you say or decide firmly that you will not do it. **2** If someone refuses something, they do not allow it or do not accept it, e.g. *The United States has refused him a visa... He offered me a second drink which I refused.*

refuse (pronounced **ref**-yoos) (noun) Refuse is rubbish or waste.

refute, refutes, refuting, refuted (verb; a formal word) To refute a theory or argument means to prove that it is wrong.

regain, regains, regaining, regained (verb) To regain something means to get it back.

regal (adjective) very grand and suitable for a king or queen, e.g. *She dined in regal style.* **regally** (adverb).

regard, regards, regarding, regarded 1 (verb) To regard someone or something in a particular way means to think of them in that way or have that opinion of them, e.g. *We all regard him as a friend... Many disapprove of the tax, regarding it as unfair.* **2** (noun) If you have a high regard for someone, you have a very good opinion of them. **3** (verb; a literary use) To regard someone in a particular way also means to look at them in that way, e.g. *She regarded him curiously for a moment.* **4** (phrases) **Regarding, as regards, with regard to,** and **in regard to** are all used to indicate what you are talking or writing about, e.g. *There was always some question regarding education.* **5** Regards is used in various expressions to express friendly feelings, e.g. *Give my regards to your husband.*

regardless (preposition or adverb) done or happening in spite of something else, e.g. *He led from the front, regardless of the danger.*

regatta, regattas (noun) A regatta is a race meeting for sailing or rowing boats.

regency, regencies (noun) A regency is a period when a country is ruled by a regent.

regenerate, regenerates, regenerating, regenerated (verb; a formal word) To regenerate a place or system means to develop and improve it after it has been declining, e.g. *a scheme to regenerate the docks area of the city.* **regeneration** (noun).

regent, regents (noun) A regent is someone who rules in place of a king or queen who is ill or too young to rule.

reggae (noun) Reggae is a type of music, originally from the West Indies, with a strong, distinctive rhythm.

regime, regimes (pronounced ray-**jeem**) (noun) A regime is a system of government, and the people who are ruling a country, e.g. *a communist regime.*

regiment, regiments (noun) A regiment is a large group of soldiers commanded by a colonel. **regimental** (adjective).

regimented (adjective) very strictly controlled, e.g. *the regimented life of the orphanage.* **regimentation** (noun).

region, regions 1 (noun) A region is a large area of land. **2** You can refer to any area or part as a region, e.g. *the pelvic region.* **3** (phrase) **In the region of** means approximately, e.g. *The scheme will cost in the region of six thousand pounds.* **regional** (adjective), **regionally** (adverb).

register, registers, registering, registered 1 (noun) A register is an official list or record of things, e.g. *the electoral register.* **2** (verb) When something is registered, it is recorded on an official list, e.g. *The car was registered in my name.* **3** If an instrument registers a measurement, it shows it. **registration** (noun).

registrar, registrars 1 (noun) A registrar is a person who keeps official records of births, marriages, and deaths. **2** At a college or university, the registrar is a senior administrative official. **3** A registrar is also a senior hospital doctor.

registration number, registration numbers (noun) The registration number of a motor vehicle is the sequence of letters and numbers on the front and back that identify it.

registry, registries (noun) A registry is a place where official records are kept.

registry office, registry offices (noun) A registry office is a place where births, marriages, and deaths are recorded, and where people can marry without a religious ceremony.

regret, regrets, regretting, re-

gretted 1 (verb) If you regret something, you are sorry that it happened. **2** (noun) If you have regrets, you are sad or sorry about something. **3** (verb) You can say that you regret something as a way of apologizing, e.g. *We regret any inconvenience to passengers.* **regretful** (adjective), **regretfully** (adverb).

regrettable (adjective) unfortunate and undesirable, e.g. *a regrettable accident.* **regrettably** (adverb).

regular, regulars 1 (adjective) even and equally spaced, e.g. *soft music with a regular beat.* **2** Regular events or activities happen often and according to a pattern, for example each day or each week, e.g. *The trains to London are fairly regular.* **3** If you are a regular customer or visitor somewhere, you go there often. **4** (noun) People who go to a place often are known as its regulars. **5** (adjective) usual or normal, e.g. *I was filling in for the regular bartender.* **6** having a well balanced appearance, e.g. *a regular geometrical shape.* **regularly** (adverb), **regularity** (noun).

regulate, regulates, regulating, regulated (verb) To regulate something means to control the way it operates, e.g. *Our water quality is closely regulated.* **regulator** (noun).

regulation, regulations 1 (noun) Regulations are official rules. **2** Regulation is the control of something, e.g. *regulation of the betting industry.*

regurgitate, regurgitates, regurgitating, regurgitated (pronounced rig-**gur**-jit-tate) (verb) To regurgitate food means to bring it back from the stomach before it is digested.

rehabilitate, rehabilitates, rehabilitating, rehabilitated (verb) To rehabilitate someone who has been ill or in prison means to help them lead a normal life. **rehabilitation** (noun).

rehearsal, rehearsals (noun) A rehearsal is a practice of a performance in preparation for the actual event.

rehearse, rehearses, rehearsing, rehearsed (verb) To rehearse a performance means to practise it in preparation for the actual event.

reign, reigns, reigning, reigned (pronounced **rain**) **1** (verb) When a king or queen reigns, he or she rules a country. **2** (noun) The reign of a king or queen is the period during which he or she reigns. **3** (verb) You can say that something reigns when it is a noticeable feature of a situation or period of time, e.g. *Panic reigned after his murder.*

rein, reins 1 (noun) Reins are the thin leather straps which you hold when you are riding a horse or controlling it. **2** (phrase) To **keep a tight rein on** someone or something means to control them firmly.

reincarnation (verb) People who believe in reincarnation believe that when you die, you are born again as another creature.

reindeer (noun) Reindeer are deer with large antlers, that live in northern areas of Europe, Asia, and America.

reinforce, reinforces, reinforcing, reinforced 1 (verb) To reinforce something means to strengthen it, e.g. *a reinforced steel barrier.* **2** If something reinforces an idea or claim, it provides evidence to support it.

reinforcement, reinforcements (noun) Reinforcements are additional soldiers sent to join an army in battle.

reinstate, reinstates, reinstating, reinstated 1 (verb) To reinstate someone means to give them back a position they have lost. **2** To reinstate something means to bring it back, e.g. *Parliament voted against reinstating capital punishment.* **reinstatement** (noun).

reiterate, reiterates, reiterating, reiterated (pronounced ree-**it**-er-ate) (verb; a formal word) If you reiterate something, you say it again. **reiteration** (noun).

reject, rejects, rejecting, rejected 1 (verb) If you reject a proposal or request, you do not accept it or agree to it. **2** If you reject a belief, political system, or way of life, you decide that it is not for you. **3** (noun) A reject is a product that cannot be used, because there is something wrong with it. **rejection** (noun).

rejoice, rejoices, rejoicing, rejoiced (verb) To rejoice means to be very pleased about something, e.g. *The country rejoiced after his downfall.*

rejoin, rejoins, rejoining, rejoined (verb) If you rejoin someone, you go back to them soon after leaving them, e.g. *She rejoined her friends in the bar.*

rejuvenate, rejuvenates, rejuvenating, rejuvenated (verb) To rejuvenate someone means to make them feel young again. **rejuvenation** (noun).

relapse, relapses (noun) If a sick person has a relapse, their health suddenly gets worse after improving.

relate, relates, relating, related 1 (verb) If something relates to something else, it is connected or concerned with it, e.g. *The statistics relate only to western Germany.* **2** If you can relate to someone, you can understand their thoughts and feelings. **3** To relate a story means to tell it.

relation, relations 1 (noun) If there is a relation between two things, they are similar or connected in some way, e.g. *This theory bears no relation to reality.* **2** Your relations are the members of your family. **3** Relations between people are their feelings and behaviour towards each other, e.g. *Relations between husband and wife had not improved.*

relationship, relationships 1 (noun) The relationship between two people or groups is the way they feel and behave towards each other. **2** A relationship is a close friendship, especially one involving romantic or sexual feelings. **3** The relationship between two things is the way in which they are connected, e.g. *the relationship between slavery and the sugar trade.*

relative, relatives 1 (adjective) compared to other things or people of the same kind, e.g.

The fighting resumed after a period of relative calm... He is a relative novice. **2** You use relative when comparing the size or quality of two things, e.g. *the relative strengths of the British and German forces.* **3** (noun) Your relatives are the members of your family.

relax, relaxes, relaxing, relaxed **1** (verb) If you relax, you become calm and your muscles lose their tension. **2** If you relax your hold, you hold something less tightly. **3** To relax something also means to make it less strict or controlled, e.g. *The rules governing student conduct were relaxed.* **relaxation** (noun).

relay, relays, relaying, relayed **1** (noun) A relay race or relay is a race between teams, with each team member running one part of the race. **2** (verb) To relay a television or radio signal means to send it on. **3** If you relay information, you tell it to someone else.

release, releases, releasing, released **1** (verb) To release someone or something means to set them free or remove restraints from them. **2** (noun) When the release of someone or something takes place, they are set free. **3** (verb) To release something also means to issue it or make it available, e.g. *He is releasing an album of love songs.* **4** (noun) A press release or publicity release is an official written statement given to reporters. **5** A new release is a new record or video that has just become available.

relegate, relegates, relegating, relegated (verb) To relegate something or someone means to give them a less important position or status. **relegation** (noun).

relent, relents, relenting, relented (verb) If someone relents, they agree to something they had previously not allowed.

relentless (adjective) never stopping and never reducing in severity, e.g. *the relentless rise of business closures.* **relentlessly** (adverb).

relevant (adjective) If something is relevant, it is connected with and is appropriate to what is being discussed, e.g. *We have passed all relevant information on to the police.* **relevance** (noun).

reliable **1** (adjective) Reliable people and things can be trusted to do what you want. **2** If information is reliable, you can assume that it is correct. **reliably** (adverb), **reliability** (noun).

reliant (adjective) If you are reliant on someone or something, you need them and depend on them, e.g. *They are not wholly reliant on charity.* **reliance** (noun).

relic, relics **1** (noun) Relics are objects or customs that have survived from an earlier time. **2** A relic is also an object regarded as holy because it is thought to be connected with a saint.

relief **1** (noun) If you feel relief, you are glad and thankful because a bad situation is over or has been avoided. **2** Relief is also money, food, or clothing provided for poor or hungry people.

relieve, relieves, relieving, relieved 1 (verb) If something relieves an unpleasant feeling, it makes it less unpleasant, e.g. *Drugs can relieve much of the pain.* **2** (a formal use) If you relieve someone, you do their job or duty for a period. **3** If someone is relieved of their duties, they are dismissed from their job.

religion, religions 1 (noun) Religion is the belief in a god or gods and all the activities connected with such beliefs. **2** A religion is a system of religious belief.

religious 1 (adjective) connected with religion, e.g. *religious worship.* **2** Someone who is religious has a strong belief in a god or gods.

religiously (adverb) If you do something religiously, you do it regularly as a duty, e.g. *He stuck religiously to the rules.*

relinquish, relinquishes, relinquishing, relinquished (pronounced ril-**ling**-kwish) (verb; a formal word) If you relinquish something, you give it up.

relish, relishes, relishing, relished 1 (verb) If you relish something, you enjoy it, e.g. *He relished the idea of getting some cash.* **2** (noun) Relish is enjoyment, e.g. *The three men ate with relish.* **3** Relish is a savoury sauce or pickle.

relive, relives, reliving, relived (verb) If you relive a past experience, you remember it and imagine it happening again.

relocate, relocates, relocating, relocated (verb) If people or businesses are relocated, they are moved to a different place. **relocation** (noun).

reluctant (adjective) If you are reluctant to do something, you are unwilling to do it. **reluctance** (noun).

reluctantly (adverb) If you do something reluctantly, you do it although you do not want to.

rely, relies, relying, relied 1 (verb) If you rely on someone or something, you need them and depend on them, e.g. *She has to rely on hardship payments.* **2** If you can rely on someone to do something, you can trust them to do it, e.g. *They can always be relied on to turn up.*

remain, remains, remaining, remained 1 (verb) If you remain in a particular place or state, you stay there or stay the same and do not change, e.g. *The three men remained silent.* **2** Something that remains still exists or is left over, e.g. *Huge amounts of weapons remain to be collected.* **3** (plural noun) The remains of something are the parts that are left after most of it has been destroyed, e.g. *the remains of an ancient mosque.* **4** You can refer to a dead body as remains, e.g. *More human remains have been unearthed today.*

remainder (noun) The remainder of something is the part that is left, e.g. *He drank the remainder of his coffee.*

remand, remands, remanding, remanded 1 (verb) If a judge remands someone who is accused of a crime, the trial is postponed and the person is ordered to come back at a later date. **2** (phrase) If someone is **on remand,** they are in prison waiting for their trial to begin.

remark, remarks, remarking, remarked 1 (verb) If you remark on something, you mention it or comment on it, e.g. *On several occasions she had remarked on the boy's improvement.* **2** (noun) A remark is something you say, often in a casual way.

remarkable (adjective) impressive and unexpected, e.g. *It was a remarkable achievement.* **remarkably** (adverb).

remarry, remarries, remarrying, remarried (verb) If someone remarries, they get married again.

remedial 1 (adjective) Remedial activities are to help someone improve their health after they have been ill. **2** Remedial exercises are designed to improve someone's ability in something, e.g. *the remedial reading class.*

remedy, remedies, remedying, remedied 1 (noun) A remedy is a way of dealing with a problem, e.g. *a remedy for colic.* **2** (verb) If you remedy something that is wrong, you correct it, e.g. *We have to remedy the situation.*

remember, remembers, remembering, remembered 1 (verb) If you can remember someone or something from the past, you can bring them into your mind or think about them. **2** If you remember to do something, you do it when you intended to, e.g. *Ben had remembered to book reservations.*

remembrance (noun) If you do something in remembrance of a dead person, you are showing that they are remembered with respect.

remind, reminds, reminding, reminded 1 (verb) If someone reminds you of a fact, they say something to make you think about it, e.g. *Remind me to buy a bottle of wine, will you?* **2** If someone reminds you of another person, they look similar and make you think of them.

reminder, reminders 1 (noun) If one thing is a reminder of another, the first thing makes you think of the second, e.g. *a reminder of better times.* **2** A reminder is a note sent to tell someone they have forgotten to do something.

reminiscent (adjective) Something that is reminiscent of something else reminds you of it.

remission (noun) When prisoners get remission for good behaviour, their sentences are reduced.

remit, remits (noun; a formal word) The remit of a person or committee is the subject or task they are responsible for, e.g. *Their remit is to research into a wide range of health problems.*

remittance, remittances (noun; a formal word) A remittance is payment for something sent through the post.

remnant, remnants (noun) A remnant is a small part of something left after the rest has been used or destroyed.

remorse (noun; a formal word) Remorse is a strong feeling of guilt. **remorseful** (adjective).

remote, remoter, remotest 1 (adjective) Remote areas are far away from places where most people live. **2** far away in time, e.g. *the remote past.* **3** If you say a person is remote, you mean they do not want to be friendly, e.g. *She is severe, solemn, and remote.* **4** If there is only a remote possibility of something happening, it is unlikely to happen. **remoteness** (noun).

remote control (noun) Remote control is a system of controlling a machine or vehicle from a distance using radio or electronic signals.

remotely (adverb) used to emphasize a negative statement, e.g. *He isn't remotely keen.*

removal 1 (noun) The removal of something is the act of taking it away. **2** A removal company transports furniture from one building to another.

remove, removes, removing, removed 1 (verb) If you remove something from a place, you take it off or away. **2** If you are removed from a position of authority, you are not allowed to continue your job. **3** If you remove an undesirable feeling or attitude, you get rid of it, e.g. *Most of her fears had been removed.* **removable** (adjective).

Renaissance (pronounced ren-**nay**-sonss) (noun) The Renaissance was a period from the 14th to 16th centuries in Europe when there was a great revival in art, literature, and learning.

renal (adjective; a technical word) concerning the kidneys, e.g. *renal failure.*

rename, renames, renaming, renamed (verb) If you rename something, you give it a new name.

render, renders, rendering, rendered (verb) You can use render to say that something is changed into a different state, e.g. *The bomb was quickly rendered harmless.*

rendezvous (pronounced **ron**-day-voo) **1** (noun) A rendezvous is a meeting, e.g. *She had a midnight rendezvous with her boyfriend.* **2** A rendezvous is also a place where you have arranged to meet someone, e.g. *The pub became a popular rendezvous for office workers.*

rendition, renditions (noun; a formal word) A rendition of a play, poem, or piece of music is a performance of it.

renew, renews, renewing, renewed 1 (verb) To renew an activity or relationship means to begin it again. **2** To renew a licence or contract means to extend the period of time for which it is valid. **renewal** (noun).

renounce, renounces, renouncing, renounced (verb; a formal word) If you renounce something, you reject it or give it up. **renunciation** (noun).

renovate, renovates, renovating, renovated (verb) If you renovate an old building or machine, you repair it and restore it to good condition. **renovation** (noun).

renowned (adjective) well known for something good, e.g. *He is by no means renowned for his humour.* **renown** (noun).

rent, rents, renting, rented 1 (verb) If you rent something, you pay the owner a regular sum of money in return for being able to use it. **2** (noun) Rent is the amount of money you pay regularly to rent land or accommodation.

rental 1 (adjective) concerned with the renting out of goods and services, e.g. *Scotland's largest video rental company.* **2** (noun) Rental is the amount of money you pay when you rent something.

rep, reps (noun; an informal word) A rep is a travelling salesperson.

repair, repairs, repairing, repaired 1 (noun) A repair is something you do to mend something that is damaged or broken. **2** (verb) If you repair something, you mend it.

repay, repays, repaying, repaid 1 (verb) To repay money means to give it back to the person who lent it. **2** If you repay a favour, you do something to help the person who helped you. **repayment** (noun).

repeal, repeals, repealing, repealed (verb) If the government repeals a law, it cancels it so that it is no longer valid.

repeat, repeats, repeating, repeated 1 (verb) If you repeat something, you say, write, or do it again. **2** If you repeat what someone has said, you tell someone else about it, e.g. *I trust you not to repeat that to anyone.* **3** (noun) A repeat is something which is done or happens again, e.g. *The BBC is to slash the number of repeats shown.* **repeated** (adjective), **repeatedly** (adverb).

repel, repels, repelling, repelled 1 (verb) If something repels you, you find it horrible and disgusting. **2** When soldiers repel an attacking force, they successfully defend themselves against it.

repellent, repellents 1 (adjective; a formal use) horrible and disgusting, e.g. *I found him repellent.* **2** (noun) Repellents are chemicals used to keep insects or other creatures away.

repent, repents, repenting, repented (verb; a formal word) If you repent, you are sorry for something bad you have done. **repentance** (noun), **repentant** (adjective).

repercussion, repercussions (noun) The repercussions of an event are the effects it has at a later time.

repertoire, repertoires (pronounced **rep**-et-twar) (noun) A performer's repertoire is all the pieces of music or dramatic parts he or she has learned and can perform.

repertory (noun) Repertory is the practice of performing a small number of plays in a theatre for a short time, using the same actors in each play.

repetition, repetitions (noun) If there is a repetition of something, it happens again, e.g. *We don't want a repetition of last week's fiasco.*

repetitive (adjective) A repetitive activity involves a lot of repetition and is boring, e.g. *dull and repetitive work.*

replace, replaces, replacing, replaced 1 (verb) When one thing replaces another, the first thing takes the place of the second. **2** If you replace something that is damaged or lost, you get a new one. **3** If you replace something, you put it back where it was before, e.g. *She replaced the receiver.*

replacement, replacements 1 (noun) The replacement for someone or something is the person or thing that takes their place. **2** The replacement of a person or thing happens when they are replaced by another person or thing.

replay, replays, replaying, replayed 1 (verb) If a match is replayed, the teams play it again. **2** (noun) A replay is a match that is played for a second time. **3** (verb) If you replay a tape or film, you play it again, e.g. *Replay the first few seconds of the tape please.*

replenish, replenishes, replenishing, replenished (verb; a formal word) If you replenish something, you make it full or complete again.

replica, replicas (noun) A replica is an accurate copy of something, e.g. *a replica of the ship.* **replicate** (verb).

reply, replies, replying, replied 1 (verb) If you reply to something, you say or write an answer. **2** (noun) A reply is what you say or write when you answer someone.

report, reports, reporting, reported 1 (verb) If you report that something has happened, you tell someone about it or give an official account of it, e.g. *He reported the theft to the police.* **2** (noun) A report is an account of an event, a situation, or a person's progress. **3** (verb) To report someone to an authority means to make an official complaint about them. **4** If you report to a person or place, you go there and say you have arrived.

reporter, reporters (noun) A reporter is someone who writes news articles or broadcasts news reports.

repossess, repossesses, repossessing, repossessed (verb) If a shop or company repossesses goods that have not been paid for, they take them back.

represent, represents, representing, represented 1 (verb) If you represent someone, you act on their behalf, e.g. *lawyers representing relatives of the victims.* **2** If a sign or symbol represents something, it stands for it. **3** To represent something in a particular way means to describe it in that way, e.g. *The popular press tends to represent him as a hero.*

representation, representations (noun) Representation is the state of being represented by someone, e.g. *Was there any student representation?*

representative, representatives 1 (noun) A representative is a person chosen to act on behalf of another person or a group. **2** (adjective) A representative selection is typical of the group it belongs to, e.g. *The photos chosen are not representative of his work.*

repress, represses, repressing, repressed 1 (verb) If you repress a feeling, you succeed in not showing or feeling it, e.g. *I couldn't repress my anger* *any longer.* **2** To repress people means to restrict their freedom and control them by force. **repression** (noun).

repressive (adjective) Repressive governments use force and unjust laws to restrict and control people.

reprieve, reprieves, reprieving, reprieved (pronounced rip-**preev**) **1** (verb) If someone who has been sentenced to death is reprieved, their sentence is changed and they are not killed. **2** (noun) A reprieve is a delay before something unpleasant happens, e.g. *The zoo won a reprieve from closure.*

reprimand, reprimands, reprimanding, reprimanded 1 (verb) If you reprimand someone, you officially tell them that they should not have done something. **2** (noun) A reprimand is something said or written by a person in authority when they are reprimanding someone.

reprisal, reprisals (noun) Reprisals are violent actions taken by one group of people against another group that has harmed them.

reproach, reproaches, reproaching, reproached (a formal word) **1** (noun) If you express reproach, you show that you feel sad and angry about what someone has done, e.g. *a long letter of reproach.* **2** (verb) If you reproach someone, you tell them, rather sadly, that they have done something wrong. **reproachful** (adjective).

reproduce, reproduces, reproducing, reproduced 1 (verb) To reproduce something means to make a copy of it. **2** When people, animals, or plants reproduce, they produce more of their own kind, e.g. *Bacteria reproduce by splitting into two.*

reproduction, reproductions 1 (noun) A reproduction is a modern copy of a painting or piece of furniture. **2** The reproduction of sound, art, or writing is the copying of it, e.g. *the increasingly high technology of music reproduction.* **3** Reproduction is the process by which a living thing produces more of its kind, e.g. *the study of animal reproduction.*

reproductive (adjective) relating to the reproduction of living things, e.g. *the female reproductive system.*

reptile, reptiles (noun) A reptile is a cold-blooded animal which has scaly skin and lays eggs. Snakes and lizards are reptiles. **reptilian** (adjective).

republic, republics (noun) A republic is a country which has a president rather than a king or queen. **republican** (noun or adjective), **republicanism** (noun).

repulsive (adjective) horrible and disgusting.

reputable (adjective) known to be good and reliable, e.g. *a well-established and reputable firm.*

reputation, reputations (noun) The reputation of something or someone is the opinion that people have of them, e.g. *The college had a good reputation.*

reputed (adjective) If something is reputed to be true, some people say that it is true, e.g. *the reputed tomb of Christ.* **reputedly** (adverb).

request, requests, requesting, requested 1 (verb) If you request something, you ask for it politely or formally. **2** (noun) If you make a request for something, you request it.

requiem, requiems (pronounced **rek**-wee-em) **1** (noun) A requiem or requiem mass is a mass celebrated for someone who has recently died. **2** A requiem is also a piece of music for singers and an orchestra, originally written for a requiem mass, e.g. *Mozart's Requiem.*

require, requires, requiring, required 1 (verb) If you require something, you need it. **2** If you are required to do something, you have to do it because someone says you must, e.g. *The rules require employers to provide training.*

requirement, requirements (noun) A requirement is something that you must have or must do, e.g. *A level English is a requirement for entry.*

requisite, requisites (a formal word) **1** (adjective) necessary for a particular purpose, e.g. *She filled in the requisite paperwork.* **2** (noun) A requisite is something that is necessary for a particular purpose.

rescue, rescues, rescuing, rescued 1 (verb) If you rescue someone, you save them from a dangerous or unpleasant situation. **2** (noun) Rescue is help which saves someone from a dangerous or unpleasant situation. **rescuer** (noun).

research, researches, researching, researched 1 (noun) Research is work that involves studying something and trying to find out facts about it. **2** (verb) If you research something, you try to discover facts about it. **researcher** (noun).

resemblance (noun) If there is a resemblance between two things, they are similar to each other, e.g. *There was a remarkable resemblance between him and Pete.*

resemble, resembles, resembling, resembled (verb) To resemble something means to be similar to it.

resent, resents, resenting, resented (verb) If you resent something, you feel bitter and angry about it. **resentment** (noun).

resentful (adjective) bitter and angry, e.g. *She felt very resentful about losing her job.* **resentfully** (adverb).

reservation, reservations 1 (noun) If you have reservations about something, you are not sure that it is right. **2** If you make a reservation, you book a place in advance. **3** A reservation is an area of land that is kept separate for a group of people to live on.

reserve, reserves, reserving, reserved 1 (verb) If something is reserved for a particular person or purpose, it is kept specially for them. **2** (noun) A reserve is a supply of something for future use. **3** In sport, a reserve is someone who is available to play in case one of the team is unable to play. **4** A nature reserve is an area of land where animals, birds, or plants are officially protected. **5** If someone shows reserve, they keep their feelings hidden. **reserved** (adjective).

reservoir, reservoirs (pronounced **rez**-ev-wahr) (noun) A reservoir is a lake used for storing water before it is supplied to people.

reshuffle, reshuffles (noun) A reshuffle is a reorganization of people or things.

reside, resides, residing, resided (pronounced riz-**zide**) (verb; a formal word) If a quality resides in something, the quality is in that thing.

residence, residences (noun; a formal word) A residence is a house.

resident, residents 1 (noun) A resident of a house or area is someone who lives there. **2** (adjective) If someone is resident in a house or area, they live there.

residential 1 (adjective) A residential area contains mainly houses rather than offices or factories. **2** providing accommodation, e.g. *residential care for the elderly.*

residue, residues (noun) A residue is a small amount of something that remains after most of it has gone, e.g. *an increase in toxic residues found in drinking water.* **residual** (adjective).

resign, resigns, resigning, resigned 1 (verb) If you resign from a job, you formally announce that you are leaving it. **2** If you resign yourself to an unpleasant situation, you realize that you have to accept it. **resigned** (adjective).

resignation, resignations 1 (noun) Someone's resignation is a formal statement of their intention to leave a job. **2** Resignation is the reluctant acceptance of an unpleasant situation or fact.

resilient (adjective) able to recover quickly from unpleasant or damaging events. **resilience** (noun).

resin, resins 1 (noun) Resin is a sticky substance produced by some trees. **2** Resin is also a chemically produced substance used to make plastics.

resist, resists, resisting, resisted 1 (verb) If you resist something, you refuse to accept it and try to prevent it, e.g. *The pay squeeze will be fiercely resisted by the unions.* **2** If you resist someone, you fight back against them.

resistance, resistances 1 (noun) Resistance to something such as change is a refusal to accept it. **2** Resistance to an attack consists of fighting back, e.g. *The demonstrators offered no resistance.* **3** Your body's resistance to germs or disease is its power to remain unharmed by them. **4** Resistance is also the power of a substance to resist the flow of an electrical current through it.

resistant 1 (adjective) opposed to something and wanting to prevent it, e.g. *People were very resistant to change.* **2** If something is resistant to a particular thing, it is not harmed or affected by it, e.g. *Certain insects are resistant to this spray.*

resolute (pronounced **rez**-ol-loot) (adjective; a formal word) Someone who is resolute is determined not to change their mind. **resolutely**

(adverb).

resolution, resolutions 1 (noun) Resolution is determination. **2** If you make a resolution, you promise yourself to do something. **3** A resolution is a formal decision taken at a meeting. **4** (a formal use) The resolution of a problem is the solving of it.

resolve, resolves, resolving, resolved 1 (verb) If you resolve to do something, you firmly decide to do it. **2** (noun) Resolve is absolute determination. **3** (verb) If you resolve a problem, you find a solution to it.

resonance, resonances 1 (noun) Resonance is sound produced by an object vibrating as a result of another sound nearby. **2** Resonance is also a deep, clear, and echoing quality of sound.

resonate, resonates, resonating, resonated (verb) If something resonates, it vibrates and produces a deep, strong sound.

resort, resorts, resorting, resorted 1 (verb) If you resort to a course of action, you do it because you have no alternative. **2** (phrase) If you do something **as a last resort,** you do it because you can find no other way of solving a problem. **3** (noun) A resort is a place where people spend their holidays.

resounding 1 (adjective) loud and echoing, e.g. *a resounding round of applause.* **2** A resounding success is a great success.

resource, resources (noun) The resources of a country, organization, or person are the materials, money, or skills they have available for use.

resourceful (adjective) A resourceful person is good at finding ways of dealing with problems. **resourcefulness** (noun).

respect, respects, respecting, respected 1 (verb) If you respect someone, you have a good opinion of their character or ideas. **2** (noun) If you have respect for someone, you respect them. **3** (verb) If you respect someone's rights or wishes, you do not do things that they would not like, e.g. *It is about time they started respecting the law.* **4** (phrase) You can say **in this respect** to refer to a particular feature, e.g. *At least in this respect we are equals.*

respectable 1 (adjective) considered to be acceptable and morally correct, e.g. *respectable families.* **2** adequate or reasonable, e.g. *a respectable rate of economic growth.* **respectability** (noun), **respectably** (adverb).

respectful (adjective) showing respect for someone, e.g. *Our children are respectful to their elders.* **respectfully** (adverb).

respective (adjective) belonging or relating individually to the people or things just mentioned, e.g. *They went into their respective rooms to pack.*

respectively (adverb) in the same order as the items just mentioned, e.g. *They finished first and second respectively.*

respiration (noun; a technical word) Your respiration is your breathing.

respiratory (adjective; a technical word) relating to breathing, e.g. *respiratory diseases.*

respite (noun; a formal word) A respite is a short rest from something unpleasant.

respond, responds, responding, responded (verb) When you respond to something, you react to it by doing or saying something.

respondent, respondents (noun) A respondent is a person who answers a questionnaire or a request for information.

response, responses (noun) Your response to an event is your reaction or reply to it, e.g. *There has been no response to his remarks yet.*

responsibility, responsibilities 1 (noun) If you have responsibility for something, it is your duty to deal with it or look after it, e.g. *The garden was to have been his responsibility.* **2** If you accept responsibility for something that has happened, you agree that you were to blame, e.g. *We must all accept responsibility for our own mistakes.*

responsible 1 (adjective) If you are responsible for something, it is your duty to deal with it and you are to blame if it goes wrong. **2** If you are responsible to someone, that person is your boss and tells you what you have to do. **3** A responsible person behaves properly and sensibly without needing to be supervised. **4** A responsible job involves making careful judgments about important matters. **responsibly** (adverb).

responsive 1 (adjective) quick to show interest and pleasure. **2** taking notice of events and reacting in an appropriate way, e.g. *The course is designed to be responsive to students' needs.*

rest, rests, resting, rested 1 (noun) The rest of something is all the remaining parts of it. **2** (verb) If you rest, you relax and do not do anything active for a while. **3** (noun) If you have a rest, you sit or lie quietly and relax.

restaurant, restaurants (pronounced **rest**-rong) (noun) A restaurant is a place where you can buy and eat a meal.

restaurateur, restaurateurs (pronounced rest-er-a-**tur**) (noun) A restaurateur is someone who owns or manages a restaurant.

restful (adjective) Something that is restful helps you feel calm and relaxed.

restless (adjective) finding it difficult to remain still or relaxed as a result of boredom or impatience. **restlessness** (noun), **restlessly** (adverb).

restore, restores, restoring, restored 1 (verb) To restore something means to cause it to exist again or to return to its previous state, e.g. *He was anxious to restore his reputation.* **2** To restore an old building or work of art means to clean and repair it. **restoration** (noun).

restrain, restrains, restraining, restrained (verb) To restrain someone or something means to hold them back or prevent them from doing what they want to.

restrained (adjective) behaving

in a controlled way.

restraint, restraints 1 (noun) Restraints are rules or conditions that limit something, e.g. *wage restraints.* **2** Restraint is calm, controlled behaviour.

restrict, restricts, restricting, restricted 1 (verb) If you restrict something, you prevent it becoming too large or varied. **2** To restrict people or animals means to limit their movement or actions. **restrictive** (adjective).

restriction, restrictions (noun) A restriction is a rule or situation that limits what you can do, e.g. *financial restrictions.*

result, results, resulting, resulted 1 (noun) The result of an action or situation is the situation that is caused by it, e.g. *As a result of the incident he got a two-year suspension.* **2** (verb) If something results in a particular event, it causes that event to happen. **3** If something results from a particular event, it is caused by that event, e.g. *The fire had resulted from carelessness.* **4** (noun) The result is also the final marks, figures, or situation at the end of an exam, calculation, or contest, e.g. *election results... The result was calculated to three decimal places.* **resultant** (adjective).

resume, resumes, resuming, resumed (pronounced riz-**yoom**) (verb) If you resume an activity or position, you return to it after a break. **resumption** (noun).

resurgence (noun) If there is a resurgence of an attitude or activity, it reappears and grows stronger. **resurgent** (adjective).

resurrect, resurrects, resurrecting, resurrected (verb) If you resurrect something, you cause it to exist again after it has disappeared or ended. **resurrection** (noun).

Resurrection (noun) In Christian belief, the Resurrection is the coming back to life of Jesus Christ three days after he had been killed.

resuscitate, resuscitates, resuscitating, resuscitated (pronounced ris-**suss**-it-tate) (verb) If you resuscitate someone, you make them conscious again after an accident. **resuscitation** (noun).

retail (noun) The retail price is the price at which something is sold in the shops. **retailer** (noun).

retain, retains, retaining, retained (verb) To retain something means to keep it. **retention** (noun).

retaliate, retaliates, retaliating, retaliated (verb) If you retaliate, you do something to harm or upset someone because they have already acted in a similar way against you. **retaliation** (noun).

retarded (adjective) If someone is retarded, their mental development is much less advanced than average.

rethink, rethinks, rethinking, rethought (verb) If you rethink something, you think about how it should be changed, e.g. *We have to rethink our strategy.*

reticent (adjective) Someone who is reticent is unwilling to tell people about things. **reticence** (noun).

retina, retinas (noun) The retina is the light-sensitive part at the back of your eyeball, which receives an image and sends it to your brain.

retinue, retinues (noun) A retinue is a group of helpers or friends travelling with an important person.

retire, retires, retiring, retired 1 (verb) When older people retire, they give up work. **2** (a formal use) If you retire, you leave to go into another room, or to bed, e.g. *She retired early with a good book.* **retired** (adjective), **retirement** (noun).

retort, retorts, retorting, retorted 1 (verb) To retort means to reply angrily. **2** (noun) A retort is a short, angry reply.

retract, retracts, retracting, retracted 1 (verb) If you retract something you have said, you say that you did not mean it. **2** When something is retracted, it moves inwards or backwards, e.g. *The undercarriage was retracted shortly after takeoff.* **retraction** (noun), **retractable** (adjective).

retreat, retreats, retreating, retreated 1 (verb) To retreat means to move backwards away from something or someone. **2** (noun) If an army moves away from the enemy, this is referred to as a retreat. **3** (verb) If you retreat from something difficult or unpleasant, you avoid doing it. **4** (noun) A retreat is a quiet, secluded place that you go to in order to rest or do things in private.

retribution (noun; a formal word) Retribution is punishment, e.g. *the threat of retribution.*

retrieve, retrieves, retrieving, retrieved (verb) If you retrieve something, you get it back. **retrieval** (noun).

retriever, retrievers (noun) A retriever is a large dog often used by hunters to bring back birds and animals which have been shot.

retrospect (noun) When you consider something in retrospect, you think about it afterwards and often have a different opinion from the one you had at the time, e.g. *In retrospect, I probably shouldn't have resigned.*

retrospective 1 (adjective) concerning things that happened in the past. **2** taking effect from a date in the past. **retrospectively** (adverb).

return, returns, returning, returned 1 (verb) When you return to a place, you go back after you have been away. **2** (noun) Your return is your arrival back at a place. **3** (verb) If you return something to someone, you give it back to them. **4** When you return a ball during a game, you hit it back to your opponent. **5** (noun) The return on an investment is the profit or interest you get from it. **6** A return is a ticket for the journey to a place and back again. **7** (phrase) If you do something **in return** for a favour, you do it to repay the favour.

reunion, reunions (noun) A reunion is a party or meeting for people who have not seen each other for a long time.

reunite, reunites, reuniting, reunited (verb) If people are reunited, they meet again after they have been separated for some time.

rev, revs, revving, revved (an informal word) **1** (verb) When you rev the engine of a vehicle, you press the accelerator to increase the engine speed. **2** (noun) The speed of an engine is measured in revolutions per minute, referred to as revs, e.g. *I noticed that the engine revs had dropped.*

Rev or **Revd** abbreviations for **Reverend.**

revamp, revamps, revamping, revamped (verb) To revamp something means to improve or repair it.

reveal, reveals, revealing, revealed 1 (verb) To reveal something means to tell people about it, e.g. *They were not ready to reveal any of the details.* **2** If you reveal something that has been hidden, you uncover it.

revel, revels, revelling, revelled (verb) If you revel in a situation, you enjoy it very much. **revelry** (noun).

revelation, revelations 1 (noun) A revelation is a surprising or interesting fact made known to people. **2** If an experience is a revelation, it makes you realize or learn something.

revenge, revenges, revenging, revenged 1 (noun) Revenge involves hurting someone who has hurt you. **2** (verb) If you revenge yourself on someone who has hurt you, you hurt them in return.

revenue, revenues (noun) Revenue is money that a government, company, or organization receives, e.g. *government tax revenues.*

revered (adjective) If someone is revered, he or she is respected and admired, e.g. *He is still revered as the father of the nation.*

reverence (noun) Reverence is a feeling of great respect.

Reverend Reverend is a title used before the name of a member of the clergy, e.g. *the Reverend George Young.*

reversal, reversals (noun) If there is a reversal of a process or policy, it is changed to the opposite process or policy.

reverse, reverses, reversing, reversed 1 (verb) When someone reverses a process, they change it to the opposite process, e.g. *They won't reverse the decision to increase prices.* **2** If you reverse the order of things, you arrange them in the opposite order. **3** When you reverse a car, you drive it backwards. **4** (noun) The reverse is the opposite of what has just been said or done. **5** (adjective) Reverse means opposite to what is usual or to what has just been described.

reversible (adjective) Reversible clothing can be worn with either side on the outside.

revert, reverts, reverting, reverted (verb; a formal word) To revert to a former state, system, or type of behaviour means to go back to it.

review, reviews, reviewing, reviewed 1 (noun) A review is an article or an item on television or radio, giving an opinion of a new book or play. **2** (verb) To review a play or book means to write an account expressing an opinion of it. **3** (noun) When there is a review of a situation or system, it is examined to decide whether changes are needed. **4** (verb) To review something means to examine it to decide whether changes are needed. **reviewer** (noun).

revise, revises, revising, revised **1** (verb) If you revise something, you alter, improve or correct it. **2** When you revise for an examination, you go over your work to learn things thoroughly. **revision** (noun).

revive, revives, reviving, revived **1** (verb) When a feeling or practice is revived, it becomes active or popular again. **2** When you revive someone who has fainted, they become conscious again. **revival** (noun).

revolt, revolts, revolting, revolted **1** (noun) A revolt is a violent attempt by a group of people to change their country's political system. **2** (verb) When people revolt, they fight against the authority that governs them. **3** If something revolts you, it is so horrible that you feel disgust.

revolting (adjective) horrible and disgusting, e.g. *The smell in the cell was revolting.*

revolution, revolutions **1** (noun) A revolution is a violent attempt by a large group of people to change the political system of their country. **2** A revolution is also an important change in an area of human activity, e.g. *the Industrial Revolution.* **3** A revolution is one complete turn in a circle.

revolutionary, revolutionaries **1** (adjective) involving great changes, e.g. *a revolutionary new cooling system.* **2** (noun) A revolutionary is a person who takes part in a revolution.

revolve, revolves, revolving, revolved **1** (verb) If something revolves round something else, it centres on that as the most important thing, e.g. *My job revolves around the telephone.* **2** When something revolves, it turns in a circle around a central point, e.g. *The moon revolves round the earth.*

revolver, revolvers (noun) A revolver is a small gun held in the hand.

revulsion (noun) Revulsion is a strong feeling of disgust or disapproval.

reward, rewards, rewarding, rewarded **1** (noun) A reward is something you are given because you have done something good. **2** (verb) If you reward someone, you give them a reward.

rewarding (adjective) Something that is rewarding gives you a lot of satisfaction.

rewind, rewinds, rewinding, rewound (verb) If you rewind a tape on a tape recorder or video, you make the tape go backwards.

rhapsody, rhapsodies (pronounced **rap**-sod-ee) (noun) A rhapsody is a short piece of music which is very passionate and flowing.

rhetoric (noun) Rhetoric is fine-sounding speech or writing that is intended to impress people.

rhetorical 1 (adjective) A rhetorical question is one which is asked in order to make a statement rather than to get an answer. **2** Rhetorical language is intended to be grand and impressive.

rheumatism (pronounced **room**-at-izm) (noun) Rheumatism is an illness that makes your joints and muscles stiff and painful. **rheumatic** (adjective).

rhino, rhinos (noun; an informal word) A rhino is a rhinoceros.

rhinoceros, rhinoceroses (noun) A rhinoceros is a large African or Asian animal with one or two horns on its nose.

rhododendron, rhododendrons (noun) A rhododendron is an evergreen bush with large coloured flowers.

rhombus, rhombuses or **rhombi** (noun) A rhombus is a shape with four equal sides and no right angles.

rhubarb (noun) Rhubarb is a plant with long red stems which can be cooked with sugar and eaten.

rhyme, rhymes, rhyming, rhymed 1 (verb) If two words rhyme, they have a similar sound, e.g. *Sally rhymes with valley.* **2** (noun) A rhyme is a word that rhymes with another. **3** A rhyme is a short poem with rhyming lines.

rhythm, rhythms 1 (noun) Rhythm is a regular movement or beat. **2** A rhythm is a regular pattern of changes, for example, in the seasons. **rhythmic** (adjective), **rhythmically** (adverb).

rib, ribs (noun) Your ribs are the curved bones that go from your backbone to your chest. **ribbed** (adjective).

ribbon, ribbons (noun) A ribbon is a long, narrow piece of cloth used for decoration.

rice (noun) Rice is a tall grass that produces edible grains.

rich, richer, richest; riches 1 (adjective) Someone who is rich has a lot of money and possessions. **2** Something that is rich in something contains a large amount of it, e.g. *Liver is particularly rich in vitamin A.* **3** Rich food contains a large amount of fat, oil, or sugar. **4** Rich colours, smells, and sounds are strong and pleasant. **5** (plural noun) Riches are valuable possessions or desirable qualities and substances, e.g. *the oil riches of the Middle East.* **richness** (noun).

richly 1 (adverb) If someone is richly rewarded, they are rewarded well with something valuable. **2** If you feel strongly that someone deserves something, you can say it is richly deserved.

rick, ricks (noun) A rick is a large pile of hay or straw.

rickets (noun) Rickets is a disease that affects children if they do not get enough Vitamin D. It makes their bones soft.

rickety (adjective) likely to collapse or break, e.g. *a rickety wooden jetty.*

rickshaw, rickshaws (noun) A rickshaw is a hand-pulled cart used in Asia for carrying passengers.

ricochet, ricochets, ricocheting

or **ricochetting, ricocheted** or **ricochetted** (pronounced **rik**-osh-ay) (verb) When a bullet ricochets, it hits a surface and bounces away from it.

rid, rids, ridding, rid 1 (phrase) When you **get rid** of something you do not want, you remove or destroy it. **2** (verb; a formal use) To rid a place of something unpleasant means to succeed in removing it.

riddle, riddles 1 (noun) A riddle is a puzzle which seems to be nonsense, but which has an entertaining solution. **2** Something that is a riddle puzzles and confuses you.

riddled (adjective) full of something undesirable, e.g. *The report was riddled with errors.*

ride, rides, riding, rode, ridden 1 (verb) When you ride a horse or a bike, you sit on it and control it as it moves along. **2** When you ride in a car, you travel in it. **3** (noun) A ride is a journey on a horse or bike or in a vehicle.

rider, riders 1 (noun) A rider is a person riding on a horse or bicycle. **2** A rider is also an additional statement which changes or puts a condition on what has already been said.

ridge, ridges 1 (noun) A ridge is a long, narrow piece of high land. **2** A ridge is also a raised line on a flat surface.

ridicule, ridicules, ridiculing, ridiculed 1 (verb) To ridicule someone means to make fun of them in an unkind way. **2** (noun) Ridicule is unkind laughter and mockery.

ridiculous (adjective) very foolish. **ridiculously** (adverb).

rife (adjective; a formal word) very common, e.g. *Unemployment was rife.*

rifle, rifles, rifling, rifled 1 (noun) A rifle is a gun with a long barrel. **2** (verb) When someone rifles something, they make a quick search through it to steal things.

rift, rifts 1 (noun) A rift between friends is a serious quarrel that damages their friendship. **2** A rift is also a split in something solid, especially in the ground.

rig, rigs, rigging, rigged 1 (verb) If someone rigs an election or contest, they dishonestly arrange for a particular person to succeed. **2** (noun) A rig is a large structure used for extracting oil or gas from the ground or sea bed. **rig up** (verb) If you rig up a device or structure, you make it quickly and fix it in place, e.g. *They had even rigged up a makeshift aerial.*

right, rights, righting, righted 1 (adjective or adverb) correct and in accordance with the facts, e.g. *That clock never tells the right time... That's absolutely right.* **2** (adjective) The right choice, action, or decision is the best or most suitable one. **3** The right people or places are those that have influence or are socially admired, e.g. *He was always to be seen in the right places.* **4** The right side of something is the side intended to be seen and to face outwards. **5** (noun) Right is used to refer to principles of morally correct behaviour, e.g. *At least he knew right from wrong.* **6** If you have a right to do something, you are morally or legally entitled to do it. **7** The right is one of the two sides of something. For example, when you look at the word 'to', the 'o' is to the right of the 't'. **8** (adjective or adverb) Right means on or towards the right side of something. **9** (noun) The Right refers to people who support the political ideas of capitalism and conservatism rather than socialism. **10** (adverb) Right is used to emphasize a precise place, e.g. *I'm right here.* **11** Right means immediately, e.g. *I had to decide right then.* **12** (verb) If you right something, you correct it or put it back in an upright position. **rightly** (adverb).

right angle, right angles (noun) A right angle is an angle of 90°.

righteous (adjective) Righteous people behave in a way that is morally good and religious.

rightful (adjective) Someone's rightful possession is one which they have a moral or legal right to. **rightfully** (adverb).

right-handed (adjective or adverb) Someone who is right-handed does things such as writing and painting with their right hand.

right-wing (adjective) believing more strongly in capitalism or conservatism, or less strongly in socialism, than other members of the same party or group. **right-winger** (noun).

rigid 1 (adjective) Rigid laws or systems cannot be changed and are considered severe. **2** A rigid object is stiff and does not bend easily. **rigidly** (adverb), **rigidity** (noun).

rigorous (adjective) very careful and thorough. **rigorously** (adverb).

rigour, rigours (noun; a formal word) The rigours of a situation are the things which make it hard or unpleasant, e.g. *the rigours of childbirth.*

rim, rims (noun) The rim of an object such as a wheel or a cup is the outside or top edge.

rind, rinds (noun) Rind is the thick outer skin of fruit, cheese, or bacon.

ring, rings, ringing, rang, rung 1 (verb) If you ring someone, you phone them. **2** When a bell rings, it makes a clear, loud sound. **3** (noun) A ring is the sound made by a bell. **4** A ring is also a small circle of metal worn on your finger. **5** A ring is also an object or group of things in the shape of a circle. **6** At a boxing match, showjumping contest, or circus, the ring is the place where the performance takes place. **7** A ring is also an organized group of criminals, e.g. *an international spy ring.* **8** (verb) To ring something means to draw a circle around it. **9** If something is ringed with something else, it has that thing all the way around it, e.g. *The courthouse was ringed with police.*

ringleader, ringleaders (noun) The ringleader is the leader of a group of troublemakers or criminals.

rink, rinks (noun) A rink is a large indoor area for ice-skating or roller-skating.

rinse, rinses, rinsing, rinsed 1

(verb) When you rinse something, you wash it in clean water. **2** (noun) A rinse is a liquid you can put on your hair to give it a different colour.

riot, riots, rioting, rioted 1 (noun) When there is a riot, a crowd of people behave noisily and violently. **2** (verb) To riot means to behave noisily and violently.

rip, rips, ripping, ripped 1 (verb) When you rip something, you tear it violently. **2** If you rip something away, you remove it quickly and violently. **3** (noun) A rip is a long split in cloth or paper.

RIP RIP is an abbreviation often written on gravestones, meaning 'rest in peace'.

ripe, riper, ripest 1 (adjective) When fruit or grain is ripe, it is fully developed and ready to be eaten. **2** If a situation is ripe for something to happen, it is ready for it. **ripeness** (noun).

ripen, ripens, ripening, ripened (verb) When crops ripen, they become ripe.

ripple, ripples, rippling, rippled 1 (noun) Ripples are little waves on the surface of calm water. **2** (verb) When the surface of water ripples, little waves appear on it. **3** (noun) If there is a ripple of laughter or applause, people laugh or applaud gently for a short time.

rise, rises, rising, rose, risen 1 (verb) If something rises, it moves upwards. **2** (a formal use) When you rise, you stand up. **3** To rise also means to get out of bed. **4** When the sun rises, it first appears. **5** The place where a river rises is where it begins. **6** If land rises, it slopes upwards. **7** If a sound or wind rises, it becomes higher or stronger. **8** If an amount rises, it increases. **9** (noun) A rise is an increase. **10** (verb) If you rise to a challenge or a remark, you respond to it rather than ignoring it, e.g. *He rose to the challenge with enthusiasm.* **11** When people rise up, they start fighting against people in authority. **12** (noun) Someone's rise is the process by which they become more powerful or successful, e.g. *his rise to fame.*

riser, risers (noun) An early riser is someone who likes to get up early in the morning.

risk, risks, risking, risked 1 (noun) A risk is a chance that something unpleasant or dangerous might happen. **2** (verb) If you risk something unpleasant, you do something knowing that the unpleasant thing might happen as a result, e.g. *If he doesn't play, he risks losing his place in the team.* **3** If you risk someone's life, you put them in a dangerous situation in which they might be killed. **risky** (adjective).

rite, rites (noun) A rite is a religious ceremony.

ritual, rituals 1 (noun) A ritual is a series of actions carried out according to the custom of a particular society or group, e.g. *This is the most ancient of the Buddhist rituals.* **2** (adjective) Ritual activities happen as part of a tradition or ritual, e.g. *fasting and ritual dancing.*

ritualistic (adjective).

rival, rivals, rivalling, rivalled 1 (noun) Your rival is the person you are competing with. **2** (verb) If something rivals something else, it is of the same high standard or quality, e.g. *They had beef good enough to rival Scotland's best.*

rivalry, rivalries (noun) Rivalry is active competition between people.

river, rivers (noun) A river is a natural feature consisting of water flowing for a long distance between two banks.

rivet, rivets (noun) A rivet is a short, round pin with a flat head which is used to fasten sheets of metal together. The other end of the rivet is hammered flat when it is in place.

riveting (adjective) If you find something riveting, you find it fascinating and it holds your attention, e.g. *I find snooker riveting.*

road, roads (noun) A road is a long piece of hard ground specially surfaced so that people and vehicles can travel along it easily.

roadworks (plural noun) Roadworks are repairs being done on a road.

roam, roams, roaming, roamed (verb) If you roam around, you wander around without any particular purpose, e.g. *Hens were roaming around the yard.*

roar, roars, roaring, roared 1 (verb) If something roars, it makes a very loud noise. **2** (noun) A roar is a very loud noise. **3** (verb) To roar with laughter or anger means to laugh or shout very noisily. **4** When a lion roars, it makes a loud, angry sound.

roast, roasts, roasting, roasted 1 (verb) When you roast meat or other food, you cook it using dry heat in an oven or over a fire. **2** (adjective) Roast meat has been roasted. **3** (noun) A roast is a piece of meat that has been roasted.

rob, robs, robbing, robbed 1 (verb) If someone robs you, they steal your possessions. **2** If you rob someone of something they need or deserve, you deprive them of it, e.g. *He robbed me of my childhood.*

robber, robbers (noun) Robbers are people who steal money or property using force or threats, e.g. *bank robbers.* **robbery** (noun).

robe, robes (noun) A robe is a long, loose piece of clothing which covers the body, e.g. *He knelt in his white robes before the altar.*

robin, robins (noun) A robin is a small bird with a red breast.

robot, robots (noun) A robot is a machine which is programmed to move and perform tasks automatically.

robust (adjective) very strong and healthy. **robustly** (adverb).

rock, rocks, rocking, rocked 1 (noun) Rock is the hard mineral substance that forms the surface of the earth. **2** A rock is a large piece of rock, e.g. *She picked up a rock and threw it into the lake.* **3** (verb) When something rocks or when you rock it, it moves regularly backwards and forwards or from side to side, e.g. *She rocked the baby.* **4** If something rocks people, it shocks and upsets them, e.g. *Palermo was rocked by a crime wave.* **5** (noun) Rock or rock music is music with simple tunes and a very strong beat. **6** Rock is also a sweet shaped into long, hard sticks, sold in holiday resorts.

rock and roll (noun) Rock and roll is a style of music with a strong beat that was especially popular in the 1950s.

rocket, rockets, rocketing, rocketed 1 (noun) A rocket is a space vehicle, usually shaped like a long pointed tube. **2** A rocket is also an explosive missile, e.g. *They fired rockets into a number of government buildings.* **3** A rocket is also a firework that explodes when it is high in the air. **4** (verb) If prices rocket, they increase very quickly.

rocking chair, rocking chairs (noun) A rocking chair is a chair on two curved pieces of wood that rocks backwards and forwards when you sit in it.

rocky (adjective) covered with rocks.

rod, rods (noun) A rod is a long, thin pole or bar, usually made of wood or metal, e.g. *a fishing rod.*

rodent, rodents (noun) A rodent is a small mammal with sharp front teeth which it uses for gnawing. Mice and squirrels are rodents.

rodeo, rodeos (noun) A rodeo is a public entertainment in which cowboys show different skills.

roe (noun) Roe is the eggs of a fish.

rogue, rogues 1 (noun) You can refer to a man who behaves dishonestly as a rogue. **2** (adjective) A rogue animal is a vicious animal that lives apart from its herd or pack.

role, roles; also spelled **rôle 1** (noun) Someone's role is their position and function in a situation or society. **2** An actor's role is the character that he or she plays, e.g. *her first leading role.*

roll, rolls, rolling, rolled 1 (verb) When something rolls or when you roll it, it moves along a surface, turning over and over. **2** When vehicles roll along, they move, e.g. *Tanks rolled into the village.* **3** If you roll your eyes, you make them turn up or go from side to side. **4** If you roll something flexible into a cylinder or ball, you wrap it several times around itself, e.g. *He rolled up the plastic bag with the money in it.* **5** (noun) A roll of paper or cloth is a long piece of it that has been rolled into a tube, e.g. *a roll of film.* **6** A roll is also a small, rounded, individually baked piece of bread. **7** A roll is also an official list of people's names, e.g. *the electoral roll.* **8** A roll on a drum is a long, rumbling sound made on it.

roll-call, roll-calls (noun) If you take a roll-call, you call a register of names to see who is present.

roller, rollers 1 (noun) A roller is a cylinder that turns round in a machine or piece of equipment. **2** Rollers are tubes which you can wind your hair around to make it curly.

rollerblade, rollerblades (noun)

Rollerblades are roller-skates which have the wheels set in one straight line on the bottom of the boot.

roller-coaster, roller-coasters (noun) A roller-coaster is a pleasure ride at a fair, consisting of a small railway that goes up and down very steep slopes.

roller-skate, roller-skates, roller-skating, roller-skated 1 (noun) Roller-skates are shoes with four small wheels underneath. **2** (verb) If you roller-skate, you move along wearing roller-skates.

rolling pin, rolling pins (noun) A rolling pin is a wooden cylinder used for rolling pastry dough to make it flat.

ROM (noun) In computing, ROM is a storage device that holds data permanently and cannot be altered by the programmer. ROM stands for 'read only memory'.

Roman Catholic, Roman Catholics 1 (adjective) relating or belonging to the branch of the Christian church that accepts the Pope in Rome as its leader. **2** (noun) A Roman Catholic is someone who belongs to the Roman Catholic church. **Roman Catholicism** (noun).

romance, romances 1 (noun) A romance is a relationship between two people who are in love with each other. **2** Romance is the pleasure and excitement of doing something new and unusual, e.g. *the romance of the American frontier.* **3** A romance is also a novel about a love affair.

Romanian, Romanians (pronounced roe-**may**-nee-an); also spelled **Rumanian 1** (adjective) belonging or relating to Romania. **2** (noun) A Romanian is someone who comes from Romania. **3** Romanian is the main language spoken in Romania.

romantic, romantics 1 (adjective or noun) A romantic person has ideas that are not realistic, for example about love or about ways of changing society, e.g. *a romantic idealist.* **2** (adjective) connected with sexual love, e.g. *a romantic relationship.* **3** Something that is romantic is beautiful in a way that strongly affects your feelings, e.g. *It is one of the most romantic ruins in Scotland.* **romantically** (adverb), **romanticism** (noun).

roof, roofs 1 (noun) The roof of a building or car is the covering on top of it. **2** The roof of your mouth or of a cave is the highest part.

roofing (noun) Roofing is material used for covering roofs.

rooftop, rooftops (noun) The rooftop is the outside part of the roof of a building.

rook, rooks 1 (noun) A rook is a large black bird. **2** In chess, a rook is a piece which can move any number of squares in a straight but not diagonal line.

room, rooms 1 (noun) A room is a separate section in a building, divided from other rooms by walls. **2** If there is plenty of room, there is a lot of space, e.g. *There wasn't enough room for his gear.*

roost, roosts, roosting, roosted 1 (noun) A roost is a place where birds rest or build their nests. **2** (verb) When birds roost, they settle somewhere for the night.

root, roots, rooting, rooted 1 (noun) The roots of a plant are the parts that grow under the ground. **2** The root of a hair is the part beneath the skin. **3** You can refer to the place or culture that you grew up in as your roots. **4** The root of something is its original cause or basis, e.g. *We got to the root of the problem.* **5** (verb) To root through things means to search through them, pushing them aside, e.g. *She rooted through his bag.* **root out** (verb) If you root something or someone out, you find them and force them out, e.g. *a major drive to root out corruption.*

rooted (adjective) developed from or strongly influenced by something, e.g. *powerful songs rooted in traditional African music.*

rope, ropes, roping, roped 1 (noun) A rope is a thick, strong length of twisted cord. **2** (verb) If you rope one thing to another, you tie them together with rope.

rosary, rosaries (noun) A rosary is a string of beads that Catholics use for counting prayers.

rose, roses 1 (noun) A rose is a large garden flower, often having many petals and a pleasant smell. Roses grow on bushes with thorny stems. **2** (noun or adjective) reddish-pink.

rosemary (noun) Rosemary is a herb with thin, spiky, greyish-green leaves and a tangy smell, used for flavouring in cooking.

rosette, rosettes (noun) A rosette is a large badge made of coloured ribbons gathered into a circle, which is worn as a prize in a competition or to support a sports team or political party.

roster, rosters (noun) A roster is a list of people who take it in turn to do a particular job, e.g. *He put himself first on the new roster for domestic chores.*

rostrum, rostrums or **rostra** (noun) A rostrum is a raised platform on which someone stands to speak to an audience or conduct an orchestra.

rosy, rosier, rosiest 1 (adjective) reddish-pink. **2** If a situation seems rosy, it is likely to be good or successful. **3** If a person looks rosy, they have pink cheeks and look healthy.

rot, rots, rotting, rotted 1 (verb) When food or wood rots, it decays and can no longer be used. **2** (noun) Rot is the condition that affects things when they rot, e.g. *The timber frame was not protected against rot.* **3** (verb) When something rots another substance, it causes it to decay, e.g. *Sugary canned drinks rot your teeth.*

rota, rotas (noun) A rota is a list of people who take turns to do a particular job.

rotate, rotates, rotating, rotated (verb) When something rotates, it turns with a circular movement, e.g. *He rotated the camera 180°.* **rotation** (noun).

rotor, rotors 1 (noun) The rotor is the part of a machine that turns. **2** The rotors or rotor blades of a helicopter are the four long flat pieces of metal on top of it which rotate and lift it off the ground.

rotten **1** (adjective) decayed and no longer of use, e.g. *The front bay window is rotten.* **2** (an informal use) of very poor quality, e.g. *I think it's a rotten idea.* **3** (an informal use) very unfair, unkind, or unpleasant, e.g. *That's a rotten thing to say!*

rouble, roubles (pronounced **roo**-bl) (noun) The rouble is the main unit of currency in Russia.

rough, rougher, roughest; roughs **1** (adjective) uneven and not smooth. **2** not using enough care or gentleness, e.g. *Don't be so rough or you'll break it.* **3** difficult or unpleasant, e.g. *Teachers have been given a rough time.* **4** approximately correct, e.g. *At a rough guess it is five times more profitable.* **5** If the sea is rough, there are large waves because of bad weather. **6** A rough town or area has a lot of crime or violence. **7** (noun or adjective) A rough or a rough sketch is a drawing or description that shows the main features but does not show the details. **roughly** (adverb), **roughness** (noun).

roulette (pronounced roo-**let**) (noun) Roulette is a gambling game in which a ball is dropped onto a revolving wheel with numbered holes in it.

round, rounder, roundest; rounds, rounding, rounded **1** (adjective) Something round is shaped like a ball or a circle. **2** complete or whole, e.g. *round numbers.* **3** (preposition or adverb) If something is round something else, it surrounds it. **4** The distance round something is the length of its circumference or boundary, e.g. *I'm about two inches larger round the waist.* **5** You can refer to an area near a place as the area round it, e.g. *There's nothing to do round here.* **6** (preposition) If something moves round you, it keeps moving in a circle with you in the centre. **7** When someone goes to the other side of something, they have gone round it. **8** (adverb) If you turn or look round, you turn so you are facing in a different direction. **9** (adverb or preposition) If you go round a place, you go to different parts of it to look at it, e.g. *We went round the museum.* **10** (adverb) When someone comes round, they visit you, e.g. *He came round with a bottle of wine.* **11** (noun) A round is one of a series of events, e.g. *After round three, two Americans shared the lead.* **12** If you buy a round of drinks, you buy a drink for each member of the group you are with. **round up** (verb) If you round up people or animals, you gather them together.

roundabout, roundabouts **1** (noun) A roundabout is a meeting point of several roads with a circle in the centre which vehicles have to travel around. **2** A roundabout is also a circular platform which rotates and which children can ride on in a park or playground. **3** A roundabout is also the same as a merry-go-round.

rounded (adjective) curved in shape, without any points or sharp edges.

round-the-clock (adjective) happening continuously.

rouse, rouses, rousing, roused 1 (verb) If someone rouses you, they wake you up. **2** If you rouse yourself to do something, you make yourself get up and do it. **3** If something rouses you, it makes you feel very emotional and excited.

rout, routs, routing, routed (rhymes with **out**) (verb) To rout your opponents means to defeat them completely and easily.

route, routes (pronounced **root**) (noun) A route is a way from one place to another.

routine, routines 1 (adjective) Routine activities are done regularly. **2** (noun) A routine is the usual way or order in which you do things. **3** A routine is also a boring repetition of tasks. **routinely** (adverb).

roving 1 (adjective) wandering or roaming, e.g. *roving gangs of youths.* **2** not restricted to any particular location or area, e.g. *a roving reporter.*

row, rows, rowing, rowed (rhymes with **snow**) **1** (noun) A row of people or things is several of them arranged in a line. **2** (verb) When you row a boat, you use oars to make it move through the water.

row, rows, rowing, rowed (rhymes with **now**) **1** (noun) A row is a serious argument. **2** (verb) If people are rowing, they are quarrelling noisily. **3** (noun) If someone is making a row, they are making too much noise.

rowdy, rowdier, rowdiest (adjective) rough and noisy.

royal, royals 1 (adjective) belonging to or involving a queen, a king, or a member of their family. **2** Royal is used in the names of organizations appointed or supported by a member of a royal family. **3** (noun; an informal use) Members of the royal family are sometimes referred to as the royals.

royalist, royalists (noun) A royalist is someone who supports their country's royal family.

royalty, royalties 1 (noun) The members of a royal family are sometimes referred to as royalty. **2** Royalties are payments made to authors and musicians from the sales of their books or records.

rub, rubs, rubbing, rubbed (verb) If you rub something, you move your hand or a cloth backwards and forwards over it. **rub out** (verb) To rub out something written means to remove it by rubbing it with a rubber or a cloth.

rubber, rubbers 1 (noun) Rubber is a strong, elastic substance made from the sap of a tropical tree or produced chemically. **2** A rubber is a small piece of rubber used to rub out pencil mistakes.

rubbish 1 (noun) Rubbish is unwanted things or waste material. **2** You can refer to nonsense or something of very poor quality as rubbish.

rubble (noun) Bits of old brick and stone are referred to as rubble.

ruby, rubies (noun) A ruby is a type of red jewel.

rucksack, rucksacks (noun) A rucksack is a bag with shoulder straps for carrying things on your back.

rudder, rudders (noun) A rudder is a vertical piece of wood or metal at the back of a boat or plane which is moved to make the boat or plane turn.

rude, ruder, rudest 1 (adjective) not polite. **2** embarrassing or offensive because of reference to sex or other bodily functions, e.g. *rude jokes.* **3** unexpected and unpleasant, e.g. *a rude awakening.* **rudely** (adverb), **rudeness** (noun).

rudimentary (adjective; a formal word) very basic and undeveloped, e.g. *He had only a rudimentary knowledge of French.*

rudiments (plural noun) When you learn the rudiments of something, you learn only the simplest and most basic things about it.

ruff, ruffs 1 (noun) A ruff is a stiff circular collar with many pleats in it, worn especially in the 16th century. **2** A ruff is also a thick band of fur or feathers around the neck of a bird or animal.

ruffle, ruffles, ruffling, ruffled 1 (verb) If you ruffle someone's hair, you move your hand quickly backwards and forwards over their head. **2** If something ruffles you, it makes you annoyed or upset. **3** (noun) Ruffles are small folds made in a piece of material for decoration.

rug, rugs 1 (noun) A rug is a small, thick carpet. **2** A rug is also a blanket which you can use to cover your knees or for sitting on outdoors.

rugby (noun) Rugby is a game played by two teams, who try to kick and throw an oval ball to their opponents' end of the pitch. Rugby League is played by professionals with 13 players in each side. Rugby Union is for amateurs with 15 players in each side.

rugged 1 (adjective) rocky, wild, and unsheltered, e.g. *the rugged west coast of Ireland.* **2** having strong features, e.g. *his rugged good looks.*

rugger (noun) Rugger is the same as rugby.

ruin, ruins, ruining, ruined 1 (verb) If you ruin something, you destroy or spoil it completely. **2** (noun) Ruin is the state of being destroyed or completely spoilt. **3** A ruin or the ruins of something refers to the parts that are left after it has been severely damaged, e.g. *the ruins of a thirteenth-century monastery.* **4** (verb) If someone is ruined, they have lost all their money.

rule, rules, ruling, ruled 1 (noun) Rules are statements which tell you what you are allowed to do. **2** (verb) To rule a country or group of people means to have power over it and be in charge of its affairs. **3** (a formal use) When someone in authority rules on a particular matter, they give an official decision about it. **4** (phrase) **As a rule,** means usually or generally, e.g. *As a rule, I eat my meals in front of the TV.* **rule out 1** (verb) If you rule out an idea or course of action, you reject it. **2** If one thing rules out another, it prevents it from happening or being possible, e.g. *The accident ruled out a future for him in football.*

ruler, rulers 1 (noun) A ruler is a person who rules a country. **2** A ruler is also a long, flat piece of wood or plastic with straight edges marked in centimetres or inches, used for measuring or drawing straight lines.

rum (noun) Rum is a strong alcoholic drink made from sugar cane juice.

Rumanian (pronounced roo-**may**-nee-an) another spelling of **Romanian.**

rumble, rumbles, rumbling, rumbled 1 (verb) If something rumbles, it makes a continuous low noise, e.g. *Another train rumbled past the house.* **2** (noun) A rumble is a continuous low noise, e.g. *the distant rumble of traffic.*

rummage, rummages, rummaging, rummaged (verb) If you rummage somewhere, you search for something, moving things about carelessly.

rumour, rumours, rumoured 1 (noun) A rumour is a story that people are talking about, which may or may not be true. **2** (verb) If something is rumoured, people are suggesting that it is has happened.

rump, rumps 1 (noun) An animal's rump is its rear end. **2** Rump or rump steak is meat cut from the rear end of a cow.

run, runs, running, ran 1 (verb) When you run, you move quickly, leaving the ground during each stride. **2** If you run away from a place, you leave it suddenly and secretly. **3** (noun) If you go for a run, you run for pleasure or exercise. **4** (verb) If you say that a road or river runs in a particular direction, you are describing its course. **5** If you run your hand or an object over something, you move it over it. **6** If someone runs in an election, they stand as a candidate, e.g. *He announced he would run for President.* **7** If you run a business or an activity, you are in charge of it. **8** If you run an experiment, a computer program, or tape, you start it and let it continue, e.g. *He ran a series of computer checks.* **9** If you run someone somewhere in a car, you drive them there, e.g. *Could you run me up to Manchester?* **10** (noun) A run is a journey somewhere, e.g. *It was quite a run to the village.* **11** (verb) If you run water, you turn on a tap to make it flow, e.g. *We heard him running the kitchen tap.* **12** If your nose is running, it is producing a lot of mucus. **13** If a newspaper runs a particular story, it publishes it. **14** If an amount is running at a particular level, it is at that level, e.g. *Inflation is currently running at 5.6%.* **15** If someone or something is running late, they have taken more time than was planned. **16** If a play, event, or contract runs for a particular time, it lasts for that time. **17** (noun) If a play or show has a run of a particular length of time, it is on for that time. **18** A run of success or failure is a series of successes or failures. **19** In cricket or baseball, a player scores one run by running between marked places on the pitch after hitting the ball. **run out** (verb) If you run out of something, you have no more left. **run over** (verb) If someone is run over, they are hit by a moving vehicle.

runaway, runaways (noun) A runaway is a person who has escaped from a place or left it secretly and hurriedly.

rundown 1 (adjective) tired and not well. **2** neglected and in poor condition. **3** (noun; an informal use) If you give someone the rundown on a situation, you tell them the basic, important facts about it.

rung, rungs (noun) The rungs on a ladder are the wooden or metal bars that form the steps.

runner, runners 1 (noun) A runner is a person who runs, especially as a sport. **2** A runner is also a person who takes messages or runs errands. **3** A runner on a plant such as a strawberry is a long shoot from which a new plant develops. **4** The runners on drawers, sledges, and ice skates are the thin strips on which they move.

runner bean, runner beans (noun) Runner beans are long green pods eaten as a vegetable, which grow on a climbing plant with red flowers.

runner-up, runners-up (noun) A runner-up is a person or team that comes second in a race or competition.

running 1 (adjective) continuing without stopping over a period of time, e.g. *a running commentary.* **2** Running water is flowing rather than standing still.

runny, runnier, runniest 1 (adjective) more liquid than usual, e.g. *Warm the honey until it becomes runny.* **2** If someone's nose or eyes are runny, liquid is coming out of them.

runt, runts (noun) The runt of a litter of animals is the smallest and weakest.

runway, runways (noun) A runway is a long strip of ground used by aeroplanes for taking off or landing.

rupee, rupees (pronounced roo-**pee**) (noun) The rupee is the main unit of currency in India, Pakistan, and some other countries.

rupture, ruptures, rupturing, ruptured 1 (noun) A rupture is a severe injury in which part of your body tears or bursts open. **2** (verb) To rupture part of the body means to cause it to tear or burst, e.g. *a ruptured spleen.*

rural (adjective) relating to or involving the countryside.

ruse, ruses (noun; a formal word) A ruse is an action which is intended to deceive someone.

rush, rushes, rushing, rushed 1 (verb) To rush means to move fast or do something quickly. **2** If you rush someone into doing something, you make them do it without allowing them enough time to think. **3** (noun) If you are in a rush, you are busy and do not have enough time to do things. **4** If there is a rush for something, there is a sudden increase in demand for it, e.g. *There was a rush for tickets.* **5** Rushes are plants with long, thin stems that grow near water.

rush hour, rush hours (noun) The rush hour is one of the busy parts of the day when most people are travelling to or from work.

rusk, rusks (noun) A rusk is a hard, dry biscuit given to babies.

Russian, Russians 1 (adjective) belonging or relating to Russia. **2** (noun) A Russian is someone who comes from Russia. **3** Russian is the main language spoken in Russia.

rust, rusts, rusting, rusted 1 (noun) Rust is a reddish-brown substance that forms on iron or steel which has been in contact with water and which is decaying gradually. **2** (verb) When a metal object rusts, it becomes covered in rust. **3** (noun or adjective) reddish-brown.

rustic (adjective) simple in a way considered to be typical of the countryside, e.g. *a rustic old log cabin.*

rustle, rustles, rustling, rustled (verb) When something rustles, it makes soft sounds as it moves. **rustling** (adjective or noun).

rusty, rustier, rustiest 1 (adjective) affected by rust, e.g. *a rusty iron gate.* **2** If someone's knowledge is rusty, it is not as good as it used to be because they have not used it for a long time, e.g. *My German is a bit rusty these days.*

rut, ruts 1 (noun) A rut is a deep, narrow groove in the ground made by the wheels of a vehicle. **2** (phrase) If someone is **in a rut,** they have become fixed in their way of doing things.

ruthless (adjective) very harsh or cruel, e.g. *a ruthless drug dealer.* **ruthlessness** (noun), **ruthlessly** (adverb).

rye (noun) Rye is a type of grass that produces light brown grain.

S s

Sabbath (noun) The Sabbath is the day of the week when members of some religious groups, especially Jews and Christians, do not work.

sable, sables (noun) Sable is a very expensive fur used for making coats and hats.

sabotage, sabotages, sabotaging, sabotaged (pronounced **sab**-ot-ahj) **1** (noun) Sabotage is the deliberate damaging of things such as machinery and railway lines. **2** (verb) If something is sabotaged, it is deliberately damaged. **saboteur** (noun).

sabre, sabres 1 (noun) A sabre is a heavy curved sword. **2** A sabre is also a light sword used in fencing.

saccharine or **saccharin** (pronounced **sak**-er-rine) (noun) Saccharine is a chemical used instead of sugar to sweeten things.

sachet, sachets (pronounced **sash**-ay) (noun) A sachet is a small closed packet, containing a small amount of something such as sugar.

sack, sacks, sacking, sacked 1 (noun) A sack is a large bag made of rough material used for carrying or storing goods. **2** (verb; an informal use) If someone is sacked, they are dismissed from their job by their employer. **3** (an informal phrase) If someone **gets the sack,** they are sacked by their employer.

sacrament, sacraments (noun) A sacrament is an important Christian ceremony such as communion or baptism.

sacred (pronounced **say**-krid) (adjective) holy, or connected with religion or religious ceremonies, e.g. *sacred ground.*

sacrifice, sacrifices, sacrificing, sacrificed (pronounced **sak**-riff-ice) **1** (verb) If you sacrifice something valuable or important, you give it up. **2** To sacrifice an animal means to kill it as an offering to a god or gods. **3** (noun) A sacrifice is the killing of an animal as an offering to a god or gods. **sacrificial** (adjective).

sacrilege (pronounced **sak**-ril-ij) (noun) Sacrilege is behaviour that shows great disrespect for something holy. **sacrilegious** (adjective).

sacrosanct (pronounced **sak**-roe-sangkt) (adjective) regarded as too important to be criticized or changed, e.g. *Freedom of the press is sacrosanct.*

sad, sadder, saddest 1 (adjective) If you are sad, you feel unhappy. **2** Something sad makes you feel unhappy, e.g. *a sad story.* **sadly** (adverb), **sadness** (noun).

sadden, saddens, saddening, saddened (verb) If something saddens you, it makes you feel sad.

saddle, saddles, saddling, saddled 1 (noun) A saddle is a leather seat that you sit on when you are riding a horse. **2** The saddle on a bicycle is the seat. **3** (verb) If you saddle a horse, you put a saddle on it.

sadism (pronounced **say**-diz-m) (noun) Sadism is the obtaining of pleasure, especially sexual pleasure, from making people suffer pain or humiliation. **sadist** (noun), **sadistic** (adjective).

safari, safaris (noun) A safari is an expedition for hunting or observing wild animals, especially in East Africa.

safari park, safari parks (noun) A safari park is a large park where wild animals such as lions roam freely.

safe, safer, safest; safes 1 (adjective) Something that is safe does not cause harm or danger. **2** If you are safe, you are not in any danger. **3** If it is safe to say something, you can say it with very little risk of being wrong. **4** (noun) A safe is a strong metal box with special locks, in which you can keep valuable things. **safely** (adverb), **safety** (noun).

safeguard, safeguards, safeguarding, safeguarded 1 (verb) To safeguard something means to protect it. **2** (noun) A safeguard is a rule or law designed to protect something or someone.

safekeeping (noun) If something is given to you for safekeeping, it is given to you to look after.

sag, sags, sagging, sagged (verb) When something sags, it hangs down loosely or sinks downwards in the middle. **sagging** (adjective).

saga, sagas (pronounced **sah**-ga) (noun) A saga is a very long story, usually with many different adventures, e.g. *a saga of rivalry and honour.*

sage, sages 1 (noun; a literary use) A sage is a very wise person. **2** Sage is also a herb used in cooking.

Sagittarius (pronounced saj-it-**tair**-ee-uss) (noun) Sagittarius is the ninth sign of the zodiac, represented by a creature half-horse, half-man holding a bow and arrow. People born between November 22nd and December 21st are born under this sign.

sail, sails, sailing, sailed 1 (noun) Sails are large pieces of material attached to a ship's mast. The wind blows against the sail and moves the ship. **2** (verb) When a ship sails, it moves across water. **3** If you sail somewhere, you go there by ship.

sailor, sailors (noun) A sailor is a member of a ship's crew.

saint, saints (noun) Saints are people honoured after their death by the Church because of their holiness.

saintly (adjective) behaving in a very good or holy way.

sake, sakes 1 (phrase) If you do something **for someone's sake,** you do it to help or please them. **2** You use **for the sake of** to say why you are doing something, e.g. *a one-off expedition for interest's sake.*

salad, salads (noun) A salad is a mixture of raw vegetables.

salami (pronounced sal-**lah**-mee) (noun) Salami is a kind of spicy sausage.

salary, salaries (noun) A salary is a regular monthly payment to an employee.

sale, sales 1 (noun) The sale of goods is the selling of them. **2** (plural noun) The sales of a product are the numbers that are sold. **3** (noun) A sale is an occasion when a shop sells things at reduced prices.

salesman, salesmen (noun) A salesman is someone who sells products for a company.

salient (pronounced **say**-lee-ent) (adjective; a formal word) The salient points or facts are the important ones.

saliva (pronounced sal-**live**-a) (noun) Saliva is the watery liquid in your mouth that helps you chew food.

sallow (adjective) Sallow skin is pale and unhealthy.

salmon, salmons or **salmon** (pronounced **sam**-on) (noun) A salmon is a large edible silver-coloured fish with pink flesh.

salmonella (pronounced sal-mon-**nell**-a) (noun) Salmonella is a kind of bacteria which can cause food poisoning.

salon, salons (noun) A salon is a place where hairdressers work.

saloon, saloons 1 (noun) A saloon is a car with a fixed roof and a separate boot. **2** In

America, a place where alcoholic drinks are sold and drunk.

salt (noun) Salt is a white substance found naturally in sea water. It is used to flavour and preserve food.

salty, saltier, saltiest (adjective) containing salt or tasting of salt.

salute, salutes, saluting, saluted **1** (noun) A salute is a formal sign of respect. Soldiers give a salute by raising their right hand to their forehead. **2** (verb) If you salute someone, you give them a salute.

salvage, salvages, salvaging, salvaged **1** (verb) If you salvage things, you save them, for example from a wrecked ship or a destroyed building. **2** (noun) You refer to things saved from a wrecked ship or destroyed building as salvage.

salvation **1** (noun) When someone's salvation takes place, they are saved from harm or evil. **2** To be someone's salvation means to save them from harm or evil.

salvo, salvos or **salvoes** (noun) A salvo is the firing of several guns or missiles at the same time.

same **1** (adjective or pronoun) If two things are the same, they look like one another. **2** Same means just one thing and not two different ones, e.g. *They were born in the same town.*

sample, samples, sampling, sampled **1** (noun) A sample of something is a small amount of it that you can try or test, e.g. *a sample of new wine.* **2** (verb) If you sample something, you try it, e.g. *I sampled his cooking.*

samurai (pronounced **sam**-oor-eye) (noun) A samurai was a member of an ancient Japanese warrior class.

sanctimonious (pronounced sank-tim-**moan**-ee-uss) (adjective) pretending to be very religious and virtuous.

sanction, sanctions, sanctioning, sanctioned **1** (verb) To sanction something means to officially approve of it or allow it. **2** (noun) Sanction is official approval of something. **3** A sanction is a severe punishment or penalty intended to make people obey the law. Sanctions are sometimes taken by countries against a country that has broken international law.

sanctity (noun) If you talk about the sanctity of something, you are saying that it should be respected because it is very important, e.g. *the sanctity of marriage.*

sanctuary, sanctuaries **1** (noun) A sanctuary is a place where you are safe from harm or danger. **2** A sanctuary is also a place where wildlife is protected, e.g. *a bird sanctuary.*

sand, sands, sanding, sanded **1** (noun) Sand consists of tiny pieces of stone. Beaches are made of sand. **2** (verb) If you sand something, you rub sandpaper over it to make it smooth.

sandal, sandals (noun) Sandals are light shoes with straps.

sandpaper (noun) Sandpaper is strong paper with a coating of sand on it. It is used for rubbing surfaces to make them smooth.

sandstone (noun) Sandstone is a type of rock formed from sand. It is often used for building.

sandwich, sandwiches, sandwiching, sandwiched 1 (noun) A sandwich is two slices of bread with a filling between them. **2** (verb) If one thing is sandwiched between two others, it is in a narrow space between them, e.g. *a dusty pit sandwiched between two modern houses.*

sandy, sandier, sandiest 1 (adjective) A sandy area is covered with sand. **2** Sandy hair is light orange-brown.

sane, saner, sanest (adjective) If someone is sane, they have a normal and healthy mind.

sanguine (pronounced **sang**-gwin) (adjective; a formal word) cheerful and confident.

sanitary (adjective) Sanitary means concerned with keeping things clean and hygienic, e.g. *improving the sanitary conditions.*

sanitary towel, sanitary towels (noun) Sanitary towels are pads of thick, soft material which women wear during their periods.

sanitation (noun) Sanitation is the process of keeping places clean and hygienic, especially by providing a sewage system and clean water supply.

sanity (noun) Your sanity is your ability to think and act normally and reasonably.

sap, saps, sapping, sapped 1 (verb) If something saps your strength or confidence, it gradually weakens and destroys it. **2** (noun) Sap is the watery liquid in plants.

sapling, saplings (noun) A sapling is a young tree.

sapphire, sapphires (noun) A sapphire is a blue precious stone.

sarcastic (adjective) saying or doing the opposite of what you really mean in order to mock or insult someone, e.g. *a sarcastic remark.* **sarcasm** (noun), **sarcastically** (adverb).

sarcophagus, sarcophagi or **sarcophaguses** (pronounced sar-**kof**-fag-uss) (noun) A sarcophagus is a stone coffin used in ancient times.

sardine, sardines (noun) A sardine is a small edible fish.

sardonic (adjective) mocking or scornful, e.g. *a sardonic grin.* **sardonically** (adverb).

sari, saris (pronounced **sah**-ree) (noun) A sari is a piece of clothing worn especially by Indian women. It consists of a long piece of material folded around the body.

sartorial (adjective; a formal word) relating to clothes, e.g. *sartorial elegance.*

sash, sashes (noun) A sash is a long piece of cloth worn round the waist or over one shoulder.

Satan (noun) Satan is the Devil.

satanic (pronounced sa-**tan**-ik) (adjective) caused by or influenced by Satan, e.g. *satanic forces.*

satchel, satchels (noun) A satchel is a leather or cloth bag with a long strap.

satellite, satellites 1 (noun) A satellite is an object sent into orbit round the earth to collect information or as part of a communications system. **2** A satellite is also a natural object in space that moves round a planet or star.

satin, satins (noun) Satin is a kind of smooth, shiny silk.

satire, satires (noun) Satire is the use of mocking or ironical humour, especially in literature, to show how foolish or wicked some people are. **satirical** (adjective).

satisfaction (noun) Satisfaction is the feeling of pleasure you get when you do something you wanted or needed to do.

satisfactory (adjective) acceptable or adequate, e.g. *a satisfactory explanation.* **satisfactorily** (adverb).

satisfy, satisfies, satisfying, satisfied 1 (verb) To satisfy someone means to give them enough of. something to make them pleased or contented. **2** To satisfy someone that something is the case means to convince them of it. **3** To satisfy the requirements for something means to fulfil them. **satisfied** (adjective).

satisfying (adjective) Something that is satisfying gives you a feeling of pleasure and fulfilment.

satsuma, satsumas (pronounced sat-**soo**-ma) (noun) A satsuma is a fruit like a small orange.

saturated 1 (adjective) very wet. **2** If a place is saturated with things, it is completely full of them. **saturation** (noun).

Saturday, Saturdays (noun) Saturday is the day between Friday and Sunday.

Saturn (noun) Saturn is the planet in the solar system which is sixth from the sun.

sauce, sauces (noun) A sauce is a liquid eaten with food to give it more flavour.

saucepan, saucepans (noun) A saucepan is a deep metal cooking pot with a handle and a lid.

saucer, saucers (noun) A saucer is a small curved plate for a cup.

saucy, saucier, sauciest (adjective) cheeky in an amusing way.

Saudi, Saudis (rhymes with **cloudy**) **1** (adjective) belonging or relating to Saudi Arabia. **2** (noun) A Saudi is someone who comes from Saudi Arabia.

sauna, saunas (pronounced **saw**-na) (noun) If you have a sauna, you go into a very hot room in order to sweat, then have a cold bath or shower.

saunter, saunters, sauntering, sauntered (verb) To saunter somewhere means to walk there slowly and casually.

sausage, sausages (noun) A sausage is a mixture of minced meat and herbs formed into a tubular shape and served cooked.

sauté, sautés, sautéing or **sautéeing, sautéed** (pronounced **soh**-tay) (verb) To sauté food means to fry it quickly in a small amount of oil or butter.

savage, savages, savaging, savaged 1 (adjective) cruel and violent, e.g. *savage fighting.* **2** (noun) If you call someone a savage, you mean that they are cruel, violent, and uncivilized. **3** (verb) If a dog or other animal savages you, it attacks you and bites you. **sav-**

agely (adverb).

savagery (noun) Savagery is cruel and violent behaviour.

save, saves, saving, saved 1 (verb) If you save someone, you rescue them or help to keep them safe, e.g. *He saved my life.* **2** If you save something, you keep it so that you can use it later, e.g. *He'd saved up enough money for the deposit.* **3** To save time, money, or effort means to prevent it from being wasted, e.g. *You could have saved us the trouble.* **4** (preposition; a formal use) Save means except, e.g. *I was alone in the house save for an old woman.*

saving, savings 1 (noun) A saving is a reduction in the amount of time or money used. **2** (plural noun) Your savings are the money you have saved.

saviour, saviours 1 (noun) If someone saves you from danger, you can refer to them as your saviour. **2** In Christianity, the Saviour is Jesus Christ.

savour, savours, savouring, savoured (verb) If you savour something, you take your time with it and enjoy it fully, e.g. *We savoured the wine.*

savoury 1 (adjective) Savoury is salty or spicy. **2** Something that is not very savoury is not very pleasant or respectable, e.g. *the less savoury aspects of life.*

saw, saws, sawing, sawed, sawn 1 Saw is the past tense of **see. 2** (noun) A saw is a tool for cutting wood. It has a blade with sharp teeth along one edge. **3** (verb) If you saw something, you cut it with a saw.

sawdust (noun) Sawdust is the fine powder produced when you saw wood.

saxophone, saxophones (noun) A saxophone is a curved metal wind instrument often played in jazz bands.

say, says, saying, said 1 (verb) When you say something, you speak words. **2** Say is used to give an example, e.g. *a maximum fee of, say, a million.* **3** (noun) If you have a say in something, you can give your opinion and influence decisions.

saying, sayings (noun) A saying is a well-known sentence or phrase that tells you something about human life.

scab, scabs (noun) A scab is a hard, dry covering that forms over a wound. **scabby** (adjective).

scaffolding (noun) Scaffolding is a temporary structure erected around buildings being built or repaired.

scald, scalds, scalding, scalded (pronounced **skawld**) **1** (verb) If you scald yourself, you burn yourself with very hot liquid or steam. **2** (noun) A scald is a burn caused by scalding.

scale, scales, scaling, scaled 1 (noun) The scale of something is its size or extent, e.g. *the sheer scale of the disaster.* **2** A scale is a set of levels or numbers used for measuring things. **3** The scale of a map is the ratio of measurements on the map to measurements in the real world, e.g. *a scale of 1:10,000.* **4** A scale is also an upward or downward sequence of musical notes. **5** (verb) If you scale something high, you climb it. **6** (noun) The scales of a fish or reptile are the small pieces of hard skin covering its body. **7** Scales are a piece of equipment used for weighing things.

scallop, scallops (noun) Scallops are edible shellfish with two flat fan-shaped shells.

scalp, scalps (noun) Your scalp is the skin under the hair on your head.

scalpel, scalpels (noun) A scalpel is a knife with a thin, sharp blade, used by surgeons.

scamper, scampers, scampering, scampered (verb) To scamper means to move quickly and lightly.

scampi (plural noun) Scampi are large prawns often eaten fried in breadcrumbs.

scan, scans, scanning, scanned 1 (verb) If you scan something, you look at all of it carefully, e.g. *I scanned the horizon to the north-east.* **2** If a machine scans something, it examines it by means of a beam of light or X-rays. **3** (noun) A scan is an examination or search by a scanner, e.g. *a brain scan.*

scandal, scandals (noun) A scandal is a situation or event that people think is shocking and immoral. **scandalous** (adjective).

Scandinavia (pronounced skan-din-**nay**-vee-a) (noun) Scandinavia is the name given to a group of countries in Northern Europe, including Norway, Sweden, Denmark, and sometimes Finland and Iceland. **Scandinavian** (noun or adjective).

scanner, scanners (noun) A scanner is a machine that examines things by means of a beam of light or X-rays. Scanners are used in hospitals, airports, and laboratories.

scant, scanter, scantest (adjective) If something receives scant attention, it does not receive enough attention.

scapegoat, scapegoats (noun) If someone is made a scapegoat, they are blamed for something, although it may not be their fault.

scar, scars, scarring, scarred 1 (noun) A scar is a mark left on your skin after a wound has healed. **2** (verb) If an injury scars you, it leaves a permanent mark on your skin. **3** If an unpleasant experience scars you, it has a permanent effect on you.

scarce, scarcer, scarcest (adjective) If something is scarce, there is not very much of it. **scarcity** (noun).

scarcely (adverb) Scarcely means hardly, e.g. *I can scarcely hear her.*

scare, scares, scaring, scared 1 (verb) If something scares you, it frightens you. **2** (noun) If something gives you a scare, it scares you. **3** If there is a scare about something, a lot of people are afraid or worried about it, e.g. *an AIDS scare.* **scared** (adjective).

scarecrow, scarecrows (noun) A scarecrow is an object shaped like a person put in a field to scare birds away.

scarf, scarfs or **scarves** (noun)

A scarf is a piece of cloth worn round your neck or head to keep you warm.

scarlet (noun or adjective) bright red.

scary, scarier, scariest (adjective; an informal word) frightening.

scathing (pronounced **skayth**-ing) (adjective) harsh and scornful, e.g. *They were scathing about his job.*

scatter, scatters, scattering, scattered 1 (verb) To scatter things means to throw or drop them all over an area. **2** If people scatter, they suddenly move away in different directions.

scattering (noun) A scattering of things is a small number of them spread over a large area, e.g. *the scattering of islands.*

scavenge, scavenges, scavenging, scavenged (verb) If you scavenge for things, you search for them among waste and rubbish. **scavenger** (noun).

scenario, scenarios (pronounced sin-**nar**-ee-oh) **1** (noun) The scenario of a film or play is a summary of its plot. **2** A scenario is also the way a situation could possibly develop in the future, e.g. *the worst possible scenario.*

scene, scenes 1 (noun) A scene is part of a play, film, or book in which a series of events happen in one place. **2** Pictures and views are sometimes called scenes, e.g. *a village scene.* **3** The scene of an event is the place where it happened. **4** A scene is also an area of activity, e.g. *the music scene.*

scenery 1 (noun) In the countryside, you can refer to everything you see as the scenery. **2** In a theatre, the scenery is the painted cloth and structures on the stage which represent the place where the action is happening.

scenic (adjective) A scenic place or route has nice views.

scent, scents, scenting, scented 1 (noun) A scent is a smell, especially a pleasant one. **2** Scent is perfume. **3** (verb) When an animal scents something, it becomes aware of it by smelling it.

sceptic, sceptics (pronounced **skep**-tik) (noun) A sceptic is someone who has doubts about things that other people believe. **sceptical** (adjective), **scepticism** (noun).

sceptre, sceptres (pronounced **sep**-ter) (noun) A sceptre is an ornamental rod carried by a king or queen as a symbol of power.

schedule, schedules, scheduling, scheduled (pronounced **shed**-yool) **1** (noun) A schedule is a plan that gives a list of events or tasks, together with the times at which each thing should be done. **2** (verb) If something is scheduled to happen, it has been planned and arranged, e.g. *Their journey was scheduled for May.*

scheme, schemes, scheming, schemed 1 (noun) A scheme is a plan or arrangement, e.g. *a development scheme.* **2** (verb) When people scheme, they make secret plans.

schism, schisms (pronounced **sizm**) (noun) A schism is a split or division within a group or organization.

schizophrenia (pronounced skit-soe-**free**-nee-a) (noun) Schizophrenia is a serious mental illness which prevents someone relating their thoughts and feelings to what is happening around them. **schizophrenic** (noun or adjective).

scholar, scholars (noun) A scholar is a person who studies an academic subject and knows a lot about it.

scholarly (adjective) having or showing a lot of knowledge.

scholarship, scholarships (noun) If you get a scholarship to a school or university, your studies are paid for by the school or university or by some other organization.

school, schools, schooling, schooled 1 (noun) A school is a place where children are educated. **2** University departments and colleges are sometimes called schools, e.g. *My oldest son is in medical school.* **3** (verb) When someone is schooled in something, they are taught it, e.g. *They were schooled in the modern techniques.* **4** (noun) You can refer to a large group of dolphins or fish as a school.

schoolchild, schoolchildren (noun) Schoolchildren are children who go to school. **schoolboy** (noun), **schoolgirl** (noun).

schooling (noun) Your schooling is the education you get at school.

schooner, schooners (noun) A schooner is a sailing ship.

science, sciences 1 (noun) Science is the study of nature and natural phenomena and the knowledge obtained about them. **2** A science is a branch of science, for example physics or biology.

science fiction (noun) Stories about events happening in the future or in other parts of the universe are called science fiction.

scientific 1 (adjective) relating to science or to a particular science, e.g. *scientific knowledge.* **2** done in a systematic way, using experiments or tests, e.g. *this scientific method.* **scientifically** (adverb).

scientist, scientists (noun) A scientist is an expert in one of the sciences who does work connected with it.

scintillating (pronounced **sin**-til-late-ing) (adjective) lively and witty, e.g. *scintillating conversation.*

scissors (plural noun) Scissors are a cutting tool with two sharp blades.

scoff, scoffs, scoffing, scoffed (verb) If you scoff, you speak in a scornful, mocking way about something.

scold, scolds, scolding, scolded (verb) If you scold someone, you tell them off.

scone, scones (pronounced **skone** or **skon**) (noun) Scones are small cakes made from flour and fat and usually eaten with butter.

scoop, scoops, scooping, scooped 1 (verb) If you scoop something up, you pick it up using a spoon or the palm of your hand. **2** (noun) A scoop is an object like a large spoon which is used for picking up food such as flour.

scooter, scooters 1 (noun) A scooter is a small, light motorcycle. **2** A child's scooter is a simple cycle which the child rides by standing on it and pushing the ground with one foot.

scope 1 (noun) If there is scope for doing something, the opportunity to do it exists. **2** The scope of something is the whole subject area which it deals with or includes.

scorch, scorches, scorching, scorched (verb) To scorch something means to burn it slightly.

scorching (adjective) extremely hot, e.g. *another scorching summer.*

score, scores, scoring, scored 1 (verb) If you score in a game, you get a goal, run, or point. **2** (noun) The score in a game is the number of goals, runs, or points obtained by the two teams. **3** (verb) To score in a game also means to record the score obtained by the players. **4** If you score a success or victory, you achieve it. **5** (noun) Scores of things means very many of them, e.g. *Ros entertained scores of celebrities.* **6** (an old-fashioned use) A score is twenty. **7** (verb) To score a surface means to cut a line into it. **8** (noun) The score of a piece of music is the written version of it. **scorer** (noun).

scorn (noun) Scorn is great contempt, e.g. *a look of scorn.*

scornful (adjective) showing contempt, e.g. *his scornful comment.* **scornfully** (adverb).

Scorpio (noun) Scorpio is the eighth sign of the zodiac, represented by a scorpion. People born between October 23rd and November 21st are born under this sign.

scorpion, scorpions (noun) A scorpion is a small tropical animal that has a long tail with a poisonous sting on the end.

Scot, Scots 1 (noun) A Scot is a person who comes from Scotland. **2** (adjective) Scots means the same as Scottish.

scotch, scotches (noun) Scotch is whisky made in Scotland. A scotch is a glass of scotch.

Scotsman, Scotsmen (noun) A Scotsman is a man who comes from Scotland. **Scotswoman** (noun).

Scottish (adjective) belonging or relating to Scotland.

scoundrel, scoundrels (noun; an old-fashioned word) A scoundrel is a man who cheats and deceives people.

scour, scours, scouring, scoured 1 (verb) If you scour a place, you look all over it in order to find something, e.g. *The police scoured the area.* **2** If you scour something such as a pan, you clean it by rubbing it with something rough.

scourge, scourges (rhymes with **urge**) (noun) A scourge is something that causes a lot of suffering, e.g. *hay fever, that scourge of summer.*

scout, scouts, scouting, scouted 1 (noun) A scout is a boy who is a member of the Scout Association, an organization for boys which aims to develop character and responsibility. **2** A scout is also someone who is sent to an area to find out the position of an enemy army. **3** (verb) If you scout around for something, you look around for it.

scowl, scowls, scowling, scowled 1 (verb) If you scowl, you frown because you are angry, e.g. *They were scowling at me.* **2** (noun) A scowl is an angry expression.

scrabble, scrabbles, scrabbling, scrabbled (verb) If you scrabble at something, you scrape at it with your hands or feet.

scramble, scrambles, scrambling, scrambled 1 (verb) If you scramble over something, you climb over it using your hands to help you. **2** (noun) A scramble is a motorcycle race over rough ground.

scrap, scraps, scrapping, scrapped 1 (noun) A scrap of something is a very small piece of it, e.g. *a scrap of cloth.* **2** (plural noun) Scraps are pieces of leftover food. **3** (verb) If you scrap something, you get rid of it, e.g. *The BBC was thinking of scrapping the series.* **4** (adjective or noun) Scrap metal or scrap is metal from old machinery or cars that can be re-used.

scrapbook, scrapbooks (noun) A scrapbook is a book in which you stick things such as pictures or newspaper articles.

scrape, scrapes, scraping, scraped 1 (verb) If you scrape something off a surface, you remove it by pulling a rough or sharp object over it, e.g. *to scrape the fallen snow off the track.* **2** If something scrapes, it makes a harsh noise by rubbing against something, e.g. *his shoes scraping across the stone ground.*

scratch, scratches, scratching, scratched 1 (verb) To scratch something means to make a small cut on it accidentally, e.g. *They were always getting scratched by cats.* **2** (noun) A scratch is a small cut. **3** (verb) If you scratch, you rub your skin with your nails because it is itching.

scratchcard, scratchcards (noun) A scratchcard is a ticket in a competition with a surface that you scratch off to show whether or not you have won a prize.

scrawl, scrawls, scrawling, scrawled 1 (verb) If you scrawl something, you write it in a careless and untidy way. **2** (noun) You can refer to careless and untidy writing as a scrawl.

scrawny, scrawnier, scrawniest (adjective) thin and bony, e.g. *a small scrawny man.*

scream, screams, screaming, screamed 1 (verb) If you scream, you shout or cry in a loud, high-pitched voice. **2** (noun) A scream is a loud, high-pitched cry.

screech, screeches, screeching, screeched 1 (verb) To screech means to make an unpleasant high-pitched noise, e.g. *The car wheels screeched.* **2** (noun) A screech is an unpleasant high-pitched noise.

screen, screens, screening, screened 1 (noun) A screen is a flat vertical surface on which a picture is shown, e.g. *a television screen.* **2** (verb) To screen a film or television programme means to show it. **3** (noun) A screen is also a vertical panel used to separate different parts of a room or to protect something. **4** (verb) If you screen someone, you put something in front of them to protect them.

screw, screws, screwing, screwed 1 (noun) A screw is a small, sharp piece of metal used for fixing things together or for fixing something to a wall. **2** (verb) If you screw things together, you fix them together using screws. **3** If you screw something onto something else, you fix it there by twisting it round and round, e.g. *He screwed the top on the ink bottle.* **screw up** (verb) If you screw something up, you twist it or squeeze it so that it no longer has its proper shape, e.g. *Amy screwed up her face.*

screwdriver, screwdrivers (noun) A screwdriver is a tool for turning screws.

scribble, scribbles, scribbling, scribbled 1 (verb) If you scribble something, you write it quickly and roughly. **2** To scribble also means to make meaningless marks, e.g. *When Caroline was five she scribbled on a wall.* **3** (noun) You can refer to something written or drawn quickly and roughly as a scribble.

scrimp, scrimps, scrimping, scrimped (verb) If you scrimp, you live cheaply and spend as little money as you can.

script, scripts (noun) The script of a play, film, or television programme is the written version of it.

scripture, scriptures (noun) Scripture refers to sacred writings, especially the Bible. **scriptural** (adjective).

scroll, scrolls (noun) A scroll is a long roll of paper or parchment with writing on it.

scrounge, scrounges, scrounging, scrounged (verb; an informal word) If you scrounge something, you get it by asking for it rather than by earning or buying it. **scrounger** (noun).

scrub, scrubs, scrubbing, scrubbed 1 (verb) If you scrub something, you clean it with a stiff brush and water. **2** (noun) If you give something a scrub, you scrub it. **3** Scrub consists of low trees and bushes.

scruff (noun) The scruff of your neck is the back of your neck or collar.

scruffy, scruffier, scruffiest (adjective) dirty and untidy, e.g. *four scruffy youths.*

scrum, scrums (noun) When rugby players form a scrum, they form a group and push against each other with their heads down in an attempt to get the ball.

scrunchie, scrunchies (noun) A scrunchie is a loop of elastic loosely covered with material which is used to hold hair in a ponytail.

scruple, scruples (pronounced **skroo**-pl) (noun) Scruples are moral principles that make you unwilling to do something that seems wrong, e.g. *The West must drop its scruples and fight back.*

scrupulous 1 (adjective) always doing what is honest or morally right. **2** paying very careful attention to detail, e.g. *a long and scrupulous search.*

scrupulously (adverb).
scrutiny (noun) If something is under scrutiny, it is being observed very carefully.
scuba diving (noun) Scuba diving is the sport of swimming underwater with tanks of compressed air on the back.
scuff, scuffs, scuffing, scuffed 1 (verb) If you scuff your feet, you drag them along the ground when you are walking. **2** If you scuff your shoes, you mark them by scraping or rubbing them.
scuffle, scuffles, scuffling, scuffled 1 (noun) A scuffle is a short, rough fight. **2** (verb) When people scuffle, they fight roughly.
scullery, sculleries (noun) A scullery is a small room next to a kitchen where washing and cleaning is done.
sculpt, sculpts, sculpting, sculpted (verb) When something is sculpted, it is carved or shaped in stone or wood.
sculptor, sculptors (noun) A sculptor is someone who makes sculptures.
sculpture, sculptures 1 (noun) A sculpture is a work of art produced by carving or shaping stone, wood, or clay. **2** Sculpture is the art of making sculptures.
scum (noun) Scum is a layer of a dirty substance on the surface of a liquid.
scurrilous (pronounced **skur**-ril-luss) (adjective) abusive and damaging to someone's good name, e.g. *scurrilous stories.*
scurry, scurries, scurrying, scurried (verb) To scurry means to run quickly with short steps.
scurvy (noun) Scurvy is a disease caused by a lack of vitamin C.
scuttle, scuttles, scuttling, scuttled 1 (verb) To scuttle means to run quickly. **2** To scuttle a ship means to sink it deliberately by making holes in the bottom.
scythe, scythes (noun) A scythe is a tool with a long handle and a curved blade used for cutting grass.
sea, seas 1 (noun) The sea is the salty water that covers much of the earth's surface. **2** A sea of people or things is a very large number of them, e.g. *a sea of red flags.*
seagull, seagulls (noun) Seagulls are common white, grey, and black birds that live near the sea.
seahorse, seahorses (noun) A seahorse is a small fish whose head resembles a horse's head.
seal, seals, sealing, sealed 1 (noun) A seal is an official mark on a document which shows that it is genuine. **2** A seal is also a piece of wax fixed over the opening of a container. The container cannot be opened without the seal being broken. **3** (verb) If you seal an envelope, you stick down the flap. **4** If you seal an opening, you cover it securely so that air, gas, or liquid cannot get through. **5** (noun) A seal is also a large mammal with flippers. Seals eat fish and live partly on land and partly in the sea.
sea lion, sea lions (noun) A sea lion is a type of large seal.
seam, seams 1 (noun) A seam

is a line of stitches joining two pieces of cloth. **2** A seam of coal is a long, narrow layer of it beneath the ground.

seaman, seamen (noun) A seaman is a sailor.

seance, seances (pronounced **say**-ahnss); also spelled **séance** (noun) A seance is a meeting in which people try to communicate with the spirits of dead people.

search, searches, searching, searched 1 (verb) If you search for something, you look for it in several places. **2** If a person is searched, for instance by the police, their body and clothing is examined to see if they are hiding anything. **3** (noun) A search is an attempt to find something.

searching (adjective) intended to discover the truth about something, e.g. *searching questions.*

searchlight, searchlights (noun) A searchlight is a powerful light whose beam can be turned in different directions.

searing (adjective) A searing pain is very sharp.

seashore (noun) The seashore is the land along the edge of the sea.

seasick (adjective) feeling sick because of the movement of a boat. **seasickness** (noun).

seaside (noun) The seaside is an area next to the sea.

season, seasons, seasoning, seasoned 1 (noun) A season is a period of the year that has particular climatic characteristics. The seasons are spring, summer, autumn, and winter. **2** A season is also a period of the year when something usually happens, e.g. *the football season... the hunting season.* **3** (verb) If you season food, you add salt, pepper, or spices to it.

seasonal (adjective) happening during one season or one time of the year, e.g. *seasonal work.*

seasoned (adjective) very experienced, e.g. *a seasoned professional.*

seasoning (noun) Seasoning is flavouring such as salt and pepper.

season ticket, season tickets (noun) A season ticket is a train or bus ticket that you can use as many times as you like within a certain period.

seat, seats, seating, seated 1 (noun) A seat is something you can sit on. **2** The seat of a piece of clothing is the part that covers your bottom. **3** (verb) If you seat yourself somewhere, you sit down. **4** If a place seats a particular number of people, it has enough seats for that number, e.g. *The theatre seats 570 people.* **5** (noun) If someone wins a seat in parliament, they are elected.

seat belt, seat belts (noun) A seat belt is a strap that you fasten across your body for safety when travelling in a car or an aircraft.

seating (noun) The seating in a place is the number or arrangement of seats there.

seaweed (noun) Plants that grow in the sea are called seaweed.

secateurs (pronounced sek-at-**turz**) (plural noun) Secateurs are small shears for pruning garden plants.

secluded (adjective) quiet and hidden from view, e.g. *a secluded bay.* **seclusion** (noun).

second, seconds, seconding, seconded 1 (adjective) The second item in a series is the one counted as number two. **2** (noun) A second is one of the sixty parts that a minute is divided into. **3** (plural noun) Seconds are goods that are sold cheaply because they are slightly faulty. **4** (verb) If you second a proposal, you formally agree with it so that it can be discussed or voted on. **secondly** (adverb).

secondary 1 (adjective) Something that is secondary is less important than something else. **2** Secondary education is education for pupils between the ages of eleven and eighteen.

secondary school, secondary schools (noun) A secondary school is a school for pupils between the ages of eleven and eighteen.

second-class 1 (adjective) Second-class things are regarded as less important than other things of the same kind, e.g. *He has been treated as a second-class citizen.* **2** (adjective or adverb) Second-class services are cheaper and therefore slower or less comfortable than first-class ones.

second cousin, second cousins (noun) Your second cousins are the children of your parents' cousins.

second-hand (adjective or adverb) Something that is second-hand has already been owned by someone else, e.g. *a second-hand car.*

second-rate (adjective) of poor quality, e.g. *a second-rate movie.*

secret, secrets 1 (adjective) Something that is secret is told to only a small number of people and hidden from everyone else, e.g. *a secret meeting.* **2** (noun) A secret is a fact told to only a small number of people and hidden from everyone else. **secretly** (adverb), **secrecy** (noun).

secret agent, secret agents (noun) A secret agent is a spy.

secretary, secretaries 1 (noun) A secretary is a person employed by an organization to keep records, write letters, and do office work. **2** Ministers in charge of some government departments are also called secretaries, e.g. *the Health Secretary.* **secretarial** (adjective).

secrete, secretes, secreting, secreted (pronounced sik-**kreet**) **1** (verb) When part of a plant or animal secretes a liquid, it produces it. **2** (a formal use) If you secrete something somewhere, you hide it. **secretion** (noun).

secretive (adjective) Secretive people tend to hide their feelings and intentions.

secret service (noun) A country's secret service is the government department in charge of espionage.

sect, sects (noun) A sect is a religious or political group which has broken away from a larger group.

sectarian (pronounced sek-**tair**-ee-an) (adjective) strongly supporting a particular sect, e.g. *a sectarian war.*

section, sections (noun) A section of something is one of the parts it is divided into, e.g. *this section of the road.*

sector, sectors 1 (noun) A sector of something, especially a country's economy, is one part of it, e.g. *the private sector.* **2** A sector of a circle is one of the two parts formed when you draw two straight lines from the centre to the circumference.

secular (adjective) having no connection with religion, e.g. *secular education.*

secure, secures, securing, secured 1 (verb; a formal use) If you secure something, you manage to get it, e.g. *They secured the rights to her story.* **2** If you secure a place, you make it safe from harm or attack. **3** To secure something also means to fasten it firmly, e.g. *One end was secured to the pier.* **4** (adjective) If a place is secure, it is tightly locked or well protected. **5** If an object is secure, it is firmly fixed in place. **6** If you feel secure, you feel safe and confident. **securely** (adverb).

security 1 (noun or adjective) Security means all the precautions taken to protect a place, e.g. *Security forces arrested one member.* **2** (noun) A feeling of security is a feeling of being safe.

sedate, sedates, sedating, sedated (pronounced sid-**date**) **1** (adjective) quiet, calm, and dignified. **2** (verb) To sedate someone means to give them a drug to make them calm or sleep. **sedately** (adverb).

sedative, sedatives (pronounced **sed**-at-tiv) **1** (noun) A sedative is a drug that calms you down or makes you sleep. **2** (adjective) having a calming or soothing effect, e.g. *antihistamines which have a sedative effect.* **sedation** (noun).

sedentary (pronounced **sed**-entree) (adjective) A sedentary occupation is one in which you spend most of your time sitting down.

sediment (noun) Sediment is solid material that settles at the bottom of a liquid.

seduce, seduces, seducing, seduced 1 (verb) To seduce someone means to persuade them to have sex. **2** If you are seduced into doing something, you are persuaded to do it because it seems very attractive.

seductive 1 (adjective) A seductive person is sexually attractive. **2** Something seductive is very attractive and tempting. **seductively** (adverb).

see, sees, seeing, saw, seen 1 (verb) If you see something, you are looking at it or you notice it. **2** If you see someone, you visit them or meet them, e.g. *I went to see my GP.* **3** If you see someone to a place, you accompany them there. **4** To see something also means to realize or understand it, e.g. *I see what you mean.* **5** If you say you will see if you can do something, you mean you will try to do it. **6** If you see that something is done, you make sure that it is done. **7** If you see to something, you deal with it. **8** See is used to say that an event takes place during a particular period of time, e.g. *The* *next couple of years saw two momentous developments.* **9** (phrases; an informal use) **Seeing that** or **seeing as** means because, e.g. *I took John for lunch, seeing as it was his birthday.* **10** (noun) A bishop's see is his diocese.

seed, seeds (noun) The seeds of a plant are the small, hard parts from which new plants can grow.

seedling, seedlings (noun) A seedling is a young plant grown from a seed.

seedy, seedier, seediest (adjective) untidy and shabby, e.g. *a seedy hotel.*

seek, seeks, seeking, sought (a formal word) **1** (verb) To seek something means to try to find it, obtain it, or achieve it, e.g. *The police were still seeking information.* **2** If you seek to do something, you try to do it, e.g. *de Gaulle sought to reunite the country.*

seem, seems, seeming, seemed (verb) If something seems to be the case, it appears to be the case or you think it is the case, e.g. *He seemed such a quiet chap.*

seeming (adjective) appearing to be real or genuine, e.g. *this seeming disregard for human life.* **seemingly** (adverb).

seep, seeps, seeping, seeped (verb) If a liquid or gas seeps through something, it flows through very slowly.

seesaw, seesaws (noun) A seesaw is a long plank supported in the middle. Two children sit on it, one on each end, and they move up and down in turn.

seething (adjective) If you are seething about something, you are very angry but it does not show.

segment, segments 1 (noun) A segment of something is one part of it. **2** The segments of an orange or grapefruit are the sections which you can divide it into. **3** A segment of a circle is one of the two parts formed when you draw a straight line across it.

segregate, segregates, segregating, segregated (verb) To segregate two groups of people means to keep them apart. **segregated** (adjective), **segregation** (noun).

seize, seizes, seizing, seized 1 (verb) If you seize something, you grab it firmly, e.g. *He seized the phone.* **2** To seize a place or to seize control of it means to take control of it quickly and suddenly. **3** If you seize an opportunity, you take advantage of it.

seizure, seizures (pronounced **seez**-yer) **1** (noun) A seizure is a sudden violent attack of an illness, especially a heart attack or a fit. **2** If there is a seizure of power, a group of people suddenly take control using force.

seldom (adverb) not very often, e.g. *They seldom speak to each other.*

select, selects, selecting, selected 1 (verb) If you select something, you choose it. **2** (adjective) of good quality, e.g. *a select gentlemen's club.* **selector** (noun).

selection, selections 1 (noun) Selection is the choosing of people or things, e.g. *the selection of parliamentary candi-*

dates. **2** A selection of people or things is a set of them chosen from a larger group. **3** The selection of goods in a shop is the range of goods available, e.g. *a good selection of wines.*

selective (adjective) choosing things carefully, e.g. *I am selective about what I eat.* **selectively** (adverb).

self, selves (noun) Your self is your basic personality or nature, e.g. *Hershey is her normal dependable self.*

self- 1 (prefix) done to yourself or by yourself, e.g. *self-help... self-control.* **2** doing something automatically, e.g. *a self-loading rifle.*

self-assured (adjective) behaving in a way that shows confidence in yourself.

self-centred (adjective) thinking only about yourself and not about other people.

self-confessed (adjective) admitting to having bad habits or unpopular opinions, e.g. *a self-confessed liar.*

self-confident (adjective) confident of your own abilities or worth. **self-confidence** (noun).

self-conscious (adjective) nervous and easily embarrassed, and worried about what other people think of you. **self-consciously** (adverb).

self-control (noun) Self-control is the ability to restrain yourself and appear calm.

self-defence (noun) Self-defence is the use of violence or special physical techniques to protect yourself when someone attacks you.

self-employed (adjective) working for yourself and organizing your own finances, rather than working for an employer.

self-esteem (noun) Your self-esteem is your good opinion of yourself.

self-evident (adjective) Self-evident facts are completely obvious and need no proof or explanation.

self-indulgent (adjective) allowing yourself to do or have things you enjoy, especially as a treat.

self-interest (noun) If you do something out of self-interest, you do it for your own benefit rather than to help other people.

selfish (adjective) caring only about yourself, and not about other people. **selfishly** (adverb), **selfishness** (noun).

selfless (adjective) putting other people's interests before your own.

self-made (adjective) rich and successful through your own efforts, e.g. *a self-made man.*

self-raising (adjective) Self-raising flour contains baking powder to make it rise.

self-respect (noun) Self-respect is a feeling of confidence and pride in your own abilities and worth.

self-righteous (adjective) convinced that you are better or more virtuous than other people. **self-righteousness** (noun).

self-service (adjective) A self-service shop or restaurant is one where you serve yourself.

self-sufficient 1 (adjective) producing or making everything you need, and so not needing to buy things. **2** able to live in a way in which you do not need other people.

sell, sells, selling, sold 1 (verb) If you sell something, you let someone have it in return for money. **2** If a shop sells something, it has it available for people to buy, e.g. *a tobacconist that sells stamps.* **3** If something sells, people buy it, e.g. *This book will sell.* **seller** (noun).

Sellotape (noun; a trademark) Sellotape is a transparent sticky tape.

semblance (noun) If there is a semblance of something, it seems to exist, although it might not really exist, e.g. *an effort to restore a semblance of normality.*

semen (pronounced **see**-men) (noun) Semen is the liquid containing sperm produced by a man's or male animal's sex organs.

semi- (prefix) half or partly, e.g. *semiskilled workers.*

semicircle, semicircles (noun) A semicircle is a half of a circle. **semicircular** (adjective).

semicolon, semicolons (noun) A semicolon is the punctuation mark (;), used to separate different parts of a sentence or to indicate a pause.

semidetached (adjective) A semidetached house is joined to another house on one side.

semifinal, semifinals (noun) The semifinals are the two matches in a competition played to decide who plays in the final. **semifinalist** (noun).

seminar, seminars (noun) A seminar is a meeting of a small number of university students or teachers to discuss a particular topic.

Senate, Senates (noun) The Senate is the smaller, more important of the two councils in the government of some countries, such as the USA.

senator, senators (noun) A senator is a member of a senate, for example in the USA.

send, sends, sending, sent 1 (verb) If you send something to someone, you arrange for it to be delivered to them. **2** To send a radio signal or message means to transmit it. **3** If you send someone somewhere, you tell them to go there or arrange for them to go. **4** If you send for someone, you send a message asking them to come and see you. **5** If you send off for something, you write and ask for it to be sent to you.

senile (adjective) If old people become senile, they become confused and cannot look after themselves. **senility** (noun).

senior, seniors 1 (adjective) The senior people in an organization or profession have the highest and most important jobs. **2** (noun) Someone who is your senior is older than you. **seniority** (noun).

senior citizen, senior citizens (noun) A senior citizen is someone receiving an old-age pension.

sensation, sensations 1 (noun) A sensation is a feeling, especially a physical feeling. **2** If something is a sensation, it causes great excitement.

sensational 1 (adjective) causing great excitement and interest. **2** (an informal use) extremely good, e.g. *a sensational party.* **sensationally** (adverb).

sense, senses, sensing, sensed 1 (noun) Your senses are the physical abilities of sight, hearing, smell, touch, and taste. 2 (verb) If you sense something, you become aware of it. 3 (noun) A sense is also a feeling, e.g. *a sense of guilt.* 4 A sense of a word is one of its meanings. 5 Sense is the ability to think and behave sensibly. 6 (phrase) If something **makes sense,** you can understand it or it seems sensible, e.g. *It makes sense to find out as much as you can.*

senseless 1 (adjective) A senseless action has no meaning or purpose, e.g. *senseless destruction.* 2 If someone is senseless, they are unconscious.

sensibility, sensibilities (noun) Your sensibility is your ability to experience deep feelings, e.g. *a man of sensibility rather than reason.*

sensible (adjective) showing good sense and judgment. **sensibly** (adverb).

sensitive 1 (adjective) If you are sensitive to other people's feelings, you understand them. 2 If you are sensitive about something, you are worried or easily upset about it, e.g. *He was sensitive about his height.* 3 A sensitive subject or issue needs to be dealt with carefully because it can make people angry or upset. 4 Something that is sensitive to a particular thing is easily affected or harmed by it. **sensitively** (adverb), **sensitivity** (noun).

sensor, sensors (noun) A sensor is an instrument which reacts to physical conditions such as light or heat.

sensual (pronounced **senss**-yool) 1 (adjective) showing or suggesting a liking for sexual pleasures, e.g. *She has a wide, sensual mouth.* 2 giving pleasure to your physical senses rather than to your mind, e.g. *the sensual rhythm of his voice.* **sensuality** (noun).

sensuous (adjective) giving pleasure through the senses. **sensuously** (adverb).

sentence, sentences, sentencing, sentenced 1 (noun) A sentence is a group of words which, when written down, begins with a capital letter and ends with a full stop. 2 In a law court, a sentence is a punishment given to someone who has been found guilty. 3 (verb) When a guilty person is sentenced, they are told officially what their punishment will be.

sentiment, sentiments 1 (noun) A sentiment is a feeling, attitude, or opinion, e.g. *I doubt my parents share my sentiments.* 2 Sentiment consists of feelings such as tenderness, romance, or sadness, e.g. *There's no room for sentiment in business.*

sentimental 1 (adjective) feeling or expressing tenderness, romance, or sadness to an exaggerated extent, e.g. *sentimental love stories.* 2 relating to a person's emotions, e.g. *things of sentimental value.* **sentimentality** (noun).

sentinel, sentinels (noun; an old-fashioned word) A sentinel is a sentry.

sentry, sentries (noun) A sentry is a soldier who keeps watch and guards a camp or building.

separate, separates, separating, separated 1 (adjective) If something is separate from something else, the two things are not connected. **2** (verb) To separate people or things means to cause them to be apart from each other. **3** If people or things separate, they move away from each other. **4** If a married couple separate, they decide to live apart. **separately** (adverb), **separation** (noun).

sepia (pronounced **see**-pee-a) (adjective or noun) deep brown, like the colour of old photographs.

September (noun) September is the ninth month of the year. It has 30 days.

septic (adjective) If a wound becomes septic, it becomes infected with poison.

sepulchre, sepulchres (pronounced **sep**-pul-ka) (noun; a literary word) A sepulchre is a large tomb.

sequel, sequels 1 (noun) A sequel to a book or film is another book or film which continues the story. **2** The sequel to an event is a result or consequence of it, e.g. *There's a sequel to my egg story.*

sequence, sequences 1 (noun) A sequence of events is a number of them coming one after the other, e.g. *the whole sequence of events that had brought me to this place.* **2** The sequence in which things are arranged is the order in which they are arranged, e.g. *Do things in the right sequence.*

sequin, sequins (noun) Sequins are small, shiny, coloured discs sewn on clothes to decorate them.

Serbian, Serbians 1 (adjective) belonging to or relating to Serbia. **2** (noun) A Serbian is someone who comes from Serbia. **3** Serbian is the form of Serbo-Croat spoken in Serbia.

Serbo-Croat (pronounced ser-boh-**kroh**-at) (noun) Serbo-Croat is the main language spoken in Serbia and Croatia.

serenade, serenades, serenading, serenaded 1 (verb) If you serenade someone you love, you sing or play music to them outside their window. **2** (noun) A serenade is a song sung outside a woman's window by a man who loves her.

serene (adjective) peaceful and calm, e.g. *She had a serene air.* **serenely** (adverb), **serenity** (noun).

serf, serfs (noun) Serfs were a class of people in medieval Europe who had to work on their master's land and could not leave without his permission.

sergeant, sergeants 1 (noun) A sergeant is a noncommissioned officer of middle rank in the army or air force. **2** A sergeant is also a police officer just above a constable in rank.

sergeant major, sergeant majors (noun) A sergeant major is a noncommissioned army officer of the highest rank.

serial, serials (noun) A serial is a story which is broadcast or published in a number of parts over a period of time, e.g. *a television serial.*

serial number, serial numbers (noun) An object's serial number is a number you can see on it which identifies it.

series 1 (noun) A series of things is a number of them coming one after the other, e.g. *a series of loud explosions.* **2** A radio or television series is a set of programmes with the same title.

serious 1 (adjective) A serious problem or situation is very bad and worrying. **2** Serious matters are important and should be thought about carefully. **3** If you are serious about something, you are sincere about it, e.g. *You are really serious about having a baby.* **4** People who are serious are thoughtful, quiet, and slightly humourless. **seriousness** (noun).

seriously 1 (adverb) You say seriously to emphasize that you mean what you say, e.g. *Seriously, though, something must be done.* **2** (phrase) If you **take something seriously,** you regard it as important.

sermon, sermons (noun) A sermon is a talk on a religious or moral subject given as part of a church service.

serpent, serpents (noun; a literary word) A serpent is a snake.

serrated (adjective) having a row of V-shaped points along the edge, like a saw, e.g. *green serrated leaves.*

servant, servants (noun) A servant is someone who is employed to work in another person's house.

serve, serves, serving, served 1 (verb) If you serve a country, an organization, or a person, you do useful work for them. **2** To serve as something means to act or be used as that thing, e.g. *the room that served as their office.* **3** If something serves people in a particular place, it provides them with something they need, e.g. *a recycling plant which serves the whole of the county.* **4** If you serve food or drink to people, you give it to them. **5** To serve customers in a shop means to help them and provide them with what they want. **6** To serve a prison sentence or an apprenticeship means to spend time doing it. **7** When you serve in tennis or badminton, you throw the ball or shuttlecock into the air and hit it over the net to start playing. **8** (noun) A serve is the act of serving in tennis or badminton.

service, services, servicing, serviced 1 (noun) A service is a system organized to provide something for the public, e.g. *the bus service.* **2** Some government organizations are called services, e.g. *the diplomatic service.* **3** The services are the army, the navy, and the air force. **4** If you give your services to a person or organization, you work for them or help them in some way, e.g. *services to the community.* **5** (verb) When a machine or vehicle is serviced, it is examined, adjusted, and cleaned so that it will continue working efficiently. **6** (noun) A service is also a religious ceremony. **7** When it is your service in a game of tennis or badminton, it is your turn to serve.

serviceman, servicemen (noun) A serviceman is a man in the army, navy, or air force.

service station, service stations (noun) A service station is a garage that sells petrol, oil, spare parts, and snacks.

servile (adjective) too eager to obey people. **servility** (noun).

serving, servings 1 (noun) A serving is a helping of food. **2** (adjective) A serving spoon or dish is used for serving food.

session, sessions 1 (noun) A session is a meeting of an official group, e.g. *the emergency session of the Supreme Court.* **2** A session is also a period during which meetings are held regularly, e.g. *the end of the parliamentary session.* **3** The period during which an activity takes place can also be called a session, e.g. *a drinking session.*

set, sets, setting, set 1 (noun) Several things make a set when they belong together or form a group, e.g. *a set of weights.* **2** In maths, a set is a collection of numbers or other things which are treated as a group. **3** (verb) If something is set somewhere, that is where it is, e.g. *The house was set back from the beach.* **4** When the sun sets, it goes below the horizon. **5** When you set the table, you prepare it for a meal by putting plates and cutlery on it. **6** When you set a clock or a control, you adjust it to a particular point or position. **7** When something such as jelly or cement sets, it becomes firm or hard. **8** (adjective) Something that is set is fixed and not varying, e.g. *a set charge.* **9** If you are set to do something, you are ready or likely to do it. **10** If you are set on doing something, you are determined to do it. **11** If a play, film, or story is set at a particular time or in a particular place, the events in it take place at that time or in that place. **12** (noun) A television set is a television. **13** The set for a play or film is the scenery or furniture on the stage or in the studio. **14** In tennis, a set is a group of six or more games. There are usually several sets in a match. **set about** (verb) If you set about doing something, you start doing it. **set off 1** (verb) When you set off, you start a journey. **2** To set something off means to cause it to start. **set out 1** (verb) When you set out, you start a journey. **2** If you set out to do something, you start trying to do it.

setback, setbacks (noun) A setback is something that delays or hinders you.

settee, settees (noun) A settee is a long comfortable seat for two or three people to sit on.

setter, setters (noun) A setter is a long-haired breed of dog originally used in hunting.

setting, settings 1 (noun) The setting of something is its surroundings or circumstances, e.g. *The Irish setting made the story realistic.* **2** The settings on a machine are the different positions to which the controls can be adjusted.

settle, settles, settling, settled 1

(verb) To settle an argument means to put an end to it, e.g. *The dispute was settled.* **2** If something is settled, it has all been decided and arranged. **3** If you settle on something or settle for it, you choose it, e.g. *We settled for orange juice and coffee.* **4** When you settle a bill, you pay it. **5** If you settle in a place, you make it your permanent home. **6** If you settle yourself somewhere, you sit down and make yourself comfortable. **7** If something settles, it sinks slowly down and comes to rest, e.g. *A black dust settled on the walls.* **settle down 1** (verb) When someone settles down, they start living a quiet life in one place. **2** To settle down means to become quiet or calm.

settlement, settlements 1 (noun) A settlement is an official agreement between people who have been involved in a conflict, e.g. *the last chance for a peaceful settlement.* **2** A settlement is also a place where people have settled and built homes.

settler, settlers (noun) A settler is someone who settles in a new country, e.g. *the first settlers in Cuba.*

seven the number 7.

seventeen the number 17. **seventeenth**

seventh, sevenths 1 The seventh item in a series is the one counted as number seven. **2** (noun) A seventh is one of seven equal parts.

seventy, seventies the number 70. **seventieth**

sever, severs, severing, severed 1 (verb) To sever something means to cut it off or cut right through it. **2** If you sever a connection with someone or something, you end it completely, e.g. *I have severed all my ties with South Africa.*

several (adjective or pronoun) Several people or things means a small number of them.

severe 1 (adjective) extremely bad or unpleasant, e.g. *severe stomach pains.* **2** stern and harsh, e.g. *Perhaps I was too severe with that young man.* **severely** (adverb), **severity** (noun).

sew, sews, sewing, sewed, sewn (pronounced **so**) (verb) When you sew things together, you join them using a needle and thread. **sewing** (noun).

sewage (noun) Sewage is dirty water and waste matter which is carried away in sewers.

sewer, sewers (noun) A sewer is a large underground channel that carries sewage to a place where it is treated to make it harmless.

sewerage (noun) Sewerage is the system by which sewage is carried away and treated.

sex, sexes 1 (noun) The sexes are the two groups, male and female, into which people and animals are divided. **2** The sex of a person or animal is their characteristic of being either male or female. **3** Sex is the physical activity by which people and animals produce young.

sexism (noun) Sexism is discrimination against the members of one sex, usually women. **sexist** (adjective or noun).

sextet, sextets (noun) A sextet

is a group of six musicians who sing or play together.

sextuplet, sextuplets (noun) Sextuplets are six children born at the same time to the same mother.

sexual 1 (adjective) connected with the act of sex or with people's desire for sex, e.g. *sexual attraction.* **2** relating to the difference between males and females, e.g. *sexual equality.* **3** relating to the biological process by which people and animals produce young, e.g. *sexual reproduction.* **sexually** (adverb).

sexual intercourse (noun) Sexual intercourse is the physical act of sex between a man and a woman.

sexuality (pronounced seks-yoo-**al**-it-ee) (noun) A person's sexuality is their ability to experience sexual feelings.

sexy, sexier, sexiest (adjective) sexually attractive or exciting, e.g. *these sexy blue eyes.*

shabby, shabbier, shabbiest 1 (adjective) old and worn in appearance, e.g. *a shabby overcoat.* **2** dressed in old, worn-out clothes, e.g. *a shabby figure crouching in a doorway.* **shabbily** (adverb).

shack, shacks (noun) A shack is a small hut.

shackle, shackles, shackling, shackled 1 (noun) In the past, shackles were two metal rings joined by a chain fastened around a prisoner's wrists or ankles. **2** (verb) To shackle someone means to put shackles on them. **3** (a literary use) If you are shackled by something, it restricts or hampers you.

shade, shades, shading, shaded 1 (noun) Shade is an area of darkness and coolness which the sun does not reach, e.g. *The table was in the shade.* **2** (verb) If a place is shaded by trees or buildings, they prevent the sun from shining on it. **3** If you shade your eyes, you put your hand in front of them to protect them from a bright light. **4** (noun) A shade is a lampshade. **5** The shades of a colour are its different forms. For example, olive green is a shade of green.

shadow, shadows, shadowing, shadowed 1 (noun) A shadow is the dark shape made when an object prevents light from reaching a surface. **2** Shadow is darkness caused by light not reaching a place. **3** (verb) To shadow someone means to follow them and watch them closely.

Shadow Cabinet (noun) The Shadow Cabinet consists of the leaders of the main opposition party, each of whom is concerned with a particular policy.

shadowy 1 (adjective) A shadowy place is dark and full of shadows. **2** A shadowy figure or shape is difficult to see because it is dark or misty.

shady, shadier, shadiest (adjective) A shady place is sheltered from sunlight by trees or buildings.

shaft, shafts 1 (noun) A shaft is a vertical passage, for example one for a lift or one in a mine. **2** A shaft of light is a beam of light.

shake, shakes, shaking, shook, shaken 1 (verb) To shake

something means to move it quickly from side to side or up and down. **2** (noun) If you give something a shake, you shake it. **3** (verb) If something shakes, it moves from side to side or up and down with small, quick movements. **4** If your voice shakes, it trembles because you are nervous or angry. **5** If something shakes you, it shocks and upsets you. **6** When you shake your head, you move it from side to side in order to say 'no'. **7** (phrase) When you **shake hands** with someone, you grasp their hand as a way of greeting them.

shaky, shakier, shakiest (adjective) rather weak and unsteady, e.g. *The UK economy is still shaky.* **shakily** (adverb).

shall 1 (verb) If I say I shall do something, I mean that I intend to do it. **2** If I say something shall happen, I am emphasizing that it will definitely happen, or I am ordering it to happen, e.g. *There shall be work and security!* **3** Shall is also used in questions when you are asking what to do, or making a suggestion, e.g. *Shall we sit down... Shall I go and check for you?*

shallow, shallower, shallowest; shallows 1 (adjective) Shallow means not deep. **2** Shallow also means not involving serious thought or sincere feelings, e.g. *a well-meaning but shallow man.* **3** (plural noun) The shallows are the shallow part of a river or lake.

sham, shams 1 (noun) Something that is a sham is not real or genuine. **2** (adjective) not real or genuine, e.g. *a sham display of affection.*

shambles (noun) If an event is a shambles, it is confused and badly organized.

shame, shames, shaming, shamed 1 (noun) Shame is the feeling of guilt or embarrassment you get when you know you have done something wrong or foolish. **2** To bring shame on someone means to make people lose respect for them, e.g. *the scenes that brought shame to English soccer.* **3** (verb) If something shames you, it makes you feel ashamed. **4** If you shame someone into doing something, you force them to do it by making them feel ashamed not to, e.g. *Two children shamed their parents into giving up cigarettes.* **5** (noun) If you say something is a shame, you mean you are sorry about it, e.g. *It's a shame you can't come round.*

shameful (adjective) If someone's behaviour is shameful, they ought to be ashamed of it. **shamefully** (adverb).

shameless (adjective) behaving in an indecent or unacceptable way, but showing no shame or embarrassment, e.g. *shameless dishonesty.* **shamelessly** (adverb).

shampoo, shampoos, shampooing, shampooed 1 (noun) Shampoo is a soapy liquid used for washing your hair. **2** (verb) When you shampoo your hair, you wash it with shampoo.

shamrock, shamrocks (noun) A shamrock is a plant with three round leaves on each stem. The shamrock is the national emblem of Ireland.

shanty, shanties 1 (noun) A shanty is a small, rough hut. **2** A sea shanty is a song sailors used to sing.

shape, shapes, shaping, shaped 1 (noun) The shape of something is the form or pattern of its outline, for example whether it is round or square. **2** A shape is something with a definite form, for example a circle, square, or triangle. **3** The shape of something such as an organization is its structure and size. **4** (verb) If you shape an object, you form it into a particular shape, e.g. *Shape the dough into an oblong.* **5** To shape something means to cause it to develop in a particular way, e.g. *events that shaped their lives.*

shapeless (adjective) not having a definite shape.

shapely, shapelier, shapeliest (adjective) A shapely woman has an attractive figure.

shard, shards (noun) A shard is a small fragment of pottery, glass, or metal.

share, shares, sharing, shared 1 (verb) If two people share something, they both use it, do it, or have it, e.g. *We shared a bottle of champagne.* **2** If you share an idea or a piece of news with someone, you tell it to them. **3** (noun) A share of something is a portion of it. **4** The shares of a company are the equal parts into which its ownership is divided. People can buy shares as an investment.

shareholder, shareholders (noun) A shareholder is a person who owns shares in a company.

shark, sharks 1 (noun) Sharks are large, powerful fish with sharp teeth. They sometimes attack people. **2** A shark is also a person who cheats people out of money.

sharp, sharper, sharpest; sharps 1 (adjective) A sharp object has a fine edge or point that is good for cutting or piercing things. **2** A sharp outline or distinction is easy to see. **3** A sharp person is quick to notice or understand things. **4** A sharp change is sudden and significant, e.g. *a sharp rise in prices.* **5** If you say something in a sharp way, you say it firmly and rather angrily. **6** A sharp sound is short, sudden, and quite loud. **7** A sharp pain is sudden and painful. **8** A sharp taste is slightly sour. **9** (adverb) If something happens at a certain time sharp, it happens at that time precisely, e.g. *You'll begin at eight o'clock sharp.* **10** (noun) In music, a sharp is a note or key a semitone higher than that described by the same letter. It is represented by the symbol (♯). **11** (adjective) A musical instrument or note that is sharp is slightly too high in pitch. **sharply** (adverb), **sharpness** (noun).

sharpen, sharpens, sharpening, sharpened 1 (verb) To sharpen an object means to make its edge or point sharper. **2** If your senses or abilities sharpen, you become quicker at noticing or understanding things. **sharpener** (noun).

shatter, shatters, shattering,

shattered 1 (verb) If something shatters, it breaks into a lot of small pieces. **2** If something shatters your hopes or beliefs, it destroys them completely. **3** If you are shattered by an event or piece of news, you are shocked and upset by it.

shattered (adjective; an informal word) completely exhausted, e.g. *He must be absolutely shattered after all that.*

shattering (adjective) making you feel shocked and upset, e.g. *a shattering event.*

shave, shaves, shaving, shaved 1 (verb) When a man shaves, he removes hair from his face with a razor. **2** (noun) When a man has a shave, he shaves. **3** (verb) If you shave off part of a piece of wood, you cut thin pieces from it.

shaven (adjective) If part of someone's body is shaven, it has been shaved, e.g. *a shaven head.*

shaver, shavers (noun) A shaver is an electric razor.

shavings (plural noun) Shavings are small, very thin pieces of wood which have been cut from a larger piece.

shawl, shawls (noun) A shawl is a large piece of woollen cloth worn round a woman's head or shoulders or used to wrap a baby in.

she (pronoun) 'She' is used to refer to a woman or girl whose identity is clear. 'She' is also used to refer to a country, a ship, or a car.

sheaf, sheaves 1 (noun) A sheaf of papers is a bundle of them. **2** A sheaf of corn is a bundle of ripe corn tied together.

shear, shears, shearing, sheared, shorn 1 (verb) To shear a sheep means to cut the wool off it. **2** (plural noun) Shears are a tool like a large pair of scissors, used especially for cutting hedges.

sheath, sheaths 1 (noun) A sheath is a covering for the blade of a knife. **2** A sheath is also a condom.

shed, sheds, shedding, shed 1 (noun) A shed is a small building used for storing things. **2** (verb) When an animal sheds hair or skin, some of its hair or skin drops off. When a tree sheds its leaves, its leaves fall off. **3** (a formal use) To shed something also means to get rid of it, e.g. *British Coal has shed 13,000 jobs in the past year.* **4** If a lorry sheds its load, the load falls off the lorry onto the road. **5** If you shed tears, you cry.

sheen (noun) A sheen is a gentle brightness on the surface of something.

sheep (noun) A sheep is a farm animal with a thick woolly coat. Sheep are kept for meat and wool.

sheepdog, sheepdogs (noun) A sheepdog is a breed of dog often used for controlling sheep.

sheepish (adjective) If you look sheepish, you look embarrassed because you feel foolish. **sheepishly** (adverb).

sheepskin (noun) Sheepskin is the skin and wool of a sheep, used for making rugs and coats.

sheer, sheerer, sheerest 1 (adjective) Sheer means complete and total, e.g. *sheer exhaustion.* **2** A sheer cliff or drop is vertical. **3** Sheer fabrics are very light and delicate.

sheet, sheets 1 (noun) A sheet is a large rectangular piece of cloth used to cover a bed. **2** A sheet of paper is a rectangular piece of it. **3** A sheet of glass, metal, or wood is a large, flat piece of it.

sheik, sheiks (pronounced **shake**); also spelled **sheikh** (noun) A sheik is an Arab chief or ruler.

shelf, shelves (noun) A shelf is a flat piece of wood, metal, or glass fixed to a wall and used for putting things on.

shell, shells, shelling, shelled 1 (noun) The shell of an egg or nut is its hard covering. **2** The shell of a tortoise, snail, or crab is the hard protective covering on its back. **3** (verb) If you shell peas or nuts, you remove their natural covering. **4** (noun) The shell of a building or other structure is its frame, e.g. *The room was just an empty shell.* **5** A shell is also a container filled with explosives that can be fired from a gun. **6** (verb) To shell a place means to fire large explosive shells at it.

shellfish, shellfish or **shellfishes** (noun) A shellfish is a small sea creature with a shell.

shelter, shelters, sheltering, sheltered 1 (noun) A shelter is a small building made to protect people from bad weather or danger. **2** If a place provides shelter, it provides protection from bad weather or danger. **3** (verb) If you shelter in a place, you stay there and are safe. **4** If you shelter someone, you provide them with a place to stay when they are in danger.

sheltered 1 (adjective) A sheltered place is protected from wind and rain. **2** If you lead a sheltered life, you do not experience unpleasant or upsetting things. **3** Sheltered accommodation is accommodation designed for old or handicapped people. It consists of a group of individual houses or flats with a caretaker to provide supervision.

shelve, shelves, shelving, shelved (verb) If you shelve a plan, you decide to postpone it for a while.

shepherd, shepherds, shepherding, shepherded 1 (noun) A shepherd is a person who looks after sheep. **2** (verb) If you shepherd someone somewhere, you accompany them there.

sheriff, sheriffs (noun) In America, a sheriff is a person elected to enforce the law in a county.

sherry, sherries (noun) Sherry is a kind of strong wine.

shield, shields, shielding, shielded 1 (noun) A shield is a large piece of a strong material like metal or plastic which soldiers or policeman carry to protect themselves. **2** If something is a shield against something, it gives protection from it. **3** (verb) To shield someone means to protect them from something.

shift, shifts, shifting, shifted 1 (verb) If you shift something, you move it. If something shifts, it moves, e.g. *to shift the rubble.* **2** (noun) A shift in an opinion or situation is a slight change. **3** (verb) If an opinion or situation shifts, it changes slightly. **4** (noun) A shift is also a set period during which people work in a factory, e.g. *the night shift.*

shilling, shillings (noun) A shilling was a unit of money equivalent to 5p.

shimmer, shimmers, shimmering, shimmered 1 (verb) If something shimmers, it shines with a faint, flickering light. **2** (noun) A shimmer is a faint, flickering light.

shin, shins, shinning, shinned 1 (noun) Your shin is the front part of your leg between your knee and your ankle. **2** (verb) If you shin up a tree or pole, you climb it quickly by gripping it with your hands and legs.

shine, shines, shining, shone 1 (verb) When something shines, it gives out or reflects a bright light, e.g. *The stars shone brilliantly.* **2** If you shine a torch or lamp somewhere, you point it there.

shingle, shingles 1 (noun) Shingle consists of small pebbles on the seashore. **2** Shingles are small wooden roof tiles. **3** Shingles is a disease that causes a painful red rash, especially around the waist.

shining 1 (adjective) Shining things are very bright, usually because they are reflecting light, e.g. *shining stainless steel tables.* **2** A shining example of something is a very good or typical example of that thing, e.g. *a shining example of courage.*

shiny, shinier, shiniest (adjective) Shiny things are bright and look as if they have been polished, e.g. *a shiny brass plate.*

ship, ships, shipping, shipped 1 (noun) A ship is a large boat which carries passengers or cargo. **2** (verb) If people or things are shipped somewhere, they are transported there.

shipment, shipments 1 (noun) A shipment is a quantity of goods that are transported somewhere, e.g. *a shipment of olive oil.* **2** The shipment of goods is the transporting of them.

shipping 1 (noun) Shipping is the transport of cargo on ships. **2** You can also refer to ships generally as shipping, e.g. *Attention all shipping!*

shipwreck, shipwrecks (noun) When there is a shipwreck, a ship is destroyed in an accident at sea, e.g. *He was drowned in a shipwreck.*

shipyard, shipyards (noun) A shipyard is a place where ships are built and repaired.

shire, shires (noun; an old-fashioned use) A shire is a county.

shirk, shirks, shirking, shirked (verb) To shirk a task means to avoid doing it.

shirt, shirts (noun) A shirt is a piece of clothing worn on the upper part of the body. It has a collar, sleeves, and buttons down the front.

shiver, shivers, shivering, shivered 1 (verb) When you shiver, you tremble slightly because you are cold or scared. **2** (noun) A shiver is a slight trembling caused by cold or fear.

shoal, shoals (noun) A shoal of fish is a large group of them swimming together.

shock, shocks, shocking, shocked 1 (noun) If you have a shock, you have a sudden upsetting experience. **2** Shock is a person's emotional and physical condition when something very unpleasant or upsetting has happened to them. **3** In medicine, shock is a serious physical condition in which the blood cannot circulate properly because of an injury. **4** A shock is also a slight movement in something when it is hit by something else, e.g. *The straps help to absorb shocks.* **5** (verb) If something shocks you, it upsets you because it is unpleasant and unexpected, e.g. *I was shocked by his appearance.* **6** You can say that something shocks you when it offends you because it is rude or immoral. **7** (noun) A shock of hair is a thick mass of it. **shocked** (adjective).

shocking 1 (adjective; an informal use) very bad, e.g. *It's been a shocking year.* **2** rude or immoral, e.g. *a shocking video.*

shoddy, shoddier, shoddiest (adjective) badly made or done, e.g. *a shoddy piece of work.*

shoe, shoes, shoeing, shod 1 (noun) Shoes are things worn on your feet. They are usually made of leather, and cover most of your foot, but not your ankle. **2** (verb) To shoe a horse means to fix horseshoes onto its hooves.

shoestring (noun) If you do something on a shoestring, you do it using very little money.

shoot, shoots, shooting, shot 1 (verb) To shoot a person or animal means to kill or injure them by firing a gun at them. **2** (noun) A shoot is an occasion when people hunt animals or birds with guns. **3** (verb) To shoot an arrow means to fire it from a bow. **4** If something shoots in a particular direction, it moves there quickly and suddenly, e.g. *They shot back into Green Street.* **5** When a film is shot, it is filmed, e.g. *The whole film was shot in California.* **6** In games such as football or hockey, to shoot means to kick or hit the ball towards the goal. **7** (noun) A shoot is also a plant that is beginning to grow, or a new part growing from a plant.

shooting, shootings (noun) A shooting is an incident in which someone is shot.

shooting star, shooting stars (noun) A shooting star is a meteor.

shop, shops, shopping, shopped 1 (noun) A shop is a place where things are sold. **2** (verb) When you shop, you go to the shops to buy things. **3** (noun) A shop is also a place where a particular type of work is done, e.g. *a bicycle repair shop.* **shopper** (noun).

shopkeeper, shopkeepers (noun) A shopkeeper is someone who owns or manages a small shop.

shoplifting (noun) Shoplifting is stealing goods from shops. **shoplifter** (noun).

shopping (noun) Your shopping is the goods you have bought from the shops.

shop steward, shop stewards (noun) A shop steward is a trade union member elected to represent the workers in a factory or office.

shore, shores, shoring, shored 1 (noun) The shore of a sea, lake, or wide river is the land along the edge of it. **2** (verb) If you shore something up, you reinforce it or strengthen it, e.g. *This will help to shore up the property market.*

shoreline, shorelines (noun) The shoreline is the edge of a sea, lake, or wide river.

shorn 1 Shorn is the past participle of **shear**. **2** (adjective) Grass or hair that is shorn is cut very short.

short, shorter, shortest; shorts 1 (adjective) not lasting very long. **2** small in length, distance, or height, e.g. *a short climb... the short road.* **3** If you are short with someone, you speak to them crossly. **4** If you have a short temper, you get angry very quickly. **5** If you are short of something, you do not have enough of it. **6** If a name is short for another name, it is a short version of it. **7** (plural noun) Shorts are trousers with short legs. **8** (adverb) If you stop short of a place, you do not quite reach it. **9** (phrase) **Short of** is used to say that a level or amount has not quite been reached, e.g. *a hundred votes short of a majority.*

shortage, shortages (noun) If there is a shortage of something, there is not enough of it.

shortbread (noun) Shortbread is a crumbly biscuit made from flour and butter.

short circuit, short circuits (noun) A short circuit is a fault in an electrical system. It happens when two points accidentally become connected and the electricity travels directly between them rather than through the complete circuit.

shortcoming, shortcomings (noun) Shortcomings are faults or weaknesses.

shortcut, shortcuts 1 (noun) A shortcut is a quicker way of getting somewhere than the usual route. **2** A shortcut is also a quicker way of doing something, e.g. *Stencils have been used as a shortcut to hand painting.*

shorten, shortens, shortening, shortened (verb) If you shorten something or if it shortens, it becomes shorter, e.g. *This might help to shorten the conversation.*

shortfall, shortfalls (noun) If there is a shortfall in something, there is less than you need.

shorthand (noun) Shorthand is a way of writing in which signs represent words or syllables. It is used to write down quickly what someone is saying.

short-list, short-lists, short-listing, short-listed 1 (noun) A short-list is a list of people selected from a larger group, from which one person is finally selected for a job or prize. **2** (verb) If someone is short-listed for a job or prize, they are put on a short-list.

shortly **1** (adverb) Shortly means soon, e.g. *I'll be back shortly.* **2** If you speak to someone shortly, you speak to them in a cross and impatient way.

short-sighted (adjective) If you are short-sighted, you cannot see things clearly when they are far away.

short-term (adjective) happening or having an effect within a short time or for a short time.

shot, shots **1** Shot is the past tense and past participle of **shoot**. **2** (noun) A shot is the act of firing a gun. **3** Someone who is a good shot can shoot accurately. **4** In football, golf, and tennis, a shot is the act of kicking or hitting the ball. **5** A shot is also a photograph or short film sequence, e.g. *I'd like to get some shots of the river.* **6** (an informal use) If you have a shot at something, you try to do it.

shotgun, shotguns (noun) A shotgun is a gun that fires a lot of small pellets all at once.

shot put (noun) In athletics, the shot put is an event in which the contestants throw a heavy metal ball called a shot as far as possible. **shot putter** (noun).

should **1** (verb) You use 'should' to say that something ought to happen, e.g. *Ward should have done better.* **2** You also use 'should' to say that you expect something to happen, e.g. *He should have heard by now.* **3** (a formal use) You can use 'should' to announce that you are about to do or say something, e.g. *I should like to express my thanks to the Professor.* **4** 'Should' is used in conditional sentences, e.g. *If they should discover the fact, what use would the knowledge be to them?* **5** 'Should' is sometimes used in 'that' clauses, e.g. *It is inevitable that you should go.* **6** If you say that you should think something, you mean that it is probably true, e.g. *I should think that's unlikely.*

shoulder, shoulders, shouldering, shouldered **1** (noun) Your shoulders are the parts of your body between your neck and the tops of your arms. **2** (verb) If you shoulder something heavy, you put it across one of your shoulders to carry it. **3** If you shoulder the responsibility or blame for something, you accept it.

shoulder blade, shoulder blades (noun) Your shoulder blades are the two large, flat, triangular bones in the upper part of your back, below your shoulders.

shout, shouts, shouting, shouted **1** (noun) A shout is a loud call or cry. **2** (verb) If you shout something, you say it very loudly, e.g. *He shouted something to his brother.*

shove, shoves, shoving, shoved **1** (verb) If you shove someone or something, you push them roughly, e.g. *He shoved his wallet into a back pocket.* **2** (noun) A shove is a rough push. **shove off** (verb; an informal use) If you tell someone to shove off, you are telling them angrily and rudely to go away.

shovel, shovels, shovelling, shovelled 1 (noun) A shovel is a tool like a spade, used for moving earth, coal, or snow. **2** (verb) If you shovel earth, coal, or snow, you move it with a shovel.

show, shows, showing, showed, shown 1 (verb) To show that something exists or is true means to prove it, e.g. *The survey showed that 29 per cent would now approve the treaty.* **2** If a picture shows something, it represents it, e.g. *The painting shows supporters and crowd scenes.* **3** If you show someone something, you let them see it, e.g. *Show me your passport.* **4** If you show someone to a room or seat, you lead them there. **5** If you show someone how to do something, you demonstrate it to them. **6** If something shows, it is visible. **7** If something shows a quality or characteristic, you can see that it has it, e.g. *Her sketches and watercolours showed promise.* **8** If you show your feelings, you let people see them, e.g. *Savage was flustered, but too proud to show it.* **9** If you show affection or mercy, you behave in an affectionate or merciful way, e.g. *the first person who showed me some affection.* **10** (noun) A show is a form of light entertainment at the theatre or on television. **11** (verb) To show a film or television programme means to let the public see it. **12** (noun) A show is an exhibition, e.g. *the Southampton Antiques Show.* **13** A show of a feeling or attitude is behaviour in which you show it, e.g. *a show of optimism.* **14** (phrase) If something is **on show,** it is being exhibited for the public to see. **show off** (verb; an informal use) If someone is showing off, they are trying to impress people. **show up 1** (verb; an informal use) If you show up, you arrive at a place where you are expected. **2** If something shows up, it can be seen clearly, e.g. *Her bones were too soft to show up on an X-ray.*

show business (noun) Show business is entertainment in the theatre, films, and TV.

showdown, showdowns (noun; an informal word) A showdown is a major argument or conflict intended to end a dispute.

shower, showers, showering, showered 1 (noun) A shower is a device which sprays you with water so that you can wash yourself. **2** If you have a shower, you wash yourself by standing under a shower. **3** (verb) If you shower, you have a shower. **4** (noun) A shower is also a short period of rain. **5** You can refer to a lot of things falling at once as a shower, e.g. *a shower of confetti.* **6** (verb) If you are showered with a lot of things, they fall on you.

showing, showings (noun) A showing of a film or television programme is a presentation of it so that the public can see it.

showjumping (noun) Showjumping is a horse-riding competition in which the horses jump over a series of high walls and fences.

show-off, show-offs (noun; an informal word) A show-off is someone who tries to impress people with their knowledge or skills.

showroom, showrooms (noun) A showroom is a shop where goods such as cars or electrical appliances are displayed.

showy, showier, showiest (adjective) large or bright and intended to impress people, e.g. *a showy house.*

shrapnel (noun) Shrapnel consists of small pieces of metal scattered from an exploding shell.

shred, shreds, shredding, shredded 1 (verb) If you shred something, you cut or tear it into very small pieces. **2** (noun) A shred of paper or material is a small, narrow piece of it. **3** If there is not a shred of something, there is absolutely none of it, e.g. *He was left without a shred of self-esteem.*

shrew, shrews (pronounced **shroo**) (noun) A shrew is a small mouse-like animal with a long pointed nose.

shrewd, shrewder, shrewdest (adjective) Someone who is shrewd is intelligent and makes good judgments. **shrewdly** (adverb).

shriek, shrieks, shrieking, shrieked 1 (noun) A shriek is a high-pitched scream. **2** (verb) If you shriek, you make a high-pitched scream.

shrift (noun) If you give someone or something short shrift, you pay very little attention to them.

shrill, shriller, shrillest (adjective) A shrill sound is unpleasantly high-pitched and piercing. **shrilly** (adverb).

shrimp, shrimps (noun) A shrimp is a small edible shellfish with a long tail and many legs.

shrine, shrines (noun) A shrine is a place of worship associated with a sacred person or object.

shrink, shrinks, shrinking, shrank, shrunk 1 (verb) If something shrinks, it becomes smaller. **2** If you shrink from something, you move away from it because you are afraid of it. **shrinkage** (noun).

shrivel, shrivels, shrivelling, shrivelled (verb) When something shrivels, it becomes dry and withered.

shroud, shrouds, shrouding, shrouded 1 (noun) A shroud is a cloth in which a dead body is wrapped before it is buried. **2** (verb) If something is shrouded in darkness or fog, it is hidden by it.

shrub, shrubs (noun) A shrub is a low, bushy plant.

shrug, shrugs, shrugging, shrugged 1 (verb) If you shrug your shoulders, you raise them slightly as a sign of indifference. **2** (noun) If you give a shrug of your shoulders, you shrug them.

shrunken (adjective; a formal use) Someone or something that is shrunken has become smaller than it used to be, e.g. *a shrunken old man.*

shudder, shudders, shuddering, shuddered 1 (verb) If you shudder, you tremble with fear or horror. **2** (noun) A shudder is a shiver of fear or horror. **3** (verb) If a machine or vehicle shudders, it shakes violently.

shuffle, shuffles, shuffling, shuffled 1 (verb) If you shuffle, you walk without lifting your feet properly off the ground. **2** (noun) A shuffle is the way someone walks when they shuffle. **3** (verb) If you shuffle about, you move about and fidget because you feel uncomfortable or embarrassed. **4** If you shuffle a pack of cards, you mix them up before you begin a game.

shun, shuns, shunning, shunned (verb) If you shun someone or something, you deliberately avoid them.

shunt, shunts, shunting, shunted (verb; an informal word) If you shunt people or things to a place, you move them there, e.g. *You are shunted from room to room.*

shut, shuts, shutting, shut 1 (verb) If you shut something, you close it. **2** (adjective) If something is shut, it is closed. **3** (verb) When a shop or pub shuts, it is closed and you can no longer go into it. **shut up** (verb; an informal expression) If you shut up, you stop talking.

shutter, shutters (noun) Shutters are hinged wooden or metal covers fitted on the outside or inside of a window.

shuttle, shuttles 1 (adjective) A shuttle service is an air, bus, or train service which makes frequent journeys between two places. **2** (noun) A shuttle is a plane used in a shuttle service.

shuttlecock, shuttlecocks (noun) A shuttlecock is the feathered object used as a ball in badminton.

shy, shyer, shyest; shies, shying, shied 1 (adjective) A shy person is nervous and uncomfortable in the company of other people. **2** (verb) When a horse shies, it moves away suddenly because something has frightened it. **3** If you shy away from doing something, you avoid doing it because you are afraid or nervous. **shyly** (adverb), **shyness** (noun).

sibling, siblings (noun; a formal word) Your siblings are your brothers and sisters.

sick, sicker, sickest 1 (adjective) If you are sick, you are ill. **2** If you feel sick, you feel as if you are going to vomit. If you are sick, you vomit. **3** (phrase) If something **makes you sick,** it makes you angry. **4** (adjective; an informal use) If you are sick of doing something, you feel you have been doing it too long. **5** (an informal use) A sick joke or story deals with death or suffering in an unpleasantly frivolous way. **sickness** (noun).

sicken, sickens, sickening, sickened (verb) If something sickens you, it makes you feel disgusted. **sickening** (adjective).

sickle, sickles (noun) A sickle is a tool with a short handle and a curved blade used for cutting grass or grain.

sickly, sicklier, sickliest 1 (adjective) A sickly person or animal is weak and unhealthy. **2** Sickly also means very unpleasant to smell, taste, or look at.

side, sides, siding, sided 1 (noun) Side refers to a position to the left or right of something, e.g. *the two armchairs on either side of the fireplace.* **2** The sides of a boundary or barrier are the two areas it separates, e.g. *this side of the border.* **3** Your sides are the parts of your body from your armpits down to your hips. **4** The sides of something are its outside surfaces, especially the surfaces which are not its front or back. **5** The sides of a hill or valley are the parts that slope. **6** (adjective) situated on a side of a building or vehicle, e.g. *the side door.* **7** A side road is a small road leading off a larger one. **8** (noun) The two sides in a war, argument, or relationship are the two people or groups involved. **9** A particular side of something is one aspect of it, e.g. *the sensitive, caring side of human nature.* **10** (verb) If you side with someone in an argument, you support them.

sideboard, sideboards (noun) A sideboard is a long, low cupboard for plates and glasses.

sideburns (plural noun) A man's sideburns are areas of hair growing on his cheeks in front of his ears.

side effect, side effects (noun) The side effects of a drug are the effects it has in addition to its main effects.

sidekick, sidekicks (noun; an informal word) Someone's sidekick is their friend who spends a lot of time with them.

sideline, sidelines (noun) A sideline is an extra job in addition to your main job.

sideshow, sideshows (noun) Sideshows are stalls at a fairground.

sidestep, sidesteps, sidestepping, sidestepped (verb) If you sidestep a difficult problem or question, you avoid dealing with it.

sidewalk, sidewalks (noun) In American English, a sidewalk is a pavement.

sideways (adverb) from or towards the side of something or someone.

siding, sidings (noun) A siding is a short railway track beside the main tracks, where engines and carriages are left when not in use.

sidle, sidles, sidling, sidled (verb) If you sidle somewhere, you walk there cautiously and slowly, as if you do not want to be noticed.

siege, sieges (pronounced **seej**) (noun) A siege is a military operation in which an army surrounds a place and prevents food or help from reaching the people inside.

sieve, sieves, sieving, sieved (pronounced **siv**) **1** (noun) A sieve is a kitchen implement used for sifting or straining things. It consists of a net attached to a ring of metal or plastic. **2** (verb) If you sieve a powder or liquid, you pass it through a sieve.

sift, sifts, sifting, sifted 1 (verb) If you sift a powdery substance, you pass it through a sieve to remove lumps. **2** If you sift through something such as evidence, you examine it all thoroughly.

sigh, sighs, sighing, sighed 1 (verb) When you sigh, you let out a deep breath. **2** (noun) A sigh is the breath you let out when you sigh.

sight, sights, sighting, sighted 1 (noun) Sight is the ability to see, e.g. *His sight was so poor that he could not follow the cricket.* **2** A sight is something you see, e.g. *It was a ghastly sight.* **3** (plural noun) Sights are interesting places which tourists visit. **4** (verb) If you sight someone or something, you see them briefly or suddenly, e.g. *He had been sighted in Cairo.* **5** (phrases) If something is **in sight,** you can see it. If it is **out of sight,** you cannot see it.

sighted (adjective) Someone who is sighted can see.

sighting, sightings (noun) A sighting of something rare is an occasion when it is seen.

sightseeing (noun) Sightseeing is visiting the interesting places that tourists usually visit. **sightseer** (noun).

sign, signs, signing, signed 1 (noun) A sign is a mark or symbol that always has a particular meaning, for example in mathematics or music. **2** A sign is also a gesture with a particular meaning. **3** A sign can also consist of words, a picture, or a symbol giving information or a warning. **4** If there are signs of something, there is evidence that it exists or is happening, e.g. *We are now seeing the first signs of recovery.* **5** (verb) If you sign a document, you write your name on it, e.g. *He hurriedly signed the death certificate.* **6** If you sign, you communicate by using sign language. **sign on 1** (verb) If you sign on for a job or course, you officially agree to do it by signing a contract. **2** When people sign on, they officially state that they are unemployed and claim benefit from the state.

signal, signals, signalling, signalled 1 (noun) A signal is a gesture, sound, or action intended to give a message to someone. **2** (verb) If you signal to someone, you make a gesture or sound to give them a message. **3** (noun) A railway signal is a piece of equipment beside the track which tells train drivers whether to stop or not.

signature, signatures (noun) If you write your signature, you write your name the way you usually write it.

significant 1 (adjective) A significant amount is a large amount. **2** Something that is significant is important, e.g. *a significant victory.* **significance** (noun), **significantly** (adverb).

signify, signifies, signifying, signified (verb) A sign or gesture that signifies something has a particular meaning, e.g. *They signified a desire to leave.*

sign language (noun) Sign language is a way of communicating using your hands, used especially by the deaf.

signpost, signposts (noun) A signpost is a road sign with information on it such as the name of a town and how far away it is.

Sikh, Sikhs (pronounced **seek**) (noun) A Sikh is a person who believes in Sikhism, an Indian religion which separated from Hinduism in the sixteenth century. Sikhs believe that there is only one God.

silence, silences, silencing, silenced 1 (noun) Silence is quietness. **2** Someone's silence about something is their failure or refusal to talk about it. **3** (verb) To silence someone or something means to stop them talking or making a noise.

silent 1 (adjective) If you are silent, you are not saying anything. **2** If you are silent about something, you do not tell people about it. **3** When something is silent, it makes no noise. **silently** (adverb).

silhouette, silhouettes (pronounced sil-loo-**ett**) (noun) A silhouette is the outline of a dark shape against a light background. **silhouetted** (adjective).

silicon (noun) Silicon is an element found in sand, clay, and stone. It is used to make parts of computers.

silk, silks (noun) Silk is a fine, soft cloth made from a substance produced by silkworms.

silkworm, silkworms (noun) Silkworms are the larvae of a particular kind of moth.

silky, silkier, silkiest (adjective) smooth and soft.

sill, sills (noun) A sill is a ledge at the bottom of a window.

silly, sillier, silliest (adjective) foolish or childish.

silt (noun) Silt is fine sand or soil which is carried along by a river.

silver 1 (noun) Silver is a valuable greyish-white metallic element used for making jewellery and ornaments. **2** Silver is also coins made from silver or from silver-coloured metal, e.g. *a handful of silver*. **3** (adjective or noun) greyish-white.

silver jubilee, silver jubilees (noun) A silver jubilee is the 25th anniversary of an important event.

silver medal, silver medals (noun) A silver medal is a medal made from silver awarded to the competitor who comes second in a competition.

silver wedding, silver weddings (noun) A couple's silver wedding is the 25th anniversary of their wedding.

silvery (adjective) having the appearance or colour of silver, e.g. *the silvery moon*.

similar 1 (adjective) If one thing is similar to another, or if two things are similar, they are like each other. **2** In maths, two triangles are similar if the angles in one correspond exactly to the angles in the other. **similarly** (adverb).

similarity, similarities (noun) If there is a similarity between things, they are similar in some way.

simile, similes (pronounced **sim**-ill-ee) (noun) A simile is an expression in which a person or thing is described as being similar to someone or something else. Examples of similes are *She runs like a deer* and *He's as white as a sheet*.

simmer, simmers, simmering, simmered (verb) When food simmers, it cooks gently at just below boiling point.

simple, simpler, simplest 1 (adjective) Something that is simple is uncomplicated and easy to understand or do. **2** Simple also means plain and not elaborate in style, e.g. *a simple coat.* **3** A simple way of life is uncomplicated. **4** Someone who is simple is mentally retarded. **5** You use 'simple' to emphasize that what you are talking about is the only important thing, e.g. *simple fear of loneliness.* **simplicity** (noun).

simple-minded (adjective) naive and unsophisticated, e.g. *simple-minded pleasures.*

simplify, simplifies, simplifying, simplified (verb) To simplify something means to make it easier to do or understand. **simplification** (noun).

simplistic (adjective) too simple or naive, e.g. *a rather simplistic approach to the subject.*

simply 1 (adverb) Simply means merely, e.g. *It was simply a question of making the decision.* **2** You use 'simply' to emphasize what you are saying, e.g. *It is simply not true.* **3** If you say or write something simply, you do it in a way that makes it easy to understand.

simulate, simulates, simulating, simulated (verb) To simulate something means to imitate it, e.g. *cast iron painted to simulate wrought iron.* **simulation** (noun).

simultaneous (adjective) Things that are simultaneous happen at the same time. **simultaneously** (adverb).

sin, sins, sinning, sinned 1 (noun) Sin is wicked and immoral behaviour. **2** (verb) To sin means to do something wicked and immoral.

since 1 (preposition, conjunction, or adverb) Since means from a particular time until now, e.g. *I've been waiting patiently since half past three.* **2** (adverb) Since also means at some time after a particular time in the past, e.g. *They split up and he has since remarried.* **3** (conjunction) Since also means because, e.g. *I'm forever on a diet, since I put on weight easily.*

sincere (adjective) If you are sincere, you say things that you really mean, e.g. *a sincere expression of friendliness.* **sincerity** (noun).

sincerely 1 (adverb) If you say or feel something sincerely, you mean it or feel it genuinely. **2** (phrase) You write **yours sincerely** before your signature at the end of a formal letter.

sinew, sinews (pronounced **sin**-yoo) (noun) A sinew is a tough cord in your body that connects a muscle to a bone.

sinful (adjective) wicked and immoral.

sing, sings, singing, sang, sung 1 (verb) When you sing, you make musical sounds with your voice, usually producing words that fit a tune. **2** When birds or insects sing, they make pleasant sounds. **singer** (noun).

singe, singes, singeing, singed 1 (verb) To singe something means to burn it slightly so that it goes brown but does not catch fire. **2** (noun) A singe is a slight burn.

single, singles, singling, singled 1 (adjective) Single means only one and not more, e.g. *A single shot was fired.* **2** People who are single are not married. **3** A single bed or bedroom is for one person. **4** A single ticket is a one-way ticket. **5** (noun) A single is a small record with one song on each side. **6** Singles is a game of tennis, badminton, or squash between just two players. **single out** (verb) If you single someone out from a group, you give them special treatment, e.g. *He'd been singled out for some special award.*

single-handed (adverb) If you do something single-handed, you do it on your own, without any help.

single-minded (adjective) A single-minded person has only one aim and is determined to achieve it.

singly (adverb) If people do something singly, they do it on their own or one by one.

singular 1 (noun) In grammar, the singular is the form of a word that refers to just one person or thing. **2** (adjective; a formal use) unusual and remarkable, e.g. *her singular beauty.* **singularity** (noun), **singularly** (adverb).

sinister (adjective) seeming harmful or evil, e.g. *something cold and sinister about him.*

sink, sinks, sinking, sank, sunk 1 (noun) A sink is a basin with taps supplying water, usually in a kitchen or bathroom. **2** (verb) If something sinks, it moves downwards, especially through water, e.g. *An Indian cargo ship sank in icy seas.* **3** To sink a ship means to cause it to sink by attacking it. **4** If an amount or value sinks, it decreases. **5** If you sink into an unpleasant state, you gradually pass into it, e.g. *These people sank into black despair.* **6** To sink something sharp into an object means to make it go deeply into it, e.g. *The tiger sank its teeth into his leg.*

sinner, sinners (noun) A sinner is someone who has committed a sin.

sinus, sinuses (noun) Your sinuses are the air passages in the bones of your skull, just behind your nose.

sip, sips, sipping, sipped 1 (verb) If you sip a drink, you drink it by taking a small amount at a time. **2** (noun) A sip is a small amount of drink that you take into your mouth.

siphon, siphons, siphoning, siphoned (pronounced **sigh**-fn); also spelled **syphon** (verb) If you siphon off a liquid, you draw it out of a container through a tube and transfer it to another place.

sir 1 (noun) Sir is a polite, formal way of addressing a man. **2** Sir is also the title used in front of the name of a knight or baronet.

siren, sirens (noun) A siren is a warning device, for example on a police car or ambulance, which makes a loud, wailing noise.

sirloin (noun) Sirloin is a prime cut of beef from the lower part of a cow's back.

sister, sisters 1 (noun) Your sister is a girl or woman who has the same parents as you.

2 A sister is a member of a female religious order. **3** In a hospital, a sister is a senior nurse who supervises a ward. **4** (adjective) Sister means closely related to something or very similar to it, e.g. *Citroen and its sister company Peugeot.*

sisterhood (noun) Sisterhood is a strong feeling of companionship between women.

sister-in-law, sisters-in-law (noun) Your sister-in-law is the wife of your brother, the sister of your husband or wife, or the woman married to your wife's or husband's brother.

sit, sits, sitting, sat 1 (verb) If you are sitting, your weight is supported by your buttocks rather than your feet. **2** When you sit or sit down somewhere, you lower your body until you are sitting. **3** If you sit an examination, you take it. **4** (a formal use) When a parliament, law court, or other official body sits, it meets and officially carries out its work.

site, sites, siting, sited 1 (noun) A site is a piece of ground where a particular thing happens or is situated, e.g. *a building site.* **2** (verb) If something is sited in a place, it is built or positioned there.

sitting, sittings 1 (noun) A sitting is one of the times when a meal is served. **2** A sitting is also one of the occasions when a parliament or law court meets and carries out its work.

sitting room, sitting rooms (noun) A sitting room is a room in a house where people sit and relax.

situated (adjective) If something is situated somewhere, that is where it is, e.g. *a town situated 45 minutes from Geneva.*

situation, situations 1 (noun) A situation is what is happening in a particular place at a particular time, e.g. *the political situation.* **2** The situation of a building or town is its surroundings, e.g. *a beautiful situation.*

six the number 6.

sixteen the number 16. **sixteenth**

sixth, sixths 1 The sixth item in a series is the one counted as number six. **2** (noun) A sixth is one of six equal parts.

sixth sense (noun) You say that someone has a sixth sense when they know something instinctively, without having any evidence of it.

sixty, sixties the number 60. **sixtieth**

sizable or **sizeable** (adjective) fairly large, e.g. *a sizable amount of money.*

size, sizes 1 (noun) The size of something is how big or small it is, e.g. *the size of the audience.* **2** The size of something is also the fact that it is very large, e.g. *the sheer size of Australia.* **3** A size is one of the standard measurements of clothes and shoes.

sizzle, sizzles, sizzling, sizzled (verb) If something sizzles, it makes a hissing sound like the sound of frying food.

skate, skates, skating, skated 1 (noun) Skates are ice skates or roller skates. **2** (verb) If you skate, you move about on ice wearing ice skates. **3** (noun) A skate is also a flat edible sea fish. **4** (verb) If you skate round a difficult subject, you avoid discussing it.

skateboard, skateboards (noun) A skateboard is a narrow board on wheels which you stand on and ride for fun.

skeleton, skeletons (noun) Your skeleton is the framework of bones in your body.

sketch, sketches, sketching, sketched 1 (noun) A sketch is a quick, rough drawing. **2** (verb) If you sketch something, you draw it quickly and roughly. **3** (noun) A sketch of a situation or incident is a brief description of it. **4** A sketch is also a short, humorous piece of acting.

sketchy, sketchier, sketchiest (adjective) giving only a rough description or account, e.g. *Details surrounding his death are sketchy.*

skew or **skewed** (pronounced **skyoo**) (adjective) in a slanting position, rather than straight or upright.

skewer, skewers, skewering, skewered 1 (noun) A skewer is a long metal pin used to hold pieces of food together during cooking. **2** (verb) If you skewer something, you push a skewer through it.

ski, skis, skiing, skied 1 (noun) Skis are long pieces of wood, metal, or plastic that you fasten to special boots so you can move easily on snow. **2** (verb) When you ski, you move on snow wearing skis.

skid, skids, skidding, skidded (verb) If a vehicle skids, it slides in an uncontrolled way, for example because the road is wet or icy.

skilful (adjective) If you are skilful at something, you can do it very well. **skilfully** (adverb).

skill, skills 1 (noun) Skill is the knowledge and ability that enables you to do something well. **2** A skill is a type of work or technique which requires special training and knowledge.

skilled 1 (adjective) A skilled person has the knowledge and ability to do something well. **2** Skilled work is work which can only be done by people who have had special training.

skim, skims, skimming, skimmed 1 (verb) If you skim something from the surface of a liquid, you remove it. **2** If something skims a surface, it moves along just above it, e.g. *seagulls skimming the waves.*

skimmed milk (noun) Skimmed milk has had the cream removed.

skin, skins, skinning, skinned 1 (noun) Your skin is the natural covering of your body. An animal skin is the skin and fur of a dead animal. **2** The skin of a fruit or vegetable is its outer covering. **3** A skin is also a solid layer which forms on the surface of a liquid. **4** (verb) If you skin a dead animal, you remove its skin. **5** If you skin a part of your body, you accidentally graze it.

skinny, skinnier, skinniest (adjective) extremely thin.

skip, skips, skipping, skipped 1 (verb) If you skip along, you move along jumping from one foot to the other. **2** (noun) Skips are the movements you make when you skip. **3** (verb) If you skip something, you miss it out or avoid doing it, e.g. *It is all too easy to skip meals.* **4** (noun) A skip is also a large metal container for holding rubbish and rubble.

skipper, skippers (noun; an informal word) The skipper of a ship or boat is its captain.

skirmish, skirmishes (noun) A skirmish is a short, rough fight.

skirt, skirts, skirting, skirted 1 (noun) A woman's skirt is a piece of clothing which fastens at her waist and hangs down over her legs. **2** (verb) Something that skirts an area is situated around the edge of it. **3** If you skirt something, you go around the edge of it, e.g. *We skirted the town.* **4** If you skirt a problem, you avoid dealing with it or talking about it, e.g. *He was skirting the real question.*

skirting, skirtings (noun) A skirting or skirting board is a narrow strip of wood running along the bottom of a wall in a room.

skittle, skittles (noun) Skittles is a game in which players roll a ball and try to knock down wooden objects called skittles.

skull, skulls (noun) Your skull is the bony part of your head which surrounds your brain.

skunk, skunks (noun) A skunk is a small black and white animal from North America which gives off an unpleasant smell when it is frightened.

sky, skies (noun) The sky is the space around the earth which you can see when you look upwards.

skylight, skylights (noun) A skylight is a window in a roof or ceiling.

skyline, skylines (noun) The skyline is the line where the sky meets buildings or the ground, e.g. *the New York City skyline.*

skyscraper, skyscrapers (noun) A skyscraper is a very tall building.

slab, slabs (noun) A slab is a thick, flat piece of something.

slack, slacker, slackest; slacks 1 (adjective) Something that is slack is loose and not firmly stretched or positioned. **2** (noun) The slack in a rope is the part that hangs loose. **3** (adjective) A slack period is one in which there is not much work to do. **4** (plural noun; an old-fashioned use) Slacks are casual trousers. **slackness** (noun).

slacken, slackens, slackening, slackened 1 (verb) If something slackens, it becomes slower or less intense, e.g. *The rain had slackened to a drizzle.* **2** To slacken also means to become looser, e.g. *Her grip slackened on Arnold's arm.*

slag, slags, slagging, slagged 1 (noun) Slag is the waste material left when ore has been melted down to remove the metal, e.g. *a slag heap.* **2** (verb; an informal use) To slag someone off means to criticize them in an unpleasant way, usually behind their back.

slalom, slaloms (pronounced

slah-lom) (noun) A slalom is a skiing competition in which the competitors have to twist and turn quickly to avoid a series of obstacles.

slam, slams, slamming, slammed 1 (verb) If you slam a door or if it slams, it shuts noisily and with great force. **2** If you slam something down, you throw it down violently, e.g. *She slammed the phone down.*

slander, slanders, slandering, slandered 1 (noun) Slander is something untrue and malicious said about someone. **2** (verb) To slander someone means to say untrue and malicious things about them. **slanderous** (adjective).

slang (noun) Slang consists of very informal words and expressions.

slant, slants, slanting, slanted 1 (verb) If something slants, it slopes, e.g. *The back can be adjusted to slant into the most comfortable position.* **2** (noun) A slant is a slope. **3** (verb) If news or information is slanted, it is presented in a biased way.

slap, slaps, slapping, slapped 1 (verb) If you slap someone, you hit them with the palm of your hand. **2** (noun) If you give someone a slap, you slap them. **3** (verb) If you slap something onto a surface, you put it there quickly and noisily.

slash, slashes, slashing, slashed 1 (verb) If you slash something, you make a long, deep cut in it. **2** (an informal use) To slash money means to reduce it greatly, e.g. *Car makers could be forced to slash prices.* **3** (noun) A slash is a diagonal line that separates letters, words, or numbers, for example in the number 340/21/K.

slat, slats (noun) Slats are the narrow pieces of wood, metal, or plastic in things such as Venetian blinds. **slatted** (adjective).

slate, slates, slating, slated 1 (noun) Slate is a dark grey rock that splits easily into thin layers. **2** Slates are small, flat pieces of slate used for covering roofs. **3** (verb; an informal use) If critics slate a play, film, or book, they criticize it severely.

slaughter, slaughters, slaughtering, slaughtered 1 (verb) To slaughter a large number of people means to kill them unjustly or cruelly. **2** (noun) Slaughter is the killing of many people. **3** (verb) To slaughter farm animals means to kill them for meat.

slave, slaves, slaving, slaved 1 (noun) A slave is someone who is owned by another person and must work for them. **2** (verb) If you slave for someone, you work very hard for them. **slavery** (noun).

slay, slays, slaying, slew, slain (verb; a literary word) To slay someone means to kill them.

sleazy, sleazier, sleaziest (adjective) A sleazy place looks dirty, run-down, and not respectable.

sled, sleds (noun) A sled is a sledge.

sledge, sledges (noun) A sledge is a vehicle on runners used for travelling over snow.

sledgehammer, sledgehammers (noun) A sledgehammer is a large, heavy hammer.

sleek, sleeker, sleekest 1 (adjective) Sleek hair is smooth and shiny. **2** Someone who is sleek looks rich and dresses elegantly.

sleep, sleeps, sleeping, slept 1 (noun) Sleep is the natural state of rest in which your eyes are closed and you are inactive and unconscious. **2** (verb) When you sleep, you rest in a state of sleep. **3** (noun) If you have a sleep, you sleep for a while, e.g. *He'll be ready for a sleep soon.* **4** (phrase) If a sick or injured animal **is put to sleep,** it is painlessly killed.

sleeper, sleepers 1 (noun) You use sleeper to say how deeply someone sleeps, e.g. *I'm a very heavy sleeper.* **2** A sleeper is a bed on a train, or a train which has beds on it. **3** Railway sleepers are the large, heavy beams that support the rails of a railway track.

sleeping bag, sleeping bags (noun) A sleeping bag is a large, warm bag for sleeping in.

sleeping pill, sleeping pills (noun) A sleeping pill or a sleeping tablet is a pill which you take to help you sleep.

sleepwalk, sleepwalks, sleepwalking, sleepwalked (verb) If you sleepwalk, you walk around while you are asleep.

sleepy, sleepier, sleepiest 1 (adjective) tired and ready to go to sleep. **2** A sleepy town or village is very quiet. **sleepily** (adverb), **sleepiness** (noun).

sleet (noun) Sleet is a mixture of rain and snow.

sleeve, sleeves (noun) The sleeves of a piece of clothing are the parts that cover your arms. **sleeveless** (adjective).

sleigh, sleighs (pronounced **slay**) (noun) A sleigh is a sledge.

slender 1 (adjective) attractively thin and graceful. **2** small in amount or degree, e.g. *the first slender hopes of peace.*

sleuth, sleuths (pronounced **slooth**) (noun; an old-fashioned word) A sleuth is a detective.

slew, slews, slewing, slewed 1 Slew is the past tense of **slay. 2** (verb) If a vehicle slews, it slides or skids, e.g. *The bike slewed into the crowd.*

slice, slices, slicing, sliced 1 (noun) A slice of cake, bread, or other food is a piece of it cut from a larger piece. **2** A slice is also a kitchen tool with a broad, flat blade, e.g. *a fish slice.* **3** (verb) If you slice food, you cut it into thin pieces. **4** To slice through something means to cut or move through it quickly, like a knife, e.g. *The ship sliced through the water.* **5** (noun) In sport, a slice is a stroke in which the player makes the ball go to one side, rather than straight ahead.

slick, slicker, slickest; slicks 1 (adjective) A slick person speaks easily and persuasively but is not sincere, e.g. *a slick TV presenter.* **2** A slick action is done quickly and smoothly, e.g. *slick passing and strong running.* **3** (noun) An oil slick is a layer of oil floating on the surface of the sea or a lake.

slide, slides, sliding, slid 1 (verb) When something slides, it moves smoothly over or against something else. **2** (noun) A slide is a small piece of photographic film which can be projected onto a screen so that you can see the picture. **3** A slide is also a small piece of glass on which you put something that you want to examine through a microscope. **4** In a playground, a slide is a structure with a steep, slippery slope for children to slide down.

slight, slighter, slightest; slights, slighting, slighted 1 (adjective) Slight means small in amount or degree, e.g. *a slight dent.* **2** (phrase) **Not in the slightest** means not at all, e.g. *This doesn't surprise me in the slightest.* **3** (adjective) A slight person has a slim body. **4** (verb) If you slight someone, you insult them by behaving rudely towards them. **5** (noun) A slight is rude or insulting behaviour. **slightly** (adverb).

slim, slimmer, slimmest; slims, slimming, slimmed 1 (adjective) A slim person is attractively thin. **2** (verb) If you are slimming, you are trying to lose weight. **3** (adjective) A slim object is thinner than usual, e.g. *a slim book.* **4** If there is only a slim chance that something will happen, it is unlikely to happen. **slimmer** (noun).

slime (noun) Slime is an unpleasant, thick, slippery substance.

slimy, slimier, slimiest 1 (adjective) covered in slime. **2** Slimy people are friendly and pleasant in an insincere way, e.g. *a slimy business partner.*

sling, slings, slinging, slung 1 (verb; an informal use) If you sling something somewhere, you throw it there. **2** If you sling a rope between two points, you attach it so that it hangs loosely between them. **3** (noun) A sling is a piece of cloth tied round a person's neck to support a broken or injured arm. **4** A sling is also a device made of ropes or cloth used for carrying things.

slip, slips, slipping, slipped 1 (verb) If you slip, you accidentally slide and lose your balance. **2** If something slips, it slides out of place accidentally, e.g. *One of the knives slipped from her grasp.* **3** If you slip somewhere, you go there quickly and quietly, e.g. *She slipped out of the house.* **4** If you slip something somewhere, you put it there quickly and quietly. **5** If something slips to a lower level or standard, it falls to that level or standard, e.g. *The shares slipped by 25p to 845p.* **6** (noun) A slip is a small mistake. **7** A slip of paper is a small piece of paper.

slipped disc, slipped discs (noun) A slipped disc is a painful condition in which one of the discs in your spine has moved out of its proper position.

slipper, slippers (noun) Slippers are loose, soft shoes that you wear indoors.

slippery 1 (adjective) smooth, wet, or greasy, and difficult to hold or walk on. **2** You describe a person as slippery when they cannot be trusted.

slipstream, slipstreams (noun) The slipstream of a car or plane is the flow of air directly behind it.

slit, slits, slitting, slit 1 (verb) If you slit something, you make a long, narrow cut in it. **2** (noun) A slit is a long, narrow cut or opening.

slither, slithers, slithering, slithered (verb) To slither somewhere means to move there by sliding along the ground in an uneven way, e.g. *The snake slithered into the water.*

sliver, slivers (noun) A sliver is a small, thin piece of something.

slob, slobs (noun; an informal word) A slob is a lazy, untidy person.

slog, slogs, slogging, slogged (verb; an informal word) If you slog at something, you work hard and steadily at it, e.g. *They are still slogging away at A level books.*

slogan, slogans (noun) A slogan is a short, easily-remembered phrase used in advertising or by a political party.

slop, slops, slopping, slopped 1 (verb) If a liquid slops, it spills over the edge of a container in a messy way. **2** (plural noun) You can refer to dirty water or liquid waste as slops.

slope, slopes, sloping, sloped 1 (noun) A slope is a flat surface that is at an angle, so that one end is higher than the other. **2** (verb) If a surface slopes, it is at an angle. **3** If something slopes, it leans to one side rather than being upright, e.g. *sloping handwriting.* **4** (noun) The slope of something is the angle at which it slopes.

sloppy, sloppier, sloppiest (an informal word) **1** (adjective) very messy or careless, e.g. *two sloppy performances.* **2** foolishly sentimental, e.g. *some sloppy love story.* **sloppily** (adverb), **sloppiness** (noun).

slot, slots, slotting, slotted 1 (noun) A slot is a narrow opening in a machine or container, for example for putting coins in. **2** (verb) When you slot something into something else, you put it into a space where it fits.

sloth, sloths (rhymes with **growth**) **1** (noun; a formal use) Sloth is laziness. **2** A sloth is an animal that lives in Central or South America. Sloths move very slowly and hang upside down from the branches of trees.

slouch, slouches, slouching, slouched (verb) If you slouch, you stand or sit with your shoulders and head drooping forwards.

slow, slower, slowest; slows, slowing, slowed 1 (adjective) moving, happening, or doing something with very little speed, e.g. *His progress was slow.* **2** (verb) If something slows, slows down, or slows up, it moves or happens more slowly. **3** (adjective) Someone who is slow is not very clever. **4** If a clock or watch is slow, it shows a time earlier than the correct one. **slowly** (adverb), **slowness** (noun).

slow motion (noun) Slow motion is movement which is much slower than normal, especially in a film, e.g. *It all seemed to happen in slow motion.*

sludge (noun) Sludge is thick mud or sewage.

slug, slugs 1 (noun) A slug is a small, slow-moving creative with a slimy body, like a snail without a shell. **2** (an informal use) A slug of an alcoholic drink such as whisky is a mouthful of it.

sluggish (adjective) moving slowly and without energy, e.g. *the sluggish waters.*

sluice, sluices, sluicing, sluiced 1 (noun) A sluice is a channel which carries water. It has an opening called a sluicegate which can be opened or closed to control the flow of water. **2** (verb) If you sluice something, you wash it by pouring water over it, e.g. *He sluiced his hands under a tap.*

slum, slums (noun) A slum is a poor, run-down area of a city.

slumber, slumbers, slumbering, slumbered (a literary word) **1** (noun) Slumber is sleep. **2** (verb) When you slumber, you sleep.

slump, slumps, slumping, slumped 1 (verb) If an amount or a value slumps, it falls suddenly by a large amount. **2** (noun) A slump is a sudden, severe drop in an amount or value, e.g. *the slump in house prices.* **3** A slump is also a time when there is economic decline and high unemployment. **4** (verb) If you slump somewhere, you fall or sit down heavily, e.g. *He slumped against the side of the car.*

slur, slurs, slurring, slurred 1 (noun) A slur is an insulting remark. **2** (verb) When people slur their speech, they do not say their words clearly, often because they are drunk or ill.

slurp, slurps, slurping, slurped (verb) If you slurp a drink, you drink it noisily.

slush (noun) Slush is wet melting snow. **slushy** (adjective).

slut, sluts (noun; an offensive word) A slut is a dirty, untidy woman, or one considered to be immoral.

sly, slyer or **slier, slyest** or **sliest 1** (adjective) A sly expression or remark shows that you know something other people do not know, e.g. *a sly smile.* **2** A sly person is cunning and good at deceiving people. **slyly** (adverb).

smack, smacks, smacking, smacked 1 (verb) If you smack someone, you hit them with your open hand. **2** (noun) If you give someone a smack, you smack them. **3** A smack is a loud, sharp noise, e.g. *He landed with a smack on the tank.* **4** (verb) If something smacks of something else, it reminds you of it, e.g. *His tale smacks of fantasy.* **5** (noun) A smack is also a small fishing boat.

small, smaller, smallest; smalls 1 (adjective) Small means not large in size, number, or amount. **2** Small means not important or significant, e.g. *small changes.* **3** (noun) The small of your back is the narrow part where your back curves slightly inwards.

smallpox (noun) Smallpox is a serious contagious disease that causes a fever and a rash.

small talk (noun) Small talk is conversation about unimportant things.

smart, smarter, smartest; smarts, smarting, smarted 1 (adjective) A smart person is clean and neatly dressed. **2** Smart means clever, e.g. *a smart idea.* **3** A smart movement is quick and sharp. **4** (verb) If a wound smarts, it stings. **5** If you are smarting from criticism or unkindness, you are feeling upset by it. **smartly** (adverb).

smarten, smartens, smartening, smartened (verb) If you smarten something up, you make it look tidier.

smash, smashes, smashing, smashed 1 (verb) If you smash something, you break it into a lot of pieces by hitting it or dropping it. **2** To smash through something such as a wall means to go through it by breaking it. **3** To smash against something means to hit it with great force, e.g. *An immense wave smashed against the hull.* **4** (noun; an informal use) If a play or film is a smash or a smash hit, it is very successful. **5** A smash is also a car crash. **6** In tennis, a smash is a stroke in which the player hits the ball downwards very hard.

smashing (adjective; an informal word) If you describe something as smashing, you mean you like it very much.

smattering (noun) A smattering of knowledge or information is a very small amount of it, e.g. *a smattering of Russian.*

smear, smears, smearing, smeared 1 (noun) A smear is a dirty, greasy mark on a surface, e.g. *a smear of blue lipstick.* **2** (verb) If something smears a surface, it makes dirty, greasy marks on it, e.g. *The blade was chipped and smeared.* **3** If you smear a surface with a greasy or sticky substance, you spread a layer of the substance over the surface. **4** (noun) A smear is also an untrue and malicious rumour.

smell, smells, smelling, smelled or **smelt 1** (noun) The smell of something is a quality it has which you perceive through your nose, e.g. *a smell of damp wood.* **2** (verb) If something smells or if you can smell it, it has a quality you can perceive through your nose, e.g. *He smelled of tobacco and garlic.* **3** (noun) Your sense of smell is your ability to smell things. **4** (verb) If you can smell something such as danger or trouble, you feel it is present or likely to happen.

smelly, smellier, smelliest (adjective) having a strong, unpleasant smell.

smelt, smelts, smelting, smelted (verb) To smelt a metal ore means to heat it until it melts, so that the metal can be extracted.

smile, smiles, smiling, smiled 1 (verb) When you smile, the corners of your mouth move outwards and slightly upwards because you are pleased or amused. **2** (noun) A smile is the expression you have when you smile.

smirk, smirks, smirking,

smirked 1 (verb) When you smirk, you smile in a sneering or sarcastic way, e.g. *The boy smirked and turned the volume up.* **2** (noun) A smirk is a sneering or sarcastic smile.

smith, smiths (noun) A smith is someone who makes things out of iron, gold, or another metal.

smitten (adjective) If you are smitten with someone or something, you are very impressed with or enthusiastic about them, e.g. *They were totally smitten with each other.*

smock, smocks (noun) A smock is a loose garment like a long blouse.

smog (noun) Smog is a mixture of fog and smoke which occurs in some cities.

smoke, smokes, smoking, smoked 1 (noun) Smoke is a mixture of gas and small particles sent into the air when something burns. **2** (verb) If something is smoking, smoke is coming from it. **3** When someone smokes a cigarette, cigar, or pipe, they suck smoke from it into their mouth and blow it out again. **4** To smoke fish or meat means to hang it over burning wood so that the smoke preserves it and gives it a pleasant flavour, e.g. *smoked bacon.* **smoker** (noun), **smoking** (noun).

smoky, smokier, smokiest (adjective) A smoky place is full of smoke.

smooth, smoother, smoothest; smooths, smoothing, smoothed 1 (adjective) A smooth surface has no roughness and no holes in it. **2** A smooth liquid or mixture has no lumps in it. **3** (verb) If you smooth something, you move your hands over it to make it smooth and flat. **4** (adjective) A smooth movement or process happens evenly and steadily, e.g. *smooth acceleration.* **5** Smooth also means successful and without problems, e.g. *staff responsible for the smooth running of the hall.* **smoothly** (adverb), **smoothness** (noun).

smother, smothers, smothering, smothered 1 (verb) If you smother a fire, you cover it with something to put it out. **2** To smother a person means to cover their face with something so that they cannot breathe. **3** To smother someone also means to give them too much love and protection, e.g. *She loved her own children, almost smothering them with love.*

smothered (adjective) completely covered with something, e.g. *a spectacular trellis smothered in climbing roses.*

smoulder, smoulders, smouldering, smouldered 1 (verb) When something smoulders, it burns slowly, producing smoke but no flames. **2** If a feeling is smouldering inside you, you feel it very strongly but do not show it, e.g. *smouldering with resentment.*

smudge, smudges, smudging, smudged 1 (noun) A smudge is a dirty or blurred mark or a smear on something. **2** (verb) If you smudge something, you make it dirty or messy by touching it.

smug, smugger, smuggest (adjective) Someone who is smug is very pleased with how good or clever they are. **smugly** (adverb), **smugness** (noun).

smuggle, smuggles, smuggling, smuggled (verb) To smuggle things or people into or out of a place means to take them there illegally or secretly.

smuggler, smugglers (noun) A smuggler is someone who smuggles goods illegally into a country.

snack, snacks (noun) A snack is a light, quick meal.

snag, snags, snagging, snagged 1 (noun) A snag is a small problem or disadvantage, e.g. *There is one snag: it is not true.* **2** (verb) If you snag your clothing, you damage it by catching it on something sharp.

snail, snails (noun) A snail is a small, slow-moving creature with a long, shiny body and a shell on its back.

snake, snakes, snaking, snaked 1 (noun) A snake is a long, thin, scaly reptile with no legs. **2** (verb) Something that snakes moves in long winding curves, e.g. *The queue snaked out of the shop.*

snap, snaps, snapping, snapped 1 (verb) If something snaps or if you snap it, it breaks with a sharp cracking noise. **2** (noun) A snap is the sound of something snapping. **3** (verb) If you snap something into a particular position, you move it there quickly with a sharp sound. **4** If an animal snaps at you, it shuts its jaws together quickly as if to bite you. **5** If someone snaps at you, they speak in a sharp, unfriendly way. **6** (adjective) A snap decision or action is taken suddenly without careful thought. **7** (noun; an informal use) A snap is a photograph taken quickly and casually.

snapshot, snapshots (noun) A snapshot is a photograph taken quickly and casually.

snare, snares, snaring, snared 1 (noun) A snare is a trap for catching birds or small animals. **2** (verb) To snare an animal or bird means to catch it using a snare.

snarl, snarls, snarling, snarled 1 (verb) When an animal snarls, it bares its teeth and makes a fierce growling noise. **2** (noun) A snarl is the noise an animal makes when it snarls. **3** (verb) If you snarl, you say something in a fierce, angry way.

snatch, snatches, snatching, snatched 1 (verb) If you snatch something, you reach out for it quickly and take it. **2** (noun) If you make a snatch at something, you reach out for it quickly to try to take it. **3** (verb) If you snatch an amount of time or an opportunity, you quickly make use of it. **4** (noun) A snatch of conversation or song is a very small piece of it.

sneak, sneaks, sneaking, sneaked 1 (verb) If you sneak somewhere, you go there quickly trying not to be seen or heard. **2** If you sneak something somewhere, you take it there secretly. **3** (noun; an informal use) A sneak is someone who tells people in authority that someone else has done something naughty or wrong.

sneaker, sneakers (noun) Sneakers are casual shoes with rubber soles.

sneaking (adjective) If you have a sneaking feeling about something or someone, you have this feeling rather reluctantly, e.g. *I had a sneaking suspicion that she was enjoying herself.*

sneaky, sneakier, sneakiest (adjective; an informal word) Someone who is sneaky does things secretly rather than openly.

sneer, sneers, sneering, sneered **1** (verb) If you sneer at someone or something, you show by your expression and your comments that you think they are stupid or inferior. **2** (noun) A sneer is the expression on someone's face when they sneer.

sneeze, sneezes, sneezing, sneezed **1** (verb) When you sneeze, you suddenly take in breath and blow it down your nose noisily, because there is a tickle in your nose. **2** (noun) A sneeze is an act of sneezing.

snide (adjective) A snide comment or remark criticizes someone in a nasty way.

sniff, sniffs, sniffing, sniffed **1** (verb) When you sniff, you breathe in air through your nose hard enough to make a sound. **2** If you sniff something, you smell it by sniffing. **3** (noun) A sniff is the noise you make when you sniff. **4** A sniff of something is a smell of it, e.g. *a sniff at the flowers.*

snigger, sniggers, sniggering, sniggered **1** (verb) If you snigger, you laugh quietly and disrespectfully, e.g. *They were sniggering at her accent.* **2** (noun) A snigger is a quiet, disrespectful laugh.

snip, snips, snipping, snipped **1** (verb) If you snip something, you cut it with scissors or shears in a single quick action. **2** (noun) A snip is a small cut made by scissors or shears.

snippet, snippets (noun) A snippet of something such as information or news is a small piece of it.

snob, snobs **1** (noun) A snob is someone who admires upper-class people and looks down on lower-class people. **2** A snob is also someone who believes that they are better than other people. **snobbery** (noun), **snobbish** (adjective).

snooker (noun) Snooker is a game played on a large table covered with smooth green cloth. Players score points by hitting different coloured balls into side pockets using a long stick.

snoop, snoops, snooping, snooped (verb; an informal word) Someone who is snooping is secretly looking round a place to find out things.

snooze, snoozes, snoozing, snoozed (an informal word) **1** (verb) If you snooze, you sleep lightly for a short time during the day. **2** (noun) A snooze is a short, light sleep.

snore, snores, snoring, snored **1** (verb) When a sleeping person snores, they make a loud noise each time they breathe. **2** (noun) A snore is the noise someone makes when they snore.

snorkel, snorkels (noun) A snorkel is a tube you can breathe through when you are swimming just under the surface of the sea. **snorkelling** (noun).

snort, snorts, snorting, snorted **1** (verb) When people or animals snort, they force breath out through their nose in a noisy way, e.g. *Sarah snorted with laughter.* **2** (noun) A snort is the noise you make when you snort.

snout, snouts (noun) An animal's snout is its nose.

snow, snows, snowing, snowed **1** (noun) Snow consists of flakes of ice crystals which fall from the sky in cold weather. **2** (verb) When it snows, snow falls from the sky.

snowball, snowballs, snowballing, snowballed **1** (noun) A snowball is a ball of snow. **2** (verb) When something such as a project snowballs, it grows rapidly.

snowdrift, snowdrifts (noun) A snowdrift is a deep pile of snow formed by the wind.

snowdrop, snowdrops (noun) A snowdrop is a small white flower which appears in early spring.

snowman, snowmen (noun) A snowman is a large mound of snow moulded into the shape of a person.

snub, snubs, snubbing, snubbed **1** (verb) To snub someone means to behave rudely towards them, especially by making an insulting remark or ignoring them. **2** (noun) A snub is an insulting remark or a piece of rude behaviour. **3** (adjective) A snub nose is short and turned-up.

snuff (noun) Snuff is powdered tobacco which people take by sniffing it up their noses.

snug (adjective) A snug place is warm and comfortable. If you are snug, you are warm and comfortable. **snugly** (adverb).

snuggle, snuggles, snuggling, snuggled (verb) If you snuggle somewhere, you cuddle up more closely to something or someone.

so **1** (adverb) So is used to refer back to what has just been mentioned, e.g. *Had he locked the car? If so, where were the keys?* **2** So is used to mean also, e.g. *He laughed, and so did Jarvis.* **3** (conjunction) 'So that' and 'so as' are used to introduce the reason for doing something, e.g. *to die so that you might live.* **4** (adverb) So can be used to mean 'therefore', e.g. *It's a bit expensive, so I don't think I will get one.* **5** So is used when you are talking about the degree or extent of something, e.g. *Why are you so cruel?* **6** So is used before words like 'much' and 'many' to say that there is a definite limit to something, e.g. *There are only so many questions that can be asked about the record.*

soak, soaks, soaking, soaked **1** (verb) To soak something or leave it to soak means to put it in a liquid and leave it there. **2** When a liquid soaks something, it makes it very wet. **3** When something soaks up a liquid, the liquid is drawn up into it.

soaked (adjective) extremely

wet.

soaking (adjective) If something is soaking, it is very wet.

soap, soaps (noun) Soap is a substance made of natural oils and fats and used for washing. **soapy** (adjective).

soap opera, soap operas (noun) A soap opera is a popular television drama serial about people's daily lives.

soar, soars, soaring, soared 1 (verb) If an amount soars, it quickly increases by a great deal, e.g. *Property prices soared.* **2** If something soars into the air, it quickly goes up into the air. **soaring** (adjective).

sob, sobs, sobbing, sobbed 1 (verb) When someone sobs, they cry in a noisy way, breathing in short breaths. **2** (noun) A sob is the noise made when you cry.

sober, soberer, soberest; sobers, sobering, sobered 1 (adjective) If someone is sober, they are not drunk. **2** Sober also means serious and thoughtful. **3** Sober colours are plain and rather dull. **4** (verb) To sober up means to become sober after being drunk. **soberly** (adverb).

sobering (adjective) Something which is sobering makes you serious and thoughtful, e.g. *the sobering lesson of the last year.*

so-called (adjective) You use so-called to say that the name by which something is called is incorrect or misleading, e.g. *the so-called great men.*

soccer (noun) Soccer is the same as football.

sociable (adjective) Sociable people are friendly and enjoy talking to other people. **sociability** (noun).

social 1 (adjective) to do with society or life within a society, e.g. *women from similar social backgrounds.* **2** to do with leisure activities that involve meeting other people. **socially** (adverb).

socialism (noun) Socialism is the political belief that the state should own industries on behalf of the people and that everyone should be equal. **socialist** (adjective or noun).

socialite, socialites (noun) A socialite is a person who goes to many fashionable, upper-class social events.

socialize, socializes, socializing, socialized; also spelled **socialise** (verb) When people socialize, they meet other people socially, for example at parties.

social security (noun) Social security is a system by which the government pays money regularly to people who have no other income or only a very small income.

social work (noun) Social work involves giving help and advice to people with serious financial or family problems. **social worker** (noun).

society, societies 1 (noun) Society is the people in a particular country or region, e.g. *a major problem in society.* **2** A society is an organization for people who have the same interest or aim. **3** Society is also rich, upper-class, fashionable people.

sociology (noun) Sociology is the study of human societies and the relationships between groups in these societies. **sociological** (adjective), **sociologist** (noun).

sock, socks (noun) Socks are pieces of clothing covering your foot and ankle.

socket, sockets 1 (noun) A socket is a place on a wall or on a piece of electrical equipment into which you can put a plug or bulb. **2** Any hollow part or opening into which another part fits can be called a socket, e.g. *eye sockets.*

sod (noun; a literary use) The sod is the surface of the ground, together with the grass and roots growing in it.

soda, sodas 1 (noun) Soda is the same as soda water. **2** Soda is also sodium in the form of crystals or a powder. It is used for baking or cleaning.

soda water, soda waters (noun) Soda water is fizzy water used for mixing with alcoholic drinks or fruit juice.

sodden (adjective) soaking wet.

sodium (noun) Sodium is a silvery-white chemical element which combines with other chemicals.

sofa, sofas (noun) A sofa is a long comfortable seat with a back and arms for two or three people.

soft, softer, softest 1 (adjective) Something soft is not hard, stiff, or firm. **2** Soft also means very gentle, e.g. *a soft breeze.* **3** A soft sound or voice is quiet and not harsh. **4** A soft colour or light is not bright. **softly** (adverb).

soft drink, soft drinks (noun) A soft drink is any cold, nonalcoholic drink.

soften, softens, softening, softened 1 (verb) If something is softened or softens, it becomes less hard, stiff, or firm. **2** If you soften, you become more sympathetic and less critical, e.g. *Phillida softened as she spoke.*

software (noun) Computer programs are known as software.

soggy, soggier, soggiest (adjective) unpleasantly wet or full of water.

soil, soils, soiling, soiled 1 (noun) Soil is the top layer on the surface of the earth in which plants grow. **2** (verb) If you soil something, you make it dirty. **soiled** (adjective).

solace (noun; a literary word) Solace is something that makes you feel less sad, e.g. *I found solace in writing.*

solar 1 (adjective) relating or belonging to the sun. **2** using the sun's light and heat as a source of energy, e.g. *a solar-powered calculator.*

solar system (noun) The solar system is the sun and all the planets, comets, and asteroids that orbit round it.

solder, solders, soldering, soldered 1 (verb) To solder two pieces of metal together means to join them with molten metal. **2** (noun) Solder is the soft metal used for soldering.

soldier, soldiers (noun) A soldier is a person in an army.

sole, soles, soling, soled 1 (adjective) The sole thing or person of a particular type is the only one of that type. **2** (noun) The sole of your foot or shoe is the underneath part. **3**

(verb) When a shoe is soled, a sole is fitted to it. **4** (noun) A sole is a flat sea-water fish which you can eat.

solely (adverb) If something involves solely one thing, it involves that thing and nothing else.

solemn (adjective) Solemn means serious rather than cheerful or humorous. **solemnly** (adverb), **solemnity** (noun).

solicitor, solicitors (noun) A solicitor is a lawyer who gives legal advice and prepares legal documents and cases.

solid, solids 1 (adjective) A solid substance or object is hard or firm, and not in the form of a liquid or gas. **2** (noun) A solid is a solid substance or object. **3** (adjective) You say that something is solid when it is not hollow, e.g. *solid steel.* **4** You say that a structure is solid when it is strong and not likely to fall down, e.g. *solid fences.* **5** You use solid to say that something happens for a period of time without interruption, e.g. *I cried for two solid days.* **solidly** (adverb).

solidarity (noun) If a group of people show solidarity, they show unity and support for each other.

soliloquy, soliloquies (pronounced sol-**lill**-ok-wee) (noun) A soliloquy is a speech in a play made by a character who is alone on the stage.

solitary 1 (adjective) A solitary activity is one that you do on your own. **2** A solitary person or animal spends a lot of time alone. **3** If there is a solitary person or object somewhere, there is only one.

solitary confinement (noun) A prisoner in solitary confinement is being kept alone in a prison cell.

solitude (noun) Solitude is the state of being alone.

solo, solos 1 (noun) A solo is a piece of music played or sung by one person alone. **2** (adjective) A solo performance or activity is done by one person alone, e.g. *my first solo flight.* **3** (adverb) Solo means alone, e.g. *to sail solo around the world.*

soloist, soloists (noun) A soloist is a person who performs a solo.

solstice, solstices (noun) A solstice is one of the two times in the year when the sun is furthest away from the equator.

soluble (adjective) A soluble substance is able to dissolve in liquid.

solution, solutions 1 (noun) A solution is a way of dealing with a problem or difficult situation, e.g. *a quick solution to our problem.* **2** The solution to a riddle or a puzzle is the answer. **3** A solution is also a liquid in which a solid substance has been dissolved.

solve, solves, solving, solved (verb) If you solve a problem or a question, you find a solution or answer to it.

solvent, solvents 1 (adjective) If a person or company is solvent, they have enough money to pay all their debts. **2** (noun) A solvent is a liquid that can dissolve other substances. **solvency** (noun).

Somali, Somalis 1 (adjective) belonging or relating to Somalia. **2** (noun) The Somalis are a group of people who live in Somalia.

sombre 1 (adjective) Sombre colours are dark and dull. **2** A sombre person is serious, sad, or gloomy.

some 1 You use some to refer to a quantity or number when you are not stating the quantity or number exactly, e.g. *There's some money on the table.* **2** You use some to emphasize that a quantity or number is fairly large, e.g. *She had been there for some days.* **3** (adverb) You use some in front of a number to show that it is not exact, e.g. *a fishing village some seven miles north.*

somebody (pronoun) Somebody means someone.

some day (adverb) Some day means at a date in the future that is unknown or that has not yet been decided.

somehow 1 (adverb) You use somehow to say that you do not know how something was done or will be done, e.g. *You'll find a way of doing it somehow.* **2** You use somehow to say that you do not know the reason for something, e.g. *Somehow it didn't feel right.*

someone (pronoun) You use someone to refer to a person without saying exactly who you mean.

somersault, somersaults (noun) A somersault is a forwards or backwards roll in which the head is placed on the ground and the body is brought over it.

something (pronoun) You use something to refer to anything that is not a person without saying exactly what you mean.

sometime 1 (adverb) at a time in the future or the past that is unknown or that has not yet been fixed, e.g. *He has to find out sometime.* **2** (adjective; a formal use) Sometime is used to say that a person had a particular job or role in the past, e.g. *a sometime actress, dancer and singer.*

sometimes (adverb) occasionally, rather than always or never.

somewhat (adverb) to some extent or degree, e.g. *The future seemed somewhat bleak.*

somewhere 1 (adverb) Somewhere is used to refer to a place without stating exactly where it is, e.g. *There has to be a file somewhere.* **2** Somewhere is used when giving an approximate amount, number, or time, e.g. *somewhere between the winter of 1989 and the summer of 1991.*

son, sons (noun) Someone's son is their male child.

sonar (noun) Sonar is equipment on a ship which calculates the depth of the sea or the position of an underwater object using sound waves.

sonata, sonatas (noun) A sonata is a piece of classical music written for the piano or for a piano and one other instrument.

song, songs (noun) A song is a piece of music with words that are sung to the music.

son-in-law, sons-in-law (noun) Someone's son-in-law is the husband of their daughter.

sonnet, sonnets (noun) A sonnet is a poem with 14 lines, in which lines rhyme according to fixed patterns.

soon, sooner, soonest (adverb) If something is going to happen soon, it will happen in a very short time.

soot (noun) Soot is black powder which rises in the smoke from a fire. **sooty** (adjective).

soothe, soothes, soothing, soothed 1 (verb) If you soothe someone who is angry or upset, you make them calmer. **2** Something that soothes pain makes the pain less severe. **soothing** (adjective).

sophisticated 1 (adjective) Sophisticated people have refined or cultured tastes or habits. **2** A sophisticated machine or device is made using advanced methods. **sophistication** (noun).

soppy, soppier, soppiest (adjective; an informal word) silly or foolishly sentimental.

soprano, sopranos (noun) A soprano is a woman, girl, or boy with a high singing voice.

sorcerer, sorcerers (pronounced **sor**-ser-er) (noun) A sorcerer is a person who performs magic by using the power of evil spirits.

sorceress, sorceresses (noun) A sorceress is a female sorcerer.

sorcery (noun) Sorcery is magic that uses the power of evil spirits.

sordid 1 (adjective) dishonest or immoral, e.g. *a rather sordid business.* **2** dirty, unpleasant, or depressing, e.g. *the sordid guest house.*

sore, sorer, sorest; sores 1 (adjective) If part of your body is sore, it causes you pain and discomfort. **2** (noun) A sore is a painful place where your skin has become infected. **3** (adjective; a literary use) 'Sore' is used to emphasize something, e.g. *in sore need of firm government.* **sorely** (adverb), **soreness** (noun).

sorrow, sorrows 1 (noun) Sorrow is deep sadness or regret. **2** Sorrows are things that cause sorrow, e.g. *the sorrows of this world.*

sorry, sorrier, sorriest 1 (adjective) If you are sorry about something, you feel sadness, regret, or sympathy because of it, e.g. *I was so sorry to hear about your husband.* **2** Sorry is used to describe people and things that are in a bad physical or mental state, e.g. *She was in a pretty sorry state when we found her.*

sort, sorts, sorting, sorted 1 (noun) The different sorts of something are the different types of it. **2** (verb) To sort things means to arrange them into different groups or sorts. **sort out** (verb) If you sort out a problem or misunderstanding, you deal with it and find a solution to it.

SOS (noun) An SOS is a signal that you are in danger and need help.

so-so (adjective) neither good nor bad, e.g. *The food is so-so.*

soufflé, soufflés (pronounced **soo**-flay); also spelled **souffle** (noun) A soufflé is a light, fluffy food made from beaten egg whites and other ingredients.

sought the past tense and past

participle of **seek**.

soul, souls 1 (noun) A person's soul is the spiritual part of them that is supposed to continue after their body is dead. **2** People also use soul to refer to a person's mind, character, thoughts, and feelings. **3** Soul can be used to mean person, e.g. *There was not a soul there.* **4** Soul is a type of pop music.

sound, sounds, sounding, sounded; sounder, soundest 1 (noun) Sound is everything that can be heard. **2** A particular sound is something that you hear. **3** (verb) If something sounds or if you sound it, it makes a noise. **4** (noun) The sound of someone or something is the impression you have of them, e.g. *I like the sound of your father's grandfather.* **5** (adjective) in good condition, e.g. *a guarantee that a house is sound.* **6** reliable and sensible, e.g. *The logic behind the argument seems sound.* **7** (verb) To sound something deep, such as a well or the sea, means to measure how deep it is. **soundly** (adverb).

sound effect, sound effects (noun) Sound effects are sounds created artificially to make a play more realistic, especially a radio play.

soundproof (adjective) If a room is soundproof, sound cannot get into it or out of it.

soup, soups (noun) Soup is liquid food made by boiling meat, fish, or vegetables in water.

sour, sours, souring, soured 1 (adjective) If something is sour, it has a sharp, acid taste. **2** Sour milk has an unpleasant taste because it is no longer fresh. **3** A sour person is bad-tempered and unfriendly. **4** (verb) If a friendship, situation, or attitude sours or if something sours it, it becomes less friendly, enjoyable, or hopeful.

source, sources 1 (noun) The source of something is the person, place, or thing that it comes from, e.g. *the source of his confidence.* **2** The source of a river or stream is the place where it begins.

south 1 (noun) The south is the direction to your right when you are looking towards the place where the sun rises. **2** The south of a place or country is the part which is towards the south when you are in the centre. **3** (adverb or adjective) South means towards the south, e.g. *The taxi headed south... the south end of the site.* **4** (adjective) A south wind blows from the south.

South America (noun) South America is the fourth largest continent. It has the Pacific Ocean on its west side, the Atlantic on the east, and the Antarctic to the south. **South American** (adjective).

south-east (noun, adverb, or adjective) South-east is halfway between south and east.

south-easterly 1 (adjective) South-easterly means to or towards the south-east. **2** A south-easterly wind blows from the south-east.

south-eastern (adjective) in or from the south-east.

southerly 1 (adjective) Southerly means to or towards the south. **2** A southerly wind blows from the south.

southern (adjective) in or from the south.

South Pole (noun) The South Pole is the place on the surface of the earth that is farthest towards the south.

southward or **southwards** **1** (adverb) Southward or southwards means towards the south, e.g. *the dusty road which led southwards.* **2** (adjective) The southward part of something is the south part.

south-west (noun, adverb, or adjective) South-west is halfway between south and west.

south-westerly **1** (adjective) South-westerly means to or towards the south-west. **2** A south-westerly wind blows from the south-west.

south-western (adjective) in or from the south-west.

souvenir, souvenirs (noun) A souvenir is something you acquire and keep to remind you of a holiday, place, or event.

sovereign, sovereigns (pronounced **sov**-rin) **1** (noun) A sovereign is a king, queen, or royal ruler of a country. **2** (adjective) A sovereign state or country is independent and not under the authority of any other country. **3** (noun) In the past, a sovereign was a coin worth £1.

sovereignty (pronounced **sov**-rin-tee) (noun) Sovereignty is the political power that a country has to govern itself.

Soviet, Soviets (pronounced **soe**-vee-et) **1** (adjective) belonging or relating to the country that used to be the Soviet Union. **2** (noun) The people and the government of the country that used to be the Soviet Union were sometimes called the Soviets.

sow, sows, sowing, sowed, sown (pronounced **soh**) (verb) To sow seeds or sow an area of land with seeds means to plant them in the ground.

sow, sows (rhymes with **now**) (noun) A sow is an adult female pig.

soya (noun) Soya flour, margarine, oil, and milk are made from soya beans.

soya bean, soya beans (noun) Soya beans are a type of edible Asian bean.

spa, spas (noun) A spa is a place where water containing minerals bubbles out of the ground. People drink or bathe in the water to improve their health.

space, spaces, spacing, spaced **1** (noun) Space is the area that is empty or available in a place, building, or container. **2** Space is the area beyond the earth's atmosphere surrounding the stars and planets. **3** A space is a gap between two things, e.g. *the space between the tables.* **4** Space can also refer to a period of time, e.g. *two incidents in the space of a week.* **5** (verb) If you space a series of things, you arrange them with gaps between them.

spaceman, spacemen (noun) A spaceman is someone who travels in space.

spaceship, spaceships (noun) A spaceship is a spacecraft that carries people through space.

space shuttle, space shuttles (noun) A space shuttle is a spacecraft designed to be used many times for travelling out into space and back again.

spacious (adjective) having or providing a lot of space, e.g. *the spacious living room.*

spade, spades 1 (noun) A spade is a tool with a flat metal blade and a long handle used for digging. **2** Spades is one of the four suits in a pack of playing cards. It is marked by a black symbol in the shape of a heart-shaped leaf with a stem.

spaghetti (pronounced spag-**get**-ee) (noun) Spaghetti consists of long, thin pieces of pasta.

span, spans, spanning, spanned 1 (noun) A span is the period of time during which something exists or functions, e.g. *looking back today over a span of forty years.* **2** (verb) If something spans a particular length of time, it lasts throughout that time, e.g. *a career that spanned 50 years.* **3** (noun) The span of something is the total length of it from one end to the other. **4** (verb) A bridge that spans something stretches right across it.

spangle, spangles, spangling, spangled 1 (verb) If something is spangled, it is covered with small, sparkling objects. **2** (noun) Spangles are small sparkling pieces of metal or plastic used to decorate clothing or hair.

Spaniard, Spaniards (pronounced **span**-yard) (noun) A Spaniard is someone who comes from Spain.

spaniel, spaniels (noun) A spaniel is a gun dog with long drooping ears and a silky coat.

Spanish 1 (adjective) belonging or relating to Spain. **2** (noun) Spanish is the main language spoken in Spain, and is also spoken by many people in Central and South America.

spank, spanks, spanking, spanked (verb) If a child is spanked, it is punished by being slapped, usually on its leg or bottom.

spanner, spanners (noun) A spanner is a tool with a specially shaped end that fits round a nut to turn it.

spar, spars, sparring, sparred 1 (verb) When boxers spar, they hit each other with light punches for exercise or practice. **2** To spar with someone also means to argue with them, but not in an unpleasant or serious way. **3** (noun) A spar is a strong pole that a sail is attached to on a yacht or ship.

spare, spares, sparing, spared 1 (adjective) extra to what is needed, e.g. *What does she do in her spare time?* **2** (noun) A spare is anything that is extra to what is needed. **3** (verb) If you spare something for a particular purpose, you make it available, e.g. *Few troops could be spared to go abroad.* **4** If someone is spared an unpleasant experience, they are prevented from suffering it, e.g. *The capital was spared the misery of an all-out train strike.*

sparing (adjective) If you are sparing with something, you use it in very small quantities. **sparingly** (adverb).

spark, sparks, sparking, sparked

1 (noun) A spark is a tiny, bright piece of burning material thrown up by a fire. 2 A spark also is a small flash of light caused by electricity. 3 A spark of feeling is a small amount of it, e.g. *that tiny spark of excitement.* 4 (verb) If something sparks, it throws out sparks. 5 If one thing sparks another thing off, it causes the second thing to start happening, e.g. *The tragedy sparked off a wave of sympathy among staff.*

sparkle, sparkles, sparkling, sparkled 1 (verb) If something sparkles, it shines with a lot of small, bright points of light. **2** (noun) Sparkles are small, bright points of light. **sparkling** (adjective).

sparrow, sparrows (noun) A sparrow is a very common, small bird with brown and grey feathers.

sparse, sparser, sparsest (adjective) small in number or amount and spread out over an area, e.g. *the sparse audience.* **sparsely** (adverb).

spartan (adjective) A spartan way of life is very simple with no luxuries, e.g. *spartan accommodation.*

spasm, spasms 1 (noun) A spasm is a sudden tightening of the muscles. **2** A spasm is also a sudden, short burst of something, e.g. *a spasm of fear.*

spasmodic (adjective) happening suddenly for short periods of time at irregular intervals, e.g. *spasmodic movements.*

spastic, spastics 1 (adjective) A spastic person is born with a disability which makes it difficult for them to control their muscles. **2** (noun) A spastic is a spastic person.

spate (noun) A spate of things is a large number of them that happen or appear in a rush, e.g. *a recent spate of first novels from older writers.*

spatial (pronounced **spay**-shl) (adjective) to do with size, area, or position.

spatter, spatters, spattering, spattered 1 (verb) If something spatters a surface, it covers the surface with drops of liquid. **2** (noun) A spatter of something is a small amount of it in drops or tiny pieces.

spawn, spawns, spawning, spawned 1 (noun) Spawn is a jelly-like substance containing the eggs of fish or amphibians. **2** (verb) When fish or amphibians spawn, they lay their eggs. **3** If something spawns something else, it causes it, e.g. *The depressed economy spawned the riots.*

speak, speaks, speaking, spoke, spoken 1 (verb) When you speak, you use your voice to say words. **2** If you speak a foreign language, you know it and can use it.

speaker, speakers 1 (noun) A speaker is a person who is speaking, especially someone making a speech. **2** A speaker on a radio or hi-fi is a loudspeaker.

spear, spears, spearing, speared 1 (noun) A spear is a weapon consisting of a long pole with a sharp point. **2** (verb) To spear something means to push a spear or other pointed object into it.

spearhead, spearheads, spear-

heading, spearheaded (verb) If someone spearheads a campaign, they lead it.

spec, specs (an informal word) **1** (plural noun) Someone's specs are their glasses. **2** (phrase) If you do something **on spec,** you do it hoping for a result but without any certainty, e.g. *He turned up at the same event on spec.*

special 1 (adjective) Something special is more important or better than other things of its kind. **2** Special describes someone who is officially appointed, or something that is needed or intended for a particular purpose, e.g. *Karen actually had to get special permission to go there.* **3** Special also describes something that belongs or relates to only one particular person, group, or place, e.g. *the special needs of the chronically sick.*

specialist, specialists 1 (noun) A specialist is someone who has a particular skill or who knows a lot about a particular subject, e.g. *a skin specialist.* **2** (adjective) having a skill or knowing a lot about a particular subject, e.g. *a specialist teacher.*

speciality, specialities (noun) A person's speciality is something they are especially good at or know a lot about, e.g. *Yorkshire puddings are her speciality.*

specialize, specializes, specializing, specialized; also spelled **specialise** (verb) If you specialize in something, you make it your speciality, e.g. *There's a shop up there specializing in ceramics.* **specialization** (noun).

specialized or **specialised** (adjective) developed for a particular purpose or trained in a particular area of knowledge, e.g. *a specialized sales team.*

specially (adverb) If something has been done specially for a particular person or purpose, it has been done only for that person or purpose.

species (pronounced **spee**-sheez) (noun) A species is a class of plants or animals whose members have the same characteristics and are able to breed with each other.

specific 1 (adjective) particular, e.g. *specific areas of difficulty.* **2** precise and exact, e.g. *She will ask for specific answers.* **specifically** (adverb).

specification, specifications (noun) A specification is a detailed description of what is needed for something, such as the necessary features in the design of something, e.g. *I like to build it to my own specifications.*

specify, specifies, specifying, specified (verb) To specify something means to state or describe it clearly and precisely, e.g. *In his will he specified that these documents were never to be removed.*

specimen, specimens (noun) A specimen of something is an example or small amount of it which gives an idea of what the whole is like, e.g. *a specimen of your writing.*

speck, specks (noun) A speck is a very small stain, mark, or amount of something.

speckled (adjective) Something that is speckled is covered in very small marks or spots.

spectacle, spectacles 1 (plural noun) Someone's spectacles are their glasses. **2** (noun) A spectacle is a strange or interesting sight or scene, e.g. *an astonishing spectacle.* **3** A spectacle is also a grand and impressive event or performance.

spectacular, spectaculars 1 (adjective) Something spectacular is very impressive or dramatic. **2** (noun) A spectacular is an impressive show or performance.

spectator, spectators (noun) A spectator is a person who is watching something.

spectra the plural of **spectrum.**

spectre, spectres 1 (noun) A spectre is a frightening idea or image, e.g. *the spectre of war.* **2** A spectre is a ghost.

spectrum, spectra or **spectrums 1** (noun) The spectrum is the range of different colours produced when light passes through a prism or a drop of water. A rainbow shows the colours in a spectrum. **2** A spectrum of opinions or emotions is a range of them.

speculate, speculates, speculating, speculated (verb) If you speculate about something, you think about it and form opinions about it based on the information available to you. **speculation** (noun).

speculative 1 (adjective) A speculative piece of information is based on guesses and opinions rather than known facts. **2** Someone with a speculative expression seems to be trying to guess something, e.g. *His mother regarded him with a speculative eye.*

speech, speeches 1 (noun) Speech is the ability to speak or the act of speaking. **2** A speech is a formal talk given to an audience. **3** In a play, a speech is a group of lines spoken by one of the characters.

speechless (adjective) Someone who is speechless is temporarily unable to speak because something has shocked them.

speed, speeds, speeding, sped or **speeded 1** (noun) The speed of something is the rate at which it moves, travels, or happens. **2** Speed is very fast movement or travel. **3** (verb) If you speed somewhere, you move or travel there quickly. **4** Someone who is speeding is driving a vehicle faster than the legal speed limit.

speedboat, speedboats (noun) A speedboat is a small, fast motorboat.

speed limit, speed limits (noun) The speed limit is the maximum speed at which vehicles are legally allowed to drive on a particular road.

speedway (noun) Speedway is the sport of racing lightweight motorcycles on special tracks.

speedy, speedier, speediest (adjective) done very quickly. **speedily** (adverb).

spell, spells, spelling, spelled or **spelt 1** (verb) When you spell a word, you name or write its letters in order. **2** When letters spell a word, they form that word when put together in a particular order. **3** If something spells a particular result, it suggests that this will be the result, e.g. *This haphazard method could spell disaster for you.* **4** (noun) A spell of something is a short period of it, e.g. *a spell of rough weather.* **5** A spell is a word or sequence of words used to perform magic. **spell out** (verb) If you spell something out, you explain it in detail, e.g. *I don't have to spell it out, do I?*

spellbound (adjective) so fascinated by something that you cannot think about anything else, e.g. *The social world in London was spellbound by the couple.*

spelling, spellings (noun) The spelling of a word is the correct order of letters in it.

spend, spends, spending, spent **1** (verb) When you spend money, you buy things with it. **2** To spend time or energy means to use it.

spent 1 (adjective) Spent describes things which have been used and therefore cannot be used again, e.g. *spent matches.* **2** If you are spent, you are exhausted.

sperm, sperms (noun) A sperm is a cell produced in the sex organ of a male animal which can enter a female animal's egg and fertilize it.

spew, spews, spewing, spewed **1** (verb) When things spew from something or when it spews them out, they come out of it in large quantities. **2** (an informal use) To spew up means to vomit.

sphere, spheres 1 (noun) A sphere is a perfectly round object, such as a ball. **2** An area of activity or interest can be referred to as a sphere of activity or interest. **spherical** (adjective).

sphinx, sphinxes (pronounced **sfingks**) **1** (noun) In mythology, the sphinx was a monster with a person's head and a lion's body. **2** A person who seems mysterious or puzzling can be called a sphinx.

spice, spices, spicing, spiced 1 (noun) Spice is powder or seeds from a plant added to food to give it flavour. **2** (verb) To spice food means to add spice to it. **3** (noun) Spice is something which makes life more exciting, e.g. *Variety is the spice of life.* **4** (verb) If you spice something up, you make it more exciting.

spicy, spicier, spiciest (adjective) strongly flavoured with spices.

spider, spiders (noun) A spider is a small insect-like creature with eight legs. Most spiders spin webs in which they catch insects for food.

spike, spikes 1 (noun) A spike is a long pointed piece of metal. **2** The spikes on a sports shoe are the pointed pieces of metal attached to the sole. **3** Some other long pointed objects are called spikes, e.g. *beautiful pink flower spikes.*

spiky, spikier, spikiest (adjective) Something spiky has sharp points.

spill, spills, spilling, spilled or **spilt 1** (verb) If you spill something or if it spills, it accidentally falls or runs out of a container. **2** If people or things spill out of a place, they come out of it in large numbers.

spillage, spillages (noun) A spillage is the spilling of something, or something that has been spilt, e.g. *the oil* *spillage in the Shetlands.*

spin, spins, spinning, spun 1 (verb) If something spins, it turns quickly around a central point. **2** (noun) A spin is a rapid turn around a central point, e.g. *clubs which put less spin on the ball.* **3** (verb) When spiders spin a web, they give out a sticky substance and make it into a web. **4** When people spin, they make thread by twisting together pieces of fibre using a machine. **5** If your head is spinning, you feel dizzy or confused.

spinach (pronounced **spin**-ij) (noun) Spinach is a vegetable with large green leaves.

spinal (adjective) to do with the spine.

spine, spines 1 (noun) Your spine is your backbone. **2** Spines are long, sharp points on an animal's body or on a plant.

spinning wheel, spinning wheels (noun) A spinning wheel is a wooden machine for spinning flax or wool.

spin-off, spin-offs (noun) A spin-off is something useful that unexpectedly results from an activity.

spinster, spinsters (noun) A spinster is a woman who has never married.

spiral, spirals, spiralling, spiralled 1 (noun) A spiral is a continuous curve which winds round and round, with each curve above or outside the previous one. **2** (adjective) in the shape of a spiral, e.g. *a spiral staircase.* **3** (verb) If something spirals, it moves up or down in a spiral curve, e.g. *The aircraft spiralled down.* **4** If an amount or level spirals, it rises or falls quickly at an increasing rate, e.g. *Prices have spiralled recently.*

spire, spires (noun) The spire of a church is the tall cone-shaped structure on top.

spirit, spirits, spiriting, spirited 1 (noun) Your spirit is the part of you that is not physical and that is connected with your deepest thoughts and feelings. **2** The spirit of a dead person is a nonphysical part that is believed to remain alive after death. **3** A spirit is a supernatural being, such as a ghost. **4** Spirit is liveliness, energy, and self-confidence, e.g. *a band full of spirit.* **5** Spirit can refer to an attitude, e.g. *his old fighting spirit.* **6** (plural noun) Spirits can describe how happy or unhappy someone is, e.g. *in good spirits.* **7** Spirits are strong alcoholic drinks such as whisky and gin. **8** (verb) If you spirit someone or something into or out of a place, you get them in or out quickly and secretly.

spirited (adjective) showing energy and courage.

spirit level, spirit levels (noun) A spirit level is a device for finding out if a surface is level. It consists of a bubble of air sealed in a tube of liquid in a wooden or metal frame.

spiritual, spirituals 1 (adjective) to do with people's thoughts and beliefs, rather than their bodies and physical surroundings. **2** to do with people's religious beliefs, e.g. *spiritual guidance.* **3** (noun) A spiritual is a religious song originally sung by Black slaves in America. **spiritually** (adverb), **spirituality** (noun).

spit, spits, spitting, spat **1** (noun) Spit is saliva. **2** (verb) If you spit, you force saliva or some other substance out of your mouth. **3** When it is spitting, it is raining very lightly. **4** (noun) A spit is a long stick made of metal or wood which is pushed through a piece of meat so that it can be hung over a fire and cooked.

spite, spites, spiting, spited **1** (phrase) **In spite of** is used to introduce a statement which makes the rest of what you are saying seem surprising, e.g. *In spite of all the gossip, Virginia stayed behind.* **2** (verb) If you do something to spite someone, you do it deliberately to hurt or annoy them. **3** (noun) If you do something out of spite, you do it to spite someone.

spiteful (adjective) A spiteful person does or says nasty things to people deliberately to hurt them.

spitting image (noun) If someone is the spitting image of someone else, they look just like them.

splash, splashes, splashing, splashed **1** (verb) If you splash around in water, your movements disturb the water in a noisy way. **2** If liquid splashes something, it scatters over it in a lot of small drops. **3** (noun) A splash is the sound made when something hits or falls into water. **4** A splash of liquid is a small quantity of it that has been spilt on something.

splatter, splatters, splattering, splattered (verb) When something is splattered with a substance, the substance is splashed all over it, e.g. *fur coats splattered with paint.*

spleen, spleens (noun) Your spleen is an organ near your stomach which controls the quality of your blood.

splendid **1** (adjective) very good indeed, e.g. *a splendid career.* **2** beautiful and impressive, e.g. *a splendid Victorian mansion.* **splendidly** (adverb).

splendour, splendours **1** (noun) If something has splendour, it is beautiful and impressive. **2** (plural noun) The splendours of something are its beautiful and impressive features.

splint, splints (noun) A splint is a long piece of wood or metal fastened to a broken limb to hold it in place.

splinter, splinters, splintering, splintered **1** (noun) A splinter is a thin, sharp piece of wood or glass which has broken off a larger piece. **2** (verb) If something splinters, it breaks into thin, sharp pieces.

split, splits, splitting, split **1** (verb) If something splits or if you split it, it divides into two or more parts. **2** If something such as wood or fabric splits, a long crack or tear appears in it. **3** (noun) A split in a piece of wood or fabric is a crack or tear. **4** A split between two things is a division or difference between them, e.g. *the split between rugby league and rugby union.* **5** (verb) If people split something, they share it between them. **split up** (verb) If two people split up, they end their relationship or marriage.

split second (noun) A split second is an extremely short period of time.

splitting (adjective) A splitting headache is very painful.

splutter, splutters, spluttering, spluttered 1 (verb) If someone splutters, they speak in a confused way because they are embarrassed. **2** If something splutters, it makes a series of short, sharp sounds.

spoil, spoils, spoiling, spoiled or **spoilt 1** (verb) If you spoil something, you prevent it from being successful or satisfactory. **2** To spoil children means to give them everything they want, with harmful effects on their character. **3** To spoil someone also means to give them something nice as a treat. **4** (plural noun) Spoils are valuable things obtained during war or as a result of violence, e.g. *the spoils of war.*

spoilsport, spoilsports (noun) A spoilsport is someone who spoils people's fun.

spoke, spokes (noun) The spokes of a wheel are the bars which connect the hub to the rim.

spokesperson, spokespersons (noun) A spokesperson is someone who speaks on behalf of another person or a group. **spokesman** (noun), **spokeswoman** (noun).

sponge, sponges, sponging, sponged 1 (noun) A sponge is a sea creature with a body made up of many cells. **2** A sponge is also part of the very light skeleton of a sponge, used for bathing and cleaning. **3** A sponge or sponge cake is a very light cake. **4** (verb) If you sponge something, you clean it by wiping it with a wet sponge.

sponsor, sponsors, sponsoring, sponsored 1 (verb) To sponsor something, such as an event or someone's training, means to support it financially, e.g. *The visit was sponsored by the London Natural History Society.* **2** If you sponsor someone who is doing something for charity, you agree to give them a sum of money for the charity if they manage to do it. **3** If you sponsor a proposal or suggestion, you officially put it forward and support it, e.g. *the Secretary of War who sponsored the Bill.* **4** (noun) A sponsor is a person or organization sponsoring something or someone. **sponsorship** (noun).

spontaneous 1 (adjective) Spontaneous acts are not planned or arranged, but are done because you feel like it. **2** A spontaneous event happens because of processes within something rather than being caused by things outside it, e.g. *spontaneous bleeding.* **spontaneously** (adverb), **spontaneity** (noun).

spoof, spoofs (noun) A spoof is something such as an article or television programme that seems to be about a serious matter but is actually a joke.

spooky, spookier, spookiest (adjective) eerie and frightening.

spool, spools (noun) A spool is a cylindrical object onto which thread, tape, or film can be wound.

spoon, spoons (noun) A spoon is an object shaped like a small shallow bowl with a long handle, used for eating, stirring, and serving food.

spoonful, spoonfuls or **spoonsful** (noun) A spoonful is the amount held by a spoon.

sporadic (adjective) happening at irregular intervals, e.g. *a few sporadic attempts at keeping a diary.* **sporadically** (adverb).

spore, spores (noun; a technical word) Spores are cells produced by bacteria and nonflowering plants such as fungi which develop into new bacteria or plants.

sporran, sporrans (noun) A sporran is a large purse made of leather or fur, worn by a Scotsman over his kilt.

sport, sports, sporting, sported **1** (noun) Sports are games and other enjoyable activities which need physical effort and skill. **2** You say that someone is a sport when they accept defeat or teasing cheerfully, e.g. *Be a sport, Minister!* **3** (verb) If you sport something noticeable or unusual, you wear it, e.g. *A German boy sported a ponytail.*

sporting **1** (adjective) relating to sport. **2** behaving in a fair and decent way.

sports car, sports cars (noun) A sports car is a low, fast car, usually with room for only two people.

sportsman, sportsmen (noun) A sportsman is a man who takes part in sports and is good at them.

sportswoman, sportswomen (noun) A sportswoman is a woman who takes part in sports and is good at them.

sporty, sportier, sportiest **1** (adjective) A sporty car is fast and flashy. **2** A sporty person is good at sports.

spot, spots, spotting, spotted **1** (noun) Spots are small, round, coloured areas on a surface. **2** Spots on a person's skin are small lumps, usually caused by an infection or allergy. **3** A spot of something is a small amount of it, e.g. *spots of rain.* **4** A place can be called a spot, e.g. *the most beautiful spot in the garden.* **5** (verb) If you spot something, you notice it. **6** (phrase) If you do something **on the spot,** you do it immediately.

spot check, spot checks (noun) A spot check is a random examination of one of a group of things.

spotless (adjective) perfectly clean. **spotlessly** (adverb).

spotlight, spotlights, spotlighting, spotlit or **spotlighted** **1** (noun) A spotlight is a powerful light which can be directed to light up a small area. **2** (verb) If something spotlights a situation or problem, it draws the public's attention to it, e.g. *a national campaign to spotlight the problem.*

spot-on (adjective; an informal expression) exactly correct or accurate.

spotted (adjective) Something spotted has a pattern of spots on it.

spotter, spotters (noun) A spotter is a person whose hobby is looking out for things of a particular kind, e.g. *a train* *spotter*.

spotty, spottier, spottiest (adjective) Someone who is spotty has spots or pimples on their skin, especially on their face.

spouse, spouses (noun) Someone's spouse is the person they are married to.

spout, spouts, spouting, spouted 1 (verb) When liquid or flame spouts out of something, it shoots out in a long stream. **2** When someone spouts what they have learned, they say it in a boring way. **3** (noun) A spout is a tube with a lip-like end for pouring liquid, e.g. *a teapot with a long spout*.

sprain, sprains, spraining, sprained 1 (verb) If you sprain a joint, you accidentally damage it by twisting it violently. **2** (noun) A sprain is the injury caused by spraining a joint.

sprawl, sprawls, sprawling, sprawled 1 (verb) If you sprawl somewhere, you sit or lie there with your legs and arms spread out. **2** A place that sprawls is spread out over a large area, e.g. *a Monday market which sprawls all over town*. **3** (noun) A sprawl is anything that spreads in an untidy and uncontrolled way, e.g. *a sprawl of skyscrapers*. **sprawling** (adjective).

spray, sprays, spraying, sprayed 1 (noun) Spray consists of many drops of liquid splashed or forced into the air, e.g. *The salt spray stung her face*. **2** Spray is also a liquid kept under pressure in a can or other container, e.g. *hair spray*. **3** (verb) To spray a liquid over something means to cover it with drops of the liquid. **4** (noun) A spray is a piece of equipment for spraying liquid, e.g. *a garden spray*. **5** A spray of flowers or leaves consists of several of them on one stem.

spread, spreads, spreading, spread 1 (verb) If you spread something out, you open it out or arrange it so that it can be seen or used easily, e.g. *He spread the map out on his knees*. **2** If you spread a substance on a surface, you put a thin layer on the surface. **3** If something spreads, it gradually reaches or affects more people, e.g. *The news spread quickly*. **4** If something spreads over a period of time, it happens regularly or continuously over that time, e.g. *His four international appearances were spread over eight years*. **5** If something such as work is spread, it is distributed evenly. **6** (noun) The spread of something is the extent to which it gradually reaches or affects more people, e.g. *the spread of Buddhism*. **7** A spread of ideas, interests, or other things is a wide variety of them. **8** A spread is soft food put on bread.

spread-eagled (adjective) Someone who is spread-eagled is lying with their arms and legs spread out.

spree, sprees (noun) A spree is a period of time spent doing something enjoyable, e.g. *a shopping spree*.

sprig, sprigs (noun) A sprig is a small twig with leaves on it.

sprightly, sprightlier, sprightli-

est (adjective) lively and active.

spring, springs, springing, sprang, sprung 1 (noun) Spring is the season between winter and summer. **2** A spring is a coil of wire which returns to its natural shape after being pressed or pulled. **3** A spring is also a place where water comes up through the ground. **4** (verb) To spring means to jump upwards or forwards, e.g. *Martha sprang to her feet.* **5** If something springs in a particular direction, it moves suddenly and quickly, e.g. *The door sprang open.* **6** (noun) A spring is an act of springing, e.g. *With a spring he had opened the door.* **7** (verb) If one thing springs from another, it is the result of it, e.g. *The failures sprang from three facts.*

springboard, springboards 1 (noun) A springboard is a flexible board on which a diver or gymnast jumps to gain height. **2** If something is a springboard for an activity or enterprise, it makes it possible for it to begin.

spring-clean, spring-cleans, spring-cleaning, spring-cleaned (verb) To spring-clean a house means to clean it thoroughly throughout.

spring onion, spring onions (noun) A spring onion is a small onion with long green shoots, often eaten raw in salads.

sprinkle, sprinkles, sprinkling, sprinkled (verb) If you sprinkle a liquid or powder over something, you scatter it over it.

sprinkling, sprinklings (noun) A sprinkling of something is a small quantity of it, e.g. *a light sprinkling of snow.*

sprint, sprints, sprinting, sprinted 1 (noun) A sprint is a short, fast race. **2** (verb) To sprint means to run fast over a short distance.

sprinter, sprinters (noun) A sprinter is an athlete who runs fast over short distances.

sprite, sprites (noun) A sprite is a type of fairy.

sprout, sprouts, sprouting, sprouted 1 (verb) When something sprouts, it grows. **2** If things sprout up, they appear rapidly, e.g. *Their houses sprouted up in that region.* **3** (noun) Sprouts are vegetables like small cabbages.

spruce, spruces; sprucer, sprucest; spruces, sprucing, spruced 1 (noun) A spruce is an evergreen tree with needle-like leaves. **2** (adjective) Someone who is spruce is very neat and smart. **3** (verb) To spruce something up means to make it neat and smart.

spur, spurs, spurring, spurred 1 (verb) If something spurs you to do something or spurs you on, it encourages you to do it. **2** (noun) Something that acts as a spur encourages a person to do something. **3** (phrase) If you do something **on the spur of the moment,** you do it suddenly, without planning it. **4** (noun) Spurs are sharp metal points attached to the heels of a rider's boots and used to urge a horse on.

spurious (pronounced **spyoor-**

ee-uss) (adjective) not genuine or real.

spurn, spurns, spurning, spurned (verb) If you spurn something, you refuse to accept it, e.g. *You spurned his last offer.*

spurt, spurts, spurting, spurted 1 (verb) When a liquid or flame spurts out of something, it comes out quickly in a thick, powerful stream. **2** (noun) A spurt of liquid or flame is a thick powerful stream of it, e.g. *a small spurt of blood.* **3** A spurt of activity or effort is a sudden, brief period of it.

spy, spies, spying, spied 1 (noun) A spy is a person sent to find out secret information about a country or organization. **2** (verb) Someone who spies tries to find out secret information about another country or organization. **3** If you spy on someone, you watch them secretly. **4** If you spy something, you notice it.

squabble, squabbles, squabbling, squabbled 1 (verb) When people squabble, they quarrel about something trivial. **2** (noun) A squabble is a quarrel.

squad, squads (noun) A squad is a small group chosen to do a particular activity, e.g. *the fraud squad.*

squadron, squadrons (noun) A squadron is a section of one of the armed forces, especially the air force.

squalid 1 (adjective) dirty, untidy, and in bad condition. **2** Squalid activities are unpleasant and often dishonest.

squall, squalls (noun) A squall is a brief, violent storm.

squalor (noun) Squalor consists of bad or dirty conditions or surroundings.

squander, squanders, squandering, squandered (verb) To squander money or resources means to waste them, e.g. *They have squandered millions of pounds.*

square, squares, squaring, squared 1 (noun) A square is a shape with four equal sides and four right angles. **2** In a town or city, a square is a flat, open place, bordered by buildings or streets. **3** (adjective) shaped like a square, e.g. *her delicate square face.* **4** (noun) The square of a number is the number multiplied by itself. For example, the square of 3, written 3^2, is 3 x 3. **5** (adjective) Square is used before units of length when talking about the area of something, e.g. *$24m^2$*. **6** Square is used after units of length when you are giving the length of each side of something square, e.g. *a towel measuring a foot square.* **7** (verb) If you square a number, you multiply it by itself.

squarely 1 (adverb) Squarely means directly rather than indirectly or at an angle, e.g. *I looked squarely in the mirror.* **2** If you approach a subject squarely, you consider it fully, without trying to avoid unpleasant aspects of it.

square root, square roots (noun) A square root of a number is a number that makes the first number when it is multiplied by itself. For example, the square roots of

25 are 5 and −5.

squash, squashes, squashing, squashed 1 (verb) If you squash something, you press it, so that it becomes flat or loses its shape. **2** (noun) If there is a squash in a place, there are a lot of people squashed in it. **3** Squash is a game in which two players hit a small rubber ball against the walls of a court using rackets. **4** Squash is also a drink made from fruit juice, sugar, and water.

squat, squats, squatting, squatted; squatter, squattest 1 (verb) If you squat down, you crouch, balancing on your feet with your legs bent. **2** A person who squats in an unused building lives there as a squatter. **3** (noun) A squat is a building used by squatters. **4** (adjective) short and thick.

squatter, squatters (noun) A squatter is a person who lives in an unused building without permission and without paying rent.

squawk, squawks, squawking, squawked 1 (verb) When a bird squawks, it makes a loud, harsh noise. **2** (noun) A squawk is a loud, harsh noise made by a bird.

squeak, squeaks, squeaking, squeaked 1 (verb) If something squeaks, it makes a short high-pitched sound. **2** (noun) A squeak is a short, high-pitched sound. **squeaky** (adjective).

squeal, squeals, squealing, squealed 1 (verb) When things or people squeal, they make long, high-pitched sounds. **2** (noun) A squeal is a long, high-pitched sound.

squeamish (adjective) easily upset by unpleasant sights or situations.

squeeze, squeezes, squeezing, squeezed 1 (verb) When you squeeze something, you press it firmly from two sides. **2** (noun) If you give something a squeeze, you squeeze it, e.g. *She gave my hand a quick squeeze.* **3** If getting into something is a squeeze, it is just possible to fit into it, e.g. *It would take four comfortably, but six would be a squeeze.* **4** (verb) If you squeeze something into a small amount of time or space, you manage to fit it in.

squelch, squelches, squelching, squelched 1 (verb) To squelch means to make a wet, sucking sound. **2** (noun) A squelch is a wet, sucking sound.

squid, squids (noun) A squid is a sea creature with a long soft body and many tentacles.

squiggle, squiggles (noun) A squiggle is a wriggly line.

squint, squints, squinting, squinted 1 (verb) If you squint at something, you look at it with your eyes screwed up. **2** (noun) If someone has a squint, their eyes look in different directions from each other.

squire, squires (noun) In a village, the squire was a gentleman who owned a large house with a lot of land.

squirm, squirms, squirming, squirmed (verb) If you squirm, you wriggle and twist your body about, usually because you are nervous or embarrassed.

squirrel, squirrels (noun) A squirrel is a small furry animal with a long bushy tail.

squirt, squirts, squirting, squirted 1 (verb) If a liquid squirts, it comes out of a narrow opening in a thin, fast stream. **2** (noun) A squirt is a thin, fast stream of liquid.

Sri Lankan, Sri Lankans (pronounced sree-**lang**-kan) **1** (adjective) belonging or relating to Sri Lanka. **2** (noun) A Sri Lankan is someone who comes from Sri Lanka.

stab, stabs, stabbing, stabbed 1 (verb) To stab someone means to wound them by pushing a knife into their body. **2** To stab at something means to push at it sharply with your finger or with something long and narrow. **3** (phrase; an informal use) If you **have a stab** at something, you try to do it. **4** (noun) You can refer to a sudden unpleasant feeling as a stab of something, e.g. *He felt a stab of guilt.*

stable, stables 1 (adjective) not likely to change or come to an end suddenly, e.g. *I am in a stable relationship.* **2** firmly fixed or balanced and not likely to move, wobble, or fall. **3** (noun) A stable is a building in which horses are kept. **stability** (noun), **stabilize** (verb).

staccato (pronounced stak-**kah**-toe) (adjective) consisting of a series of short, sharp, separate sounds.

stack, stacks, stacking, stacked 1 (noun) A stack of things is a pile of them, one on top of the other. **2** (verb) If you stack things, you arrange them one on top of the other in a pile. **3** (plural noun; an informal use) If someone has stacks of something, they have a lot of it.

stadium, stadiums (noun) A stadium is a sports ground with rows of seats around it.

staff, staffs, staffing, staffed 1 (noun) The staff of an organization are the people who work for it. **2** (verb) To staff an organization means to find and employ people to work in it. **3** If an organization is staffed by particular people, they are the people who work for it.

stag, stags (noun) A stag is an adult male deer.

stage, stages, staging, staged 1 (noun) A stage is a part of a process that lasts for a period of time. **2** In a theatre, the stage is a raised platform where the actors or entertainers perform. **3** (verb) If someone stages a play or event, they organize it and present it or take part in it.

stagecoach, stagecoaches (noun) A stagecoach is a large carriage pulled by horses which used to carry passengers and mail.

stagger, staggers, staggering, staggered 1 (verb) If you stagger, you walk unsteadily because you are ill or drunk. **2** If something staggers you, it amazes you. **3** If events are staggered, they are arranged so that they do not all happen at the same time. **staggering** (adjective).

stagnant (adjective) Stagnant water is not flowing and is unhealthy and dirty.

stag night, stag nights (noun) A stag night is a party for a man who is about to get married, which only men go to.

staid (adjective) serious and dull.

stain, stains, staining, stained 1 (noun) A stain is a mark on something that is difficult to remove. **2** (verb) If a substance stains something, the thing becomes marked or coloured by it.

stained glass (noun) Stained glass is coloured pieces of glass held together with strips of lead.

stainless steel (noun) Stainless steel is a metal made from steel and chromium which does not rust.

stair, stairs (noun) Stairs are a set of steps inside a building going from one floor to another.

staircase, staircases (noun) A staircase is a set of stairs.

stairway, stairways (noun) A stairway is a set of stairs.

stake, stakes, staking, staked 1 (phrase) If something is **at stake,** it might be lost or damaged if something else is not successful, e.g. *The whole future of the company was at stake.* **2** (plural noun) The stakes involved in something are the things that can be lost or gained. **3** (verb) If you say you would stake your money, life, or reputation on the success or truth of something, you mean you would risk it, e.g. *He is prepared to stake his own career on this.* **4** (noun) If you have a stake in something such as a business, you own part of it and its success is important to you. **5** A stake is a pointed wooden post that can be hammered into the ground.

stale, staler, stalest (adjective) Stale food or air is no longer fresh.

stalemate 1 (noun) Stalemate is a situation in which neither side in an argument or contest can win. **2** In chess, stalemate is a situation in which a player cannot make any move permitted by the rules, so that the game ends and no-one wins.

stalk, stalks, stalking, stalked (pronounced **stawk**) **1** (noun) The stalk of a flower or leaf is its stem. **2** (verb) To stalk a person or animal means to follow them quietly in order to catch, kill, or observe them. **3** If someone stalks into a room, they walk in a stiff, proud, or angry way.

stall, stalls, stalling, stalled 1 (noun) A stall is a large table containing goods for sale or information. **2** (plural noun) In a theatre, the stalls are the seats at the lowest level, in front of the stage. **3** (verb) When a vehicle stalls, the engine suddenly stops. **4** If you stall when someone asks you to do something, you try to avoid doing it until later.

stallion, stallions (noun) A stallion is an adult male horse that can be used for breeding.

stamina (noun) Stamina is the physical or mental energy needed to do something for a very long time.

stammer, stammers, stammering, stammered 1 (verb) When someone stammers, they speak with difficulty, repeating words and sounds and hesitating awkwardly. **2** (noun) Someone who has a stammer tends to stammer when they speak.

stamp, stamps, stamping, stamped 1 (noun) A stamp is a small piece of gummed paper which you stick on a letter or parcel before posting it. **2** A stamp is also a small block with a pattern cut into it. You press it onto an inky pad and make a mark with it on paper. The mark is also called a stamp. **3** (verb) If you stamp a piece of paper, you make a mark on it using a stamp. **4** If you stamp, you lift your foot and put it down hard on the ground. **5** (noun) If something bears the stamp of a particular quality or person, it shows clear signs of that quality or of the person's style or characteristics. **stamp out** (verb) To stamp something out means to put an end to it, e.g. *the battle to stamp out bullying in schools.*

stampede, stampedes, stampeding, stampeded 1 (verb) When a group of animals stampede, they run in a wild, uncontrolled way. **2** (noun) A stampede is a group of animals stampeding.

stance, stances (noun) Your stance on a particular matter is your attitude and way of dealing with it, e.g. *He takes no particular stance on animal rights.*

stand, stands, standing, stood 1 (verb) If you are standing, you are upright, your legs are straight, and your weight is supported by your feet. When you stand up, you get into a standing position. **2** If something stands somewhere, that is where it is, e.g. *The house stands alone on the top of a small hill.* **3** If you stand something somewhere, you put it there in an upright position, e.g. *Stand the containers on bricks.* **4** If a decision or offer stands, it is still valid, e.g. *My offer still stands.* **5** You can use 'stand' when describing the state or condition of something, e.g. *Youth unemployment stands at 35%.* **6** If a letter stands for a particular word, it is an abbreviation for that word. **7** If you say you will not stand for something, you mean you will not tolerate it. **8** If something can stand a situation or test, it is good enough or strong enough not to be damaged by it. **9** If you cannot stand something, you cannot bear it, e.g. *I can't stand that woman.* **10** (phrase) When someone **stands trial,** they are tried in a court of law. **11** (noun) A stand is a stall or very small shop outdoors or in a large public building. **12** A stand is a large structure at a sports ground, where the spectators sit to watch what is happening. **13** A stand is a piece of furniture designed to hold something, e.g. *an umbrella stand.* **stand by 1** (verb) If you stand by to provide help or take action, you are ready to do it if necessary. **2** If you stand by while something happens, you do nothing to stop it. **stand in** (verb) If you stand in for someone, you take their place while they are ill or away.

stand out (verb) If something stands out, it can be easily noticed or is more important than other similar things. **stand up 1** (verb) If something stands up to rough treatment, it remains undamaged or unharmed. **2** If you stand up to someone who is criticizing or attacking you, you defend yourself.

standard, standards 1 (noun) A standard is a level of quality or achievement that is considered acceptable, e.g. *The work is not up to standard.* **2** (plural noun) Standards are moral principles of behaviour. **3** (adjective) usual, normal, and correct, e.g. *The practice became standard procedure for most companies.*

stand-by, stand-bys 1 (noun) A stand-by is something available for use when you need it, e.g. *a useful stand-by.* **2** (adjective) A stand-by ticket is a cheap ticket that you buy just before a theatre performance or a flight if there are any seats left.

stand-in, stand-ins (noun) A stand-in is someone who takes a person's place while the person is ill or away.

standing 1 (adjective) permanently in existence or used regularly, e.g. *a standing joke.* **2** (noun) A person's standing is their status and reputation. **3** Standing is used to say how long something has existed, e.g. *a friend of 20 years' standing.*

standpoint, standpoints (noun) If you consider something from a particular standpoint, you consider it from that point of view, e.g. *from a military standpoint.*

standstill (noun) If something comes to a standstill, it stops completely.

stanza, stanzas (noun) A stanza is a verse of a poem.

staple, staples, stapling, stapled 1 (noun) Staples are small pieces of wire that hold sheets of paper firmly together. **2** (verb) If you staple sheets of paper, you fasten them together with staples. **3** (adjective) A staple food forms a basic part of someone's everyday diet.

star, stars, starring, starred 1 (noun) A star is a large ball of burning gas in space that appears as a point of light in the sky at night. **2** A star is also a shape with four, five, or more points sticking out in a regular pattern. **3** Famous actors, sports players, and musicians are referred to as stars. **4** (verb) If an actor or actress stars in a film or if the film stars that person, he or she has one of the most important parts in it. **5** (plural noun) The horoscope in a newspaper or magazine can be referred to as the stars, e.g. *I'm a Virgo, but don't read my stars every day.*

starboard (adjective or noun) The starboard side of a ship is the right-hand side when you are facing the front.

starch, starches, starching, starched 1 (noun) Starch is a substance used for stiffening fabric such as cotton and linen. **2** (verb) To starch fabric means to stiffen it with starch. **3** (noun) Starch is a carbohydrate found in food such as bread and potatoes.

stare, stares, staring, stared 1 (verb) If you stare at something, you look at it for a long time. **2** (noun) A stare is a long fixed look at something.

starfish, starfishes or **starfish** (noun) A starfish is a flat, star-shaped sea creature with five limbs.

stark, starker, starkest 1 (adjective) harsh, unpleasant and plain, e.g. *the stark choice.* **2** (phrase) If someone is **stark-naked,** they have no clothes on at all.

starling, starlings (noun) A starling is a common European bird with shiny dark feathers.

start, starts, starting, started 1 (verb) To start means to begin. To start doing something means to begin doing it, e.g. *The new season starts in September... Suzy started crying.* **2** (noun) The start of something is the point or time at which it begins. **3** (verb) If you start a machine or car, you operate the controls to make it work. **4** If you start, your body suddenly jerks because of surprise or fear. **5** (noun) If you do something with a start, you do it with a sudden jerky movement because of surprise or fear, e.g. *I awoke with a start.*

starter, starters (noun) A starter is a small quantity of food served as the first part of a meal.

startle, startles, startling, startled (verb) If something sudden and unexpected startles you, it surprises you and makes you slightly frightened. **startled** (adjective), **startling** (adjective).

starve, starves, starving, starved 1 (verb) If people are starving, they are suffering from a serious lack of food and are likely to die. **2** To starve a person or animal means to prevent them from having any food. **3** (an informal use) If you say you are starving, you mean you are very hungry. **4** If someone or something is starved of something they need, they are suffering because they are not getting enough of it, e.g. *The hospital was starved of cash.* **starvation** (noun).

stash, stashes, stashing, stashed (verb; an informal word) If you stash something away in a secret place, you store it there to keep it safe.

state, states, stating, stated 1 (noun) The state of something is its condition, what it is like, or its circumstances. **2** (phrase) If you are **in a state,** you are nervous or upset and unable to control your emotions. **3** (noun) Countries are sometimes referred to as states, e.g. *the state of Denmark.* **4** Some countries are divided into regions called states which make some of their own laws, e.g. *the State of Vermont.* **5** You can refer to the government or administration of a country as the state. **6** (adjective) A state ceremony involves the ruler or leader of a country. **7** (verb) If you state something, you say it or write it, especially in a formal way.

stately home, stately homes (noun) A stately home is a

very large old house which belongs to an upper-class family.

statement, statements 1 (noun) A statement is something you say or write when you give facts or information in a formal way. **2** A statement is also a document provided by a bank showing all the money paid into and out of an account.

state school, state schools (noun) A state school is a school financed by the local authority and government.

statesman, statesmen (noun) A statesman is an important and experienced politician.

static 1 (adjective) never moving or changing, e.g. *The temperature remains fairly static.* **2** (noun) Static is an electrical charge caused by friction. It builds up in metal objects.

station, stations, stationing, stationed 1 (noun) A railway station is a building and platforms where trains stop for passengers. **2** A bus or coach station is a place where some buses start their journeys. **3** A radio station is the frequency on which a particular company broadcasts. **4** (an old-fashioned use) A person's station is their position or rank in society. **5** (verb) Someone who is stationed somewhere is sent there to work or do a particular job, e.g. *Her husband was stationed in Vienna.*

stationary (adjective) not moving, e.g. *a stationary car.*

stationery (noun) Stationery is paper, pens, and other writing equipment.

statistic, statistics 1 (noun) Statistics are facts obtained by analysing numerical information. **2** Statistics is the branch of mathematics that deals with the analysis of numerical information. **statistical** (adjective).

statistician, statisticians (pronounced stat-iss-**tish**-an) (noun) A statistician is a person who studies or works with statistics.

statue, statues (noun) A statue is a sculpture of a person.

stature 1 (noun) Someone's stature is their height and size. **2** Someone's stature is also their importance and reputation, e.g. *the desire to gain international stature.*

status, statuses (pronounced **stay**-tuss) **1** (noun) A person's status is their position and importance in society. **2** Status is also the official classification given to someone or something, e.g. *I am not sure what your legal status is.*

status quo (pronounced stay-tuss **kwoh**) (noun) The status quo is the situation that exists at a particular time, e.g. *They want to keep the status quo.*

statute, statutes (noun) A statute is a law. **statutory** (adjective).

staunch, stauncher, staunchest (adjective) A staunch supporter is a strong and loyal supporter.

stave, staves, staving, staved 1 (noun) In music, a stave is the five lines that music is written on. **2** (verb) If you stave something off, you try to delay or prevent it.

stay, stays, staying, stayed 1 (verb) If you stay in a place, you do not move away from it, e.g. *She stayed in bed until noon.* **2** If you stay at a hotel or a friend's house, you spend some time there as a guest or visitor. **3** If you stay in a particular state, you continue to be in it, e.g. *I stayed awake the first night.* **4** (noun) A stay is a short time spent somewhere, e.g. *a very pleasant stay in Cornwall.*

stead (noun) Something that will stand someone in good stead will be useful to them in the future.

steady, steadier, steadiest; steadies, steadying, steadied 1 (adjective) continuing or developing gradually without major interruptions or changes, e.g. *a steady rise in profits.* **2** firm and not shaking or wobbling, e.g. *O'Brien held out a steady hand.* **3** A steady look or voice is calm and controlled. **4** Someone who is steady is sensible and reliable. **5** (verb) When you steady something, you hold on to prevent it from shaking or wobbling. **6** When you steady yourself, you control and calm yourself. **steadily** (adverb).

steak, steaks 1 (noun) Steak is a good-quality beef without much fat. **2** A fish steak is a large piece of fish.

steal, steals, stealing, stole, stolen 1 (verb) To steal something means to take it without permission and without intending to return it. **2** To steal somewhere means to move there quietly and secretively.

stealth (rhymes with **health**) (noun) If you do something with stealth, you do it quietly and secretively. **stealthy** (adjective), **stealthily** (adverb).

steam, steams, steaming, steamed 1 (noun) Steam is the hot vapour formed when water boils. **2** (adjective) Steam engines are operated using steam as a means of power. **3** (verb) If something steams, it gives off steam. **4** To steam food means to cook it in steam. **steamy** (adjective).

steam-engine, steam-engines (noun) A steam-engine is any engine that uses the energy of steam to produce mechanical work.

steamer, steamers 1 (noun) A steamer is a ship powered by steam. **2** A steamer is a container with small holes in the bottom in which you steam food.

steed, steeds (noun; a literary word) A steed is a horse.

steel, steels, steeling, steeled 1 (noun) Steel is a very strong metal containing mainly iron with a small amount of carbon. **2** (verb) To steel yourself means to prepare to deal with something unpleasant.

steel band, steel bands (noun) A steel band is a group of people who play music on special metal drums.

steep, steeper, steepest; steeps, steeping, steeped 1 (adjective) A steep slope rises sharply and is difficult to go up. **2** A steep increase is large and sudden. **3** (verb) To steep something in a liquid means to soak it thoroughly. **steeply** (adverb).

steeped (adjective) If a person or place is steeped in a particular quality, they are deeply affected by it, e.g. *an industry steeped in tradition.*

steeple, steeples (noun) A steeple is a tall pointed structure on top of a church tower.

steeplechase, steeplechases (noun) A steeplechase is a long horse race in which the horses jump over obstacles such as hedges and water jumps.

steer, steers, steering, steered 1 (verb) To steer a vehicle or boat means to control it so that it goes in the right direction. **2** To steer someone towards a particular course of action means to influence and direct their behaviour or thoughts. **3** (noun) A steer is a castrated bull.

stem, stems, stemming, stemmed 1 (noun) The stem of a plant is the long thin central part above the ground that carries the leaves and flowers. **2** The stem of a glass is the long narrow part connecting the bowl to the base. **3** (verb) If a problem stems from a particular situation, that situation is the original starting point or cause of the problem. **4** If you stem the flow of something, you restrict it or stop it from spreading, e.g. *to stem the flow of refugees.*

stench, stenches (noun) A stench is a very strong, unpleasant smell.

stencil, stencils, stencilling, stencilled 1 (noun) A stencil is a piece of card or metal with a design cut out of it. You rest the stencil on a surface and put paint or ink over the cutout area to create a pattern on the surface. **2** (verb) To stencil a design on a surface means to create it using a stencil.

step, steps, stepping, stepped 1 (noun) If you take a step, you lift your foot and put it down somewhere else. **2** (verb) If you step in a particular direction, you move your foot in that direction. **3** (noun) A step is one of a series of actions that you take in order to achieve something. **4** A step is also a raised flat surface, usually one of a series that you can walk up or down. **5** (verb) If someone steps down or steps aside from an important position, they resign.

step- (prefix) If a word like 'father' or 'sister' has 'step-' in front of it, it shows that the family relationship has come about because a parent has married again, e.g. *stepfather... stepsister.*

stepping stone, stepping stones 1 (noun) Stepping stones are a line of large stones that you walk on to cross a shallow river. **2** A stepping stone is a job or event that is regarded as a stage in your progress, especially in your career.

stereo, stereos 1 (adjective) A stereo record or music system is one in which the sound is directed through two speakers. **2** (noun) A stereo is a piece of equipment that reproduces sound from records, tapes, or CDs directing the sound through two speakers.

stereotype, stereotypes, stereotyping, stereotyped 1 (noun) A stereotype is a fixed image or set of characteristics that people consider to represent a particular type of person or thing, e.g. *He doesn't live up to the stereotype of the ideal man.* **2** (verb) If you stereotype someone, you assume they are a particular type of person and will behave in a particular way.

sterile 1 (adjective) Sterile means completely clean and free from germs. **2** A sterile person or animal is unable to produce offspring. **sterility** (noun).

sterilize, sterilizes, sterilizing, sterilized; also spelled **sterilise 1** (verb) To sterilize something means to make it completely clean and free from germs, usually by boiling it or treating it with an antiseptic. **2** If a person or animal is sterilized, they have an operation that makes it impossible for them to produce offspring.

sterling 1 (noun) Sterling is the money system of Great Britain. **2** (adjective) excellent in quality, e.g. *Volunteers are doing sterling work.*

stern, sterner, sternest; sterns 1 (adjective) very serious and strict, e.g. *a stern father... a stern warning.* **2** (noun) The stern of a boat is the back part.

steroid, steroids (noun) Steroids are chemicals that occur naturally in your body. Sometimes sportsmen illegally take them as drugs to improve their speed or strength.

stethoscope, stethoscopes (noun) A stethoscope consists of earpieces connected to a hollow tube and a small disc. A doctor uses a stethoscope to listen to a patient's heart and breathing.

stew, stews, stewing, stewed 1 (noun) A stew consists of small pieces of savoury food cooked together slowly in a liquid. **2** (verb) To stew meat, vegetables, or fruit means to cook them slowly in a liquid.

steward, stewards 1 (noun) A steward is a man who works on a ship or plane looking after passengers and serving meals. **2** A steward is also a person who helps to direct the public at a race, march, or other event.

stewardess, stewardesses (noun) A stewardess is a woman who works on a ship or plane looking after passengers and serving meals.

stick, sticks, sticking, stuck 1 (noun) A stick is a long, thin piece of wood. **2** A stick of something is a long, thin piece of it, e.g. *a stick of celery.* **3** (verb) If you stick a long or pointed object into something, you push it in. **4** If you stick one thing to another, you attach it with glue or sticky tape. **5** If one thing sticks to another, it becomes attached and is difficult to remove. **6** If a movable part of something sticks, it becomes fixed and will no longer move or work properly, e.g. *My gears keep sticking.* **7** (an informal use) If you stick something somewhere, you put it there. **8** If you stick to something, you keep to it and do not change to something else, e.g. *He should have stuck to the old ways of doing things.* **9** When people stick together, they stay together and support each other. **stick out 1** (verb) If something sticks out, it projects from something else. **2** To stick out also means to be very noticeable. **stick up 1** (verb) If something sticks up, it points upwards from a surface. **2** (an informal use) If you stick up for a person or principle, you support or defend them.

sticker, stickers (noun) A sticker is a small piece of paper or plastic with writing or a picture on it, that you stick onto a surface.

sticking plaster, sticking plasters (noun) A sticking plaster is a small piece of fabric that you stick over a cut or sore to protect it.

stick insect, stick insects (noun) A stick insect is an insect with a long cylindrical body and long legs, which looks like a twig.

sticky, stickier, stickiest 1 (adjective) A sticky object is covered with a substance that can stick to other things, e.g. *sticky hands*. **2** Sticky paper or tape has glue on one side so that you can stick it to a surface. **3** (an informal use) A sticky situation is difficult or embarrassing to deal with. **4** Sticky weather is unpleasantly hot and humid.

stiff, stiffer, stiffest 1 (adjective) Something that is stiff is firm and not easily bent. **2** If you feel stiff, your muscles or joints ache when you move. **3** Stiff behaviour is formal and not friendly or relaxed. **4** Stiff also means difficult or severe, e.g. *stiff competition for places*. **5** A stiff breeze is blowing strongly. **6** (adverb; an informal use) If you are bored stiff or scared stiff, you are very bored or very scared. **stiffly** (adverb), **stiffness** (noun).

stiffen, stiffens, stiffening, stiffened 1 (verb) If you stiffen, you suddenly stop moving and your muscles become tense, e.g. *I stiffened with tension*. **2** If your joints or muscles stiffen, they become sore and difficult to bend or move. **3** If fabric or material is stiffened, it is made firmer so that it does not bend easily.

stifle, stifles, stifling, stifled (pronounced **sty**-fl) **1** (verb) To stifle something means to stop it from happening or continuing, e.g. *Martin stifled a yawn*. **2** If the atmosphere stifles you, you feel you cannot breathe properly. **stifling** (adjective).

stigma, stigmas (noun) If something has a stigma attached to it, people consider it unacceptable or a disgrace, e.g. *the stigma of mental illness*.

stile, stiles (noun) A stile is a step on either side of a wall or fence to enable you to climb over.

stiletto, stilettos (noun) Stilettos are women's shoes with very high, narrow heels.

still, stiller, stillest; stills 1 (adverb) If a situation still exists, it has continued to exist and it exists now. **2** If something could still happen, it might happen although it has not happened yet. **3** 'Still' emphasizes that something is the case in spite of other things, e.g. *Whatever you think of him, he's still your father*. **4**

(adverb or adjective) Still means staying in the same position without moving, e.g. *Sit still... The air was still.* **5** (adjective) A still place is quiet and peaceful with no signs of activity. **6** (noun) A still is a photograph taken from a cinema film or video. **stillness** (noun).

stillborn (adjective) A stillborn baby is dead when it is born.

stilt, stilts 1 (noun) Stilts are long upright poles on which a building is built, for example on wet land. **2** Stilts are also two long pieces of wood or metal on which people balance and walk.

stilted (adjective) formal, unnatural, and rather awkward, e.g. *a stilted conversation.*

stimulant, stimulants (noun) A stimulant is a drug or other substance that makes your body work faster, increasing your heart rate and making it difficult to sleep.

stimulate, stimulates, stimulating, stimulated 1 (verb) To stimulate something means to encourage it to begin or develop, e.g. *to stimulate discussion.* **2** If something stimulates you, it gives you new ideas and enthusiasm. **stimulating** (adjective), **stimulation** (noun).

stimulus, stimuli (noun) A stimulus is something that causes a process or event to begin or develop.

sting, stings, stinging, stung 1 (verb) If a creature or plant stings you, it pricks your skin and injects a substance which causes pain. **2** (noun) A creature's sting is the part it stings you with. **3** (verb) If a part of your body stings, you feel a sharp tingling pain there. **4** If someone's remarks sting you, they make you feel upset and hurt.

stink, stinks, stinking, stank, stunk 1 (verb) Something that stinks smells very unpleasant. **2** (noun) A stink is a very unpleasant smell.

stint, stints (noun) A stint is a period of time spent doing a particular job, e.g. *a three-year stint in the army.*

stipulate, stipulates, stipulating, stipulated (verb; a formal word) If you stipulate that something must be done, you state clearly that it must be done. **stipulation** (noun).

stir, stirs, stirring, stirred 1 (verb) When you stir a liquid, you move it around using a spoon or a stick. **2** To stir means to move slightly. **3** If something stirs you, it makes you feel strong emotions, e.g. *The power of the singing stirred me.* **4** (noun) If an event causes a stir, it causes general excitement or shock.

stirring, stirrings 1 (adjective) causing excitement, emotion, and enthusiasm, e.g. *a stirring account of the action.* **2** (noun) If there is a stirring of emotion, people begin to feel it.

stirrup, stirrups (noun) Stirrups are two metal loops hanging by leather straps from a horse's saddle, which you put your feet in when riding.

stitch, stitches, stitching, stitched 1 (verb) When you stitch pieces of material together, you use a needle and thread to sew them together. **2** (noun) A stitch is one of the pieces of thread that can be seen where material has been sewn. **3** (verb) To stitch a wound means to use a special needle and thread to hold the edges of skin together. **4** (noun) A stitch is one of the pieces of thread that can be seen where a wound has been stitched, e.g. *He had eleven stitches in his lip.* **5** If you have a stitch, you feel a sharp pain at the side of your abdomen, usually because you have been running or laughing.

stoat, stoats (noun) A stoat is a small wild animal with a long body and brown fur.

stock, stocks, stocking, stocked **1** (noun) Stocks are shares bought as an investment in a company. **2** (verb) A shop that stocks particular goods keeps a supply of them to sell. **3** (noun) A shop's stock is the total amount of goods it has for sale. **4** (verb) If you stock a shelf or cupboard, you fill it with food or other things. **5** (noun) If you have a stock of things, you have a supply ready for use. **6** The stock an animal or person comes from is the type of animal or person they are descended from, e.g. *She was descended from Scots Highland stock.* **7** Stock is a liquid made from boiling meat, bones, or vegetables together in water. Stock is used as a base for soups, stews, and sauces. **8** (adjective) A stock expression or way of doing something is one that is commonly used. **stock up** (verb) If you stock up with something, you buy a supply of it.

stockbroker, stockbrokers (noun) A stockbroker is a person whose job is to buy and sell shares for people who want to invest money.

stock exchange, stock exchanges (noun) A stock exchange is a place where there is trading in stocks and shares, e.g. *the New York Stock Exchange.*

stocking, stockings (noun) Stockings are long pieces of thin clothing that cover a woman's leg.

stock market, stock markets (noun) The stock market is the organization and activity involved in buying and selling stocks and shares.

stockpile, stockpiles, stockpiling, stockpiled **1** (verb) If someone stockpiles something, they store large quantities of it for future use. **2** (noun) A stockpile is a large store of something.

stocktaking (noun) Stocktaking is the counting and checking of all a shop's or business's goods.

stocky, stockier, stockiest (adjective) A stocky person is rather short, but broad and solid-looking.

stoke, stokes, stoking, stoked (verb) To stoke a fire means to keep it burning by moving or adding fuel.

stomach, stomachs, stomaching, stomached **1** (noun) Your stomach is the organ inside your body where food is digested. **2** You can refer to the front part of your body below your waist as your stomach. **3** (verb) If you cannot stomach something, you strongly dislike it and cannot accept it.

stone, stones, stoning, stoned 1 (noun) Stone is the hard solid substance found in the ground and used for building. **2** A stone is a small piece of rock. **3** You can refer to a jewel as a stone, e.g. *a diamond ring with three stones.* **4** The stone in a fruit such as a plum or cherry is the large seed in the centre. **5** (verb) To stone something or someone means to throw stones at them. **6** (noun) A stone is also a unit of weight equal to 14 pounds or about 6.35 kilograms.

stoned (adjective; an informal word) affected by drugs.

stony, stonier, stoniest 1 (adjective) Stony ground is rough and contains a lot of stones or rocks. **2** If someone's expression is stony, it shows no friendliness or sympathy.

stool, stools 1 (noun) A stool is a seat with legs but no back or arms. **2** A stool is also a lump of faeces.

stoop, stoops, stooping, stooped 1 (verb) If you stoop, you stand or walk with your shoulders bent forwards. **2** If you would not stoop to something, you would not disgrace yourself by doing it.

stop, stops, stopping, stopped 1 (verb) If you stop doing something, you no longer do it. **2** If an activity or process stops, it comes to an end or no longer happens. **3** If a machine stops, it no longer functions or it is switched off. **4** To stop something means to prevent it. **5** (phrase) To **put a stop to** something means to prevent it from happening or continuing. **6** (verb) If people or things that are moving stop, they no longer move. **7** (noun) A stop is a place where a bus, train, or other vehicle stops during a journey. **8** If something that is moving comes to a stop, it no longer moves. **9** (verb) If you stop somewhere, you stay there for a short while.

stoppage, stoppages (noun) If there is a stoppage, people stop work because of a disagreement with their employer.

stopper, stoppers (noun) A stopper is a piece of glass, plastic, or cork that fits into the neck of a jar or bottle.

stopwatch, stopwatches (noun) A stopwatch is a watch that can be started and stopped by pressing buttons. Stopwatches are used to time events.

storage (noun) The storage of something is the keeping of it somewhere until it is needed.

store, stores, storing, stored 1 (noun) A store is a shop. **2** (verb) When you store something somewhere, you keep it there until it is needed. **3** (noun) A store of something is a supply kept for future use. **4** A store is also a place where things are kept while they are not used. **5** (phrase) Something that is **in store for** you is going to happen to you in the future.

storeroom, storerooms (noun) A storeroom is a room where things are kept until they are needed.

storey, storeys (noun) A storey of a building is one of its floors or levels.

stork, storks (noun) A stork is

a very large white and black bird with long red legs and a long bill.

storm, storms, storming, stormed 1 (noun) When there is a storm, there is heavy rain, a strong wind, and often thunder and lightning. **2** If something causes a storm, it causes an angry or excited reaction, e.g. *His words caused a storm of protest.* **3** (verb) If someone storms out, they leave quickly, noisily, and angrily. **4** To storm means to say something in a loud, angry voice, e.g. *'It's a fiasco!' he stormed.* **5** If people storm a place, they attack it. **stormy** (adjective).

story, stories 1 (noun) A story is a description of imaginary people and events written or told to entertain people. **2** The story of something or someone is an account of the important events that have happened to them, e.g. *his life story.*

stout, stouter, stoutest 1 (adjective) rather fat. **2** thick, strong, and sturdy, e.g. *stout walking shoes.* **3** determined, firm, and strong, e.g. *He can outrun the stoutest opposition.* **stoutly** (adverb).

stove, stoves (noun) A stove is a piece of equipment for heating a room or for cooking.

stow, stows, stowing, stowed 1 (verb) If you stow something somewhere or stow it away, you store it until it is needed. **2** If someone stows away in a ship or plane, they hide in it to go somewhere secretly without paying.

straddle, straddles, straddling, straddled 1 (verb) If you straddle something, you stand or sit with one leg on either side of it. **2** If something straddles a place, it crosses it, linking different parts together, e.g. *The town straddles a river.*

straight, straighter, straightest 1 (adjective or adverb) continuing in the same direction without curving or bending, e.g. *the straight path... Amy stared straight ahead of her.* **2** upright or level rather than sloping or bent, e.g. *Keep your arms straight.* **3** (adverb) immediately and directly, e.g. *We will go straight to the hotel.* **4** (adjective) neat and tidy, e.g. *Get this room straight.* **5** honest, frank, and direct, e.g. *They wouldn't give me a straight answer.*

straightaway (adverb) If you do something straightaway, you do it immediately.

straighten, straightens, straightening, straightened 1 (verb) To straighten something means to remove any bends or curves from it. **2** To straighten something also means to make it neat and tidy. **3** To straighten out a confused situation means to organize and deal with it.

straightforward 1 (adjective) easy and involving no problems. **2** honest, open, and frank.

strain, strains, straining, strained 1 (noun) Strain is worry and nervous tension. **2** If a strain is put on something, it is affected by a strong force which may damage it. **3** (verb) To strain something means to force it or use it more than is reasonable or normal. **4** If you strain a muscle, you injure it by moving awkwardly. **5** (noun) You can refer to an aspect of someone's character as a strain. **6** You can refer to distant sounds of music as strains of music. **7** (verb) To strain food means to pour away the liquid from it. **8** (noun) A particular strain of plant is a variety of it, e.g. *strains of rose.*

strained 1 (adjective) worried and anxious. **2** If a relationship is strained, people feel unfriendly and do not trust each other.

strait, straits 1 (noun) You can refer to a narrow strip of sea as a strait or the straits, e.g. *the Straits of Dover.* **2** (plural noun) If someone is in a bad situation, you can say they are in difficult straits.

straitjacket, straitjackets (noun) A straitjacket is a special jacket used to tie the arms of a violent person tightly around their body.

strait-laced (adjective) having a very strict and serious attitude to moral behaviour.

strand, strands 1 (noun) A strand of thread or hair is a single long piece of it. **2** You can refer to a part of a situation or idea as a strand of it, e.g. *the different strands of the problem.*

stranded (adjective) If someone or something is stranded somewhere, they are stuck and cannot leave.

strange, stranger, strangest 1 (adjective) unusual or unexpected. **2** not known, seen, or experienced before, e.g. *alone in a strange country.* **strangely** (adverb), **strangeness** (noun).

stranger, strangers 1 (noun) A stranger is someone you have never met before. **2** If you are a stranger to a place or situation, you have not been there or experienced it before.

strangle, strangles, strangling, strangled (verb) To strangle someone means to kill them by squeezing their throat. **strangulation** (noun).

strangled (adjective) A strangled sound is unclear and muffled.

stranglehold, strangleholds (noun) To have a stranglehold on something means to have control over it and prevent it from developing.

strap, straps, strapping, strapped 1 (noun) A strap is a narrow piece of leather or cloth, used to fasten or hold things together. **2** (verb) To strap something means to fasten it with a strap.

strapping (adjective) tall, strong, and healthy-looking.

strata the plural of **stratum**.

strategic (pronounced strat-**tee**-jik) (adjective) planned or intended to achieve something or to gain an advantage, e.g. *a strategic plan.* **strategically** (adverb).

strategy, strategies 1 (noun) A strategy is a plan for achieving something. **2** Strategy is the skill of planning the best way to achieve something, especially in war. **strategist** (noun).

stratum, strata (noun) The strata in the earth's surface are the different layers of rock.

straw, straws 1 (noun) Straw is the dry, yellowish stalks from cereal crops. **2** A straw is a hollow tube of paper or plastic which you use to suck a drink into your mouth. **3** (phrase) If something is **the last straw,** it is the latest in a series of bad events and makes you feel you cannot stand any more.

strawberry, strawberries (noun) A strawberry is a small red fruit with tiny seeds in its skin.

stray, strays, straying, strayed 1 (verb) When people or animals stray, they wander away from where they should be. **2** (adjective) A stray dog or cat is one that has wandered away from home. **3** (noun) A stray is a stray dog or cat. **4** (adjective) Stray things are separated from the main group of things of their kind, e.g. *a stray piece of lettuce.* **5** (verb) If your thoughts stray, you stop concentrating.

streak, streaks, streaking, streaked 1 (noun) A streak is a long mark or stain. **2** (verb) If something is streaked with a colour, it has lines of the colour in it. **3** (noun) If someone has a particular streak, they have that quality in their character. **4** (verb) To streak somewhere means to move there very quickly. **streaky** (adjective).

stream, streams, streaming, streamed 1 (noun) A stream is a small river. **2** You can refer to a steady flow of something as a stream, e.g. *a constant stream of people.* **3** (verb) To stream somewhere means to move in a continuous flow in large quantities, e.g. *Rain streamed down the windscreen.* **4** (noun) In a school, a stream is a group of children of the same age and ability.

streamer, streamers (noun) A streamer is a long, narrow strip of coloured paper used for decoration.

streamline, streamlines, streamlining, streamlined 1 (verb) To streamline a vehicle, aircraft, or boat means to improve its shape so that it moves more quickly and efficiently. **2** To streamline an organization means to make it more efficient by removing parts of it.

street, streets (noun) A street is a road in a town or village, usually with buildings along it.

strength, strengths 1 (noun) Your strength is your physical energy and the power of your muscles. **2** Strength can refer to the degree of someone's confidence or courage. **3** You can refer to power or influence as strength, e.g. *The campaign against pit closures gathered strength.* **4** Someone's strengths are their good qualities and abilities. **5** The strength of an object is the degree to which it can stand rough treatment. **6** The strength of a substance is the amount of other substances that it contains, e.g. *coffee with sugar and milk in it at the correct strength.* **7** The strength of a feeling or opinion is the degree to which it is felt or supported. **8** The strength of a relationship is its degree of closeness or success. **9** The strength of a group is the total number of people in it. **10** (phrase) If people do something **in strength,** a lot of them do it together, e.g. *The press were here in strength.*

strengthen, strengthens, strengthening, strengthened 1 (verb) To strengthen something means to give it more power, influence, or support and make it more likely to succeed. **2** To strengthen an object means to improve it or add to its structure so that it can withstand rough treatment.

strenuous (pronounced **stren**-yoo-uss) (adjective) involving a lot of effort or energy. **strenuously** (adverb).

stress, stresses, stressing, stressed 1 (noun) Stress is worry and nervous tension. **2** Stresses are strong physical forces applied to an object. **3** (verb) If you stress a point, you emphasize it and draw attention to its importance. **4** (noun) Stress is emphasis put on a word or part of a word when it is pronounced, making it slightly louder. **stressful** (adjective).

stretch, stretches, stretching, stretched 1 (verb) Something that stretches over an area extends that far. **2** (noun) A stretch of land or water is an area of it. **3** A stretch of time is a period of time. **4** (verb) When you stretch, you hold out part of your body as far as you can. **5** To stretch something soft or elastic means to pull it to make it longer or bigger.

stretcher, stretchers (noun) A stretcher is a long piece of material with a pole along each side, used to carry an injured person.

strewn (adjective) If things are strewn about, they are scattered about untidily, e.g. *The costumes were strewn all over the floor.*

stricken (adjective) severely affected by something unpleasant.

strict, stricter, strictest 1 (adjective) Someone who is strict controls other people very firmly. **2** A strict rule must always be obeyed absolutely. **3** The strict meaning of something is its precise and accurate meaning. **4** You can use strict to describe someone who never breaks the rules or principles of a particular belief, e.g. *a strict Muslim.*

strictly 1 (adverb) Strictly means only for a particular purpose, e.g. *I was in it strictly for the money.* **2** (phrase) You say **strictly speaking** to correct a statement or add more precise information, e.g. *Somebody pointed out that, strictly speaking, electricity was a discovery, not an invention.*

stride, strides, striding, strode, stridden 1 (verb) To stride along means to walk quickly with long steps. **2** (noun) A stride is a long step; also the length of a step.

strident (pronounced **stry**-dent) (adjective) loud, harsh, and unpleasant.

strife (noun) Strife is trouble, conflict, and disagreement.

strike, strikes, striking, struck 1

(noun) If there is a strike, people stop working as a protest. **2** A hunger strike is a refusal to eat anything as a protest. A rent strike is a refusal to pay rent. **3** (verb) To strike someone or something means to hit them. **4** If an illness, disaster, or enemy strikes, it suddenly affects or attacks someone. **5** (noun) A strike is a military attack, e.g. *the threat of American air strikes.* **6** (verb) If a thought strikes you, it comes into your mind. **7** When a clock strikes, it makes a sound to indicate the time. **8** To strike a deal with someone means to come to an agreement with them. **9** If someone strikes oil or gold, they discover it in the ground. **10** If you strike a match, you rub it against something to make it burst into flame. **strike off** (verb) If a professional person is struck off for bad behaviour, their name is removed from an official register and they are not allowed to practise their profession. **strike up** (verb) To strike up a conversation or friendship means to begin it.

striker, strikers 1 (noun) Strikers are people who are refusing to work as a protest. **2** In football, a striker is a player whose function is to attack and score goals rather than to defend.

striking (adjective) very noticeable because of being unusual or very attractive. **strikingly** (adverb).

string, strings, stringing, strung 1 (noun) String is thin cord made of twisted threads. **2** You can refer to a row or series of similar things as a string of them, e.g. *a string of islands... a string of injuries.* **3** The strings of a musical instrument are tightly stretched lengths of wire or nylon which vibrate to produce the notes. **4** (plural noun) The section of an orchestra consisting of stringed instruments is called the strings. **string along** (verb; an informal use) To string someone along means to deceive them. **string out 1** (verb) If things are strung out, they are spread out in a long line. **2** To string something out means to make it last longer than necessary.

stringed (adjective) A stringed instrument is one with strings, such as a guitar or violin.

stringent (adjective) Stringent laws, rules, or conditions are very severe or are strictly controlled, e.g. *stringent financial checks.*

strip, strips, stripping, stripped 1 (noun) A strip of something is a long, narrow piece of it. **2** (verb) If you strip, you take off all your clothes. **3** To strip something means to remove whatever is covering its surface. **4** To strip someone of their property or rights means to take their property or rights away from them officially. **5** (noun) A comic strip is a series of drawings which tell a story. **6** A football team's strip is the clothes worn by the team when playing a match.

stripe, stripes (noun) Stripes are long, thin lines, usually of different colours. **striped** (adjective).

stripper, strippers (noun) A stripper is an entertainer who does striptease.

striptease (noun) Striptease is a form of entertainment in which someone takes off their clothes gradually to music.

strive, strives, striving, strove, striven (verb) If you strive to do something, you make a great effort to achieve it.

stroke, strokes, stroking, stroked 1 (verb) If you stroke something, you move your hand smoothly and gently over it. **2** (noun) If someone has a stroke, they suddenly lose consciousness as a result of a blockage or rupture in a blood vessel in the brain. A stroke can result in damage to speech and paralysis. **3** The strokes of a brush or pen are the movements that you make with it. **4** The strokes of a clock are the sounds that indicate the hour. **5** A swimming stroke is a particular style of swimming. **6** (phrase) If you have **a stroke of luck,** then you are lucky and something good happens to you.

stroll, strolls, strolling, strolled 1 (verb) To stroll along means to walk slowly in a relaxed way. **2** (noun) A stroll is a slow, pleasurable walk.

strong, stronger, strongest 1 (adjective) Someone who is strong has powerful muscles. **2** You also say that someone is strong when they are confident and have courage. **3** Strong objects are able to withstand rough treatment. **4** Strong also means great in degree or intensity, e.g. *a strong wind.* **5** A strong argument or theory is supported by a lot of evidence. **6** If a group or organization is strong, it has a lot of members or influence. **7** You can use strong to say how many people there are in a group, e.g. *The audience was about two dozen strong.* **8** Your strong points are the things you are good at. **9** A strong economy or currency is financially stable and successful. **10** A strong liquid or drug contains a lot of a particular substance. **11** (adverb) If someone or something is still going strong, they are still healthy or working well after a long time. **strongly** (adverb).

stronghold, strongholds 1 (noun) A stronghold is a place that is held and defended by an army. **2** A stronghold of an attitude or belief is a place in which the attitude or belief is strongly held.

structure, structures, structuring, structured 1 (noun) The structure of something is the way it is made, built, or organized. **2** A structure is something that has been built or constructed. **3** If something has structure, it is properly organized, e.g. *The days have no real structure.* **4** (verb) To structure something means to arrange it into an organized pattern or system. **structural** (adjective), **structurally** (adverb).

struggle, struggles, struggling, struggled 1 (verb) If you struggle to do something, you try hard to do it in difficult circumstances. **2** (noun) Something that is a struggle is difficult to achieve and takes a lot of effort. **3** (verb) When people struggle, they twist and move violently during a fight. **4** (noun) A struggle is a fight.

strum, strums, strumming, strummed (verb) To strum a guitar means to play it by moving your fingers backwards and forwards across all the strings.

strut, struts, strutting, strutted 1 (verb) To strut means to walk in a stiff, proud way with your chest out and your head high. **2** (noun) A strut is a piece of wood or metal which strengthens or supports part of a building or structure.

stub, stubs, stubbing, stubbed 1 (noun) The stub of a pencil or cigarette is the short piece that remains when the rest has been used. **2** The stub of a cheque or ticket is the small part that you keep. **3** (verb) If you stub your toe, you hurt it by accidentally kicking something.

stubble 1 (noun) The short stalks remaining in the ground after a crop is harvested are called stubble. **2** If a man has stubble on his face, he has very short hair growing there because he has not shaved recently.

stubborn 1 (adjective) Someone who is stubborn is determined not to change their opinion or course of action. **2** A stubborn stain is difficult to remove. **stubbornly** (adverb), **stubbornness** (noun).

stuck 1 (adjective) If something is stuck in a particular position, it is fixed or jammed and cannot be moved, e.g. *His car's stuck in a snowdrift.* **2** If you are stuck, you are unable to continue what you were doing because it is too difficult. **3** If you are stuck somewhere, you are unable to get away.

stuck-up (adjective; an informal word) proud and conceited.

stud, studs 1 (noun) A stud is a small piece of metal fixed into something. **2** A male horse or other animal that is kept for stud is kept for breeding purposes.

studded (adjective) decorated with small pieces of metal or precious stones.

student, students (noun) A student is a person studying at university or college.

studied (adjective) A studied action or response has been carefully planned and is not natural, e.g. *She sipped her glass of white wine with studied boredom.*

studio, studios 1 (noun) A studio is a room where a photographer or painter works. **2** A studio is also a room containing special equipment where records, films, or radio or television programmes are made.

studious (pronounced **styoo**-dee-uss) (adjective) spending a lot of time studying.

studiously (adverb) carefully and deliberately, e.g. *She was studiously ignoring me.*

study, studies, studying, studied 1 (verb) If you study a particular subject, you spend time learning about it. **2** (noun) Study is the activity of studying a subject, e.g. *the se-*

rious study of medieval archaeology. **3** Studies are subjects which are studied, e.g. *media studies.* **4** (verb) If you study something, you look at it carefully, e.g. *He studied the map in silence.* **5** (noun) A study is a piece of research on a particular subject, e.g. *a detailed study of the world's most violent people.* **6** A study in a house is a room used for writing, reading, and studying.

stuff, stuffs, stuffing, stuffed 1 (noun) You can refer to a substance or group of things as stuff. **2** (verb) If you stuff something somewhere, you push it there quickly and roughly. **3** If you stuff something with a substance or objects, you fill it with the substance or objects.

stuffing (noun) Stuffing is a mixture of small pieces of food put inside poultry or a vegetable before it is cooked.

stuffy, stuffier, stuffiest 1 (adjective) very formal and old-fashioned. **2** If it is stuffy in a room, there is not enough fresh air.

stumble, stumbles, stumbling, stumbled 1 (verb) If you stumble while you are walking or running, you trip and almost fall. **2** If you stumble when speaking, you make mistakes when pronouncing the words. **3** If you stumble across something or stumble on it, you find it unexpectedly.

stump, stumps, stumping, stumped 1 (noun) A stump is a small part of something that is left when the rest has been removed, e.g. *the stump of a dead tree.* **2** In cricket, the stumps are the three upright wooden sticks that support the bails, forming the wicket. **3** (verb) If a question or problem stumps you, you cannot think of an answer or solution.

stun, stuns, stunning, stunned 1 (verb) If you are stunned by something, you are very shocked by it. **2** To stun a person or animal means to knock them unconscious with a blow to the head.

stunning (adjective) very beautiful or impressive, e.g. *a stunning first novel.*

stunt, stunts, stunting, stunted 1 (noun) A stunt is an unusual or dangerous and exciting action that someone does to get publicity or as part of a film. **2** (verb) To stunt the growth or development of something means to prevent it from developing as it should.

stupendous (adjective) very large or impressive, e.g. *a stupendous amount of money.*

stupid, stupider, stupidest (adjective) showing lack of good judgment or intelligence and not at all sensible. **stupidity** (noun).

sturdy, sturdier, sturdiest (adjective) strong and firm and unlikely to be damaged or injured, e.g. *a sturdy chest of drawers.*

sturgeon (pronounced **stur**-jon) (noun) A sturgeon is a large edible fish. Its eggs are also eaten and are known as caviar.

stutter, stutters, stuttering, stuttered 1 (noun) Someone who has a stutter finds it difficult to speak smoothly and often repeats sounds through being unable to complete a word. **2** (verb) When someone stutters, they hesitate or repeat sounds when speaking.

sty, sties 1 (noun) A sty is the same as a pigsty. **2** A sty or stye is an infection in the form of a small red swelling on a person's eyelid.

style, styles, styling, styled 1 (noun) The style of something is the general way in which it is done or presented, often showing the attitudes of the people involved. **2** A person or place that has style is smart, elegant, and fashionable. **3** The style of something is its design, e.g. *new windows that fit in with the style of the house.* **4** (verb) To style a piece of clothing or a person's hair means to design and create its shape.

stylish (adjective) smart, elegant, and fashionable. **stylishly** (adverb).

suave (pronounced **swahv**) (adjective) charming, polite, and confident, e.g. *a suave Italian.*

sub- 1 (prefix) Sub- is used at the beginning of words that have 'under' as part of their meaning, e.g. *submarine.* **2** Sub- is also used to form nouns that refer to the parts into which something is divided, e.g. *Subsection 2 of section 49... a particular subgroup of citizens.*

subconscious 1 (noun) Your subconscious is the part of your mind that can influence you without your being aware of it. **2** (adjective) happening or existing in someone's subconscious and therefore not directly realized or understood by them, e.g. *a subconscious fear of rejection.* **subconsciously** (adverb).

subcontinent, subcontinents (noun) A subcontinent is a large mass of land, often consisting of several countries, and forming part of a continent, e.g. *the Indian subcontinent.*

subdue, subdues, subduing, subdued 1 (verb) If soldiers subdue a group of people, they bring them under control by using force, e.g. *It would be quite impossible to subdue the whole continent.* **2** To subdue a colour, light, or emotion means to make it less bright or strong.

subdued 1 (adjective) rather quiet and sad. **2** not very noticeable or bright.

subject, subjects, subjecting, subjected 1 (noun) The subject of writing or a conversation is the thing or person being discussed. **2** In grammar, the subject is the word or words representing the person or thing doing the action expressed by the verb. For example, in the sentence 'My cat keeps catching birds', 'my cat' is the subject. **3** A subject is an area of study. **4** (verb) To subject someone to something means to make them experience it, e.g. *He was subjected to constant interruption.* **5** (noun) The subjects of a country are the people who live there. **6** (adjective) Someone or something that is subject to something is affected by it, e.g. *He was subject to attacks at various times.*

subjective (adjective) influenced by personal feelings and opinion rather than based on fact or rational thought.

sublime (adjective) Something that is sublime is wonderful and affects people emotionally, e.g. *sublime music.*

submarine, submarines (noun) A submarine is a ship that can travel beneath the surface of the sea.

submerge, submerges, submerging, submerged 1 (verb) To submerge means to go beneath the surface of a liquid. **2** If you submerge yourself in an activity, you become totally involved in it.

submission, submissions 1 (noun) Submission is a state in which someone accepts the control of another person, e.g. *Now he must beat us into submission.* **2** The submission of a proposal or application is the act of sending it for consideration.

submissive (adjective) behaving in a quiet, obedient way.

submit, submits, submitting, submitted 1 (verb) If you submit to something, you accept it because you are not powerful enough to resist it. **2** If you submit an application or proposal, you send it to someone for consideration.

subordinate, subordinates, subordinating, subordinated 1 (noun) A person's subordinate is someone who is in a less important position than them. **2** (adjective) If one thing is subordinate to another, it is less important, e.g. *Non-elected officials are subordinate to elected leaders.* **3** (verb) To subordinate one thing to another means to treat it as being less important.

subscribe, subscribes, subscribing, subscribed 1 (verb) If you subscribe to a particular belief or opinion, you support it or agree with it. **2** If you subscribe to a magazine, you pay to receive regular copies. **subscriber** (noun).

subscription, subscriptions (noun) A subscription is a sum of money that you pay regularly to belong to an organization or to receive regular copies of a magazine.

subsequent (adjective) happening or coming into existence at a later time than something else, e.g. *the December uprising and the subsequent political violence.* **subsequently** (adverb).

subservient (adjective) Someone who is subservient does whatever other people want them to do.

subside, subsides, subsiding, subsided 1 (verb) To subside means to become less intense or quieter, e.g. *Her excitement suddenly subsided.* **2** If water or the ground subsides, it sinks to a lower level.

subsidence (noun) If a place is suffering from subsidence, parts of the ground have sunk to a lower level.

subsidiary, subsidiaries (pronounced sub-**sid**-yer-ee) **1** (noun) A subsidiary is a company which is part of a larger company. **2** (adjective) treated as being of less importance and additional to another thing, e.g. *Drama is offered as a subsidiary subject.*

subsidize, subsidizes, subsidizing, subsidized; also spelled **subsidise** (verb) To subsidize something means to provide part of the cost of it, e.g. *He feels the government should do much more to subsidize films.* **subsidized** (adjective).

subsidy, subsidies (noun) A subsidy is a sum of money paid to help support a company or provide a public service.

substance, substances 1 (noun) Anything which is a solid, a powder, a liquid, or a paste can be referred to as a substance. **2** If a speech or piece of writing has substance, it is meaningful or important, e.g. *a good speech, but there was no substance.*

substantial 1 (adjective) very large in degree or amount, e.g. *a substantial pay rise.* **2** large and strongly built, e.g. *a substantial stone building.*

substantially (adverb) Something that is substantially true is generally or mostly true.

substitute, substitutes, substituting, substituted 1 (verb) To substitute one thing for another means to use it instead of the other thing or to put it in the other thing's place. **2** (noun) If one thing is a substitute for another, it is used instead of it or put in its place. **substitution** (noun).

subterfuge, subterfuges (pronounced **sub**-ter-fyooj) (noun) Subterfuge is the use of deceitful or dishonest methods.

subtitle, subtitles (noun) A film with subtitles has a printed translation of the dialogue at the bottom of the screen.

subtle, subtler, subtlest (pronounced **sut**-tl) **1** (adjective) very fine, delicate, or small in degree, e.g. *a subtle change.* **2** using indirect methods to achieve something. **subtly** (adverb), **subtlety** (noun).

subtract, subtracts, subtracting, subtracted (verb) If you subtract one number from another, you take away the first number from the second. **subtraction** (noun).

suburb, suburbs (noun) A suburb is an area of a town or city that is away from its centre.

suburban 1 (adjective) relating to a suburb or suburbs. **2** dull and conventional.

suburbia (noun) You can refer to the suburbs of a city as suburbia.

subversive, subversives 1 (adjective) intended to destroy or weaken a political system, e.g. *subversive activities.* **2** (noun) Subversives are people who try to destroy or weaken a political system. **subversion** (noun).

subvert, subverts, subverting, subverted (verb; a formal word) To subvert something means to cause it to weaken, fail, or be destroyed, e.g. *a cunning campaign to subvert the music industry.*

subway, subways 1 (noun) A subway is a footpath that goes underneath a road. **2** In American English, a subway is an underground railway.

succeed, succeeds, succeeding, succeeded 1 (verb) To succeed means to achieve the result you intend. **2** To succeed someone means to be the next person to have their job. **3** If one thing succeeds another, it comes after it in time, e.g. *The explosion was succeeded by a crash.* **succeeding** (adjective).

success, successes 1 (noun) Success is the achievement of something you have been trying to do. **2** Someone who is a success has achieved an important position or made a lot of money. **successful** (adjective), **successfully** (adverb).

succession, successions 1 (noun) A succession of things is a number of them occurring one after the other. **2** (phrase) If something happens a number of weeks, months, or years **in succession,** it happens that number of times without a break, e.g. *Borg won Wimbledon five years in succession.* **3** (noun) When someone becomes the next person to have an important position, you can refer to this event as their succession to this position, e.g. *his succession to the throne.*

successive (adjective) occurring one after the other without a break, e.g. *nine successive defeats.*

successor, successors (noun) Someone's successor is the person who takes their job when they leave.

succinct (pronounced **suk-singkt**) (adjective) expressing something clearly and in very few words. **succinctly** (adverb).

succulent (adjective) Succulent food is juicy and delicious.

succumb, succumbs, succumbing, succumbed (verb) If you succumb to something, you are unable to resist it any longer, e.g. *She never succumbed to his charms.*

such 1 (adjective or pronoun) You use 'such' to refer to the person or thing you have just mentioned, or to someone or something similar, e.g. *Naples or Palermo or some such place.* **2** (phrase) You can use **such as** to introduce an example of something, e.g. *herbal teas such as camomile.* **3** (adjective) 'Such' can be used for emphasizing, e.g. *I have such a terrible sense of guilt.* **4** (phrase) You can use **such as it is** to indicate that something is not great in quality or quantity, e.g. *The action, such as it is, is set in Egypt.* **5** You can use **such and such** when you want to refer to something that is not specific, e.g. *A good trick is to ask whether they have seen such and such a film.*

suchlike (adjective or pronoun) used to refer to things similar to those already mentioned, e.g. *shampoos, talcs, toothbrushes, and suchlike.*

suck, sucks, sucking, sucked 1 (verb) If you suck something, you hold it in your mouth and pull at it with your cheeks and tongue, usually to get liquid out of it. **2** To suck something in a particular direction means to draw it there with a powerful force. **3** (an informal use) To suck up to someone means to do things to please them in order to obtain praise or approval.

sucker, suckers 1 (noun; an informal use) If you call someone a sucker, you mean that they are easily fooled or cheated. **2** Suckers are pads on the bodies of some animals and insects which they use to cling to a surface.

suckle, suckles, suckling, suckled (verb) When a mother suckles a baby, she feeds it with milk from her breast.

suction 1 (noun) Suction is the force involved when a substance is drawn or sucked from one place to another. **2** Suction is the process by which two surfaces stick together when the air between them is removed, e.g. *They stay there by suction.*

Sudanese (pronounced soo-dan-**neez**) **1** (adjective) belonging or relating to the Sudan. **2** (noun) A Sudanese is someone who comes from the Sudan.

sudden (adjective) happening quickly and unexpectedly, e.g. *a sudden cry.* **suddenly** (adverb), **suddenness** (noun).

sue, sues, suing, sued (verb) To sue someone means to start a legal case against them, usually to claim money from them.

suede (pronounced **swayd**) (noun) Suede is a thin, soft leather with a rough surface.

suffer, suffers, suffering, suffered 1 (verb) If someone is suffering pain, or suffering as a result of an unpleasant situation, they are badly affected by it. **2** If something suffers as a result of neglect or an unfavourable situation, its condition or quality becomes worse, e.g. *The bus service is suffering.* **sufferer** (noun), **suffering** (noun).

suffice, suffices, sufficing, sufficed (verb; a formal word) If something suffices, it is enough or adequate for a purpose.

sufficient (adjective) If a supply or quantity is sufficient for a purpose, there is enough of it available. **sufficiently** (adverb).

suffix, suffixes (noun) A suffix is a group of letters which is added to the end of a word to form a new word, for example '-ology' or '-itis'.

suffocate, suffocates, suffocating, suffocated (verb) To suffocate means to die as a result of having too little air or oxygen to breathe. **suffocation** (noun).

suffrage (noun) Suffrage is the right to vote in political elections.

suffragette, suffragettes (noun) A suffragette was a woman who, at the beginning of this century, was involved in the campaign for women to be given the right to vote.

suffused (adjective; a literary word) If something is suffused with light or colour, light or colour has gradually spread over it.

sugar (noun) Sugar is a sweet substance used to sweeten food and drinks.

suggest, suggests, suggesting, suggested 1 (verb) If you suggest a plan or idea to someone, you mention it as a possibility for them to consider. **2** If something suggests a particular thought or impression, it makes you think in that way or gives you that impression, e.g. *Nothing you say suggests he is mentally ill.*

suggestion, suggestions 1 (noun) A suggestion is a plan or idea that is mentioned as a possibility for someone to consider. **2** A suggestion of something is a very slight indication or faint sign of it, e.g. *a suggestion of awe.*

suggestive 1 (adjective) Something that is suggestive of a particular thing gives a slight hint or sign of it. **2** Suggestive remarks or gestures make people think about sex.

suicidal 1 (adjective) People who are suicidal want to kill themselves. **2** Suicidal behaviour is so dangerous that it is likely to result in death, e.g. *a mad suicidal attack.*

suicide (noun) People who commit suicide deliberately kill themselves.

suit, suits, suiting, suited 1 (noun) A suit is a matching jacket and trousers or skirt. **2** (verb) If a situation or course of action suits you, it is appropriate or acceptable for your purpose. **3** If a piece of clothing or a colour suits you, you look good when you are wearing it. **4** If you do something to suit yourself, you do it because you want to and without considering other people. **5** (noun) In a court of law, a suit is a legal action taken by one person against another. **6** A suit is one of four different types of card in a pack of playing cards. The four suits are hearts, clubs, diamonds, and spades.

suitable (adjective) right or acceptable for a particular purpose or occasion. **suitability** (noun), **suitably** (adverb).

suitcase, suitcases (noun) A suitcase is a case in which you carry your clothes when you are travelling.

suite, suites (pronounced **sweet**) **1** (noun) In a hotel, a suite is a set of rooms. **2** A suite is a set of matching furniture or bathroom fittings.

suited (adjective) right or appropriate for a particular purpose or person, e.g. *He is well suited to be minister for the arts.*

suitor, suitors (noun; an old-fashioned word) A woman's suitor is a man who wants to marry her.

sulk, sulks, sulking, sulked (verb) Someone who is sulking is showing their annoyance by being silent and moody. **sulky** (adjective).

sullen (adjective) behaving in a bad-tempered and disagreeably silent way, e.g. *a sullen and resentful workforce.*

sulphur (noun) Sulphur is a pale yellow nonmetallic element which burns with a very unpleasant smell.

sultan, sultans (noun) In some Muslim countries, the ruler of the country is called the sultan.

sultana, sultanas 1 (noun) Sultanas are dried grapes. **2** A sultana is also the wife of a sultan.

sum, sums, summing, summed 1 (noun) A sum is an amount of money. **2** In arithmetic, a sum is a calculation. **3** The sum of something is the total amount of it. **sum up** (verb) If you sum something up, you briefly describe its main points.

summarize, summarizes, summarizing, summarized; also spelled **summarise** (verb) To summarize something means to give a short account of its main points.

summary, summaries 1 (noun) A summary of something is a short account of its main points. **2** (adjective) A summary action is done without delay or careful thought, e.g. *Summary executions are common.* **summarily** (adverb).

summer, summers (noun) Summer is the season between spring and autumn.

summit, summits 1 (noun) The summit of a mountain is its top. **2** A summit is a meeting between leaders of different countries to discuss particular issues.

summon, summons, summoning, summoned 1 (verb) If someone summons you, they order you to go to them. **2** If you summon up strength or energy, you make a great effort to be strong or energetic.

summons, summonses 1 (noun) A summons is an official order to appear in court. **2** A summons is an order to go to someone, e.g. *The result was a summons to Downing Street.*

sumptuous (adjective) Something that is sumptuous is magnificent and obviously very expensive.

sum total (noun) The sum total of a number of things is all of them added or considered together.

sun, suns, sunning, sunned 1 (noun) The sun is the star providing heat and light for the planets revolving around it in our solar system. **2** You refer to heat and light from the sun as sun, e.g. *We need a bit of sun.* **3** (verb) If you sun yourself, you sit in the sunshine.

sunbathe, sunbathes, sunbathing, sunbathed (verb) If you sunbathe, you sit in the sunshine to get a suntan.

sunburn (noun) Sunburn is sore red skin on someone's body due to too much exposure to the rays of the sun. **sunburnt** (adjective).

sundae, sundaes (pronounced **sun**-day) (noun) A sundae is a dish of ice cream with cream and fruit or nuts.

Sunday, Sundays (noun) Sunday is the day between Saturday and Monday.

Sunday school, Sunday schools (noun) Sunday school is a special class held on Sundays to teach children about Christianity.

sundial, sundials (noun) A sundial is an object used for telling the time, consisting of a pointer which casts a shadow on a flat base marked with the hours.

sundry 1 (adjective) Sundry is used to refer to several things or people of various sorts, e.g. *sundry journalists and lawyers.* **2** (phrase) **All and sundry** means everyone.

sunflower, sunflowers (noun) A sunflower is a tall plant with very large yellow flowers.

sunglasses (plural noun) Sunglasses are spectacles with dark lenses that you wear to protect your eyes from the sun.

sunken 1 (adjective) having sunk to the bottom of the sea, a river, or lake, e.g. *sunken* *ships.* **2** A sunken object or area has been constructed below the level of the surrounding area, e.g. *a sunken garden.* **3** curving inwards, e.g. *Her cheeks were sunken.*

sunlight (noun) Sunlight is the bright light produced when the sun is shining. **sunlit** (adjective).

sunny, sunnier, sunniest (adjective) When it is sunny, the sun is shining.

sunrise, sunrises (noun) Sunrise is the time in the morning when the sun first appears, and the colours produced in the sky at that time.

sunset, sunsets (noun) Sunset is the time in the evening when the sun disappears below the horizon, and the colours produced in the sky at that time.

sunshine (noun) Sunshine is the bright light produced when the sun is shining.

sunstroke (noun) Sunstroke is an illness caused by spending too much time in hot sunshine.

suntan, suntans (noun) If you have a suntan, the sun has turned your skin brown. **suntanned** (adjective).

super 1 (adjective) very nice or very good, e.g. *a super party.* **2** Super is used to describe something that is larger or better than similar things, e.g. *a European super state.*

superb (adjective) very good indeed. **superbly** (adverb).

supercilious (pronounced soo-per-**sill**-ee-uss) (adjective) If you are supercilious, you behave in a scornful way towards other people because you think they are inferior to you.

superficial 1 (adjective) involving only the most obvious or most general aspects of something, e.g. *a superficial knowledge of music.* **2** not having a deep, serious, or genuine interest in anything, e.g. *a superficial and rather silly woman.* **3** Superficial wounds are not very deep or severe. **superficially** (adverb).

superfluous (pronounced soo-**per**-floo-uss) (adjective; a formal word) unnecessary or no longer needed.

superhuman (adjective) having much greater power or ability than is normally expected of humans, e.g. *superhuman strength.*

superimpose, superimposes, superimposing, superimposed (verb) To superimpose one image on another means to put the first image on top of the other so that they are seen as one image.

superintendent, superintendents 1 (noun) A superintendent in the police force is an officer above the rank of inspector. **2** A superintendent is a person whose job is to be responsible for a particular thing, e.g. *the superintendent of prisons.*

superior, superiors 1 (adjective) better or of higher quality than other similar things. **2** in a position of higher authority than another person. **3** showing too much pride and self-importance, e.g. *Jerry smiled in a superior way.* **4** (noun) Your superiors are people who are in a higher position than you in society or an organization. **superiority** (noun).

superlative, superlatives (pronounced soo-**per**-lat-tiv) **1** (noun) In grammar, the superlative is the form of an adjective which indicates that the person or thing described has more of a particular quality than anyone or anything else. For example, 'quicker', 'best', and 'easiest' are all superlatives. **2** (adjective; a formal use) very good indeed, e.g. *a superlative performance.*

supermarket, supermarkets (noun) A supermarket is a shop selling food and household goods arranged so that you can help yourself and pay for everything at a till by the exit.

supernatural 1 (adjective) Something that is supernatural, for example ghosts or witchcraft, cannot be explained by normal scientific laws. **2** (noun) You can refer to supernatural things as the supernatural.

superpower, superpowers (noun) A superpower is a very powerful and influential country such as the USA.

supersede, supersedes, superseding, superseded (pronounced soo-per-**seed**) (verb) If something supersedes another thing, it replaces it because it is more modern.

supersonic (adjective) A supersonic aircraft can travel faster than the speed of sound.

superstar, superstars (noun) You can refer to a very famous entertainer or sports player as a superstar.

superstition, superstitions (noun) Superstition is a belief in things like magic and powers that bring good or bad luck. **superstitious** (adjective).

supervise, supervises, supervising, supervised (verb) To supervise someone means to check and direct what they are doing to make sure that they do it correctly. **supervision** (noun), **supervisor** (noun).

supper, suppers (noun) Supper is a meal eaten in the evening or a snack eaten before you go to bed.

supplant, supplants, supplanting, supplanted (verb; a formal word) To supplant someone or something means to take their place, e.g. *He really could supplant the man who sat behind the desk.*

supple (adjective) able to bend and move easily.

supplement, supplements, supplementing, supplemented 1 (verb) To supplement something means to add something to it to improve it, e.g. *Many village men supplemented their wages by fishing for salmon.* **2** (noun) A supplement is something that is added to something else to improve it.

supplementary (adjective) added to something else to improve it, e.g. *supplementary doses of vitamin E.*

supplier, suppliers (noun) A supplier is a firm which provides particular goods.

supply, supplies, supplying, supplied 1 (verb) To supply someone with something means to provide it or send it to them. **2** (noun) A supply of something is an amount available for use, e.g. *the world's* *supply of precious metals.* **3** (plural noun) Supplies are food and equipment for a particular purpose.

support, supports, supporting, supported 1 (verb) If you support someone, you agree with their aims and want them to succeed. **2** If you support someone who is in difficulties, you are kind, encouraging, and helpful to them. **3** If something supports an object, it is underneath it and holding it up. **4** (noun) A support is an object that is holding something up. **5** (verb) To support someone or something means to prevent them from falling by holding them. **6** (noun) Financial support is money that is provided for someone or something. **7** (verb) To support someone financially means to provide them with money. **supporter** (noun), **supportable** (adjective).

supportive (adjective) A supportive person is kind, encouraging, and helpful to someone who is in difficulties.

suppose, supposes, supposing, supposed 1 (verb) If you suppose that something is the case, you think that it is likely, e.g. *I supposed that would be too obvious.* **2** (phrase) You can say **I suppose** when you are not entirely certain or enthusiastic about something, e.g. *Yes, I suppose he could come.* **3** (conjunction) You can use 'suppose' or 'supposing' when you are considering or suggesting a possible situation or action, e.g. *Supposing he were to break down under interrogation?* **4** (phrase) If something **is supposed** to be done, it should be done, e.g. *You are supposed to report it to the police.* **5** If something **is supposed** to happen, it is planned or expected to happen, e.g. *It was supposed to be this afternoon.* **6** Something that **is supposed** to be the case is generally believed or thought to be so, e.g. *Wimbledon is supposed to be the best tournament of them all.*

supposed (adjective) Supposed is used to express doubt about something that is generally believed, e.g. *the supposed culprit.* **supposedly** (adverb).

supposition, suppositions (noun) A supposition is something that is believed or assumed to be true, e.g. *Her supposition was absolutely correct.*

suppress, suppresses, suppressing, suppressed 1 (verb) If an army or government suppresses an activity, it prevents people from doing it. **2** If someone suppresses a piece of information, they prevent it from becoming generally known. **3** If you suppress your feelings, you stop yourself expressing them. **suppression** (noun).

supremacy (pronounced soo-**prem**-mass-ee) (noun) If a group of people has supremacy over others, it is more powerful than the others.

supreme 1 (adjective) Supreme is used as part of a title to indicate the highest level of an organization or system, e.g. *the Supreme Court.* **2** Supreme is used to emphasize the greatness of something, e.g. *the supreme achievement of the* *human race.* **supremely** (adverb).

surcharge, surcharges (noun) A surcharge is an additional charge.

sure, surer, surest 1 (adjective) If you are sure about something, you have no doubts about it. **2** If you are sure of yourself, you are very confident. **3** If something is sure to happen, it will definitely happen. **4** (phrase) If you **make sure** about something, you check it or take action to see that it is done. **5** (adjective) Sure means reliable or accurate, e.g. *a sure sign that something is wrong.* **6** (interjection) Sure is an informal way of saying 'yes', e.g. *'Can I come too?' — 'Sure.'*

surely (adverb) Surely is used to emphasize the belief that something is the case, e.g. *Surely these people here knew that?*

surf (noun) Surf is the white foam that forms on the top of waves when they break near the shore.

surface, surfaces, surfacing, surfaced 1 (noun) The surface of something is the top or outside area of it. **2** The surface of a situation is what can be seen easily rather than what is hidden or not immediately obvious. **3** (verb) If someone surfaces, they come up from under water to the surface.

surfboard, surfboards (noun) A surfboard is a long narrow lightweight board used for surfing.

surfeit (pronounced **sur**-fit) (noun) If there is a surfeit of something, there is too much of it.

surfing (noun) Surfing is a sport which involves riding towards the shore on the top of a large wave while standing on a surfboard.

surge, surges, surging, surged 1 (noun) A surge is a sudden great increase in the amount of something, e.g. *a surge of panic.* **2** (verb) If something surges, it moves suddenly and powerfully, e.g. *The soldiers surged forwards.*

surgeon, surgeons (noun) A surgeon is a doctor who performs operations.

surgery, surgeries 1 (noun) Surgery is medical treatment involving cutting open part of the patient's body to treat the damaged part. **2** The room or building where a doctor or dentist works is called a surgery. **3** A period of time during which a doctor is available to see patients is called surgery, e.g. *evening surgery.*

surgical (adjective) used in or involving a medical operation, e.g. *surgical gloves.* **surgically** (adverb).

surly, surlier, surliest (adjective) rude and bad-tempered. **surliness** (noun).

surmise, surmises, surmising, surmised (verb; a formal word) To surmise something means to guess it, e.g. *I surmised it was of French manufacture.*

surmount, surmounts, surmounting, surmounted 1 (verb) To surmount a difficulty means to manage to solve it. **2** (a formal use) If something is surmounted by a particular thing, that thing is on top of it, e.g. *The island is surmounted by a huge black castle.*

surname, surnames (noun) Your surname is your last name which you share with other members of your family.

surpass, surpasses, surpassing, surpassed (verb; a formal word) To surpass someone or something means to be better than them.

surplus, surpluses (noun) If there is a surplus of something there is more of it than is needed.

surprise, surprises, surprising, surprised 1 (noun) A surprise is an unexpected event. **2** Surprise is the feeling caused when something unexpected happens. **3** (verb) If something surprises you, it gives you a feeling of surprise. **4** If you surprise someone, you do something they were not expecting. **surprising** (adjective).

surreal (adjective) very strange and dreamlike.

surrender, surrenders, surrendering, surrendered 1 (verb) To surrender means to stop fighting and agree that the other side has won. **2** (noun) Surrender is a situation in which one side in a fight agrees that the other side has won and gives in. **3** (verb) If you surrender to a temptation or feeling, you let it take control of you. **4** To surrender something means to give it up to someone else, e.g. *The gallery director surrendered his keys.*

surreptitious (pronounced sur-rep-**tish**-uss) (adjective) A surreptitious action is done secretly or so that no-one will notice, e.g. *a surreptitious glance.* **surreptitiously** (adverb).

surrogate, surrogates 1 (adjective) acting as a substitute for someone or something. **2** (noun) A surrogate is a person or thing that acts as a substitute.

surround, surrounds, surrounding, surrounded 1 (verb) To surround someone or something means to be situated all around them. **2** (noun) The surround of something is its outside edge or border.

surrounding, surroundings 1 (adjective) The surrounding area of a particular place is the area around it, e.g. *the surrounding countryside.* **2** (plural noun) You can refer to the area and environment around a place or person as their surroundings, e.g. *very comfortable surroundings.*

surveillance (pronounced sur-**vay**-lanss) (noun) Surveillance is the close watching of a person's activities by the police or army.

survey, surveys, surveying, surveyed 1 (verb) To survey something means to look carefully at the whole of it. **2** To survey a building or piece of land means to examine it carefully in order to make a report or plan of its structure and features. **3** (noun) A survey of something is a detailed examination or investigation of it, often in the form of a report.

surveyor, surveyors (noun) A surveyor is a person whose job is to survey buildings or land.

survival, survivals (noun) Survival is being able to continue living or existing in spite of great danger or difficulties, e.g. *There was no hope of survival.*

survive, survives, surviving, survived (verb) To survive means to continue to live or exist in spite of a great danger or difficulties, e.g. *a German monk who survived the shipwreck.* **survivor** (noun).

susceptible (adjective) If you are susceptible to something, you are likely to be influenced or affected by it, e.g. *Elderly people are more susceptible to infection.* **susceptibility** (noun).

suspect, suspects, suspecting, suspected 1 (verb) If you suspect something, you think that it is likely or is probably true, e.g. *I suspected that the report would be sent.* **2** If you suspect something, you have doubts about its reliability, e.g. *He suspected her intent.* **3** If you suspect someone of doing something wrong, you think that they have done it. **4** (noun) A suspect is someone who is thought to be guilty of a crime. **5** (adjective) If something is suspect, it cannot be trusted or relied upon, e.g. *a rather suspect holy man.*

suspend, suspends, suspending, suspended 1 (verb) If something is suspended, it is hanging from somewhere, e.g. *the television set suspended above the bar.* **2** To suspend an activity or event means to delay it or stop it for a while. **3** If someone is suspended from their job, they are told not to do it for a period of time, usually as a punishment.

suspender, suspenders (noun) Suspenders are fastenings which hold up a woman's stockings.

suspense (noun) Suspense is a state of excitement or anxiety caused by having to wait for something.

suspension 1 (noun) The suspension of something is the delaying or stopping of it. **2** A person's suspension is their removal from a job for a period of time, usually as a punishment.

suspicion, suspicions 1 (noun) Suspicion is the feeling of not trusting someone or the feeling that something is wrong. **2** A suspicion is a feeling that something is likely to happen or is probably true, e.g. *the suspicion that more could have been achieved.*

suspicious 1 (adjective) If you are suspicious of someone, you do not trust them. **2** Suspicious is used to describe things that make you think that there is something wrong with a situation, e.g. *suspicious circumstances.* **suspiciously** (adverb).

sustain, sustains, sustaining, sustained 1 (verb) To sustain something means to continue it or maintain it for a period of time, e.g. *Their team-mates were unable to sustain the challenge.* **2** If something sustains you, it gives you energy and strength, e.g. *Custer swallowed his beer to sustain him.* **3** (a formal use) To sustain an injury or loss means to suffer it.

sustenance (noun; a formal word) Sustenance is food and drink.

swab, swabs, swabbing, swabbed 1 (noun) A swab is a small piece of cotton wool used for cleaning a wound. **2** (verb) To swab something means to clean it using a large mop and a lot of water. **3** To swab a wound means to clean it or take specimens from it using a swab.

swagger, swaggers, swaggering, swaggered 1 (verb) To swagger means to walk in a proud, exaggerated way. **2** (noun) A swagger is an exaggerated walk.

swallow, swallows, swallowing, swallowed 1 (verb) If you swallow something, you make it go down your throat and into your stomach. **2** When you swallow, you move your throat muscles as if you were swallowing something, especially when you are nervous. **3** (noun) A swallow is a bird with pointed wings and a long forked tail.

swamp, swamps, swamping, swamped 1 (noun) A swamp is an area of permanently wet land. **2** (verb) If something is swamped, it is covered or filled with water. **3** If you are swamped by things, you have more than you are able to deal with, e.g. *She was swamped with calls.* **swampy** (adjective).

swan, swans (noun) A swan is a large bird with a very long neck. Swans are usually white and live on rivers or lakes.

swap, swaps, swapping, swapped (rhymes with **stop**) (verb) To swap one thing for another means to replace the first thing with the second, often by making an exchange with another person, e.g. *a pack of cigarettes which I swapped for some eggs.*

swarm, swarms, swarming, swarmed 1 (noun) A swarm of insects is a large group of them flying together. **2** (verb) When bees or other insects swarm, they fly together in a large group. **3** If people swarm somewhere, a lot of people go there quickly and at the same time, e.g. *the crowds of office workers who swarm across London Bridge.* **4** If a place is swarming with people, there are a lot of people there.

swarthy, swarthier, swarthiest (adjective) A swarthy person has a dark complexion.

swashbuckling (adjective) Swashbuckling is used to describe people who have the exciting behaviour or appearance of pirates.

swastika, swastikas (pronounced **swoss**-tik-ka) (noun) A swastika is a symbol in the shape of a cross with each arm bent over at right angles. It was the official symbol of the Nazis in Germany, but in India it is a good luck sign.

swat, swats, swatting, swatted (verb) To swat an insect means to hit it sharply in order to kill it.

swathe, swathes (rhymes with **bathe**) **1** (noun) A swathe is a long strip of cloth that is wrapped around something, e.g. *swathes of white silk.* **2** A swathe of land is a long strip of it.

swathed (adjective) If someone is swathed in something, they are wrapped in it, e.g. *She was swathed in towels.*

sway, sways, swaying, swayed **1** (verb) To sway means to lean or swing slowly from side to side. **2** If something sways you, it influences your judgment. **3** (noun; a literary use) Sway is the power to influence people, e.g. *under the sway of more powerful neighbours.*

swear, swears, swearing, swore, sworn **1** (verb) To swear means to say words that are considered to be very rude or blasphemous. **2** If you swear to something, you state solemnly that you will do it or that it is true. **3** If you swear by something, you firmly believe that it is a reliable cure or solution, e.g. *Some women swear by extra vitamins.*

swearword, swearwords (noun) A swearword is a word which is considered to be rude or blasphemous, which people use when they are angry.

sweat, sweats, sweating, sweated **1** (noun) Sweat is the salty liquid produced by your sweat glands when you are hot or afraid. **2** (verb) When you sweat, sweat comes through the pores in your skin in order to lower the temperature of your body.

sweater, sweaters (noun) A sweater is a knitted piece of clothing covering your upper body and arms.

sweatshirt, sweatshirts (noun) A sweatshirt is a piece of clothing made of thick cotton, covering your upper body and arms.

sweaty (adjective) covered or soaked with sweat.

swede, swedes (noun) A swede is a large round root vegetable with yellow flesh and a brownish-purple skin.

Swede, Swedes (noun) A Swede is someone who comes from Sweden.

Swedish **1** (adjective) belonging or relating to Sweden. **2** (noun) Swedish is the main language spoken in Sweden.

sweep, sweeps, sweeping, swept **1** (verb) If you sweep the floor, you use a brush to gather up dust or rubbish from it. **2** To sweep things off a surface means to push them all off with a quick, smooth movement. **3** If something sweeps from one place to another, it moves there very quickly, e.g. *A gust of wind swept over the terrace.* **4** If an attitude or new fashion sweeps a place, it spreads rapidly through it, e.g. *a phenomenon that is sweeping America.* **5** (noun) If you do something with a sweep of your arm, you do it with a wide curving movement of your arm.

sweeping **1** (adjective) A sweeping curve or movement is long and wide. **2** A sweeping statement is based on a general assumption rather than on careful thought. **3** affecting a lot of people to a great extent, e.g. *sweeping changes.*

sweet, sweeter, sweetest; sweets **1** (adjective) containing a lot of sugar, e.g. *a mug of sweet tea.* **2** (noun) Things such as toffees, chocolates, and mints are sweets. **3** A sweet is a dessert. **4** (adjective) pleasant and satisfying, e.g. *sweet success.* **5** A sweet smell is soft and fragrant. **6** A sweet sound is gentle and tuneful. **7** attractive and delightful, e.g. *a sweet little baby.* **sweetly** (adverb), **sweetness** (noun).

sweet corn (noun) Sweet corn is a long stalk covered with juicy yellow seeds that can be eaten as a vegetable.

sweeten, sweetens, sweetening, sweetened (verb) To sweeten food means to add sugar, honey, or another sweet substance to it.

sweetener, sweeteners (noun) A sweetener is a very sweet, artificial substance that can be used instead of sugar.

sweetheart, sweethearts 1 (noun) You can call someone who you are very fond of 'sweetheart'. **2** A young person's sweetheart is their boyfriend or girlfriend.

sweet pea, sweet peas (noun) Sweet peas are delicate, very fragrant climbing flowers.

sweet tooth (noun) If you have a sweet tooth, you like sweet food very much.

swell, swells, swelling, swelled, swollen 1 (verb) If something swells, it becomes larger and rounder, e.g. *It causes the abdomen to swell.* **2** If an amount swells, it increases in number. **3** (noun) The regular up and down movement of the waves at sea can be called a swell.

swelling, swellings 1 (noun) A swelling is an enlarged area on your body as a result of injury or illness. **2** The swelling of something is an increase in its size.

sweltering (adjective) If the weather is sweltering, it is very hot.

swerve, swerves, swerving, swerved (verb) To swerve means to suddenly change direction to avoid colliding with something.

swift, swifter, swiftest; swifts 1 (adjective) happening or moving very quickly, e.g. *a swift glance.* **2** (noun) A swift is a bird with narrow crescent-shaped wings. **swiftly** (adverb).

swig, swigs, swigging, swigged (an informal word) **1** (verb) To swig a drink means to drink it in large mouthfuls, usually from a bottle. **2** (noun) If you have a swig of a drink, you take a large mouthful of it.

swill, swills, swilling, swilled 1 (verb) To swill something means to pour water over it to clean it, e.g. *Swill the can out thoroughly.* **2** (noun) Swill is a liquid mixture containing waste food that is fed to pigs.

swim, swims, swimming, swam, swum 1 (verb) To swim means to move through water using various movements with parts of the body. **2** (noun) If you go for a swim, you go into water to swim for pleasure. **3** (verb) If things are swimming, it seems as if everything you see is moving and you feel dizzy. **swimmer** (noun).

swimming (noun) Swimming is the activity of moving through water using your arms and legs.

swimming bath, swimming baths (noun) A swimming bath is a public swimming pool.
swimming costume, swimming costumes (noun) A swimming costume is the clothing worn by a woman when she goes swimming.
swimming pool, swimming pools (noun) A swimming pool is a large hole that has been tiled and filled with water for swimming.
swimming trunks (plural noun) Swimming trunks are shorts worn by a man when he goes swimming.
swimsuit, swimsuits (noun) A swimsuit is a swimming costume.
swindle, swindles, swindling, swindled 1 (verb) To swindle someone means to deceive them to obtain money or property. **2** (noun) A swindle is a trick in which someone is cheated out of money or property. **swindler** (noun).
swine, swines 1 (noun; an old-fashioned use) Swine are pigs. **2** (an informal use) If you call someone a swine, you mean they are nasty and spiteful.
swing, swings, swinging, swung 1 (verb) If something swings, it moves repeatedly from side to side from a fixed point. **2** If someone or something swings in a particular direction, they turn quickly or move in a sweeping curve in that direction. **3** (noun) A swing is a seat hanging from a frame or a branch, which moves backwards and forwards when you sit on it. **4** A swing in opinion is a significant change in people's opinion.
swipe, swipes, swiping, swiped 1 (verb) To swipe at something means to try to hit it making a curving movement with the arm. **2** (noun) To take a swipe at something means to swipe at it. **3** (verb; an informal use) To swipe something means to steal it. **4** To swipe a credit card means to pass it through a machine that electronically reads the information stored in the card.
swirl, swirls, swirling, swirled (verb) To swirl means to move quickly in circles, e.g. *The black water swirled around his legs.*
swish, swishes, swishing, swished 1 (verb) To swish means to move quickly through the air making a soft sound, e.g. *The curtains swished back.* **2** (noun) A swish is the sound made when something swishes.
Swiss 1 (adjective) belonging or relating to Switzerland. **2** (noun) A Swiss is someone who comes from Switzerland.
switch, switches, switching, switched 1 (noun) A switch is a small control for an electrical device or machine. **2** (verb) To switch to a different task or topic means to change to it. **3** (noun) A switch is a change, e.g. *a switch in routine.* **4** (verb) If you switch things, you exchange one for the other. **switch off** (verb) To switch off a light or machine means to stop it working by pressing a switch. **switch on** (verb) To switch on a light or

machine means to start it working by pressing a switch.

switchboard, switchboards (noun) The switchboard in an organization is the part where all telephone calls are received.

swivel, swivels, swivelling, swivelled 1 (verb) To swivel means to turn round on a central point. **2** (adjective) A swivel chair or lamp is made so that you can move the main part of it while the base remains in a fixed position.

swollen (adjective) Something that is swollen has swelled up.

swoon, swoons, swooning, swooned (verb; a literary word) To swoon means to faint as a result of strong emotion.

swoop, swoops, swooping, swooped (verb) To swoop means to move downwards through the air in a fast curving movement, e.g. *A flock of pigeons swooped low over the square.*

swop another spelling of **swap**.

sword, swords (noun) A sword is a weapon consisting of a very long blade with a short handle.

swordfish, swordfishes or **swordfish** (noun) A swordfish is a large sea fish with a long upper jaw.

sworn (adjective) If you make a sworn statement, you swear that everything in it is true.

swot, swots, swotting, swotted (an informal word) **1** (verb) To swot means to study or revise very hard. **2** (noun) A swot is someone who spends too much time studying. **3** (verb) If you swot up on a subject you find out as much about it as possible in a short time.

sycamore, sycamores (pronounced **sik**-am-mor) (noun) A sycamore is a tree that has large leaves with five points.

syllable, syllables (noun) A syllable is part of a word that contains a single vowel sound and is pronounced as a unit. For example, 'book' has one syllable and 'reading' has two.

syllabus, syllabuses or **syllabi** (noun) The subjects that are studied for a particular course or examination are called the syllabus.

symbol, symbols (noun) A symbol is a shape, design, or idea that is used to represent something, e.g. *The fish has long been a symbol of Christianity.*

symbolic (adjective) Something that is symbolic has a special meaning that is considered to represent something else, e.g. *The card is symbolic of new beginnings.*

symbolize, symbolizes, symbolizing, symbolized; also spelled **symbolise** (verb) If a shape, design, or idea symbolizes something, it is regarded as being a symbol of it, e.g. *In China and Japan the carp symbolizes courage.* **symbolism** (noun).

symmetrical (adjective) If something is symmetrical, it has two halves which are exactly the same, except that one half is like a reflection of the other half. **symmetrically** (adverb).

symmetry (noun) Something that has symmetry is symmetrical.

sympathetic 1 (adjective) A sympathetic person shows kindness and understanding to other people. **2** If you are sympathetic to a proposal or an idea, you approve of it.

sympathize, sympathizes, sympathizing, sympathized; also spelled **sympathise** (verb) To sympathize with someone who is in difficulties means to show them understanding and care.

sympathizer, sympathizers; also spelled **sympathiser** (noun) People who support a particular cause can be referred to as sympathizers.

sympathy, sympathies 1 (noun) Sympathy is kindness and understanding towards someone who is in difficulties. **2** If you have sympathy with someone's ideas or actions, you agree with them. **3** (phrase) If you do something **in sympathy** with someone, you do it to show your support for them.

symphony, symphonies (noun) A symphony is a piece of music for an orchestra, usually in four movements.

symptom, symptoms 1 (noun) A symptom is something wrong with your body that is a sign of an illness. **2** Something that is considered to be a sign of a bad situation can be referred to as a symptom of it, e.g. *another symptom of the racism sweeping across the country.* **symptomatic** (adjective).

synagogue, synagogues (pronounced **sin**-a-gog) (noun) A synagogue is a building where Jewish people meet for worship and religious instruction.

synchronize, synchronizes, synchronizing, synchronized (pronounced **sing**-kron-nize); also spelled **synchronise 1** (verb) To synchronize two actions means to do them at the same time and speed. **2** To synchronize watches means to set them to show exactly the same time as each other.

syndicate, syndicates (noun) A syndicate is an association of business people formed to carry out a particular project.

syndrome, syndromes 1 (noun) A syndrome is a medical condition characterized by a particular set of symptoms, e.g. *Down's syndrome.* **2** You can refer to a typical set of characteristics as a syndrome, e.g. *the syndrome of sex discrimination, harassment, and exploitation.*

synod, synods (noun) A synod is a council of church leaders which meets regularly to discuss religious and moral issues.

synonym, synonyms (noun) If two words have the same or a very similar meaning, they are synonyms.

synonymous 1 (adjective) Two words that are synonymous have the same or very similar meanings. **2** If two things are closely associated, you can say that one is synonymous with the other, e.g. *New York is synonymous with the Statue of Liberty.*

synopsis, synopses (noun) A synopsis is a summary of a book, play, or film.

syntax (noun) The syntax of a language is its grammatical

rules and the way its words are arranged.
synthetic (adjective) made from artificial substances rather than natural ones.
syphon another spelling of **siphon.**
Syrian, Syrians (pronounced **sirr**-ee-an) **1** (adjective) belonging or relating to Syria. **2** (noun) A Syrian is someone who comes from Syria.
syringe, syringes (pronounced sir-**rinj**) (noun) A syringe is a hollow tube with a plunger and a fine hollow needle. Syringes are used for injecting or extracting liquids.
syrup, syrups (noun) Syrup is a thick sweet liquid made by boiling sugar with water.
system, systems 1 (noun) A system is an organized way of doing or arranging something according to a fixed plan or set of rules. **2** People sometimes refer to the government and administration of the country as the system. **3** You can also refer to a set of equipment as a system, e.g. *an old stereo system.* **4** In biology, a system of a particular kind is the set of organs that perform that function, e.g. *the immune system.*
systematic (adjective) following a fixed plan and done in an efficient way, e.g. *a systematic study.* **systematically** (adverb).

T t

tab, tabs (noun) A tab is a small piece of paper or cloth that is attached to something, especially a garment.
tabby, tabbies (noun) A tabby is a cat whose fur has grey, brown, or black stripes.
tabernacle, tabernacles (pronounced **tab**-er-nak-kl) (noun) A tabernacle is a place of Christian worship not called a church.
table, tables, tabling, tabled 1 (noun) A table is a piece of furniture with a flat horizontal top supported by one or more legs. **2** A table is a set of facts or figures arranged in rows or columns. **3** (verb) If you table something such as a proposal, you say formally that you want it to be discussed.
tablecloth, tablecloths (noun) A tablecloth is a cloth used to cover a table.
tablespoon, tablespoons (noun) A tablespoon is a large spoon used for serving food; also the amount that a tablespoon contains.
tablet, tablets 1 (noun) A tablet is any small, round pill made of powdered medicine. **2** A stone tablet is a slab of stone with words cut into it.
table tennis (noun) Table tennis is a game for two or four people in which you use bats to hit a small hollow ball over

a low net across a table.

tabloid, tabloids (noun) A tabloid is a newspaper with small pages, short news stories, and lots of photographs.

taboo, taboos 1 (noun) A taboo is a social custom that some words, subjects, or actions must be avoided because they are considered embarrassing or offensive, e.g. *We have a powerful taboo against boasting.* **2** A taboo is a religious custom that forbids people to do something. **3** (adjective) forbidden or disapproved of, e.g. *a taboo subject.*

tacit (pronounced **tass**-it) (adjective) understood or implied without actually being said or written. **tacitly** (adverb).

taciturn (pronounced **tass**-it-urn) (adjective) Someone who is taciturn does not talk very much and so seems unfriendly.

tack, tacks, tacking, tacked 1 (noun) A tack is a short nail with a broad, flat head. **2** (verb) If you tack something to a surface, you nail it there with tacks. **3** If you tack a piece of fabric, you sew it with long loose stitches. **4** (noun) If you change tack, you start to use a different method for dealing with something.

tackle, tackles, tackling, tackled 1 (verb) If you tackle a difficult task, you start dealing with it in a determined way. **2** If you tackle someone in a game such as football, you try to get the ball away from them. **3** (noun) A tackle in sport is an attempt to get the ball away from your opponent. **4** (verb) If you tackle someone about something, you talk to them about it in order to get something changed or dealt with. **5** (noun) Tackle is the equipment used for fishing.

tacky, tackier, tackiest 1 (adjective) slightly sticky to touch, e.g. *The cream feels tacky to the touch.* **2** (an informal use) badly made and unpleasant, e.g. *tacky furniture.*

tact (noun) Tact is the ability to see when a situation is difficult or delicate and to handle it without upsetting people. **tactful** (adjective), **tactfully** (adverb), **tactless** (adjective), **tactlessly** (adverb).

tactic, tactics 1 (noun) Tactics are the methods you use to achieve what you want. **2** Tactics are also the ways in which troops and equipment are used in order to win a battle. **tactical** (adjective), **tactically** (adverb).

tactile (adjective) involving the sense of touch.

tadpole, tadpoles (noun) Tadpoles are the larvae of frogs and toads. They are black with round heads and long tails and live in water.

taffeta (pronounced **taf**-fit-a) (noun) Taffeta is a stiff, shiny fabric that is used mainly for making women's clothes.

tag, tags, tagging, tagged 1 (noun) A tag is a small label made of cloth, paper, plastic, or leather. **2** (verb) If you tag along with someone, you go with them or behind them.

tail, tails, tailing, tailed 1 (noun) The tail of an animal, bird, or fish is the part extending beyond the end of its body. **2**

Tail can be used to mean the end or concluding part of something, e.g. *the tail of the plane.* **3** (plural noun) If a man is wearing tails, he is wearing a formal jacket which has two long pieces hanging down at the back. **4** (verb; an informal use) If you tail someone, you follow them in order to find out where they go and what they do. **5** (adjective or adverb) The tails side of a coin is the side which does not have a person's head.

tailback, tailbacks (noun) A tailback is a long queue of traffic stretching back from whatever is blocking the road.

tailor, tailors, tailoring, tailored **1** (noun) A tailor is a person who makes, alters, and repairs clothes, especially for men. **2** (verb) If something is tailored for a particular purpose, it is specially designed for it.

tailor-made (adjective) suitable for a particular person or purpose, or specifically designed for them.

taint, taints, tainting, tainted **1** (verb) To taint something means to spoil it by adding something undesirable to it. **2** (noun) A taint is an undesirable quality in something which spoils it.

take, takes, taking, took, taken **1** (verb) Take is used to show what action or activity is being done, e.g. *Amy took a bath... She took her driving test.* **2** If something takes a certain amount of time, or a particular quality or ability, it requires it, e.g. *He takes three hours to get ready.* **3** If you take something, you put your hand round it and hold it or carry it, e.g. *Here, let me take your coat.* **4** If you take someone somewhere, you drive them there by car or lead them there. **5** If you take something that is offered to you, you accept it, e.g. *He had to take the job.* **6** If you take the responsibility or blame for something, you accept responsibility or blame. **7** If you take something that does not belong to you, you steal it. **8** If you take pills or medicine, you swallow them. **9** If you can take something painful, you can bear it, e.g. *We can't take much more of this.* **10** If you take someone's advice, you do what they say you should do. **11** If you take a person's temperature or pulse, you measure it. **12** If you take a car or train, or a road or route, you use it to go from one place to another. **take after** (verb) If you take after someone in your family, you look or behave like them. **take in** **1** (verb) If someone is taken in, they are deceived. **2** If you take something in, you understand it. **take off** (verb) When an aeroplane takes off, it leaves the ground and begins to fly. **takeoff** (noun). **take over** (verb) To take something over means to start controlling it. **takeover** (noun).

takeaway, takeaways **1** (noun) A takeaway is a shop or restaurant that sells hot cooked food to be eaten elsewhere. **2** A takeaway is a hot cooked meal bought from a takeaway.

takings (plural noun) Takings

are the money that a shop, theatre, or cinema gets from selling its goods or tickets.

talc (noun) Talc is the same as talcum powder.

talcum powder (noun) Talcum powder is a soft perfumed powder used for absorbing moisture on the body.

tale, tales (noun) A tale is a story.

talent, talents (noun) Talent is the natural ability to do something well. **talented** (adjective).

talisman, talismans (pronounced **tal**-iz-man) (noun) A talisman is an object which you believe has magic powers to protect you or bring luck.

talk, talks, talking, talked 1 (verb) When you talk, you say things to someone. **2** If people talk, especially about other people's private affairs, they gossip about them, e.g. *She wouldn't have him at home because the neighbours might talk.* **3** (noun) Talk is discussion or gossip. **4** (verb) If you talk on or about something, you make an informal speech about it. **5** (noun) A talk is an informal speech about something. **talk down** (verb) If you talk down to someone, you talk to them in a way that shows that you think you are more important or clever than them.

talkative (adjective) talking a lot.

tall, taller, tallest 1 (adjective) of more than average or normal height. **2** having a particular height, e.g. *He's six feet tall.*

tally, tallies, tallying, tallied 1 (noun) A tally is an informal record of amounts which you keep adding to as you go along, e.g. *He ended with a reasonable goal tally last season.* **2** (verb) If numbers or statements tally, they are exactly the same or they give the same results or conclusions.

Talmud (pronounced **tal**-mood) (noun) The Talmud consists of the books containing the ancient Jewish ceremonies and civil laws.

talon, talons (noun) Talons are sharp, hooked claws, especially of a bird of prey.

tambourine, tambourines (noun) A tambourine is a percussion instrument made up of a skin stretched tightly over a circular frame with small round pieces of metal around the edge.

tame, tamer, tamest; tames, taming, tamed 1 (adjective) A tame animal or bird is not afraid of people and is not violent towards them. **2** Something that is tame is uninteresting and lacks excitement or risk, e.g. *The report was pretty tame.* **3** (verb) If you tame people or things, you bring them under control. **4** To tame a wild animal or bird means to train it to be obedient and live with humans.

tamper, tampers, tampering, tampered (verb) If you tamper with something, you interfere or meddle with it.

tampon, tampons (noun) A tampon is a firm, specially shaped piece of cotton wool that a woman places inside her vagina to absorb the blood during her period.

tan, tans, tanning, tanned 1 (noun) If you have a tan, your skin is darker than usual because you have been in the sun. **2** (verb) To tan an animal's hide means to turn it into leather by treating it with chemicals. **3** (adjective) Something that is tan is of a light yellowish-brown colour.

tandem, tandems (noun) A tandem is a bicycle designed for two riders sitting one behind the other.

tang, tangs (noun) A tang is a strong, sharp smell or flavour, e.g. *the tang of lemon.* **tangy** (adjective).

tangent, tangents 1 (noun) A tangent of a curve is any straight line that touches the curve at one point only. **2** (phrase) If you **go off at a tangent,** you start talking or thinking about something that is not completely relevant to what has gone before.

tangerine, tangerines 1 (noun) A tangerine is a type of small sweet orange with a loose rind. **2** (noun or adjective) reddish-orange.

tangible (pronounced **tan**-jib-bl) (adjective) clear or definite enough to be easily seen, felt, or noticed, e.g. *tangible proof.*

tangle, tangles, tangling, tangled 1 (noun) A tangle is a mass of things such as hairs, lines, or fibres knotted or coiled together and difficult to separate. **2** (verb) If you are tangled in wires or ropes, you are caught or trapped in them so that it is difficult to get free.

tango, tangos (noun) A tango is a Latin American dance using long gliding steps and sudden pauses.

tank, tanks 1 (noun) A tank is a large container for storing liquid or gas. **2** A tank is also an armoured military vehicle which moves on tracks and is equipped with guns or rockets.

tankard, tankards (noun) A tankard is a large metal mug used for drinking beer.

tanker, tankers (noun) A tanker is a ship, lorry, or aeroplane designed to carry large quantities of gas or liquid, e.g. *a petrol tanker.*

tantalizing or **tantalising** (adjective) Something that is tantalizing makes you feel hopeful and excited, although you know that you probably will not be able to have what you want, e.g. *a tantalizing glimpse of riches to come.*

tantamount (adjective) If you say that something is tantamount to something else, you mean that it is almost the same as it, e.g. *That would be tantamount to treason.*

tantrum, tantrums (noun) A tantrum is a noisy and sometimes violent outburst of temper, especially by a child.

Tanzanian, Tanzanians (pronounced tan-zan-**nee**-an) **1** (adjective) belonging or relating to Tanzania. **2** (noun) A Tanzanian is someone who comes from Tanzania.

tap, taps, tapping, tapped 1 (noun) A tap is a device that you turn in order to control the flow of liquid or gas from a pipe or container. **2** (verb) If you tap something or tap on it, you hit it lightly. **3** (noun) A tap is the action of hitting something lightly; also the sound that this action makes. **4** (verb) If a telephone is tapped, a device is fitted to it so that someone can listen secretly to the calls.

tap-dancing (noun) Tap-dancing is a type of dancing in which the dancers wear special shoes with pieces of metal on the toes and heels which click against the floor.

tape, tapes, taping, taped 1 (noun) Tape is plastic ribbon covered with a magnetic substance and used to record sounds, pictures, and computer information. **2** A tape is a cassette or spool with magnetic tape wound round it. **3** (verb) If you tape music, sounds, or television pictures, you record them using a tape recorder or a video recorder. **4** (noun) Tape is a long, thin strip of fabric that is used for binding or fastening. **5** Tape is also a strip of sticky plastic which you use for sticking things together. **6** (verb) If you tape one thing to another, you attach them using sticky tape.

tape measure, tape measures (noun) A tape measure is a strip of plastic or metal that is marked off in inches or centimetres and used for measuring things.

taper, tapers, tapering, tapered 1 (verb) Something that tapers gradually becomes thinner towards one end. **2** (noun) A taper is a thin candle.

tape recorder, tape recorders (noun) A tape recorder is a machine used for recording sounds onto magnetic tape, and for reproducing these sounds.

tapestry, tapestries (noun) A tapestry is a piece of heavy cloth with designs embroidered on it.

tar (noun) Tar is a thick, black, sticky substance which is used in making roads.

tarantula, tarantulas (pronounced tar-**rant**-yoo-la) (noun) A tarantula is a large, hairy poisonous spider.

target, targets 1 (noun) A target is something which you aim at when firing weapons. **2** The target of an action or remark is the person or thing at which it is directed, e.g. *You become a target for our hatred.* **3** Your target is the result that you are trying to achieve.

tariff, tariffs 1 (noun) A tariff is a tax that a government collects on imported goods. **2** A tariff is any list of prices or charges.

tarmac (noun) Tarmac is a material used for making road surfaces. It consists of crushed stones and tar.

tarnish, tarnishes, tarnishing, tarnished 1 (verb) If metal tarnishes, it becomes stained and loses its shine. **2** If something tarnishes your reputation, it spoils it and causes people to lose their respect for you.

tarot (pronounced **tar**-roh) (noun) A tarot card is one of a special pack of cards used for fortune-telling.

tarpaulin, tarpaulins (noun) A tarpaulin is a sheet of heavy waterproof material used as a protective covering.

tarragon (noun) Tarragon is a

herb with narrow green leaves used in cooking.

tarry, tarries, tarrying, tarried (verb; an old-fashioned word) To tarry means to wait, or to stay somewhere for a little longer.

tart, tarts; tarter, tartest 1 (noun) A tart is a pastry case with a sweet filling. **2** (adjective) Something that is tart is sour or sharp to taste. **3** A tart remark is unpleasant and cruel.

tartan, tartans (noun) Tartan is a woollen fabric from Scotland with checks of various colours and sizes, depending on which clan it belongs to.

tartar (noun) Tartar is a hard, crusty substance that forms on teeth.

task, tasks (noun) A task is any piece of work which has to be done.

tassel, tassels (noun) A tassel is a tuft of loose threads tied by a knot and used for decoration.

taste, tastes, tasting, tasted 1 (noun) Your sense of taste is your ability to recognize the flavour of things in your mouth. **2** The taste of something is its flavour. **3** If you have a taste of food or drink, you have a small amount of it to see what it is like. **4** (verb) When you can taste something in your mouth, you are aware of its flavour. **5** If you taste food or drink, you have a small amount of it to see what it is like. **6** If food or drink tastes of something, it has that flavour. **7** (noun) If you have a taste for something, you enjoy it, e.g. *a taste for publicity*. **8** If you have a taste of something, you experience it, e.g. *my first taste of defeat.* **9** A person's taste is their choice in the things they like to buy or have around them, e.g. *His taste in music is great.*

taste bud, taste buds (noun) Your taste buds are the little points on the surface of your tongue which enable you to taste things.

tasteful (adjective) attractive and elegant. **tastefully** (adverb).

tasteless 1 (adjective) vulgar and unattractive. **2** A tasteless remark or joke is offensive. **3** Tasteless food has very little flavour.

tasty, tastier, tastiest (adjective) having a pleasant flavour.

tatters (plural noun) Clothes that are in tatters are badly torn. **tattered** (adjective).

tattoo, tattoos, tattooing, tattooed 1 (verb) If someone tattoos you or tattoos a design on you, they draw it on your skin by pricking little holes and filling them with coloured dye. **2** (noun) A tattoo is a picture or design tattooed on someone's body. **3** A tattoo is also a public military display of exercises and music.

tatty, tattier, tattiest (adjective) worn out or untidy and rather dirty.

taught the past tense and past participle of **teach**.

taunt, taunts, taunting, taunted 1 (verb) To taunt someone means to speak offensively to them about their weaknesses or failures in order to make them angry or upset. **2** (noun)

A taunt is an offensive remark intended to make a person angry or upset.

Taurus (noun) Taurus is the second sign of the zodiac, represented by a bull. People born between April 20th and May 20th are born under this sign.

taut (adjective) stretched very tight, e.g. *taut wires.*

tavern, taverns (noun; an old-fashioned word) A tavern is a pub.

tawdry, tawdrier, tawdriest (pronounced **taw**-dree) (adjective) cheap, gaudy, and of poor quality.

tawny (noun or adjective) brownish-yellow.

tax, taxes, taxing, taxed 1 (noun) Tax is an amount of money that citizens have to pay to the government so that it can provide public services such as health care and education. **2** (verb) If a sum of money is taxed, a proportion of it has to be paid to the government. **3** If goods are taxed, a proportion of their price has to be paid to the government. **4** If a person or company is taxed, they have to pay a proportion of their income to the government. **5** If something taxes you, it makes heavy demands on you, e.g. *They must be told not to tax your patience.* **taxation** (noun).

taxi, taxis, taxiing, taxied 1 (noun) A taxi or taxicab is a car with a driver which you hire to take you to where you want to go. **2** (verb) When an aeroplane taxis, it moves slowly along the runway before taking off or after landing.

tea, teas 1 (noun) Tea is the dried leaves of an evergreen shrub found in Asia. **2** Tea is a drink made by brewing the leaves of the tea plant in hot water; also a cup of this. **3** Tea is also any drink made with hot water and leaves or flowers, e.g. *peppermint tea.* **4** Tea is a meal taken in the late afternoon or early evening.

tea bag, tea bags (noun) A tea bag is a small paper bag with tea leaves in it which is placed in boiling water to make tea.

teach, teaches, teaching, taught 1 (verb) If you teach someone something, you give them instructions so that they know about it or know how to do it. **2** If you teach a subject, you help students learn about a subject at school, college, or university. **teacher** (noun), **teaching** (noun).

teak (noun) Teak is a hard wood which comes from a large Asian tree.

team, teams, teaming, teamed 1 (noun) A team is a group of people who play together against another group in a sport or game. **2** (verb) If you team up with someone, you join them and work together with them.

teamwork (noun) Teamwork is the ability of a group of people to work well together.

teapot, teapots (noun) A teapot is a round pot with a handle, a lid, and a spout.

tear, tears, tearing, tore, torn Sense 1 rhymes with **peer** and the other senses rhyme with **hair**. **1** (noun) Tears are the drops of salty liquid that come out of your eyes when you cry. **2** (verb) If you tear something, it is damaged by being pulled so that a hole appears in it. **3** (noun) A tear in something is a hole that has been made in it. **4** (verb) If you tear somewhere, you rush or race there, e.g. *He tore through busy streets in a high-speed chase.*

tearaway, tearaways (noun) A tearaway is someone who is wild and uncontrollable.

tearful (adjective) about to cry or crying gently. **tearfully** (adverb).

tease, teases, teasing, teased 1 (verb) If you tease someone, you deliberately make fun of them or embarrass them because it amuses you. **2** (noun) Someone who is a tease enjoys teasing people.

teaspoon, teaspoons (noun) A teaspoon is a small spoon used for stirring drinks; also the amount that a teaspoon holds.

teat, teats 1 (noun) A teat is a nipple on a female animal. **2** A teat is also a piece of rubber or plastic that is shaped like a nipple and fitted to a baby's feeding bottle.

tech, techs (noun; an informal word) A tech is a technical college.

technical 1 (adjective) involving machines, processes, and materials used in industry, transport, and communications. **2** skilled in practical and mechanical things rather than theories and ideas. **3** involving a specialized field of activity, e.g. *I never understood the technical jargon.*

technical college, technical colleges (noun) A technical college is a college where you can study technical subjects, usually as part of the qualifications and training required for a particular job.

technicality, technicalities 1 (noun) The technicalities of a process or activity are the detailed methods used to do it. **2** A technicality is a point that is based on a strict interpretation of a law or a set of rules.

technically (adverb) If something is technically true or correct, it is true or correct when you consider only the facts, rules, or laws, but may not be important or relevant in a particular situation, e.g. *Technically, they were not supposed to drink on duty.*

technician, technicians (noun) A technician is someone whose job involves skilled practical work with scientific equipment.

technique, techniques 1 (noun) A technique is a particular method of doing something, e.g. *these techniques of manufacture.* **2** Technique is skill and ability in an activity which is developed through training and practice, e.g. *Jim's unique vocal technique.*

technology, technologies 1 (noun) Technology is the study of the application of science and scientific knowledge for practical purposes in industry, farming, medicine, or business. **2** A technology is a particular area of activity that requires scientific methods and knowledge, e.g. *computer technology.* **technological** (adjective), **technologically** (adverb).

teddy, teddies (noun) A teddy or teddy bear is a stuffed toy that looks like a friendly bear.

tedious (pronounced **tee**-dee-uss) (adjective) boring and lasting for a long time, e.g. *the tedious task of cleaning.*

tedium (pronounced **tee**-dee-um) (noun) Tedium is the quality of being boring and lasting for a long time, e.g. *the tedium of unemployment.*

tee, tees, teeing, teed 1 (noun) A tee is the small wooden or plastic peg on which a golf ball is placed before the golfer first hits it. **2** (verb) To tee off means to hit the golf ball from the tee.

teem, teems, teeming, teemed 1 (verb) If a place is teeming with people or things, there are a lot of them moving about. **2** If it teems, it rains very heavily, e.g. *The rain was teeming down.*

teenage 1 (adjective) aged between thirteen and nineteen. **2** typical of people aged between thirteen and nineteen, e.g. *teenage fashion.* **teenager** (noun).

teens (plural noun) Your teens are the period of your life when you are between thirteen and nineteen years old.

tee shirt another spelling of **T-shirt.**

teeter, teeters, teetering, teetered (verb) To teeter means to shake or sway slightly in an unsteady way and seem about to fall over.

teeth the plural of **tooth.**

teethe, teethes, teething, teethed (rhymes with **breathe**) (verb) When babies are teething, their teeth are starting to come through, usually causing them pain.

teetotal (pronounced tee-**toe**-tl) (adjective) Someone who is teetotal never drinks alcohol. **teetotaller** (noun).

telecommunications (noun) Telecommunications is the science and activity of sending signals and messages over long distances using electronic equipment.

telegram, telegrams (noun) A telegram is a message sent by telegraph.

telegraph (noun) The telegraph is a system of sending messages over long distances by means of electrical or radio signals.

telepathy (pronounced til-**lep**-ath-ee) (noun) Telepathy is direct communication between people's minds. **telepathic** (adjective).

telephone, telephones, telephoning, telephoned 1 (noun) A telephone is a piece of electrical equipment for talking directly to someone who is in a different place. **2** (verb) If you telephone someone, you speak to them using a telephone.

telephone box, telephone boxes (noun) A telephone box is a type of small shelter in the street where there is a public telephone.

telescope, telescopes (noun) A telescope is a long instrument shaped like a tube which has lenses which make distant objects appear larger and nearer.

teletext (noun) Teletext is an

electronic system that broadcasts pages of information onto a television set.

televise, televises, televising, televised (verb) If an event is televised, it is filmed and shown on television.

television, televisions (noun) A television is a piece of electronic equipment which receives pictures and sounds by electrical signals over a distance.

tell, tells, telling, told 1 (verb) If you tell someone something, you let them know about it. **2** If you tell someone to do something, you order, instruct, or advise them to do it. **3** If you can tell something, you are able to judge correctly what is happening or what the situation is, e.g. *I could tell he was scared.*

teller, tellers (noun) A teller is a person who receives or gives out money in a bank.

telling (adjective) Something that is telling has an important effect, often because it shows the true nature of a situation, e.g. *a telling account of the war.*

telltale (adjective) A telltale sign reveals information, e.g. *the sad, telltale signs of a recent accident.*

telly, tellies (noun; an informal word) A telly is a television.

temerity (pronounced tim-**mer**-it-ee) (noun) If someone has the temerity to do something, they do it even though it upsets or annoys other people, e.g. *She had the temerity to call him Bob.*

temp, temps (noun; an informal word) A temp is a secretary who works for short periods of time in different places.

temper, tempers, tempering, tempered 1 (noun) Your temper is the frame of mind or mood you are in. **2** A temper is a sudden outburst of anger. **3** (phrase) If you **lose your temper**, you become very angry. **4** (verb) To temper something means to make it more acceptable or suitable, e.g. *justice tempered with mercy.*

temperament, temperaments (pronounced **tem**-pra-ment) (noun) Your temperament is your nature or personality, shown in the way you react towards people and situations, e.g. *an artistic temperament.*

temperamental (adjective) Someone who is temperamental has moods that change often and suddenly.

temperate (adjective) A temperate place has weather that is neither extremely hot nor extremely cold.

temperature, temperatures 1 (noun) The temperature of something is how hot or cold it is. **2** Your temperature is the temperature of your body.

tempest, tempests (noun; a literary word) A tempest is a violent storm.

tempestuous (pronounced tem-**pest**-yoo-uss) (adjective) violent or strongly emotional e.g. *a tempestuous affair.*

template, templates (noun) A template is a shape or pattern cut out in wood, metal, plastic, or card which you draw or cut around to reproduce that shape or pattern.

temple, temples 1 (noun) A temple is a building used for the worship of a god in various religions, e.g. *a Buddhist temple.* **2** Your temples are the flat parts on each side of your forehead.

tempo, tempos or **tempi 1** (noun) The tempo of something is the speed at which it happens, e.g. *the slow tempo of change.* **2** (a technical use) The tempo of a piece of music is its speed.

temporary (adjective) lasting for only a short time. **temporarily** (adverb).

tempt, tempts, tempting, tempted 1 (verb) If you tempt someone, you try to persuade them to do something by offering them something they want. **2** If you are tempted to do something, you want to do it but you think it might be wrong or harmful, e.g. *He was tempted to reply with sarcasm.*

temptation, temptations 1 (noun) Temptation is the state you are in when you want to do or have something, even though you know it might be wrong or harmful. **2** A temptation is something that you want to do or have, even though you know it might be wrong or harmful, e.g. *There is a temptation to ignore the problem.*

ten the number 10. **tenth**

tenacious (pronounced tin-**nay**-shuss) (adjective) determined and not giving up easily. **tenaciously** (adverb), **tenacity** (noun).

tenant, tenants (noun) A tenant is someone who pays rent for the place they live in, or for land or buildings that they use. **tenancy** (noun).

tend, tends, tending, tended 1 (verb) If something tends to happen, it happens usually or often. **2** If you tend someone or something, you look after them, e.g. *the way we tend our cattle.*

tendency, tendencies (noun) A tendency is a habit, trend, or type of behaviour that happens very often, e.g. *a tendency to be critical.*

tender, tenderest; tenders, tendering, tendered 1 (adjective) Someone who is tender has gentle and caring feelings. **2** If someone is at a tender age, they are young and do not know very much about life. **3** Tender meat is easy to cut or chew. **4** If a part of your body is tender, it is painful and sore. **5** (verb) If someone tenders an apology or their resignation, they formally offer it. **6** (noun) A tender is a formal offer to supply goods or to do a job for a particular price.

tendon, tendons (noun) A tendon is a strong cord of tissue which joins a muscle to a bone.

tendril, tendrils (noun) Tendrils are short, thin stems which grow on climbing plants and attach them to walls.

tenement, tenements (pronounced **ten**-em-ent) (noun) A tenement is a large house or building divided into many flats.

tenet, tenets (noun) The tenets of a theory or belief are the main ideas it is based upon.

tenner, tenners (noun; an informal word) A tenner is a ten-pound note.

tennis (noun) Tennis is a game

played by two or four players on a rectangular court in which a ball is hit by players over a central net.

tenor, tenors 1 (noun) A tenor is a man who sings the second lowest part in four-part harmony. **2** (adjective) A tenor recorder, saxophone, or other musical instrument has a range of notes of a fairly low pitch. **3** (noun) The tenor of something is the general meaning or mood that it expresses, e.g. *the general tenor of the book.*

tense, tenser, tensest; tenses, tensing, tensed 1 (adjective) If you are tense, you are worried and nervous and cannot relax. **2** A tense situation or period of time is one that makes people nervous and worried. **3** If your body is tense, your muscles are tight. **4** (verb) If you tense, or if your muscles tense, your muscles become tight and stiff. **5** (noun) The tense of a verb is the form which shows whether you are talking about the past, present, or future.

tension, tensions 1 (noun) Tension is the feeling of nervousness or worry that you have when something difficult, dangerous, or important is happening. **2** The tension in a rope or wire is how tightly it is stretched.

tent, tents (noun) A tent is a shelter made of canvas or nylon held up by poles and pinned down with pegs and ropes.

tentacle, tentacles (noun) The tentacles of an animal such as an octopus are the long, thin parts that it uses to feel and hold things.

tentative (adjective) acting or speaking cautiously because of being uncertain or afraid. **tentatively** (adverb).

tenterhooks (plural noun) If you are on tenterhooks, you are nervous and excited about something that is going to happen.

tenuous (pronounced **ten**-yoo-uss) (adjective) If an idea, connection, or relation is tenuous, it is so slight and weak that it may not really exist or may easily cease to exist, e.g. *a very tenuous friendship.*

tenure, tenures (pronounced **ten**-yoor) **1** (noun) Tenure is the legal right to live in a place or to use land or buildings for a period of time. **2** Tenure is the period of time during which someone holds an important job, e.g. *His tenure ended in 1993.*

tepee, tepees (pronounced **tee**-pee) (noun) A tepee is a cone-shaped tent of animal skins used by North American Indians.

tepid (adjective) Tepid liquid is only slightly warm.

term, terms, terming, termed 1 (noun) A term is a fixed period of time, e.g. *her second term of office.* **2** A term is one of the periods of time that each year is divided into at a school or college. **3** A term is a name, expression, or word used for a particular thing. **4** (plural noun) The terms of an agreement are the conditions that have been accepted by the people involved in it. **5** If you express something in particular terms, you express it using a particular type of language or in a way that clearly shows your attitudes, e.g. *The young priest spoke of her in glowing terms.* **6** (phrase) If you **come to terms with** something difficult or unpleasant, you learn to accept it. **7** (verb) To term something means to give it a name or to describe it, e.g. *He termed my performance memorable.*

terminal, terminals 1 (adjective) A terminal illness or disease cannot be cured and causes death gradually. **2** (noun) A terminal is a place where vehicles, passengers, or goods begin or end a journey. **3** A computer terminal is a keyboard and a visual display unit that is used to put information into or get information out of a computer. **terminally** (adverb).

terminate, terminates, terminating, terminated (verb) When you terminate something or when it terminates, it stops or ends. **termination** (noun).

terminology, terminologies (noun) The terminology of a subject is the set of special words and expressions used in it.

terminus, terminuses (pronounced **ter**-min-uss) (noun) A terminus is a place where a bus or train route ends.

termite, termites (noun) Termites are small white tropical insects that feed on wood.

tern, terns (noun) A tern is a small black and white sea bird with long wings and a forked tail.

terrace, terraces 1 (noun) A terrace is a row of houses joined together by their side walls. **2** A terrace is a flat area of stone next to a building where people can sit.

terracotta (noun) Terracotta is a type of reddish-brown unglazed pottery.

terrain (noun) The terrain of an area is the type of land there, e.g. *the region's hilly terrain.*

terrapin, terrapins (noun) A terrapin is a type of small freshwater turtle.

terrestrial (adjective) involving the earth or land.

terrible 1 (adjective) serious and unpleasant, e.g. *a terrible illness.* **2** (an informal use) very bad or of poor quality, e.g. *Paddy's terrible haircut.*

terribly (adverb) very or very much, e.g. *I am terribly sad.*

terrier, terriers (noun) A terrier is a small, short-bodied dog.

terrific 1 (adjective; an informal use) very pleasing or impressive, e.g. *a terrific film.* **2** great in amount, degree, or intensity, e.g. *a terrific blow on the head.* **terrifically** (adverb).

terrify, terrifies, terrifying, terrified (verb) If something terrifies you, it makes you feel extremely frightened.

territorial (adjective) involving or relating to the ownership of a particular area of land or water.

territory, territories 1 (noun) The territory of a country is the land that it controls. **2** An animal's territory is an area which it regards as its own and defends when other animals try to enter it.

terror, terrors 1 (noun) Terror

is great fear or panic. **2** A terror is something that makes you feel very frightened.

terrorism (noun) Terrorism is the use of violence for political reasons. **terrorist** (noun or adjective).

terrorize, terrorizes, terrorizing, terrorized; also spelled **terrorise** (verb) If someone terrorizes you, they frighten you by threatening you or being violent to you.

terse, terser, tersest (adjective) A terse comment or statement is short and rather unfriendly.

tertiary (pronounced **ter**-sharee) **1** (adjective) third in order or importance. **2** Tertiary education is education at university or college level.

test, tests, testing, tested 1 (verb) When you test something, you try it to find out what it is, what condition it is in, or how well it works. **2** If you test someone, you ask them questions to find out how much they know. **3** (noun) A test is a deliberate action or experiment to find out whether something works or how well it works. **4** A test is also a set of questions or tasks given to someone to find out what they know or can do.

testament, testaments 1 (noun; a legal use) A testament is the same as a will. **2** A testament is also a copy of either the Old or the New Testament of the Bible.

test case, test cases (noun) A test case is a legal case that becomes an example for deciding other similar cases.

testicle, testicles (noun) A man's testicles are the two sex glands that produce sperm.

testify, testifies, testifying, testified 1 (verb) When someone testifies, they make a formal statement, especially in a court of law, e.g. *Ismay later testified at the British inquiry.* **2** To testify to something means to show that it is likely to be true, e.g. *a consultant's certificate testifying to her good health.*

testimonial, testimonials (pronounced tess-tim-**moh**-nee-al) (noun) A testimonial is a statement saying how good someone or something is.

testimony, testimonies (noun) A person's testimony is a formal statement they make, especially in a court of law.

testing (adjective) Testing situations or problems are very difficult to deal with, e.g. *It is a testing time for his team.*

test match, test matches (noun) A test match is one of a series of international cricket or rugby matches.

testosterone (pronounced tess-**toss**-ter-rone) (noun) Testosterone is a male hormone that produces male characteristics.

test tube, test tubes (noun) A test tube is a small cylindrical glass container that is used in chemical experiments.

tetanus (pronounced **tet**-nuss) (noun) Tetanus is a painful infectious disease caused by germs getting into wounds.

tether, tethers, tethering, tethered 1 (verb) If you tether an animal, you tie it to a post. **2** (phrase) If you are **at the end of your tether**, you are extremely tired and have no more patience or energy left to deal with your problems.

Teutonic (pronounced tyoo-**tonn**-ik) (adjective; a formal word) involving or related to German people.

text, texts 1 (noun) The text of a book is the main written part of it, rather than the pictures or index. **2** Text is any written material. **3** A text is a book or other piece of writing used for study or an exam at school or college. **textual** (adjective).

textbook, textbooks (noun) A textbook is a book about a particular subject that is intended for students to use.

textile, textiles (noun) A textile is a woven cloth or fabric.

texture, textures (noun) The texture of something is the way it feels when you touch it.

Thai, Thais 1 (adjective) belonging or relating to Thailand. **2** (noun) A Thai is someone who comes from Thailand. **3** Thai is the main language spoken in Thailand.

than 1 (preposition or conjunction) You use 'than' to link two parts of a comparison, e.g. *She was older than me.* **2** You use 'than' to link two parts of a contrast, e.g. *Players would rather play than train.*

thank, thanks, thanking, thanked (verb) When you thank someone, you show that you are grateful for something, usually by saying 'thank you'.

thankful (adjective) happy and relieved that something has happened. **thankfully** (adverb).

thankless (adjective) A thankless job or task involves doing a lot of hard work that other people do not notice or are not grateful for, e.g. *Soccer referees have a thankless task.*

thanks 1 (plural noun) When you express your thanks to someone, you tell or show them how grateful you are for something. **2** (phrase) If something happened **thanks to** someone or something, it happened because of them, e.g. *I'm as prepared as I can be, thanks to you.* **3** (interjection) You say 'Thanks' to show that you are grateful for something.

thanksgiving 1 (noun) Thanksgiving is an act of thanking God, especially in prayer or in a religious ceremony. **2** In the United States, Thanksgiving is a public holiday in the autumn.

thank you You say 'thank you' to show that you are grateful to someone for something.

that, those 1 (adjective or pronoun) 'That' or 'those' is used to refer to things or people already mentioned or known about, e.g. *That man was waving.* **2** (conjunction) 'That' is used to introduce a clause, e.g. *I said that I was coming home.* **3** (pronoun) 'That' is also used to introduce a relative clause, e.g. *I followed Alex to a door that led inside.*

thatch, thatches, thatching, thatched 1 (noun) Thatch is straw and reeds used to make roofs. **2** (verb) To thatch a roof means to cover it with thatch.

thaw, thaws, thawing, thawed 1 (verb) When snow or ice

thaws, it melts. **2** (noun) A thaw is a period of warmer weather in winter when snow or ice melts. **3** (verb) When you thaw frozen food, or when it thaws, it becomes unfrozen. **4** When people who are unfriendly thaw, they begin to be more friendly and relaxed.

the (adjective) The definite article 'the' is used when you are talking about something that is known about, that has just been mentioned, or that you are going to give details about.

theatre, theatres (pronounced **theer**-ter) **1** (noun) A theatre is a building where plays and other entertainments are performed on a stage. **2** Theatre is work such as writing, producing, and acting in plays. **3** An operating theatre is a room in a hospital designed and equipped for surgical operations.

theatrical (pronounced thee-**at**-rik-kl) **1** (adjective) involving the theatre or performed in a theatre, e.g. *his theatrical career.* **2** Theatrical behaviour is exaggerated, unnatural, and done for effect. **theatrically** (adverb).

thee (pronoun; an old-fashioned word) Thee means you.

theft, thefts (noun) Theft is the crime of stealing.

their (adjective) Their refers to something belonging or relating to people or things, other than yourself or the person you are talking to, which have already been mentioned, e.g. *It was their fault.*

theirs (pronoun) Theirs refers to something belonging or relating to people or things, other than yourself or the person you are talking to, which have already been mentioned, e.g. *Amy had been Helen's friend, not theirs.*

them (pronoun) Them refers to things or people, other than yourself or the people you are talking to, which have already been mentioned, e.g. *He picked up the pillows and threw them to the floor.*

theme, themes 1 (noun) A theme is a main idea or topic which is expressed or developed in writing, painting, film, or music, e.g. *the main theme of the book.* **2** A theme is also a tune, especially one played at the beginning and end of a television or radio programme.

themselves 1 (pronoun) Themselves is used when people, other than yourself or the person you are talking to, do an action and are affected by it, e.g. *They got themselves into this mess.* **2** Themselves is used to emphasize 'they'.

then (adverb) at a particular time in the past or future, e.g. *I'd left home by then.*

theologian, theologians (pronounced thee-ol-**loe**-jee-an) (noun) A theologian is someone who studies religion and the nature of God.

theology (noun) Theology is the study of religion and God. **theological** (adjective).

theoretical 1 (adjective) based on or to do with ideas of a subject rather than the practical aspects. **2** not proved to exist or be true. **theoretically** (adverb).

theory, theories 1 (noun) A theory is an idea or set of ideas that is meant to explain something, e.g. *Darwin's theory of evolution.* **2** Theory is the set of rules, principles, and ideas that a particular subject or skill is based upon. **3** (phrase) You use **in theory** to say that although something is supposed to happen, it may not in fact happen, e.g. *In theory, prices should rise by 2%.*

therapeutic (pronounced ther-ap-**yoo**-tik) **1** (adjective) If something is therapeutic, it helps you to feel happier and more relaxed, e.g. *Laughing is therapeutic.* **2** In medicine, therapeutic treatment is designed to treat a disease or to improve a person's health.

therapy (noun) Therapy is the treatment of mental or physical illness, often without the use of drugs or operations. **therapist** (noun).

there 1 (adverb) in, at, or to that place, point, or case, e.g. *He's sitting over there.* **2** (pronoun) There is used to say that something exists or does not exist, or to draw attention to something, e.g. *There are flowers on the table.*

thereby (adverb; a formal word) as a result of the event or action mentioned, e.g. *They had recruited 200 new members, thereby making the day worthwhile.*

therefore (adverb) as a result.

thermal 1 (adjective) to do with or caused by heat, e.g. *thermal energy.* **2** Thermal clothes are specially designed to keep you warm in cold weather.

thermometer, thermometers (noun) A thermometer is an instrument for measuring the temperature of a room or a person's body.

thermostat, thermostats (noun) A thermostat is a device used to control temperature, for example on a central heating system.

thesaurus, thesauruses (pronounced this-**saw**-russ) (noun) A thesaurus is a reference book in which words with similar meanings are grouped together.

these the plural of **this.**

thesis, theses (pronounced **thee**-siss) (noun) A thesis is a long piece of writing, based on research, that is done as part of a university degree.

they 1 (pronoun) They refers to people or things, other than you or the people you are talking to, that have already been mentioned, e.g. *They married two years later.* **2** They is sometimes used instead of 'he' or 'she' where the sex of the person is unknown or unspecified. Some people consider this to be incorrect, e.g. *Someone could have a nasty accident if they tripped over that.*

thick, thicker, thickest 1 (adjective) Something thick has a large distance between its two opposite surfaces. **2** If something is a particular amount thick, it measures that amount between its two sides. **3** Thick means growing or grouped closely together and in large quantities, e.g. *thick dark hair.* **4** Thick liquids contain little water and do not flow easily, e.g. *thick soup.* **5** (an informal use) A thick person is stupid or slow to understand things.

thicken, thickens, thickening, thickened (verb) If something thickens, it becomes thicker, e.g. *The clouds thickened.*

thicket, thickets (noun) A thicket is a small group of trees growing closely together.

thief, thieves (noun) A thief is a person who steals.

thieving (noun) Thieving is the act of stealing.

thigh, thighs (noun) Your thighs are the top parts of your legs, between your knees and your hips.

thimble, thimbles (noun) A thimble is a small metal or plastic cap that you put on the end of your finger to protect it when you are sewing.

thin, thinner, thinnest; thins, thinning, thinned 1 (adjective) Something that is thin is much narrower than it is long. **2** A thin person or animal has very little fat on their body. **3** Thin liquids contain a lot of water, e.g. *thin soup.* **4** (verb) If you thin something such as paint or soup, you add water or other liquid to it.

thing, things 1 (noun) A thing is an object, rather than a plant, an animal, a human being, or something abstract. **2** (plural noun) Your things are your clothes or possessions.

think, thinks, thinking, thought 1 (verb) When you think about ideas or problems, you use your mind to consider them. **2** If you think something, you have the opinion that it is true or the case, e.g. *I think she has a secret boyfriend.* **3** If you think of something, you remember it or it comes into your mind. **4** If you think a lot of someone or something, you admire them or think they are good.

third, thirds 1 The third item in a series is the one counted as number three. **2** (noun) A third is one of three equal parts.

Third World (noun) The poorer countries of Africa, Asia, and South America can be referred to as the Third World.

thirst, thirsts 1 (noun) If you have a thirst, you feel a need to drink something. **2** A thirst for something is a very strong desire for it, e.g. *a thirst for money.* **thirsty** (adjective), **thirstily** (adverb).

thirteen the number 13. **thirteenth**

thirty, thirties the number 30. **thirtieth**

this, these 1 (adjective or pronoun) This is used to refer to something or someone that is nearby or has just been mentioned, e.g. *This is Robert.* **2** This is used to refer to the present time or place, e.g. *I've been on holiday this week.*

thistle, thistles (noun) A thistle is a wild plant with prickly-edged leaves and purple flowers.

thong, thongs (noun) A thong is a long narrow strip of leather.

thorn, thorns (noun) A thorn is one of many sharp points growing on some plants and trees.

thorny, thornier, thorniest 1

(adjective) covered with thorns. **2** A thorny subject or question is difficult to discuss or answer.

thorough (pronounced **thur**-ruh) **1** (adjective) done very carefully and completely, e.g. *a thorough examination.* **2** A thorough person is very careful and methodical in what they do. **thoroughly** (adverb).

thoroughbred, thoroughbreds (noun) A thoroughbred is an animal that has parents that are of the same high quality breed.

thoroughfare, thoroughfares (noun) A thoroughfare is a main road in a town.

those the plural of **that**.

thou (pronoun; an old-fashioned word) Thou means you, when you are talking to only one person.

though 1 (conjunction) despite the fact that, e.g. *Meg felt better, even though she knew it was the end.* **2** if, e.g. *It looks as though you were right.*

thought, thoughts 1 Thought is the past tense and past participle of **think**. **2** (noun) A thought is an idea that you have in your mind. **3** Thought is the activity of thinking, e.g. *She was lost in thought.* **4** Thought is a particular way of thinking or a particular set of ideas, e.g. *this school of thought.*

thoughtful 1 (adjective) When someone is thoughtful, they are quiet and serious because they are thinking about something. **2** A thoughtful person remembers what other people want or need, and tries to be kind to them. **thoughtfully** (adverb).

thoughtless (adjective) A thoughtless person forgets or ignores what other people want, need, or feel. **thoughtlessly** (adverb).

thousand, thousands the number 1000. **thousandth**

thrash, thrashes, thrashing, thrashed 1 (verb) To thrash someone means to beat them by hitting them with something. **2** To thrash someone in a game, contest, or fight means to defeat them completely. **3** To thrash out a problem or an idea means to discuss it in detail until a solution is reached.

thread, threads, threading, threaded 1 (noun) A thread is a long, fine piece of cotton, silk, nylon, or wool. **2** The thread on something such as a screw or the top of a container is the raised spiral line of metal or plastic round it. **3** The thread of an argument or story is an idea or theme that connects the different parts of it. **4** (verb) When you thread something, you pass thread, magnetic tape, or cord through it. **5** If you thread your way through people or things, you carefully make your way through them.

threadbare (adjective) Threadbare cloth or clothing is old and thin.

threat, threats 1 (noun) A threat is a statement that someone will harm you, especially if you do not do what they want. **2** Anything or anyone that seems likely to harm you can be called a threat. **3** If there is a threat of something unpleasant happening, it is very possible that it will happen.

threaten, threatens, threatening, threatened 1 (verb) If you threaten to harm someone or threaten to do something that will upset them, you say that you will do it. **2** If someone or something threatens a person or thing, they are likely to harm them.

three the number 3.

threesome, threesomes (noun) A threesome is a group of three.

threshold, thresholds (pronounced **thresh**-hold) **1** (noun) The threshold of a building or room is the doorway, or the floor in the doorway. **2** The threshold of something is the lowest amount, level, or limit at which something happens or changes, e.g. *the tax threshold.*

thrice (adverb; an old-fashioned word) If you do something thrice, you do it three times.

thrift (noun) Thrift is the practice of saving money and not wasting things.

thrifty, thriftier, thriftiest (adjective) A thrifty person saves money and does not waste things.

thrill, thrills, thrilling, thrilled 1 (noun) A thrill is a sudden feeling of great excitement, pleasure, or fear; also any event or experience that gives you such a feeling. **2** (verb) If something thrills you, or you thrill to it, it gives you a feeling of great pleasure and excitement. **thrilled** (adjective), **thrilling** (adjective).

thriller, thrillers (noun) A thriller is a book, film, or play that tells an exciting story about dangerous or mysterious events.

thrive, thrives, thriving, thrived or **throve** (verb) When people or things thrive, they are healthy, happy, successful, or strong. **thriving** (adjective).

throat, throats 1 (noun) Your throat is the back of your mouth and the top part of the passages inside your neck. **2** Your throat is also the front part of your neck.

throb, throbs, throbbing, throbbed 1 (verb) If a part of your body throbs, you feel a series of strong beats or dull pains. **2** If something throbs, it vibrates and makes a loud, rhythmic noise, e.g. *The engines throbbed.*

throes 1 (plural noun) Throes are a series of violent pangs, pain, or convulsions, e.g. *death throes.* **2** (phrase) If you are **in the throes of** something, you are deeply involved in it.

thrombosis, thromboses (pronounced throm-**boe**-siss) (noun) A thrombosis is a blood clot which blocks the flow of blood in the body. Thromboses are dangerous and often fatal.

throne, thrones 1 (noun) A throne is a ceremonial chair used by a King or Queen on important official occasions. **2** The throne is a way of referring to the position of being King or Queen.

throng, throngs, thronging, thronged 1 (noun) A throng is a large crowd of people. **2** (verb) If people throng somewhere or throng a place, they go there in great numbers, e.g. *Hundreds of city workers thronged the scene.*

throttle, throttles, throttling, throttled (verb) To throttle someone means to kill or injure them by squeezing their throat.

through 1 (preposition) moving all the way from one side of something to the other, e.g. *a path through the woods.* **2** because of, e.g. *He had been exhausted through lack of sleep.* **3** during, e.g. *He has to work through the summer.* **4** If you go through an experience, it happens to you, e.g. *I don't want to go through that again.* **5** (adjective) If you are through with something, you have finished doing it or using it.

throughout 1 (preposition) during, e.g. *I stayed awake throughout the night.* **2** (adverb) happening or existing through the whole of a place, e.g. *The house was painted brown throughout.*

throve the past tense of **thrive.**

throw, throws, throwing, threw, thrown 1 (verb) When you throw something you are holding, you move your hand quickly and let it go, so that it moves through the air. **2** If you throw yourself somewhere, you move there suddenly and with force, e.g. *We threw ourselves on the ground.* **3** To throw someone into an unpleasant situation means to put them there, e.g. *It threw them into a panic.* **4** If something throws light or shadow on something else, it makes that thing have light or shadow on it. **5** If you throw yourself into an activity, you become actively and enthusiastically involved in it.

throwback, throwbacks (noun) A throwback is something which has the characteristics of something that existed a long time ago, e.g. *Everything about her was a throwback to the fifties.*

thrush, thrushes 1 (noun) A thrush is a small brown songbird. **2** Thrush is a fungal disease of the mouth or of the vagina.

thrust, thrusts, thrusting, thrust 1 (verb) If you thrust something somewhere, you push or move it there quickly with a lot of force. **2** (noun) A thrust is a sudden forceful movement. **3** (verb) If you thrust your way somewhere, you move along, pushing between people or things. **4** (noun) The main thrust of an activity or idea is the most important part of it, e.g. *the general thrust of his argument.*

thud, thuds, thudding, thudded 1 (noun) A thud is a dull sound, usually made by a solid, heavy object hitting something soft. **2** (verb) If something thuds somewhere, it makes a dull sound, usually by hitting something else.

thug, thugs (noun) A thug is a very rough and violent person.

thumb, thumbs, thumbing, thumbed 1 (noun) Your thumb is the short, thick finger on the side of your hand. **2** (verb) If someone thumbs a lift, they stand at the side of the road and stick out their thumb until a driver stops and gives them a lift.

thump, thumps, thumping, thumped 1 (verb) If you thump someone or something, you hit them hard with your fist. **2** If something thumps somewhere, it makes a fairly loud, dull sound, usually when it hits something else. **3** When your heart thumps, it beats strongly and quickly. **4** (noun) A thump is a hard hit, e.g. *a great thump on the back.* **5** A thump is also a fairly loud, dull sound.

thunder, thunders, thundering, thundered 1 (noun) Thunder is a loud cracking or rumbling noise caused by expanding air which is suddenly heated by lightning. **2** (verb) When it thunders, a loud cracking or rumbling noise occurs in the sky after a flash of lightning. **3** (noun) Thunder is any loud rumbling noise, e.g. *the distant thunder of bombs.* **4** (verb) If something thunders, it makes a loud continuous noise, e.g. *The helicopter thundered low over the trees.*

thunderbolt, thunderbolts (noun) A thunderbolt is a flash of lightning, accompanied by thunder.

thunderous (adjective) A thunderous noise is very loud, e.g. *thunderous applause.*

Thursday, Thursdays (noun) Thursday is the day between Wednesday and Friday.

thus (a formal word) **1** (adverb) in this way, e.g. *I sat thus for nearly half an hour.* **2** therefore, e.g. *Critics were thus able to denounce him.*

thwart, thwarts, thwarting, thwarted (verb) To thwart someone or their plans means to prevent them from doing or getting what they want.

thy (adjective; an old-fashioned word) Thy means your.

thyme (pronounced **time**) (noun) Thyme is a bushy herb with very small leaves.

tiara, tiaras (pronounced tee-**ah**-ra) (noun) A tiara is a semicircular crown of jewels worn by a woman on formal occasions.

Tibetan, Tibetans 1 (adjective) belonging or relating to Tibet. **2** (noun) A Tibetan is someone who comes from Tibet.

tic, tics (noun) A tic is a twitching of a group of muscles, especially the muscles in the face.

tick, ticks, ticking, ticked 1 (noun) A tick is a written mark to show that something is correct or has been dealt with. **2** (verb) To tick something written on a piece of paper means to put a tick next to it. **3** When a clock ticks, it makes a regular series of short sounds as it works. **4** (noun) The tick of a clock is the series of short sounds it makes when it is working. **5** A tick is a tiny, blood-sucking, insect-like creature that usually lives on the bodies of people or animals. **ticking** (noun). **tick off** (verb; an informal expression) If you tick someone off, you speak angrily to them because they have done something wrong.

ticket, tickets (noun) A ticket is a piece of paper or card which shows that you have paid for a journey or have paid to enter a place of entertainment.

tickle, tickles, tickling, tickled 1 (verb) When you tickle someone, you move your fingers lightly over their body in order to make them laugh. **2** If something tickles you, it amuses you or gives you pleasure, e.g. *Simon is tickled by the idea.*

tidal (adjective) to do with or produced by tides, e.g. *a tidal estuary.*

tidal wave, tidal waves (noun) A tidal wave is a very large wave, often caused by an earthquake, that comes over land and destroys things.

tide, tides, tiding, tided 1 (noun) The tide is the regular change in the level of the sea on the shore, caused by the gravitational pull of the sun and the moon. **2** The tide of opinion or fashion is what the majority of people think or do at a particular time. **3** A tide of something is a large amount of it, e.g. *the tide of anger and bitterness.* **tide over** (verb) If something will tide someone over, it will help them through a difficult period of time.

tidings (plural noun; a formal word) Tidings are news.

tidy, tidier, tidiest; tidies, tidying, tidied 1 (adjective) Something that is tidy is neat and arranged in an orderly way. **2** Someone who is tidy always keeps their things neat and arranged in an orderly way. **3** (verb) To tidy a place means to make it neat by putting things in their proper place. **4** (adjective; an informal use) A tidy amount of money is a fairly large amount of it.

tie, ties, tying, tied 1 (verb) If you tie one thing to another or tie it in a particular position, you fasten it using cord of some kind. **2** If you tie a knot or a bow in a piece of cord or cloth, you fasten the ends together to make a knot or bow. **3** (noun) A tie is a long, narrow piece of cloth worn around the neck under a shirt collar and tied in a knot at the front. **4** (verb) Something or someone that is tied to something else is closely linked with it, e.g. *40,000 British jobs are tied to the project.* **5** (noun) A tie is a connection or feeling that links you with a person, place, or organization, e.g. *I had very close ties with the family.* **6** (verb) If you tie with someone in a competition or game, you have the same number of points.

tied up (adjective) If you are tied up, you are busy.

tier, tiers (noun) A tier is one of a number of rows or layers of something, e.g. *Take the stairs to the upper tier.*

tiff, tiffs (noun) A tiff is a small unimportant quarrel.

tiger, tigers (noun) A tiger is a large carnivorous animal of the cat family. It comes from Asia and has an orange coloured coat with black stripes.

tight, tighter, tightest 1 (adjective) fitting closely, e.g. *The shoes are too tight.* **2** firmly fastened and difficult to move, e.g. *a tight knot.* **3** stretched or pulled so as not to be slack, e.g. *a tight cord.* **4** (adverb) held firmly and securely, e.g.

He held me tight. **5** (adjective) A tight plan or arrangement allows only the minimum time or money needed to do something, e.g. *Our schedule tonight is very tight.* **tightly** (adverb), **tightness** (noun).

tighten, tightens, tightening, tightened 1 (verb) If you tighten your hold on something, you hold it more firmly. **2** If you tighten a rope or chain, or if it tightens, it is stretched or pulled until it is straight. **3** If someone tightens a rule or system, they make it stricter or more efficient.

tightrope, tightropes (noun) A tightrope is a tightly-stretched rope on which an acrobat balances and performs tricks.

tights (plural noun) Tights are a piece of clothing made of thin stretchy material that fit closely round a person's hips, legs, and feet.

tile, tiles, tiling, tiled 1 (noun) A tile is a small flat square piece of something, for example, slate, carpet, or cork, that is used to cover surfaces. **2** (verb) To tile a surface means to fix tiles to it. **tiled** (adjective).

till, tills, tilling, tilled 1 (preposition or conjunction) Till means the same as until. **2** (noun) A till is a drawer or box in a shop where money is kept, usually in a cash register. **3** (verb) To till the ground means to plough it for raising crops.

tiller, tillers (noun) In a boat, the tiller is the handle fixed to the top of the rudder for steering.

tilt, tilts, tilting, tilted 1 (verb) If you tilt an object or it tilts, it changes position so that one end or side is higher than the other. **2** (noun) A tilt is a position in which one end or side of something is higher than the other.

timber, timbers 1 (noun) Timber is wood that has been cut and prepared ready for building and making furniture. **2** The timbers of a ship or house are the large pieces of wood that have been used to build it.

time, times, timing, timed 1 (noun) Time is what is measured in hours, days, and years, e.g. *What time is it?* **2** Time is used to mean a particular period or point, e.g. *I enjoyed my time in London.* **3** If you say it is time for something or it is time to do it, you mean that it ought to happen or be done now, e.g. *It is time for a change.* **4** Times is used after numbers to indicate how often something happens, e.g. *I saw my father four times a year.* **5** Times is used after numbers when you are saying how much bigger, smaller, better, or worse one thing is compared to another, e.g. *The Belgians drink three times as much beer as the French.* **6** Times is used in arithmetic to link numbers that are multiplied together, e.g. *Two times three is six.* **7** (verb) If you time something for a particular time, you plan that it should happen then, e.g. *We could not have timed our arrival better.* **8** If you time an activity or action, you measure how long it lasts.

timeless (adjective) Something timeless is so good, beautiful, or perfect that it cannot be affected by the passing of time or by changes in fashion.

timely (adjective) happening at just the right time, e.g. *a timely appearance.*

timer, timers (noun) A timer is a device that measures time, especially one that is part of a machine.

timescale, timescales (noun) The timescale of an event is the length of time during which it happens.

timetable, timetables 1 (noun) A timetable is a plan of the times when particular activities or jobs should be done. **2** A timetable is a list of the times when particular trains, boats, buses, or aeroplanes arrive and depart.

timid (adjective) shy and having no courage or self-confidence. **timidly** (adverb), **timidity** (noun).

timing 1 (noun) Someone's timing is their skill in judging the right moment at which to do something. **2** The timing of an event is when it actually happens.

timpani (pronounced **tim**-pan-ee) (plural noun) Timpani are large drums with curved bottoms that are played in an orchestra.

tin, tins 1 (noun) Tin is a soft silvery-white metal. **2** A tin is a metal container which is filled with food and then sealed in order to preserve the food. **3** A tin is a small metal container which may have a lid, e.g. *a cake tin.*

tinder (noun) Tinder is small pieces of dry wood or grass that burn easily and can be used for lighting a fire.

tinge, tinges (noun) A tinge of something is a small amount of it, e.g. *a tinge of envy.* **tinged** (adjective).

tingle, tingles, tingling, tingled 1 (verb) When a part of your body tingles, you feel a slight prickling feeling in it. **2** (noun) A tingle is a slight prickling feeling. **tingling** (noun or adjective).

tinker, tinkers, tinkering, tinkered 1 (noun) A tinker is a person who travels from place to place mending metal pots and pans or doing other small repair jobs. **2** (verb) If you tinker with something, you make a lot of small adjustments to it in order to repair or improve it, e.g. *All he wanted was to tinker with engines.*

tinkle, tinkles, tinkling, tinkled 1 (verb) If something tinkles, it makes a sound like a small bell ringing. **2** (noun) A tinkle is a sound like that of a small bell ringing.

tinned (adjective) Tinned food has been preserved by being sealed in a tin.

tinsel (noun) Tinsel is long threads with strips of shiny paper attached, used as a decoration at Christmas.

tint, tints, tinting, tinted 1 (noun) A tint is a small amount of a particular colour, e.g. *a distinct tint of green.* **2** (verb) If a person tints their hair, they change its colour by adding a weak dye to it. **tinted** (adjective).

tiny, tinier, tiniest (adjective) extremely small.

tip, tips, tipping, tipped 1 (noun) The tip of something long and thin is the end of it, e.g. *a fingertip.* **2** (verb) If you tip an object, you move it so that it is no longer horizontal or upright. **3** If you tip something somewhere, you pour it there quickly or carelessly. **4** (noun) A tip is a place where rubbish is dumped. **5** If you give someone such as a waiter a tip, you give them some money to thank them for their services. **6** A tip is also a useful piece of advice or information. **tipped** (adjective).

tipple, tipples (noun) A person's tipple is the alcoholic drink that they normally drink.

tipsy, tipsier, tipsiest (adjective) slightly drunk.

tiptoe, tiptoes, tiptoeing, tiptoed (verb) If you tiptoe somewhere, you walk there very quietly on your toes.

tirade, tirades (pronounced tie-**rade**) (noun) A tirade is a long, angry speech in which you criticize someone or something.

tire, tires, tiring, tired 1 (verb) If something tires you, it makes you use a lot of energy so that you want to rest or sleep. **2** If you tire of something, you become bored with it. **tired** (adjective), **tiredness** (noun).

tireless (adjective) Someone who is tireless has a lot of energy and never seems to need a rest.

tiresome (adjective) A person or thing that is tiresome makes you feel irritated or bored.

tiring (adjective) Something that is tiring makes you tired.

tissue, tissues (pronounced **tiss**-yoo) **1** (noun) The tissue in plants and animals consists of cells that are similar in appearance and function, e.g. *scar tissue... dead tissue.* **2** Tissue is thin paper that is used for wrapping breakable objects. **3** A tissue is a small piece of soft paper that you use as a handkerchief.

tit, tits (noun) A tit is a small European bird, e.g. *a blue tit.*

titillate, titillates, titillating, titillated (verb) If something titillates someone, it pleases and excites them, especially in a sexual way. **titillation** (noun).

title, titles 1 (noun) The title of a book, play, or piece of music is its name. **2** Someone's title is a word that describes their rank, status, or job, e.g. *My official title is Design Manager.* **3** A title in a sports competition is the position of champion, e.g. *the European featherweight title.*

titled (adjective) Someone who is titled has a high social rank and has a title such as 'Princess', 'Lord', 'Lady', or 'Sir'.

titter, titters, tittering, tittered (verb) If you titter, you laugh in a way that shows you are nervous or embarrassed.

TNT (noun) TNT is a type of powerful explosive. It is an abbreviation for 'trinitrotoluene'.

to 1 (preposition) 'To' is used to indicate the place that someone or something is moving towards or pointing at, e.g. *They are going to China.* **2** 'To' is used to indicate the limit of something, e.g. *Goods* *to the value of £500.* **3** 'To' is used in ratios and rates when saying how many units of one type there are for each unit of another, e.g. *I only get about 18 miles to the gallon from it.* **4** (adverb) If you push or shut a door to, you close it but do not shut it completely.

toad, toads (noun) A toad is an amphibian that looks like a frog but has a drier skin and lives less in the water.

toadstool, toadstools (noun) A toadstool is a type of poisonous fungus.

toast, toasts, toasting, toasted **1** (noun) Toast is slices of bread made brown and crisp by cooking at a high temperature. **2** (verb) If you toast bread, you cook it at a high temperature so that it becomes brown and crisp. **3** If you toast yourself, you sit in front of a fire so that you feel pleasantly warm. **4** (noun) To drink a toast to someone means to drink an alcoholic drink in honour of them. **5** (verb) To toast someone means to drink an alcoholic drink in honour of them.

toaster, toasters (noun) A toaster is a piece of electrical equipment used for toasting bread.

tobacco (noun) Tobacco is the dried leaves of the tobacco plant which people smoke in pipes, cigarettes, and cigars.

tobacconist, tobacconists (noun) A tobacconist is a shop where tobacco, cigarettes, and cigars are sold.

toboggan, toboggans (noun) A toboggan is a flat seat with two wooden or metal runners, used for sliding over the snow.

today **1** (adverb or noun) Today means the day on which you are speaking or writing. **2** Today also means the present period of history, e.g. *all of today's problems.*

toddle, toddles, toddling, toddled (verb) To toddle means to walk in short, quick steps, as a very young child does.

toddler, toddlers (noun) A toddler is a small child who has just learned to walk.

to-do, to-dos (noun) A to-do is a situation in which people are very agitated, confused, or annoyed, e.g. *It's just like him to make such a to-do about a baby.*

toe, toes **1** (noun) Your toes are the five movable parts at the end of your foot. **2** The toe of a shoe or sock is the part that covers the end of your foot.

toff, toffs (noun; an informal, old-fashioned word) A toff is a rich person or one from an aristocratic family.

toffee, toffees (noun) Toffee is a sticky, chewy sweet made by boiling sugar and butter together with water.

toga, togas (noun) In ancient Rome, a toga was a long loose robe.

together **1** (adverb) If people do something together, they do it with each other. **2** If two things happen together, they happen at the same time. **3** If things are joined or fixed together, they are joined or fixed to each other. **4** If things or people are together, they are very near to each other.

togetherness (noun) Togetherness is a feeling of closeness and friendship.

toil, toils, toiling, toiled 1 (verb) When people toil, they work hard doing unpleasant, difficult, or tiring tasks or jobs. **2** (noun) Toil is unpleasant, difficult, or tiring work.

toilet, toilets 1 (noun) A toilet is a large bowl, connected by a pipe to the drains, which you use when you want to get rid of urine or faeces. **2** A toilet is a small room containing a toilet.

toiletries (plural noun) Toiletries are the things you use when cleaning and taking care of your body, such as soap and talc.

token, tokens 1 (noun) A token is a piece of paper or card that is worth a particular amount of money and can be exchanged for goods, e.g. *record tokens.* **2** Tokens are flat round pieces of metal or plastic that can sometimes be used instead of money. **3** If you give something to someone as a token of your feelings for them, you give it to them as a way of showing those feelings. **4** (adjective) If something is described as token, it shows that there is something required but it is not being treated as important, e.g. *a token contribution to your fees.*

told Told is the past tense and past participle of **tell.**

tolerable 1 (adjective) able to be borne or put up with. **2** fairly satisfactory or reasonable, e.g. *a tolerable salary.*

tolerance 1 (noun) A person's tolerance is their ability to accept or put up with something which may not be enjoyable or pleasant for them. **2** Tolerance is the quality of allowing other people to have their own attitudes or beliefs, or to behave in a particular way, even if you do not agree or approve, e.g. *religious tolerance.* **tolerant** (adjective).

tolerate, tolerates, tolerating, tolerated 1 (verb) If you tolerate things that you do not approve of or agree with, you allow them. **2** If you can tolerate something, you accept it, even though it is unsatisfactory or unpleasant. **toleration** (noun).

toll, tolls, tolling, tolled 1 (noun) The death toll in an accident is the number of people who have died in it. **2** A toll is a sum of money that you have to pay in order to use a particular bridge or road. **3** (verb) When someone tolls a bell, it is rung slowly, often as a sign that someone has died.

tom, toms (noun) A tom is a male cat.

tomahawk, tomahawks (noun) A tomahawk is a small, light axe used by North American Indians.

tomato, tomatoes (noun) A tomato is a small round red fruit, used as a vegetable and often eaten raw in salads.

tomb, tombs (noun) A tomb is a large grave for one or more corpses.

tomboy, tomboys (noun) A tomboy is a girl who likes playing rough or noisy games.

tome, tomes (noun; a formal word) A tome is a very large heavy book.

tomorrow 1 (adverb or noun) Tomorrow means the day after today. **2** You can refer to the future, especially the near future, as tomorrow.

ton, tons 1 (noun) A ton is a unit of weight equal to 2240 pounds or about 1016 kilograms. **2** (plural noun; an informal use) If you have tons of something, you have a lot of it.

tonal (adjective) involving the quality or pitch of a sound or of music.

tone, tones, toning, toned 1 (noun) Someone's tone is a quality in their voice which shows what they are thinking or feeling. **2** The tone of a musical instrument or a singer's voice is the kind of sound it has. **3** The tone of a piece of writing is its style and the ideas or opinions expressed in it, e.g. *I was shocked at the tone of your leading article.* **4** A tone is a lighter, darker, or brighter shade of the same colour, e.g. *The whole room is painted in two tones of orange.* **tone down** (verb) If you tone down something, you make it less forceful or severe.

tone-deaf (adjective) unable to sing in tune or to recognize different tunes.

tongs (plural noun) Tongs consist of two long narrow pieces of metal joined together at one end. You press the pieces together to pick an object up.

tongue, tongues 1 (noun) Your tongue is the soft part in your mouth that you can move and use for tasting, licking, and speaking. **2** A tongue is also a language. **3** Tongue is the cooked tongue of an ox.

tonic, tonics 1 (noun) Tonic or tonic water is a colourless, fizzy drink that has a slightly bitter flavour and is often mixed with alcoholic drinks. **2** A tonic is a medicine that makes you feel stronger, healthier, and less tired. **3** You can refer to anything that makes you feel stronger or more cheerful as a tonic, e.g. *It was a tonic just being with her.*

tonight (adverb or noun) Tonight is the evening or night that will come at the end of today.

tonne, tonnes (pronounced **tun**) (noun) A tonne is a unit of weight equal to 1000 kilograms.

tonsil, tonsils (noun) Your tonsils are the two small, soft lumps in your throat at the back of your mouth.

tonsillitis (pronounced ton-sil-**lie**-tiss) (noun) Tonsillitis is a painful swelling of your tonsils caused by an infection.

too 1 (adverb) also or as well, e.g. *You were there too.* **2** more than a desirable, necessary, or acceptable amount, e.g. *a man who had taken too much to drink.*

tool, tools 1 (noun) A tool is any hand-held instrument or piece of equipment that you use to help you do a particular kind of work. **2** A tool is an object, skill, or idea that is needed or used for a particular purpose, e.g. *You can use the survey as a bargaining tool in the negotiations.*

toot, toots, tooting, tooted (verb) If a car horn toots, it produces a short sound.

tooth, teeth 1 (noun) Your teeth are the hard enamel-covered objects in your mouth that you use for biting and chewing food. **2** The teeth of a comb, saw, or zip are the parts that stick out in a row on its edge.

toothpaste (noun) Toothpaste is a substance which you use to clean your teeth.

top, tops, topping, topped 1 (noun) The top of something is its highest point, part, or surface. **2** (adjective) The top thing of a series of things is the highest one, e.g. *the top deck of a bus.* **3** (noun) The top of a bottle, jar, or tube is its cap or lid. **4** A top is a piece of clothing worn on the upper half of your body. **5** A top is a toy with a pointed end on which it spins. **6** (verb) If someone tops a poll or popularity chart, they do better than anyone else in it, e.g. *It has topped the best seller lists in almost every country.* **7** If something tops a particular amount, it is greater than that amount, e.g. *The temperature topped 90°.*

top hat, top hats (noun) A top hat is a tall hat with a narrow brim that men wear on special occasions.

topic, topics (noun) A topic is a particular subject that you write about or discuss.

topical (adjective) involving or related to events that are happening at the time you are speaking or writing.

topping, toppings (noun) A topping is food that is put on top of other food in order to decorate it or add to its flavour.

topple, topples, toppling, toppled (verb) If something topples, it becomes unsteady and falls over.

top-secret (adjective) meant to be kept completely secret.

topsy-turvy (adjective) in a confused state, e.g. *My life was truly topsy-turvy.*

torch, torches 1 (noun) A torch is a small electric light carried in the hand and powered by batteries. **2** A torch is also a long stick with burning material wrapped around one end.

torment, torments, tormenting, tormented 1 (noun) Torment is extreme pain or unhappiness. **2** A torment is something that causes extreme pain and unhappiness, e.g. *It's a torment to see them staring at me.* **3** (verb) If something torments you, it causes you extreme unhappiness.

torn 1 Torn is the past participle of **tear**. **2** (adjective) If you are torn between two or more things, you cannot decide which one to choose and this makes you unhappy, e.g. *a woman torn between reason and passion.*

tornado, tornadoes or **tornados** (pronounced tor-**nay**-doh) (noun) A tornado is a violent storm with strong circular winds around a funnel-shaped cloud.

torpedo, torpedoes, torpedoing, torpedoed (pronounced tor-**pee**-doh) **1** (noun) A torpedo is a tube-shaped bomb that travels underwater and explodes when it hits a target. **2** (verb) If a ship is torpedoed, it is hit, and usually sunk, by a torpedo.

torrent, torrents 1 (noun) When a lot of water is falling very rapidly, it can be said to be falling in torrents. **2** A torrent of speech is a lot of it directed continuously at someone, e.g. *torrents of abuse.*

torrential (adjective) Torrential rain pours down very rapidly and heavily.

torrid 1 (adjective) Torrid weather is very hot and dry. **2** A torrid love affair is one in which people show very strong emotions.

torso, torsos (noun) Your torso is the main part of your body, excluding your head, arms, and legs.

tortoise, tortoises (noun) A tortoise is a slow-moving reptile with a large hard shell over its body into which it can pull its head and legs for protection.

tortuous 1 (adjective) A tortuous road is full of bends and twists. **2** A tortuous piece of writing is long and complicated.

torture, tortures, torturing, tortured 1 (noun) Torture is great pain that is deliberately caused to someone in order to punish them or get information from them. **2** (verb) If someone tortures another person, they deliberately cause that person great pain in order to punish them or get information. **3** To torture someone also means to cause them to suffer mentally, e.g. *Memory tortured her.* **torturer** (noun).

Tory, Tories (noun) A Tory is a member or supporter of the Conservative Party.

toss, tosses, tossing, tossed 1 (verb) If you toss something somewhere, you throw it there lightly and carelessly. **2** If you toss a coin, you decide something by throwing a coin into the air and guessing which side will face upwards when it lands. **3** If you toss your head, you move it suddenly backwards, especially when you are angry, annoyed, or want your own way. **4** To toss means to move repeatedly from side to side, e.g. *We tossed and turned and tried to sleep.*

tot, tots, totting, totted 1 (noun) A tot is a very young child. **2** A tot of strong alcohol such as whisky is a small amount of it. **3** (verb) To tot up numbers means to add them together.

total, totals, totalling, totalled 1 (noun) A total is the number you get when you add several numbers together. **2** (verb) When you total a set of numbers or objects, you add them all together. **3** If several numbers total a certain figure, that is the figure you get when all the numbers are added together, e.g. *Their debts totalled over £300,000.* **4** (adjective) Total means complete, e.g. *a total failure.* **totally** (adverb).

totalitarian (pronounced toe-tal-it-**tair**-ee-an) (adjective) A totalitarian political system is one in which one political party controls everything and does not allow any other parties to exist. **totalitarianism**

(noun).

tote, totes, toting, toted (verb; an informal word) To tote a gun means to carry it.

totem pole, totem poles (noun) A totem pole is a long wooden pole with symbols and pictures carved and painted on it. Totem poles are made by some North American Indians.

totter, totters, tottering, tottered (verb) When someone totters, they walk in an unsteady way.

toucan, toucans (pronounced **too**-kan) (noun) A toucan is a large tropical bird with a very large beak.

touch, touches, touching, touched 1 (verb) If you touch something, you put your fingers or hand on it. **2** When two things touch, their surfaces come into contact, e.g. *Their knees were touching.* **3** (noun) Your sense of touch is your ability to tell what something is like by touching it. **4** (verb) If you are touched by something, you are emotionally affected by it, e.g. *I was touched by his thoughtfulness.* **5** (noun) A touch is a detail which is added to improve something, e.g. *finishing touches.* **6** A touch of something is a small amount of it, e.g. *a touch of mustard.* **7** (phrase) If you are **in touch** with someone, you are in contact with them.

touchdown, touchdowns (noun) Touchdown is the landing of an aircraft.

touching (adjective) causing feelings of sadness and sympathy.

touchy, touchier, touchiest 1 (adjective) If someone is touchy, they are easily upset, offended, or irritated. **2** A touchy subject is one that needs to be dealt with carefully, because it might upset or offend people.

tough, tougher, toughest 1 (adjective) A tough person is strong and independent and able to put up with hardship. **2** A tough substance is difficult to break. **3** A tough task, problem, or way of life is difficult or full of hardship. **toughly** (adverb), **toughness** (noun), **toughen** (verb).

toupee, toupees (pronounced **too**-pay) (noun) A toupee is a small wig worn by a man to cover a bald patch on his head.

tour, tours, touring, toured 1 (noun) A tour is a long journey during which you visit several places. **2** A tour is a short trip round a place such as a city or famous building. **3** (verb) If you tour a place, you go on a journey or a trip round it.

tourism (noun) Tourism is the business of providing services for people on holiday, for example hotels and sightseeing trips.

tourist, tourists (noun) A tourist is a person who visits places for pleasure or interest.

tournament, tournaments (noun) A tournament is a sports competition in which players who win a match play further matches, until just one person or team is left.

tourniquet, tourniquets (pronounced **toor**-nik-kay) (noun)

A tourniquet is a strip of cloth tied tightly round a wound in order to stop it bleeding.

tousled (adjective) Tousled hair is untidy.

tout, touts, touting, touted 1 (verb) If someone touts something, they try to sell it. **2** If someone touts for business or custom, they try to obtain it in a very direct way, e.g. *volunteers who spend days touting for donations.* **3** (noun) A tout is someone who sells tickets outside a sports ground or theatre, charging more than the original price.

tow, tows, towing, towed 1 (verb) If a vehicle tows another vehicle, it pulls it along behind it. **2** (noun) To give a vehicle a tow means to tow it.

towards 1 (preposition) in the direction of, e.g. *He turned towards the door.* **2** about or involving, e.g. *My feelings towards Susan have changed.* **3** as a contribution for, e.g. *a huge donation towards the new opera house.* **4** near to, e.g. *We sat towards the back.*

towel, towels (noun) A towel is a piece of thick, soft cloth that you use to dry yourself with.

towelling (noun) Towelling is thick, soft cloth that is used for making towels.

tower, towers, towering, towered 1 (noun) A tower is a tall, narrow building, sometimes attached to a larger building such as a castle or church. **2** (verb) Someone or something that towers over other people or things is much taller than them. **towering** (adjective).

town, towns 1 (noun) A town is a place with many streets and buildings where people live and work. **2** Town is the central shopping and business part of a town rather than the suburbs, e.g. *She has gone into town.*

towpath, towpaths (noun) A towpath is a path along the side of a canal or river.

toxic (adjective) poisonous, e.g. *toxic waste.*

toxin, toxins (noun) A toxin is a poison, especially one produced by bacteria and very harmful to plants, people, and other living creatures.

toy, toys, toying, toyed 1 (noun) A toy is any object made to play with. **2** (verb) If you toy with an idea, you consider it without being very serious about it, e.g. *She toyed with the idea of telephoning him.* **3** If you toy with an object, you fiddle with it, e.g. *Jessica was toying with her glass.*

trace, traces, tracing, traced 1 (verb) If you trace something, you find it after looking for it, e.g. *Police are trying to trace the owner.* **2** To trace the development of something means to find out or describe how it developed. **3** If you trace a drawing or a map, you copy it by covering it with a piece of transparent paper and drawing over the lines underneath. **4** (noun) A trace is a sign which shows you that someone or something has been in a place, e.g. *No trace of his father had been found.* **5** A trace of something is a very small amount of it. **tracing**

(noun).

track, tracks, tracking, tracked 1 (noun) A track is a narrow road or path. **2** A railway track is a strip of ground with rails on it that a train travels along. **3** A track is also a piece of ground, shaped like a ring, which horses, cars, or athletes race around. **4** (adjective) In an athletics competition, the track events are the races on a running track. **5** (plural noun) Tracks are marks left on the ground by a person or animal, e.g. *the deer tracks by the side of the path.* **6** (verb) If you track animals or people, you find them by following their footprints or other signs that they have left behind. **track down** (verb) If you track down someone or something, you find them by searching for them.

track record, track records (noun) The track record of a person or a company is their past achievements or failures, e.g. *the track record of the film's star.*

tracksuit, tracksuits (noun) A tracksuit is a loose, warm suit of trousers and a top, worn for outdoor sports.

tract, tracts 1 (noun) A tract of land or forest is a large area of it. **2** A tract is a pamphlet which expresses a strong opinion on a religious, moral, or political subject. **3** A tract is a system of organs and tubes in an animal's or person's body that has a particular function, e.g. *the digestive tract.*

traction (noun) Traction is a form of medical treatment given to an injured limb which involves pulling it gently for long periods of time using a system of weights and pulleys.

tractor, tractors (noun) A tractor is a vehicle with large rear wheels that is used on a farm for pulling machinery and other heavy loads.

trade, trades, trading, traded 1 (noun) Trade is the activity of buying, selling, or exchanging goods or services between people, firms, or countries. **2** (verb) When people, firms, or countries trade, they buy, sell, or exchange goods or services. **3** (noun) Someone's trade is the kind of work they do, especially when it requires special training in practical skills, e.g. *a joiner by trade.* **4** (verb) If you trade things, you exchange them, e.g. *Their mother had traded her rings for a few potatoes.*

trademark, trademarks (noun) A trademark is a name or symbol that a manufacturer always uses on its products. Trademarks are usually protected by law so that no-one else can use them.

trader, traders (noun) A trader is a person whose job is to trade in goods, e.g. *a timber trader.*

tradesman, tradesmen (noun) A tradesman is a person, for example a shopkeeper, whose job is to sell goods.

trade union, trade unions (noun) A trade union is an organization of workers that tries to improve the pay and conditions in a particular industry.

tradition, traditions (noun) A

tradition is a custom or belief that has existed for a long time without changing.

traditional 1 (adjective) Traditional customs or beliefs have existed for a long time without changing, e.g. *her traditional Indian dress.* **2** A traditional organization or institution is one in which older methods are used rather than modern ones, e.g. *a traditional school.* **traditionally** (adverb).

traditionalist, traditionalists (noun) A traditionalist is someone who supports the established customs and beliefs of their society, and does not want to change them.

traffic, traffics, trafficking, trafficked 1 (noun) Traffic is the movement of vehicles or people along a route at a particular time. **2** Traffic in something such as drugs is an illegal trade in them. **3** (verb) Someone who traffics in drugs or other goods buys and sells them illegally.

traffic light, traffic lights (noun) Traffic lights are the set of red, amber, and green lights at a road junction which control the traffic.

traffic warden, traffic wardens (noun) A traffic warden is a person whose job is to make sure that cars are not parked in the wrong place.

tragedy, tragedies (pronounced **traj**-id-ee) **1** (noun) A tragedy is an event or situation that is disastrous or very sad. **2** A tragedy is a serious story or play, that usually ends with the death of the main character.

tragic 1 (adjective) Something tragic is very sad because it involves death, suffering, or disaster, e.g. *a tragic accident.* **2** Tragic films, plays, and books are sad and serious, e.g. *a tragic love story.* **tragically** (adverb).

trail, trails, trailing, trailed 1 (noun) A trail is a rough path across open country or through forests. **2** A trail is a series of marks or other signs left by someone or something as they move along. **3** (verb) If you trail something or it trails, it drags along behind you as you move, or it hangs down loosely, e.g. *a small plane trailing a banner.* **4** If someone trails along, they move slowly, without any energy or enthusiasm. **5** If a voice trails away or trails off, it gradually becomes more hesitant until it stops completely.

trailer, trailers (noun) A trailer is a small vehicle which can be loaded with things and pulled behind a car.

train, trains, training, trained 1 (noun) A train is a number of carriages or trucks which are pulled by a railway engine. **2** (verb) If you train, you learn how to do a particular job, e.g. *She trained as a serious actress.* **3** If you train for a sports match or a race, you prepare for it by doing exercises. **4** (noun) A train of thought is a connected series of thoughts, e.g. *I don't want to break his train of thought.* **5** A train of vehicles or people is a line or group following behind something or someone, e.g. *a train of wives and girl-*

friends. **training** (noun).

trainee, trainees (noun) A trainee is someone who is being taught how to do a job.

trainers (plural noun) Trainers are special shoes worn for running or jogging.

trait, traits (noun) A trait is a particular characteristic, quality, or tendency, e.g. *a very British trait.*

traitor, traitors (noun) A traitor is someone who betrays their country or the group which they belong to.

trajectory, trajectories (pronounced traj-**jek**-tor-ee) (noun) The trajectory of an object moving through the air is the curving path that it follows.

tram, trams (noun) A tram is a vehicle which runs on rails along the street and is powered by electricity from an overhead wire.

tramp, tramps, tramping, tramped 1 (noun) A tramp is a person who has no home, no job, and very little money. **2** (verb) If you tramp from one place to another, you walk with slow, heavy footsteps. **3** (noun) A tramp is also a long country walk, e.g. *I took a long, wet tramp through the fine woodlands.*

trample, tramples, trampling, trampled 1 (verb) If you trample on something, you tread heavily on it so that it is damaged. **2** If you trample on someone or on their rights or feelings, you behave in a way that shows you don't care about them.

trampoline, trampolines (noun) A trampoline is a piece of gymnastic apparatus consisting of a large piece of strong cloth held taut by springs in a frame.

trance, trances (noun) A trance is a mental state in which someone seems to be asleep but is conscious enough to be aware of their surroundings and to respond to questions and commands.

tranquil (pronounced **trang**-kwil) (adjective) calm and peaceful, e.g. *tranquil lakes... I have a tranquil mind.* **tranquillity** (noun).

tranquillizer, tranquillizers; also spelled **tranquilliser** (noun) A tranquillizer is a drug that makes people feel less anxious or nervous.

trans- (prefix) Trans means across, through, or beyond, e.g. *transatlantic.*

transaction (noun) A transaction is a business deal which involves buying and selling something.

transcend, transcends, transcending, transcended (verb) If one thing transcends another, it goes beyond it or is superior to it, e.g. *Her beauty transcends all barriers.*

transcribe, transcribes, transcribing, transcribed (verb) If you transcribe something that is spoken or written, you write it down, copy it, or change it into a different form of writing, e.g. *These letters were often transcribed by his wife Patti.*

transcript, transcripts (noun) A transcript of something that is spoken is a written copy of it.

transfer, transfers, transferring, transferred 1 (verb) If you transfer something from one place to another, you move it, e.g. *They transferred the money to the Swiss account.* **2** (noun) The transfer of something is the movement of it from one place to another. **3** (verb) If you transfer to a different place or job, or are transferred to it, you move to a different place or job within the same organization. **4** (noun) A transfer is also a piece of paper with a design on one side which can be ironed or pressed onto cloth, paper, or china. **transferable** (adjective).

transfixed (adjective) If a person is transfixed by something, they are so impressed or frightened by it that they cannot move, e.g. *Price stood transfixed at the sight of that tiny figure.*

transform, transforms, transforming, transformed (verb) If something is transformed, it is changed completely, e.g. *The frown is transformed into a smile.* **transformation** (noun).

transfusion, transfusions (noun) A transfusion or blood transfusion is a process in which blood from a healthy person is injected into the body of another person who is badly injured or ill.

transient (pronounced **tran**-zee-ent) (adjective) Something transient does not stay or exist for very long, e.g. *transient emotions.* **transience** (noun).

transistor, transistors 1 (noun) A transistor is a small electrical device in something such as a television or radio which is used to control electric currents. **2** A transistor or a transistor radio is a small portable radio.

transit 1 (noun) Transit is the carrying of goods or people by vehicle from one place to another. **2** (phrase) People or things that are **in transit** are travelling or being taken from one place to another, e.g. *damage that had occurred in transit.*

transition, transitions (noun) A transition is a change from one form or state to another, e.g. *the transition from war to peace.*

transitional (adjective) A transitional period or stage is one during which something changes from one form or state to another.

transitive (adjective) In grammar, a transitive verb is a verb which has an object.

transitory (adjective) lasting for only a short time.

translate, translates, translating, translated (verb) To translate something that someone has said or written means to say it or write it in a different language. **translation** (noun), **translator** (noun).

translucent (adjective) If something is translucent, light passes through it so that it seems to glow, e.g. *translucent petals.*

transmission, transmissions 1 (noun) The transmission of something involves passing or sending it to a different place or person, e.g. *the transmission of infectious diseases.* **2** The transmission of television or radio programmes is the broadcasting of them. **3** A transmission is a broadcast.

transmit, transmits, transmitting, transmitted 1 (verb) When a message or an electronic signal is transmitted, it is sent by radio waves. **2** To transmit something to a different place or person means to pass it or send it to the place or person, e.g. *the clergy's role in transmitting knowledge.* **transmitter** (noun).

transparency, transparencies 1 (noun) A transparency is a small piece of photographic film which can be projected onto a screen. **2** Transparency is the quality that an object or substance has if you can see through it.

transparent (adjective) If an object or substance is transparent, you can see through it. **transparently** (adverb).

transpire, transpires, transpiring, transpired 1 (verb; a formal use) When it transpires that something is the case, people discover that it is the case, e.g. *It transpired that he had flown off on holiday.* **2** When something transpires, it happens, e.g. *You start to wonder what transpired between them.*

transplant, transplants, transplanting, transplanted 1 (noun) A transplant is the process of removing something from one place and putting it in another, e.g. *a man who needs a heart transplant.* **2** (verb) When something is transplanted, it is moved to a different place.

transport, transports, transporting, transported 1 (noun) Vehicles that you travel in are referred to as transport, e.g. *public transport.* **2** Transport is the moving of goods or people from one place to another, e.g. *The prices quoted include transport costs.* **3** (verb) When goods or people are transported from one place to another, they are moved there.

transportation (noun) Transportation is the transporting of people and things from one place to another.

transvestite, transvestites (noun) A transvestite is a person who enjoys wearing clothes normally worn by people of the opposite sex.

trap, traps, trapping, trapped 1 (noun) A trap is a piece of equipment or a hole that is carefully positioned in order to catch animals or birds. **2** A trap is a trick that is intended to catch or deceive someone. **3** (verb) Someone who traps animals catches them using traps. **4** If you trap someone, you trick them so that they do or say something which they did not want to. **5** If you are trapped somewhere, you cannot move or escape because something is blocking your way or holding you down. **6** If you are trapped, you are in an unpleasant situation that you cannot easily change, e.g. *I'm trapped in an unhappy marriage.*

trap door, trap doors (noun) A trap door is a small horizontal door in a floor, ceiling, or stage.

trapeze, trapezes (noun) A trapeze is a bar of wood or metal hanging from two ropes on which acrobats and gymnasts swing and perform skilful movements.

trappings (plural noun) The trappings of a particular rank, position, or state are the clothes or equipment that go with it.

trash (noun) Trash is rubbish, e.g. *He picks up your trash on Mondays.*

trauma, traumas (pronounced **traw**-ma) (noun) A trauma is a very upsetting experience which causes great stress, e.g. *the trauma of his mother's death.*

traumatic (adjective) A traumatic experience is very upsetting.

travel, travels, travelling, travelled 1 (verb) To travel means to go from one place to another. **2** (noun) Travel is the act of travelling, e.g. *air travel.* **3** (plural noun) Someone's travels are the journeys that they make to places a long way from their home, e.g. *my travels in the Himalayas.* **4** (verb) When something reaches one place from another, you say that it travels there, e.g. *Gossip travels fast.* **traveller** (noun), **travelling** (adjective).

traveller's cheque, traveller's cheques (noun) Traveller's cheques are cheques for use abroad. You buy them at home and then exchange them when you are abroad for foreign currency.

traverse, traverses, traversing, traversed (verb; a formal word) If you traverse an area of land or water, you go across it or over it, e.g. *They have traversed the island from the west coast.*

travesty, travesties (noun) A travesty of something is a very bad or ridiculous representation or imitation of it, e.g. *British salad is a travesty of freshness.*

trawl, trawls, trawling, trawled (verb) When fishermen trawl, they drag a wide net behind a ship in order to catch fish.

trawler, trawlers (noun) A trawler is a fishing boat that is used for trawling.

tray, trays (noun) A tray is a flat object with raised edges which is used for carrying food or drinks.

treacherous 1 (adjective) A treacherous person is likely to betray you and cannot be trusted. **2** The ground or the sea can be described as treacherous when it is dangerous or unreliable, e.g. *treacherous mountain roads.* **treacherously** (adverb).

treachery (noun) Treachery is behaviour in which someone betrays their country or a person who trusts them.

treacle (noun) Treacle is a thick, sweet, sticky syrup used to make cakes and toffee, e.g. *treacle tart.*

tread, treads, treading, trod, trodden 1 (verb) If you tread on something, you walk on it or step on it. **2** If you tread something into the ground or into a carpet, you crush it in by stepping on it, e.g. *bubblegum that has been trodden into the pavement.* **3** (noun) A person's tread is the sound they make with their feet as they walk, e.g. *his heavy tread.* **4** The tread of a tyre or shoe is the pattern of ridges on it that stops it slipping.

treadmill, treadmills (noun) Any task or job that you must keep doing even though it is unpleasant or tiring can be referred to as a treadmill, e.g. *My life is one constant treadmill of making music.*

treason (noun) Treason is the crime of betraying your country, for example by helping its enemies.

treasure, treasures, treasuring, treasured 1 (noun) Treasure is a collection of gold, silver, jewels, or other precious objects, especially one that has been hidden, e.g. *buried treasure.* **2** Treasures are valuable works of art, e.g. *the finest art treasures in the world.* **3** (verb) If you treasure something, you are very pleased that you have it and regard it as very precious, e.g. *He treasures his friendship with her.* **treasured** (adjective).

treasurer, treasurers (noun) A treasurer is a person who is in charge of the finance and accounts of an organization.

treasury (noun) The Treasury is the government department that deals with the country's finances.

treat, treats, treating, treated 1 (verb) If you treat someone in a particular way, you behave that way towards them. **2** If you treat something in a particular way, you deal with it that way or see it that way, e.g. *We are now treating this case as murder.* **3** When a doctor treats a patient or an illness, he or she gives them medical care and attention. **4** If something such as wood or cloth is treated, a special substance is put on it in order to protect it or give it special properties, e.g. *The carpet's been treated with a stain protector.* **5** (noun) If you give someone a treat, you buy or arrange something special for them which they will enjoy, e.g. *my birthday treat.* **treatment** (noun).

treatise, treatises (pronounced **tree**-tiz) (noun) A treatise is a long formal piece of writing about a particular subject.

treaty, treaties (noun) A treaty is a written agreement between countries in which they agree to do something or to help each other.

treble, trebles, trebling, trebled 1 (verb) If something trebles or is trebled, it becomes three times greater in number or amount. **2** (adjective) Treble means three times as large or three times as strong as previously, e.g. *Next year we can raise treble that amount.*

tree, trees (noun) A tree is a large plant with a hard woody trunk, branches, and leaves.

trek, treks, trekking, trekked 1 (verb) If you trek somewhere, you go on a long and difficult journey. **2** (noun) A trek is a long and difficult journey.

trellis, trellises (noun) A trellis is a frame made of horizontal and vertical strips of wood or metal and used to support plants.

tremble, trembles, trembling, trembled 1 (verb) If you tremble, you shake slightly, usually because you are frightened or cold. **2** If something trembles, it shakes slightly. **3** If your voice trembles, it sounds unsteady, usually because you are frightened or upset. **trembling** (adjective).

tremendous 1 (adjective) large or impressive, e.g. *It was a tremendous performance.* **2** (an informal use) very good or pleasing, e.g. *tremendous fun.* **tremendously** (adverb).

tremor, tremors 1 (noun) A tremor is a shaking movement of your body which you cannot control. **2** A tremor is an unsteady quality in your voice, for example when you are upset. **3** A tremor is also a small earthquake.

trench, trenches (noun) A trench is a long narrow channel dug into the ground.

trenchant (pronounced **trent**-shent) (adjective) Trenchant writing or comments are bold and firmly expressed.

trend, trends (noun) A trend is a change towards doing or being something different.

trendy, trendier, trendiest (adjective; an informal word) Trendy things or people are fashionable.

trepidation (noun; a formal word) Trepidation is fear or anxiety, e.g. *He saw the look of trepidation on my face.*

trespass, trespasses, trespassing, trespassed (verb) If you trespass on someone's land or property, you go onto it without their permission. **trespasser** (noun).

tresses (plural noun; an old-fashioned word) A woman's tresses are her long flowing hair.

trestle, trestles (noun) A trestle is a wooden or metal structure that is used as one of the supports for a table.

tri- (prefix) three, e.g. *tricycle.*

trial, trials 1 (noun) A trial is the legal process in which a judge and jury decide whether a person is guilty of a particular crime after listening to all the evidence about it. **2** A trial is also an experiment in which something is tested, e.g. *Trials of the drug start next month.*

triangle, triangles 1 (noun) A triangle is a shape with three straight sides. **2** A triangle is also a percussion instrument consisting of a thin steel bar bent in the shape of a triangle. **triangular** (adjective).

triathlon, triathlons (pronounced tri-**ath**-lon) (noun) A triathlon is a sports contest in which athletes compete in three different events.

tribe, tribes (noun) A tribe is a group of people of the same race, who have the same customs, religion, language, or land, especially when they are thought to be primitive. **tribal** (adjective).

tribulation, tribulations (noun; a formal word) Tribulation is trouble or suffering, e.g. *the trials and tribulations of a female football star.*

tribunal, tribunals (pronounced try-**byoo**-nl) (noun) A tribunal is a special court or committee appointed to deal with particular problems, e.g. *an industrial tribunal.*

tributary, tributaries (noun) A tributary is a stream or river that flows into a larger river.

tribute, tributes 1 (noun) A

tribute is something said or done to show admiration and respect for someone, e.g. *Police paid tribute to her courage.* **2** If one thing is a tribute to another, it is the result of the other thing and shows how good it is, e.g. *His success has been a tribute to hard work.*

trice (noun) If someone does something in a trice, they do it very quickly.

trick, tricks, tricking, tricked 1 (verb) If someone tricks you, they deceive you. **2** (noun) A trick is an action done to deceive someone. **3** Tricks are clever or skilful actions done in order to entertain people, e.g. *magic tricks.*

trickery (noun) Trickery is deception, e.g. *China accuses Hong Kong of trickery.*

trickle, trickles, trickling, trickled 1 (verb) When a liquid trickles somewhere, it flows slowly in a thin stream. **2** When people or things trickle somewhere, they move there slowly in small groups or amounts. **3** (noun) A trickle of liquid is a thin stream of it. **4** A trickle of people or things is a small number or quantity of them.

tricky, trickier, trickiest (adjective) difficult to do or deal with.

tricycle, tricycles (noun) A tricycle is a vehicle similar to a bicycle but with two wheels at the back and one at the front.

trifle, trifles, trifling, trifled 1 (noun) A trifle also means a little, e.g. *He seemed a trifle annoyed.* **2** Trifles are things that are not very important or valuable. **3** A trifle is a cold pudding made of layers of sponge cake, fruit, jelly, and custard. **4** (verb) If you trifle with someone or something, you treat them in a disrespectful way, e.g. *He was not to be trifled with.*

trifling (adjective) small and unimportant.

trigger, triggers, triggering, triggered 1 (noun) The trigger of a gun is the small lever which is pulled in order to fire it. **2** (verb) If something triggers an event or triggers it off, it causes it to happen.

trigonometry (pronounced trig-gon-**nom**-it-ree) (noun) Trigonometry is the branch of mathematics that is concerned with calculating the angles of triangles or the lengths of their sides.

trill, trills, trilling, trilled (verb) If a bird trills, it sings with short high-pitched repeated notes.

trillion, trillions (noun; an informal word) Trillions of things means an extremely large number of them. Formerly, a trillion meant a million million.

trilogy, trilogies (noun) A trilogy is a series of three books or plays with the same characters or subject.

trim, trimmer, trimmest; trims, trimming, trimmed 1 (adjective) neat, tidy, and attractive. **2** (verb) To trim something means to clip small amounts off it. **3** (noun) If something is given a trim, it is cut a little, e.g. *All styles need a trim every six to eight weeks.* **4** (verb) If you trim off parts of something, you cut them off because they are not needed, e.g. *Trim off the excess marzipan.* **5** (noun) A trim on something is a decoration on it, especially along its edges, e.g. *a fur trim.* **trimmed** (adjective).

trimming, trimmings (noun) Trimmings are extra parts added to something for decoration or as a luxury, e.g. *bacon and eggs with all the trimmings.*

trinity (noun) In the Christian religion, the Trinity is the joining of God the Father, God the Son, and God the Holy Spirit.

trinket, trinkets (noun) A trinket is a cheap ornament or piece of jewellery.

trio, trios 1 (noun) A trio is a group of three musicians who sing or play together; also a piece of music written for three instruments or singers. **2** Any group of three things or people together can be referred to as a trio.

trip, trips, tripping, tripped 1 (noun) A trip is a journey made to a place. **2** (verb) If you trip, you catch your foot on something and fall over. **3** If you trip someone or trip them up, you make them fall over by making them catch their foot on something.

tripe (noun) Tripe is the stomach lining of a pig, cow, or ox, which is cooked and eaten.

triple, triples, tripling, tripled 1 (adjective) consisting of three things or three parts, e.g. *the Triple Alliance.* **2** (verb) If you triple something or if it triples, it becomes three times greater in number or size.

triplet, triplets (noun) Triplets are three children born at the same time to the same mother.

tripod, tripods (pronounced **try**-pod) (noun) A tripod is a stand with three legs used to support something like a camera or telescope.

tripper, trippers (noun) A tripper is a tourist or someone on an excursion.

trite (adjective) dull and unoriginal, e.g. *his trite novels.*

triumph, triumphs, triumphing, triumphed 1 (noun) A triumph is a great success or achievement. **2** Triumph is a feeling of great satisfaction when you win or achieve something. **3** (verb) If you triumph, you win a victory or succeed in overcoming something.

triumphal (adjective) done or made to celebrate a victory or great success, e.g. *a triumphal return to Rome.*

triumphant (adjective) Someone who is triumphant feels very happy because they have won a victory or have achieved something, e.g. *a triumphant shout.*

trivia (plural noun) Trivia are unimportant or uninteresting things.

trivial (adjective) Something trivial is unimportant.

troll, trolls (noun) A troll is an imaginary creature in Scandinavian mythology that lives in caves or mountains and is believed to turn to stone at daylight.

trolley, trolleys 1 (noun) A trolley is a small table on wheels. **2** A trolley is a small cart on wheels used for carrying heavy objects, e.g. *a supermarket trolley*.

trombone, trombones (noun) A trombone is a brass wind instrument with a U-shaped slide which you move to produce different notes.

troop, troops, trooping, trooped 1 (noun) Troops are soldiers. **2** A troop of people or animals is a group of them. **3** (verb) If people troop somewhere, they go there in a group.

trooper, troopers (noun) A trooper is a low-ranking soldier in the cavalry.

trophy, trophies (noun) A trophy is a cup or shield given as a prize to the winner of a competition.

tropical (adjective) belonging to or typical of the tropics, e.g. *a tropical island*.

tropics (plural noun) The tropics are the hottest parts of the world between two lines of latitude, the Tropic of Cancer, 23½° north of the equator, and the Tropic of Capricorn, 23½° south of the equator.

trot, trots, trotting, trotted 1 (verb) When a horse trots, it moves at a speed between a walk and a canter, lifting its feet quite high off the ground. **2** (noun) When a horse breaks into a trot, it starts trotting. **3** (verb) If you trot, you run or jog using small quick steps.

trotter, trotters (noun) A pig's trotters are its feet.

trouble, troubles, troubling, troubled 1 (noun) Troubles are difficulties or problems. **2** (phrase) If you are **in trouble,** you are in a situation where you may be punished because you have done something wrong. **3** (noun) If there is trouble, people are quarrelling or fighting, e.g. *There was more trouble after the match.* **4** (verb) If something troubles you, it makes you feel worried or anxious. **5** If you trouble someone for something, you disturb them in order to ask them for it, e.g. *I'm sorry to trouble you again.* **troubling** (adjective), **troubled** (adjective).

troublesome (adjective) causing problems or difficulties, e.g. *a troublesome teenager*.

trough, troughs (pronounced **troff**) (noun) A trough is a long, narrow container from which animals drink or feed.

trounce, trounces, trouncing, trounced (verb) If you trounce someone, you defeat them completely.

troupe, troupes (pronounced **troop**) (noun) A troupe is a group of actors, singers, or dancers who work together and often travel around together.

trousers (plural noun) Trousers are a piece of clothing covering the body from the waist down, enclosing each leg separately.

trout (noun) A trout is a type of freshwater fish.

trowel, trowels 1 (noun) A trowel is a small garden tool with a curved, pointed blade used for planting or weeding. **2** A trowel is a small tool with a flat blade used for spreading cement or plaster.

truant, truants 1 (noun) A truant is a child who stays away from school without permission. **2** (phrase) If children

play truant, they stay away from school without permission. **truancy** (noun).

truce, truces (noun) A truce is an agreement between two people or groups to stop fighting for a short time.

truck, trucks 1 (noun) A truck is a large motor vehicle used for carrying heavy loads. **2** A truck is an open vehicle used for carrying goods on a railway.

truculent (pronounced **truk**-yoo-lent) (adjective) bad-tempered and aggressive. **truculence** (noun).

trudge, trudges, trudging, trudged 1 (verb) If you trudge, you walk with slow, heavy steps. **2** (noun) A trudge is a slow tiring walk, e.g. *the long trudge home.*

true, truer, truest 1 (adjective) A true story or statement is based on facts and is not made up. **2** (phrase) If something **comes true,** it actually happens. **3** (adjective) True is used to describe things or people that are genuine, e.g. *She was a true friend.* **4** True feelings are sincere and genuine. **truly** (adverb).

truffle, truffles 1 (noun) A truffle is a soft, round sweet. **2** A truffle is also a round mushroom-like fungus which grows underground and is considered very good to eat.

trump, trumps (noun) In a game of cards, trumps is the suit with the highest value.

trumpet, trumpets, trumpeting, trumpeted 1 (noun) A trumpet is a brass wind instrument with a narrow tube ending in a bell-like shape. **2** (verb) When an elephant trumpets, it makes a sound like a very loud trumpet.

truncated (adjective) Something that is truncated is made shorter.

truncheon, truncheons (pronounced **trunt**-shn) (noun) A truncheon is a short, thick stick that policemen carry as a weapon.

trundle, trundles, trundling, trundled (verb) If you trundle something or it trundles somewhere, it moves or rolls along slowly.

trunk, trunks 1 (noun) The trunk of a tree is the main stem from which the branches and roots grow. **2** Your trunk is the main part of your body, excluding your head, neck, arms, and legs. **3** An elephant's trunk is its long flexible nose. **4** A trunk is a large, strong case or box with a hinged lid used for storing things. **5** (plural noun) A man's trunks are his bathing pants or shorts.

truss, trusses, trussing, trussed 1 (verb) To truss someone or truss them up means to tie them up so that they cannot move. **2** (noun) A truss is a supporting belt with a pad worn by a man with a hernia.

trust, trusts, trusting, trusted 1 (verb) If you trust someone, you believe that they are honest and will not harm you. **2** If you trust someone to do something, you believe they will do it successfully or properly. **3** If you trust someone with something, you give it to them or tell it to them, e.g. *One member of the group cannot be* *trusted with the secret.* **4** If you do not trust something, you feel that it is not safe or reliable, e.g. *I didn't trust my arms and legs to work.* **5** (noun) Trust is the responsibility you are given to deal with or look after important, valuable, or secret things, e.g. *He had built up a position of trust.* **6** A trust is a financial arrangement in which an organization looks after and invests money for someone. **trusting** (adjective).

trustee, trustees (noun) A trustee is someone who is allowed by law to control money or property they are keeping or investing for another person.

trustworthy (adjective) A trustworthy person is reliable and responsible and can be trusted.

trusty, trustier, trustiest (adjective) Trusty things and animals are considered to be reliable because they have always worked well in the past, e.g. *a trusty black labrador.*

truth, truths 1 (noun) The truth is the facts about something, rather than things that are imagined or made up, e.g. *I know she was telling the truth.* **2** A truth is an idea or principle that is generally accepted to be true, e.g. *the basic truths in life.*

truthful (adjective) A truthful person is honest and tells the truth. **truthfully** (adverb).

try, tries, trying, tried 1 (verb) To try to do something means to make an effort to do it. **2** (noun) A try is an attempt to do something. **3** (verb) If you try something, you use it, do it, or experience it in order to test how useful, effective, or enjoyable it is, e.g. *Howard wanted me to try the wine.* **4** (noun) A try of something is a test of it, e.g. *You gave it a try.* **5** In rugby, a try is scored when someone carries the ball over the goal line of the opposing team and touches the ground with it. **6** (verb) When a person is tried, they appear in court and a judge and jury decide if they are guilty after hearing the evidence.

trying (adjective) Something or someone trying is difficult to deal with and makes you feel impatient or annoyed.

tryst, trysts (pronounced **trist**) (noun) A tryst is an appointment or meeting, especially between lovers in a quiet, secret place.

tsar, tsars (pronounced **zar**); also spelled **czar** (noun) A tsar was a Russian emperor between 1547 and 1917.

tsarina, tsarinas (pronounced zah-**ree**-na); also spelled **czarina** (noun) A tsarina was a female tsar or the wife of a tsar.

tsetse fly, tsetse flies (pronounced **tset**-tsee) (noun) A tsetse fly is an African fly that feeds on blood and causes serious diseases in people and animals.

T-shirt, T-shirts; also spelled **tee shirt** (noun) A T-shirt is a simple short-sleeved cotton shirt with no collar.

tub, tubs (noun) A tub is a wide circular container.

tuba, tubas (noun) A tuba is a large brass musical instrument that can produce very low notes.

tubby, tubbier, tubbiest (adjective) rather fat.

tube, tubes 1 (noun) A tube is a round, hollow pipe. **2** A tube is a soft metal or plastic cylindrical container with a screw cap at one end, e.g. *a tube of toothpaste.* **tubing** (noun).

tuberculosis (pronounced tyoo-ber-kyoo-**low**-siss) (noun) Tuberculosis is a serious infectious disease affecting the lungs.

tubular (adjective) in the shape of a tube.

TUC an abbreviation for 'Trades Union Congress', which is an association of trade unions.

tuck, tucks, tucking, tucked 1 (verb) If you tuck something somewhere, you put it there so that it is safe or comfortable, e.g. *She tucked the letter into her handbag.* **2** If you tuck a piece of fabric into or under something, you push the loose ends inside or under it to make it tidy. **3** If something is tucked away, it is in a quiet place where few people go, e.g. *a little croft house tucked away in a valley.*

Tudor, Tudors (noun) Tudor was the family name of the English monarchs who reigned from 1485 to 1603.

Tuesday, Tuesdays (noun) Tuesday is the day between Monday and Wednesday.

tuft, tufts (noun) A tuft of something such as hair is a bunch of it growing closely together.

tug, tugs, tugging, tugged 1 (verb) To tug something means to give it a quick, hard pull. **2** (noun) A tug is a quick, hard pull, e.g. *He felt a tug at his arm.* **3** A tug is also a small, powerful boat which tows large ships.

tug of war (noun) A tug of war is a sport in which two teams test their strength by pulling against each other on opposite ends of a rope.

tuition (noun) Tuition is the teaching of a subject, especially to one person or to a small group.

tulip, tulips (noun) A tulip is a brightly-coloured spring flower.

tumble, tumbles, tumbling, tumbled 1 (verb) To tumble means to fall with a rolling or bouncing movement. **2** (noun) A tumble is a fall.

tumbler, tumblers (noun) A tumbler is a drinking glass with straight sides.

tummy, tummies (noun; an informal word) Your tummy is your stomach.

tumour, tumours (pronounced **tyoo**-mur) (noun) A tumour is a mass of diseased or abnormal cells that has grown in a person's or animal's body.

tumultuous (adjective) A tumultuous event or welcome is very noisy because people are happy or excited.

tuna (pronounced **tyoo**-na) (noun) Tuna are large fish that live in warm seas and are caught for food.

tundra (noun) The tundra is a vast treeless Arctic region.

tune, tunes, tuning, tuned 1 (noun) A tune is a series of musical notes arranged in a particular way. **2** (verb) To tune a musical instrument means to adjust it so that it produces the right notes. **3** To tune an engine or machine means to adjust it so that it works well. **4** If you tune to a particular radio or television station you turn or press the controls to select the station you want to listen to or watch. **5** (phrase) If your voice or an instrument is **in tune,** it produces the right notes.

tuneful (adjective) having a pleasant and easily remembered tune.

tuner, tuners (noun) A piano tuner is a person whose job it is to tune pianos.

tunic, tunics (noun) A tunic is a sleeveless garment covering the top part of the body.

Tunisian, Tunisians (pronounced tyoo-**niz**-ee-an) **1** (adjective) belonging or relating to Tunisia. **2** (noun) A Tunisian is someone who comes from Tunisia.

tunnel, tunnels, tunnelling, tunnelled 1 (noun) A tunnel is a long underground passage. **2** (verb) To tunnel means to make a tunnel.

turban, turbans (noun) A turban is a head-covering worn by a Hindu, Muslim, or Sikh man, consisting of a long piece of cloth wound round his head.

turbot (pronounced **tur**-bot) (noun) A turbot is a large, flat fish that is caught for food.

turbulent 1 (adjective) A turbulent period of history is one where there is much confusion, uncertainty, and possibly violent change. **2** Turbulent air or water currents make sudden changes of direction. **turbulence** (noun).

tureen, tureens (pronounced tur-**reen**) (noun) A tureen is a large dish with a lid for serving soup.

turf, turves; turfs, turfing, turfed (noun) Turf is short thick even grass and the layer of soil beneath it. **turf out** (verb; an informal expression) To turf someone out means to force them to leave a place.

turgid (pronounced **tur**-jid) (adjective; a literary word) A turgid play, film, or piece of writing is difficult to understand and rather boring.

Turk, Turks (noun) A Turk is someone who comes from Turkey.

turkey, turkeys (noun) A turkey is a large bird kept for food; also the meat of this bird.

Turkish 1 (adjective) belonging or relating to Turkey. **2** (noun) Turkish is the main language spoken in Turkey.

turmoil (noun) Turmoil is a state of confusion, disorder, or great anxiety, e.g. *Europe is in a state of turmoil.*

turn, turns, turning, turned 1 (verb) When you turn, you move so that you are facing or going in a different direction. **2** When you turn something or when it turns, it moves or rotates so that it faces in a different direction or is in a different position. **3** (noun) A turn is an act of turning something so that it faces in a different direction or is in a different position. **4** (verb) If you turn your attention or thoughts to someone or something, you start thinking about them or discussing them. **5** When something turns or is turned into something else, it becomes something different, e.g. *A hobby can be turned into a career.* **6** (noun) A turn is a change in the way something is happening or being done, e.g. *Her career took a turn for the worse.* **7** If it is your turn to do something, you have the right, chance, or duty to do it. **8** (phrase) **In turn** is used to refer to people, things, or actions that are in sequence one after the other. **turn down** (verb) If you turn down someone's request or offer, you refuse or reject it. **turn up 1** (verb) If someone or something turns up, they arrive or appear somewhere. **2** If something turns up, it is found or discovered.

turncoat, turncoats (noun) A turncoat is a person who leaves one political party or group for an opposing one.

turning, turnings (noun) A turning is a road which leads away from the side of another road.

turning point, turning points (noun) A turning point is the moment when decisions are taken and events start to move in a different direction.

turnip, turnips (noun) A turnip is a round root vegetable with a white or yellow skin.

turnout, turnouts (noun) The turnout at an event is the number of people who go to it.

turnover, turnovers 1 (noun) The turnover of people in a particular organization or group is the rate at which people leave it and are replaced by others. **2** The turnover of a company is the value of the goods or services sold during a particular period.

turnstile, turnstiles (noun) A turnstile is a revolving mechanical barrier at the entrance to places like football grounds or zoos.

turpentine (noun) Turpentine is a strong-smelling colourless liquid used for cleaning and for thinning paint.

turps (noun) Turps is turpentine.

turquoise (pronounced **tur**-kwoyz) **1** (noun or adjective) light bluish-green. **2** (noun) Turquoise is a bluish-green stone used in jewellery.

turret, turrets (noun) A turret is a small narrow tower on top of a larger tower or other buildings.

turtle, turtles (noun) A turtle is a large reptile with a thick shell covering its body and flippers for swimming. It lays its eggs on land but lives the rest of its life in the sea.

tusk, tusks (noun) The tusks of an elephant, wild boar, or walrus are the pair of long curving pointed teeth it has.

tussle, tussles (noun) A tussle is an energetic fight, struggle, or argument between two people, especially about something they both want.

tutor, tutors, tutoring, tutored 1 (noun) A tutor is a teacher at a college or university. **2** A tutor is a private teacher. **3** (verb) If someone tutors a person or subject, they teach that person or subject.

tutorial, tutorials (noun) A tutorial is a teaching session involving a tutor and a small group of students.

tutu, tutus (pronounced **too**-too) (noun) A tutu is a short stiff skirt worn by female ballet dancers.

TV, TVs 1 (noun) TV is television. **2** A TV is a television set.

twang, twangs, twanging, twanged 1 (noun) A twang is a sound like the one made by pulling and then releasing a tight wire. **2** (verb) If a tight wire or string twangs or you twang it, it makes a sound as it is pulled and then released. **3** (noun) A twang is a nasal quality in a person's voice.

tweak, tweaks, tweaking, tweaked 1 (verb) If you tweak something, you twist it or pull it. **2** (noun) A tweak of something is a short twist or pull of it.

twee (adjective) sweet and pretty but in bad taste or sentimental.

tweed, tweeds (noun) Tweed is a thick woollen cloth.

tweet, tweets, tweeting, tweeted 1 (verb) When a small bird tweets, it makes a short, high-pitched sound. **2** (noun) A tweet is a short high-pitched sound made by a small bird.

tweezers (plural noun) Tweezers are a small tool with two arms, used for pulling out hairs or picking up small objects.

twelve the number 12. **twelfth**

twenty, twenties the number 20. **twentieth**

twice (adverb) Twice means two times.

twiddle, twiddles, twiddling, twiddled (verb) To twiddle something means to twist it or turn it quickly.

twig, twigs (noun) A twig is a very small thin branch growing from a main branch of a tree or bush.

twilight (pronounced **twy**-lite) **1** (noun) Twilight is the time after sunset when it is just getting dark. **2** The twilight of something is the final stages of it, e.g. *the twilight of his career.*

twin, twins 1 (noun) If two people are twins, they have the same mother and were born on the same day. **2** Twin is used to describe two similar things that are close together or happen together, e.g. *the little twin islands.*

twine, twines, twining, twined 1 (noun) Twine is strong smooth string. **2** (verb) If you twine one thing round another, you twist or wind it round.

twinge, twinges (noun) A twinge is a sudden, unpleasant feeling, e.g. *a twinge of jealousy.*

twinkle, twinkles, twinkling, twinkled 1 (verb) If something twinkles, it sparkles or seems to sparkle with an unsteady light, e.g. *Her green eyes twinkled.* **2** (noun) A twinkle is a sparkle or brightness that something has.

twirl, twirls, twirling, twirled (verb) If something twirls, or if you twirl it, it spins or twists round and round.

twist, twists, twisting, twisted 1 (verb) When you twist something you turn one end of it in one direction while holding the other end or turning it in the opposite direction. **2** (noun) A twist is a twisting action or motion. **3** (verb) When something twists or is twisted, it moves or bends into a strange shape. **4** If you twist a part of your body, you injure it by turning it too sharply or in an unusual direction, e.g. *I've twisted my ankle.* **5** If you twist something that someone has said, you change the meaning slightly. **6** (noun) A twist in a story or film is an unexpected development or event, especially at the end, e.g. *Each day now seemed to bring a new twist to the story.*

twisted 1 (adjective) Something twisted has been bent or moved into a strange shape, e.g. *a tangle of twisted metal.* **2** If someone's mind or behaviour is twisted, it is unpleasantly abnormal, e.g. *He's bitter and twisted.*

twit, twits (noun; an informal word) A twit is a silly person.

twitch, twitches, twitching, twitched 1 (verb) If you twitch, you make little jerky movements which you cannot control. **2** If you twitch something, you give it a little jerk in order to move it. **3** (noun) A twitch is a little jerky movement.

twitter, twitters, twittering, twittered (verb) When birds twitter, they make short high-pitched sounds.

two the number 2.

two-faced (adjective) A two-faced person is not honest in the way they behave towards other people.

twofold (adjective) Something twofold has two equally important parts or reasons, e.g. *Their concern was twofold: personal and political.*

twosome, twosomes (pronounced **too**-sum) (noun) A twosome refers to two people or things that are usually seen together.

two-time, two-times, two-timing, two-timed (verb; an informal expression) If you two-time your boyfriend or girlfriend, you deceive them, by having a romantic relationship with someone else without telling them.

tycoon, tycoons (noun) A tycoon is a person who is successful in business and has become rich and powerful.

type, types, typing, typed 1 (noun) A type of something is a class of it that has common features and belongs to a larger group of related things, e.g. *What type of dog should we get?* **2** A particular type of person has a particular appearance or quality, e.g. *the arty, academic, sensitive types.* **3** (verb) If you type something, you use a typewriter or word processor to write it.

typewriter, typewriters (noun) A typewriter is a machine with a keyboard with individual keys which are pressed to produce letters and numbers on a page.

typhoid (pronounced **tie**-foyd) (noun) Typhoid, or typhoid fever, is an infectious disease caused by dirty water or food. It produces fever and can kill.

typhoon, typhoons (noun) A typhoon is a very violent tropical storm.

typhus (noun) Typhus is an infectious disease transmitted by lice or mites. It results in fever, severe headaches, and a skin rash.

typical (adjective) showing the most usual characteristics or behaviour. **typically** (adverb).

typify, typifies, typifying, typified (verb) If something typifies a situation or thing, it is characteristic of it or a typical example of it, e.g. *This story is one that typifies our times.*

typing (noun) Typing is the work or activity of producing something on a typewriter.

typist, typists (noun) A typist is a person whose job is typing.

tyrannosaurus, tyrannosauruses (pronounced tir-ran-oh-**saw**-russ) (noun) The tyrannosaurus was a very large meat-eating dinosaur which walked upright on its hind legs.

tyranny, tyrannies 1 (noun) A tyranny is cruel and unjust rule of people by a person or group, e.g. *the evils of Nazi tyranny.* **2** You can refer to harsh inhuman force as tyranny, e.g. *the tyranny of drugs.* **tyrannical** (adjective).

tyrant, tyrants (noun) A tyrant is a person who treats the people he or she has authority over cruelly and unjustly.

tyre, tyres (noun) A tyre is a thick ring of rubber fitted round each wheel of a vehicle and filled with air.

U u

ubiquitous (pronounced yoo-**bik**-wit-tuss) (adjective) Something that is ubiquitous seems to be everywhere at the same time, e.g. *the ubiquitous jeans.*

udder, udders (noun) A cow's udder is the baglike organ that hangs below its body and produces milk.

UFO, UFOs (noun) A UFO is a strange object seen in the sky, which some people believe to be a spaceship from another planet. UFO is an abbreviation for 'unidentified flying object'.

Ugandan, Ugandans (pronounced yoo-**gan**-dan) **1** (adjective) belonging or relating to Uganda. **2** (noun) A Ugandan is someone who comes from Uganda.

ugly, uglier, ugliest (adjective) very unattractive in appearance.

UK an abbreviation for **United Kingdom**.

ulcer, ulcers (noun) An ulcer is a sore area on the skin or inside the body, which takes a long time to heal, e.g. *stomach ulcers.*

ulterior (pronounced ul-**teer**-ee-or) (adjective) If you have an ulterior motive for doing something, you have a hidden reason for it.

ultimate 1 (adjective) final or eventual, e.g. *Olympic gold is the ultimate goal.* **2** most important or powerful, e.g. *the ultimate ambition of any player.* **3** (noun) You can refer to the best or most advanced example of something as the ultimate, e.g. *This hotel is the ultimate in luxury.* **ultimately** (adverb).

ultimatum, ultimatums (pronounced ul-tim-**may**-tum) (noun) An ultimatum is a warning stating that unless someone meets your conditions, you will take action against them.

ultra- (prefix) Ultra- is used to form adjectives describing something as having a quality to an extreme degree, e.g. *the ultra-competitive world of sport today.*

ultramarine (noun or adjective) bright blue.

ultrasonic (adjective) An ultrasonic sound has a very high frequency that cannot be heard by the human ear.

ultraviolet (adjective) Ultraviolet light is not visible to the human eye. It is a form of radiation that causes your skin to darken after exposure to sunlight.

umbilical cord, umbilical cords (pronounced um-**bil**-lik-kl) (noun) The umbilical cord is the tube of blood vessels which connects an unborn baby to its mother and through which the baby receives nutrients and oxygen.

umbrella, umbrellas (noun) An umbrella is a device that you use to protect yourself from the rain. It consists of a folding frame covered in cloth attached to a long stick.

umpire, umpires, umpiring, umpired 1 (noun) The umpire in cricket or tennis is the person who makes sure that the game is played according to the rules. **2** (verb) If you umpire a game, you are the umpire.

umpteen (adjective; an informal word) very many, e.g. *tomatoes and umpteen other plants.* **umpteenth** (adjective).

un- (prefix) Un- is added to the beginning of many words to form a word with the opposite meaning, e.g. *an uncomfortable chair... He unlocked the door.*

unabashed (adjective) not ashamed, embarrassed, or discouraged by something, e.g. *Mildred was continuing unabashed.*

unabated (adjective or adverb) continuing without any reduction in intensity or amount, e.g. *The noise continued unabated.*

unable (adjective) If you are unable to do something, you cannot do it.

unacceptable (adjective) very bad or of a very low standard.

unaccompanied (adjective) alone.

unaccustomed (adjective) If you are unaccustomed to something, you are not used to it.

unaffected 1 (adjective) not changed in any way by a particular thing, e.g. *unaffected by the recession.* **2** behaving in a natural and genuine way, e.g. *the most down-to-earth unaffected person I've ever met.*

unaided (adverb or adjective) without help, e.g. *He was incapable of walking unaided.*

unambiguous (adjective) An

unambiguous statement has only one meaning.

unanimous (pronounced yoon-**nan**-nim-mus) (adjective) When people are unanimous, they all agree about something. **unanimously** (adverb), **unanimity** (noun).

unannounced (adjective) happening unexpectedly and without warning.

unarmed (adjective) not carrying any weapons.

unassuming (adjective) modest and quiet.

unattached (adjective) An unattached person is not married and is not having a steady relationship.

unattended (adjective) not being watched or looked after, e.g. *an unattended handbag.*

unauthorized or **unauthorised** (adjective) done without official permission, e.g. *unauthorized parking.*

unavoidable (adjective) unable to be prevented or avoided.

unaware (adjective) If you are unaware of something, you do not know about it.

unawares (adverb) If something catches you unawares, it happens when you are not expecting it.

unbalanced 1 (adjective) slightly mad. **2** An unbalanced account of something is an unfair one because it emphasizes some things and ignores others.

unbearable (adjective) Something unbearable is so unpleasant or upsetting that you feel you cannot stand it, e.g. *The pain was unbearable.* **unbearably** (adverb).

unbeatable (adjective) Something that is unbeatable is the best thing of its kind.

unbelievable 1 (adjective) extremely great or surprising, e.g. *unbelievable courage.* **2** so unlikely that you cannot believe it. **unbelievably** (adverb).

unborn (adjective) not yet born.

unbroken (adjective) continuous or complete, e.g. *ten days of almost unbroken sunshine.*

uncanny (adjective) strange and difficult to explain, e.g. *an uncanny resemblance.*

uncertain 1 (adjective) not knowing what to do, e.g. *For a minute he looked uncertain.* **2** doubtful or not known, e.g. *The outcome of the war was uncertain.* **uncertainty** (noun).

unchallenged (adjective) accepted without any questions being asked, e.g. *We can't let this enormous theft go unchallenged.*

uncharacteristic (adjective) not typical or usual, e.g. *My father reacted with uncharacteristic speed.*

uncle, uncles (noun) Your uncle is the brother of your mother or father or the husband of your aunt.

unclean (adjective) dirty and likely to cause disease, e.g. *unclean water.*

unclear (adjective) confusing and not obvious.

uncomfortable 1 (adjective) If you are uncomfortable, you are not physically relaxed and feel slight pain or discomfort. **2** Uncomfortable also means slightly worried or embarrassed. **uncomfortably** (adverb).

uncommon 1 (adjective) not happening often or not seen

often. **2** unusually great, e.g. *She had read Cecilia's last letter with uncommon interest.* **uncommonly** (adverb).

uncompromising (adjective) determined not to change an opinion or aim in any way, e.g. *an uncompromising approach to life.* **uncompromisingly** (adverb).

unconcerned (adjective) not interested in something or not worried about it.

unconditional (adjective) with no conditions or limitations, e.g. *a full three-year unconditional guarantee.* **unconditionally** (adverb).

unconscious 1 (adjective) Someone who is unconscious is in a state similar to sleep as a result of a shock, accident, or injury. **2** If you are unconscious of something, you are not aware of it. **unconsciously** (adverb).

unconventional (adjective) not behaving in the same way as most other people.

unconvinced (adjective) not at all certain that something is true or right, e.g. *Some critics are unconvinced by the plan.*

uncouth (pronounced un-**kooth**) (adjective) bad-mannered and unpleasant.

uncover, uncovers, uncovering, uncovered 1 (verb) If you uncover a secret, you find it out. **2** To uncover something means to remove the cover or lid from it.

undaunted (adjective) If you are undaunted by something disappointing, you are not discouraged by it.

undecided (adjective) If you are undecided, you have not yet made a decision about something.

undemanding (adjective) not difficult to do or deal with, e.g. *undemanding work.*

undeniable (adjective) certainly true, e.g. *undeniable evidence.* **undeniably** (adverb).

under 1 (preposition) below or beneath. **2** You can use 'under' to say that a person or thing is affected by a particular situation, condition, or state, e.g. *The country was under threat.* **3** If someone studies or works under a particular person, that person is their teacher or their boss. **4** less than, e.g. *under five miles... children under the age of 14.* **5** (phrase) **Under way** means already started, e.g. *A murder investigation is already under way.*

under- (prefix) Under- is used in words that describe something as not being provided to a sufficient extent or not having happened to a sufficient extent.

underarm 1 (adjective) under your arm, e.g. *underarm hair.* **2** (adverb) If you throw a ball underarm, you throw it without raising your arm over your shoulder.

undercarriage, undercarriages (noun) The undercarriage of an aircraft is the part, including the wheels, that supports the aircraft when it is on the ground.

underclothes (plural noun) Your underclothes are the clothes that you wear under your other clothes and next to your skin.

undercover (adjective) involving secret work to obtain information, e.g. *a police undercover operation.*

undercurrent, undercurrents (noun) An undercurrent is a weak, partly hidden feeling that may become stronger later.

undercut, undercuts, undercutting, undercut (verb) To undercut someone's prices means to sell a product more cheaply than they do.

underdeveloped (adjective) An underdeveloped country does not have modern industries, and usually has a low standard of living.

underdog, underdogs (noun) The underdog in a competition is the person who seems likely to lose.

underestimate, underestimates, underestimating, underestimated (verb) If you underestimate something or someone, you do not realize how large, great, or capable they are.

underfoot (adjective or adverb) under your feet, e.g. *the icy ground underfoot.*

undergo, undergoes, undergoing, underwent, undergone (verb) If you undergo something unpleasant, it happens to you.

underground 1 (adjective) below the surface of the ground. **2** (noun) The underground is a railway system in which trains travel in tunnels below ground. **3** (adjective) secret, unofficial, and usually illegal.

undergrowth (noun) Small bushes and plants growing under trees are called the undergrowth.

underhand (adjective) secret and dishonest, e.g. *underhand behaviour.*

underlie, underlies, underlying, underlay, underlain (verb) The thing that underlies a situation is the cause or basis of it. **underlying** (adjective).

underline, underlines, underlining, underlined 1 (verb) If something underlines a feeling or a problem, it emphasizes it. **2** If you underline a word or sentence, you draw a line under it.

underling, underlings (noun) An underling is someone who is less important than someone else in rank or status.

undermine, undermines, undermining, undermined (verb) To undermine an idea, feeling, or system means to make it less strong or secure.

underneath 1 (preposition) below or beneath. **2** (adjective) The underneath part of something is the part that touches or faces the ground. **3** (adverb or preposition) Underneath describes feelings and qualities that do not show in your behaviour, e.g. *I knew that underneath she was afraid.*

underpants (plural noun) Underpants are a piece of clothing worn by men and boys under their trousers.

underpass, underpasses (noun) An underpass is a road or footpath that goes under a road or railway.

underpin, underpins, underpinning, underpinned (verb) If something underpins something else, it helps it to continue by supporting and strengthening it.

underprivileged (adjective)

Underprivileged people have less money and fewer opportunities than other people.

underrate, underrates, underrating, underrated (verb) If you underrate someone, you do not realize how clever or valuable they are.

understand, understands, understanding, understood 1 (verb) If you understand what someone says, you know what they mean. **2** If you understand a situation, you know what is happening and why. **3** If you say that you understand that something is the case, you mean that you have heard that it is the case, e.g. *I understand that she's a lot better now.*

understandable (adjective) If something is understandable, people can easily understand it. **understandably** (adverb).

understanding, understandings 1 (noun) If you have an understanding of something, you have some knowledge about it. **2** (adjective) kind and sympathetic. **3** (noun) An understanding is an informal agreement between people.

understatement, understatements (noun) An understatement is a statement that does not say fully how true something is, e.g. *To say I was pleased was an understatement.*

understudy, understudies (noun) An understudy is someone who has learnt a part in a play so that they can act it if the main actor or actress is ill.

undertake, undertakes, undertaking, undertook, undertaken (verb) When you undertake a task or job, you agree to do it. **undertaking** (noun).

undertaker, undertakers (noun) An undertaker is someone whose job is to prepare bodies for burial and arrange funerals.

undertone, undertones 1 (noun) If you say something in an undertone, you say it very quietly. **2** If something has undertones of a particular kind, it indirectly suggests ideas of this kind, e.g. *unsettling undertones of violence.*

undervalue, undervalues, undervaluing, undervalued (verb) If you undervalue something, you think it is less important than it really is.

underwater 1 (adverb or adjective) beneath the surface of the sea, a river, or a lake. **2** (adjective) designed to work in water, e.g. *an underwater camera.*

underwear (noun) Your underwear is the clothing that you wear under your other clothes, next to your skin.

underwent the past tense of **undergo.**

undesirable (adjective) unwelcome and likely to cause harm, e.g. *undesirable behaviour.*

undid the past tense of **undo.**

undisputed (adjective) definite and without any doubt, e.g. *the undisputed champion.*

undivided (adjective) If you give something your undivided attention, you concentrate on it totally.

undo, undoes, undoing, undid, undone 1 (verb) If you undo something that is tied up, you untie it. **2** If you undo something that has been done, you reverse the effect of it.

undoing (noun) If something is someone's undoing, it is the cause of their failure.

undoubted (adjective) You use undoubted to emphasize something, e.g. *The event was an undoubted success.* **undoubtedly** (adverb).

undress, undresses, undressing, undressed (verb) When you undress, you take off your clothes.

undue (adjective) greater than is reasonable, e.g. *undue violence.* **unduly** (adverb).

undulating (adjective; a formal word) moving gently up and down, e.g. *undulating hills.*

undying (adjective) lasting forever, e.g. *his undying love for his wife.*

unearth, unearths, unearthing, unearthed (verb) If you unearth something that is hidden, you discover it.

unearthly (adjective) strange and unnatural.

uneasy (adjective) If you are uneasy, you feel worried that something may be wrong. **unease** (noun), **uneasily** (adverb), **uneasiness** (noun).

unemployed 1 (adjective) without a job, e.g. *an unemployed mechanic.* **2** (noun) The unemployed are all the people who are without a job.

unemployment (noun) Unemployment is the state of being without a job.

unending (adjective) Something unending has continued for a long time and seems as if it will never stop, e.g. *unending joy.*

unenviable (adjective) An unenviable situation is one that you would not like to be in.

unequal 1 (adjective) An unequal society does not offer the same opportunities and privileges to all people. **2** Unequal things are different in size, strength, or ability.

uneven 1 (adjective) An uneven surface is not level or smooth. **2** not regular or consistent, e.g. *six lines of uneven length.* **unevenly** (adverb).

uneventful (adjective) An uneventful period of time is one when nothing interesting happens.

unexpected (adjective) Something unexpected is surprising because it was not thought likely to happen. **unexpectedly** (adverb).

unfailing (adjective) continuous and not weakening as time passes, e.g. *his unfailing cheerfulness.*

unfair (adjective) not right, fair, or just. **unfairly** (adverb).

unfaithful (adjective) If someone is unfaithful to their lover or the person they are married to, they have a sexual relationship with someone else.

unfamiliar (adjective) If something is unfamiliar to you, or if you are unfamiliar with it, you have not seen or heard it before.

unfit 1 (adjective) If you are unfit, your body is not in good condition because you have not been taking regular exercise. **2** Something that is unfit for a particular purpose is not suitable for that purpose.

unfold, unfolds, unfolding, unfolded 1 (verb) When a situation unfolds, it develops and becomes known. **2** If you unfold something that has been folded, you open it out so that it is flat.

unforeseen (adjective) happening unexpectedly.

unforgettable (adjective) Something unforgettable is so good or so bad that you are unlikely to forget it. **unforgettably** (adverb).

unforgivable (adjective) Something unforgivable is so bad or cruel that it can never be forgiven or justified.

unfortunate 1 (adjective) Someone who is unfortunate is unlucky. **2** If you describe an event as unfortunate, you mean that it is a pity that it happened, e.g. *an unfortunate accident.* **unfortunately** (adverb).

unfounded (adjective) Something that is unfounded has no evidence to support it, e.g. *unfounded allegations.*

ungainly (adjective) moving in an awkward or clumsy way.

unhappy, unhappier, unhappiest 1 (adjective) sad and depressed. **2** not pleased or satisfied, e.g. *I am unhappy at being left out.* **3** If you describe a situation as an unhappy one, you are sorry that it exists, e.g. *an unhappy state of affairs.* **unhappily** (adverb), **unhappiness** (noun).

unhealthy 1 (adjective) likely to cause illness, e.g. *an unhealthy lifestyle.* **2** An unhealthy person is often ill.

unheard-of (adjective) never having happened before and therefore surprising or shocking.

unhinged (adjective) Someone who is unhinged is mentally ill.

unicorn, unicorns (noun) A unicorn is an imaginary animal that looks like a white horse with a straight horn growing from its forehead.

unidentified (adjective) You say that someone or something is unidentified when nobody knows who or what they are.

uniform, uniforms 1 (noun) A uniform is a special set of clothes worn by people at work or school. **2** (adjective) Something that is uniform does not vary but is even and regular throughout. **uniformity** (noun).

unify, unifies, unifying, unified (verb) If you unify a number of things, you bring them together. **unification** (noun).

unilateral (adjective) A unilateral decision or action is one taken by only one of several groups involved in a particular situation. **unilaterally** (adverb).

unimaginable (adjective) impossible to imagine or understand properly, e.g. *a fairyland of unimaginable beauty.*

unimportant (adjective) having very little significance or importance.

uninhabited (adjective) An uninhabited place is a place where nobody lives.

uninhibited (adjective) If you are uninhibited, you behave freely and naturally and show your true feelings.

unintelligible (adjective; a formal word) impossible to understand.

uninterested (adjective) If you

are uninterested in something, you are not interested in it.

uninterrupted (adjective) continuing without breaks or interruptions, e.g. *uninterrupted views.*

union, unions 1 (noun) A union is an organization of workers that aims to improve the working conditions, pay, and benefits of its members. **2** When the union of two things takes place, they are joined together to become one thing.

unique (pronounced yoo-**neek**) **1** (adjective) being the only one of its kind. **2** If something is unique to one person or thing, it concerns or belongs to that person or thing only, e.g. *trees and vegetation unique to the Canary islands.* **uniquely** (adverb), **uniqueness** (noun).

unisex (adjective) designed to be used by both men and women, e.g. *unisex clothing.*

unison (noun) If a group of people do something in unison, they all do it together at the same time.

unit, units 1 (noun) If you consider something as a unit, you consider it as a single complete thing. **2** A unit is a group of people who work together at a particular job, e.g. *the Scottish drugs intelligence unit.* **3** A unit is also a machine or piece of equipment which has a particular function, e.g. *a remote control unit.* **4** A unit of measurement is a fixed standard that is used for measuring things.

unite, unites, uniting, united (verb) If a number of people unite, they join together and act as a group.

United Kingdom (noun) The United Kingdom consists of Great Britain and Northern Ireland.

unity (noun) Where there is unity, people are in agreement and act together for a particular purpose.

universal (adjective) concerning or relating to everyone in the world or every part of the universe, e.g. *Music and sports programmes have a universal appeal.* **universally** (adverb).

universe, universes (noun) The universe is the whole of space, including all the stars and planets.

university, universities (noun) A university is a place where students study for degrees.

unjust (adjective) not fair or reasonable. **unjustly** (adverb).

unjustified (adjective) If a belief or action is unjustified, there is no good reason for it.

unkempt (adjective) untidy and not looked after properly, e.g. *unkempt hair.*

unkind (adjective) unpleasant and rather cruel. **unkindly** (adverb), **unkindness** (noun).

unknown 1 (adjective) If someone or something is unknown, people do not know about them or have not heard of them. **2** (noun) You can refer to the things that people in general do not know about as the unknown.

unlawful (adjective) not legal, e.g. *the unlawful use of drugs.*

unleaded (adjective) Unleaded petrol has a reduced amount of lead in it in order to reduce the pollution from cars.

unleash, unleashes, unleashing, unleashed (verb) When a powerful or violent force is unleashed, it is released.

unless (conjunction) You use unless to introduce the only circumstances in which something will not take place or is not true, e.g. *Unless it was raining, they played in the little garden.*

unlike (preposition) If one thing is unlike another, the two things are different.

unlikely 1 (adjective) If something is unlikely, it is probably not true or probably will not happen. **2** strange and unexpected, e.g. *an unlikely combination of poet, duck expert and yachtsman.*

unlimited (adjective) If a supply of something is unlimited, you can have as much as you want or need.

unload, unloads, unloading, unloaded (verb) If you unload things from a container or vehicle, you remove them.

unlock, unlocks, unlocking, unlocked (verb) If you unlock a door or container, you open it by turning a key in the lock.

unlucky (adjective) Someone who is unlucky has bad luck. **unluckily** (adverb).

unmarked (adjective) with no marks of damage or injury.

unmistakable or **unmistakeable** (adjective) Something unmistakable is so obvious that it cannot be mistaken for something else. **unmistakably** (adverb).

unmitigated (adjective; a formal word) You use unmitigated to describe a situation or quality that is completely bad, e.g. *an unmitigated disaster.*

unmoved (adjective) not emotionally affected, e.g. *He is unmoved by criticism.*

unnatural 1 (adjective) strange and rather frightening because it is not usual, e.g. *There was an unnatural stillness.* **2** artificial and not typical, e.g. *My voice sounded high-pitched and unnatural.* **unnaturally** (adverb).

unnerve, unnerves, unnerving, unnerved (verb) If something unnerves you, it frightens or startles you. **unnerving** (adjective).

unobtrusive (adjective) Something that is unobtrusive does not draw attention to itself.

unoccupied (adjective) If a house is unoccupied, there is nobody living in it.

unofficial (adjective) without the approval or permission of a person in authority, e.g. *unofficial strikes.* **unofficially** (adverb).

unorthodox (adjective) unusual and not generally accepted, e.g. *an unorthodox theory.*

unpack, unpacks, unpacking, unpacked (verb) When you unpack, you take everything out of a suitcase or bag.

unpaid 1 (adjective) If you do unpaid work, you do not receive any money for doing it. **2** An unpaid bill has not yet been paid.

unpalatable 1 (adjective) Unpalatable food is so unpleasant that you can hardly eat it. **2** An unpalatable idea is so unpleasant that it is difficult to accept.

unparalleled (adjective) greater than anything else of its kind, e.g. *an unparalleled success.*

unpleasant 1 (adjective) Something unpleasant causes you to have bad feelings, for example by making you uncomfortable, upset, or frightened. **2** An unpleasant person is unfriendly or rude.

unpopular (adjective) disliked by most people, e.g. *an unpopular idea.*

unprecedented (pronounced un-**press**-id-en-tid) (adjective; a formal word) Something that is unprecedented has never happened before or is the best of its kind so far.

unpredictable (adjective) If someone or something is unpredictable, you never know how they will behave or react.

unprepared (adjective) If you are unprepared for something, you are not ready for it and are therefore surprised or at a disadvantage when it happens.

unproductive (adjective) not producing anything useful.

unqualified 1 (adjective) having no qualifications or not having the right qualifications for a particular job, e.g. *dangers posed by unqualified doctors.* **2** total, e.g. *an unqualified success.*

unquestionable (adjective) so obviously true or real that nobody can doubt it, e.g. *His devotion is unquestionable.* **unquestionably** (adverb).

unravel, unravels, unravelling, unravelled 1 (verb) If you unravel something such as a twisted and knotted piece of string, you unwind it so that it is straight. **2** If you unravel a mystery, you work out the answer to it.

unreal (adjective) so strange that you find it difficult to believe.

unrealistic 1 (adjective) An unrealistic person does not face the truth about something or deal with it in a practical way. **2** Something unrealistic is not true to life, e.g. *an unrealistic picture.*

unreasonable (adjective) unfair and difficult to deal with or justify, e.g. *an unreasonable request.* **unreasonably** (adverb).

unrelated (adjective) Things that are unrelated have no connection with each other.

unrelenting (adjective) continuing in a determined way without caring about any hurt that is caused, e.g. *unrelenting criticism.*

unreliable (adjective) If people, machines, or methods are unreliable, you cannot rely on them.

unremitting (adjective) continuing without stopping.

unrest (noun) If there is unrest, people are angry and dissatisfied.

unrivalled (adjective) better than anything else of its kind, e.g. *an unrivalled range of health and beauty treatments.*

unroll, unrolls, unrolling, unrolled (verb) If you unroll a roll of cloth or paper, you open it up and make it flat.

unruly (adjective) difficult to control, organize, or keep tidy, e.g. *unruly children.*

unsatisfactory (adjective) not good enough.

unscathed (adjective) not injured or harmed as a result of a dangerous experience.

unscrew, unscrews, unscrewing, unscrewed (verb) If you unscrew something, you remove it by turning it or by removing the screws that are holding it.

unscrupulous (adjective) willing to behave dishonestly in order to get what you want.

unseemly (adjective) Unseemly behaviour is not suitable for a particular situation and shows a lack of control and good manners, e.g. *an unseemly squabble.*

unseen (adjective) You use unseen to describe things that you cannot see or have not seen.

unsettle, unsettles, unsettling, unsettled (verb) If something unsettles you, it makes you restless or worried.

unshakable or **unshakeable** (adjective) An unshakable belief is so strong that it cannot be destroyed.

unsightly (adjective) very ugly, e.g. *an unsightly scar.*

unskilled (adjective) Unskilled work does not require any special training.

unsolicited (adjective) given or happening without being asked for.

unsound 1 (adjective) If a conclusion or method is unsound, it is based on ideas that are likely to be wrong. **2** An unsound building is likely to collapse.

unspeakable (adjective) very unpleasant.

unspecified (adjective) You say that something is unspecified when you are not told exactly what it is, e.g. *It was being stored in some unspecified place.*

unspoken (adjective) An unspoken wish or feeling is one that is not mentioned to other people.

unstable 1 (adjective) likely to change suddenly and create difficulty or danger, e.g. *The political situation in Moscow is unstable.* **2** not firm or fixed properly and likely to wobble or fall.

unsteady 1 (adjective) having difficulty in controlling the movement of your legs or hands, e.g. *unsteady on her feet.* **2** not held or fixed securely and likely to fall over. **unsteadily** (adverb).

unstuck (adjective) If something comes unstuck, it becomes separated from the thing that it was stuck to.

unsuccessful (adjective) If you are unsuccessful, you do not succeed in what you are trying to do. **unsuccessfully** (adverb).

unsuitable (adjective) not right or appropriate for a particular purpose. **unsuitably** (adverb).

unsuited (adjective) not appropriate for a particular task or situation.

unsung (adjective) You use unsung to describe someone who is not appreciated or praised for their good work, e.g. *George is the unsung hero of the club.*

unsure (adjective) uncertain or doubtful.

unsuspecting (adjective) having no idea of what is happening or going to happen, e.g. *His horse escaped and collided with an unsuspecting cyclist.*

untangle, untangles, untan-

gling, untangled (verb) If you untangle something that is twisted together, you undo the twists.

untenable (adjective; a formal word) A theory, argument, or position that is untenable cannot be successfully defended.

unthinkable (adjective) so shocking or awful that you cannot imagine it to be true.

untidy, untidier, untidiest (adjective) not neat or well arranged.

untie, unties, untying, untied (verb) If you untie something, you undo the knots in the string or rope around it.

until 1 (preposition or conjunction) If something happens until a particular time, it happens before that time and stops at that time, e.g. *The shop stayed open until midnight... She waited until her husband was asleep.* **2** If something does not happen until a particular time, it does not happen before that time and only starts happening at that time, e.g. *It didn't rain until the middle of the afternoon... It was not until they arrived that they found out who he was.*

untimely (adjective) happening too soon or sooner than expected, e.g. *his untimely death.*

unto (preposition; an old-fashioned word) Unto means the same as to, e.g. *Nation shall speak peace unto nation.*

untold (adjective) You use untold to emphasize how great or extreme something is, e.g. *The island possessed untold wealth.*

untouched 1 (adjective) not changed, moved, or damaged, e.g. *a small village untouched by tourism.* **2** If a meal is untouched, none of it has been eaten.

untoward (adjective) unexpected and causing difficulties, e.g. *no untoward problems.*

untrue (adjective) not true.

unused 1 (adjective; pronounced un-**yoozd**) not yet used. **2** (pronounced un-**yoost**) If you are unused to something, you have not often done or experienced it.

unusual (adjective) Something that is unusual does not occur very often. **unusually** (adverb).

unveil, unveils, unveiling, unveiled (verb) When someone unveils a new statue or plaque, they draw back a curtain that is covering it.

unwarranted (adjective; a formal word) not justified or not deserved, e.g. *unwarranted fears.*

unwelcome (adjective) not wanted, e.g. *an unwelcome visitor... unwelcome news.*

unwell (adjective) If you are unwell, you are ill.

unwieldy (adjective) difficult to move or carry because of being large or an awkward shape.

unwilling (adjective) If you are unwilling to do something, you do not want to do it. **unwillingly** (adverb).

unwind, unwinds, unwinding, unwound 1 (verb) When you unwind after working hard, you relax. **2** If you unwind something that is wrapped round something else, you undo it.

unwise (adjective) foolish or not sensible.

unwitting (adjective) Unwitting describes someone who becomes involved in something without realizing what is really happening, e.g. *her unwitting victims.* **unwittingly** (adverb).

unworthy (adjective; a formal word) Someone who is unworthy of something does not deserve it.

unwrap, unwraps, unwrapping, unwrapped (verb) When you unwrap something, you take off the paper or covering around it.

unwritten (adjective) An unwritten law is one which is generally understood and accepted without being officially laid down.

up 1 (adverb or preposition) towards or in a higher place, e.g. *He ran up the stairs... high up in the mountains.* **2** towards or in the north, e.g. *I drove up to Birmingham.* **3** (preposition) If you go up a road or river, you go along it. **4** (adjective) If you are up, you are not in bed. **5** (adverb) If an amount of something goes up, it increases. **6** (adjective) If a period of time is up, it has come to an end. **7** (preposition) You use 'up to' to say how large something can be or what level it has reached, e.g. *traffic jams up to 10 miles long.* **8** (an informal use) If someone is up to something, they are secretly doing something they should not be doing. **9** If it is up to someone to do something, it is their responsibility.

up-and-coming (adjective) Up-and-coming people are likely to be successful.

upbringing (noun) Your upbringing is the way that your parents have taught you to behave.

update, updates, updating, updated (verb) If you update something, you make it more modern or add new information to it, e.g. *He had failed to update his will.*

upgrade, upgrades, upgrading, upgraded (verb) If a person or their job is upgraded, they are given more responsibility or status and usually more money.

upheaval, upheavals (noun) An upheaval is a big change which causes a lot of trouble.

uphill 1 (adverb) If you go uphill, you go up a slope. **2** (adjective) An uphill task requires a lot of effort and determination.

uphold, upholds, upholding, upheld (verb) If someone upholds a law or a decision, they support and maintain it.

upholstery (noun) Upholstery is the soft covering on chairs and sofas that makes them comfortable.

upkeep (noun) The upkeep of something is the continual process and cost of keeping it in good condition.

upland, uplands 1 (adjective) An upland area is an area of high land. **2** (noun) Uplands are areas of high land.

uplifting (adjective) making you feel happy.

up-market (adjective) sophisticated and expensive.

upon 1 (preposition; a formal use) Upon means on, e.g. *I stood upon the stair.* **2** You use 'upon' when mentioning an event that is immediately followed by another, e.g. *Upon entering the hall he took a quick glance round.* **3** If an event is upon you, it is about to happen, e.g. *The football season is upon us once more.*

upper, uppers 1 (adjective) referring to something that is above something else, or the higher part of something, e.g. *the upper arm.* **2** (noun) The upper of a shoe is the top part.

upper class, upper classes (noun) The upper classes are people who belong to a very wealthy or aristocratic group in a society.

uppermost 1 (adjective or adverb) on top or in the highest position, e.g. *the uppermost leaves... Lay your arms beside your body with the palms turned uppermost.* **2** (adjective) most important, e.g. *His family is now uppermost in his mind.*

upright 1 (adjective or adverb) standing or sitting up straight, rather than bending or lying down. **2** behaving in a very respectable and moral way.

uprising, uprisings (noun) If there is an uprising, a large group of people begin fighting against the existing government to bring about political changes.

uproar (noun) If there is uproar or an uproar, there is a lot of shouting and noise, often because people are angry.

uproot, uproots, uprooting, uprooted 1 (verb) If someone is uprooted, they have to leave the place where they have lived for a long time. **2** If a tree is uprooted, it is pulled out of the ground.

upset, upsets, upsetting, upset 1 (adjective) unhappy and disappointed. **2** (verb) If something upsets you, it makes you feel worried or unhappy. **3** If you upset something, you turn it over or spill it accidentally. **4** (noun) A stomach upset is a slight stomach illness caused by an infection or by something you have eaten.

upshot (noun) The upshot of a series of events is the final result.

upside down (adjective or adverb) the wrong way up.

upstage, upstages, upstaging, upstaged (verb) If someone upstages you, they draw people's attention away from you by being more attractive or interesting.

upstairs 1 (adverb) If you go upstairs in a building, you go up to a higher floor. **2** (noun) The upstairs of a building is its upper floor or floors.

upstart, upstarts (noun) If you call someone an upstart, you mean that they have risen too quickly to an important position and are too arrogant.

upstream (adverb) towards the source of a river, e.g. *They made their way upstream.*

upsurge (noun) An upsurge of something is a sudden large increase in it.

uptake (noun) You can say that someone is quick on the uptake if they understand things quickly.

uptight (adjective; an informal word) tense or annoyed.

up-to-date 1 (adjective) being the newest thing of its kind. **2** having the latest information.

up-to-the-minute (adjective) Up-to-the-minute information is the latest available information.

upturn, upturns (noun) An upturn in a situation is an improvement in it.

upturned 1 (adjective) pointing upwards, e.g. *rain splashing down on her upturned face.* **2** upside down, e.g. *an upturned bowl.*

upwards (adverb) towards a higher place, e.g. *People stared upwards and pointed.* **upward** (adjective).

uranium (pronounced yoo-**ray**-nee-um) (noun) Uranium is a radioactive metal used to produce nuclear energy and weapons.

Uranus (noun) Uranus is the planet in the solar system which is seventh from the sun.

urban (adjective) relating to a town or city.

urbane (adjective) well-mannered, relaxed, and comfortable in social situations.

Urdu (pronounced **oor**-doo) (noun) Urdu is the official language of Pakistan. It is also spoken by many people in India.

urge, urges, urging, urged 1 (noun) If you have an urge to do something, you have a strong wish to do it. **2** (verb) If you urge someone to do something, you try hard to persuade them to do it.

urgent (adjective) needing to be dealt with as soon as possible. **urgently** (adverb), **urgency** (noun).

urinal, urinals (pronounced yoor-**rye**-nl) (noun) A urinal is a bowl or trough fixed to the wall in a men's public toilet for men to urinate in.

urinate, urinates, urinating, urinated (pronounced **yoor**-rin-ate) (verb) When you urinate, you go to the toilet and get rid of urine from your body.

urine (pronounced **yoor**-rin) (noun) Urine is the waste liquid that you get rid of from your body when you go to the toilet.

urn, urns (noun) An urn is a decorated container that is used to hold the ashes of a person who has been cremated.

us (pronoun) A speaker or writer uses us to refer to himself or herself and one or more other people, e.g. *Why don't you tell us?*

US or **USA** an abbreviation for 'United States of America'.

usage (noun) Usage is the degree to which something is used, or the way in which it is used.

use, uses, using, used 1 (verb) If you use something, you do something with it in order to do a job or achieve something, e.g. *May I use your phone?* **2** If you use someone, you take advantage of them by making them do things for you. **3** (noun) The use of something is the act of using it, e.g. *the use of force.* **4** If you have the use of something, you have the ability or permission to use it. **5** If you find a use for something, you find a purpose for it. **usable** or **useable** (adjective), **user** (noun).

used 1 (verb; pronounced **yoost**) Something that used to be done or used to be true was done or was true in the past. **2** (phrase) If you are **used to** something, you are familiar with it and have often experienced it. **3** (adjective; pronounced **yoozd**) A used object has had a previous owner.

useful (adjective) If something is useful, you can use it in order to do something or to help you in some way. **usefully** (adverb), **usefulness** (noun).

useless 1 (adjective) If something is useless, you cannot use it because it is not suitable or helpful. **2** If a course of action is useless, it will not achieve what is wanted.

usher, ushers, ushering, ushered 1 (verb) If you usher someone somewhere, you show them where to go by going with them. **2** (noun) An usher is a person who shows people where to sit at a wedding or a concert.

USSR an abbreviation for 'Union of Soviet Socialist Republics', a country which was made up of a lot of smaller countries including Russia, but which is now broken up.

usual 1 (adjective) happening, done, or used most often, e.g. *his usual seat.* **2** (phrase) If you do something **as usual,** you do it in the way that you normally do it. **usually** (adverb).

usurp, usurps, usurping, usurped (pronounced yoo-**zerp**) (verb; a formal word) If someone usurps another person's job, title, or position, they take it when they have no right to do so.

utensil, utensils (pronounced yoo-**ten**-sil) (noun) Utensils are tools, e.g. *cooking utensils.*

uterus, uteruses (pronounced **yoo**-ter-russ) (noun; a formal word) A woman's uterus is her womb.

utility, utilities 1 (noun) The utility of something is its usefulness. **2** A utility is a service, such as water or gas, that is provided for everyone.

utilize, utilizes, utilizing, utilized; also spelled **utilise** (verb; a formal word) To utilize something means to use it. **utilization** (noun).

utmost (adjective) used to emphasize a particular quality, e.g. *I have the utmost respect for Richard.*

utter, utters, uttering, uttered 1 (verb) When you utter sounds or words, you make or say them. **2** (adjective) Utter means complete or total, e.g. *scenes of utter chaos.* **utterly** (adverb).

utterance, utterances (noun) An utterance is something that is said, e.g. *his first utterance.*

V v

v an abbreviation for **versus.**

vacant 1 (adjective) If something is vacant, it is not occupied or being used. **2** If a job or position is vacant, no-one holds it at present. **3** A vacant look suggests that someone does not understand something or is not very intelligent. **vacancy** (noun), **vacantly** (adverb).

vacate, vacates, vacating, vacated (verb; a formal word) If you vacate a room or job, you leave it and it becomes available for someone else.

vacation, vacations 1 (noun) A vacation is the period between academic terms at a university or college, e.g. *the summer vacation.* **2** In American English, a vacation is a holiday.

vaccinate, vaccinates, vaccinating, vaccinated (pronounced **vak**-sin-ate) (verb) To vaccinate someone means to give them a vaccine, usually by injection, to protect them against a disease. **vaccination** (noun).

vaccine, vaccines (pronounced **vak**-seen) (noun) A vaccine is a substance made from the germs that cause a disease and is given to people to make them immune to that disease.

vacuum, vacuums, vacuuming, vacuumed (pronounced **vak**-yoom) **1** (noun) A vacuum is a space containing no air, gases, or other matter. **2** (verb) If you vacuum something, you clean it using a vacuum cleaner.

vacuum cleaner, vacuum cleaners (noun) A vacuum cleaner is an electric machine which cleans by sucking up dirt.

vagina, vaginas (pronounced vaj-**jie**-na) (noun) A woman's vagina is the passage that connects her outer sex organs to her womb.

vagrant, vagrants (noun) A vagrant is a person who moves from place to place, and has no home or regular job. **vagrancy** (noun).

vague, vaguer, vaguest (pronounced **vayg**) **1** (adjective) If something is vague, it is not expressed or explained clearly, or you cannot see or remember it clearly, e.g. *vague statements.* **2** Someone looks or sounds vague if they are not concentrating or thinking clearly. **vaguely** (adverb), **vagueness** (noun).

vain, vainer, vainest 1 (adjective) A vain action or attempt is one which is not successful, e.g. *He made a vain effort to cheer her up.* **2** A vain person is very proud of their looks, intelligence, or other qualities. **3** (phrase) If you do something **in vain,** you do not succeed in achieving what you intend. **vainly** (adverb).

vale, vales (noun; a literary word) A vale is a valley.

valentine, valentines 1 (noun) Your valentine is someone you love and send a card to on Saint Valentine's Day, February 14th. **2** A valentine or a valentine card is the card you send to the person you love on Saint Valentine's Day.

valet, valets (pronounced **val**-lit) (noun) A valet is a male servant who is employed to look after another man, particularly caring for his clothes.

valiant (adjective) very brave. **valiantly** (adverb).

valid 1 (adjective) Something that is valid is based on sound reasoning. **2** A valid ticket or document is one which is officially accepted. **validity** (noun).

validate, validates, validating, validated (verb) If something validates a statement or claim, it proves that it is true or correct.

valley, valleys (noun) A valley is a long stretch of land between hills, often with a river flowing through it.

valour (noun) Valour is great bravery.

valuable, valuables 1 (adjective) Something that is valuable has great value. **2** (plural noun) Valuables are things that you own that cost a lot of money.

valuation, valuations (noun) A valuation is a judgment about how much money something is worth or how good it is.

value, values, valuing, valued 1 (noun) The value of something is its importance or usefulness, e.g. *information of great value.* **2** The value of something you own is the amount of money that it is worth. **3** The values of a group or a person are the moral principles and beliefs that they think are important, e.g. *the values of liberty and equality.* **4** (verb) If you value something, you think it is important and you appreciate it. **5** When experts value something, they decide how much money it is worth. **valued** (adjective), **valuer** (noun).

valve, valves 1 (noun) A valve is a part attached to a pipe or tube which controls the flow of gas or liquid. **2** A valve is a small flap in your heart or in a vein which controls the flow and direction of blood.

vampire, vampires (noun) In horror stories, vampires are corpses that come out of their graves at night and suck the blood of living people.

van, vans (noun) A van is a covered vehicle larger than a car but smaller than a lorry used for carrying goods.

vandal, vandals (noun) A vandal is someone who deliberately damages or destroys things, particularly public property. **vandalize** or **vandalise** (verb), **vandalism** (noun).

vane, vanes (noun) A vane is a flat blade that is part of a mechanism for using the energy of the wind or water to drive a machine.

vanguard (pronounced **van**-gard) (noun) If someone is in the vanguard of something they are in the most advanced part of it.

vanilla (noun) Vanilla is a flavouring for food such as ice cream, which comes from the pods of a tropical plant.

vanish, vanishes, vanishing, vanished (verb) If something vanishes, it disappears or ceases to exist, e.g. *The moon vanished behind a cloud.*

vanity (noun) Vanity is a feeling of excessive pride about your looks or abilities.

vanquish, vanquishes, vanquishing, vanquished (pronounced **vang**-kwish) (verb; literary word) To vanquish someone means to defeat them completely.

vapour (noun) Vapour is a mass of tiny drops of water or other liquids in the air, which looks like mist.

variable, variables 1 (adjective) Something that is variable is likely to change at any time. **2** (noun) In any situation, a variable is something in it that can change. **3** In maths, a variable is a symbol such as x which can represent any value or any one of a set of values. **variability** (noun).

variance (noun) If one thing is at variance with another, the two seem to contradict each other.

variant, variants 1 (noun) A variant of something has a different form from the usual one, for example *gaol* is a variant of *jail.* **2** (adjective) alternative or different.

variation, variations 1 (noun) A variation is a change from the normal or usual pattern, e.g. *a variation of the same route.* **2** A variation is a change in level, amount, or quantity, e.g. *a large variation in demand.*

varicose veins (plural noun) Varicose veins are swollen painful veins in the legs.

varied (adjective) of different types, quantities, or sizes.

variety, varieties 1 (noun) If something has variety, it consists of things which are not all the same. **2** A variety of things is a number of different kinds of them, e.g. *a wide variety of readers.* **3** A variety of something is a particular type of it, e.g. *a new variety of celery.* **4** Variety is a form of entertainment consisting of short unrelated acts, such as singing, dancing, and comedy.

various (adjective) Various means of several different types, e.g. *trees of various sorts.* **variously** (adverb).

varnish, varnishes, varnishing, varnished 1 (noun) Varnish is a liquid which when painted onto a surface gives it a hard clear shiny finish. **2** (verb) If you varnish something, you paint it with varnish.

vary, varies, varying, varied 1 (verb) If things vary, they change, e.g. *Weather patterns vary greatly.* **2** If you vary something, you introduce changes in it, e.g. *Vary your routes as much as possible.* **varied** (adjective).

vascular (adjective) relating to tubes or ducts that carry fluids within animals or plants.

vase, vases (noun) A vase is a glass or china jar for flowers.

vasectomy, vasectomies (pronounced vas-**sek**-tom-ee) (noun) A vasectomy is an operation to sterilize a man by cutting the tube that carries the sperm.

Vaseline (noun; a trademark) Vaseline is a soft clear jelly made from petroleum and used as an ointment or as grease.

vast (adjective) extremely large. **vastly** (adverb), **vastness** (noun).

vat, vats (noun) A vat is a large container for liquids.

VAT (noun) VAT is a tax which is added to the costs of making or providing goods and services. VAT is an abbreviation for 'value-added tax'.

vault, vaults, vaulting, vaulted (rhymes with **salt**) **1** (noun) A vault is a strong secure room, often underneath a building, where valuables are stored, or underneath a church where people are buried. **2** A vault is an arched roof, often found in churches. **3** (verb) If you vault over something, you jump over it using your hands or a pole to help.

VCR an abbreviation for 'video cassette recorder'.

VDU, VDUs (noun) A VDU is a monitor screen attached to a computer or word processor. VDU is an abbreviation for 'visual display unit'.

veal (noun) Veal is the meat from a calf.

veer, veers, veering, veered (verb) If something which is moving veers in a particular direction, it suddenly changes course, e.g. *The aircraft veered sharply to one side.*

vegan, vegans (pronounced **vee**-gn) (noun) A vegan is someone who does not eat any food made from animal products, such as meat, eggs, cheese, or milk.

vegetable, vegetables 1 (noun) Vegetables are edible roots or leaves such as carrots or cabbage. **2** (adjective) Vegetable is used to refer to any plants in contrast to animals or minerals, e.g. *vegetable life.*

vegetarian, vegetarians (noun) A vegetarian is a person who does not eat meat, poultry, or fish. **vegetarianism** (noun).

vegetation (noun) Vegetation is the plants in a particular area.

vehement (pronounced **vee**-iment) (adjective) Someone who is vehement has strong feelings or opinions and expresses them forcefully, e.g. *He wrote a letter of vehement protest.* **vehemence** (noun), **vehemently** (adverb).

vehicle, vehicles (pronounced **vee**-ik-kl) **1** (noun) A vehicle is a machine, often with an engine, used for transporting people or goods. **2** A vehicle is something used to achieve a particular purpose or as a means of expression, e.g. *The play seemed an ideal vehicle for his music.* **vehicular** (adjective).

veil, veils (rhymes with **male**) (noun) A veil is a piece of thin, soft cloth that women sometimes wear over their heads.

vein, veins (rhymes with **rain**) **1** (noun) Your veins are the tubes in your body through which your blood flows to your heart. **2** Veins are the thin lines on leaves or on insects' wings. **3** A vein of a metal or a mineral is a layer of it in rock. **4** Something that is in a particular vein is in that style or mood, e.g. *in a more serious vein.*

velocity (noun; a technical word) Velocity is the speed at which something is moving in a particular direction.

velvet (noun) Velvet is a very soft material which has a thick layer of fine short threads on one side. **velvety** (adjective).

vendetta, vendettas (noun) A vendetta is a long-lasting bitter quarrel which results in people or organizations trying to harm each other.

vending machine, vending machines (noun) A vending machine is a machine which provides things such as drinks sweets, or cigarettes when you put money in it.

vendor, vendors (noun) A vendor is a person who sells something.

veneer 1 (noun) You can refer to a superficial quality that someone has as a veneer of that quality, e.g. *a veneer of calm.* **2** Veneer is a thin layer of wood or plastic used to cover a surface.

venerable 1 (adjective) A venerable person is someone you treat with respect because they are old and wise. **2** Something that is venerable is impressive because it is old or important historically.

'enerate, venerates, venerating, venerated (verb; a formal word) If you venerate someone, you feel great respect for them. **veneration** (noun).

engeance 1 (noun) Vengeance is the act of harming someone because they have harmed you. **2** (phrase) If something happens **with a vengeance,** it happens to a much greater extent than was expected, e.g *It began to rain again with a vengeance.*

enison (noun) Venison is the meat from a deer.

enom 1 (noun) The venom of a snake, scorpion, or spider is its poison. **2** Venom is a feeling of great bitterness or spitefulness towards someone, e.g. *He was glaring at me with venom.* **venomous** (adjective).

ent, vents, venting, vented 1 (noun) A vent is a hole in something through which gases and smoke can escape and fresh air can enter, e.g. *air vents.* **2** (verb) If you vent strong feelings, you express them, e.g. *She wanted to vent her anger upon me.* **3** (phrase) If you **give vent** to strong feelings, you express them, e.g. *Pamela gave vent to a lot of bitterness.*

ventilate, ventilates, ventilating, ventilated (verb) To ventilate a room means to allow fresh air into it. **ventilated** (adjective), **ventilation** (noun).

ventilator, ventilators (noun) A ventilator is a machine that helps people breathe when they cannot breathe naturally, for example if they are very ill.

ventriloquist, ventriloquists (pronounced ven-**trill**-o-kwist) (noun) A ventriloquist is an entertainer who can speak without moving their lips so that the words seem to come from a dummy or a puppet. **ventriloquism** (noun).

venture, ventures, venturing, ventured 1 (noun) A venture is something new which involves the risk of failure or of losing money, e.g. *a successful venture in television films.* **2** (verb) If you venture something such as an opinion, you say it cautiously or hesitantly because you are afraid it might be foolish or wrong, e.g. *I would not venture to agree.* **3** If you venture somewhere that might be dangerous, you go there.

venue, venues (pronounced **ven**-yoo) (noun) The venue for an event is the place where it will happen.

Venus (noun) Venus is the planet in the solar system which is second from the sun.

veranda, verandas (pronounced ver-**ran**-da); also spelled **verandah** (noun) A veranda is a platform with a roof that is attached to an outside wall of a house at ground level.

verb, verbs (noun) In grammar, a verb is a word that expresses actions and states, for example 'be', 'become', 'take', and 'run'.

verbal 1 (adjective) You use verbal to describe things connected with words and their use, e.g. *verbal attacks on referees.* **2** Verbal describes things which are spoken rather than written, e.g. *a verbal agreement.* **verbally** (adverb).

verdict, verdicts 1 (noun) In a law court, a verdict is the decision which states whether a prisoner is guilty or not guilty. **2** If you give a verdict on something, you give your opinion after thinking about it.

verge, verges, verging, verged 1 (noun) The verge of a road is the narrow strip of grassy ground at the side. **2** (phrase) If you are **on the verge** of something, you are going to do it soon or it is likely to happen soon, e.g. *on the verge of crying.* **3** (verb) Something that verges on something else is almost the same as it, e.g. *dark blue that verged on purple.*

verify, verifies, verifying, verified (verb) If you verify something, you check that it is true, e.g. *None of his statements could be verified.* **verifiable** (adjective), **verification** (noun).

veritable (adjective) You use veritable to emphasize that something is really true, even if it seems as if you are exaggerating, e.g. *a veritable jungle of shops.*

vermin (plural noun) Vermin are small animals or insects such as rats and cockroaches which carry disease and damage crops.

vernacular, vernaculars (pronounced ver-**nak**-yoo-lar) (noun) The vernacular of a particular country or district is the language widely spoken there.

verruca, verrucas (pronounced ver-**roo**-ka) (noun) A verruca is a small hard infectious growth rather like a wart. I most commonly occurs on the feet.

versatile (adjective) If someone is versatile, they have many different skills. **versatility** (noun).

verse, verses 1 (noun) Verse i another word for poetry. **2** A verse is one part of a poem song, or chapter of the Bible.

versed (adjective) If you ar versed in something, yo know a lot about it.

version, versions 1 (noun) A version of something is a form of it in which some details ar different from earlier or late forms, e.g. *a cheaper version c the aircraft.* **2** Someone's ver sion of an event is their per sonal description of what hap pened.

versus (preposition) Versus i used to indicate that two pe ple or teams are competin against each other.

vertebra, vertebrae (pr

nounced **ver**-tib-bra) (noun) Vertebrae are the small bones which form a person's or animal's backbone.

vertical (adjective) Something that is vertical points straight up and forms a ninety-degree angle with the surface on which it stands. **vertically** (adverb).

vertigo (noun) Vertigo is a feeling of dizziness caused by looking down from a high place.

verve (noun) Verve is lively and forceful enthusiasm.

very 1 (adjective or adverb) Very is used before words to emphasize them, e.g. *very bad dreams... the very end of the book.* **2** (phrase) You use **not very** to mean that something is the case only to a small degree, e.g. *You're not very like your sister.*

vessel, vessels 1 (noun) A vessel is a ship or large boat. **2** (a literary use) A vessel is also any bowl or container in which a liquid can be kept. **3** A vessel is also a thin tube along which liquids such as blood or sap move in animals and plants.

vest, vests (noun) A vest is a piece of underwear worn for warmth on the top half of the body.

vestige, vestiges (pronounced **vest**-ij) (noun; a formal word) If there is not a vestige of something, then there is not even a little of it left, e.g. *They have a vestige of strength left.*

vestry, vestries (noun) The vestry is the part of the church building where a priest or minister changes into their official clothes.

vet, vets, vetting, vetted 1 (noun) A vet is a doctor for animals. **2** (verb) If you vet someone or something, you check them carefully to see if they are acceptable, e.g. *He refused to let them vet his speeches.*

veteran, veterans 1 (noun) A veteran is someone who has served in the armed forces, particularly during a war. **2** A veteran is also someone who has been involved in a particular activity for a long time, e.g. *a veteran of 25 political campaigns.*

veterinary (pronounced **vet**-er-in-ar-ee) (adjective) Veterinary is used to describe the work of a vet and the medical treatment of animals.

veterinary surgeon, veterinary surgeons (noun) A veterinary surgeon is the same as a vet.

veto, vetoes, vetoing, vetoed 1 (verb) If someone in authority vetoes something, they say no to it. **2** (noun) Veto is the right that someone in authority has to say no to something, e.g. *Dr Baker has the power of veto.*

vexed (adjective) If you are vexed, you are annoyed, worried, or puzzled.

VHF (noun) VHF is a range of high radio frequencies. VHF is an abbreviation for 'very high frequency'.

via 1 (preposition) If you go to one place via another, you travel through that place to get to your destination, e.g. *He drove directly from Bonn via Paris.* **2** Via also means done or achieved by making use of a particular thing or person, e.g. *to follow proceedings via newspapers or television.*

viable (pronounced **vy**-a-bl) (adjective) Something that is viable is capable of doing what it is intended to do without extra help or financial support, e.g. *a viable business.* **viability** (noun).

viaduct, viaducts (noun) A viaduct is a long high bridge that carries a road or railway across a valley.

vibes (plural noun; an informal word) Vibes are the emotional reactions that you feel a person has towards you, or the atmosphere that a place has.

vibrant (adjective) Something or someone that is vibrant is full of life, energy, and enthusiasm. **vibrantly** (adverb), **vibrancy** (noun).

vibrate, vibrates, vibrating, vibrated (verb) If something vibrates, it moves a tiny amount backwards and forwards very quickly. **vibration** (noun).

vicar, vicars (noun) A vicar is a priest in the Church of England.

vicarage, vicarages (noun) A vicarage is a house where a vicar lives.

vice, vices 1 (noun) A vice is a serious moral fault in someone's character, such as greed, or a weakness, such as smoking. **2** Vice is criminal activities connected with drugs, prostitution, pornography, or gambling. **3** A vice is a tool with a pair of jaws that hold an object tightly while it is being worked on.

vice- (prefix) Vice- is used before a title or position to show that the holder is the deputy of the person with that title or position, e.g. *vice-president.*

vice versa Vice versa is used to indicate that the reverse of what you have said is also true, e.g. *Wives criticize their husbands, and vice versa.*

vicinity (pronounced vis-**sin**-it-ee) (noun) If something is in the vicinity of a place, it is in the surrounding or nearby area.

vicious (adjective) cruel and violent. **viciously** (adverb), **viciousness** (noun).

victim, victims (noun) A victim is someone who has been harmed or injured by someone or something.

victor, victors (noun) The victor in a fight or contest is the person who wins.

Victorian (adjective) Victorian describes things that happened or were made during the reign of Queen Victoria.

victory, victories (noun) A victory is a success in a battle or competition. **victorious** (adjective).

video, videos, videoing, videoed 1 (noun) Video is the recording and showing of films and events using a video recorder, video tape, and a television set. **2** A video is a sound and picture recording which can be played back on a television set. **3** A video is also a video recorder. **4** (verb) If you video something, you record it on magnetic tape for later viewing.

video recorder, video recorders (noun) A video recorder or video cassette recorder is machine for recording and playing back programmes from television.

vie, vies, vying, vied (verb; a formal word) If you vie with someone, you compete to do something sooner than or better than they do.

Vietnamese (pronounced vyet-nam-**meez**) **1** (adjective) belonging or relating to Vietnam. **2** (noun) A Vietnamese is someone who comes from Vietnam. **3** Vietnamese is the main language spoken in Vietnam.

view, views, viewing, viewed 1 (noun) Your views are your personal opinions, e.g. *his political views.* **2** (verb) If you view something in a particular way, you think of it in that way, e.g. *They viewed me with contempt.* **3** (noun) A view is everything you can see from a particular place. **4** (phrase) You use **in view of** to specify the main fact or event influencing your actions or opinions, e.g. *He wore a lighter suit in view of the heat.* **5** If something is **on view**, it is being shown or exhibited to the public.

viewer, viewers (noun) Viewers are the people who watch television.

viewpoint, viewpoints 1 (noun) Your viewpoint is your attitude towards something. **2** A viewpoint is a place from which you get a good view of an area or event.

vigil, vigils (pronounced **vij**-jil) (noun) A vigil is a period of time, especially at night, when you stay quietly in one place, for example because you are making a political protest or praying.

vigilant (adjective) careful and alert to danger or trouble.

vigilante, vigilantes (pronounced vij-il-**ant**-ee) (noun) Vigilantes are unofficially organized groups of people who try to protect their community and catch and punish criminals.

vigorous (adjective) energetic or enthusiastic. **vigorously** (adverb), **vigour** (noun).

Viking, Vikings (noun) The Vikings were groups of seamen from Scandinavia who attacked villages in parts of north-western Europe from the 8th to the 11th centuries.

vile, viler, vilest (adjective) unpleasant or disgusting, e.g. *a vile accusation... a vile smell.*

villa, villas (noun) A villa is a house, especially a pleasant holiday home in a country with a warm climate.

village, villages (noun) A village is a collection of houses and other buildings in the countryside. **villager** (noun).

villain, villains (noun) A villain is someone who harms others or breaks the law. **villainous** (adjective), **villainy** (noun).

vindicate, vindicates, vindicating, vindicated (verb; a formal word) If someone is vindicated, their views or ideas are proved to be right, e.g. *My friend's instincts have been vindicated.*

vindictive (adjective) Someone who is vindictive is deliberately hurtful towards someone, often as an act of revenge. **vindictiveness** (noun).

vine, vines (noun) A vine is a

trailing or climbing plant which winds itself around and over a support, especially one which produces grapes.

vinegar (noun) Vinegar is a sharp-tasting liquid made from sour wine, beer, or cider, which is used for salad dressing. **vinegary** (adjective).

vineyard, vineyards (noun) A vineyard is an area of land where grapes are grown.

vintage, vintages 1 (adjective) A vintage wine is a good quality wine which has been stored for a number of years to improve its quality. **2** Vintage describes something which is the best or most typical of its kind, e.g. *a vintage guitar*. **3** (noun) A vintage is a grape harvest of one particular year and the wine produced from it. **4** (adjective) A vintage car is one made between 1918 and 1930.

vinyl (noun) Vinyl is a strong plastic used to make things such as furniture and floor coverings.

viola, violas (pronounced vee-**oh**-la) (noun) A viola is a musical instrument with four strings. It is similar to a violin, but larger and with a lower pitch.

violate, violates, violating, violated 1 (verb) If you violate an agreement, law, or promise, you break it. **2** If you violate someone's peace or privacy, you disturb it. **3** If you violate a place, especially a holy place, you treat it with disrespect or violence. **violation** (noun).

violence 1 (noun) Violence is behaviour which is intended to hurt or kill people. **2** If you do or say something with violence, you use a lot of energy in doing or saying it, often because you are angry.

violent 1 (adjective) If someone is violent, they try to hurt or kill people. **2** A violent event happens unexpectedly and with great force. **3** Something that is violent is said, felt, or done with great force. **violently** (adverb).

violet, violets 1 (noun) A violet is a plant with dark purple flowers. **2** (noun or adjective) bluish purple.

violin, violins (noun) A violin is a musical instrument with four strings that is held under the chin and played with a bow. **violinist** (noun).

VIP, VIPs (noun) VIPs are famous or important people. VIP is an abbreviation for 'very important person'.

viper, vipers (noun) Vipers are poisonous snakes found in Europe, Africa, and Asia.

virgin, virgins 1 (noun) A virgin is someone who has never had sexual intercourse. **2** (adjective) Something that is virgin is fresh and unused, e.g. *virgin land*. **3** (noun) The Virgin, or the Blessed Virgin, is a name given to Mary, the mother of Jesus Christ. **virginity** (noun).

virginal 1 (adjective) Someone who is virginal looks young and innocent. **2** Something that is virginal is fresh and clean and looks as if it has never been used. **3** (noun) The virginal was a keyboard instrument popular in the 16th and 17th centuries.

Virgo (noun) Virgo is the sixth sign of the zodiac, represented by a girl. People born between August 23rd and September 22nd are born under this sign.

virile (adjective) A virile man has all the qualities that a man is traditionally expected to have, such as strength, forcefulness, and sexuality. **virility** (noun).

virtual (pronounced **vur**-tyool) (adjective) Virtual means that something has all the characteristics of a particular thing, but it is not formally recognized as being that thing, e.g. *The country is in a virtual state of war.* **virtually** (adverb).

virtual reality (noun) Virtual reality is a situation or setting that has been created by a computer and that looks real to the person using it.

virtue, virtues 1 (noun) Virtue is thinking and doing what is morally right and avoiding what is wrong. **2** A virtue is a good quality in someone's character. **3** A virtue of something is an advantage, e.g. *the virtue of neatness.* **4** (a formal phrase) **By virtue of** means because of, e.g. *The article stuck in my mind by virtue of one detail.*

virtuoso, virtuosos or **virtuosi** (pronounced vur-tyoo-**oh**-zoh) (noun) A virtuoso is someone who is exceptionally good at something, particularly playing a musical instrument.

virtuous (adjective) behaving with or showing moral virtue.

virus, viruses (pronounced **vie**-russ) **1** (noun) A virus is a kind of germ that can cause disease. **2** A virus in a computer system is a program that alters or damages the information stored there. **viral** (adjective).

visa, visas (noun) A visa is an official stamp, usually put in your passport, that allows you to visit a particular country.

viscount, viscounts (pronounced **vie**-kount) (noun) A viscount is a British nobleman. **viscountess** (noun).

visibility (noun) You use visibility to say how far or how clearly you can see in particular weather conditions.

visible 1 (adjective) able to be seen. **2** noticeable or evident, e.g. *There was little visible excitement.* **visibly** (adverb).

vision, visions 1 (noun) Vision is the ability to see clearly. **2** A vision is a mental picture, in which you imagine how things might be different, e.g. *the vision of a possible future.* **3** Vision is also imaginative insight, e.g. *a total lack of vision and imagination.* **4** A vision is also a mental picture or hallucination that someone has as a result of divine inspiration, madness, or drugs. **visionary** (noun or adjective).

visit, visits, visiting, visited 1 (verb) If you visit someone, you go to see them and spend time with them. **2** If you visit a place, you go to see it. **3** (noun) A visit is a trip to see a person or place. **visitor** (noun).

visor, visors (pronounced **vie**-zor) (noun) A visor is a transparent movable shield attached to a helmet, which can be pulled down to protect the eyes or face.

visual (adjective) relating to sight, e.g. *visual problems.*

visualize, visualizes, visualizing, visualized (pronounced **viz**-yool-eyes); also spelled **visualise** (verb) If you visualize something, you form a mental picture of it.

vital 1 (adjective) necessary or very important, e.g. *vital evidence.* **2** energetic, exciting, and full of life, e.g. *an active and vital life outside school.* **vitally** (adverb).

vitality (noun) People who have vitality are energetic and lively.

vitamin, vitamins (noun) Vitamins are organic compounds which you need in order to remain healthy. They occur naturally in food.

vitriolic (adjective; a formal word) Vitriolic language or behaviour is full of bitterness and hate.

vivacious (pronounced viv-**vay**-shuss) (adjective) A vivacious person is attractively lively and high-spirited. **vivacity** (noun).

vivid (adjective) very bright in colour or clear in detail, e.g. *vivid red paint... vivid memories.* **vividly** (adverb), **vividness** (noun).

vivisection (noun) Vivisection is the act of cutting open living animals for medical research.

vixen, vixens (noun) A vixen is a female fox.

vocabulary, vocabularies 1 (noun) Someone's vocabulary is the total number of words they know in a particular language. **2** The vocabulary of a language is all the words in it.

vocal (adjective) You say that someone is vocal if they express their opinions strongly and openly.

vocation, vocations 1 (noun) A vocation is a strong wish to do a particular job, especially one which involves serving other people. **2** A vocation is also a profession or career.

vocational (adjective) Vocational is used to describe the skills needed for a particular job or profession, e.g. *vocational training.*

vociferous (pronounced voe-**sif**-fer-uss) (adjective; a formal word) Someone who is vociferous speaks a lot, or loudly, because they want to make a point strongly, e.g. *vociferous critics.* **vociferously** (adverb).

vodka, vodkas (noun) Vodka is a strong clear alcoholic drink which originally came from Russia.

vogue (pronounced **vohg**) (phrase) If something is **the vogue** or **in vogue,** it is fashionable and popular, e.g. *Colour photographs became the vogue.*

voice, voices, voicing, voiced 1 (noun) Your voice is the sounds produced by your vocal cords, or the ability to make such sounds. **2** (verb) If you voice an opinion or an emotion, you say what you think or feel, e.g. *A range of opinions were voiced.*

void, voids 1 (noun) A void is a situation which seems empty because it has no interest, excitement, or value, e.g. *Cats fill a very large void in your life.* **2** A void is also a large empty hole or space, e.g. *His* *feet dangled in the void.*

volatile (adjective) liable to change often and unexpectedly, e.g. *The situation at work is volatile.*

volcanic (adjective) A volcanic region has many volcanoes or was created by volcanoes.

volcano, volcanoes (noun) A volcano is a hill or mountain with an opening through which lava, gas, and ash burst out from inside the earth onto the surface.

vole, voles (noun) Voles are small animals like mice with short tails. They live in fields and near rivers.

volition (noun; a formal word) If you do something of your own volition, you do it because you have decided for yourself, without being persuaded by others, e.g. *He attended of his own volition.*

volley, volleys 1 (noun) A volley of shots or gunfire is a lot of shots fired at the same time. **2** In tennis, a volley is a stroke in which the player hits the ball before it bounces.

volleyball (noun) Volleyball is a game in which two teams hit a large ball back and forth over a high net with their hands. The ball is not allowed to bounce on the ground.

volt, volts (noun) A volt is a unit used to measure the force of an electric current.

voltage, voltages (noun) The voltage of an electric current is its force measured in volts.

volume, volumes 1 (noun) The volume of something is the amount of space it contains or occupies. **2** The volume of something is also the amount of it that there is, e.g. *a large volume of letters.* **3** The volume of a radio, TV, or record player is the strength of the sound that it produces. **4** A volume is a book, or one of a series of books.

voluminous (pronounced vol-**loo**-min-uss) (adjective) very large or full in size or quantity, e.g. *voluminous skirts.*

voluntary 1 (adjective) Voluntary actions are ones that you do because you choose to do them and not because you have been forced to do them. **2** Voluntary work is done by people who are not paid for what they do. **voluntarily** (adverb).

volunteer, volunteers, volunteering, volunteered 1 (noun) A volunteer is someone who does work for which they are not paid, e.g. *a volunteer for Friends of the Earth.* **2** A volunteer is also someone who chooses to join the armed forces, especially during wartime. **3** (verb) If you volunteer to do something, you offer to do it rather than being forced into it. **4** If you volunteer information, you give it without being asked.

voluptuous (pronounced vol-**lupt**-yoo-uss) (adjective) A voluptuous woman has a figure which is considered to be sexually exciting. **voluptuously** (adverb), **voluptuousness** (noun).

vomit, vomits, vomiting, vomited 1 (verb) If you vomit, food and drink comes back up from your stomach and out through your mouth. **2** (noun) Vomit is partly digested food and drink that has come back up from someone's stomach and out through their mouth.

voodoo (noun) Voodoo is a form of magic practised in the Caribbean, especially in Haiti.

vote, votes, voting, voted 1 (noun) Someone's vote is their choice in an election, or at a meeting where decisions are taken. **2** When a group of people have a vote, they make a decision by allowing each person in the group to say what they would prefer. **3** In an election, the vote is the total number of people who have made their choice, e.g. *the average Tory vote.* **4** (verb) When people vote, they indicate their choice or opinion, usually by writing on a piece of paper or by raising their hand. **5** (noun) If people have the vote, they have the legal right to vote in an election. **6** (verb) If you vote that a particular thing should happen, you are suggesting it should happen, e.g. *I vote that we all go to Holland.* **voter** (noun).

vouch, vouches, vouching, vouched 1 (verb) If you say that you can vouch for something, you mean that you have evidence from your own experience that it is true or correct. **2** If you say that you can vouch for someone, you mean that you are sure that you can guarantee their good behaviour or support, e.g. *Her employer will vouch for her.*

voucher, vouchers (noun) A voucher is a piece of paper that can be used instead of money to pay for something.

vow, vows, vowing, vowed 1 (verb) If you vow to do something, you make a solemn promise to do it, e.g. *He vowed to do better in future.* **2** (noun) A vow is a solemn promise.

vowel, vowels (noun) A vowel is a sound made without your tongue touching the roof of your mouth or your teeth, or one of the letters a, e, i, o, u, which represent such sounds.

voyage, voyages (noun) A voyage is a long journey on a ship or in a spacecraft. **voyager** (noun).

vulgar 1 (adjective) socially unacceptable or offensive, e.g. *vulgar language.* **2** showing a lack of taste or quality, e.g. *the most vulgar person who ever existed.* **vulgarity** (noun), **vulgarly** (adverb).

vulnerable (adjective) weak and without protection. **vulnerably** (adverb), **vulnerability** (noun).

vulture, vultures (noun) A vulture is a large bird which lives in hot countries and eats the flesh of dead animals.

vying the present participle of **vie**.

W w

wacky, wackier, wackiest (adjective; an informal word) odd or crazy, e.g. *wacky clothes.*

wad, wads 1 (noun) A wad of papers or banknotes is a thick bundle of them. **2** A wad of something is a lump of it, e.g. *a wad of cotton wool.*

waddle, waddles, waddling,

waddled (verb) When a duck or a fat person waddles, they walk with short, quick steps, swaying slightly from side to side.

wade, wades, wading, waded 1 (verb) If you wade through water or mud, you walk slowly through it. **2** If you wade through a book or document, you spend a lot of time and effort reading it because you find it dull or difficult.

wader, waders (noun) Waders are long waterproof rubber boots worn by fishermen.

wafer, wafers 1 (noun) A wafer is a thin, crisp, sweet biscuit often eaten with ice cream. **2** A wafer is also a thin disc of special bread used in the Christian service of Holy Communion.

waffle, waffles, waffling, waffled (pronounced **wof**-fl) **1** (verb) When someone waffles, they talk or write a lot without being clear or without saying anything of importance. **2** (noun) Waffle is vague and lengthy speech or writing. **3** A waffle is a thick, crisp pancake with squares marked on it often eaten with syrup poured over it.

waft, wafts, wafting, wafted (pronounced **wahft**) (verb) If a sound or scent wafts or is wafted through the air, it moves gently through it.

wag, wags, wagging, wagged 1 (verb) When a dog wags its tail, it shakes it repeatedly from side to side. **2** If you wag your finger, you move it repeatedly up and down.

wage, wages, waging, waged 1 (noun) A wage or wages is the regular payment made to someone each week for the work they do, especially for manual or unskilled work. **2** (verb) If a person or country wages a campaign or war, they start it and carry it on over a period of time.

wager, wagers (noun) A wager is a bet.

wagon, wagons; also spelled **waggon 1** (noun) A wagon is a strong four-wheeled vehicle for carrying heavy loads, usually pulled by a horse or tractor. **2** Wagons are also the containers for freight pulled by a railway engine.

waif, waifs (pronounced **wayf**) (noun) A waif is a young, thin person who looks hungry and homeless.

wail, wails, wailing, wailed 1 (verb) To wail means to cry loudly with sorrow or pain. **2** (noun) A wail is a long, unhappy cry.

waist, waists (noun) Your waist is the middle part of your body where it narrows slightly above your hips.

waistcoat, waistcoats (noun) A waistcoat is a sleeveless piece of clothing, often worn under a suit or jacket, which buttons up the front.

wait, waits, waiting, waited 1 (verb) If you wait, you spend time, usually doing little or nothing, before something happens. **2** If something can wait, it is not urgent and can be dealt with later. **3** (noun) A wait is a period of time before something happens. **4** (phrase) If you **can't wait** to do something, you are very excited and eager to do it. **5** (verb) If you wait on people in a restaurant, it is your job to serve them food.

waiter, waiters (noun) A waiter is a man who works in a restaurant, serving people with food and drink.

waiting list, waiting lists (noun) A waiting list is a list of people who have asked for something which cannot be given to them immediately, for example medical treatment.

waitress, waitresses (noun) A waitress is a woman who works in a restaurant, serving people with food and drink.

waive, waives, waiving, waived (pronounced **wave**) (verb) If someone waives something such as a rule or a right, they decide not to insist on it being applied.

wake, wakes, waking, woke, woken 1 (verb) When you wake or when something wakes you, you become conscious again after being asleep. **2** (noun) The wake of a boat or other object moving in water is the track of waves it leaves behind it. **3** A wake is a gathering of people who have got together to mourn someone's death. **4** (phrase) If one thing follows **in the wake of** another, it follows it as a result of it, or in imitation of it, e.g. *a project set up in the wake of last year's riots.* **wake up 1** (verb) When you wake up or something wakes you up, you become conscious again after being asleep. **2** If you wake up to a dangerous situation, you become aware of it.

waken, wakens, wakening, wakened (verb; a literary word) When you waken someone, you wake them up.

walk, walks, walking, walked 1 (verb) When you walk, you move along by putting one foot in front of the other on the ground. **2** If you walk away with or walk off with something such as a prize, you win it or achieve it easily. **3** (noun) A walk is a journey made by walking, e.g. *We'll have a quick walk.* **4** Your walk is the way you walk, e.g. *his rolling walk.* **walk out 1** (verb) If you walk out on someone, you leave them suddenly. **2** If workers walk out, they go on strike.

walkabout, walkabouts (noun) A walkabout is an informal walk amongst crowds in a public place by royalty or by some other well-known person.

walker, walkers (noun) A walker is a person who walks, especially for pleasure or to keep fit.

walking stick, walking sticks (noun) A walking stick is a wooden stick which people can lean on while walking.

Walkman (noun; a trademark) A Walkman is a small cassette player with lightweight headphones, which people carry around so that they can listen to music while they are doing something like walking.

walk of life, walks of life (noun) The walk of life that you come from is the position you have in society and the kind of job you have.

walkover, walkovers (noun; an

informal word) A walkover is a very easy victory in a competition or contest.

walkway, walkways (noun) A walkway is a passage between two buildings for people to walk along.

wall, walls 1 (noun) A wall is one of the vertical sides of a building or a room. **2** A wall is a long, narrow vertical structure made of stone or brick that surrounds or divides an area of land. **3** A wall is also a lining or membrane enclosing a bodily cavity or structure, e.g. *the wall of the womb.*

wallaby, wallabies (noun) A wallaby is an animal like a small kangaroo.

wallet, wallets (noun) A wallet is a small, flat case made of leather or plastic, used for keeping paper money and sometimes credit cards.

wallop, wallops, walloping, walloped (verb; an informal word) If you wallop someone, you hit them very hard.

wallow, wallows, wallowing, wallowed 1 (verb) If you wallow in an unpleasant feeling or situation, you allow it to continue longer than is reasonable or necessary because you are getting a kind of enjoyment from it, e.g. *We're wallowing in misery.* **2** When an animal wallows in mud or water, it lies or rolls about in it slowly for pleasure.

wallpaper, wallpapers (noun) Wallpaper is thick coloured or patterned paper for pasting onto the walls of rooms in order to decorate them.

walnut, walnuts 1 (noun) A walnut is an edible nut with a wrinkled shape and a hard, round, light-brown shell. **2** Walnut is wood from the walnut tree which is often used for making expensive furniture.

walrus, walruses (noun) A walrus is an animal which lives in the sea and which looks like a large seal with a tough skin, coarse whiskers, and two tusks.

waltz, waltzes, waltzing, waltzed 1 (noun) A waltz is a dance which has a rhythm of three beats to the bar. **2** (verb) If you waltz with someone, you dance a waltz with them. **3** (an informal use) If you waltz somewhere, you walk there in a relaxed and confident way.

wan (rhymes with **on**) (adjective) pale and tired-looking.

wand, wands (noun) A wand is a long, thin rod that magicians wave when they are performing tricks and magic.

wander, wanders, wandering, wandered 1 (verb) If you wander in a place, you walk around in a casual way. **2** If your mind wanders or your thoughts wander, you lose concentration and start thinking about other things. **wanderer** (noun).

wane, wanes, waning, waned (verb) If a condition, attitude, or emotion wanes, it becomes gradually weaker.

wangle, wangles, wangling, wangled (verb; an informal word) If you wangle something that you want, you manage to get it by being crafty or persuasive.

want, wants, wanting, wanted **1** (verb) If you want something, you feel a desire to have it or a need for it to happen. **2** (an informal use) If something wants doing, there is a need for it to be done, e.g. *Her hair wants cutting.* **3** If someone is wanted, the police are searching for them, e.g. *John was wanted for fraud.* **4** (noun; a formal use) A want of something is a lack of it.

wanting (adjective) If you find something wanting or if it proves wanting, it is not as good in some way as you think it should be.

wanton (adjective) A wanton action deliberately causes unnecessary harm, damage, or waste, e.g. *wanton destruction.*

war, wars, warring, warred **1** (noun) A war is a period of fighting between countries or states when weapons are used and many people may be killed. **2** A war is also competition between groups of people, or a campaign against something, e.g. *a trade war... the war against crime.* **3** (verb) When two countries war with each other, they are fighting a war against each other. **warring** (adjective).

warble, warbles, warbling, warbled (verb) When a bird warbles, it sings pleasantly with high notes.

ward, wards, warding, warded **1** (noun) A ward is a room in a hospital which has beds for several people who need similar treatment. **2** A ward is an area or district which forms a separate part of a political constituency or local council. **3** A ward or a ward of court is a child who is officially put in the care of an adult or a court of law, because their parents are dead or because they need protection. **4** (verb) If you ward off a danger or an illness, you do something to prevent it from affecting or harming you.

-ward or **-wards** (suffix) -ward and -wards form adverbs or adjectives that show the way something is moving or facing, e.g. *homeward... westwards.*

warden, wardens **1** (noun) A warden is a person in charge of a building or institution such as a youth hostel or prison. **2** A warden is an official who makes sure that certain laws or rules are obeyed, e.g. *a game warden.*

warder, warders (noun) A warder is a person who is in charge of prisoners in a jail.

wardrobe, wardrobes **1** (noun) A wardrobe is a tall cupboard in which you can hang your clothes. **2** Someone's wardrobe is their collection of clothes.

ware, wares **1** (noun) Ware is manufactured goods of a particular kind, e.g. *kitchenware.* **2** Someone's wares are the things they sell, usually in the street or in a market.

warehouse, warehouses (noun) A warehouse is a large building where raw materials or manufactured goods are stored.

warfare (noun) Warfare is the activity of fighting a war.

warhead, warheads (noun) A warhead is the front end of a bomb or missile, where the explosives are carried.

warlock, warlocks (noun) A warlock is a male witch.

warm, warmer, warmest; warms, warming, warmed 1 (adjective) Something that is warm has some heat, but not enough to be hot, e.g. *a warm day.* **2** Warm clothes or blankets are made of a material which protects you from the cold. **3** Warm colours or sounds are pleasant and make you feel comfortable and relaxed. **4** A warm person is friendly and affectionate. **5** (verb) If you warm something, you heat it up gently so that it stops being cold. **warmly** (adverb). **warm up** (verb) If you warm up for an event or an activity, you practise or exercise gently to prepare for it.

warmth 1 (noun) Warmth is a moderate amount of heat. **2** Someone who has warmth is friendly and affectionate.

warn, warns, warning, warned 1 (verb) If you warn someone about a possible problem or danger, you tell them about it in advance so that they are aware of it, e.g. *I warned him what it would be like.* **2** If you warn someone not to do something, you advise them not to do it, in order to avoid possible danger or punishment, e.g. *I have warned her not to train for 10 days.* **warn off** (verb) If you warn someone off, you tell them to go away or to stop doing something.

warning, warnings (noun) A warning is something said or written to tell people of a possible problem or danger.

warp, warps, warping, warped 1 (verb) If something warps or is warped, it becomes bent, often because of the effect of heat or water. **2** If something warps someone's mind or character, it makes them abnormal or corrupt.

warrant, warrants, warranting, warranted 1 (verb; a formal use) If something warrants a particular action, it makes the action seem necessary, e.g. *no evidence to warrant a murder investigation.* **2** (noun) A warrant is an official document which gives permission to the police to do something, e.g. *a warrant for his arrest.*

warranty, warranties (noun) A warranty is a guarantee, e.g. *a three-year warranty.*

warren, warrens (noun) A warren is a group of holes under the ground connected by tunnels, which rabbits live in.

warrior, warriors (noun) A warrior is a fighting man or soldier, especially in former times.

warship, warships (noun) A warship is a ship built with guns and used for fighting in wars.

wart, warts (noun) A wart is a small, hard piece of skin which can grow on someone's face or hands.

wartime (noun) Wartime is a period of time during which a country is at war.

wary, warier, wariest (adjective) cautious and on one's guard, e.g. *Michelle is wary of marriage.* **warily** (adverb).

was a past tense of **be**.

wash, washes, washing, washed 1 (verb) If you wash something, you clean it with water and soap. **2** (noun) The wash is all the clothes and bedding that are washed together at one time, e.g. *a typical family's weekly wash.* **3** (verb) If you wash, you clean yourself using soap and water. **4** If something is washed somewhere, it is carried there gently by water, e.g. *The infant Arthur was washed ashore.* **5** (noun) The wash in water is the disturbance and waves produced at the rear of a moving boat. **6** (phrase) If you **wash your hands of** something, you refuse to have anything more to do with it. **wash up 1** (verb) If you wash up, you wash the dishes, pans, and cutlery used in preparing and eating a meal. **2** If something is washed up on land, it is carried by a river or sea and left there, e.g. *A body had been washed up on the beach.*

washer, washers (noun) A washer is a thin, flat ring of metal or plastic which is placed over a bolt before the nut is screwed on, in order to make a tighter connection.

washing (noun) Washing consists of clothes and bedding which need to be washed or are in the process of being washed and dried.

washing machine, washing machines (noun) A washing machine is a machine for washing clothes in.

washing-up (noun) If you do the washing-up, you wash the dishes, pans, and cutlery which have been used in the cooking and eating of a meal.

wasp, wasps (noun) A wasp is an insect with yellow and black stripes across its body, which can sting like a bee.

wastage (noun) Wastage is loss and misuse of something, e.g. *wastage of resources.*

waste, wastes, wasting, wasted 1 (verb) If you waste time, money, or energy, you use too much of it on something that is not important or necessary. **2** If you waste an opportunity, you do not take advantage of it when it is available. **3** If you say that something is wasted on someone, you mean that it is too good, too clever, or too sophisticated for them, e.g. *This book is wasted on us.* **4** (noun) If an activity is a waste of time, money, or energy, it is not important or necessary. **5** Waste is the use of more money or some other resource than is necessary. **6** Waste is also material that is no longer wanted, or material left over from a useful process, e.g. *nuclear waste.* **7** (adjective) unwanted and unusable in its present form, e.g. *waste paper.* **8** Waste land is land which is not used or looked after by anyone. **waste away** (verb) If someone is wasting away, they are becoming very thin and weak because they are ill or not eating properly.

wasted (adjective) unnecessary, e.g. *a wasted journey.*

wasteful (adjective) extravagant or causing waste by using resources in a careless and inefficient way.

wasteland, wastelands (noun) A wasteland is land which is of no use because it is infertile or has been misused.

wasting (adjective) A wasting disease is one that gradually reduces the strength and health of the body.

watch, watches, watching, watched 1 (noun) A watch is a small clock usually worn on a strap on the wrist. **2** (verb) If you watch something, you look at it for some time and pay close attention to what is happening. **3** If you watch a situation, you pay attention to it or are aware of it, e.g. *I had watched Jimmy's progress with interest.* **4** If you watch over someone or something, you care for them. **5** (noun) A watch is a period of time during which a guard is kept over something. **watch out 1** (verb) If you watch out for something, you keep alert to see if it is near you, e.g. *Watch out for more fog and ice.* **2** If you tell someone to watch out, you are warning them to be very careful.

watchdog, watchdogs 1 (noun) A watchdog is a dog used to guard property. **2** A watchdog is a person or group whose job is to make sure that companies do not act illegally or irresponsibly.

watchful (adjective) careful to notice everything that is happening, e.g. *the watchful eye of her father.*

watchman, watchmen (noun) A watchman is a person whose job is to guard property.

water, waters, watering, watered 1 (noun) Water is a clear, colourless, tasteless, and odourless liquid that is necessary for all plant and animal life. **2** You use water or waters to refer to a large area of water, such as a lake or sea, e.g. *the black waters of the lake.* **3** (verb) If you water a plant or an animal, you give it water to drink. **4** If your eyes water, you have tears in them because they are hurting. **5** If your mouth waters, it produces extra saliva, usually because you think of or can smell something appetizing. **water down** (verb) If you water something down, you make it weaker.

watercolour, watercolours 1 (noun) Watercolours are paints for painting pictures, which are diluted with water or put on the paper using a wet brush. **2** A watercolour is a picture which has been painted using watercolours.

watercress (noun) Watercress is a small plant which grows in streams and pools. Its leaves taste hot and are eaten in salads.

waterfall, waterfalls (noun) A waterfall is water from a river or stream as it flows over the edge of a steep cliff in hills or mountains and falls to the ground below.

waterfront, waterfronts (noun) A waterfront is a street or piece of land next to an area of water such as a river or harbour.

watering can, watering cans (noun) A watering can is a container with a handle and a long spout, which you use to water plants.

waterlogged (adjective) Land that is waterlogged is so wet that the soil cannot contain any more water, so that some water remains on the surface of the ground.

watermelon, watermelons (noun) A watermelon is a large, round fruit which has a hard green skin and red juicy flesh with a lot of black seeds.

waterproof, waterproofs 1 (adjective) not letting water pass through, e.g. *waterproof clothing.* **2** (noun) A waterproof is a coat which keeps water out.

watershed, watersheds (noun) A watershed is an event or period which marks a turning point or the beginning of a new way of life, e.g. *a watershed in European history.*

water-skiing (noun) Water-skiing is the sport of skimming over the water on skis while being pulled by a boat.

water table, water tables (noun) The water table is the level below the surface of the ground at which water can be found.

watertight 1 (adjective) Something that is watertight does not allow water to pass through. **2** An agreement or an argument that is watertight has been so carefully put together that nobody should be able to find a fault in it.

waterway, waterways (noun) A waterway is a canal, river, or narrow channel of sea which ships or boats can sail along.

waterworks (noun) A waterworks is the system of pipes, filters, and tanks where the public supply of water is stored and cleaned, and from where it is distributed.

watery 1 (adjective) pale or weak, e.g. *a watery smile.* **2** Watery food or drink contains a lot of water or is thin like water.

watt, watts (pronounced **wot**) (noun) A watt is a unit of measurement of electrical power.

wave, waves, waving, waved 1 (verb) If you wave your hand, you move it from side to side, usually to say hello or goodbye. **2** If you wave someone somewhere or wave them on, you make a movement with your hand to tell them which way to go. **3** If you wave something, you hold it up and move it from side to side, e.g. *The doctor waved a piece of paper at him.* **4** (noun) A wave is a ridge of water on the surface of the sea caused by wind or by tides. **5** A wave is the form in which some types of energy such as heat, light, or sound travel through a substance. **6** A wave of sympathy, alarm, or panic is a steady increase in it which spreads through you or through a group of people. **7** A wave is an increase in a type of activity or behaviour, e.g. *the crime wave.*

wavelength, wavelengths (noun) A wavelength is the distance between the same point on two adjacent waves of energy. **2** A wavelength is the size of radio wave which a particular radio station uses to broadcast its programmes.

waver, wavers, wavering, wavered 1 (verb) If you waver or if your confidence or beliefs waver, you are no longer as firm, confident, or sure in your beliefs, e.g. *Benn has never wavered from his beliefs*

2 If something wavers, it moves slightly, e.g. *The gun did not waver in his hand.*

wavy, wavier, waviest (adjective) having waves or regular curves, e.g. *wavy hair.*

wax, waxes, waxing, waxed 1 (noun) Wax is a solid, slightly shiny substance made of fat or oil and used to make candles and polish. **2** Wax is also the sticky yellow substance in your ears. **3** (verb) If you wax a surface, you treat it or cover it with a thin layer of wax, especially in order to polish it. **4** (a formal use) If you wax eloquent, you talk in an eloquent way.

way, ways 1 (noun) A way of doing something is the manner of doing it, e.g. *an excellent way of cooking meat.* **2** The ways of a person or group are their customs or their normal behaviour, e.g. *Their ways are certainly different.* **3** The way you feel about something is your attitude to it or your opinion about it. **4** If you have a way with people or things, you are very skilful at dealing with them. **5** The way to a particular place is the route that you take to get there. **6** If you go or look a particular way, you go or look in that direction, e.g. *She glanced the other way.* **7** (phrase) If something or someone is **in the way,** they prevent you from moving freely or seeing clearly. **8** (noun) If you divide something a number of ways, you divide it into that number of parts. **9** Way is used with words such as 'little' or 'long' to say how far off in distance or time something is, e.g. *They lived a long way away.* **10** (phrase) You say **by the way** when adding something to what you are saying, e.g. *By the way, I asked Beryl to drop in.* **11** If you **go out of your way** to do something, you make a special effort to do it.

wayside (phrase) If someone or something **falls by the wayside,** they fail in what they are trying to do, or become forgotten and ignored.

wayward (adjective) difficult to control and likely to change suddenly, e.g. *your wayward husband.*

WC, WCs (noun) A WC is a toilet. WC is an abbreviation for 'water closet'.

we (pronoun) A speaker or writer uses we to refer to himself or herself and one or more other people, e.g. *We are going to see Eddie.*

weak, weaker, weakest 1 (adjective) not having much strength, e.g. *weak from lack of sleep.* **2** If something is weak, it is likely to break or fail, e.g. *Russia's weak economy.* **3** If you describe someone as weak, you mean they are easily influenced by other people. **weakly** (adverb).

weaken, weakens, weakening, weakened 1 (verb) If someone weakens something, they make it less strong, powerful, or certain. **2** If someone weakens, they become less certain about something.

weakling, weaklings (noun) A weakling is a person who lacks physical strength or who is weak in character or health.

weakness, weaknesses 1 (noun) Weakness is lack of moral or physical strength. **2** If you have a weakness for something, you have a great liking for it, e.g. *a weakness for whisky*.

wealth 1 (noun) Wealth is the large amount of money or property which someone owns. **2** A wealth of something is a lot of it, e.g. *a wealth of information*.

wealthy, wealthier, wealthiest (adjective) having a large amount of money, property, or other valuable things.

wean, weans, weaning, weaned (verb) To wean a baby or animal means to start feeding it food other than its mother's milk.

weapon, weapons 1 (noun) A weapon is an object used to kill or hurt people in a fight or war. **2** A weapon is anything which can be used to get the better of an opponent, e.g. *Surprise was his only weapon*. **weaponry** (noun).

wear, wears, wearing, wore, worn 1 (verb) When you wear something such as clothes, make-up, or jewellery, you have them on your body or face. **2** If you wear a particular expression, it shows on your face. **3** (noun) You can refer to clothes that are suitable for a particular time or occasion as a kind of wear, e.g. *beach wear*. **4** (verb) If something wears, it becomes thinner, weaker, or worse in condition. **5** (noun) Wear is the amount or type of use that something has and which causes damage or change to it, e.g. *signs of wear*. **wear down** (verb) If you wear people down, you weaken them by repeatedly doing something or asking them to do something. **wear off** (verb) If a feeling such as pain wears off, it gradually disappears. **wear out** (verb) When something wears out or when you wear it out, it is used so much that it becomes thin, weak, and no longer usable.

wear and tear (noun) Wear and tear is the damage caused to something by normal use.

wearing (adjective) Someone or something that is wearing makes you feel extremely tired.

weary, wearier, weariest; wearies, wearying, wearied 1 (adjective) very tired. **2** (verb) If you weary of something, you become tired of it. **wearily** (adverb), **weariness** (noun).

weasel, weasels (noun) A weasel is a small wild anima with a long, thin body and short legs.

weather, weathers, weathering weathered 1 (noun) The weather is the condition o the atmosphere at any particular time. **2** (verb) If something such as rock or woo weathers, it changes colour o shape as a result of being exposed to the wind, rain, o sun. **3** If you weather a problem or difficulty, you com through it safely. **4** (phrase) I you are **under the weather** you feel slightly ill.

weather forecast, weathe forecasts (noun) A weathe forecast is a statement sayin what the weather will be like the next day or for the next few days.

weather vane, weather vanes (noun) A weather vane is a metal object on the roof of a building which turns round in the wind and shows which way the wind is blowing.

weave, weaves, weaving, wove, woven 1 (verb) To weave cloth means to make it by crossing threads over and under each other, especially by using a machine called a loom. **2** (noun) The weave of cloth is the way in which the threads are arranged and the pattern that they form, e.g. *a tight weave.* **3** (verb) If you weave your way somewhere, you go there by moving from side to side through and round the obstacles.

weaver, weavers (noun) A weaver is a person who weaves cloth.

web, webs 1 (noun) A web is a fine net of threads that a spider makes from a sticky substance which it produces in its body. **2** A web is a complicated structure or pattern, e.g. *a web of corruption.*

webbed (adjective) Webbed feet have the toes connected by a piece of skin.

wed, weds, wedding, wedded or **wed** (verb; an old-fashioned word) If you wed someone or if you wed, you get married.

wedding, weddings (noun) A wedding is a marriage ceremony.

wedge, wedges, wedging, wedged 1 (verb) If you wedge something, you force it to remain there by holding it there tightly, or by fixing something next to it to prevent it from moving, e.g. *I shut the shed door and wedged it with a log of wood.* **2** (noun) A wedge is a piece of something such as wood, metal, or rubber with one pointed edge and one thick edge which is used to wedge something. **3** A wedge is a piece of something that has a thick triangular shape, e.g. *a wedge of cheese.*

wedlock (noun; an old-fashioned word) Wedlock is the state of being married.

Wednesday, Wednesdays (noun) Wednesday is the day between Tuesday and Thursday.

wee, weer, weest (adjective; a Scottish word) very small.

weed, weeds, weeding, weeded 1 (noun) A weed is a wild plant that prevents cultivated plants from growing properly. **2** (verb) If you weed a place, you remove the weeds from it. **weed out** (verb) If you weed out unwanted things, you get rid of them.

week, weeks 1 (noun) A week is a period of seven days, especially one beginning on a Sunday and ending on a Saturday. **2** A week is also the number of hours you spend at work during a week, e.g. *a 35-hour week.* **3** The week can refer to the part of a week that does not include Saturday and Sunday, e.g. *They are working during the week.*

weekday, weekdays (noun) A weekday is any day except Saturday and Sunday.

weekend, weekends (noun) A weekend is Saturday and Sunday.

weekly, weeklies 1 (adjective or adverb) happening or appearing once a week. **2** (noun) A weekly is a newspaper or magazine that is published once a week.

weep, weeps, weeping, wept 1 (verb) If someone weeps, they cry. **2** If something such as a wound weeps, it oozes blood or other liquid.

weevil, weevils (noun) A weevil is a type of beetle which eats grain, seeds, or plants.

weigh, weighs, weighing, weighed 1 (verb) If something weighs a particular amount, that is how heavy it is. **2** If you weigh something, you measure how heavy it is using scales. **3** If you weigh facts or words, you think about them carefully before coming to a decision or before speaking. **4** If a problem weighs on you or weighs upon you, it makes you very worried. **weigh down 1** (verb) If a load weighs you down, it stops you moving easily. **2** If you are weighed down by a difficulty, it is making you very worried. **weigh up** (verb) If you weigh up a person or a situation, you make an assessment of them.

weight, weights, weighting, weighted 1 (noun) The weight of something is its heaviness. **2** A weight is a metal object which has a certain known heaviness. Weights are used with sets of scales in order to weigh things. **3** You can refer to any heavy object as a weight. **4** (verb) If you weight something or weight it down, you make it heavier, often so that it cannot move. **5** (noun) The weight of something is its large amount or importance which makes it hard to fight against or contradict, e.g. *the weight of the law.* **6** (phrase) If you **pull your weight,** you work just as hard as other people involved in the same activity.

weighted (adjective) A system that is weighted in favour of a particular person or group is organized in such a way that this person or group will have an advantage.

weightlifting (noun) Weightlifting is the sport of lifting heavy weights in competition or for exercise. **weightlifter** (noun).

weighty, weightier, weightiest (adjective) serious or important, e.g. *a weighty problem.*

weir, weirs (rhymes with **near**) (noun) A weir is a low dam which is built across a river to raise the water level, control the flow of water, or change its direction.

weird, weirder, weirdest (pronounced **weerd**) (adjective) strange or odd. **weirdly** (adverb).

weirdo, weirdos (pronounced **weer**-doe) (noun; an informal word) If you call someone a weirdo, you mean they behave in a strange way.

welcome, welcomes, welcoming, welcomed 1 (verb) If you welcome a visitor, you greet them in a friendly way when they arrive. **2** 'Welcome' can be said as a greeting to a visitor who has just arrived. **3** (noun) A welcome is a greeting to a visitor, e.g. *a warm welcome.* **4** (adjective) If someone is welcome at a place, they will be warmly received there. **5** If something is welcome, it brings pleasure or is accepted gratefully, e.g. *a welcome rest.* **6** If you tell someone they are welcome to something or welcome to do something, you mean you are willing for them to have or to do it. **7** (verb) If you welcome something, you approve of it and support it, e.g. *He welcomed the decision.* **welcoming** (adjective).

weld, welds, welding, welded (verb) To weld two pieces of metal together means to join them by heating their edges and fixing them together so that when they cool they harden into one piece. **welder** (noun).

welfare 1 (noun) The welfare of a person or group is their general state of health, comfort, and prosperity. **2** Welfare services are provided to help with people's living conditions and financial problems, e.g. *welfare workers.*

welfare state (noun) The welfare state is a system in which the government uses money from taxes to provide health care and education services, and to give benefits to people who are old, unemployed, or sick.

well, better, best; wells, welling, welled 1 (adverb) If something goes well, it happens in a satisfactory way, e.g. *The interview went well.* **2** in a good, skilful, or pleasing way, e.g. *He draws well.* **3** thoroughly and completely, e.g. *well established.* **4** kindly, e.g. *We treat our employees well.* **5** If something may well or could well happen, it is likely to happen. **6** (adjective) If you are well, you are healthy. **7** (adverb) You use well to emphasize an adjective, adverb, or phrase, e.g. *He was well aware of that.* **8** (phrase) **As well** means also, e.g. *He was a bus driver as well.* **9 As well as** means in addition to, e.g. *a meal which includes meat or fish, as well as rice.* **10** If you say you **may as well** or **might as well** do something, you mean you will do it although you are not keen to do it. **11** (noun) A well is a hole drilled in the ground from which water, oil, or gas is obtained. **12** (verb) If tears well or well up, they appear in someone's eyes.

well-advised (adjective) sensible or wise, e.g. *Bill would be well-advised to retire.*

well-balanced (adjective) sensible and without serious emotional problems, e.g. *a well-balanced happy teenager.*

wellbeing (noun) Someone's wellbeing is their health and happiness.

well-earned (adjective) thoroughly deserved.

well-heeled (adjective; an informal word) wealthy.

well-informed (adjective) having a great deal of knowledge about a subject or subjects.

wellington, wellingtons (noun) Wellingtons or wellington boots are long waterproof rubber boots.

well-meaning (adjective) A

well-meaning person tries to be helpful but is often unsuccessful.

well-off (adjective; an informal word) quite wealthy.

well-to-do (adjective) quite wealthy.

well-worn 1 (adjective) A well-worn expression or saying has been used too often and has become boring. **2** A well-worn object or piece of clothing has been used and worn so much that it looks old and shabby.

welly, wellies (noun; an informal word) Wellies are wellingtons.

Welsh 1 (adjective) belonging or relating to Wales. **2** (noun) Welsh is a language spoken in parts of Wales.

Welshman, Welshmen (noun) A Welshman is a man who comes from Wales. **Welshwoman** (noun).

welt, welts (noun) A welt is a raised mark on someone's skin made by a blow from something like a whip or a stick.

welter (noun; a formal word) A welter of things is a large number of them that happen or appear together in a state of confusion, e.g. *a welter of rumours.*

wench, wenches (noun; an old-fashioned word) A wench is a woman or young girl.

wept the past tense and past participle of **weep.**

were a past tense of **be.**

werewolf, werewolves (noun) In horror stories, a werewolf is a person who changes into a wolf.

west 1 (noun) The west is the direction in which you look to see the sun set. **2** The west of a place or country is the part which is towards the west when you are in the centre, e.g. *the west of Scotland.* **3** (adverb or adjective) West means towards the west. **4** (adjective) A west wind blows from the west. **5** (noun) The West refers to the countries of North America and western and southern Europe.

westerly (adjective) Westerly means to or towards the west, e.g. *France's most westerly region.*

western, westerns 1 (adjective) in or from the west. **2** coming from or associated with the countries of North America and western and southern Europe, e.g. *western dress.* **3** (noun) A western is a book or film about life in the west of America in the nineteenth century.

West Indian, West Indians (noun) A West Indian is someone who comes from the West Indies.

westward or **westwards** (adverb) Westward or westwards means towards the west, e.g. *He stared westwards towards the clouds.*

wet, wetter, wettest; wets, wetting, wet or **wetted 1** (adjective) If something is wet, it is covered in water or another liquid. **2** If the weather is wet, it is raining. **3** If something such as paint, ink, or cement is wet, it is not yet dry or solid. **4** (an informal use) If you say someone is wet, you mean they are weak and lack enthusiasm, energy, or confidence, e.g. *Don't be so wet!* **5** (verb)

To wet something means to put water or some other liquid over it. **6** If people wet themselves or wet their beds, they urinate in their clothes or bed because they cannot control their bladder. **wetness** (noun).

wet suit, wet suits (noun) A wet suit is a close-fitting rubber suit which a diver or someone taking part in water sports wears to keep his or her body warm.

whack, whacks, whacking, whacked (verb) If you whack someone or something, you hit them hard.

whale, whales (noun) A whale is a very large sea mammal which breathes out water through a hole on the top of its head.

whaling (noun) Whaling is the work of hunting and killing whales for oil or food.

wharf, wharves (pronounced **worf**) (noun) A wharf is a platform beside a river or the sea, where ships load or unload.

what 1 (pronoun) What is used in questions, e.g. *What time is it?* **2** What is used in indirect questions and statements, e.g. *I don't know what you mean.* **3** What can be used at the beginning of a clause to refer to something with a particular quality, e.g. *It is impossible to decide what is real and what is invented.* **4** (adjective) What can be used at the beginning of a clause to show that you are talking about the whole amount that is available to you, e.g. *Their spouses try to earn what money they can.* **5** You say 'what' to emphasize an opinion or reaction, e.g. *What nonsense!* **6** (phrase) You say **what about** at the beginning of a question when you are making a suggestion or offer, e.g. *What about a drink?*

whatever 1 (pronoun) You use whatever to refer to anything or everything of a particular type, e.g. *He said he would do whatever he could.* **2** (conjunction) You use whatever to mean no matter what, e.g. *Whatever happens, you have to behave decently.* **3** (adverb) You use whatever to emphasize a negative statement or a question, e.g. *You have no proof whatever... Whatever is wrong with you?* **4** (pronoun) You use whatever when you do not know the precise nature of something, e.g. *Whatever it is, I don't like it.*

whatsoever (adverb) You use whatsoever to emphasize a negative statement, e.g. *I have no memory of it whatsoever.*

wheat (noun) Wheat is a cereal plant grown for its grain which is used to make flour.

wheel, wheels, wheeling, wheeled 1 (noun) A wheel is a circular object which turns on a rod attached to its centre. Wheels are fixed underneath vehicles so that they can move along. **2** The wheel of a car is its steering wheel. **3** (verb) If you wheel something such as a bicycle, you push it. **4** If someone or something wheels, they move round in the shape of a circle, e.g. *Cameron wheeled around and hit him.*

wheelbarrow, wheelbarrows (noun) A wheelbarrow is a

small cart with a single wheel at the front, used for carrying things in the garden.

wheelchair, wheelchairs (noun) A wheelchair is a chair with wheels in which sick, injured, or disabled people can move around.

wheeze, wheezes, wheezing, wheezed (verb) If someone wheezes, they breathe with difficulty, making a whistling sound, usually because they have a chest complaint such as asthma. **wheezy** (adjective).

whelk, whelks (noun) A whelk is a snail-like shellfish with a strong shell and a soft edible body.

when 1 (adverb) You use when to ask what time something happened or will happen, e.g. *When are you leaving?* **2** (conjunction) You use when to refer to a time in the past, e.g. *I met him when I was sixteen.* **3** You use when to introduce the reason for an opinion, comment, or question, e.g. *How did you pass the exam when you hadn't studied for it?* **4** When is used to mean although, e.g. *He drives when he could walk.*

whence (adverb or conjunction; an old-fashioned word) Whence means from where.

whenever (conjunction) Whenever means at any time, or every time that something happens, e.g. *I still go on courses whenever I can.*

where 1 (adverb) You use where to ask which place something is in, is coming from, or is going to, e.g. *Where is Philip?* **2** (conjunction) You use where to refer to the place in which something is situated or happening, e.g. *I don't know where we are.* **3** (conjunction, pronoun, or adverb) You use where when asking about or referring to something, e.g. *I hardly know where to begin.* **4** (conjunction) Where can introduce a clause that contrasts with the other part of the sentence, e.g. *A teacher will be listened to, where a parent might not.*

whereabouts 1 (noun) The whereabouts of a person or thing is the place where they are. **2** (adverb) You use whereabouts when you are asking more precisely where something is, e.g. *Whereabouts in Scotland are you from?*

whereas (conjunction) Whereas introduces a comment that contrasts with the other part of the sentence, e.g. *Her eyes were blue, whereas mine were brown.*

whereby (pronoun; a formal word) Whereby means by which, e.g. *a new system whereby you pay the bill quarterly.*

whereupon (conjunction; a formal word) Whereupon means at which point, e.g. *His enemies rejected his message, whereupon he tried again.*

wherever 1 (conjunction) Wherever means in every place or situation, e.g. *Alex heard the same thing wherever he went.* **2** You use wherever to show that you do not know where a place or person is, e.g. *the nearest police station, wherever that is.*

wherewithal (noun) If you have the wherewithal to do

something, you have enough money to do it.

whet, whets, whetting, whetted (phrase) To **whet someone's appetite** for something, means to increase their desire for it.

whether (conjunction) You use whether when you are talking about two or more alternatives, e.g. *I don't know whether that's true or false.*

whey (rhymes with **day**) (noun) Whey is the watery liquid that is separated from the curds in sour milk when cheese is made.

which 1 (adjective or pronoun) You use which to ask about alternatives or to refer to a choice between alternatives, e.g. *Which room are you in?* **2** (pronoun) Which at the beginning of a clause identifies the thing you are talking about or gives more information about it, e.g. *certain wrongs which exist in our society.*

whichever (adjective or pronoun) You use whichever when you are talking about different alternatives or possibilities, e.g. *Make your pizzas round or square, whichever you prefer.*

whiff, whiffs 1 (noun) A whiff of something is a slight smell of it. **2** A whiff is also a slight sign or trace of something, e.g. *a whiff of criticism.*

while, whiles, whiling, whiled 1 (conjunction) If something happens while something else is happening, the two things happen at the same time. **2** While also means but, e.g. *Men tend to gaze more, while women dart quick glances.* **3** (noun) A while is a period of time, e.g. *a little while earlier.* **4** (phrase) If an action or activity is **worth your while,** it will be helpful or useful to you if you do it. **while away** (verb) If you while away the time in a particular way, you pass the time that way because you have nothing else to do.

whilst (conjunction) Whilst means the same as while.

whim, whims (noun) A whim is a sudden desire or fancy.

whimper, whimpers, whimpering, whimpered 1 (verb) When children or animals whimper, they make soft, low, unhappy sounds. **2** If you whimper something, you say it in an unhappy or frightened way, as if you are about to cry.

whimsical (adjective) unusual and slightly playful, e.g. *an endearing, whimsical charm.*

whine, whines, whining, whined 1 (verb) To whine means to make a long, high-pitched noise, especially one which sounds sad or unpleasant. **2** (noun) A whine is the noise made by something or someone whining. **3** (verb) If someone whines about something, they complain about it in an annoying way.

whinge, whinges, whinging or **whingeing, whinged** (verb) If someone whinges about something, they complain about it in an annoying way.

whinny, whinnies, whinnying, whinnied (verb) When a horse whinnies, it neighs softly.

whip, whips, whipping, whipped 1 (noun) A whip is a thin piece of leather or rope attached to a handle, which is used for hitting people or animals. **2** (verb) If you whip a person or animal, you hit them with a whip. **3** When the wind whips something, it strikes it. **4** If you whip something out or off, you take it out or off very quickly, e.g. *She had whipped off her glasses.* **5** If you whip cream or eggs, you beat them until they are thick and frothy or stiff. **whip up** (verb) If you whip up a strong emotion, you make people feel it, e.g. *The thought whipped up his temper.*

whiplash injury, whiplash injuries (noun) A whiplash injury is a neck injury caused by your head suddenly jerking forwards and then back again, for example in a car accident.

whippet, whippets (noun) A whippet is a small, thin dog used for racing.

whirl, whirls, whirling, whirled 1 (verb) When something whirls, or when you whirl it round, it turns round very fast. **2** (noun) You can refer to a lot of intense activity as a whirl of activity.

whirlpool, whirlpools (noun) A whirlpool is a small circular area in a river or the sea where the water is moving quickly round and round so that objects floating near it are pulled into its centre.

whirlwind, whirlwinds 1 (noun) A whirlwind is a tall column of air which spins round and round very fast. **2** (adjective) more rapid than usual, e.g. *a whirlwind tour.*

whirr, whirrs, whirring, whirred; also spelled **whir 1** (verb) When something such as a machine whirrs, it makes a series of low sounds so fast that it sounds like one continuous sound. **2** (noun) A whirr is the noise made by something whirring.

whisk, whisks, whisking, whisked 1 (verb) If you whisk someone or something somewhere, you take them there quickly, e.g. *We were whisked away into a private room.* **2** If you whisk eggs or cream, you stir air into them quickly. **3** (noun) A whisk is a kitchen tool used for quickly stirring air into eggs or cream.

whisker, whiskers (noun) The whiskers of an animal such as a cat or mouse are the long, stiff hairs near its mouth.

whisky, whiskies (noun) Whisky is a strong alcoholic drink made from grain such as barley.

whisper, whispers, whispering, whispered 1 (verb) When you whisper, you talk to someone very quietly, using your breath and not your throat. **2** (noun) If you talk in a whisper, you whisper.

whist (noun) Whist is a card game for four players in which one pair of players tries to win more tricks than the other pair.

whistle, whistles, whistling, whistled 1 (verb) When you whistle a tune or whistle, you produce a clear musical sound by forcing your breath out between your lips. **2** If something whistles, it makes a loud, high sound, e.g. *The kettle whistled.* **3** (noun) A whistle is the sound something or someone makes when they whistle. **4** A whistle is also a small metal tube that you blow into to produce a whistling sound.

whit (noun; a formal use) You say 'not a whit' or 'no whit' to emphasize that something is not the case at all, e.g. *It does not matter one whit to the customer.*

white, whiter, whitest; whites 1 (noun or adjective) White is the lightest possible colour. **2** Someone who is white has a pale skin and is of European origin. **3** (adjective) If someone goes white, their face becomes very pale because they are afraid, shocked, or ill. **4** White coffee contains milk or cream. **5** (noun) The white of an egg is the transparent liquid surrounding the yolk. **whiteness** (noun).

white lie, white lies (noun) A white lie is a harmless lie, especially one told to prevent someone's feelings from being hurt.

whitewash 1 (noun) Whitewash is a mixture of lime and water used for painting walls white. **2** A whitewash is an attempt to hide unpleasant facts, e.g. *the refusal to accept official whitewash in the enquiry.*

whither (adverb or conjunction; an old-fashioned word) Whither means to what place.

whiting (noun) A whiting is a sea fish related to the cod.

whittle, whittles, whittling, whittled (verb) If you whittle a piece of wood, you shape it by shaving or cutting small pieces off it. **whittle away** or **whittle down** (verb) To whittle away at something or to whittle it down means to make it smaller or less effective, e.g. *The 250 entrants had been whittled down to 34.*

whizz, whizzes, whizzing, whizzed; also spelled **whiz** (verb; an informal word) If you whizz somewhere, you move there quickly, e.g. *We whizzed across the King's Road.*

who 1 (pronoun) You use who when you are asking about someone's identity, e.g. *Who gave you that black eye?* **2** Who at the beginning of a clause refers to the person or people you are talking about, e.g. *a shipyard worker who wants to be a postman.*

whoa (pronounced **woh**) (interjection) Whoa is a command used to slow down or stop a horse.

whoever 1 (pronoun) Whoever means the person who, e.g. *Whoever bought it for you has to make the claim.* **2** Whoever also means no matter who, e.g. *I pity him, whoever he is.* **3** Whoever is used in questions as an emphatic form of who, e.g. *Whoever thought of such a thing?*

whole, wholes 1 (noun or adjective) The whole of something is all of it, e.g. *the whole of Africa... Have the whole cake.* **2** (adverb) in one piece, e.g. *He swallowed it whole.* **3** (phrase) You use **as a whole** to emphasize that you are talking about all of something, e.g. *The country as a whole is in a very odd mood.* **4** You say **on the whole** to mean that something is generally true, e.g. *On the whole, we should be glad they are gone.* **wholeness** (noun).

wholehearted (adjective) enthusiastic and totally sincere, e.g. *wholehearted approval.* **wholeheartedly** (adverb).

wholemeal (adjective) Wholemeal flour is made from the complete grain of the wheat plant, including the husk.

wholesale 1 (adjective or adverb) Wholesale refers to the activity of buying goods cheaply in large quantities and selling them again, especially to shopkeepers, e.g. *We buy fruit and vegetables wholesale.* **2** (adjective) Wholesale also means done to an excessive extent, e.g. *the wholesale destruction of wild plant species.* **wholesaler** (noun).

wholesome (adjective) good and likely to improve your life, behaviour, or health, e.g. *good wholesome entertainment.*

wholly (pronounced **hoe**-lee) (adverb) completely.

whom (pronoun) Whom is the object form of 'who', e.g. *the girl whom Albert would marry.*

whoop, whoops, whooping, whooped 1 (verb) If you whoop, you shout loudly in a happy or excited way. **2** (noun) A whoop is a loud cry of happiness or excitement, e.g. *whoops of delight.*

whooping cough (pronounced **hoop**-ing) (noun) Whooping cough is an acute infectious disease which makes people cough violently and produce a loud sound when they breathe.

whore, whores (pronounced **hore**) (noun; an offensive word) A whore is a prostitute, or a woman believed to act like a prostitute.

whose 1 (pronoun) You use whose to ask who something belongs to, e.g. *Whose gun is this?* **2** You use whose at the beginning of a clause which gives information about something relating or belonging to the thing or person you have just mentioned, e.g. *a wealthy gentleman whose marriage is breaking up.*

why (adverb or pronoun) You use why when you are asking about the reason for something, or talking about it, e.g. *Why did you do it?.. He wondered why she suddenly looked happier.*

wick, wicks (noun) The wick of a candle is the cord in the middle, which you set alight.

wicked 1 (adjective) very bad, e.g. *a wicked thing to do.* **2** mischievous in an amusing or attractive way, e.g. *a wicked sense of humour.* **wickedly** (adverb), **wickedness** (noun).

wicker (adjective) A wicker basket or chair is made from twigs, canes, or reeds that have been woven together.

wicket, wickets 1 (noun) In cricket, the wicket is one of the two sets of stumps and bails at which the bowler aims the ball. **2** The grass between the wickets on a cricket pitch is also called the wicket.

wide, wider, widest 1 (adjective) measuring a large distance from one side to the other. **2** (adverb) If you open or spread something wide, you open it to its fullest extent. **3** (adjective) If there is a wide variety, range, or selection of something, there are many different kinds of it, e.g. *a wide range of colours.* **widely** (adverb).

wide-awake (adjective) completely awake.

widen, widens, widening, widened 1 (verb) If something widens or if you widen it, it becomes bigger from one side to the other. **2** You can say that something widens when it becomes greater in size or scope, e.g. *the opportunity to widen your outlook.*

wide-ranging (adjective) extending over a variety of different things or over a large area, e.g. *a wide-ranging survey.*

widespread (adjective) existing or happening over a large area or to a great extent, e.g. *the widespread use of chemicals.*

widow, widows (noun) A widow is a woman whose husband has died.

widowed (adjective) If someone is widowed, their husband or wife has died.

widower, widowers (noun) A widower is a man whose wife has died.

width, widths (noun) The width of something is the distance from one side or edge to the other.

wield, wields, wielding, wielded (pronounced **weeld**) **1** (verb) If you wield a weapon or tool, you carry it and use it. **2** If someone wields power, they have it and are able to use it.

wife, wives (noun) A man's wife is the woman he is married to.

wig, wigs (noun) A wig is a false head of hair worn to cover someone's own hair or to hide their baldness.

wiggle, wiggles, wiggling, wiggled 1 (verb) If you wiggle something, you move it up and down or from side to side with small jerky movements. **2** (noun) A wiggle is a small jerky movement or line.

wigwam, wigwams (noun) A wigwam is a kind of tent used by North American Indians.

wild, wilder, wildest; wilds 1 (adjective) Wild animals, birds, and plants live and grow in natural surroundings and are not looked after by people. **2** Wild land is natural and uncultivated, e.g. *wild areas of countryside.* **3** (noun) The wild is a free and natural state of living, e.g. *There are about 200 left in the wild.* **4** The wilds are remote areas where few people live, far away from towns. **5** (adjective) Wild weather or sea is stormy and rough. **6** Wild behaviour is excited and uncontrolled, e.g. *wild with excitement.* **7** A wild idea or scheme is original and crazy. **wildly** (adverb).

wilderness, wildernesses (noun) A wilderness is an area of natural land which is not cultivated.

wildfire (noun) If something spreads like wildfire, it spreads very quickly.

wild-goose chase, wild-goose chases (noun) A wild-goose chase is a hopeless or useless search.

wildlife (noun) Wildlife means

wild animals and plants.

Wild West (noun) The Wild West was the western part of the United States when it was first being settled by Europeans.

wiles (plural noun) Wiles are clever or crafty tricks used to persuade people to do something.

wilful 1 (adjective) Wilful actions or attitudes are deliberate and often intended to hurt someone, e.g. *wilful damage*. **2** Someone who is wilful is obstinate and determined to get their own way, e.g. *a wilful little boy*. **wilfully** (adverb).

will, wills, willing, willed 1 (verb) You use will to form the future tense, e.g. *Robin will be quite annoyed*. **2** You use will to say that you intend to do something, e.g. *I will not deceive you*. **3** You use will when inviting someone to do or have something, e.g. *Will you have another coffee?* **4** You use will when asking or telling someone to do something, e.g. *Will you do me a favour?.. You will do as I say*. **5** You use will to say that you are assuming something to be the case, e.g. *As you will have gathered, I was surprised*. **6** (noun) Will is the determination to do something, e.g. *the will to win*. **7** If something is the will of a person or group, they want it to happen, e.g. *the will of the people*. **8** (phrase) If you can do something **at will**, you can do it whenever you want. **9** (verb) If you will something to happen, you try to make it happen by mental effort, e.g. *I willed my eyes to open*. **10** (noun) A will is a legal document in which you say what you want to happen to your money and property when you die. **11** (verb) If you will something to someone, you leave it to them when you die, e.g. *Penbrook Farm is willed to her*.

willing 1 (adjective) If you are willing to do something, you will do it if someone wants you to. **2** Someone who is willing is eager and enthusiastic, e.g. *a willing helper*. **willingly** (adverb), **willingness** (noun).

willow, willows (noun) A willow or willow tree is a tree with long, thin branches and narrow leaves that often grows near water.

wilt, wilts, wilting, wilted 1 (verb) If a plant wilts, it droops because it needs more water or is dying. **2** If someone wilts, they gradually lose strength or confidence, e.g. *James visibly wilted under pressure*.

wily, wilier, wiliest (pronounced **wie**-lee) (adjective) clever and cunning.

wimp, wimps (noun; an informal word) If you call someone a wimp, you mean they are feeble and timid.

win, wins, winning, won 1 (verb) If you win a fight, game, or argument, you defeat your opponent. **2** (noun) A win is a victory in a game or contest. **3** (verb) If you win a prize, you get it as a reward for succeeding in something. **4** If you win something you want, such as approval or support, you succeed in getting it

win over (verb) If you win someone over, you persuade them to support you.

wince, winces, wincing, winced (verb) When you wince, the muscles of your face tighten suddenly because of pain, fear, or distress.

winch, winches, winching, winched 1 (noun) A winch is a machine used to lift heavy objects. It consists of a cylinder around which a rope or chain is wound. **2** (verb) If you winch an object or person somewhere, you lift, lower, or pull them using a winch.

wind, winds (rhymes with **tinned**) **1** (noun) A wind is a current of air moving across the earth's surface. **2** Your wind is the ability to breathe easily, e.g. *Brown had recovered her wind.* **3** Wind is air swallowed with food or drink, or gas produced in your stomach, which causes discomfort. **4** The wind section of an orchestra is the group of musicians who play wind instruments.

wind, winds, winding, wound (rhymes with **mind**) **1** (verb) If a road or river winds in a particular direction, it twists and turns in that direction. **2** When you wind something round something else, you wrap it round it several times. **3** When you wind a clock or machine or wind it up, you turn a key or handle several times to make it work. **wind up 1** (verb) When you wind up something such as an activity or a business, you finish it or close it. **2** If you wind up in a particular place, you end up there.

windfall, windfalls (noun) A windfall is a sum of money that you receive unexpectedly.

wind instrument, wind instruments (noun) A wind instrument is an instrument you play by using your breath, for example a flute, an oboe, or a trumpet.

windmill, windmills (noun) A windmill is a machine for grinding grain or pumping water. It is driven by vanes or sails turned by the wind.

window, windows (noun) A window is a space in a wall or roof or in the side of a vehicle, usually with glass in it so that light can pass through and people can see in or out.

window box, window boxes (noun) A window box is a long, narrow container on a windowsill in which plants are grown.

windowsill, windowsills (noun) A windowsill is a ledge along the bottom of a window, either on the inside or outside of a building.

windpipe, windpipes (noun) Your windpipe is the tube which carries air into your lungs when you breathe.

windscreen, windscreens (noun) The windscreen of a vehicle is the glass at the front through which the driver looks.

windsurfing (noun) Windsurfing is the sport of moving along the surface of the sea or a lake standing on a board with a sail on it.

windswept (adjective) A windswept place is exposed to strong winds, e.g. *a windswept* *beach.*

windy, windier, windiest (adjective) If it is windy, there is a lot of wind.

wine, wines (noun) Wine is the red or white alcoholic drink which is normally made from grapes.

wing, wings 1 (noun) A bird's or insect's wings are the parts of its body that it uses for flying. **2** An aeroplane's wings are the long, flat parts on each side that support it while it is in the air. **3** A wing of a building is a part which sticks out from the main part or which has been added later. **4** A wing of an organization, especially a political party, is a group within it with a particular role or particular beliefs, e.g. *the left wing of the party.* **5** (plural noun) The wings in a theatre are the sides of the stage which are hidden from the audience. **winged** (adjective).

wink, winks, winking, winked 1 (verb) When you wink, you close one eye briefly, often as a signal that something is a joke or a secret. **2** (noun) A wink is the closing of your eye when you wink.

winkle, winkles (noun) A winkle is a small sea-snail with a hard shell and a soft edible body.

winner, winners (noun) The winner of a prize, race, or competition is the person or thing that wins it.

winning 1 (adjective) The winning team or entry in a competition is the one that has won. **2** (plural noun) Your winnings are the money you have won in a competition or by gambling. **3** (adjective) attractive and charming, e.g. *a winning smile.*

winter, winters (noun) Winter is the season between autumn and spring.

wintry (adjective) Something wintry has features that are typical of winter, e.g. *the wintry dawn.*

wipe, wipes, wiping, wiped 1 (verb) If you wipe something, you rub its surface lightly to remove dirt or liquid. **2** If you wipe dirt or liquid off something, you remove it using a cloth or your hands, e.g. *Dot wiped the tears from her eyes.* **wipe out** (verb) To wipe out people or places means to destroy them completely.

wire, wires, wiring, wired 1 (noun) Wire is metal in the form of a long, thin, flexible thread which can be used to make or fasten things or to conduct an electric current. **2** (verb) If you wire one thing to another, you fasten them together using wire. **3** If you wire something or wire it up, you connect it so that electricity can pass through it. **wired** (adjective).

wireless, wirelesses (noun; an old-fashioned word) A wireless is a radio.

wiring (noun) The wiring in a building is the system of wires that supply electricity to the rooms.

wiry, wirier, wiriest 1 (adjective) Wiry people are thin but with strong muscles. **2** Wiry things are stiff and rough to the touch, e.g. *wiry hair.*

wisdom 1 (noun) Wisdom is

the ability to use experience and knowledge in order to make sensible decisions or judgments. **2** If you talk about the wisdom of an action or a decision, you are talking about how sensible it is.

wisdom tooth, wisdom teeth (noun) Your wisdom teeth are the four molar teeth at the back of your mouth which grow much later than other teeth.

wise, wiser, wisest 1 (adjective) Someone who is wise can use their experience and knowledge to make sensible decisions and judgments. **2** (phrase) If you say that someone is **none the wiser** or **no wiser,** you mean that they know no more about something than they did before, e.g. *I left the conference none the wiser.*

wisecrack, wisecracks (noun) A wisecrack is a clever remark, intended to be amusing but often unkind.

wish, wishes, wishing, wished 1 (noun) A wish is a longing or desire for something, often something difficult to achieve or obtain. **2** A wish is something desired or wanted, e.g. *That wish came true two years later.* **3** (plural noun) Good wishes are expressions of hope that someone will be happy or successful, e.g. *best wishes on your birthday.* **4** (verb) If you wish to do something, you want to do it, e.g. *We wished to return.* **5** If you wish something were the case, you would like it to be the case, but know it is not very likely, e.g. *I wish I were tall.*

wishbone, wishbones (noun) A wishbone is a V-shaped bone in the breast of most birds.

wishful thinking (noun) If someone's hope or wish is wishful thinking, it is unlikely to come true.

wishy-washy (adjective; an informal word) If a person or their ideas are wishy-washy, then their ideas are not firm or clear, e.g. *wishy-washy reasons.*

wisp, wisps 1 (noun) A wisp of grass or hair is a small, thin, untidy bunch of it. **2** A wisp of smoke is a long, thin streak of it. **wispy** (adjective).

wistful (adjective) sadly thinking about something, especially something you want but cannot have, e.g. *A wistful look came into her eyes.* **wistfully** (adverb).

wit, wits 1 (noun) Wit is the ability to use words or ideas in an amusing and clever way. **2** Wit means sense, e.g. *They haven't got the wit to realize what they're doing.* **3** (plural noun) Your wits are the ability to think and act quickly in a difficult situation, e.g. *the man who lived by his wits.* **4** (phrase) If someone is **at their wits' end,** they are so worried and exhausted by problems or difficulties that they do not know what to do.

witch, witches (noun) A witch is a woman claimed to have magic powers and to be able to use them for good or evil.

witchcraft (noun) Witchcraft is the skill or art of using magic powers, especially evil ones.

witch doctor, witch doctors (noun) A witch doctor is a

man in some societies, especially in Africa, who appears to have magic powers.

with 1 (preposition) With someone means in their company, e.g. *He was at home with me.* **2** With is used to show who your opponent is in a fight or competition, e.g. *next week's game with Chelsea.* **3** With can mean using or having, e.g. *Apply the colour with a brush... a bloke with a moustache.* **4** With is used to show how someone does something or how they feel, e.g. *She looked at him with hatred.* **5** With can mean concerning, e.g. *a problem with her telephone bill.* **6** With is used to show support, e.g. *Are you with us or against us?*

withdraw, withdraws, withdrawing, withdrew, withdrawn 1 (verb) If you withdraw something, you remove it or take it out, e.g. *He withdrew the money from his bank.* **2** If you withdraw to another place, you leave where you are and go there, e.g. *He withdrew to his study.* **3** If you withdraw from an activity, you back out of it, e.g. *They withdrew from the conference.*

withdrawal, withdrawals 1 (noun) The withdrawal of something is the act of taking it away, e.g. *the withdrawal of Russian troops.* **2** The withdrawal of a statement is the act of saying formally that you wish to change or deny it. **3** A withdrawal is an amount of money you take from your bank or building society account.

withdrawal symptoms (plural noun) Withdrawal symptoms are the unpleasant effects suffered by someone who has suddenly stopped taking a drug to which they are addicted.

withdrawn 1 Withdrawn is the past participle of **withdraw. 2** (adjective) unusually shy or quiet.

wither, withers, withering, withered 1 (verb) When something withers or withers away, it becomes weaker until it no longer exists. **2** If a plant withers, it wilts or shrivels up and dies.

withering (adjective) A withering look or remark makes you feel ashamed, stupid, or inferior.

withhold, withholds, withholding, withheld (verb; a formal word) If you withhold something that someone wants, you do not let them have it.

within 1 (preposition or adverb) Within means in or inside. **2** (preposition) Within can mean not going beyond certain limits, e.g. *Stay within the budget.* **3** Within can mean before a period of time has passed, e.g. *You must write back within fourteen days.*

without 1 (preposition) Without means not having, feeling, or showing, e.g. *Didier looked on without emotion.* **2** Without can mean not using, e.g. *You can't get in without a key.* **3** Without can mean not in someone's company, e.g. *He went without me.* **4** Without can indicate that something does not happen when something else happens, e.g. *Stone signalled the ship, again with-*

out response.

withstand, withstands, withstanding, withstood (verb) When something or someone withstands a force or action, they survive it or do not give in to it, e.g. *ships designed to withstand the North Atlantic winter.*

witness, witnesses, witnessing, witnessed 1 (noun) A witness is someone who has seen an event such as an accident and can describe what happened. **2** A witness is also someone who appears in a court of law to say what they know about a crime or other event. **3** A witness is also someone who writes their name on a document that someone else has signed, to confirm that it is really that person's signature. **4** (verb; a formal use) If you witness an event, you see it.

witticism, witticisms (pronounced **wit**-tiss-izm) (noun) A witticism is a clever and amusing remark or joke.

witty, wittier, wittiest (adjective) amusing in a clever way, e.g. *this witty novel.* **wittily** (adverb).

wives the plural of **wife**.

wizard, wizards (noun) A wizard is a man in a fairy story who has magic powers.

wizened (pronounced **wiz**-nd) (adjective) having a wrinkled skin, especially with age, e.g. *a wizened old man.*

wobble, wobbles, wobbling, wobbled (verb) If something wobbles, it shakes or moves from side to side because it is loose or unsteady, e.g. *a cyclist who wobbled into my path.*

wobbly (adjective) unsteady, e.g. *a wobbly table.*

woe, woes (a literary word) **1** (noun) Woe is great unhappiness or sorrow. **2** (plural noun) Someone's woes are their problems or misfortunes.

wok, woks (noun) A wok is a large bowl-shaped metal pan used for Chinese-style cooking.

woke the past tense of **wake**.

woken the past participle of **wake**.

wolf, wolves; wolfs, wolfing, wolfed 1 (noun) A wolf is a wild animal related to the dog that hunts in packs and kills other animals for food. **2** (verb; an informal use) If you wolf food or wolf it down, you eat it up quickly and greedily.

woman, women 1 (noun) A woman is an adult female human being. **2** Woman can refer to women in general, e.g. *man's inhumanity to woman.*

womanhood (noun) Womanhood is the state of being a woman rather than a girl, e.g. *on the verge of womanhood.*

womb, wombs (pronounced **woom**) (noun) A woman's womb is the part inside her body where her unborn baby grows.

wombat, wombats (pronounced **wom**-bat) (noun) A wombat is a short-legged furry Australian animal which eats plants.

wonder, wonders, wondering, wondered 1 (verb) If you wonder about something, you think about it with curiosity or doubt. **2** If you wonder at something, you are surprised and amazed at it, e.g. *He wondered at her anger.* **3** (noun)

Wonder is a feeling of surprise and amazement. **4** A wonder is something or someone that surprises and amazes people, e.g. *the wonders of science.*

wonderful 1 (adjective) making you feel very happy and pleased, e.g. *It was wonderful to be together.* **2** very impressive, e.g. *Nature is a wonderful thing.* **wonderfully** (adverb).

wondrous (adjective; a literary word) amazing and impressive.

wont (rhymes with **don't**) (adjective; an old-fashioned word) If someone is wont to do something, they do it often, e.g. *a gesture he was wont to use when preaching.*

woo, woos, wooing, wooed 1 (verb) If you woo people, you try to get them to help or support you, e.g. *attempts to woo the women's vote.* **2** (an old-fashioned use) When a man woos a woman, he tries to get her to marry him.

wood, woods 1 (noun) Wood is the substance which forms the trunks and branches of trees. **2** A wood is a large area of trees growing near each other.

wooded (adjective) covered in trees, e.g. *a wooded area nearby.*

wooden (adjective) made of wood, e.g. *a wooden box.*

woodland, woodlands (noun) Woodland is land that is mostly covered with trees.

woodpecker, woodpeckers (noun) A woodpecker is a climbing bird with a long, sharp beak that it uses to drill holes into trees to find insects.

woodwind (adjective) Woodwind instruments are musical instruments such as flutes, oboes, clarinets, and bassoons, that are played by being blown into.

woodwork 1 (noun) Woodwork refers to the parts of a house, such as stairs, doors or window-frames, that are made of wood. **2** Woodwork is the craft or skill of making things out of wood.

woodworm, woodworm or **woodworms 1** (noun) Woodworm are the larvae of a kind of beetle. They make holes in wood by feeding on it. **2** Woodworm is damage caused to wood by woodworm making holes in it.

woody, woodier, woodiest 1 (adjective) Woody plants have hard tough stems. **2** A woody area has a lot of trees in it.

woof, woofs (noun) A woof is the sound that a dog makes when it barks.

wool, wools 1 (noun) Wool is the hair that grows on sheep and some other animals. **2** Wool is also yarn spun from the wool of animals which is used to knit, weave, and make such things as clothes, blankets, and carpets.

woollen, woollens 1 (adjective) made from wool. **2** (noun) Woollens are clothes made of wool.

woolly, woollier, woolliest 1 (adjective) made of wool or looking like wool, e.g. *a woolly hat.* **2** If you describe people or their thoughts as woolly, you mean that they seem confused and unclear.

word, words, wording, worded

1 (noun) A word is a single unit of language in speech or writing which has a meaning. **2** A word can mean something brief said, such as a remark, statement, or conversation, e.g. *a word of praise... Could I have a word?* **3** A word can also be a message, e.g. *The word is that Sharon is exhausted.* **4** Your word is a promise, e.g. *He gave me his word.* **5** A word can mean a command, e.g. *Wait till I give the word.* **6** (verb) When you word something, you choose your words in order to express your ideas accurately or acceptably, e.g. *the best way to word our invitations.* **7** (plural noun) The words of a play or song are the spoken or sung text.

wording (noun) The wording of a piece of writing or a speech is the words used in it, especially when these words have been carefully chosen to have a certain effect.

word processor, word processors (noun) A word processor is an electronic machine which has a keyboard and a visual display unit and which is used to produce, store, and organize printed material.

work, works, working, worked **1** (verb) People who work have a job which they are paid to do, e.g. *My husband works for a national newspaper.* **2** (noun) People who have work or who are in work have a job which they are paid to do, e.g. *She's trying to find work.* **3** Work is the tasks that have to be done. **4** (verb) When you work, you do the tasks that your job involves. **5** (noun) A work is something done or made, e.g. *a work of art.* **6** (verb) To work the land means to cultivate it. **7** If someone works a machine, they control or operate it. **8** If a machine works, it operates properly and effectively, e.g. *The radio doesn't work.* **9** If something such as an idea or a system works, it is successful, e.g. *The housing benefit system is not working.* **10** If something works its way into a particular position, it gradually moves there, e.g. *The cable had worked loose.* **11** (noun) A works is a place where something is made by an industrial process, e.g. *the old steel works.* **12** (plural noun) Works are large scale building, digging, or general construction activities, e.g. *road works.* **work out** **1** (verb) If you work out a solution to a problem, you find the solution. **2** If a situation works out in a particular way, it happens in that way. **work up** **1** (verb) If you work up to something, you gradually progress towards it. **2** If you work yourself up or work someone else up, you make yourself or the other person very upset or angry about something. **worked up** (adjective).

workable (adjective) Something workable can operate successfully or can be used for a particular purpose, e.g. *a workable solution.*

workaholic, workaholics (noun) A workaholic is a person who finds it difficult to stop working and do other things.

worker, workers (noun) A worker is a person employed in a particular industry or business, e.g. *a defence worker.*
workforce, workforces (noun) The workforce is the number of people who work in a particular industry, company, region, or country.
workhouse, workhouses (noun) In the past a workhouse was a building to which very poor people were sent and made to work in return for food and shelter.
working, workings 1 (adjective) Working people have jobs which they are paid to do. **2** Working can mean related to, used for, or suitable for work, e.g. *the working week... working conditions.* **3** Working can mean sufficient to be useful or to achieve what is required, e.g. *a working knowledge of Hebrew.* **4** (plural noun) The workings of a piece of equipment, an organization, or a system are the ways in which it operates, e.g. *the workings of the European Union.*
working class, working classes (noun) The working class or working classes are the group of people in society who do not own much property and who do jobs which involve physical rather than intellectual skills.
workload, workloads (noun) The workload of a person or a machine is the amount of work that they have to do.
workman, workmen (noun) A workman is a man whose job involves using physical rather than intellectual skills.
workmanship (noun) Workmanship is the skill with which something is made or a job completed.
workmate, workmates (noun) Someone's workmate is the fellow worker with whom they do their job.
workout, workouts (noun) A workout is a session of physical exercise or training.
workshop, workshops 1 (noun) A workshop is a room or building that contains tools or machinery used for making or repairing things, e.g. *an engineering workshop.* **2** A workshop on a particular subject is a period of discussion or practical work in which a group of people learn about the subject, e.g. *a theatre workshop.*
world, worlds 1 (noun) The world is the earth, the planet we live on. **2** You can use world to refer to people generally, e.g. *The eyes of the world are upon me.* **3** Someone's world is the life they lead and the things they experience, e.g. *We come from different worlds.* **4** (adjective) World is used to describe someone or something that is one of the best or most important of its kind, e.g. *a world leader.* **5** (noun) A world is a division or section of the earth, its history, or its people, such as the Arab World, or the Ancient World. **6** A particular world is a field of activity and the people involved in it, e.g. *the world of football.* **7** (phrase) If you **think the world** of someone, you like or admire them very much.
worldly, worldlier, worldliest 1 (adjective) relating to the ordi-

nary activities of life rather than spiritual things, e.g. *opportunities for worldly pleasures.* **2** experienced and knowledgeable about life.

world war, world wars (noun) A world war is a war that involves countries all over the world.

worldwide (adjective) throughout the world, e.g. *a worldwide increase in skin cancers.*

worm, worms, worming, wormed 1 (noun) A worm is a small thin animal without bones or legs, which lives in the soil or off other creatures. **2** A worm is an insect such as a beetle or moth at a very early stage in its life. **3** (verb) If you worm an animal, you give it medicine in order to kill the worms that are living as parasites in its intestines. **worm out** (verb) If you worm information out of someone, you gradually persuade them to give you it.

worn 1 Worn is the past participle of **wear**. **2** (adjective) damaged or thin because of long use. **3** looking old or exhausted, e.g. *Her husband looks frail and worn.*

worn-out 1 (adjective) used until it is too thin or too damaged to be of further use, e.g. *a worn-out cardigan.* **2** extremely tired, e.g. *You must be worn-out after the drive.*

worried (adjective) unhappy and anxious about a problem or about something unpleasant that might happen.

worry, worries, worrying, worried 1 (verb) If you worry, you feel anxious, fearful, and uneasy about a problem or about something unpleasant that might happen. **2** If something worries you, it causes you to feel uneasy or fearful, e.g. *a puzzle which had worried her all her life.* **3** If you worry someone with a problem, you disturb or bother them by telling them about it, e.g. *I didn't want to worry the boys with this.* **4** If a dog worries sheep or other animals, it frightens or harms them by chasing them or biting them. **5** (noun) Worry is a feeling of unhappiness and unease caused by a problem or by thinking of something unpleasant that might happen, e.g. *the major source of worry.* **6** A worry is a person or thing that causes you to feel anxious or uneasy, e.g. *Inflation is the least of our worries.* **worrying** (adjective).

worse 1 (adjective or adverb) Worse is the comparative form of **bad** and **badly. 2** If someone who is ill gets worse, they become more ill than before. **3** (phrase) If someone or something is **none the worse** for something, they have not been harmed by it, e.g. *He appeared none the worse for the accident.*

worsen, worsens, worsening, worsened (verb) If a situation worsens, it becomes more difficult or unpleasant, e.g. *My relationship with my mother worsened.*

worse off (adjective) If you are worse off, you have less money or are in a more unpleasant situation than before, e.g. *There are people much worse off than me.*

worship, worships, worship-

ping, worshipped 1 (verb) If you worship a god, you show your love and respect by praying or singing hymns. **2** If you worship someone or something, you love them or admire them very much. **3** (noun) Worship is the feeling of respect, love, or admiration you feel for something or someone. **worshipper** (noun).

worst (adjective or adverb) Worst is the superlative of **bad** and **badly**.

worth 1 (preposition) If something is worth a sum of money, it has that value, e.g. *a house worth £85,000.* **2** If something is worth doing, it deserves to be done. **3** (noun) A particular amount of money's worth of something is the quantity of it that you can buy for that money, e.g. *£5's worth of petrol.* **4** Someone's worth is the value, usefulness, or importance they are considered to have.

worthless (adjective) having no real value or use, e.g. *a worthless piece of junk.*

worthwhile (adjective) important enough to justify the time, money, or effort spent on it, e.g. *a worthwhile career.*

worthy, worthier, worthiest (adjective) If someone or something is worthy of something, they deserve it, e.g. *a worthy champion.*

would 1 (verb) You use would to say what someone thought was going to happen, e.g. *We were sure it would be a success.* **2** You use would when you are referring to the result or effect of a possible situation, e.g. *If readers can help I would be most grateful.* **3** You use would when referring to someone's willingness to do something, e.g. *I wouldn't change places with him if you paid me.* **4** You use would in polite questions, e.g. *Would you like some lunch?*

would-be (adjective) wanting to be or claiming to be, e.g. *a would-be pop singer.*

wound, wounds, wounding, wounded 1 (noun) A wound is an injury to part of your body, especially a cut in your skin and flesh. **2** (verb) If someone wounds you, they damage your body using a gun, knife, or other weapon. **3** If you are wounded by what someone says or does, your feelings are hurt. **wounded** (adjective).

wow (interjection) Wow is an expression of admiration or surprise.

WPC, WPCs (noun) A WPC is a female member of the police force. WPC is an abbreviation for 'woman police constable'.

wrangle, wrangles, wrangling, wrangled 1 (verb) If you wrangle with someone, you argue noisily or angrily, often about something unimportant. **2** (noun) A wrangle is an argument that is difficult to settle. **wrangling** (noun).

wrap, wraps, wrapping, wrapped 1 (verb) If you wrap something or wrap something up, you fold a piece of paper or cloth tightly around it to cover or enclose it. **2** If you wrap paper or cloth round something, you put or fold the paper round it. **3** If you wrap your arms, fingers, or legs round something, you coil them round it. **wrap up** (verb) If you wrap up, you put warm clothes on.

wrapped up (adjective; an informal use) If you are wrapped up in a person or thing, you give that person or thing all your attention.

wrapper, wrappers (noun) A wrapper is a piece of paper, plastic, or foil which covers and protects something that you buy, e.g. *sweet wrappers.*

wrapping, wrappings (noun) Wrapping is the material used to cover and protect something.

wrath (pronounced **roth**) (noun; a literary word) Wrath is great anger, e.g. *the wrath of his father.*

wreak, wreaks, wreaking, wreaked (pronounced **reek**) (verb) To wreak havoc or damage means to cause it.

wreath, wreaths (pronounced **reeth**) (noun) A wreath is an arrangement of flowers and leaves, often in the shape of a circle, which is put on a grave as a sign of remembrance for the dead person.

wreck, wrecks, wrecking, wrecked 1 (verb) If someone wrecks something, they break it, destroy it, or spoil it completely. **2** If a ship is wrecked, it has been so badly damaged that it can no longer sail. **3** (noun) A wreck is a ship, car, plane, or other vehicle which has been badly damaged in an accident. **4** If you say someone is a wreck, you mean that they are in a very poor physical or mental state of health and cannot cope with life. **wrecked** (adjective).

wreckage (noun) Wreckage is what remains after something has been badly damaged or destroyed.

wren, wrens (noun) A wren is a very small brown songbird.

wrench, wrenches, wrenching, wrenched 1 (verb) If you wrench something, you give it a sudden and violent twist or pull, e.g. *Nick wrenched open the door.* **2** If you wrench a limb or a joint, you twist and injure it. **3** (noun) A wrench is a metal tool with parts which can be adjusted to fit around nuts or bolts to loosen or tighten them. **4** If a parting from someone or something is a wrench, it is a painful parting to make.

wrest, wrests, wresting, wrested (pronounced **rest**) (verb; a formal word) If you wrest something from someone else you take it from them violently or with effort, e.g. *to try and wrest control of the island from the Mafia.*

wrestle, wrestles, wrestling, wrestled 1 (verb) If you wrestle someone or wrestle with them, you fight them by holding or throwing them, but not hitting them. **2** When you wrestle with a problem, you try to deal with it. **wrestler** (noun).

wrestling (noun) Wrestling is a sport in which two people fight and try to win by throwing or pinning their opponent to the ground.

wretch, wretches (noun; an old-fashioned word) A wretch is someone who is thought to be wicked or very unfortunate.

wretched (pronounced **ret**-shid) **1** (adjective) very unhappy or unfortunate, e.g. *a wretched childhood.* **2** (an informal use) You use wretched to describe something or someone you feel angry about or dislike, e.g. *a wretched bully.*

wriggle, wriggles, wriggling, wriggled 1 (verb) If someone wriggles, they twist and turn their body or a part of their body using quick movements, e.g. *He wriggled his arms and legs.* **2** If you wriggle somewhere, you move there by twisting and turning, e.g. *I wriggled out of the van.*

wring, wrings, wringing, wrung 1 (verb) When you wring a wet cloth or wring it out, you squeeze the water out of it by twisting it. **2** If you wring your hands, you hold them together and twist and turn them, usually because you are worried or upset. **3** If someone wrings a bird's neck, they kill the bird by twisting and breaking its neck.

wrinkle, wrinkles, wrinkling, wrinkled 1 (noun) Wrinkles are lines in someone's skin, especially on the face, which form as they grow old. **2** (verb) If something wrinkles, folds or lines develop on it, e.g. *silk so rich it doesn't wrinkle.* **3** When you wrinkle your nose, forehead, or eyes, you tighten the muscles in your face so that the skin folds into several lines. **wrinkled** (adjective), **wrinkly** (adjective).

wrist, wrists (noun) Your wrist is the part of your body between your hand and your arm which bends when you move your hand.

writ, writs (noun) A writ is a legal document that orders a person to do or not to do a particular thing.

write, writes, writing, wrote, written 1 (verb) When you write something, you use a pen or pencil to form letters, words, or numbers on a surface. **2** If you write something such as a poem, a book, or a piece of music, you create it. **3** When you write to someone or write them a letter, you express your feelings in a letter. **4** When someone writes something such as a cheque, they put the necessary information on it and sign it. **write down** (verb) If you write something down, you record it on a piece of paper. **write up** (verb) If you write up something, you write a full account of it, often using notes that you have previously made.

writer, writers 1 (noun) A writer is a person who writes books, stories, or articles as a job. **2** The writer of something is the person who wrote it.

writhe, writhes, writhing, writhed (pronounced **rieth**) (verb) If you writhe, you twist and turn your body, often because you are in pain.

writing, writings 1 (noun) Writing is something that has been written or printed, e.g. *Apply in writing for the information.* **2** Your writing is the way you write with a pen or pencil. **3** Writing is also a piece of written work, especially the style of language used, e.g. *witty writing.* **4** An author's writings are his or her written works.

written 1 Written is the past participle of **write. 2** (adjective) taken down in writing, e.g. *a written agreement.*

wrong, wrongs, wronging, wronged 1 (adjective) not working properly or unsatisfactory, e.g. *There was something wrong with the car.* **2** not correct or truthful, e.g. *the wrong answer.* **3** bad or immoral, e.g. *It is wrong to kill people.* **4** (noun) A wrong is an unjust action or situation, e.g. *the wrongs of our society.* **5** (verb) If someone wrongs you, they treat you in an unfair or unjust way. **wrongly** (adverb).

wrongful (adjective) A wrongful act is regarded as illegal, unfair, or immoral, e.g. *wrongful imprisonment.*

wrought iron (noun) Wrought iron is a pure type of iron that is formed into decorative shapes.

wry (adjective) A wry expression shows that you find a situation slightly amusing because you know more about it than other people. **wryly** (adverb).

X x

X, x 1 X is used to represent the name of an unknown or secret person or place, e.g. *The victim was referred to as Mr X throughout Tuesday's court proceedings.* **2** People sometimes write X on a map to mark a precise position. **3** X is used to represent a kiss at the bottom of a letter, a vote on a ballot paper, or the signature of someone who cannot write.

xenophobia (pronounced zen-nof-**foe**-bee-a) (noun) Xenophobia is a fear or strong dislike of people from other countries, e.g. *the xenophobia of the British public.* **xenophobic** (adjective).

Xerox, Xeroxes (pronounced **zeer**-roks) (a trademark) **1** (noun) A Xerox is a machine that makes photographic copies of sheets of paper with writing or printing on them. **2** A Xerox is also a copy made by a Xerox machine.

Xmas (noun; an informal word) Xmas means the same as Christmas.

X-ray, X-rays, X-raying, X-rayed 1 (noun) An X-ray is a stream of radiation of very short wavelength that can pass through some solid materials. X-rays are used by doctors to examine the bones or organs inside a person's body. **2** An X-ray is a picture made by sending X-rays through someone's body in order to examine the inside of it. **3** (verb) If you are X-rayed, a picture is made of the inside of your body by passing X-rays through it.

xylophone, xylophones (pronounced **zy**-lo-fone) (noun) A xylophone is a musical instrument made of a row of wooden bars of different lengths. It is played by hitting the bars with special hammers.

Y y

yacht, yachts (pronounced **yot**) (noun) A yacht is a boat with sails or an engine, used for racing or for pleasure trips.

yachting (noun) Yachting is the sport or activity of sailing a yacht.

yachtsman, yachtsmen (noun) A yachtsman is a man who sails a yacht. **yachtswoman** (noun).

yak, yaks (noun) A yak is a type of long-haired long-horned ox found mainly in the mountains of Tibet.

yam, yams (noun) A yam is a root vegetable which grows in tropical regions. It is also called a sweet potato.

yank, yanks, yanking, yanked 1 (verb) If you yank something, you pull or jerk it suddenly with a lot of force. **2** (noun; an informal use) A Yank is an American.

Yankee, Yankees (noun) A Yankee is the same as a Yank.

yap, yaps, yapping, yapped (verb) If a dog yaps, it barks with a high-pitched sound.

yard, yards 1 (noun) A yard is a unit of length equal to 36 inches or about 91.4 centimetres. **2** A yard is also an enclosed area that is usually next to a building and is often used for a particular purpose, e.g. *a ship repair yard.*

yardstick, yardsticks (noun) If you use someone or something as a yardstick, you use them as a standard against which to judge other people or things, e.g. *He had no yardstick by which to judge university.*

yarn, yarns 1 (noun) Yarn is thread used for knitting or making cloth. **2** (an informal use) A yarn is a story that someone tells, often with invented details to make it more interesting or exciting.

yashmak, yashmaks (noun) A yashmak is a veil that some Muslim women wear over their faces when they are in public.

yawn, yawns, yawning, yawned (verb) When you yawn, you open your mouth wide and take in more air than usual. You often yawn when you are tired or bored.

yawning (adjective) A yawning gap or opening is very wide.

ye (an old word) **1** (pronoun) Ye used to mean 'you'. **2** (adjective) Ye also used to mean 'the'.

yeah (interjection; an informal word) Yeah means 'yes'.

year, years 1 (noun) A year is a period of twelve months or 365 days (366 days in a leap year), which is the time taken for the earth to make one revolution around the sun. **2** A year is also a period of twelve consecutive months on which administration or organization is based, e.g. *the current financial year.* **3** (phrase) If something happens **year in, year out,** it happens every year, e.g. *a tradition kept up year in, year out.* **yearly** (adjective or adverb).

yearling, yearlings (noun) A yearling is an animal between one and two years old.

yearn, yearns, yearning, yearned (rhymes with **learn**) (verb) If you yearn for something, you want it very much indeed, e.g. *He yearned to sleep.* **yearning** (noun).

yeast, yeasts (noun) Yeast is a kind of fungus which is used to make bread rise, and to make liquids ferment in order to produce alcohol.

yell, yells, yelling, yelled 1 (verb) If you yell, you shout loudly, usually because you are angry, excited, or in pain. **2** (noun) A yell is a loud shout.

yellow, yellower, yellowest; yellows, yellowing, yellowed 1 (noun or adjective) Yellow is the colour of buttercups, egg yolks, or lemons. **2** (verb) When something yellows or is yellowed, it becomes yellow, often because it is old. **3** (adjective; an informal use) If you say someone is yellow, you mean they are cowardly. **yellowish** (adjective).

yellow fever (noun) Yellow fever is a serious infectious disease that is found in tropical countries. It causes fever and jaundice.

yelp, yelps, yelping, yelped 1 (verb) When people or animals yelp, they give a sudden, short cry. **2** (noun) A yelp is a sudden, short cry.

yen 1 (noun) The yen is the main unit of currency in Japan. **2** If you have a yen to do something, you have a strong desire to do it, e.g. *Mike had a yen to try cycling.*

yes (interjection) You use yes to agree with someone, to say that something is true, or to accept something.

yesterday 1 (noun or adverb) Yesterday is the day before today. **2** You also use yesterday to refer to the past, e.g. *Leave yesterday's sadness behind you.*

yet 1 (adverb) If something has not happened yet, it has not happened up to the present time, e.g. *It isn't quite dark yet.* **2** If something should not be done yet, it should not be done now, but later, e.g. *Don't switch off yet.* **3** Yet can mean there is still a possibility that something can happen, e.g. *We'll make a soldier of you yet.* **4** You can use yet when you want to say how much longer a situation will continue, e.g. *The service doesn't start for an hour yet.* **5** (conjunction) You can use yet to introduce a fact which is rather surprising, e.g. *He isn't a smoker yet he always carries a lighter.* **6** (adverb) Yet can be used for emphasis, e.g. *She'd changed her mind yet again.*

yeti, yetis (pronounced **yet**-tee) (noun) A yeti, or abominable snowman, is a large hairy apelike animal which some people believe exists in the Himalayas.

yew, yews (noun) A yew is an evergreen tree with bright red berries.

Yiddish (noun) Yiddish is a language derived mainly from German, which many Jewish people of European origin speak.

yield, yields, yielding, yielded 1 (verb) If you yield to someone or something, you stop resisting and give in to them, e.g. *Russia recently yielded to US pressure.* **2** If you yield something that you have control of or responsibility for, you surrender it, e.g. *They refused to yield control of their weapons.* **3** If something yields, it breaks or gives way, e.g. *The handle would yield to her grasp.* **4** To yield something means to produce it, e.g. *One season's produce yields food for the following year.* **5** (noun) A yield is an amount of food, money, or profit produced from a given area of land or from an investment.

yippee (interjection) 'Yippee!' is an exclamation of happiness or excitement.

yob, yobs (noun; an informal word) A yob is a noisy, badly behaved boy or young man.

yodel, yodels, yodelling, yodelled (pronounced **yoe**-dl) (verb) When someone yodels, they sing normal notes with high quick notes in between. This style of singing is associated with the Swiss and Austrian Alps.

yoga (pronounced **yoe**-ga) (noun) Yoga is a Hindu method of mental and physical exercise or discipline.

yogurt, yogurts; also spelled **yoghurt** or **yoghourt** (pronounced **yog**-gurt) (noun) Yogurt is a slightly sour thick liquid made from milk that has had bacteria added to it.

yoke, yokes 1 (noun) A yoke is a wooden bar attached to two collars which is laid across the necks of animals such as oxen to hold them together, and to which a plough or other tool may be attached. **2** (a literary use) If people are under a yoke of some kind, they are being oppressed, e.g. *two women who escape the yoke of insensitive men.*

yokel, yokels (pronounced **yoe**-kl) (noun) If you call someone a yokel, you mean they live in the country, and you think they are rather stupid and old-fashioned.

yolk, yolks (rhymes with **joke**) (noun) The yolk of an egg is the yellow part in the middle of the egg.

Yom Kippur (pronounced yom kip-**poor**) (noun) Yom Kippur is an annual Jewish religious holiday, which is a day of fasting and prayers. It is also called the Day of Atonement.

yonder (adverb or adjective; an old word) over there, e.g. *There's an island yonder.*

yore (an old-fashioned phrase) **Of yore** means existing a long time ago, e.g. *nostalgia for the days of yore.*

Yorkshire pudding, Yorkshire puddings (noun) Yorkshire pudding is a kind of baked batter made of flour, milk, and eggs, and usually eaten with roast beef.

you 1 (pronoun) You refers to the person or group of people that a person is speaking or writing to. **2** You also refers to people in general, e.g. *You can get a two-bedroom villa for £80,000.*

young, younger, youngest 1 (adjective) A young person, animal, or plant has not lived very long and is not yet mature. **2** (noun) The young are young people in general. **3** The young of an animal are its babies.

youngster, youngsters (noun) A youngster is a child or young person.

your 1 (adjective) Your means belonging or relating to the person or group of people that someone is speaking to, e.g. *I do like your name.* **2** Your is used to show that something belongs or relates to people in general, e.g. *Your driving ability is affected by just one or two drinks.*

yours (pronoun) Yours refers to something belonging or relating to the person or group of people that someone is speaking to, e.g. *His hair is longer than yours.*

yourself, yourselves 1 (pronoun) Yourself is used when the person being spoken to does the action and is affected by it, e.g. *Why can't you do it yourself?* **2** Yourself is used to emphasize 'you', e.g. *Do you yourself want a divorce?*

youth, youths 1 (noun) Someone's youth is the period of their life before they are a fully mature adult. **2** Youth is the quality or condition of being young and often inexperienced. **3** A youth is a boy or young man. **4** The youth are young people thought of as a group, e.g. *the youth of today.* **youthful** (adjective).

youth hostel, youth hostels (noun) A youth hostel is a place where young people can stay cheaply when they are on holiday.

yo-yo, yo-yos (noun) A yo-yo is a round wooden or plastic toy attached to a piece of string. You play by making the yo-yo rise and fall on the string.

Yugoslav, Yugoslavs (pronounced **yoo**-goe-slahv) **1** (adjective) belonging or relating to the country that used to be known as Yugoslavia. **2** (noun) A Yugoslav is someone who came from the country that used be known as Yugoslavia.

Yule (noun; an old word) Yule means Christmas.

yuppie, yuppies (noun) If you say people are yuppies, you think they are young, middle-class, and earn a lot of money which they spend on themselves.

Z z

Zambian, Zambians (pronounced **zam**-bee-an) **1** (adjective) belonging or relating to Zambia. **2** (noun) A Zambian is someone who comes from Zambia.

zany, zanier, zaniest (adjective) odd and ridiculous, e.g. *zany humour.*

zap, zaps, zapping, zapped (an informal word) **1** (verb) To zap someone means to kill them, usually by shooting, e.g. *He would zap the skinny cop with the moustache.* **2** To zap also means to go somewhere quickly.

zeal (noun) Zeal is very great enthusiasm. **zealous** (adjective).

zealot, zealots (pronounced **zel**-lot) (noun) A zealot is a person who acts with very great enthusiasm, especially in following a political or religious cause.

zebra, zebras (noun) A zebra is a type of African wild horse with black and white stripes over its body.

zebra crossings, zebra crossings (noun) A zebra crossing is a place where people can cross the road safely. The road is marked with black and white stripes.

Zen or **Zen Buddhism** (noun) Zen is a form of Buddhism that concentrates on learning through meditation and intuition.

zenith (noun; a literary use) The zenith of something is the time when it is at its most successful or powerful, e.g. *the zenith of his military career.*

zero, zeros or **zeroes, zeroing, zeroed 1** Zero is the number 0. **2** Zero is freezing point, 0° Centigrade. **3** (adjective) Zero means there is none at all of a particular thing, e.g. *His chances are zero.* **4** (verb) To zero in on a target means to aim at or to move towards it, e.g. *She had an instinct for zeroing in on the money.*

zest 1 (noun) Zest is a feeling of pleasure and enthusiasm, e.g. *zest for life.* **2** Zest is a quality which adds extra flavour, interest, or charm to something, e.g. *brilliant ideas to add zest to your wedding list.* **3** The zest of an orange or lemon is the outside of the peel which is used to flavour food or drinks.

zigzag, zigzags, zigzagging, zigzagged 1 (noun) A zigzag is a line which has a series of sharp, angular turns to the right and left in it, like a continuous series of 'W's. **2** (verb) To zigzag means to move forward by going at an angle first right and then left, e.g. *He zigzagged his way across the racecourse.*

Zimbabwean, Zimbabweans (pronounced zim-**bahb**-wee-an) **1** (adjective) belonging or relating to Zimbabwe. **2** (noun) A Zimbabwean is someone who comes from Zimbabwe.

zinc (noun) Zinc is a bluish-white metal used in alloys and to coat other metals to stop them rusting.

zing (noun; an informal word) Zing is a quality in something that makes it lively or interesting, e.g. *There's a real zing around the studio.*

zip, zips, zipping, zipped 1 (noun) A zip is a long narrow fastener with two rows of teeth that are closed or opened by a small clip pulled between them. **2** (verb) When you zip something or zip it up, you fasten it using a zip.

zipper, zippers (noun) A zipper is the same as a zip.

zodiac (pronounced **zoe**-dee-ak) (noun) The zodiac is an imaginary strip in the sky which contains the planets and stars which astrologers think are important influences on people. It is divided into 12 sections, each with a special name and symbol.

zombie, zombies 1 (noun; an informal use) If you refer to someone as a zombie, you mean that they seem to be unaware of what is going on around them and to act without thinking about what they are doing. **2** In voodoo, a zombie is a dead person who has been brought back to life by witchcraft.

zone, zones (noun) A zone is an area that has particular features or properties, e.g. *a war zone.*

zoo, zoos (noun) A zoo is a place where live animals are kept so that people can look at them.

zoology (pronounced zoo-**ol**-loj-jee) (noun) Zoology is the scientific study of animals. **zoological** (adjective), **zoologist** (noun).

zoom, zooms, zooming, zoomed 1 (verb) To zoom means to move very quickly, e.g. *They zoomed to safety.* **2** If a camera zooms in on something, it gives a close-up picture of it.

Zulu, Zulus (pronounced **zoo**-loo) **1** (noun) The Zulus are a group of black people who live in southern Africa. **2** Zulu is the language spoken by the Zulus.

COLLINS GEM

Clear and simple meanings

■

Spelling help given in full

■

Examples of actual word use from the Bank of English

BANK *of* ENGLISH

This dictionary has been created using
COLLINS UNIQUE LANGUAGE DATABASE

£2.50 net in UK

ISBN 0-00-470903-9